# Handbook of Research on Interdisciplinary Preparation for Equitable Special Education

Dena D. Slanda
*University of Central Florida, USA*

Lindsey Pike
*University of Central Florida, USA*

A volume in the Advances in Educational Technologies and Instructional Design (AETID) Book Series

Published in the United States of America by
IGI Global
Information Science Reference (an imprint of IGI Global)
701 E. Chocolate Avenue
Hershey PA, USA 17033
Tel: 717-533-8845
Fax:  717-533-8661
E-mail: cust@igi-global.com
Web site: http://www.igi-global.com

Copyright © 2023 by IGI Global.  All rights reserved. No part of this publication may be reproduced, stored or distributed in any form or by any means, electronic or mechanical, including photocopying, without written permission from the publisher. Product or company names used in this set are for identification purposes only. Inclusion of the names of the products or companies does not indicate a claim of ownership by IGI Global of the trademark or registered trademark.
Library of Congress Cataloging-in-Publication Data

Names: Slanda, Dena, 1977- editor. | Pike, Lindsey, 1986- editor.
Title: Handbook of research on interdisciplinary preparation for equitable
   special education / Dena Slanda, and Lindsey Pike, Editor.
Description: Hershey, PA : Information Science Reference, [2023] | Includes
   bibliographical references and index. | Summary: "This book explores and
   highlights interdisciplinary personnel preparation to advance special
   education and enhance outcomes for students with disabilities, providing
   theories and frameworks, examples, and discussions around innovations
   and lessons-learned from interdisciplinary preparation programs and/or
   practices"-- Provided by publisher.
Identifiers: LCCN 2022039876 (print) | LCCN 2022039877 (ebook) | ISBN
   9781668464380 (hardcover) | ISBN 9781668464397 (ebook)
Subjects: LCSH: Children with disabilities--Education. | Educational
   equalization. | Interdisciplinary approach in education. | Special
   education.
Classification: LCC LC4019 .I536 2023  (print) | LCC LC4019  (ebook) | DDC
   371.9--dc23/eng/20220922
LC record available at https://lccn.loc.gov/2022039876
LC ebook record available at https://lccn.loc.gov/2022039877

This book is published in the IGI Global book series Advances in Educational Technologies and Instructional Design (AETID) (ISSN: 2326-8905; eISSN: 2326-8913)

British Cataloguing in Publication Data
A Cataloguing in Publication record for this book is available from the British Library.

All work contributed to this book is new, previously-unpublished material. The views expressed in this book are those of the authors, but not necessarily of the publisher.

For electronic access to this publication, please contact: eresources@igi-global.com.

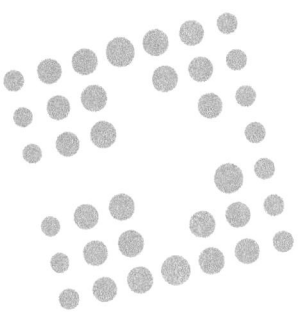

# Advances in Educational Technologies and Instructional Design (AETID) Book Series

Lawrence A. Tomei
Robert Morris University, USA

ISSN:2326-8905
EISSN:2326-8913

## Mission

Education has undergone, and continues to undergo, immense changes in the way it is enacted and distributed to both child and adult learners. In modern education, the traditional classroom learning experience has evolved to include technological resources and to provide online classroom opportunities to students of all ages regardless of their geographical locations. From distance education, Massive-Open-Online-Courses (MOOCs), and electronic tablets in the classroom, technology is now an integral part of learning and is also affecting the way educators communicate information to students.

The **Advances in Educational Technologies & Instructional Design (AETID) Book Series** explores new research and theories for facilitating learning and improving educational performance utilizing technological processes and resources. The series examines technologies that can be integrated into K-12 classrooms to improve skills and learning abilities in all subjects including STEM education and language learning. Additionally, it studies the emergence of fully online classrooms for young and adult learners alike, and the communication and accountability challenges that can arise. Trending topics that are covered include adaptive learning, game-based learning, virtual school environments, and social media effects. School administrators, educators, academicians, researchers, and students will find this series to be an excellent resource for the effective design and implementation of learning technologies in their classes.

## Coverage

- Higher Education Technologies
- Adaptive Learning
- Educational Telecommunications
- Collaboration Tools
- Social Media Effects on Education
- E-Learning
- Online Media in Classrooms
- Curriculum Development
- Digital Divide in Education
- Game-Based Learning

IGI Global is currently accepting manuscripts for publication within this series. To submit a proposal for a volume in this series, please contact our Acquisition Editors at Acquisitions@igi-global.com or visit: http://www.igi-global.com/publish/.

The Advances in Educational Technologies and Instructional Design (AETID) Book Series (ISSN 2326-8905) is published by IGI Global, 701 E. Chocolate Avenue, Hershey, PA 17033-1240, USA, www.igi-global.com. This series is composed of titles available for purchase individually; each title is edited to be contextually exclusive from any other title within the series. For pricing and ordering information please visit http://www.igi-global.com/book-series/advances-educational-technologies-instructional-design/73678. Postmaster: Send all address changes to above address. Copyright © 2023 IGI Global. All rights, including translation in other languages reserved by the publisher. No part of this series may be reproduced or used in any form or by any means – graphics, electronic, or mechanical, including photocopying, recording, taping, or information and retrieval systems – without written permission from the publisher, except for non commercial, educational use, including classroom teaching purposes. The views expressed in this series are those of the authors, but not necessarily of IGI Global.

## Titles in this Series

*For a list of additional titles in this series, please visit: www.igi-global.com/book-series/advances-educational-technologies-instructional-design/73678*

*Shaping Online Spaces Through Online Humanities Curricula*
Julie Tatlock (Mount Mary University, USA)
Information Science Reference • © 2023 • 290pp • H/C (ISBN: 9781668440551) • US $215.00

*Cases on Effective Universal Design for Learning Implementation Across Schools*
Frederic Fovet (Royal Roads University, Canada)
Information Science Reference • © 2023 • 300pp • H/C (ISBN: 9781668447505) • US $215.00

*Engaging Students With Disabilities in Remote Learning Environments*
Peter Griswold (William Paterson University, USA) Manina Urgolo Huckvale (William Paterson University, USA) and Kelly McNeal (William Paterson University, USA)
Information Science Reference • © 2023 • 305pp • H/C (ISBN: 9781668455036) • US $215.00

*Enhancing Education Through Multidisciplinary Film Teaching Methodologies*
Jason D. DeHart (University of Tennessee, Knoxville, USA)
Information Science Reference • © 2023 • 289pp • H/C (ISBN: 9781668453940) • US $215.00

*Handbook of Research on Advancing Teaching and Teacher Education in the Context of a Virtual Age*
Aaron Samuel Zimmerman (Texas Tech University, USA)
Information Science Reference • © 2023 • 405pp • H/C (ISBN: 9781668484074) • US $270.00

*Technology Integration and Transformation in STEM Classrooms*
Christie Martin (University of South Carolina – Columbia, USA) Drew Polly (University of North Carolina – Charlotte, USA) and Bridget T. Miller (University of South Carolina, USA)
Information Science Reference • © 2023 • 335pp • H/C (ISBN: 9781668459201) • US $215.00

*Advancing STEM Education and Innovation in a Time of Distance Learning*
Roberto Alonso González-Lezcano (Universidad CEU San Pablo, Spain)
Information Science Reference • © 2023 • 359pp • H/C (ISBN: 9781668450536) • US $205.00

*Promoting Next-Generation Learning Environments Through CGScholar*
Matthew Montebello (University of Malta, Malta)
Information Science Reference • © 2023 • 310pp • H/C (ISBN: 9781668451243) • US $215.00

701 East Chocolate Avenue, Hershey, PA 17033, USA
Tel: 717-533-8845 x100 • Fax: 717-533-8661
E-Mail: cust@igi-global.com • www.igi-global.com

# List of Contributors

**Achola, Edwin** / *California State University, Long Beach, USA* .................................................................... 526
**Adams, David** / *California State Polytechnic University, Humboldt, USA* ........................................................ 65
**Alvayero Ricklefs, Mariana** / *Northern Illinois University, USA* ................................................................. 318
**Anderson, Jill** / *California State Polytechnic University, Humboldt, USA* ........................................................ 65
**Bao, Wenjing** / *University of Oregon, USA* ............................................................................................ 111
**Bengtson, Ed** / *University of Arkansas, USA* .......................................................................................... 505
**Bonati, Michelle L.** / *SUNY Plattsburgh, USA* ......................................................................................... 21
**Brown, Jennifer A.** / *University of Georgia, USA* ................................................................................... 237
**Bruhn, Allison L.** / *University of Iowa, USA* .......................................................................................... 420
**Bueno, Sydney A.** / *University of Wisconsin-Stevens Point, USA* ................................................................. 85
**Chang, Ya-Chih** / *California State University, Los Angeles, USA* ............................................................... 177
**Chatlos, Suzannah B.** / *SUNY Plattsburgh, USA* ..................................................................................... 21
**Collins, Brett** / *San Francisco State University, USA* ............................................................................. 468
**Cook, Amy** / *University of Massachusetts, Boston, USA* .......................................................................... 359
**Crain, Marina R.** / *University of Oregon, USA* ...................................................................................... 111
**Cramer, Elizabeth D.** / *Florida International University, USA* .................................................................. 374
**Crutchfield, Jandel** / *University of Texas at Arlington, USA* .................................................................... 495
**Datchuk, Shawn** / *University of Iowa, USA* .......................................................................................... 420
**De Arment, Serra** / *Virginia Commonwealth University, USA* ...................................................................... 1
**Denning, Christopher** / *University of Massachusetts, Boston, USA* ............................................................ 359
**Dixon, Maria V.** / *Arizona State University, USA* ................................................................................... 254
**Ehrhardt, Kristal E.** / *Western Michigan University, USA* ....................................................................... 130
**Erwin-Davidson, Lisa N.** / *California State University, Fullerton, USA* ...................................................... 198
**Fabian Freire, Ana Paula** / *Florida International University, USA* ........................................................... 374
**Foster, Elizabeth A.** / *West Chester University, USA* ............................................................................. 85
**Frazier, Kimberly** / *University of Arkansas, USA* .................................................................................. 505
**Friesen, Amber** / *San Francisco State University, USA* .......................................................................... 468
**Fryling, Mitch** / *California State University, Los Angeles, USA* ............................................................... 177
**Gallo, Rosalia F.** / *Florida International University, USA* ..................................................................... 374
**Gonzalez, Liana** / *Florida International University, USA* ........................................................................ 374
**Green, Ambra L.** / *University of Texas at Arlington, USA* ....................................................................... 495
**Hagans, Kristi S.** / *California State University, Long Beach, USA* ............................................................ 296
**Harris, Chaiqua A.** / *Northwestern University, USA* .............................................................................. 219
**Hayden, Laura** / *University of Massachusetts, Boston, USA* .................................................................... 359
**Hepperlen, Renee A.** / *School of Social Work, University of St. Thomas, USA* ............................................... 42

**Hermoso, Jocelyn Clare Reyno** / *San Francisco State University, USA* .................................. 468
**Hines, Rebecca A.** / *University of Central Florida, USA* .................................................. 277
**Hoeh, Emily** / *SUNY Plattsburgh, USA* ........................................................................ 21
**Hopper, Chris** / *California State Polytechnic University, Humboldt, USA* ........................ 65
**Hughes, Delaney** / *California State Polytechnic University, Humboldt, USA* ................... 65
**Hunter, Tameeka** / *Florida International University, USA* .............................................. 505
**Ingelin, Bonnie L.** / *School of Education, University of St. Thomas, USA* ....................... 42
**Jamanis, Shanna** / *Nazareth College, USA* .................................................................... 155
**Jennings, R. Lanai** / *Marshall University, USA* ............................................................ 440
**King, Alison** / *Longwood University, USA* ...................................................................... 1
**King, Seth A.** / *University of Iowa, USA* ...................................................................... 420
**Kraemer, Bonnie** / *San Diego State University, USA* .................................................... 396
**Kucharczyk, Suzanne** / *University of Arkansas, USA* ................................................... 505
**Kupzyk, Sara** / *University of Nebraska, Omaha, USA* ................................................... 342
**LaLonde, Kate B.** / *Western Michigan University, USA* ................................................ 130
**Lambros, Katina M.** / *San Diego State University, USA* ............................................... 396
**Lehal, Jasmine Kaur** / *San Diego State University, USA* ............................................... 396
**Lieberman-Betz, Rebecca G.** / *University of Georgia, USA* ......................................... 237
**McCloud, Paige** / *University of Central Florida, USA* .................................................. 277
**McKee, Aja** / *California State University, Fullerton, USA* ............................................. 198
**Mitsch, Maryssa Kucskar** / *San Francisco State University, USA* ................................ 468
**Moise, Danica** / *University of Central Florida, USA* .................................................... 277
**Moore, Erika** / *University of Central Florida, USA* ...................................................... 277
**Murphy, Kristin M.** / *University of Massachusetts, Boston, USA* ................................. 359
**Myck-Wayne, Janice** / *California State University, Fullerton, USA* ............................. 198
**Nelson, Bergen B.** / *Virginia Commonwealth University, USA* ....................................... 1
**Newkirk-Turner, Brandi L.** / *Jackson State University, USA* ....................................... 219
**Nordness, Philip D.** / *University of Nebraska, Omaha, USA* ........................................ 342
**O'Brien, Matthew J.** / *University of Iowa, USA* .......................................................... 420
**Patricelli, Miyoko** / *University of Oregon, USA* ........................................................... 111
**Paz, Jennica L.** / *San Diego State University, USA* ....................................................... 396
**Perkins, Whitney D.** / *Jackson State University, USA* .................................................. 219
**Perryman, Kristi L.** / *University of Arkansas, USA* ..................................................... 505
**Peterson, Stephanie** / *Western Michigan University, USA* ............................................ 130
**Pham, Andy V.** / *Florida International University, USA* ............................................... 374
**Poling, Alan** / *Western Michigan University, USA* ....................................................... 130
**Powers, Kristin** / *California State University, Long Beach, USA* ................................. 526
**Price, Sarah Kye** / *Virginia Commonwealth University, USA* ........................................ 1
**Prohn, Seb M.** / *Virginia Commonwealth University, USA* ............................................ 1
**Richards-Tutor, Catherine** / *California State University, Long Beach, USA* ............... 296
**Romig, John Elwood** / *University of Texas at Arlington, USA* ..................................... 495
**Rotheram-Fuller, Erin** / *Arizona State University, USA* ............................................. 254
**Ruland, Kalyn** / *California State Polytechnic University, Humboldt, USA* ..................... 65
**Santos, Ann Marie** / *University of Iowa, USA* ............................................................. 420
**Shire, Stephanie Yoshiko** / *University of Oregon, USA* ................................................ 111
**Speight, Renee** / *University of Arkansas, USA* ............................................................. 505

**Spence, Christine M.** / *Virginia Commonwealth University, USA* .................................................................. 1
**Squires, Maureen E.** / *SUNY Plattsburgh, USA* ........................................................................................ 21
**Stansberry Brusnahan, L. Lynn** / *School of Education, University of St. Thomas, USA* .................. 42
**Stone-MacDonald, Angi** / *California State University, San Bernadino, USA* ................................... 359
**Stroebel, Sandra S.** / *Marshall University, USA* ..................................................................................... 440
**Summy, Sarah** / *Western Michigan University, USA* ............................................................................ 130
**Symon, Jennifer B.** / *California State University, Los Angeles, USA* ................................................. 177
**Taylor, Heather E.** / *California State Polytechnic University, Pomona, USA* ..................................... 85
**Thomas, Johanna** / *University of Arkansas, USA* ................................................................................. 505
**Towson, Jacqueline** / *University of Central Florida, USA* .................................................................. 277
**Tran, Teresa** / *San Diego State University, USA* ................................................................................... 396
**Vail, Cynthia O.** / *University of Geogia, USA* ....................................................................................... 237
**Valdez, Melaina A.** / *California State Polytechnic University, Humboldt, USA* ................................ 65
**Van Boxtel, Joanne M.** / *California State Polytechnic University, Pomona, USA* ............................ 85
**VanDerwall, Rena** / *Western Michigan University, USA* .................................................................... 130
**Vogler-Elias, Dawn** / *Nazareth College, USA* ...................................................................................... 155
**Wiegand, Sarah D.** / *New Mexico State University, USA* .................................................................. 237
**Wiles, Jennifer E.** / *Jackson State University, USA* ............................................................................. 219
**Wyatt, Maris** / *Virginia Commonwealth University, USA* ..................................................................... 1
**Xu, Yaoying** / *Virginia Commonwealth University, USA* ....................................................................... 1
**Yarbrough, Dana** / *Virginia Commonwealth University, USA* ............................................................... 1

# Table of Contents

**Preface** ............................................................................................................................................. xxiv

**Chapter 1**
Supporting Children With High-Intensity Needs Through Interdisciplinary Personnel Preparation ..... 1
    *Yaoying Xu, Virginia Commonwealth University, USA*
    *Alison King, Longwood University, USA*
    *Sarah Kye Price, Virginia Commonwealth University, USA*
    *Christine M. Spence, Virginia Commonwealth University, USA*
    *Serra De Arment, Virginia Commonwealth University, USA*
    *Bergen B. Nelson, Virginia Commonwealth University, USA*
    *Maris Wyatt, Virginia Commonwealth University, USA*
    *Dana Yarbrough, Virginia Commonwealth University, USA*
    *Seb M. Prohn, Virginia Commonwealth University, USA*

**Chapter 2**
Interdisciplinary Pre-Service Professional Preparation Through Video Modeling ............................. 21
    *Suzannah B. Chatlos, SUNY Plattsburgh, USA*
    *Emily Hoeh, SUNY Plattsburgh, USA*
    *Michelle L. Bonati, SUNY Plattsburgh, USA*
    *Maureen E. Squires, SUNY Plattsburgh, USA*

**Chapter 3**
Enhancing Professionals' Interdisciplinary Competencies: Meeting the Needs of Children With
Disabilities From Diverse Communities .............................................................................................. 42
    *L. Lynn Stansberry Brusnahan, School of Education, University of St. Thomas, USA*
    *Renee A. Hepperlen, School of Social Work, University of St. Thomas, USA*
    *Bonnie L. Ingelin, School of Education, University of St. Thomas, USA*

**Chapter 4**
Collaborative Preparation of Special Educators and Adapted Physical Educators ............................. 65
    *Jill Anderson, California State Polytechnic University, Humboldt, USA*
    *David Adams, California State Polytechnic University, Humboldt, USA*
    *Chris Hopper, California State Polytechnic University, Humboldt, USA*
    *Melaina A. Valdez, California State Polytechnic University, Humboldt, USA*
    *Delaney Hughes, California State Polytechnic University, Humboldt, USA*
    *Kalyn Ruland, California State Polytechnic University, Humboldt, USA*

**Chapter 5**
Interdisciplinary Special Education and APE Teacher Preparation Using Evidence-Based, High-Leverage Practices ............................................................................................................................. 85
    *Heather E. Taylor, California State Polytechnic University, Pomona, USA*
    *Joanne M. Van Boxtel, California State Polytechnic University, Pomona, USA*
    *Elizabeth A. Foster, West Chester University, USA*
    *Sydney A. Bueno, University of Wisconsin-Stevens Point, USA*

**Chapter 6**
Preparing a New Generation of Early Autism Educators: An Interdisciplinary Personnel Preparation Grant .................................................................................................................................... 111
    *Marina R. Crain, University of Oregon, USA*
    *Wenjing Bao, University of Oregon, USA*
    *Miyoko Patricelli, University of Oregon, USA*
    *Stephanie Yoshiko Shire, University of Oregon, USA*

**Chapter 7**
Interdisciplinary Training in Special Education and Behavior Analysis to Meet the Needs of Students With Autism Spectrum Disorder ....................................................................................... 130
    *Kate B. LaLonde, Western Michigan University, USA*
    *Kristal E. Ehrhardt, Western Michigan University, USA*
    *Sarah Summy, Western Michigan University, USA*
    *Stephanie Peterson, Western Michigan University, USA*
    *Rena VanDerwall, Western Michigan University, USA*
    *Alan Poling, Western Michigan University, USA*

**Chapter 8**
Autism From Multiple Perspectives: Developing Interdisciplinary Changemakers ........................ 155
    *Shanna Jamanis, Nazareth College, USA*
    *Dawn Vogler-Elias, Nazareth College, USA*

**Chapter 9**
Partners in Improving Social Communication in Children With Disabilities in Urban Early Childhood Settings .......................................................................................................................... 177
    *Ya-Chih Chang, California State University, Los Angeles, USA*
    *Jennifer B. Symon, California State University, Los Angeles, USA*
    *Mitch Fryling, California State University, Los Angeles, USA*

**Chapter 10**
Interdisciplinary Training for Early Childhood Special Educators and Speech Language Pathology Candidates ........................................................................................................................................ 198
    *Lisa N. Erwin-Davidson, California State University, Fullerton, USA*
    *Aja McKee, California State University, Fullerton, USA*
    *Janice Myck-Wayne, California State University, Fullerton, USA*

**Chapter 11**
A Model for the Interprofessional Preparation of Speech-Language Pathologists and School
Counselors: Effectively Serving Children With Disabilities ............................................................... 219
    *Brandi L. Newkirk-Turner, Jackson State University, USA*
    *Whitney D. Perkins, Jackson State University, USA*
    *Jennifer E. Wiles, Jackson State University, USA*
    *Chaiqua A. Harris, Northwestern University, USA*

**Chapter 12**
An Interdisciplinary Case-Based Approach to Preservice Interprofessional Training ...................... 237
    *Rebecca G. Lieberman-Betz, University of Georgia, USA*
    *Jennifer A. Brown, University of Georgia, USA*
    *Cynthia O. Vail, University of Geogia, USA*
    *Sarah D. Wiegand, New Mexico State University, USA*

**Chapter 13**
Interprofessional SLP and Educator Collaboration to Improve Communication for Students With
Complex Disabilities ............................................................................................................................ 254
    *Erin Rotheram-Fuller, Arizona State University, USA*
    *Maria V. Dixon, Arizona State University, USA*

**Chapter 14**
Exceptional Education and Language Disorders: Interdisciplinary Collaboration to Create New
Experts in Special Education .............................................................................................................. 277
    *Rebecca A. Hines, University of Central Florida, USA*
    *Erika Moore, University of Central Florida, USA*
    *Danica Moise, University of Central Florida, USA*
    *Paige McCloud, University of Central Florida, USA*
    *Jacqueline Towson, University of Central Florida, USA*

**Chapter 15**
Interdisciplinary Training in Intensive Intervention for Students With Disabilities and Multi-
Lingual Youth ...................................................................................................................................... 296
    *Kristi S. Hagans, California State University, Long Beach, USA*
    *Catherine Richards-Tutor, California State University, Long Beach, USA*

**Chapter 16**
Preparing Pre-Service Teachers to Work With English Learners With Special Education Needs ..... 318
    *Mariana Alvayero Ricklefs, Northern Illinois University, USA*

**Chapter 17**
Interdisciplinary Preparation to Meet the Emotional and Behavioral Health Needs of Diverse
Students ................................................................................................................................................ 342
    *Sara Kupzyk, University of Nebraska, Omaha, USA*
    *Philip D. Nordness, University of Nebraska, Omaha, USA*

**Chapter 18**
Interdisciplinary Special Educator and School Counselor Preparation: Supporting Equitable Student Outcomes in the COVID-19 Era .................................................................................................... 359
    *Kristin M. Murphy, University of Massachusetts, Boston, USA*
    *Laura Hayden, University of Massachusetts, Boston, USA*
    *Amy Cook, University of Massachusetts, Boston, USA*
    *Christopher Denning, University of Massachusetts, Boston, USA*
    *Angi Stone-MacDonald, California State University, San Bernadino, USA*

**Chapter 19**
Collaborative Preparation in Equity-Based Practices to Support Minoritized Students With High-Intensity Needs .......................................................................................................................................... 374
    *Elizabeth D. Cramer, Florida International University, USA*
    *Andy V. Pham, Florida International University, USA*
    *Liana Gonzalez, Florida International University, USA*
    *Rosalia F. Gallo, Florida International University, USA*
    *Ana Paula Fabian Freire, Florida International University, USA*

**Chapter 20**
Interdisciplinary Support Teams to Enhance Social Emotional and Behavioral Outcomes for Students With Disabilities: Project BEAMS .................................................................................................. 396
    *Katina M. Lambros, San Diego State University, USA*
    *Bonnie Kraemer, San Diego State University, USA*
    *Jennica L. Paz, San Diego State University, USA*
    *Teresa Tran, San Diego State University, USA*
    *Jasmine Kaur Lehal, San Diego State University, USA*

**Chapter 21**
Creating and Sustaining Collaborative Professional Development in Special Education: Lessons From the Interdisciplinary Training Project in Special Education and School Psychology (SP2) ..... 420
    *Seth A. King, University of Iowa, USA*
    *Ann Marie Santos, University of Iowa, USA*
    *Matthew J. O'Brien, University of Iowa, USA*
    *Allison L. Bruhn, University of Iowa, USA*
    *Shawn Datchuk, University of Iowa, USA*

**Chapter 22**
Lessons Learned: Equipping Interdisciplinary Scholars to Provide a Continuum of Mental and Behavioral Health Supports ................................................................................................................... 440
    *R. Lanai Jennings, Marshall University, USA*
    *Sandra S. Stroebel, Marshall University, USA*

**Chapter 23**
Social Emotional Development and Early Childhood Mental Health: Special Education and Social Work Collaboration ........................................................................................................................... 468
    *Maryssa Kucskar Mitsch, San Francisco State University, USA*
    *Brett Collins, San Francisco State University, USA*
    *Amber Friesen, San Francisco State University, USA*
    *Jocelyn Clare Reyno Hermoso, San Francisco State University, USA*

**Chapter 24**
Introducing a Collaborative Training Program for Special Educators and School Social Workers ... 495
    *John Elwood Romig, University of Texas at Arlington, USA*
    *Ambra L. Green, University of Texas at Arlington, USA*
    *Jandel Crutchfield, University of Texas at Arlington, USA*

**Chapter 25**
Teaming for Transition: A Model for Interdisciplinary, Collaborative Preparation of Secondary Education Professionals ........................................................................................................................ 505
    *Suzanne Kucharczyk, University of Arkansas, USA*
    *Kimberly Frazier, University of Arkansas, USA*
    *Tameeka Hunter, Florida International University, USA*
    *Kristi L. Perryman, University of Arkansas, USA*
    *Johanna Thomas, University of Arkansas, USA*
    *Renee Speight, University of Arkansas, USA*
    *Ed Bengtson, University of Arkansas, USA*

**Chapter 26**
A Model for Interdisciplinary Preparation in Culturally-Responsive, Evidence-Based Transition Planning ............................................................................................................................................... 526
    *Kristin Powers, California State University, Long Beach, USA*
    *Edwin Achola, California State University, Long Beach, USA*

**Compilation of References** ............................................................................................................ 545

**About the Contributors** ................................................................................................................. 631

**Index** ................................................................................................................................................. 652

# Detailed Table of Contents

**Preface** .................................................................................................................................. xxiv

**Chapter 1**
Supporting Children With High-Intensity Needs Through Interdisciplinary Personnel Preparation ..... 1
    *Yaoying Xu, Virginia Commonwealth University, USA*
    *Alison King, Longwood University, USA*
    *Sarah Kye Price, Virginia Commonwealth University, USA*
    *Christine M. Spence, Virginia Commonwealth University, USA*
    *Serra De Arment, Virginia Commonwealth University, USA*
    *Bergen B. Nelson, Virginia Commonwealth University, USA*
    *Maris Wyatt, Virginia Commonwealth University, USA*
    *Dana Yarbrough, Virginia Commonwealth University, USA*
    *Seb M. Prohn, Virginia Commonwealth University, USA*

This chapter addresses potential challenges and opportunities of developing innovative programs in interdisciplinary personnel preparation in special education and related services. The mission of this chapter is to advocate for an interdisciplinary personnel preparation model in special education and related services, particularly for serving young children with significant disabilities and their families from high-need communities. First, an interdisciplinary conceptual framework that guides the model is illustrated. Second, the authors demonstrate essential components of the model with evidence and highlight the features of the model. Finally, three program examples of the model are presented to provide evidence-based strategies for serving children with high-intensity needs and their families. The chapter concludes with recommendations for future directions.

**Chapter 2**
Interdisciplinary Pre-Service Professional Preparation Through Video Modeling ............................. 21
    *Suzannah B. Chatlos, SUNY Plattsburgh, USA*
    *Emily Hoeh, SUNY Plattsburgh, USA*
    *Michelle L. Bonati, SUNY Plattsburgh, USA*
    *Maureen E. Squires, SUNY Plattsburgh, USA*

Preparation of pre-service professionals to work in the field of special education requires explicitly taught approaches to collaboration as a part of a multidisciplinary team. The authors' faculty learning community provides a model to emanate the skills, knowledge, and dispositions of a high-functioning collaborative team expected from pre-service professionals through a mock individualized education program (IEP) team video series. Issues (origin story), solutions (video modeling), and areas of future research (mock interdisciplinary student teams) will be discussed. A description of Cox's (n.d.) 16 recommendations to frame a faculty learning community, video production, and other relevant topics for potential implementation will also be included. The faculty learning community and its video modeling products are presented as an exemplar for interdisciplinary, cross-departmental/institutional expertise to model a positive student-centered mock IEP team.

**Chapter 3**
Enhancing Professionals' Interdisciplinary Competencies: Meeting the Needs of Children With Disabilities From Diverse Communities .................................................................................................. 42
    *L. Lynn Stansberry Brusnahan, School of Education, University of St. Thomas, USA*
    *Renee A. Hepperlen, School of Social Work, University of St. Thomas, USA*
    *Bonnie L. Ingelin, School of Education, University of St. Thomas, USA*

This chapter introduces interprofessional competencies and an assessment that can guide preparation and impact competency of interdisciplinary professionals working in special education to meet the needs of children with disabilities and families from diverse communities. Additionally, this chapter highlights examples of integrated preparation approaches that allow interdisciplinary professionals to learn about each other's discipline to advance their knowledge and skills to meet the needs of young children with disabilities from multicultural communities. These practices include: (a) virtual learning communities; (b) professional development micro credentials awarded by digital badges; (c) subject matter expert panels; and (d) combined field experiences.

**Chapter 4**
Collaborative Preparation of Special Educators and Adapted Physical Educators .............................. 65
    *Jill Anderson, California State Polytechnic University, Humboldt, USA*
    *David Adams, California State Polytechnic University, Humboldt, USA*
    *Chris Hopper, California State Polytechnic University, Humboldt, USA*
    *Melaina A. Valdez, California State Polytechnic University, Humboldt, USA*
    *Delaney Hughes, California State Polytechnic University, Humboldt, USA*
    *Kalyn Ruland, California State Polytechnic University, Humboldt, USA*

Adapted physical education (APE) is an important, but often overlooked, component of a well-rounded education experience and provides a variety of benefits for student's health, well-being, and educational achievement. Interdisciplinary teacher preparation in special education (SPED) and APE can facilitate collaborative learning and prepare preservice educators to implement high-quality holistic education and participate in multidisciplinary teams. The objective of this chapter is to provide an overview of the importance of APE within educational programming and outline strategies for interdisciplinary education. These strategies include interdisciplinary instructional and community programing and implantation of action research. Providing opportunities to engage in purposeful multidisciplinary groups in teacher preparation programs prepares students to effectively step into their future roles as educators.

**Chapter 5**
Interdisciplinary Special Education and APE Teacher Preparation Using Evidence-Based, High-Leverage Practices .................................................................................................................................. 85
    *Heather E. Taylor, California State Polytechnic University, Pomona, USA*
    *Joanne M. Van Boxtel, California State Polytechnic University, Pomona, USA*
    *Elizabeth A. Foster, West Chester University, USA*
    *Sydney A. Bueno, University of Wisconsin-Stevens Point, USA*

Preparing teachers to teach in inclusive, interdisciplinary settings is critical for teacher preparation programs if all students are to have access to general education curriculum. High-leverage practices have been proven to academically benefit students with disabilities. Using a continuous improvement cycle, the programs discussed in this chapter integrated evidence-based, high-leverage practices deliberately into special education and adapted physical education programs using an interdisciplinary approach. An audit at the program and course levels was completed and high-leverage practices and competencies were then integrated into teacher education courses where gaps were identified. Preservice teacher data was collected pre and post program to measure the effectiveness of the integration of these evidence-based practices into the programs. The steps the authors took to complete this work are detailed to be of use to other teacher preparation programs.

**Chapter 6**
Preparing a New Generation of Early Autism Educators: An Interdisciplinary Personnel
Preparation Grant ............................................................................................................................ 111
    *Marina R. Crain, University of Oregon, USA*
    *Wenjing Bao, University of Oregon, USA*
    *Miyoko Patricelli, University of Oregon, USA*
    *Stephanie Yoshiko Shire, University of Oregon, USA*

Despite young children with autism spectrum disorders (ASD) making up larger portions of early intervention caseloads and classrooms, many educators and related service providers do not receive explicit training and practical experience in supporting these students until they encounter them on caseloads. This chapter provides an example of a personnel preparation program emphasizing interdisciplinary training of early intervention (EI)/Early childhood special education (ECSE) service providers and speech-language pathologists (SLPs) to serve young children with ASD. Specifically, the chapter will discuss the Preparing a New Generation of Early Autism Educators (PANGEA) personnel preparation grant (H325K180170), funded through the Office of Special Education Programs (OSEP) at the U.S. Department of Education. Descriptions and rationales for required competencies, coursework, and practicum will be described as well as induction support. Finally, the chapter will review strengths and positive outcomes, challenges, and future directions for similar interdisciplinary grants.

**Chapter 7**
Interdisciplinary Training in Special Education and Behavior Analysis to Meet the Needs of
Students With Autism Spectrum Disorder ....................................................................................... 130
    *Kate B. LaLonde, Western Michigan University, USA*
    *Kristal E. Ehrhardt, Western Michigan University, USA*
    *Sarah Summy, Western Michigan University, USA*
    *Stephanie Peterson, Western Michigan University, USA*
    *Rena VanDerwall, Western Michigan University, USA*
    *Alan Poling, Western Michigan University, USA*

This chapter describes the value of providing interdisciplinary graduate training in special education and behavior analysis to prepare professionals to meet the high intensity needs of students with autism spectrum disorder (ASD). Within the chapter, we provide a detailed description of the development, goals, and implementation of a master's-level interdisciplinary training program. The program was developed by special education and behavior analysis faculty at Western Michigan University (WMU). Scholars admitted into the program obtained a master's degree in special education or behavior analysis and met the requirements to become a Board Certified Behavior Analyst (BCBA). Special education scholars also met the requirements for a teaching endorsement in ASD. The program was supported by a personnel preparation grant funded by the Department of Education, Office of Special Education Programs (OSEP; Ehrhardt et al., 2017) and directed by Kristal Ehrhardt.

**Chapter 8**
Autism From Multiple Perspectives: Developing Interdisciplinary Changemakers........................... 155
　*Shanna Jamanis, Nazareth College, USA*
　*Dawn Vogler-Elias, Nazareth College, USA*

Autism is the fastest-growing category for public education across the United States, however there is a continued shortage of highly qualified professionals. Supporting children with autism requires specialized knowledge and skills in evidence-based practices. Although a majority of individuals on the autism spectrum are supported by professionals from multiple disciplines, focus on autism in pre-service preparation is often developed without an interdisciplinary focus and without viewing autism through multiple lenses. This chapter shares the development, framework, multi-year outcomes, lessons learned and future direction for an interdisciplinary professional preparation program in autism. The program's conceptual framework includes disability studies, neurodiversity, and intersections with diversity, equity, and inclusion. Participants are guided to examine differing perspectives, collaborate across disciplines, and consistently reflect upon their own practice to develop the skills of reflective practitioners and changemakers in autism.

**Chapter 9**
Partners in Improving Social Communication in Children With Disabilities in Urban Early
Childhood Settings............................................................................................................................. 177
　*Ya-Chih Chang, California State University, Los Angeles, USA*
　*Jennifer B. Symon, California State University, Los Angeles, USA*
　*Mitch Fryling, California State University, Los Angeles, USA*

This present chapter describes the focus and aims of the partners in improving social communication in early childhood special education (PISCES) program at California State University, Los Angeles (Cal State LA). The chapter begins with an overview of the aims and focus of the PISCES program in general; providing an interdisciplinary and collaborative training experience to graduate students in early childhood special education and applied behavior analysis who provide services to minimally verbal children with disabilities. After describing the context of the University, the shared experiences of students in the two programs are described in detail. These shared experiences include coursework, fieldwork, and PISCES specific activities. After describing the PISCES program, the authors consider some of the lessons learned, and importantly, how some features of the PISCES program can be sustained going forward. The chapter concludes with a call for ongoing, community-based action research to further inform service provision with early childhood special education populations.

**Chapter 10**
Interdisciplinary Training for Early Childhood Special Educators and Speech Language Pathology
Candidates.......................................................................................................................................... 198
　*Lisa N. Erwin-Davidson, California State University, Fullerton, USA*
　*Aja McKee, California State University, Fullerton, USA*
　*Janice Myck-Wayne, California State University, Fullerton, USA*

This chapter informs readers of a collaborative five-year grant, project activity based communication (ABC), between the College of Education, Department of Special Education and the College of Communications, Department of Communication Sciences and Disorders. The purpose of this collaboration was to respond to the call for delivering high-quality preservice training to early childhood special educators and speech-language pathology candidates. A collaborative and cross-disciplinary approach was taken in the design of the instructional framework, the delivery of coursework, and the selection of professional development opportunities. The instructional framework is meant to prepare and educate pre-professionals on how to collaborate successfully while applying best practices of universal design for learning that support all preschoolers, with and without high-intensity needs in an inclusive preschool environment. This work is funded through a 325K personnel preparation development grant by the US Department of Education in the Office of Special Education Programs (OSEP).

### Chapter 11
A Model for the Interprofessional Preparation of Speech-Language Pathologists and School Counselors: Effectively Serving Children With Disabilities ............................................................. 219
    *Brandi L. Newkirk-Turner, Jackson State University, USA*
    *Whitney D. Perkins, Jackson State University, USA*
    *Jennifer E. Wiles, Jackson State University, USA*
    *Chaiqua A. Harris, Northwestern University, USA*

Project CALIPSO was an interdisciplinary personnel preparation project for speech-language pathology and school counseling graduate students.. A primary focus of the project was preparing scholars to serve children with communication disorders and concomitant challenges in areas such as social-emotional development and behavior. Shared coursework, collaborative clinical experiences, and other activities were used to prepare the scholars to address the needs of children with disabilities as well as design and deliver services to parents and teachers to increase the likelihood for optimal child outcomes. Through this collaborative model, scholars were guided to consider the whole child and were provided specialized opportunities to develop holistic approaches to supporting children with disabilities.

### Chapter 12
An Interdisciplinary Case-Based Approach to Preservice Interprofessional Training ...................... 237
    *Rebecca G. Lieberman-Betz, University of Georgia, USA*
    *Jennifer A. Brown, University of Georgia, USA*
    *Cynthia O. Vail, University of Geogia, USA*
    *Sarah D. Wiegand, New Mexico State University, USA*

This chapter focuses on an innovative interdisciplinary training to support preservice professionals in provision of early intervention services to young children with high-intensity needs and their families. A brief review of the literature on interprofessional education in early intervention/early childhood special education practice fields, adult learning, and case-based methods of instruction is presented. Building on that foundation, a two-year, interdisciplinary personnel preparation program is described, with specific emphasis on a two-day interprofessional training event. During the training interdisciplinary faculty and families delivered content on early intervention and used a progressing case study to allow students to apply newly learned content in interdisciplinary teams. Lessons learned and implications for future training to support interdisciplinary collaboration among professionals and families are discussed.

**Chapter 13**
Interprofessional SLP and Educator Collaboration to Improve Communication for Students With
Complex Disabilities..................................................................................................................................254
 *Erin Rotheram-Fuller, Arizona State University, USA*
 *Maria V. Dixon, Arizona State University, USA*

Students with complex disabilities require coordinated care to address communication challenges. Speech-language pathologists (SLPs) and educators are in a unique position to jointly support the communication goals of these students through interprofessional clinical practice (IPCP). Unfortunately, most professionals are not prepared during training, nor supported in professional settings, to engage in IPCP. Foundational requirements and best practices in the literature suggest that professionals need guidance, training, and ongoing institutional support to effectively collaborate. Existing interprofessional education (IPE) and IPCP models show promise in training professionals to work more effectively together before and after they enter the field, but they are not prevalent nor well-evaluated enough yet in education to draw strong conclusions. Key characteristics, strategies, and benefits of existing training and practice models for SLPs and educators are reviewed, and an applied example is presented on best practices for collaboratively implementing an AAC device.

**Chapter 14**
Exceptional Education and Language Disorders: Interdisciplinary Collaboration to Create New
Experts in Special Education ....................................................................................................................277
 *Rebecca A. Hines, University of Central Florida, USA*
 *Erika Moore, University of Central Florida, USA*
 *Danica Moise, University of Central Florida, USA*
 *Paige McCloud, University of Central Florida, USA*
 *Jacqueline Towson, University of Central Florida, USA*

With 71% of students with disabilities (SWD) eligible for speech/language services and dismal outcomes in reading for SWD, the exceptional student education program at a large Florida university created a partnership with the speech/language program to educate new practitioners who are well prepared to support SWD's language and literacy needs. This chapter describes the creation of a partnership undergraduate program at a large Florida university that prepares students for special education and language disorders. The non-certification track in the Exceptional Education Program features coursework in the School of Communication Sciences and Disorders, which is not typically available to education majors. Students graduate with an undergraduate degree in exceptional student education and a certificate in language development and disorders after the program. The authors present specific course and program components and the theoretical framework anchoring the partnership.

**Chapter 15**
Interdisciplinary Training in Intensive Intervention for Students With Disabilities and Multi-
Lingual Youth ............................................................................................................................................296
 *Kristi S. Hagans, California State University, Long Beach, USA*
 *Catherine Richards-Tutor, California State University, Long Beach, USA*

This chapter describes an interdisciplinary training project funded by OSEP to support school psychology and dual credential teacher candidates to effectively work with and provide inclusive educational supports to students with disabilities, including multilingual youth, with intensive academic needs. The authors describe the need for the project and provide an overview of the conceptual framework and training components, such as didactic and experiential learning, as well as key elements of the project, including evidence-based assessment and instruction and culturally responsive and sustaining practices. Formative and summative measures used to measure candidate outcomes are described, and preliminary results are provided.

**Chapter 16**
Preparing Pre-Service Teachers to Work With English Learners With Special Education Needs..... 318
    *Mariana Alvayero Ricklefs, Northern Illinois University, USA*

This chapter reports a mixed methods research study with preservice teachers (PSTs) enrolled in different teacher credentialing programs at a public university in the Midwestern United States. The purpose of the study is twofold: to explore PSTs' self-efficacy and outcome expectancy beliefs to teach and assess English Learners with special education needs and to explore the relationship between PSTs' self-efficacy and outcome expectancy beliefs and with demographic and experiential factors. The findings of the study demonstrate that most PSTs did not feel capable or prepared to teach and assess English Learners with disabilities. The chapter ends with implications for collaborative teacher education and research.

**Chapter 17**
Interdisciplinary Preparation to Meet the Emotional and Behavioral Health Needs of Diverse Students.................................................................................................................................................. 342
    *Sara Kupzyk, University of Nebraska, Omaha, USA*
    *Philip D. Nordness, University of Nebraska, Omaha, USA*

Although interdisciplinary teaming within a multi-tiered system of support is valuable, barriers to collaboration exist among professionals because of competing standards, lack of understanding roles, and lack of common language. These challenges may relate to how pre-service training is arranged. Training is usually provided in separate programs with little overlap in courses and field experiences. Interprofessional education (IPE) is a potential means of addressing the siloed approach. The goal of this chapter is to describe an IPE preparation program designed to develop scholars to meet the emotional and behavioral health needs of diverse students. Participating scholars complete a plan of study that includes shared coursework and courses that are unique to their field, participate in a weekly professional seminar, and take part in an interdisciplinary practicum experience. The authors also offer recommendations for university programs seeking to create interdisciplinary opportunities for pre-service professionals.

**Chapter 18**
Interdisciplinary Special Educator and School Counselor Preparation: Supporting Equitable
Student Outcomes in the COVID-19 Era....................................................................................... 359
    *Kristin M. Murphy, University of Massachusetts, Boston, USA*
    *Laura Hayden, University of Massachusetts, Boston, USA*
    *Amy Cook, University of Massachusetts, Boston, USA*
    *Christopher Denning, University of Massachusetts, Boston, USA*
    *Angi Stone-MacDonald, California State University, San Bernadino, USA*

The purpose of this chapter is to provide readers with a rationale and blueprint for interdisciplinary programs like Project TLC, which prepare preservice special educators alongside school adjustment counselors. First, the authors discuss the rationale for Project TLC, including the current state of

K-12 student mental health and social emotional learning, particularly in the context of public health and racial pandemics and issues pertaining to personnel shortages and attrition in both teaching and counseling. Then, the authors outline the blueprint of an interdisciplinary program including strategies for recruitment and retention of diverse students and a plan for shared coursework, fieldwork, and other learning opportunities that buoy graduate student development and preparation for serving students as collaborative colleagues. Throughout, the authors present the Project TLC blueprint with considerations for how this interdisciplinary training approach that utilizes faculty expertise and partnerships within local school communities can be translated into other communities.

**Chapter 19**
Collaborative Preparation in Equity-Based Practices to Support Minoritized Students With High-Intensity Needs.................................................................................................................................. 374
    *Elizabeth D. Cramer, Florida International University, USA*
    *Andy V. Pham, Florida International University, USA*
    *Liana Gonzalez, Florida International University, USA*
    *Rosalia F. Gallo, Florida International University, USA*
    *Ana Paula Fabian Freire, Florida International University, USA*

The purpose of this chapter is to provide an overview of the development and implementation of a currently running, interdisciplinary program between school psychology and special education within a Hispanic-serving institution. Due to critical shortages of school psychologists and special educators across the country, novel practices in interdisciplinary collaborative training may aid in recruitment and retention efforts while enhancing service delivery for racially, ethnically, and linguistically diverse (RELD) students with high intensity needs. The chapter highlights approaches and components including (1) focus on an equity-based and integrated framework for personnel preparation, (2) recruitment and retention activities to attract diverse scholars, (3) planning and delivery of shared collaborative coursework and field experiences, (4) reflection of the lessons learned, and (5) recommendations to other preparation programs in providing interdisciplinary training and support to RELD personnel.

**Chapter 20**
Interdisciplinary Support Teams to Enhance Social Emotional and Behavioral Outcomes for Students With Disabilities: Project BEAMS ................................................................................... 396
    *Katina M. Lambros, San Diego State University, USA*
    *Bonnie Kraemer, San Diego State University, USA*
    *Jennica L. Paz, San Diego State University, USA*
    *Teresa Tran, San Diego State University, USA*
    *Jasmine Kaur Lehal, San Diego State University, USA*

This chapter highlights Project BEAMS (Behavioral Emotional and Mental Health Supports in Schools), an interdisciplinary personnel preparation program at San Diego State University. Project BEAMS is a five-year training grant funded by the Office of Special Education Programs (OSEP) to improve the preparation of school psychologists (SP) and special educators (SE) to deliver intensive, yet coordinated, interventions to address behavior and mental health. This chapter describes the training components and collaborative learning activities (e.g., core research-based courses, monthly project seminars, clinical practicum, summer institutes, and co-attendance at research conferences) that enable special educators and school psychologists to form teams that enhance academic, social-emotional, and behavioral outcomes for students with disabilities.

**Chapter 21**
Creating and Sustaining Collaborative Professional Development in Special Education: Lessons
From the Interdisciplinary Training Project in Special Education and School Psychology (SP2)..... 420
    *Seth A. King, University of Iowa, USA*
    *Ann Marie Santos, University of Iowa, USA*
    *Matthew J. O'Brien, University of Iowa, USA*
    *Allison L. Bruhn, University of Iowa, USA*
    *Shawn Datchuk, University of Iowa, USA*

Shortages in personnel qualified to address the academic, behavioral, and mental health needs of people with disabilities are well documented. The limited interdisciplinary training professionals in special education and related disciplines receive greatly exacerbates the challenges faced by exceptional populations, particularly in regions that have historically struggled to provide sufficient access to special education services. This chapter describes the Interdisciplinary Training Project in Special Education and School Psychology (SP2), a federally funded, interdisciplinary program that combines elements of the School Psychology, Special Education, and Applied Behavior Analysis programs at the University of Iowa. Specific sections describe the national and state-level context supporting the development of SP2, identify the components designed to promote interdisciplinary knowledge and competence, and delineate challenges associated with creating and maintaining interdisciplinary programs.

**Chapter 22**
Lessons Learned: Equipping Interdisciplinary Scholars to Provide a Continuum of Mental and
Behavioral Health Supports ..................................................................................................................... 440
    *R. Lanai Jennings, Marshall University, USA*
    *Sandra S. Stroebel, Marshall University, USA*

This chapter outlines important lessons learned while implementing Marshall University's interdisciplinary personnel development program. Motivated by the intense needs of youth with disabilities in Appalachia and the shortage of qualified personnel to address these needs, the program employed evidence-based models to train school counselors, school psychologists, and special educators. Factors found to be essential include finding evidence-based interventions appropriate for all disciplines, early intense training, while acknowledging differences in entry skills and knowledge of interdisciplinary scholars, exposing scholars to a continuum of tiered school-based supports including working together across disciplines, modeling and attending to self-care of scholars, and acquiring partnerships for sustainability. These factors were important in successfully training the scholars to provide services to children with intensely complex social, emotional, and behavioral needs. Also included are suggestions for improving training based on the authors' reflections and feedback from scholars.

**Chapter 23**
Social Emotional Development and Early Childhood Mental Health: Special Education and Social
Work Collaboration ................................................................................................................................. 468
    *Maryssa Kucskar Mitsch, San Francisco State University, USA*
    *Brett Collins, San Francisco State University, USA*
    *Amber Friesen, San Francisco State University, USA*
    *Jocelyn Clare Reyno Hermoso, San Francisco State University, USA*

This chapter describes Project Adversity and Resiliency Interventions for Social Emotional Development in Early Childhood (Project ARISE), a preservice interdisciplinary training for early childhood special education (ECSE) and social workers (SW) to support young children and their families with high-intensity social emotional needs who require early childhood mental health support (ECMH) through collaborative and inclusive services. One key to understanding why many young children continue to be excluded from inclusive settings is understanding the differences between disciplines, as well as systemic inequities. To address these challenges, the program honors a holistic and interrelated development approach within the tenets of ECMH. This chapter begins with an overview of the program's essential theoretical frameworks. Then, the chapter shares key elements that define the program. Finally, the chapter shares reflections and next steps for interdisciplinary programmatic development.

**Chapter 24**
Introducing a Collaborative Training Program for Special Educators and School Social Workers ... 495
    *John Elwood Romig, University of Texas at Arlington, USA*
    *Ambra L. Green, University of Texas at Arlington, USA*
    *Jandel Crutchfield, University of Texas at Arlington, USA*

This chapter introduces Project Match Made in Schools (Project MMS). Project MMS is funded by a H325K grant from the U.S. Department of Education, Office of Special Education Programs. The project provides interdisciplinary training for special educators and social workers. Scholars in the special education program pursue initial teacher licensure in special education. Special education and social work scholars share six hours of coursework, are paired together for field experiences, and participate in interdisciplinary research apprenticeships. This chapter describes the components of Project MMS and highlights some challenges and successes the project personnel have experienced.

**Chapter 25**
Teaming for Transition: A Model for Interdisciplinary, Collaborative Preparation of Secondary Education Professionals .................................................................................................................. 505
    *Suzanne Kucharczyk, University of Arkansas, USA*
    *Kimberly Frazier, University of Arkansas, USA*
    *Tameeka Hunter, Florida International University, USA*
    *Kristi L. Perryman, University of Arkansas, USA*
    *Johanna Thomas, University of Arkansas, USA*
    *Renee Speight, University of Arkansas, USA*
    *Ed Bengtson, University of Arkansas, USA*

This chapter, developed by faculty who self-organized as an interdisciplinary, collaborative team in the implementation of these two 325K projects, Teaming for Transition, funded at the University of Arkansas, describes a shared, core focus to better prepare professionals to support youth with disabilities in transition to adulthood. The authors share how across disciplines of Special Education, Communication Disorders, Vocational Rehabilitation, School Counseling, Social Work, and School Administration, the projects Teaming for Transition and Teaming for Transition – Preparing Youth for Work and Community have been designed and implemented around a shared framework, using innovative online learning technologies, with an inquiry-based approach to understanding the challenges of transition for youth in Arkansas and beyond. They share lessons learned and implications for faculty seeking to de-silo across programs, colleges, and disciplines.

### Chapter 26
A Model for Interdisciplinary Preparation in Culturally-Responsive, Evidence-Based Transition Planning .................................................................................................................................. 526

*Kristin Powers, California State University, Long Beach, USA*
*Edwin Achola, California State University, Long Beach, USA*

Over the past seven years, we have provided intensive training to cohorts of school psychology and special education graduate students. Through rigorous shared coursework, in-person and virtual learning, coordinated school-based fieldwork, and enhanced study (conference attendance, seminar participation, case study completions) scholars gained the skills to establish and sustain culturally responsive, evidence-based transition services for students with disabilities, including those high-intensity needs. This chapter describes the steps the co-authors took to enhance the training and service delivery of school psychologists and special education teachers to provide effective transition services.

**Compilation of References** ............................................................................................................ 545

**About the Contributors** ................................................................................................................. 631

**Index** ............................................................................................................................................... 652

# Preface

## OVERVIEW AND DESCRIPTION

Today's K-12 classrooms are more inclusive and diverse than ever before with the majority of students with disabilities (SWDs) spending 80% or more of their day in a general education setting (USDOE, 2022). Educators are not alone when working with students with disabilities. They have the support of a team of professionals, and they can tap into that support to better serve student's academic, behavioral, and social/emotional needs. Researchers and scholars focused on inclusive and equitable education continue to point to the need for interdisciplinary models of collaboration across the field, including within preparation (e.g., McLeskey et al., 2017; Ronfeldt et al., 2015). Research, development, and implementation of interdisciplinary models and practices improve the delivery of content, supports, and services to all students, especially those with disabilities, and advance the cause of equitable education. To further the ability of professionals to collaborate effectively and support the varying challenges faced by students with high-intensity needs HIN, educator preparation programs can be redesigned and re-envisioned to be more collaborative. Interdisciplinary preparation ensures educators enter the field or further their professional learning ready to support students through intentional collaboration. The collection of chapters in this book affords readers a valuable resource for engaging in this type of preparation program development and enhancement through theories, frameworks, program structures, and practices.

Multiple professionals are involved in the development and implementation of academic and behavioral supports for students with disabilities and HIN. In this way, the pool of stakeholders connected to enhancing special education reaches far beyond the special education teacher. The chapters in this book present and discuss theory, research, and practice related to the preparation of personnel from multiple fields within interdisciplinary models to advance and enhance education for students with disabilities and HIN. Chapter authors have backgrounds in a range of professions and contexts related to special education and contribute their diverse perspectives and experiences to the book. In collaborating to improve the education and services provided to students with disabilities, each professional involved in the interdisciplinary team brings their own field perspectives, expertise, and strengths. Leveraging these assets as resources catalyzes more comprehensive and targeted practices in educating and supporting students with disabilities. Each chapter in this book also includes discussion about how interdisciplinary preparation practices can be a lever for enhancing educational equity related to disability and the additional intersecting identities of students across cultural, linguistic, and economic diversity. This book serves as a collection of valuable perspectives, practices, experiences, outcomes, and lessons-learned in interdisciplinary preparation, which can move the field forward through innovation and the advancement of equity in education.

Preface

## BOOK'S PURPOSE AND USES

A key goal for this edited book is to support the development of professional preparation practices that are collaborative, interdisciplinary, and sustainable. As such, the reach of this work extends across fields and from pre-service to professional through the career span. The interdisciplinary focus of this work creates appeal and value for a wide range of personnel involved in undergraduate/graduate level professional preparation in universities/colleges, districts, and alternative educator certification programs. This includes special education and general education, educational leadership and administration preparation, and preparation personnel in the fields of school psychology, social work, school counseling, physical education, early childhood, English as a Second Language, speech-language pathology, occupational therapy, and physical therapy. The chapters in this book also support in-service professional learning for all related professions as efforts are made to develop and sustain interdisciplinary collaboration within schools.

## ORGANIZATION OF THE BOOK

This book is organized into 26 chapters.

### Chapter 1: Supporting Children With High-Intensity Needs Through Interdisciplinary Personnel Preparation

Yaoying Xu, Alison King, Sarah Kye Price, Christine M. Spence, Serra De Arment, Bergen B. Nelson, Maris Wyatt, Dana Yarbrough, Seb M. Prohn

This chapter addresses potential challenges and opportunities of developing innovative programs in interdisciplinary personnel preparation in special education and related services. The mission of this chapter is to advocate for an interdisciplinary personnel preparation model in special education and related services, particularly for serving young children with significant disabilities and their families from high-need communities.

### Chapter 2: Interdisciplinary Pre-Service Professional Preparation Through Video Modeling

Suzannah B. Chatlos, Emily Hoeh, Michelle L. Bonati, Maureen E. Squires

The authors' faculty learning community provides a model to emanate the skills, knowledge, and dispositions of a high-functioning collaborative team expected from pre-service professionals through a mock Individualized Education Program (IEP) team video series. A description of Cox's (n.d.) 16 recommendations to frame a faculty learning community, video production, and other relevant topics for potential implementation is also included.

### Chapter 3: Enhancing Professionals' Interdisciplinary Competencies – Meeting the Needs of Children With Disabilities From Diverse Communities

L. Lynn Stansberry Brusnahan, Renee A. Hepperlen, Bonnie L. Ingelin

This chapter introduces interprofessional competencies and an assessment that can guide preparation and impact competency of interdisciplinary professionals working in special education to meet the needs of children with disabilities and families from diverse communities. Additionally, this chapter highlights examples of integrated preparation approaches that allow interdisciplinary professionals to learn about each other's discipline to advance their knowledge and skills to meet the needs of young children with disabilities from multicultural communities.

## Chapter 4: Collaborative Preparation of Special Educators and Adapted Physical Educators

Jill Anderson, David Adams, Chris Hopper, Melaina A. Valdez, Delaney Hughes, Kalyn Ruland

Adapted physical education (APE) is an important, but often overlooked, component of a well-rounded education experience and provides a variety of benefits for student's health, well-being, and educational achievement. Interdisciplinary teacher preparation in special education (SPED) and APE can facilitate collaborative learning and prepare preservice educators to implement high-quality holistic education and participate in multidisciplinary teams. The objective of this chapter is to provide an overview of the importance of APE within educational programming and outline strategies for interdisciplinary education.

## Chapter 5: Interdisciplinary Special Education and APE Teacher Preparation Using Evidence-Based, High-Leverage Practices

Heather E. Taylor, Joanne M. Van Boxtel, Elizabeth A. Foster, Sydney A. Bueno

Using a continuous improvement cycle, the programs discussed in this chapter integrated evidence-based, high-leverage practices deliberately into special education and adapted physical education programs using an interdisciplinary approach. An audit at the program and course levels was completed and high-leverage practices and competencies were then integrated into teacher education courses where gaps were identified. Preservice teacher data was collected pre and post program to measure the effectiveness of the integration of these evidence-based practices into the programs.

## Chapter 6: Preparing a New Generation of Early Autism Educators – An Interdisciplinary Personnel Preparation Grant

Marina R. Crain, Wenjing Bao, Miyoko Patricelli, Stephanie Yoshiko Shire

This chapter provides an example of a personnel preparation program emphasizing interdisciplinary training of Early Intervention (EI)/Early Childhood Special Education (ECSE) service providers and Speech-Language Pathologists (SLPs) to serve young children with ASD. Descriptions and rationales for required competencies, coursework, and practicum will be described as well as induction support. Finally, the chapter will review strengths and positive outcomes, challenges, and future directions for similar interdisciplinary grants.

## Chapter 7: Interdisciplinary Training in Special Education and Behavior Analysis to Meet the Needs of Students With Autism Spectrum Disorder

Kate B. LaLonde, Kristal E. Ehrhardt, Sarah Summy, Stephanie Peterson, Rena VanDerwall, Alan Poling

## Preface

This chapter describes the value of providing interdisciplinary graduate training in special education and behavior analysis to prepare professionals to meet the high intensity needs of students with autism spectrum disorder (ASD). Within the chapter, we provide a detailed description of the development, goals, and implementation of a master's-level interdisciplinary training program. The program was developed by special education and behavior analysis faculty at Western Michigan University (WMU).

### Chapter 8: Autism From Multiple Perspectives – Developing Interdisciplinary Changemakers

Shanna Jamanis, Dawn Vogler-Elias

This chapter shares the development, framework, multi-year outcomes, lessons learned and future direction for an interdisciplinary professional preparation in autism. The program's conceptual framework includes disability studies, neurodiversity, and intersections with diversity, equity, and inclusion. Participants are guided to examine differing perspectives, collaborate across disciplines, and consistently reflect upon their own practice to develop the skills of reflective practitioners and changemakers in autism.

### Chapter 9: Partners in Improving Social Communication in Children With Disabilities in Urban Early Childhood Settings

Ya-Chih Chang, Jennifer B. Symon, Mitch Fryling

This chapter describes the focus and aims of the PISCES program which provides an interdisciplinary and collaborative training experience to graduate students in Early Childhood Special Education and Applied Behavior Analysis who provide services to minimally verbal children with disabilities. The authors discuss some of the lessons learned, and importantly, how some features of the PISCES program can be sustained going forward. The chapter concludes with a call for ongoing, community-based action research to further inform service provision with early childhood special education populations.

### Chapter 10: Interdisciplinary Training for Early Childhood Special Educators and Speech Language Pathology Candidates

Lisa N. Erwin-Davidson, Aja McKee, Janice Myck-Wayne

A collaborative and cross-disciplinary approach was taken in the design of the instructional framework, delivery of coursework, and selection of professional development opportunities for a high-quality preservice training to Early Childhood Special Educators and Speech-Language Pathology candidates. The instructional framework is meant to prepare and educate pre-professionals on how to collaborate successfully while applying best practices of Universal Design for Learning that support all preschoolers, with and without high-intensity needs in an inclusive preschool environment.

### Chapter 11: A Model for the Interprofessional Preparation of Speech-Language Pathologists and School Counselors – Effectively Serving Children With Disabilities

Brandi L. Newkirk-Turner, Whitney D. Perkins, Jennifer E. Wiles, Chaiqua A. Harris

Project CALIPSO was an interdisciplinary personnel preparation project for speech-language pathology and school counseling graduate students. A primary focus of the project was preparing scholars to serve children with communication disorders and concomitant challenges in areas such as social-emotional development and behavior. Through this collaborative model, scholars were guided to consider the whole child and were provided specialized opportunities to develop holistic approaches to supporting children with disabilities.

## Chapter 12: An Interdisciplinary Case-Based Approach to Preservice Interprofessional Training

Rebecca G. Lieberman-Betz, Jennifer A. Brown, Cynthia O. Vail, Sarah D. Wiegand

This chapter focuses on an innovative interdisciplinary training to support preservice professionals in provision of early intervention services to young children with high-intensity needs and their families. A two-year, interdisciplinary personnel preparation program is described, with specific emphasis on a two-day interprofessional training event. During the training interdisciplinary faculty and families delivered content on early intervention and used a progressing case study to allow students to apply newly learned content in interdisciplinary teams.

## Chapter 13: Interprofessional SLP and Educator Collaboration to Improve Communication for Students With Complex Disabilities

Erin Rotheram-Fuller, Maria V. Dixon

Speech-language pathologists (SLPs) and educators are in a unique position to jointly support the communication goals of these students through Interprofessional Clinical Practice (IPCP). This chapter presents key characteristics, strategies, and benefits of existing training and practice models for SLPs and educators are reviewed, and an applied example is presented on best practices for collaboratively implementing an AAC device.

## Chapter 14: Exceptional Education and Language Disorders – Interdisciplinary Collaboration to Create New Experts in Special Education

Rebecca A. Hines, Erika Moore, Danica Moise, Paige McCloud, Jacqueline Towson

This chapter describes the creation of a partnership undergraduate program at a large Florida university that prepares students for special education and language disorders. The non-certification track in the Exceptional Education Program features coursework in the School of Communication Sciences and Disorders. Students graduate with an undergraduate degree in exceptional student education and a certificate in language development and disorders after the program. The authors present specific course and program components and the theoretical framework anchoring the partnership.

## Chapter 15: Interdisciplinary Training in Intensive Intervention for Students With Disabilities and Multi-lingual Youth

Kristi Hagans, Catherine Richards-Tutor

Preface

This chapter describes an interdisciplinary training project funded by OSEP to support school psychology and dual credential teacher candidates to effectively work with and provide inclusive educational supports to students with disabilities, including multilingual youth, with intensive academic needs. The authors discuss the need for the project, provide an overview of the conceptual framework and training components, and highlight key elements of the project, including evidence-based assessment and instruction, and culturally responsive and sustaining practices.

## Chapter 16: Preparing Pre-Service Teachers to Work With English Learners With Special Education Needs

Mariana Alvayero Ricklefs

This chapter reports a mixed methods research study with preservice teachers (PSTs) enrolled in different teacher credentialing programs at a public university in the Midwestern United States. The purpose of the study is twofold: to explore PSTs' self-efficacy and outcome expectancy beliefs to teach and assess English Learners with special education needs, and to explore the relationship between PSTs' self-efficacy and outcome expectancy beliefs, and with demographic and experiential factors.

## Chapter 17: Interdisciplinary Preparation to Meet the Emotional and Behavioral Health Needs of Diverse Students

Sara Kupzyk, Philip D. Nordness

The goal of this chapter is to describe an interprofessional education (IPE) program designed to develop scholars to meet the emotional and behavioral health needs of diverse students. Participating scholars complete a plan of study that includes shared coursework and courses that are unique to their field, participate in a weekly professional seminar, and take part in an interdisciplinary practicum experience. The authors also offer recommendations for university programs seeking to create interdisciplinary opportunities for pre-service professionals.

## Chapter 18: Interdisciplinary Special Educator and School Counselor Preparation – Supporting Equitable Student Outcomes in the COVID-19 Era

Kristin M. Murphy, Laura Hayden, Amy Cook, Christopher Denning, Angi Stone-MacDonald

The purpose of this chapter is to provide readers with a rationale and blueprint for interdisciplinary programs like Project TLC, which prepares preservice special educators alongside school adjustment counselors. Throughout, the authors present the Project TLC blueprint with considerations for how this interdisciplinary training approach that utilizes faculty expertise and partnerships within local school communities can be translated into other communities.

## Chapter 19: Collaborative Preparation in Equity-Based Practices to Support Minoritized Students With High-Intensity Needs

Elizabeth D. Cramer, Andy V. Pham, Liana Gonzalez, Rosalia F. Gallo, Ana Paula Fabian Freire

The purpose of this chapter is to provide an overview of the development and implementation of a currently running, interdisciplinary program between school psychology and special education within a Hispanic-Serving Institution. The chapter highlights approaches and components including: (1) focus on an equity-based and integrated framework for personnel preparation, (2) recruitment and retention activities to attract diverse scholars, (3) planning and delivery of shared collaborative coursework and field experiences, (4) reflection of the lessons learned, and (5) recommendations to other preparation programs in providing interdisciplinary training and support to racially, ethnically, and linguistically diverse personnel.

## Chapter 20: Interdisciplinary Support Teams to Enhance Social Emotional and Behavioral Outcomes for Students With Disabilities – Project BEAMS

Katina M. Lambros, Bonnie Kraemer, Jennica L. Paz, Teresa Tran, Jasmine Kaur Lehal

This chapter highlights an interdisciplinary personnel preparation program at San Diego State University to improve the preparation of school psychologists (SP) and special educators (SE) to deliver intensive, yet coordinated, interventions to address behavior and mental health. The authors describe the training components and collaborative learning activities that enable special educators and school psychologists to form teams that enhance academic, social-emotional, and behavioral outcomes for students with disabilities.

## Chapter 21: Creating and Sustaining Collaborative Professional Development in Special Education – Lessons From the Interdisciplinary Training Project in Special Education and School Psychology (SP2)

Seth A. King, Ann Marie Santos, Matthew J. O'Brien, Allison L. Bruhn, Shawn Datchuk

This chapter describes an interdisciplinary training project in special education and school psychology (SP2) that combines elements of the School Psychology, Special Education, and Applied Behavior Analysis programs at the University of Iowa. Specific sections describe the national and state-level context supporting the development of SP2, identify the components designed to promote interdisciplinary knowledge and competence, and delineate challenges associated with creating and maintaining interdisciplinary programs.

## Chapter 22: Lessons Learned – Equipping Interdisciplinary Scholars to Provide a Continuum of Mental and Behavioral Health Supports

R. Lanai Jennings, Sandra S. Stroebel

This chapter outlines important lessons learned while implementing Marshall University's interdisciplinary personnel development program. The program employed evidence-based models to train school counselors, school psychologists, and special educators. Factors important to successfully training the scholars to provide services to children with intensely complex social, emotional, and behavioral needs are discussed. Also included are suggestions for improving training based on the authors' reflections and feedback from scholars.

*Preface*

## Chapter 23: Social Emotional Development and Early Childhood Mental Health – Special Education and Social Work Collaboration

Maryssa Kucskar Mitsch, Brett Collins, Amber Friesen, Jocelyn Clare Reyno Hermoso

This chapter describes a preservice interdisciplinary training program for early childhood special education (ECSE) and social workers (SW) to support young children and their families with high-intensity social emotional needs who require early childhood mental health support (ECMH) through collaborative and inclusive services. The program honors a holistic and interrelated development approach within the tenets of ECMH. The chapter shares the program's essential theoretical frameworks, key elements that define the program, and reflections and next steps for interdisciplinary programmatic development.

## Chapter 24: Introducing a Collaborative Training Program for Special Educators and School Social Workers

John Elwood Romig, Ambra L. Green, Jandel Crutchfield

This chapter introduces Project Match Made in Schools (Project MMS) which provides interdisciplinary training for special educators and social workers. Scholars in the special education program pursue initial teacher licensure in special education. Special education and social work scholars share six hours of coursework, are paired together for field experiences, and participate in interdisciplinary research apprenticeships. This chapter describes the components of Project MMS and highlights some challenges and success the project personnel have experienced.

## Chapter 25: Teaming for Transition – A Model for Interdisciplinary, Collaborative Preparation of Secondary Education Professionals

Suzanne Kucharczyk, Kimberly Frazier, Tameeka Hunter, Kristi L. Perryman, Johanna Thomas, Renee Speight, Ed Bengtson

This chapter describes the implementation of two interdisciplinary preparation programs at the University of Arkansas with a shared focus on preparing professionals to support youth with disabilities in transition to adulthood. The project works across disciplines of Special Education, Communication Disorders, Vocational Rehabilitation, School Counseling, Social Work, and School Administration using innovative online learning technologies with an inquiry-based approach to understand the challenges of transition for youth in Arkansas and beyond. The authors share lessons learned and implications for faculty seeking to de-silo across programs, colleges, and disciplines.

## Chapter 26: A Model for Interdisciplinary Preparation in Culturally-Responsive, Evidence-Based Transition Planning

Kristin Powers, Edwin Achola

Over the past seven years, we have provided intensive training to cohorts of school psychology and special education graduate students. This chapter describes the steps the co-authors took to enhance the training and service delivery of school psychologists and special education teachers to provide effective transition services.

*Handbook of Research on Interdisciplinary Preparation for Equitable Special Education* is one of the first edited books to focus on the interdisciplinary and interprofessional preparation of special educators, administrators, general educators, and related service personnel. As such, this text provides researchers and educators with evidence and exemplars which can be used to build or enhance their own preparation programming to be collaborative, interdisciplinary, and interprofessional. The book editors are proud to facilitate the sharing of expertise, research, and experiences from scholars, researchers, and teacher/professional educators involved in interdisciplinary professional preparation, including several programs funded by the U.S. Office of Special Education Programs (OSEP). The concept and contents of this publication illustrate the importance of collaboration across disciplines to enhance the knowledge, skills, and dispositions of education professionals as they enter the field to improve outcomes for *all* students, including those with disabilities. Both the contributing authors and the editors hope this work serves as an impetus for continuing conversation, collaboration, and innovation to enhance educational equity.

*Dena D. Slanda*
*University of Central Florida, USA*

*Lindsey Pike*
*University of Central Florida, USA*

## REFERENCES

McLeskey, J., Barringer, M.-D., Billingsley, B., Brownell, M., Jackson, D., Kennedy, M., Lewis, T., Maheady, L., Rodriguez, J., Scheeler, M. C., Winn, J., & Ziegler, D. (2017). *High-leverage practices in special education.* Council for Exceptional Children and CEEDAR Center.

Ronfeldt, M., Farmer, S. O., McQueen, K., & Grissom, J. A. (2015). Teacher collaboration in instructional teams and student achievement. *American Educational Research Journal, 52*(3), 475–514. doi:10.3102/0002831215585562

U.S. Department of Education. (2022). *43rd annual report to Congress on the implementation of the Individuals with Disabilities Education Act, 2021.* https://sites.ed.gov/idea/files/43rd-arc-for-idea.pdf

# Chapter 1
# Supporting Children With High-Intensity Needs Through Interdisciplinary Personnel Preparation

**Yaoying Xu**
Virginia Commonwealth University, USA

**Alison King**
https://orcid.org/0000-0002-9879-6590
Longwood University, USA

**Sarah Kye Price**
Virginia Commonwealth University, USA

**Christine M. Spence**
https://orcid.org/0000-0002-6158-7082
Virginia Commonwealth University, USA

**Serra De Arment**
https://orcid.org/0000-0001-7752-7108
Virginia Commonwealth University, USA

**Bergen B. Nelson**
Virginia Commonwealth University, USA

**Maris Wyatt**
https://orcid.org/0000-0003-3551-3810
Virginia Commonwealth University, USA

**Dana Yarbrough**
Virginia Commonwealth University, USA

**Seb M. Prohn**
Virginia Commonwealth University, USA

## ABSTRACT

*This chapter addresses potential challenges and opportunities of developing innovative programs in interdisciplinary personnel preparation in special education and related services. The mission of this chapter is to advocate for an interdisciplinary personnel preparation model in special education and related services, particularly for serving young children with significant disabilities and their families from high-need communities. First, an interdisciplinary conceptual framework that guides the model is illustrated. Second, the authors demonstrate essential components of the model with evidence and highlight the features of the model. Finally, three program examples of the model are presented to provide evidence-based strategies for serving children with high-intensity needs and their families. The chapter concludes with recommendations for future directions.*

DOI: 10.4018/978-1-6684-6438-0.ch001

## INTRODUCTION

The rationale for interdisciplinary personnel preparation is supported by the literature and practice. In the field of special education, effective team collaboration is an essential feature of the Individuals with Disabilities Education Act (IDEA) that is well described in the educational literature (Bruder et al., 2019; Dettmer et al., 2009; Friend & Cook, 2010; Snell & Janney, 2005; Stayton, 2015) and early intervention/early childhood special education (EI/ECSE) standards (Division for Early Childhood of the Council for Exceptional Children, 2020), as well as clinical guidelines (Adams et al., 2013). Several studies established empirical support for the role of collaboration in promoting exemplary schools, increased parent involvement, increased student inclusion and mental health support, and improved child outcomes (Frauenholtz et al., 2017; Hunt et al., 2004; McLaughlin, 2002; Sandall et al., 2009; Shannon & Bylsma, 2004). In the field of EI/ECSE, interdisciplinary personnel preparation is especially critical because programs and services for young children with disabilities or developmental delays, by their nature, almost always involve a team representing different disciplines in addition to the child's primary caregivers (DEC Recommended Practices, 2014). The National Research Panel on Preschool Education found comparable results in terms of teacher education effects on young children's development and learning (National Research Council, 2001). Yet, there remains a critical shortage of EI/ECSE personnel qualified to provide services for young children with disabilities and children who experience emotional difficulties.

There is an identified need for individuals who are well prepared in their professions yet who are also uniquely prepared to engage diverse knowledge, skills, and dispositions of professionals through an interdisciplinary lens (Coiro et al, 2016; Pfeiffer et al., 2019; Weiss et al., 2020). Individuals who are educated using an interdisciplinary framework are more likely to incorporate multiple perspectives when developing, implementing, and evaluating potential interventions (Coiro et al, 2016; Pfeiffer et al., 2019). Pfeiffer et al. (2019) demonstrated that interprofessional education leads to interprofessional practice. National survey results found that prior training in collaboration was a predictor of engaging in interprofessional practice during the development and implementation of special education services (Pfeiffer et al., 2019).

Given the needs for interdisciplinary preparation in special education and related services, particularly related to EI/ECSE, in this chapter we discuss and demonstrate an interdisciplinary personnel preparation model that involves multiple disciplines, including special education, social work, physical therapy, speech-language pathology, occupational therapy, and medicine. Three objectives for the interdisciplinary preparation are addressed: (1) To improve the quality of personnel working with young children with high-intensity needs; (2) To increase the knowledge, skills, and dispositions of pre-service professionals in evidence-based strategic interprofessional practices; and (3) To promote cultural humility and cultural competence to better support the diverse needs of children with disabilities and their families.

## CHALLENGES

The challenge remains that the individuals on interdisciplinary teams vary in regard to their educational background, clinical experiences, knowledge of the roles and responsibilities of other professionals on the team, and level of confidence in implementing strategies on how to effectively collaborate when providing support to students and families (Jane-Griffiths et al., 2020; Wallace et al., 2020). Despite the increase in research surrounding the benefits of interdisciplinary collaboration, pre-service programs continue to provide minimal content on how to develop and maintain partnerships (Almendingen et al, 2021). Thus, upon entry into the field, professionals reported a lack of knowledge and confidence in regard to the appropriate steps on how to develop and maintain interdisciplinary collaborative partnerships (Archibald, 2017; Da Fonte & Barton-Arwood, 2017). Additionally, once they enter the field, professionals continue to face persistent systemic barriers within school systems that impede their ability to collaborate (Archibald, 2017; Da Fonte & Barton-Arwood, 2017; Wallace et al., 2020). It is critical for pre-service programs to imbed programs, courses, and experiences to prepare pre-service personnel using interdisciplinary modes of instruction because interprofessional collaboration is essential to the success of children and students who receive special education services, and interprofessional collaboration requires skills and practice.

Interdisciplinary collaboration is a recommended practice for infants and young children with disabilities, and ensuring special education services delivered in least restrictive environments requires effective teamwork to support desired outcomes for young children with disabilities, including those with high-intensity needs (Odom et al., 2004). It is challenging to provide high-quality services to children with severe medical, behavioral, and emotional disabilities (Chen et al., 2009). Providing high quality services means learning when and how to rely on both disciplinary and shared interdisciplinary expertise.

COVID-19 created additional unexpected challenges as well as opportunities for developing innovative programs. There is no doubt COVID-19 will have long-term impact on young children, particularly children with disabilities and with emotional or behavioral difficulties and their families. It takes coordinated and collaborative efforts from all aspects of the society to provide positive and effective intervention services to mitigate the risk for mental health issues of these children (Hoagwood & Kelleher, 2020). Now, more than ever, it is imperative to consider the most effective, interdisciplinary models of service and support.

## BENEFITS

Applying intensive intervention approaches within EI and ECSE services further optimizes opportunities to achieve the greatest impact on developmental outcomes for young children with high-intensity needs. However, research and the expressed needs of professionals indicate that EI/ECSE personnel are not fully prepared to meet the needs of young children such as those with autism, motor development challenges, and significant emotional and behavioral or mental health difficulties (Hemmeter, et al., 2016; Lerman et al., 2004; Osofsky & Lieberman, 2011). As more young children with significant disabilities are included with their typically developing peers in natural learning environments and inclusive programs, EI/ECSE professionals and related services providers need to work directly with a child and the child's family across settings. They also learn to teach in diverse community contexts through systematic supervision linked to the curriculum and focused instruction on intensive and individualized interventions for young children with significant disabilities or children who experience emotional difficulties.

Individuals working in early childhood must understand social and emotional development for young children, attachment, adverse childhood experiences, toxic stress, resilience, trauma, the impact of social-emotional difficulties, and strategies to support mental health (Hemmeter et al., 2021; Klawetter & Frankel, 2018; Sciaraffa et al., 2018; Shonkoff & Gardner, 2012; Williams & Mulrooney, 2021). There is also a growing body of research exploring the role of personnel preparation in bias and exclusionary discipline practices in early childhood (Davis et al., 2020; Neitzel, 2018), home visiting (Roggman et al., 2016), and supporting young children who have experienced trauma (Bartlett & Smith, 2019).

Well-prepared personnel are needed to work with young children with disabilities in high-need communities and in diverse least restrictive environments. National, state, and local data clarify the need for personnel who understand effects of poverty on young children's development, work effectively with families and other agencies, address resource access, and improve services to ensure developmental progress and academic success of children (Coleman et al., 2020; Magnuson & Waldfogel, 2005; Reed, 2012). Together, these factors require EI/ECSE personnel to be culturally competent while also skilled in working directly with infants and young children with disabilities in varied community settings. EI/ECSE personnel needs to be well-prepared to assess, identify, and provide culturally responsive supports and resources to diverse children and families. They need to be equipped with knowledge, skills, and dispositions in designing learning environments that promote optimal progress for all young children, in linking assessment to instruction and monitoring programming effectiveness, and in collaborating with families and professionals from diverse backgrounds.

## CONCEPTUAL FRAMEWORK

The interdisciplinary model described in this chapter embeds the *Pyramid Early Intervention Model* (Fox et al., 2003; Hemmeter et al., 2006; Hemmeter et al., 2021) in the *Learning to Teach in Community* (Hammerness et al., 2005) framework within the bioecological context. The goal is to build and strengthen the path between high quality personnel preparation and optimal outcomes of young children with disabilities and their families, particularly children with high-intensity needs and children from high-need communities. The Pyramid Model is a tiered framework of research-based practices that has been applied in early childhood learning settings to teach young children social-emotional skills, particularly by preventing or reducing challenging behaviors. The tiers of the Pyramid Model start with universal practices through nurturing and responsive relationships and high-quality supportive environments provided for all age-appropriate children. Then targeted supports are provided to promote social-emotional competencies for children who are at risk due to environmental and/or biological factors. Individualized and intensive interventions may be needed for children who need additional support (TACSEI, 2018). The *Learning to Teach in Community* framework (Hammerness et al., 2005) builds on research about cognitive science and effective teacher education (Darling-Hammond & Bransford, 2005 NRC, 2000), and shows how "…new teachers learn to teach in a community that enables them to develop a *vision* for their practice; a set of *understandings* about teaching, learning, and children; *dispositions* about how to use this knowledge; *practices* that allow them to act on their intentions and beliefs; and *tools* that support their efforts" (Hammerness et al., 2005, p. 385).

The bioecological model emphasizes the relationship of children and their families and how this relationship impacts child development. The bioecological model values the multi-layered interrelationship between and among individuals, communities, and the society (Center for Child and Family Well-being, 2021). Through interdisciplinary cohort and community-based learning, the interdisciplinary model prepares personnel across disciplines such as special education and social work to develop adaptive dispositions, cognitive and metacognitive skills that address the fundamental problems of learning to teach, contribute to lifelong learning, and promote sustained professional commitment (De Arment et al., 2013). Further, this model intends to transfer the knowledge, skills, and dispositions of EI/ECSE

*Figure 1.*

**Learning to Teach in Community**

- Shared Coursework
- Series of Seminars
- Coordinated Fieldwork

*Interdisciplinary Practices* — *Interdisciplinary* — *Interdisciplinary Tools*

Child

Family

School

Community

*Understanding* — *Dispositions*

Vision: Optimal Child and Family Outcomes

personnel to optimal child outcomes in learning and development through the *Pyramid Early Intervention Model* (Fox et al., 2003; Hemmeter et al., 2006; Hemmeter et al., 2021) with systematic and focused instruction across developmental, educational, and social aspects. See figure 1.

To illustrate, the *Learning to Teach in Community* serves as the framework within which the Pyramid Model is incorporated, and this framework is applied to the multi-layered contexts emphasized by the bioecological model. As demonstrated in Figure 1, the focus of our programs presented in this chapter is the interdisciplinary collaboration across all levels through shared coursework, series of seminars, and coordinated fieldwork (shown as the triangle).

## ADULT LEARNING PRINCIPLES

In our interdisciplinary model we apply evidence-based adult learning principles focused on addressing student preconceptions to learning, acquisition of knowledge for deep understanding, and the development of lifelong learning towards the development of adaptive expertise (De Arment et al., 2013; NRC, 2000). The adult learning principles align well with the *Learning to Teach in Community* framework because we emphasize competencies of adult learners in developing a vision of serving young children with disabilities and their families as well as empowering them with knowledge and skills in culturally relevant contexts, which further strengthen their dispositions in their practices. Adults come into higher education with many life experiences, different forms or levels of education, and varied cultural backgrounds that have influence in their perception and motivation (Conner et al., 2018; Shaw et al., 2012). The accumulation of experiences and the variation in the quality of those experiences can increase the heterogeneity of adult learners. Different from children or adolescents, adult learners come to higher education with a well-developed sense of their identity (Knowles et al., 2005). Adults as learners usually

*Figure 2.*

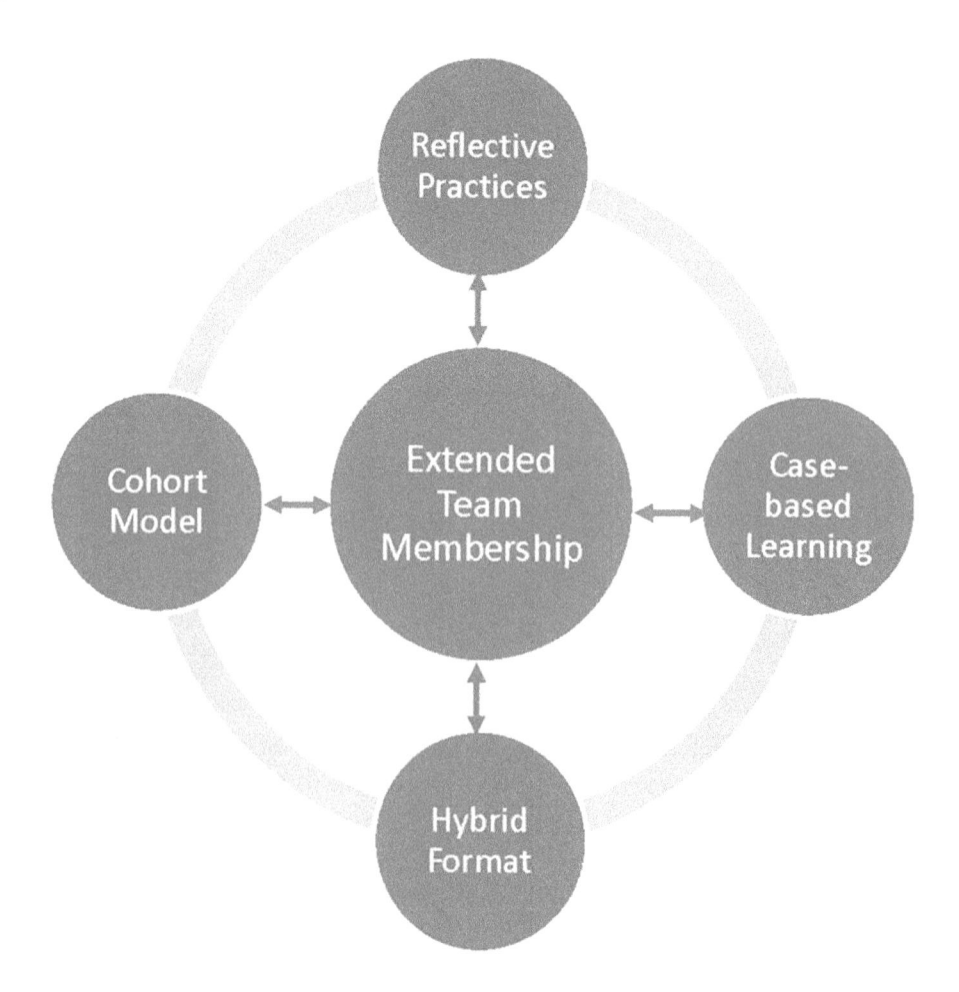

have a strong sense of responsibility for what, why, and how they learn (McDaniel, 2020). Brookfield (1986) explained that adults learn best when they feel the need to learn and when they have a sense of responsibility for what, why, and how they learn. He also pointed out the value of past experience for adult learners because they "use experience as a resource in learning so the learning content and process must bear a perceived and meaningful relationship to past experience" (p.31). Similarly, Knowles' theory of andragogy is a constructivist approach to learning that involves facilitating adults to draw their experience and to create new learning based on previous understandings (Cox, 2015). To summarize, adult learners with strong knowledge, skills, and dispositions will have a better vision and deeper understanding of the diverse communities and people they serve.

To support adult learners as they bring an expanding pool of experience that can be used as a resource for that learning, we incorporate the following adult learning principles into the program: extended team membership, reflective practices, case-based learning, hybrid course format, and cohort model (See figure 2). As illustrated by Figure 2, these principles are interactive and interrelated with one informing another as a dynamic system instead of a static linear relationship, with the collaborative team as the essential gear. Extended team membership provides both inter- and intra-personal information of team members which informs the functioning of other factors such as reflective practices, case-based learning, hybrid course format, and cohort model. On the other hand, the interaction between and among the other factors will further strengthen team membership through deeper understanding of the community they serve and adaptive expertise they develop.

## Extended Team Membership

Research on teamwork confirms the critical importance of effective communications and shared knowledge and skills between and among interdisciplinary team members, particularly for serving children with disabilities and their families. However, pre-service teacher preparation programs rarely provide opportunities for students to form teams that remain together across the program (Bransford et al., 2000). Often times when we form teams, we tend to identify surface-level constructs such as training discipline, race, age, or educational background, which can be easily recognized and documented. Some deep-level factors such as personality, attitudes, or approaches to learning which are considered underlying psychological variables would only be discovered after an extended interaction with someone (Bell, 2007; Rosen et al., 2018). To increase and improve inter-personal communication, an extended team membership through collaborative work would be necessary.

An innovative component of our model is an extended team experience through shared coursework including group assignments, coordinated clinical experiences, and ongoing seminars provided by interdisciplinary specialists that include multiple disciplines such as EI/ECSE, social work, physical therapy, speech-language pathology, occupational therapy, and pediatrics. Students work as a team by collaborating with community partners and families on a shared group assignment identified by the interdisciplinary faculty team.

## Reflective Practices

Reflective practice is an effective approach to preparing teacher candidates as reflective thinkers and problem solvers through clinical experiences (deBettencourt & Nagro, 2019; Tripp & Rich, 2012). For pre-service teacher candidates, their reflective practices are more likely to translate to professional routines upon entering the workforce if they occurred in authentically diverse settings (Etscheidt et al., 2012; Moore, 2003). As Crawford et al. (2012) suggested, teacher candidates become competent and confident to recognize their own strengths and limits by reflecting on their clinical teaching experiences while learning and refining instructional decision-making skills. Clinical field experiences are critical for all teacher candidates, particularly special education candidates through supervised implementation of best practices in serving children and students with disabilities (Sayeski & Paulsen, 2012).

Using the *Learning to Teach in Community* framework, our interdisciplinary personnel preparation model incorporates systematic supervised learning in diverse environments to enhance program students' evidence-based practices for positive child outcomes. Throughout the program, students are offered numerous opportunities to reflect on specific competencies as a result of their in-depth understanding and skill development in the field.

## Case-Based Learning

Case-based pedagogy is used in a number of professions (e.g., law, medicine, and business) to link research and practice. The use of cases in teacher education has been accepted as a promising instructional method for creating authentic learning environments (Akbulut & Hill, 2020; Koury et al., 2009; Levin, 2001). However, case methodology without specific teaching supports is not effective (Levin, 2002; Whitcomb, 2002). With scaffolding and feedback from interdisciplinary team members, case-based learning can help teachers move from simplistic to more mature perspectives about teaching and learning (Goodwin, 2002; Hammerness et al., 2002; Kantar & Massouh, 2015; Roeser, 2002), modeling the benefit of interprofessional dialogue embedded in the learning process.

To provide consistency and continuity across courses, the interdisciplinary faculty team works with parent mentors to develop video case studies (one infant- and one preschool-focused) that include children with significant disabilities and their families, particularly families who are culturally and/or linguistically diverse and who are living in poverty. Dilemmas about collaboration, use of Universal Design for Learning (UDL) principles, and high-intensity needs of young children and families are portrayed in the context of assessment, program planning, and progress monitoring through interdisciplinary teamwork from multiple perspectives.

## Hybrid Course Format

Before the COVID-19 pandemic, a hybrid course referred to a course where online elements replaced some of face-to-face teaching, sometimes this format also was referred to as a "blended" course (Leh, 2002). A hybrid or blended course was designed to integrate online and classroom pedagogy to promote active independent learning (Sandoz, 2007). Additionally, hybrid courses offer flexibilities as a solution to quantity and quality issues in special education teacher preparation. Since the pandemic, a hybrid course may also refer to a course with synchronous and asynchronous online teaching. Hybrid course delivery format has become more common, given the scheduling differences between programs, curriculum requirements, as well as the trend of more and more non-traditional candidates who are part-time students due to their full-time employment status (Crais et al., 2004). To address these barriers, shared coursework, along with the shared group assignments, are offered in hybrid formats within our model.

In addition, the COVID-19 pandemic has caused the largest disruption to the traditional education system across all levels. Blended or hybrid courses that consist of both face-to-face and online sessions are the trend in instructional delivery, particularly during the post-pandemic era (Kara, 2021). This combination of face-to-face and online classes provides flexibility and prepares students for the realities of online collaboration in their careers (Lim & Yoon, 2008) with no loss of learning required knowledge and skills (Ivey & Reed, 2011).

## Cohort Model

Rooted in group development and adult learning theory, cohort model instruction has been considered best practice in the fields such as multicultural education, special education, and social work (Lee et al., 2018; Personnel Improvement Center, 2011). The cohort design and its intended outcomes open opportunities for building connections among professionals from diverse fields of scholarship with their own professional knowledge and experience combined knowledge with a shared fundamental premise: access and accommodation to ensure all individuals receive equitable services.

Learning cohorts encourage intercultural interactions between and among learners which promotes inclusivity and meaningful integration of diverse learners. Research on learning in cohorts suggests increased development in critical thinking skills (Chairs et al., 2002; Holloway & Alexandre, 2012), knowledge base (Mukeredzi, 2014), self-examination of own knowledge (Tisdell et al., 2002), motivation to learn more (Swayze & Jakeman, 2014), and changes in learner perspectives (Mello, 2016).

## PROGRAM EXAMPLES

In this section we demonstrate three project examples applying the interdisciplinary personnel preparation conceptual framework. *Project Connect* is a collaboration that involves three disciplines: EI/ECSE, social work, and pediatrics. *Project Bridge* is a collaboration among EI/ECSE, physical therapy, and pediatrics. *Project Link* is a speech-language pathology program that involves multiple disciplines such as social work, physical therapy, EI/ECSE, and occupational therapy.

## Project Connect

Project Connect is an interdisciplinary project preparing students from Master of Education in Special Education leading to licensure in special education-early childhood serving infants and children birth through ages five and Master of Social Work (MSW) leading to licensure in clinical social work. As a cohort model, all project students receive 11 seminars provided by the interdisciplinary faculty team from EI/ECSE, social work (SW), pediatrics, and the university's Center for Excellence in Developmental Disabilities, the Partnership for People with Disabilities (PPD), as well as practitioners from communities. As illustrated by the previous interdisciplinary framework, the seminars are planned to build strong foundational knowledge, skills, and dispositions of EI/ECSE personnel in serving infants and young children with significant disabilities and their families within culturally and socially appropriate contexts. The project implementation team intentionally plans for seminar topics that address the contextual factors of working with young children with high-intensity needs and their families who are from high needs communities to ensure high quality professional preparation. To remain flexible and responsive to students' needs in the COVID-19 era, seminars are offered in a synchronous online format allowing students and seminar providers to readily come together without the challenges of travel time, parking, and competing schedules. Further, the project interdisciplinary team identifies shared coursework between the two programs from which students select four courses, for a total of 10 credit hours of interdisciplinary coursework during their professional practice preparation. Courses offer options in delivery mode so that students can make selections based on interests and modality preferences.

Project Connect also develops a series of group assignments across EI/ECSE and SW throughout the students' program of study. The series of shared group assignments intends to help students from EI/ECSE and SW work together as a collaborative team on the shared goals and outcomes of children with disabilities, including high-intensity needs, and their families from high needs communities. For example, the first shared group assignment of the series focuses on gathering valid, reliable, and culturally relevant data on a child with a disability and the child's family. This assignment is convergent by nature and interdisciplinary by design. Each group consists of three members including two EI/ECSE students and one SW student. The team works collaboratively for a child who has a significant disability or emotional difficulties and the child's family. In addition to project faculty from ECSE and MSW, Project Connect includes a parent of a child with disabilities as a family mentor. The family mentor is identified through the PPD's Center for Family Involvement (CFI) and works closely with other key personnel throughout the project. Guided by the Council for Exceptional Children's Division for Early Childhood (DEC) Recommended Practices (2014), the Project Connect team collects assessment information from multiple sources, using multiple measures and adopting multiple assessment methods. This assignment takes place during the second semester of each cohort. Students are encouraged to maximize the affordances of online collaboration tools such as Google Docs and video conferencing platforms in developing their assignments. These digital collaborations not only support assignment efficiency, they also mirror the realities of professional interdisciplinary practice in the wake of COVID-19.

The second shared group assignment focuses on linking the assessment to intervention planning based on the information collected through the convergent assessment. This assignment helps build project students' interdisciplinary competencies through shared knowledge and skills across the disciplines and guides students to design high quality IEP/IFSP goals and objectives that are meaningful, integrative, and measurable (Mclean, 2016; Noonan & McCormick, 2014). This shared group assignment includes planning for essential components such as shared team environments, UDL principles, embedded learning opportunities for children with significant disabilities, and individualized instructional strategies for intensive interventions within least restrictive or natural environments. This assignment is completed during the third semester of the project and similarly encourages virtual collaborative practices among students.

The last shared group assignment is the implementation of the instructional planning developed through group assignment 2. Using the planning matrix developed in assignment 2, project students work as small groups to implement the intervention strategies during their coordinated clinical experience. This assignment takes at least 8 weeks in the fieldwork for students to implement an intervention, collect data, monitor progress of the target child, and adjust intervention when needed. This assignment is completed during project students' last semester.

Furthermore, Project Connect team identifies two coordinated clinical field experiences across educational, developmental, medical, and social aspects throughout the project. The first coordinated field experience takes place during the first year to provide an orientation to students from multiple perspectives about typical and atypical infant and toddler development. This coordinated field experience consists of 100 hours including 65-hour onsite observations of child development centers (particularly infant and toddler programs), home care programs, foster care services, Children's Treatment Center, Intensive

Care Unit (NICU), the NICU follow-up clinic, the Child Development Clinic, the Care Connections for Children, and child welfare programs. In addition to the onsite observations, Project Connect students share their reflections via blogs and small group discussions within their hybrid coursework. The second coordinated clinical experience happens during the last semester when EI/ECSE students are conducting their preschool externship and SW students are completing their clinical work in the field. A minimum number of 200 clinical hours (8-12 weeks) are expected during the second coordinated clinical experience. Since the COVID-19 pandemic, clinical work expectations have shifted to reflect current practice in the field. For example, ECSE students in the preschool externship accomplish fieldwork hours through virtual contact with children and their families when these practices are being implemented in schools. Increasingly, students are experiencing clinical practice that employs virtual modes of connecting with families and related services providers reflecting a shift away from pre-pandemic expectations of in-person meetings.

## Project Bridge

Project Bridge is an interdisciplinary project preparing students from Master of Education in Special Education leading to licensure in special education-early childhood serving infants and children birth through ages five and Doctor of Physical Therapy (DPT) leading to licensure in Physical Therapy. Project Bridge attempts to build and strengthen the path from high quality EI /ECSE and related services personnel preparation to the optimal learning and developmental outcomes of young children with significant disabilities and their families. Project Bridge focuses on preparing students across disciplines with shared knowledge and skills in education, physical therapy, and medicine leading to strong dispositions with the ultimate goal to promote the quality of life for young children with significant disabilities and their families. Project Bridge is designed to enhance the existing pre-service personnel preparation program in EI/ECSE and Physical Therapy (PT).

The DPT curriculum is a 3-year program. Typically, 20-30% of the admitted PT students indicate a strong interest in pediatric PT and they would like to learn about the role of pediatrics in the DPT curriculum. The availability of ample pediatric clinical experiences and need for pediatric physical therapists in the state makes the DPT program an excellent choice for applicants who are interested in dedicating their career to pediatric PT. Through interdisciplinary seminars provided by faculty from EI/ECSE, PT, and pediatrics, along with community partners, Project Bridge strengthens DPT's curriculum with a stronger pediatric component and educational connection for long term outcomes of children with disabilities.

The existing EI/ECSE course sequences align with Project Bridge to better scaffold students' learning within the related context. As a cohort model, Project Bridge students begin their studies with an orientation to EI/ECSE and community engagement. This foundation sets the stage for subsequent community-based learning, with the emphasis on natural learning environments, collaboration with community partners and families, cultural competence, and professional reflection.

To help project students bridge research to practice, Project Bridge requires that all EI/ECSE candidates take a 1-credit seminar course on research in action focusing on EI/ECSE, prior to their externships. This online course includes five synchronous meetings via video conference, but maximizes flexibility for students through a predominantly asynchronous format. The course includes three components: (1) comprehensive literature review on an intervention selected by the project student that is relevant and timely given the context of COVID-19, (2) research design with an operationalized research question and hypothesis based on the literature review, and (3) pilot study that consists of data collection, analysis, and a virtual poster presentation.

In preparation for their research in action, project students practice this process in the hybrid assessment course taken during the second semester, using project video case studies (infant and preschool age) on language sample collection to generate present levels of performance and identified goals/objectives. Three students (2 ECSE; 1 PT) work as a team through flexible synchronous and asynchronous collaboration approaches to develop an intervention and data collection plan. Each team presents their plans and receives constructive feedback from instructors and peers. Each team also works with the family liaison to identify a child with significant disabilities and the child's family.

Using linked assessment to intervention strategies they have learned through the case studies, each team develops an intervention and data collection plan for the child and the caregiver using an interdisciplinary teamwork approach through shared knowledge and skills across disciplines. Over a minimum of 8 weeks, data are collected and reviewed weekly and the team documents data-based decisions. During two externships (infant and preschool), the pilot study that students developed during their research in action seminar is generalized to other infants or young children within daily routines. Students are responsive to evolving practice models within either externship following COVID-19; in some cases adapting implementation of their research plans for telepractice (EI) or virtual teaching (ECSE) practices. Project students collect and analyze data on a regular basis to make data-based decisions to inform ongoing instructional practice.

## Program Link

Project Link is a Speech-Language Pathology program offering Master of Science in Communication Sciences and Disorders (CSD). The program is accredited by the Council on Academic Accreditation in Audiology Speech-Language Pathology of the American Speech-Language Hearing Association. Project Link is designed as an interdisciplinary model involving occupational therapy (OT), PT, SW, and EI/ECSE. Project Link students are prepared for entry-level practice as a speech-language pathologist working with diverse populations of adults and children in educational and healthcare settings.

Project Link is unique in that the Infant and Toddler Connection (ITC), a local early intervention program, is housed in the university Speech, Hearing and Learning Services (SHLS) clinic giving graduate students direct access to the expertise of EI providers. Additionally, the university's Speech-Language Pathology (SLP) graduate students are required to participate in EI evaluations and desk eligibilities each semester on campus. Graduate students work with Developmental Specialists, Teachers for the Deaf/Hard-of-Hearing, Occupational Therapists, Physical Therapists, and Social Workers throughout their program.

In addition, the Developmental Specialists at ITC conduct simulations with the students on phone interviews and explain evaluation results to families. Each semester students have the opportunity to complete their clinical hours providing direct services in the natural environment with an SLP who is employed by both the university and the ITC. The ITC director and two case managers are able to present to the students in two courses – *Initial Practicum in SLP* and *Language Disorders in Infants and Preschool-Age Children*.

The SHLS clinic also employs an Audiologist and students gain a deeper understanding of the field by observing diagnostic sessions with children and adults. The SLP graduate students participate in a monthly support group meeting for those affected by hearing loss. They prepare presentations with the

Audiologist on topics such as *Strategies for Better Communication, What is an Audiogram,* or *Making the Most of Your Night Out.* The local 4-H sponsors a three-day summer camp for children with hearing loss ages 9 - 18 called *Camp Loud & Clear.* The camp is open for children who use any communication methodology including American Sign Language, Cued Speech, Bilingual-Bimodal, as well as Listening and Spoken Language. Graduate students have the opportunity to gain clinical experience working with children who have a hearing loss as well as how to work with sign language interpreters during the three-day intensive camp.

The university also offers a campus-based two-year non-degree post-secondary certificate program for individuals ages 18 – 25 with high-intensity needs such as intellectual disabilities and Autism Spectrum Disorder. The certificate program is designed to provide work-based learning experiences in both job-readiness instructional training lab and on-site jobs with task instruction provided by job coaches over multiple semesters. Furthermore, the program provides a research opportunity for graduate students on the effectiveness of interventions in post-secondary transition programs for individuals with intellectual disabilities. The certificate program involves graduate students from Special Education (SPED), School Counseling, and SLP to participate in the interventions provided to the certificate students. The SPED and SLP graduate students plan sessions together weekly and implement their plans for the certificate students together using the interdisciplinary team approach. The sessions take place on the university campus and frequently moves from a classroom to the university lawn, local restaurants, or the university fitness center. The graduate students gain valuable experience in joint planning and implementation of activities with emerging adult students with disabilities and a deeper understanding of the unique opportunities presented by interdisciplinary approaches to service delivery.

The CSD students participate each semester in Clinical Therapy (CT) Teams. Each team is guided by one of the faculty or clinical educators and is composed of four graduate students. The students have monthly meetings and assignments designed to provide a deeper understanding of the link between the local community, families, and the children being served at SHLS and in the local ITC by interdisciplinary teams as illustrated in the conceptual framework of the program. In the spring, the assignments consist of monthly seminars presented by various interdisciplinary specialists suggested by the outgoing cohort. For example, students suggested presentations on (a) trauma-informed care by a clinical social worker; (b) sensory integration by an occupational therapist; and (c) behavior management by a special education professor with extensive experience in working with children who have emotional and behavioral difficulties. Students build on their knowledge of the developmental, educational, and social aspects of interdisciplinary practice by meeting with their CT teams after the presentations to discuss the topics and the benefits of collaborating with those professionals on the measurable outcomes of their clients.

Adaptations to each of the distinct components of Project Link are made during the height of the COVID pandemic to allow maximum flexibility to students in obtaining their required clinical hours to meet CAA standards, but also to continue their interdisciplinary experiences. CAA has made temporary accommodations to supervision requirements allowing for remote supervision of student clinicians. The SHLS clinic and ITC continue to serve clients and families using telepractice. The clinic has converted two therapy rooms to telepractice suites complete with green screens and state of the art equipment. The ITC teams and therapy sessions continue via telepractice with collaboration with OT, PT, Developmental Specialists, SLP graduate students, and Social Workers. Once the clinic opens again, the use of telepractice continues.

Clinical Educators that provide supervision are issued iPads for supervision and all student clinicians receive additional education and training on telepractice during the pandemic. Two of the faculty have had training and experience using telepractice allowing for a quick transition to online services. The CSD program creates a one-credit optional course offered one time per year on *Telepractice Service Delivery in the Helping Professions* for students that is also open for current practitioners. The course is popular with over 35 students taking the course since it has been offered.

Other program adjustments are made to not only provide clinical experiences for students, but to continue to serve the community. For example, the university Audiologist has developed a drive-thru service for hearing aid cleaning and consultations to maintain social distancing. The support group for adults with hearing loss continue in an online format with a great deal of computer support services provided by the university and the students.

## CONCLUSION

In this chapter, we have demonstrated an interdisciplinary personnel preparation model and offered three examples building from the model. Although each program example varies in focused disciplines, they share the similar conceptual framework that embeds the *Pyramid Early Intervention Model* (Fox et al., 2003; Hemmeter et al., 2006; Hemmeter et al., 2021) in the *Learning to Teach in Community* (Hammerness et al., 2005) framework within the bioecological context. Adult learning principles such as extended team membership, reflective practices, case-based learning, hybrid course format, and cohort model are incorporated into each of the project models. Given the widely practiced interdisciplinary models in EI/ECSE and related fields, additional scientific evidence is needed to document the effects of these models on developmental and educational outcomes of children with disabilities and their families, particularly since the onset of the COVID-19 pandemic.

## REFERENCES

Adams, R. C., Tapia, C., Murphy, N. A., Norwood, K. W. Jr, Adams, R. C., Burke, R. T., Friedman, S. L., Houtrow, A. J., Kalichman, M. A., Kuo, D. Z., Levy, S. E., Turchi, R. M., & Wiley, S. E.Council on Children with Disabilities. (2013). Early Intervention, IDEA Part C Services, and the Medical Home: Collaboration for Best Practice and Best Outcomes. *Pediatrics*, *132*(4), e1073–e1088. doi:10.1542/peds.2013-2305 PMID:24082001

Akbulut, M. S., & Hill, J. R. (2020). Case-based pedagogy for teacher education: An instructional model. *Contemporary Educational Technology*, *12*(2), 1-17. doi:10.30935/cedtech/8937

Almendingen, K., Molin, M., & Šaltytė Benth, J. (2021). Preparedness for interprofessional learning: An exploratory study among health, social care, and teacher education programs. *Journal of Research in Interprofessional Practice and Education*, *11*(1), 1–11. doi:10.22230/jripe.2021v11n1a309

Archibald, L. M. (2017). SLP-educator classroom collaboration: A review to inform reason-based practice. *Autism & Developmental Language Impairments*, *2*. doi:10.1177/2396941516680369

Bartlett, J. D., & Smith, S. (2019). The role of early care and education in addressing early childhood trauma. *American Journal of Community Psychology*, *64*(3-4), 359–372. doi:10.1002/ajcp.12380 PMID:31449682

Bell, S. T. (2007). Deep-level composition variables as predictors of team performance: A meta-analysis. *The Journal of Applied Psychology*, *92*(3), 595–615. doi:10.1037/0021-9010.92.3.595 PMID:17484544

Bransford, J. D., Brown, A. L., & Cocking, R. R. (2000). *How people learn: Brain, mind, experience, and school*. National Resource Council.

Brookfield, S. D. (1986). *Understanding and facilitating adult learning*. Jossey-Bass.

Bruder, M. B., Catalino, T., Chiarello, L. A., Mitchell, M. C., Deppe, J., Gundler, D., Kemp, P., LeMoine, S., Long, T., Muhlenhaupt, M., Prelock, P., Schefkind, S., Stayton, V., & Ziegler, D. (2019). Finding a common lens: Competencies across professional disciplines providing early childhood intervention. *Infants and Young Children*, *32*(4), 280–293. doi:10.1097/IYC.0000000000000153

Chairs, M. J., McDonald, B. J., Shroyer, P., Urbanski, B., & Vertin, D. (2002). Meeting the graduate education needs of Minnesota extension educators. *Journal of Extension*, *40*(4). http://www.joe.org/joe/2002august/rb4.shtml

Chen, D., Klein, M. D., & Minor, L. (2009). Interdisciplinary perspectives in early intervention: Professional development in multiple disabilities through distance education. *Infants and Young Children*, *22*(2), 146–158. doi:10.1097/IYC.0b013e3181a030e0

Coiro, M. J., Kotchick, B. A., & Preis, J. (2016). Youth social skills groups: A training platform for promoting graduate clinician interprofessional competence. *Journal of Interprofessional Education & Practice*, *4*, 89–92. doi:10.1016/j.xjep.2016.04.004

Coleman, H. M., Xu, Y., & De Arment, S. (2020). Empowering diverse families. *International Journal of Early Childhood Special Education*, *12*(1), 702077. doi:10.20489/intjecse

Conner, L. R., Richardson, S., & Murphy, A. L. (2018). Teaching note: Using adult learning principles for evidence-based learning in a BSW research course. *The Journal of Baccalaureate Social Work*, *23*(1), 355–365. doi:10.18084/1084-7219.23.1.355

Cox, E. (2015). Coaching and adult learning: Theory and practice. *New Directions for Adult and Continuing Education*, *2015*(148), 27–38. doi:10.1002/ace.20149

Crais, E. R., Boone, H. A., Harrison, M., Freund, P., Downing, K., & West, T. (2004). Interdisciplinary personnel preparation: Graduates' use of targeted practices. *Infants and Young Children*, *17*(1), 82–92. doi:10.1097/00001163-200401000-00010

Crawford, S., O'Reilly, R., & Luttrell, S. (2012). Assessing the effects of integrating the reflective framework for teaching in physical education (RFTPE) on the teaching and learning of undergraduate sport studies and physical education students. *Reflective Practice*, *13*(1), 115–129. doi:10.1080/14623943.2011.626025

Da Fonte, M. A., & Barton-Arwood, S. M. (2017). Collaboration of general and special education teachers: Perspectives and strategies. *Intervention in School and Clinic*, *53*(2), 99–106. doi:10.1177/1053451217693370

Darling-Hammond, L., & Berry, B. (2006). Highly qualified teachers for all. *Educational Leadership*, *64*(3), 14–20.

Davis, A. E., Perry, D. F., & Rabinovitz, L. (2020). Expulsion prevention: Framework for the role of infant and early childhood mental health consultation in addressing implicit biases. *Infant Mental Health Journal, 41*, 327-339.

De Arment, S., Reed, E., & Wetzel, A. (2013). Promoting adaptive expertise: A conceptual framework for special educator preparation. *Teacher Education and Special Education, 36*(1), 217–230. doi:10.1177/0888406413489578

deBettencourt, L. U., & Nagro, S. A. (2019). Tracking special education teacher candidates' reflective practices over time. *Remedial and Special Education, 40*(5), 277–288. doi:10.1177/0741932518762573

Dettmer, P., Thurston, L. P., Knackendoffel, A., & Dyck, N. J. (2009). *Collaboration, consultation, and teamwork for students with special needs* (6th ed.). Pearson Education, Inc.

Division for Early Childhood. (2014). *DEC recommended practices in early intervention/early childhood special education 2014*. Retrieved from http://www.dec-sped.org/recommendedpractices

Division for Early Childhood of the Council for Exceptional Children. (2020). *Initial practice-based professional preparation standards for early interventionists/early childhood special educators (EI/ECSE) (initial birth through age 8)*. Retrieved from: https://exceptionalchildren.org/standards/initial-practice-based-standards-early-interventionists-early-childhood-special-educators

Etscheidt, S., Curran, C. M., & Sawyer, C. M. (2012). Promoting reflection in teacher preparation programs: A multilevel model. *Teacher Education and Special Education, 35*(1), 7–26. doi:10.1177/0888406411420887

Fox, L., Dunlap, G., Hemmeter, M. L., Joseph, G. E., & Strain, P. S. (2003). The teaching pyramid: A model for supporting social competence and preventing challenging behavior in young children. *Young Children, 58*(4), 48–53.

Frauenholtz, S., Mendenhall, A. N., & Moon, J. (2017). Role of school employees' mental health knowledge in interdisciplinary collaborations to support the academic success of students experiencing mental distress. *Children & Schools, 39*(2), 71–79. doi:10.1093/cs/cdx004

Friend, M., & Cook, L. (2010). *Interactions: Collaboration skills for school professionals* (6th ed.). Pearson.

Goodwin, A. L. (2002). The case of one child: Making the shift from personal knowledge to professionally informed practice. *Teaching Education, 13*(2), 137–154. doi:10.1080/1047621022000007558

Hammerness, K., Darling-Hammond, L., Bransford, J., Berliner, D., Cochran-Smith, M., McDonald, M., & Zeichner, K. (2005). How teachers learn and develop. In L. Darling Hammond & J. Bransford (Ed.), Preparing teachers for a changing world: What teachers should learn and be able to do (pp. 358–389). Jossey-Bass.

Hammerness, K., Darling-Hammond, L., & Shulman, L. (2002, April 10-14). *Towards expert thinking: How case-writing contributes to the development of theory-based professional knowledge in student-teachers*. Paper presented at the Annual Meeting of the American Educational Research Association, Seattle, WA.

Hemmeter, M. L., Ostrosky, M., & Fox, L. (2006). Social and emotional foundations for early learning: A conceptual model for intervention. *School Psychology Review*, *35*(4), 583–601. doi:10.1080/0279601 5.2006.12087963

Hemmeter, M. L., Ostrosky, M. M., & Fox, L. K. (2021). *Unpacking the Pyramid Model: A practical guide for preschool teachers*. Brookes Publishing.

Hemmeter, M. L., Snyder, P. A., Fox, L., & Algina, J. (2016). Evaluating the implementation of the Pyramid Model for Promoting Social-Emotional Competence in early childhood classrooms. *Topics in Early Childhood Special Education*, *36*(3), 133–146. doi:10.1177/0271121416653386

Hoagwood, K. E., & Kelleher, K. J. (2020). A Marshall plan for children's mental health after COVID-19. *Psychiatric Services (Washington, D.C.)*, *71*(12), 1216–1217. doi:10.1176/appi.ps.202000258 PMID:32933414

Holloway, E., & Alexandre, L. (2012). Crossing boundaries in doctoral education: Relational learning, cohort communities, and dissertation committees. *New Directions for Teaching and Learning*, *131*, 85-97.

Hunt, P., Soto, G., Maier, J., Liboiron, N., & Bae, S. (2004). Collaborative teaming to support preschoolers with severe disabilities who are placed in general education early childhood programs. *Topics in Early Childhood Special Education*, *24*(3), 123–142. doi:10.1177/02711214040240030101

Ivey, C., & Reed, E. (2011). An examination of learning formats on interdisciplinary teamwork knowledge, skills, and dispositions. *Interdisciplinary Journal of Teaching and Learning*, *1*, 43–55.

Jane-Griffiths, A., Alsip, J., Hart, S. R., Round, R. L., & Brady, J. (2021). Together we can do so much: A systematic review and conceptual framework of collaboration in schools. *Canadian Journal of School Psychology*, *36*(1), 59–85.

Jones, P., & West, E. A. (2010). Moving toward a hybrid teacher education course: Supporting the theory to practice challenge in special education. *Journal of Special Education Technology*, *25*(2), 45–56. doi:10.1177/016264341002500204

Kantar, L., & Massouh, A. (2015). Case-based learning: What traditional curricula fail to teach. *Nurse Education Today*, *35*(8), e8–e14. doi:10.1016/j.nedt.2015.03.010 PMID:25842004

Kara, A. (2021). Covid-19 pandemic and possible trends for the future of higher education: A Review. *Journal of Education and Educational Development*, *8*(1), 9–26. doi:10.22555/joeed.v8i1.183

Klawetter, S., & Frankel, K. (2018). Infant mental health: A lens for maternal and child mental health disparities. *Journal of Human Behavior in the Social Environment*, *28*(5), 557–569. doi:10.1080/1091 1359.2018.1437495

Knowles, M. S., Holton, E. E., & Swanson, R. A. (2005). *The adult learner: The definitive classic in adult education and human resource development*. Elsevier. doi:10.4324/9780080481913

Koury, K., Hollingsead, C., Fitzgerald, G., Miller, K., Mitchem, K., Tsai, H., & Zha, S. (2009). Case-based instruction in different delivery contexts: The impact of time in cases. *Journal of Interactive Learning Research*, *20*(4), 445–467.

Lee, A., Poch, R., Smith, A., Kelly, M. D., & Leopold, H. (2018). Intercultural pedagogy: A faculty learning cohort. *Education in Science, 177*, 1–14.

Leh, A. S. C. (2002). Action research in hybrid courses and their online communities. *Educational Media International, 39*, 31–38.

Lerman, D. C., Vorndran, C. M., Addison, L., & Contrucci Kuhn, S. (2004). Preparing teachers in evidence-based practices for young children with autism. *School Psychology Review, 33*(4), 510–526.

Levin, B. B. (2001). *Energizing teacher education and professional development with problem- based learning*. ASCD.

Levin, B. B. (2002). *Case studies of teacher development: An in-depth look at how thinking about pedagogy develops over time*. Erlbaum.

Lim, D. H., & Yoon, S. W. (2008). Team learning and collaboration between online and blended learner groups. *Performance Improvement Quarterly, 21*, 59–72. doi:10.1002/piq.20031

Magnuson, K. A., & Waldfogel, J. (2005). Early childhood care and education: Effects on ethnic and racial gaps in school readiness. *The Future of Children, 15*(1), 169–196.

McDaniel, E. A. (2020). Faculty collaboration for better teaching: Adult learning principles applied to teaching improvement. *To Improve the Academy, 6*, 94-102.

McLaughlin, M. (2002). Examining special and general education collaborative practices in exemplary schools. *Journal of Educational & Psychological Consultation, 13*, 279–283.

McLean, M. (2016). A history of the DEC Recommended Practices. *DEC Recommended Practices Monograph Series, 1*, 1–10.

Mello, L. V. (2016). Fostering postgraduate student engagement: Online resources supporting self-directed learning in a diverse cohort. *Research in Learning Technology, 24*(1). DOI: doi:10.3402/rlt.v24.29366

Moore, R. (2003). Reexamining the field experiences of teacher candidate. *Journal of Teacher Education, 54*, 31–42. doi:10.1177/ 0022487102238656

Mukeredzi, T. G. (2014). Re-envisioning teaching practice: Student teacher learning in a cohort model of practicum in a rural South African context. *International Journal of Educational Development, 39*, 100–109.

National Research Council. (2001). *Eager to learn: Educating our preschoolers*. National Academies Press.

Neitzel, J. (2018). Research to practice: Understanding the role of implicit bias in early childhood disciplinary practices. *Journal of Early Childhood Teacher Education, 39*, 232–242.

Noonan, M. J., & McCormick, L. (2014). *Teaching Young Children with Disabilities in Natural Environments* (2nd ed.). Brookes Publishing Co., Inc.

Odom, S. L., Vitztum, J., Wolery, R., Lieber, J., Sandall, S., Hanson, M. J., ... Horn, E. (2004). Preschool inclusion in the United States: A review of research from an ecological systems perspective. *Journal of Research in Special Educational Needs, 4*(1), 17–49. doi:10.1111/J.1471-3802.2004.00016.x

Osofsky, J. D., & Liebrmam, A. F. (2011). A call for integrating a mental health perspective into systems of care for abused and neglected infants and young children. *The American Psychologist*, *66*(2), 120–128.

Personnel Improvement Center. (2011). *Practice brief summer 2011*. Retrieved from http://personnelcenter.org/documents/Special%20Education-Related%20Personnel%20Preparation%20Partnerships-HEADINGS.pdf

Pfeiffer, D. L., Pavelko, S. L., Hahs-Vaughn, D. L., & Dudding, C. C. (2019). A national survey of speech-language pathologists' engagement in interprofessional collaborative practice in schools: Identifying predictive factors and barriers to implementation. *Language, Speech, and Hearing Services in Schools*, *50*(4), 639–655.

Reed, E. (2012). Education of low income children in US. In J. E. Banks (Ed.), *Encyclopedia of Diversity in Education*. Sage.

Roeser, R. (2002). Bringing a "whole adolescent" perspective to secondary teacher education: A case study of the use of an adolescent case study. *Teaching Education*, *13*(2), 155–178.

Roggman, L. A., Peterson, C. A., Chazan-Cohen, R., Ispa, J., Decker, K. B., Hughes-Belding, K., Cook, G. A., & Wallotton, C. D. (2016). Preparing home visitors to partner with families of infants and toddlers. *Journal of Early Childhood Teacher Education*, *37*, 301–313.

Rosen, M., Diazgranados, D., Dietz, A., Benishek, L. E., Thompson, D., Pronovost, P. J., & Weaver, S. J. (2018). Teamwork in healthcare: Key discoveries enabling safer, high- quality care. *The American Psychologist*, *73*(4), 433–450.

Sandall, S., Hemmeter, M. L., Smith, B. J., & McLean, M. (2009). *DEC Recommended Practices: A Comprehensive Guide for Practical Application in Early Intervention/Early Childhood Special Education. Division for Early Childhood of the Council for Exceptional Children*. Sopris West.

Sandoz, J. (2007). Teaching in the 21st century: Pedagogies for the evolving brain. In J. A. Chambers (Ed.), *Selected papers from the 18th international conference on College Teaching and Learning* (pp. 167-187). Jacksonville, FL: Florida State College at Jacksonville.

Sayeski, K., & Paulsen, K. (2012). Student teacher evaluations of cooperating teachers as indices of effective mentoring. *Teacher Education Quarterly*, *39*, 117–130.

Sciaraffa, M. A., Zeanah, P. D., & Zeanah, C. H. (2018). Understanding and promoting resilience in the context of adverse childhood experiences. *Early Childhood Education Journal*, *46*, 343–353.

Shannon, G. S., & Bylsma, P. (2004). *Characteristics of improved school districts: Themes from research*. Washington State Department of Education.

Shaw, T. V., Lee, B. R., & Wulczyn, F. (2012). "I thought I 'hated' data": Preparing MSW students for data- driven practice. *Journal of Teaching in Social Work*, *32*(1), 78–89. doi:10.1080/08841233.2012.640599

Shonkoff, J. P., & Garner, A. S. (2012). The lifelong effects of early childhood adversity and toxic stress. *Pediatrics*, *129*(1), e232–e246.

Snell, M. E., & Janney, R. (2005). *Collaborative teaming* (2nd ed.). Paul H. Brooks Publishing Co.

Stayton, V. D. (2015). Preparation of early childhood special educators for inclusive and interdisciplinary settings. *Infants and Young Children, 28*, 113–122.

Swayze, S., & Jakeman, R. C. (2014). Student perceptions of communication, connectedness, and learning in a merged cohort course. *The Journal of Continuing Higher Education, 62*(2), 102–111.

Technical Assistance Center on Social Emotional Intervention for Young Children (TACSEI). (2018). *Learn about the Pyramid Model.* http://challengingbehavior.fmhi.usf.edu/do/pyramid_model.htm

Tisdell, E. J. (2002). High tech meets high touch: Cohort learning online in graduate higher education. In R. Orem (Ed.), *Proceedings of the 21st Midwest Research-to-Practice Conference in Adult, Continuing and Community Education, DeKalb, Illinois, October 9-11, 2002* (pp. 114-119). Retrieved from https://www.cedu.niu.edu/reps/Document/Midwest_Conference_Papers_part2.pdf

Tripp, T. R., & Rich, P. J. (2012). The influence of video analysis on the process of teacher change. *Teaching and Teacher Education, 28*, 728–739. doi:10.1016/j.tate.2012.01.011

Wallace, E., Senter, R., Peterson, N., Dunn, K. T., & Chow, J. (2020). How to establish a language-rich environment through a collaborative SLP–teacher partnership. *Teaching Exceptional Children.*

Weiss, D., Cook, B., & Eren, R. (2020). Transdisciplinary approach practicum for speech-language pathology and special education graduate students. *Journal of Autism and Developmental Disorders, 50*(10), 3661–3678.

Whitcomb, J. A. (2002). Composing dilemma cases: An opportunity to understand moral dimensions of teaching. *Teaching Education, 13*(2), 125–135.

Williams, D. S., & Mulrooney, K. (2021). Guardians in the nursery: The role of early childhood educators in fostering infant and young children's positive mental health. *Zero to Three Journal, 41*(3), 10–16.

# Chapter 2
# Interdisciplinary Pre-Service Professional Preparation Through Video Modeling

**Suzannah B. Chatlos**
https://orcid.org/0000-0001-7347-8361
*SUNY Plattsburgh, USA*

**Emily Hoeh**
https://orcid.org/0000-0003-4164-7612
*SUNY Plattsburgh, USA*

**Michelle L. Bonati**
https://orcid.org/0000-0002-6139-888X
*SUNY Plattsburgh, USA*

**Maureen E. Squires**
*SUNY Plattsburgh, USA*

## ABSTRACT

*Preparation of pre-service professionals to work in the field of special education requires explicitly taught approaches to collaboration as a part of a multidisciplinary team. The authors' faculty learning community provides a model to emanate the skills, knowledge, and dispositions of a high-functioning collaborative team expected from pre-service professionals through a mock individualized education program (IEP) team video series. Issues (origin story), solutions (video modeling), and areas of future research (mock interdisciplinary student teams) will be discussed. A description of Cox's (n.d.) 16 recommendations to frame a faculty learning community, video production, and other relevant topics for potential implementation will also be included. The faculty learning community and its video modeling products are presented as an exemplar for interdisciplinary, cross-departmental/institutional expertise to model a positive student-centered mock IEP team.*

DOI: 10.4018/978-1-6684-6438-0.ch002

# INTRODUCTION

The following chapter outlines an approach to create and model interdisciplinary pre-service professional preparation with representation from personnel with a range of expertise in the field of special education. In this approach, an interdisciplinary team of faculty, also known as a faculty learning community (FLC), model and learn from each other to enhance professional knowledge and skills. These experiences include the development of an FLC and the creation of a video case study series to model interdisciplinary professional roles and engagement within special education and related fields. Professionals across various fields related to education might consider this project as an exemplar for organizing, facilitating, and evaluating the overall impacts of a shared and interdisciplinary learning experience.

The interdisciplinary and inter-professional FLC that was established developed the following collaborative goals:

1. Compose video models for pre-service professionals that represent inter-professional expertise to support students with high-intensity academic, social-emotional, and behavioral needs;
2. Model a positive collaborative approach to special education team meetings (i.e., Individualized Education Program team meetings, Functional Behavioral Assessment data analysis with behavior planning, Individualized Education Program goal development and selection of support services) for pre-service professionals' future careers; and
3. Distribute video models for pre-service professionals across a range of disciplines.

This interdisciplinary and inter-professional project-based approach to collaboration stemmed from the need for quality models of individualized education program (IEP) team meetings for pre-service professionals. Additionally, faculty were interested in establishing a stronger partnership between pre-service professional preparation programs and continuity in the use of discipline-specific terminology and practice. In this particular FLC project, then, the *IEP team* was used as a broad term most universally accepted in special education. Specifically, *IEP team* was used as a replacement for the Committee on Special Education (CSE) referenced in the *New York State Handbook Guide to Quality Individualized Education Program* (IEP) *Development and Implementation* (University of the State of New York: The State Department of Education, 2010).

In sum, this chapter will serve as an example to support the need for interdisciplinary and inter-professional approaches to preparing future service providers for students with disabilities and the stakeholders who support them.

# BACKGROUND

## Collaboration in Higher Education through Faculty Learning Communities (FLCs)

One of the essential prerequisites to interdisciplinary collaboration in higher education is interdisciplinary education (Petri, 2010). As part of this interdisciplinary education, faculty from separate disciplines develop an understanding of the knowledge, skills, roles, and inherent value of other disciplines. The ability to model and effectively teach pre-professional students how to collaborate within the complex field of special education to serve the needs of children with disabilities is not possible in isolation.

Creating a faculty learning community (FLC) is one method for supporting the interdisciplinary education of special education and its related service professional disciplines in higher education. An FLC involves a small group of faculty voluntarily joining together to actively engage in a professional development process to promote teaching and learning (Richlin & Cox, 2004). FLCs have been found to result in several benefits for participating faculty members, including enhanced instructional practices (Hirst et al., 2021; Shulman, 1986), more productive scholarly outputs (Richlin & Cox, 2004), and the development of collegial relationships across discipline boundaries (Glowacki-Dudka & Brown, 2007). In being a part of an FLC, faculty members can develop the skills necessary to model collaborative practices.

While FLCs are specific to the context of higher education, the concept of a professional learning community has existed within K-12 education since the 1970s, where administrators and educators were encouraged to engage in reflective practice, capacity building, and collective learning (Stoll et al., 2006). Stoll et al. (2006) note five features of professional learning communities, including: (1) shared values and vision, (2) collective responsibility, (3) reflective personal inquiry, (4) collaboration, and (5) group and individual learning. These core features align with the purpose and goals of our FLC to translate our reflective practice into improved outcomes for our respective pre-professional students.

## Collaboration in Special Education and the IEP Process (P-12)

The Individuals with Disabilities Education Improvement Act of 2004 (IDEIA, 2004) requires forming a multidisciplinary team to interpret assessment data as part of the special education service evaluation and reevaluation processes. A multidisciplinary team is defined within the IDEIA Part C regulations as "the involvement of two or more separate disciplines or professions" (IDEIA, 2004, Section 303.24). However, multidisciplinary models of assessment, goal development, and service delivery may lead to siloed and fragmented approaches that confuse families and limit the effectiveness of interventions (Friend & Cook, 2017; Woodruff & McGonigel, 1988). Educators and related service professionals often conduct their assessments, develop and draft Individualized Education Program (IEP) goals, and implement services following an IEP meeting independent of each other (Dillon et al., 2021). IEP meetings within this multidisciplinary approach are less collaborative. They reflect a consultative approach, where educators and related service personnel are viewed as experts in their specific areas who report discipline-specific assessment findings and recommendations for services. The student's family members are passive recipients rather than actively engaged in the IEP process. In short, while a multidisciplinary approach meets the minimum legal expectations, other collaborative structures can offer increased benefits. Interdisciplinary approaches in particular consider the needs of the whole child while breaking down silos to produce better outcomes for integrating and coordinating services provided across discipline areas of expertise. Interdisciplinary or transdisciplinary collaboration provides an opportunity for change, bringing forward an improved educational opportunity for students and the learning community (Solone et al., 2020).

*Figure 1. Continuum of Collaborative Teaming*

[Figure 1: Continuum of Collaborative Teaming — arrow from "Limited Collaboration" to "Extensive Collaboration" with three team types: Multidisciplinary Team (Siloed expertise), Interdisciplinary Team (Complementary goals and services), and Transdisciplinary Team (Shared goals and services across disciplines).]

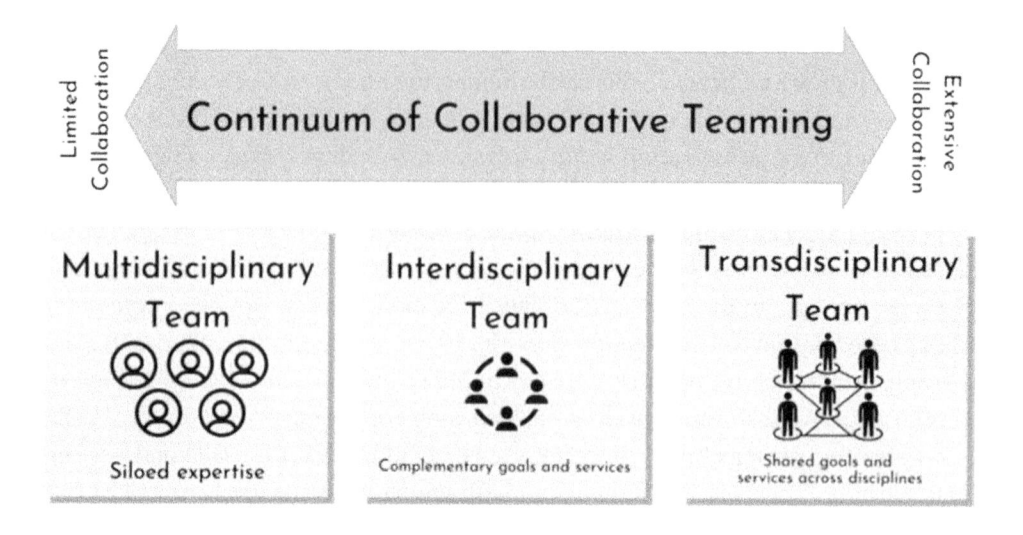

## Interdisciplinary Approaches: Continuity in Service Delivery for P-12 Students with Disabilities

Friend and Cook (2017) define collaboration as a process "for direct interaction between at least two coequal parties voluntarily engaged in shared decision making as they work toward a common goal," (p. 5). Interprofessional collaboration is an expectation within the standards of the various professional organizations that serve students under IDEIA. These include professional organizations of special educators, general educators, speech language pathologists (SLP), audiologists, occupational therapists (OT), physical therapists (PT), and school psychologists (i.e., American Occupational Therapy Association, 2021; American Physical Therapy Association, 2019; Council for Clinical Certification in Audiology and Speech-Language Pathology of the American Speech-Language-Hearing Association, 2018; Council for Exceptional Children, 2015; National Association of School Psychologists, 2020). Collaboration is also one of the four domains of high leverage practices that all special educators should demonstrate proficiency in knowledge and skills (McLeskey et al., 2017). In a review of best practices for professionals in a collaborative school setting, Solone and colleagues (2020) put forward four areas of necessary skills and considerations for effective teams: mutual goals, shared resources, shared responsibility, and synergy.

As noted previously, collaborative approaches in special education vary along a continuum. On one end of the continuum is multidisciplinary collaboration; interdisciplinary collaboration sits at the middle of the continuum; and transdisciplinary collaboration falls at the other end of the continuum (see Figure 1).

During multidisciplinary collaboration, entirely independent assessment, goal development, and service delivery take place. Each discipline contributes to the process, but without coordination or significant input from other team members (Dillon et al., 2021; Friend & Cook, 2017). Lack of coordination in multidisciplinary collaboration means students have less opportunity to receive services, because only one expert delivers interventions and strategies. For example, when an SLP provides language therapy outside of the general education classroom without the special education teacher and general education teacher being present, these teachers cannot utilize the strategies and interventions throughout the student's school day and at home.

During interdisciplinary collaboration, educators, related service providers, and the family benefit from an increased understanding of the knowledge and skills that support mutual goals developed within the team (Friend & Cook, 2017; Woodruff & McGonigel, 1988). Imagine the potential outcomes for a student who receives services for interrelated goals reinforced across the school day by all team members compared to a student who receives language therapy for 20 minutes twice per week in isolation. Families can also incorporate strategies and supports outside of school to maximize positive outcomes. Students with complex support needs have been found to have increased academic engagement in general education classrooms when IEP team members engage in interdisciplinary collaboration (Kuntz & Carter, 2021).

At the other end of the collaborative continuum lies transdisciplinary collaboration. Transdisciplinary collaboration involves the same processes found within interdisciplinary collaboration, but with the addition of role release and responsibilities, where team members regularly deliver services performed by other disciplines under that practitioner's supervision and support (Friend & Cook, 2017; Woodruff & McGonigel, 1988). Given the limited time and resources of related services personnel, interdisciplinary collaboration may be a more feasible approach (Dillon et al., 2021).

## Modeling Collaboration for Pre-Service Professionals

Although the professional standards and benefits of collaboration are widely known, university faculty across disciplines that instruct on the development and implementation of a child's IEP often develop their curricula and teach within programs with limited interaction across disciplines. Additionally, pre-professional programs typically provide preparation within each specialized profession, with little to no opportunity for pre-service professionals to develop the interdisciplinary knowledge and collaboration skills needed to more effectively engage in the IEP process (Dobbs-Oates & Wachter Morris, 2016; Sisti & Robledo, 2021). Pre-professional programs can consider how to model and explicitly teach the skills needed to form high-functioning interdisciplinary collaborative teams to meet the individual needs of students with disabilities (Miller & Stayton, 2006).

Collaboration involves the ability to communicate effectively as well as to actively listen and facilitate understanding of the mutual goals of the collaborative team, the roles and responsibilities of each member, and processes to monitor and communicate progress (Friend & Cook, 2017). To effectively collaborate, a professional must exhibit problem solving, communication, and interpersonal skills (Kampwirth & Powers, 2016). Examples of problem solving skills include establishing rapport, identifying the problem, analyzing why the problem is occurring, and developing a plan to ameliorate the problem and set goals. Examples of collaborative communication skills include attending, active listening, reframing, empathy, keeping a goal orientation, and asking questions. Examples of collaborative interpersonal skills include forging positive relationships, conveying competence and confidence, and projecting the idea that the situation is going to improve.

Faculty can incorporate a broad range of approaches to develop interdisciplinary collaboration skills. All approaches should include explicit instruction of effective communication skills, group dynamics, meeting facilitation (Beck & DeSutter, 2020), collaborative goal setting, and implementation of embedded instruction and service delivery (Friend & Cook, 2017).

Specific research-based strategies for teaching collaboration skills include problem-based learning (Tseng et al., 2016), service-learning (Osterholt & Barratt, 2011; Neeper & Dymond, 2020), simulations

(Mueller et al., 2019); and video modeling (McLeskey et al., 2017). Video modeling is a promising approach to scaffold pre-professional students in learning foundational collaboration skills before students engage in a problem-based learning experience, service-learning, or a simulation that requires students to demonstrate these skills. Video modeling of interdisciplinary work among education-related professionals, paired with debriefing, can fill a gap in the preparation of pre-service professionals. Modeling of such effective interdisciplinary structures illustrates to pre-service professionals that diverse providers working together for a single student/client can be practical - not simply an aspirational goal.

## Video Modeling

Bandura's social learning theory (1971) asserts that observational learning occurs through competent models via four processes: (1) attending to critical features of the model, (2) retaining a memory of what was observed, (3) reproducing the skills observed, and (4) reinforcing performance of the skills to increase motivation. Observational learning can occur in-person or virtually; however, Bandura noted the effectiveness of televised models because of their power to hold people's attention. Video modeling is a familiar format and extensively-researched teaching approach for observational learning in the field of P-12 special education for students with disabilities (e.g., Boon et al., 2020; Hein et al., 2019), but its use as a pedagogical tool in pre-professional programs is also increasing.

Analysis of video models of classroom practices followed by discussion and reflection is a staple of teacher preparation programs (Baecher & Connor, 2010; Burden et al., 2010). Pre-service teachers benefit from observational learning opportunities from video models to develop pedagogical knowledge and effective instructional practices (Dieker et al., 2009). Increasingly, video models of instructional methods are available online via subscriptions, such as ATLAS (Accomplished Teaching, Learning, and Schools; National Board for Professional Teaching Standards, 2022), and for free through the High Leverage Practices for Special Educators Video Series (Kennedy et al., 2018).

Video modeling is a valued pedagogical tool within pre-professional programs to support observational learning focused on students developing discipline-specific skills. These models can occur by recording, live authentic demonstrations of skills (Kennedy et al., 2018), or scripted and simulated role-plays (Burden et al., 2010; Giles et al., 2014). Students in speech-language pathology pre-professional programs may subscribe to the Master Clinician Network (n.d.) to view videos of speech-language pathologists (SLP) providing therapy services to children. SLP faculty can also subscribe to AphasiaBank (n.d.) and supervise pre-professionals' use of the video database. Occupational and physical therapy pre-professional programs may use the video database available via subscription from the International Clinical Educators Video Library (International Clinical Educators Learning Center, 2022). Other programs may produce their own collection of video models of practices to use in their programs, similar to recommendations within the field of teacher education (Dymond & Bentz, 2006). For professionals who will work in school settings to serve the needs of students with disabilities eligible under IDEIA, video modeling ensures educators and related service personnel acquire the expertise to contribute to comprehensive IEPs.

# INTERDISCIPLINARY PRE-SERVICE PROFESSIONAL PREPARATION

## Issues, Controversies, Problems

Two major underlying challenges to interdisciplinary pre-service professional preparation are narrow perspectives of pre-professional preparation and limited educational resources. Both of these challenges will be discussed next.

### Narrow Perspectives of Pre-Professional Preparation

As discussed above, multidisciplinary teams represent the legal minimum for fulfilling the requirements of IDEIA. However, if teams of professionals from across disciplines are to provide continuity of support and services, then interdisciplinary collaboration is necessary. A multidisciplinary team within the context of multidisciplinary collaboration involves members of different disciplines who conduct their activities (assessments) independently, bringing discipline-specific skills, knowledge, and terminology to describe students' needs as they relate to their own specific disciplines (King-Sears et al., 2015). By broadening the perspectives of often siloed service providers and establishing a foundation for interdisciplinary approaches for pre-professional service providers, there is a natural gateway of access for novice professionals to follow and model for future school-based team meetings. The following section will outline issues faced by programs preparing pre-service professionals to work in the field of special education for interdisciplinary collaboration engaging in IEP processes.

An interdisciplinary collaboration of school-based professionals provides a multidisciplinary student support team, or IEP team, with not only an increased level of support or resources but perhaps more importantly a broader understanding of the child as a whole person. Service providers can be organized as core team members such as general education teachers, special education teachers, and family members, as well as additional members such as social workers, school psychologists, administrators, occupational therapists, speech therapists, physical therapists, school nurses, and community agents bringing a variety of perspectives that must work in tandem to improve student outcomes (King-Sears et al., 2015). IEP teams can prevent disjointed programming by aligning expertise and ensuring continuity in service delivery. In a survey of 17 teachers and administrators through interviews, Woods et al. (2018) identified two critical voices in the identification of students with disabilities through the multidisciplinary team: elementary-level general and special education educators (Buell et al., 1999, as cited in Woods et al., 2018). Additionally, it was found that administrators still perceived those same educators as two separate entities (Woods et al., 2018). Kosko and Wilkins (2009) noted that general educators may feel insufficiently prepared or given insufficient opportunities to collaborate with special educators, possibly leading to significantly less competence in participating in interdisciplinary meetings held by IEP teams. Pfeiffer and colleagues (2019) reflect on the need for pre-professional students to participate in collaborative learning opportunities integrated across disciplines and colleges. An *IEP team* is tasked with meeting the needs of students in schools and therefore must work across various disciplines to efficiently work together (Giordano et al., 2019).

The interdisciplinary preparation of pre-service professionals will naturally allow academics an opportunity to gain knowledge and skills in a variety of areas of expertise, learning from each other and related fields. By modeling this level of interdisciplinary collaboration for pre-service professionals, the foundation is established to support novice pre-service professionals with the knowledge, skills, and dispositions to eventually enhance outcomes for P-12 students through multidisciplinary school-based teams. The interdisciplinary collaborative process affords an opportunity to gain experience in successfully navigating collegial relationships while simultaneously gaining knowledge of and ideally respect for other disciplines (Dillon et al., 2021). The Council for Exceptional Children targets collaboration as one of the four areas of high-leverage practice in P-12 classrooms for special education teachers (McLeskey et al., 2017), supported by researchers documenting positive impacts on student outcomes (Ronfeldt et al., 2015). By broadening the perspectives of pre-service professionals (i.e., special and general educators), interdisciplinary collaboration opens up opportunities to consider the needs of the whole child while breaking down silos to produce better outcomes for integrating and coordinating services provided across discipline-specific areas of expertise.

The preparation of pre-service professionals through the lens of the interdisciplinary and interprofessional model of support to enhance service delivery for students with disabilities reflects the ideal scenario of continuity for school-based interdisciplinary teams. Preparation programs for pre-service professionals can consider how to model and explicitly teach the skills needed to form high-functioning collaborative teams, with the end goal of meeting the individual needs of students with disabilities (Miller & Stayton, 2006). For example, special education teachers and speech-language pathologists are two professionals represented on collaborative multidisciplinary teams with close interaction and partnerships in schools. Woods and colleagues (2018) argue there are limited collaborative university training programs, courses, and/or practica for these two professions. Pre-professional programs typically focus on each specialized discipline, with little to no opportunity to build interdisciplinary knowledge and collaboration skills needed to effectively engage in the IEP process (Dobbs-Oates & Wachter Morris, 2016).

Finally, as discussed above, terminology used in team meetings can vary from member to member (or from state to state), resulting in reduced collaborative potential. Discipline-specific language is used to efficiently and effectively communicate with other professionals. However, using discipline-specific jargon can serve as a barrier to effective interdisciplinary communication (McLaughlin et al., 2017). The use of jargon without clear explanations has also been found to marginalize parents during the IEP process and amplify perceived power imbalances (Singh & Keese, 2020). Ineffective communication by the professionals on the IEP team decreases parental engagement in the process.

Creating continuity in terminology for members of a interdisciplinary team might provide an avenue to eliminate intimidating educational jargon as a barrier to communication between members of the team and support for families (Woods et al., 2018). Roncaglia (2018) found in a case study analysis that an effective working relationship with families required expertise positively shared focusing on evidence-based practice rather than professional judgments. Additionally, approaches such as predictively scheduled focused meetings with external personnel provided an opportunity to work collaboratively, broadening the individual perspective and opening a dialogue for holistically and consistently integrated support across different contexts. The authors' work also aimed to remove the barrier of unfamiliarity with those involved in the team, leading to a potential for inequalities between those on the interdisciplinary team. One of Nooteboom et al.'s (2022) nine recommendations for a team discussion is to ensure a safe team climate by approaching topics with an "open and curious attitude, equality, and mutual respect, familiarity, and a positive atmosphere with a focus on learning" (p. 8).

## Limited Educational Resources

Video modeling has made an essential contribution to various pre-professional preparation programs to support the development of discipline-specific skills (e.g., Giles et al., 2014). However, examples of video modeling that supports interdisciplinary collaboration among the education and related services disciplines are limited. This is surprising given the central role that interdisciplinary collaboration plays during IEP meetings, where professionals across disciplines determine eligibility for special education services, develop individualized goals, and plan for service delivery. In short, interdisciplinary collaboration should be a critical component of video models, because this collaboration is required for effective special education service development and delivery. Nonetheless, only one study has investigated the use of simulated IEP meeting video models (Burden et al., 2010).

Issues of privacy and confidentiality create a significant barrier to creating video models during actual IEP meetings. A possible explanation for the very limited literature base may relate to challenges in obtaining parental/guardian permission to video record IEP meetings with the legal mandates of parental/guardian rights for confidentiality (Burden et al., 2010). As a result, simulated IEP videos may be a more feasible approach.

Another challenge of developing these educational resources is that specific terminology exists within departments of education in different states for special education policies and regulation. As a result, developing generic videos of applicable skills for IEP development may be limited in their usefulness.

Although exemplars of IEP simulation video models are typically not available, educational IEP simulation design principles can be followed to create video models (Mueller et al., 2019). These principles focus on three aspects of the simulation, which can be adapted to develop video models with utility across disciplines (Hoeh et al., in press). Mueller et al.'s (2019) first principle is to create videos for common and unusual challenges professionals will likely experience. The second principle is to incorporate content that demonstrates specific interdisciplinary collaboration and discipline-specific skills. The third principle is to focus on developing simulations of practices that will result in positive outcomes for K-12 students. With these principles, faculty members can create video models for engaging in interdisciplinary collaboration during IEP meetings.

As mentioned previously, Burden et al. (2010) conducted the only study examining the use of simulated IEP meeting video cases to support the engagement level of special educators during team meetings. The authors noted that the simulated meeting videos enhanced the reflection and discussions of the pre-service teachers and increased their comfort level to participate in actual IEP meetings (Burden et al., 2010). This further reinforces one of the main issues faced by the FLC members: the need for quality models of IEP team meetings for pre-service professionals across disciplines.

## SOLUTIONS AND RECOMMENDATIONS

The previously-described concerns clearly demonstrate a lack of training opportunities for pre-service professionals to practice their interdisciplinary collaborative skills and the negative impact these missed opportunities have for pre-service professionals, professionals, and (most importantly), P-12 students with disabilities and their families. The following section will outline solutions and recommendations to support the limited number of resources for video case models in special education as well as recommendations for preparing pre-service professionals to be collaborative and effective, so that they can transition to novice service providers with the skills needed to participate and contribute to an interdisciplinary team.

Specifically, the challenges discussed above served as a catalyst for the authors' faculty learning community (FLC) video modeling project. First, an origin story briefly details the grassroots efforts of a voluntary FLC. The authors' accomplishment was developing three video models addressing the nuances of an interdisciplinary team as a support for students with disabilities and their families. In all, the FLC's development and creation of video models offers a possible solution to the challenges and problems academics face in instruction of interdisciplinary collaboration and modeling of such collaboration for pre-service professionals.

## Origin Story

As addressed in the previous section, there are a limited number of resources for video models of IEP meetings in special education and related fields (Burden et al., 2010). In addition, the COVID-19 pandemic resulted in moving course work to an asynchronous online format in the spring of 2020 for the FLC's pre-professional programs, which required flexible teaching and learning activities for graduate special/childhood education majors. Faculty from special education, childhood education, field placement offices, and adjunct faculty, along with external departments of psychology, communication, and an external faculty member from an outside institution representing occupational therapy recognized this time as an opportunity to work collaboratively in training pre-service professionals to ensure continuity in collaboration and broadening professional perspectives with the intention of more efficiently and effectively preparing pre-service professionals for the field of special education.

Faculty members thus established an interdisciplinary and inter-professional faculty learning community (FLC) with a focus on creating video models to foster growth in community (Glowacki-Dudka & Brown, 2007), pedagogy (Hirst et al., 2021), and scholarship (Richlin & Cox, 2004). The FLC joined together faculty from two universities representing the disciplines of special education, general education, school psychology, speech-language pathology, and occupational therapy.

## Development of the FLC

The authors developed their faculty learning community (FLC) following Cox's (n.d.) framework for collaboration and professional development in order to create a mock video case study series to model interdisciplinary professional roles and engagement within special education and related fields. This video series was designed for training pre-service professionals. In Table 1, the FLC's actions for each step of Cox's (n.d.) framework are described.

Cox's (n.d.) 16 recommendations provided the framework for successful interaction during the development and subsequent revision of the video models, which will be described next. These video-based materials were created for use in teacher education and related service provider education fields across institutions. Video modeling was selected as the method of delivery as an evidence-based practice (i.e., expert demonstrations of the specific procedures of instructional practices; Dieker et al., 2009).

*Table 1. Cox's 16 Recommendations for Conducting a Faculty Learning Community (FLC)*

| Cox's (n.d.) 16 Recommendations | FLC Actions |
|---|---|
| 1. Limit membership | FLC was limited to eight team members to ensure adequate interaction between members. |
| 2. Make membership voluntary | FLC team members were invited to volunteer based on their area of expertise. Bringing various stakeholders together on a voluntary basis allowed for motivated members to complete the project successfully. |
| 3. Consider associated partners (consultants) | One of the collaborating university's Center for Teaching Excellence was contacted for mentorship and distribution of knowledge. |
| 4. Develop a multidisciplinary team | Eight areas of expertise (four departments, two universities). Institution 1 (seven areas of expertise, three departments: Areas of expertise included Special Education, Secondary Education, a Field Placement Office, Adjunct Faculty, School Psychology, Communication Sciences and Disorders, and Department Chairs. Institution 2: Area of expertise was Occupational Therapy. The multidisciplinary team that was developed included a variety of professionals with public school and college teaching experience. Having different perspectives present during the creation of multidisciplinary team video models allowed members to do more than just play a role. The team members were able to draw upon their previous experience in the public school setting to provide realistic video models based on authentic processes during the meeting process. |
| 5. Schedule planned meetings | A mutually agreed upon schedule was developed with consideration for full-time and adjunct teaching schedules, childcare, and departmental/university needs. |
| 6. Build a social community | Social community was built via networking within the FLC and across institutions, prioritizing teaching topics or content, and focusing on shared scholarship. |
| 7. Have an FLC facilitator | FLC leader fostered the development of shared goals, facilitated the FLC process, solicited comments and feedback from team members, organized project materials, and maintained lines of communication. |
| 8. Members should have shared governance in objectives, goals, and content | Team members shared the decision making in content reviewed in the video series and also shared professional readings. |
| 9. Obtain and maintain a commitment to the FLC | The facilitator took charge of this role through consistent communication, maintaining team member commitment. |
| 10. Assess the FLC's impact on professional development and the FLC components | Representing the Scholarship of Teaching and Learning (SoTL), team members reflected on the impact of the FLC on faculty development. Five team members completed a shared discussion group based on the selected texts using three levels of text protocol (School Reform Initiative, 2017). |
| 11. Use an approach that contributes to the Scholarship of Teaching and Learning (SoTL) | Documented the FLC process in published manuscripts and book chapters. Additionally, Boyer's Model of Scholarship (1990) was taken into consideration. Boyer's Model of Scholarship (1990) includes the practice of teaching, sharing about teaching, scholarly teaching, and scholarship of teaching and learning. |
| 12. Present FLC outcomes on campus or at conferences | FLC team members presented locally (to colleagues) through one of the participating university's Center for Teaching Excellence. In addition, FLC members presented at a state-level conference. Both presentations outlined the FLC's process of organizing, facilitating, and evaluating the overall impacts of a shared learning experience. |
| 13. Blend the modality of meetings (including in-person and online modalities) | Using in-person meetings allowed for small group discussions and planning and gave members the opportunity to work jointly on this project. Whole group discussions and video recordings completed via video conferencing allowed FLC members to develop the content and provide information for students to view. |
| 14. Provide rewards, recognition, and celebrations | The FLC facilitator arranged for university-level recognition letters from administrators at the universities to be sent to FLC members. |
| 15. Embed the FLC within the institution's Teaching and Learning Center | Mentorship from one of the participating university's Center for Teaching Excellence was obtained. At the end of the project, the FLC shared their process and product with the Center for Teaching Excellence. |
| 16. Adapt the FLC to fit the institution's culture and faculty needs | The first university emphasizes collaborative faculty projects and scholarship; as a result, the institution's culture was in line with the FLC focus. The FLC also allowed for flexible engagement based on personal and professional needs and areas of expertise. |

## Creation of Video Models and Intended Student Learning Outcomes

In the Spring 2021 semester, the FLC worked collaboratively to design a case study for K-6 students with severe disabilities and subsequently develop simulated IEP team meeting video models. The team based the video models on a psychological report, an Individualized Education Program (IEP), and supporting assessment documents on an actual child from a previous case management load. The team wrote scripts for the multidisciplinary team meetings and recorded three main videos. Notably, the authors' interdisciplinary collaborative team prioritized the family perspective as an equal voice and stakeholder in the discussion and in the video models.

With pre-service professionals as the target audience, the team worked to model typical procedures of a multidisciplinary team as well, such as introductions, reviewing basic parent/guardian and student rights through due process safeguards, and follow-up expectations for the family and staff. These videos centered on what to expect in an IEP team meeting from a variety of perspectives, including the student, family, chairperson, school psychologist, general education teacher, special education teacher, related service providers, and parent advocate. The multidisciplinary team also worked through the FLC process to establish common terminology and practices to emphasize and model with the authors' pre-service professionals within their individual preparation programs.

The FLC members selected the scenarios for the videos following the educational simulation design principles adapted from medical education and described by Mueller et al.'s (2019) research on simulated IEP meetings to include: (a) common and rare challenges special educators are likely to encounter, (b) the varied, specific skill sets needed, and (c) scenarios that will positively impact student outcomes. Based on the simulation design principles (Mueller et al., 2019), the FLC developed a case of a child with high-intensity needs across multiple domains and disciplines (academic, social-emotional, behavioral) using an authentic school psychology evaluation report. The aim of this case study was to provide modeling of the use of an interdisciplinary framework to support students with high-intensity needs through prevention and intervention techniques. Three scenarios for the initial videos were selected, including a reevaluation meeting, an IEP annual review meeting in which annual goals and services were established, and a meeting focused on sharing the results of a Functional Behavioral Assessment (FBA) and developing a Positive Behavior Intervention Plan (BIP). The case of this particular child and these three scenarios align with the simulation design principles by including both common and rare challenges of IEP meetings, including two common purposes for IEP meetings (reevaluation and annual review) and a less common meeting (FBA/BIP-focused IEP).

The scenarios required varied and specific skill sets via interdisciplinary collaboration and discipline-specific knowledge for video analysis. The intended pre-professional service provider learning outcomes, interdisciplinary skills, and strategies included the types of data collected; the documentation described; specific instructional, therapeutic, and support strategies described; the legal requirements enacted; and the interpersonal communication skills used. Team members also selected IEPs as the scenarios that could positively impact pre-service professionals and their future students and clients by strengthening their skills for interdisciplinary collaboration and their self-efficacy for engaging in IEP meetings. Some of the authors' approaches paired with the video analysis included group discussions and written reflections with prompts intended to highlight specific collaborative and communication skills. Similar to Mueller et al.'s (2019) approach to creating IEP simulations, the FLC ensured that the videos could be utilized across multiple courses and disciplines.

Each of the three videos for the FLC's video series took approximately one month to develop. For each video, the team first met to review the psychological report materials, assign roles and responsibilities, and determine topics to be included or highlighted during the video models. Mock meetings, which were kept to a manageable level of content at approximately 20-25 minutes, were then scripted. By pre-determining the learning objectives for each meeting (e.g., "Who attends a IEP team meeting?"), FLC members could ensure that appropriate topics were covered in the authors' scripts. Mock meetings, held through Zoom, were recorded on two computers so that shots of both the individual speaker as well as the entire IEP team could be captured. The FLC then test ran, reported, edited, and captioned the videos using Screencast-O-Matic (an online video editing software) for distribution to classes as instructional materials.

The video models were intended for eventual use across courses in school psychology, special education, communication, and occupational therapy. The FBA/BIP video case model was initially introduced in a combined childhood special education masters program during a special education assessment course as well as in a school psychology graduate course on behavioral interventions. The choice to target elementary education pre-professional teachers was prioritized based on the typical pre-referral processes in special education. The intention was to create an awareness of perspective and expertise across disciplines and universities represented through a set of interdisciplinary video-based team meetings.

The second major intention of the FLC video modeling project was to highlight the importance of continuity of services. Faculty were interested in establishing a stronger partnership between pre-service professional preparation programs and continuity in the use of discipline-specific terminology and practice. Following Cox's 16 recommendations for FLCs (n.d.), a limited number of faculty team members were invited to volunteer based on expertise. The authors' emphasis was to establish an interdisciplinary team to build a community with shared governance and a professional social community. Using this approach, the authors developed an FLC to meet their professional needs, in turn addressing topics such as consistency in discipline-specific terminology and practices. The FLC team was comprised of a small group of five faculty representing special education, general education, and psychology, including adjunct academics. The FLC team completed two shared readings and a structured discussion using the Three Levels of Text Protocol (School Reform Initiative, 2017) based on state-specific special education policies and procedures in special education. A detailed description of the FLC process, implementation of Cox's 16 recommendations (n.d.), text selection, and faculty learning outcomes are included in Hoeh et al. (in press).

In sum, this FLC was developed with a central focus of creating a culture of communication and interdisciplinary collaboration. Furthermore, the FLC had a shared vision for service delivery supporting P-12 students with disabilities and their stakeholders. Nonetheless, this was only an initial project developed by the FLC. In the next section, the authors address future directions that the FLC plans to address, as well as wider future research trends others may wish to pursue.

## IMPLICATIONS FOR RESEARCH AND PRACTICE

As previously described, faculty engaged in the faculty learning community (FLC) video modeling project faced two underlying challenges: narrow perspectives of pre-professional preparation and limited educational resources. These faculty also discovered features of their experience that made the project beneficial. Such insights emerged from personal reflection and structured collaborative dialogue following Cox's (n.d.) framework. Implications for future research and current practice surfaced from analysis of both the issues and solutions.

Regarding research, this group of faculty intends to replicate use of the FBA/BIP video. This will likely be done in a graduate education course on prosocial behavior as well as a graduate school psychology course on behavioral interventions. The impact of the video modeling will be measured by graduate student pre- and post- questionnaires on FBAs and BIPs or a focus group discussion. This will serve as the second cohort of students to engage in the video modeling project. Undergraduate and graduate students may also be invited to participate in future research projects on video simulations. This would expand research opportunities for members of the established Teacher Education Student Research Group (TESRG). The TESRG pairs volunteer-students with volunteer-faculty based on similar research interests. Faculty members mentor students through research design, implementation, and reporting.

Regarding practice, these faculty have a multi-pronged approach to enhancing both professional preparation activities and FLC experiences. Such suggestions range from curriculum revisions to collaboration with other divisions on campus to securing administrative support for ongoing development in these fields.

Typically, pre-service professional preparation programs have content-specific courses taught by respective faculty members. This means that students studying to become Speech-Language Pathologists (SLP) enroll in the equivalent of a Special Education foundations course ("Teaching Students with Speech-Language-Disabilities Preschool-12") separate from students studying to become K-12 teachers ("Introduction to Special Education"). However, this arrangement at the authors' college recently changed. By cross-listing both courses and assigning a single instructor, pre-service teachers and pre-service SLPs have the opportunity to learn from each other. For example, they can share how IEP development applies to various school-based professions. Some degree programs also offer electives in related professional fields so that students experience cross-disciplinary frameworks and practices before graduation. For example, at one of the FLC universities, the BA/MST Adolescence Education program encourages students to take an elective from the Special Education, School Psychology, or Educational Leadership programs. Likewise, students in the graduate School Psychology program often take an elective in the Special Education department. Providing students with opportunities for interdisciplinary collaboration during their professional preparation sets the stage for this same interdisciplinary collaboration once students are licensed/certified professionals.

Another curricular implication is to develop more video models of simulated IEP team meetings. For example, videos could focus on Early Intervention, a student at the secondary level, or transition planning. These videos could also center around different referral areas than the ones in the initial case study.

Finally, the FLC has plans to extend the use of the video models to allow pre-service professionals to practice interdisciplinary collaboration skills themselves. As discussed above, interdisciplinary collaboration skills include competence in problem solving (e.g., identifying the problem, developing a plan), communication (e.g., reframing, active listening, asking questions), and interpersonal interactions (e.g., conveying competence and confidence; Kampwirth & Powers, 2016).

Hoover (2013) attributes the lack of skills and training in collaboration to a lack of adequate resources and professional development, among other factors. In order to address these barriers, Hoover (2013) offers a six-point collaborative model: shared leadership, coherent vision, comprehensive planning, adequate resources, sustained implementation, and continuous evaluation of team efficiency and productivity. The FLC curated video series aims to address some of the barriers to collaboration by modeling for pre-service professionals. In this plan, FLC faculty would develop instructional material for running simulated interdisciplinary IEP team meetings for pre-service professionals in preparation programs. After viewing a video model, students would assume the role of an IEP team member in a mock meeting with students across training programs. After the simulation, they would debrief the experience and reflect on their participation. These types of experiences for pre-service professionals would provide explicit modeling and instruction in shared leadership (data-based instructional decisions), coherent vision (student-centered IEP development), comprehensive planning (development of IEP goals), and a sustained implementation (comprehensive representation of student supports).

In addition to curriculum revision, there are implications for broader interdisciplinary collaboration. This could include inviting faculty from other school-related professional preparation programs (like social work or counseling) to join the FLC. Additionally, partnerships could be forged with university-based resources such as a Center for Teaching Excellence; a center on ethics; or a Center for Diversity, Equity, and Inclusion. In the case of the FLC's main university, each of these centers is already established on campus and have similar goals: to support faculty professional development and to enhance inclusive practices on campus. University-based preparation programs may consider partnerships with community organizations such as The Arc Alliance (ARC), Autism Speaks, The National Down Syndrome Society (NDSS), or related school based organizations (e.g., Boards of Cooperative Educational Services [BOCES]), branching out to supports beyond the more traditional school-based setting. Such partnerships would incorporate the expertise of diverse professionals and could promote FLC engagement across multiple professions. This is in line with Cox's (n.d.) third recommendation in framing an FLC: to consider associated partners.

Equally important is administrative support. Leaders who value interdisciplinary collaboration, curriculum development, and research must allocate the necessary resources. Effective interdisciplinary collaborative work requires time. Designing an effective video model includes securing redacted documents; writing scripts; designing related assignments and scoring guides; recording, editing, and producing videos; coordinating the use of video models with instructors; and collecting and analyzing data. Administrators could support course releases for faculty engaged in the design of video models. Administrators could also consider creative funding streams so that faculty and instructional technology teams can collaborate on video model projects. This would marry expertise in multiple areas, thereby enhancing the video model product. Administrators (and faculty) may also want to reconceptualize degree program or department configurations to eliminate silos and promote interdisciplinary curriculum design and research opportunities. Such innovation will need the support of numerous administrative offices, as decisions about teaching load, faculty lines, funding, and other crucial conversations would need to occur. If form follows function, then restructuring to promote interdisciplinary collaboration may be effective.

A myriad of interdisciplinary collaboration opportunities exist. Here, the authors outlined possible future directions for both research and professional practice. The benefit of such collaboration is clear for faculty and pre-service professionals. The intent is that such interdisciplinary collaboration carries over when graduate students become certified-licensed professionals and results in positive outcomes for P-12 students. More work is needed to add to the extant literature in this area.

## CONCLUSION

An FLC provides higher education faculty with a sense of professional community, shared responsibility for preparing pre-service professionals, and models of best practice to use in their respective areas of expertise. This FLC's focus was to prepare video modeling materials for pre-service professionals with a common set of values around service delivery, collaboration, communication, and respect for a variety of perspectives. These video models were intended for use in respective courses across training programs, and preliminary feedback from students was positive. In the summer of 2021, FLC members met via an online video conference platform to discuss their thoughts on the project, analyze student responses to survey questions about the videos, conduct textual analysis, and develop next steps.

Faculty debriefed on the benefits of professional development, learning, and engaging in collaborative opportunities through the creation of the FLC video series. The benefits include working with providers in numerous disciplines, across various levels, and with multiple departments/colleges. The authors' FLC took an integrated approach across disciplines (general education, special education, school psychology, speech-language pathology, and occupational therapy) in developing interdisciplinary and inter-professional preparation practices. Interdisciplinary and inter-professional participation constituted a powerful component of this project, as it promotes the ideal P-12 special education experience: to include a variety of service providers working together to provide an appropriate, quality education for all students, including those with disabilities.

In developing these materials, faculty learned from other fields and advanced their own knowledge. More importantly, the team's materials were intended for pre-service professionals to learn from each other and improve their own knowledge and skills in forming teams to enhance service delivery, and therefore outcomes (academic, social-emotional, and behavioral) for P-12 students with disabilities.

## ACKNOWLEDGMENT

The authors would like to acknowledge the support of their FLC members. Although not all FLC members were involved in the authorship of this chapter, their work and expertise across fields was integral in the success of the FLC and the creation of the video models.

## REFERENCES

American Occupational Therapy Association. (2021). Standards of practice for occupational therapy. *The American Journal of Occupational Therapy*, *75*(Supplement_3), 7513410030. doi:10.5014/ajot.2021.75S3004 PMID:34939642

American Physical Therapy Association. (2019). *HOD S06-20-35-29: The standards of practice for physical therapy.* APTA. https://www.apta.org/apta-and-you/leadership-and-governance/policies/standards-of-practice-pt

AphasiaBank. (n.d.) *AphasiaBank.* AphasiaBank. https://aphasia.talkbank.org/

Baecher, L. H., & Connor, D. J. (2010). "What do you see?" Using video analysis of classroom practice in a preparation program for teachers of students with learning disabilities. *Insights on Learning Disabilities*, 7(2), 5–18.

Bandura, A. (1971). *Social learning theory*. General Learning Press.

Beck, S. J., & DeSutter, K. (2020). An examination of group facilitator challenges and problem-solving techniques during IEP team meetings. *Teacher Education and Special Education*, 43(2), 127–143. doi:10.1177/0888406419839766

Boon, R. T., Urton, K., Grunke, M., & Ko, E. H. (2020). Video modeling interventions for students with learning disabilities: A systematic review. *Learning Disabilities (Weston, Mass.)*, 18(1), 49–69.

Boyer, E. (1990). Scholarship reconsidered: Priorities of the professoriate. Carnegie Foundations for the Advancement of Teaching. Princeton University Press.

Buell, M., Hallam, R., Gamel-McCormick, M., & Scheer, S. (1999). A survey of general and special education teachers' perceptions and inservice needs concerning inclusion. *International Journal of Disability Development and Education*, 46(2), 143–156. doi:10.1080/103491299100597

Burden, R., Tinnerman, L., Lunce, L., & Runshe, D. (2010). Video case studies: Preparing teachers for inclusion. *Teaching Exceptional Children Plus*, 6(4), 2–11.

Council for Clinical Certification in Audiology and Speech-Language Pathology of the American Speech-Language-Hearing Association. (2018). 2020 Standards for the Certificate of Clinical Competence in Speech-Language Pathology. ASHA. www.asha.org/certification/2020-SLP-Certification-Standards

Council for Exceptional Children. (2015). What every special educator must know: Professional ethics and standards. *CEC*. https://exceptionalchildren.org/standards/professional-practice-guidelines

Cox, M. D. (n.d.). *Faculty learning communities: 16 recommendations for FLCs*. Center for Teaching Excellence. Miami University. https://miamioh.edu/cte/faculty-staff/flcs/index.html

Dieker, L. A., Lane, H. B., Allsopp, D. H., O'Brien, C., Butler, T. W., Kyger, M., Louvin, L., & Fenty, N. S. (2009). Evaluating video models of evidence-based instructional practices to enhance teacher learning. *Teacher Education and Special Education*, 32(3), 180–196. doi:10.1177/0888406409334202

Dillon, S., Armstrong, E., Goudy, L., Reynolds, H., & Scurry, S. (2021). Improving special education service delivery through interdisciplinary collaboration. *Teaching Exceptional Children*, 54(1), 36–43. doi:10.1177/00400599211029671

Dobbs-Oates, J., & Wachter Morris, C. (2016). The case for interprofessional education in teacher education and beyond. *Journal of Education for Teaching*, 42(1), 50–65. doi:10.1080/02607476.2015.1131363

Dymond, S., & Bentz, J. (2006). Using digital videos to enhance teacher preparation. *Teacher Education and Special Education*, 29(2), 98–112. doi:10.1177/088840640602900202

Friend, M., & Cook, L. (2017). *Interactions: Collaboration skills for school professionals* (8th ed.). Pearson.

Giles, A. K., Carson, N. E., Breland, H. L., Coker-Bolt, P., & Bowman, P. J. (2014). Use of simulated patients and reflective video analysis to assess occupational therapy students' preparedness for fieldwork. *The American Journal of Occupational Therapy, 68*(S2), S57–S66. doi:10.5014/ajot.2014.685S03 PMID:25397940

Giordano, K., LoCascio, S., & Inoa, R. (2019). Special education placement: An interdisciplinary case study. *Journal of Cases in Educational Leadership, 22*(2), 14–25. doi:10.1177/1555458919828422

Glowacki-Dudka, M., & Brown, M. P. (2007). Professional development through faculty learning communities. *New Horizons in Adult Education and Human Resource Development, 21*(1-2), 29–39. doi:10.1002/nha3.10277

Hein, R., & Els, J. OBrien, K., Anasi, S., Pascuzzi, K., Blanchard, S., & Bollmann, E. (2019). Effectiveness of video modeling in children with Autism Spectrum Disorder (ASD). *American Journal of Occupational Therapy, 73*(S1), NA. http://dx.doi.org.webdb.plattsburgh.edu:2048/10.5014/ajot.2019.73S1-PO3039

Hirst, R. A., Anderson, K. L., Packard, B. W. L., Liotta, L. J., Bleakley, B. H., Lombardi, P. J., & Burkholder, K. C. (2021). Faculty learning at the individual and group level: A multi-year analysis of an interdisciplinary science faculty learning community focused on inclusive teaching and mentoring. *Journal of College Science Teaching, 50*(6), 20–30.

Hoeh, E., Bonati, L. M., Chatlos, S., Squires, M., & Countermine, B. (in press). Stop, collaborate, and listen: A faculty learning community developed to address gaps in pre-service education about interdisciplinary collaboration. *International Journal for the Scholarship of Teaching and Learning*.

Hoover, J. J. (2013). *Linking assessment to instruction in Multi-Tiered Models: A teacher's guide to selecting reading, writing, and mathematics interventions.* Pearson.

Individuals with Disabilities Education Improvement Act, Pub. L. 101-476. 20 U.S.C. § 303.24. (2004). https://sites.ed.gov/idea/regs/c/a/303.24

International Clinical Educators Learning Center. (2022) *ICE Learning Center.* https://www.icelearningcenter.com/

Kampwirth, T. J., & Powers, K. M. (2016). *Collaborative consultation in the schools: Effective practices for students with learning and behavior problems* (5th ed.). Pearson.

Kennedy, M. J., Peeples, K. N., Romig, J. E., Mathews, H. M., & Rodgers, W. J. (2018). Welcome to our new series on high-leverage practices for students with disabilities. https://highleveragepractices.org/welcome-our-new-series-high-leverage-...

King-Sears, M. E., Janney, R., & Snell, M. E. (2015). *Collaborative teaming: Teachers' guides to inclusive practices* (3rd ed.). Brookes.

Kosko, K. W., & Wilkins, J. L. (2009). General educators' in-service training and their self-perceived ability to adapt instruction for students with IEPs. *Professional Educator, 33*(2). https://eric.ed.gov/?id=EJ988196

Kuntz, E. M., & Carter, E. W. (2021). Effects of a collaborative planning and consultation framework to increase participation of students with severe disabilities in general education classes. *Research and Practice for Persons with Severe Disabilities*, *46*(1), 35–52. doi:10.1177/1540796921992518

Master Clinician Network. (n.d.) *Master Clinician Network*. https://www.masterclinician.org/

McLaughlin, T. W., Budd, J., & Clendon, S. (2017). The Child and Youth Profile: A toolkit to facilitate cross-disciplinary educational planning. *Kairaranga*, *18*(1), 3–11. doi:10.54322/kairaranga.v18i1.217

McLeskey, J., Barringer, M.-D., Billingsley, B., Brownell, M., Jackson, D., Kennedy, M., Lewis, T., Maheady, L., Rodriguez, J., Scheeler, M. C., Winn, J., & Ziegler, D. (2017). *High-leverage practices in special education.* Council for Exceptional Children and CEEDAR Center. https://highleveragepractices.org/four-areas-practice-k-12/collaboration

Miller, P. S., & Stayton, V. D. (2006). Interdisciplinary teaming in teacher preparation. *Teacher Education and Special Education*, *29*(1), 56–68. doi:10.1177/088840640602900107

Mueller, T. G., Massafra, A., Robinson, J., & Peterson, L. (2019). Simulated Individualized Education Program meetings: Valuable pedagogy within a preservice special educator program. *Teacher Education and Special Education*, *42*(3), 209–226. doi:10.1177/0888406418788920

National Association of School Psychologists. (2020). *Model for comprehensive and integrated school psychological services*. Author.

National Board for Professional Teaching Standards. (2022). *ATLAS: Accomplished Teaching, Learning, and Schools.* National Board for Professional Teaching Standards. https://www.nbpts.org/support/atlas/

Neeper, L. S., & Dymond, S. K. (2020). Incorporating service-learning in special education coursework: Experiences of university faculty. *Teacher Education and Special Education*, *43*(4), 343–357. doi:10.1177/0888406420912373

Nooteboom, L.A., Mulder, E.A., Vermeiren, R.R. JM, Eilander, J., van den Driesschen

Osterholt, D. A., & Barratt, K. (2011). A case for a collaborative classroom. *About Campus: Enriching the Student Learning Experience*, *16*(2), 20–26. doi:10.1002/abc.20057

Petri, L. (2010). Concept analysis of interdisciplinary collaboration. *Nursing Forum*, *45*(2), 73–82. doi:10.1111/j.1744-6198.2010.00167.x PMID:20536755

Pfeiffer, D. L., Pavelko, S. L., Hahs-Vaughn, D. L., & Duddinge, C. C. (2019). A national survey of Speech-Language Pathologists' engagement in interprofessional collaborative practice in schools: Identifying predictive factors and barriers to implementation. *Language, Speech, and Hearing Services in Schools*, *50*(4), 639–655. doi:10.1044/2019_LSHSS-18-0100 PMID:31411947

Richlin, L., & Cox, M. D. (2004). Developing scholarly teaching and the scholarship of teaching and learning through faculty learning communities. *New Directions for Teaching and Learning*, *2004*(97), 127–135. doi:10.1002/tl.139

Roncaglia, I. (2018). Transdisciplinary approaches embedded through PERMA with Autistic individual: A case study. *Psychological Thought, 11*(2), 224–233. doi:10.5964/psyct.v11i2.306

Ronfeldt, M., Farmer, S. O., McQueen, K., & Grissom, J. A. (2015). Teacher collaboration in instructional teams and student achievement. *American Educational Research Journal, 52*(3), 475–514. doi:10.3102/0002831215585562

School Reform Initiative. (2017). *Three levels of text protocol*. https://www.schoolreforminitiative.org/download/three-levels-of-text-protocol/

Shulman, L. S. (1986). Those who understand: Knowledge growth in teaching. *Educational Researcher, 15*(2), 4–14. doi:10.3102/0013189X015002004

S.I, Kuiper, C.H.Z. (2022). Practical recommendations for youth care professionals to improve evaluation and reflection during multidisciplinary team discussions: An action research project. *International Journal of Integrated Care, 22*(1). . doi:10.5334/ijic.5639

Singh, S., & Keese, J. (2020). Applying systems-based thinking to build better IEP relationships: A case for relational coordination. *Support for Learning, 35*(3), 359–371. doi:10.1111/1467-9604.12315

Sisti, M. K., & Robledo, J. A. (2021). Interdisciplinary collaboration practices between education specialists and related service providers. *The Journal of Special Education Apprenticeship, 10*(1), 1–19. https://scholarworks.lib.csusb.edu/josea/vol10/iss1/5

Solone, C. J., Thornton, B. E., Chiappe, J. C., Perez, C., Rearick, M. K., & Falvey, M. A. (2020). Creating collaborative schools in the United States: A review of best practices. *International Electronic Journal of Elementary Education, 12*(3), 283–292. doi:10.26822/iejee.2020358222

Stoll, L., Bolam, R., McMahon, A., Wallace, M., & Thomas, S. (2006). Professional learning communities: A review of the literature. *Journal of Educational Change, 7*(4), 221–258. doi:10.100710833-006-0001-8

Tseng, H., Gardner, T., & Yeh, H.-T. (2016). Enhancing students' self-efficacy, elaboration, and critical thinking skills in a collaborative educator preparation program. *Quarterly Review of Distance Education, 17*(2), 15–28.

University of the State of New York, The State Education Department. (2010). *Guide to quality Individualized Education Program (IEP) development and implementation*. http://www.p12.nysed.gov/specialed/publications/iepguidance/IEPguideDec2010.pdf

Woodruff, G., & McGonigel, M. J. (1988). *Early intervention team approaches: The transdisciplinary model*. Council for Exceptional Children, Office of Educational Research and Improvement (ED). https://files.eric.ed.gov/fulltext/ED302971.pdf

Woods, A. D., Morrison, F. J., & Palincsar, A. S. (2018). Perceptions of communication practices among stakeholders in special education. *Journal of Emotional and Behavioral Disorders, 26*(4), 209–224. doi:10.1177/1063426617733716

## KEY TERMS AND DEFINITIONS

**Collaboration:** Two or more co-equal parties working together toward a shared goal.

**Committee on Special Education (CSE):** A multi-disciplinary IEP team as referenced in New York State.

**Faculty Learning Community (FLC):** A small group of faculty that voluntarily joined together to actively engage in a professional development process to promote teaching and learning.

**Interdisciplinary Collaboration:** During interdisciplinary collaboration, assessment, goal development, and service delivery take place in a coordinated nature, involving significant input from all team members.

**Multidisciplinary Collaboration:** During multidisciplinary collaboration, entirely independent assessment, goal development, and service delivery take place.

**Multidisciplinary Team:** A school-based team that includes two or more separate disciplines or professions.

**Video Modeling:** An instructional method that uses videos of competent models to teach skills to observers.

# Chapter 3
# Enhancing Professionals' Interdisciplinary Competencies:
## Meeting the Needs of Children With Disabilities From Diverse Communities

**L. Lynn Stansberry Brusnahan**
*School of Education, University of St. Thomas, USA*

**Renee A. Hepperlen**
*School of Social Work, University of St. Thomas, USA*

**Bonnie L. Ingelin**
*School of Education, University of St. Thomas, USA*

## ABSTRACT

*This chapter introduces interprofessional competencies and an assessment that can guide preparation and impact competency of interdisciplinary professionals working in special education to meet the needs of children with disabilities and families from diverse communities. Additionally, this chapter highlights examples of integrated preparation approaches that allow interdisciplinary professionals to learn about each other's discipline to advance their knowledge and skills to meet the needs of young children with disabilities from multicultural communities. These practices include: (a) virtual learning communities; (b) professional development micro credentials awarded by digital badges; (c) subject matter expert panels; and (d) combined field experiences.*

Interprofessional education occurs "when two or more professions learn with, from, and about each other to improve collaboration and the quality of care" (Centre for the Advancement of Interprofessional Education, 2006, p. 1). Interprofessional or interdisciplinary competencies can guide practitioners across multiple fields about effective ways to work together and integrate knowledge and experience. In this chapter, we introduce interprofessional competencies that guide the preparation of interdisciplinary professionals working to meet the needs of young children who have or are at risk for developmental delays

DOI: 10.4018/978-1-6684-6438-0.ch003

or disabilities. While this chapter focuses on supporting pre-service professionals working with young children with disabilities, this framework is applicable to any special education population. Working with children with disabilities requires input from professionals in multiple fields, but the need to collaborate intensifies when providing support and services to young children and their families from diverse communities (Cook & Friend, 2010). Thus, we provide examples of integrated preparation approaches that allow interdisciplinary professionals to learn about each other's discipline and advance their knowledge and skills to meet the needs of young children with disabilities and their families, specifically from immigrant and refugee communities. We highlight vignettes with distinct examples and lessons learned from engaging in interdisciplinary preparation between early childhood special education and social work.

## INTERPROFESSIONAL COMPETENCIES

Federal regulations, such as the Individuals with Disabilities Education Act (IDEA), established the necessity of multidisciplinary collaboration to support the growth and development of children and their families. Likewise, the Council for Exceptional Children's (CEC) Division of Early Childhood's (DEC) recommended practices highlight teaming and collaboration for practitioners as an effective way to improve the development of young children with delays or disabilities. The siloed services initially offered by early intervention (EI) and early childhood special education (ECSE) professionals have evolved to a recognition that multiple people with varied perspectives must be mobilized to provide optimal services to young children and their families (Bricker et al., 2022).

To support EI/ECSE interprofessional work, the U.S. Department of Education's Office of Special Education Programs (OSEP) Early Childhood Personnel Center was tasked with developing interprofessional competencies. Using a sampling of seven EI/ECSE service provider professional standards, the group developed four common training competencies, which include (1) coordination and collaboration; (2) family-centered practice; (3) evidence-based intervention; and (4) professionalism (Bruder et al., 2019; Early Childhood Personnel Center, 2020). Although these competencies mention coordination and collaboration and represent areas of consistent knowledge, skills, and dispositions, they do not provide specific "interdisciplinary" competencies.

Due to a lack of interdisciplinary competencies, the EI/ECSE literature suggests that preparation programs turn to interprofessional competencies and practices developed in health education as a model for interdisciplinary education (Bricker et al., 2022). The Institute of Medicine's (2001) recognition of the need to develop skills to effectively communicate and coordinate care led to the formation of the Interprofessional Education Collaborative (IPEC). In 2016, due to a lack of clarity about outcomes in interdisciplinary education, a consortium of U.S. professional associations representing six disciplines created Interprofessional Education Collaborative core competencies.

With the vision of enhanced interprofessional collaborative practice, the IPEC competencies serve to frame dialogue for interprofessional education and collaborative practice. These competencies support team-based care and provide direction for professional schools of health care. These competencies are a catalyst to improve service provision and enhance outcomes. After publishing the original competencies, IPEC (2021) convened multidisciplinary working groups to review and update these competencies to provide the best available evidence and research related to interdisciplinary education and collaborative practice; review common definitions for competence and competency; and ensure the competency framework accurately reflects the most up to date research, policy, and practice.

Table 1. *IPEC Interprofessional Education Competency and Description*

| Competency | IPEC Description | Adapted IP Description |
|---|---|---|
| Values/Ethics for Interprofessional Practice | Work with individuals of other professions to maintain a culture of mutual respect and shared values, | Work with individuals of other professions to maintain a culture of mutual respect and shared values. |
| Roles / Responsibilities | Use the knowledge of one's own role and those of other professions to appropriately assess and address the health care needs of patients and to promote and advance the health of populations. | Use the knowledge of one's own role and those of other professions to appropriately assess and address the developmental and social/emotional needs of children and their families to promote growth and development. |
| Interprofessional Communication | Communicate with patients, families, communities, and professionals in health and other fields. | Communicate with children, families, communities, and professionals in health, social welfare, and education. |
| Teams and Teamwork | Apply relationship-building values and the principles of team dynamics to perform effectively in different team roles to plan, deliver, and evaluate patient/population centered care and population health programs and policies that are safe, timely, efficient, effective, and equitable. | Apply relationship-building values and the principles of team dynamics to perform effectively in different team roles to plan, deliver, and evaluate a child's development, through family-centered approaches using evidence-based practices. |

IPEC (2016) Interprofessional Education Competency and Description, p. 10

IPEC established four domains areas for competencies to support professional development, which include (1) values and ethics of interprofessional practice; (2) roles and responsibilities; (3) interprofessional communication; and (4) teams and teamwork. These competencies focus on the experience of being a member of a professional team and emphasize interactions and dynamics. Table 1 includes the original health care descriptions of the interprofessional education competencies with adapted classification for addressing the needs of young children with disabilities and their families.

Figure 1 illustrates the components of interdisciplinary competency focused on placing the interests of children with disabilities and their families at the center of interprofessional practice. These components include (a) communicating; (b) problem solving; (c) making informed decisions; (d) collaborating; (e) respecting privacy and maintaining confidentiality; (f) creating mutually trusting relationships; (g) engaging in teamwork; and (h) embracing diversity. These components and interdisciplinary competency are vital with the increased numbers of children qualifying for EI/ECSE services from diverse communities (Early Childhood Technical Assistance Center, 2020; U.S. Department of Education, 2022).

Like trends in K-12 education (de Brey et al., 2019), the proportion of young children in EI/ECSE who are Asian, Black, or of two or more races has increased (IDEA Data Center, 2022). Data trends also indicate a growing number of immigrants and refugees (U.S. Census Bureau, 2021). The U.S. Immigrant Learning Center (2019) estimates there are 44 million or one in eight foreign-born individuals in the U.S. These individuals, born outside the country, could be either immigrants or refugees. Immigrants are individuals who relocate from another country (United Nations Department of Economic and Social Affairs, 1998). The United Nations (1951) defines refugees as those who leave a country due to tyranny associated with race, religion, social identity, or political beliefs.

Immigrant and refugee families of children with special needs face unique challenges as they navigate the educational system for their child with a disability. Parents and caregivers are motivated to support their children but sometimes struggle to understand the complexities of the U.S. public education system, leading to disparities in access (Miller & Nguyen, 2014). U.S. disability policies focus on individual values

*Figure 1.*

Circular diagram with center: "Center Interprofessional Practice on Interests of Young Children with Disabilities and their Families"

Surrounding circles (clockwise):
- Communicate (Tools & Techniques)
- Problem Solve (Shared Responsibility)
- Base Intervention Decisions on Understanding of Responsibilities
- Collaborate
- Embrace Diversity, Respect Cultures & Values
- Create Trusting Relationships (Ethical Conduct, Honesty & Integrity)
- Engage in Teamwork
- Respect Privacy and Maintain Confidentiality

of personal choice and independence, which often diverges from immigrant and refugee understandings of disability, resulting in limited requests and access from services providers, such as education (Hasnain, 2010). When children qualify for services, families may not fully comprehend their role with the professionals who enter their homes and provide suggestions and support. Refugee families often experience oppression and possible exposure to trauma in their home country, a sequel of which can include mental health concerns for both the parents and children (Miller & Nguyn, 2014). These experiences highlight the importance of the interdisciplinary work of early childhood special educators and social workers to support immigrant and refugee children with disabilities and their families by (1) enhancing families' understanding of the educational system; (2) collaborating to improve the quality of care; and (3) focusing on the children and their families' needs. With EI/ECSE programs serving an increasingly diverse group of children with disabilities and their families, training programs should ensure the next generation of EI/ECSE professionals have the knowledge, skills, and attitudes to effectively engage and work with families from a variety of different backgrounds (Bruder et al., 2019).

*Table 2. IPC Revised Questions*

---

"I am able to..."
1. Choose communication tools and techniques that facilitate effective team interactions.
2. Place the interests of children with disabilities and their families at the center of interprofessional practice.
3. Engage other professionals in shared problem-solving appropriate to the specific care situation.
4. Respect the privacy of children and their families while maintaining confidentiality in the delivery of team-based care.
5. Inform care decisions by integrating the knowledge and experience of other professions appropriate to the educational situation.
6. Embrace the diversity that characterizes the educational team.
7. Apply leadership practices that support effective collaborative practice.
8. Respect the cultures and values of other educational professions.
9. Engage other educational professionals to constructively manage disagreements about children and their families' care.
10. Develop a trusting relationship with other team members.
11. Use strategies that improve the effectiveness of interprofessional teamwork and team-based educational services.
12. Demonstrate high standards of ethical conduct in my contributions to team-based services.
13. Use available evidence to inform effective teamwork and team-based practices.
14. Act with honesty and integrity in relationships with other team members.
15. Understand the responsibilities and expertise of other professions.
16. Maintain competence in my own profession appropriate to my level of training.

---

## Interprofessional Competency Assessment

Interdisciplinary competencies can guide the development of professional knowledge and skills and build an understanding of equitable practices and collaboration across fields (McLeskey et al., 2017; Miller & Stein, 2018; Ronfeldt et al., 2015). Competency in interprofessional practice requires the utilization of a competency-based assessment. A comprehensive assessment approach can determine and measure a professional's interdisciplinary skills and help define proficiency in interprofessional practice. Competency assessment can guide interdisciplinary preparation and monitor the success of interdisciplinary education. Based on the original IPEC core competency statements, a competency self-assessment tool was created (Dow et al., 2014). The initial assessment's creators gave the authors permission to edit the IPEC tool for use outside the health profession to suit the education field. The IPEC instrument assesses competencies related to collaborative practice through individual self-assessment. The assessment results of this instrument can inform interdisciplinary program planning and track the effects of programming on interprofessional competency. Table 2 includes the 16 edited interdisciplinary competency items. The response options for these statements are a 5-point scale from strongly disagree to strongly agree.

## Interprofessional Preparation Practices

Higher education can use IPEC competencies in preparation programs to guide professional collaboration activities. Interdisciplinary personnel preparation in early intervention is critical to improving practice and providing exemplary services to children with special needs and their families (Crais et al., 2004). Interprofessional training for education settings, which is in the nascent stage of development, has much to learn from the interprofessional education medical literature that has over 40 years of research supporting best practices in education and field experience (Thistlethwaite et al., 2010). In a scoping review, two identified interprofessional education design components included integrated curriculum and extracurricular models (Grace, 2021). Integrated models include phased interprofessional education and conceptual model application (Grace, 2021). Extracurricular models add interprofessional education experiences, such as an additional field or clinical experiences. To provide efficient, high-quality interdisciplinary personnel preparation, it is essential to embed and align content, practices, and field experiences in preservice training to an interdisciplinary team-based approach.

It is vitally important that personnel preparation programs address educational equity by improving the preparation of interdisciplinary preservice professionals who can enhance outcomes for young children with disabilities and their families. Figure 2 provides a framework to ensure interdisciplinary preservice professionals (e.g., both special educators and social workers), who work with children with educational needs, are well-prepared and demonstrate growth in interprofessional competencies. In this section, we present how organizations involved in training and education can engage in advanced interprofessional development and discuss several professional preparation practices aligned to interdisciplinary preparation and competency. These include (a) virtual learning communities; (b) professional development micro credentials awarded by digital badges; (c) subject matter guest speaker panels; and (d) combined field experiences. As this program is in the early stages of implementation, it focuses on conceptualization of the training rather than specific outcomes.

## Virtual Learning Communities

A way to prepare professionals from multiple disciplines in interdisciplinary preparation is through professional learning communities (PLCs) (Battersby, 2019; Stanley et al., 2014). With technological advances, a virtual learning community can be conceptualized from the perspective of professional learning communities of practice (Wenger, 2001). Virtual learning communities (VLCs) are professional development groups that embody all the characteristics of traditional PLCs, but participants meet virtually through an online platform (e.g., Zoom) (Rolandson & Ross-Hekkel, 2022). VLCs support the needs of working adults and rural communities with virtual participation expanding opportunities beyond the immediate area surrounding the training facility and those who can attend in-person meetings.

In a VLC, individuals from a variety of professional backgrounds, who share vocation or common interests or goals, can collectively interact, learn, and share or obtain knowledge on topics such as how to engage in interprofessional collaboration (Chiu et al., 2006; Chunngam et al., 2014; Hung & Cheng, 2013). Online communities provide spaces for professionals to combat isolation, discuss teaching and learning, experience professional camaraderie, collaborate, and seek input and diverse perspectives from other professionals (Matzat, 2013; McConnell et al., 2013; Rickels & Brewer, 2017; Rolandson & Ross-Hekkel, 2022). A VLC can include informal learning (e.g., curriculum not approved through a university process) and pedagogy focused on more practical than theoretical applications (Andreatos, 2007). Members of a practice community are motivated to exchange best practices, problems, and experiences that support "knowledge flows" between disciplines (van Winkelen, 2003). Through these communities, professionals can gain conceptual understanding and skills in research-based interventions. In VLCs, interdisciplinary preservice professionals can interact and engage in capacity-building structured training and activities and achieve the advanced knowledge and essential skills necessary to provide effective interventions and services for children with disabilities and their families.

Interdisciplinary preservice preparation programs can utilize VLCs and host collaborative meetings to encourage critical and strategic cross-discipline thinking about educational goals, priorities, and challenges. Content in VLCs can contribute to collaborative professionals who have the vision to address educational disparities and provide equitable opportunities to children with disabilities and their families. Table 3 includes an example of a yearly calendar for a VLC focused on the interdisciplinary preparation of early childhood special educators and social workers to work with children with disabilities, specifically

*Figure 2.*

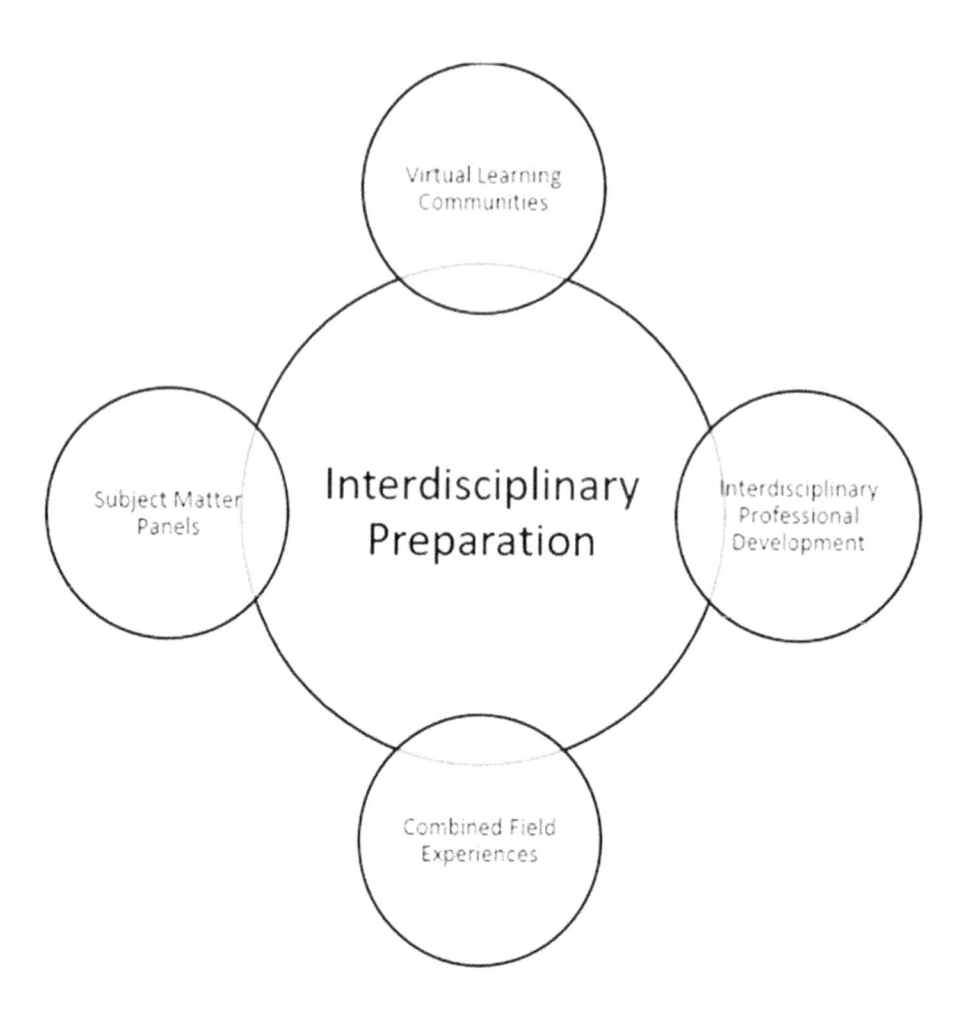

A diagram showing "Interdisciplinary Preparation" in the center, surrounded by four circles: Virtual Learning Communities (top), Interdisciplinary Professional Development (right), Combined Field Experiences (bottom), and Subject Matter Panels (left).

from families from diverse communities, including immigrants and refugees. With the goal of creating professionals with interdisciplinary competency, VLC professional development sessions can target interdisciplinary competencies framed in problem-solving around case studies and other activities. The structured learning opportunities provided in the training program outlined in this chapter considers the application of the University of Washington's learning cycle (i.e., introduce, prepare, enact, analyze) to prepare interdisciplinary preservice professionals. This model supports knowledge and skill development to provide high-quality collaborative services and support to families and their children with disabilities. Table 4 includes an example of how to implement learning cycle steps.

Vignette 1 highlights a VLC focused on supporting the growth and understanding of the roles and responsibilities of ECSE and SW professionals with a focus on a specific interprofessional competency following the outline of the University of Washington's learning cycle steps.

*Table 3. Virtual Learning Community Calendar Example*

| |
|---|
| VLC 1. Building a Professional Learning Community (recent graduates' panel) |
| VLC 2. Engaging in Beneficial Interdisciplinary Practice (professional panel) |
| VLC 3. Identifying Disability Characteristics in Young Children (linked to micro credential) |
| VLC 4. Focusing on Social and Emotional Mental Health and Family Quality of Life (linked to micro credential) |
| VLC 5. Becoming Trauma-Informed (linked to micro credential) |
| VLC 6. Experiencing Interdisciplinary Collaboration (discuss field experiences) |
| VLC 7. Addressing Behavior from a Cultural and Trauma-Informed Perspective (linked to micro credential) |
| VLC 8. Understanding Immigrants and Refugee Family Needs (diverse family panel) |
| VLC 9. Engaging in Personal Self Care (linked to micro credential) |

## Vignette 1

### Virtual Learning Community

**Virtual Learning Community**: Engaging in Beneficial Interdisciplinary Practice

**IPEC Competency**: Understand the responsibilities and expertise of other professions.

**VLC Objective:** Articulate the role and responsibilities of ECSE and SW professionals and ways in which they can beneficially collaborate to provide support and services to children who have or are at-risk for developmental delays or disabilities and their families, including those from immigrant and refugee communities.

1. **Introduce.** To begin this activity, the VLC facilitator introduces the IPEC competency. Then, the facilitator asks participants to explain the rationale and the importance of understanding other professionals' roles and interdisciplinary collaboration in supporting children with disabilities and their families.
2. **Prepare.** After reviewing the IPEC competency and articulating the rationale for understanding other professionals' roles and collaboration, the facilitator assigns preservice professionals to small group discussion breakouts with equal numbers from the two disciplines. In these breakouts, the facilitator asks participants to share examples of the actual function of their profession and stereotypes about their profession. Once they complete this discussion, the facilitator merges the small groups back into a large group to share information on the roles and stereotypes of each profession.
3. **Enact.** The facilitator introduces a case study. The facilitator asks the preservice professionals to discuss the roles and responsibilities of their profession regarding supporting the family in the case study using the information discussed in the introductory activity and breakout sessions in small

*Table 4. Learning Cycle Steps in Virtual Learning Community*

| |
|---|
| 1. **Introduce.** Select an interprofessional competency to investigate collectively during VLC and select informational resources and an activity to support that investigation. Prepare a case study with a problem to solve linked to the targeted VLC topic. |
| 2. **Prepare.** Collaboratively overview the focused interprofessional competency and targeted topic during the VLC meeting. |
| 3. **Enact.** Collaboratively discuss the enactment of the focused interprofessional competency in the context of the targeted topic and case study and the preservice professionals' fields. |
| 4. **Analyze.** Analyze how focused interprofessional competency can be approached collaboratively through informed practices to impact children with disabilities and their families highlighted in the case studies. |

groups. The facilitator challenges the groups to find ways the two professions can beneficially collaborate to meet the needs of the child and their family.

**Case Study.** You are collaboratively working with the family of an 18-month-old boy who was born extremely prematurely, leading to complications and Cerebral Palsy. The parents are refugees from Somalia. In a recent visit, the mother expressed interest in learning how she and her family can interact with and engage her son in activities. She said her family often does everything for him, like bring him his favorite toy or feed him. She notes that requesting items and feeding are something that he has been working on developing for some time. She also states that the family has had ongoing challenges with accessing services (e.g., healthcare, related services, education) and wondered if there is anything that the professional might suggest.

- How could an individual in your profession support this family?
- How could you beneficially collaborate with other professionals to meet the needs of this family?
  4. **Analyze.** After a specified time, the facilitator merges the small groups back into a large group to share information on the case study discussion. The group discusses how they can collaboratively leverage each profession's knowledge and skills to address this family's needs and concerns, highlighting evidence-based and family-centered practices.

## Professional Development Micro Credentials

When providing preservice professionals working with interprofessional opportunities, universities struggle with how to do this without contributing to the requirement for more credits, which cost more money. One way to provide advanced interdisciplinary professional development opportunities is to create non-credit-based micro credentials focused on targeted competencies. Competency-based micro credentials are mini certificates that offer knowledge and assessment of targeted skills (Elliott et al., 2014). Micro credentials can be awarded through digital badges, which are a validated indicator of competency (Randall & West, 2020). Badges provide professionals with an efficient way to offer evidence and a more comprehensive picture of advanced competency to others (Cheng et al., 2018; Young et al., 2019). Higher education awards digital badges when preservice professionals complete the content and pass assessments to demonstrate proficiency in the micro credential's targeted knowledge, skills, and standards. The objective of using micro credentials in interdisciplinary preparation is to increase knowledge of implementing collaborative practices to address educational disparities and improve positive outcomes for children with disabilities and their families.

Because there is a divergence emerging between traditional in-person schooling and the fast-growing demands of digital culture, especially in circumstances as a pandemic, virtual formats of professional development meet the needs of educators who view attending an in-person class to learn as unnecessary with the online realm as the preferred learning environment. Benefits of micro credentials include competency, flexibility, and cost efficiency (Hunt et al., 2020). Options are important as statistics reveal the least prevalent topics of professional development for educators is teaching students with disabilities and English Language Learners (Cox et al., 2016; National Center for Educational Research, 2017).

Micro credentials can co-educate preservice professionals across multiple disciplines (e.g., special educators and social workers) and be used to help guide learning in the VLCs (Cheng et al., 2018; Young et al., 2019). In most cases, micro credentials do not have to go through university curriculum approval

*Table 5. Micro Credential Topic Examples*

| |
|---|
| 1. **Identifying Disability Characteristics in Young Children to Gain Access to Meaningful and Effective Early Intervention Educationally and Medically.** Preservice professionals learn the medical and educational criteria for disability areas and how to support the social, emotional, and behavioral needs of children and their families. Preservice professionals learn that working with young children and their families requires a specialized set of competencies firmly grounded in the developmental and relational needs of the earliest years. |
| 2. **Focusing on Social and Emotional Mental Health and Family Quality of Life to Support Immigrant and Refugee Children and Families.** Preservice professionals engage in topics including family quality of life and family systems theory. Preservice professionals consider how these various aspects can impact the experiences of families from immigrant and refugee backgrounds caring for a child with disabilities and high intensity needs. |
| 3. **Becoming Trauma-Informed to Meet the Needs of Immigrant and Refugee Children and Families.** Preservice professionals learn about immigrant and refugee trauma related to war, torture, resettlement, and intergenerational trauma. Preservice professionals learn trauma-informed practices to support young children and their families from immigrant and refugee backgrounds. |
| 4. **Addressing Behavior from a Cultural and Trauma-Informed Perspective to Provide Culturally and Linguistically Sustaining Practices to Support Children and Families.** Preservice professionals learn how to work with children and their families in accessible, effective, and culturally and linguistically sustaining ways to address challenging behaviors by utilizing culturally responsive practices from the educational field and cultural humility from social work. |
| 5. **Engaging in Personal Self Care to Support the Emotional Wellbeing of Early Childhood Professionals.** Preservice professionals learn about compassion fatigue and burnout. Preservice professionals complete an inventory to assess compassion fatigue and burnout and develop a self-care plan to support ongoing engagement in their professions. |

process (Selwyn, 2008) if they are not intentionally structured or intended for the purpose of licensing or certification (Hemphill & Leskowitz, 2013).

Micro credentials can be structured for preservice professionals to develop skills and acquire knowledge to improve interdisciplinary professional practice. Preservice professionals from multiple fields can take these micro credentials collaboratively. Programs can combine a series of these interdisciplinary micro credentials to lead to a macro credential. Program developers should embed the interdisciplinary micro credentials with research-based practices, standards from each field (ECSE, SW, IPEC), and high-leverage approaches (Martin et al., 2019). To award a micro credential, the training must include an assessment of competency in targeted skills. Table 5 includes examples of micro credential topics based on collaborating with other professions to meet the interdisciplinary needs of culturally diverse, including refugee and immigrants, children with social, emotional, and behavioral needs who may have experienced trauma and their families.

Vignette 2 highlights a micro credential for ECSE and SW professionals with a focus on addressing behavior from a cultural and trauma-informed perspective that follows the outline of the University of Washington's learning cycle steps.

## Vignette 2

### Micro Credentials

**Micro Credential:** Addressing Behavior from a Cultural and Trauma-Informed Perspective to Provide Culturally and Linguistically Sustaining Practices to Support Children and Families.

**IPEC Competency:** Use strategies that improve the effectiveness of interprofessional teamwork and team-based educational services.

**Micro Credential Objective.** Interdisciplinary professionals (e.g., special educators and social workers) will articulate how culture and trauma influence interpretations of behavior and utilize culturally and linguistically sustaining practices when addressing behaviors.

1. **Introduce.** The micro credential requires preservice professionals to complete a pre-test based on the targeted IPEC competency and objectives to assess current knowledge on the training topic.
2. **Prepare.** In this micro-credential course, awarded by a digital badge, preservice interdisciplinary professionals learn how to understand maladaptive and challenging behavior from a multi-culturally diverse lens. The rationale is that without adequate knowledge and understanding of how culture and trauma affect behavior, children's behaviors can be misinterpreted, and strategies may be put into place that does not meet the needs of the child and/or their family. Thus, this micro credential introduces antecedents, behavior serves a function, consequences, the escalation cycle, an ABC-Diversity iceberg, functional behavior assessment, and a behavior intervention planning process.
3. **Enact.** In the micro credential, preservice professionals complete case studies and learn to identify antecedents that trigger or cue behaviors and consequences that serve to maintain, increase, or decrease behaviors.

**Case Study.** Mx. Rodriguez's student is engaging in behaviors that are disrupting the learning in the classroom. Because the student's behavior is interfering with the teacher's ability to meet the educational needs of the individual student as well as the peers, Mx. Rodriguez has implemented a variety of behavioral interventions to address the behaviors, but they have failed to work. Mx. Rodriguez does not understand the function of the behavior or understand the cultural community of which the child is a member. Behavior – adaptive (i.e., beneficial to child), maladaptive (i.e., disadvantageous to child), and challenging (i.e., problematic in specific context) —is learned. Behavior can be cued or triggered by antecedents and maintained, increased, or decreased by the consequences of a behavior. Mx. Rodriguez will be more successful in modifying the student's behavior once there is an understanding of the escalation cycle, ABC-Diversity iceberg, and the function of the behavior. The school social worker is part of the team working on a functional behavior assessment and behavior intervention plan. The social worker has met with the family on multiple occasions and has some background information on the trauma the child has recently experienced.

- How might culture influence interpretations of the child's behavior?
- How might trauma influence interpretations of the child's behavior?
- How could the special education teacher and social worker collaborate in the assessment and behavior plan creation for the child?
- Once determining the function of the behavior, what culturally and linguistically sustaining practices might address the child's behaviors?
    4. **Analyze.** The micro credential requires preservice professionals to complete a post-test based on the targeted IPEC competency and objectives to assess current knowledge on the training topic. Preservice professionals also complete a qualitative exit survey assessment to share significant learning and how the information impacts children with disabilities.

## Subject Matter Guest Speaker Panels

In addition to learning about specialized content that supports EI/ECSE in virtual learning communities and micro credentials, invited panels of guest speakers provide information. These professionals and parents discuss working professionally in the field and provide additional opportunities for preservice professionals to engage in professional development with emerging research and evidence-based practices. Panels can include recent graduates of the interdisciplinary programs to discuss their experiences in a learning community, professionals in the field to share interprofessional experiences and provide tips for working collaboratively, and children with disabilities and their families to share their experiences. The panel discussions build interdisciplinary skills and focus on research-based interventions, effective practice-based skills, and equitable access. Vignette 3 highlights a subject matter guest speaker panel with a focus on understanding immigrants and refugee family needs that follows the outline of the University of Washington's learning cycle steps.

## Vignette 3

### Subject Matter Guest Speaker Panel Example

**Subject Matter Panel:** Understanding Immigrants and Refugee Family Needs Panel

**IPEC Competency:** Place the interests of children with disabilities and their families at the center of interprofessional practice.

**Panel Objective:** To learn about the interdisciplinary needs of children with disabilities and their families from parents and caregivers from diverse communities, including immigrant and refugees.

1. **Introduce.** Using professional networks, the facilitators recruit parents and caregivers of young children with disabilities from diverse communities to talk with the preservice professionals. The facilitators provide panelists with several discussion prompts to consider before the interdisciplinary meeting with the preservice professionals.
2. **Prepare.** The facilitators provide information to preservice professionals about the importance of providing family-centered care that emphasizes open communication and teamwork with parents and caregivers as essential team members.
3. **Enact.** Rather than using a case study, the preservice professionals hear from parents and caregivers of children with disabilities about their experiences with EI/ECSE. The facilitator guides the discussion utilizing prompts such as
    - Provide background information on your child, including when you first had concerns about their development.
    - Describe how you received information about EI/ECSE and your experiences working with your child's team members.
    - Describe your family's strengths in meeting the needs of your child's disability. Describe areas where you require support to meet your child's needs.
    - Share any challenges faced to get your child's needs met and receive support for their development.
    - Do you think any challenges were based on your social identities and communities? For example, did being an immigrant or refugee hinder your child from receiving equitable services?
4. **Analyze.** Following the panel, facilitators place preservice professionals into interdisciplinary breakout rooms to discuss questions related to the presentation. These discussion questions include questions such as
    - What stood out to you about the presentations?
    - What do you identify as a strength of these families?

◦ How might interdisciplinary professionals leverage our communication and teamwork skills to more effectively meet the needs of immigrant and refugee families and support families who may face additional barriers based on their social identities?

## Field Experiences

"Field experience" means an opportunity in which preservice professionals may observe licensed professionals working with children and their families and engage in activities such as collaboration, assessment, or instruction (Professional Educator Licensing Standards Board [PELSB], 2020). Field experiences are an important part of license programs, such as teacher preparation and social work, with national program accreditation and standards establishing its importance (Council for Exceptional Children Division of Early Childhood, 2020; Council on Social Work Education, 2015; 2022). Field experiences provide preservice professionals with hands-on opportunities to practice the skills they learn in their preparation programs and learn from professionals in the field. Field experiences allow preservice educators to connect the conceptual and theoretical knowledge obtained during coursework to real-life settings (Hanline, 2010).

Of the many things learned in field experiences, one key element is how to collaborate with other professionals from different disciplines. When working with children with disabilities and their families, professionals do not work independently and often collaborate with many professionals. However, many preservice professionals do not feel prepared to collaborate effectively with other professionals and families (Hanline, 2010). Universities often structure programs to focus solely on one discipline to help support the preservice professional's ability to meet the specific state licensure requirements (Geer & Hamill, 2007), which does little to support their ability to learn collaboratively or how to work in a collaborative setting. To fully support children with disabilities and their families, professionals need interdisciplinary experiences (Robertson et al., 2022). Programs need to develop creative ways for preservice professionals from different programs to learn the collaborative skills they will need to successfully provide services to children and their families (Geer & Hamill, 2007; Robertson et al. 2022).

One way to help support preservice professionals' understanding of collaboration across disciplines is to set up collaborative field experiences. Field experiences provide preservice professionals from different disciplines, such as special education and social work, opportunities to learn each other's roles and practice working together. These types of placements might be a change for universities as they work through coordination with other university programs and departments to create these opportunities (Hawkins et al., 2008). However, collaborative field experiences offer a rich opportunity for preservice professionals to share ideas about intervention design and resources as well as form a better understanding of their future careers (Hawkins et al. 2008). These experiences also help future professionals to network in their future fields as they work together across disciplines (Robertson et al. 2022). The focus of field experiences will depend on the disciplines. Table 6 includes examples of focus areas for field experiences based on an EI/ECSE focus, which include (1) screenings; (2) assessments; (3) collaborative planning; and (4) coaching sessions.

Another essential aspect of compelling collaborative field experiences is working with internship or student teaching (i.e., school districts) locations to find the best joint placements for preservice professionals. For example, a university preparation program working on field experiences for early childhood special educators and social workers would need to work directly with the school districts to find locations that foster collaborative working relationships for preservice professionals (Hawkins et al. 2008).

*Table 6. Field Experience Focus Areas*

| |
|---|
| 1. **Screenings** – During interprofessional preparation, preservice professionals can observe and be collaboratively involved in the screening process. Special education screenings are done as part of the Child Find process to support the identification of children with disabilities (IDEA, 2004). Providing a screening experience allows preservice professionals the opportunity to see how professionals across different disciplines work with children and their families from the beginning of the early intervention and special education process.<br>2. **Assessments** - During interprofessional preparation, preservice professionals can observe and be collaboratively involved in assessments. Children undergo an assessment process at various times in the special education process, including an initial evaluation for eligibility for services and a reevaluation every three years. This is an important process for preservice professionals to observe as it provides an opportunity to see how a collaborative assessment functions and best supports the needs of children and their families.<br>3. **Collaborative Planning** - During interprofessional preparation, preservice professionals can observe and collaborate in planning. When professionals across disciplines jointly plan it helps to support the unique needs of children from diverse cultures and linguistic backgrounds (Robertson et al., 2012), including immigrant and refugee children and their families. This planning process allows professionals across disciplines to have a cohesive plan to best support children and their families. Being a part of these planning sessions allowed preservice professionals to observe this process from a collaborative perspective.<br>4. **Coaching Sessions** - During interprofessional preparation, preservice professionals can observe and participate in lessons or coaching sessions. For example, preservice professionals can observe home visits that revolve around supporting children and families through coaching sessions. These coaching sessions often involve a single provider as part of the primary service provider model. These sessions result from the collaborative planning that occurs between all service providers. The preservice professionals see how the planning sessions are enacted in practice along with collaboration with families to best support the needs of young children and their families. |

Relationships with organizations and school districts are important to have appropriate and meaningful placements for all preservice professionals. Strategic placements help create future professionals able to meet the specific needs of children and their families (Robertson et al., 2022). The connections with organization and school districts also helps to create field experiences that meets the needs of these organizations and not just the preservice professionals (Robertson et al., 2022). Placements should link to the licensing requirements for all preservice professionals involved. This prevents these placements from being additional work for preservice professionals and instead are just a basic requirement (Hawkins et al. 2008). Vignette 4 highlights an example of the process to set up collaborative field experiences.

## Vignette 4

### Field Experiences

Two university professors, one from the School of Education and the other from the School of Social Work, wants to create a collaborative field experience opportunity for preservice professionals from their respective fields (early childhood special education and social work). They have had many conversations about how this will benefit preservice professionals as they prepare to support the unique needs of children with disabilities and their families. First, they plan a meeting with their perspective field placement offices to find sites with which both departments already have relationships that could best support their preservice professionals. The social worker professor realizes that in talking with the field placement office that this process might be more of a challenge for his social work preservice professionals as they have less choice in their field placements. This is still possible for the preservice social work professionals, but it will take planned partnerships with school districts to create meaningful working relationships. The last thing either professor wants is to create added work for their preservice professionals. The professors decide to meet with a school district team about their partnership. The professors meet with the school district's special education director and the district social work coordinator. These district professionals have many questions about this collaborative process. Their first question centers on basic things such as how many hours would be included. The social work coordinator asks if all the hours need to be collaborative as their school district social workers are not assigned solely to early childhood special education but to a large group of students. The special education director is curious about how this will work since they use the primary service delivery model for home visits for young children, meaning that only an early childhood special education teacher or a social worker would be going on these visits. During this meeting, everyone is excited about these collaborative field experiences, but to be effective experiences, they will need to work together now during the initial setup and throughout the process. They will also need to keep in communication and make changes from year to year to continue improving these experiences for students.

After preservice professionals engage in collaborative field experiences, they should discuss these experiences to learn across disciplines and knowledge areas (Kekoni et al., 2022). Research on a facilitated online discussion board between interdisciplinary preservice professionals (e.g., special education and early childhood majors) found that preservice professionals often shared across disciplines, providing thoughtful self-reflectional comments to one another (Geer & Hamill, 2007). These types of collaborative discussions support preservice professionals in better understanding the roles and responsibilities of each field and how to build a collaborative environment to support the needs of children with disabilities. Since interaction with other fields can be minimal as preservice professionals complete their course work, these discussions are important to help build collaborative skills needed in practice (Geer & Hamill, 2007). Discussing interdisciplinary work has been shown to bring unique perspective and skills to the work as well as both role clarity and role flexibility (Siegel et al., 2020). There are many ways to have these discussions, including the growing use of technology. These preservice professional discussions can occur through live (i.e., synchronous) virtual sessions where there is an opportunity to talk freely about field experiences as well follow provided prompts about how the IPEC competencies relate to what they learned in their collaborative field experiences and how it will apply to their future careers. VLC can provide preservice professionals multiple opportunities to discuss their field experiences many different times during meetings so they can learn from each other about their field experiences and build their collaborative skills.

## DISCUSSION

This chapter provides a conceptual framework for developing interdisciplinary training to prepare special educators and social workers to work with children with disabilities and their families. It emphasizes using interprofessional competencies to guide knowledge and skill development to support professional collaborations targeted on working with diverse cultures, specifically individuals and families from immigrant and refugee populations. In developing this material, the authors adapted interprofessional competencies from the medical field to align with educational needs and wove these adapted competencies into the VLC meetings. Competency discussions in VLC meetings allow preservice professionals to fully engage in interprofessional conversations to develop their knowledge and skills. As a component of evaluating the effectiveness of this program, the authors use pre- and post-test data from the interprofessional competency assessment, listed in Table 2 to evaluate outcomes. To date, this program has completed one of the five planned cohorts and does not yet have a robust sample size to report student outcomes. However, the medical field, with a more established history of interprofessional training, can offer some insight. A systematic review of medical interprofessional training outcomes (Riskiyana et al., 2018) concluded that collaborative competencies showed improvements. This review highlighted that case study discussions were a frequently used and effective method to learn interprofessional competencies, consistent with this program's use of these methods (Riskiyana et al., 2018). Other researchers (Lapkin et al., 2013) have argued for a more meaningful integration of interprofessional learning to include experiential learning, which is consistent with this program's integrated field opportunities, which allows for intentional and applied interprofessional experiences. As interprofessional learning is in the early stages of development in education, it is essential to develop programs to examine what works and for whom. The goal of interprofessional training is to improve the care and support children with disabilities and their families receive.

## CONCLUSION

In this chapter, we highlighted how interprofessional competencies can provide guidance to the preparation of interdisciplinary preservice professionals working with children who have or are at-risk for developmental delays or disabilities. Utilizing the revised IPEC competencies can help guide the preparation and impact competency of interdisciplinary professionals, together with those working to meet the needs of populations from diverse communities, which include refugees and immigrants. Integrating competencies into preparation programs allows interdisciplinary professionals to learn about each other's discipline and advance their knowledge and skills to meet the diverse populations they serve.

## REFERENCES

Alim, H. S., & Paris, D. (2017). What is culturally sustaining pedagogy and why does it matter. In D. Paris & H. S. Alim (Eds.), *Culturally sustaining pedagogies: Teaching and learning for justice in a changing world* (pp. 1–21). Teachers College Press.

Andreatos, A. (2007). Virtual communities and their importance for informal learning. *International Journal of Computers*, *2*(1), 9–47.

Battersby, S. L. (2019). Reimagining music teacher collaboration: The culture of professional learning communities as professional development within schools and districts. *General Music Today*, *33*(1), 15–23. doi:10.1177/1048371319840653

Bricker, D. D., Felimban, H. S., Lin, F. Y., Stegenga, S. M., & Storie, S. O. M. (2022). A proposed framework for enhancing collaboration in early intervention/early childhood special education. *Topics in Early Childhood Special Education*, *41*(4), 240–252. doi:10.1177/0271121419890683

Bruder, M. B., Catalino, T., Chiarello, L. A., Mitchell, M. C., Deppe, J., Gundler, D., Kemp, P., LeMoine, S., Long, T., Muhlenhaupt, M., Prelock, P., Schefkind, S., Stayton, V., & Ziegler, D. (2019). Finding a common lens: Competencies across professional disciplines providing early childhood intervention. *Infants and Young Children*, *32*(4), 280–293. doi:10.1097/IYC.0000000000000153

Centre for the Advancement of Interprofessional Education. (2006). CAIPE re-issues its statement on the definition and principles of interprofessional education. *CAIPE.* www.caipe.org/resources/publications/archived-publications/caipe-2006-re-issues-its-statement-on-the-definition-and-principles-of-interprofessional-education

Cheng, Z., Watson, S. L., & Newby, T. J. (2018). Goal setting and open digital badges in higher education. *TechTrends*, *62*(2), 190–196. doi:10.100711528-018-0249-x

Chiu, C., Hsu, M., & Wang, E. (2006). Understanding knowledge sharing in virtual communities: An integration of social capital and social cognitive theories. *Decision Support Systems*, *42*(3), 1872–1888. doi:10.1016/j.dss.2006.04.001

Chunngam, B., Chanchalor, S., & Murphy, E. (2014). Membership, participation and knowledge building in virtual communities for informal learning. *British Journal of Educational Technology*, *45*(5), 863–879. doi:10.1111/bjet.12114

Cook, L., & Friend, M. (2010). The state of the art of collaboration on behalf of students with disabilities. *Journal of Educational & Psychological Consultation*, *20*(1), 1–8. doi:10.1080/10474410903535398

Council for Exceptional Children Division for Early Childhood. (2020). Initial practice-based professional preparation standards for early interventionists/early childhood special educators (EI/ECSE) (initial birth through age 8). *Exceptional Children.* https://exceptionalchildren.org/standards/initial-practice-based-standards-early-interventionists-early-childhood-special-educators

Council on Social Work Education. (2015). Educational Policy and Accreditation Standards. *CSWE.* https://www.cswe.org/accreditation/standards/2015-epas/

Council on Social Work Education. (2022). Educational Policy and Accreditation Standards. *CSWE.* https://www.cswe.org/accreditation/standards/2022-epas/

Cox, S., Parmer, R., Strizek, G., & Thomas, T. (2016). Documentation for the 2011–12 Schools and Staffing Survey (NCES 2016-817). U.S. Department of Education. *National Center for Education Statistics.* https://nces.ed.gov/pubsearch

Crais, E. R., Boone, H. A., Harrison, M., Freund, P., Downing, K., & West, T. (2004). Interdisciplinary personnel preparation: Graduates' use of targeted practices. *Infants and Young Children*, *17*(1), 82–92. doi:10.1097/00001163-200401000-00010

de Brey, C., Musu, L., McFarland, J., Wilkinson-Flicker, S., Diliberti, M., Zhang, A., Branstetter, C., & Wang, X. (2019). Status and trends in the education of racial and ethnic groups 2018 (NCES 2019-038). *U.S. Department of Education. Washington, DC: National Center for Education Statistics.* https://nces.ed.gov/pubsearch/

Division for Early Childhood. (2014). DEC recommended practices. *DEC.* http://www.dec-sped.org/recommendedpractices

Division of Early Childhood. (2015). DEC recommended practices: Enhancing services for young children with disabilities and their families. *DEC Recommended Practices Monograph Series, 1.*

Dow, A. W., DiazGranados, D., Mazmanian, P. E., & Retchin, S. M. (2014). An exploratory study of an assessment tool derived from the competencies of the interprofessional education collaborative. *Journal of Interprofessional Care, 28*(4), 299–304. doi:10.3109/13561820.2014.891573 PMID:24593327

Early Childhood Personnel Center. (2020). Cross-disciplinary competencies. *ECPTCA.* https://ecpcta.org/cross-disciplinary-competencies/

Early Childhood Technical Assistance Center. (2020). Part C. *ECTA Center.* https://ectacenter.org/partc/partc.asp

Elliott, R., Clayton, J., & Iwata, J. (2014). Exploring the use of microcredentialing and digital badges in learning environments to encourage motivation to learn and achieve. In B. Hegarty, J. McDonald, & S.-K. Loke (Eds.), *Rhetoric and Reality: Critical perspectives on educational technology. Proceedings ascilite Dunedin 2014* (pp. 703–707).

Gay, G. (2010). Acting on beliefs in teacher education for cultural diversity. *Journal of Teacher Education, 61*(1-2), 143–152. doi:10.1177/0022487109347320

Geer, C., & Hamill, L. E. E. (2007). An online interdisciplinary discussion: Promoting collaboration between early childhood and special education preservice teachers. *Journal of Technology and Teacher Education, 15*(4), 533–553.

Grace, S. (2021). Models of interprofessional education for healthcare students: A scoping review. *Journal of Interprofessional Care, 35*(5), 771–783. doi:10.1080/13561820.2020.1767045 PMID:32614628

Hanline, M. F. (2010). Preservice teachers' perceptions of field experiences in inclusive preschool settings: Implications for personnel preparation. *Teacher Education and Special Education, 33*(4), 335–351. doi:10.1177/0888406409360144

Hasnain, R. (2010). Brokering the culture gap. *Forced Migration Review,* (35), 32.

Hawkins, R. O., Kroeger, S. D., Musti-Rao, S., Barnett, D. W., & Ward, J. E. (2008). Preservice training in response to intervention: Learning by doing an interdisciplinary field experience. *Psychology in the Schools, 45*(8), 745–762. doi:10.1002/pits.20339

Hemphill, D., & Leskowitz, S. (2013). DIY activists: Communities of practice, cultural dialogism, and radical knowledge sharing. *Adult Education Quarterly, 63*(1), 51–77. doi:10.1177/0741713612442803

Hung, S., & Cheng, M. (2013). Are you ready for knowledge sharing? An empirical study of virtual communities. *Computers & Education, 62,* 8–17. doi:10.1016/j.compedu.2012.09.017

Hunt, T., Carter, R., Zhang, L., & Yang, S. (2020). Micro-credentials: The potential of personalized professional development. *Development and Learning in Organizations.*

IDEA Data Center. (2022). IDEA Part C: Child count and settings. *IDEA.* https://idc.clicdata.com/v/sqKIRJeKdg2J

Immigrant Learning Center. (2019). Quick immigration statistics: United States. *ILL.* https://www.ilctr.org/quick-us-immigration-statistics/?gclid =Cj0KCQjw0JiXBhCFARIsAOSAKqCF54aQDel0ea1sGcfe7LgS78q9brz5n12 e3mgGbdkdq-8ZLAcrZ2gaAlu9EALw_wcB

Individuals With Disabilities Education Act, 20 U.S.C. §§ 1400 et seq. (1994; 2006; 2012)

Individuals with Disabilities Education Act. (2022). *2021 Annual report to Congress on IDEA.* https://sites.ed.gov/idea/department-submits-the-43rd-annual-report-to-congress-idea

Individuals with Disabilities Education Act of 2004, 20 U.S.C. 1400 *et seq.* (2004). https://sites.ed.gov/idea/statuteregulations/

Institute of Medicine. (2001). Crossing the Quality Chasm. *Health Systems (Basingstoke, England)*, 21.

Interprofessional Education Collaborative. (2016) Core competencies for interprofessional collaborative practice: 2016 update. *Interprofessional Education Collaborative.* https://ipec.memberclicks.net/assets/2016-Update.pdf

Interprofessional Education Collaborative. (2021). Press release: IPEC announces working group members for core competencies revision update of IPEC core competencies to begin June 2021. *IEC.* https://www.ipecollaborative.org/assets/press-release/IPEC_Press-Release_2021-05-04_CCR-WG-Announcement.pdf

Kekoni, T., Kainulainen, A., Tiilikainen, E., Mäki-Petäjä-Leinonen, A., Mönkkönen, K., & Vanjusov, H. (2022). Integrative learning through the interdisciplinary social law clinic—Learning experiences of law and social work students. *Social Work Education*, 1–15. doi:10.1080/02615479.2022.2102163

Ladson-Billings, G. (1995). But that's just good teaching! The case for culturally relevant pedagogy. *Theory into Practice*, *34*(3), 159–165. doi:10.1080/00405849509543675

Lapkin, S., Levett-Jones, T., & Gilligan, C. (2013). A systematic review of the effectiveness of interprofessional education in health professional programs. *Nurse Education Today*, *33*(2), 90–102. doi:10.1016/j.nedt.2011.11.006 PMID:22196075

Martin, F., Ritzhaupt, A., Kumar, S., & Budhrani, K. (2019). Award-winning faculty online teaching practices: Course design, assessment and evaluation, and facilitation. *The Internet and Higher Education*, *42*, 34–43. doi:10.1016/j.iheduc.2019.04.001

Matzat, U. (2013). Do blended virtual learning communities enhance teachers' professional development more than purely virtual ones? A large scale empirical comparison. *Computers & Education*, *60*(1), 40–51. doi:10.1016/j.compedu.2012.08.006

McConnell, T. J., Parker, J. M., Eberhardt, J., Koehler, M. J., & Lundeberg, M. A. (2013). Virtual professional learning communities: Teachers' perceptions of virtual versus face-to-face professional development. *Journal of Science Education and Technology*, *22*(3), 267–277. doi:10.100710956-012-9391-y

McLeskey, J., Barringer, M. D., Billingsley, B., Brownell, M., & Jackson, D. (2017). *High-leverage practices in special education.* Council for Exceptional Children & CEEDAR Center.

Miller, G. E., & Nguyen, V. (2014). Family school partnering to support new immigrant and refugee families with children with disabilities. In L. Lo & D. B. Hiatt-Michael (Eds.), *Promising practices to empower culturally and linguistically diverse families of children with disabilities* (pp. 67–84).

Miller, R., & Stein, K. V. (2018). Building competencies for integrated care: Defining the landscape. *International Journal of Integrated Care, 17*(6), 6. doi:10.5334/ijic.3946

National Center for Educational Research. (2017). Characteristics of public and private elementary and secondary school teachers in the United States: Results from the 2011–12 schools and staffing survey. *NCES 2013-314.* https://nces.ed.gov/

Professional Education Licensing and Standards Board [PELSB] (2020). *Rules relating to teacher preparation program and unit approval 8705.0100. PELSB.* https://mn.gov/pelsb/board/rulemaking/program-unit-rules/

Randall, D. L., & West, R. E. (2020). Who cares about open badges? An examination of principals' perceptions of the usefulness of teacher open badges in the United States. *Open Learning*, 1–19. doi:10.1080/02680513.2020.1752166

Rickels, D. A., & Brewer, W. D. (2017). Facebook band director's group: Member usage behaviors and perceived satisfaction for meeting professional development needs. *Journal of Music Teacher Education, 26*(3), 77–92. doi:10.1177/1057083717692380

Riskiyana, R., Claramita, M., & Rahayu, G. R. (2018). Objectively measured interprofessional education outcome and factors that enhance program effectiveness: A systematic review. *Nurse Education Today, 66*, 73–78. doi:10.1016/j.nedt.2018.04.014 PMID:29684835

Robertson, P., McCaleb, K. N., & McFarland, L. A. (2022). Preparing all educators to serve students with extensive support needs: An interdisciplinary approach. *New Educator, 18*(1-2), 87–109. doi:10.1080/1547688X.2022.2055248

Robertson, P. M., García, S. B., McFarland, L. A., & Rieth, H. J. (2012). Preparing culturally and linguistically responsive special educators: It "does" take a village. *Interdisciplinary Journal of Teaching and Learning, 2*(3), 115–130.

Rolandson, D. M., & Ross-Hekkel, L. E. (2022). Virtual professional learning communities: A case study in rural music teacher professional development. *Journal of Music Teacher Education, 31*(3), 81–94. doi:10.1177/10570837221077430

Ronfeldt, M., Owens Farmer, S., & Grissom, J. A. (2015). Teacher collaboration in instructional teams and student achievement. *American Educational Research Journal, 52*(3), 475–514. doi:10.3102/0002831215585562

Selwyn, N. (2008). Realising the potential of new technology? Assessing the legacy of New Labour's ICT agenda 1997–2007. *Oxford Review of Education, 34*(6), 701–712. doi:10.1080/03054980802518920

Siegel, D. H., Smith, M. C., & Melucci, S. C. (2020). Teaching social work students about homelessness: An interdisciplinary interinstitutional approach. *Journal of Social Work Education, 56*(sup1), S59-S71. doi:10.1080/10437797.2020.1741479

Stanley, A. M., Snell, A., & Edgar, S. (2014). Collaboration as effective musical professional development: Success stories from the field. *Journal of Music Teacher Education, 24*(1), 76–88. doi:10.1177/1057083713502731

Thistlethwaite, J., & Moran, M. (2010). Learning outcomes for interprofessional education (IPE): Literature review and synthesis. *Journal of Interprofessional Care, 24*(5), 503–513. doi:10.3109/13561820.2010.483366 PMID:20718596

United Nations Department of Economic and Social Affairs. (1998). Recommendations on statistics of international migration, Revision 1. *United Nations Publication, Sales No. E.98.XVII.14.* https://unstats.un.org/unsd/publication/SeriesM/SeriesM_58rev1E.pdf

United Nations, High Commissioner for Refugees. (1951). Relating to the status of refugees. *UN.* https://www.unhcr.org/en-us/3b66c2aa10

University of Washington. (n.d.). The learning cycle. *Inspire Washington.* https://inspirewashington.edu/index.php/the-learning-cycle/

U.S. Census Bureau. (2021). American community survey tables on the foreign born by subject. *USCB.* https://www.census.gov/topics/population/foreign-born/guidance/acs-guidance/acs-by-subject.html

U.S. Congress. (1975, November 29). Education for All Handicapped Children Act of 1975. *Public Law*, •••, 94–142.

U.S. Congress. (1990). Individuals with Disabilities Act 1990. *Public Law*, 101–476.

U.S. Congress. (1997). Individuals with Disabilities Act 1997. *Public Law*, 105–117.

U.S. Congress. (2004). Individuals with Disabilities Act 2004. *Public Law*, 114–195.

U.S. Department of Education. (2022). Part C child count and setting. *USDE.* https://www2.ed.gov/programs/osepidea/618-data/static-tables/index.html

U.S. Immigrant Learning Center. (2019). Retrieved from: https://www.ilctr.org/quick-us-immigration-statistics/

van Winkelen, C. (2003). Inter-organizational communities of practice. *Henley Knowledge Management Forum.* https://www.elearningeuropa.info/en/article/Inter-Organizational-Communities-of-Practice

Wenger, E. (2001). Supporting communities of practice: A survey of community-oriented technologies. Retrieved from http://www.ewenger.com/tech/

Young, D., West, R. E., & Nylin, T. A. (2019). Value of open microcredentials to earners and issuers: A case study of national instruments open badges. *International Review of Research in Open and Distributed Learning, 20*(5), 104–121. doi:10.19173/irrodl.v20i5.4345

## ADDITIONAL READING

Fisher-Borne, M., Cain, J. M., & Martin, S. L. (2015). From mastery to accountability: Cultural humility as an alternative to cultural competence. *Social Work Education*, *34*(2), 165–181. doi:10.1080/02615479.2014.977244

Harkins Monaco, E. A., Fuller, M., & Stansberry Brusnahan, L. L. (2021). *Diversity, autism, and developmental disabilities: Guidance for the culturally responsive educator. Prism Series, 13*. Council for Exceptional Children.

Interprofessional Education Collaborative. (2016). *Core competencies for interprofessional collaborative practice: 2016 update*. Interprofessional Education Collaborative.

## KEY TERMS AND DEFINITIONS

**Competency Based Assessment:** Evaluation, often directed by regulatory bodies, to determine students' knowledge, skills, abilities, or behaviors linked to professional practice.

**Culturally and Linguistically Sustaining Practices:** Practices that draw upon, infuse, and affirm students' existing social identities, schema, experiences, funds of knowledge, and perspectives to optimally facilitate learning that provides racial and cultural equity and expands opportunities for historically marginalized students (Alim & Paris, 2017; Gay, 2010; Ladson-Billings, 1995).

**Digital Badges:** Badges provided virtually (e.g., online), which provide professionals with an efficient way to offer evidence of specific knowledge to others.

**Early Intervention:** Intervention that consists of services and supports provided in natural environments (e.g., homes) to young children with developmental delays and disabilities age zero until the age of three and their families.

**Early Childhood Special Education:** Education that incorporates services and supports to meet the needs of preschool students with developmental delays and disabilities in various environments, including but not limited to classrooms, community childcare centers, and homes.

**Field Experience:** Experiences that allow preservice professionals (e.g., university students) to practice their professional skills in applied settings. For this article, it considers only educational settings.

**Interdisciplinary Practice:** Practice that integrates methods, knowledge, skills, and perspectives of different disciplines to develop innovative solutions to complex needs.

**Interprofessional Competencies:** Knowledge, skills, abilities, and behaviors that support effective and innovative collaboration between professional disciplines.

**Interprofessional Education Collaborative (IPEC):** A collective of health professional groups that aim to support interactive training of future health professionals toward enhanced team-based care.

**Micro Credentials:** Mini certificates that offer knowledge and assessment of targeted skills. Micro credentials can be awarded through digital badges.

**Social Work:** Aa helping profession that seeks to strengthen individual and societal well-being and support people in fulfilling their basic needs. The professional discipline recognizes six foundational values of service, social justice, dignity and worth of the person, importance of human relationships, integrity, and competence.

**Virtual Learning Community:** Professional development groups, which have the same characteristics of professional learning communities, where participants meet virtually using an online platform (e.g., Zoom).

# Chapter 4
# Collaborative Preparation of Special Educators and Adapted Physical Educators

**Jill Anderson**
https://orcid.org/0000-0002-0058-6502
*California State Polytechnic University, Humboldt, USA*

**David Adams**
*California State Polytechnic University, Humboldt, USA*

**Chris Hopper**
*California State Polytechnic University, Humboldt, USA*

**Melaina A. Valdez**
*California State Polytechnic University, Humboldt, USA*

**Delaney Hughes**
*California State Polytechnic University, Humboldt, USA*

**Kalyn Ruland**
*California State Polytechnic University, Humboldt, USA*

## ABSTRACT

*Adapted physical education (APE) is an important, but often overlooked, component of a well-rounded education experience and provides a variety of benefits for student's health, well-being, and educational achievement. Interdisciplinary teacher preparation in special education (SPED) and APE can facilitate collaborative learning and prepare preservice educators to implement high-quality holistic education and participate in multidisciplinary teams. The objective of this chapter is to provide an overview of the importance of APE within educational programming and outline strategies for interdisciplinary education. These strategies include interdisciplinary instructional and community programing and implantation of action research. Providing opportunities to engage in purposeful multidisciplinary groups in teacher preparation programs prepares students to effectively step into their future roles as educators.*

## INTRODUCTION

Physical education (PE) is part of a well-rounded K-12 educational experience (Every Student Succeeds

DOI: 10.4018/978-1-6684-6438-0.ch004

Act, 2015). The Individuals with Disabilities Education Act (2004) protects the rights of all students to a free and appropriate education within the least-restrictive environment. For students with disabilities many times the least-restrictive environment is in a modified PE class, such as adapted physical education (APE). Within APE, students are provided the same, modified or different curriculum based on prior assessments and academic goals established by the multidisciplinary individualized education programming (IEP) team. Though APE is an important component of educational experiences that can support development in multiple domains of learning (e.g. psychomotor, affective, and cognitive), APE professionals are often overlooked in the IEP process. Implementing interdisciplinary educational components in teacher preparation programs can serve as a tool to improve depth and breadth of learning and collaborative communication skills that will serve future educators well for working in multidisciplinary teams. One of the most significant challenges all teachers face is identifying effective instructional strategies and determining the activity that best supports the learning of the student (Montgomery & Smith, 2015). Action research, first coined by Lewin (1946), is the process of the teacher identifying a problem (e.g., identifying effective instructional strategies) in their classroom and coming up with relevant solutions. Bringing educators from different focus areas (e.g., APE and special education [SPED]) together in action research and practical application through programming can serve a critical need to prepare future educators in SPED and related services for working effectively together and providing appropriate curriculum to all students.

The faculty at Cal Poly Humboldt recognized the unique opportunity to design and implement a multifaceted interdisciplinary program for teacher preparation in SPED and APE to improve the career readiness of future teachers. In the state of California, teacher credential programs are primarily post-baccalaureate. This system provids an opportunity to move students though the interdisciplinary program in cohorts. These cohorts have shared experience in coursework, student teaching, and community based field work that incorporates knowledge and skills necessary for the acquisition of both an Education Specialist teaching credential and an APE added authorization. The elements of Cal Poly Humboldts interdisciplinary program have been intentionally designed to consistently draw on both specializations, providing students the opportunity to work collaboratively and develop a thorough understanding of the complementary nature of providing special education and related services to their future students with disabilities. This chapter will examine Cal Poly Humboldt's interdisciplinary framework for supporting the preparation of special educators and adapted physical educators through the following objectives:

**Objective One:** Provide an overview of APE and how APE teachers play an important role in interdisciplinary teams providing SPED services.

**Objective Two:** Examine how an interdisciplinary approach that includes physical activity (PA) can enhance student service delivery which improves educational outcomes for students with disabilities.

**Objective Three:** Present key design components in action research in an interdisciplinary teacher preparation program in SPED and APE.

**Objective Four:** Present practical examples of how SPED teachers and APE teachers can collaboratively design curriculum to enhance the academic, social emotional, and behavior outcomes for students with disabilities using action research models.

**Objective Five:** Provide examples of how a series of community engagement activities that include SPED and APE candidates can support recruitment into the professions.

# BACKGROUND

## Physical Education and Adapted Physical Education

The overall mission of PE and APE programs alike is to help students, including those with disabilities, to develop independent PA behaviors in community settings and thus empower them to be active across their lifespan. To achieve this level of independence in activity participation, a variety of knowledge and skills are necessary, including motor skills, social skills, affective development, and application of knowledge. Despite the well-documented positive outcomes of (A)PE and legislation protecting the subject area, (A)PE as a curriculum is not considered a core subject, and, in some instances, administrators may perceive PE as a lower priority, compared to other content areas (Barroso et al., 2005; Stevens-Smith et al., 2006). Further, in some states, PE at the elementary level is taught by general and SPED classroom teachers who are not prepared by their teacher preparation programs to implement high-quality PE for students with disabilities. Historically, general PE had neglected students with disabilities in integrated classes, and restricted access to facilities and equipment (Holland & Haegele, 2020; Richards & Wilson, 2020). This creates a challenge for APE teachers who must contend with assumptions placed on them related to general PE that they may not be able to control.

## Importance of Adapted Physical Education as a Special Education Related Service

Many health promoting organizations including Centers for Disease Control and Prevention (CDC, 2022), recommend 60 minutes of PA per day for children and adolescents to achieve associated health benefits. PA is any bodily movement that requires energy expenditure (CDC, 2022). For students with disabilities, engaging in PA provides opportunities for improvements in social interactions (Jobling, 2001), body composition (LeMura & Maziekas, 2002), bone health (Daly, 2007), psychological health (Trost, 2005), academic performance and lower absenteeism (Springboard to Active Schools, 2017). Positive outcomes from PA and exercise have also been observed in individual populations, such as autism spectrum disorder. For example, the National Professional Center for Autism Spectrum Disorder in 2015 identified exercise as an evidence-based practice (EBP) and researchers have reported a reduction in stereotypical behaviors (Oriel et al., 2011; Petrus et al., 2008), aggressive behaviors (Oriel et al., 2011), and body mass index (Neely et al., 2014), as well as improved motor coordination (Batey et al., 2013; Curtin et al., 2014), mental health (Biddle et al., 2019), academic performance (Neely et al., 2014; Oriel et al., 2011), social interactions, and quality of life (Rimmer & Rowland, 2008). A fundamental component of APE is the development of motor skills. Motor skill development is a facilitating factor for PA participation in later childhood and adulthood (Barnett et al., 2009; Fisher et al., 2005; Okely et al., 2001). As a result, APE is an important tool to support lifelong health of children with disabilities.

Physical inactivity leads to many adverse health outcomes including increased risk for obesity (Kohl 3rd et al., 2012). Children who experience obesity are more likely to have increased negate social experiences, health outcomes, and educational outcomes compared to their peers who are not categorized as obese (Carey et al., 2015). Furthermore, young children categorized as obese are more likely to be categorized as obese in later childhood and further into adulthood (Cunningham et al., 2014; Quattrin, et al., 2005). As a population health concern, obesity is easier to mitigate through prevention than treatment (Goldfield et al., 2002), with PA shown to facilitate prevention in children (Brown et al., 2019).

Individuals with disabilities are at increased risk for adverse health outcomes in many cases, due to reduced independence and access to accessible community recreation (Rimmer et al., 2010). Highly-qualifies APE teachers not only provide exceptional education in the classroom, but also provide support for students to engage in out of school PA (Lytle et al., 2010). This component of the APE profession is becoming increasingly important over recent years, as many schools have decreased time PE/APE is offered. When these reductions in PE/APE time occur, students lose valuable time in PA during their school day, and do not make up for this lost activity in their leisure time outside of school hours (Meyer et al., 2011). As a result, it is important for APE teachers to be prepared to bring high-quality evidence into IEP meetings that support students' needs for APE services.

APE can take place in a variety of settings (e.g., general PE, APE classroom, home, and hospital); thus, APE teachers need to be able to provide instruction to students one-on-one, as well as in small and large classroom settings. Additionally, APE professionals must be able to promote activity beyond the education setting to provide successful transition services. Transition planning, which prepares students with an IEP not only to transition between schools but also from the education system into adult life, plays a critical role in the APE professionals ability to support lifelong PA engagement habits for their students. Transition plans are the place for the APE professional to incorporate the practical skills that will be necessary to engage in PA during the students leisure time. This leisure time activity, or activities that students enjoy and participate in outside of education settings, will be key in supporting their students' health and wellbeing across the lifespan. To establish student support needs for both in the education setting and within their leisure time, APE teachers assess and evaluate movement and behavioral skills of children with disabilities using standardized (formal) and alternative (informal) assessments. Through these assessments, valid and reliable data can be collected and used to develop a motor and behavior profile for each student. The motor and behavioral profile represents the student's present level of academic performance which will, in turn, identify service qualifications and support needs, as well as inform academic APE goals for the student's IEP development and implementation. The ability to collect, analyze, and communicate data to a variety of collaborators with varying levels of knowledge in APE assessment is a critical component of APE teacher preparation. Collaborative education wherein APE teachers can gain knowledge of IEP development from SPED educators and SPED educators can gain a knowledge of how to engage with APE data can symbiotically support higher level skills in participating in IEP teams.

Bringing together multidisciplinary IEP teams is critical for supporting students' growth and development, as the goals in one area (e.g., APE) can be developed to support goals in other areas (e.g., SPED). However, despite the documented value of APE for student growth and development, APE teachers are often not invited to IEP meetings and must advocate for themselves and their students to be included. Additionally, caregivers of children with disabilities may not be fully informed about the availability and purpose of APE nor their rights in requesting APE services in their child's IEP. As a result, APE teachers need to be trained in the skills and services they provide in the classroom, in communication with all members of multidisciplinary IEP teams, including families and caregivers of students, and as advocates for their students to receive APE. Collaborative education between SPED and APE teachers can support the knowledge sharing on the impacts of quality APE services and joint advocacy for the provision of these important educational opportunities to support student growth, development, and achievement.

## Interdisciplinary Teacher Preparation

A critical component of student learning is the ability to translate knowledge and skills to a variety of settings (Holland et al., 2019). This translation serves to solidify learning and student development. Educators can work together to effectively provide opportunities for interdisciplinary learning to occur and support achievement in all areas. An ample amount of evidence shows the importance of PE and APE for supporting the physical, intellectual, and sociocultural health of children with disabilities as well as the aligning advocacy work of organizations (e.g., National Professional Development Center on Autism Spectrum Disorder and What Works Clearinghouse). Nevertheless, there is a gap in the translation of research to practice in both PE (Knudson, 2005) and APE (McNamara, 2020). This gap has left APE and SPED professionals alike without supportive training in coordinating their educational efforts to support cross-disciplinary learning. Integrating purposeful opportunities to develop the tangible and nontangible skills necessary to be effective on multidisciplinary teams and provide high-quality interdisciplinary education will develop well-rounded professionals in SPED services.

The need for interdisciplinary collaboration in SPED preservice educator programs has been long identified as a critical component for future teacher success (Dillon et al., 2021; Hernandez, 2013). Additionally, in the field of APE, researchers have reported that many preservice or new to the field APE teachers use trial and error, instead of proven practices (Colombo-Dougovito, 2015). McNamara (2020) also reported that APE teachers with more experience have lower perceptions of the usefulness of research to guide their daily practices. This indicates that the low levels of teacher engagement with proven practices only decrease as they progress in their careers. University preservice teaching programs have the opportunity, at small and large scales, to infuse collaborative, evidence-based, and interdisciplinary learning. At the individual course level, faculty can use current research and EBPs to help preservice teacher candidates gain the skills and abilities needed to meet the educational needs of students with disabilities. Criteria established in the manual on standards for EBP in SPED (Council of Exceptional Children, 2014), EBP in philosophy in APE (Hutzler, 2011; Jin & Yun, 2010), and reports from the CEEDAR center to identify EBPs provide guidance for inclusion in an interdisciplinary preparation program. To best prepare future teachers, university preservice teaching programs (e.g., PE teacher education) need to provide multiple opportunities across settings (e.g., general PE, APE, and community-based programming) where students are provided opportunities to connect theory to practice in the development and understanding of how to select, design, and implement appropriate interventions for groups and individual students with varying support needs. In this regard, Adams et al. (in-press) reported that APE teachers identified selecting, designing, and implementing interventions as well as hands-on experience as the most significant area of improvement needed within their preservice teaching program at the university undergraduate and graduate levels.

A longstanding goal in APE has been connecting cognitive learning and PA (Cratty, 1989). This is based on the premise that reinforcement of academic content in a PA setting provides value-added benefits to reinforce learning goals. Special educators and adapted physical educators who work independently may not be able to make this connection. However, providing learning opportunities where preservice educators can learn from each other's experience and expertise and work together to assess, plan, implement, and reevaluate programming can train educators to see these connections and work together to make them a reality. APE activities help develop skills that improve socialization, waiting and taking turns, communication, self-regulation strategies, and enhancement in self-efficacy (Güvendi & İlhan, 2017). In this context, the focus of collaborative activities between the APE teachers and SPED teach-

*Table 1. Knowledge and skills that SPED and APE teachers can learn from each other, as identified by preservice educators in an interdisciplinary program.*

| Knowledge and Skills SPED Teachers can Gain from APE Colleagues | Knowledge and Skills SPED and APE Teachers can Gain From Eachother | Knowledge and Skills APE Teachers can Gain from SPED Colleagues |
|---|---|---|
| 1. Overall mission of APE as it relates to a healthy lifestyle.<br>2. The impact of PA engagement on student achievement.<br>3. Broad understanding of PE goals that may be represented in state PE content standards.<br>4. Motor development sequences during the elementary school years.<br>5. Familiarity with APE assessment domains and techniques.<br>6. Overview of APE services and programs available.<br>7. Overview of transition planning as it pertains to PA engagement. | 1. Behavior and classroom management strategies.<br>2. Development of interdisciplinary goals.<br>3. Supporting the holistic growth and development of their students.<br>4. How to effectively communicate across disciplines. | 1. Broad understanding of subject matter content standards in SPED.<br>2. Familiarity with assessment domains and techniques in SPED.<br>3. Overview of educational services and programs available.<br>4. Overview of transition planning, as it pertains to life preparation.<br>5. Strategies to participate effectively in IEP teams. |

ers should be developed for implementing cross-disciplinary self-regulation skills within individualized instruction to improve student achievement. Collaborating with an adapted physical educator on specific learning targets can help promote a student's ability to generalize skills in other classrooms, community, and independent living settings (Roth et al., 2016).

Additionally, academic goals set by a SPED teacher can be embedded and pursued in an APE setting (Whinnery et al., 2016). For example, students with an early math goal, specifically for counting, can practice rote counting in the APE setting by counting repetitions and set numbers throughout a workout. Number sense and representation can also be a focus through the use of both small and large manipulatives in a PA setting that correspond with a particular number (e.g., a number four on a basket demonstrating that a student needs to throw four balls into it). Other early math skills, such as spatial sense, measurement, and emerging addition and subtraction problems, can be learned through sport games such as bowling, frisbee golf, and basketball. Literacy skills are another area that can also be united between a SPED teacher and an adapted physical educator. For students with early reading goals, the use of words that can be represented visually or phonetically can be worked on through sport activities. For example, the game of "HORSE", where students are shooting basketballs into a hoop; with each miss, a student must add a letter to the word. Activities such as marching, jumping, and stomping may also provide a student with an early reading skill of rhythm and cadence. When working on literacy goals, a student may also access improvements in sequencing, prediction, and early problem solving through multistep games and PAs.

A continual challenge for teacher education programs is how to decide on essential content knowledge for the beginning teacher. The professional field of SPED includes a vast array of subfield specialty areas. In a crowded curriculum for the prospective SPED teacher, there is often limited space for content in APE. Preservice educators in an interdisciplinary SED and APE program identified knowledge and skills that SPED and APE teachers can benefit from learning from each other. Table one below includes these components.

The interdisciplinary SPED and APE program at Cal Poly Humboldt is designed around supporting preservice educators in not only working together but also learning from each other to develop the knowledge and skills outlined in table one above. The remainder of the chapter will detail how the program at Cal Poly Humboldt has supported that learning through the incorporation of interdisciplinary coursework, strategies (e.g., action research that will support educators in developing best practices in education), and interdisciplinary programming.

## MAIN FOCUS OF THE CHAPTER

### Designing Interdisciplinary Programs

#### Interdisciplinary Coursework

Teacher preparation programs can incorporate interdisciplinary opportunities for preservice SPED and APE teachers in multiple ways, including sharing content courses or varying class examples and interdisciplinary seminars and conferences. APED and APE preparation programs have overlapping content areas that may provide opportunities to share courses. For example, instead of a separate behavior management course, the Cal Poly Humboldt interdisciplinary program identified opportunities to have scholars in both programs take the same course together. This provides opportunities for the preservice educators to have prolonged interactions with each other and learn from the unique examples they can bring in from their respective student teaching experiences. Incorporating a variety of examples in courses that cannot be shared in as another strategy to infuse interdisciplinary learning into teacher preparation programs. For example, in a course that covers legislation related to SPED services, courses focused on APE can include SPED-related examples and vice versa. This prompts conversations about how the components of SPED and related services work together as part of a whole and build awareness in how to understand and communicate with professionals in other areas of SPED.

At Cal Poly Humboldt, shared interdisciplinary seminars and conferences have been utilized as viable avenues to provide collaborative learning and leadership experiences for preservice teachers. Through these knowledge sharing opportunities, preservice educators can identify topics they believe are key for other professionals to understand about their field and develop and deliver presentations to interdisciplinary groups. Like coursework integration, these opportunities foster conversation and idea sharing on implementation in different settings, and will go beyond to develop leadership skills in how to both learn from and teach their peers. An important component of working on multidisciplinary teams, such as IEP teams, is to be able to recognize the knowledge and skills professionals bring to the table and those that they can learn from others, and be able to communicate effectively in both situations. Providing opportunities for preservice educators to practice both teaching and actively learning from each other will prepare them well for these collaborations in their future careers. As part of this integrated work, targeted educational strategies, such as Action research, can be utilized to strengthen preservice educators skills in applying their knowledge to the classroom.

Action Research and Benefits of the Model within preservice programs and for professional teachers
During the 2020/2021 school year 7.2 million or 15% of students qualified for services under IDEA (National center for Education Statistics, 2022). These numbers suggest that SPED teachers and APE teachers will play a critical role in educating and determining appropriate services for each student. To support students understanding of appropriate services Cal Poly Humboldt follows an action research model (Adams et al., 2022) that allows students to identify and implement best practices for their students

across settings. The following sections provide an overview of action research, as well as the teaching behaviors each student or cohort will complete within the interdisciplinary program at Cal Poly Humboldt. It should also be noted that while the examples of action research focus primarily on behaviors associated with APE, we believe the Cal Poly Humbodlt interdisciplinary model prepares future SPED and APE teachers to complete the below teaching behaviors across academic settings.

Action research provides opportunities for future teachers within both SPED and APE to critically examine their own teaching behaviors and focus on effective approaches to learning (Mertler, 2019). McNiff (2017) stated that, when teachers conduct action research, they will reflect on their own teaching behaviors by asking questions, such as "what am I doing," "what are the intended goals I am attempting to accomplish," "how can I improve the learning environment for my students." This reflective questioning supports Lewin's (1946) statement that research conducted within the context (e.g., classroom) where the problem existed was essential to determining a solution for that problem or bringing about some level of change (Mertler, 2020). Researchers have since defined action research as a systematic inquiry that teachers, administrators or others conduct with the interest of gathering information on topics related to how their schools operate and how those teaching behaviors or other factors impact student learning (Mertler, 2009; Mills, 2000; Schmuck, 1997). Mills (2000) went on to report that action research provides practitioners with new knowledge of how to improve current practices or resolve existing issues with the main goal of improving the lives of students. Finally, action research is distinctive in that the teacher is the main researcher as opposed to traditional research where a researcher may come into a classroom, observe a teacher interacting with their students, and try to explain those interactions (McNiff, 2017).

Established within master degree programs and teacher pre-service education programs (Zambo & Zambo, 2007) in the 1990's, action research places an emphasis on the preparation of preservice teachers with the most effective methods to impact student outcomes (Cochran-Smith & Lytle, 1990; Noffke, 1997; Scheeler et al., 2016). The model accomplishes this by having teachers reflect on their own teaching behaviors and how those behaviors impact the learning of their students (Vaughan & Burnaford, 2016). Through these times of reflection, teachers can critically analyze the teacher-student interactions within their classroom, challenge traditional practices, and begin to take risks (Mills, 2000). Further, action research places the teacher at the center of the research and allows them to become agents of change for their students (Vaughan & Brunaford, 2016). Adams et al. (2022) identified a systematic and cyclical action research model that encompasses the following teaching behaviors: (a) Observation; (b) data collection; (c) selecting, designing, and implementing interventions; (d) analyzing data; (e) reporting data; (f) reflection of data. Figure 1 illustrates the teaching behaviors within the action research model.

## Teaching Behaviors of Action Research

### Observation

Systematic observation is the first teaching behavior within the model. Green (2019) defined this step as the process of teachers identifying appropriate academic goals for their class and students, based on systematic and continuous observation. Specifically, during this time, SPED and APE teachers should use observation of their class and individual students to determine how their own teaching behaviors (e.g., setting and activity choice) and expectations (e.g., individual task and group task) impact the learning environment. Table 2 provides an illustration of an observation checklist APE teachers could apply within their classroom to better understand their student's behaviors.

*Figure 1. Action research teaching behaviors for teachers*

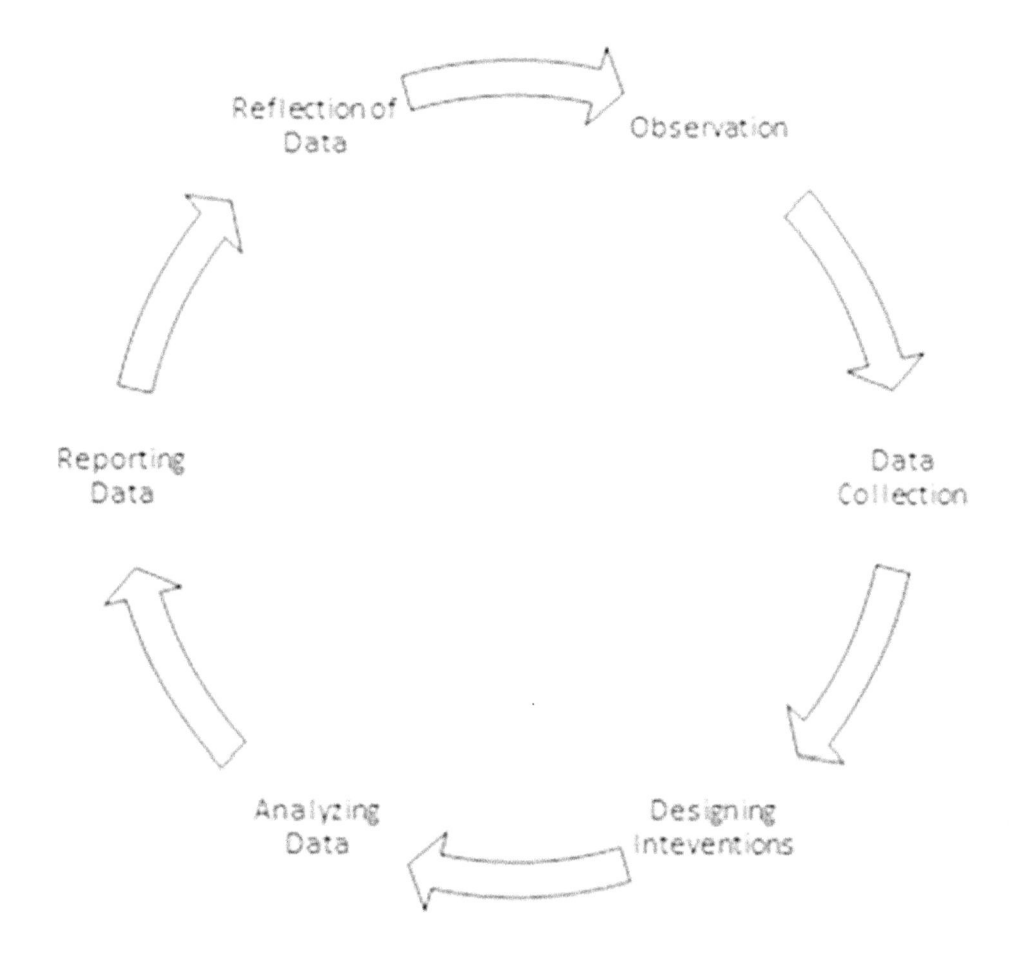

*Table 2. Teacher observation checklist for whole class and individual students for soccer Activity*

| Date: 6-16-2022 Setting: Outdoor | Activity: Soccer<br>Assigned Task: Individual and Small Group Practice and Game Play |
|---|---|
| **Class Notes**<br>Engagement Level H/L<br>Accommodation Needed Y/N<br>Modification Needed Y/N | **Notes**: 70-80% of class were not engaged during the dribbling activity. Accommodation activity for next class includes an attacking goal and defending goal for students and keep students moving throughout activity. Also, provide more examples for students of possible attacking moves for students to apply during activity. |
| **Individual Student Notes**<br>Engagement Level H/L<br>Accommodation Needed Y/N<br>Modification Needed Y/N | **Notes:** Jason was on-task for 10% of the dribbling activity and struggled when performing the attacking moves. Accommodation activity: Allow Jason practice time prior to beginning the activity and provide visual cues to support his understanding of the different attacking moves for the upcoming activity. |

*Table 3. Alternative assessment for the free-throw basketball shot*

| Major Component | Verbal Prompt | Completed/Notes |
|---|---|---|
| 1. Feet shoulder width apart and facing the basket. | Feet shoulder width apart | Completed: Y/N<br>Notes: |
| 2. Knees bent at 45 degree angle. | Knees bent | Completed: Y/N<br>Notes: |
| 3. Ball placed in the dominant hand with fingers spread. | Fingers spread | Completed: Y/N<br>Notes: |
| 4. Non-dominant hand is placed on the side of the ball. | Support the ball | Completed: Y/N<br>Notes: |
| 5. Eyes on the basket/bath elbows bent at 90 degrees. | Eyes up, elbows bent | Completed: Y/N<br>Notes: |
| 6. Ball released above the head towards the basket. | Shoot | Completed: Y/N<br>Notes: |

## Data Collection

The second teaching behavior within the model is data collection. Successful SPED and APE teachers will need to be able to administer valid and reliable assessments with their students through standardized and alternative assessments. For example, APE teachers wanting to assess their students' ability to perform a variety of gross motor skills may use the *Test of Gross Motor Development* (Ulrich, 2018). Additionally, APE teachers wanting to assess aerobic capacity, muscle strength and endurance, as well as flexibility, may use the Fitnessgram (Plowman & Meredith, 2017). Additionally, SPED teachers will need to have a good understanding of teacher-developed alternative assessments, such as systematic direct observation, rubrics, task-analysis, and portfolios. These alternative assessments allow teachers to collect data that may not have been available through the use of standardized assessments. For example, a SPED teacher wanting to assess an individual student's ability to complete a free-throw shot for basketball could use a task analysis where each major component of the skill is listed in order. Additionally, at this stage SPED and APE teachers will need to determine a systematic approach to collecting data. The Cal Poly Humboldt encourages students to utilize a number of different types of single case designs during this phase. Single-case design is the process of the researcher determining if a functional relationship exist based on the implementation of an environmental variable and a behavior change (Cooper et al., 2020). Table 3 below provides an example of task analysis that includes verbal prompts, as well as a recording system and area for taking notes that SPED teachers can use when assessing a student free-throw shooting.

## Selecting, Designing, and Implementing Interventions

The third teaching behavior within the model is selecting, designing, and implementing interventions. The ability to support individuals, as well as the whole class's needs in the classroom, is a vital skill that all successful teachers will need to be able to demonstrate. To accomplish this, SPED and APE teachers will need to have a strong understanding of research and what practices have proven to be effective in supporting students' needs across multiple contexts. Prior to implementing an intervention, SPED and APE teachers should have collected consistent and stable data (e.g., three-five days) on the class or individual student to determine a trend in behavior. Following this data collection, SPED and APE teachers can begin to determine the most appropriate types of intervention for their class or individual students. For example, for a class or student who struggles with engaging in activities during the class due to a lack of motivation, the teacher may want to implement a reward system, such as a group contingency. Group contingencies allow the class to work for a reward contingent on the class, small squads or an individual student meeting a predetermined outcome (Lavay et al., 2016; Patrick, 1998). For example, the (A)PE teacher could allow the students the opportunity to pick the ending activity for the class based on the whole class completing the required activities. Additionally, for students who struggle engaging in activities during class due to a lack of understanding of how to perform the movement, a visual cue may be more appropriate. Visual cues can consist of task analysis, rubrics, pictures, and videos (e.g., video-based instruction). Using these visual cues may support the students understanding of the critical elements needed to complete the required movement(s). Moreover, visual cues allow students the opportunity to self-evaluate their own performances with the support of the SPED and APE teacher to identify corrections needed for future performances.

## Analyzing Data

The fourth teaching behavior within the model is analyzing data. SPED and APE teachers who analyze data will better understand how their own teaching behaviors are impacting their students' academic performance. To accomplish this SPED and APE, teachers will need to review the data to support future feedback provided to the class or individual student (Horvat et al., 2019). Additionally, providing class and individual student data in graphs allows for the student and all members of the multidisciplinary team to make objective observations based on the data presented, as graphing provides unbiased feedback. For example, an APE teacher may have implemented a visual cue (i.e., rubric) as the intervention to support their students' understanding of the free throw shot for the game of basketball. To appropriately analyze the data collected, both the APE teacher would want to consider the variability of the data (i.e., measures reveal inconsistent responding), immediacy of effect (i.e., percentage of change once the intervention is introduced), overlapping data (i.e., overlap of data once intervention has been introduced), and trend or overall direction of the (Ledford et al., 2018). Figure 2 provides a graphical representation of the data collected by the APE teacher, as well as indicators for variability, immediacy, overlap, and the trend within the data. Following the procedures the authors listed above allows for SPED and APE teachers to make sound defensible decisions to support their class and students performance within the classroom.

## Reporting Data

Step five within the model is reporting data. Within this step, SPED and APE teachers have the opportunity to highlight how the class or individual is performing. These opportunities can take place during faculty meetings, parent conferences or IEP meetings. For example, in Figure 2, the SPED or APE teacher could speak to the variability of data in the first four class periods. Additionally, the SPED and APE teacher could point out to the student, parents, and multidisciplinary team about the immediacy of effect during the intervention phase where there was an immediate improvement in the number of free throws made. Finally, the SPED and APE teacher could point out that there is no overlapping data present from one phase to the next, and that the trend in data in the intervention phase demonstrates a positive increase in performance. Reporting this type of data provides evidence for what the SPED and APE teacher is doing in the class and demonstrates that consistent data is being collected and decisions

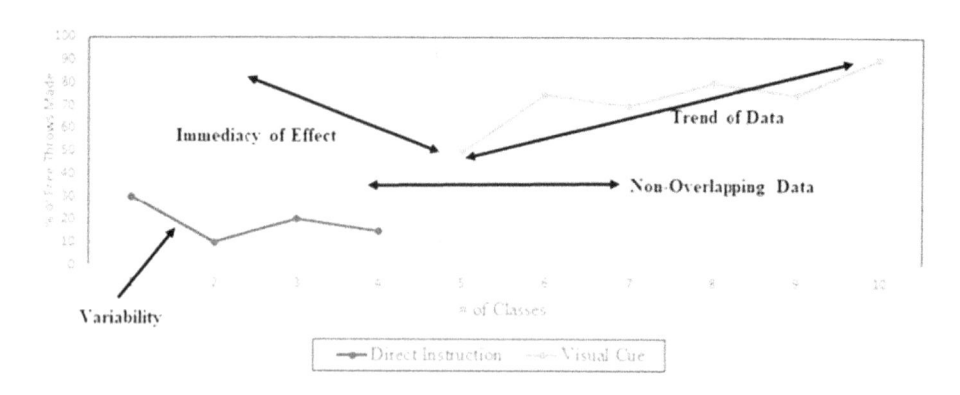

*Figure 2. Graphical representation of data collected and included key terms of reporting*

are being made based on that data. Moreover, presenting this information within the multidisciplinary team meeting (e.g., IEP meeting) provides opportunities for other teachers to follow the same model of instruction and use of interventions to support the student throughout the school day.

## Reflection of Data

The final teaching behavior within the model is reflection of data. When teachers consistently engage in reflection, they are able to make informed decisions, based on their own decisions, perceptions, and the data collected. Taggart and Wilson (1999) described the reflection process as a time where teachers make informed and logical decisions, based on their own beliefs, experiences, perceptions, and the data collected. Additionally, Korthagen (2001) stated that teachers who engage in reflection prevent themselves from settling on traditional practices. Finally, teachers who reflect on data consistently will be better able to select and design appropriate curriculum and establish appropriate academic goals for their class and individual students across multiple contexts. As part of Cal Poly Humboldts interdisciplinary program, preservice educators were provided opportunities to apply action research within their student teaching and as a tool to inform their leadership in interdisciplinary community based programs.

## Interdisciplinary Community Based Programming

Accessible PA and recreation opportunities for individuals with disabilities are often limited due to physical and social barriers to participation (Rimmer et al., 2010). Developing and implementing accessible community programming at universities can be mutually beneficial for the community and preservice educators. For the community, the programming provides not only opportunities for PA engagement, but also building connectivity and social support amongst the community members. For the preservice educators, these programs offer real world opportunities to apply the knowledge they are building and action research procedures to assess, develop, and implement a variety of instructional strategies and programs. Furthermore, these programs offer opportunities to engage with peers, families, and key community members that support recreation (e.g., Special Olympics director, and Parks and Recreation Professionals).

*Collaborative Preparation of Special Educators and Adapted Physical Educators*

Cal Poly Humboldt integrated a variety of community based programs to support the development of SPED and APE preservice educators. One viable model Cal Poly Humboldt uses is engaging preservice educators on multiple levels to build leadership skills through a scaffolded organization model. This scaffolded model includes contributions from faculty, preservice educators, and undergraduate students in various programs. A faculty member serves as the lead of the program, mentoring the preservice educators, managing the logistical components of the program, and supporting recruitment and engaging with the community. Undergraduate majors from a variety of programs volunteer for or enroll in a course connected to community programs where they serve as instructional support, working one-on-one or two-on-one pairs with community members (i.e., children and/or adults with disabilities). These pairs are then brought together into groups based on age, with preservice educators serving as group leaders. As the group leader, the preservice educator is responsible for planning and implementing the activity for that session and mentoring the undergraduate students from other programs, which models how teachers work with paraeducators in the field. This structure provides opportunities for undergraduate students to build skills for their future careers and strengthen understanding of how to engage with diverse populations and for preservice educators to build leadership skills working with teams to support their students. Additionally, opening up program engagement to undergraduate students from across majors, these programs can serve as a pathway for recruiting students in teacher preparation programs by providing them exposure to what professionals in education do as well as an opportunity to build relationships with current preservice educators and teacher preparation program faculty.

These programs are not only for PE and APE preservice teachers, but should engage future educators from all areas of education (e.g., SPED, General Education, and Occupational Therapy), as the skills in collaborating with other professionals, implementing adapted instruction, and communicating with families and community members are translational across service areas. These opportunities to take leadership roles in a program that necessitates communicating with peers in other service areas provides an opportunity to learn how to speak the language of professionals in other service areas to form effective multidisciplinary groups. This is a valuable opportunity for scholars to share their knowledge and skills with each other in real world settings, fostering respect and holistic programming. At Cal Poly Humboldt, students in preservice programs in Secondary, SPED, and APE programs have engaged as leaders of community programs, and undergraduates in education, kinesiology, child development, and recreation administration, among other programs, have participated as instructional support. This interdisciplinary engagement has improved the quality of the programming offered as well as the educational outcomes of students in the Cal Poly Humboldt programs.

One of the cornerstones of fostering engagement in community programs is for the participants to enjoy the activities in which they are engaging (Shields et al., 2021). At Cal Poly Humboldt, programs have been designed to put equal emphasis on enjoyment as well as motor skill and fitness development to foster continued participation both in structured programs and independently. Traditional swim and gym programs are implemented in the spring and summer, with time in the program split between land-based skills in the gym and water-based skills in the pool on campus. Sports programs are run in collaboration with the local Special Olympic chapter to provide basketball, bocce, and Unified Sports programming. These programs focus primarily on youth with disabilities and their typically developing peers. Adults with disabilities are engaged in transitional programming that engages participants in gym and community-based recreation facilities, which implements not only activity skills, but also skills for independently navigating these recreational facilities.

Another aspect of programming is adventure programming. These programs engage individuals with disabilities and their families in activities that take advantage of the local recreational opportunities in nature. Kayaking and Stand-Up Paddle Boarding programs at a lagoon and surfing program were put on with the support of Cal Ply Humboldt Center Activities. Center Activities served as partners providing the trained kayak instructors and lifeguards needed to support a safe program, while the program facilitators were the preservice educators. Additionally, Cal Poly Humboldt Student Recreation Center supported a rock-climbing program which provided climbing and belaying instructors' support and access to the indoor climbing wall. Many of the families that have engaged in adventure programming were doing those activities with their family member with a disability for the first time and on multiple occasions. This engagement led to the family incorporating those activities into their lives as things they do together on their own.

Including a variety of community programming into teacher preparation programs supports the development of concrete and soft skills that future educators will need to be effective in their careers. Bringing in students from a variety of teacher preparation programs to facilitate the programs provides practical situations in which to build communication skills that will be necessary for effective engagement in multidisciplinary teams. Incorporating action research into program refinement facilitates high-quality instruction and continuous improvement in educational strategies. Furthermore, working in these groups allows the scholars to learn from each other and benefit from the specific knowledge and skills that are established in other preparation programs. Engaging directly with community members will also provide practical experience in communicating with families of children with disabilities and recreation professionals in the community. Further, using a scaffolded program design provides a leadership opportunity for scholars in teacher preparation programs that they otherwise would not have during their program. In addition to these benefits for preservice educators already in the teacher preparation program, these community based programs provide a pathway for recruiting students from a variety of backgrounds and majors into teacher preparation programs.

## FUTURE RESEARH DIRECTIONS

The interdisciplinary program faculty at Cal Poly Humboldt feel strongly about the importance of interdisciplinary collaboration at all levels when supporting and determining academic goals for students, including those with disabilities. For this reason, the faculty have implemented the above action research model into a number of classes and fieldwork opportunities. Within these classes, students go through each of the above steps of the action research model and use a type of single case design (e.g., withdrawal design, multiple baseline design, and multiple treatment designs) to guide the students data collection and designing of graphs for analyzing and reporting data. Single case design was determined to be a more appropriate design based on the number of low-incidence disabilities within the public schools and the opportunity for future teachers to detect, analyze, and determine functional relationships between environmental variables and behavior changes within a class or individual students. Additionally, faculty encourage students to present their data at the university colloquium, as well as district and state SPED and APE conferences. In addition, a number of events that include special Olympics, unified sports, rock climbing, and surfing will continue to be offered with the intention of providing future SPED and APE teachers strong examples of how physical activity can support the overall development in social and communication skills, cognitive skills, and physical skills for students with disabilities Doing this,

Cal Poly Humboldt faculty will continue to prepare those students as future professionals in SPED and APE with the knowledge and ability to correctly advocate for their students and programs, when faced with possible program cuts or increased student caseloads.

Overall, the interdisciplinary program model at Cal Poly Humboldt has provided more opportunities for preservice educators to develop their skills and learn in dynamic environments. Since this program's implementation, the relationships between our faculty and teachers in the school districts have strengthened (from additional communications and collaborations), improving the content of the courses and preservice educators' preparation for interdisciplinary student teaching placements. This improved preparation has in turn resulted in increased satisfaction of student teaching performance as indicated by meteor teacher evaluations. Additionally, the interdisciplinary program has provided opportunities to host more community based programs providing improved community collections between the University and local community as well as increased social support among community members. The implementation of an interdisciplinary program at Cal Poly Humboldt has had marked benefits for student learning, job preparation, and community building, showcasing the potential and importance of interdisciplinary teacher preparation programs in the future.

## CONCLUSION

Provision of appropriate educational services to students with disabilities has always been a cornerstone of K-12 education. Successful implementation of this education depends on the professionals from multiple disciplines working together to develop each student's IEP, which requires preservice teacher to be trained in the skills necessary to work in these teams. Historically, APE, while a recognized related service, has been often overlooked as part of the IEP team. Current trends in APE indicate increased professional advocacy for recognition of the value and importance of APE as part of the IEP. Incorporating interdisciplinary education and opportunities to engage in multidisciplinary skills into teacher preparation programs is a viable way to support mutual understanding of different fields and communication and collaborative skills to work together in support of student success.

## ACKNOWLEDGMENT

This program was supported by the United States Department of Education, Office of Special Education Programs Grant Number: H325K180135.

## REFERENCES

Adams, D., Bittner, M., Lavay, B., & Silliman-French., L. (in-press). Adapted physical education teachers' prior training and current use of action research to monitor student progress. *Palaestra*.

Barnett, L. M., Van Beurden, E., Morgan, P. J., Brooks, L. O., & Beard, J. R. (2009). Childhood motor skill proficiency as a predictor of adolescent physical activity. *The Journal of Adolescent Health, 44*(3), 252–259. doi:10.1016/j.jadohealth.2008.07.004 PMID:19237111

Barroso, C. S., McCullum-Gomez, C., Hoelscher, D. M., Kelder, S. H., & Murray, N. G. (2005). Self-reported barriers to quality physical education by physical education specialists in Texas. *The Journal of School Health*, *75*(8), 313–319. doi:10.1111/j.1746-1561.2005.tb07348.x PMID:16179081

Batey, C. A., Missiuna, C. A., Timmons, B. W., Hay, J. A., Faught, B. E., & Cairney, J. (2013). Self-efficacy toward physical activity and the physical activity behavior of children with and without developmental coordination disorder. *Human Movement Science*, *36*, 258–271. doi:10.1016/j.humov.2013.10.003 PMID:24345354

Biddle, S. J., Ciaccioni, S., Thomas, G., & Vergeer, I. (2019). Physical activity and mental health in children and adolescents: An updated review of reviews and an analysis of causality. *Psychology of Sport and Exercise*, *42*, 146–155. doi:10.1016/j.psychsport.2018.08.011

Brown, T., Moore, T. H., Hooper, L., Gao, Y., Zayggh, A., Ijaz, S., Elwenspoke, M., Foxen, S. C., Magee, L., O'Malley, C., Water, E., & Summerbell, C. D. (2019). Interventions for preventing obesity in children. *Cochrane Database of Systematic Reviews*, *7*(7). doi:10.1002/14651858.CD001871.pub4 PMID:31332776

Carey, F. R., Singh, G. K., Brown, H. S. III, & Wilkinson, A. V. (2015). Educational outcomes associated with childhood obesity in the United States: Cross-sectional results from the 2011–2012 National Survey of Children's Health. *The International Journal of Behavioral Nutrition and Physical Activity*, *12*(S1), S3. doi:10.1186/1479-5868-12-S1-S3 PMID:26222699

Center for Disease Control. (2022). Physical activity guidelines for Americans. *CDC*.

Cochran-Smith, M., & Lytle, S. L. (1990). Research on teaching and teacher research: The issues that divide. *Educational Researcher*, *19*(2), 2–11. doi:10.3102/0013189X019002002

Colombo-Dougovito, A. M. (2015). "Try to do the best you can:" How pre-service APE specialists experience teaching students with autism spectrum disorder. *International Journal of Special Education*, *30*(3), 160–176.

Cooper, J. O., Heron, T. E., & Heward, W. L. (2020). *Applied behavior analysis*. doi:10.26741/abaespana/2020.cooper3e

Council of Exceptional Children. (2014). CEC standards for evidence-based practices. *CEC*.

Cratty, B. J. (1989). *Adapted physical education in the mainstream*. Love Publishing Company.

Cunningham, S. A., Kramer, M. R., & Narayan, K. M. (2014). Incidence of childhood obesity in the United States. *The New England Journal of Medicine*, *370*(5), 403–411. doi:10.1056/NEJMoa1309753 PMID:24476431

Curtin, C., Jojic, M., & Bandini, L. G. (2014). Obesity in children with autism spectrum disorder. *Harvard Review of Psychiatry*, *22*(2), 93–103. doi:10.1097/HRP.0000000000000031 PMID:24614764

Daly, R. M. (2007). The effect of exercise on bone mass and structural geometry during growth. *Optimizing Bone Mass and Strength*, *51*, 33–49. doi:10.1159/000103003 PMID:17505118

Dillon, S., Armstrong, E., Goudy, L., Reynolds, H., & Scurry, S. (2021). Improving Special Education Service Delivery Through Interdisciplinary Collaboration. *Teaching Exceptional Children, 54*(1), 36–43. doi:10.1177/00400599211029671

Every Student Succeeds Act. (2015). Every Student Succeeds Act. *ESSA*. https://www.ed.gov/essa?src=ft

Fisher, A., Reilly, J. J., Kelly, L. A., Montgomery, C., Williamson, A., Paton, J. Y., & Grant, S. (2005). Fundamental movement skills and habitual physical activity in young children. *Medicine and Science in Sports and Exercise, 37*(4), 684–688. doi:10.1249/01.MSS.0000159138.48107.7D PMID:15809570

Goldfield, G. S., Raynor, H. A., & Epstein, L. H. (2002). Treatment of pediatric obesity.

Green, D. J. (2019). Are state-level physical education programs aching student learning? Ace Fitness. https://www.acefitness.org/education-and-resources/professional/certified/august-2019/7345/are-state-level-physical-education-programs-tracking-student-learning/

Güvendi, B., & İlhan, E. L. (2017). Effects of adapted physical activity applied on intellectual disability students toward level of emotional adjustment, self-managing and the socialization: Parent and teacher interactive research. *Journal of Human Sciences, 14*(4), 3879–3894. doi:10.14687/jhs.v14i4.4812

Hernandez, S. J. (2013). Collaboration in Special Education: Its History, Evolution, and Critical Factors Necessary for Successful Implementation. *Online submission, 3*(6), 480-498.

Holland, S. K., & Haegele, J. A. (2020). Socialization experiences of first-year adapted physical education teachers with a master's degree. *Adapted Physical Activity Quarterly; APAQ, 37*(3), 304–323. doi:10.1123/apaq.2019-0126 PMID:32534449

Holland, S. K., Holland, K., Haegele, J. A., & Alber-Morgan, S. R. (2019). Making it stick: Teaching students with autism to generalize physical education skills. *Journal of Physical Education, Recreation & Dance, 90*(6), 32–39. doi:10.1080/07303084.2019.1614120

Horvat, M., Kelly, L., Block, M., & Croce, R. (2019). *Developmental and adapted physical activity assessment* (2nd ed.). Human Kinetics. doi:10.5040/9781718209244

Hutzler, Y. S. (2011). Evidence-based practice and research: A challenge to the development of adapted physical activity. *Adapted Physical Activity Quarterly; APAQ, 28*(3), 189–209. doi:10.1123/apaq.28.3.189 PMID:21725114

Individuals with Disabilities Education Act. (2004). https://sites.ed.gov/idea/about-idea/

Jin, J., & Yun, J. (2010). Evidence-based practice in adapted physical education. *Journal of Physical Education, Recreation & Dance, 81*(4), 50–54. doi:10.1080/07303084.2010.10598465

Jobling, A. (2001). Life be in it: Lifestyle choices for active leisure. *Down's Syndrome: Research and Practice, 6*(3), 117–122. doi:10.3104/perspectives.102 PMID:11501213

Kohl, H. W. III, Craig, C. L., Lambert, E. V., Inoue, S., Alkandari, J. R., Leetongin, G., & Kahlmeier, S.Lancet Physical Activity Series Working Group. (2012). The pandemic of physical inactivity: Global action for public health. *Lancet, 380*(9838), 294–305. doi:10.1016/S0140-6736(12)60898-8 PMID:22818941

Korthagen, F. (2001). A reflection on reflection. In *Linking practice and theory* (pp. 67–84). Routledge. doi:10.4324/9781410600523-9

Lavay, B., French, R., & Henderson, H. (2016). *Positive behavior management in physical activity settings* (3rd ed.). Human Kinetics.

Ledford, J. R., Lane, J. D., & Severini, K. E. (2018). Systematic use of visual analysis for assessing outcomes in single case design studies. *Brain Impairment*, *19*(1), 4–17. doi:10.1017/BrImp.2017.16

LeMura, L. M., & Maziekas, M. T. (2002). Factors that alter body fat, body mass, and fat-free mass in pediatric obesity. In *Database of abstracts of reviews of effects (DARE): Quality-assessed reviews*. Centre for Reviews and Dissemination. doi:10.1097/00005768-200203000-00016

Lewin, K. (1946). Action research and minority problems. *The Journal of Social Issues*, *2*(4), 34–46. doi:10.1111/j.1540-4560.1946.tb02295.x

Lytle, R., Lavay, B., & Rizzo, T. (2010). What is a highly qualified adapted physical education teacher? *Journal of Physical Education, Recreation & Dance*, *81*(2), 40–50. doi:10.1080/07303084.2010.10598433

McNamara, S. (2020). Universal design for learning in physical education. *Adapted Physical Activity Quarterly; APAQ*, *37*(2), 235–237. doi:10.1123/apaq.2020-0016

McNiff, J. (2017). Action research: All you need to know. *Sage (Atlanta, Ga.)*.

Mertler, C. A. (2019). *Action research: Improving schools and empowering educators*. Sage Publications.

Meyer, U., Kriemler, S., Roth, R., Zahner, L., Gerber, M., Puder, J., & Hebestreit, H. (2011). Contribution of physical education to overall physical activity. *Scandinavian Journal of Medicine & Science in Sports*, *23*, 600–606. doi:10.1111/j.1600-0838.2011.01425.x PMID:22151355

Mills, G. E. (2000). *Action research: A guide for the teacher researcher*. Prentice-Hall, Inc.

Montgomery, C., & Smith, L. C. (2015). Bridging the gap between researchers and practitioners. *Die Unterrichtspraxis/Teaching German*, *48*(1), 100-113.

National Center for Education Statistics. (2022). Students With Disabilities Condition of Education. *U.S. Department of Education, Institute of Education Sciences*. https://nces.ed.gov/programs/coe/indicator/cgg

Neely, L., Rispoli, M., Gerow, S., & Ninci, J. (2014). Effects of antecedent exercise on academic engagement and stereotypy during instruction. *Behavior Modification*, *39*(1), 98–116. doi:10.1177/0145445514552891 PMID:25271070

Noffke, S. E. (1997). Professional, personal, and political dimensions of action research. *Review of Research in Education*, *22*(1), 305–343. doi:10.3102/0091732X022001305

Okely, A. D., Booth, M. L., & Patterson, J. W. (2001). Relationship of physical activity to fundamental movement skills among adolescents. *Medicine and Science in Sports and Exercise*, *33*(11), 1899–1904. doi:10.1097/00005768-200111000-00015 PMID:11689741

Oriel, K. N., George, C. L., Peckus, R., & Semon, A. (2011). The effects of aerobic exercise on academic engagement in young children with autism spectrum disorder. *Pediatric Physical Therapy*, *23*(2), 187–193. doi:10.1097/PEP.0b013e318218f149 PMID:21552085

Patrick, C. A., Ward, P., & Crouch, D. W. (1998). Effects of holding students accountable for social behaviors during volleyball games in elementary physical education. *Journal of Teaching in Physical Education*, *17*(2), 143–156. doi:10.1123/jtpe.17.2.143

Petrus, C., Adamson, S. R., Block, L., Einarson, S. J., Sharifnejad, M., & Harris, S. R. (2008). Effects of exercise interventions on stereotypic behaviours in children with autism spectrum disorder. *Physiotherapy Canada. Physiotherapie Canada*, *60*(2), 134–145. doi:10.3138/physio.60.2.134 PMID:20145777

Plowman, S. A., & Meredith, M. D. (2017). *FitnessGram/ActivityGram reference guide* (5th ed.). The Cooper Institute.

Quattrin, T., Liu, E., Shaw, N., Shine, B., & Chiang, E. (2005). Obese children who are referred to the pediatric endocrinologist: Characteristics and outcome. *Pediatrics*, *115*(2), 348–351. doi:10.1542/peds.2004-1452 PMID:15687443

Richards, K. A. R., & Wilson, W. J. (2020). Recruitment and initial socialization into adapted physical education teacher education. *European Physical Education Review*, *26*(1), 54–69. doi:10.1177/1356336X18825278

Rimmer, J., & Rowland, J. (2008). Physical activity for youth with disabilities: A critical need in an underserved population. *Developmental Neurorehabilitation*, *11*(2), 141–148. doi:10.1080/17518420701688649 PMID:18415819

Rimmer, J. H., Chen, M. D., McCubbin, J. A., Drum, C., & Peterson, J. (2010). Exercise intervention research on persons with disabilities: What we know and where we need to go. *American Journal of Physical Medicine & Rehabilitation*, *89*(3), 249–263. doi:10.1097/PHM.0b013e3181c9fa9d PMID:20068432

Roth, K., Zittel, L., Pyfer, J., & Auxter, D. (2016). *Principles and methods of adapted physical education & recreation*. Jones & Bartlett Learning.

Scheeler, M. C., Budin, S., & Markelz, A. (2016). The role of teacher preparation in promoting evidence-based practice in schools. *Learning Disabilities (Weston, Mass.)*, *14*(2), 171–187.

Schmuck, R. A. (1997). *Practical action research for change*. Skylight Training and Publishing.

Shields, N., Bruder, A. M., & Cleary, S. L. (2021). An exploratory content analysis of how physiotherapists perceive barriers and facilitators to participation in physical activity among adults with disability. *Physiotherapy Theory and Practice*, *37*(1), 149–157. doi:10.1080/09593985.2019.1623957 PMID:31172868

Springboard to Active Schools. (2017). *Strengthen physical education in schools*. National Network of Public Health Institutes.

Stevens-Smith, D. A., Fisk, W., Williams, F. K., & Barton, G. (2006). Principals' perceptions of academic importance and accountability in physical education. *International Journal of Learning*, *13*(2), 7–20. doi:10.18848/1447-9494/CGP/v13i02/44632

Taggart, G. L., & Wilson, A. P. (1999). Promoting reflective thinking in teachers: 44 action strategies. *Quality Assurance in Education.*

Trost, S. G. (2005). Report: Discussion paper for the development of recommendations for children's and youth's participation in health promoting physical activity.

Ulrich, D. A. (2018). *TGMD-3: Test of gross motor development.* Pro-Ed.

Vaughan, M., & Burnaford, G. (2016). Action research in graduate teacher education: A review of the literature 2000–2015. *Educational Action Research, 24*(2), 280–299. doi:10.1080/09650792.2015.1062408

Whinnery, S. B., Whinnery, K. W., & Eddins, D. (2016). A Strategy for Embedding Functional Motor and Early Numeracy Skill Instruction into Physical Education Activities. *Physical Disabilities: Education and Related Services, 35*(1), 17–27. doi:10.14434/pders.v35i1.20499

Zambo, D., & Zambo, R. (2007). Action research in an undergraduate teacher education program: What promises does it hold? *Action in Teacher Education, 28*(4), 62–74. doi:10.1080/01626620.2007.10463430

## KEY TERMS AND DEFINITIONS

**Action Research:** A systematic approach teachers implement to identify and solve academic issues within their own classroom.

**Adapted Physical Education:** The provision of individualized physical education services to meet a student's needs.

**Community Programming:** Instructional program that incorporates members of the community as participants.

**Interdisciplinary Education:** Incorporation of knowledge and skills from multiple specialty areas into one educational program.

**Multidisciplinary Teams:** Groups of professionals with varying skillsets and roles in education and related services that work together to provide support for student growth, development, and achievement.

**Physical Education:** Instruction in motor skills, fitness, games, and sports with emphasis in development in psychomotor, affective, and cognitive domains.

**Special Education:** An instructional setting where individual academic goals are established for each student and teachers implement evidence-based practices to best support the needs of those students.

# Chapter 5
# Interdisciplinary Special Education and APE Teacher Preparation Using Evidence-Based, High-Leverage Practices

**Heather E. Taylor**
*California State Polytechnic University, Pomona, USA*

**Joanne M. Van Boxtel**
*California State Polytechnic University, Pomona, USA*

**Elizabeth A. Foster**
*West Chester University, USA*

**Sydney A. Bueno**
https://orcid.org/0000-0002-6241-4407
*University of Wisconsin-Stevens Point, USA*

## ABSTRACT

*Preparing teachers to teach in inclusive, interdisciplinary settings is critical for teacher preparation programs if all students are to have access to general education curriculum. High-leverage practices have been proven to academically benefit students with disabilities. Using a continuous improvement cycle, the programs discussed in this chapter integrated evidence-based, high-leverage practices deliberately into special education and adapted physical education programs using an interdisciplinary approach. An audit at the program and course levels was completed and high-leverage practices and competencies were then integrated into teacher education courses where gaps were identified. Preservice teacher data was collected pre and post program to measure the effectiveness of the integration of these evidence-based practices into the programs. The steps the authors took to complete this work are detailed to be of use to other teacher preparation programs.*

DOI: 10.4018/978-1-6684-6438-0.ch005

## INTRODUCTION

This chapter will address the following themes related to interdisciplinary program and course revisions in the authors' special education and adapted physical education programs:

1) Interdisciplinary and inter-professional preparation to enhance service delivery for students with disabilities; and
2) integrated preparation approaches that allow personnel to cross disciplines, learn from each other and other fields to advance their own knowledge and skills to enhance outcomes for K-12 students.

Examples will be shown of the curriculum audit that was used at the program and course levels to strategically integrate high-leverage practices along with details about the key interdisciplinary assignments that were developed and implemented throughout the programs. A gap analysis matrix will highlight key competencies that were integrated into teacher education courses where gaps were identified. The authors will present samples of preservice teacher data that was collected pre- and post-program to measure the effectiveness of the integration of these practices into the preservice programs. The steps the authors took to complete this work are detailed to be of use to other teacher preparation programs to increase interdisciplinary learning and collaboration between programs. The objectives of this chapter are to a) detail the process the authors followed to integrate high-leverage practices deliberately into the special education and adapted physical education programs using an interdisciplinary approach, and b) provide exemplars and sample data to demonstrate effectiveness of a continuous improvement model for replication in other teacher preparation programs to continue to provide high quality teachers and quality content for students with disabilities.

Per federal legislation, the Individuals with Disabilities Education Improvement Act (IDEA) explains education for students with an eligible disability. The IDEA defines special education in Section 300.39(a)(1) as: specially designed instruction, at no cost to the parents, to meet the unique needs of a child with a disability, including—

i. Instruction conducted in the classroom, in the home, in hospitals and institutions, and in other settings; and
ii. Instruction in physical education. (2004)

This definition is imperative because of the inclusion of physical education (PE) instruction within a special education program for students with disabilities. IDEA (2004) requires that students with disabilities who have an individualized education program (IEP) have access to specially designed PE to meet their unique needs as determined appropriately by their education team. Typically, the special education teacher is responsible for academic and/or behavioral instruction and support in the classroom and serves in a dual role of IEP case manager for their students. Often the special education teacher is responsible for preparing, implementing, and progress monitoring IEP goals in collaboration with service providers within the school setting. Therefore, special education teachers need to be aware and knowledgeable about PE and Adapted Physical Education (APE). Our interdisciplinary approach applied within higher education between two separate pre-service programs, special education (i.e., Education Specialist) and APE, emphasizes the importance of collaboration of educators early on for new teacher candidates.

IDEA further provides guidance by defining what PE is in Section 300.39(b)(2):

## Interdisciplinary Special Education and APE Teacher Preparation Using Evidence

i. The development of—
   a. Physical and motor fitness;
   b. Fundamental motor skills and patterns; and
   c. Skills in aquatics, dance, and individual and group games and sports (including intramural and lifetime sports); and
ii. Includes special physical education, adapted physical education, movement education, and motor development. (2004)

The significance of this definition is the quality of content and instruction that should be provided to students with disabilities within PE and APE. CDC (2020) reported that per the Results from the School Health Policies and Practices Study in 2016, 52% of students with intellectual disabilities and 86% of students with a chronic physical disability or otherwise long-term disabilities were exempted from participating in their PE programs. Insufficient access to PE and APE for students with disabilities leads to lower levels of physical activity and fitness and health indicators (United States Department of Education, 2011). Participation within PE and APE for students with disabilities is influenced by many factors such as limited support networks, appropriate facilities and equipment, experienced staff, and physical limitations (Taheri et al., 2017; United States Department of Education, 2011). Through interdisciplinary collaboration, outcomes and special education service delivery for students with disabilities can be improved (de Oliveira et al., 2020; McLeskey et al., 2017; Scruggs & Mastropieri, 2017).

Both Education Specialist (ES) and APE teachers need to be able to specially design instruction appropriately for students with disabilities through providing proper adaptations. Appropriate adaptations are designed and implemented successfully across settings when IEP teams collaborate and work as an interdisciplinary team (Dillon, et al., 2021). Most IEP teams work collaboratively to share reports on assessments and IEP goal development (Sisti & Robledo, 2021). However, in order to adapt academic content, methodology or delivery of instruction to meet the needs of students with disabilities, a more in-depth interdisciplinary approach needs to be utilized, one where professionals share decision making and practice (Anderson, 2013).

This chapter will address how institutes of higher education (IHEs) can develop and build into existing programs an interdisciplinary approach to pre-service preparation to instill a collaboration mindset early on within the education program of future educators and service providers. This interdisciplinary approach between professionals within education is also supported by many professional standards such as the Adapted Physical Education National Standards (Kelly, 2019), American Speech Language Hearing Association (2020), Council for Exceptional Children (2020), and the Society of Health and Physical Educators (SHAPE) America, (2017).

## BACKGROUND

The interdisciplinary work between the two programs was supported by a U.S. Department of Education, Office of Special Education Programs Personnel Development grant. The focus of these personnel development grants is to help meet "state-identified needs for adequate numbers of fully certified personnel to service children with disabilities by supporting competitive awards to provide research-based training and professional development to prepare special education, related services, early intervention, and regular education personnel to work with children with disabilities" (Office of Special Education

Programs, n.d.). The authors targeted the development of interdisciplinary work between the ES and APE teacher preparation programs. These programs are situated within a large, culturally and linguistically diverse, urban service area in Southern California and the university is designated federally as a Hispanic-Serving Institution. It is crucial that candidates within the two programs are equipped with high-leverage and culturally responsive practices as most will be serving the richly diverse surrounding communities once they are teachers within the field.

## Conceptual Framework

The conceptual framework involved a continuous improvement cycle (CIC) during strategic planning framed by three core, essential questions as outlined by Shakman et al. (2017). Applying this framework was central to the program redesign to improve both the Education Specialist and APE programs with lasting interdisciplinary service delivery preparation for all candidates, not just candidates served by the OSEP grant. The three guiding questions were: a) What problem are we trying to solve? (b) What changes might we introduce and why?, and (c) How will we know that a change is actually an improvement? (Shakman et al., 2017). A conceptual model is summarized in the figure below.

The authors began the CIC process by consulting key CEEDAR Center Innovation Configurations (IC) in key domains aligned to grant deliverables. The CEEDAR Center, a federally funded Technical Assistance and Dissemination (TA&D) Center, had developed numerous ICs to promote evidence-based practices in teacher preparation. The ICs are an extremely useful tool to use to evaluate teacher preparation programs and to guide professional development. The intention of ICs is to improve teacher education with the ultimate goal of improving student improvement (CEEDAR, n.d.).

The ICs selected were *Evidence-based Practices for Students with Severe Disabilities* (Browder, et al., 2014), *Literacy Instruction for Students with Multiple and Severe Disabilities* (Orlando & Ruppar, 2016), and *Universal Design for Learning* (Israel, Ribuffo, & Smith, 2014). To answer the question 'What changes might we introduce and why?', the authors engaged in several phases of program design and alignment to the Council for Exceptional Children (CEC) high leverage practices (HLPs). The HLPs are organized around four areas of practice: 1) collaboration; 2) assessment; 3) social/emotional/behavioral; and 4) instruction. Table 1 details the HLPs within each area of practice.

Finally, to answer the question 'How will we know that a change is actually an improvement?', the authors created two capstone measures: a) an intervention symposium survey that included a peer evaluation of presentation skills and b) a digital portfolio.

## PROGRAM REDESIGN METHODS

**What problems are we trying to solve?** To begin, a matrix was created that included the approved grant competencies that the authors intended to integrate into the ES and APE programs. The project competencies were developed for the grant proposal using the CEEDAR Center ICs. The identified competencies were: a) focused instruction, b) intense, individualized interventions with interdisciplinary approaches, c) improved student outcomes, d) inclusion support, and e) teacher performance expectations for education specialists and adapted physical education teachers as defined by the state accreditation body. Figure 2 below demonstrates the format of the matrix.

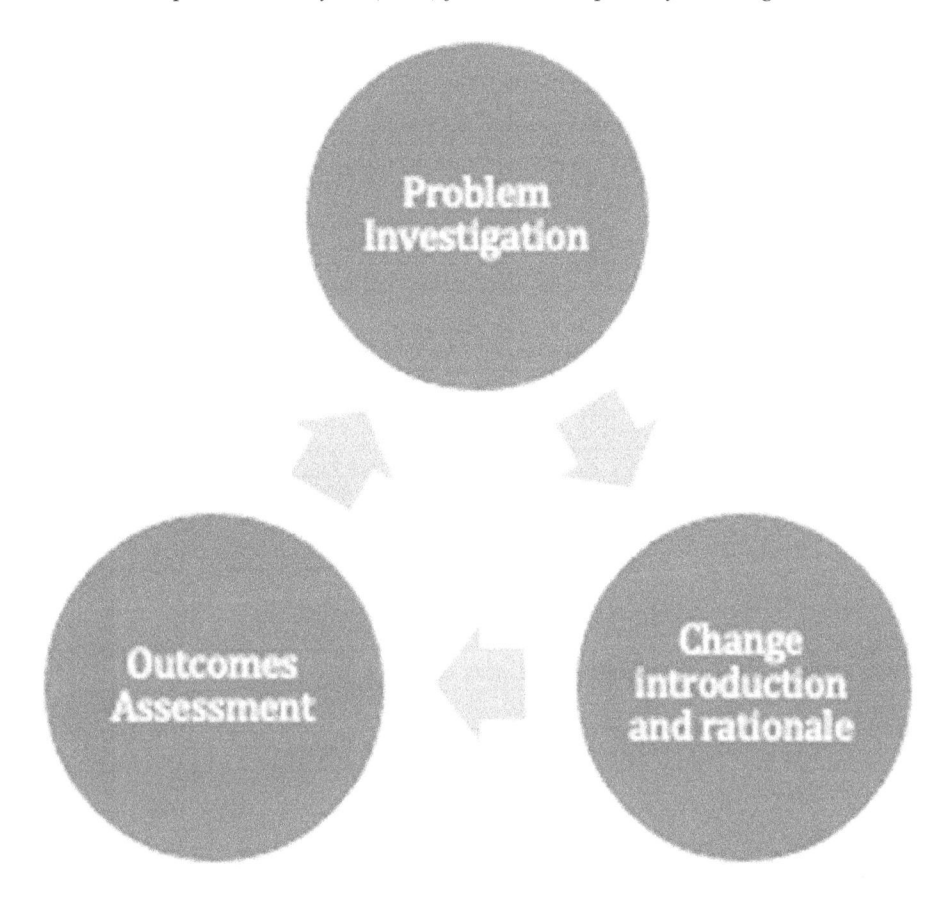

*Figure 1. Continuous Improvement Cycle (CIC) for Interdisciplinary Redesign*

## Program Competencies

**What changes might we introduce and why?** Following the IC-focused matrix, the established project competencies were then cross referenced with the following:

1. Aligned California Teacher Performance Expectations (TPEs) (2016)
2. CEEDAR Center Innovation Configuration *Evidence-based Practices for Students with Severe Disabilities*
3. Council for Exceptional Children (CEC) High-Leverage Practices
4. California Adapted Physical Education Added Authorization Standards

Early cross-referencing was completed using current program courses. Courses where the competencies could be primarily aligned were listed from both the APE and ES programs. From this list, assignments to evaluate candidate proficiency of each competency based on evidence-based practices were included. After discussion, additional courses were included where competencies could be incorporated, as well as potential assignments that could assess scholar proficiency. Curriculum planning efforts

*Table 1. Council for Exceptional Children High-Leverage Practices*

| |
|---|
| Collaboration |
| HLP 1: Collaborate with Professionals to Increase Student Success |
| HLP 2: Organize and Facilitate Effective Meetings with Professionals and Families |
| HLP 3: Collaborate with Families to Support Student Learning and Secure Needed Services |
| Assessment |
| HLP 4: Use Multiple Sources of Information to Develop a Comprehensive Understanding of a Student's Strengths and Needs |
| HLP 5: Interpret and Communicate Assessment Information with Stakeholders to Collaboratively Design and Implement Educational Programs |
| HLP 6: Use Student Assessment Data, Analyze Instructional Practices, and Make Necessary Adjustments that Improve Student Outcomes |
| Social/Emotional/Behavioral |
| HLP 7: Establish a Consistent, Organized, and Respectful Learning Environment |
| HLP 8: Provide Positive and Constructive Feedback to Guide Students' Learning and Behavior |
| HLP 9: Teach Social Behaviors |
| HLP 10: Conduct Functional Behavioral Assessments to Develop Individual Student Behavior Support Plans |
| Instruction |
| HLP 11: Identify and Prioritize Long- and Short-Term Learning Goals |
| HLP 12: Systematically Design Instruction Toward a Specific Learning Goal |
| HLP 13: Adapt Curriculum Tasks and Materials for Specific Learning Goals |
| HLP 14: Teach Cognitive and Metacognitive Strategies to Support Learning and Independence |
| HLP 15: Provide Scaffolded Supports |
| HLP 16: Use Explicit Instruction |
| HLP 17: Use Flexible Grouping |
| HLP 18: Use Strategies to Promote Active Student Engagement |
| HLP 19: Use Assistive and Instructional Technologies |
| HLP 20: Provide Intensive Instruction |
| HLP 21: Teach Students to Maintain and Generalize New Learning Across Time and Settings |
| HLP 22: Provide Positive and Constructive Feedback to Guide Students' Learning and Behavior |

*Note.* https://highleveragepractices.org/.

included integrating CEC HLPs, instruction in evidence-based practices, and information from federal TA&D resources were examined and implemented throughout courses (https://osepideasthatwork.org/find-center-or-grant).

## COURSE REDESIGN METHODS

### Course Audits

After all alignment tasks were completed, project faculty conducted course audits to assess courses for evidence-based, inclusive, and collaborative practices. This was completed using the CEEDAR Center

*Figure 2. Project Competency Matrix*

Project SEEDS Education Specialist Competencies
Exceptional Support Needs (ESN--Mild/Mod) Extensive Support Needs (EXN-Mod/Sev)

| Project SEEDS: Education Specialist Competencies | Aligned California TPEs | CEEDAR Center Innovation Configuration (IC) for Teacher Prep | CEC High Leverage Practices | Aligned California APE Added Authorization Standards | APE (Possible courses in ( ) | EDSP (Possible courses in ( ) | Assignment |
|---|---|---|---|---|---|---|---|
| **1. Focused Instruction: #1.** Scholars will identify & implement evidence-based practices for teaching both academic and function skills including: a) most to least prompting; b) backward chaining; c) mnemonics; d) constant time delay; e) use of visual displays. #2. Scholars will integrate technology to teach academic skills to learners with high-intensity needs. #3. Scholars will incorporate the Universal Design for Learning (UDL) framework into lessons/instructional units & deliver systematic instruction both in specialized and inclusive settings. | TPE 1, TPE3, TPE 4, TPE 6, TPE 7, TPE 8, TPE 9 | Universal Design for Learning; Supporting content learning with technology for students with disabilities; Evidence Based Practices for Students with Severe Disabilities | Instruction (HLP11-22) | APE AA 6, APE AA 13 | 4340: APE Program Development and Implementation (UDL principles, technology instruction and assessment) 4050S/4050AS: Adapted Physical Education Fieldwork; Lesson Plan (UDL differentiation lessons; technology for lesson implementation, PM, tracking data) (IRIS Modules) | 5334: Intensive intervention with struggling student; MS assistive technology and intervention planning in-class assignment 5340: Differentiation (#3 Unit map with UDL Principles) 5302: Ed. Students with Dis (#3 UDL Comp. Observation report) | (5334: possible UDL reading lesson planning for inclusive settings; AT piece included) 5334: EBP reading strategies, progress monitoring; technology integration Key Assessments and Fieldwork Experiences in: EDU 5302 EDU 5332 EDU 5342 EDU 532: EDU 5334 EDU 5336 EDU 5320 EDU 5340 |

IC *Evidence-Based Practices for Students with Moderate/Severe Disabilities* Rubric. This rubric, located in the Appendix of the IC, included 16 *Essential Elements of Instruction* that were discussed within the IC (Table 2).

An audit was conducted on 20 courses between the APE and ES programs. Each syllabus was assessed for the above *Essential Elements of Instruction* and their level of implementation. Each element was separated into *how to teach, what to teach,* and *how to support* elements. Within each element, the authors self-scored each syllabus based on an implementation score of 0 (no evidence); 1 (one piece of evidence); 2 (two pieces of evidence); or 3 (several pieces of evidence).

A goal was established for each essential element to have at least one course in Level 2 and one course in Level 3 from each program. The rubrics were analyzed to establish an arc of learning throughout a candidate's time in the program, with earlier courses scoring in the Level 1 area and more advanced courses falling in Level 2 or Level 3 categories as candidates' skills become more advanced prior to clinical practice (student teaching). It was decided that for any essential elements that scored at an Implementation Level of 0, a focus would be placed on revising coursework to integrate the lacking essential component throughout coursework. It was found that all essential components were covered in coursework in both programs, so no course revisions were necessary.

*Table 2. CEEDAR Essential Elements of Instruction*

| How to Teach |
|---|
| Systematic Instruction |
| Self-Directed Instruction |
| Peer-Tutors |
| Technology |
| What to Teach |
| Academics |
| Daily Living |
| Job and Community |
| Self-Determination |
| Communication and Social Skills |
| How to Support |
| Team Planning |
| Assistive Technology |
| Peer Supports |
| Paraprofessionals |
| Inclusive Setting |
| Positive Behavior Support |
| Home-School Collaboration |

*Note.* https://ceedar.education.ufl.edu/wp-content/uploads/2014/09/IC-3_FINAL_03-03-15.pdf

## Integrated Assignments

In this stage of development, faculty worked together to redesign program syllabi and develop interdisciplinary assignments, field experiences, and seminars between the ES and APE programs and where shared learning between program faculty occurred. Six courses were redesigned to include interdisciplinary assignments. A summary of the course redesign work is presented in Table 3 below.

The first redesigned assignment for the ES law course and an APE fieldwork course was a mock IEP meeting. Collaboration opportunities emerged as APE candidates participated as service providers and motor skills experts and ES candidates led the meetings as case managers and academic/behavioral/social skills experts. A second integrated assignment involved the ES and APE program's assessment methods course where candidates were given the option to assess a student in the APE program's motor development clinic. APE students conducted assessment within this field work experience with the on-campus clinic. After performing the standardized assessment with a clinic participant, the candidates also interviewed family members to gain a holistic summary of the K-22 focus student's strengths, interests, preferences, and needs. Finally, a third interdisciplinary collaboration was integrated into three methods courses: the APE program's student with disabilities fieldwork course, the ES program's transition and collaboration course, and the ES program's assessment methods course. Intentional collaboration opportunities were cultivated between APE and ES candidates through the designing of interdisciplinary service delivery for transition-aged youth. Candidates engaged in the person-centered transition planning

*Table 3. Interdisciplinary Assignments and Service Delivery Competencies*

| Interdisciplinary Assignments | Course | Program | Interdisciplinary Service Delivery Focus |
|---|---|---|---|
| Mock IEP | Law Class | ES | Collaborative case management & decision-making for academics, behavior & motor skills experts |
| | APE Fieldwork Course | APE | |
| Assessment Case Study | Assessment Course<br>Assessment Course | ES<br>APE | Expertise with standardized assessment administration and interpretation; parent/family input |
| Person-centered transition plan | Transition & Collaboration Course | ES | Person-Centered transition planning; Strengths-based goals for academic, behavioral, and physical education domains |
| | Assessment Course | ES | |
| | APE Fieldwork Course | APE | |

process (National Parent Center on Transition and Employment, 2022) with a K-22 student focus student who received services from the APE program's motor skills clinic. Candidates worked to develop a transition plan for a student who would be transitioning from preschool to elementary school; elementary school to middle school; middle school to high school; or postsecondary transition. Candidates in the transition course took the lead as case managers and organized the assessments and reporting. Candidates in the assessment course practiced student-centered transition assessments and interviews with parents and student(s). Candidates from the APE course completed assessments in motor skills and discussed student goals and objectives, including transition into community and adulthood regarding their motor skills, fitness, and health aspects.

## Integrated Symposium

The two programs also developed an Intervention Symposium, which is now held each Spring semester and involves three methods courses: a) literacy intervention, b) math intervention, and c) APE motor skills intervention. Through the symposium, candidates come together to engage in a scholarly poster presentation where each candidate presents fieldwork interventions that they developed over the semester in their respective courses. The scientific posters candidates developed were based on an action research cycle of intervention assessment, intervention lessons, and progress monitoring of a K-12 student with a need in the area of literacy, math, or motor skills. The overarching goals of the symposium are to: a) have candidates practice intervention cycles, data collection, and progress monitoring, b) learn from one another in an interdisciplinary setting, and c) be confident in leading data discussions with others based on interventions.

## Adapted PE

For the APE motor skills intervention, candidates utilized an on-campus, community-based, experiential clinic to learn about a participant with disabilities through interviewing the parents or guardians and then performing movement assessments. Based on the results of the assessment tests, candidates then selected four specific movement areas (e.g., locomotor skill, object control/ball skill, fitness skill, balance skill etc.) in which the participants with disabilities were behind their peers in performing. Once these four skills were selected and approved by the course instructor and with insight and collaboration from the participant's family, the candidate then began to develop interventions to address the areas of need within the movement skill in order to increase performance and skill element attainment.

The interventions were implemented twice a week for one hour throughout eight weeks. During this time, the APE candidate assessed their participants on their lesson objectives related to each of the four skills in order to progress monitor their skill performance and to examine if the interventions were working to address the participant's needs and areas that needed to be improved on to increase proper performance of the skill. The interventions implemented were individualized based on the participants' needs and their skill levels. Interventions implemented ranged from: backward chaining, task analysis, step by step teaching of skill components, use of motivational equipment, visuals and video prompting, positive behavior supports, prompting and cueing, modeling, and activity modifications.

At the end of the eight weeks, the APE candidates prepared research posters which provided information about their participant, interventions used, and then data related to pre- and post-testing and also progress monitoring of the participant's skill development across the eight weeks (Figure 3). Candidates provided an oral presentation at the symposium and reflected on their experience to their peers.

## Literacy and Math

For both the literacy intervention and math intervention course candidates worked 1:1 with a student who was struggling either in any area of reading or in specific mathematics domains. Most candidates selected a K-22 student who received special education support during the school day, though a student at-risk was also acceptable. Candidates first assessed the current reading and/or math skills of the target student and reviewed any earlier assessments they may have access to. With scaffolded support from the course instructor in the reading course, they analyzed these assessments to determine the students' strengths and areas of need in reading. Similarly, with the mathematics course, candidates identified a targeted math domain to address with an aligned, evidence-based intervention.

From the assessment information, the ES candidates developed an individualized intervention plan for their target student and implemented it over the course of six weeks, using progress monitoring to gauge student progress and make adjustments as needed. Near the end of the term, they reviewed all their collected data to determine the overall effectiveness of their intervention and completed an extensive reflection on the experience. From this information, the candidates developed and presented their findings on a scientific poster at the symposium (Figures 4 and 5). Candidates enrolled in both courses during the same semester were given the option to prepare a combined literacy and mathematics intervention poster on the same focus student.

Unique to the symposium experience, peer evaluations are included using Likert scales and short responses (Table 3). Students rotate through presentations and complete peer evaluations through a QR code form posted throughout the presentation room. The added level of accountability of peer evaluations completed real-time during poster presentations provided candidates with anonymous, authentic feedback on their presentation skills.

In addition, all candidates completed an exit ticket on a Google form to provide program instructors with anonymous, authentic feedback on the entire experience in support of the continuous improvement cycle and perceived mastery of select evidence-based practices (Table 4). Adjustments to the symposium are undertaken each year to address candidate feedback.

*Interdisciplinary Special Education and APE Teacher Preparation Using Evidence*

*Figure 3. Intervention Symposium Motor Skills Poster Sample*

Instructors completed comprehensive evaluations of the intervention case studies using an Anchor Assignment rubric. The final grade was based on several rubric elements of the intervention and symposium including poster content, supplemental evidence such as progress monitoring data and interest inventories, literature discussions, goal setting, and an average peer evaluation score.

*Figure 4. Intervention Symposium Literacy Poster Sample*

*Figure 5. Intervention Symposium Math Poster Sample*

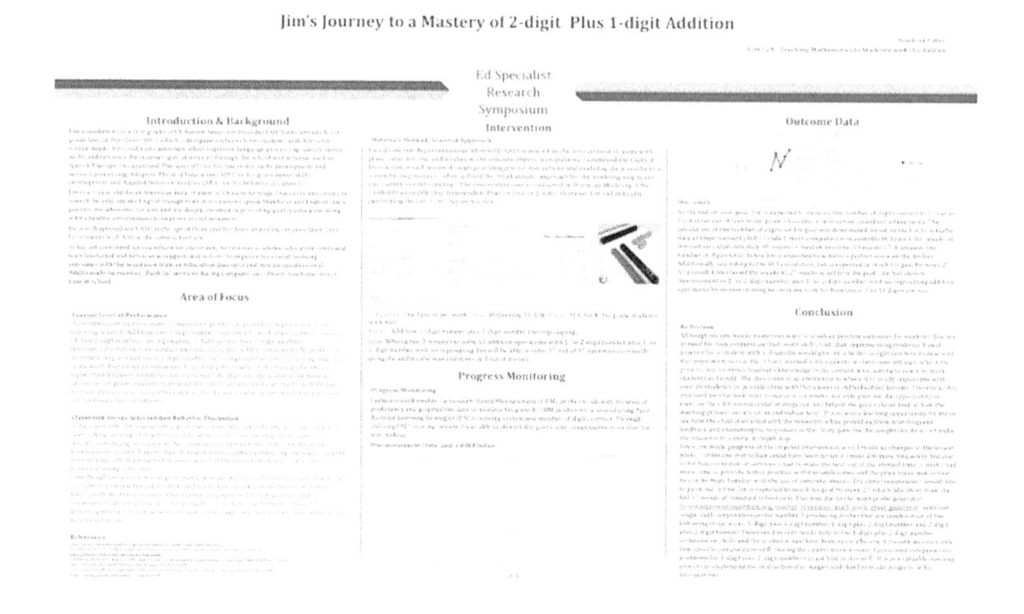

*Table 3. Intervention Symposium Peer Evaluation Questions*

| |
|---|
| 1) Presenter engaged effectively with participants. <br> 2) Presenter demonstrated knowledge of subject matter/course content and case study findings. |
| 3) Presenter was effective in answering questions. |
| 4) Presenter managed time allotted for the presentation effectively. |
| 5) Presenter was dressed professionally. <br> 6) Any comments about the presenter? |

## INTERDISCIPLINARY EXPERIENCES

Educational support of students with disabilities is multidimensional and is best constructed by applying multiple perspectives through various pedagogical approaches and ways of thinking (Astleitner, 2018; Shogren, Luckasson, & Schalock, 2020). Advances in critical thought processes for teacher candidates can occur through the use of interdisciplinary instruction and can be applied within the education field (Repko, 2011). This integration and synthesis of different perspectives (Ashby & Exter, 2019) is why planned interdisciplinary experiences were part of the program implementation of the ES and APE teacher candidates.

## Mentoring and Support

Project faculty placed an emphasis on innovative ways to mentor candidates with a focus on equity and access for all candidates. Candidates received targeted mentoring and support throughout their time in the ES and APE programs. All project faculty integrate culturally and linguistically responsive mentoring into their respective programs to ensure engagement of all candidates. This included identifying with candidates and honoring candidate assets, lived experiences, and backgrounds while working with them

*Table 4. Intervention Symposium Evaluation Questions*

| |
|---|
| 1) This assignment was effective in helping me understand and apply course content. |
| 2) This assignment was effective in preparing me how to use multiple sources of information to develop comprehensive understanding of a student's strengths and needs (HLP4). |
| 3) This assignment was effective in preparing me to communicate assessment information with stakeholders (i.e., IEP Team members, parents, colleagues, administrators) to collaboratively design and implement educational programs (HLP5). |
| 4) This assignment was effective in preparing me to use assessment data, analyze instructional practices, and make necessary adjustments that improve student outcomes (HLP6). |
| 5) This assignment was effective in preparing me how to identify and prioritize long- and short-term learning goals (HLP11). |
| 6) This assignment was effective in preparing me how to systematically design instruction toward a specific learning goal (HLP12). |
| 7) This assignment was effective in preparing me how to adapt curriculum tasks and materials for specific learning goals (HLP13). |
| 8) This assignment was effective in preparing me how to provide intensive instruction (HLP20). |
| 9) What were the strengths of this assignment? What was your biggest take-away? |
| 10) What were the weaknesses of this assignment? What could be improved for future students? |
| 11) Is there anything else you would like us to know? |

to ensure their success (González et al., 2005; Rios-Aguilar & Kiyama, 2018). Careful attention was also given to best practices for teaching adult learners (Bransford, Brown, & Cocking, 2000).

Mentoring occurred both formally and informally during candidates' time in the program. Formal mentoring, through advising sessions and collaboration meetings occurred on a regular basis to ensure that candidates were on track to complete their respective programs, typically occurring once or twice a semester. Individual program plans were created for each candidate with their assigned faculty advisor. An action plan was also created for any candidate that needed additional academic support. Through this process, candidates and faculty formed professional relationships that were beneficial to the mentoring process.

Informal mentoring occurred in large and small interdisciplinary groups or individually and was often focused on individual candidate situations. This type of mentoring was more organic and developed from the strong professional relationships that were formed during the formal mentoring sessions. Informal mentoring occurred in many different spaces including during office hours, before and after courses, during collaboration meetings, or during professional development workshop breaks. Informal mentoring topics ranged from how to approach an assignment for a course to how to approach an issue with a paraprofessional out in the field.

Ad hoc mentoring also occurred during the project such as when "just in time" support was given to an internship teacher struggling in an unsupportive placement. (An intern teacher is a teacher hired on a temporary, intern credential who is attending courses while they are teaching full-time). The project was able to support the candidate by funding an exemplary graduate of the ES program to assist her in setting up her classroom efficiently and establishing a daily routine. In another instance, candidates asked for additional support with writing weekly lesson plans for students with intensive support needs. To further address this need, faculty planned and implemented a lesson planning workshop highlighting the work of an in-service exemplary teacher to all the teacher candidates. During COVID school closures, mentoring occurred remotely and was more informal at the request of candidates. Candidates would most often want to meet and just talk through what was happening at their school sites, the university, and the greater community. During this time, we were able to partner with the campus Mind Heart Research Lab, where research takes place on total health and wellness, and hold a group remote meditation for stress-relief.

## Collaboration Meetings

Having two preservice preparation programs run side by side with each other does not truly promote interdisciplinary learning and experiences. Therefore, it was imperative to plan opportunities for the ES and APE teacher candidates to meet and collaborate together on various topics to examine their perspectives and learn from others' thoughts and feelings. At one of the first collaboration meetings, as a team building exercise, candidates stood in a circle and played "Ask Me a Question". APE candidates could ask any special education question they had and vice versa. Many had never interacted with their service provider counterparts prior to the interdisciplinary project and they learned a great deal about the joys and challenges of one another's professions and experiences they have each had. Furthermore, discussion would follow on ways to address the challenges shared by the APE and ES candidates and positive problem solving began early on within their program which will hopefully continue within their teacher career. This activity was routinely identified as one of the most valuable by the candidates.

*Table 5. Semester Collaborative Meeting Topic Schedule*

| Fall Year 2 | Competency #1 | Focused Instruction |
|---|---|---|
| Spring Year 2 | Competency #2 | Intense, Individualized Interventions with Interdisciplinary-based Approaches |
| Fall Year 3 | Competency #2 | Technology Supports including AAC |
| Spring Year 3 | Competency #4 | Inclusion Support |
| Fall Year 4 | Competency #1 | Focused Instruction |
| Spring Year 4 | Competency #2 | Intense, Individualized Interventions with Interdisciplinary-based Approaches |
| Fall Year 5 | Competency #3 | Improved Outcomes: IEP goal and objective writing; progress monitoring |
| Spring Year 5 | Competency #4 | Inclusion Support |

Note. Year 1 was a planning year for grant activities so no collaborative meetings were held.

Shared topics were selected each semester within the programs based on project competencies. Many times, the topics were based on issues within the field of education where no single answer could be presented to solve the problem nor would any specific textbook be able to cover the topic. These topics were discussed at the collaborative meeting sessions with different perspectives from the ES and APE candidates. The ES and APE candidates shared their experiences, content within their perspective field, and then reflected on interdisciplinary learning.

Table 5 below details topics that were used as the starting point for the collaborative meetings. IEP goal and objective writing was one area since many districts and IEP programs require different specifics to be provided. This topic then expanded into the best ways and how to progress monitor students with disabilities on IEP goals and show progress or data to the parents and IEP team. Another discussion topic was augmentative and alternative communication (AAC) devices used by students with disabilities. To expand on communication, another collaborative meeting discussion was based on behavior supports and positive behavior interventions for students within special education, including APE services.

Some collaborative meetings started off with the candidates reading an article or case study and then reflecting on their perspectives based on the information provided in small heterogeneous groups. Video clips or movies were also shown to get the candidates thinking and reflecting to share their thoughts and emotional reactions to what they watched. This opportunity then allowed for an open, honest dialogue to naturally occur between the different disciplines. This led the candidates to reflectively integrate and synthesize different perspectives which allowed an increase in their understanding and incorporated various ideas and actions steps to approach issues and problems.

Through these collaborative meetings, candidates developed an appreciation of differences but also similarities between disciplines which aided in problem solving and further expanded their structural knowledge at a more personal level. The collaborative meetings provided opportunities for significant learning (Fink, 2003) through meaningful and lasting social interaction experiences. These experiences expanded learning, caring, and the application of foundational knowledge that the candidates had obtained through course work. Candidates have reported increased awareness of their interdisciplinary colleagues when out at school sites. It has made collaborative work with other service providers a priority for them as they see the value in interdisciplinary teaming for the benefit of their K-22 students.

## Technology Analysis

As technology is integrated within education settings for both teacher and student use more fully, it is imperative that preservice teachers receive instruction and experience using technology that can benefit learning outcomes and provide accessibility for students with disabilities. Within special education, technology can be used to support student learning or it can be used by the student to increase their expression of ideas (Alharbi, 2018). Research has supported the beneficial uses of technology for students with disabilities; however, teachers are often not fully prepared to incorporate technology within their classrooms (Zilz & Pang, 2021). One of the goals of the project was to develop teachers that were fully confident with using both educational technology and assistive technology, including visuals and communication devices to ensure accessibility for their students.

During the course of the project, iPads were furnished to each candidate to become comfortable with educational technology and explore options for assistive technology and AAC. During collaboration meetings, candidates were tasked with exploring technology that they would find useful and demonstrating the possible uses of the technology tool to the larger group. Apps and online platforms included visuals for learning and communication, communication tools for non-verbal students, assistive technology tools (low and high tech) for a wide range of students, and health and fitness tools. Interdisciplinary discussions would then take place as a whole group as to how apps could be used to better integrate special education and APE services for students. For instance, visual communication and behavior support apps could be used by both direct service providers and special education teachers to communicate between the two different settings to provide more consistency for behavior and communication supports. Other technology was discussed that could integrate APE and special education services into collaborative service models, such as task cards that were collaboratively created or using GoNoodle in the classroom for student work breaks while also working on APE goals.

## Professional Development

An important goal of the project was to support candidates along a path to becoming teacher-leaders. During their time in the ES and APE programs, professional development opportunities were created for candidates to write proposals and present at national conferences. Candidates had the option to present with faculty on project competencies or create their own proposals. Three cohorts of students presented sessions with project faculty on their experiences in the program and their perceptions of how interdisciplinary and collaboration impacted their teaching practice as in-service teachers. In addition, two candidates also presented at a national conference on the importance of interdisciplinary knowledge when advocating for students across settings. They spoke from their own lived experiences as neurodiverse students and developed a transition toolkit for teachers to use when working with students that they shared with session participants.

*Table 6. HLP Area Survey Results – Prepared and Very Prepared*

| HLP Area | Pre-survey | Post-Survey |
|---|---|---|
| Collaboration | 75% | 91% |
| Assessment | 30% | 91% |
| Social/Emotional/Behavioral | 39% | 84% |
| Instruction | 54% | 86% |

## SOLUTIONS AND RECOMMENDATIONS

### Measuring Impact

**How will we know that a change is actually an improvement?** To analyze the impact that the CIC changes had on the teacher preparation programs, candidate pre- and post-program surveys, as well as focus groups, were conducted by an external evaluator. The external evaluator surveyed candidates during their first and last semesters in the credential program. Candidates would also be invited to participate in a focus group during their last semester in their program. The culminating experience in each program was the creation of an e-portfolio by each candidate which was also used as an evaluation measure to examine the candidate and program improvements.

### Pre and Post Program Survey

Using the HLPs as a framework for survey questions, pre- and post-surveys were emailed to candidates enrolled in the ES credential and APE programs. The survey measured candidates' perceived level of preparedness in the four areas of practice: Collaboration, Social/Emotional/Behavioral, Instruction, and Assessment. The pre-survey was emailed each semester by the external evaluator. Ninety-five candidates received the pre-survey with 37 candidates participating, which is a response rate of 42%. The post-survey had a lower response rate of ~16% with a total of 7 of 45 candidates participating. The surveys were identical and consisted of 21 questions, three related to consent and demographics and 17 questions asked candidates to identify "the degree to which they feel prepared…" using a Likert scale. The Likert scale ranged from very prepared, prepared, somewhat prepared, and not prepared. A matrix format was used to ask the overall preparedness for several different skills associated with the HLP areas of practice. The final question on the survey asked participants to identify their experience working with students with disabilities before starting the credential program.

Post-surveys revealed an increase in the perceived level of preparedness for all HLP areas of practice. The largest increases were in the areas of Assessment and Social/Emotional/Behavioral (Table 6). The matrix format of the questions gave further information on what skills participants felt the most prepared for each HLP area.

### Collaboration

Four matrix questions asked participants to rate themselves on collaboration including the following skills: the ability to effectively communicate, facilitate meetings, work in a team, and collaborate with

*Table 7. Assessment Survey Results – Prepared and Very Prepared*

| Assessment | Pre-survey | Post-Survey |
|---|---|---|
| Collect data | 30% | 91% |
| Assess students | 50% | 83% |
| Use Assessments to Make Decisions | 50% | 80% |
| Interpret data | 39% | 71% |
| Use data to improve student outcomes | 42% | 91% |

others. In the pre-survey, 73% of the participants felt prepared or very prepared to collaborate with teachers, paraprofessionals, and related service personnel. While only 55% felt prepared or very prepared to collaborate with parents. The post-survey showed an increase of preparedness in the areas of teachers, related personnel, and parents, at 85%. Preparedness working with paraprofessionals was the only area that did not show an increase, which provided valuable programmatic feedback.

## Assessment

Assessment is the HLP area of practice that showed the greatest overall improvement from the pre- to post-surveys. Participants were asked to rate the degree to which they were prepared to use assessment in five categories: to collect data, assess students and use the assessments to make decisions, interpret data, and use data to improve student outcomes. The areas of collecting data and using data to improve student outcomes had the largest increases. Ninety-one percent of participants rated themselves prepared or very prepared on the post-survey in these two skills.

## Social/Emotional/Behavioral

Four matrix questions on the survey aligned with the social/emotional/behavioral HLPs. All skills addressed in the survey showed an increase in preparedness on the post-survey (Table 8). Several questions asked participants to rate themselves on implementing strategies for social and communication skills including implementing social narratives, peer tutoring, and teaching social and communication skills. Implementing social narratives had the largest increase with 100% of participants rating themselves prepared or very prepared on the post-survey.

Emotional skills addressed in the survey included increasing student learning by establishing a consistent, organized, and respectful learning environment. Sixty percent of participants rated themselves prepared or very prepared in the pre-survey this increased to 86% on the post-survey.

Eight different evidence-based practices in the behavioral domain were covered in a matrix question including: non-aversive techniques; differential reinforcement of alternative behaviors; functional communication training; antecedent strategies; implementing positive behavior support systems; conducting functional behavior assessment; developing an individual student support plan; and providing positive and constructive feedback. The two skills that had the largest increase, from 27% on the pre-survey to 86% on the post-survey, were conducting a functional behavior assessment and developing an individual student support plan.

*Table 8. Social/Emotional/Behavioral Survey Results – Prepared and Very Prepared*

| Social | Pre-survey | Post-Survey |
|---|---|---|
| Social Narratives | 32% | 100% |
| Peer tutoring | 32% | 87% |
| Social and Communication Skills | 41% | 71% |
| **Emotional** | **Pre-survey** | **Post-Survey** |
| Increase Student Learning | 60% | 86% |
| **Behavioral** | **Pre-survey** | **Post-Survey** |
| Non-aversive Techniques | 36% | 86% |
| Differential Reinforcement - alternative behaviors | 33% | 86% |
| Functional Communication Training | 33% | 86% |
| Antecedent Strategies | 33% | 86% |
| Implementing PBIS | 58% | 86% |
| Conducting an FBA | 27% | 86% |
| Developing an Individual Student Support Plan | 27% | 86% |
| Providing Feedback | 64% | 86% |

## Instruction

Participants were asked to rate themselves on the extent to which they feel prepared to systematically design instruction and use instructional strategies and adaptations. Participants were also asked to rate the degree to which they feel prepared to increase student learning using several strategies including providing intensive instruction; promoting active student engagement; using flexible grouping; using explicit instruction; providing scaffolded support; as well as teaching cognitive and metacognitive strategies. All skills in this area of practice increased on the post-survey and three areas showed 100% of participants reported feeling prepared or very prepared (Table 9).

*Table 9. Instructional Survey Results – Prepared and Very Prepared*

| Instruction | Pre-survey | Post-Survey |
|---|---|---|
| Systematically Design Instruction | 12% | 100% |
| Use Instructional Strategies | 70% | 86% |
| Use Assistive and Instructional Technology | 40% | 86% |
| Providing Intensive Instruction | 49% | 86% |
| Promoting Active Student Engagement | 69% | 100% |
| Use Flexible Grouping | 57% | 86% |
| Use Explicit Instruction | 57% | 100% |
| Provide Scaffolded Support | 57% | 86% |
| Teach Cognitive and Metacognitive Strategies | 42% | 86% |

*Table 10. Focus group Questions and Themes*

| Focus group Question | Theme 1 | Theme 2 | Theme 3 |
|---|---|---|---|
| Features of the Program | Relationships with advisors | Relationships with peers (sense of community) | Conferences and Professional Development |
| Assistive and Instructional Technology | Google | Zoom | Apps |
| Interdisciplinary coursework | Collaboration | Understanding | Student support |

## Focus Groups

Focus groups were held with completers each semester. Participants were asked three questions: 1) What features of the program were most effective to you as a scholar? 2) What technology and distance learning techniques or strategies were most effective for you as a candidate? and 3) How did the interdisciplinary coursework change your outlook on professional collaboration? The focus groups were recorded on zoom and then transcribed for analysis. A content analysis was completed and themes emerged from each question (Table 10).

The features of the program that participants identified as most effective were relationships with advisors, relationships with peers, and finally, the opportunities to attend conferences and professional developments. Participants identified mentoring and support from their advisors as the number one feature that helped them be successful in the program. When discussing relationships with advisors, participants noted that they were asked how things were going with the program and if something wasn't working out, the advisors worked to correct the problem. For instance, participants identified a time they wanted to learn more information on behavior management and the program advisors invited a teacher to come and give a presentation on the subject in one of their advising meetings.

Participants identified the technology and distance learning strategies that were most effective for them including Google, Zoom, and iPad apps. Participants in the focus groups discussed that they used technologies in the program that they would use on the job, such as Google and Zoom. They also found benefit in the many apps that they were introduced to in the program. Participants stated that many of the apps they could immediately use in their classrooms or with their students with disabilities when hired in a teaching position.

When asked how the interdisciplinary coursework changed their outlook on professional collaboration, participants said the opportunity for collaboration with peers was important and helpful in informing their outlook on professional collaboration. Participants discussed the collaborative effort among interdisciplinary peers helped them understand each professionals' role and how to better communicate with others on the IEP team. The focus group participants concluded that the interdisciplinary coursework helped them improve their collaboration skills to also better support student needs.

## Culminating Experience: E-portfolio

The last phase of design work culminated with the implementation of an e-portfolio to assess candidate competencies with interdisciplinary elements and state Teacher Performance Expectation (TPE) elements. A digital platform available to all university students (i.e., Portfolium) was selected for this purpose as it continued to be available to candidates after graduation and it allowed candidates to embed links to their

*Table 11. E-portfolio Rubric Scale*

| Score | Standard Competency | Descriptors |
| --- | --- | --- |
| 3 | Met standard with distinction | Extensive indicators of candidate's TPE knowledge and application |
| 2 | Met standard satisfactorily | At least 3 indicators of candidate's TPE knowledge and application |
| 1- 0 | Standard not met or not satisfactory | Few to no indicators of candidate's TPE knowledge and application; revised examples needed by the reviewer |

digital portfolios in their resumes and social media accounts such as LinkedIn. The authors designed the interdisciplinary evaluation rubric using TPE standards and input from an advisory board, who highly recommended the utility of a digital portfolio for a seamless transition into the district-provided induction programs.

Similar to e-portfolio assessment designs for pre-service special and inclusive education (Lambe et al., 2013), candidates were required to select and present evidence of their learning of key interdisciplinary and TPE competencies acquired through the program. The TPE domains were assigned as required e-portfolio headers so that the e-portfolio could be used across the program with all candidates, not just project candidates. Narratives of artifacts presented detailed specifics about discrete competencies. Links to sample evidence were included: (a) copies of program anchor assignments, (b) video lessons, (c) graphics/tools created during the clinical practice phase, (e) lesson plans, (f) completed observational evaluations from clinical practice supervisors, and (g) the Individualized Transition Plan (ITP) used for induction.

An e-portfolio assessment rubric was created by project faculty where a bank of possible evidence/artifacts was listed for each TPE element. Though not prescriptive, there were a few elements that were required artifacts such as supervisor evaluations in clinical practice, lesson plans, and several anchor assignments from methods courses. Candidates completed the e-portfolios during their clinical practice phase. For the ES program, a clinical practice seminar was implemented for the e-portfolio creation and evidence gathering. For the APE program, the e-portfolio was completed within a specific course that candidates took while they were in their clinical practice (i.e., student teaching). Through this course, candidates would meet four times throughout the semester to work on preparing their e-portfolios and to also provide peer feedback on each other's e-portfolios. Candidates were encouraged to include 3-5 samples of evidence for each TPE element. Final e-portfolios were evaluated by the program faculty using a scale of 0-3 for evidence provided. Table 11 below details the scale.

## Discussion

The CEC HLPs (2017) and the CEEDAR Center IC (Browder et al., 2014) were used as tools to guide the development and implementation of the project competencies in the areas of focused instruction, intense interventions, improved student outcomes, inclusion support, and meeting state credentialing standards. The competencies provided a clearer lens to reflect and revise course outcomes within the ES and APE programs, which resulted in positive program changes. Sustained program changes included a more rigorous integration of evidence-based practices and a clear focus on interdisciplinary, intensive instruction. Changes to both programs also include dedicated pre-service teacher instruction and practice on improving K-22 student outcomes through student progress data collection and analysis. Lastly, inclusion advocacy has become standard discussion in the programs as well as pre-service teacher learning and practicing behavior and communication supports for students with disabilities in inclusive settings.

Restructuring teacher preparation programming with an interdisciplinary approach is a substantial undertaking; however, through this approach, integration of HLPs into existing coursework can be completed collaboratively (Patti & McLeskey, 2019) and strategically through a conceptual framework (Shakman, 2017). By making curriculum and assignment revisions, candidates can develop a deeper knowledge of the HLPs if they are coupled with experience to use the HLPs that have been covered throughout the courses, such as in the integrated symposium. Revisions of student learning outcomes or objectives within teacher preparation courses related to HLPs and current literature ensure that candidates are assessed on their understanding and application of HLPs prior to entering the teaching field. Interdisciplinary opportunities between the two programs provided through the collaborative meetings, technology review, and professional development aided in the development of collaboration between the two programs and were added as additional features within the programs that yielded positive and impactful results.

## FUTURE RESEARCH DIRECTIONS

Preparing teachers to teach in inclusive, interdisciplinary settings is critical for teacher preparation programs if all students are to have access to the general education curriculum. HLPs have been proven to academically benefit students with disabilities and provide research-based approaches for improving outcomes. Teaching pre-service teachers about access to the general curriculum as a springboard to inclusive education is a way teacher educator programs can address common barriers to inclusion from a strengths-based versus a deficit-based view of disability. For example, Olson and Roberts (2020) interviewed teacher educators and discovered they faced common barriers to preparing candidates for inclusive settings for students with significant disabilities such as: a) lack of inclusive placements, (b) misalignment between coursework and fieldwork, (c) educational stakeholders' knowledge and beliefs, and (d) isolated teacher preparation programs with limited shared experiences. However, these teacher educators all held a vision of inclusive education as an "ethical compass to advocate for equitable practices even in the midst of barriers..." (Olson & Roberts, 2020, p. 172). Research in how to nurture an interdisciplinary, inclusive vision through preparation and professional development with a commitment to a shared goal of inclusion can also address resistance to inclusion by general education teachers (Mortier, 2020).

### Top Ten Action Steps

While the work described in this chapter applies to our specific university and ES and APE programs, there are actionable steps that can be generalized to other programs to promote strong interdisciplinary teacher preparation with strong foundations in evidence-based, high-leverage practices. Below is out top 10 list of action steps that can increase interdisciplinary collaboration through program review and revision:

1. Create collaborative partnerships with colleagues in other programs. We can't expect our candidates to collaborate if we do not!
2. Research high-leverage practices in special education.

3. Create program course review rubrics that include high-leverage practices and criteria for measurement.
4. Complete an interdisciplinary course audit. Collaboration is key –an interdisciplinary review of program courses strengthens the process.
5. Analyze the results of the course audit and develop actionable ways to address current gaps in high-leverage practices.
6. Determine where in program courses integrated assignments would be beneficial to candidate learning.
7. Develop integrated assignments that use the strengths in each program.
8. Create interdisciplinary experiences for candidates that are culturally responsive to their needs. Be sure these experiences include ongoing opportunities for formal and informal mentoring, collaboration, and discussion.
9. Be intentional with frequent opportunities for authentic formal and informal feedback about your program from your candidates.
10. Assess and review your interdisciplinary progress, including collecting feedback from program completers. Make adjustments as needed to continue to successfully prepare teachers to work as interdisciplinary teams for the ultimate benefit of all K-12 students with disabilities.

## CONCLUSION

Ongoing analysis and revisions to higher education teacher preparation programs are crucial for addressing educational trends and issues that arise to better prepare teacher candidates for inclusive classrooms. Systematically training teachers through implementing and practicing HLPs through interdisciplinary learning can drastically have an impact on supporting K-12 student learning, especially for students with disabilities (McLeskey & Brownell, 2015). Engaging in the continuous improvement cycle through a systematic integration of HLPs into teacher preparation programs can ensure teachers enter the field ready to meet the challenges of inclusive education with proven strategies and approaches for collaborative service delivery.

## ACKNOWLEDGMENT

This research was supported by the U.S. Department of Education, Office of Special Education Programs [Grant Number H325K170102].

## REFERENCES

Alharbi, A. (2018). Perceptions of using assistive technology for students with disabilities in the classroom. *International Journal of Special Education*, *33*(1), 129–139.

SHAPE America. (2017). National standards for initial physical education teacher education. https://www.shapeamerica.org/accreditation/upload/2017-SHAPE-America-Initial-PETE-Standards-and-Components.pdf

American Speech-Language-Hearing Association. (2020). Standards and implementation procedures for the certificate of clinical competence in speech-language pathology. *ASLHA.* https://www.asha.org/Certification/2020-SLP-Certification-Standards/

Anderson, E. M. (2013). Preparing the next generation of early childhood teachers: The emerging role of interprofessional education and collaboration in teacher education. *Journal of Early Childhood Teacher Education, 34*(1), 23–35. doi:10.1080/10901027.2013.758535

Ashby, I., & Exter, M. (2019). Designing for interdisciplinarity in higher education: Considerations for instructional designers. *TechTrends, 63*(2), 202–208. doi:10.100711528-018-0352-z

Astleitner, H. (2018). Multidimensional engagement in learning-An integrated instructional design approach. *Journal of Institutional Research, 7*(1), 6–32. doi:10.9743/JIR.2018.1

Bransford, J., Brown, A. L., & Cocking, R. R. (Eds.). (2000). *How people learn: Brain, mind, experience and schools.* National Academy Press.

Browder, D. M., Wood, L., Thompson, J., & Ribuffo, C. (2014). *Evidence-based practices for students with severe disabilities* (Document No. IC-3). University of Florida, Collaboration for Effective Educator, Development, Accountability, and Reform Center. https://ceedar.education.ufl.edu/tools/innovation-configurations/

California Commission on Teacher Credentialing. (2016, June). *Preliminary Education Specialist teaching credential preconditions, program standards, and teaching performance expectations.* CTC. https://www.ctc.ca.gov/docs/default-source/educator-prep/standards/adopted-tpes-2016.pdf

CEEDAR Center. (n.d.) The CEEDAR Center Innovation Configuration Guidelines. *CEEDAR Center.* https://ceedar.education.ufl.edu/wp-content/uploads/2014/08/IC-Guidelines.pdf

Centers for Disease Control and Prevention. (2020, June 24). Inclusive school physical education and physical activity. *CDC.* https://www.cdc.gov/healthyschools/physicalactivity/inclusion_pepa.htm

Council for Exceptional Children. (2020). Initial practice-based professional preparation standards for special educators. *CEC.* https://exceptionalchildren.org/standards/initial-practice-based-professional-preparation-standards-special-educators

Council for Exceptional Children. (n.d.). High Leverage Practices for students with disabilities. *CEC.* https://highleveragepractices.org/

de OliveiraP. S.van MunsterM. D. A.de SouzaJ. V.LiebermanL. J. (2020). Adapted physical education collaborative consulting: A systematic literature review. Journal of Teaching in Physical Education, 39, 165–175.

Dillon, S., Armstrong, E., Goudy, L., Reynolds, H., & Scurry, S. (2021). Improving special education service delivery through interdisciplinary collaboration. Teaching Exceptional Children, 54(1), 36–43.

Fink, L. D. (2003). *Creating significant learning experiences: An integrated approach to designing college courses*. Jossey-Bass.

González, N., Moll, L. C., & Amanti, C. (Eds.). (2005). Funds of knowledge: Theorizing practices in households, communities, and classrooms. Routledge.

Individuals With Disabilities Education Act, 20 U.S.C. § 1400 (2004).

Israel, M., Ribuffo, C., & Smith, S. (2014). *Universal Design for Learning: Recommendations for teacher preparation and professional development (Document No. IC-7)*. University of Florida, Collaboration for Effective Educator, Development, Accountability, and Reform Center website: https://ceedar.education.ufl.edu/tools/innovation-configurations/

Kelly, L. E. (Ed.). (2019). *Adapted physical education national standards* (3rd ed)Human Kinetics.

Lambe, J., McNair, V., & Smith, R. (2013). Special educational needs, e-learning and the reflective e-portfolio: Implications for developing and assessing competence in pre-service education. *Journal of Education for Teaching*, 39(2), 181–196.

McLeskey, J., Barringer, M-D., Billingsley, B., Brownell, M., Jackson, D., Kennedy, M., Lewis, T., Maheady, L., Rodriguez, J., Scheeler, M. C., Winn, J., & Ziegler, D. (2017). High-leverage practices in special education. *Council for Exceptional Children and CEEDAR Center*.

McLeskey, J., & Brownell, M. (2015). *High-leverage practices and teacher preparation in special education* (Document No. PR-1). University of Florida, Collaboration for Effective Educator, Development, Accountability, and Reform Center website: https://ceedar.education.ufl.edu/tools/best-practice-review/

Mortier, K. (2020). Communities of practice: A conceptual framework for inclusion of students with significant disabilities. *International Journal of Inclusive Education*, 24(3), 329–340. https://doi.org/10.1080/13603116.2018.1461261

National Parent Center on Transition and Employment (2022). Person-Centered Planning. *Pacer*. https://www.pacer.org/transition/learning-center/independent-community-living/person-centered.asp.

The Office of Special Education Programs. (2011). *Creating Equal Opportunities for Children and Youth with Disabilities to Participate in Physical Education and Extracurricular Athletics*.Office of Special Education and Rehabilitative Services.

Office of Special Education Programs. (n.d.) Personnel Preparation Program Description. *U.S. Department of Education*. https://www2.ed.gov/print/programs/osepprep/index.html

Olson, A. J., & Roberts, C. A. (2020). Navigating barriers as special education teacher educators. *Research and Practice for Persons with Severe Disabilities*, 45(3), 161–177. https://doi.org/10.1177/1540796920914969

Orlando, A., & Ruppar, A. (2016). *Literacy instruction for students with multiple and severe disabilities who use augmentative/alternative communication* (Document No. IC-16). University of Florida, Collaboration for Effective Educator, Development, Accountability, and Reform Center. https://ceedar.education.ufl.edu/tools/innovation-configurations/

Patti, A. L., & McLeskey, J. (2019). The role of high-leverage practices in Special Education Teacher Preparation. *Teacher Education Division of the Council for Exceptional Children*. https://tedcec.org/wp-content/uploads/2019/11/TED-Brief-1-HLPs-PDF.pdf

Repko, A. (2011). *Interdisciplinary research: Process and theory* (2nd ed.). Sage Publications.

Rios-Aguilar, C., & Kiyama, J. M. (Eds.). (2018). *Funds of knowledge in higher education: Honoring students' cultural experiences and resources as strength*. Routledge.

Scruggs, T. E., & Mastropieri, M. A. (2017). Making inclusion work with co-teaching. Teaching Exceptional Children, 49(4), 284–293. https://doi.org/10.1177/0040059916685065

Shakman, K., Bailey, J., & Breslow, N. (2017). *A primer for continuous improvement in schools and districts*. Teacher & Leadership Programs.

Shogren, K. A., Luckasson, R., & Schalock, R. L. (2020). Using a multidimensional model to analyze context and enhance personal outcomes. *Intellectual and developmental disabilities, 58*(2), 95-110.

Sisti M. K., & Robledo, J. A. (2021). Interdisciplinary collaboration practices between education specialists and related service providers. *The Journal of Special Education Apprenticeship, 10*(1), 5.

Taheri, A., Perry, A., & Minnes, P. (2017). Exploring factors that impact activity participation of children and adolescents with severe developmental disabilities. *Journal of Intellectual Disability Research, 61*(12), 1151–1161.

Zilz, W., & Pang, Y. (2021). Application of assistive technology in inclusive classrooms. Disability and Rehabilitation. Assistive Technology, 16(7), 684–686.

# Chapter 6
# Preparing a New Generation of Early Autism Educators:
## An Interdisciplinary Personnel Preparation Grant

**Marina R. Crain**
*University of Oregon, USA*

**Wenjing Bao**
*University of Oregon, USA*

**Miyoko Patricelli**
*University of Oregon, USA*

**Stephanie Yoshiko Shire**
*University of Oregon, USA*

## ABSTRACT

*Despite young children with autism spectrum disorders (ASD) making up larger portions of early intervention caseloads and classrooms, many educators and related service providers do not receive explicit training and practical experience in supporting these students until they encounter them on caseloads. This chapter provides an example of a personnel preparation program emphasizing interdisciplinary training of early intervention (EI)/Early childhood special education (ECSE) service providers and speech-language pathologists (SLPs) to serve young children with ASD. Specifically, the chapter will discuss the Preparing a New Generation of Early Autism Educators (PANGEA) personnel preparation grant (H325K180170), funded through the Office of Special Education Programs (OSEP) at the U.S. Department of Education. Descriptions and rationales for required competencies, coursework, and practicum will be described as well as induction support. Finally, the chapter will review strengths and positive outcomes, challenges, and future directions for similar interdisciplinary grants.*

DOI: 10.4018/978-1-6684-6438-0.ch006

## INTRODUCTION

The Preparing a New Generation of Early Autism Educators (PANGEA) program at University of Oregon is an H325K personnel preparation grant funded through the Office of Special Education Programs (OSEP) at the U.S. Department of Education (H325K180170: PI Shire, Co-PI Patricelli). The purpose of Project PANGEA is to provide interdisciplinary pre-service training, focusing on explicitly training future special educators (Early Intervention (EI) master's program) and future Speech Language Pathologists (SLPs: Communication Disorders and Sciences (CDS) master's program) to serve young children with disabilities such as autism spectrum disorder (ASD). Project PANGEA seeks to address the nation-wide shortage of highly trained practitioners focused on supporting young children with disabilities by: (a) recruiting and graduating a diverse pool of high-quality scholars, (b) preparing well-trained EI/Early Childhood Special Education (ECSE) professionals who can provide high quality services to young children with high intensity needs and their families, and(c) providing induction support to graduates.

The PANGEA project grant has provided funding for a total of 29 scholars to date with an additional 9 scholars who will complete the program by the 22/23 academic year. Scholars are guided through a series of coursework and practical experiences to develop proficiency in delivering high-quality interventions to young children with ASD while also expanding skills for working on interdisciplinary teams.

## BACKGROUND

Within both the fields of EI/ECSE and CDS, there are ongoing and critical shortages of personnel to meet the needs of children with disabilities. Currently, reports based on responses from 49 states/territories indicated significant shortages of ECSE personnel for serving children under IDEA Part B (ages 3-21), with most states identifying shortages of both SLPs and special educators (CEC, 2020). In a report by the National Association of State Directors of Special Education (Sopko, 2010), 40 of 41 states responding identified significant shortages in personnel to provide services through IDEA Part C (ages birth to 3). Surveys conducted at both the national and state level demonstrate that school districts and contractors experience difficulty finding personnel to fill positions in EI/ECSE (AAEE, 2021). Project PANGEA works to address this personnel shortage by matriculating providers prepared to enter the field of special education and meet necessary requirements for state and national certification in their respective professional organizations.

The prevalence of ASD is estimated at 1 in 44 children in the US, and data indicates that children are being diagnosed at earlier ages (Maenner et al., 2021; Shaw et al., 2021). Because children with ASD are being diagnosed at earlier ages, they are more likely to enroll special education services during the early intervention years. It is increasingly likely that early career special educators and related service providers will encounter children with ASD on their caseloads and in their classrooms. It is necessary to prepare EI/ECSE providers entering the field to support children with ASD in core areas of need including social communication and interaction as well as regulation (Masi et al., 2017). Tager-Flusberg & Kasari (2013) estimated that 30% of children diagnosed with ASD are preverbal and working on developing functional spoken language through age five. There is, however, considerable evidence to show that young children with ASD who participate in high-quality, evidence-based interventions, can make significant growth in communication and other core domains of development (e.g., Kasari et al., 2021). While the research into evidence-based interventions is promising, there continues to be a research-to-practice gap impacting use of evidence-based ASD interventions by practitioners in community settings. In these settings, evidence-based, efficacious interventions for ASD are rarely adopted, and when implemented, fidelity and sustainability are often a challenge (Dingfelder & Mandell, 2011). While there is robust evidence that community practitioners can effectively implement high quality interventions when trained, they may lack access to training, coaching, and materials to implement such interventions. Therefore, it is critical to capitalize on pre-service opportunities to learn and practice implementation of these evidence-based interventions in highly supportive environments before entering the field. Project PANGEA utilizes coursework and practical experiences to provide scholars with knowledge of and scaffolded experiences to implement evidence-based interventions for children with ASD.

Because evidence-based interventions often address nonverbal communication and functional language use, core target areas for children with ASD, SLPs and EI/ECSE practitioners are crucial members of intervention teams (APA, 2013). The Individuals with Disabilities Education Act (IDEA) federally mandates interdisciplinary services for all children receiving special education services (IDEA, 2004). The Early Childhood Personal Center (TECPC), Council of Exceptional Children (CEC), and the American Speech and Hearing Association (ASHA) all identify collaboration and teaming as standards for preparation or clinical competence (CEC, 2015; Council for Clinical Certification in Audiology and Speech-Language Pathology of the American Speech-Language-Hearing Association, 2018; Bruder et al., 2019). ASHA identifies interprofessional problem solving and planning as a priority when working with clients with ASD (ASHA, 2006). Despite expectations for EI/ECSE providers and SLPs to bring their respective training and skills to interdisciplinary teams to support students with ASD, there is little evidence of emphasis that pre-service programs are emphasizing interdisciplinary training or teaming. A survey of university faculty working in personnel preparation programs across early intervention disciplines found that significantly less content and emphasis was placed on teaming practices and service coordination across disciplines compared to other evidence-based early intervention practices such as family-centered practice (Bruder and Dunst, 2005). A 2015 survey of CDS program directors found only 22% of responding programs included interdisciplinary coursework, while 70% reported that interdisciplinary cases were incorporated into case-based analysis or case stimulations as part of coursework (Francois et al., 2015). It may be presumptive to assume that pre-service students will naturally acquire skills for interdisciplinary practice over the course of their preparation programs without systematic, targeted coursework and teaming experiences. Project PANGEA incorporates structured interdisciplinary teaming opportunities throughout the graduate program to better prepare scholars to work as part of interdisciplinary teams upon program completion.

## PROJECT PANGEA

Project PANGEA funding includes one year of tuition support for approximately seven scholars per year. The first cohort of scholars served as a pilot cohort, providing important feedback on coursework, courseload and scheduling, and effectiveness of teaming opportunities.

In order to tailor the program to best develop interdisciplinary skills, resources were allocated to allow for expert and community involvement in addition to a planning year. Developers of project PANGEA incorporated input from both a community advisory board and an academic advisory board. The community advisory board, consisting of parents of children with ASD, autistic community members, and local practitioners, provided important perspectives and feedback to ensure relevance to community practice. Autistic community members were a priority for inclusion on the advisory board as they have invaluable input for future interventionists who may support children with ASD (Courchesne et al., 2022). The academic advisory board consisted of ASD researchers and policy experts who supported development of course content and training experiences. The board reviewed the program structure and course syllabi to ensure that scholars in both EI/ECSE and CDS programs were accessing required content for their respective programs while also gaining necessary knowledge and skills in interdisciplinary teaming and implementing evidence-based practices. Examples of revisions from the community panel and academic advisory board include revision of PANGEA competencies from eight competencies to four primary competencies and four secondary competencies, addition of an experience portfolio to scholar documentation requirements, and increasing systematic assessment experience.

## Framework

Project PANGEA is based on a transactional model of child development, in which development takes place through continuous bi-directional interactions between a child and their environment (Sameroff, 2009) and a family systems model (Minuchin, 1974; Guralnick, 2011). As educators and caregivers spend the most time with young children, they are integral to the child's environment and are positioned to provide frequent opportunities for learning. Families are an essential component of the early intervention process. The framework of this project emphasizes a responsive, individualized approach to children and their families to support gains in core developmental domains where children with ASD demonstrate a need for support, including social engagement, social communication and regulation. In the context of Project PANGEA, this framework is utilized as a foundation to train PANGEA scholars to support young children with disabilities and their families (See figure 1).

Project PANGEA emphasizes development of teaming skills through coursework explicitly addressing target skills, group projects and activities, and interdisciplinary practicum opportunities. Effective communication, collaborative work, and flexibility have been identified as critical soft skills for special educators to utilize when working in teams, particularly in supporting inclusive education (Fernandes et al., 2021). As scholars develop skills in provision of evidence-based practices, they are also expected to develop soft skills that support interdisciplinary special education partnership. These skills are addressed in practicum opportunities of increasing complexity beginning with partnerships supporting individual children to functioning as a team to prepare and implement an early intervention classroom program.

## Competencies

Competency areas for Project PANGEA were selected based on shared philosophies of the University of Oregon EI/ECSE and CDS programs as well as best practices for interdisciplinary teaming and evidence-based interventions for EI/ECSE services to meet the diverse needs of children with ASD. Competencies were identified based on recommendations from governing bodies such as the Division for Early Childhood (DEC) and ASHA, as well as researchers and experts in the field of ASD (ASHA, 2006; DEC, 2014). To meet the project's goals of preparing well-trained personnel to work with young children with ASD, Project PANGEA emphasizes four key primary competency areas and four secondary competency areas (see Table 1). Project PANGEA coursework and practical experiences were then selected, tailored, or designed to facilitate mastery of the key primary competency areas over the course of the program.

*Figure 1. Project PANGEA Theoretical Framework*

**Theoretical Framework of UO's EI and CDS Master's Training Programs:** transactional (Sameroff, 2000; Sameroff & Chandler, 1975) and family systems (Minuchin, 1974; Guralnick, 2011) models

↓

Training for supporting young children with disabilities (including ASD) & their caregivers

↓

**1. Training of Project PANGEA Scholars**
- EI/ECSE & CDS competencies
- Interdisciplinary coursework focused on supporting young children with ASD and their caregivers
- Three field placements with young children with ASD
- Specialized training for ASD evidence-based practices
- Training and opportunities to experience and practice interdisciplinary teaming
- Opportunities for research, leadership, and advocacy
- Instruction on coaching and supporting diverse families

**2. Highly Qualified EI & CDS Educators**
- 35 Project PANGEA graduates obtain employment in EI/ECSE settings that serve children with ASD
- Project PANGEA graduates receive ongoing induction support and professional development opportunities to continue high-quality work focused on interdisciplinary teaming and supporting young children with ASD and their families.

**3. Positive Impact on Special Education**
- Reduction in shortage of high quality EI & CDS educators to meet the needs of the growing number of children with ASD
- EI & CDS educators prepared to work on interdisciplinary teams
- Improved satisfaction for families of children in EI/ECSE
- Improved special education and school readiness outcomes for young children with special needs including ASD
- Improved behavioral outcomes leading to more children with disabilities included successfully in regulary education settings

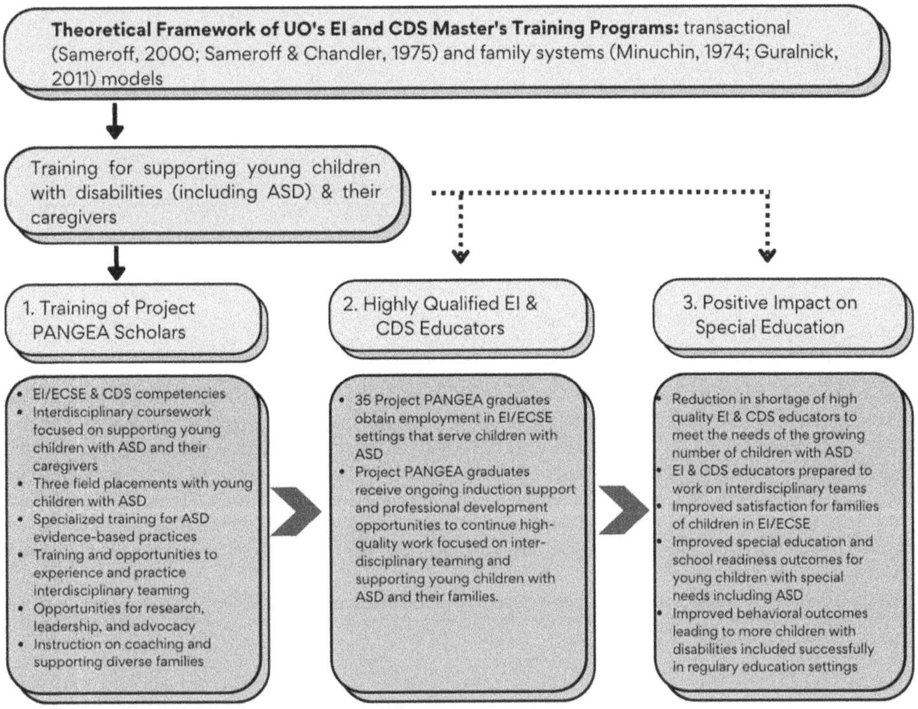

## Coursework and Practical Experiences

### Shared Coursework

In addition to the required series of coursework for their respective EI/ECSE and CDS programs, PANGEA scholars participate together in several courses intended to build their theoretical and practical knowledge in interprofessional practice and providing evidence-based interventions to young children with ASD. These courses (see Table 2) were either developed or adapted for Project PANGEA. The sequence is designed to systematically build scholars' skills alongside practical experiences. Coursework begins with a focus on understanding foundational knowledge focused on the development of core early childhood skills (e.g., social communication, regulation, play) and how development may be delayed or different for young children ASD. Scholars are then introduced to assessments and to measure core developmental domains and a range of approaches to intervention. Emphasis is placed on their respective evidence base to address the core challenges experienced by many young children with ASD. Later coursework builds upon this foundation by highlighting the application of practices to support children's engagement and regulation in everyday interactions. Scholars are also systematically given opportunities to increase independence in utilizing teaming practices and knowledge translation practices each term.

*Table 1. Project PANGEA competencies*

| Primary Competencies |
|---|
| **A. Typical and Atypical Development** |
| Scholars demonstrate knowledge across and within domains of typical child development, delayed development, and patterns of atypical development associated with pediatric disabilities. Scholars understand the heterogeneity of skills associated with ASD and exhibit a particular expertise in skill domains with research evidence that indicates differences or delays often experienced by young children with ASD including social engagement, behavioral regulation, play, joint attention, and social communication. |
| **B. Infant, Toddler and Preschool Assessment** |
| Scholars correctly select technically adequate assessment measures matched to the skill domain(s) they seek to measure. Scholars use this information for planning and evaluating interventions, with added focus on measures commonly used to assess core domains for young children with ASD. PANGEA scholars graduate with knowledge in assessing both child and caregiver behavior in order to effectively generate evidence-based intervention plans. |
| **C. Design, Implement, and Evaluate Evidence-Based Interventions** |
| Based on assessment information, PANGEA scholars develop individualized intervention plans. Scholars apply the information they have learned about child development and use the assessment data to write individualized, developmentally appropriate goals for children. Scholars demonstrate skill in selecting and implementing evidence-based intervention strategies that lead to improved learning and developmental outcomes of young children with disabilities with a specific emphasis on the intense instructional needs of young children with ASD. Scholars incorporate evidence-based strategies that foster social-communication (including the use of assistive technology, AAC modalities), play, emotional and behavior regulation, and academic development into their direct instruction and intervention. Scholars also demonstrate the ability to share intervention strategies with caregivers to support the above domains. Scholars demonstrate the knowledge and ability to monitor child, family, and program outcomes through a variety of objective data-driven measures. |
| **D. Interdisciplinary and Interagency Collaboration** |
| PANGEA scholars understand how the professional roles and responsibilities of interdisciplinary EI/ECSE team members complement one another and demonstrate the ability to engage with and work alongside professionals from different disciplines who provide services to children with ASD and their families. Scholars demonstrate exemplary professional behavior supportive of collaborative relationships and demonstrate skills for serving various EI/ECSE roles, including service coordination, consulting, and coaching. Scholars understand and flexibly apply multiple models of collaboration to meet the unique learning and developmental needs of children with disabilities, including ASD. |
| **Secondary Competencies** |
| **E. Foundations in Early Childhood Early Intervention/Early Childhood Special Education** |
| Specific to ASD, PANGEA scholars demonstrate a working understanding of the spectrum of EI/ECSE models ranging from developmental/relational intervention through those based in applied behavior analysis (ABA), including the history and development of experimental studies exploring atypical development which inform the intervention landscape. Relative to these, scholars understand various teaming models, including the roles of practitioners within multi-disciplinary intervention teams supporting children with ASD in educational settings. |
| **F. Family Involvement** |
| PANGEA scholars identify cultural, socioeconomic, ethical, political, linguistic, and historical factors as well as beliefs, values, and practices of individual families that influence the development of the child and access to effective ASD services. Scholars use this knowledge to collaborate with families with the goal of providing natural and inclusive EI/ECSE services that are family-guided, foster a sense of belonging through family and peer relationships, and develop skills needed for academic success. Scholars employ adult learning principles to help caregivers become active members of the assessment and intervention process. |
| **G. Research Application** |
| PANGEA scholars will use current research related to young children with ASD and interdisciplinary teaming to guide professional practices. Scholars will evaluate evidence-based practices. |
| **H. Leadership and Advocacy** |
| PANGEA scholars develop skills relevant to translating research related to ASD and teaming into practice and advocate for evidence-based practices when interacting with, providing training to, or supporting EI/ECSE colleagues, families, community members, and other important stakeholders. Scholars advocate for children with ASD and their families while participating in EI/ECSE programs and during transition to school-age services. Scholars provide leadership in the collaborative development of community-based services and resources. |

*Table 2. Shared coursework of PANGEA scholars*

| Course | Course Description | PANGEA competencies |
|---|---|---|
| CDS 665 | **Language Disorders in Young Children**<br>Coursework competencies include knowledge of the principles and methods of assessment and intervention of language delay/disorder in young children and application of evidence-based methods that best account for linguistic and cultural correlates and individualized contexts and service provision. | • Typical and atypical early development<br>• Interdisciplinary/interagency collaboration<br>• Infant, toddler, preschool assessment |
| SPED 680 | **Foundations in Early Childhood & EI**<br>Coursework competencies include foundations of early intervention, and typical and atypical child development from cross disciplinary perspectives. | • Foundations in EI/ECSE<br>• Typical and atypical early development<br>• Interdisciplinary/interagency collaboration<br>• Leadership & advocacy |
| SPED 686 | **Autism & EI**<br>This course introduces scholars to core early childhood developmental domains including strengths and needs experienced by young children with ASD. Scholars are introduced to assessment of these domains and a range of intervention approaches including perspectives of self-advocates and caregivers. | • Typical and atypical early development<br>• Family involvement<br>• Infant, toddler, preschool assessment<br>• Design, implement, and evaluate evidence-based practices<br>• Research application |
| SPED 610 | **Autism Intervention I and II**<br>These courses build upon the scholars' practical experiences and are taken concurrent to the summer Preschool BOOST classroom experience. The courses provide a deeper dive into regulation and engagement profiles of young children with ASD | • Family involvement<br>• Interdisciplinary/interagency collaboration<br>• Infant, toddler, preschool assessment<br>• Design, implement, and evaluate evidence-based interventions<br>• Leadership & advocacy |
| SPED 610 | **BOOST Transdisciplinary Teaming**<br>This course is taken concurrent to the BOOST Preschool Experience to provide structured support for weekly review and revision of the scholars' implementation of the preschool program. | • Foundations in EI/ECSE<br>• Interdisciplinary/interagency collaboration<br>• Infant, toddler, preschool assessment<br>• Design, implement, and evaluate evidence-based interventions<br>• Leadership & advocacy<br>• Research application |

## Seminars and Supported Practicum Experiences

Along with shared coursework, Project PANGEA includes several required seminar courses and practical experiences developed specifically to address project competencies and facilitate opportunities for interdisciplinary teaming. These courses include a combination of course lectures, group work, and practical experience with young children with ASD outside of regular required coursework and practicum experiences. These experiences provide PANGEA scholars with training in intervention and accommodation strategies to support engagement and regulation of young children with ASD.

## JASPER Seminar and Practicum

The Joint Attention, Symbolic Play, Engagement, and Regulation (JASPER) intervention is a naturalistic developmental behavioral intervention that promotes development of play diversity and complexity, joint engagement, and social communication (Kasari et al., 2021). The JASPER seminar, taken in the fall quarter, emphasizes early childhood development in core domains including communication, play skills, social engagement, and regulation. Scholars learn how skills in these four domains may differ in children on the autism spectrum. They then learn to assess, set goals, and utilize the JASPER intervention to address skills in these core developmental domains. JASPER has an extensive research base demonstrating efficacy/effectiveness in over 10 published randomized controlled trials utilizing clinician-child interventions and has been shown to be effective when implemented by caregivers (e.g., Kasari et al., 2014) and by teachers and paraprofessionals (e.g., Chang et al., 2016; Shire et al., 2018). The JASPER framework consists of (a) planning developmentally appropriate play opportunities, (b) being an active and responsive play partner, (c) establishing and expanding play activities, and (d) monitoring progress and adjusting targets and interventions as needed (Chang & Shire, 2020). Because of its extensive research-base and effectiveness being implemented by caregivers and community practitioners, JASPER is an optimal intervention to train pre-service EI/ECSE specialists and SLPs to prepare them for working with children with high intensity needs. The JASPER seminar includes a practicum experience where scholars participate in provide 1:1 intervention in an early intervention classroom for children with ASD located on campus.

## Interdisciplinary Opportunities in JASPER Seminar

During the seminar, scholars work in dyads to implement the JASPER intervention with a an assigned child in the partner early intervention classroom. Scholars are required to briefly assess their assigned child, establish play and social communication targets, and provide intervention tailored to the child's level. Scholars work with EI students in short 1:1 sessions with support from a supervisor knowledgeable in JASPER. Because scholars do not work with their student at the same time, they must communicate effectively and efficiently to share assessment results, identify mastered skills, choose targets, and plan intervention. Students are given some time to collaborate during JASPER sessions but must also manage their time effectively to collaborate outside of the course. Additionally, partners gain experience in defining roles and splitting up responsibilities (e.g. sending lists of needed materials to supervisors and documenting sessions).

## Assessment Seminar and Practicum

The assessment seminar provides opportunities for scholars to practice conducting assessments, analyzing results, and recommending targets. For cohorts 2 and 3 of PANGEA, the assessment seminar focused on ASD assessment, with practicum experience in the University of Oregon ASD clinic. During cohorts 4 and 5 of PANGEA, scholars attended seminars and participated in practicum related to AAC assessment. AAC is the use of alternative communication modalities for individuals who are unable to meet their daily communication needs through spoken language as a result of a disability (Beukelman & Mirenda, 2013). AAC modalities can include a spectrum of tools including gestures, signs, picture boards, writing, and speech generating devices (SGDs; Beukelman & Mirenda, 2013). Research findings indicate that AAC interventions can have positive effects on communication and behavior outcomes of children with ASD (Ganz et al., 2012). When SGDs are included with interventions, minimally verbal early communicators with ASD can increase use of spontaneous utterances, new words, and comments (Kasari et al., 2014). The PANGEA AAC experience includes introducing a foundation in types of AAC, AAC assessment, matching system features to child needs, and device selection. During the practicum portion of the experience, scholars work collaboratively in a supported setting to complete remote AAC assessments via tele-health.

*Table 3. Required planning components of BOOST seminar*

| | |
|---|---|
| Programming | · Lesson Plans – circle, art, outdoor play, 1:1 centers (e.g., JASPER), snack<br>· Entry assessment<br>· Target Selection<br>· Data collection |
| Caregiver/Family Involvement | · Introduction/Welcome information & forms<br>· Home to school communication systems<br>· Progress update reports<br>· Strategies to utilize at home |
| Classroom management | · Environmental Arrangement<br>· Transitions<br>· Supports for engagement and regulation<br>· Team member roles and responsibilities<br>· Classroom schedules and routines |

### Interdisciplinary Opportunities

During the ASD and AAC assessment experiences, PANGEA scholars work in small teams or as a whole group to plan and conduct assessments. Scholars are supported in assigning roles and responsibilities during assessments such as logistics (managing technology, data collection) and conducting assessment tasks. During this time, PANGEA faculty support students in combining expertise between the two fields to effectively conduct an interdisciplinary assessment. This is an excellent opportunity for scholars to engage in flexibility in roles and work on the various types of collaboration that can take place on interdisciplinary teams such as consultation, coaching, planning, and co-treatment.

## BOOST Curriculum Planning Seminar

The BOOST curriculum planning course is designed to prepare PANGEA scholars for their BOOST preschool field practicum to take place over the summer. The BOOST program is a classroom-based program for preschool-aged students with ASD. Over the course of the seminar, scholars work in interdisciplinary groups to develop a multi-week preschool program emphasizing the development of social engagement, play skills, and social communication that maximizes learning opportunities during all parts of the program day. Instruction and guidance are provided to facilitate development of a high-quality classroom-based intervention setting for young children with ASD. The seminar emphasizes the many components necessary for interdisciplinary classroom planning, from intervention planning to environmental setup and staff assignments (See Table 3).

### Interdisciplinary Opportunities

Over the course of the BOOST planning seminar scholars are instructed in strategies for facilitating interdisciplinary teaming. Scholars are split into two groups and are expected to coordinate weekly group meetings as well as define group expectations and norms. The planning seminar includes a responsive teaming support component, wherein teaming strategies and soft skills are selected for focus based on student performance and feedback. Soft skills that have been addressed include facilitating effective meetings, time management, and communication within and between groups. While working in planning groups, scholars develop group problem solving skills and continue to practice capitalizing on knowledge and experience of team members from various disciplines.

## BOOST Classroom Experience

The BOOST classroom experience takes place during the summer term and lasts for five weeks. Scholars utilize the plans created during the BOOST curriculum planning seminar to select materials, arrange the classroom environment, and prepare for students. The first week of the BOOST program consists of small groups of PANGEA scholars completing entry assessments with each child participant. Entry assessments are utilized to determine a baseline and select targets in the areas of play, communication, and engagement. The final four weeks of the BOOST program consist of implementation of the preschool classroom program. Up to 7 child participants attend BOOST for two hours, three days per week. EI/ECSE PANGEA scholars attend every day of the program and CDS scholars attend one day per week each. Support and supervision are provided by faculty and graduate students throughout the program. Supervisors assist scholars by providing support for instruction implementation including priming and environmental set up, coaching and support while children are present, and support for reflection and revision. Classroom management supports provided by BOOST supervisors include identifying and assigning roles and responsibilities, adjusting schedules as needed, and ensuring materials are adequately prepped. Supervisors provide coaching related to programming throughout the day by modeling and giving live feedback to troubleshoot diminishing engagement and regulation and directing scholars' attention to students or activities that may need additional support. BOOST supervisors model and coach behavior management and communication strategies using spoken language and AAC. Lastly, supervisors take notes and record activities for PANGEA scholars to reflect on during team meetings and for related coursework.

### Boost Transdisciplinary Teaming Seminar

The BOOST Transdisciplinary teaming seminar is taken in conjunction with the summer BOOST preschool experience. PANGEA scholars meet weekly with BOOST supervisors to plan, reflect, and revise classroom programming as a team. During transdisciplinary team meetings, supervisors facilitate reflection and problem solving to improve the classroom environment, increase interdisciplinary practices, and encourage application of evidence-based practices to support classroom engagement, social communication, and regulation. These discussions stress the importance of problem solving by identifying changes that practitioners can make within the intervention setting to support children in these areas.

### Interdisciplinary Opportunities

The BOOST classroom experience is the culminating experience and requires scholars to employ interdisciplinary teaming skills to work as a cohort group in a setting similar to what they may experience upon entering the field. Scholars must coordinate communication amongst themselves as well as with supervisors. They have opportunities to develop skills in delineating responsibilities, appropriately dividing workload, and supporting accountability for themselves and others. The unpredictable nature of the preschool classroom setting promotes practicing flexibility and asking for assistance. Scholars continue to engage in group problem solving and increase independence in utilizing group discussions to identify problems and formulate solutions. Interpersonal skills such as building positive working relationships and interpersonal problem solving are also highlighted over the course of the BOOST program.

## Induction

After matriculation from their graduate programs, PANGEA scholars are supported in their early career placements by the PANGEA project team. Many educators entering the EI/ECSE field report feeling under-prepared (Bruder et al., 2009). Special educators also report feeling less prepared to provide direct services to students with severe disabilities, especially in addressing long-term curriculum needs (Ruppar et al., 2016). In addition to instructional practices, early career teachers report needing support in collaboration and interaction with other adults and managing various roles (Billingsley et al., 2009). Guidance provided through induction support can help new special education teachers apply knowledge and improve practices, which can help to reduce attrition of special educators (Billingsley, et al., 2019). PANGEA induction support provides ongoing opportunities to increase preparedness and effectiveness for early career educators by building on the pre-service specialist knowledge and targeted experiences. PANGEA project faculty engage in follow-up communication with program graduates during their early years in educational settings. The PANGEA program also provides opportunities for collaboration, access to new research, and access to resources such as online training that graduates can utilize to support their professional development.

## DISCUSSION

Four cohorts of scholars have completed Project PANGEA to date. The program is on track to exceed expected enrollment. The nature of the program has resulted in high levels of interested applicants, allowing for a competitive field of candidates with various backgrounds and experiences applying for and enrolling in the program. This has led to the selection of scholars who articulate a solid commitment to entering the field to work specifically in early intervention programs supporting scholars with high-intensity needs. Scholars enrolled in the program include first generation students, scholars from historically marginalized populations, and scholars with disabilities (including neurodiverse scholars). Follow-up communication with candidates who have now completed Project PANGEA indicates promising early career outcomes, with program graduates taking positions supporting student populations relevant to PANGEA focus areas. This includes supporting young children with ASD in clinic, university research, and school settings. Further, several graduates from the first two graduated cohorts report serving early communicators in early childhood through middle school through the provision of classroom services and consultation focused on AAC. By observing scholar development the first several cohorts, the Project PANGEA team has identified strengths of the program, lessons learned, and directions for future interdisciplinary grants.

## Strengths of Project PANGEA

Throughout project PANGEA, the program has been able to capitalize on expertise and knowledge from instructors and supervisors across CDS, EI/ECSE, and K-12 Special Education programs at the University of Oregon. Scholars attend classes, seminars, and lectures presented by specialists in multiple disciplines,

*Figure 2. PANGEA knowledge to practice process*

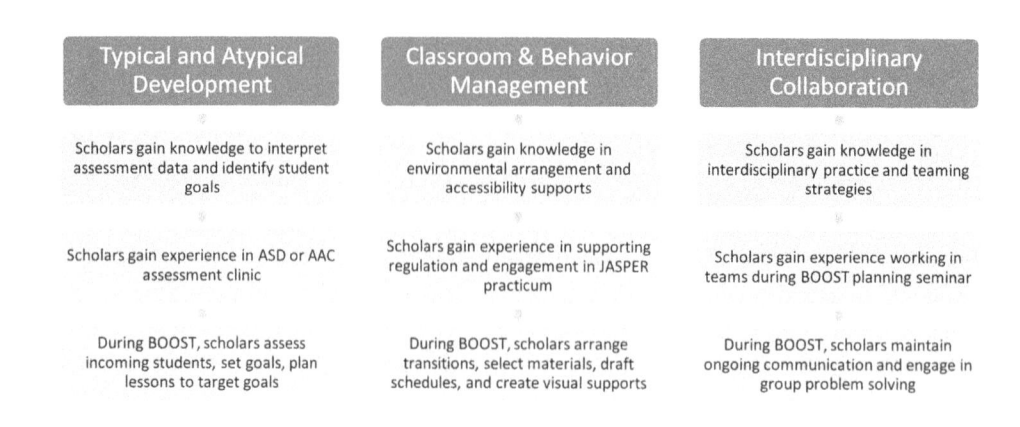

| Typical and Atypical Development | Classroom & Behavior Management | Interdisciplinary Collaboration |
|---|---|---|
| Scholars gain knowledge to interpret assessment data and identify student goals | Scholars gain knowledge in environmental arrangement and accessibility supports | Scholars gain knowledge in interdisciplinary practice and teaming strategies |
| Scholars gain experience in ASD or AAC assessment clinic | Scholars gain experience in supporting regulation and engagement in JASPER practicum | Scholars gain experience working in teams during BOOST planning seminar |
| During BOOST, scholars assess incoming students, set goals, plan lessons to target goals | During BOOST, scholars arrange transitions, select materials, draft schedules, and create visual supports | During BOOST, scholars maintain ongoing communication and engage in group problem solving |

including school psychologists, speech-language pathologists, special education teachers, and board-certified behavior analysts. These coordinated efforts both model interdisciplinary teaming and provide a diversity of perspectives, instructional methods, and knowledge to support scholars' learning. Beyond learning and interacting with a variety of specialties during their coursework, PANGEA scholars also participate in enriching practical experiences they may not otherwise have exposure to in a pre-service program. These opportunities require scholars to reflect upon the many components of their training to date and systematically merge those knowledge and skills (see figure 2). Scholars have commented that this level of critical thinking and teaming required to develop and implement their own classroom programming has been invaluable as they step into professional roles as ECSE lead classroom teachers, EI/ECSE specialists, and school based SLPs.

Beyond the positive impact to community resulting from more highly trained interventionists entering the field, Project PANGEA has resulted in additional positive community impacts. Practicum opportunities have provided PANGEA scholars with opportunities to serve community members directly (e.g. providing direct intervention and assessment to children and families, participating in in-service activities with local ECE practitioners). These interactions have resulted in favorable relationships between university departments, community organizations, and families of young children with disabilities. Multiple families involved in PANGEA practical intervention or classroom experiences have expressed positive attitudes regarding their intervention experiences and have returned when additional opportunities to participate with Project PANGEA have become available. These programs have further served a need in the local community by providing evidence-based interventions during a time when children eligible for early intervention services may be awaiting services due to wait lists or experience service disruptions during transitions or school closures.

A further strength of the program is the flexible and responsive nature of programming that results in differentiation of instruction and experiences between the two graduate programs and the varying backgrounds and levels of expertise of PANGEA scholars. As Project PANGEA has attracted strong candidates, many scholars enter the program with a wealth of prior experience in fields related to child development or early intervention (e.g., preschool teachers, teaching assistants, early interventionists, registered behavior technicians, paraprofessionals). Each cohort's programming requires unique tailoring to ensure that all participants can capitalize on their current knowledge while filling in knowledge in other competency areas. To encourage self-reflection and support faculty decision making, each PANGEA scholar selects key competencies to focus on developing as an individual. These scholar-selected areas of growth, in conjunction with faculty observed areas of need, are used to support adjustments to the PANGEA program. Differences in coursework between programs result in varying expertise levels in many areas. PANGEA scholars take 15 units of coursework together that emphasize PANGEA competencies. However, scholars in each graduate program get more breadth or depth of content in some target areas. For example, all PANGEA scholars take a Language Disorders in Young Children and learn about AAC in the Autism and Early Intervention Course; CDS scholars have coursework and practical experiences specific to their program that gives them a deeper understanding of those topics. Alternatively, in addition to the Foundations in Early Childhood and Early Intervention that all PANGEA scholars take, EI/ECSE scholars take additional coursework resulting in deeper knowledge of family-guided early intervention and behavior management. EI/ECSE scholars also gain more breadth across development areas, while CDS scholars focus in depth on communication. To best support these differences between the two programs, the project team adjusts each year, particularly within the JASPER seminar courses, to (a) provide enough training for all scholars to participate in assessments and programming and (b) offer insight into how interdisciplinary teams can utilize their differing areas of expertise to collaborate and consult effectively. This differentiation allows for dynamic programming to better prepare scholars as they transition into careers in the field.

## Lessons Learned

The PANGEA project team has made several adjustments to improve interdisciplinary teaming experiences during the project. Both the EI/ECSE and CDS programs are intensive, with master's program requirements including high credit loads of both coursework and practical experiences each term. Therefore, cross program scheduling is a significant challenge that must be addressed by the project directors for each cohort to create space and time for interdisciplinary participation and teaming. For instance, scholars are asked in spring term to meet in small interdisciplinary groups each week to work on the development of components of the BOOST summer preschool classroom. Mixed availability can make equitable distribution of the work more challenging. Similarly, due to the multiple clinic experiences planned for CDS scholars during the summer term, it is challenging for CDS scholars to participate in more than one day a week of the BOOST preschool program. This also results in less balance of responsibilities between EI/ECSE and CDS PANGEA scholars when implementing the BOOST program and communication challenges between scholars. Project supervisors have continued to revise these components of the program to include more explicit teaming and communication content, support scheduling, and facilitate distribution of project roles and responsibilities.

The PANGEA practical experience sequence has undergone several revisions over the past four years. These changes were made based on feedback from advisory boards and scholar cohorts in conjunction with needs identified by PANGEA faculty. The practical experiences were intended to align with coursework starting with a foundational understanding of development and ASD, understanding how to assess core developmental domains, and then setting goals to plan intervention. The program originally planned to have the JASPER seminar, a seminar and practicum experience centering around parent coaching, and the BOOST planning seminar and classroom experience. Feedback and Covid-19 resulted in necessary shifts in the applied experiences of Project PANGEA where cohorts 2 and 3 received a mix of in person and remote content as local health and safety regulations permitted. Scholars in these two cohorts worked with video case studies in team seminars. Based on clinic and supervisor availability, cohorts 4 and 5 have the opportunity to engage in an assessment experience focused on supporting evaluation for AAC. This AAC assessment experience involves working directly with families to gather information to assess fit for an AAC system and coaching to support initial implementation. Project PANGEA, therefore, has shifted to a practical experience sequence with a greater focus on supporting early communicators both within the clinician-child interventions (e.g., JASPER) followed by assessment experiences (e.g., AAC experience) and then the BOOST preschool program experience.

Interdisciplinary teaming is one of four core competencies in Project PANGEA. The importance of course content explicitly reviewing teaming models and strategies for working as a member of a team has been reinforced by the pattern of strengths and challenges demonstrated by scholars in the first four program cohorts. The project team has revised this content each year based on scholar experiences to provide additional content as well as opportunities to put teaming skills to practice during PANGEA experiences. Although Project PANGEA was designed to provide scholars with information to understand the scope of practice of various disciplines (e.g., Foundation of EI/ECSE coursework, Language Disorders coursework, BOOST teaming), it became clear that more explicit instruction is required to support systematic connection of those materials, especially when considering the areas of overlap between different specialties and collaborating between generalist practitioners (e.g., ECSE providers) and specialist providers (SLPs, Board Certified Behavior Analysts, etc.). Providing explicit examples, guided discussions, and opportunities for group problem solving have been helpful in supporting scholars to understand areas of overlap and divergence between speech-language pathologist and early interventionist roles. Given that PANGEA scholars are likely to enter early career placements that utilize interdisciplinary teaming, maximizing opportunities for them to understand their roles and responsibilities and strategies for consultation and collaboration are vital to creating effective practitioners.

In addition to improving scholars' understanding of interdisciplinary teaming models, PANGEA scholars have required guidance in navigating interpersonal aspects of working on teams. During the BOOST curriculum planning seminar, PANGEA scholars are split into mixed groups of CDS and EI/ECSE majors and meet weekly outside of class to plan the BOOST program. Feedback and performance from scholars during this course have demonstrated a need to address soft skills related to successful professional practice more overtly. Skills the project team has observed a need to emphasize include time management, critical thinking, conflict resolution, and accountability. Activities to promote the use of these skills are incorporated into PANGEA seminars. In future interdisciplinary pre-service programming, embedding explicit instruction and expectations for these skills during the planning stages may help to develop critical soft skills for scholars entering the field.

When addressing each of these areas of personnel development, the PANGEA project team noted the value of balancing support with space for scholars to learn through experience. Finding an appropriate balance proved to be a challenge and requires adjustment based on each cohort's needs. During coursework and seminars, support is provided in the form of templates, detailed rubrics, and real-world examples. During practical experiences, support is provided through modeling and in-person coaching. Project faculty and supervisors determine appropriate areas to pull back support to allow PANGEA scholars opportunities to increase independence and utilize self-reflection and problem-solving. Scholars are then supported in group discussions and written reflection assignments to identify what went well and what changes could be made to their practice to better serve clients. During practical experiences, particularly in the BOOST preschool program, the project team regularly re-evaluates when to provide direct support and when to allow for experiential learning. For example, when supporting BOOST preschoolers with regulation and engagement, the supervisors began with more intensive support (e.g., modeling), especially for moments of dysregulation including externalizing behaviors (e.g., throwing, self-injury) to support the children's success in the classroom. As scholars successfully took on strategy implementation, supervisors faded either to less intensive supports (e.g., verbal reminders, environmental supports) or no support when independent implementation occurred.

## Future Directions

The PANGEA project team has identified several areas of consideration for future interdisciplinary grants. First, is the personalization of learning targets for cohorts and individuals. Later PANGEA cohorts have been asked to identify, in both group and individual written reflections, the competency areas they feel are strengths and the areas they would like to grow more skills. This has been helpful in tailoring seminars and practical experiences to meet the needs of individual scholars. Second, is consideration of opportunities to include pre-service students in other specialties, such as school psychologists or behavior analysts. Practitioners working in early intervention will likely work on teams with many specialties, and opportunities to iron out scope of practice and team member responsibilities in a supported environment would provide benefit in preparing students for these settings. Lastly, community partnerships for PANGEA practicum experiences have taken place in clinic settings or in self-contained special education classrooms, rather than inclusive settings. While scholars develop skills that can be utilized in inclusive settings (e.g., clear and consistent classroom transitions, environmental supports for engagement, arranging opportunities for communication initiation), exploration of practicum opportunities in inclusive settings could be considered in future programs.

## CONCLUSION

Project PANGEA has provided one example for increasing explicit interdisciplinary opportunities in graduate pre-service programs. The project has successfully graduated four cohorts of scholars to date who are focused on supporting young children with high-intensity needs. The project has delivered coursework and practical experiences for future ECSE and SLP providers focused on providing evidence-based, developmentally appropriate and personalized instructional supports for young children with ASD, specifically those who are early communicators. This work has been conducted in the context of interdisciplinary teaming and collaboration which has demonstrated opportunities for learning and growth that push students to integrate the knowledge and skills from their programs to create meaningful programming for young children with ASD. This is a demanding task from which several challenges have arisen as scholars plan, test, and revise their team plans. Future interdisciplinary programs would benefit from addressing soft skills needed for working on teams, emphasizing teaming models and scopes of practice of various disciplines, and individualizing scholar learning targets specific to teaming.

## ACKNOWLEDGMENTS

This personnel preparation grant was supported by the Office of Special Education Programs at the U.S. Department of Education [OSEP: H325K180170, PI: Shire, Co-I: Patricelli.]. Project PANGEA activities were supported by past co-directors Dr. Heather Moore and Lori Hornfelt.

## REFERENCES

American Association for Employment in Education. (2021). *Educator supply and demand report 2020-2021*. [Data set]. AAEE.

American Psychiatric Association. (2013). *Diagnostic and statistical manual of mental disorders* (5th ed.).

American Speech-Language-Hearing Association. (2006). Guidelines for speech-language pathologists in diagnosis, assessment, and treatment of autism spectrum disorders across the lifespan. *ASHA*. https://www.asha.org/members/deskref-journal/deskref/default

Beukelman, D. R., & Mirenda, P. (2013). *Augmentative and alternative communication: Supporting children and adults with complex communication needs* (4th ed.). Paul H. Brookes Pub.

Billingsley, B., Bettini, E., & Jones, N. D. (2019). Supporting special education teacher induction through high-leverage practices. *Remedial and Special Education*, *40*(6), 365–379. doi:10.1177/0741932518816826

Billingsley, B. S., Griffin, C. C., Smith, S. J., Kamman, M., & Israel, M. (2009). *A review of teacher induction in special education: Research, practice, and technology solutions.* (NCIPP Doc. RS-1).

Bruder, M., & Dunst, C. (2005). Personnel preparation in recommended early intervention practices: Degree of emphasis across disciplines. *Topics in Early Childhood Special Education*, *25*(1), 25–33. doi:10.1177/02711214050250010301

Bruder, M. B., Catalino, T., Chiarello, L. A., Cox Mitchell, M., Deppe, J., & Gundler, D. (2019). Finding a common lens: Competencies across professional disciplines providing early childhood intervention. *Infants and Young Children*, *32*(4), 280–293. doi:10.1097/IYC.0000000000000153

Bruder, M. B., Mogro-Wilson, C. M., Stayton, V. D., & Dietrich, S. L. (2009). The national status of in-service professional development systems for early intervention and early childhood special education practitioners. *Infants and Young Children*, *22*(1), 13–20. doi:10.1097/01.IYC.0000343333.49775.f8

Chang, Y., & Locke, J. (2016). A systematic review of peer-mediated interventions for children with autism spectrum disorder. *Research in Autism Spectrum Disorders*, *27*, 1–10. doi:10.1016/j.rasd.2016.03.010 PMID:27807466

Chang, Y., & Shire, S. (2020). Promoting play in early childhood programs for children with ASD: Strategies for educators and practitioners. *Teaching Exceptional Children*, *52*(2), 66–76. doi:10.1177/0040059919874305

Council for Clinical Certification in Audiology and Speech-Language Pathology of the American Speech Language Hearing Association. (2018). 2020 standards for the certificate of clinical competence in speech-language pathology. *ASHA*. www.asha.org/certification/2020-slp-certification-standards

Council for Exceptional Children (CEC). (2015). What every special educator must know: Professional ethics and standards. *CEC*.

Council for Exceptional Children (CEC). (2020). *Shortages of Special Education Teachers and Early Intervention Providers: Issue Brief.* Special Education Legislative Summit. https://exceptionalchildren.org/sites/default/files/2020-07/2020-TeacherShortageBrief.pdf

Courchesne, V., Tesfaye, R., Mirenda, P., Nicholas, D., Mitchell, W., Singh, I., Zwaigenbaum, L., & Elsabbagh, M. (2022). Autism Voices: A novel method to access first-person perspective of autistic youth. *Autism*, *26*(5), 1123–1136. doi:10.1177/13623613211042128 PMID:34482746

Dingfelder, H. E., & Mandell, D. S. (2011). Bridging the research-to-practice gap in autism intervention: An application of diffusion of innovation theory. *Journal of Autism and Developmental Disorders*, *41*(5), 597–609. doi:10.100710803-010-1081-0 PMID:20717714

Division for Early Childhood. (2014). DEC recommended practices in early intervention/early childhood special education 2014. *DEC*. http://www.dec-sped.org/recommendedpractices

Ferndandes, P. R. S., Jardim, J., & Lopes, M. C. S. (2021). The soft skills of special education teachers: Evidence from the literature. *Education Sciences*, *11*(3), 125. doi:10.3390/educsci11030125

Francois, J. R., Coufal, K. L., & Subramanian, A. (2015). Student preparation for professional practice in early intervention. *Communication Disorders Quarterly*, *36*(3), 177–186. doi:10.1177/1525740114543349

Ganz, J. B., Earles-Vollrath, T. L., Heath, A. K., Parker, R. I., Rispoli, M. J., & Duran, J. B. (2012). A Meta-Analysis of Single Case Research Studies on Aided Augmentative and Alternative Communication Systems with Individuals with Autism Spectrum Disorders. [ERIC.]. *Journal of Autism and Developmental Disorders*, *42*(1), 60–74. doi:10.100710803-011-1212-2 PMID:21380612

Guralnick, M. (2011). Why early intervention works: A systems perspective. *Infants and Young Children*, *24*(1), 6–28. doi:10.1097/IYC.0b013e3182002cfe PMID:21532932

Individuals with Disabilities Education Act, 20 U.S.C. § 1400 (2004).

Kasari, C., Gulsrud, A. C., Shire, S. Y., & Strawbridge, C. (2021). *The JASPER model for children with autism: Promoting joint attention, symbolic play, engagement, and regulation.* The Guilford Press.

Kasari, C., Lawton, K., Shih, W., Barker, T. V., Landa, R., Lord, C., Orlich, F., King, B., Wetherby, A., & Senturk, D. (2014). Caregiver-mediated intervention for low-resourced preschoolers with autism: An RCT. *Pediatrics*, *134*(1), e72–e79. doi:10.1542/peds.2013-3229 PMID:24958585

Maenner, M. J., Shaw, K. A., Bakian, A. V., Bilder, D. A., Durkin, M. S., Esler, A., Furnier, S. M., Hallas, L., Hall-Lande, J., Hudson, A., Hughes, M. M., Patrick, M., Pierce, K., Poynter, J. N., Salinas, A., Shenouda, J., Vehorn, A., Warren, Z., Constantino, J. N., DiRienzo, M., ... Cogswell, M. E. (2021). Prevalence and Characteristics of Autism Spectrum Disorder Among Children Aged 8 Years - Autism and Developmental Disabilities Monitoring Network, 11 Sites, United States, 2018. *Morbidity and mortality weekly report. Surveillance summaries (Washington, D.C.: 2002), 70*(11), 1–16. doi:10.15585/mmwr.ss7011a1

Masi, A., DeMayo, M. M., Glozier, N., & Guastella, A. J. (2017). An Overview of Autism Spectrum Disorder, Heterogeneity and Treatment Options. *Neuroscience Bulletin, 33*(2), 183–193. doi:10.100712264-017-0100-y PMID:28213805

Minuchin, S. (1974). *Families and Family Therapy*. Harvard University Press. doi:10.4159/9780674041127

Ruppar, A. L., Neeper, L. S., & Dalsen, J. (2016). Special education teachers' preparedness to teach students with severe disabilities. *Research and Practice for Persons with Severe Disabilities, 41*(4), 273–286. doi:10.1177/1540796916672843

Sameroff, A. (2009). The transactional model. In A. Sameroff (Ed.), *The transactional model of development: How children and contexts shape each other* (pp. 3–21). American Psychological Association. doi:10.1037/11877-001

Shaw, K. A., Maenner, M. J., Bakian, A. V., Bilder, D. A., Durkin, M. S., Furnier, S. M., Hughes, M. M., Patrick, M., Pierce, K., Salinas, A., Shenouda, J., Vehorn, A., Warren, Z., Zahorodny, W., Constantino, J. N., DiRienzo, M., Esler, A., Fitzgerald, R. T., Grzybowski, A., Hudson, A., & Cogswell, M. E. (2021). Early Identification of Autism Spectrum Disorder Among Children Aged 4 Years - Autism and Developmental Disabilities Monitoring Network, 11 Sites, United States, 2018. *Morbidity and mortality weekly report. Surveillance summaries (Washington, D.C.: 2002), 70*(10), 1–14. doi:10.15585/mmwr.ss7010a1

Shire, S. Y., Shih, W., & Kasari, C. (2018). Brief report: Caregiver strategy implementation—advancing spoken communication in children who are minimally verbal. *Journal of Autism and Developmental Disorders, 48*(4), 1228–1234. doi:10.100710803-017-3454-0 PMID:29313178

Sopko, K. (2010). *Workforce preparation to serve children who receive part C services: Brief Policy Analysis*. Project Forum at National Association of School of State Directors of Special Education. https://www.yumpu.com/en/document/view/37973326/here-national-association-of-state-directors-of-special-education

Tager-Flusberg, H., & Kasari, C. (2013). Minimally verbal school-aged children with autism spectrum disorder: The neglected end of the spectrum. *Autism Research, 6*(6), 468–478. doi:10.1002/aur.1329 PMID:24124067

U.S. Department of Education. OSERS. (2022, March 28). About OSEP. *OSEP.* https://www2.ed.gov/about/offices/list/osers/osep/about.html

## KEY TERMS AND DEFINITIONS

**Autism Spectrum Disorder:** Autism Spectrum Disorder (ASD) refers to a group of disorders characterized by deficits in social communication and interaction, and restricted interests and repetitive behaviors.

**Early Intervention/Early Childhood Special Education:** Early Intervention/Early Childhood Special Education (EI/ECSE) provides support for infants, toddlers and preschool-age children with special needs and their families.

**Office of Special Education Programs:** The Office of Special Education Programs (OSEP) is within the U.S. Department of Education. It focuses on improving educational outcomes for people with disabilities ages birth through 21.

**Preverbal:** Refers to young children who are not yet using spoken language to communicate. Preverbal children may utilize gestures, vocalizations, and eye gaze instead of spoken words to communicate.

**Regulation:** A process of adjusting behaviors to given situations.

**Social Communication:** Social communication includes the use of both verbal and nonverbal communication directed at a communication partner to share and/or request.

**Social engagement:** A state of active participation in a shared activity with others.

**Speech-Language Pathologists (SLP):** Specialists who treat speech, language and/or related problems.

**Transactional Model of Child Development:** A model explaining that child development is a result of bi-directional interactions between a child and their environment.

# Chapter 7
# Interdisciplinary Training in Special Education and Behavior Analysis to Meet the Needs of Students With Autism Spectrum Disorder

**Kate B. LaLonde**
https://orcid.org/0000-0002-9161-765X
*Western Michigan University, USA*

**Kristal E. Ehrhardt**
*Western Michigan University, USA*

**Sarah Summy**
*Western Michigan University, USA*

**Stephanie Peterson**
*Western Michigan University, USA*

**Rena VanDerwall**
*Western Michigan University, USA*

**Alan Poling**
*Western Michigan University, USA*

## ABSTRACT

*This chapter describes the value of providing interdisciplinary graduate training in special education and behavior analysis to prepare professionals to meet the high intensity needs of students with autism spectrum disorder (ASD). Within the chapter, we provide a detailed description of the development, goals, and implementation of a master's-level interdisciplinary training program. The program was developed by special education and behavior analysis faculty at Western Michigan University (WMU). Scholars admitted into the program obtained a master's degree in special education or behavior analysis and met the requirements to become a Board Certified Behavior Analyst (BCBA). Special education scholars also met the requirements for a teaching endorsement in ASD. The program was supported by a personnel preparation grant funded by the Department of Education, Office of Special Education Programs (OSEP; Ehrhardt et al., 2017) and directed by Kristal Ehrhardt.*

DOI: 10.4018/978-1-6684-6438-0.ch007

## THE NEED FOR INTERDISCIPLINARY TRAINING IN SPECIAL EDUCATION AND BEHAVIOR ANALYSIS

Currently, the United States is experiencing a concerning convergence in special education services for students with autism spectrum disorder (ASD); teacher attrition is increasing at a rate parallel to the increasing rate of students with disabilities. Forty-nine states and the District of Columbia report shortages of special educators (U.S. Department of Education, 2022). The special educator shortage has resulted in some states using long-term substitutes for special education teachers, most of whom have *no* teacher training and some only have a high school diploma (HECSE, 2021). As teacher attrition increases, so does the number of students with ASD entering public school (U.S. Department of Education, 2020). In 2020-21, ASD was the fourth-most prevalent disability category for students aged 6 through 21 years served under IDEA, Part B, accounting for 12% of all students served (National Center for Education Statistics, 2022). Unfortunately, the multi-faceted problem of the special education teacher shortage negatively affects outcomes for students (CEEDAR Center, 2020).

Given the severity of the special education teacher shortage across the country, federal-level solutions are needed. One federal-level strategy for addressing the special education teacher shortage is the Office of Special Education Programs (OSEP) Personnel Development to Improve Services and Results for Children with Disabilities program (PDP). The PDP supports personnel preparation and professional development of qualified personnel to work with infants or toddlers with disabilities and to serve and support children with disabilities. The purpose of the PDP is to help address state-identified needs for qualified personnel and to ensure personnel have the necessary skills and knowledge, derived from practices that have been determined through scientifically based research and experience, to be successful in serving those children. There are three types of PDP investments; one of these grants, *325K: Interdisciplinary Approaches to Preparation of Special Education, Early Intervention, and Related Services Personnel Serving Children with Disabilities who Have High-Intensity Needs*, provides funding for master's-level training. To qualify for the funding, a preparation program must be an interdisciplinary collaboration between two or more disciplines.

The interdisciplinary training program described in this chapter was possible, in part, because of OSEP PDP funding. Western Michigan University received PDP funding to develop and implement an interdisciplinary training program designed to increase the number of qualified personnel available to meet the unique and intense needs of students with ASD. The high intensity needs of children with ASD often arise because they exhibit challenging behaviors that are not part of the defining features of the disorder, as well as the kinds of behavioral excesses and deficits required for the diagnosis (Heute et al., 2014). Students with ASD are characterized by restricted and repetitive behaviors/interests and impairments in social communication (American Psychiatric Association; DSM-5) and have increased susceptibility to emotional and behavioral difficulties, including anxiety emotional dysregulation, inattention, and disruptive behaviors (Baker & Blacher, 2019; Leyfer et al., 2006; Samson et al., 2014). These behavioral excesses and deficits pose unique challenges in educational settings. Teachers report that the greatest challenges of instructing students with autism are behavior difficulties and inappropriate social skills (Teffs & Whitbread, 2009). Additionally, students with ASD can demonstrate deficits in observational learning (Townley-Cochran et al., 2015), which hinders their passive learning. Because of these characteristics of students with ASD, teachers must use specialized, evidence-based practices (EBPs) to serve them effectively (Scheurmann et al., 2003).

*Table 1. Interdisciplinary Preparation in Autism Project Goals*

| Goal |
| --- |
| 1. Develop and implement an interdisciplinary program in which the Special Education and Behavior Analysis faculty at WMU work together to increase the number of competent and credentialed professionals available to use evidence-based practices (EBP) in meeting the high intensity needs of students with autism spectrum disorder (ASD). |
| 2. Recruit, admit, prepare, and graduate 24 scholars, 12 with a master's degree in special education and a teaching endorsement in ASD and 12 with a master's degree in behavior analysis and expertise in providing school-based services, all prepared to take the Behavior Analysis Certification Board certification examination. |
| 3. Establish and implement a collaborative induction program to support program graduates and their employing agencies. |

Fortunately, a substantial number of EBPs for addressing the high-intensity needs of students with ASD have been developed and evaluated. Most EBPs that meet these needs are based on the principles of applied behavior analysis (ABA; Steinbrenner, 2020). Table 1 provides a list of the 27 EBPs for individuals with ASD that professional organizations have identified. There is general agreement that teacher preparation programs should emphasize EBPs (Scheeler et al., 2016), but research indicates that fewer than 10% of the strategies used in school-based programs with students with ASD are based on scientifically based practices (Locke et al., 2019). Teachers' failure to use EBPs negatively affects students' educational achievement (Ouellette et al., 2019), can lead to student regression (Barnhill et al., 2011), and increases teacher burnout (Ouellette et al., 2019). General and special education teachers often report apprehension and a lack of confidence when students with ASD are included in their classrooms (Anglim et al., 2017), which results in increased stress and feelings of inadequacy — factors associated with teacher attrition (Billingsley & Bettini, 2019; Ouellette et al., 2019). Providing special education teachers with targeted training in behavior analysis and effective instruction is an obvious way to increase the likelihood of them staying in the field and succeeding in their efforts to instruct students with ASD and other disabilities.

## Special Education Services for Students with ASD

Once a student with ASD has been identified as having a disability and is eligible for special education services, a multidisciplinary team collaborates with the student's family to develop an individual education plan (IEP). To ensure the IEP is carried out effectively, the "IEP team must develop an IEP calculated to enable a student to make academic and/or functional progress that is appropriate considering the student's capabilities" (Yell & Katsiyannis, 2019, p. 314). This means that IEP teams need to focus on the components of an IEP that will demonstrate that a student is making progress, including conducting assessments, developing ambitious and measurable IEP goals, using data-based progress monitoring systems, collecting, and reacting to data (e.g., engaging in data-based decision making) (Yell & Bateman, 2018). Although special education teacher preparation programs commonly include instruction on using assessment data to develop ambitious and realistic IEP goals, reports indicate that coursework in assessment, EBPs for students with ASD, and data literacy is sporadic, embedded into existing courses, or only offered at the graduate level (e.g., Wagner et al., 2017; DeLuca & Klinger, 2010; Chesley & Jordan, 2012). Therefore, it is probable that special educators instructing students with ASD will have little, or perhaps no formal training in data collection, graphing, or data-based instructional decision making. The research on instructing teachers in reading and interpreting academic data (e.g., curriculum-based measurement) is limited and effective interventions for instructing teachers how to do so are surprisingly unknown (Wagner et al., 2017).

## Behavior Analysts in Schools

Applied behavior analysis graduate students are trained to use EBPs, and school districts are increasingly seeking BCBAs to help meet the high-intensity needs of students with ASD and other disabilities (Shepley & Grisham-Brown, 2018). The Behavior Analysis Certification Board (BACB) reports that 12.46% of BCBAs are working in education, second only to those working with individuals with ASD. The role of school-based BCBAs is multidimensional and specific roles and responsibilities depend on the setting (e.g., early childhood, elementary, secondary classrooms, center-based programs), the specific needs of a district or school, and the funding source (Shepley & Grisham-Brown, 2018). School-based BCBAs may struggle to identify their specific roles and responsibilities because of vague job descriptions, being the only BCBA employed by a district or school, and lack of experience working in educational settings (Layden, 2022). Although federal-level policies (e.g., Individuals with Disabilities Education Act Amendments of 2004 [IDEA]) have mandated the use of behavior analytic practices (e.g., Functional Behavioral Assessments) in schools for students with disabilities, research indicates that behavior analysts frequently have difficulty working effectively in schools. Some of these barriers include BCBAs lacking familiarity with foundational elements of special education (e.g., cornerstone laws, individual educational planning, academic assessment, curriculum development, job demands faced by teachers), lack of experience working as part of an educational team, and their use of behavior-analytic jargon (Critchfield et al., 2017). Schools are unique and complex environments that require specialized skills and knowledge that are typically not included in behavior-analytic graduate training programs (Brodhead, 2015; Layden, 2022).

School-based BCBAs will be members of multi- and interdisciplinary groups and should understand the roles and responsibilities of other members of that team (e.g., speech pathologists, paraprofessionals, school social workers, and special education teachers). They also should be familiar with Multi-tiered Systems of Support (MTSS), Positive Behavior Intervention and Support (PBIS), and Individualized Education Plan (IEP) teams (Giangreco et al., 2021). However, it is highly probable that many behavior analysts will not receive systematic instruction in several areas of special education. To become a BCBA, individuals must complete coursework from a college or university with an ABAI Verified Course Sequence (VCS). To establish a VCS, a training program must demonstrate how its coursework aligns with the Behavior Analyst Certification Board BCBA Task List. The BCBA Task List does not include knowledge or skills on educational assessment (e.g., curriculum-based measurement), MTSS, PBIS, or IEPs (Behavior Analyst Certification Board, 2017; Giangreco et al., 2021). Although it is tenable that behavior-analytic graduate training programs include instruction on these topics, it is highly probable that students do not graduate with a breadth of knowledge or skills in this area (unless they attended a training program within a special education department).

## The Need for Interdisciplinary Training in Special Education and Behavior Analysis

Many ongoing issues within special education call for preparing special education teachers and behavior analysts together. When students with ASD are included in educational settings, teachers often lack the knowledge and skills necessary to effectively instruct and manage behavior (e.g., Lindsay et al., 2013; Anglim et al., 2017), which unfortunately can lead to students not achieving education outcomes (Yell & Katsiyannis, 2019), teacher attrition and burnout (Ouellette et al., 2019), and ligation (Katsiyannis et al., 2016). An overview of special education litigation in 2015 found that ASD was the most litigated disability category (Katsiyannis et al., 2016). Special educators commonly do not receive instruction on how to use evidence-based strategies for students with ASD (Locke et al., 2019) or how to evaluate intervention effectiveness using student data (Wagner et al., 2017). In fact, in some cases, implementing interventions based on applied behavior analysis is discouraged by stakeholders unfamiliar with the full scope of these interventions (Pennington, 2022). Conversely, behavior analysts are trained to implement and evaluate evidence-based interventions but do not commonly receive systematic instruction in educational systems, including MTSS, PBIS, or IEPs (Giangreco et al., 2021). Special education and applied behavior analysis preparation programs are often siloed, which leads to graduates entering the field with a specialized skill set with little to no formal training in specific skills needed to collaborate on education teams (i.e., MTSS, PBIS, and IEP teams) (Giangreco et al., 2021; Brodhead, 2015). To demonstrate this disconnect, of the 24 Association of Behavior Analysis Intervention (ABAI)-accredited master's programs in the United States, only four programs are housed within special education colleges, include general or special education in their program description, or mention field experiences in educational settings (Association of Behavior Analysis Intervention, 2022).

There are economic costs associated with special education teachers and school-based BCBAs being inadequately prepared to collaborate to meet the high-intensity needs of students with ASD. Educators who feel inadequate in their positions often leave the field, which undermines student achievement in literacy and math, hurts the overall effectiveness of teachers in schools, and consumes valuable staff time and resources. Urban and rural schools are affected most by inadequate training and teacher attrition, and these schools frequently cannot fill their vacancies, resulting in the most vulnerable students being taught by unqualified teachers (Mason-Williams et al., 2017). Carver-Thomas & Darling-Hammond (2017) estimate the cost of one teacher leaving the field to be $20,000, and older estimates place the national cost of new teacher turnover at $2.2 billion per year (Alliance for Excellent, 2014), which likely has increased substantially.

In recent years, there has been a call to action for behavior analysis training programs to include explicit instruction on collaboration skills (Boivin et al., 2021; Brodhead 2015; Shepley et al., 2017). Professional collaboration is more than simply working on a shared student case with other educators and practitioners. In the context of education, collaboration includes working directly with at least one other person towards a mutual goal and can be defined as a cooperative process among members of a team, requiring trust and respect, clearly defined and equitable roles with shared responsibilities, commitment, and accountability among all members (Bock et al., 2011). Collaboration also requires group members to have knowledge of their own, as well as other team members', roles, including their general training, experience, and professional scope of practice (Boivin et al., 2015; Brodhead, 2015). In school settings, collaboration is not an option but rather an expectation (Bock et al., 2011). Therefore, behavior-analytic training programs should explicitly train scholars to be effective and collaborative team members in education settings, including members of MTSS, PBIS and IEP teams. It is promising that behavior analysts are discussing the need for interdisciplinary training because studies indicate that behavior-analytic coursework has not provided adequate training in the application of behavior analytic interventions in educational settings (Schreck et al., 2016; Schreck & Mazur, 2008). A good case can certainly be made that the best place to learn about educating children with ASD is a special education graduate program. Moreover, interdisciplinary training, which is intended to give trainees "a common core of knowledge and skills while having discipline-specific expertise" (Stayton & Bruder, 1999, p. 64) is a recommended and effective practice in many areas, including early childhood special education (DEC, 2014; Mickelson et al., 2021).

## BUILDING AN INTERDISCIPLINARY PROGRAM

Faculty from two colleges at Western Michigan University collaborated to develop and implement an interdisciplinary training program to prepare teachers and behavior analysts to work together to meet the high-intensity needs of students with ASD. In the sections below, the authors present the conceptual framework, goals of the interdisciplinary project, outcomes, and reflections on the project. The authors hope that faculty from typically siloed colleges and/or departments can use the detailed description of the project as a blueprint to develop and implement interdisciplinary programs to meet the needs of high-intensity special education students. The interdisciplinary training program described includes special education and behavior analysis, but a similar framework could be used by various fields including speech-language pathology, adaptive physical education, counseling, and social work, to name a few.

### Developing a Conceptual Framework and Project Goals

To begin, the faculty had to determine the goals of the interdisciplinary training program. Three goals, provided in Table 2, were selected. The faculty then developed a conceptual framework for the project that was appropriate for pursuing those goals. Figure 1 depicts that conceptual framework. It comprised six components: 1) interdisciplinary core coursework, 2) competency-based coursework and field experiences, 3) scholars implementing and evaluating EBPs with students with ASD, 4) interdisciplinary projects, 5) activities that resulted in scholars meeting the certification requirements to become a BCBA (all scholars) and an ASD teacher (special education scholars only), and 6) an induction program. By having meaningful experiences across the six program components, graduates of the program would be trained to be effective school personnel able to meet the high-intensity needs of students with ASD. Figure 2 depicts the sequence of activities completed over the five-year funding period as scholars were exposed to the six components of the conceptual framework.

### Aligning Professional Competencies Across Disciplines

To maximally benefit students with ASD, special educators and behavior analysts should attain general competency in (a) applied behavior analysis, (b) EBPs that benefit students with ASD, (c) collaboration within interdisciplinary teams (e.g., MTSS, PBIS, and IEP teams), (d) data-driven decision-making, (e) coaching and supervision of teachers and paraeducators, and (f) professional self-care skills. They also should become experts in utilizing the 27 EBPs recognized by the National Clearinghouse on Autism Evidence & Practice (NPDC; Steinbrenner et al., 2020).

To develop an interdisciplinary graduate training program in special education and behavior analysis, the faculty had to consider the professional standards and competencies across the two disciplines. To obtain the ASD teaching endorsement, special education scholars need to demonstrate competencies listed in the CEC Advanced Specialty Set: Special Education Developmental Disabilities and Autism

*Figure 1. Interdisciplinary in Autism Project Conceptional Framework*

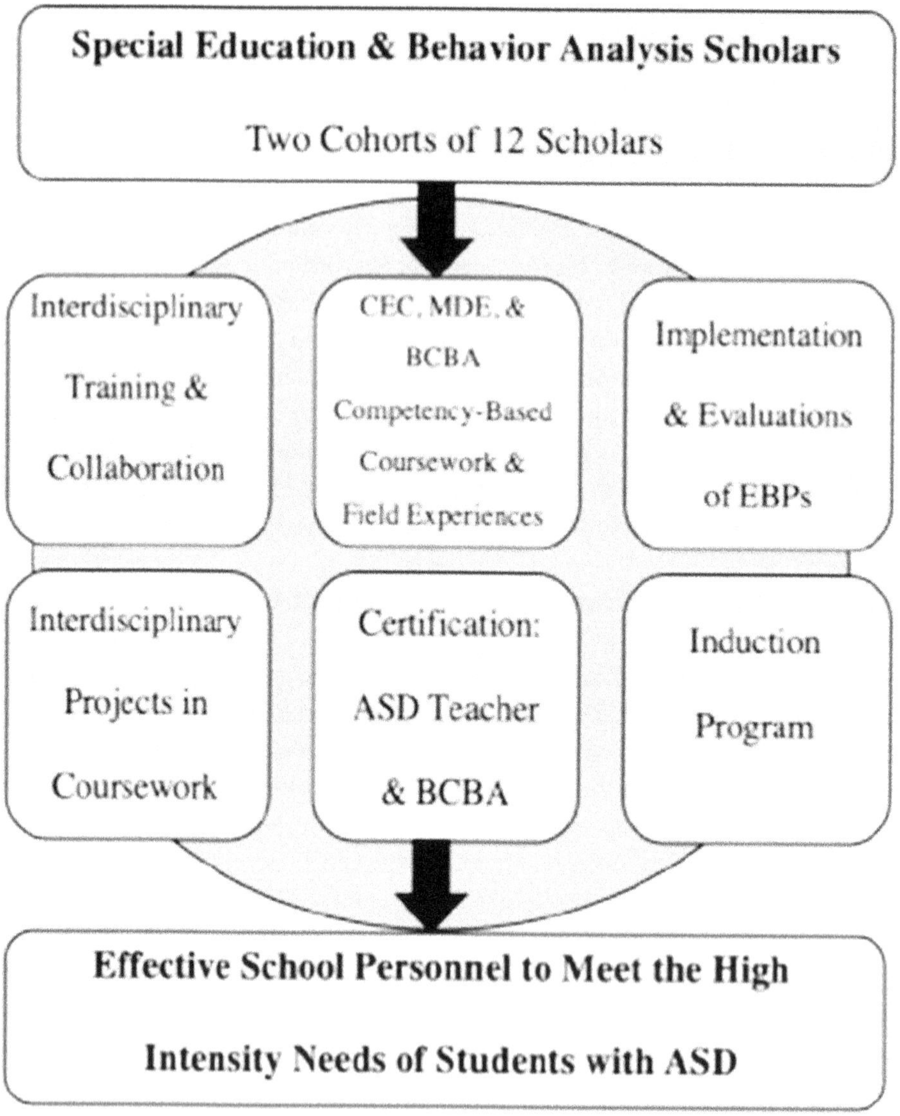

```
┌─────────────────────────────────────────────────┐
│   Special Education & Behavior Analysis Scholars │
│            Two Cohorts of 12 Scholars            │
└─────────────────────────────────────────────────┘
                        ↓
┌──────────────┐  ┌──────────────┐  ┌──────────────┐
│Interdisciplinary│ │CEC, MDE, &  │ │Implementation│
│  Training &  │  │    BCBA      │  │ & Evaluations│
│ Collaboration│  │Competency-Based│ │   of EBPs   │
│              │  │ Coursework & │  │              │
│              │  │Field Experiences│              │
└──────────────┘  └──────────────┘  └──────────────┘
┌──────────────┐  ┌──────────────┐  ┌──────────────┐
│Interdisciplinary│ │Certification:│ │  Induction  │
│  Projects in │  │ ASD Teacher  │  │   Program   │
│  Coursework  │  │    & BCBA    │  │              │
└──────────────┘  └──────────────┘  └──────────────┘
                        ↓
┌─────────────────────────────────────────────────┐
│  Effective School Personnel to Meet the High    │
│     Intensity Needs of Students with ASD        │
└─────────────────────────────────────────────────┘
```

Spectrum Disorder Specialist (CEC, 2015) and meet the state's requirements for the ASD endorsement, which includes coursework, various K-12 fieldwork experiences, and passing the Michigan Test for Teacher Certification (MTTC) in ASD. Similarly, to become a BCBA, scholars need to demonstrate the competencies listed in the BCBA Task List (5th ed.; BACB, 2017), complete specific coursework and supervised fieldwork and pass the BCBA examination.

It was important to determine the degree to which special education scholars needed to master the behavior analytic competencies (beyond those required by the BACB) and the degree to which behavior analysis scholars needed to demonstrate mastery of special education competencies (i.e., CEC standards). Ideally, there should be a great deal of overlap in the professional standards, but certainly

*Figure 2. The sequence of Activities Completed Across 5-year Project*

| Activity | Funding (April 2018) Sp | Year 1 (2018-19) Su | Year 1 F | Year 1 Sp | Year 2 (2019-20) Su | Year 2 F | Year 2 Sp | Year 3 (2020-21) Su | Year 3 F | Year 3 Sp | Year 4 (2021-22) Su | Year 4 F | Year 4 Sp | Year 5 (2022-23) Su | Year 5 F |
|---|---|---|---|---|---|---|---|---|---|---|---|---|---|---|---|
| Planning and development of program | x | x | x | | | | | | | | | | | | |
| Scholar recruitment | C1 | | | | | | C2 | | | | | | | | |
| Scholars complete coursework | | | | | C1 | | | | | | | | | | |
| | | | | | | | | | | C2 | | | | | |
| Scholars complete supervised fieldwork | | | | | C1 | | | | | | | | | | |
| | | | | | | | | | | C2 | | | | | |
| Scholars complete applied research | | | | | | | C1 | | | | | C2 | | | |
| Scholars graduate | | | | | | | | | C1 | | | | | | C2 |
| Scholars take MTTC | | | | | | | C1 | | | | | C2 | | | |
| Scholars take BCBA examination | | | | | | | | | C1 | | | | | C2 | |
| Faculty revise program based on data | | x | | x | x | | x | x | x | x | x | | | | |
| Generate Reports for OSEP | | | x | | x | | | x | | | | x | x | x | |

there is discipline-specific knowledge and skill that may not be necessary for all scholars to master. An interdisciplinary crosswalk of CEC and BCBA professional standards was created to guide the development of the various program components and is displayed in Figure 3.

*Table 2. Evidence-Based Practices for Individuals with ASD*

| Evidence-Based Practices ||
|---|---|
| Antecedent-Based Intervention | Prompting |
| Cognitive Behavioral Intervention | Reinforcement |
| Differential Reinforcement Procedures | Response Interruption/Redirection |
| Discrete Trial Training | Scripting |
| Exercise | Self-Management |
| Extinction | Social Narratives |
| Functional Behavior Assessment | Social Skills Training |
| Functional Communication Training | Structured Play Groups |
| Modeling | Task Analysis |
| Naturalistic Intervention | Technology-Aided Instruction |
| Parent-Implemented Intervention | Time Delay |
| Peer-Mediated Instruction and Intervention | Video Modeling |
| Picture Exchange Communication System | Visual Support |
| Pivotal Response Training | |

*Figure 3. BACB and CEC Competency Crosswalk*

|  |  | Behavior Analyst Certification Board Standards ||||||||
|---|---|---|---|---|---|---|---|---|---|
|  |  | Philosophical Underpinnings | Concepts & Principles | Measurement, Data Display & Interpretations | Experimental Design | Ethics | Behavioral Assessment | Behavior-Change Procedures (EBPs) | Selecting and Implementing Interventions | Personnel Supervision and Management |
| CEC Competencies | Assessment |  |  |  |  |  | X |  |  |  |
|  | Curricular Content Knowledge |  |  | X |  |  |  |  | X |  |
|  | Programs, Services & Outcomes |  |  |  |  |  |  | X | X |  |
|  | Research and Inquiry |  |  |  | X |  |  |  |  |  |
|  | Leadership and Policy |  |  |  |  |  |  |  |  | X |
|  | Professional & Ethical Practice |  |  |  |  | X |  |  |  | X |
|  | Collaboration |  |  |  |  |  |  |  |  | X |

Following the development of the interdisciplinary crosswalk of professional standards, faculty reviewed syllabi to identify the CEC and BACB standards covered in specific courses. The faculty discussed the extent and manner that each standard was covered in a course, which allowed faculty to determine an appropriate sequence of courses and determine which courses would be included in the core curriculum if two courses met the same professional standards. For example, each department's VCS included a course on behavior-change procedures (i.e., EBPs). The special education course focuses on the application of EBPs in school settings for students with ASD and the behavior analysis course focuses on the application of EBPs in clinical settings for a variety of disorders and disabilities.

In general, it was not hard to arrange courses that met the requirements of the standards of the two professions in which IPA students received training. However, there were some challenges. For instance, both behavior analysts and special educators need to be aware of and abide by standards of ethical conduct. The ethics code for behavior analysts (Behavior Analysis Certification Board, 2014; 2020) is lengthy, detailed, and prescriptive. The CEC (2015) ethics code promulgated for special education at that time is, in marked contrast, a one-page document that presents 12 general ethical principles. In addition to the substantial difference in these documents, ethical issues being discussed in the two disciplines in which IPA was in effect differed. The ethics course that IPA scholars were to take was offered in the psychology department and, therefore, could easily have been inappropriate for special education scholars. Fortunately, however, it was possible to arrange a special section of the course for IPA students, and the instructor was careful to target material relevant to both special education and behavior analysis. In the absence of external funding, however, such flexibility might well be impossible to achieve.

## Interdisciplinary Core Curriculum and Projects

Several strategies were used to increase opportunities for interdisciplinary collaboration and based on best practices in interdisciplinary training. The first strategy was to admit scholars into the program as cohorts, which creates a built-in community of support. Completing educational programs as a cohort has been shown to be a predictor of program completion, more so than gender, race, and first-generation student status (Bista & Cox, 2014). Social connections allow scholars to bond with each other to ac-

*Table 3. Interdisciplinary Core Coursework*

| Interdisciplinary Core | |
|---|---|
| SPED 5300: *Introduction to Special Education* | SPED 6370: *Single Subject Research in ABA* |
| PSY 6100: *Conditioning and Learning* | SPED 6391: *Instructional Practices in Schools Settings for Students with Autism* |
| SPED 6380: *Applications of Behavior Analysis in Special Education* | PSY 6270: *Supervision and ABA* |
| PSY 6260: *Behavioral Assessment* | PSY 6050: *Professional and Ethical Issues in Psychology* |
| SPED 6390: *Evidence Based Instructional Practices: Autism* | |

complish a common goal, such as completing their degree program. IPA scholars had two built-in communities of support; the interdisciplinary cohort that encompassed scholars from both departments and a smaller discipline-specific cohort. The interdisciplinary cohort completed a set of courses, called the interdisciplinary core curriculum, together. Table 3 lists the interdisciplinary core curriculum. The shared coursework focused on 1) theoretical underpinnings of applied behavior analysis in special education and applied behavior analysis, 2) evidence-based assessment, 3) evidence-based instructional practices with an emphasis on the application of these practices in school settings, 4) applications of research in special education and; 5) ethics and supervision and ABA.

Interdisciplinary projects were embedded within the core curriculum. The aim of these projects was to increase collaboration when selecting, implementing, and evaluating EBPs for students with ASD. In many ways, these assignments mimicked how professionals collaborate as members of IEP teams. For example, in *SPED 6390 and SPED 6391*, scholars collaborated in small interdisciplinary groups to complete case studies that included selecting appropriate assessments, generating student learning targets from assessments, drafting an instructional lesson plan that included EBPs, and developing data collection procedures. Scholars completed assignments individually and as small groups and, in both cases, had time to provide each other with feedback on their projects, including the feasibility of the intervention and data collection procedures in a school setting, the jargon used within the instructional program, and whether the plan aligned with the 27 EBPs for students with ASD. Another interdisciplinary project included scholars working together to develop professional development training on specific EBPs (e.g., prompting, visual supports, token economies). Scholars developed a behavioral skills training (BST) intended for general and special education teachers and support staff (e.g., paraprofessionals). Scholars first presented the BST to the class and received peer and instructor feedback and subsequently presented the BST to personnel in their field placements, increasing the use of EBPs in schools. Each group uploaded their training materials to a shared folder so they could be used in the future.

## Supervised Fieldwork

A major component of the interdisciplinary program was intensive school-based fieldwork experiences. These experiences included competencies for the two certifications (i.e., BCBA and ASD endorsement). All special education scholars were employed full-time and completed most of the fieldwork in their classrooms, which included early childhood, elementary and secondary special education or general education classrooms, or center-based programs. When possible, behavior analysis students completed their supervised hours in an IPA special education teacher's classroom or in special education settings in which faculty had established partnerships. Activities they performed included implementing behavior change procedures with students, attending individual and group supervision meetings, and completing all necessary paperwork to document these activities.

## Applied Research to Improve Outcomes for Students with ASD

To meet the requirements for a master's degree, scholars in each department completed a capstone (special education) or thesis (behavior analysis) project. Scholars designed and implemented a single-case research study. The independent variable was one of the EBPs they learned about in their coursework. Each study focused on improving educational outcomes for students with ASD or evaluating staff training procedures to increase the fidelity of EBPs implemented by school personnel (e.g., paraprofessionals).

## Professional Development Activities

Professional Development Activities were developed that addressed current issues in special education and behavior analysis and provided additional opportunities for interdisciplinary collaboration and social connectedness. These activities were designed to broaden the knowledge base of scholars by addressing topics highly relevant to, but not emphasized in, the program. These activities included a speaker series that featured distinguished university or community members who work in the field of ASD. The speaker series included special education administrators, university faculty with expertise in ASD, and a panel of ASD practitioners and family members of students with ASD. Other professional development activities included visits to education settings to highlight various applications of behavior analytic intervention for students with ASD. One visit was to a center-based program that utilized an interdisciplinary team focused on implementing behavior analytic interventions. The second visit was to a private ASD center that provided 1:1 behavior analytic service to clients with ASD, offered family training, and collaborated with the client's IEP teams. During the visits, scholars discussed diverse topics with a panel of professionals. Lastly, a handful of social events were hosted by IPA faculty, including program barbeques and informal dinners before evening classes.

## RECRUITING AND RETAINING DIVERSE SCHOLARS

There has been an increase in the number of culturally diverse students receiving special education services. For example, the prevalence of Hispanic and Black students with ASD has increased over the last two decades (Nevison & Zahorodny, 2019). As the K-12 student population grows more diverse, the teaching force remains largely White and female. Data from the National Center for Education Statistics (NCES, 2022) show that White teachers made up 79% of the total K–12 teaching workforce in public elementary and secondary schools during the 2017-2018 school year whereas 9% were Hispanic and 7% were Black. The field of behavior analysis also lacks diversity. Only recently has the BACB started collecting and reporting data on the race and ethnicity of BCBAs. As of January 2022, 70% of BCBAs and BCBA-Ds were White and 85% were female (BACB, 2022).

Increasing diversity in these fields has important implications for students' academic and social-emotional outcomes. Decades of research highlight countless inequalities that certain groups of students encounter in educational settings. For example, White children with higher socioeconomic status are more often diagnosed with ASD at an early age than children who are Black, Latino, Asian, or from lower-income families, and therefore are more likely to receive valuable early autism-specific intervention services (Wiggins et al., 2020). Nonetheless, overall, White children from wealthy families are less likely to receive special education services. The term *significant disproportionality* describes the increased likelihood of students from certain racial and ethnic groups (e.g., students of color, English Language Learners) receiving special education, being placed in more restrictive educational settings, and being disciplined at markedly higher rates than White students (National Center for Learning Disabilities, 2020).

Diversifying the fields of special education and behavior analysis can mitigate these inequalities and can have a positive effect on all students. For example, teachers of color can improve the academic performance of students of color by as much as 3 to 6 percentile points compared to students without such teachers (Dee, 2004). There are also social-emotional benefits to having a more diverse teaching force, especially for males of color who are more likely to be chronically absent, suspended, or expelled if they have a White teacher compared to a Black teacher (Lindsay, 2016).

Professionals in education and behavior analysis have issued a call to action to diversify the fields and ensure that teachers and behavior analysts are culturally competent (e.g., Carter Andrews et al., 2019). Conners and colleagues (2019) surveyed BCBAs to assess whether their graduate training included content on providing ABA services to clients/students of different racial and ethnic backgrounds, religious and spiritual backgrounds, and sexual orientations, and found that fewer than 50% of respondents indicated they received training in these areas. Recommendations for developing culturally responsive curricula and training for behavior analysts are just starting to emerge (Mathur & Rodriguez, 2021).

Although it is beyond the scope of the current chapter to examine the multitude of systemic barriers that hinder diversifying the fields of education and behavior analysis, it is important to consider these barriers when planning an interdisciplinary training program. College students of color are less likely to enroll in teacher preparation programs than their White peers, even though overall college enrollment for students of color has increased over the past two decades (NCES, 2020). People of color encounter unique barriers when deciding to enter and stay in the teaching field (Carver-Thomas, 2017). These barriers include perceptions of student loan debt relative to a teaching salary (Rothstein & Rouse, 2011), financial burdens and responsibilities that limit the number of classes students of color can take each semester and delay program completion (Santos & Haycock, 2016), and dissatisfaction with lack of faculty diversity (Osler, 2016). It is probable that students of color face these same barriers when considering behavior analysis as a field of study.

## Recruitment and Retention Strategies

When planning recruitment and retention strategies, IPA faculty considered the barriers mentioned above and implemented five strategies shown to attract candidates from groups historically underrepresented based on race, color, national origin, gender, age, or disability (Podolsky et al., 2019; Hart-Baldridge, 2020). **First**, students received funding because of the OSEP training grant. Stipends have been shown to be necessary to recruit, retain, and graduate members of groups that have traditionally been under-represented (Banks & Doly, 2019).

**Second**, scholars received consistent and appropriate advising. Quality advising is considered one of the most crucial aspects of a scholar's interaction and engagement with university faculty and plays an important role in retention (Podolsky et al., 2019). Social support for scholars through advising and mentoring can enhance retention and program completion; this is especially true for at-risk groups including first-generation and low-income students who lack other resources for dealing with the challenges of completing advanced degrees (Hart-Baldridge, 2020). All admitted scholars had a primary faculty advisor from their department and a secondary advisor from the other department. At the beginning of the program, IPA faculty held an orientation that established the foundation of a professional learning community and outlined program expectations. In addition, faculty held regularly scheduled advising meetings with individual scholars to monitor progress and offer guidance. At the monthly IPA meetings, faculty reviewed student progress and, if needed, developed individualized support plans for scholars.

**Third**, regular interactions with faculty were arranged because students who meet often with faculty are more likely to persist and graduate (Podolsky et al., 2019). Scholars and faculty interacted each week. First, IPA faculty conducted most fieldwork supervision, thus scholars and faculty interacted regularly. Additionally, group supervision was arranged weekly or bi-weekly, which provided another touch point between faculty and scholars.

**Fourth**, unnecessary and burdensome institutional bureaucratic requirements were reduced as much as possible because such requirements lead students to develop a negative attitude toward their university. Negative experiences with units like the financial aid office can cause scholars to become disillusioned about the institution and less likely to finish their program (Hart-Baldridge, 2020; Roberts & Styron, 2010). Whenever possible and appropriate, as noted, the project's graduate assistant completed business paperwork for scholars and registered them in courses. In addition, the graduate assistant frequently emailed scholars to ask about their experiences and any assistance they needed. The assistant also informally met with them before evening classes to offer support and inquire about ongoing challenges.

**Last**, IPA faculty taught all courses within the interdisciplinary core curriculum. The classroom is the primary place for scholars to engage with peers and faculty, especially for non-residential scholars and scholars working part- or full-time while earning their degree, who may not be involved in other campus activities, events, or organizations (O'Keeffe, 2013). All courses within the interdisciplinary core curriculum had no more than 15 students. By design, small classes and scheduled activities encouraged faculty-student interactions, which must have a positive effect on student success and retention (Podolsky et al., 2019).

## BEST PRACTICES TO SUPPORT INTERDISCIPLINARY PRACTICE IN THE FIELD

The success of novice teachers should be a shared responsibility but, too often, it is not. Historically, the primary task of teacher preparation programs was to ensure that its graduates acquire and demonstrate a set of essential starter skills that would enable them to begin teaching, in a competent manner, on the first day of school. The districts and schools around the country that hire Educator Preparation Institutions graduates typically have a new teacher orientation or induction program in place that provides support and guidance and sometimes offers professional development that fills in the missing gaps in the new teacher's knowledge and skills (Ronfeldt & McQueen, 2017). Such programs, if implemented well, can decrease attrition (Kutsyurbua & Walker, 2015). With few exceptions, teacher preparation programs and school districts do not coordinate efforts aimed at strengthening the hand-off of novice teachers from preservice preparation programs to their first few years in the classroom.

Teachers receiving comprehensive induction elements report higher job satisfaction, improved teaching practices and pedagogical methods, and increased student achievement (Ingersoll et al., 2019).

*Interdisciplinary Training in Special Education and Behavior Analysis*

Research is suggesting that early-career BCBAs share the challenges that special education teachers face, resulting in high attrition rates (Plantiveau et al., 2018). Therefore, it is reasonable to assume that an induction program would similarly benefit teachers and behavior analysts. After the components of the interdisciplinary training program were in place, faculty began to develop an induction program for graduates. The induction program, which is still being refined, has two major components: 1) support for district partners and 2) a professional network program.

## Supporting Local Districts to Meet the Needs of Students with ASD

District partners were an integral part of ensuring that IPA was successful. District partners helped recruit scholars into the program, provided opportunities for fieldwork experiences, and participated in the speaker series. The IPA faculty regularly meet with district partners to determine school needs, share information, and gather data on how coursework and professional development activities can be improved. IPA faculty work with district partners to fill special education vacancies, which has included special education undergraduates completing their internships as long-term substitutes. This required collaboration with MDE, which was facilitated by faculty. Additionally, with approval from MDE, the special education faculty started an expedited teaching program that will allow individuals with a bachelor's degree to obtain a special education teaching certificate for K-12 and an endorsement in learning disabilities, emotional impairment, or ASD.

## Professional Network Program

IPA faculty are currently developing and implementing a professional network program. The program will include three components intended to support IPA graduates and to improve future interdisciplinary training programs. The professional network program includes 1) providing continuing education events targeted to special educators and school-based BCBAs, 2) providing ongoing advising and mentoring to IPA alumni, and 3) ongoing data collection for continuous program improvement for future interdisciplinary programs.

IPA faculty became a sponsor for Michigan's State Continuing Education Clock Hours (SCECH) to provide continuing education credits for special education teachers and an Authorized Continuing Education (ACE) provider to provide continuing education (CE) credits for BCBAs. All continuing education events will be free-of-charge for IPA alumni and their employers and cost a small fee for community members not associated with IPA. The CE events will allow IPA alumni to stay current in their certifications and reduce the effort and cost of doing so. The continuing education events will foster skill development and encourage graduates to remain current in EBPs for individuals with ASD. The CE events will use best practices for continuing education by focusing on specific content (e.g., a specific EBP) and incorporating active learning. All CE events will include collaboration, emphasize the use of effective practice models, provide expert support, and provide feedback and time for reflection (Darling-Hammond et al., 2017). The topics covered in CE events will be based on reviews of current trends and issues in special education and applied behavior analysis and by surveying alumni.

# REFLECTING ON AN INTERDISCIPLINARY TRAINING PROGRAM

## Progress Towards Program Goals

Overall, the IPA program was successful. Many of the project's goals were achieved and the faculty are making significant progress toward others. The interdisciplinary team has spent time reflecting on the successes of the program and identified areas for improvement. These reflections have led to a handful of recommendations for other faculty members who intend to develop and implement interdisciplinary training programs, in particular programs that train scholars in special education and behavior analysis.

The first goal was to develop an interdisciplinary training program in special education and behavior analysis. Developing the program required aligning professional standards across two disciplines, developing an interdisciplinary core curriculum and fieldwork experiences, embedding interdisciplinary projects within the coursework, and providing opportunities for scholars to conduct applied research to improve educational outcomes for students with ASD. Each of these activities was successfully completed. The faculty implemented changes between the cohorts based on scholar and faculty feedback. These changes included adding a co-taught seminar course at the start of the program, extending the number of semesters needed to accrue BCBA hours, and adjusting the presentation of behavior analysis course content to solidify the application of behavior analytic principles in educational settings.

The faculty believe a strength of the program was the number of opportunities scholars had for engaging in interdisciplinary collaboration. In part, this was accomplished by carefully planning course assignments and intentionally grouping scholars. A common theme in the feedback from scholars was how the interdisciplinary coursework and projects increased behavior analysts' knowledge and understanding of the numerous responsibilities of special education teachers. For example, prior to joining IPA, most of the behavior analyst scholars noted they were unaware of all of the responsibilities that special education teachers have, and that course discussions and projects allowed them to better understand the demands placed on special education teachers. This, in turn, impacted their approach to collaboration, intervention selection, and data collection procedures. Likewise, special education scholars frequently stated that prior to IPA they did not understand the complexities of treatment planning, especially for students who engage in challenging behavior, and stated that the interdisciplinary coursework increased their confidence in working in multi- and interdisciplinary teams at their school. Another huge success of the program was graduating highly competent special education teachers and behavior analysts who are experts in applying EBPs to meet the high intensity needs of students with ASD. All scholars who completed the program met or exceeded the competencies in implementing EBPs with students in K-12, which substantially increased the number of students with ASD who received high-quality services, and subsequently demonstrated improved academic and social outcomes. These improvements were demonstrated in scholars' applied projects that were completed in coursework, fieldwork, and master's projects.

It was important to recruit, admit, and graduate 24 scholars, including members from groups that have traditionally been underrepresented based on race, color, national origin, gender, age, or disability. In some ways, this goal was met while in other ways, the faculty fell short. Table 4 displays IPA scholar information and outcome data. Twenty-nine scholars were admitted into the program and all but three successfully finished the program within 2.5 years. Two scholars from the first cohort left the program within a year to pursue careers outside of education, and the third individual never started the program (this is described in more detail below). Of the 26 program completers, 16 were admitted into the special education program and 10 into the behavior analysis program. Some scholars entered the program with

## Interdisciplinary Training in Special Education and Behavior Analysis

*Table 4. Scholar Demographics and Outcomes*

|  | Cohort 1 (*n*=10) | Cohort 2 (*n*=16) | Total (*n*=26) |
|---|---|---|---|
| Program |  |  |  |
| Special Education | 6 | 10 | 16 |
| Behavior Analysis | 4 | 6 | 10 |
| Gender |  |  |  |
| Female | 9 | 15 | 24 |
| Male | 1 | 1 | 2 |
| Member from Underrepresented Group | 4 | 3 | 7 |
| *Certification Obtained |  |  |  |
| Master's degree (n=24) | 13/13 | 11/11 | 24/24 |
| BCBA (n=10) | 7/10 | n/a | 7/10 |
| ASD (n=12) | 2/6 | 4/6 | 6/12 |
| Working with students with disabilities | 10/10 | 16/16 | 26/26 |

a master's degree and/or the ASD teaching endorsement, which is reflected by the ratios presented in Table 4. Twenty-four scholars earned a master's degree in special education or behavior analysis. At the time of writing this chapter, only cohort 1 alumni are eligible to take the BCBA exam and, of those 10 scholars, seven have taken it and 100% have passed. This pass rate is significantly higher than the 2021 national pass rate of 66% (BACB website, retrieved 6/17/22).

Special education scholars are eligible to take the ASD endorsement test (i.e., MTTC) after they have completed most of their endorsement coursework. Two of the six scholars in cohort 1 took and passed the ASD test. Four of the six scholars in cohort 2 have taken and passed the test and two scholars report they plan to take it within the next three months. All program completers currently report working with students with disabilities and indicate that they use behavior-analytic strategies daily or weekly. Behavior analysts who work in clinics typically have a higher salary than teachers with comparable experience, and the faculty feared that some of the special education graduates would leave the teaching profession. Unfortunately, this fear was merited. After completing the program, two special education teachers sought and found employment in private ABA centers. Moreover, three special education scholars were immediately promoted to administrative positions. Although these individuals will likely have a robust impact on educational and behavioral outcomes for students with special needs in these administrative positions, these promotions, and the career shifts of two students, created vacancies within special education classrooms amid a special education teacher shortage. A downside of high-quality interdisciplinary training is that it can have harmful unintended consequences. Nonetheless, providing interdisciplinary training in areas with substantial pay differences poses the threat of graduates concentrating on the more lucrative area, and this is something that should be considered when developing interdisciplinary training programs.

Seven of the 26 (27%) program completers were members of groups that have traditionally been underrepresented based on race, color, national origin, gender, age, or disability. Of these seven scholars, six were admitted into the behavior analysis program. All special education scholars were white females, highlighting how the program fell short of *pulling in* teachers of color (Carter Andrews et al., 2019). The faculty have started to identify and analyze the variables that led to the lack of diversity in special education applicants. One factor to consider is the lack of diversity in the faculty (Carter Andrews et al., 2019). When the program was conceived and first implemented, there was one Black IPA faculty. She was a member of the behavior analysis program, which seemingly contributed to the successful recruitment of diverse behavior analysis students. Unfortunately, she left WMU soon after the program started.

The program implemented five strategies (e.g., Podolsky et al., 2019; Hart-Baldridge, 2020) to attract a diverse pool of candidates, but more is clearly needed. When recruiting the first cohort of students, program faculty hosted informational webinars with two Historically Black Colleges and Universities (HBCUs), but these efforts unfortunately did not result in any applications. It is possible that on-campus informational sessions would prove more effective in recruiting teachers of color, which is intended for future requirement efforts. For such efforts to be effective, faculty need to carefully consider historical and contemporary factors that influence the recruitment and retention of teachers of color. To recruit teachers of color into a master's-level interdisciplinary program, there needs to be a pool of candidates to draw upon. The program faculty have made efforts to increase diversity in the undergraduate teacher preparation programs. One effort is applying for support from the U.S. Department of Education Teacher Quality Partnership (TQP) program.

The third goal of the program was to develop an induction program to support local districts and IPA alumni. The faculty are currently working to achieve this goal. The faculty collected data on their needs and adjusted coursework to be responsive to their issues (e.g., increased rates of challenging behavior since the return to in-person learning after the COVID-19 hiatus). Additionally, the faculty are currently implementing the components of the induction program, which were delayed due to COVID-19. The faculty have submitted grants to secure financial support for diverse special education teachers and behavior analysts, submitted applications to be a provider for CEs for both teacher and behavior analyst credentials, and have implemented an ongoing data collection system to be responsive to IPA alumni, which will allow for careful planning of CE events and mentoring activities.

## Challenges Encountered

Although many of the project objectives were accomplished, the faculty encountered substantial challenges, which may arise in other interdisciplinary training programs. For that reason, the faculty share these challenges and provide tenable solutions for similar programs to consider when designing interdisciplinary projects.

### Impact of COVID-19

The COVID-19 pandemic made it difficult or impossible to carry out some planned aspects of the project and its sequelae, as well as the threat of its continuation, poses general challenges for special educators and behavior analysts. Although everyone hopes that the scourge of COVID-19 will soon be behind, that is not assured. Even if it soon ends, the COVID-19 pandemic has significantly and typically negatively affected more than 50 million public school students (Office of Civil Rights, 2021). In a recent survey, parents of children with ASD were more than three times as likely as other parents to report negative changes in their children due to the pandemic (Gevova et al., 2021). Parents of children with ASD frequently reported concerns related to their child's behavioral regression, therapy disruption, meltdowns, and lack of desire to return to school (Genova et al., 2021). As the country returns to in-person learning, it is likely that many students with ASD will have exacerbated needs resulting from the pandemic. Well-trained special education teachers and behavior analysts, such as the 26 IPA graduates, need to be available in meeting those needs. The cost to the federal government for educating each of them was $45,469, which is a bargain. But the IPA graduates are but a small drop in a large and growing bucket.

## Challenges in Supervised Fieldwork

Some of the challenges confronted were not entirely due to COVID-19. One consistent challenge was ensuring special education scholars met the fieldwork requirements for BCBA certification. The fieldwork requirements for BCBAs posed many challenges for the special education faculty and scholars and similar, although lesser, challenges for behavior analysis faculty and students. All of the behavior analysis students were traditional students, giving them more open time than employed teachers to acquire supervised hours.

Scholars reported that it was valuable for them to discuss these issues in group supervision sessions and to learn how their peers were applying what they learned in their courses during their fieldwork. However, given the BCBA requirements, group supervision was capped at half of the monthly supervision hours. Therefore, faculty needed to meet individually with scholars for two to three hours each month. This was difficult to accomplish with special education scholars because they were teaching full-time and could not always debrief after an observation, which meant individual supervision needed to take place during their planning period or after school. The intense supervision requirements, on top of taking two courses each semester, meant scholars had program requirements four nights a week. The faculty feel, and fear, that such rigorous training contributed to teacher stress and burnout.

Given the difficulties that special education scholars, who were full-time teachers, faced in receiving the supervised field experiences required to become BCBAs; the effort required for faculty to provide such feedback; and the knowledge that teachers do not have to be BCBAs to be good behavior analysts or well-versed in the use of EBPs, the faculty have come to question the value of all scholars earning the BCBA. Holding the BCBA is neither necessary nor sufficient for teachers to use behavioral principles and procedures effectively

## Impact on Teacher Shortage

As noted, two of the special education scholars have shifted to behavior analysis positions and three have moved into administrative roles. Although these job changes do not prevent the people who made them from providing valuable service to students with ASD, they do remove quality special education teachers from the classroom. This is contrary to an important objective of IPA: Increasing the number of well-trained special educators. Currently, the faculty are working to mitigate contributing to the special education teacher shortage through systematic collaboration with local district partners. This past year, the special education faculty placed undergraduate teacher candidates in IPA scholars' classrooms to complete their fieldwork for their initial special education endorsement.

## CONCLUSION

Despite the various challenges that were encountered over the five years, the faculty continue to recognize the value of interdisciplinary preparation in special education and behavior analysis and are enthusiastic about continuing such training. Although it is not easy for faculty and administrators to offer such programs, or for students to succeed in them, both are possible and well worth the effort. Securing funds to support students is a critical aspect of this effort that must be taken very seriously. Training grants are one option. Establishing partnerships with local districts, which provide financial support for students in training, is another. It isn't easy to obtain money to support students, or to train them well, but nothing worthwhile is easy. And funding well-trained students is worthwhile. To the extent that IPA has done that, it is a success.

## REFERENCES

Alliance for Excellent Education. (2014). On the Path to Equity: Improving the Effectiveness of Beginning Teachers. Alliance for Excellent Education: Washington, D.C.

American Psychiatric Association. (2013). *Diagnostic and Statistical Manual of Mental Disorders: Diagnostic and Statistical Manual of Mental Disorders* (5th ed.). American Psychiatric Association.

Anglim, J., Prendeville, P., & Kinsella, W. (2017). The self-efficacy of primary teachers in supporting the inclusion of children with autism spectrum disorder. *Educational Psychology in Practice*, *34*(1), 1–16. doi:10.1080/02667363.2017.1391750

Behavior Analyst Certification Board. (n.d.) Board Certified Behavior Analyst. [Data set]. BACB. https://www.bacb.com/bacb-certificant-data/

Behavior Analyst Certification Board. (2017). *BCBA task list* (5th ed.). Authors.

Behavior Analyst Certification Board. (2020). Ethics code for behavior analysts. *BACB*. https://bacb.com/wp-content/ethics-code-for-behavior-analysts/

Behavior Analyst Certification Board. (2014). Professional and ethical compliance code for behavior analysts. *BACB*. https://www.bacb.com/wp-content/uploads/2020/05/BACB-Compliance-Code-english_190318.pdf

Baker, B. L., & Blacher, J. (2020). Brief Report: Behavior disorders and social skills in adolescents with autism spectrum disorder: Does IQ matter? *Journal of Autism and Developmental Disorders*, *50*(6), 2226–2233. doi:10.100710803-019-03954-w PMID:30888552

Banks, T., & Doly, J. (2019). Mitigating barriers to persistence: A review of efforts to improve retention and graduation rates for students of color in higher education. *Higher Education Studies*, *9*(1), 118–131. doi:10.5539/hes.v9n1p118

Barnhill, G. P., Polloway, E. A., & Sumutka, B. M. (2011). A survey of personnel preparation practices in autism spectrum disorders. *Focus on Autism and Other Developmental Disabilities*, *26*(2), 75–86. doi:10.1177/1088357610378292

Billingsley, B., & Bettini, E. (2019). Special education teacher attrition and retention: A review of the literature. *Review of Educational Research*, *89*(5), 697–744. doi:10.3102/0034654319862495

Bock, S. J., Michalak, N., & Brownlee, S. (2011). Collaboration and consultation: The first steps. In C. G. Simpson & J. P. Bakken (Eds.), *Collaboration: A multidisciplinary approach to educating students with disabilities* (pp. 3–15). Prufrock Press.

Boivin, B., Ruane, J., Quigley, S. P., Harper, J., & Weiss, M. J. (2021). Interdisciplinary collaboration training: An example of preservice training series. *Behavior Analysis in Practice*, *14*(4), 1223–1236. doi:10.100740617-021-00561-z PMID:34868824

Brodhead, M. T. (2015). Maintaining professional relationships in an interdisciplinary setting: Strategies for navigating nonbehavioral treatment recommendations for individuals with autism. *Behavior Analysis in Practice*, *8*(10), 70–78. doi:10.100740617-015-0042-7 PMID:27703885

Carver-Thomas, D. (2017). Diversifying the field: Barriers to recruiting and retaining teachers of color and how to overcome them. ERIC. https://files.eric.ed.gov/fulltext/ED582730.pdf

Carver-Thomas, D., & Darling-Hammond, L. (2017). *Teacher turnover: Why it matters and what we can do about it*. Learning Policy. https://learningpolicyinstitute.org/product/teacher-turnover-report doi:10.54300/454.278

Carter Andrews, D. J., Castro, E., Cho, C. L., Petchauer, E., Richmond, G., & Floden, R. (2019). Changing the narrative on diversifying the teaching workforce: A look at the historical and contemporary factors that inform recruitment and retention of teachers of color. *Journal of Teacher Education, 70*(1), 6-12. https:// doi:10.1177/0022487118812418

CEEDAR Center. (2020). Preparing and retaining effective special education teachers: Short term strategies for long-term solutions (A policy brief). *CEEDAR Center*. https://ceedar.education.ufl.edu/wp-content/uploads/2020/01/CEEDAR-GTL-Shortages-Brief.pdf

Chesley, M. G., & Jordan, J. (2012). What's missing from teacher prep. *Educational Leadership*, *69*(8), 41–45.

Conners, B., Johnson, A., Duarte, J., Murriky, R., & Marks, K. (2019). Future directions of training and fieldwork in diversity issues in applied behavior analysis. *Behavior Analysis in Practice*, *12*(4), 767–776. doi:10.100740617-019-00349-2 PMID:31976288

Council for Exceptional Children (CEC). (2015). *What every special educator must know: Professional ethics and standards*. CEC..

Critchfield, T. S., Doepke, K. J., & Epting, L. K. (2017). Normative emotional responses to behavior analysis jargon or how not to use words to win friends and influence people. *Behavior Analysis in Practice*, *7*(2), 1–10. doi:10.100740617-016-0161-9 PMID:28630814

Dee, T. (2004). Teachers, race and student achievement in a randomized experiment. *The Review of Economics and Statistics*, *86*(1), 195–210. https://www.nber.org/system/files/working_papers/w8432/w8432.pdf. doi:10.1162/003465304323023750

DeLuca, C., & Klinger, D. A. (2010). Assessment literacy development: Identifying gaps in teachers candidates' learning. *Assessment in Education: Principles, Policy & Practice, 17*(4), 419–438. doi:10.1080/0969594X.2010.516643

Division for Early Childhood (DEC). (2014). DEC recommended practices in early intervention/early childhood special education 2014. *DEC.* https://divisionearlychildhood.egnyte.com/dl/7urLPWCt5U

Ehrhardt, K., Curiel, E., Frieder, J., Ross, D., & Summy, S. (2017). *Interdisciplinary Preparation in Autism. Office of Special Education Programs (OSEP) Preparation of Special Education.* Early Intervention, and Related Service Leadership Personnel Grant.

Gevova, H. M., Arora, A., & Botticeelo, A. L. (2021). *Effects of school closures resulting from COVID-19 in autistic and neurotypical children.* Frontiers in Education., doi:10.3389/feduc.2021.761485

Giangreco, M. F., Pennington, R. C., & Walker, V. L. (2021). Conceptualizing and utilizing board certified behavior analysts as related service providers in inclusion-oriented schools. *Remedial and Special Education*, •••, 1–13. doi:10.1177/07419325211063610

Hart-Baldridge, E. (2020). Faculty advisor perspectives of academic advising. *NACADA Journal, 40*(1), 10–22. doi:10.12930/NACADA-18-25

Higher Education Consortium for Special Education (HECSE) (2021, February). The shortage of special education teachers and higher education faculty. *HECSE.*

Huete, J., Schmidt, J., & Lopez-Arvizu, D. (2014). Behavioral disorders in young children with autism spectrum disorder. In J. Tarbox, D. R. Dixon, P. Sturmey, & J. L. Matson (Eds.), *Handbook of Early Intervention for Autism Spectrum Disorders* (pp. 717–752). Springer. doi:10.1007/978-1-4939-0401-3_26

Individuals with Disabilities Education Act, 20 U.S.C. § 1400 (2004).

Katsiyannis, A., Counts, J., Popham, M., Ryan, J., & Butzer, M. (2016). Litigation and students with disabilities: An Overview of cases from 2015. *NAASP Bulletin, 100*(1), 287–298. doi:10.1177/0192636516664827

Kutsyuruba, B., & Walker, K. (2015). The role of trust in developing teacher leaders through early-career induction and mentoring programs. *Antistasis, 5*(1), 32-36. Retrieved from https://journals.lib.unb.ca/index.php/antistasis/article/view/22859 https://www.ncsl.org/research/education/tackling-teacher-and-principal-shortages-in-rural-areas.aspx

Layden, S. J. (2022). Creating a professional network: A statewide model to support school-based behavior analysts. *Behavior Analysis in Practice.* doi:10.100740617-022-00700-0 PMID:35371415

Leyfer, O. T., Folstein, S. E., Bacalman, S., Davis, N. O., Dinh, E., Morgan, J., Tager-Flusberg, H., & Lainhart, J. E. (2006). Comorbid psychiatric disorders in children with autism: Interview development and rates of disorders. *Journal of Autism and Developmental Disorders, 36*(7), 849–861. doi:10.100710803-006-0123-0 PMID:16845581

Lindsay, C. A. (2016). Teacher race and school discipline. *Education Next, 17*(1), 72–78. https://www.educationnext.org/teacher-race-and-school-discipline-suspensions-research/

Lindsay, S., Proulx, M., Thomson, N., & Scott, H. (2013). Educators' challenges of including children with autism spectrum disorders in mainstream classrooms. *International Journal of Disability Development and Education*, *60*(4), 347–362. doi:10.1080/1034912X.2013.846470

Locke, J., Lawson, G. M., Beidas, R. S., Aarons, G. A., Xie, M., Lyon, A. R., Stahmer, A., Seidman, M., Frederick, L., Oh, C., Spaulding, C., Dorsey, S., & Mandell, D. S. (2019). Individual and organizational factors that affect implementation of evidence-based practices for children with autism in public schools: A cross-sectional observational study. *Implementation Science; IS*, *14*(29), 29. doi:10.118613012-019-0877-3 PMID:30866976

Mason-Williams, L., Bettini, E., Peyton, D., Harvey, A., Rosenberg, M., & Sindelar, P. T. (2020). Rethinking shortages in special education: Making good on the promise of an equal opportunity for students with Disabilities. *Teacher Education and Special Education*, *43*(1), 45–62. doi:10.1177/0888406419880352

Mathur, S. K., & Rodriguez, K. A. (2021). Cultural responsiveness curriculum for behavior analysts: A meaningful step towards social justice. *Behavior Analysis in Practice*. doi:10.100740617-021-00579-3

National Center for Education Statistics. (2022, May). Characteristics of public school teachers. *Condition of Education*. U.S. Department of Education, Institute of Education Sciences. *NCES*. https://nces.ed.gov/programs/coe/pdf/2021/clr_508c.pdf

National Center for Education Statistics. (2022). Students With Disabilities. *Condition of Education*. U.S. Department of Education, Institute of Education Sciences. *NCES*. https://nces.ed.gov/programs/coe/indicator/cgg

National Center for Learning Disabilities. (2020). Significant disproportionality in special education: Current trends and actions for impact. *NCLD*. https://www.ncld.org/sigdispro/

Nevison, C., & Zahorodny, W. (2019). Race/ethnicity-resolved time trends in United States ASD prevalence estimates from IDEA and ADDM. *Journal of Autism and Developmental Disorders*, *49*(12), 4721–4730. doi:10.100710803-019-04188-6 PMID:31435818

O'Keeffe, P. (2013). A sense of belonging: Improving student retention. *College Student Journal*, *47*(4), 605–613.

Office for Civil Rights. (2021). Education in a pandemic: The disparate impact of COVID-19 on America's students. https://www2.ed.gov/about/offices/list/ocr/docs/20210608-impacts-of-covid19.pdf

Osler, J. (2016). Beyond brochures: Practicing "soul care" in the recruitment of teachers of color. *San Francisco: San Francisco Teacher Residency*. http://www.wcstonefnd.org/wp-content/uploads/2016/12/SFTR-SoulCare-Final1.pdf

Ouellette, R. R., Pellecchia, M., Beidas, R. S., Wideman, R., Xie, M., & Mandell, D. S. (2019). Boon or Burden: The effect of implementing evidence-based practices on teachers' emotional exhaustion. *Administration and Policy in Mental Health*, *46*(1), 62–70. doi:10.100710488-018-0894-6 PMID:30225662

Pennington, R. (2022). Applied behavior analysis: A valuable partner in special education. *Teaching Exceptional Children*, *54*(4), 315–317. doi:10.1177/00400599221079130

Plantiveau, C., Dounavi, K., & Virues-Ortega, J. (2018). High levels of burnout among early-career board-certified behavior analysts with low collegial support in the work environment. *European Journal of Behavior Analysis*, *19*(2), 195–207. doi:10.1080/15021149.2018.1438339

Podolsky, A., Kini, T., Darling-Hammond, L., & Bishop, J. (2019). Strategies for attracting and retaining educators: What does the evidence say? *Education Policy Analysis Archives*, *27*(38), 1–47. doi:10.14507/epaa.27.3722

Roberts, J., & Styron, R. (2010). Student satisfaction and persistence: Factors vital to student retention. *Research in Higher Education*, *6*(3), 1–18.

Ronfeldt, M., & McQueen, K. (2017). Does new teacher induction really improve retention? *Journal of Teacher Education*, *68*(4), 394–410. doi:10.1177/0022487117702583

Rothstein, J., & Rouse, C. E. (2011). Constrained after college: Student loans and early-career occupational choices. *Journal of Public Economics*, *91*(1-2), 149–163. doi:10.1016/j.jpubeco.2010.09.015

Samson, A. C., Phillips, J. M., Parker, K. J., Shah, S., Gross, J. J., & Hardan, A. Y. (2014). Emotion dysregulation and the core features of autism spectrum disorder. *Journal of Autism and Developmental Disorders*, *44*(7), 1766–1772. doi:10.100710803-013-2022-5 PMID:24362795

Santos, J. L., & Haycock, K. (2016). Fixing America's college attainment problems: It's about more than affordability. *The Education Trust*. https://edtrust.org/wp-content/uploads/2014/09/FixingAmericasCollegeAttainmentProblem_EdTrust.pdf

Scheeler, M. C., Budin, S., & Markelz, A. (2016). The role of teacher preparation in promoting evidence-based practices in schools. *Learning Disabilities (Weston, Mass.)*, *14*(2), 171–187. https://files.eric.ed.gov/fulltext/EJ1118433.pdf

Scheibel, G., & Watling, R. (2016). Collaborating with behavior analysts on the autism service delivery team. *OT Practice*, *21*(7), 15–19.

Scheuermann, B., Webber, J., Boutot, E. A., & Goodwin, M. (2003). Problems with personnel preparation in autism spectrum disorders. *Focus on Autism and Other Developmental Disabilities*, *18*(3), 97–206. https://journals.sagepub.com/doi/pdf/10.1177/108835760301800 3080. doi:10.1177/10883576030180030801

Schreck, K. A., Karunaratne, Y., Zane, T., & Wilford, H. (2016). Behavior analysts' use of and beliefs in treatment for people with autism: A 5-year follow-up. *Behavioral Interventions*, *31*(4), 355–376. doi:10.1002/bin.1461

Schreck, K. A., & Mazur, K. (2008). Behavior analysts' use of and beliefs in treatments for people with autism. *Behavioral Interventions*, *23*(3), 201–212. doi:10.1002/bin.264

Shepley, C., Allday, R. A., Crawford, D., Pence, R., Johnson, M., & Winstead, O. (2017). Examining the emphasis on consultation in behavior analyst preparation programs. *Behavior Analysis: Research and Practice*, *17*(4), 381–392. doi:10.1037/bar0000064

Shepley, C., & Grisham-Brown, J. (2018). Applied behavior analysis in early childhood education: An overview of policies, research, blended practices, and the curriculum framework. *Behavior Analysis in Practice, 12*(1), 235–246. doi:10.100740617-018-0236-x PMID:30918790

Stayton, V., & Bruder, M. B. (1999). Early intervention personnel preparation for the new millennium: Early childhood special education. *Infants and Young Children, 12*(1), 59–69. doi:10.1097/00001163-199907000-00009

Steinbrenner, J. R., Hume, K., Odom, S. L., Morin, K. L., Nowell, S. W., Tomaszewski, B., Szendrey, S., McIntyre, N. S., Yücesoy-Özkan, S., & Savage, M. N. (2020). *Evidence-based practices for children, youth, and young adults with autism.* The University of North Carolina at Chapel Hill, Frank Porter Graham Child Development Institute, National Clearinghouse on Autism Evidence and Practice Review Team. https://ncaep.fpg.unc.edu/sites/ncaep.fpg.unc.edu/files/imce/documents/EBP%20Report%202020.pdf

Teffs, E., & Whitbread, K. M. (2009). Level of Preparation of General Education Teachers to Include Students with Autism Spectrum Disorders. *Current Issues in Education (Tempe, Ariz.), 12,* https://cie.asu.edu/ojs/index.php/cieatasu/article/view/172

Townley-Cochran, D., Leaf, J. B., Taubman, M., Leaf, R., & McEachin, J. (2015, September). Observational Learning for Students Diagnosed with Autism: A Review Paper. *Review Journal of Autism and Developmental Disorders, 2*(3), 262–272. doi:10.100740489-015-0050-0

U.S. Department of Education. (2022). Office of Special Education and Rehabilitative Services, Office of Special Education Programs, 43rd Annual Report to Congress on the Implementation of the Individuals with Disabilities Education Act. *USDE.*

U.S. Department of Education, Office of Special Education and Rehabilitative Services, Office of Special Education Programs. (2020). "IDEA Part B Child Count Collection" 2008-09 to 2011-12, "IDEA Part B Child Count and Educational Environments Collection" 2012-13 to 2018-19. *EDFacts Data Warehouse (EDW).* https://sites.ed.gov/idea/osep-fast-facts-children-with-autism-20/

United States., & Job Accommodation Network (U.S.). (2011). *The ADA Amendments Act of 2008.* Morgantown, WV: U.S. Dept. of Labor, Office of Disability Employment Policy, Job Accommodation Network.

Wagner, D. L., Hammerschmidt-Snidarich, S. M., Espin, C. A., Seifert, K., & McMaster, K. L. (2017). Pre-service teachers' interpretation of CBM progress monitoring data. *Learning Disabilities Research & Practice, 32*(1), 22–31. doi:10.1111/ldrp.12125

Wiggins, L. D., Durkin, M., Esler, A., Lee, L.-C., Zahorodny, W., Rice, C., Yeargin-Allsopp, M., Dowling, N. F., Hall-Lande, J., Morrier, M. J., Christensen, D., Shenouda, J., & Baio, J. (2020). Disparities in documented diagnoses of autism spectrum disorder based on demographic, individual, and service factors. *Autism Research, 13*(3), 464–473. doi:10.1002/aur.2255 PMID:31868321

Yell, M. L., & Bateman, D. F. (2018). Free appropriate public education and Endrew F. v. Douglas County School District (2017): Implication for personnel preparation. *Teacher Education and Special Education*, *42*(1), 6–17. doi:10.1177/0888406417754239

Yell, M. L., & Katsiyannis, A. (2019). The Supreme Court and special education. *Intervention in School and Clinic*, *54*(5), 311–318. doi:10.1177/1053451218819256

# Chapter 8
# Autism From Multiple Perspectives:
## Developing Interdisciplinary Changemakers

**Shanna Jamanis**
*Nazareth College, USA*

**Dawn Vogler-Elias**
*Nazareth College, USA*

## ABSTRACT

*Autism is the fastest-growing category for public education across the United States, however there is a continued shortage of highly qualified professionals. Supporting children with autism requires specialized knowledge and skills in evidence-based practices. Although a majority of individuals on the autism spectrum are supported by professionals from multiple disciplines, focus on autism in pre-service preparation is often developed without an interdisciplinary focus and without viewing autism through multiple lenses. This chapter shares the development, framework, multi-year outcomes, lessons learned and future direction for an interdisciplinary professional preparation program in autism. The program's conceptual framework includes disability studies, neurodiversity, and intersections with diversity, equity, and inclusion. Participants are guided to examine differing perspectives, collaborate across disciplines, and consistently reflect upon their own practice to develop the skills of reflective practitioners and changemakers in autism.*

## INTRODUCTION

Meet Michael, an eleven-year-old boy in the fifth grade. According to school and medical evaluations, he has been diagnosed with autism and intellectual disability. For the upcoming school year, Michael has been placed in a specialized classroom designed for children on the autism spectrum. This year, the class will have a new teacher, Ms. Blake, who is experienced in working in special education yet has

DOI: 10.4018/978-1-6684-6438-0.ch008

had minimal formal professional development in the area of autism. Michael's classroom is supported by a team that includes a social worker, speech-language pathologist, music therapist, and occupational therapist. Each of these professionals spends time within the classroom providing push-in or group-based lessons as well as individual therapy for most of the students in the classroom. Because the support professionals all have caseloads that include many students across several schools, Michael's team rarely has time to meet in person.

Michael's speech primarily consists of repeated phrases from his favorite television program featuring a talking train. These phrases are often in narrative form with a variety of intonations and voice impressions that sound similar to the characters on the television program. Michael's parents have indicated they often do not understand what he is trying to communicate. During the upcoming year, the team, led by the speech-language pathologist, will introduce an iPad mini with the TouchChat program to augment Michael's communication. Michael's speech-language pathologist will be the primary professional to introduce and teach him to use this device.

At school, Michael appears to enjoy math the most, particularly content that involves operations, measurement, and patterns. However, the team is perplexed that Michael consistently becomes frustrated during math class as they implement the scripted math modules, even when the content is similar to that in some of the math-based computer games that he seeks out on his own. Michael often comes to school without having his homework completed. His parents have indicated that they must both work together with Michael for at least two hours in order to complete the homework worksheets. When Michael is upset at school, he will often scream, "I must go home now," repeatedly and attempt to hit or spit on adults or other students who approach him.

At home, bedtime usually takes over an hour. Michael has a routine of jumping on a trampoline, doing a 10-minute relaxation session of yoga, washing his face, brushing his teeth, and writing numbers. It takes him a while to fall asleep, but once he is sleeping, he will sleep all night. However, if the family does not complete the entire routine, Michael becomes upset. When the parents consulted the school team about bedtime help, Michael's teacher recommended they try a visual checklist that he responds well to at school.

At both school and home, Michael often takes items apart, including clocks, computers, televisions, and thermostats. Both parents and teachers have walked back into the room and found Michael sitting in the midst of dismantled devices, examining them excitedly.

Although Michael is a unique human being with his own unique fingerprint, this may sound like a typical story about someone on the autism spectrum. After hearing about Michael, you may be wondering, what is the outcome for a child like Michael? Will he ever be able to live independently? In what kind of job could he excel, or could he even have a job? What will Michael's relationships look like in the future, and what support will he need? It is not unusual to hear stories about autism that characterize individuals with the difficulties and barriers that they face. Alternately, we may also encounter stories about individuals on the autism spectrum who have overcome great obstacles to reach "normalcy" or whose strengths are so extraordinary that we can't relate to them as human beings. Or read stories about good Samaritans reaching out to offer kindness by taking them to the prom, offering them a job, or giving them a chance to play on a sports team. How do these stories shape professional beliefs and perceptions of autism? Are there voices missing from these stories, or are they otherwise incomplete? What might professionals gain from learning about how to shift perspectives and consider Michael's story in a different way?

*Autism From Multiple Perspectives*

Table 1. Children ages 3–21 being served under IDEA

| Disability | 2016–2017 | 2017–2018 | 2018–2019 | 2019–2020 | 2020–2021 |
|---|---|---|---|---|---|
| All | 6,802,000 | 6,964,000 | 7,132,000 | 7,282,000 | 7,183,000 |
| Autism | 661,000 | 710,000 | 762,000 | 803,000 | 828,000 |

This chapter presents the development, framework, multi-year outcomes, lessons learned, and future work for the Interdisciplinary Specialty Program in Autism (I-SPAN) project. I-SPAN is an interdisciplinary graduate-level program that was developed and continues to be informed through data gathered from professionals and families of people on the autism spectrum. The program is a collaborative project between the School of Education (SOE) and the School of Health and Human Services (SHHS) at a small, independent, comprehensive institution that supports graduate students working in special education, music education, art education, literacy education, TESOL, speech-language pathology, occupational therapy, physical therapy, higher education student affairs administration, art and music therapy, and social work. Over 100 participants have completed I-SPAN at this time.

## RATIONALE FOR INTERDISCIPLINARY PROFESSIONAL PREPARATION

The U.S. Department of Education (2020) noted that the percentage of students with disabilities that are identified with autism doubled between 2008–2009 and 2018–2019; it is the fastest-growing category for public education across the United States. Most recently, Maenner, et al. (2021) released data suggesting a 1:44 prevalence rate for children identified with autism. Young boys are four times more likely than girls to be identified with autism spectrum disorder (ASD). Prevalence was similar by race and ethnicity, but at some sites, children who were Hispanic were less likely to be identified as having ASD than children who were non-Hispanic. The higher proportion of children who are black compared with children who are white or Hispanic classified as being diagnosed with an intellectual disability was consistent with previous findings (Maenner et al., 2021). In the last 10 years, the total number of children being served under IDEA increased by 12.2%. The number of children on the autism spectrum being served under IDEA increased by 82.0% (National Center for Education Statistics, 2021). Table 1 shows the rate of growth for the last five years.

Increased awareness and better screening options are potentially a cause for these increases. Undoubtedly, many more children are being identified with ASD, and students on the autism spectrum are less likely to be included in general education settings, putting them at risk for experiencing more isolation than neurotypical peers (Office of Special Education Programs, 2020). There is a critical need to increase the number of highly qualified professionals across multiple disciplines to provide person-centered and evidence-based support for individuals with ASD within the school setting.

Given the increased prevalence of autism and the fact that children with autism are more at risk for academic failure with challenges in communication, behaviors, and social relationships, there is a need to prepare professionals from multiple disciplines to support this group of children. Furthermore, professionals from various disciplines must learn to work together and understand their individual roles in interdisciplinary teams within the educational system. Holding certification in a specific area, such as special education or speech-language pathology, does not ensure that professionals are adequately prepared to support children with autism. Most professional degrees are generalized in nature and must prepare professionals to work with individuals across a range of ages with a range of abilities or challenges. Specifically, most licensure options are multi-categorical and do not include specializations in autism (Scheuermann et al., 2003). The National Research Council (2001) reported that most teachers received minimal to no education in their teacher education programs on evidence-based strategies for children with ASD. This report concluded there is a lack of specialized training in autism in pre-service professional programs, yet children with ASD are most likely to receive services in schools within the community. With increased expectations for more inclusive school models, general and special education teachers are expected to collaborate to serve students on the autism spectrum. While time management and communication are critical, teachers also identified gaps in content knowledge as a factor in being able to effectively collaborate to support children on the autism spectrum (Brock et al., 2014; Da Fonte & Barton-Arwood, 2017). Brock et al. (2014) surveyed 456 teachers and administrators and found that teachers were not very confident in their implementation of evidence-based practices and ability to address the important issues of high-needs students with ASD. Yet, teachers do demonstrate an interest in receiving specialized training in ASDs, and as a result, most teachers pursue training through professional development opportunities in an attempt to rectify this gap (Brock et al., 2014; Lerman et al., 2004). The challenge with the professional development model, or specialist training, is that it is often completed in response to a specific problem, such as litigation or the school district's need to qualify a professional to deliver services to children with ASD (Scheuermann et al., 2003). In addition, most professional development opportunities are limited in scope and depth; furthermore, they support a single theory of supporting individuals with ASD (Scheuermann et al., 2003).

In a survey distributed to teachers across New York State, approximately half of the respondents indicated that they were not aware of the current best practices in supporting children with autism (Saddler, 2012). Most participants had received training through professional development but had not taken a course focusing on students with ASD; 71.7% indicated they wanted specific preparation in their undergraduate or graduate programs on evidence-based practices for children with ASD (Saddler, 2012). These findings are consistent with the recommendations from the New York State Interagency Task Force on Autism (2010), which reported that "teachers need specialized training and expertise to meet the unique educational needs of preschool and school-aged students with ASD" (p. 21). In another survey distributed to institutions of higher education that offered graduate-level programs in speech-language pathology, 45% of the respondents reported dedicated coursework to ASD (Battaglia et al., 2013). Coursework varied from one to three credit courses, and only one institution required the coursework; however, 91% of respondents reported serving clients with autism (Battaglia et al., 2013). When the authors reviewed publicly available data for institutions that did not respond, only one institution offered coursework dedicated to autism, indicating a need for increased pre-service professional preparation regarding autism in speech-language pathology programs (Battaglia et al., 2013).

To serve individuals on the autism spectrum effectively, interdisciplinary collaboration is critical, given the complex differences that individuals on the spectrum may experience. Yet, interprofessional collaborative practice can be difficult to implement, particularly when there are barriers to doing this work. Pre-service professionals are often not prepared to understand the roles of other professionals or effective collaboration as part of an interdisciplinary team (Almendingen et al., 2021). Pfeiffer et al. (2019) examined collaboration between speech-language pathologists (SLPs) and other school-based professionals and found that there were fairly low percentages of SLPs engaging in collaborative work. Barriers included time constraints and scheduling, resistance from other professionals, and lack of support from administrators, further emphasizing the importance of pre-service professionals engaging in collaborative learning opportunities that are integrated across programs and colleges (Pfeiffer et al., 2019). Certain professionals, such as speech-language pathologists and educators, may uniquely complement one another when collaborating to be able to provide differentiated support within the classroom to meet the needs of children with complex communication needs, such as those on the autism spectrum (Archibald, 2017).

While effective collaboration is a key element of equity in education, there are differences in how it is described and utilized to support children. Griffiths et al. (2020) conducted an extensive review and analysis of collaboration literature and identified eight common key constructs that led to collaboration: (a) open communication, (b) trust, (c) mutual respect, (d) shared goals, (e) common understanding, (f) shared responsibility, (g) active participation, and (h) shared decision making. Based on their review, collaboration can be defined as a

*complex process built on trust, open communication, and mutual respect (relationship building), with all members focused on shared goals and responsibility with a common understanding (shared values), who are actively participating with a sense of shared responsibility (active engagement) and decision making. (p. 64)*

Their "building blocks" conceptual model suggests that collaboration is a dynamic model across multiple stakeholders and systems, which further indicates the importance of preparing pre-service professionals to work across these systems.

Bronstein's (2003) model for interdisciplinary collaboration has been utilized regularly in the field of social work and includes the following components: (a) interdependence, (b) newly created professional activities, (c) flexibility, (d) collective ownership of goals, and (e) reflection on the process. Additionally, interdisciplinary collaboration has been identified as a shared process characterized by "professionals from multiple disciplines with shared objectives, decision-making, responsibility, and power working together" (Petri, 2010, p. 80). Petri (2010) further emphasized the importance of interprofessional education in promoting effective interdisciplinary collaboration because it allows professionals from different fields of study to understand other disciplines and acknowledge the value of all disciplines in collaborative support models. *Interprofessional education* is defined as what happens when participants from two or more professions learn about, from, and with each other to enable effective collaboration and improve health outcomes (Department of Human Resources for Health, 2010). Professionals such as educators, speech-language pathologists, occupational therapists, physical therapists, and social workers should be involved in supporting and guiding families through the process of understanding the complex needs of children with ASD diagnoses (NRC, 2001). As stated earlier, most personnel preparation programs for professionals working with all developmental levels consist of a generalized certification and do not offer participants the opportunities to understand the complexities of the autism diagnosis nor provide a scope and depth in evidence-based support (NRC, 2001; Simpson, 2004). In addition, children diagnosed with autism who have complex academic, social, emotional, and behavioral needs typically require a variety of related special education services, with the most common services being speech and language therapy and occupational therapy (Wei et al., 2014). Given that most children diagnosed with autism will receive multiple related services, schools require interdisciplinary teams to best support them, which means that personnel preparation programs must prepare participants to collaborate across disciplines (Simpson, 2004). Providing a specialty program that allows pre-service participants to engage in interdisciplinary collaboration will lead to improved collaborative professional practice in supporting individuals with autism.

Thinking point: How do you think this information impacts how Michael is supported in his educational setting?

## DEVELOPMENT OF THE PROGRAM

### Local Needs Assessment Survey

At the local level, a school personnel and family needs assessment survey resulted in similar findings related to professional perceptions of preparedness (Jamanis & Vogler-Elias, 2014). For example, when asked to rate themselves on a scale of 1 (*not prepared at all*) to 5 (*well prepared*), school personnel provided an average self-rating of 2.84, while families indicated an average rating of 3.76 for the professionals supporting their children. Most school personnel reported that they had very little pre-service professional preparation in the area of autism. Section 3004 of New York State Education Law now requires all pre-service professionals serving children diagnosed with autism to complete at least three hours of coursework in their programs in the area of autism; however, there continues to be no state certificate of specialization in autism (New York State Education Department, 2006). While this allows for increased awareness and understanding of autism, it does not adequately prepare professionals to support children with autism. There continues to be a need for all personnel involved in public education to have access to pre-service professional programs that will prepare them to appropriately serve children with autism (New York State Interagency Task Force on Autism, 2010). Additionally, given the increasing practice of providing special education programs and services to children with disabilities in inclusive classrooms, where multiple professionals are required to interact with one another, there is a growing need for interdisciplinary pre-service professional preparation.

Given the need for interdisciplinary preparation in autism, the authors developed I-SPAN and implemented a pilot program in the first year at their university. This institution is uniquely designed to support interdisciplinary preparation, as it is a small, independent, comprehensive institution with a number of graduate programs across disciplines. There are four academic divisions at the institution that include both a School of Education and a School of Health and Human Services. Graduate programs across both divisions house approximately 10 master's degree programs that initially had an interest in participating in an autism specialization option. Students across these programs were able to integrate a three-course sequence into their graduate programs and obtain a local specialization in autism. While their graduate programs included special education-focused coursework, none of the programs highlighted autism as a specific area of training in their coursework or clinical experiences. The goals for the pilot program were (a) to see if it met local professional preparation needs in the community and (b) to determine what resources were necessary to grow the program.

Program assessment data indicated that participants felt more prepared to support individuals on the autism spectrum after participating in the three-course sequence. Prior to beginning coursework, participants were asked to complete an entry survey where they utilized a scale of 1–4 to self-report their level of understanding in multiple areas related to supporting individuals on the autism spectrum. Upon completion, the participants completed an exit survey. All participants indicated a higher level of understanding in all content areas on the exit survey, with an overall mean score increased from 2.07

*Figure 1. Changemaker framework for student learning*
Source: Nazareth College (2021)

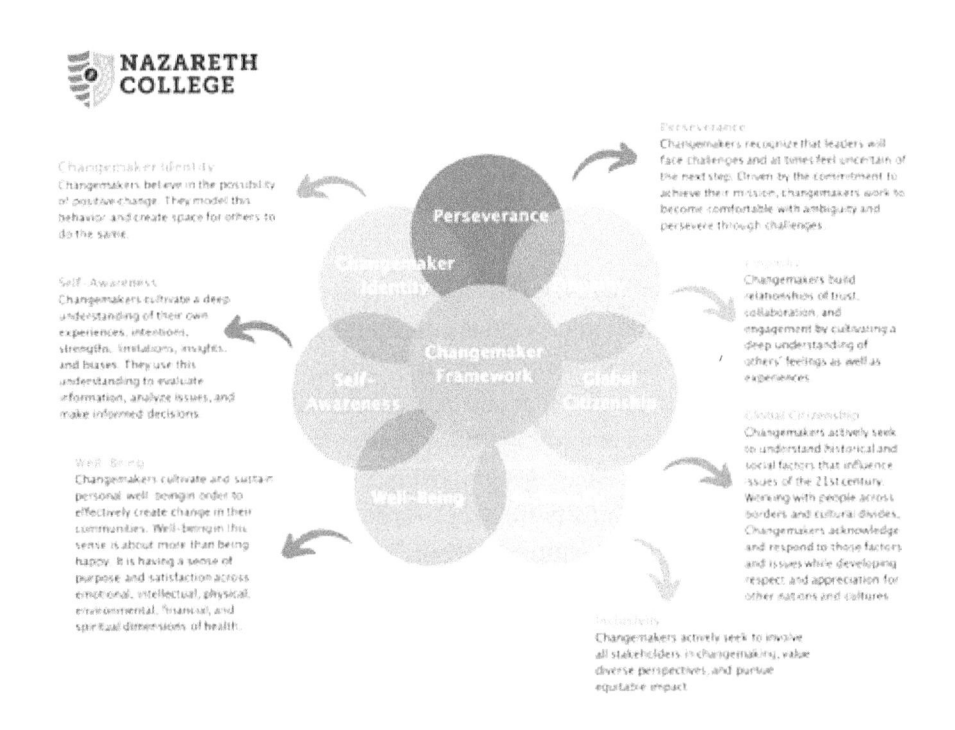

(entry survey) to 3.63 (exit survey). In the second year of implementation, the number of participants doubled, and the authors were able to apply for a Department of Education Office of Special Programs Personnel Preparation grant to support I-SPAN participants across multiple disciplines, including special education, speech-language pathology, occupational therapy, physical therapy, and social work.

## Conceptual Framework

I-SPAN's conceptual framework is grounded in multiple perspectives, both from western and global ideologies with opportunities to study these multiple perspectives. The conceptual framework, illustrated in figure 2, includes disability studies, Neurodiversity, and intersections with diversity, equity, and inclusion. The conceptual framework is supported by the institution's changemaker framework: *changemakers* are defined as "anyone who takes action to address a problem, activates others, and works towards solutions for the good of all" (Rahman et al., 2016). As illustrated in figure 1, changemakers continuously notice challenges and cultivate solutions in the family, community, workplace, sector, country, and world, creating a more resilient and inclusive future.

I-SPAN participants are guided to examine differing perspectives, collaborate across disciplines, and consistently reflect upon their own practice to develop the skills of reflective practitioners and changemakers in autism. Additionally, a key feature of I-SPAN is the inclusion of the autistic voice and experience in the curriculum and program projects. Participants are required to utilize autistic narratives as expert resources for their projects throughout the program. This specialization program does not utilize a single theory approach, so participants study the effectiveness of multiple evidence-based support for individuals on the autism spectrum.

When I-SPAN was conceptualized, the authors utilized input from key stakeholders, such as local autism community organizations, families, and individuals on the autism spectrum. These stakeholders serve on an advisory board for the program and continue to influence its evolution. The advisory board members have reviewed and rated the I-SPAN curricula, assisted with recruitment, evaluated the capstone projects, and have been guest experts in the courses.

## Disability Studies

*Disability studies* is a growing academic discipline that examines disability as physical or psychological impairment and as a social, cultural, interpersonal, and political phenomenon, as well as the lived experience of people who identify with disability (Goodley, 2016; Syracuse University, 2022). It is interdisciplinary in nature, as it does not draw from one particular field of study. Rather, disability studies examines the socially constructed ideas of disability through the lens of fields such as history, sociology, law, policy studies, economics, anthropology, geography, philosophy, theology, gender studies, media studies, architecture, and art (Syracuse University, 2022). As defined, disability through a medical model lens conceptualizes it as a "pathological condition intrinsic to the individual" and requires an approach that is focused on changing the individual and "fixing" disability (Valle & Connor, 2019). The terms "disability" and "impairment" are considered the same in this model. Conversely, disability viewed through a social model lens distinguishes "impairments" as "variations that exist in human behavior, appearance, functioning, sensory acuity, and cognitive processing" (Linton, 1998, p. 2) and "disability" as a socially constructed idea that occurs as a result of an interaction between the individual with an impairment and environmental barriers such as negative attitudes, inaccessible transportation and public buildings, and limited social support (World Health Organization, 2022). Participants in I-SPAN examine the history of autism as a disability and the influence of various paradigms, including the medical model and social model theoretical frameworks, on the current conceptualization of autism. They are required to analyze autism research, diagnosis, and treatment through these multiple perspectives and, in particular, to deeply understand the impact of these paradigms on the lived experience of individuals and their families.

## Neurodiversity Movement

There is a growing trend in Autistic self-advocacy to consider Autism from a neurodiverse perspective and to better integrate the strengths of individuals on the autism spectrum into our society (i.e., Armstrong, 2011; Autistic Self-Advocacy Network, 2022; Dawson et al., 2007; Silberman, 2013). Neurodiversity asserts that atypical (or neurodivergent) neurological development is a normal difference that is to be recognized and respected as any other biological variation (Armstrong, 2011) and has grown from the field of Disability Studies. Given the variability in beliefs about the causes of autism, intervention options and whether it should be considered a disability or a difference in thinking and processing, professionals must also be abreast of the multiple perspectives that permeate the field. I-SPAN's conceptual framework is grounded in neurodiversity, and participants explore multiple facets of autism through this perspective.

*Figure 2. I-SPAN conceptual framework*

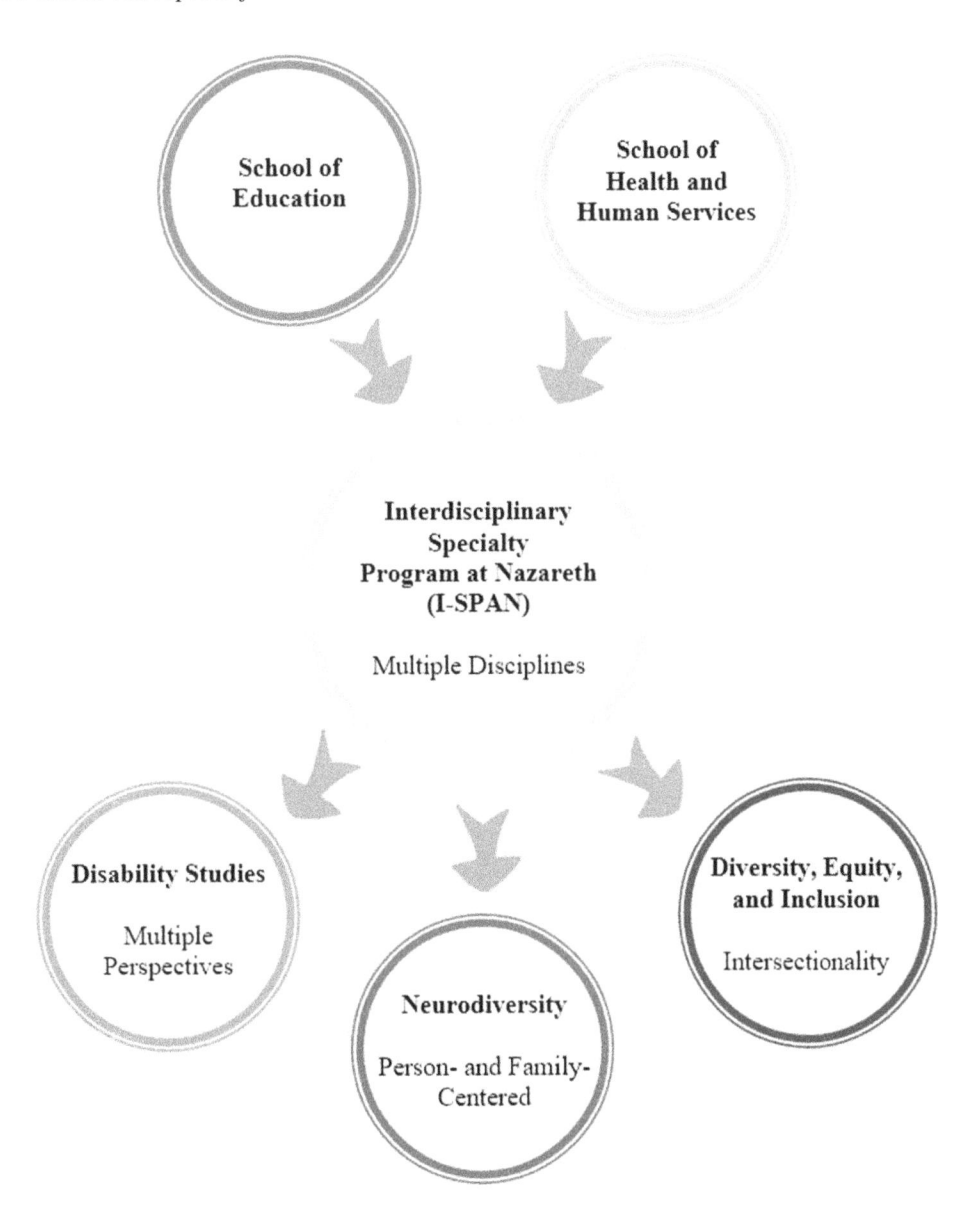

## Diversity, Equity, and Inclusion

The autistic experience intersects with other dimensions of diversity, such as ethnicity, religion, gender, nationality, handedness, and sexual orientation, and thus, should be examined in the context of diversity, equity, and inclusion. The CDC's recent report suggested that overall ASD prevalence was similar by race and ethnicity, with the exception of Hispanic children who were less likely to be identified as having ASD than White or Black children. The higher proportion of Black children compared with White and Hispanic children classified as having an intellectual disability was consistent with previous findings (CDC, 2021). Black children experience racial disparities in diagnosis and access to intervention, as they are more likely to receive a late diagnosis or misdiagnosis and are diagnosed with intellectual disabilities as a comorbidity at a higher rate (Constantino et al., 2020).

Furthermore, ASD is 4.2 times more prevalent among boys than girls (CDC, 2021) and there is emerging research examining the female autism phenotype and camouflaging, suggesting that our current diagnostic criteria may be missing the female expression of autism (Hull et al., 2020). Warrier et al. (2020) found elevated rates of autism in the transgender and gender-diverse community. They describe four important findings: (a) transgender and gender-diverse individuals were 3.03 to 6.36 times as likely to be autistic than were cisgender individuals after controlling for age and educational attainment; (b) transgender and gender-diverse individuals scored significantly higher on self-report measures of autistic traits, systemizing and sensory sensitivity and scored significantly lower on empathy traits compared to cisgender individuals; (c) in two datasets with available data, transgender and gender-diverse individuals had elevated rates of multiple other neurodevelopmental and psychiatric conditions; and (d) exploratory analysis identified that transgender and gender-diverse individuals were more likely to report that they suspected they had undiagnosed autism (p. 6). Why are these important intersections? The legacy of historical beliefs about race, gender, culture, and ability are intertwined in complex ways and impact the way autism is viewed today. Understanding this allows I-SPAN participants to consider intersectionality in their own professional practice and the potential biases that exist in diagnosis, access to support, intervention, and the ability for autistic individuals to participate in life opportunities such as education, employment, marriage, and parenting. I-SPAN's focus is to prepare leaders in autism who will create a more equitable space in their professional practice.

Thinking point: How might these perspectives influence the way Michael's teachers and therapists view him?

## CURRICULAR HIGHLIGHTS

I-SPAN is a three-course sequence and leads to a local certificate of specialization in autism. The first course explores the contemporary conceptualization of autism from multiple perspectives, including the history, diagnosis, characteristics, interdisciplinary practice, family experience, and current research. Participants collaborate in interdisciplinary partner groups and engage in a family experience project where they are placed in the position of *learners,* and families serve as *experts*. Emphasis is placed on examining the lived experiences of individuals with autism as they interact with the societal expectations of "normalcy" and reflecting on their observations through interdisciplinary reflective discussion circles and journals. Table 2 outlines the student learning outcomes and key assignments for the course.

The second course focuses on examining evidence-based support for individuals on the autism spectrum. This course focuses on evaluating and implementing support for younger children with autism, as well as older children and adults using an interdisciplinary and person-centered model. Participants explore support across a variety of disciplines to gain familiarity and understanding of professional practices outside of their own disciplines. Many participants are engaged in clinical experiences in their graduate programs at this point in the program, so their work in this course is integrated into that experience. The co-directors of I-SPAN collaborate with various graduate program directors to ensure that participants are in clinical experiences with students on the autism spectrum, thus fulfilling the experiential components for both their graduate programs and I-SPAN. This model of collaboration and cross-pollination is a model for interdisciplinary practice in higher education. A significant project-based experiential learn-

*Table 2. AUT 660 Student learning outcomes and key assignments*

| AUT 660 Exploring Autism from Multiple Perspectives Student Learning Outcomes | Key Assignments |
|---|---|
| • Discuss classification, etiology, and prevalence of autism.<br>• Develop appropriate approaches to identification/screening and assessment for children on the autism spectrum.<br>• Describe the nature of inter-professional team practice in working with individuals on the autism spectrum.<br>• Describe individual and cultural considerations for individuals on the autism spectrum.<br>• Discuss multiple perspectives related to the assessment, characteristics, and intervention for children on the autism spectrum. | • **Reading reactions:** Weekly journal reactions to reading assignments.<br>• **Family experience project:** The purpose of this project is to allow participants to engage in family experiences to gain a perspective on how families live with autism and to and to recognize the strengths that families use in supporting the family member with autism and to recognize the challenges families face in multiple social contexts. Their role in this project is that of a learner and observer, rather than a professional. They complete a pre- and post-journal that reflects upon their learning. In addition, participants present their findings in roundtables made up of their peers and families.<br>• **Future exploration annotated bibliography:** participants create an annotated bibliography that provides resources for an area of autism that they would like to explore further to develop their own leadership skills in the field of autism. The bibliography is used to develop the final capstone project in the AUT 662 course.<br>• **Perspective final paper:** Participants analyze their own understanding of autism and how their perspectives have changed or been solidified throughout the course. As they consider their growth, they are required to provide evidence to support their perspectives, using the articles, discussions, experiences, assignments, and class activities. |

ing component connected to this course allows participants to apply or observe evidence-based support in action, followed by an evaluation of their effectiveness and professional reflection. This experiential component allows participants to observe, plan, implement, and reflect on evidence-based support in action with actual students. Being able to individualize support and also respond to unanticipated challenges builds skills for future use as professionals and members of teams supporting individuals with autism. Again, the emphasis is on the process of selecting and evaluating support rather than utilizing a certain technique or intervention philosophy, such as applied behavior analysis. Table 3 outlines the student learning outcomes and key assignments for this course.

The final course includes an exploration of current topics in autism, including the representation of autism in literature, film, and the media. Participants examine socially constructed ideas about autism

*Table 3. AUT 661 student learning outcomes and key assignments*

| AUT 661 Autism Support Across the Lifespan Student Learning Outcomes | Key Assignments |
|---|---|
| • Identify, analyze, and assess the evidence supporting various conceptual intervention frameworks for autism spectrum disorders.<br>• Evaluate the integrity and quality of evidence regarding the assessment and treatment of individuals with autism spectrum disorders.<br>• Apply an interprofessional lens in case-based reviews for individuals with autism in order to promote improved outcomes of care.<br>• Reflect on how to integrate evidence with clinical expertise and family or client values when implementing evidence-based practice for assessment and intervention for individuals with autism spectrum disorders. | • **Reading reactions:** Weekly journal reactions to reading<br>• **Interview analysis:** Participants work in pairs to interview one parent of a child on the spectrum and one professional who works with individuals on the spectrum about how they evaluate support and interventions for individuals on the autism spectrum. They use the interview data in class to explore qualitative data analysis.<br>• **Support analysis project:** participants select, research, implement, and reflect on one support or intervention that is within their professional scope of practice. The support analysis is shared or presented as part of a professional panel. In addition, they complete a formal written project.<br>• **Snapshot intervention presentation:** Participants present a summary and critical reflection of the available evidence for a selected type of support or intervention, as well as present professional questions to engage their peers. |

*Table 4. AUT 662 Student learning outcomes and key assignments*

| AUT 662 Autism: A Contemporary Lens Student Learning Outcomes | Key Assignments |
|---|---|
| • Describe individual and cultural considerations for working with individuals with autism spectrum disorders.<br>• Explore issues of power structures, hierarchies, and stereotypes that may impact outcomes for Autistic individuals.<br>• Synthesize multiple levels of research in order to develop unique, person-centered, and evidence-based support for the local autism community. | • **Comprehensive I-SPAN examination:** One component of the successful completion of I-SPAN is a comprehensive examination to assess program student learning outcomes. Participants must achieve 85% competency on the exam for successful completion of the program.<br>• **Capstone project:** The I-SPAN capstone project includes the research and development of unique, person-centered, and evidence-based support within their scope of practice for the local autism community. The project is presented at a community exhibition that key stakeholders are invited to attend. It is open to the general public. Projects are assessed by individuals in the local autism community, peer ratings, and instructor feedback. |

from a neurodiverse philosophy. The final course includes a capstone project that allows participants to integrate their learning experiences and research to design a product that benefits the autism community. Table 4 outlines the student learning outcomes and key assignments for this course. The authors will share student learning outcomes and details about the projects in the next section.

## PROGRAM OUTCOMES

I-SPAN was developed eight years ago and continues to have healthy enrollment, often with the courses being enrolled to capacity or over capacity. Participants continue to complete an entry and exit survey each year where they self-assess their level of preparation in key areas, such as diagnosis, implementation of evidence-based support, and advocacy. Upon completion of I-SPAN, participants consistently indicate a higher level of preparedness. Since the first pilot year, there have been 162 participants across 14 disciplines who have completed the specialization. Table 5 shows the various disciplines represented in I-SPAN across academic years.

I-SPAN participants have designed and implemented a variety of projects to give back to the autism community. Participants begin to construct their projects in the first I-SPAN course by developing an annotated bibliography related to an area of autism that they are passionate about and have a desire to learn more about. They spend the next several months researching that area and providing a rationale for the need. In the final I-SPAN course, they utilize their research to construct a project that will meet the needs of the autism community and present their project at a community exhibition. Members from a variety of community stakeholders, including Autistic individuals, families, professionals, and higher education staff and faculty, provide feedback on the projects. A sample of project titles and abstracts is included in Table 6.

The authors collected data on the effectiveness of the program through a survey of I-SPAN completers and graduate students who did not participate in the I-SPAN program (i.e., non-completers). Results indicated that the majority of I-SPAN completers and non-completers work in educational settings (see a specific breakdown in Table 4). I-SPAN completers indicated that they spend 87% of their time in special education settings and, more specifically, 57% of their time working with students diagnosed with autism. In comparison, non-completers indicated they spent 74% of their time in special education

*Table 5. Disciplines represented in I-SPAN across academic years*

| Academic Year | Represented Disciplines |
|---|---|
| 2013–2014 | Creative arts therapy<br>Music education<br>Early childhood and childhood inclusive education<br>Speech-language pathology |
| 2014–2015 | Adolescence inclusive education<br>Early childhood and childhood inclusive education<br>Music education<br>Music therapy<br>Speech-language pathology |
| 2015–2016 | Art education<br>Adolescence inclusive education<br>Early childhood and childhood inclusive education<br>Music education<br>Speech-language pathology<br>Social work |
| 2016–2017 | Adolescence inclusive education<br>Art education<br>Early childhood and childhood inclusive education<br>Music education<br>Physical therapy<br>Speech-language pathology<br>Social work |
| 2017–2018 | Adolescence inclusive education<br>Early childhood and childhood inclusive education<br>Music education<br>Speech-language pathology<br>Social work<br>TESOL |
| 2018–2019 | Adolescence inclusive education<br>Early childhood and childhood inclusive education<br>Higher education student affairs administration<br>Music education<br>Speech-language pathology<br>Social work |
| 2019–2020 | Adolescence inclusive education<br>Early childhood and childhood inclusive education<br>Music education<br>Occupational therapy<br>Speech-language pathology<br>Social work |
| 2020–2021 | Adolescence inclusive education<br>Early childhood and childhood inclusive education<br>Literacy education<br>Music education<br>Occupational therapy<br>Speech-language pathology<br>Social work |
| 2021–2022 | Adolescence inclusive education<br>Early childhood and childhood inclusive education<br>Higher education student affairs administration<br>Music education<br>Speech-language pathology<br>Social work<br>TESOL |
| 2022–2023 | Adolescence inclusive education<br>Art education<br>Early childhood/childhood inclusive education<br>Higher education student affairs administration<br>Music education<br>Nursing<br>Speech-language pathology |
| Total different disciplines | 14 |

*Note.* Inclusive education includes general and special education certifications. All graduate education programs are dual certification programs.

*Table 6. Sample I-SPAN capstone projects*

| Project Title | Abstract |
|---|---|
| Connecting 4 Kids: A community effort | Primary school is often when autistic students begin to receive related services provided by their school district. Families with children on the spectrum begin their journey of gaining knowledge about autism as they gather resources and support that best meet the needs of their child, especially after a recent diagnosis. Places in which families may gather information predominantly arise from pediatricians, educators, and the Internet. The provision of a direct link between the autism community and the school in which the child attends can strengthen relationships and provide consistent and specific interventions or other support for the child to be successful in their primary years. The purpose of this capstone is to connect families in the district and provide support in areas in which parents are seeking. A survey will be sent out to the families of students that obtain an individualized education plan to gather topics to guide the discussion and needed support. To provide a full experience to parents, special education teachers, therapists, community support, and self-advocates, as well as make-and-take sessions, will be readily available. This monthly meeting is called Connecting 4 Kids (C4K) and is to create a positive collaborative community in the school district to establish foundational and essential life skills. |
| Collaborate to communicate! | In current literature, multiple researchers have found that paraprofessionals and similar disciplines lack formal personnel training. This can have a significant impact on the overall performance of a student with different communication and learning needs. The purpose of this workshop is to educate paraprofessionals, one-to-one aides, and any other disciplines who work with neurodiverse individuals and support their communication needs. By using a person-centered approach, along with collaboration with professionals, families, and neurodiverse individuals, participants will learn how to support the communication needs of their students better. Efficient training, practice, and feedback will be provided. Personnel will learn and implement skills to promote social communication, interaction, and the development of meaningful friendships. Through building, learning, and gaining a new perspective on communication support, paraprofessionals, and similar professions of individuals with alternative learning styles will be better equipped to support communication and become advocates for neurodiversity. As both neurotypicals and neurodiverse individuals collaborate to communicate, barriers to communication can be overcome, and meaningful connections can be made. |
| Addressing accessibility of early intervention resources for culturally and linguistically diverse families of children with autism | This literature review aims to examine the existing research on the barriers to accessing early intervention information and services for culturally and linguistically diverse (CLD) families of children with autism. Early intervention has significant outcomes on the development of a child with autism. For CLD children at risk of autism, early intervention contributes to early detection and screening. Since CLD individuals are more likely to be diagnosed at a later age or misdiagnosed, early intervention proves crucial to the administration of accurate evaluations and implementation of appropriate treatments. The known outcomes of early intervention for children with autism justify the need to investigate the barriers preventing CLD families from reaping these benefits. Numerous studies revealed that linguistic differences, access to reliable information, poor interactions with healthcare providers, and the cultural stigma surrounding disabilities contributed to the lack of CLD families receiving early intervention for the child with or at risk for autism. |
| Students with autism in the instrumental music classroom | Teaching someone on the autism spectrum is common in general music teaching, but teachers of music ensembles rarely see these students. If they do encounter these students, many new service teachers feel unprepared when entering the workforce. They are uncomfortable in these unfamiliar situations and worry about providing the adequate support and attention their students deserve. This literature review and presentation will challenge new and seasoned music teachers to be more inclusive in their ensemble music classes. Interventions will be reviewed at length to help the students receive the attention they deserve. Cheat sheets, curriculum, and intervention samples will also be discussed. |
| Crisis child care and autism: An in-service for social service providers | Additional training is needed for social service professionals working directly with children diagnosed with or displaying symptoms of autism spectrum disorder (ASD) in crisis childcare settings. An interactive In-service training was created to first explore staff biases and stereotypes of the autism population before providing introductory education specific to children with ASD. Lastly, the Inservice is designed to equip staff with crisis intervention skills for the program to keep the child(ren) safe and remain in the program. By becoming self-aware by debunking stereotypes and providing education on critical information related to the uniqueness of children with ASD, staff will increase their confidence in providing care. Ultimately resulting in the normalization of the population utilizing emergency childcare services and increased access to the service. |

settings and 40% of their time working with students diagnosed with autism. Employment setting data are shown in Table 7.

Both completers and non-completers reported utilizing a variety of evidence-based interventions covered in the I-SPAN coursework, including evidence-based practices reviewed in the National Standards Project Phase 2 (2015). Regardless of whether they completed I-SPAN or not, all survey respondents

*Table 7. I-SPAN Completer and Non-Completer Employment Data*

| Employment Setting | I-SPAN Completers | I-SPAN Non-Completers |
|---|---|---|
| School (public or private) | 22 (59%) | 62 (60%) |
| Alternative or center-based school | 5 (14%) | 6 (6%) |
| Hospital or medical | 2 (5%) | 8 (7%) |
| Preschool | 3 (8%) | 9 (9%) |
| Clinic or early intervention | 5 (14%) | 19 (18%) |

indicated that they utilize evidence-based strategies on a daily basis. Non-completers likely did not receive sufficient pre-service preparation to employ autism-specific evidence-based strategies and support.

In qualitative responses about job satisfaction, I-SPAN completers indicated strength in the interdisciplinary classroom-based experiences. For example, one respondent said,

*The collaboration among disciplines is extremely important in my current employment because most students received more than one therapy; many of them receive co-treats. I feel more confident collaborating having completed the I-SPAN program.*

I-SPAN completers also become advocates for neurodiversity in their employment settings as shared by one respondent,

*I feel like I have a good mindset regarding the autism population, which not all my coworkers have. I have a strong understanding of neurodiversity which helps me find the strengths in my students and advocate for their needs.*

Finally, they become changemakers and known as specialists within their buildings related to autism, as shared by another respondent,

*After completing the program, I have held numerous professional learning opportunities for colleagues within my district. I have become a go-to person for support. Through the program, I was able to learn more about a neurodiverse perspective and about the types of EBP that best support my clients.*

In the next section, the authors will share lessons learned from developing a pilot program to obtaining and managing a multi-year Department of Education Personnel Preparation grant at a small private comprehensive institution. They will also present new, innovative ideas to advance interdisciplinary special education preparation in response to the current context of higher education.

Thinking point: How would a program like this prepare Michael's team to better support him?

## LESSONS LEARNED

Higher education is in a constant state of flux and is experiencing significant declines in enrollment, particularly in small, private institutions (Fischer, 2022). As a result, there is a great deal of changeover in leadership that leads to structural changes at the institutional level. Most institutions of higher education are not designed to implement interdisciplinary preparation, particularly in traditional academia, yet to successfully design and sustain an interdisciplinary, collaborative practice, a program must have institutional support. Without this support and messaging from academic leadership, programs are more likely to occur within disciplinary hierarchies, and it is easy to dismiss the importance of collaboration (Banach & Couse, 2012). One lesson learned as the authors developed and grew I-SPAN was that there was a strong need to advocate for the program at multiple levels, including departmental, divisional, and institutional. To create an interdisciplinary program, one must be persistent, particularly as leadership comes and goes, and policies change frequently. Academia is not designed for interdisciplinary collaboration, so there will be challenges when working across divisions that require frequent communication, advocacy for funding, and quick problem-solving capabilities. One way that the authors addressed these challenges was to work closely with the graduate admissions office and graduate program directors to develop a recruitment strategy to ensure all incoming graduate students received information about participating in I-SPAN.

While institutions are not traditionally designed for interdisciplinary collaboration, nor are students. The authors found that graduate students entered the program entrenched in their own disciplines or considered themselves to be well-versed outside their scope of practice. In order to support them in understanding the value and expertise of other disciplines in serving individuals on the autism spectrum, the authors placed an intentional focus on interdisciplinary collaboration throughout the coursework. Students were often grouped in heterogeneous groups for projects as "experts" in their own discipline, assignments were intentional in exploring and researching interprofessional education and interdisciplinary collaboration, and they were consistently required to seek the expertise of their colleagues and expand their perspectives to include disciplines outside of their own. As a result, students began to understand that it was not possible to effectively serve individuals on the autism spectrum without the support of their colleagues in other disciplines. Additionally, they were guided into experiences that provided them the opportunity to explore other perspectives, such as the lived experiences of individuals on the autism spectrum.

An important lesson that the authors learned was the inclusion of multiple perspectives, particularly the voices of individuals on the autism spectrum as experts. As I-SPAN evolved, the authors worked to challenge academia's position on what expertise is by requiring students to include articles, autobiographies, blogs, stories, and other narratives written or shared by the Autistic Community in addition to peer-reviewed references. Students participated in a family experience project that allowed them to collaborate with families, with families serving as teachers or experts. A variety of autistic self-advocates presented multiple times throughout the program, and as the program evolved, more students that self-identified as individuals on the autism spectrum enrolled in I-SPAN. This dynamic allowed the instructors an opportunity to reconsider how the courses were delivered and shifted their pedagogy to include more neurodiverse methods of instruction.

## FUTURE DIRECTIONS

Looking to the future, there are three areas of focus to continue to develop autism changemakers. The lessons learned, as well as external forces within higher education, the world, and the community, have informed and highlighted the need for new and innovative models, expanding audiences, and ensuring carryover from classroom to community settings. Institutions of higher education are engaged in strategic planning in response to threats such as enrollment decline and rising costs. In order for programs like I-SPAN to sustain, the program must be embedded within the institution's strategic priorities, which requires an openness to programmatic change and innovation. Specifically, the authors will focus future work with I-SPAN on expanding the diversity of cohorts, reexamining the delivery modality for coursework, and increasing the embedded clinical opportunities within the program.

To date, I-SPAN has included 14 different disciplines, with a primary focus on students who are pre-service professionals. There have been a handful of students who are currently practicing professionals who complete I-SPAN, but the majority of each cohort are students who have not yet entered the workforce in their chosen field. Given the current shortage of school-based professionals combined with the increasing rates of students with autism, the need for highly qualified professionals has become increasingly critical for school-age children. One way to meet this need is to focus on professional development or continuing education for already certified and working professionals. Partnerships with school systems and agencies could allow qualified professionals, such as the teacher Ms. Blake mentioned previously in the case study, to gain specialized knowledge about autism-specific interventions and support. A cohort model could allow these professionals to study together and complete projects that will specifically respond to current challenges and needs within their organization and earn a micro-credential or advanced certificate in the area of Autism. New and varied disciplines could also be included in this type of model, including school psychologists, paraprofessionals, physical education teachers, and school administrators.

An area that has emerged as an expansive audience is the increasing number of students who self-identify as autistic openly within the classroom setting. Supporting and including self-advocates as students provides for rich learning for all within the classroom community. Often the students are learning about themselves and what it will mean in their career and life to be a professional, as well as an advocate. Intentional pedagogical techniques must be infused to ensure that the autistic student voices are heard, valued, and appreciated, yet also balancing that there is no expectation or requirement for sharing or supporting the learning of others within the classroom beyond what is expected of all students.

Along with diversifying the disciplines that participate in I-SPAN, considering alternate delivery models is another way to reach a broader audience. Specifically, the inclusion of participants from a national or international audience can target training in areas where there is a greater need for specialized training in the area of autism. If I-SPAN content were presented in a fully online or hybrid format, it might also allow for school or organization cohorts to participate more readily, particularly in remote, rural, or under-resourced areas where there may be limited opportunities for professional development in the area of autism. Parents and caregivers could also participate in this type of format, given some limitations that they may have with participating in a fully in-person model.

Lastly, there is increasing evidence in the professional development literature that treatment efficacy is beneficial in the professional development process (e.g., Johnson et al., 2021). In the future, building in more opportunities for practice and feedback on skills utilized within therapeutic and classroom-based contexts would support students in employing skills after the professional development is completed. Participants can be observed implementing an intervention or completing an efficacy checklist to ensure that the intervention is being employed in the way it was intended. This can also provide rich opportunities for feedback and self-reflection.

## CONCLUSION

In conclusion, let's revisit Michael's story from another perspective. What if the school team viewed Michael's use of language from his favorite television program as a strength revealing his ability to use symbolic language in a creative and functional way instead of as repetitive behavior that needs to be stopped or reduced? Additionally, the team might consider Michael's prompted use of the iPad mini as a beginning in Michael's repertoire of technology skills as well as an opportunity to scaffold social connections.

Michael's nighttime routine could be viewed as an innovative way that Michael and his family have co-created a way to regulate the environment. Perhaps some of the tools that Michael uses at home can be carried over to the school. The team can embrace his family as collaborators and experts in understanding Michael's needs and consider providing some of the strategies used at home within the school instead of the other way around. What if the team considered Michael's ability to follow visual prompts and schedules as an important employment prerequisite skill? They could recognize his ability to follow directions and complete a routine from start to finish and teach Michael how to construct visual schedules to use across multiple settings.

What if the team noticed Michael's strengths in mathematical memory skills and his gift of distinguishing patterns in things as assets in a number of employment settings, such as electrical or mechanical engineering, computer repair, or manufacturing? This flip in thinking may inspire the team to construct learning experiences for Michael that would develop his employment skills while also educating local business partners about autism and employment-based support and perhaps even showing them the assets a person like Michael can bring to the workplace. After all, seeing a thermostat from the inside does offer quite a different perspective than seeing it from the outside.

But how does a team do this? It's not only about flipping the story but also about listening to individuals on the autism spectrum and including their voices in the conversation. They must truly recognize and accept that Michael knows what it means to be autistic, and the team may not. It is also acknowledging that autism is a spectrum with a wide range of complex differences in thinking, communicating, and behaving. It means finding specific ways to listen to families as they share what works best for their children and what doesn't work for them as a family. The team will need to work together to recognize that there may be barriers that make autism difficult for families and that families have very different experiences, acknowledging that it may not be autism that is the problem but rather the influence of incomplete stories about autism.

Most importantly, the team needs to realize that Michael is the expert on Michael. They must listen to him as he shows them what is working and what is not working and embed his interests into all aspects of his activities so that he can experience joy, which is something we all have a right to experience each and every day. They need to be able to accept Michael as a diverse human being and see his possibilities, including everything he is right now, transforming their own perceptions about autism and deconstructing inaccurate paradigms about autistic potential. They need to be able to flip the story.

How are we helping them do this? Our interdisciplinary program is designed to bring professionals together across disciplines like education, speech-language pathology, creative arts therapy, and several others to collaborate as we work to transform these perceptions about autism. In this program, they are able to integrate community and family-based experiences as they develop expertise in supporting individuals on the autism spectrum in their various disciplines. Voices of people on the autism spectrum are an essential source of information in understanding the lived experience of autism.

## ACKNOWLEDGMENTS

This research was supported by award H325K160049 through the Office of Special Education Programs in the U.S. Department of Education.

## REFERENCES

Almendingen, K., Molin, M., & Benth, J. (2021). Professional roles and interprofessional collaboration: Health, social and education programme students' self-perceived learning outcome. *Journal of Research in Interprofessional Practice and Education*, *11*(1). Advance online publication. doi:10.22230/jripe.2021v11n1a309

Archibald, L. M. (2017). SLP–educator classroom collaboration: A review to inform reason-based practice. *Autism & Developmental Language Impairments*, *2*. Advance online publication. doi:10.1177/2396941516680369

Armstrong, T. (2011). *The power of neurodiversity: Unleashing the advantages of your differently wired brain*. Da Capo Press.

Autistic Self-Advocacy Network. (2022). About autism. *Autistic Advocacy*. https://autisticadvocacy.org/about-autism/

Banach, M., & Couse, L. J. (2012). Interdisciplinary co-facilitation of support groups for parents of children with autism: An opportunity for professional preparation. *Social Work with Groups*, *35*(4), 313–329. doi:10.1080/01609513.2012.671103

Battaglia, D., Domingo, R., & Moravcik, G.-M. (2013). Autism related curriculum in New York state graduate speech language pathology programs. *Excelsior (Oneonta, N.Y.)*, *8*(1), 53–64.

Brock, M. E., Huber, H. B., Carter, E. W., Juarez, A. P., & Warren, Z. E. (2014). Statewide assessment of professional development needs related to educating students with autism spectrum disorders. *Focus on Autism and Other Developmental Disabilities*, *29*(2), 67–79. doi:10.1177/1088357614522290

Bronstein, L. (2003). A model for interdisciplinary collaboration. *Social Work*, *48*(3), 297–306. doi:10.1093w/48.3.297 PMID:12899277

Constantino, J. N., Abbacchi, A. M., Saulnier, C., Klaiman, C., Mandell, D. S., Zhang, Y., Hawks, Z., Bates, J., Klin, A., Shattuck, P., Molholm, S., Fitzgerald, R., Roux, A., Lowe, J. K., & Geschwind, D. H. (2020). Timing of the diagnosis of autism in African American children. *Pediatrics*, *146*(3), e20193629. doi:10.1542/peds.2019-3629 PMID:32839243

Da Fonte, M. A., & Barton-Arwood, S. M. (2017). Collaboration of general and special education teachers: Perspectives and strategies. *Intervention in School and Clinic*, *53*(2), 99–106. doi:10.1177/1053451217693370

Dawson, M., Soulières, I., Gernsbacher, M. A., & Mottron, L. (2007). The level and nature of autistic intelligence. *Psychological Science*, *18*(8), 657–662. doi:10.1111/j.1467-9280.2007.01954.x PMID:17680932

Department of Human Resources for Health. (2010). Framework for action on interprofessional education and collaborative practice (WHO/HRH/HPN/10.3). WHO Press, World Health Organization.

Fischer, K. (2022). The shrinking of higher ed. *The Chronicle of Higher Education.* https://www.chronicle.com/article/the-shrinking-of-higher-ed

Goodley, D. (2016). *Disability studies an interdisciplinary introduction* (2nd ed.). Sage Publications Limited.

Griffiths, A.-J., Alsip, J., Hart, S. R., Round, R. L., & Brady, J. (2020). Together we can do so much: A systematic review and conceptual framework of collaboration in schools. *Canadian Journal of School Psychology, 36*(1), 59–85. doi:10.1177/0829573520915368

Hull, L., Petrides, K. V., & William, M. (2020). The female autism phenotype and camouflaging: A narrative review. *Review Journal of Autism and Developmental Disorders, 7*(4), 306–317. doi:10.100740489-020-00197-9

Jamanis, S., & Vogler-Elias, D. (2014). *Examining parent and professional survey results for preservice professional preparation in autism spectrum disorders.* Nazareth College of Rochester.

Johnson, A., Soares, L., & Gutierrez de Blume, A. (2021). Professional development for working with students with autism spectrum disorders and teacher self-efficacy. *Georgia Educational Researcher, 18*(1), 1–25. doi:10.20429/ger.2021.180101

Lerman, D. C., Vorndran, C. M., Addison, L., & Kuhn, S. (2004). Preparing teachers in evidence-based practices for young children with autism. *School Psychology Review, 33*(4), 510–526. doi:10.1080/02796015.2004.12086265

Linton, S. (1998). *Claiming disability: Knowledge and identity.* New York University Press.

Maenner, M. J., Shaw, K. A., Bakian, A. V., Bilder, D. A., Durkin, M. S., Essler, A., Fournier, S. M., Hallas, L., Hall-Lande, J., Hudson, A., Hughes, M. M., Patrick, M., Pierce, K., Poynter, J. M., Salinas, A., Shenouda, J., Vehorm, A., Spivey, M. H., Pettygrove, S., ... Cogswell, M. E. (2021). Prevalence and characteristics of autism spectrum disorder among children aged 8 years: Autism and Developmental Disabilities Monitoring Network, 11 Sites, United States, 2018. *Surveillance Summaries, 70*(11), 1–16. doi:10.15585/mmwr.ss7011a1 PMID:34855725

National Center for Education Statistics. (2021). Findings and conclusions: National standards project, phase 2. *Digest of Education Statistics.* https://nces.ed.gov/programs/digest/d21/tables/dt21_204.30.asp

National Resource Council. (2001). *Educating children with autism.* National Academy Press.

New York State Education Department. (2006). Syllabus (outline) and application for approval as a provider of training or course work in the needs of children with autism. *NYSED.* https://www.highered.nysed.gov/ocue/documents/appsyllabus.pdf

New York State Interagency Task Force on Autism. (2010). New York state interagency task force on autism. *NYSED.* http://www.opwdd.ny.gov/opwdd_community_connections/autism_platform/interagency_task_force_on_autism

Office of Special Education Programs. (2020). Fast facts: Children identified with autism. *OSEP.* https://sites.ed.gov/idea/osep-fast-facts-children-with-autism-20/

Petri, L. (2010). Concept analysis of interdisciplinary collaboration. *Nursing Forum, 45*(2), 73–82. doi:10.1111/j.1744-6198.2010.00167.x PMID:20536755

Pfeiffer, D. L., Pavelko, S. L., Hahs-Vaughn, D. L., & Dudding, C. C. (2019). A national survey of speech-language pathologists' engagement in interprofessional collaborative practice in schools: Identifying predictive factors and barriers to implementation. *Language, Speech, and Hearing Services in Schools, 50*(4), 639–655. doi:10.1044/2019_LSHSS-18-0100 PMID:31411947

Rahman, R., Herbst, K., & Mobley, P. (2016). *More than simply "doing good": A definition of changemaker.* Ashoka Changemaker Learning Lab. http://changemakers.com/learning-lab

Saddler, K. (2012). How prepared are New York's teachers to work with students with autism spectrum disorders? *Exceptional Individuals, 35*, 8–12.

Scheuermann, B., Webber, J., Boutot, E., & Goodwin, M. (2003). Problems with personnel preparation in autism spectrum disorders. *Focus on Autism and Other Developmental Disabilities, 18*(3), 197–206. doi:10.1177/10883576030180030801

Silberman, S. (2013). Neurodiversity rewires conventional thinking about brains. *Wired.* https://www.wired.com/2013/04/neurodiversity/

Simpson, R. L. (2004). Finding effective intervention and personnel preparation practices for students with autism spectrum disorders. *Exceptional Children, 70*(2), 135–144. doi:10.1177/001440290407000201

Syracuse University. (2022). Disability Studies at Syracuse University. *Syracuse University.* https://soe.syr.edu/disability-studies/

U.S. Department of Education. (2020). OSEP fast facts: Children identified with autism. *USDE.* https://sites.ed.gov/idea/osep-fast-facts-children-with-autism-20/

Valle, J., & Connor, D. (2019). *Rethinking disability: A disability studies approach to inclusive practices.* Routledge. doi:10.4324/9781315111209

Warrier, V., Greenberg, D. M., Weir, E., Buckingham, C., Smith, P., Lai, M. C., Allison, C., & Baron-Cohen, S. (2020). Elevated rates of autism, other neurodevelopmental and psychiatric diagnoses, and autistic traits in transgender and gender-diverse individuals. *Nature Communications, 11*(1), 3959. doi:10.103841467-020-17794-1 PMID:32770077

Wei, X., Wagner, M., Christiano, E. R., Shattuck, P., & Yu, J. W. (2014). Special education services received by students with autism spectrum disorders from preschool through high school. *The Journal of Special Education, 48*(3), 167–179. doi:10.1177/0022466913483576 PMID:25419002

World Health Organization. (2022). International classification of functioning, disability and health (ICF). *WHO.* https://www.who.int/standards/classifications/international-classification-of-functioning-disability-and-health

## KEY TERMS AND DEFINITIONS

**Autism:** A developmental disability that affects how individuals experience the world around them, including communication, thinking, and sensory differences.

**Changemaker:** Anyone who takes action to address a problem, activates others, and works towards solutions for the good of all.

**Interdisciplinary Collaboration:** A shared process characterized by professionals from multiple disciplines with shared objectives, decision-making, responsibility, and power working together.

**Interprofessional Education:** What happens when participants from two or more professions learn about, from, and with each other to enable effective collaboration and improve health outcomes.

**Medical Model of Disability:** Views as a result of the individual person's physical or mental limitations with a focus on finding a cure or normalization.

**Neurodiversity:** The idea that people experience and interact with the world around them in many different ways; there is no one right way of thinking, learning, and behaving, and differences are not viewed as deficits.

**Professional Preparation:** A combination of courses or work experience designed to prepare and qualify individuals to be effective within the teaching profession.

**Social Model of Disability:** the framework that emphasizes societal limits on a person, not their disability.

# Chapter 9
# Partners in Improving Social Communication in Children With Disabilities in Urban Early Childhood Settings

**Ya-Chih Chang**
*California State University, Los Angeles, USA*

**Jennifer B. Symon**
*California State University, Los Angeles, USA*

**Mitch Fryling**
*California State University, Los Angeles, USA*

## ABSTRACT

*This present chapter describes the focus and aims of the partners in improving social communication in early childhood special education (PISCES) program at California State University, Los Angeles (Cal State LA). The chapter begins with an overview of the aims and focus of the PISCES program in general; providing an interdisciplinary and collaborative training experience to graduate students in early childhood special education and applied behavior analysis who provide services to minimally verbal children with disabilities. After describing the context of the University, the shared experiences of students in the two programs are described in detail. These shared experiences include coursework, fieldwork, and PISCES specific activities. After describing the PISCES program, the authors consider some of the lessons learned, and importantly, how some features of the PISCES program can be sustained going forward. The chapter concludes with a call for ongoing, community-based action research to further inform service provision with early childhood special education populations.*

DOI: 10.4018/978-1-6684-6438-0.ch009

# INTRODUCTION

Professionals from a variety of disciplines provide support to young, minimally verbal children and their families with disabilities, including children with autism spectrum disorders (ASD) across home, school, and community settings. Early childhood special education (ECSE) teachers and applied behavior analysis (ABA) professionals are often at the forefront in supporting this population. They are also expected to work together to best support these children and families. However, individuals in these professions (ECSE and ABA) often have distinct disciplinary knowledge and ways of communicating about service provision (e.g., their roles vary, and they write and target different types of goals). They may also work in different settings and often have distinct funding streams for services. These theoretical and foundational differences in training and aims often leave children with disabilities and families without cohesive support.

Effective collaboration is fundamental to promote positive outcomes for children with disabilities and their families (Dillon et al., 2021; McLeskey et al., 2017), and given the common occurrence of these two disciplines working together in the field, it is critical that training on interdisciplinary collaboration is emphasized in preservice training programs for both disciplines. For these reasons and more, the authors felt it was important to pursue a training program, Partners in Improving Social Communication in Early Childhood Special Education (PISCES), focused on interdisciplinary collaboration among preservice ECSE teachers and applied behavior analysts in an urban, minority-serving institution whose students support diverse, under-resourced families within and surrounding the metropolitan area.

Collaboration can be complex and requires clear communication from all parties involved. The chapter aims to address how the PISCES program promotes interdisciplinary collaboration between ECSE and ABA to effectively support young children with disabilities and their families. First, the chapter provides an overview of relevant literature and challenges in the field in effective interdisciplinary collaboration between the two disciplines, including theoretical differences (e.g., behavioral vs. developmental), curriculum and skills, discipline-specific terminologies, and roles and responsibilities. Second, the context of the preservice training program is presented through a description of the public urban university, participant scholars, and the faculty. Third, the chapter provides a detailed description of the components of the program (including shared coursework and other features). Lastly, lessons learned and future implications are presented in the conclusion.

# LITERATURE REVIEW

## Theoretical Differences

Training in early childhood emphasizes developmentally appropriate practices for education services for young children with and without disabilities. Assessments, goals, and interventions are determined based on children's developmental levels, which requires knowledge and clear understanding of typical child development. In this sense one might imagine that professionals in ECSE may place emphasis on selecting developmentally appropriate goals, and in articulating their work in a developmental context. On the other hand, ABA professionals conduct their work from a behavior analytic theoretical foundation. Following from this, it would make sense that ABA professionals might place emphasis on measuring behavior in an objective manner, assuring there is careful progress monitoring including graphing and visual analysis, assessment of environmental factors related to behavioral targets, technical fading procedures, and more. Given this, it would also make sense that workers in the area of ECSE may often place relatively less emphasis on the strengths of ABA, and that ABA professionals may often place relatively less emphasis on the strengths of ECSE (see Greer & Ross, 2008 for examples of behavioral work integrating developmental context). These theoretical differences represent both a challenge and opportunity for the promotion of interdisciplinary collaboration.

## Curriculum and Skills

There are various considerations related to the curriculum and skills targeted in both ECSE and ABA training programs. Research has shown that teachers often report feeling less confident and struggle managing challenging behavior in the classroom and school settings (Gilliam & Reyes, 2018; O'Grady & Ostrosky, 2021). They may request additional support from the experts in the field, namely in the areas of creating data collection systems and assessing and designing effective intervention for challenging behavior, which are strengths of the ABA professionals. While teacher training programs include courses on positive behavior support and intervention for challenging behavior, they often have a limited scope and do not include comprehensive behavioral assessment and intervention training. For example, detailed coverage of how disruptive behaviors may inadvertently result from how adults prevent (proactive approaches) and respond to (reactive) student maladaptive behaviors may be missing. In terms of antecedent based strategies, many challenging behaviors can be prevented from proper design of lesson plans and intentional planning for embedded teaching opportunities (e.g., Symon et al., 2019). In terms of reactive strategies, without understanding communicative functions of behavior, teachers may respond to maladaptive behaviors by inadvertently reinforcing them (e.g., McKerchar & Thompson, 2004). ECSE teacher candidates complete a course on behavior support early in their training program, however, their participation in the shared fieldwork course with ABA colleagues, which is only provided as part of the PISCES program and under the supervision of faculty with expertise in ABA, provides them the opportunity to practice and apply the concepts and strategies (more on this below).

Considerations related to adaptations and modifications to curriculum, and age and developmentally appropriate skills are also present in ABA training programs. With respect to the PISCES project, with a specific focus on early childhood populations, considerable knowledge and skills related to childhood development are necessary for optimal service provision. As referred to above, knowledge and related skills in this area impact all work – assessment, goal setting, intervention, and more. While this topic is partly a reflection of theoretical differences among ECSE and ABA professionals, this theoretical difference also impacts curriculum and subsequent skill development. Despite general recognition that understanding development is important for practice, specific course content pertaining to human development is not required by common ABA certification and accreditation bodies.

## Discipline Specific Terminologies

Terminology in special education and ABA are highly specialized, and this presents a challenge and opportunity related to interdisciplinary collaboration. Special education terminology often pertains to legal requirements and documents for students with disabilities, such as Individualized Education Program (IEP) and Least Restrictive Environment (LRE). Beyond this, special education is full of various models, which may differ by state or geographic location, may remain in practice for brief periods of time while others sustain, are used by few educators while others are used by many. In other words, there are likely differences in language among professionals *within* ECSE depending on the model or framework of the individual, setting, etc. On the other hand, ABA is well known for using very specific, technical language, which is coherent with its theoretical foundations and basic research and is used consistently across the discipline. For example, terms like reinforcement, extinction, stimulus control, mand, tact, and intraverbal are specific terms used in unique ways by behavior analysts. Interestingly, behavior analysts have long been concerned about terms being off-putting to others (e.g., Rolider et al., 1998; Witt et al., 1994) and have conducted research that confirms these worries (e.g., Becirevic et al., 2016; Critchfield et al., 2017a, 2017b; but see Normand & Donohue, 2022 for recent results that conflict with this general concern).

While professionals from each of the respective disciplines may not fully understand the language and terminology used by the other, the good news is that collaborative, interdisciplinary efforts might not require this. Indeed, professionals from each discipline benefit from learning to "speak the same language" particularly in a collaborative context but recognizing that there is often some amount of "speaking differently about the same thing" can also be a good first step. In addition, it is important that graduates from both programs learn to use more "family-friendly language" to communicate, particularly since both professions work with families in supporting their children with disabilities. Knowing their respective field's terminology is important but learning to communicate with shared language will improve communication and collaboration, ultimately providing the best support for the child.

## Roles and Responsibilities

ECSE teachers and applied behavior analysts often serve in different roles and provide intervention in different settings. Teachers are responsible for designing lessons and supporting all students in their classrooms which can include inclusive or specialized instruction. ABA professionals, on the other hand, often provide assessment, intervention, and consultation in home, community or school settings and their role is to focus on a particular client on their caseload. When both ECSE teachers and ABA professionals are working in the same classroom there can sometimes be a conflict regarding these different roles and responsibilities. For example, an ABA professional may recommend a strategy or intervention that is difficult to incorporate in the context of the larger classroom context, and an ECSE teacher may use practices that are at odds with the ABA support being provided. Moreover, a lack of understanding of each profession's respective roles and responsibilities may lead to recommending practices that are not feasible to the other. For example, an ABA professional could recommend an intervention that while evidence-based, requires more resources that the ECSE teacher has available to them in the absence of the ABA service provider. Successful collaboration requires an understanding and consideration of the respective profession's roles and responsibilities.

## OVERVIEW OF PROJECT PISCES

The PISCES program includes cohorts of scholars taking courses full time across four semesters, or two academic years along with one summer course. Scholars take courses in their respective degree training programs at the same time they participate in the PISCES grant. Their courses include seminars and various fieldwork opportunities aligned with their professional roles at schools and in agencies working in the community (e.g., providing home-based ABA services, conducting directed student teaching in an ECSE setting).

## University Context

California State University, Los Angeles (Cal State LA) is a public university within the broader California State University system which constitutes a total of 23 campuses across the western state. The Cal State LA campus is in metropolitan Eastern Los Angeles. Cal State LA educates over 26,000 students including approximately 22,000 undergraduates and more than 3,500 graduate students. The student population includes many who are first-generation college students (63%), with approximately 90% who are from underrepresented ethnic backgrounds, with the majority being Latinx (73.6%).

The geographical context is fundamental to the work in the PISCES program. Most generally, it is noted that highly trained teachers and related service professionals are often lacking within communities that serve minority and underrepresented families (Imazeki & Goe, 2009). This often is the result of these communities and schools not receiving proper attention and support at various levels. This provides an additional challenge in that the students and families with the highest needs have less access to professionals and teachers who have the expertise to support young children in school and educational settings. The PISCES program faculty and students are deeply committed to meeting the needs of the community, and most students in the program end up working in the region upon graduation. Thus, this is not a mere matter of service, but one pertaining to educational and social equity for this population of children and their families.

## Project PISCES Scholars

The students in the PISCES program are enrolled in either the Master of Arts in Special Education, option in Early Childhood Special Education program or the Master of Science in Counseling, option in Applied Behavior Analysis program at Cal State LA. Prior to entering the programs, students in the PISCES program were interviewed about their interest in working with young children with disabilities, including ASD, in urban high need communities, their past and/or current activities related to ECSE or ABA, and their attitudes and receptivity in collaboration with other disciplines. Additionally, they also had to complete a written application that included three questions asking them why they were applying to the program. Based on student interviews and their written responses to the application, they may have been accepted for participation. Each funded year, the PISCES program accepted 10-14 scholars, for a total of 39 scholars across the four years of the project.

Accepted PISCES scholars were diverse across variables such as gender, age, years of previous work experience, linguistic background, ethnicity, and culture. In addition to their personal backgrounds, the group of scholars displays a range of professional experiences in working with children with disabilities. Scholars' professional backgrounds include serving as behavior interventionists, classroom paraprofessionals, teaching assistants, classroom teachers, family members of ASD, and case supervisors. While enrolled as full-time graduate students, PISCES scholars were employed part-time or full-time within school districts, behavioral agencies, or the like providing direct support to children with disabilities. This diversity enhanced opportunities to expand perspectives and share knowledge between scholars and faculty.

## Faculty on Project PISCES

Tenured university faculty served as coordinators and advisors for the PISCES program. The faculty involved coordinated all aspects of the program including designing the course sequence, recruitment, interview and selection of scholars, identifying and coordination of panel experts, coordinating fieldwork site placements, and design of research and data collection for future outcomes and program evaluations. The faculty members involved with the PISCES project are all housed within the Division of Special Education and Counseling and include one faculty dedicated to ECSE and teacher education, and two faculty with expertise in ABA (and who are Board Certified Behavior Analysts[R]). Regarding teaching the courses within the project sequence, the instructors include full and tenured faculty as well as part-time instructors.

## COMPONENTS OF PROJECT PISCES

### Project PISCES Shared Coursework

As indicated above, the primary focus of Project PISCES is interdisciplinary collaboration between ECSE and ABA professionals. We have identified four critical areas that need to be considered to promote interdisciplinary collaboration: 1) recognizing theoretical differences (e.g., behavioral vs. developmental), 2) understanding curriculum and skills, 3) learning discipline-specific terminologies and jargon, and 4) understanding roles and responsibilities (See Literature Review above for details).

Students in the PISCES program complete four shared semester courses where they earn a University Certificate in Autism Spectrum Disorders in addition to their master's degree. These four shared courses heavily emphasize interdisciplinary collaboration and discuss how the two disciplines can "speak the same language" to better support families of children with disabilities, and specifically what each of their discipline-specific roles are in home and educational settings. The four shared courses include 1) an assessment course, 2) an intervention course, 3) an augmentative and alternative communication (AAC) course, and 4) a fieldwork course in autism spectrum disorders. The courses are developmentally sequenced to address the challenges that ECSE teachers and behaviorists face in the field. First, assessments help both teachers and behaviorists determine meaningful and developmentally appropriate goals for children with disabilities. Once the goals are determined, evidence-based strategies are identified to support these children. Additionally, a subset of these children may require the use of AAC, particularly for children who are pre-verbal or minimally verbal. Lastly, fieldwork allows students from both programs to practice the different skills gained in the courses, including assessment, goal development, implementing evidence-based strategies, and the use of AAC as appropriate.

One of the main skills that is emphasized in all courses is the creation of developmentally appropriate goals for children with disabilities. ECSE teachers are taught to write goals for children's Individual Educational Programs (IEP) or Individual Family Service Plans (IFSP) while ABA professionals providing behavior interventions for children with ASD create goals aligned with requirements through a behavioral agency, school, insurance company, etc. The goals that are developed provide insight into the behaviors and skills those developing them feel are most important to address and are written in terms aligned with their theoretical viewpoint and funding source (e.g., school, agency, insurance). However, how goals are written, and their foci drive the intervention and creation of teaching opportunities. Thus, it is important for students from both disciplines to be able to co-develop and co-write developmentally appropriate goals with the respective discipline, to better support the children with disabilities. Thus, this skill is emphasized in all shared courses.

Furthermore, within each of the shared courses, scholars participate in targeted collaborative, interdisciplinary experiences. Scholars are taught to recognize who their audience is and present materials in layman and family-friendly terms, especially across disciplines without discipline-specific language. In the section below, we will elaborate on the shared coursework as it is the foundation for much of the work in the program. For each shared course, we provide the rationale as to why the course is included in Project PISCES and how interdisciplinary collaboration is emphasized.

## Shared Course 1: Assessment Course

### Creating Comprehensive Assessments

It is well known that the assessment of skills drives the creation of goals and sets the foundation of appropriate interventions. A comprehensive assessment is recommended for the most accurate and effective intervention plan (McConnell & Rahn, 2016). Comprehensive assessments include multiple measures that focus on various skill domains of the child such as communication, social, behavioral, adaptive, motor, and cognitive skills. They also include a thorough assessment of the context and family values that affect the child. A thorough assessment includes both formative and summative (e.g., standardized, norm-referenced, and teacher-created tools) assessments along with direct observations.

In addition to an initial assessment, effective collaboration between educational team members includes *on-going* communication and progress monitoring between teachers, related service providers (e.g., occupational, speech, behavioral, physical therapists), and family members (Bricker et al., 2022). This way, an individual's culture, language, and background are considered throughout the assessment process. Ongoing interdisciplinary collaboration is central to this work.

### Opportunities Related to Project PISCES

As outlined above, teachers and ABA therapists often share students/clients yet lack positive collaborative practice for several reasons such as working from different theoretical perspectives, being overly focused on different skill areas, limited skills, lack of time to coordinate, or no overlap between settings. In terms of skill assessment, the team members are often not included in the full assessment process, or they focus only on their own areas of expertise. Or, in another common scenario, different professionals independently assess the same domain areas without knowledge of the other. Early childhood educators often use norm-referenced, standardized, criterion-based, and teacher-made assessments to determine areas of need along developmental domains such as cognitive, communication, motor, and adaptive skills. ABA therapists, on the other hand, most often use direct observational assessments designed to measure and understand behavior (e.g., Peterson & Neef, 2020). Each of these types of assessment tools provides valuable input to gain a deeper understanding of how a child communicates, learns, and behaves across settings and with different communicative partners and other contextual factors.

Differences in assessment practices are not only a matter of standardization vs. observational methods, however. An additional opportunity relates to the type of assessment each discipline contributes within a comprehensive evaluation. This knowledge is often critical when creating developmentally appropriate goals while also considering how culture, family values, and language impact the needs of a particular learner. Of note, several developmental assessments are used by ECSE professionals, yet they are not commonly used in ABA. In the assessment course scholars are introduced to various assessments including standardized assessments (e.g., Mullen Scales of Early Learning; Mullen, 1995), comprehensive assessments (e.g., Transdisciplinary Play-Based Assessment; Linder, 2008), developmental screening (e.g., Ages and Stages Questionnaires, Third Edition; Squires & Bricker, 2009) and teacher assessments of developmental domains (e.g., Short Play and Communication Evaluation; Shire et al., 2018). Assessment reliability and validity are discussed, as well as language and cultural considerations. This is particularly important given the diverse children and families the scholars worked with, and the focus on minimally verbal children under this training program.

## Interdisciplinary Collaboration Activities in the Assessment Course

Throughout the semester, scholars participate in weekly small group activities comprised of both ECSE and ABA students. These small groups are deliberately mixed to provide opportunities for interdisciplinary collaboration. On a weekly basis, scholars are expected to participate in different interdisciplinary activities. For example, in this course scholars are introduced to writing Specific, Measurable, Attainable, Routine-based, Tied to a functional priority (SMART) goals (Jung, 2007). Different case scenarios are presented, and scholars are expected to co-write family-friendly, developmentally appropriate SMART goals as IEP team members would in the field. They also role-play and practice administering assessments with each other. Lastly, for the signature assignment, scholars in mixed groups co-develop an assessment tool that they are expected to pilot in an early childhood setting. During the semester, scholars use the assessment tool and collect data on a child with disabilities and present their findings.

## **Shared Course 2: Intervention Course**

## Co-designing Evidence Based Practice Interventions

Interventions in the ASD course is included in the PISCES shared coursework and are fundamental to both sets of professionals. Being involved in early childhood more generally requires having strong knowledge and understanding of ASD considering the growing number of individuals who receive this diagnosis. Indeed, the numbers of those diagnosed with ASD has continued to rise (Center for Disease Control, 2021). Whether they choose a position specific to supporting individuals with ASD or a position that provides support to a broader population, there would likely be a substantial number of those with ASD in their classrooms or on their caseloads. Having a clear understanding of the core features of ASD and a strong knowledge of evidence-based practice (EBP) is essential for those at the master's level in special education and ABA. There are many strategies and interventions purported for ASD, including those with little or no evidence to support their use (e.g., Foxx & Mulick, 2015). While many therapies have received strong empirical support, many additional strategies are commonly used in classrooms and educational settings and embedded into teaching practice, despite their lack of clear promising evidence (e.g., Cihon et al., 2020). For this reason, it is important for scholars to distinguish between practices that are evidence-based and those which are not empirically supported.

## Opportunities Related to Project PISCES

The intervention course presents strategies that merge candidate strengths as they learn about and practice using fidelity measures on conducting preference assessments and implementing different EBP interventions including Discrete Trial Training (e.g., Smith, 2001), Pivotal Response Training (e.g., Koegel et al., 2009), and Joint Attention, Social Play, Emotional Regulation (JASPER; Chang & Shire, 2019; Kasari et al., 2021). This allows for merging the developmental and behavioral approaches (i.e., Naturalistic Developmental Behavioral Interventions) leading to a shared philosophy between the scholars and a chance to share terminology and perspectives.

## Interdisciplinary Collaboration Activities in the Intervention Course

During this course scholars have assigned readings and independently access university resources to conduct their own literature searches to identify research articles of EBP that have support for improving social behavior, communication skills, and prosocial behaviors as well as collaborative practice and partnership. Using the articles they find, they work in small groups throughout the semester to discuss and interpret how the findings would be adapted for school, home, and community settings. Student learning outcomes include articulating fidelity of implementation measures across interventions to improve skills. Throughout the course, they role-play the use of fidelity measures and collect data while practicing the strategies. Discussions and practice adapting the interventions across school and home and community settings are provided as graduates often take on leadership and supervisory roles within their schools, districts, and agencies. Additionally, scholars are placed into small interdisciplinary working groups throughout the semester to share perspectives, discuss the application of research studies, and prepare and present a professional development training session. They jointly develop professional development trainings for targeted audiences of their choice (e.g., paraprofessionals, family members, peers) and embed EBP into the content. The training must include clear goals for the audience, be interactive, include EBP, and contain an assessment component. They also must include consideration of socio-cultural awareness and implications for practice. Through these collaborative assignments and discussions, scholars work in diverse teams to offer perspective from their training programs, their roles, and their personal cultures.

## Shared Course 3: Augmentative and Alternative Communication Course

## Supporting Students with Augmentative and Alternative Communication

Considering delays or challenges in social communication are primary symptoms of children with ASD (American Psychiatric Association, 2013), most individuals on the autism spectrum are provided with goals targeting improved communication skills. An estimated 30% of individuals with ASD remain nonverbal even after receiving early intervention (Tager-Flusberg & Kasari, 2013). These individuals will require or benefit from augmentative and alternative communication (AAC) systems to communicate. Therefore, all professionals working with students with ASD should have familiarity with and some expertise in this area as they frequently work on a team with Speech-Language Pathologists (SLPs). Through the course on AAC, students learn about ecological and environmental assessment and the importance of designing and creating various AAC arrays using low- and high-tech systems for a variety of learners across settings. The PISCES program emphasizes young learners who are preverbal or minimally verbal. The AAC course provides content focused on this often-underrepresented group (e.g., Kasari et al., 2014; Koegel, et. al, 2020).

## Opportunities Related to Project PISCES

Both ECSE and ABA professionals alike benefit from learning about diverse types of AAC to support individuals who may benefit from them. They practice using various ecological assessments within various contexts across home, school, and community settings while embedded learning opportunities across routines. In this course scholars learn about core and fringe vocabulary that would be most useful for a target individual to participate within various activities and routines to create the several types of arrays for AAC devices. As part of the array, scholars are challenged to target teaching communication to get needs met (e.g., request or terminate activities, select between choices) and to interact with peers. Additionally, scholars demonstrate their skills in creating teaching opportunities targeting social functions (e.g., greeting, commenting, complimenting, etc.) including between peers.

## Interdisciplinary Collaboration Activities in the AAC Course

The course focused on AAC allows scholars to work in small educational teams to assess and develop diverse types of AAC devices to create a meaningful system for communication. From their diverse experiences in the field and in schools, scholars contribute to the feasibility of each system and offer suggestions of individualization across various case studies. This targets the aim of professionals from two disciplines sharing how the different settings impact the communication opportunities for a learner. In pairs and in small groups, scholars practice creating, using, and sharing their AAC arrays. They practice communicating with different partners and provide feedback to each other. One signature assignment includes a case study where scholars select a routine, assess the individual and contextual variables, design a lesson or activity plan and create the AAC array. The signature case study assignment and associated lesson/activity plan must include communication opportunities for the target individual to communicate as independently as possible within the lesson/routine. Furthermore, the AAC display and lesson/activity plan must also include opportunities for the target individual to communicate for social interactions. In other words, scholars must demonstrate their ability to create purposeful and meaningful social opportunities that do not serve to get their needs met or to request. Specifically, scholars must embed creative suggestions for the children to target social opportunities such as greeting, commenting, sustain conversation, complimenting, asking a question, or such directed toward a communicative partner by using their AAC. Throughout the course, scholars meet with colleagues from both disciplines to share feedback and suggestions for each other's AAC development to provide them perspectives and collaboration on the assignments.

## **Shared Course 4: Fieldwork Course**

### Interdisciplinary Collaboration in Educational Settings

The autism fieldwork experience serves as the final collaborative course where PISCES scholars work in various settings supporting children with ASD. PISCES students in the ECSE program are placed or are currently working in inclusive or special education preschool classrooms while those in the ABA program are either placed or currently working in home, classroom, or community settings providing behavioral services. Throughout the semester fieldwork course scholars receive individual supervised site visits, participate in group supervision meetings, and complete signature assignments.

A university supervisor observes the master's degree candidate in their classroom or place of work while supporting individuals with ASD multiple times over the course of the semester. Prior to each individual site visit the candidate submits a lesson plan or activity/routine plan aligned with the activities they will focus on during the visit. Classroom examples include a circle time routine, small group, table-top centers, outdoor play activities, or whole group instruction. ABA candidates demonstrate their creativity in using EBP across varied academic, social, community, or daily activities. Routines range considerably and have focused on activities such as table-top structured games, academic work, mealtime routine, extracurricular class (karate, art, dance) daily activities (meal preparation, walking or caring for a pet), and more. Through the lesson/activity plan, the candidate demonstrates their skills in creating a lesson for a small or large group of students, while targeting one or more individuals with ASD. Within each lesson or activity plan students identify the targeted goals which are aligned with state standards or preschool foundations (California Department of Education, 2022) and developed from assessments to show how they deliberately create learning opportunities to target these goals. The candidate can include the materials they would use, as well as the data they propose to collect during the lesson/activity and prompting levels they are planning to use.

## Opportunities Related to Project PISCES and Interdisciplinary Collaboration Activities

Whole Group Supervision Meetings

Scholars participate in six whole group supervision meetings throughout the semester. During the group seminars, PISCES scholars meet with the university supervisor who is a tenured faculty member with expertise in ASD and a Board-Certified Behavior Analyst at the doctoral level (BCBA-D). During the group supervision meetings scholars (who serve in different roles, and who have different training backgrounds and experience) take turns to share perspectives on their assessment, proposed goals, intervention designs, data collection and outcomes. During each group meeting, scholars take turns sharing information about their cases and the instructor facilitates brainstorming between scholars to offer suggestions, ideas, insight, and strategies. Family variables and diverse or unique needs are considered as well as gaining awareness and appreciation for working in a setting other than what they are used to. These activities are designed to foster interdisciplinary perspective-taking. They are also designed to provide opportunities for scholars to take leadership roles. Scholars practice communicating with others outside their areas of expertise and learn to translate professional jargon into more friendly terminology. Effective communication skills are critical as students take on more supervisory and consultative roles in fieldwork practicum, and when they graduate and take on leadership positions in districts, agencies, and sites.

## Signature Assignment

The autism fieldwork course involves conducting a case study, where each scholar selects a target child with ASD, completes an assessment of skills and behavior, develops goals and a data collection system, designs and then implements an intervention. Scholars must consider the child, family, system and cultural context and their relevance. Scholars collect on-going data to measure progress and use data to inform their practice. For the final portion of the case study assignment scholars present their data and write further recommendations and next steps for intervention and evaluation. In addition to the signature assignment, self-reflection is valuable for our scholars to determine aspects of their work that aligns with their personal goals and their growth as a professional. They are required to view themselves via video recording while interacting with students/clients and to identify their strengths and areas of growth.

## Other Shared Experiences

The scholars in the PISCES program have several shared experiences outside of their shared coursework. These experiences served to further build community among the scholars as well as provided important, supplementary educational experiences that go beyond their shared coursework. These include annual interdisciplinary collaboration seminars, additional research and scholarly opportunities and support, and regular "check-in" meetings.

### Interdisciplinary Collaboration Seminars

Scholars in the PISCES program attend annual seminars focusing on several topics related to interdisciplinary collaboration. These seminars are organized by the faculty involved, and always pertain to the aims of the PISCES program - they are interdisciplinary and collaborative, community-oriented, and focus on core areas pertinent to holistic services delivery for young children with ASD.

For example, one of the seminars focused on IEP meetings for minimally verbal children in early childhood educational settings. This seminar included representatives from a range of professions and disciplines, including school psychology, speech-language pathology, early childhood special education, early childhood general education, and an applied behavior analyst. For this seminar, PISCES faculty created two case vignettes for the panelists to consider, and these were given to panelists in advance of the seminar so they could prepare their thoughts regarding how their respective discipline might begin to approach the case. During the seminar, PISCES faculty facilitated a dialogue among the panelists, with a particular aim to emphasize how particular disciplines consider distinct factors. There were many opportunities for scholars to ask questions leading to elaborate discussions among the panelists and scholars. Discussions often occasioned rich conversation that would not be occasioned in the context of a classroom. For example, this seminar generated an important interdisciplinary discussion of bilingual or multilingual language environments, and how such environments impact assessment and goal setting for minimally verbal students in early childhood settings.

An additional seminar focused on community resources for families. This seminar involved three panelists, including a parent advocate of a child with disabilities, an advocate from a non-profit organization, and a coordinator from a community-based program. In this seminar each panelist shared their experience and role in the community as an advocate, and in particular considered lessons or key issues they would like PISCES scholars to be aware of. This was important as many professionals who support minimally verbal children in early childhood settings have a limited understanding of community resources and focus primarily on their particular areas of service provision. Panelists provided a wealth of information during this seminar, shared their experiences with each other and scholars, and more. Scholars were especially appreciative of the information shared during this seminar and indicated the families they work with frequently ask them questions about resources, questions that they do not always feel equipped to answer. The seminar helped PISCES scholars embrace their own roles as future advocates for their students and clients.

These are just examples of seminars organized for scholars in the PISCES program. Other seminars included caregivers' experiences in the early intervention and education systems and California Autism Professional Training and Information Network (CAPTAIN) resources for families, teachers, and service providers. These seminars are an important part of the PISCES program, and they generate meaningful conversation and occasion unique learning opportunities for scholars.

## Research and Scholarly Activity

Scholars in the PISCES program receive guidance and financial support to attend and participate in professional conferences throughout their time in the program. PISCES program faculty disseminate potential conference information to scholars regularly and encourage scholars to consider submitting proposals of projects that might be presented. Faculty help organize groups of scholars who are interested in different topics, conduct searches for literature that may inform their work, and guide them through the proposal. The COVID-19 pandemic shifted a significant amount of this work to have more of a focus on reviewing literature and making recommendations for practitioners (e.g., rather than more traditional single-case design research in ABA). While scholars benefit from increased exposure to content related to their respective field of practice and PISCES grant more generally, they also develop and hone non-disciplinary scholarly skills. For example, skills related to searching for topics, reading and summarizing articles, writing an abstract for a submission, paraphrasing key points for a poster presentation, are developed and refined through scholars' experiences in the PISCES program. Furthermore, exposure to recent research in their fields provided education and a deeper understanding of evidence-based practice and current issues in the field. They also are exposed to various researchers and professionals, allowing them to make connections as they may be considering career and further education opportunities.

## Regular PISCES "check-in" Meetings

Scholars attend regular "check-in" meetings throughout the semester. The check-in is a form of community of practice that allows scholars from the same and different cohorts to share their experiences. The meetings also allow faculty to check-in with scholars to ensure that they are making satisfactory progress in completing their respective degree programs and grant requirements. Additionally, frequent individual check-in meetings are scheduled between faculty and scholars as needed. Most of the scholars are first-generation graduate students, and this community of practice and individual mentorship is important for the retention of culturally and ethnically diverse students (Davidson & Foster-Johnson, 2001).

## Community Advisory Board Meetings

An important annual component of the PISCES program includes an annual community advisory board meeting. Here the program evaluator meets with grant personnel, the college dean, division chair, school district administrators, ECSE teachers, early interventionists, regional center coordinators, school psychologists, speech therapists, applied behavior analysts, and faculty in the PISCES program. The advisory board provides opportunities for discussion and collaboration, including updates on current needs of the field and how the programs can support service provision and preservice training (e.g., potential curricular developments). The meetings inform faculty practice and refine the program. The feedback was particularly important during the challenging times associated with the COVID-19 pandemic. Specifically, the community advisory board provides invaluable input in addressing the rapid, shifting needs of the field during the COVID-19 pandemic. The group is collaborative and uses a problem-solving approach to mediate challenges of dealing with assessment, applications of evidence-based practices, and working with families while all experiences shifted from face to face to virtual formats. The shift included additional training in courses that cover the use of different online synchronous and asynchronous instructional tools and programs (e.g., Zoom, Google Classroom, Microsoft TEAMS, Nearpod) and modified assignments that allowed scholars to observe children in virtual classrooms. Special accommodations are made with teachers who are receptive in allowing scholars to observe their virtual classrooms during this time.

The community advisory board was informed that one of the favorite aspects of the PISCES program that scholars shared at their exit interviews was having the opportunities to discuss experiences from different perspectives. The scholars found these opportunities to be informative and contributed to their positive interdisciplinary collaboration. Based on this feedback from scholars, the program is now systematically collecting qualitative data (e.g., videorecorded discussions) from the autism fieldwork seminars to determine the elements (e.g., mixed grouping of students, discipline-specific perspectives) that contribute to scholars' attitudes towards and experiences with interdisciplinary collaboration and teaming.

## LESSONS LEARNED AND RECOMMENDATIONS

Many lessons were learned from the PISCES program. Generally, it is noted that both students and faculty from the professional disciplines are dedicated to supporting children with disabilities and their families, particularly those from under-resourced and under-served communities. Beyond this, the deliberate and intentional efforts embedded into the program to promote skills required for effective interdisciplinary collaboration have been successful. This includes improved communication (e.g., speaking similar language around goals), appreciation and perspective-taking of disciplinary differences and roles, and hoping to have further collaborative experienced in their practice. Moreover, the PISCES program provided scholars from underrepresented groups to gain specialized experience and knowledge giving them potential benefit in the job market. This in turn provides many children, families, and individuals within the greater Los Angeles region with access to highly qualified and well-trained early education special educators and applied behavior analysts. All of this has occasioned considerations of how the program might sustain some of the features of the PISCES program going forward for both preservice ECSE and ABA masters level candidates even after the program is no longer funded.

The master's candidates in both programs, particularly those in the ABA program, had to take additional courses to earn the added certificate in ASD through their participation in the PISCES program. The logistics of requiring extra coursework on top of an already full course load required significant determination and persistence from the scholars. While these scholars committed to this as part of their participation in the PISCES program, they were provided with a tuition waiver for doing so. Without external funding, it may be more difficult for candidates to commit to taking additional courses considering their full course load and working schedules. Given this, the challenge then shifts towards how the positive collaborative features of the PISCES program might be integrated into the existing ECSE and ABA curricula in some way. Recommendations for sustainability are presented below.

## Curricula

There are several university courses that offer opportunities for integrating the interdisciplinary collaboration fostered in the PISCES program into the existing coursework for each discipline. For example, students in the ABA program are required to take a course titled "Analysis and Application of Verbal Behavior", which centers on a behavioral approach to language and cognition, broadly speaking. Much of the research and concepts reviewed in this course focus on language skills of students with language delays and scholars might benefit from a stronger interdisciplinary focus. For example, the course could include a project where students are required to collaborate with professionals from related disciplines to develop a comprehensive language assessment and intervention plan. The course might also consider naturalistic developmental and behavioral interventions, which are coherent with the principles of ABA (e.g., Schreibman et al., 2015), and ask students to develop support plans that incorporate this work in some way. More generally, students in the course could be exposed to general developmental assessments (e.g., Developmental Assessment of Young Children; Voress et al., 2012) and articulate how these may be helpful in developing language programming for the children they serve. Content related to AAC could also be integrated in this course.

A similar opportunity to include interdisciplinary collaborative experiences is included in the course entitled "Behavioral Consultation". This course focuses on behavior analytic approaches to consultation, a broad topic with plenty of opportunities for interdisciplinary collaboration and partnership. While behavioral consultation can sometimes focus on teaching others to implement behavior interventions plans (e.g., as with the common "behavioral skills training" packages), consultation can and often *should* include working with professionals from other disciplines who may inform the work of those providing ABA services. Indeed, interdisciplinary consultation is not only best practice but required in many instances (BACB, 2017).

Like the suggestions presented for the ABA program, infusing the collaborative opportunities from the PISCES program into the ECSE curriculum may yield special educators with stronger skills in understanding and managing challenging behaviors and addressing comprehension needs. With this focus, ECSE candidates would gain opportunities throughout their coursework through shared activities, assignments, and courses. This would require deliberate cross planning by faculty of courses in both programs. Course activities would need to be deliberate and thoughtful to include the needs of special educators, such as behavioral strategies to work with small and large groups of students, instead of only one-on-one models. Another possibility for these interdisciplinary cross-training models could be co-teaching with instructors from both programs. Within a semester course, faculty from different programs could co-teach a few weeks together to model and highlight the importance of collaboration and share knowledge from their respective fields. Collaborative co-teaching models in higher education have been shown to benefit students from different programs, particularly on collaboration and team-teaching (Dresher & Chang, 2022). More specifically, topics such as developmental and multidisciplinary assessments, developmentally appropriate SMART goals, and naturalistic developmental behavioral interventions could be taught and discussed in co-taught lectures and seminars for ECSE and ABA students. These topics and skills set the foundation of the intersection between ECSE and ABA.

## Fieldwork

In thinking about the existing curriculum of both the Master of Science in ABA and Master of Arts in ECSE programs, it seems that fieldwork courses might be an optimal place to consider some of the content from the PISCES Program. For example, in the ABA program scholars currently complete three semesters of fieldwork, where they receive both group and individual supervision. Scholars not only complete hours of supervised clinical practice during these courses, but they also have specific skills and competency requirements during each semester. It seems possible that competencies related to the PISCES program could be included and beneficial for all students. For example, students could be required to conduct an interdisciplinary assessment and behavior support plan, where they specifically demonstrate how the knowledge and expertise of other disciplines (e.g., ECSE, SLP) is incorporated into the behavior plan. In addition to including new skill competencies, the current competencies targeted during these fieldwork courses might be modified / re-aligned so that they focus on areas in the PISCES program. For example, scholars in the ABA program are currently required to conduct a behavioral consultation competency. While completing the competency students could be required to incorporate information from professionals within related disciplines who provide services to their clients/patients to demonstrate their experience in collaborating with professionals outside ABA.

ECSE scholars take three semester courses of fieldwork, where they receive individual and group supervision from university instructors. In these fieldwork courses, scholars complete the required clinical hours (aligned with state requirements), demonstrate their competence aligned to standards and teaching performance expectations for their credential and master's degree. Interdisciplinary collaboration is heavily emphasized in ECSE programs. In fact, one of the eight content topics included in the Division of Early Childhood (DEC) Recommended Practices (2014) includes Teaming and Collaboration. Currently in their final fieldwork experience, ECSE scholars participate in an IEP meeting and write a reflection about the process and their experience. The assignment was created deliberately for scholars to reflect on the IEP process and their collaboration efforts with different related service providers. Many lessons from the PISCES program can be incorporated into this assignment, particularly when the collaboration involves ECSE and ABA.

In addition to these increased requirements for interdisciplinary collaboration, it may also be possible to re-design one of the three fieldwork experiences for *both* ABA and ECSE scholars, so they all complete their required hours and specific competencies at shared clinical sites. Within each PISCES cohort, scholars were placed individually at various school sites and came together during supervision seminars to discuss their clinical cases. Through participant feedback, scholars mentioned that the group seminars were helpful for brainstorming ideas and intervention strategies in supporting their individual students, yet their feedback also showed that intentional placement at shared sites would afford them with opportunities to observe how colleagues worked with the students. This model allows scholars to provide more specific and immediate suggestions to one another. Possibly, even model strategies for one another as appropriate.

## Certificate Programs

PISCES scholars from both programs pursued the Post-Baccalaureate University Certificate in Autism Spectrum Disorders as part of their participation in the PISCES program. Thinking about the future and ways to sustain the beneficial aspects of the PISCES program, the Certificate in Autism Spectrum

Disorders may be re-imagined. At present, this university certificate program requires the completion of a baccalaureate and involves four courses, including a final fieldwork experience focused on ASD. As mentioned earlier in this chapter, completing the certificate program required ABA candidates to complete four courses beyond the master's degree, and required ECSE candidates to complete one additional fieldwork course.

Going forward, faculty and other leaders in the College of Education should consider how to be more intentional with this certificate program. For example, perhaps the certificate could be revised to include optional courses from the ABA program to make it more feasible and desirable for the ABA candidates to complete in the context of their existing program requirements. Students in the ECSE program or more general Special Education "strand" of the certificate could take the AAC course (in Special Education), while students in the ABA program take the Analysis of Verbal Behavior course (in Counseling). Faculty teaching these two courses could consider the overarching, shared aims of the program and tailor the courses accordingly (while continuing to meet accreditation needs, etc.). Although scheduling may present a challenge, specific shared experiences could be planned for students in these two courses, to target the interdisciplinary competencies in PISCES.

Another possibility regarding generating reliable interest in the ASD certificate program without earning stipends to support their work may pertain to supervision. Scholars in the ABA program are largely interested in becoming Board Certified Behavior Analysts. To promote their interest, faculty supervisors in the Autism fieldwork, which is a part of the ASD certificate, could provide additional hours of supervision and supervised practice toward the ABA candidates BCBA(R) requirements.

## Resources and Faculty

The feasibility of pursuing any of the ideas mentioned above requires resources, faculty expertise, creativity, and commitment. As mentioned previously, collaborative co-teaching models are promising methodologies to infuse interdisciplinary content into programs in higher education (Drescher & Chang, 2022) and the benefits to the professionals and individuals whom they support could be profound. Administrative support to encourage creative co-teaching and collaborative partnerships between faculty from different programs is necessary for sustainability. For example, coordination of scheduling for co-teaching courses, development of shared clinical practicum sites, and creation of new interdisciplinary programs all require administration support to facilitate and navigate through institutional policies and guidelines. To overcome the barriers associated with interdisciplinary collaboration, faculty commitment from different programs would include significant co-planning, flexibility, and teaming. It would also require a shift in culture toward enhanced collaboration among a few faculty to create the model. To sustain these collaborative programs, additional buy-in and support (e.g., willingness to teach these courses) from more faculty in the program and administration would be required.

Additionally, professional development for university and fieldwork site supervisors focused on interdisciplinary collaboration is needed. All supervisors are qualified and experienced in their respective fields; and interdisciplinary collaboration would be emphasized throughout clinical fieldwork and explicitly addressed in supervision. Collaborative teaming and partnerships should be explicit in the fieldwork syllabus and addressed in supervision, along with discipline specific competencies. To cultivate this deeper understanding of the values of the program, the college would also need to commit to the investment of supervisors, from the hiring process (e.g., individual teaching philosophy are aligned to program values) and to provide additional ongoing professional development and training.

Finally, from the participant scholar feedback and faculty interest, creating an autism center located on or near campus would afford scholars opportunities to experience a shared worksite. Such a center would provide a formal training site for teachers and ABA to work together while providing resources for the local individuals, families, and community.

## FUTURE RESEARCH DIRECTIONS

The courses, seminars, and activities in the PISCES program addressed challenges and opportunities that professionals in ECSE and ABA experience. To continue to improve the interprofessional collaboration in the schools, home, and communities, stronger collaboration with school administrators and other community stakeholders is warranted. Future projects should include more community-partnered participatory research (Jones & Wells, 2007), where community stakeholders and academic partners collaboratively plan, develop, and implement research-informed programs. This approach strengthens community-academic relationships as both organization entities have equal input in decision-making as they work collaboratively to address real-world challenges schools face in supporting children with disabilities.

Future systematic studies can provide qualitative and quantitative outcomes of the interdisciplinary training program. Namely, studies exploring the process of interdisciplinary teaming could be captured through qualitative processes to identify components or themes that are most relevant for collaboration. Scholars' experience, confidence, and competence in their use of collaborative techniques and EBP in ASD could be reported and measured to determine program efficacy. The results of these studies would shape future programming and program development of interdisciplinary training programs and ultimately enhance the support for young children with disabilities, their families, and educational team members.

## CONCLUSION

The PISCES program addressed the critical need for more training and opportunities in interdisciplinary collaboration, specifically for ECSE teachers and ABA professionals who support diverse populations of young children with disabilities in under-served and under-resourced communities. This program not only addressed the critical skills that are needed in the field of education but also provided high-quality professionals in ECSE and ABA to address the educational and social inequities that are often seen in this population of diverse children. The sustainment of the program, or even the core components of interdisciplinary collaboration, will be of utmost importance to continue the invaluable services and supports that the program provides to young children with disabilities, their families, and the surrounding communities.

## ACKNOWLEDGMENT

This work was supported by the Department of Education, Office of Special Education Programs (H325K180154).

# REFERENCES

American Psychiatric Association. (2013). *Diagnostic and statistical manual of mental disorders* (5th ed.). APA.

Becirevic, A., Critchfield, T. S., & Reed, D. D. (2016). On the social acceptability of behavior-analytic terms: Crowdsourced comparisons of lay and technical language. *The Behavior Analyst*, *39*(2), 305–317. doi:10.100740614-016-0067-4 PMID:31976979

Bricker, D. D., Felimban, H. S., Lin, F. Y., Stegenga, S. M., & Storie, S. O. M. (2022). A proposed framework for enhancing collaboration in early intervention/early childhood special education. *Topics in Early Childhood Special Education*, *41*(4), 240–252. doi:10.1177/0271121419890683

California Department of Education. (2022). California Preschool Learning Foundations. *CDE*. https://www.cde.ca.gov/sp/cd/re/psfoundations.asp

Center for Disease Control. (2021). Autism prevalence higher in CDC's ADDM Network: Improvements being made in identifying children with autism early. *CDC*. https://www.cdc.gov/media/releases/2021/p1202-autism.html

Chang, Y. C., & Shire, S. (2019). Promoting play in early childhood programs for children with ASD: Strategies for educators and practitioners. *Teaching Exceptional Children*, *52*(2), 66–76. doi:10.1177/0040059919874305

Cihon, J. H., Milne, C. M., Leaf, J., Ferguson, J. L., & Leaf, R. (2020). Fad treatments in autism intervention. *Education and Training in Autism and Developmental Disabilities*, *5*(4), 466–475.

Critchfield, T. S., Becirevic, A., & Reed, D. D. (2017a). On the social validity of behavior-analytic communication: A call for research and description of one method. *Analysis of Verbal Behavior*, *33*(1), 1–23. doi:10.100740616-017-0077-7 PMID:30854284

Critchfield, T. S., Doepke, K. J., Epting, L. K., Becirevic, A., Reed, D. D., Fienup, D. F., Kremsreiter, J. L., & Ecott, C. L. (2017b). Normative emotional responses to behavior analysis jargon: How not to use words to win friends and influence people. *Behavior Analysis in Practice*, *10*(2), 97–106. doi:10.100740617-016-0161-9 PMID:28630814

Davidson, M. N., & Foster-Johnson, L. (2001). Mentoring in the preparation of graduate researchers of color. *Review of Educational Research*, *71*(4), 549–574. doi:10.3102/00346543071004549

Dillon, S., Armstrong, E., Goudy, L., Reynolds, H., & Scurry, S. (2021). Improving special education service delivery through interdisciplinary collaboration. *Teaching Exceptional Children*, *54*(1), 36–43. doi:10.1177/00400599211029671

Division for Early Childhood. (2014). DEC recommended practices in early intervention/early childhood special education. *DEC*. http://www.dec-sped.org/recommendedpractices

Drescher, T., & Chang, Y. C. (2022). Benefits of Collaborative Teaching Models in Teacher Education Programs: Sharing disability knowledge and promoting inclusion. *Teacher Development*, *26*(2), 151–165. doi:10.1080/13664530.2022.2032299

Gilliam, W. S., & Reyes, C. R. (2018). Teacher decision factors that lead to preschool expulsion. *Infants and Young Children*, *31*(2), 93–108. doi:10.1097/IYC.0000000000000113

Greer, R. D., & Ross, D. E. (2008). Verbal behavior analysis: Inducing and expanding new verbal capabilities in children with language delays. In Pearson. Foxx, R. M., & Mulick, J. A. (Eds.) (2015). Controversial therapies for autism and intellectual disabilities.

Imazeki, J., & Goe, J. (2009). *The distribution of highly qualified, experienced teachers: Challenges and opportunities. TQ Research and Policy Brief*. National Comprehensive Center for Teacher Quality.

Jones, L., & Wells, K. (2007). Strategies for academic and clinician engagement in community-participatory partnered research. *Journal of the American Medical Association*, *297*(4), 407–410. doi:10.1001/jama.297.4.407 PMID:17244838

Jung, L. A. (2007). Writing SMART objectives and strategies that fit the ROUTINE. *Teaching Exceptional Children*, *39*(4), 54–58. doi:10.1177/004005990703900406

Kasari, C., Gulsrud, A. C., Shire, S. Y., & Strawbridge, C. (2021). *The JASPER model for children with autism: promoting joint attention, symbolic play, engagement, and regulation*. Guilford Publications.

Kasari, C., Kaiser, A., Goods, K., Nietfeld, J., Mathy, P., Landa, R., Murphy, S., & Almirall, D. (2014). Communication interventions for minimally verbal children with autism: A sequential multiple assignment randomized trial. *Journal of the American Academy of Child and Adolescent Psychiatry*, *53*(6), 635–646. doi:10.1016/j.jaac.2014.01.019 PMID:24839882

Koegel, L. K., Bryan, K. M., Su, P. L., Vaidya, M., & Camarata, S. (2020). Definitions of nonverbal and minimally verbal in research for autism: A systematic review of the literature. *Journal of Autism and Developmental Disorders*, *50*(8), 2957–2972. doi:10.100710803-020-04402-w PMID:32056115

Koegel, R. L., Vernon, T., & Koegel, L. K. (2009). Improving social initiations in young children using reinforcers and embedded social interactions. *Journal of Autism and Developmental Disorders*, *39*(9), 1240–1251. doi:10.100710803-009-0732-5 PMID:19357942

Linder, T. (2008). *Transdisciplinary Play-Based Assessment: A Functional Approach to Working with Young Children* (2nd ed.). Paul H. Brookes.

McConnell, S. R., & Rahn, N. L. (2016). Assessment in early childhood special education. In *Handbook of early childhood special education* (pp. 89–106). Springer. doi:10.1007/978-3-319-28492-7_6

McKerchar, P. M., & Thompson, R. H. (2004). A descriptive analysis of potential reinforcement contingencies in the preschool classroom. *Journal of Applied Behavior Analysis*, *37*(4), 431–443. doi:10.1901/jaba.2004.37-431 PMID:15669403

McLeskey, J., Barringer, M-D., Billingsley, B., Brownell, M., Jackson, D., Kennedy, M., Lewis, T., Maheady, L., Rodriguez, J., Scheeler, M. C., Winn, J., & Ziegler, D. (2017, January). High-leverage practices in special education. *Council for Exceptional Children & CEEDAR Center*.

Mullen, E. M. (1995). *Mullen Scales of Early Learning*. American Guidance Service.

Normand, M. P., & Donohue, H. E. (2022). Behavior analytic jargon does not seem to influence treatment acceptability ratings. *Journal of Applied Behavior Analysis*, *55*(4), 1294–1305. doi:10.1002/jaba.953 PMID:36131368

O'Grady, C., & Ostrosky, M. M. (2021). Suspension and Expulsion: Early Educators' Perspectives. *Early Childhood Education Journal*, 1–11.

Peterson, S., & Neef, N. (2020). Functional behavioral assessment. In J. O. Cooper, T. E. Heron, & W. L. Heward, Applied behavior analysis (3rd Ed.) (pp. 628-654). Pearson.

Rolider, A., Axelrod, S., & Van Houten, R. (1998). Don't speak behaviorism to me: How to clearly and effectively communicate behavioral interventions to the general public. *Child & Family Behavior Therapy*, *20*(2), 39–56. doi:10.1300/J019v20n02_03

Schreibman, L., Dawson, G., Stahmer, A. C., Landa, R., Rogers, S. J., McGee, G. G., Kasari, C., Ingersoll, B., Kaiser, A., Bruinsma, Y., McNerney, E., Wetherby, A., & Halladay, A. (2015). Naturalistic developmental behavioral interventions: Empirically validated treatments for autism spectrum disorder. *Journal of Autism and Developmental Disorders*, *45*(8), 2411–2428. doi:10.100710803-015-2407-8 PMID:25737021

Shire, S. Y., Shih, W., Chang, Y. C., & Kasari, C. (2018). Short Play and Communication Evaluation: Teachers' assessment of core social communication and play skills with young children with autism. *Autism*, *22*(3), 299–310. doi:10.1177/1362361316674092 PMID:29671644

Smith, T. (2001). Discrete Trial Training in the treatment of Autism. *Focus on Autism and Other Developmental Disabilities*, *16*(2), 86–92. doi:10.1177/108835760101600204

Squires, J., & Bricker, D. (2009). Ages & Stages Questionnaires®, Third Edition (ASQ®-3): A Parent-Completed Child Monitoring System. Paul H. Brookes Publishing Co., Inc.

Symon, J. B., Bruinsma, Y., & McNerney, E. M. (2019). Antecedent Strategies, In Bruinsma, Y., Boettcher, M. Stahmer, A., Schreibman, L., (Eds.). Naturalistic Developmental Behavioral Interventions: An Overview and Practical Application. Brookes Publishing Co.

Tager-Flusberg, H., & Kasari, C. (2013). Minimally verbal school-aged children with autism spectrum disorder: The neglected end of the spectrum. *Autism Research*, *6*(6), 468–478. doi:10.1002/aur.1329 PMID:24124067

Voress, J. K., Maddox, T., & Hammill, D. D. (2012). *Developmental Assessment of Young Children* (2nd ed.). Pearson.

Witt, J. C., Moe, G., Gutkin, T. B., & Andrews, L. (1984). The effect of saying the same thing in different ways: The problem of language and jargon in school-based consultation. *Journal of School Psychology*, *22*(4), 361–367. doi:10.1016/0022-4405(84)90023-2

# Chapter 10
# Interdisciplinary Training for Early Childhood Special Educators and Speech Language Pathology Candidates

**Lisa N. Erwin-Davidson**
*California State University, Fullerton, USA*

**Aja McKee**
*California State University, Fullerton, USA*

**Janice Myck-Wayne**
*California State University, Fullerton, USA*

## ABSTRACT

*This chapter informs readers of a collaborative five-year grant, project activity based communication (ABC), between the College of Education, Department of Special Education and the College of Communications, Department of Communication Sciences and Disorders. The purpose of this collaboration was to respond to the call for delivering high-quality preservice training to early childhood special educators and speech-language pathology candidates. A collaborative and cross-disciplinary approach was taken in the design of the instructional framework, the delivery of coursework, and the selection of professional development opportunities. The instructional framework is meant to prepare and educate pre-professionals on how to collaborate successfully while applying best practices of universal design for learning that support all preschoolers, with and without high-intensity needs in an inclusive preschool environment. This work is funded through a 325K personnel preparation development grant by the US Department of Education in the Office of Special Education Programs (OSEP).*

This chapter informs readers of a collaborative and interdisciplinary approach to training early childhood special education (ECSE) teachers and preservice speech and language pathologists (SLPs) on how to

DOI: 10.4018/978-1-6684-6438-0.ch010

co-support young students with high-intensity learning needs in an inclusive preschool environment. The instructional framework is aligned with the Comprehensive System of Personnel Development outlined by the Early Childhood Personnel Center and is designed to prepare and educate preprofessionals on how to successfully collaborate and best apply principles and practices of Universal Design for Learning (UDL) to support preschoolers with and without disabilities. Project ABC (Activity-Based Communication) is a collaboration between the College of Education ECSE credential program and the College of Communications Department of Communication Sciences and Disorders (CSD).

The chapter defines Project ABC, provides the rationale for a cross-disciplinary approach to personnel preparation, presents the components of the instructional framework, and describes how the learning outcomes of Project ABC scholars will be measured and monitored. This work is funded through a $325,000 personnel preparation development grant by the U.S. Department of Education's Office of Special Education Programs.

## PROJECT ABC

Project ABC is a 5-year project providing interdisciplinary training to cohorts of ECSE teacher candidates and SLP candidates. The aims of Project ABC are twofold: (a) to improve the effectiveness of early intervention, early childhood special education, and speech language pathology services and supports in bettering learning outcomes of young children with high-intensity communication needs, and (b) to increase the quality of early inclusive education for young children with high-intensity learning needs. The iterative nature of the project is designed to address the critical need to recruit and retain high-quality early educators and increase the knowledge and skills of Assistive Technology (AT)/Augmentative and Alternative Communication (AAC) in ESCEs and SLPs, and accomplishes this by offering an interdisciplinary training program between the ECSE credential master's program and the CSD master's program (e.g., see Figure 1).

Project ABC seeks to accomplish these aims through collaborative training and instructional content. Training and seminars are designed to guide preservice professionals in the preparing, planning, and understanding of how to implement augmentative and alternative communication (AAC) across daily preschool routines to support the early language, literacy, and communication development of young children with intensive communication and learning needs.

## THE NEED FOR PROJECT ABC

According to the 2017 report to Congress on the Individuals with Disabilities in Education Act (IDEA; U.S. Department of Education, 2017), almost half (43%) of preschoolers with disabilities had a speech or language impairment as their primary disability and 37.6% had a developmental delay (DD) as their primary disability. Given these numbers, early educators should expect to serve children who need access to aided AAC to promote their cognitive development. However, this is not always the case (Lieber et al., 2008).

Unfortunately, most preschool-aged children with DD who may require aided AAC are still educated in separate settings (Kleinert et al., 2015), where they face all the same challenges as their peers in inclusive settings yet have limited opportunity to learn language from or with same-age peers. In an

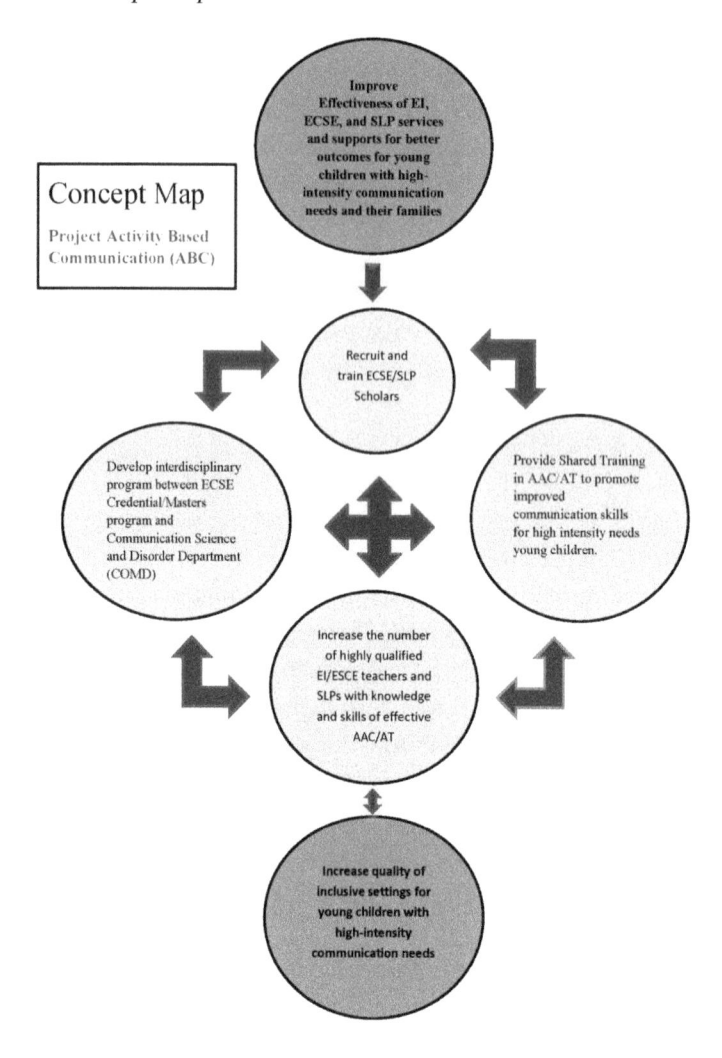

*Figure 1. Project ABC Concept Map*

**Concept Map**
Project Activity Based Communication (ABC)

- Improve Effectiveness of EI, ECSE, and SLP services and supports for better outcomes for young children with high-intensity communication needs and their families
- Recruit and train ECSE/SLP Scholars
- Develop interdisciplinary program between ECSE Credential/Masters program and Communication Science and Disorder Department (COMD)
- Provide Shared Training in AAC/AT to promote improved communication skills for high intensity needs young children.
- Increase the number of highly qualified EI/ESCE teachers and SLPs with knowledge and skills of effective AAC/AT
- Increase quality of inclusive settings for young children with high-intensity communication needs

inclusive classroom serving children with and without disabilities, all students are expected to learn from knowledgeable others, including classroom teachers, instructional aides, visiting family members, related service providers, and same-age peers. No matter the makeup of the preschool classroom, standard practices require all educators serving the classroom to know how to provide the necessary supports and services so all students develop school readiness skills for academic achievement (National Professional Development Center on Inclusion, 2012). Thus, there is an ongoing need for preservice education to offer integrated trainings (Tegler et al., 2019) to meet the needs of students with and without disabilities, all of whom are expected to learn together in their preschool settings.

Project ABC designed an interdisciplinary personnel preparation instructional framework to meet this need. In particular, the project director identified a need to build ECSE and SLP candidates' AAC-related knowledge and skills to address the complex and diverse learning needs of all children. Additionally, project faculty wished to instruct early educators and preservice SLPs to reduce the reported social marginalization of preschoolers with complex communication needs. The reasons for this marginalization may be due to a limited number of communication partners or the lack of physical and adapted access to places where children without disabilities are playing (Østvik et al., 2017).

The work of Project ABC focuses on preservice training in early childhood education classrooms because evidence points to the need for preschool teachers to have education and experience in integrating aided AAC successfully (von Tetzchner et al., 2009). Project ABC wished to address this problem because classroom teachers are likely the first people to identify children in the classroom who may struggle to socially engage or fully participate in their early learning curricula (Light & McNaughton, 2014).

Unfortunately, young children with complex communication needs may not be enrolled in inclusive preschool classrooms. Instead, children who cannot speak in conventional ways may be labeled "moderately to severely disabled" and placed in more restrictive educational settings, even at the start of their educational journey. The U.S. Department of Education (2017) reported children labeled moderately to severely disabled had fewer opportunities to engage in the general education environment than their nondisabled peers. Additionally, students labeled as moderately to severely disabled may present with concomitant visual and hearing impairments that require other forms of AT to allow students' full participation in their preschool curricula. Without early educators who know how to maximize language development for daily interactions with nondisabled peers, children with complex communication needs face another layer of challenges when they may already face a variety of opportunity and access barriers.

The faculty members directing Project ABC understand the benefits of high-quality instruction, which promotes cognitive and language development for all language learners, including dual language learners (Jacoby & Lesaux, 2017). Likewise, high-quality educators need to have an understanding of the intersection between a child's cultural-linguistic environment, social-cultural communication expectations, and how to appropriately represent the aided language. To that end, a majority of the scholars chosen for the project are bilingual, and represent the racial diversity of the region (3 scholars are African-American, 4 Asian, 19 Hispanic/Latinx, 2 Middle Eastern-North African, 13 White). Scholars are trained on how to create daily lessons that are culturally-linguistically sensitive, and to provide frequent, equitable, and successful learning opportunities for all children (Rafferty et al., 2003). Early educators need to be trained to recognize children with complex communication or high-intensity learning needs and need AAC. If the children have to wait for an AAC specialist for a formal assessment, the classroom educators can begin to teach language in various forms (e.g., graphic symbols, tactual symbols, sign language) and provide a means for children to socialize, express basic needs and wants to regulate their behavior, and participate in educational curricula.

Project ABC recognized the need to instruct scholars to not only take steps to eliminate opportunity and access barriers, but to also learn about, practice, and implement the evidence-based communication partner strategies that facilitate early language and communication skills into assigned fieldwork (Biggs et al., 2018; Kent-Walsh et al., 2010, 2015; O'Neill et al., 2018). Project faculty wanted to teach scholars how to incorporate non-electronic and electronic aided AAC systems into classroom settings for facilitating communication behaviors, expanding vocabulary growth, and developing grammar (Justice et al., 2018). In so doing, Project ABC faculty wanted to build scholars knowledge and skills for creating numerous language learning opportunities for a culturally and linguistically diverse group of preschoolers with a wide range of cognitive, sensorimotor, and communicative abilities.

## Development of Project ABC

Faculty members who developed the Project ABC instructional curriculum understood the critical role of early childhood educators and speech language pathologists in supporting and coordinating services to maximize children's positive learning outcomes (Richardson-Gibbs & Klein, 2014). Project faculty wished to ensure early educators and preservice SLPs understood successful learning outcomes for students with severe disabilities in early and inclusive educational settings should include: (a) a focus on a child's strengths, (b) a positive attitude from educators, (c) increased understanding of the importance of communication among the child's team, (d) collaboration between the providers and the parent(s), and, (e) a willingness to embed language and early literacy into daily instruction and existing routines rather than removing children from their classroom for SLP services, or a "pull-out model" (Cross et al., 2004).

In 2006, an estimated 12% of young children who received special education services in the United States experienced significant communication delays (Binger & Light, 2006). These percentages were higher among children with high-intensity needs such as autism spectrum disorder, cognitive impairment, deafness/blindness and severe physical impairments (Beukelman & Mirenda, 2012; Binger & Light, 2006). In developing the Project ABC coursework, faculty members highlighted the need for early educators to have knowledge of and skills in AAC, and agreed AAC methods were an effective way to support young children in developing communication skills (Branson & Demchak, 2009). It was also necessary for project faculty to inform preservice SLPs that the American Speech Language and Hearing Association outlined the roles and responsibilities of SLPs with respect to AAC and its impact on children's early learning and language outcomes in the Technical Report published in 2004. Even though there is minimal consensus on who must implement AAC assessments, there is solid evidence and expert testimony that assessment should be an intercollaborative process for fostering language and literacy development, especially for children with severe and multiple disabilities (Ogletree, 2017).

A factor in developing the coursework for the project was awareness of the national and local problems of relying solely on district-or school-wide AAC specialists. Some of these issues included: (a) the appointed AAC specialists may not be known to the student they are assessing and may be unable to achieve the level of engagement reported by the parents or the student's primary educators; (b) young children with complex communication and learning needs may not perform well with unknown adults or in unfamiliar environments, which make it difficult to obtain a true assessment of the child's skills (Soto & Zangari, 2009); and (c) the AAC specialist may not receive adequate information from the preschool classroom's SLP about the student's language development, current communication level, or literacy level.

Conversely, approaches involving adults familiar with the child can support successful AAC assessments (Downing et al., 2015; Soto & Zangari, 2009). Project ABC wished to convey to scholars that partnering with professionals educated in assistive technology (e.g., classroom teachers, SLPs, OTs, educational technologists) may be the best combination for evaluating the need for AAC in a classroom environment in which access to preacademic or academic curricula is imperative (Center on Disability, California State University-Northridge, 2018; Costigan & Light, 2010; DePaepe & Wood, 2001; Downing et al., 2015).

Interprofessional collaboration was thus an important concept to emphasize in the instructional framework. Consequently, there was significant discussion about the local challenges of district-wide SLPs being designated as the *sole* assessor and provider of AAC service delivery in schools. An AAC service delivery model that does not include frequent communication partner training in children's naturalistic settings to develop the language of social communication between peers and with adults (i.e., how to support communication interactions, make comments, or ask questions) has limited effectiveness for aided AAC users (Barker et al., 2013; Kent-Walsh et al., 2010, 2015). Children not only need instruction for communicating basic needs and wants but also to learn enough vocabulary to more fully participate in their preacademic and academic curricula, as federally mandated by IDEA. A service delivery model requiring young children to wait months for AAC assessments creates an added and unreasonable delay in language instruction for daily classroom communication.

Finally, Project ABC faculty sought to debunk the myth that aided AAC prevents speech and language development; in fact, research findings have suggested the opposite (Romski et al., 2015). In developing project coursework, faculty members knew myth-debunking would be a powerful way to provide scholars with the evidence and counter arguments they may need when speaking with families, administrators, and fellow educators on a daily basis. Scholars need to learn the accumulated evidence supporting early implementation of AAC into educational programming for the ongoing development of language for daily communication (e.g., Williams et al., 2008), and understand early AAC intervention has repeatedly demonstrated a reduction in the potential lifelong impact of a communication disability (Drager et al., 2010; Kent-Walsh et al., 2015; Romski et al., 2015).

In summary, there is no doubt children with complex communication and learning needs will continue to enroll in early education classrooms, necessitating the development of a workforce ready to address these needs. The project faculty steeped themselves in literature on early childhood education from the last 30 years, and understood the necessity of incorporating unaided and aided AAC into early learning environments to develop young children's communication, language, and early literacy skills (Romski et al., 2015).

## Filling the Gap to Address the Need for Interdisciplinary Implementation of AT and AAC

Twelve years ago, Costigan and Light (2010) found preservice certification programs offered minimal content on AAC. At that time, a significant percentage of preservice graduate programs (18–38% of SLP programs, 76% of Special Education Teacher (SET) programs, and 100% of OT programs) failed to offer an AAC course. Between 2008 and 2019, there has been a substantial increase in the number of academic programs offering preservice AAC training (Johnson & Prebor, 2019; Ratcliff et al., 2008). However, the type of AAC instruction and the amount of AAC clinical experience students are expected to document by graduation may vary by university program. As a result, preservice clinicians may still enter the workforce with minimal to no knowledge of the benefits of AAC or how to implement AAC for students with complex communication needs.

The work of Project ABC is informed by the work outlined in the Early Childhood Personnel Center (ECPC)'s Family-Centered Practice and Intervention/Instruction, in addition to current research findings on implementing AAC with preschool-aged children who require early language, literacy, and communication instruction to fully participate in early educational curricula. The Project ABC team recognized this gap in AAC knowledge and skills and wished to fill it by teaching early childhood special educators and preservice SLPs how appropriate instruction with appropriate tools can make a significant difference in children's educational outcomes. Appropriate instruction was deemed a collaborative one in which scholars are taught how to function as an interdisciplinary team and learn to instruct very young children, both those with and without disabilities, how to learn together in a shared space 4 to 5 days a week. Project ABC considers the classroom a shared learning space providing family-centered and culturally and linguistically responsive services.

A shared learning space requires universal access to the tools, materials, and strategies young children need to engage with, and benefit from, their educational curricula. Project ABC trains ECSE teachers and preservice SLPs on these AT and AAC tools by incorporating AT and AAC basic training into the coursework. Project ABC considers this training necessary because it addresses the need for the interdisciplinary implementation of AT and AAC, in which scholars learn to apply the tools, strategies, and techniques necessary for young children, especially those with complex communication and high intensity learning needs, to more fully participate in their daily preschool education.

## DISCUSSION

Project ABC's instructional framework is designed to develop scholars' cross-disciplinary competencies through collaboration. The faculty members who co-deliver the instruction understand the importance of training preservice educators on building successful collaborations, as highlighted in Dinnebeil (2014) and Dinnebeil et al. (2009). Project ABC focuses on the cross-disciplinary competencies identified by Bruder et al., (2018) and published by the ECPC's Family-Centered Practice and Intervention/Instruction (ECPC, 2020).

## INSTRUCTIONAL FRAMEWORK OF PROJECT ABC

Focusing on cross-disciplinary professional competencies helps faculty coordinate and collaborate on coursework to ensure scholars receive instruction supporting high-quality inclusive preschool education. This type of coursework is one approach for solving the lack of high-quality teacher and SLP training on inclusion reported in the literature over 15 years ago (e.g., Barton & Smith, 2015). For example, the preliminary credentials program offered to Project ABC scholars incorporates specific interdisciplinary strategies and practices related to the successful inclusion of all young children.

Cross-disciplinary collaboration is also supported by more recent research findings suggesting AAC users' language outcomes are "catalyzed by collaboration" (Zangari, 2016, p. 151). There is now sufficient evidence in the field of AAC that better communication outcomes come from better trained communication partners (e.g., Kent-Walsh et al., 2015). In fact, an expert panel on interprofessional collaborative practice (Interprofessional Education Collaborative, 2011) suggested the core competencies Project ABC referenced when building coursework and seminars supporting collaborative classroom work for a variety of reasons, including collaborating with other service providers and co-developing individualized language, literacy, and communication goals embedded into daily classroom instruction. Project ABC strives to move from cross-disciplinary collaboration to interdisciplinary collaboration. The framework of implementation is listed below.

All Project ABC scholars collaborate on four components, including: (a) shared coursework, (b) shared seminars, (c) selected fieldwork, and (d) professional development. Project scholars are enrolled in the grant for two years. ECSE scholars are required to complete coursework and fieldwork to obtain their credentials to teach in California and preservice SLPs must complete the selected coursework to earn their master's degree. Project ABC scholars participate in four shared courses: two from the ECSE credential program and two from the CSD master's program. The selected and overlapping fieldwork provides hands-on experiential opportunities and the shared seminars cover a total of six identified areas of need. Scholars spend approximately 30 hours in the shared seminars. In the area of professional development, scholars join a professional organization related to their field that supports further training and contributes to retention in their chosen discipline. In the shared coursework, fieldwork, seminars, and professional development, the blending of both practices and assumptions from both disciplines are presented and explored resulting in interdisciplinary experiences and development for all scholars. Each of the four components is explained in further detail next.

## Shared Coursework

Project ABC scholars co-enroll in the following semester-long courses: (a) a special education course focused on learning to collaborate with families of children with disabilities, (b) a special education course focused on inclusive practices in early childhood education, (c) a CSD graduate service-learning course and introductory seminar on augmentative and alternative communication, and (d) a CSD graduate seminar on autism spectrum disorder. The coursework was intentionally designed for interdisciplinary training and adult learning, using the How People Learn (HPL) theory (Iris Center, n.d.) through a community-centered lens.

Each course focuses on developing shared knowledge and skills for supporting the inclusive education of young children with high-intensity communication and learning needs. In addition, one shared course is a foundational class that focuses on effectively partnering with culturally and linguistically diverse families who have children with disabilities. This course examines characteristics of family systems; functional assessment of family needs, cultural concerns and priorities. Scholars learn about families' valued roles in the IFSP/IEP process with an emphasis on effective communication, collaboration skills, and identification of community resources. Scholars are also expected to apply the principles of UDL (CAST, 2018) and learn how to embed AT and AAC into daily classroom routines. Scholars are taught how to engage young learners in early learning experiences, how to graphically represent language for preliterate learners, and how to provide a means of expression and communication that may need to linguistically shift between home and preschool. (e.g., see Table 1).

## Shared Seminars

In addition to semester-long coursework, scholars are required to attend five seminars annually. These seminars are designed in an interdisciplinary manner with faculty from both communication disorders and special education intertwining the work and theoretical foundations from both disciplines.. These seminars aim to codevelop knowledge around teaching early language concepts and early-emergent literacy instruction while embedding AT and AAC. The seminars are co-led by faculty from both departments, which allows for the modeling of collaboration and coteaching. The instructional components teach scholars classroom strategies that limit or eliminate the professional, practical, opportunity, and philosophical barriers that often occur in segregated education.

Seminars are designed to provide time and space for in-depth topics of collaboration and instruction on early language and literacy development using AAC. For example, scholars learn how to implement a Tier 1 (set of highly useful, and frequently used words that can be broadly learned and used by all students in a classroom) (CDE, 2022; Geist et al., 2016; Greenwood et al., 2014). The Center for Literacy

*Table 1. Shared Coursework Description*

| | |
|---|---|
| **SPED course**<br>Inclusive Education | Introduces the concepts, strategies, and legislation for including children with disabilities alongside their typically developing peers in natural environments. Emphasis includes best practices such as Universal Design for Learning (UDL), environmental assessment, the use of AT to support inclusion (PEATs Suite and LAMP), and collaboration with families and school personnel. |
| **SPED course**<br>Working with Families with Children with Special Needs | A foundational class that focuses on effectively partnering with diverse families that have children with disabilities. Course examines characteristics of family systems; functional assessment of family needs, concerns and priorities. The families' role in the IFSP/IEP and transition. There is an emphasis on effective communication, collaborative skills and identification of community resources. |
| **COMMD course**<br>Augmentative and Alternative Communication (AAC) | Course includes historical service delivery approaches; symbol sets and systems; assessment and management strategies for persons with severe physical; and speech impairments; advocacy approaches for the disabled |
| **COMD course**<br>Autism Spectrum Disorder in Speech-Language Pathology | This class will focus on communication disorders in children with autism spectrum disorders (current theories, diagnostic process, co-occurring conditions, the role of speech-language pathologists in multidisciplinary approaches to assessment and intervention planning, critical review of relevant research). Emphasis placed on the development of critical thinking and analytical skills related to the assessment and treatment of communication disorders in children with autism spectrum disorders. |

and Disability Studies at the University of North Carolina, Chapel Hill, defines this small set of words as the Universal Core, "a set of 36 highly useful single words that can be used alone or in combination to communicate for a range of purposes on countless topics with a wide variety of communication partners" (Project Core, n.d., para.1).

Cross-disciplinary collaboration is required when scholars participate in these seminars. Specific seminar topics include: (a) inclusion and consultation/collaboration strategies, (b) principles and practices of UDL, including application of AT/AAC, (c) literacy with AT and AAC, (d) working with very young children with high-intensity needs, (e) working with high-need families who represent diverse cultural-linguistic backgrounds, and (f) writing an Individual Family Service Plan (IFSP) and an Individualized Education Program (IEP) to support inclusion (ECPC, 2020). These five required seminars are described in detail next.

## Inclusion and Consultation/Collaboration Strategies

The content of this seminar fills a big gap in ECSE teacher education by preparing ECSE teachers and preservice SLPs to provide direct and consultative services to children in their classrooms. Classrooms are where collaboration frequently takes place with other educators, childcare personnel, and related service providers (Bruder & Dunst, 2005; Campbell & Halbert, 2002; Frankel, 2006). Cross-disciplinary competences are explored and discussed (ECPC, 2020; Whipple, 2014), including different types of inclusive classroom teaching strategies and co-teaching approaches (Richardson-Gibbs & Klein, 2014), and the various types, phases, and stages of itinerant consulting models (Friend et al., 2010). In addition, examples of interpersonal skills are discussed since they are needed to promote effective collaboration (Bruder et al., 2018; Dinnebeil et al., 2009; Friend et al., 2010; Pretti-Frontczak & Bricker, 2004). This seminar allows for the instructors to model the merging of cross-disciplinary competencies, strategies, and approaches.

## Principles and Practices of UDL, Including Application of AT/AAC

This seminar instructs scholars on how to apply the principles of Universal Design for Learning (UDL) that are federally mandated through the Every Child Succeeds Act (ESSA). Scholars learn how the UDL framework guides the design of children's assessments, goals, access to materials, and methods of instruction, as supported by the Individuals with Disabilities Act, Part B. CSD and ECE scholars need to know-how to accommodate the needs and abilities of all learners through the introductory use of various types of AT and with a range of aided AAC systems (e.g., no-tech, light-tech, mid-tech, high-tech). For example, scholars may explore the basic operational functions of several communication applications and speech generating devices. Operational skills include: (a) learning how to set up devices for alternate input, such as for eye gaze, head movements, or single/dual switches when direct access is not possible; (b) learning how to organize and edit pages to improve access to both core and personalized language without excess effort and fatigue; and, (c) learning key tips to personalize communication pages in ways that are age-appropriate and culturally-linguistically sensitive for young learners and their families. Understanding these concepts and practices in an interdisciplinary manner is important for a thorough implementation of AT/AAC once scholars enter schools to work with young children. The activities or experiences completed by scholars and demonstrated by instructors model the interweaving of the respective knowledge and skills of each discipline.

Specific content includes learning how to meet the ESSA mandate so young children with special needs have access to and can work towards grade-level (i.e., preschool) core standards (Kameenui & Simmons, 1999; Nolet & McLaughlin, 2005; Ruffino et al., 2006). Incorporation of UDL in an early childhood curriculum focuses on creating engaging learning environments and adopting practices that allow for the access and participation of all children, regardless of individual, cultural, or linguistic differences (Hanna, 2005).

For example, scholars are provided with various aided language applications on the iPad that not only demonstrate how robust vocabulary can be organized for early language learners, but also to show how different languages can be added, graphic symbols changed for cultural-racial authenticity, and alternate access inputs changed or customized. Scholars are taught how to customize/edit the main or secondary page to include the 36 Universal Core vocabulary (English and other languages as needed) as an easily accessible start to a broad base of communication support for students and teachers who share space 3-6 hours a day in an inclusive classroom. Scholars are also taught how to link to additional pages in an aided language application that allow access to hundreds of more core and personalized vocabulary.

Scholars learn about other early learning supports available on the iPad that can address all students' learning needs in an inclusive classroom, thus applying principles of UDL from the start. Specific seminars allow scholars to pair-up and role play using non-electronic and electronic-aided AAC systems to practice teaching early language concepts during daily classroom routines. At specified times, scholars take aided AAC systems to their practicum sites and implement the learned language facilitation and communication partner strategies, such as aided language input, to support children's language learning for daily communication. In follow-up seminars, scholars debrief their experience with faculty who help to problem-solve and plan for the next instructional period. Overall, this seminar content explores how a preschool curriculum incorporates UDL at the beginning of the school year, preemptively planning for all students, instead of adopting it after the fact, or in a scrambled reaction to a student with specific needs.

## Literacy with AT and AAC

The literacy with AT and AAC seminar introduces scholars to the foundational components of early-emergent literacy learning for young children. Faculty collaborate and co-present on creating a monthly theme for educators and SLPs to co-create weekly lesson plans addressing IEP goals and incorporating the necessary components of early and emergent literacy instruction (e.g., alphabet identification, phonological awareness, concepts about print, print has meaning, language comprehension, and communication). For example, early childhood special educators and preservice SLPs are intentionally paired to learn how to teach children language and literacy on aided AAC systems using a variety of communication partner strategies, including aided language input. Scholars are introduced to adaptive tools and applications, light-tech voiced output devices, and electronic aided language systems that allow alternative access methods (e.g., switches, head mice, eye gaze) so any child can participate in literacy activities throughout the school day and at the same time as nondisabled peers (Beck, 2002).

Additionally, all scholars are taught that every child should have access to the alphabet in a way that works best for their sensorimotor capabilities. In this way, scholars are taught that all young children, regardless of disability type, should participate in daily classroom letter-sound exploration with opportunities for early writing. For example, scholars are introduced to websites and iPad applications teachers and students can access in everyday practice. These applications, such as Tar Heel Reader (https://tarheelreader.org) and BookCreator, provide alternative access for reading books and practicing early writing. Websites are also provided to scholars supporting ongoing professional development on literacy development, such as Tarheel Shared Reader (https://www.sharedreader.org) and https://praacticalaac.org/tag/preschool/.

## Working with Very Young Children with High-Intensity Needs

The overall focus of this seminar is on four areas of need: medical, physical, learning, and social emotional (Horn & Kang, 2012). Specific content focuses on the implementation of additional supports to provide a meaningful and individualized curriculum within the context of fully inclusive and natural environments. For example, faculty instruct scholars on developing learning outcomes, daily living skills, community membership, and relationship formation for young children with multiple disabilities (Snell & Brown, 2011). Participants will apply their learning from previous seminars, such as UDL practices, to support the effective use of aided AAC in increasing early communication for young children with multiple disabilities (Campbell et al., 2006; Udvari-Solner et al., 2004).

Scholars learn strategies to better engage families who may be struggling to support their young children with high-intensity needs.. These strategies include (a) solutions-oriented approaches enlisting positive behavior supports (Peckham-Hardin, as cited in Richardson-Gibbs & Klein, 2014), (b) sensitivity and awareness training on how to work with families who may have cultural differences around discipline, use of AAC, or disability, (c) strategies on how to empower families (Edwards & Da Font, 2012) to advocate for their child and become participatory change agents in their childs' school and community (Hsaio et al., 2018).

This seminar reviews evidence-based practices (EBP) related to working with culturally and linguistically diverse families (Lynch & Hanson, 2011; Stockman, Boult, & Robinson, 2004). Further, faculty discuss these practices related to early childhood second language acquisition (Tabors, 2008) and deliver appropriate seminar content related to general early childhood settings situated in culturally diverse regions (Pretti-Frontczak & Bricker, 2004; Sexton et al., 2002). Additionally, this seminar is informed by the work of Haberman (2005), which identified the developing characteristics of teachers successful at working in underresourced communities and schools with culturally diverse populations. Hughes (2010) contended that to work in classrooms of such-schools, teachers need to understand the cultural communities they teach and learn culturally-sensitive strategies and techniques for successfully supporting families who live in or are at risk for poverty (Payne, 2005). An upcoming seminar will provide content and fieldwork to address topics related to working with high-need families in underresourced school districts.

## Writing IFSPs and IEPs to Support Inclusion

This seminar focuses on teaching scholars how to embed AT/AAC into daily routines (Sandall & Schwartz, 2008), beginning with the co-creation of goals addressing individual needs and supports for developing early language, literacy, and communication. Preschoolers' communication and language skills are essential for cognitive development, social-emotional competency, and reasoning. Writing individualized goals for children with more intense learning needs means educators prepare and plan to lay a strong foundation for teaching vocabulary, the conventions of language construction, and the essential building blocks of reading and writing (California Department of Education, 2008; Meloy & Schachner, 2019). Project ABC scholars are guided in writing functional IFSPs and IEPs aligned with core preschool learning standards and include classroom activities supported by a sound rationale addressing individualized learning needs in a classroom environment. In this seminar, scholars complete the IRIS IEP modules (https://iris.peabody.vanderbilt.edu/module/iep01/), which provide guidance on developing high-quality IEPs for students with disabilities (Bruder et al., 2018; Horn et al., 2002; McWilliam, 2010).

In sum, these five seminars were developed in collaboration with faculty from special education, and communication sciences and disorders to provide additional training beyond scholars' coursework. With a focus on early-emergent literacy and AT/AAC instruction, scholars have a chance to further develop their knowledge and participate together in hands-on activities. These hands-on activities expand into fieldwork, with scholars from both disciplines participating in community-based programs and practicing the skills they have learned.

## **Selected Fieldwork**

Project ABC includes three revised fieldwork components and one new fieldwork experience to increase scholars' competence in collaboration, consultation, and service to classrooms related to comprehensive and inclusive programming and promoting interdisciplinary knowledge of AT/AAC. Scholars participate in community-based programs serving young children with disabilities, such as childcare centers, private preschools, and Head Start and state preschool classrooms. Dinnebeil (2014) contended that although ECSE teachers are prepared to work directly with children, ECSE teacher candidates receive minimal preparation to serve as consultants or coaches to other teachers and service providers; Project ABC prepares scholars for this type of work.

During their fieldwork experience with preschoolers, ECSE scholars are required to conduct an applied UDL assignment in which they plan, implement, and evaluate interactive social-communication activities (e.g., CARA's Kit, a resource of the Council of Exceptional Children's Division for Early Childhood; Dinnebeil et al., 2013). For example, scholars may complete the Universal Design for Play Tool (Ruffino et al., 2006). These planned activities focus on the scholars' use of specific research-based, play-based, and social communication skills. During the evaluation phase of this assignment, scholars evaluate their skills and the skills of their classroom students, collect qualitative information, and compare data over time to track progress and make intervention modifications as needed.

## Professional Development

Project ABC scholars develop their professional knowledge and skills in several ways. First, scholars are expected to complete all 12 professional development modules produced by Project Core at the Center for Literacy & Disability Studies at the University of North Carolina-Chapel Hill. Completion of these modules is meant to establish a foundation of shared knowledge on early language and literacy instruction. The 12 modules provide practical and evidence-based tips for adult learners without prior knowledge of AAC or how to deliver communication, language, and literacy instruction using aided AAC systems. Scholars work in interdisciplinary groups to discuss the content of the modules and co-plan strategies and instructional techniques to implement aided AAC in their classrooms.

Second, Project ABC scholars are expected to attend at least one professional development opportunity at the national, state, or local level (e.g., Division for Early Childhood, National Association for the Education of Young Children, American Speech Language and Hearing Association, California State University, Northridge AT Conference) to develop a network of colleagues, participate in selected sessions, and earn professional development hours. Conferences are an effective form of professional development. In fact, Marlow (2009) identified factors contributing to teacher development, with professionals and leaders reporting that presentation and attendance at conferences can create a sense of community, encourage professional networking, and enhance professional growth and identity. Our data from previous grants suggest that preservice and beginning teachers developed a sense of belonging to a larger professional community.

Attending conferences provides beginning teachers opportunities to learn from experts from around the country and world. While little research has been conducted on the impact of conference attendance on beginning teachers, a few studies have suggested attending major conferences can broaden their vision and understanding of the field (Sickel & Hanuscin, 2010). Project ABC scholars are encouraged to also join a professional organization related to their field. This activity supports the training and retention of high quality educators and service providers. Each of these aforementioned professional learning opportunities was chosen because they support the overall objectives of Project ABC and provide a shared foundation of knowledge and skills.

## WAYS WE MEASURE AND TRACK OUTCOMES

Inherent in the instructional curricula is the expectation that scholars complete both formative and summative evaluations. The formative assessments during semester coursework and seminars include: (a) oral, written, or recorded responses and reflections to assignments and required service-learning experiences; (b) reports on concepts learned through group projects; (c) co-development of lesson plans focused on embedding AAC into daily activities; and (d) collaborating on the development of individualized goals for facilitating children's early language, literacy, and communication. An example of a formative assessment used in the AAC service-learning course is the requirement of scholars to learn how to use VoiceThread as a way of co-creating asynchronous presentations to share with the whole class. VoiceThread allows the use of textual or voice-recorded discussion threads for commenting and interactive learning. Assigned groups collaborate to share what they observed in classrooms or learned from teachers and make connections to what was learned in the course.

Currently, Project ABC is halfway through the grant cycle and data continue to be collected. Anecdotal findings over the last 3 years indicate scholars have become quite adept at identifying AAC myths or instructional misconceptions still pervasive among educators, service-providers, and families. As a result of these observations and rich VoiceThread discussions, several students solved this problem by co-creating handouts for their service classrooms that dispelled AAC myths or listed evidence-based communication partner strategies in easy-to-read formats.

Summative assessments are used to measure scholars' competencies at the completion of semester courses and topic-focused seminars. For example, at the beginning and the end of the early literacy seminars offered in the spring of each year, scholars are expected to complete K-W-L charts (graphic organizers) to: (a) organize and assess their prior knowledge of the topic, (b) pose (wh) questions about what they want to know about the topic, and (c) identify at least three things they learned and will adopt the following week in their preschool classroom. These self-evaluation charts are often collected at the conclusion of the seminar and compared to the seminar instructor's assessment. Other summative assessments include graded end-of-class projects that either assess a scholar's ability to develop classroom lessons embedding AAC or their ability to co-write language and early literacy goals using assistive technology and aided AAC as tools for facilitating language and literacy development across progress monitoring periods and annually. Further summative assessments include ratings and scores on fieldwork competencies, performance ratings during clinical rounds, and other graded and faculty-produced evaluations to identify competency in required teaching or clinical skills.

There is a specific requirement of each ECSE scholar to develop an action research plan (ARP) for use as both a formative and summative assessment of the intended outcomes of Project ABC. Additionally, ECSE scholars are required to complete a culminating portfolio. The completed portfolio serves as a collective representation of artifacts related to performance measures; these artifacts demonstrate the learning and growth outcomes of the children with disabilities to whom the scholar attended in early intervention and preschool.

Last, all Project ABC scholars have the opportunity to provide periodic feedback on the project itself. For example, scholars evaluate the project objectives, the components of the project (i.e., courses, seminars, professional development, induction, and fieldwork), the ECSE credential program, and university and school mentor effectiveness. Quantitative and qualitative data are collected through seminar evaluation surveys, course evaluations, scholar reflections, and post-project assessments. These assessment tools track scholars' identified knowledge and skills as they enter and exit the program. The instructional and training strategies and collaborative activities that demonstrate effectiveness after the analysis of the aforementioned assessments will be institutionalized into the ECSE credential program by placement into ECSE credential course and fieldwork. The Project ABC advisory board annually evaluates project objectives using pre-post scholar self-assessment data, CSU Qualtrics data from employers, and course assignments. The advisory board provides feedback on the professional development activities, and an external reviewer evaluates grant objectives and Project ABC scholars' perceptions of the efficacy of the ECSE programs.

## CONCLUSION

Project ABC is a 5-year project providing interdisciplinary training to cohorts of SLP candidates and ECSE teacher candidates. Project ABC provides high-quality, evidence-based instructional content and collaborative training to help preservice ECSE teachers and SLPs understand how to work together to serve young children with disabilities and their families on AT/AAC interventions. In doing so, they support language and communication development for children with complex communication and learning needs.

Project ABC components such as shared coursework, selected fieldwork, shared seminars, and professional development provide interdisciplinary training to scholars of both disciplines in several ways. Scholars overlap across four courses: two in the ECSE credential program and two in the SLP program. Scholars also work together in selected fieldwork, providing them the opportunity to share what they are learning by engaging in hands-on experience. Project ABC scholars also engage with each other in five seminars developed with interdisciplinary content by faculty from both disciplines. Lastly, professional development in each field provides additional training and retention in the respective discipline. These components, along with the assessment of scholars to better understand the outcomes of the grant, make Project ABC a comprehensive and much-needed project for increasing well-trained ECSE and SLPs in school settings.

## REFERENCES

American Speech-Langauge-Hearing Association. (2004). *Roles and responsibilities of speech-language pathologists with respect to augmentative and alternative communication: Technical report.* ASLHA. https://asha.org/policy

Barker, R. M., Akaba, S., Brady, N. C., & Thiemann-Bourque, K. (2013). Support for AAC use in preschool, and growth in language skills, for young children with developmental disabilities. *Augmentative and Alternative Communication*, 29(4), 334–346. doi:10.3109/07434618.2013.848933 PMID:24229337

Barton, E. E., & Smith, B. J. (2015). *The preschool inclusion toolbox: How to build and lead a high-quality program.* Brookes Publishing.

Beck, J. (2002). Emerging literacy through assistive technology. *Teaching Exceptional Children*, 35(2), 44–48. doi:10.1177/004005990203500206

Beukelman, D. R., & Mirenda, P. (2012). *Principles of assessment in augmentative & alternative communication: Supporting children & adults with complex communication needs* (4th ed.). Paul H. Brookes Publishing.

Biggs, E. E., Carter, E. W., & Gilson, C. B. (2018). A scoping review of the involvement of children's communication partners in aided augmentative and alternative communication modeling interventions. *American Journal of Speech-Language Pathology*, 28(2), 743–758. doi:10.1044/2018_AJSLP-18-0024 PMID:31039322

Binger, C., & Light, J. (2006). Demographics of preschoolers who require AAC. *Language, Speech, and Hearing Services in Schools*, 37(3), 200–208. doi:10.1044/0161-1461(2006/022) PMID:16837443

Branson, D., & Demchak, M. (2009). The use of augmentative and alternative communication methods with infants and toddlers with disabilities: A research review. *Augmentative and Alternative Communication, 25*(4), 274–286. doi:10.3109/07434610903384529 PMID:19883287

Bruder, M. B., & Dunst, C. J. (2005). Personnel preparation in recommended early intervention practices: Degree of emphasis across discipline. *Topics in Early Childhood Special Education, 25*(1), 25–33. doi:10.1177/02711214050250010301

Bruder, M. B., Long, T., & Rhodes, T. (2018). *Cross-disciplinary competencies: Serving the whole child* [PowerPoint slides]. Early Childhood Personnel Center. https://www.aucd.org/docs/webinars/PresentationSlides_ECPC%20Cross%20Disciplinary%20Core%20%20Personnel%20Competencies_.pdf

California Department of Education. (2008). *California preschool learning foundations, volume 1*. CDE. https://www.cde.ca.gov/sp/cd/re/documents/preschoollf.pdf

California Department of Education. (2022). *Multi-Tiered System of Supports*. CDE. https://www.cde.ca.gov/ci/cr/ri

Campbell, P. H., & Halbert, J. (2002). Between research and practice: Provider perspectives on early intervention. *Topics in Early Childhood Special Education, 22*(4), 213–226. doi:10.1177/027112140202200403

Campbell, P. H., Milbourne, S., Dugan, L. M., & Wilcox, M. J. (2006). A review of the evidence on practices for teaching young children to use assistive technology devices. *Topics in Early Childhood Special Education, 26*(1), 3–13. doi:10.1177/02711214060260010101

CAST. (2018). *Universal design for learning guidelines, version 2.2*. https://pillars.taylor.edu/cgi/viewcontent.cgi?article=1003&context=ett-conference

Center on Disability. California State University-Northridge. (2018). *Assistive Technology Certificate Program* [Course syllabus]. https://canvas.csun.edu/courses/47382

Costigan, F. A., & Light, J. (2010). A review of preservice training in augmentative and alternative communication for speech-language pathologists, special education teachers, and occupational therapists. *Assistive Technology, 22*(4), 200–212. doi:10.1080/10400435.2010.492774 PMID:21306066

Cross, A. F., Traub, E. K., Hutter-Pishgahi, L., & Shelton, G. (2004). Elements of successful inclusion for children with significant disabilities. [TECSE]. *Topics in Early Childhood Special Education, 24*(3), 169–183. doi:10.1177/02711214040240030401

DePaepe, P. A., & Wood, L. A. (2001). Collaborative practices related to augmentative and alternative communication: Currently personnel preparation programs. *Communication Disorders Quarterly, 22*(2), 77–86. doi:10.1177/152574010102200203

Dinnebeil, L., Boat, M., & Bae, Y. (2013). Integrating principles of universal design into early childhood curriculum. *Dimensions in Early Childhood, 41*(1), 3–13.

Dinnebeil, L., Petti-Frontczak, K., & McInerney, W. (2009). A consultative itinerant approach to service delivery: Considerations for the early childhood community. *Language, Speech, and Hearing Services in Schools*, *40*(4), 435–445. doi:10.1044/0161-1461(2008/08-0028) PMID:18952808

Dinnebeil, L. A. (2014). Top-down and bottom-up thinking comprehensively about support for early childhood inclusion. *Young Exceptional Children*, *17*(3), 48–50. doi:10.1177/1096250614542175

Downing, J. E., Hanreddy, A., & Peckham-Hardin, K. D. (2015). *Teaching communication skills to students with severe disabilities* (3rd ed.). Paul H. Brookes Publishing.

Drager, K., Light, J., & McNaughton, D. (2010). Effects of AAC interventions on communication and language for young children with complex communication needs. *Journal of Pediatric Rehabilitation Medicine*, *3*(4), 303–310. doi:10.3233/PRM-2010-0141 PMID:21791864

Early Childhood Personnel Center. (2020). https://ecpcta.org

Edwards, C. C., & Da Font, A. (2012). The 5-point plan: Fostering successful partnerships with families of students with disabilities. *Teaching Exceptional Children*, *44*(30), 6–13. doi:10.1177/004005991204400301

Frankel, E. B. (2006). The knowledge, skills and personal qualities of early childhood resource consultants as agents of change. *Exceptionality Education Canada*, *16*(2), 35–58.

Friend, M., Cook, L., Hurley-Chamberlain, D., & Shamberger, C. (2010). Co-teaching: An illustration of the complexity of collaboration in special education. *Journal of Educational & Psychological Consultation*, *20*(1), 9–27. doi:10.1080/10474410903535380

Geist, L., Erickson, K. A., Greer, C., Hatch, P., & Erwin-Davidson, L. (2016). *Core vocabulary for students with significant cognitive disabilities: Essential tools, teaching strategies and assessment components*. Session presented at the annual meeting of the International Association for Augmentative and Alternative Communication, Toronto, Canada.

Greenwood, C. R., Carta, J. J., Goldstein, H., Kaminski, R. A., McConnell, S. R., & Atwater, J. (2014). The center for response to intervention in early childhood: Developing evidence-based tools for a multitier approach to preschool language and early literacy instruction. *Journal of Early Intervention*, *36*(4), 246-262. https://doi doi:10.1177/1053815115581209

Haberman, M. (2005). *Star teachers: The ideology and best practice of effective teachers of diverse children and youth in poverty*. Haberman Educational Foundation.

Hanna, E. I. (2005). *Inclusive design for maximum accessibility: A practical approach to universal design (PEM research rep. no. 05-04)*. Pearson Educational Measurement.

Horn, E., Lieber, J., Sandall, S. R., Schwartz, I., & Li, S. (2002). Supporting young children's IEP goals in inclusive settings through embedded learning opportunities. *Topics in Early Childhood Special Education*, *20*(4), 208–223. doi:10.1177/027112140002000402

Horn, E. M., & Kang, J. (2012). Supporting young children with multiple disabilities: What do we know and what do we still need to learn? *Topics in Early Childhood Special Education*, *31*(4), 241–248. doi:10.1177/0271121411426487 PMID:24574575

Hsiao, Y.-J., Higgins, K., & Diamond, L. (2018). Parent empowerment: Respecting their voices. *Teaching Exceptional Children*, *51*(1), 43–53. doi:10.1177/0040059918790240

Hughes, J. (2010). What teacher preparation programs can do to better prepare teachers to meet the challenges of educating students living in poverty. *Action in Teacher Education*, *32*(1), 54–64. doi:10.1080/01626620.2010.10463542

Interprofessional Education Collaborative. (2011). *Core competencies for interprofessional collaborative practice: Report of an expert panel*. IEC. https://www.aacom.org/docs/default-source/insideome/ccrpt05-10-11.pdf

Iris Center. (n.d.). *IRIS & adult learning theory*. IRIS. https://iris.peabody.vanderbilt.edu/_archive/iris-and-adult-learning-theory/

Jacoby, J. W., & Lesaux, N. K. (2017). Language and literacy instruction in preschool classes that serve Latino dual language learners. *Early Childhood Research Quarterly*, *40*, 77–86. doi:10.1016/j.ecresq.2016.10.001

Johnson, R. K., & Prebor, J. (2019). Update on preservice training in augmentative and alternative communication for speech-language pathologists. *American Journal of Speech-Language Pathology*, *28*(2), 536–549. doi:10.1044/2018_AJSLP-18-0004 PMID:31136246

Justice, L. M., Jiang, H., & Strasser, K. (2018). Linguistic environment of preschool classrooms: What dimensions support children's language growth? *Early Childhood Research Quarterly*, *42*, 79–92. doi:10.1016/j.ecresq.2017.09.003

Kameenui, E., & Simmons, D. (1999). *Toward successful inclusion of students with disabilities: The architecture of instruction*. The Council for Exceptional Children. https://files.eric.ed.gov/fulltext/ED429381.pdf

Kent-Walsh, J., Binger, C., & Malani, M. (2010). Teaching partners to support the communication skills of young children who use AAC: Lessons from the ImPAACT program. *Early Childhood Services (San Diego, Calif.)*, *4*(3), 155–170.

Kent-Walsh, J., Murza, K. A., Malani, M. D., & Binger, C. (2015). Effects of communication partner instruction on the communication of individuals using AAC: A meta-analysis. *Augmentative and Alternative Communication*, *31*(4), 271–284. doi:10.3109/07434618.2015.1052153 PMID:26059542

Kleinert, H., Towles-Reeves, E., Quenemoen, R., Thurlow, M., Fluegge, L., Weseman, L., & Kerbel, A. (2015). Where students with the most significant cognitive disabilities are taught: Implications for general curriculum access. *Exceptional Children*, *81*(3), 312–328. doi:10.1177/0014402914563697

Lieber, J., Horn, E., Palmer, S., & Fleming, K. (2008). Access to the general education curriculum for preschoolers with disabilities: Children's school success. *Exceptionality*, *16*(1), 18–32. doi:10.1080/09362830701796776

Light, J., & McNaughton, D. (2014). Communicative competence for individuals who require augmentative and alternative communication: A new definition for a new era of communication? *Augmentative and Alternative Communication, 30*(1), 1–18. doi:10.3109/07434618.2014.885080 PMID:30952185

Lynch, E., & Hanson, M. (2011). *Developing cross-cultural competence: A guide for working with children and their families* (4th ed.). Brookes Publishing.

Marlow, M. (2009). Supporting teacher professional identity through mentoring activities. *Research in Higher Education*, 2.

McWilliam, R. A. (2010). *Routines-based early intervention: Strategies for supporting young children with disabilities*. Brookes Publishing.

Meloy, B., & Schachner, A. (2019). *Early childhood essentials: A framework for aligning child skills and educator competencies*. Learning Policy Institute. https://learningpolicyinstitute.org/sites/default/files/product-files/Early_Childhood_Essentials_Framework_REPORT.pdf

National Professional Development Center on Inclusion. (2012). [Data set]. NPDCI. https://fpg.unc.edu/projects/national-professional-development-center-inclusion

Nolet, V., & McLaughlin, M. (2005). *Accessing the general curriculum: Including students with disabilities in standards-based reform* (2nd ed.). Corwin Press. doi:10.4135/9781483329253

O'Neill, T., Light, J., & Pope, L. (2018). Effects of interventions that include aided augmentative and alternative communication input on the communication of individuals with complex communication needs: A meta-analysis. *Journal of Speech, Language, and Hearing Research: JSLHR, 61*(7), 1743–1765. doi:10.1044/2018_JSLHR-L-17-0132 PMID:29931287

Ogletree, B. T. (2017). Meaningful moves toward independence. *ASHA Leader, 22*(2). doi:10.1044/leader.OV.22022017.np

Østvik, J., Ytterhus, B., & Balandin, S. (2017). Friendship between children using augmentative and alternative communication and peers: A systematic literature review. *Journal of Intellectual & Developmental Disability, 42*(4), 403–415. doi:10.3109/13668250.2016.1247949

Payne, R. K. (2005). A framework for understanding poverty (4th ed.). aha! Process.

Pretti-Frontczak, K., & Bricker, D. (2004). *An activity-based approach to early intervention* (3rd ed.). Brookes Publishing.

Project Core. (n.d.). Universal core communication systems. *Project Core*. https://www.project-core.com/communication-systems

Rafferty, Y., Piscitelli, V., & Boettcher, C. (2003). The impact of inclusion on language development and social competence among preschoolers with disabilities. *Exceptional Children, 69*(4), 467–479. doi:10.1177/001440290306900405

Ratcliff, A., Koul, R., & Lloyd, L. L. (2008). Preparation in augmentative and alternative communication: An update for speech-language pathology training. *American Journal of Speech-Language Pathology*, *17*(1), 48–59. doi:10.1044/1058-0360(2008/005) PMID:18230813

Richardson-Gibbs, A. M., & Klein, M. D. (2014). *Making preschool inclusion work*. Brookes Publishing.

Romski, M., Sevcik, R. A., Barton-Hulsey, A., & Whitmore, A. S. (2015). Early intervention and AAC: What a difference 30 years makes. *Augmentative and Alternative Communication*, *31*(3), 181–202. doi:10.3109/07434618.2015.1064163 PMID:26153901

Ruffino, A. G., Mistrett, S. G., Tomita, M., & Hajare, P. (2006). The Universal Design for Play Tool: Establishing validity and reliability. *Journal of Special Education Technology*, *21*(4), 25–38. doi:10.1177/016264340602100404

Sandall, S., & Schwartz, I. (2008). *Building blocks for teaching preschoolers with special needs* (2nd ed.). Brookes Publishing.

Sexton, D., Snyder, P., Lobman, M., & Daly, T. (2002). Comparing the developmentally appropriate practice (DAP) beliefs of practitioners in general and special early childhood service settings. *Teacher Education and Special Education*, *25*(3), 247–261. doi:10.1177/088840640202500305

Sickel, A., & Hanuscin, D. (2010). A new chapter: How NSTA student chapters can support preservice teachers and prepare them for the challenges ahead. *Science and Children*, *48*(2), 71–75.

Snell, M. E., & Brown, F. (2011). *Instruction of students with severe disabilities*. Pearson.

Soto, G., & Zangari, C. (2009). *Practically speaking: Language, literacy, & academic development for students with AAC needs*. Brookes Publishing.

Stockman, I. J., Boult, J., & Robinson, G. (2004). Multicultural issues in academic and clinical education: A cultural mosaic. *ASHA Leader*, *9*(13), 6–22. doi:10.1044/leader.FTR5.09132004.6

Tabors, P. O. (2008). *One child, two languages: A guide for early childhood educators of children learning English as a second language* (2nd ed.). Brookes Publishing.

Tegler, H., Pless, M., Johansson, M. B., & Sonnander, K. (2019). Speech and language pathologists' perceptions and practises of communication partner training to support children's communication with high-tech speech generating devices. *Disability and Rehabilitation. Assistive Technology*, *14*(6), 581–589. doi:10.1080/17483107.2018.1475515 PMID:29790394

Udvari-Solner, A., Causton-Theoharis, J., & York-Barr, J. (2004). Developing adaptations to promote participation in inclusive environments. In *Orelove, F.P., Sobsey, D., & Dilberman, R.K. of Educating children with multiple disabilities: A collaborative approach, 4*. Brookes Publishing.

U.S. Department of Education. (2017). *39th Annual Report to Congress on the Implementation of the Individuals with Disabilities Education Act, 2017*. [Data set]. https://files.eric.ed.gov/fulltext/ED591108.pdf

von Tetzchner, S., Brekke, K., Sjøthun, B., & Grindheim, E. (2009). Constructing preschool communities of learners that afford alternative language development. *Augmentative and Alternative Communication*, *21*(2), 82–100. doi:10.1080/07434610500103541

Whipple, W. (2014). *Key principles of early intervention and effective practices: A crosswalk with statements from discipline-specific literature.* Early Childhood TA Center. https://ectacenter.org/~pdfs/topics/eiservices/KeyPrinciples Matrix_01_30_15.pdf

Williams, M., Krezman, C., & McNaughton, D. (2008). Reach for the stars: Five principles for the next 25 years of AAC. *Augmentative and Alternative Communication, 24*(3), 94–206. doi:10.1080/08990220802387851

Zangari, C. (2016). Looking back to move forward: 25 years of thinking about AAC and language. *Perspectives of the ASHA Special Interest Groups, 1*(12), 144–152. doi:10.1044/persp1.SIG12.144

# Chapter 11
# A Model for the Interprofessional Preparation of Speech-Language Pathologists and School Counselors:
## Effectively Serving Children With Disabilities

**Brandi L. Newkirk-Turner**
*Jackson State University, USA*

**Whitney D. Perkins**
*Jackson State University, USA*

**Jennifer E. Wiles**
*Jackson State University, USA*

**Chaiqua A. Harris**
*Northwestern University, USA*

## ABSTRACT

*Project CALIPSO was an interdisciplinary personnel preparation project for speech-language pathology and school counseling graduate students.. A primary focus of the project was preparing scholars to serve children with communication disorders and concomitant challenges in areas such as social-emotional development and behavior. Shared coursework, collaborative clinical experiences, and other activities were used to prepare the scholars to address the needs of children with disabilities as well as design and deliver services to parents and teachers to increase the likelihood for optimal child outcomes. Through this collaborative model, scholars were guided to consider the whole child and were provided specialized opportunities to develop holistic approaches to supporting children with disabilities.*

DOI: 10.4018/978-1-6684-6438-0.ch011

## INTRODUCTION

Effectively serving school-age children who have complex, high-intensity needs requires training of professionals with interdisciplinary expertise and advanced or specialized training in cross-disciplinary design and delivery of evidence-based instruction and intensive individualized intervention. Project **C**ounseling **A**nd **L**anguage/Literacy **I**n **P**ublic **S**chools and **O**ther educational settings (CALIPSO) was designed to address national, state, and district shortages of personnel who are fully qualified to serve children with disabilities who have high intensity needs by providing interdisciplinary, team-based training to graduate-level speech-language pathology (SLP) scholars and school counselor (SC) scholars to support the needs of school-age children with high intensity language, literacy, and social emotional needs in public schools and other educational settings. This interdisciplinary program is a collaborative effort between the Department of Communicative Disorders' speech-language pathology graduate program and the Department of Counseling, Rehabilitation, and Psychometric Services' school counseling graduate program at a minority-serving university in Mississippi.

## HIGH QUALITY INTERDISCIPLINARY PREPARATION IN MISSISSIPPI AND SIMILAR STATES

High quality interdisciplinary preparation of healthcare and academic professionals may be an effective strategy for addressing some of the complex issues in the state of Mississippi. Mississippi consistently ranks at the lowest quadrants of many polls on various measures of health and well-being, and academics -- putting many of the state's children at highest risks for disabilities and academic difficulties. For example, using 16 measures across four domains (economic well-being, education, health, family and community), Mississippi's overall ranking is 48 of the 50 states (Children's Foundation of Mississippi, 2020). Considered in this ranking are measures such as percent/rate of children in poverty (27%), young children ages three and four not in school (47%), low birth weight babies (12%), and children living in high poverty areas (24%).

More recent data used to determine America's Health Rankings shows that Mississippi continues to be near last place in the nation for three of five social determinants of children's health (#47 for physical environment, #49 for health outcomes, and #50 for health behaviors; United Health Foundation, 2021). For the remaining two social determinants of child health, Mississippi is ranked in the bottom half (#38 for clinical care and #40 for social and economic factors; United Health Foundation, 2021). These rankings have supported the characterization of Mississippi as the state with the most challenges for women, infants, and children (United Health Foundation, 2018).

Indeed, national data show that a significant proportion of infants born in Mississippi enter the world with health challenges. The 2021 March of Dimes Report Card shows that in Mississippi, a state that received a F rating, 14% of babies are born pre-term (March of Dimes, 2021; CDC, 2022). This means that 14% of the state's children start life at high risk for serious health problems such as breathing and eating difficulties. Pre-term babies are more likely to require early intervention and special education services and experience long term effects including learning problems and socio-emotional difficulties (University of Kentucky, nd). The percentage is even higher (17.4%) for babies born to Black/African American mothers. In fact, the preterm birth rate for Black/African American mothers is 44% higher than the rate of other women who give birth to children in Mississippi.

These are noteworthy statistics because children who are born preterm are considered to be at high risk for developmental disabilities including communication disorders and future academic problems. There is a suggestive link between preterm birth and later academic difficulties of children in Mississippi. In regard to reading, the average scores of students in Mississippi on national reading tests show that school-age children in Mississippi read at lower levels than students in most other states at grades four and eighth (NAEP, 2017). Although there has been a slight increase in scores in recent years (NAEP, 2019), the average scores from Mississippi have been consistently below the national average since 1992. Scores are particularly low for Black and Hispanic children, children who qualify for free or reduced lunch, children from urban cities, small towns, and rural communities, and students with disabilities (NAEP, 2017).

Measures of academic achievement like reading have been linked to attendance such that children who have high rates of absenteeism are more likely to have poorer metrics on measures of student success (Ansari & Gottfried, 2021; Ansari & Pianta, 2019). Based on this correlation, it is not surprising that Mississippi has a high chronic school absentee rate (14%) with rates highest at the high school level, eighth grade, and kindergarten. Rates for some districts are as high as 26% and are as high as 62% in individual schools (Mississippi Department of Education; MDE, 2016). While the Mississippi Department of Education does not report the rate of absenteeism as a function of disability, data elsewhere have shown that children with disabilities are particularly susceptible to school absences (Center for Learning Disabilities, 2017). State-level data also indicate that although overall high school graduation rates in the state are increasing (88% in 2022) and dropout rates are decreasing (8% in 2022), these same metrics for children with disabilities are considerably lower (59% graduation rate in 2022) and higher (18% dropout rate in 2022; Mississippi Department of Education, 2022).

Taken together, these data suggest that many children who are born, raised, and educated in Mississippi – particularly those who have disabilities – may be at elevated risks for academic difficulties. In the state of Mississippi and other states that have similar profiles of populations with complex needs resulting from poverty, poor health behaviors and outcomes, and lower rates of literacy and academic achievement, having more concerted efforts to prepare personnel through interdisciplinary models may be an effective strategy for improving outcomes of school children who have disabilities and complex needs that cannot be effectively addressed by professionals who work in a siloed manner.

## PROJECT CALIPSO

Project CALIPSO was designed to prepare speech-language pathology and school counseling graduate students to meet the needs of children with disabilities in Mississippi, and the project was inspired by findings in the literature that show that students with disabilities such as speech/language impairments, hearing impairments, and autism often struggle academically, behaviorally, emotionally, and socially (Gage, Lerheimer & Goran, 2012). Students with these disabilities often exhibit higher rates of acting out and problem behaviors (Hollo & Chow, 2015), have lower quality of friendships with peers (Brinton, Fujiki, & Robinson, 2005; Cook & Howell, 2014; Lyons & Roulstone, 2018; Redmond, 2011), experience social exclusion, and decreased social acceptance or sense of belonging in school (Cook & Howell, 2014; Lyons & Roulstone, 2018), are suspended and expelled from school more often, are given harsher sanctions for behavior (U.S. Department of Civil Rights, 2016), have higher rates of school absenteeism (Redmond & Hosp, 2018), are subjected to bullying and peer victimization (Cook & Howell, 2014;

Lyons & Roulstone, 2018; Redmond, 2011; U.S. Department of Education Office for Civil Rights, 2018), demonstrate higher rates of anxiety and shyness and lower rates of measures of well-being such as negative feelings, difficulties with relationships and forming friendships, lower self-esteem, lower social acceptance, and lower social confidence (Cook & Howell, 2014; Durkin, Toseeb, Botting, Pickles, & Conti-Ramsden, 2017; Lyons & Roulstone, 2018; Redmond, 2011).

Although the benefits of collaborations among school professionals are clear, the reality is that many graduate education programs continue the tradition of discipline-specific teaching with minimal or no focus on interdisciplinary training. Standards set forth in teacher education, counselor education, and speech-language pathology acknowledge the benefits of interprofessional practice (IPP), yet data show that collaborative service delivery in schools is still a challenge for many disciplines. For example, the American Speech-Language, Hearing Association (ASHA) 2016 Schools Survey reported that in elementary schools, only about 20% of SLPs engaged in IPP for assessments once a week or more, less than half (45%) engaged in IPP for intervention, 33% engaged in IPP team meetings, and less than 20% engaged in IPP report writing. In a more recent ASHA IPP survey, 62% of ASHA members reported that they had not had any formal training in IPP. Just under half of school-based speech-language pathologists (49%) indicated that they felt very prepared to effectively participate on IPP teams, and just 22% of ASHA members said they felt very prepared to effectively lead an IPP team of multiple professionals (ASHA, 2021).

Owing to these findings, we recognized a need for a project that prepared fully-qualified, interdisciplinary service providers to collaboratively address not only the academic needs of Mississippi's children with disabilities, but also their social-emotional needs that support and increase the likelihood of improved academic achievement, positive behavior and relationships, successful conflict resolution, safe and supportive school environments, attendance, and graduation. Recognizing the benefits of collaborative, team-based services for children with disabilities (e.g., exposure to multiple perspectives, more effective interventions, role sharing and role releasing), we designed and implemented Project CALIPSO with the goal of benefitting children with disabilities by preparing graduate students for interprofessional practice.

## Speech-Language Pathology and School Counseling

Project CALIPSO reflects an interdisciplinary pairing of professionals that has not been extensively discussed in the literature – speech-language pathologists and school counselors. In designing the project, we recognized that the overlapping roles and responsibilities of the two professions, as well as discipline-specific knowledge and skills, could be leveraged to provide and form interdisciplinary teams of professionals that can enhance academic, social-emotional, and behavior outcomes for students with disabilities, particularly those with speech/language impairments, hearing impairments, and autism. Figure A shows a depiction of some of these discipline-specific and shared roles and responsibilities, as depicted by a Project CALIPSO scholar.

Our project provides a model for pairing two disciplines that have not traditionally been paired in interprofessional models. The pairing of speech-language pathologists and school counselors overcomes gaps in knowledge and skills that result from both professions' tradition of discipline-specific teaching with minimal or no focus on interdisciplinary training. With the rising numbers of students with disabilities in schools, school personnel often face challenges in addressing the overall emotional, social, and academic needs of these students and lack training on how to effectively intervene with this popula-

## A Model for the Interprofessional Preparation of Speech-Language Pathologists and School Counselors

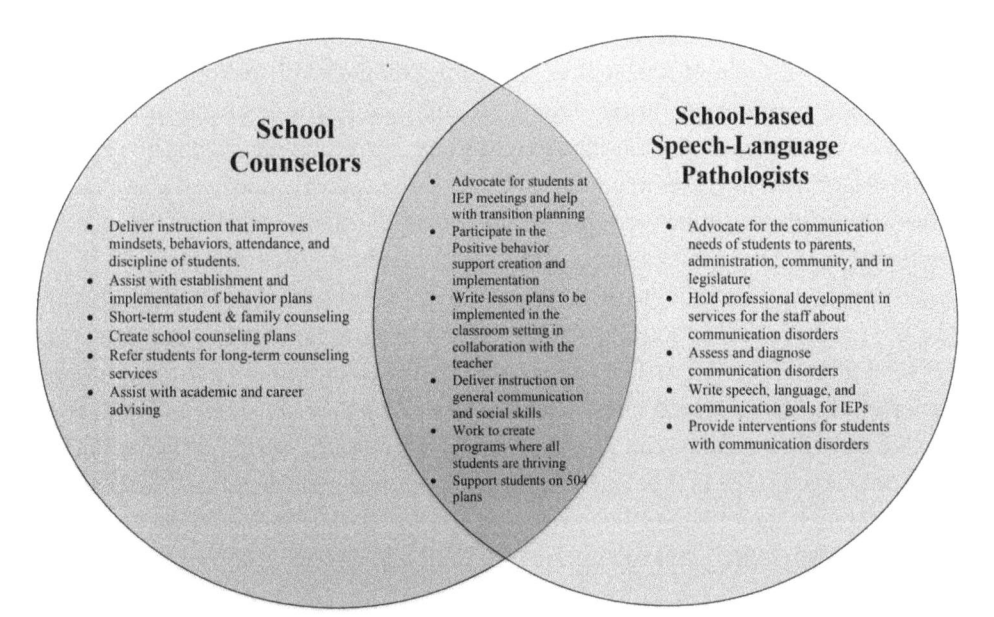

*Figure 1. Roles and Responsibilities of School Counselors and Speech-Language Pathologists*

**School Counselors**
- Deliver instruction that improves mindsets, behaviors, attendance, and discipline of students.
- Assist with establishment and implementation of behavior plans
- Short-term student & family counseling
- Create school counseling plans
- Refer students for long-term counseling services
- Assist with academic and career advising

**Overlap**
- Advocate for students at IEP meetings and help with transition planning
- Participate in the Positive behavior support creation and implementation
- Write lesson plans to be implemented in the classroom setting in collaboration with the teacher
- Deliver instruction on general communication and social skills
- Work to create programs where all students are thriving
- Support students on 504 plans

**School-based Speech-Language Pathologists**
- Advocate for the communication needs of students to parents, administration, community, and in legislature
- Hold professional development in services for the staff about communication disorders
- Assess and diagnose communication disorders
- Write speech, language, and communication goals for IEPs
- Provide interventions for students with communication disorders

tion. For example, one study showed that about 30% of speech-language pathologists lack the comfort and training to manage bullying and peer victimization of children with disabilities (Ofe et al., 2016). Additionally, many speech-language pathologists reportedly lack skills to offer counseling support to children with disabilities.

Although ASHA considers counseling as an integral part of practice for speech-language pathologists, practitioners report lacking the skills needed to effectively incorporate this component into their practice (Atkins, 2007). Beck and Verticchio (2014) noted that only a few programs in speech-language pathology offer coursework in counseling and graduates are not well equipped in the area of basic counseling interventions. Along these same lines, Luterman (2006) reported that over 80% of speech-language pathologists expressed a need for more training and experiences in the area of counseling. Although ASHA considers counseling to be within the speech-language pathologist's scope of practice, many still hesitate to incorporate counseling into practice (Holland and Nelson, 2020). DiLollo and Neimeyer (2020) suggest that speech-language pathologists' feelings of inadequacy contribute to frustration and reluctance to include counseling as part of their service delivery. An additional contributing factor is that practitioners report lacking the skills needed to effectively incorporate this component into their practice (Atkins, 2007). This is likely related to only a small fraction of speech-language pathology graduate programs offering coursework in counseling, preventing speech-language pathologists from feeling well equipped in basic counseling interventions (Beck and Verticchio, 2014).

Limitations also exist in the preparation of school counselors. For example, the literature notes that school counselors historically have had limited contact with students with disabilities due to a lack of training in working with students with disabilities (Hall, 2015). It has been noted in the literature that school counseling graduate programs typically do not have specific courses about special education (Hall, 2015) or about the wide range disabilities that school-age children may have (e.g., speech/language impairment, hearing impairment, autism) even though the American School Counselor Association's position statement, *The School Counselor and Students with Disabilities* (ASCA, 2022), clearly defines roles and responsibilities for school counselors concerning students with disabilities. Nevertheless, there still appears to be some limitations in the education and training of graduate-level school counselor preparation programs. As a check, an examination of the core curriculum in master-level school counselor programs in Mississippi revealed that a foundational course in special education is not required by most programs. The lack of formal coursework in special education likely contributes to school counselors not feeling well equipped to support students with a range of disabilities in schools.

A collaborative project with speech-language pathologists and school counselors presents an opportunity to add a unique preparation model to the literature and to higher education practices. A review of the literature has revealed only one article about collaborations involving these two professionals. This article is Barnes et al. (2003), which noted that because of changes in roles and standards regarding inclusion, diverse settings, teaming, and service delivery models, the services that are offered by these two professions are very parallel in their approaches and could benefit from collaborative efforts to offer more efficient and enriching services. We agree with Barnes et al. (2003) that because of the similarities in current models of school counseling and speech-language pathology interventions in regards to environment, methods, professional relationships, scheduling, behavior management, curriculum development and evaluations, by working together, speech-language pathologists and school counselors could offer a more strengthened support for students who need specialized interventions and supports.

## Theoretical and Practical Underpinnings of Project CALIPSO

Inspired by some of the observations of Barnes et al. (2003), the design of Project CALIPSO was based on a model posited by the Interprofessional Education Collaborative (IPEC; 2016) and focused on IPEC's four core competencies: values/ethics, roles/responsibilities, interprofessional communication, and teams and teamwork. These four competencies were woven throughout the project. Work with each cohort of our CALIPSO scholars always began with activities that addressed IPEC's first two core competences (values/ethics, roles/responsibilities) and involved learning about both professions' scope of practice, roles and responsibilities, and code of ethics. By design, the learning activities allowed scholars to identify and appreciate the roles of both professions and to create a culture of mutual respect and shared values related to working with children with disabilities. As shown in Figure A, scholars were engaged in discussions and assignments that allowed them to discover how the two disciplines have different yet similar roles in working with school-age children, including those who have disabilities. Ultimately, scholars were supported to use the knowledge of their own role and that of the other discipline to appropriately assess and address the communication, socio-emotional, and behavioral needs of school-age children with disabilities. As part of this, scholars were guided to recognize their own limitations in skills, knowledge, and abilities and by doing so, appreciate the contributions of other professions and recognize the need for them.

Helping scholars to be able to communicate about limitations in having singular disciplinary perspectives relates to the second IPEC core competency, Interprofessional Communication. As part of this competency, scholars were guided to effectively communicate with children, parents, teachers, other professionals using communication tools and techniques, language and terminology that were appropriate to the context. Given that the project involved graduate students from two different disciplines who were learning to use professional jargon, helping the scholars to clearly communicate with others and

## A Model for the Interprofessional Preparation of Speech-Language Pathologists and School Counselors

with each other, avoiding discipline-specific jargon, whenever possible, was an important component of this competency. Additionally, this competency also supported scholars to actively listen, provide feedback, and respectfully respond to the ideas of other team members to maintain positive interprofessional relationships. The final competency, teams and teamwork, was interwoven in all aspects of the project, guiding the scholars to apply principles of team dynamics to effectively perform on teams that assess and address the needs of school-age children with disabilities.

Beyond the IPEC model, the limitations in the graduate-level training of speech-language pathologists and school counselors were considered when designing Project CALIPSO. To fill in for the curricular gaps of both programs, we were intentional to include what is important but missing from the two curricula. For the speech-language pathology students, this was counseling and effective behavior management, and for the school counselor students, this was special education and exposure to a wider range of disabilities.

Finally, in designing Project CALIPSO, we were intentional in including literacy as a major component of the project and as a primary instructional and intervention approach that scholars would learn to use. A literacy-based framework that includes storybooks, narratives, and social stories appealed to us and was selected as a primary instructional and intervention context for language and social-emotional development because it allows speech-language pathologists and school counselors to provides services in a context that addresses one of Mississippi's greatest challenges and one of MDE's legislative priorities: literacy. Mississippi's Literacy-Based Promotion Act requires school districts to provide scientifically-based reading instruction, to regularly monitor progress, and to provide intensive reading instruction and intervention for students who exhibit substantial deficiency in reading in kindergarten and first through third grades, and to retain third grade students who are not reading on grade level. Given the high stakes of literacy testing in Mississippi, the adoption of the Literacy-Based Promotion Act created an opportunity for all educators to play a role in the literacy development of school-age children, including those with disabilities. We recognized that within this inclusive approach, speech-language pathologists can draw on their extensive training in child development, assessment, and in providing high-quality, evidence-based speech, language and literacy interventions and services for children with disabilities. Likewise, school counselors can draw on their expertise in child development, identification and intervention of children's academic and social-emotional needs in an effort to removes barriers to learning, planning and implementing interventions that target developing skills and behaviors that are critical for academic achievement, and team-teaching using methods that recognizes that students learn in multiple ways.

Drawing on the unique and overlapping skill sets of speech-language pathologists and school counselors, the specific literacy-based approach selected for Project CALIPSO was bibliotherapy. Bibliotherapy is the use of books to help individuals solve problems. The approach is guided by an adult who scaffolds the student to read and comprehend the story language, and make connections, including personal connections, with the literature or the book (Regan & Page, 2008). Bibliotherapy has been shown to be an effective way to explore alternative problem solving, foster emotional wellness, relieve emotional pressure, improve self-concept, help in planning a more appropriate course of action, foster motivation, deal with emotional and psychological concerns, and aid in social skill development (Forgan, 2002). Specifically, when used with children with disabilities, research has shown that bibliotherapy helps children cope with grief, social stressors, depression (Gregory, Canning, Lee, & Wise, 2004) and problem solving (Forgan, 2002), and other social-emotional skills.

## Components of Project CALIPSO

Shared coursework, collaborative clinical experiences, and other activities were used to prepare speech-language pathology scholars and school counselor scholars in our project. Embedded in our instructional and clinical activities were the four IPEC core competencies. Through the shared coursework, collaborative clinical experiences, and other activities, we prepared our scholars to address the language, literacy, and social-emotional needs of children with disabilities, as well as to design and deliver services to parents and teachers through parent and teacher trainings to increase the likelihood for optimal child outcomes. In the next sections, we provide some examples of each of the three components of Project CALIPSO: shared coursework, collaborative clinical experiences, and other activities.

## Coursework

In the courses associated with Project CALIPSO, scholars from both graduate programs were enrolled, and Project CALIPSO faculty from both programs facilitated collaborative coursework and learning experiences, aligning with the IPE teams and teamwork core competencies. Each cohort of students began the project with a special topics course that focused on children with disabilities, the role of speech-language pathologists and counselors, and interprofessional practice. Through the course, scholars were introduced to special education laws, scopes of practice for both disciplines, codes of ethics, roles and responsibilities of both professions, and various conditions and disabilities that may impact school-age children. Project faculty planned lessons to teach scholars about the conditions, including the impact of each condition on speech, language, literacy, social-emotional development, and behavior. At the conclusion of each lesson, scholars were assigned learning activities that allow them to further learn how to support children with disabilities through interprofessional collaboration. Learning activities included participating on discussion boards, writing opinion papers (e.g., Down syndrome and facial cosmetic surgery for adolescents) and reflection papers, creating anti-bullying campaigns designed to support children with disabilities and social stories, designing classroom problem-solving tools, conducting interviews with parents of children with disabilities, and working through case studies.

An example of a unit in the special problems course is the childhood hearing loss unit. During this unit, an audiology faculty member provided an interactive lecture that included a detailed description of childhood hearing loss, prevalence, and incidence of childhood hearing loss and discussed the impacts of hearing loss on auditory skills, speech, receptive and expressive language skills, literacy, academic performance, social-emotional development, behavior, career readiness and/or college preparedness. By discussing a wide array of impacted areas beyond audition, scholars from speech-language pathology and school counseling had the opportunity to understand the needs that children with hearing loss have that may extend beyond what has traditionally been considered within their scope of practice. The discussion was intended to help scholars further recognize unmet and unaddressed needs that students with hearing loss may have, as well as help them to identify other professionals that may also have a role on an interdisciplinary team of support professionals. After the interactive lesson, scholars were paired or grouped with interdisciplinary partners to complete learning activities to expand their knowledge.

Beyond the special topics course, the scholars were enrolled in two counseling courses: one that was taught by a school counseling faculty member and one that was taught by an audiologist. Both courses were intended to promote holistic support of children with disabilities through interprofessional collaboration. This was accomplished through collaborative course assignments and projects that the scholars completed in small interdisciplinary groups or as a speech-language pathology/school counselor dyad. Through group work, we were able to fortify our scholars' competencies in teams and team work as well as interprofessional communication.

## Case Studies

Case studies were used in each of the Project CALIPSO courses as a key strategy for teaching and learning because they promote problem-based learning and analytical thinking (Herreid et al., 2011). Case studies were used to introduce complex cases and teach new concepts, assessment methods, and intervention approaches to scholars. An example of a case study that was used in this way is below.

*Andrea, a six- year- old African American first grade student who has been diagnosed with Generalized Anxiety and has a moderate sensorineural hearing loss and a related speech-language disorder, experiences panic attacks that began after the death of her twin brother. The school counselor utilizes play therapy and Positive Behavioral Interventions and Supports (PBIS) to assist with the underlying emotions of grief and to decrease Andrea's panic attacks. Play therapy allows the student to uproot those unconscious feelings and express them through play and PBIS encourages the decrease in panic attacks. The speech-language pathologist also uses play-based therapy and shared storybook reading to address language goals such as planning sequences of pretend events using temporal terms such as next, then, before, after as well as expanding her vocabulary.*

Case studies such as the one above were used by project faculty who were facilitating the learning experience to guide scholars through the assessment approaches leading to the child's diagnosis, selection of appropriate goals for the child, intervention methods, and additional ways to support the child in a classroom environment.

Case studies were also used to promote problem solving, clinical analyses, decision making in complex student profiles, and interprofessional collaboration. Scholars worked together through the scenarios and as part of case study activities, scholars were asked to always consider their discipline-specific role in meeting the needs of the student as well as how both disciplines can collaboratively meet the needs of the student. Examples are:

*Speech-Language/Hearing/Trauma:* Courtney is a eight-year-old Hispanic female that was diagnosed with a moderate sensorineural hearing loss at 5 months old. Courtney is a second-grade student in a public school district, and she wears two hearing aids to school daily. Her teachers describe her as active, busy and inattentive. Courtney is 60% intelligible to her family and friends, and 50% intelligible to her peers and teachers. She does not interact well with her peers and has frequent meltdowns at recess. Teachers often have to separate Courtney from the class due to safety concerns for the other children. Courtney exhibits behaviors such as pulling other children's hair, yelling at the teacher, and getting out of her seat to move. Courtney also has difficulty with following multi-step directions and is struggling socially and academically in school. Courtney struggles with math word problems, reading comprehension, phonological skills, and written communication. Courtney's mom is a single parent that lives with her aunt. She has limited transportation and often catches the city bus to commute to work. Mom has reported that Courtney's brother was recently sent to jail. Recently, her mom has observed the same behaviors at home. Her mom is quite anxious and concerned about Courtney's behavior and wants to be proactive regarding a plan to help Courtney address her needs.

Identify the key team members that need to be involved in creating and implementing a plan for Courtney. Please include the role that each key member plays in creating and/or implementing the plan. Based on the *Individuals with Disabilities Education Improvement Act of 2004* (IDEA), what type of plan would be relevant to Courtney's educational experience? In what ways can the key team members support each other in practice? Play therapy with dolls can be used to discover a child's emotions and reactions to situations. Identify a listening, language, social-emotional (at home and at school), and behavioral situation that this child is experiencing that can be more deeply explored through play therapy. What obstacles may impact the ability to implement interprofessional practice? What are some solutions to overcome those obstacles? Identify some ways that you can coach the parent to support the child's needs holistically.

*Truancy dropout/teasing bullying:* Jordan is a 16-year-old African American male that attends a local high school in a rural area. Jordan was diagnosed with a fluency disorder at age 5. Jordan exhibits pauses, syllable repetitions, and secondary characteristics of stuttering including eye twitches. Jordan has been teased most of his primary and secondary school years. Jordan has recently entered 10th grade. He has missed 30 days of school and is in jeopardy of failing the 10th grade. Jordan still receives services for his fluency disorder, however due to children teasing him about his disorder he does not like to attend therapy. He often skips school at the designated time for therapy. The truancy officer has made attempts to investigate the reason for the habitual absences with Jordan's parents. Jordan's parents work full-time and were unaware of his habitual absences. Recently, Jordan mentioned to a friend that he is considering dropping out of school.

Identify the key team members that need to be involved in creating and implementing a plan for Jordan. Please include the role that each key member plays in creating and/or implementing the plan. In what ways can the key team members support each other in practice? Identify ways that speech-language pathologists and school counselors in high school can work together to create a more inclusive environment to reduce bullying. Identify ways that you can support the parents in the home environment. Identify alternative ways that Jordan can access speech-language services. What obstacles may impact the ability to implement interprofessional practice? What are some solutions to overcome those obstacles?

In some cases, videos were used to facilitate interaction and discussion around the case study and case studies were typically paired with readings from articles or textbooks. Case studies typically ended with a written paper or an oral presentation with opportunity for further discussion. Throughout Project CALIPSO, a goal was to provide students with as many opportunities as possible to work through case studies to prepare them for the heterogeneity of the school-age population of children with disabilities that they will encounter in their professional careers.

## Collaborative Clinical Experiences

Project CALIPSO was designed to not only include interprofessional education, but also the opportunity to apply the knowledge gained in clinical practice. The clinical experiences of Project CALIPSO primarily focused on three clinical activities: parent and teacher training sessions, the development and implementation of behavioral observation and modification plans, and the development of speech-language and literacy plans with a specific focus on social-emotional skills. Each clinical activity was intentionally designed to provide scholars with opportunities to fortify their IPEC competencies as well as develop knowledge and skills in working with different populations and to allow scholars to consider the whole child in their intervention approaches. Four clinical experiences will be described in detail for readers who may wish to replicate this aspect of the project.

One clinical experience involved the speech-language pathology and school counselor scholars collaborating to prepare and implement parent support sessions to help them to support the needs of the whole child by working with parents. For this experience, the target parent population was parents of children with autism spectrum disorders (ASD). Two project faculty – one from speech-language pathology and one from school counseling – spearheaded this clinical experience. Working with the scholars, it was decided to focus on parents of children with ASD because of the significant challenges for this population brought on by the COVID-19 pandemic and the observation that the instant change of routine brought feelings of fear and uncertainty to many of our clients. After expanding their knowledge of ASD, scholars from both disciplines planned sessions designed around specific topics that were intended to help families cope with the impacts of COVID-19. In addition to our goal of creating sessions that were beneficial to the parents, a primary intent of the clinical experience was to provide opportunities to the students to strengthen their skills in two IPEC core competency areas: interprofessional communication and team and teamwork.

The topics included explaining COVID-19 to your child, self-care, children with disabilities and their siblings, and assertiveness training. The purpose of the first session was to support parents to explain COVID-19 to their children using social stories. Components of social stories were discussed, and parents were guided to create or use social stories to help their children understand their emotions, promote a sense of safety, re-establish stability in the midst of uncertainty, and reinforce positive behavior. The purpose of the self-care session was to provide resources for parents/caregivers to explore self-care strategies to promote a well-balanced life. Scholars gave information about and examples of negative and positive coping strategies. The session ended with scholars providing resources that were specific to parents and children with ASD. The siblings session was designed to provide ways to incorporate siblings in everyday routines, interactions, and activities involving the child with ASD. As part of the session, scholars introduced the book *My Brother Charlie* by Holly Robinson Peete and Ryan Elizabeth Peete, which is told from the perspective of a sibling of a boy with autism. The book was used to provide the sibling's perspective of having a sibling with autism to support parents to manage life with children with and without disabilities. The session ended with parents discussing their typical day and the application of the strategies discussed during the session. The final session, assertiveness training, focused on forms of behavior and providing ways that children with ASD can maintain an appropriate balance between aggression and passivity. Scholars also led discussions about how parents can enhance their children's social skills despite the limitations on social interactions due to the COVID-19 pandemic.

The local autism center was the site of another clinical experience that was designed to provide scholars with direct experiences working with children with autism. The school counselor and speech-language pathology scholars were paired to create thematic lesson plans that addressed speech-language and social-emotional skills for school-age children with ASD attending a summer camp. Lesson plans included a sensory activity, and a 3D craft and an outdoor activity addressing the goals that addressed the child's language and social-emotional skills. In addition to implementing the lesson plans, scholars were also guided to recognize the children's need for break and how to use mindfulness techniques to help the children regulate themselves, how to promote positive behavior, and to expand language skills and communication in a naturalistic setting.

Another clinical experience for the project involved training early childhood teachers on two intervention approaches: shared storybook reading and bibliotherapy. Shared storybook reading is an intervention approach used by speech-language pathologists to provide a naturalistic context of language learning to intentionally and strategically expose children to vocabulary, grammar, story grammar, and the use of language (Ezell & Justice, 2005). As previously discussed, bibliotherapy is a counseling technique and refers to the use of books to help individuals solve problems. The approach is guided by an adult who scaffolds the student to read and comprehend the story language, and make connections, including personal connections, with the literature or the book (Regan & Page, 2008). Combining the interventions of shared storybook reading and bibliotherapy, scholars were paired and tasked with creating lesson plans based on a storybook that could be used to address three target areas: emergent literacy skills, language and vocabulary, and social-emotional skills. Each lesson plan included a shared storybook reading that included concepts about print activities, a picture walk, explicit vocabulary instruction, wh-questions, mini lesson that targeted language and social-emotional skills, a 3D craft, and ideas of carryover of skills. Each scholar-pair was assigned to a project faculty member and worked together to create lesson plans for two different preschool classrooms. Lesson plans consisted of very specific instructions (e.g., "Say....," "Point to...," "Turn the page and say...") for the teacher so that the teacher could implement the activity with as much fidelity to the intervention approaches as possible. In addition to the lesson plan, the book, all materials associated with the lesson plan (i.e., craft materials, mini-lesson materials), and an instructional video which showed the scholars implementing the lesson plan were provided to the teachers.

The final clinical experience for the project took place at the speech-language pathology program's on-campus speech, language, and hearing clinic. For this experience, speech-language pathology and school counseling scholars were paired and assigned to pediatric clients with communication disorders and concomitant behavioral issues. Drawing on past coursework and Positive Behavioral Intervention and Supports training, scholars created behavioral modification plans for selected clients in the clinic after reviewing client's files and reviewing a series of sessions. Following a period of observation, the scholars worked in a team approach to design, implement, and measure the success of behavioral plans for selected children. Debriefing sessions that were facilitated by project faculty were held to allow scholars to discuss the outcomes and impact of the behavior modification plan. As shown by each of the clinical experiences, scholars from both disciplines had the opportunity to enhance skills germane to their discipline as well as skills traditionally thought to be outside their discipline, aligning with IPEC core competency of roles/responsibilities. Further, each experience allowed the scholars to address sub competencies related to values/ethics (e.g., ethical conduct), interprofessional communication (e.g., using respectful language appropriate for a given difficult situation), and teams and teamwork (e.g., integrate the knowledge and experience of other professionals to inform care).

## OTHER COLLABORATIVE LEARNING EXPERIENCES

Other collaborative learning experiences were interspersed throughout the project to ensure that the scholars had opportunities across the project to hone their interprofessional practice knowledge and skills. Workshops taught by external experts were held to expand scholars' knowledge and skills in the areas of positive behavioral interventions and supports, students with disabilities, high-risk students, and dropout prevention. Workshops included break-out sessions, collaborative activities, and homework and other opportunities to extend learning. Scholars also attended professional conferences for both disciplines including the American Speech, Language, Hearing Association convention, the American

School Counselor Association conference, and the state association conferences for both professions. Some scholars also presented at professional conferences. For example, one group of scholars presented at a local conference on strategies to manage children's trauma, hunger, academic, and behavioral issues related to COVID-19.

Another Project CALIPSO learning experience was the group book reading and discussion activity. Books were selected by project faculty based on the book's relation to both professions. Examples of books were *Glow Kids* by Nicholas Kardaras, *Autobiography of a Face* by Lucy Grealy, and *Wonder* by R. J. Palacio. Scholars were responsible for either leading or participating in discussions with the project faculty members serving as discussion facilitators. Project faculty were intentional about linking the information from the book to areas of speech-language pathology and/or school counseling, making a case for interprofessional practice as often as possible. The book discussion activity was typically linked to other readings or was extended with learning activities or other experiences. For example, at the conclusion of *Glow Kids*, a book about the dangers of screen time, scholars participated in a service project at the local children's museum where they facilitated activities with children and provided resources (e.g., informational pamphlets) to parents about screen time and alternative ways of entertaining and teaching children.

## SUMMARY

Project CALIPSO was an interdisciplinary personnel preparation project for speech-language pathology and school counseling graduate students who participated in two years of shared courses, collaborative assignments, and clinical experiences that were designed to increase the number and improve the quality of personnel who had the knowledge and skills necessary to serve children and youth with disabilities, including those with high-intensity needs. A primary focus of the project was children with communication disorders and concomitant difficulties in areas such as social-emotional development and behavior. Components of the project were detailed in this chapter with a specific focus on shared courses that used case studies as a primary instructional method, collaborative clinical experiences, and other learning activities. Through this collaborative model, scholars were guided to consider the whole child and were provided specialized opportunities to develop holistic approaches to supporting children with disabilities.

We recognize that effective collaboration between speech-language pathologists and school counselors is critical in achieving the academic, social, behavioral and communication goals for students (Sisti & Robledo, 2021). By leveraging the distinct and overlapping skills of speech-language pathologists and school counselors, the project taught graduate-level scholars to collaboratively work in a way that allows them to offer a more strengthened system of support for children and youth who need specialized interventions and supports. To end the chapter, we discuss lessons learned, we offer suggestions to others who are interested in this type of work, and we provide directions for future research.

## LESSONS, SUGGESTIONS, AND DIRECTION FOR RESEARCH

At our institution, the speech-language pathology graduate program and the school counseling graduate program are structured very differently. The speech-language pathology program typically has its courses and clinical practicum experiences during the day, so students typically do not have full-time jobs. In contrast, the school counseling graduate program's courses are in the evening to accommodate a working student population. The different structures of the program necessitated careful and advanced planning of program activities. We learned to plan early and to take advantage of short spans of available time (e.g., 1-hour sessions each week instead of longer sessions), evening times, and intersessions.

The COVID-19 pandemic occurred during the first year of the program requiring project faculty to shift many of the activities to an online format. We took advantage of virtual tools (e.g., Zoom class sessions, online conferences and webinars, e-portfolios) during the first year of the pandemic to minimize disruption. We found ourselves being creative and coming up with innovative ways to meet our project goals. Beyond the first year of the pandemic, we took what we learned about virtual tools during the peak of the pandemic and used them, as necessary and for convenience, while re-introducing face-to-face activities.

Our recruitment efforts were designed to recruit diverse students for the project. A minimum of two graduate informational sessions were held in the speech-language pathology program to recruit students for the program and share details about Project CALIPSO. Current graduate students on Project CALIPSO were utilized at the graduate informational sessions to share their experiences on the project. The school counseling program participated in graduate informational fairs and recruitment events. Scholars from each program were required to submit an application that included a summary of their background, career goals, interest in working with children, and their views on interdisciplinary collaboration in the education and clinical setting.

As a result of our efforts, we recruited and enrolled diverse students on Project CALIPSO. Our scholars were diverse on a range of factors including race and ethnicity, gender, age, neurodiversity, academic background, and geographical background. All factors of diversity added value to the project but the neurodiverse students, in particular, provided perspectives and insights about people with disabilities that we may not have had without their participation. Based on our experiences, we suggest that all projects seek to have as diverse of a scholar population as possible. As projects enroll diverse students, we suggest that project personnel are intentional about honoring the diversity and different perspectives that scholars bring to the project. For example, on our project, project personnel were typically responsible for pairing and grouping scholars for collaborative work. This helped to ensure that the scholars were getting opportunities to collaborate with different scholars throughout the project. During group work, project personnel monitored scholars' interpersonal communication and collaborative styles. If project personnel observed difficulties with communication or collaboration, issues were addressed, used as teachable moments, and scholars were re-focused on the goal of effective interprofessional collaboration. Project personnel also were intentional about structuring lectures and discussions in ways that encouraged and provided all scholars an opportunity to participate and contribute.

Finally, as previously mentioned, the existing literature is lacking studies about interprofessional practice involving speech-language pathologists and school counselors. An older article by Barnes, Friehe, and Radd (2003) provides a compelling argument for collaboration between speech-language pathologists and school counselors. We believe that the successes of Project CALIPSO add to that argument and the project provides a model of interprofessional practice that is worthy of research and further exploration. Future studies should examine and document the benefits of this interprofessional model and document the positive impacts that it has on children with disabilities, their families, and school communities.

*A Model for the Interprofessional Preparation of Speech-Language Pathologists and School Counselors*

## ACKNOWLEDGMENTS

The contents of this chapter were developed under a grant from the U.S. Department of Education, #H325K180188. However, those contents do not necessarily represent the policy of the U.S. Department of Education, and you should not assume endorsement by the Federal Government. We would like to acknowledge all of the Project CALIPSO scholars who participated on this project, and particularly, Kat Yates whose Venn diagram assignment was used in Figure A. Additionally, we extend gratitude to the project's clinical partners and our colleagues who assisted with the project, especially Dr. Betty Sutton, Dr. Ronica Arnold Branson, and William Davis.

## REFERENCES

American School Counselor Association. (2022). The school counselor and students with disabilities. *ASCA*. https://www.schoolcounselor.org/Standards-Positions/Position-Statements/ASCA-Position-Statements/The-School-Counselor-and-Students-with-Disabilitie

American Speech-Language-Hearing Association. (2016). Scope of Practice in Speech- Language Pathology [Scope of Practice]. *ASHA*. https://www.asha.org/policy/

American Speech-Language-Hearing Association. (2021). *Interprofessional practice survey results*. https://www.asha.org/siteassets/surveys/2021-interprofessional-practice-survey-results.pdf

American Speech-Language-Hearing Association. (n.d.). *Caseload/Workload* (Practice Portal). https://www.asha.org/practice-portal/professional-issues/caseload-and-workload/

Ansari, A., & Gottfried, M. A. (2021). The grade level and cumulative outcome of absenteeism. *Child Development*, 92(4), 548–564. doi:10.1111/cdev.13555 PMID:33739441

Ansari, A., & Pianta, R. C. (2019). School absentee in the first decade of education and outcomes in adolescents. *Journal of School Psychology*, 76, 48–61. doi:10.1016/j.jsp.2019.07.010 PMID:31759468

Atkins, C.P. (2007). Graduate SLP/Aud Clinicians on Counseling: Self-Perceptions and Awareness of Boundaries.

Barnes, P. E., Friehe, M. J. M., & Radd, T. R. (2003). Collaboration between speech-language pathologists and school counselors. *Communication Disorders Quarterly*, 24(3), 137–142. doi:10.1177/15257401030240030501

Beck, A. R., & Verticchio, H. (2018). Effectiveness of a Method for Teaching Self-Compassion to Communication Sciences and Disorders Graduate Students. *American Journal of Speech-Language Pathology*, 27(1), 192–206. doi:10.1044/2017_AJSLP-17-0060 PMID:29383372

Brinton, B., Fujiki, M., & Robinson, L. A. (2005). Life on a Tricycle: A Case Study of Language Impairment From 4 to 19. *Topics in Language Disorders*, 25(4), 338–352. doi:10.1097/00011363-200510000-00009

Center for Disease Control. (2022). Percentage of births born preterm by states. *CDC.* https://www.cdc.gov/nchs/pressroom/sosmap/preterm_births/preterm.htm

Center for Disease Control (n.d.). *Disability impacts Mississippi.* 2022 MS Disability and Health State Profile (cdc.gov). *CDC.*

Center for Disease Control. (n.d.). *Disability and health U.S. state profile data for Mississippi (adults 18+ years of age).* [Data set]. https://www.cdc.gov/ncbddd/disabilityandhealth/impacts/mississippi.html

Center for Learning Disabilities. (2017). The State of Learning Disabilities: Understanding the 1 in 5. *CDC.* https://www.ncld.org/wp-content/uploads/2017/03/Executive-Summary.Fin_.03142017.pdf

Children's Foundation of Mississippi. (2020). *2020 Mississippi kids count factbook.* [Data set].https://childrensfoundationms.org/research/kidscount2020/

Conti-Ramsden, G., Durkin, K., Toseeb, U., Botting, N., & Pickles, A. (2018). Education and employment outcomes of young adults with a history of developmental language disorder. *International Journal of Language & Communication Disorders, 53*(2), 237–255. doi:10.1111/1460-6984.12338 PMID:29139196

Cook, S., & Howell, P. (2014). Bullying in children and teenagers who stutter and the relation to self-esteem, social acceptance, and anxiety. *Perspectives on Fluency and Fluency Disorders, 24*(2), 46–57. doi:10.1044/ffd24.2.46

DiLollo, A., & Neimeyer, R. A. (2022). *Counseling in speech-language pathology and audiology: Reconstructing personal narratives* (2nd ed.). Plural Publishing.

Ezell, H. K., & Justice, L. M. (2005). *Shared storybook reading: Building young children's language and emergent literacy skills.* Paul H. Brookes Publishing Co.

Forgan, J. W. (2002). Using bibliotherapy to teach problem solving. *Intervention in School and Clinic, 38*(2), 75–82. doi:10.1177/10534512020380020201

Gage, N. A., Lierheimer, K. S., & Goran, L. (2012). Characteristics of students with high-incidence disabilities broadly defined. *Journal of Disability Policy Studies, 23*(3), 168–178. doi:10.1177/1044207311425385

Gregory, R. J., Schwer Canning, S., Lee, T. W., & Wise, J. C. (2004). Cognitive bibliotherapy for depression: A Meta-Analysis. *Professional Psychology, Research and Practice, 35*(3), 275–280. doi:10.1037/0735-7028.35.3.275

Hall, J. (2015). The school counselor and special education: Aligning training with practice. *The Professional Counselor, 5*(2), 217–224. doi:10.15241/jgh.5.2.217

Herreid, C. F., Schiller, N. A., Herreid, K. F., & Wright, C. (2011). In case you are interested: Results of a survey of case study teachers. *Journal of College Science Teaching, 40,* 7–80.

Holland, A., & Nelson, R. (2020). *Counseling in communication disorders* (3rd ed.). Plural Publishing.

Hollo, A., & Chow, J. C. (2015). Communicative Functions of Problem Behavior for Students with High-Incidence Disabilities. *Beyond Behavior, 24*(3), 23–30. doi:10.1177/107429561502400304

Interprofessional Education Collaborative. (2016). Core competencies for interprofessional collaborative practice: Report of an expert panel. *IEC.* https://www.asha.org/siteassets/uploadedfiles/interprofessional-collaboration-core-competency.pdf

Katz, L. A., Maag, A., Fallon, K. A., Blenkarn, K., & Smith, M. K. (2010). What makes a caseload (un)manageable? School-based speech language pathologists speak. *Language, Speech, and Hearing Services in Schools, 41*(2), 139–151. doi:10.1044/0161-1461(2009/08-0090) PMID:19755641

Kim, N., & Lambie, G. W. (2018). Burnout and implications for professional school counselors. *The Professional Counselor, 8*(3), 277–294. https://tpcjournal.nbcc.org/burnout-and-implications-for-professional-school-counselors/. doi:10.15241/nk.8.3.277

Luterman, D. (2006). The counseling relationship. *ASHA Leader, 11*(4), 8–33. doi:10.1044/leader.FTR3.11042006.8

Lyons, R., & Roulstone, S. (2018). Well-Being and Resilience in Children With Speech and Language Disorders. *Journal of Speech, Language, and Hearing Research: JSLHR, 61*(2), 324–344. doi:10.1044/2017_JSLHR-L-16-0391 PMID:29374284

March of Dimes. (2021). *Rate of PreTerm Births.* https://www.marchofdimes.org/Peristats/tools/prematurityprofile.aspx?reg=99

Mississippi Department of Education. (2022, June). *4-year graduation rates.* [Data set]. https://www.mdek12.org/sites/default/files/Offices/MDE/OEA/OPR/2022/grad_dropout_rates_2022_report.pdf

National Assessment of Educational Progress (2017). *State performance compared to the nation.* State Profiles. nationsreportcard.gov

National Assessment of Educational Progress. (2019). *State performance compared to the nation.* [Data set]. https://www.nationsreportcard.gov/profiles/stateprofile?chort=1&sub=RED&sj=AL&sfj=NP&st=MN&year=2019R3

National Center for Education Statistics. (2022). Students with disabilities. *NCES.* https://nces.ed.gov/fastfacts/display.asp?id=64

Ofe, E. E., Plumb, A. M., Plexico, L. W., & Haak, N. J. (2016). School-based speech-language pathologists' knowledge and perceptions of autism spectrum disorder and bullying. *Language, Speech, and Hearing Services in Schools, 47*(1), 59–76. doi:10.1044/2015_LSHSS-15-0058 PMID:26812936

Redmond, S. M. (2011). Peer victimization among students with specific language impairment, attention-deficit/hyperactivity disorder, and typical development. *Language, Speech, and Hearing Services in Schools, 42*(4), 520–535. doi:10.1044/0161-1461(2011/10-0078) PMID:21844400

Regan, K., & Page, P. (2008). "Character" building: Using literature to connect with youth. *Reclaiming Youth and Children: The Journal of Strength-Based Interventions, 16,* 37–43.

Sisti, M., & Robledo, J. (2021). Interdisciplinary Collaboration Practices between Education Specialists and Related Service Providers. *The Journal of Special Education Apprenticeship, 10*(1), 1–22.

Spencer, E. J., Goldstein, H., & Kaminski, R. (2012). Teaching Vocabulary in Storybooks: Embedding Explicit Vocabulary Instruction for Young Children. *Young Exceptional Children*, *15*(1), 18–32. doi:10.1177/1096250611435367

Tang, K. S., Fortner, K. M., & Morgan, R. D. (2021). School counselors and special education teachers involvement in leadership activities at their school sites. *Journal of Leadership, Equity, &. Research*, *7*(3), 1–17.

United Health Foundation. (2018). America's health rankings: Health of women and children report 2018. *UHF*. https://assets.americashealthrankings.org/app/uploads/2018ahrannual_020419.pdf

United Health Foundation. (2021). America's health rankings: Health of women and children report 2021. *UHF*. https://assets.americashealthrankings.org/app/uploads/state-summaries-healthofwomenandchildren-2021.pdf

United States Department of Education Office for Civil Rights. (2016). School Climate and Safety. *USDE*. https://www2.ed.gov/about/offices/list/ocr/docs/school-climate-and-safety.pdf

University of Kentucky HealthCare. (n.d.). Short and long-term effects of preterm birth. *UKH*. https://ukhealthcare.uky.edu/wellness-community/health-information/short-long-term-effects-preterm-birth

# Chapter 12
# An Interdisciplinary Case-Based Approach to Preservice Interprofessional Training

**Rebecca G. Lieberman-Betz**
*University of Georgia, USA*

**Jennifer A. Brown**
*University of Georgia, USA*

**Cynthia O. Vail**
*University of Geogia, USA*

**Sarah D. Wiegand**
*New Mexico State University, USA*

## ABSTRACT

*This chapter focuses on an innovative interdisciplinary training to support preservice professionals in provision of early intervention services to young children with high-intensity needs and their families. A brief review of the literature on interprofessional education in early intervention/early childhood special education practice fields, adult learning, and case-based methods of instruction is presented. Building on that foundation, a two-year, interdisciplinary personnel preparation program is described, with specific emphasis on a two-day interprofessional training event. During the training interdisciplinary faculty and families delivered content on early intervention and used a progressing case study to allow students to apply newly learned content in interdisciplinary teams. Lessons learned and implications for future training to support interdisciplinary collaboration among professionals and families are discussed.*

## INTRODUCTION

Interdisciplinary teaming and collaboration are established and recommended practices within the field of Early Intervention (EI) for infants and toddlers with developmental delays and disabilities (Council

DOI: 10.4018/978-1-6684-6438-0.ch012

for Exceptional Children-Division for Early Childhood [DEC], 2014; 2020). Effective collaborative practices between professionals and families are necessary to meet the often complex developmental and health needs of young children served through Part C of the Individuals with Disabilities Education Improvement Act (IDEA, 2004). Professional organizations guiding the practices of early interventionists, speech language pathologists, occupational therapists, and physical therapists emphasize interprofessional practice and collaboration with families in professional standards and recommended practices (DEC, American Speech-Language-Hearing Association [ASHA], American Physical Therapy Association [APTA], American Occupational Therapy Association [AOTA]). However, many preservice preparation programs continue to train future providers within disciplinary "silos" (King et al., 2016), with limited opportunities for cross-disciplinary electives or additional practicum placements due to tightly scheduled programs of study. Unfortunately, a lack of interprofessional opportunities at the preservice level may limit the preparedness of newly trained EI providers to effectively collaborate across disciplines and with families to support infants and toddlers with high-intensity needs. In response, it is incumbent upon those engaged in training early intervention and related services providers to develop feasible and effective interprofessional training opportunities that could be implemented across a variety of preservice training programs and models.

Development and implementation of interdisciplinary personnel preparation programs has been supported through US Department of Education Office of Special Education Programs (OSEP) grant awards. However, funding for such programs is limited by the amount of federal dollars available (only a small percentage of programs are funded each year) and is not typically used to sustain a program once it has been established. Therefore, it is important to find ways to extend the reach of such grants by developing innovative practices and strategies for interdisciplinary training that can be implemented outside the parameters of the original funded personnel preparation program. This chapter describes one example of an interprofessional training event developed for preservice EI providers as part of a larger OSEP-funded interdisciplinary preparation program for early intervention/early childhood special education (EI/ECSE) and speech-language pathology (SLP) graduate students. The full program model took two years to complete, and provided students with joint coursework and applied experiences integrated into their disciplinary programs of study. As part of the grant-funded program, a brief weekend-long interdisciplinary training event was developed and implemented during the second summer of the two-year program. The training event included additional students in the fields of physical and occupational therapy and used a case-based application to support practice of teaming and collaboration skills. The interdisciplinary training incorporated principles of adult learning by connecting content to real-life applications using problem-based case studies. This is deemed a critical strategy for adult learners (Bryan et al, 2009; Daley, 2001; Steinberg & Vinjamuri, 2014) and gives relevance to the content. Steinberg and Vinjamuri (2014) highlight the concepts of scaffolding "opportunities to critique applicability of multiple perspectives" and hands-on learning "opportunities to immediately apply evidence-based practice examples" as key adult learning principles (p. 372); these key principles were intentionally woven into the training. This chapter highlights this innovative interdisciplinary training (hereafter referred to as the Interprofessional Practice Summer Institute) as a way to extend the reach of grant-funded programs so greater numbers of practitioners are ready to provide EI services to young children with high-intensity needs using an interdisciplinary framework. The following section provides a brief review of interprofessional education in EI/ECSE fields of practice, with focus on interdisciplinary training and practice standards of professional organizations such as DEC, ASHA, APTA, and AOTA.

## Interprofessional Education in Early Intervention

Interdisciplinary education provides the foundation for interdisciplinary collaboration as practicing EI professionals. Part C early intervention services are frequently provided by EI/ECSE providers, SLPs, physical therapists (PTs), and occupational therapists (OTs; Raspa et al., 2010). Each of these disciplinary professions are guided by professional standards and/or codes from their respective professional organization. The Early Childhood Personnel Center identified commonalities across the disciplines specific to EI service delivery (Bruder et al., 2019). This crosswalk illustrated competency areas in coordination and collaboration, family-centered practice, data-based intervention/instruction, and professionalism. DEC (professional organization for EI/ECSE), ASHA (professional organization for SLP), APTA (professional organization for PT), and AOTA (professional organization for OT) each have specific guidelines or standards for interdisciplinary professional collaboration – ASHA, APTA, and AOTA specifically included the term "interdisciplinary" to refer to teaming, and DEC specified collaborating with professionals. Recognizing the importance of interdisciplinary practice starting at the preservice level, these organizations also support or require interdisciplinary education experiences, often referred to as interprofessional education, in preservice training programs (e.g., ASHA, 2022).

Interdisciplinary education opportunities focus on promoting relationships, learning experiences, and shared application across two or more disciplines with the intended goal of increasing knowledge, skills, and beliefs/attitudes for collaborative teaming (Center for Advancement of Interprofessional Education [CAIPE], 2002). Program evaluation results of interdisciplinary education experiences suggest improved student outcomes related to teaming practices, as well as knowledge and perceptions of other disciplines (Guraya & Barr, 2018; Kilgo et al., 2017). Early intervention interdisciplinary education activities have ranged in the depth, breadth, and intensity of content delivery, as well as the method of instruction. Some examples representing the range include workshops, brief trainings, applied activities, shared practicum experiences, and interdisciplinary personnel preparation programs. The level of intentionality and focus on collaboration and teaming also ranges from implicit (e.g., students from different disciplines learning early intervention content together) to explicit (e.g., students from different disciplines learning specifically about teaming along with early intervention content). Few studies focus on EI practice settings, or include EI/ECSE students in trainings with other related service providers.

Expanding early intervention interdisciplinary education experiences to represent the disciplines that frequently provide Part C services (e.g., EI/ECSE, SLP, PT, OT) is important to prepare students to provide the professional collaboration that is needed for effective service delivery. Including families and caregivers within those training experiences further prepares students to provide family-centered services and engage with families in ways that support their capacity for promoting their children's development. Identifying and exploring meaningful and effective interdisciplinary education activities that fit within and complement the individual disciplinary degree programs is essential for early intervention interdisciplinary education to move from an ideal scenario in theory to a feasible and effective regularly occurring practice. Expanding promising practices in interdisciplinary education, such as shared learning and application through case-based learning, provides a relevant context to support both learning about teaming as well as learning about specific early intervention content.

## Adult Learning and Case-Based Methods of Instruction

Adult learning principles provide a bedrock for faculty and professional development providers as they develop and implement interprofessional learning activities and professional development opportunities for both preservice and in-service teachers and EI providers across disciplines. The term andragogy was used by Knowles (1984) to describe assumptions of adult learning including active participation, self-directedness, and solution-centered. According to a research synthesis by Trivette and colleagues (2009), active participation in the learning process is the most effective common element of adult learning methods. Furthermore, adults are motivated to learn when they see the relevance of the learning activity and their previous experience is respected and built upon (self-directedness), and when there is a problem to solve (solution-centered; Bryan et al., 2009). Experiential learning connects content and theory to real life applications, providing the context to apply evidence-based practice principles and problem-focused approaches (Steinberg& Vinjamuri, 2009). Importantly, the extant literature indicates that learning experiences that are well-structured, practical, and collaborative have the best learning outcomes (McCall, et al., 2018).

Case-based instruction generally incorporates many of the adult learning principles outlined above (active participation, self-directedness, and solution-centered). According to Lyons and Bandura (2020), empirical research over the past several decades supports the use of case-based instruction in many fields including law, business/management, medicine, nursing, public administration, teacher education, social work, and engineering. The method is effective in improving teamwork, problem-solving, reflective skills, creativity, and professional judgement. Moreover, college faculty who used case-based instruction reported that learners demonstrated stronger critical thinking skills, were better able to make connections across content areas, developed deeper understanding of concepts, and were better able to view an issue from multiple perspectives (Lundeberg & Yadav, 2006).

Case-based instruction is a strategy well-suited for building common knowledge and skills among interprofessional teams. The case-based instruction process is linked to skill development in analysis, problem solving, active listening, collaboration, and compromise (Lyons & Bandura, 2020). Knowledge integration is continuous and unfolds as the case proceeds, requiring integrative thinking by the individual and team. These are critical skills needed to work well in interprofessional teams. Snyder and McWilliam (2003) provide evidence that case method instruction is an effective strategy to increase competence in family-centered practices among early intervention preservice students. They indicate that case method instruction promotes problem solving, decision making, reflection, and application of skills through use of case stories depicting real life dilemmas that EI providers encounter. This instructional process aligns with the components described by andragogy including the importance of active participation (occurring through discussion of cases), self-directedness (supported through presentation of relevant content in cases and reflection), and solution-centeredness (required by case discussions and decision making). McWilliam (2000) developed multiple case stories that can be applied to both preservice and professional development in early intervention and interprofessional teaming. These stories are generally unresolved and are accompanied by discussion questions. Case stories such as these can be adapted for use in multiple ways. Later in this chapter, a description is provided of how such a case can be adapted to unfold in a progressive manner to provide the context for preservice EI providers to apply newly acquired content and problem solve in fully collaborative teams.

*An Interdisciplinary Case-Based Approach to Preservice Interprofessional Training*

## PRESERVICE INTERPROFESSIONAL TRAINING

Interprofessional experiences at the preservice level are vitally important to preparing an early intervention workforce ready to collaborate with professionals representing other disciplines as well as with families. The following sections describe an interdisciplinary personnel preparation program for graduate students in EI/ECSE and SLP, a component of that program designed to provide intensive in-person training in interprofessional practice across multiple disciplines, and a model for virtual implementation of the intensive training.

## An Interdisciplinary Personnel Preparation Program

In recognition of the importance of interdisciplinary training at the preservice level, an OSEP-funded personnel preparation program was developed and implemented for EI/ECSE and SLP graduate students. The focus of the program was to prepare providers at the graduate level to support children with high-intensity needs through interdisciplinary teaming and collaboration. The program involved key interdisciplinary faculty (EI/ECSE and SLP); project-specific courses focused on young children with high-intensity needs and cross-disciplinary collaboration; development of program-specific competencies; integration of professional standards across discipline areas; an advisory stakeholder team; and community collaboration. The goal of the personnel preparation program was to increase students' knowledge and use of evidence-based practices in interdisciplinary EI/ECSE services, as well as students' competence in building collaborative partnerships to increase community capacity to provide high-quality services for young children with high-intensity needs and their families. Knowledge competencies were developed specifically for the program, and were in alignment with professional standards from ASHA and DEC. Those competencies focused on five program areas including: Young Children with Complex Needs, Families, Interdisciplinary Collaboration, Team-Based Problem Solving, and Embedded Evidence-Based Practices.

The two-year preservice program model involved four key elements: (a) interdisciplinary training, (b) joint coursework for EI/ECSE and SLP students, (c) joint clinical experiences, and (d) an interprofessional summer institute. *Interdisciplinary training* was foundational to the program and was threaded throughout each additional element. *Joint courses* were integrated into discipline-specific programs of study and focused on work with infants, toddlers, and families; communication and language development, assessment, and intervention; deaf-blindness; and collaboration, coaching, and consultation. Syllabi created for the joint courses specified the program competencies addressed through the course content; students maintained online portfolios tracking specific courses, assignments, and experiences that contributed to their growth of knowledge for each competency. Efforts were made to reduce redundancy and overlap with courses taken in discipline-specific programs of study by creating embedded modules and modifying course requirements. For example, EI/ECSE and SLP scholars were required to take a course on preschool language assessment and intervention. However, EI/ECSE students were required to take an additional communication course, while SLP students were required to attend only a subset of sessions on augmentative and alternative communication embedded in that additional course because the majority of the course content was gained from their required courses for the SLP program. Such innovative modifications allowed students to complete courses required for their discipline-specific programs of study, as well as courses required for the interdisciplinary personnel program.

*Joint clinical experiences* provided opportunities for students to work on interdisciplinary teams to collaborate with one another, professionals, and families in real-world applications of learned competencies. The experiences took place in students' first, second, and final full semesters and included a variety of experiences including implementation of a transdisciplinary play-based assessment (first fall semester), community-based intervention projects involving mentorship from project personnel and professionals in the field (first spring semester), and capstone projects to demonstrate accumulated knowledge and leadership skills (final spring semester). Intervention and capstone projects were determined based on student interest and availability of collaborative opportunities with partners in the community, including families. Joint intervention projects carried out by students included supporting inclusion in an early care and education center; developing an augmentative communication system for a child receiving Part C early intervention services; contributing to the development and implementation of a community play group for infants, toddlers, and preschoolers with disabilities; and coaching parents to support play with their child in the natural environment. Student capstone projects included development of: curriculum materials for a community playgroup for young children with disabilities; materials to support caregivers to provide language learning opportunities to preschoolers with disabilities; and a welcome module for families whose children were transitioning from Part C EI to preschool special education services. Other capstone projects involved person-centered transition planning from Part C to preschool special education services with the state technical assistance center for sensory impairments, and development of a tutorial for practitioners on augmentative and alternative communication.

The final key element of the interdisciplinary personnel preparation program was an *Interprofessional Practice (IPP) Summer Institute* that took place during the second summer of the two-year personnel preparation program. The following sections provide an overview of the institute, as well as detailed descriptions of planning, structure, and implementation of institute activities.

## The Interprofessional Practice (IPP) Summer Institute

The purpose of the IPP Summer Institute was to provide an opportunity to learn and apply content focused on provision of EI services to infants and toddlers with developmental delays and disabilities and their families through a progressing case study of an infant and family receiving Part C EI services. The IPP Summer Institute provided a brief yet intensive collaborative opportunity for grant-funded scholars to team with one another, with students from other preservice preparation programs, as well as with interdisciplinary faculty and families. The institute was developed and implemented by interdisciplinary faculty, two doctoral graduate assistants, and family members of an individual with complex needs. The institute faculty team consisted of project key personnel in EI/ECSE and SLP programs; program-affiliated faculty in the fields of SLP, physical therapy, and occupational therapy; and a "featured speaker" in the field of occupational therapy with expertise in teaming and collaboration. Student objectives for the IPP Summer Institute were to: (1) demonstrate skills in developing and implementing interdisciplinary plans collaboratively with team members representing a variety of disciplines to address outcomes for children with complex needs across developmental domains; (2) demonstrate knowledge of team-based problem-solving approaches to expand knowledge and skills in working with children with complex needs; (3) demonstrate skills in making evidence-based decisions to promote positive outcomes for children with complex needs and their families; and (4) demonstrate skills in self-reflection throughout experiences in problem-solving, teaming, and service delivery. These objectives aligned with the five competency areas of the interdisciplinary personnel preparation program to provide students opportunities to increase and

### An Interdisciplinary Case-Based Approach to Preservice Interprofessional Training

apply knowledge in: working with young children with complex needs and families, interdisciplinary collaboration, team-based problem solving, and evidence-based practices.

The IPP Summer Institute was designed to take place over a two-and-half day period – for example, a Friday evening to a Sunday afternoon. The interdisciplinary team developing the institute decided on this timeframe to increase feasibility of participation of students from other graduate programs not funded through the personnel preparation grant. PT and OT faculty affiliated with the grant and involved in the development of the institute were able to nominate students from their preservice programs who expressed interest in working with pediatric populations. In this way, the IPP Summer Institute included EI/ECSE, SLP, PT, and OT students in a fully interprofessional training experience. Furthermore, facilitators of the institute represented these four disciplinary areas (two EI/ECSE faculty, two SLP faculty, two PT faculty, three OT faculty, and two doctoral students in EI/ECSE) as well as a mother and sibling of an individual with complex needs. Facilitators of the institute took on several roles. First, faculty and family members formally presented new content in workshop-style sessions to students. Next, facilitators remained available to students during case-based application blocks in order to answer questions. Finally, six facilitators were assigned the role of "family member" (one for each interdisciplinary team) to participate in the decision-making process as part of the case-based application. The following paragraphs provide a more detailed description of the organization and activities of the IPP Summer Institute.

## Organization and Activities of the IPP Summer Institute

All students and facilitators of the IPP Summer Institute arrived at the institute venue on a Friday evening; the meeting launched with introductions and a group dinner. Following introductions, two facilitators led the group in relationship building exercises to encourage team-building to support the case-based application activities on the following day. After the team-building activities, the first evening concluded. The following full day was composed of alternating content blocks and blocks of time for pre-assigned interdisciplinary teams to apply new content to a progressing case study. There were four content blocks, during which one to two facilitators presented topics on their area of expertise as it related to working in early intervention. Content Block I featured a PT faculty member speaking about the neonatal intensive care unit, the transition from hospital to home, and family stressors. An OT faculty member presented content around feeding for young children with complex needs. The first content block lasted for 75 minutes. After this first content block, students were given 45 minutes to work in their assigned interdisciplinary teams on the case-based application. Students were all presented with the same foundational case story in hardcopy form to begin their discussion. However, each team was also provided (in hardcopy) a different scenario for the child and family that was relevant to the content they had just been presented. To support the problem-solving process that was required of each team through their case study, teams were provided with a guide loaded into an online portfolio. The problem-solving process guide required teams to address a series of questions to help make decisions about their case. The guide also prompted students at a specific point to call over their assigned family member to engage in the decision-making process as part of the fully collaborative team.

Content Block II (75 minutes in length) consisted of a parent and sibling presentation on their experiences with their child/sibling with complex needs and perspectives on working with professionals to support the child. This second block also consisted of a presentation by the IPP Summer Institute featured speaker, an OT faculty member not affiliated with the personnel preparation grant, who spoke about teaming and collaboration. After this second block of presentations, teams met again for 30 minutes after being presented with the next segment of their progressing case. Students and facilitators then broke for lunch. Upon return, presenters for Content Block III (60 minutes in length) focused on assistive technology (the featured speaker), and positioning and mobility (a second PT faculty member). Teams then worked on their cases for an hour after being presented with the next segment of their case. The final block (Content Block IV) consisted of a presentation on augmentative and alternative communication by an SLP faculty member. After the 30-minute presentation, teams worked on their case study for an hour after receiving the final segment of the case study. After the final block of time allotted for work on case studies, concluding remarks were made by the featured speaker, who provided perspectives on interdisciplinary teaming and collaboration, including moving collaboration beyond EI into school settings. Students and facilitators were then provided a break and time to socialize before dinner.

The final day of the institute was a half day during which students presented their cases and completed evaluative activities. After breakfast, teams were given 45 minutes to prepare their presentations. Over the course of two hours, each team shared the main issues addressed in their case, including characteristics of the child and family, and decisions made on how best to support the child and family. To promote engagement, the students were provided with a form with three prompts (what questions do you have, what surprised you, what would you do differently) for students to fill out during each presentation. After each presentation, the entire group of students and facilitators engaged in discussion around the case. This provided opportunities for students to engage in dialogue with the facilitators (faculty, family members, and doctoral students) on interdisciplinary teaming and problem-solving. After presentations, teams were given time to debrief with one another. Additional evaluative activities such as measures of attitudes and beliefs about interprofessional practice, focus groups, and exit surveys took place to understand impacts of the IPP Summer Institute and collect information about how to improve future trainings. The following section outlines in more detail the development and implementation of the case-study application during the IPP Summer Institute.

## Development and Implementation of a Case-Study Application

Several months prior to the IPP Summer Institute, the facilitators met to brainstorm ideas for the case studies and develop a problem-solving guide to accompany each section of the case studies. Facilitators discussed the desired length of the problem-solving guide and developed questions to facilitate interdisciplinary teaming and collaboration. They also considered the best way to include family members as interdisciplinary team members and to simulate family-centered practices. Although facilitators acknowledged it would have been beneficial to have someone role-play a "family member" for the entirety of the case-based application, it was decided that it would be most supportive of students' learning to allow them to participate in their professional capacity during the case instead of having a student take on the role of family member. Because institute facilitators were also serving as content experts, it was important they remained available to other groups for the majority of the time. In EI practice, teams do meet without families present; it was therefore determined that including a "family member" during important points in decision-making reflected key aspects of authentic teaming and collaboration in EI while also considering the resources available for the IPP Summer Institute.

The result of this initial planning meeting was a problem-solving process document for teams to work through for each content block. After establishing the guide to support problem-solving, teaming, and collaboration within teams, six case-studies were developed. All six cases originated from a case study entitled "Little Things That Count" by Johnson and Reilly (1993), which describes a little girl named

*An Interdisciplinary Case-Based Approach to Preservice Interprofessional Training*

Megan who was born three and a half months early weighing less than two pounds. Using the initial section of this case study and the newly developed problem-solving process guide as a reference, two doctoral graduate assistants developed six progressing case studies, each resulting in different diagnoses and trajectories for Megan and her family. The diagnoses for Megan described across the cases included deaf-blindness, a cleft palate, cerebral palsy, hydrocephalus, autism spectrum disorder, and a congenital limb defect. While each story unfolded differently, all cases contained information related to the following content: (1) transition to home, feeding, and family stressors; (2) teaming/collaboration and family perspectives; (3) assistive technology and positioning/mobility; and (4) alternative and augmentative communication. Each case study was broken into five segments. The first segment was the initial case study, identical for each group; the following four segments focused on a content block and featured a problem for the team of students to work through. Each segment of the case study described Megan at different ages and highlighted her strengths and challenges, as well as her family life at that specific time (see Table 1 for highlights from three of the case studies).

As students worked in their interdisciplinary teams after each content block, the problem-solving process guide prompted them to determine the main issue for Megan and her family presented in that particular segment. Students were to: identify family priorities, list information they needed and immediate action steps to be taken, identify the main goal that needed to be achieved to support the child and family, and note any outside resources required. Next, the guide directed student teams to develop at least two ideas that could be presented to the "family member" who was assigned for each team prior to the institute. The problem-solving process guide then prompted student teams to present their ideas to the family member; once the family member had indicated their choice of ideas, the teams were prompted to continue filling out the guide by listing the steps and strategies needed, along with their evidence base, to carry out the family's preference.

Along with each case study, the two graduate assistants developed an IFSP for Megan to provide teams with more context and family information. The IFSP was provided at a specific point in the case, which varied across teams. In addition, the student teams were provided with resources such as the faculty PowerPoint presentations along with any accompanying documents. Every segment of the case study was designed so that interdisciplinary teams would discuss the problem presented and use the presentations, resources provided, evidence-based research, and family input to fill out their problem-solving process guide. Before being finalized, the IPP Summer Institute facilitators reviewed the case studies and the graduate assistants made changes based on the feedback provided.

In preparation for the IPP Summer Institute, the graduate assistant associated with the personnel preparation program created online portfolios for use during case study work. Each team had their own folder, and all IPP Summer Institute Facilitators had access to each one. Each folder contained four blank problem-solving guides, the PowerPoint presentations, associated handouts from each presenter, and directions for completing the problem-solving guide. Each case study was printed out, divided by segment, and placed in manila envelopes to be handed to teams after the appropriate content block. The IFSPs were provided to teams and included in the same manila envelope as the segment of the case study when it would be used for discussion and problem-solving. Once a team received their hard copy of the IFSP, the graduate assistant also added the IFSP to the team's online folder. The teams were provided two laminated cards, one that read, "need facilitator support" and another that read, "need family input." The cards were designed for teams to hold up when they needed general support from a facilitator and when they needed their specific family member to come to their table and provide input. Additionally, all facilitators were provided a physical folder which included the case studies, instructions for facilitators,

*Table 1. Content blocks and associated dilemmas presented across three progressing case studies*

| Content Block (Length) | Topics Addressed | Example Case 1 | Example Case 2 | Example Case 3 |
|---|---|---|---|---|
| I (75min) | 1. Transition from NICU to home and Family Stressors<br>2. Feeding | CA: 4mos; AA: 15days<br>1. Mom remains in hospital with Megan when dad returns to work; once home mom does most of the care herself; mom is exhausted.<br>2. Megan born with cleft lip and palate; mom is overwhelmed with feeding without support from hospital feeding specialist; mom is concerned with inadequate weight gain. | CA: 6mos; AA: 2.5mos<br>1. Megan diagnosed with hydrocephalus and shunt placed; primary language is Spanish, with limited availability of interpreters at the hospital; mom afraid to take Megan home due to medical needs; shunt failure after arriving home; financial challenges.<br>2. Megan sent home with oxygen and a feeding tube. | CA: 5mos; AA: 1.5mos<br>1. Megan born with severe Fibular Hemimelia; also diagnosed with hydrocephalus requiring surgery to drain excess fluid; parents need to decide on course of action to address limb length differences; dad misses too much work due to Megan's surgeries and is fired; finances stress dad, as do his fears of being able to care for a child with disabilities.<br>2. No feeding issues noted. |
| II (75min) | 1. Family Perspectives<br>2. Teaming and Collaboration | CA: 14mos; AA: 10.5mos<br>1. Dad is leaving mom, and mom needs to return to work; toddler's grandmother is moving in with the family to support mom.<br>2. Part C primary service provider (PSP) is moving and will no longer be able to work with the family, and they will need to determine a new PSP for the family; mom is afraid to have a new PSP at the same time she is returning to work. | CA: 12mos; AA: 8.5mos<br>1. Megan is off oxygen, but still needs feeding tube; Mom frustrated with limited availability of interpreters for medical visits.<br>2. Part C PSP is bilingual; notices mom rarely speaks to Megan in Spanish, dad and rest of family rarely speak to Megan at all; PSP discovers doctor informed family it would be best to speak to Megan only in English due to likelihood of intellectual disability. | CA: 7mos; AA: 3.5mos<br>1. Family is busy with hospital appointments, which is overwhelming to dad; Doctors recommended amputation to address Fibular Hemimelia; dad cried when relaying this information to the PSP, and is afraid Megan will be bullied due to this difference.<br>2. Family is having difficulties making Part C home visits on time, or is having to cancel altogether due to the number of medical appointments for Megan. |
| III (60min) | 1. Assistive Technology<br>2. Positioning and Mobility | CA: 20mos; AA: 16.5mos<br>1. Eating and communication concerns; motor skills impact self-feeding.<br>2. Megan is cruising along furniture, but not yet walking. | CA: 20mos; AA: 16.5mos<br>1. Megan not yet self-feeding and needs assistance to drink from a sippy cup.<br>2. Megan army crawls on belly, and prefers to "lay around"; moderate to severe delays across cognitive, motor, and speech/language domains. | CA: 18mos; AA: 14.5mos<br>1. Parents decided on partial amputation of Megan's leg and had her fit with a prosthetic.<br>2. Megan is receiving physical therapy services at the hospital, and parents do not want to include gross motor outcomes on the IFSP, preferring instead to focus on cognitive (e.g., play) and language areas. |
| IV (30min) | 1. Augmentative and Alternative Communication | CA:33mos<br>Megan using 30 words or word approximation, but is very difficult to understand. | CA: 30mos<br>Megan not yet using single words, or receptively identifying colors or pictures of objects/feelings; SLP brings up possibility of getting an AAC device; family concerned about how to program a device and cost. | CA: 26mos<br>Megan has a vocabulary of about 10 single words, and uses gestures and signs to communicate some wants and needs; family is eager for her to develop more language skills, and are open to ideas about how to do so. |

Note. NICU = neonatal intensive care unit; CA = chronological age; AA = adjusted age; SLP = speech language pathologist; AAC = augmentative and alternative communication.

### An Interdisciplinary Case-Based Approach to Preservice Interprofessional Training

and a detailed agenda for the weekend. Facilitators who were designated as family members received a highlighted case study for their team, the accompanying IFSP, and specific instructions regarding their role as family member.

The second and third days of the IPP Summer Institute took place inside a large conference room with large round tables provided. Each team was assigned a table where they were able to listen to the presentations together and then work as a team to complete their problem-solving process guides at the designated times. IPP Summer Institute facilitators sat at two tables at the back of the room where they would watch for teams to raise their cards, indicating they either needed general assistance or input from their family member.

As described earlier, the second day of the IPP Summer Institute consisted of content blocks and time for teams to work on their cases. After the first content block, the teams were provided the initial case study along with the first segment of their individualized case study. Teams were given time to work through their problem-solving process guide and were also instructed to decide who would be the appropriate primary service provider (PSP) for the family from the information they were given. Students were instructed to discuss what they knew about the family and the disciplines represented in their team to come up with a plan for who would act as the PSP for their case. During each work time the students would fill out their problem-solving process guide until they reached the point where they needed to call over their family member for input. The facilitator playing the family member was instructed to stay in character during this time. Once the family member made their decision about the preferred course of action for the child and family, the team could continue working through the problem-solving process guide. The case study work time consisted of students looking up resources, discussing their case as a team, and filling out their guide. After Content Block IV the teams were given time to complete their final problem-solving process guide. If they had time left, students were instructed to work on their team presentations for the next day.

Following the presentations on the third day, students participated in evaluative activities. This included an IPP Summer Institute evaluation with both closed and open-ended questions, as well as focus group interviews. On the written evaluation, students were asked what they liked most about the institute. Many students wrote they enjoyed collaborating as a team, learning about other disciplines, and getting experience on an interdisciplinary team. One student wrote, "[I] thoroughly enjoyed working in a collaborative team with different disciplines (OT, PT, special educators). I feel like this was great practice working with an interprofessional team." Another student noted, "We have talked about collaboration extensively in class, but truly being able to do so in a model setting has been a unique experience." Focus group interviews revealed similar sentiments. One student shared, "I like that it [the IPP Summer Institute] gives us the opportunity to share our experiences and teach others what we do and what we're about as well as getting their information." Another student said, "I thought it was nice because we've done mock collaboration in the classroom where an SLP would pretend to be a PT or an OT, but it was different to have someone that actually has that training to be able to do it." Overall, the evaluative measures revealed students were very satisfied with the IPP Summer Institute. Students provided helpful feedback, such as noting they would have liked more time to complete the problem-solving process guides and more resources to complete them.

## Taking the Summer Institute Virtual

The IPP Summer Institute was initially developed as an in-person training event. However, faculty of the personnel preparation program made the decision to hold the second IPP Summer Institute virtually due to timing with the COVID-19 global pandemic. Although the overall structure and content of the second IPP Summer Institute remained the same, this switch to virtual implementation required additional planning for the faculty, family, and doctoral student facilitators to make modifications allowing for meaningful engagement between students and all facilitators. This section describes modifications made in development and implementation of this second virtual institute.

First, feedback provided by students who participated in the first IPP Summer Institute led to changes in some of the content and organization of the second virtual institute. For example, feedback indicated some students did not have as much background knowledge of the use of the PSP model in EI services; therefore, a brief presentation on the PSP model and early intervention was provided on the first evening of the virtual institute. Additionally, some students indicated they needed more time to work in teams on the case-based application, and would like more resources provided to support their decision making. In response, students were provided longer blocks of time to discuss cases, and presenters were asked to provide additional resources and web-based links that could be uploaded into teams' online portfolios prior to the institute.

Next, the IPP Summer Institute was adapted to a virtual format. For this initial implementation, a university-based event planner was hired to collaborate with facilitators to run registration activities; create virtual rooms for team meetings; come up with team-building exercises that could be done virtually; and create online team and facilitator folders to upload all case study segments, IFSPs, problem-solving guides, resources, and contact information for IPP Summer Institute Facilitators and "family members". The event planner also helped move students and facilitators in and out of the appropriate virtual meeting rooms. It was decided each interdisciplinary student team would have a designated facilitator who they could contact with general or technical questions. Three individuals served in this role of designated team facilitator and remained available on the virtual platform for the majority of the institute. As with the in-person institute, facilitators (who included authentic family partners) were assigned as family members and asked to be on call to act in this role or to answer any content specific questions; however, they were not required to remain on the virtual platform beyond their presentation during content blocks. Instructions for how to contact these facilitators for questions and designated family members for decisions on cases were provided to teams. IPP Summer Institute Facilitators were asked their preference for being contacted directly by students or to have students contact their designated facilitator, who would then contact the requested person to log into the virtual platform to meet with the team. Each team designated a student lead to contact facilitators when needed.

Finally, evaluative activities were adapted to take place on the virtual platform (i.e., focus groups) or through an online survey platform (i.e., interprofessional attitudes and beliefs measure and exit survey). Overall, students who took part in the virtual IPP Summer Institute shared similar thoughts and takeaways as students who took part in the in-person institute. In their virtual focus groups one student shared,

*I found it interesting that a lot of us had the same ideas and how, like, overlapping our fields were as well. And I think that we don't get a lot of coursework on working with other disciplines, so I found this experience very interesting.*

### An Interdisciplinary Case-Based Approach to Preservice Interprofessional Training

Another student said, "I definitely think it gave me a greater understanding of the depth and breadth of knowledge that other providers have and can contribute to the interdisciplinary team." When asked what they liked about the IPP Summer Institute on the written evaluation one student wrote, "I loved having the opportunity to engage in interdisciplinary collaboration! After discussing this topic over the past year, it was wonderful to have hands on experience." Another student shared they liked, "hearing perspectives from different professions such as OT, PT, SLP, and SPED Teachers." In addition, 100% of students either agreed or strongly agreed they felt engaged given the virtual format of the institute.

## LESSONS LEARNED AND FUTURE DIRECTIONS

An intensive interdisciplinary training event focused on teaming and collaboration in EI practice settings was developed and implemented as part of a federally funded personnel preparation program. Interdisciplinary (EI/ECSE, SLP, PT, and OT) key and affiliated program personnel worked together to provide content knowledge and real-world application of that knowledge using case-stories in an intensive delivery format. Initial implementation of the IPP Summer Institute was in-person, while a second institute was conducted virtually. This section describes some lessons learned in development and delivery of the trainings, as well as possible future directions for work in this area.

Engagement with interdisciplinary facilitators played a key role in the development and implementation of the IPP Summer Institute. First, engagement with interdisciplinary faculty in development of the institute enabled involvement of students outside of the EI/ECSE and SLP personnel preparation program. Additionally, the planning process allowed for identification of appropriate and needed content across four discipline-specific programs (EI/ECSE, SLP, PT, and OT) to target in content blocks, and to identify the individuals who would present that content to students. Collaboration with interdisciplinary facilitators in the planning process helped identify the most efficient and feasible format for the institute across all programs – in this case, a two-and-a-half-day institute delivered over a weekend. Finally, faculty from PT and OT programs were able to identify students to invite to participate in the program based on content they already had as part of their training. This enabled participation in the IPP Summer Institute by students representing four disciplines, providing a unique and rich interdisciplinary training experience.

Due to the COVID-19 pandemic, the institute was implemented virtually the second time it was offered. Although there were initial concerns about providing the institute in this format, virtual delivery allowed for flexibility for facilitators (e.g., reducing the need for travel, reducing the time commitment across the weekend), and also allowed students from different states to attend. Based on feedback from students and measures of satisfaction, there were few substantive differences in outcomes between the in-person and virtual delivery formats. The ability to provide such a training event in-person or virtually may prove important as flexibility in delivery modality optimizes participation for students and faculty.

The IPP Summer Institute was developed as part of a grant-funded program. However, the brief format of the institute and the option to deliver it virtually may increase the feasibility to offer a similar training opportunity independent of grant funding. Future directions for implementation might be to examine the feasibility of embedding such trainings into existing programs of study to support interdisciplinary collaboration prior to professionals entering the field. Additional work may be conducted to adapt the institute for in-service professionals to increase skills around interdisciplinary teaming and collaboration, including with families. Exploration of these possibilities may bolster the capacity of the early intervention workforce to engage in interdisciplinary collaboration within the context of family-centered services for young children with disabilities and their families.

## CONCLUSION

The need for preservice interdisciplinary training of EI professionals is paramount to a workforce ready to collaborate with other professionals and families upon entering the field. Many current preservice programs prepare EI service professionals within disciplinary silos, with limited opportunities for meaningful collaboration with students training in other EI fields of practice. A lack of interprofessional experiences at the preservice level has ramifications for the effectiveness of the EI workforce in collaborating with other professionals and families to best serve young children with high-intensity needs. This chapter described a model for a brief yet intensive interdisciplinary training, which incorporated best practices for adult learners and used a progressing case study so students could apply newly learned content to real-world EI scenarios. The content of the institute focused on areas most relevant to early intervention, and the structure enabled students to work in interdisciplinary teams and draw from their own area of expertise to support the problem-solving process necessitated by the case. Students then presented their cases to students and training facilitators, enabling discussion with an interdisciplinary group of students, faculty, and family members. Additional insight was provided on how to provide this model of training virtually, as well as lessons learned and future directions for those involved in preparing or training EI professionals. Young children served through Part C early intervention services often have delays or disabilities requiring expertise and collaboration from professionals representing multiple disciplines. To best serve children and families, it is important the professionals entering early intervention have the skill set necessary to engage in interdisciplinary collaboration upon entering the field; as those involved in preservice preparation, it is incumbent upon us to find ways that are effective, efficient, and feasible to prepare them to do so.

## ACKNOWLEDGMENT

We would like to thank our partners in the development and implementation of the IPP Summer Institute including family members of individuals with disabilities, university faculty, and doctoral students. This work would not have been possible without their willingness to share their time, expertise, and perspectives on supporting young children with high intensity needs and their families.

This work was supported by the Office of Special Education Programs of the United States Department of Education [grant number H325K170036]. However, the work described in this chapter does not necessarily represent the policy of the U.S. Department of Education, and one should not assume endorsement by the Federal Government. Project Officer: Anita Vermeer.

## REFERENCES

American Speech-Language-Hearing Association. (2022). Strategic pathway to excellence. *ASHA*. https://www.asha.org/about/strategic-pathway/

Bagatell, N., & Broggi, M. (2014). Occupational therapy and physical therapy students' perceptions of a short-term interprofessional education module. *Education Special Interest Section Quarterly*, *24*(2), 1–4.

Barton, E. E., Moore, H. W., & Squires, J. K. (2012). Preparing speech language pathology students to work in early childhood. *Topics in Early Childhood Special Education*, *32*(1), 4–13. doi:10.1177/0271121411434567

Bruder, M. B., Catalino, T., Chiarello, L., Mitchell, M., Deppe, J., Gundler, D., Kemp, P., LeMoine, S., Long, T., Muhlenhaupt, M., Prelock, P., Schefkind, S., Stayton, V., & Ziegler, D. (2019). Finding a common lens: Competencies across professional disciplines providing early childhood intervention. *Infants and Young Children*, *32*(4), 280–293. doi:10.1097/IYC.0000000000000153

Bryan, R. L., Kreutre, M. W., & Brownson, R. C. (2009). Integrating adult learning principles into training for public health practice. *Health Promotion Practice*, *10*(4), 557–563. doi:10.1177/1524839907308117 PMID:18385488

Center for Advancement of Interprofessional Education. (CAIPE; 2002). *Interprofessional education: Today, yesterday, and tomorrow – a review* (Barr, H.). Higher Education Academy, Learning and Teaching Support Network for Health Sciences & Practice, Occasional Paper 1.

Council for Exceptional Children and The Division for Early Childhood. (2020). Initial practice-based professional preparation standards for early interventionists/early childhood special educators (EI/ECSE) (initial birth through age 8). *Exceptional Children*. https://exceptionalchildren.org/standards/initial-practice-based-standards-early-interventionists-early-childhood-special-educators

Daley, B. J. (2001). Learning and professional practice: A study of four professions. *Adult Education Quarterly*, *52*(1), 39–54. doi:10.1177/074171360105200104

Division for Early Childhood. (2014). DEC recommended practices in early intervention/early childhood special education 2014. *DEC*. http://www.dec-sped.org/recommendedpractices

Guraya, S. Y., & Barr, H. (2018). The effectiveness of interprofessional education in healthcare: A systematic review and meta-analysis. *The Kaohsiung Journal of Medical Sciences*, *34*(3), 160–165. doi:10.1016/j.kjms.2017.12.009 PMID:29475463

Kilgo, E. D., Jennifer, L., Aldridge, J., Vogtle, L., Ronilo, W., & Bruton, A. (2017). Teaming, collaboration, and case-based learning: A transdisciplinary approach to early intervention/education. *Case Studies Journal*, *6*(6), 7–12.

King, G., Orchard, C., Khalili, H., & Avery, L. (2016). Refinement of the Interprofessional Socialization and Valuing Scale (ISVS-21) and development of 9-item equivalent versions. *The Journal of Continuing Education in the Health Professions*, *36*(3), 171–177. doi:10.1097/CEH.0000000000000082 PMID:27583993

Knowles, M. S. (Ed.). (1984). *Andragogy in action*. Jossey-Bass.

Lundeberg, M. A., & Yadav, A. (2006). Assessment of case study teaching: Where do we go from here? Part 1. *Journal of College Science Teaching*, *35*(5), 10–13.

Lyons, P., & Bandura, R. P. (2020). Skills needs, integrative pedagogy and case-based instruction. *Journal of Workplace Learning*, *32*(7), 473–487. doi:10.1108/JWL-12-2019-0140

McCall, R. C., Padron, K., & Andrews, C. (2018). Evidence-based instructional strategies for adult learners: A review of the literature. *Codex: the Journal of the Louisiana Chapter of the ACRL, 4*(4), 29–47.

McWilliam, P. J. (2000). *Lives in Progress: Case Stories in Early Intervention.* Paul H. Brookes.

Raspa, M., Hebbeler, K., Bailey, D. B. Jr, & Scarborough, A. A. (2010). Service provider combinations and the delivery of early intervention services to children and families. *Infants and Young Children, 23*(2), 132–144. doi:10.1097/IYC.0b013e3181d230f9

Snyder, P., & McWilliam, P. J. (2003). Using case method of instruction effectively in early intervention personnel preparation. *Infants and Young Children, 16*(4), 284–295. doi:10.1097/00001163-200310000-00003

Steinberg, D. M., & Vinjamuri, M. K. (2014). Activating adult-learning principles through small groups in preparing social work students to achieve CSWE research competencies. *Journal of Teaching in Social Work, 34*(4), 363–383. doi:10.1080/08841233.2014.937890

Trivette, C. M., Dunst, C. J., Hamby, D. W., & O'Herin, C. E. (2009). Characteristics and consequences of adult learning methods and strategies, *Research Brief, 3*(1). Tots n Tech Research Institute.

## KEY TERMS AND DEFINITIONS

**Adult Learning Strategies:** Approaches that recognize and support the learning needs of adults. Adult learning strategies stem from the work on andragogy (adult learning theory). Adult learning strategies include self-direction, connecting content to learners' experience, practical application, active involvement, and solution-focused problem-solving.

**Case-Based Instruction:** An approach to teaching and learning focused on practical application through a case study. It involves active learning practices where learners approach real-world scenarios that encourage applying knowledge to make decisions in the case. Case-based instruction is one type of problem-based learning.

**Early Intervention:** Services and supports provided to infants and toddlers with developmental delays or disabilities and their families to support development. Early intervention services provided through Part C of IDEA are specifically designed to increase family capacity to support child development in natural environments (e.g., locations and activities in which the child and family typically participate).

**Experiential Learning:** Learning by active engagement in the process of doing along with reflection about the learning experience. Experiential learning involves hands-on application in actual or simulated situations.

**Interdisciplinary:** A teaming model where providers from different professional disciplines collaborate together to provide integrated approaches. Sometimes referred to as interprofessional.

**Interprofessional Training:** Preservice and/or professional developmental teaching and learning experiences that include providers from different professions/disciplines as recipients and/or presenters. Interprofessional training often includes content specifically designed from an interdisciplinary/interprofessional framework.

**Professional Standards:** Practices, skills, ethics, and/or qualifications set forth by a professional body representing the respective profession or discipline. Professional standards guide the behaviors of the individuals as well as the collective within a profession.

# Chapter 13
# Interprofessional SLP and Educator Collaboration to Improve Communication for Students With Complex Disabilities

**Erin Rotheram-Fuller**
*Arizona State University, USA*

**Maria V. Dixon**
*Arizona State University, USA*

## ABSTRACT

*Students with complex disabilities require coordinated care to address communication challenges. Speech-language pathologists (SLPs) and educators are in a unique position to jointly support the communication goals of these students through interprofessional clinical practice (IPCP). Unfortunately, most professionals are not prepared during training, nor supported in professional settings, to engage in IPCP. Foundational requirements and best practices in the literature suggest that professionals need guidance, training, and ongoing institutional support to effectively collaborate. Existing interprofessional education (IPE) and IPCP models show promise in training professionals to work more effectively together before and after they enter the field, but they are not prevalent nor well-evaluated enough yet in education to draw strong conclusions. Key characteristics, strategies, and benefits of existing training and practice models for SLPs and educators are reviewed, and an applied example is presented on best practices for collaboratively implementing an AAC device.*

## INTRODUCTION

There has been a steady increase in the number of children receiving special education services under

DOI: 10.4018/978-1-6684-6438-0.ch013

the Individuals with Disabilities Education Act for the last decade (NCES, 2022). As the demand for special education teachers and related services personnel (e.g., Speech-Language Pathology, Occupational Therapy, Physical Therapy, Applied Behavioral Analysts) is increasing across the United States, there is a critical shortage of professionals trained in interprofessional Clinical Practice (IPCP) to meet the demand (U.S. Department of Education, 2022). While it takes support from multiple professionals to meet the social, behavioral, academic, speech, and physical needs of children with disabilities with high-intensity needs, most professionals work in isolation (Pfeiffer et al., 2019). Ensuring that special educators and related service professionals use a collaborative, inclusive approach in service delivery for students with special needs requires re-envisioning training and education at the pre-professional stage, as well as providing ongoing guidance and institutional support in schools. Both the American Speech-Language-Hearing Association (Arner et. al, 2022) and Council for Exceptional Children (CEC Standards, 2020) recognize this need and have provided discipline-specific guidance for speech-language pathologists (SLPs) and special education professionals, by encouraging collaborative practice within their professional standards. However, both training for and engagement in IPCP remains limited. This chapter will examine the key characteristics of interprofessional training and practice models that have been used effectively with SLPs and educators to support the communication skills of students with disabilities with high intensity needs.

## BACKGROUND

### Defining Interprofessional Education and Clinical Practice

Interprofessional Clinical Practice (IPCP; WHO, 2010) is a term used to describe the collaboration process between multiple professionals around common clinical goals. There have been several other terms to describe the professional collaboration. These include collaboration, interprofessional practice, multidisciplinary, integrated services, and interdisciplinary practice. Unfortunately, these terms can represent different activities yielding sometimes unique outcomes (Lord et al., 2020), so IPCP will be used to specifically focus on the professional collaborative process where at least two professionals engage in service provision together to improve outcomes around the communication and literacy needs of children with disabilities with high intensity needs.

Interprofessional Education (IPE; Barr et al., 2005) is the training of multiple related professionals in collaborative training activities before they get into practice. IPE is an opportunity for training programs to model the collaboration process (Heisler & Thousand, 2021), as well as improve the collaborative skills of faculty as well as students (Goldberg, 2015). IPE can include many types of collaborative activities, but are focused on teaching trainees overarching competencies for engaging in interprofessional collaboration (Interprofessional Education Collaborative Expert Panel, 2011; 2016). It is important to consider IPE as a precursor to IPCP, as IPE prepares professionals at the pre-professional stage to both value and engage in interprofessional collaboration.

The idea of interprofessional education and practice is not new. These were first introduced in the 1960s (Powers, 1965), and have largely focused on medical professions until the last decade (Ogletree, 2017). There has been a shift in the field of disabilities toward a focus on IPCP, where comprehensive care for children with disabilities has been recognized as increasingly important (Rosanoff et al., 2015). Professionals are urged to view the child holistically, with multiple needs served by different professionals jointly developing goals and cooperatively determining service provision. Especially for students with complex health and education needs, more coordination is required to ensure consistent and comprehensive support. It has also been found that "state education standards (such as Common Core State Standards) are best achieved when all professionals integrate their services, communicate, evaluate, and train together to support students' success" (Nunez, 2015).

Guidance regarding fundamental underlying principles and core interprofessional competencies of IPCP was established by the IPEC Expert Panel (2011; updated in 2016). IPEC's underlying principles of IPCP suggest that professionals should be (a) patient/family-centered, (b) community/population oriented, (c) relationship-focused, (d) process-oriented, (e) linked to developmentally appropriate learning activities, (f) focused on ensuring that educational strategies and behavioral assessments match developmental level, (g) able to be integrated across the learning continuum, (h) applicable across practice settings, (i) applicable across professions, (j) stated in a common and meaningful language, and (k) outcome-driven (IPEC Expert Panel, 2011).

As IPCP has gained traction, additional professional organizations, such as the National Center for Interprofessional Practice and Education (https://nexusipe.org/; established in 2021), have been established to update and monitor guidelines for IPCP. These kinds of organizations help keep professionals current on the literature and engage in an ongoing research process to ensure the most efficacious IPCP strategies. Progress monitoring tools are being used to evaluate addressing IPCP within training programs, as well as performance within the field.

## SLP and Educator Collaboration Opportunities

Speech-Language Pathologists (SLPs) and special education teachers are in a unique position to work together in addressing the communication goals for children with disabilities in schools (Suleman et al., 2014). Communication interventions are most effective when applied in multiple contexts, and having professionals who work collaboratively can improve the consistent and rapid acquisition of skills (Glover, et al. 2015). Communication goals can impact the child's academic performance and social engagement with peers, both of which are foundations for educational success. Communication goals and interventions can be jointly established for the classroom, as well as during speech-language therapy sessions, with ongoing progress monitoring in each setting. It is critical that both professionals know what the other is doing, understand each other's teaching objectives and methods, and can provide consistent ongoing support to help students reach their goals most effectively and efficiently (Suleman et al., 2014). This collaboration yields improved access to appropriate education and longer-term successful outcomes for the child and their families.

### Educators

Educators have the most time with their students and are able to assess communication and academic skills through regular academic assessment tools. Within a classroom of students, teachers have the opportunity to recognize when students are falling below standardized grade-level content and identify students early who may be struggling. They can then refer students to appropriate professionals, such as SLPs, for more extensive evaluation.

Educator surveys have shown that teachers are eager for more collaboration skills (Berry et al., 2011) and that they have positive perceptions of the SLPs expertise, role, and opportunities to collaborate

(Shaughnessy & Sanger, 2005). In a survey of K-12 teachers' collaboration, teachers reported SLPs as their most important collaborators, with 47% of teachers reporting daily, and 42% reporting weekly collaboration with SLPs (Sisti & Robledo, 2021). In a study by Zagona and colleagues (2017), general education (n=33) and special education (n=10) teachers were surveyed about their impressions of inclusion and collaboration. Teachers reported feeling unprepared for collaboration with colleagues who did not share their same philosophy and were especially uncomfortable collaborating around students with significant disabilities. However, special educators were more frequently trained and more comfortable with collaboration than general education teachers (Zagona et al., 2017).

Despite the desire for more skills in collaboration, most professional training programs are taught independently (Shoffner & Wachter Morris, 2010). Thus, the onus is often on professionals already in the field to gain additional professional development on ways to collaborate in practice. There are guides for teachers, however, that identify the roles and responsibilities of different professionals within schools (e.g. Leader-Janssen et al., 2012) to highlight opportunities for collaboration and guide teachers on where to turn for support for different needs of students with disabilities. There are also guides for teachers on strategies to engage in IPCP, with practical steps on how to collaborate with SLPs in schools (Bauer et al., 2010). These steps range from 'being creative' to 'soliciting specific support from SLPs and other stakeholders about the collaboration process.'

## Speech-Language Pathologists

SLPs are essential collaborators in communication skills. SLPs are skilled in both assessment and intervention (Apel, 2002) of language development and skills and can assess foundational skills including phonological awareness (Gillon, 2002), morphology, word recognition, reading development (DeKemel, 2003), reading fluency (Kamhi, 2003), and reading comprehension. These assessment results can be opportunities for both teachers and SLPs to review assessment data and determine interventions together that would best address students' needs.

The service delivery models of an SLP can be varied, however, providing both direct services, as well as consultation, training, or collaborative support (Kamhi, 2003). In a large survey of SLPs, it was found that the majority of students received pull-out services, regardless of disability or focus (Brandel & Frome Loeb, 2011; Mullen & Schooling, 2010). Similarly, in another survey of 617 SLPs, few SLPs engaged in IPCP (8% during evaluations, 43% during eligibility meetings, and 14% during interventions) in their current practice. There were three factors predicting the use of IPCP: 1) training in collaboration, 2) years of experience, and 3) educational setting (Pfeiffer et al., 2019). Therefore, to increase the likelihood of educators and SLPs engaging in IPCP, it seems critical to begin training these two professionals together so that both are prepared to engage in collaborative service delivery models in the field.

## COMMUNICATION CHALLENGES FOR STUDENTS WITH HIGH-INTENSITY NEEDS

Educators and SLPs have unique expertise to support the complex communication needs of students with disabilities. Children with high-intensity needs (also known as a severe disability) often need support in multiple areas, such as academic, physical, communication, and/or social skills. Children are considered to have a severe disability when developmental functioning is characterized by delays in reaching developmental milestones or limitations in one or more of the following domains: cognition, motor performance, vision, hearing and speech, and behavior (Developmental Disabilities Assistance and Bill of Rights Act of 2000). Children with high-intensity needs also often show limited adaptive abilities ranging from needing assistance in some areas (such as feeding, dressing, and basic self-care) to full dependence for everyday living activities (Westling et al., 2015). They may present with significant limitations in intellectual functioning (e.g., learning, reasoning, and problem solving; American Psychiatric Association, 2013). Additional medical concerns can co-occur with severe disabilities, such as heart defects, seizures, physical differences, etc., as well as sensory impairments (Westling et al., 2015), which require multiple professionals with unique expertise to support the child.

Communication can be significantly impaired amongst children with disabilities with high-intensity needs. Communication challenges are the most common problems identified in school-aged children (Bryan et al, 2015) and can vary dramatically between individuals (Ogletree, 2017). Communication consists of comprehension (receptive language) and use (expressive language), and impairments can affect either receptive or expressive language (or both), and severity can range from mild to profound. Receptive communication is the ability to receive and accurately interpret incoming messages. Receptive communication challenges range from an inability to understand the core meaning of messages to difficulty interpreting figurative and other non-literal language (e.g., joking or sarcasm; Beukelman & Mirenda, 2013). Expressive language specifically refers to spoken (verbalizations or vocalizations), or symbol systems, such as written, gestural, picture, sign language, and augmentation and alternative communication (AAC) modalities (Beukelman & Mirenda, 2013). Similar to receptive communication challenges, expressive communication challenges can range from no functional use of communication to producing communication effectively, but without complex structure or nuance.

Working with children with high intensity needs who have little to no verbal expressive skills represents an ideal opportunity to use IPCP. Augmentative and alternative communication (AAC) that assist students in expressing themselves include low-tech and high-tech tools such as picture communication systems and speech generating devices (SGDs) (Light & McNaughton, 2015). Determinants of the appropriate AAC approach depend on several factors, including cognition, physical abilities, and ease of access. Low-tech tools are easily created, accessible in a variety of settings, and are relatively easy to train communication partners (Light et al., 2019). High-tech tools, such as speech-generating devices (SGDs), can also support students with minimal verbal communication. While teachers, parents, and other related professionals are adept with the use of smartphones and tablets, familiarity with specific applications can be a barrier. Issues related to a professional's competency in usage can lead to the device not being used effectively or at all across settings (Ganz, 2014; Light et al., 2019). Thus, teachers, SLPs, families, and other related professionals should work together to determine the best tool, as well as ensure that all are trained on how to use it.

## CHALLENGES IN INTERPROFESSIONAL EDUCATION AND PRACTICE

When considering successful IPCP implementation, there are two barriers to overcome; those in the pre-professional realm and those in the professional educational setting. Before professionals even get into the field, university programs do not traditionally train or support students in developing interprofessional understanding or skills. Programs within universities are often organized by specific degree disciplines, and these are not traditionally interprofessional in nature (Shoffner & Wachter Morris, 2010).

In order to allow students to learn across disciplines, programs must embrace IPE by organizing learning opportunities across programs, and overcoming scheduling, sequencing, and focused program thinking to allow flexibility in student coursework or clinical opportunities (Frenk et al., 2010; Goldberg, 2015).

Unfortunately, there is also not always institutional support for IPE programs. All training programs have unique competencies that are considered essential to ensure minimal proficiency within any field. Interprofessional competencies are often undervalued relative to those profession-specific skills (Frenk et al., 2010), and there has to be a commitment from both administration and faculty to ensure true integration and value of IPE for it to be successful. The training of professionals remains largely siloed (Kunze & Machalicek, 2022), and there are limited professional guidelines about how to fully integrate IPE into training programs. Although the literature is expanding, concrete steps for training programs should be clear and institutional support must be in place before programs try to add these additional interprofessional competencies.

Once professionals get into the field, additional barriers arise to implementing truly collaborative IPCP. The most often noted issues are the amount of time, the competing workload, and the fragmented services that interfere with the necessary time needed to dedicate to collaborative partnerships (Bauer et al., 2010; Phoenix et al., 2020). SLPs have large caseloads, and teachers have many students within their classrooms with competing time demands. In a survey of SLPs, they identified the most frequent barriers to IPCP as scheduling or time constraints (48%), resistance from other professionals (23%), and a lack of support from the administration (11%; Pfeiffer et al., 2019). Unless there is clear institutional support for the collaborative process and dedicated time and resources to the process, it will be difficult to add to the already overwhelmed schedules of most professionals.

Treatment-focused work is also largely reimbursement-focused, and professionals, by design, work independently so that all of their activities can be funded. It remains to be seen whether we can overcome this reimbursement model to fully integrate our services and still financially support expertise from multiple professionals around one child while working together (Ogletree, 2017).

It is clear that there are challenges in effectively meeting the diverse communication goals of students with disabilities with high intensity needs, and that multiple professionals are needed to most efficiently and effectively provide comprehensive support to reach those goals. In addition, there are well-defined barriers to both pre-professional training in interprofessional skills (using IPE), as well as in the successful implementation of IPCP in educational settings. Thus, three hypotheses were developed to guide an examination of the existing research literature on IPCP within education, especially on IPCP between SLPs and educators.

**Hypothesis One:** Using IPCP will produce faster and more global gains in communication goals.

**Hypothesis Two:** By increasing effective interprofessional training opportunities, professionals will be more likely to use IPCP in the field.

**Hypothesis Three:** There are foundational conditions and characteristics that must be present to encourage and support IPCP in educational settings.

## Examining Hypothesis One: IPCP Augments Communication Support Strategies

Language development is key to students' abilities to engage in school academically and socially (Adolf & Hogan, 2019; Chow & Wehby, 2018; Dickenson et al., 2010; Durkin & Conti-Ramsden, 2010; Yew & O'Kearney, 2015). Without communication, students struggle to engage in other activities within the classroom and social structure of their classes. SLPs, teachers, and related service providers can jointly intervene in both receptive and expressive language challenges. While SLPs have specific expertise in building communication skills, teachers also have knowledge of how to foster communication within the classroom, build vocabulary, and engage peers with one another. These two professionals have the opportunity to not only contribute their own expertise to support the student but also to learn from one another and jointly use strategies to support communication in both the classroom and in pull-out speech sessions. Four established strategies are described below that can help support communication (Pentimonti et al., 2017), as well as opportunities for how teachers and SLPs can effectively collaborate and use them to support a student more holistically:

1. **Modeling:** SLPs and teachers can present the target communication (e.g. word, gesture) to the child to repeat. Using modeling consistently across contexts can be part of a joint intervention both in the classroom and within clinical settings.
2. **Expansion:** Expansion refers to providing related words to augment a one-word utterance or incomplete message from a child. Using the expansion technique models multi-word communication, and teaches related terms and important ideas about the original utterance. For example, if a student says "cup" when requesting a cup, the teacher could respond "I would like a cup of water, please" to show the student how to complete the sentence with additional details. If both teachers and SLPs are using expansion methods regularly, the student is able to recognize more quickly how to elaborate on shorter utterances, as well as realize that the expectation for longer utterances is expected across contexts and not just in the classroom or speech session.
3. **Wh-questions:** Children presented with wh-questions are able to get an idea across without the challenges of sentence formulation. The complexity of wh-questions is a consideration with progression from simpler (e.g., what?) to more challenging questions (e.g., why?). Teachers and SLPs can discuss the level of question that might be best to ask a student and be consistent across settings so that the student becomes comfortable with easier questions (e.g. what?) before harder questions are posed. Both professionals may have good ideas and experience to draw upon to make these decisions on the level of questions to ask, but their consistency across adults asking the same types of questions can help in the more rapid acquisition of skills.
4. **Scaffolding:** Scaffolding involves providing a framework for the student to respond correctly, with less support over time, as the child learns the different components of communication. For example, initially, a child may need most of the words provided in a sentence frame. As the skill progresses, the child may be able to produce more of the sentence independently. While teachers may see multiple examples of the student's abilities each day and be able to adjust to their growing independence, an SLP who only sees the student once or twice per week may stay consistent with providing more scaffolding than the student may need and slow down progress. When the teacher and SLP communicate regularly, they can adapt the amount of scaffolding provided so that growth seen within the classroom can continue to be built within speech sessions as well.

Receptive and expressive communication is the foundation of multiple academic and social skills, and it is an important foundational target for students who may be struggling in multiple areas. Students with communication challenges can also have additional physical impairments, such as vision, motor skills, or attention challenges that can impact these academic abilities. IPCP for communication skills is key, as traditional means of teaching communication to children with high-intensity needs are not always accessible, or effective. It is critical to use additional strategies to improve the comprehension and production of language that capitalizes on different modalities (words, gestures, pictures, etc.). Academic texts can be shortened, used repeatedly, and symbols and pictures can be added to aid comprehension (Jerome, 2020). Both electronic and low-tech tools are also available for communication. For example, sentence frames allow the child to supply a word or picture to express a need or idea, without having to independently produce the entire sentence to get the message across successfully. This kind of scaffolding can be faded as the student gains more skills in producing ideas. While teachers may not be trained in more specialized communication techniques, they have the opportunity to observe students' learning and growth on a daily basis and continue to increase the complexity of demands to meet that growth.

There is considerable evidence supporting the use of IPCP, and growing evidence for its use in schools, especially for communication goals for students with high-intensity needs. Overall, several different target skills have been improved as a result of IPCP. A team including a physical therapist and applied behavior analyst were able to jointly improve the motor skills (overhand throwing) of a student with autism (Coleburn et al., 2017). Similarly, team-based approaches were also found to be more effective for oral aversion (Edwards et al., 2015), where multiple medical, sensory, and behavior issues could be addressed by individuals with different expertise. Focusing on SLP and teacher collaborations, specifically, studies have shown successful improvements in vocabulary, and phonological awareness (Archibald, 2017; Lund et al., 2020), as well as improved communication skills across multiple settings (Cooper-Duffy & Eaker, 2017). However, there was mixed support for oral language gains (Archibald, 2017). Even though not all skills were demonstrably improved as a result of SLP and teacher collaborative practice, progress was not hindered, so the practice of IPCP was still recommended.

## EXAMINING HYPOTHESIS TWO: EFFECTIVE IPE LEADS TO INCREASED USE OF IPCP

Strong IPE programs provide pre-professionals with model-based, overt, and dedicated instruction paired with meaningful collaborative clinical experiences (Coufal & Scherz, 2013). The IPEC Expert Panel (2011) identified four core competencies needed in IPE: 1) values and ethics for interprofessional practice, 2) roles and responsibilities for professional collaboration, 3) interprofessional communication, and 4) interprofessional teamwork and team-based care. The first competency suggests that "values and ethics are patient centered with a community/population orientation, grounded in a sense of shared purpose to support the common good in health care, and reflect a shared commitment to creating safer, more efficient, and more effective systems of care" (p. 23). The second competency of roles and responsibilities involves understanding the expertise of other related professionals and coming to a shared agreement on the different aspects of student/patient care that each professional will lead. Interprofessional communication refers to developing effective communication skills with other professionals to help the team work most efficiently towards student/patient goals. Finally, interprofessional teamwork and team-based care involve cooperation and interdependence to reach shared student/patient goals (IPEC Expert Panel, 2011; 2016). Pre-professionals who attend quality IPE programs and leave with these four core competencies are ideally both more interested in and have the skills to engage with related professionals on cases. Knowing the roles and expertise of other related professionals before entering the field also helps professionals better recognize the limits of their own expertise and when and where to seek guidance and support from others.

Additional guidelines have been established within the research for developing IPE programs (Barr & Low, 2012), with six common tenets that appear key to education programs (Dobbs-Oates & Wachter Morris, 2016).

1. Interprofessional teamwork is central to students' learning
2. All stakeholders are involved in the planning
3. Outcomes from students' interprofessional learning are defined as competencies or capabilities and curricula planned accordingly
4. Teacher and practice supervisors optimize interactive opportunities for students to learn with, from, and about each other's professions
5. Every effort is made to include student groups for professions likely to work in the same settings in their subsequent careers
6. Objectives, content, and learning methods during IPE lay the foundation for continuing professional development (Barr and Low, 2012)

These guidelines have been successfully implemented in health professions to establish cross-disciplinary programs, with professional organizations and infrastructure built around these core competencies, but this has not been as diffused in education professions. Teachers and SLPs are ideal partners in IPE, as they focus on core communication skills, and have regular opportunities to interact and build joint treatment plans for students in educational settings. Since these two professions are likely to interact regularly in practice, building these tenets within both programs early removes many potential barriers to their collaboration.

Goldberg (2015) also suggests a 3-stage learning model, where there is 1) exposure to IPE, then 2) immersion into IPE, and finally 3) development of competence (ready for IPCP). Pulling these two models together, it seems that pre-professional training activities can be organized around the guidelines above, but move students through the sequence of exposure-immersion-competence to get students ready to collaborate in practice. In the first stage, course content and readings should encourage broad information about multiple disciplines and perspectives. The second stage asks students to engage in IPCP within their training program director, and allows them practice (and opportunities for guidance) in collaborating with others in related fields. Finally, after multiple practice opportunities, students can move into the stage where they are ready to implement IPCP independently within practice.

Some IPE learning activities have been studied and shown that they help to advance IPCP competencies. Collaborative coursework, assignments, debates, readings, and case-based discussions or planning expose students to both the research on IPCP as well as the practice of engaging in cross-discipline perspective-taking (Abu-Rish et al., 2012). Similarly, reflective practice allows students to take an active role in considering their own communication and collaboration styles, and how to most effectively work with others (Richard et al., 2019). However, the effectiveness of many of these strategies has not been extensively studied. Collaborative clinical practicum opportunities are the most common and well-evaluated IPE activities within the literature. Practicum opportunities provide collaborative clinical experiences to both SLP trainees and student teachers, to work together to solve complex challenges for students within a classroom setting.

Collaborative practicum opportunities have been shown to support a wide range of skill development amongst trainees, including increasing professional vocabularies, and curricular knowledge and reducing the use of professional jargon (Suleman et al., 2014; Wilson, McNeill, & Gillon, 2016), as well as improved speech and literacy outcomes of the students receiving support from collaborating practicum students (Wilson, McNeill, & Gillon, 2019). Students who engaged in collaborative practicum experiences also showed improved knowledge, comfort with, and openness to collaboration (Weiss, Cook, & Eren, 2020) as well as increased understanding of professional roles and expertise, improved communication skills to support shared decision-making, understanding of interdependence in supporting children's learning, and flexibility to implement alternative instructional practices (Wilson, McNeill, & Gillon, 2017).

It is clear that collaborative training activities support collaboration skill development, but also promote collaboration in the field. SLPs who were trained using IPE were five times more likely to co-teach when in practice (Brandel & Frome Loeb, 2011). Unfortunately, even though IPE can improve collaboration, it does not always improve attitudes toward other professionals (Hammick et al., 2007). For most effectiveness, it seems that IPE programming should occur at the beginning and throughout SLP and teacher training (Stehle Wallace et al., 2022), and that there needs to be institutional support to sustain IPE efforts.

## EXAMINING HYPOTHESIS THREE: KEY CHARACTERISTICS CAN PROMOTE THE SUCCESSFUL USE OF IPCP

Once professionals enter the field, collaboratively trained personnel can serve as a model emphasizing IPCP across disciplines to support positive outcomes for children with high-intensity needs. Those who have learned about and engaged in interprofessional collaboration during their pre-professional training are more likely to feel comfortable engaging in similar activities in the field, and school administrators may want to consider this in the hiring process. However, while having individuals who are prepared for IPCP in training is beneficial, there are several additional key characteristics that have been identified in the literature that make IPCP more likely to be successful. As a foundation, school norms should be set to encourage collaboration instead of isolation (resources to support collaborative time, invitations to all related professionals for meetings on student goals, etc.). While there is growing research on IPCP within schools, and specifically between SLPs and educators, the research that has been done often uses different measures to assess its success, and therefore cannot always be directly compared. However, these core characteristics (which are sometimes referred to by slightly different, but related terms) cut across school settings and professions, and highlight fundamental conditions that may be necessary to engage in IPCP effectively.

### Characteristics of Effective Partnerships

Several studies have explored the characteristics of effective interprofessional clinical partnerships. There are many terms used to describe the different components by different authors, however, the themes are similar across studies (see Table 1 for a sample of studies discussing effective partnership characteristics). Themes emerge around relationships, communication, time and effort to work together, shared focus, clear roles and responsibilities, and integrating complementary skills. However, it is important to note (as is shown in the table), that there can be considerable overlap between themes, and that some are more clearly distinct than others. When two concepts do share some meaning, the barriers between cells have been removed to highlight this overlap.

Relationships refer to concepts ranging from interpersonal respect, trust, and professional partnerships (Borg & Drange, 2019; Heisler & Thousand, 2021; Kunze & Machalicek, 2022; Volkers, 2016). It is difficult to partner with others unless those key aspects of the professional relationship exist. Each professional brings unique expertise to the collaboration, and by building a respectful exchange, and learning about the expertise and abilities of others, it is possible to truly utilize the skills of both partners to reach client-focused goals. It is far less likely that a teacher and SLP will work together when they do not make an initial effort to build the relationship and become more confident in the skills, knowledge, and communication styles of the other. Being able to be open and honest with concerns or challenges hinges on their ability to interact comfortably within their relationship.

The second key characteristic that is repeatedly mentioned throughout the literature on IPCP is communication between professionals. While respectful relationships are the goal, effective communication is an essential step to achieving those relationships and engaging in meaningful and productive meetings. Communication and relationships are often mentioned interchangeably, as using clear communication (Volkers, 2016), or even leadership skills (such as positive management skills; Banach & Couse, 2012; Kunze & Machalicek, 2022; Nancarrow et al., 2013) underlie effective relationships. Ultimately, effective listening skills are also essential, and being able to communicate respectfully and with a clear purpose. For example, if a teacher seeks the advice of an SLP with a student who needs support expanding one-word utterances, it is important that the SLP listens carefully to the challenge being presented, and is clear about how it is impacting the student within the class. The teacher may not explain the program in the same terms the SLP would use, but both need to be able to listen closely and understand the challenge in their own terms so that they can solve it together.

Time and effort to work together share several other related terms, such as effective and efficient process (Cooper-Duffy & Eaker, 2017), joint time (Archibald, 2017), and opportunities to plan (Pratt et al., 2017). Volkers (2016), suggests that collaborators need to be in "close proximity with ongoing interaction" with one another (p. 44). While proximity may be ideal, intentionality in setting joint planning time seems to be the common underlying requirement. Many educational settings do not have more than one SLP assigned (and sometimes that SLP is assigned to multiple schools). Teachers are also required to be in the classroom, attending to students throughout the day, with only brief lunch or preparatory periods as opportunities to leave their classroom. Thus, it can be challenging for teachers and SLPs to find a common time and space to work together. In an ideal collaboration, they would be able to check in briefly, and regularly on progress and adjust interventions as needed. But if the two professionals are unable to find a common time to discuss cases, it can substantially delay decision-making and ongoing progress. Given their challenging schedules, both educators and SLPs must be dedicated to the collaborative practice to make the time and effort to keep it going.

A shared focus on the student/patient goals (Cooper-Duffy & Eakers, 2017; Volkers, 2016) is another common element across several reports. This sense of interdependency (Cropanzano & Mitchell, 2005) creates a shared philosophy (D'Armour et al., 2005; Nancarrow et al., 2013) and cooperation on a joint task (Stehle Wallace et al., 2021; Watts & Jones, 2000). The overarching focus on the student allows professionals from multiple disciplines to target their communications and expertise to only those topics most relevant to the student. By focusing on those target issues, the team can work more efficiently and effectively toward student goals. This also has the potential to help the student to work on goals in multiple settings, and reach goals more quickly, and with better generalization across settings (McGinty & Justice, 2006; Moore & Montgomery, 2008; Pershey & Rapking, 2003). A shared focus on the student goals also helps to reduce the time needed to collaborate, as the goal helps organize the discussion, and keep both professionals working in service to that goal. Having clear and commonly agreed upon goals by both teachers and SLPs is the first step in this process though, so both need to be included in the initial goal development process.

Clear roles and responsibilities (Archibald, 2017; Cooper-Duffy & Eaker, 2017; Volkers, 2016) are at the core of all professional collaborations. Unfortunately, education professionals are often trained in silos and are therefore not always aware of each other's focus and expertise. Being explicit about what each team member brings to the table, and where they will each take the lead at the outset of team planning can be vital to an effective partnership where the contribution of each member is valued. Assumptions about the role and expertise of each team member can undermine the partnership (an assumption about roles might be that SLPs only know about speech and communication, so they should not be asked about literacy skills). Therefore, it is important to outline the expectations of the roles and responsibilities from the outset of the collaboration. By each professional sharing their expertise and clarifying what actions they will take within the collaboration, the expectations are known to all, and trust and respect are built within the partnership from the outset.

Finally, knowledge and skills (Archibald, 2017; Stehle Wallace et al., 2021) are also mentioned as key characteristics of successful partnerships. This involves not only being able to identify professional expertise within one's profession, but also the ability to share knowledge effectively, and use multiple service delivery models, such as consultation or coaching to help increase the skills of others, and actively participate in the partnership. SLPs often engage in speech therapy sessions outside of the classroom, so they do not have an opportunity to share their expertise, strategies, or skills unless they actively find ways to do this within the classroom, or with the teacher during collaboration sessions. Similarly, teachers are often isolated within their classroom, so others do not see their skills with the students. Both professionals have an opportunity and obligation to share their knowledge and skills so that they become resources for collaboration to help students achieve their goals more effectively and efficiently.

## IPCP Service Delivery Models

While IPCP involves the partnership of two related professionals focused on student/patient goals, there is also the question of how those professionals can best work together to reach the students' needs. The traditional model of SLP service delivery has been pull-out services (Brandel & Frome Loeb, 2011; Mullen & Schooling, 2010), but SLPs are encouraged to try more integrated models, such as in-class therapy, which has specifically been shown to increase therapeutic outcomes with language challenges (Archibald, 2017). Several alternatives to pull-out services are available, such as consultation, co-teaching, small group intervention within classrooms, and providing information to other stakeholders (Archibald, 2017).

Co-teaching will be discussed in more detail, as four types of co-teaching arrangements have been shown to effectively support students when SLPs and teachers work together (Devecchi & Nevin, 2010; Heisler & Thousand, 2021).

1. *Supportive co-teaching* (one professional is the leader while the other provides targeted supports; Villa & Thousand, 2016; Villa et al., 2013)
2. *Parallel co-teaching* (students are divided and teacher and SLP each instruct a group simultaneously; Villa & Thousand, 2016; Villa et al., 2008, 2013)

*Table 1. Characteristics of Effective Partnerships*

| Source | Volkers, 2016 | Archibald, 2017 | Cooper-Duffy & Eaker, 2017 | Stehle Wallace, Senter, Peterson, Dunn, & Chow, 2021 | Kunze & Machalicek, 2022 | Common Themes |
|---|---|---|---|---|---|---|
| Characteristics for Effective Partnerships | Building respectful relationships | | Communication and interpersonal relationships | | Partnership | Relationships |
| | Using Clear Communication | | | Integration and removing boundaries for collaboration | Leadership Skills | Communication |
| | Close proximity with ongoing interaction | Joint time | Effective and efficient process | Coordination adjusting work habits or perspectives to ensure teamwork | Collaborative | Time and Effort to Work Together |
| | Focusing on client goals | | Goal setting | Cooperation on a joint task | Interdependency Shared philosophy | Shared Focus |
| | Defining roles Sharing responsibilities | Roles and responsibilities | Roles and responsibilities | | | Roles and Responsibilities |
| | | Knowledge and skills | Collaborative problem-solving | Cross-fertilization of knowledge and skills | Professional Identity | Knowledge and Skills |
| | | Resources | | | | |
| | | | Evaluation | | | |

3. *Complementary Co-teaching* (whole group instruction with one professional enhancing the material being presented by the other using visuals or examples; Villa & Thousand, 2016; Villa et al., 2010; Villa et al., 2013)
4. *Team Co-Teaching* (SLPs and teachers take on all teaching activities together, in planning, implementing lessons, and assessing students; Villa & Thousand, 2016; Villa et al., 2013)

Co-teaching has been found to increase treatment integrity and intensity to achieve improved outcomes (Moore & Montgomery, 2008). This makes sense, as students are not pulled out of regular class times, and interventions can be infused throughout the school day, instead of being isolated to a brief pull-out speech session. Both professionals working together also keep both accountable to maintain fidelity to the intervention while the other is in the room and can both observe and support one another. Students are also able to generalize and maintain gains in communication skills (McGinty & Justice, 2006; Pershey & Rapking, 2003) when they are receiving interventions in multiple settings, and with multiple providers, as they do not respond only to one person under specific circumstance (the SLP within the speech session alone).

While there are many different types of service delivery options when working in collaboration, no one service delivery model seems to be superior to others (Archibald, 2017). Teachers and SLPs are urged to decide what will work best in their setting based on the resources and data that they have about their students (Archibald, 2017). However, it is clear that in addition to improved student gains in acquiring skills, there is evidence to show that professionals also enjoy and feel like the process of IPCP is effective (Bruce & Bashinski, 2017; Phoenix et al., 2020). A collaborative effort between SLPs and Occupational Therapists reported that students received more timely services, and increased the capacity of both professionals (Phoenix et al., 2020). Similarly, collaborations between SLPs and physical therapists showed more seamless care for their clients in addition to improvements in student skills (Sylvester, Ogletree, & Lunnen, 2017). Thus, there is considerable potential for IPCP between SLPs and educators to address communication challenges at school.

## AAC DEVICE USE AS AN IPCP OPPORTUNITY

Students needing augmentative and alternative communication (AAC) devices represent a specific opportunity for educators and SLPs to collaborate (Leatherman & Wegner, 2022). AAC devices not only allow for communication for those students who are minimally verbal but also underpin reading and writing skills (Ganz, 2014). AAC devices refer to a range of electronic devices that can be programmed to represent specific vocabulary and have buttons or picture icons that can be pushed by the individual student to communicate. Using AAC devices has been shown to have positive effects on communication, especially with those with complex needs (Light & McNaughton, 2015). There is a process to receive an AAC device, where students must be assessed for the need for a device, identify which type of device, and then the device must be programmed, and maintained. Ideally, the device should accompany the student in all settings (school, home, community, etc.), so the ability and mode of communication is consistent, and there are real-life opportunities to apply it (Light & McNaughton, 2015). Thus, this represents a unique opportunity for all stakeholders in a child's life to work together to know how to maintain the device and use it to its highest potential in each setting.

The use of AAC devices needs to be implemented and supported by a team to ensure consistency and generalization (DePaepe & Wood, 2001; Ganz, 2014). Everyone needs to know how to use the device, and when and how it should be used to access the curriculum or community. SLPs can recognize the need for an AAC device and have a role in the assessment and goal setting, as well as identify AAC options and provide training and support to others in the child's life who need to use the device with the child (Ganz, 2014). Teachers, on the other hand, can help decide when and how to infuse the AAC device into the classroom to help the student access the curriculum, as well as encourage AAC use in multiple settings and monitor progress (Ganz, 2014). Teachers also help other students in the class understand and accept the use of the AAC device with their peers.

To support AAC use in schools, there are both fundamental skills and collaborative practices needed. All stakeholders in the child's life need to know both how to use and maintain the AAC device, as well as how to work with others to provide consistent support to the child. Families, SLPs, and teachers (at a minimum) should work together, with clear and ongoing communication between the team (DePaepe & Wood, 2001).

## FUTURE RESEARCH DIRECTIONS

To improve IPE and IPCP, there must be a continued study of both the preparation for, and engagement in interprofessional practice. While there have been a series of tools created to document the impact of interprofessional training and activities, they have not been extensively studied or validated. Some examples of measures are below, and represent opportunities for those engaging in IPE and IPCP to more systematically study the measures, as well as compare program components.

1. Readiness for Interprofessional Learning Scale (RIPLS; McFayden, Webster, & Maclaren, 2006). This tool includes a 5-point rating scale with four subscales: Teamwork and collaboration, negative professional identity, positive professional identity, and roles and responsibilities.
2. Assessment of Interprofessional Team Collaboration (AITCS; Orchard et al., 2012). This tool includes a 5-point rating scale with three sub-categories: Partnership/shared decision-making, cooperation, and coordination.
3. Interprofessional collaborative competency attainment survey (ICCAS; Archibald, Trumpower, & MacDonald, 2014). This self-report tool includes 20 items on communication, collaboration, roles and responsibilities, collaborative patient-family-centered approach, conflict management/resolution, and team functioning.
4. Interprofessional Professionalism Assessment (IPA; Frost et al., 2019). This observational rating scale includes 26 items on interprofessional professionalism to be used by faculty observing students during clinical practice.

In addition to systematically measuring IPCP success, there are also gaps in our understanding of which delivery models work best under which professional conditions. Continuing to explore the IPCP core characteristics and service models under different professional conditions can help clarify when and how to establish IPCP in a new educational setting. Given the advantages of educators and SLPs using IPCP to support communication challenges for students with high-needs disabilities, more roadmaps are needed to guide professionals in best practices for implementation within their setting.

## CONCLUSION

Complex needs require coordinated care to help support students with disabilities with high intensity needs within schools. Unfortunately, while this movement towards professional integration is recommended by both ASHA and CEC, most professionals continue to work in isolation. Existing research suggests that participating in interprofessional collaboration during training (such as in IPE) does increase the use of IPCP in the field (Brandel & Frome Loeb, 2011; Stehle Wallace et al., 2022). However, there are additional foundational characteristics and institutional supports that need to be in place to truly integrate IPCP into schools. Key characteristics of collaboration include effective communication, building trusting and effective relationships, understanding roles and responsibilities, focusing on interdependent student goals, and building knowledge and skills to best support their students. When these characteristics are in place, and the time and resources are provided to allow collaborations to occur, communication goals can be achieved faster, and with greater generalization (Glover, et al. 2015; McGinty & Justice, 2006; Moore & Montgomery, 2008; Pershey & Rapking, 2003).

## ACKNOWLEDGMENT

This research was supported by the United States Department of Education, Office of Special Education Programs (grant number H325K210006).

## REFERENCES

Abu-Rish, E., Kim, S., Choe, L., Varpio, L., Malik, E., White, A. A., & Zierler, B. (2012). Current trends in interprofessional education of health science students: A literature review. *Journal of Interprofessional Care*, *26*(6), 444–451. doi:10.3109/13561820.2012.715604 PMID:22924872

Adlof, S. M., & Hogan, T. P. (2019). If we don't look, we won't see: Measuring language development to inform literacy instruction. *Policy Insights from the Behavioral and Brain Sciences, 6*(2), 210–217. doi:10.1177/2372732219839075

American Psychiatric Association. (2013). *Diagnostic and statistical manual of mental disorders* (5th ed.). doi:10.1176/appi.books.9780890425596

Apel, K. (2002). Serving students with spoken and written language challenges. *ASHA Leader*, *7*(1), 6–7. doi:10.1044/leader.FTR1.07012002.6

Archibald, D., Trumpower, D., & MacDonald, C. J. (2014). Validation of the interprofessional collaborative competency attainment survey (ICCAS). *Journal of Interprofessional Care*, *28*(6), 553–558. doi:10.3109/13561820.2014.917407 PMID:24828620

Archibald, L. (2017). SLP-educator classroom collaboration: A review to inform reason-based practice. *Autism & Developmental Language Impairments*, *2*, 1–17. doi:10.1177/2396941516680369

Arner, L., Barreca, J., Cosbey, J., Prasad, A., Schlessman, A., & Stephenson, P. (2022). *Joint statement on interprofessional collaborative goals in school-based practice.* American Occupational Therapy Association, American Physical Therapy Association, American Speech-Language-Hearing Association. Retrieved from https://webnew.ped.state.nm.us/wp-content/uploads/2022/03/Joint-Statement-on-Interprofessional-Collaborative-Goals-in-School-Based-Practice-2022-2-17.pdf

Banach, M., & Couse, L. J. (2012). Interdisciplinary co-facilitation of support groups for parents of children with Autism: An opportunity for professional preparation. *Social Work with Groups*, *35*(4), 313–329. doi:10.1080/01609513.2012.671103

Barr, H., Koppel, I., Reeves, S., Hammick, M., & Freeth, D. (2005). *Effective Interprofessional Education*. Blackwell Publishing Ltd., doi:10.1002/9780470776445

Barr, H., & Low, H. (2012). *Interprofessional education in pre-registration courses: A CAIPE guide for commissioners and regulators of education.* CAIPE. Retrieved from https://www.caipe.org/resources/publications/caipe-publications/caipe-2012-ipe-pre-registration-courses-caipe-guide-commissioners-regulators-eduction-barrh-low-h-howkins-e

Bauer, K. L., Iver, S. N., Boon, R. T., & Fore, C. (2010). 10 ways for classroom teachers to collaborate with speech-language pathologists. *Intervention in School and Clinic*, *45*(5), 333–337. doi:10.1177/1053451208328833

Berry, A. B., Petrin, R. A., Gravelle, M. L., & Farmer, T. W. (2011). Issues in special education teacher recruitment, retention, and professional development: Considerations in supporting rural teachers. *Rural Special Education Quarterly*, *30*(4), 3–11. doi:10.1177/875687051103000402

Beukelman, D., & Mirenda, P. (2013). *Augmentative and alternative communication: Supporting children & adults with complex communication needs* (4th ed.). Paul H. Brookes Publishing. https://www.asha.org/njc/definition-of-communication-and-appropriate-targets/

Borg, E., & Drange, I. (2019). Interprofessional collaboration in school: Effects on teaching and learning. *Improving Schools*, *22*(3), 251–266. doi:10.1177/1365480219864812

Brandel, J., & Frome Loeb, D. (2011). Program intensity and service delivery models in the schools: SLP survey results. *Language, Speech, and Hearing Services in Schools*, *42*(4), 461–490. doi:10.1044/0161-1461(2011/10-0019 PMID:21616986

Bruce, S. M., & Bashinski, S. M. (2017). The Trifocus Framework and interprofessional collaborative practice in severe disabilities. *American Journal of Speech-Language Pathology*, *26*(2), 162–180. doi:10.1044/2016_AJSLP-15-0063 PMID:28514472

Bryan, K., Garvani, G., Gregory, J., & Kilner, K. (2015). Language difficulties and criminal justice: The need for earlier identification. *International Journal of Language & Communication Disorders*, *50*(6), 763–775. doi:10.1111/1460-6984.12183 PMID:26344062

Chow, J. C., & Wehby, J. H. (2018). Associations between language and problem behavior: A systematic review and correlational meta-analysis. *Educational Psychology Review*, *30*(1), 61–82. doi:10.100710648-016-9385-z

Colebourn, J. A., Golub-Victor, A. C., & Paez, A. (2017). Developing overhand throwing skills for child with autism with a collaborative approach in school-based therapy. *Pediatric Physical Therapy*, *29*(3), 262–269. doi:10.1097/PEP.0000000000000405 PMID:28654501

Cooper-Duffy, K., & Eaker, K. (2017). Effective team practices: Interprofessional contributions to communication issues with a parent's perspective. *American Journal of Speech-Language Pathology*, *26*(2), 181–192. doi:10.1044/2016_AJSLP-15-0069 PMID:28514473

Coufal, K. L., & Scherz, J. (2013). *Interprofessional education in communication sciences and disorders*. Retrieved from https://www.asha.org/enews/accessacademics.html

Council for Exceptional Children. (2020). *Initial practice-based professional preparation standards for special educators*. Retrieved from https://exceptionalchildren.org/standards/initial-practice-based-professional-preparation-standards-special-educators

Cropanzano, R., & Mitchell, M. S. (2005). Social exchange theory: An interdisciplinary review. *Journal of Management*, *31*(6), 874–900. doi:10.1177/0149206305279602

D'Armour, D., Ferrada-Videla, M., San Martin Rodriguez, L., & Beaulieu, M. (2005). The conceptual basis for interprofessional collaboration: Core concepts and theoretical frameworks. *Journal of Interprofessional Care*, *19*(1), 116–131. doi:10.1080/13561820500082529 PMID:16096150

DeKemel, K. P. (2003). *Intervention in language arts: A practical guide for speech-language pathologists*. Butterworth Heinemann.

DePaepe, P. A., & Wood, L. A. (2001). Collaborative practices related to augmentative and alternative communication: Current personnel preparation programs. *Communication Disorders Quarterly*, *22*(2), 77–86. doi:10.1177/152574010102200203

Devecchi, C., & Nevin, A. (2010). Leadership for inclusive schools and inclusive school leadership. *Advances in Educational Administration*, *11*, 211–241. doi:10.1108/S1479-3660(2010)0000011014

Developmental Disabilities Assistance and Bill of Rights Act of. 2000, Pub. L. No. 106-402, § 102(8). https://www.congress.gov/106/plaws/publ402/PLAW-106publ402.pdf

Dickenson, D. K., Golinkoff, R. M., & Hirsh-Pasek, K. (2010). Speaking out for language: Why language is central to reading development. *Educational Researcher*, *39*(4), 305–310. doi:10.3102/0013189X10370204

Dobbs-Oates, J., & Wachter Morris, C. (2016). The case for interprofessional education in teacher education and beyond. *Journal of Education for Teaching*, *42*(1), 50–65. doi:10.1080/02607476.2015.1131363

Durkin, K., & Conti-Ramsden, G. (2010). Young people with specific language impairment: A review of social and emotional functioning in adolescence. *Child Language Teaching and Therapy*, *26*(2), 105–121. doi:10.1177/0265659010368750

Edwards, S., McGrath Davis, A., Ernst, L., Sitzman, B., Bruce, A., Keeler, D., Almadhoun, O., Mousa, H., & Hyman, P. (2015). Interdisciplinary strategies for treating oral aversions in children. *Journal of Parental and Entreal Nutrition*, *39*(8), 899–909. doi:10.1177/0148607115609311 PMID:26487751

Frenk, J., Chen, L., Bhutta, Z. A., Cohen, J., Crisp, N., Evans, T., Fineberg, H., Garcia, P., Ke, Y., Kelley, P., Kistnasamy, B., Meleis, A., Naylor, D., Pablos-Mendez, A., Reddy, S., Scrimshaw, S., Sepulveda, J., Serwadda, D., & Zurayk, H. (2010). Health professions for a new century: Transforming education to strengthen health systems in an independent world. *Lancet*, *376*(9756), 1923–1958. doi:10.1016/S0140-6736(10)61854-5 PMID:21112623

Frost, J. S., Hammer, D. P., Nunez, L. M., Adams, J. L., Chesluk, B., Grus, C., Harvison, N., McGuinn, K., Mortensen, L., Nishimoto, J. H., Palatta, A., Richmond, M., Ross, E. J., Tegzes, J., Ruffin, A. L., & Bentley, J. P. (2019). The intersection of professionalism and interprofessional care: Development and initial testing of the interprofessional professionalism assessment (IPA). *Journal of Interprofessional Care*, *33*(1), 102–115. doi:10.1080/13561820.2018.1515733 PMID:30247940

Ganz, J. B. (2014). Interdisciplinary issues and collaboration in assessment and treatment. In *Aided Augmentative Communication for Individuals with Autism Spectrum Disorders, Autism and Child Psychopathology Series*. Springer Science Business Media. doi:10.1007/978-1-4939-0814-1_4

Gillon, G. (2002). Phonological awareness intervention for children. From the research laboratory to the clinic. *ASHA Leader*, *7*(22), 4–5, 16–17. doi:10.1044/leader.FTR2.07222002.4

Glover, A., McCormack, J., & Smith-Tamaray, M. (2015). Collaboration between teachers and speech and language therapists: Services for primary school children with speech, language and communication needs. *Child Language Teaching and Therapy*, *31*(3), 363–382. doi:10.1177/0265659015603779

Goldberg, L. R. (2015). The importance of interprofessional education for students in communication sciences and disorders. *Communication Disorders Quarterly*, *36*(2), 121–125. doi:10.1177/1525740114544701

Hammick, M., Freeth, D., Koppel, S., Reeves, S., & Barr, H. (2007). A best evidence systematic review of interprofessional education: BEME Guide No. 9. *Medical Teacher*, *29*(735), 735–751. doi:10.1080/01421590701682576 PMID:18236271

Heisler, L. A., & Thousand, J. S. (2021). A guide to co-teaching for the SLP: A tutorial. *Communication Disorders Quarterly*, *42*(2), 122–127. doi:10.1177/1525740119886310

Interprofessional Education Collaborative Expert Panel. (2011). *Core competencies for interprofessional collaborative practice: Report of an expert panel.* Washington, DC: Interprofessional Education Collaborative. https://ipec.memberclicks.net/assets/2011-Original.pdf

Interprofessional Education Collaborative Expert Panel. (2016). *Core competencies for interprofessional collaborative practice: 2016 update.* Washington, DC: Interprofessional Education Collaborative. https://ipec.memberclicks.net/assets/2016-Update.pdf

Jerome, M. K., & Ainsworth, M. K. (2020). Literacy acquisition for students with severe disabilities: Making it happen through assistive technology. *Teaching Exceptional Children*, *53*(1), 80–83. doi:10.1177/0040059920945590

Kamhi, A. G. (2003). The role of the SLP in improving reading fluency. *ASHA Leader*, *8*(7), 6–8. doi:10.1044/leader.FTR1.08072003.6

Kunze, M., & Machalicek, W. (2022). Interdisciplinary teams: A model to support students with autism. *Psychology in the Schools*, *59*(7), 1350–1362. doi:10.1002/pits.22618

Leader-Janssen, E., Swain, K. D., Delkamiller, J., & Ritzman, M. J. (2012). Collaborative relationships for general education teachers working with students with disabilities. *Journal of Instructional Psychology*, *39*(2), 112–118.

Leatherman, E., & Wegner, J. (2022). Augmentative and alternative communication in the classroom: Teacher practices and experiences. *Journal of Speech. Language and Hearing in the Schools*, *53*(3), 874–893. doi:10.1044/2022_LSHSS-21-00125 PMID:35699256

Light, J., & McNaughton, D. (2015). Designing AAC research and intervention to improve outcomes for individuals with complex communication needs. *Augmentative and Alternative Communication*, *31*(2), 85–96. doi:10.3109/07434618.2015.1036458 PMID:25904008

Light, J., McNaughton, D., & Caron, J. (2019). New and emerging AAC technology supports for children with complex communication needs and their communication partners: State of the science and future research directions. *Augmentative and Alternative Communication*, *35*(1), 26–41. doi:10.1080/07434618.2018.1557251 PMID:30648902

Lord, C., Charman, T., Havdahl, A., Carbone, P., Anagnostou, E., Boyd, B., Carr, T., de Vries, P. J., Dissanayake, C., Divan, G., Freitag, C. M., Gotelli, M. M., Kasari, C., Knapp, M., Mundy, P., Plank, A., Scahill, L., Servili, C., Shattuck, P., ... McCauley, J. B. (2022). The lancet commission on the future of care and clinical research in autism. *Lancet*, *399*(10321), 271–334. doi:10.1016/S0140-6736(21)01541-5 PMID:34883054

Lund, E., Young, A., & Yarbrough, R. (2020). The effects of co-treatment on concept development in children with Down syndrome. *Communication Disorders Quarterly*, *41*(3), 176–187. doi:10.1177/1525740119827264

McFadyen, A. K., Webster, V. S., & Maclaren, W. M. (2006). The test-retest reliability of a revised version of the Readiness for Interprofessional Learning Scale (RIPLS). *Journal of Interprofessional Care*, *20*(6), 633–639. doi:10.1080/13561820600991181 PMID:17095441

McGinty, A., & Justice, L. (2006). Predictors of print knowledge in children with specific language impairment: Experiential and developmental factors. *Journal of Speech, Language, and Hearing Research: JSLHR*, *52*(1), 81–97. doi:10.1044/1092-4388(2008/07-0279) PMID:18723595

Moore, B., & Montgomery, J. (2008). *Making a difference for America's children: Speech-Language pathologists in public schools*. Pro-Ed.

Mullen, R., & Schooling, T. (2010). The National outcomes measurement system for pediatric speech-language pathology. *Language, Speech, and Hearing Services in Schools*, *41*(1), 44–60. doi:10.1044/0161-1461(2009/08-0051) PMID:19833827

Nancarrow, S. A., Booth, A., Ariss, S., Smith, T., Enderby, P., & Roots, A. (2013). Ten principles of good interdisciplinary team work. *Human Resources for Health*, *11*(19), 1–11. doi:10.1186/1478-4491-11-19 PMID:23663329

National Center for Education Statistics. (2022). *Students With Disabilities. Condition of Education*. U.S. Department of Education, Institute of Education Sciences. Retrieved October 17, 2022, from https://nces.ed.gov/programs/coe/indicator/cgg

Nunez, L. (2015). Achieving Quality and Improved Outcomes Through Interprofessional Collaboration. *ASHA Leader Live*. Retrieved from https://leader.pubs.asha.org/do/10.1044/2021-0902-interprofessional-collaboration-outcomes?utm_source=TrendMD&utm_medium=cpc&utm_campaign=The_ASHA_Leader_TrendMD_0

Ogletree, B. T. (2017). Addressing the communication and other needs of persons with severe disabilities through engaged interprofessional teams: Introduction to a clinical forum. *American Journal of Speech-Language Pathology*, *26*(2), 157–161. doi:10.1044/2017_AJSLP-15-0064 PMID:28514471

Orchard, C. A., King, G. A., Khalili, H., & Bezzina, M. B. (2012). Assessment of Interprofessional Team Collaboration Scale (AITCS): Development and testing of the instrument. *The Journal of Continuing Education in the Health Professions*, *32*(1), 58–67. doi:10.1002/chp.21123 PMID:22447712

Pentimonti, J. M., Justice, L. M., Yeomans-Maldonado, G., McGinty, A. S., Slocum, L., & O'Connell, A. (2017). Teachers' use of high-and low-support scaffolding strategies to differentiate language instruction in high-risk/economically disadvantaged settings. *Journal of Early Intervention*, *39*(2), 125–146. doi:10.1177/1053815117700865

Pershey, M. G., & Rapking, C. I. (2003). A survey of collaborative speech-language service delivery under large caseload conditions in an urban school district in the United States. *Journal of Speech-Language Pathology and Audiology*, *27*, 211–220.

Pfeiffer, D., Pavelko, S., Hahs-Vaughn, D., & Duddinge, C. (2019). A national survey of speech-language pathologists' engagement in interprofessional collaborative practice in schools: Identifying predictive factors and barriers to implementation. *Language, Speech, and Hearing Services in Schools*, *50*(4), 639–655. doi:10.1044/2019_LSHSS-18-0100 PMID:31411947

Phoenix, M., Dix, L., DeCola, C., Eisen, I., & Campbell, W. (2020). Health professional-educator collaboration in the delivery of school-based tiered support services: A qualitative case study. *Child: Care, Health and Development*, *47*(3), 367–376. doi:10.1111/cch.12849 PMID:33432659

Powers, L. S. (1965). Interprofessional education and medicolegal conflict as seen from the other side. *Journal of Medical Education*, *40*, 233–244. PMID:14254289

Pratt, S. M., Imbody, S. M., Wolf, L. D., & Patterson, A. L. (2017). Co-planning in co-teaching: A practical solution. *Intervention in School and Clinic*, *32*(4), 243–249. doi:10.1177/1053451216659474

Richard, A., Gagnon, M., & Careau, E. (2019). Using reflective practice in interprofessional education and practice: A realist review of its characteristics and effectiveness. *Journal of Interprofessional Care*, *33*(5), 424–436. doi:10.1080/13561820.2018.1551867 PMID:30513235

Rosanoff, M. J., Daniels, A. M., & Shih, A. (2015). Autism: A (key) piece of the global mental health puzzle. *Global Mental Health (Cambridge, England)*, *2*, e2. doi:10.1017/gmh.2014.7 PMID:28596851

Shaughnessy, A., & Sanger, D. (2005). Kindergarten teachers' perceptions of language and literacy development, speech-language pathologists, and language interventions. *Communication Disorders Quarterly*, *26*(2), 67–84. doi:10.1177/15257401050260020601

Shoffner, M., & Wachter Morris, C. A. (2010). Preparing preservice English teachers and school counselor interns for future collaboration. *Teaching Education*, *21*(2), 185–197. doi:10.1080/10476210903183894

Sisti, M. K., & Robledo, J. A. (2021). Interdisciplinary collaboration practices between education specialists and related service providers. *The Journal of Special Education Apprenticeship*, *10*(1), 1–19.

Stehle Wallace, E., Senter, R., Peterson, N., Dunn, K. T., & Chow, J. (2022). How to Establish a Language-Rich Environment Through a Collaborative SLP–Teacher Partnership. *Teaching Exceptional Children*, *54*(3), 166–176. doi:10.1177/0040059921990690

Suleman, S., McFarlane, L., Pollock, K., Schneider, P., Leroy, C., & Skoczylas, M. (2014). Collaboration: More than 'working together': An exploratory study to determine effect of interprofessional education on awareness and application of models of specialized service delivery by student speech-language pathologists and teachers. *Canadian Journal of Speech Language Pathology and Audiology*, *37*, 298–307.

Sylvester, L., Ogletree, B. T., & Lunnen, K. (2017). Cotreatment as a vehicle for interprofessional collaborative practice: Physical therapists and speech-language pathologists collaborating in the care of children with severe disabilities. *American Journal of Speech-Language Pathology, 26*(2), 206–216. doi:10.1044/2017_AJSLP-15-0179 PMID:28514475

U.S. Department of Education. (2022). *Fact sheet: The U.S. Department of Education Announces Partnerships Across States, School Districts, and Colleges of Education to Meet Secretary Cardona's Call to Action to Address the Teacher Shortage.* Retrieved from https://www.ed.gov/coronavirus/factsheets/teacher-shortage

Villa, R., & Thousand, J. S. (2016). *A guide to co-teaching PD resources center.* Corwin.

Villa, R. A., Thousand, J. S., & Nevin, A. I. (2008). *A guide to co-teaching: Practical tips for facilitating student learning.* Corwin.

Villa, R. A., Thousand, J. S., & Nevin, A. I. (2010). *Collaborating with students in instruction and decision making.* Corwin.

Villa, R. A., Thousand, J. S., & Nevin, A. I. (2013). *A guide to co-teaching: New lessons and strategies to facilitate student learning* (3rd ed.). Corwin.

Volkers. (2016). Bridging the professional divide: Along with clear benefits, interprofessional collaboration can bring misunderstandings. Six bridge-builders share their strategies. *ASHA Leader, 21*(11), 41-50. doi:10.1044/leader.FTR1.21112016.40

Watts, B., & Jones, S. (2000). Inter-professional practice and action research: Commonalities and parallels. *Educational Action Research, 8*(2), 377–382. doi:10.1080/09650790000200126

Weiss, D., Cook, B., & Eren, R. (2020). Transdisciplinary approach practicum for speech-language pathology and special education graduate students. *Journal of Autism and Developmental Disorders, 50*(10), 3661–3678. doi:10.100710803-020-04413-7 PMID:32076959

Westling, D., Fox, L., & Carter, E. (2015). *Teaching students with severe disabilities.* Pearson.

Wilson, L., McNeill, B. C., & Gillon, G. T. (2016). A comparison of inter-professional education programs in preparing prospective teachers and speech and language pathologists for collaborative language–literacy instruction. *Reading and Writing, 29*(6), 1179–1201. doi:10.100711145-016-9631-2

Wilson, L., McNeill, B. C., & Gillon, G. T. (2017). Inter-professional education of prospective speech–language therapists and primary school teachers through shared professional practice placements. *International Journal of Language & Communication Disorders, 52*(4), 426–439. doi:10.1111/1460-6984.12281 PMID:27624388

Wilson, L., McNeill, B. C., & Gillon, G. T. (2019). Understanding the effectiveness of student speech-language pathologists and student teachers co-working during inter-professional school placements. *Child Language Teaching and Therapy, 35*(2), 125–143. doi:10.1177/0265659019842203

World Health Organization. (2010). *Framework for action on interprofessional education and collaborative practice.* Retrieved from http://whqlibdoc.who.int/hq/2010/WHO_HRH_HPN_10.3_eng.pdf?ua=1

Yew, S. G. K., & O'Kearney, R. (2015). The role of early language difficulties in the trajectories of conduct problems across childhood. *Journal of Abnormal Child Psychology*, *43*(8), 1515–1527. doi:10.100710802-015-0040-9 PMID:26105208

Zagona, A. L., Kurth, J. A., & MacFarland, S. Z. C. (2017). Teachers' views of their preparation for inclusive education and collaboration. *Teacher Education and Special Education*, *40*(3), 163–178. doi:10.1177/0888406417692969

# Chapter 14
# Exceptional Education and Language Disorders:
## Interdisciplinary Collaboration to Create New Experts in Special Education

**Rebecca A. Hines**
*University of Central Florida, USA*

**Erika Moore**
*University of Central Florida, USA*

**Danica Moise**
*University of Central Florida, USA*

**Paige McCloud**
*University of Central Florida, USA*

**Jacqueline Towson**
*University of Central Florida, USA*

## ABSTRACT

*With 71% of students with disabilities (SWD) eligible for speech/language services and dismal outcomes in reading for SWD, the exceptional student education program at a large Florida university created a partnership with the speech/language program to educate new practitioners who are well prepared to support SWD's language and literacy needs. This chapter describes the creation of a partnership undergraduate program at a large Florida university that prepares students for special education and language disorders. The non-certification track in the Exceptional Education Program features coursework in the School of Communication Sciences and Disorders, which is not typically available to education majors. Students graduate with an undergraduate degree in exceptional student education and a certificate in language development and disorders after the program. The authors present specific course and program components and the theoretical framework anchoring the partnership.*

DOI: 10.4018/978-1-6684-6438-0.ch014

## INTRODUCTION

Language, precisely oral language skills, are the precursors to both emergent and later literacy skills, and language development deficits in children can lead to reading deficits. Preparing future educators and other pre-service professionals to understand typical linguistic construction is critical to aid in identifying children who are not achieving essential language development milestones, which are indicators for subsequent academic progress.

According to the U.S. Department of Education's 43rd Annual Report to congress, 71% of students with disabilities (SWD) fall into a category qualifying them for speech and language services (U.S. Department of Education, 2021). In 2019, the most prevalent disability categories receiving speech-language services were developmental delay (40.1%) for children ages three through five and specific learning disability (37.1%) for students ages 6 through 21. Under IDEA Part B, 39.9% of students ages 3 through 5 and 16.3% of students ages 6 through 21 were in the primary disability category of speech or language impairment. Additionally, 11.8% of students ages three through five and 11% of students ages six through 21 received special education services in the disability category of Autism Spectrum Disorder (ASD) (U.S. Department of Education, 2021).

Educators are often the first to recognize a delay or deficit in a particular skill. Additionally, a teacher's impact is vital in facilitating language development in young children, directly contributing to later literacy skills. Considering these high stakes, the ability of teachers and related personnel to support language and early literacy skill development is crucial (McDonnell et al., 2014; Odom & Wolery, 2003), especially for young children. Communication disorders are considered to be a high incidence disability category for infants, toddlers, and preschoolers. When children experience deficits in oral language, they usually carry them into the elementary classroom, leading to persistent deficits in reading and writing skills (NICHD, 2005). These oral language skills, which include receptive and expressive language and vocabulary, combine with phonological skills in kindergarten to account for approximately half of the variance in reading comprehension in second grade and later in eighth grade (Catts et al., 2014).

Essentially, speech-language pathologists (SLPs) evaluate, diagnose, and treat speech, language and swallowing disorders. Children with speech/language impairment (SLI) and developmental delays comprise the largest segment of children served under IDEA Parts C and B. For infants and toddlers, 89% received their early intervention services primarily in the home (U.S. Department of Education, 2021). However in school settings, SLPs partner with a team to provide students who qualify for services with a range of support. The interdisciplinary collaboration described in this chapter was created with the understanding that increasing training in language development and disorders for educators of all types, parents, non-profit and early childhood employees, and others working with young children can lead to increased recognition of language disorders, more support for students who struggle with language skills, and more specific training in skills that lead to literacy for SWD.

## BACKGROUND

The 1975 Education for All Handicapped Children Act cleared the way for SWD to have a place in schools and support their needs. From its inception, a core component of this law was a collaboration with related support systems in the special education field and included related services in a child's individualized education plan (IEP). An amendment to the legislation in 1986 formally required all states to offer interdisciplinary educational services to disabled toddlers, infants, and their families. In the 1990s and early 2000s, the Regular Education Initiative placed more emphasis on achievement and accountability and moved schools in a progressively more inclusive and interdisciplinary direction for serving SWD. Because of the legislative acts and support from the government, support for students with special needs increased by the 2018-2019 school year. According to the Office of Special Education Programs (OSEP), the number of students with disabilities served in a regular classroom for at least part of the day rose to 95% (OSEP, 2021).

Several studies dating back to the 1980s address the need for institutions to restructure Teacher Education Programs to include cross-disciplinary collaboration (Allen-Maeres & Pugach, 1982; Humes & Hohenshil, 1987; Prasse &, 1982; Pugach & Allen-Maeres, 1985). However, a quick scan through various teacher education degrees and course offerings shows that the common practice is to provide school professionals with specialized training separately. This traditional way of preparation allows for little to no cross-disciplinary collaboration.

## Time for Change

Due to teaching certification shortages across the country, qualified teachers of SWD are decreasing rather than adapting. States like Arizona and Florida are taking aggressive measures to fill teaching positions, including bypassing college requirements, and placing persons directly in classrooms with no education training and, sometimes, no four-year college degree. For instance, Florida has approved legislation that reduces certification requirements for veterans. The results from surveys conducted by the Florida Education Association displayed that the teaching shortage in the state doubled between 2016 and 2022 (Florida Education Association, 2022). Because of these shortages, Veterans Can Teach H.B. 573 was passed in Florida in early 2022, reducing requirements for Veterans to fill these vacancies with five-year temporary teaching certifications even when they do not have a college degree. To address teaching shortages in Arizona, legislators have followed suit in reducing requirements for teachers by passing SB 1159, which allows individuals without bachelor's degrees to enter the classroom as a teacher while they pursue a career in education.

As alternative options increase and teacher education enrollment decreases, professionals with expertise in special education in the classroom are also declining. According to the American Association of Colleges of Teacher Education (AACTE, 2022), supplying enough special education teachers each year into the workforce is only a portion of the challenge faced in special education. Despite educational reform efforts, interest in special education continues to decrease while teacher attrition increases, resulting in a national price tag nearing $8 billion (Sutcher et al., 2020). The American educational system has emphasized a critical need for more practitioners to work with SWD as the number of students with disabilities is rising. For example, the Centers for Disease Control and Prevention (CDC) reported that, as of 2018, one in 44 children are diagnosed with ASD as opposed to one in 88 a decade prior (National Center on Birth Defects and Developmental Disabilities, Centers for Disease Control and Prevention, 2022). With this shortage of well-qualified professionals to work with students with special needs and changes in the composition of today's student population, there is an increasing need for specialists to work with children with disabilities in school and beyond. Building new opportunities in higher education to attract pre-service professionals into the field is critical.

## INTERDISCIPLINARY PROGRAMS AND SPECIAL EDUCATION

In the field of early intervention, there is a consensus dated back to the late 1990s that interdisciplinary approaches to personnel preparation are best practice (Kilgo & Bruder, 1997, Stayton & Bruder, 1999; Welch et al., 1992). Interdisciplinary preparation allows professionals to establish a common core of knowledge and skills across disciplines that complement their specific expertise (Kilgo & Bruder, 1997; Stayton & Bruder, 1999).

The Center for Teacher Education at the University of Wisconsin-Milwaukee, a pioneer program in the efforts to restructure teacher education to foster cross-disciplinary preparation for educational professionals (Pugach, 1992), developed a program unifying general education and special education. Following Pugach's (1992) efforts, Welch and Sheridan (1993) shared a re-conceptualized approach to teacher preparation implemented in the Graduate School of Education at the University of Utah. Their initiative to implement three components (educational partnerships, collaborative educational problem solving, and the STEP Project) within their teacher education program allowed their students to assimilate the skills to establish academic partnerships to teach students with disabilities.

The most innovative component is the Site-Based Transdisciplinary Educational Partnerships (STEP) Project, a federal-funded project to provide various professional preparation programs opportunities to apply instructional techniques collaboratively during field experiences. The university formed transdisciplinary teams through a partnership between the university and public education, comprising student volunteers from the Department of Educational Psychology, Educational Administration, Educational Studies, and Special Education.

In the same way, the National Association for the Education of Young Children (NAEYC) guided the field in developing and submitting blended programs for accreditation review in its 2003 edition of *Preparing Early Childhood Professionals: NAEYC's Standards for Programs* (Hyson, 2003). Building upon their research, Miller and Stayon (2006) described an interdisciplinary, blended program designed for a degree program developed by intentionally blending philosophy and content from two or more professions with a new comprehensive curriculum and a multi-disciplinary faculty team.

Another illustration of an interdisciplinary approach to early intervention is a university-community collaboration initiative between the University of North Carolina at Charlotte and the North Carolina Consortium of Partnership: Families, Newborn Intensive Care Units (NICUs), and Community Programs (Smith, 2010). The grant-funded program prepared students and professionals from various disciplines (special education, psychology, sociology, nursing) to meet the complex and unique needs of premature infants and toddlers by providing them with interdisciplinary preparation provided by community-based professionals. The one-year training program comprised two content courses and an intensive practicum experience that met competencies and standards for the state Infant, Toddler, and Family Specialist (ITFS) certificate and the state Birth-Kindergarten (B-K) blended license. In addition, academic credit applies to their degree requirements based on the student's course of study.

Another unique collaboration in early childhood is a partnership between the University of Michigan-Dearborn Early Childhood Teacher Education program, Oakwood Healthcare Inc., and its Center for Exceptional Families described by Silverman et al. (2010). The transdisciplinary program focused on preparing early childhood educators to work with children with disabilities in inclusive education settings. Students are co-taught and mentored by clinicians, teachers, and university faculty. During the program, students observe health professionals provide diagnostic assessments, individual therapy, and

## Exceptional Education and Language Disorders

family therapy. During their fieldwork, they plan and implement inclusive activities with the clinicians, teachers, and faculty.

In focusing on inclusion in education, Able-Boone et al. (2002) developed a collaborative interdisciplinary program for graduate students in early childhood special education, school psychology, and speech and hearing science. Before entering their first semester of graduate school, students engaged in interdisciplinary coursework and field experiences with instructors across disciplines focusing on inclusive practices. Lam (2005) also developed a graduate-level course to prepare pre-service educators to work with families with children with disabilities. The multi-disciplinary approach for students in special education, deaf education, social work, psychology, and counseling was co-designed and co-taught and contained collaborative training, family involvement training, and multi-disciplinary group assignments. In addition, Kilgo (2006) articulated a similar program for master-level students at the University of Alabama at Birmingham. The program is a collaboration of faculty from education, communication disorders, occupational therapy, physical therapy, and nursing disciplines.

More recently, Dobbs-Oates and Wachter Morris (2016) incorporated interprofessional education (IPE) into a pre-service educational program for special educators and school counselors. The Center for the Advancement of Interprofessional Education (CAIPE) (Barr, 2002) defines interprofessional education as "Occasions when two or more professions learn with, from and about each other to improve collaboration and the quality of care" (p. 6). The researchers implemented the practice in a large Midwestern university by linking two existing courses and redesigning a one-course unit. They found the merge a viable format for educator training as it did not require additional resources from the institution. Additionally in 2019, OSEP awarded the University of Nevada $1.3 million for the development of an interdisciplinary personnel preparation program for Early Childhood Special Education and Speech-Language Pathology (Russell, 2019). The master's degree program emphasizes serving young children with autism with high-intense communication needs. At the completion of the program scholars will be qualified for a state or national certification in Early Childhood Special education or Speech Language Pathology. The program's first cohort begined in 2020.

Some programs, such as the Deaf and Hard of Hearing track at Texas Christian University (TCU), focus on specific disabilities. For example, the TCU program is focused primarily on ensuring that Deaf Education pre-service teachers receive training in communication sciences disorders and specifically addresses working with persons with hearing loss (Texas Christian University). Alternatively, Hofstra University in New York offers a master's teacher certification program for teachers of students with speech-language disabilities. Still, it requires an undergraduate degree in Speech-Language Pathology or equivalent (Hofstra University, n.d.).

Many of the programs mentioned above highlight the need and significance of the development of interdisciplinary programs. Nevertheless, a call to develop more interdisciplinary collaboration in teacher preparation programs still exists. The OSEP-K Grants for the master's level began requiring interdisciplinary preparation in 2018. However, this training, like most, is only at the graduate level. Therefore, there is a need for more undergraduate programs to establish more program partnerships. The partnerships discussed in this chapter offer stakeholders tangible examples of collaborations and strategies that can be implemented on the undergraduate level to prepare individuals entering the profession to meet the needs of the field.

The professional standards of organizations such as the Council for Exceptional Children (CEC) and the Division for Early Childhood (DEC) also support and promote the professional unification and intentional blending of philosophy and content (Stayton, 2015). These organizations understand that preparing personnel working with children in special education is becoming more critical as the educational system strives toward inclusion. Additionally, the prevalence of children diagnosed with ASD in the last decade makes it vital. When teacher education programs do not offer special education coursework to all school professionals and degree programs, their graduates are not well prepared to serve all students (Mason-Williams et al., 2020); this is a disservice to the field. School professionals who are uninformed in special education create a gap between what professionals contribute to the classroom and what students and their families require for success.

Data from the U.S. Department of Education (2017) suggests an overwhelming need for more language and literacy support in the classroom. For example, in Florida's early childhood enrollment, of the 42,908 children served through IDEA Part B, ages 3-5 years, 29% receive speech and language impairments services. In addition, 55% of those students fall under developmental delay eligibility, which often includes communication impairments (U.S. Department of Education, 2017). The need for enhanced instruction in communication and language prompted a partnership with the speech/language program at a large Florida university when opening a new non-certification program track in exceptional student education.

## PROGRAM STRUCTURE AND DELIVERY

Before the new program track, exceptional student education majors at the University of Central Florida only completed four courses specific to working with students with disabilities because of changes in the legislation of the early 2000s. Shortly after the No Child Left Behind (NCLB) and Individuals with Disabilities Education Act (IDEA) authorization, modifications in the certification track in exceptional student education included more reading and general education requirements (U.S. Department of Education, 2021). As a result, the program moved away from coursework specializing in disabilities. The University replaced these courses with additional reading and Teaching English to Speakers of Other Languages (TESOL) coursework aligned with State requirements. While this change allowed for more intensive reading instruction, SWD in the surrounding service areas continued to underachieve in this area almost twenty years later.

Data from the Florida Department of Education (2020) revealed that during the 2018-2019 school year, 20% of SWD were proficient in reading, and only 14% were competent in the 2020-2021 school year. The scores of students in surrounding districts were similar to the State reading achievement rate at 20% in the 2021-2022 school year for SWD and 57% for non-SWD. The new interdisciplinary partnership track increased the number of courses focused on special education to eight and added a reading course focused on SWD. The Reading Instruction in Exceptional Education course provides students with the knowledge, tools, and skills necessary to confidently select, use, and monitor reading strategies and interventions. In addition, the new interdisciplinary track included three courses and one lab in Language Development and Disorders. By offering this option, the program addressed the comorbidity of poor literacy and poor language skills rather than focusing on traditional reading instruction. The new track creates a path for graduates to apply for teaching certification, but unlike the traditional track, students must explore requirements and apply on their own for certification. The track also allows for professional opportunities with non-profits that serve persons with disabilities and nontraditional education agencies serving SWD.

*Exceptional Education and Language Disorders*

## Partnering Programs

The University of Central Florida has a Communication Sciences and Disorders (CSD) program within the College of Health Professions and Sciences. The CSD program offers both a Bachelor of Science and Bachelor of Arts in CSD and an average of 400 undergraduate students enrolled in any year. Unlike many CSD programs, the program is not a restricted access undergraduate degree, meaning anyone meeting the minimum requirements can declare this major and complete the degree requirements. This program prepares students with the foundational knowledge to pursue many career paths. The primary careers for undergraduates in CSD are speech-language pathology and audiology, which require graduate degrees in most states for licensure and national certification through the American Speech-Language-Hearing Association (ASHA). However, in Florida, graduates of the program can work in the public school setting as speech-language therapists (SLTs) for up to two years before being accepted into a master's program. After two years, they have up to five years to complete their graduate degree. Other career paths include applied behavior analysis, traditional and special education, the healthcare industry, non-profit or governmental agencies, and more.

The undergraduate Exceptional Student Education (special education) program, a part of the College of Community Innovation and Education's School of Teacher Education, was relaunched in 2017 after six years of suspended enrollment while the decision was made on whether to continue offering an undergraduate degree. The program enrollment was zero by the 2016 school year, and they offered students interested in special education only a minor in the subject and dual certification with Elementary Education. Ultimately, the program faculty voted to reinstate the program with the agreement that the relaunch would include a "community-embedded" focus. The program grew from 11 students in 2017 to over 100 in 2022. With the program's growth came a recognition that many students were interested in new areas of education and working with persons with disabilities beyond traditional teaching. The new Learning and Language track, an alternative to the traditional certification track, was approved at the University in 2019 and launched in 2020. Approximately half of the initial cohort of 35 students reported on an informal advising survey they do not plan to teach, while the other half intend to apply for certification after graduation.

## History of Collaboration

Collaboration between the Communication Sciences and Disorders program and the Exceptional Student Education program already existed at the University, making the new interdisciplinary program track a more straightforward partnership than others may encounter. In addition, two federally funded grant projects were in place at the graduate level before they created the new undergraduate program track. Project ASD, *Preparing Special Educators and Speech-Language Practitioners in Autism Spectrum Disorders,* is an Office of Special Education-funded personnel preparation project that has been in place since 2004. The project extends financial and academic support to individuals seeking Master's Degrees in either Exceptional Student Education or Communication Sciences and Disorders and includes a Certificate in ASD. The collaborative project has supported over 370 scholars in earning Master's Degrees and completing certification in Exceptional Student Education and State Endorsement in ASD.

Project SPEECH, *Speech-Language Pathologists and Exceptional Educators Collaboration for Children with High-Intensity Needs* is another OSEP-funded project at the university designed to provide training in intensive interventions through an interdisciplinary approach. The university's traditional

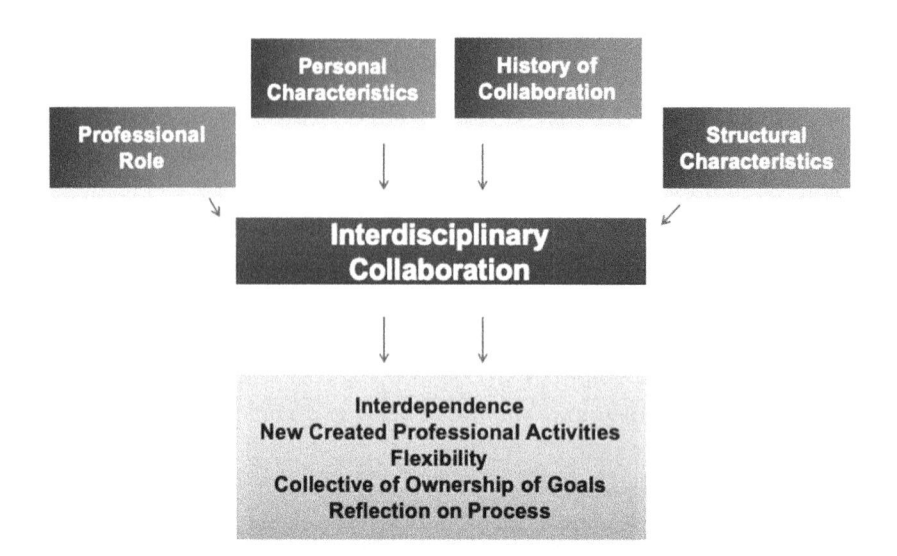

*Figure 1. Model for Interdisciplinary Collaboration. Adapted from Bronstein (2003)*

graduate programs in special education and communication disorders have been enhanced by an interdisciplinary partnership that includes collaborative field-based experiences in high-need school settings (Project Speech, 2022).

Like the existing Masters' collaborative programs, the undergraduate Learning and Language Program is interdependent, with exceptional student education graduates earning a degree in exceptional education from the School of Teaching and Learning and a certificate in Language Development and Disorders from the School of Communication Sciences and Disorders. The new interdisciplinary track offers students an alternative to the certification track and enhanced training in working with SWD. The track increased the number of courses focused on special education to eight and added a reading course focused on SWD. In addition, the new interdisciplinary track includes three courses and one lab in Language Development and Disorders. By offering this option, the new program track addressed the comorbidity of poor literacy and poor language skills rather than focusing on traditional reading instruction. Figure 2 shows key concepts from course syllabi in the traditional reading courses and those from the language disorder track.

## Theoretical Framework

Bronstein's (2003) Model for Interdisciplinary Collaboration provides the theoretical underpinnings for this collaboration. As seen in Figure 1, professional role, personal characteristics, structural characteristics, and a history of collaboration influence the model. The mentioned skills lead to interdependence, newly created professional activities, flexibility, collective ownership of goals, and reflection on the process. The Bronstein (2003) model was adopted to highlight the benefits of integrating special education and communication sciences and disorders, leading to more specialized personnel entering the special education workforce.

*Figure 2. Key content from traditional university reading courses taken by special education majors and content from language disorder courses in the interdisciplinary special education track*

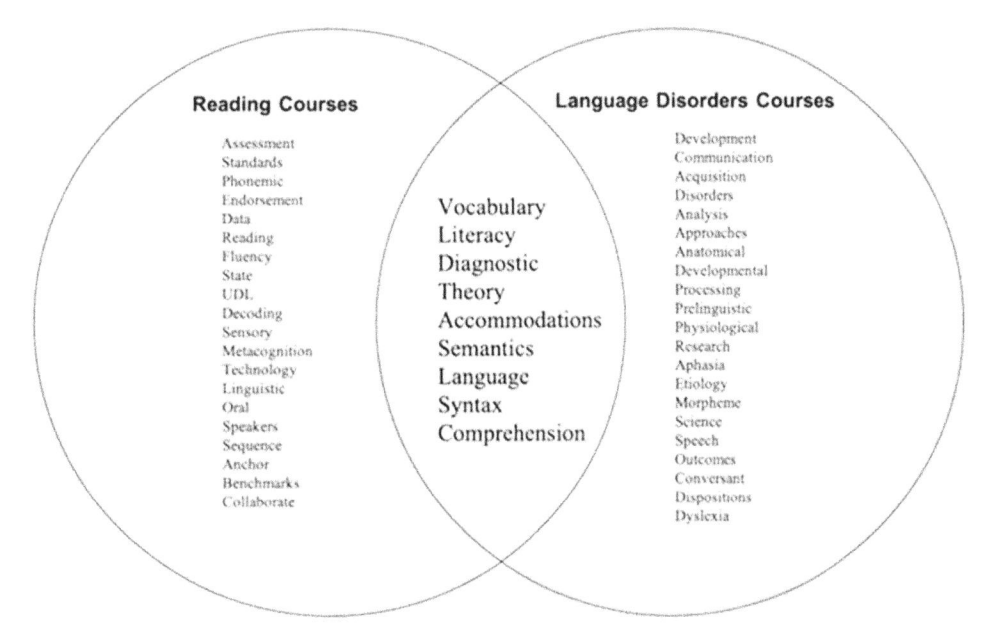

## Online Coursework and Field Experiences

Field experience is the most influential element of teacher preparation (Grant-Smith et al., 2018; Shelton et al., 2020). However, given the rapid shift from face-to-face instruction to remote learning in the early days of the COVID-19 pandemic, educators had to reimagine the practice in higher education quickly. In the past, virtual field experiences (Wilkens et al., 2014), 3D virtual learning environments (Tuncer, 2020), and virtual simulators (Billingsley et al., 2019) were merely supplements to authentic learning. Today, the use of Information and Communication Technology (ICT) to prepare pre-service teachers has become a substantial part of teacher preparation worldwide (Gaudin & Chalies, 2015). In addition, the wide-ranging use of multimedia technology in teacher preparation has enabled instructors to provide future teachers with a high-quality virtual experience that bridges theory-to-practice (Peterson-Ahmed, 2018).

Students have flexibility in the program because university coursework is offered online. This flexibility allows full-time working professionals access to a degree and is ideal for paraprofessionals and other school staff who want to become classroom teachers. In addition, with 18% of classrooms already filled with teachers who gained entry through alternative certification (NCES, 2018), the track offers a pathway for those who wish to not only teach but who specifically wish to enter the profession with skills beyond teachings in a traditional teacher preparation program.

## Remote Community-Embedded Approach

Virtual field experiences have been a part of pre-service teacher preparation programs for over ten years (Compton et al., 2009; Hixon & So, 2009; Wilkens et al., 2014). Using technology to foster an environment that parallels traditional field experiences enables pre-service personnel to practice the skills needed in the profession and explore the career from anywhere (Briant & Crowther, 2020). High-quality virtual field experiences that prepare practitioners to work in diverse and inclusive learning environments are essential. Field experience emphasizes experiential education by allowing students to remotely teach and observe learning and instruction using asynchronous video-conferencing technology. This approach to teacher preparation benefits pre-service teachers by (a) exposing them to various learning/teaching settings and styles, (b) encouraging reflexivity, (c) preparing them cognitively, and (d) providing them with first-hand experience with technology integration (Vu & Fisher, 2021).

The Learning and Language track provides community-embedded virtual field experiences as an effective experiential learning opportunity. Through a collaborative university-school partnership, students take part in a Learning Lab, tutoring elementary students at a local inclusive school. The Learning Lab is a "drop-in" model where classroom teachers can invite university students to address individual elementary students' needs on a one-on-one basis with explicit instructions during the instructional day. University students sign up for two-hour blocks at their convenience using a web-based scheduling program. The entire project design runs through a Google Site, Google Classroom, and Google Form. These platforms offer easy accessibility for all participants and require low maintenance by university staff.

A session begins with the elementary students logging into Zoom via a link provided by their teacher. Next, the Learning Lab coach pairs a university student with a student in the classroom. They then directed the student and the tutor to a Zoom breakout room to begin their session. The Learning Lab coach can view each breakout room's audio and video status through the Zoom breakout room feature. In addition, the Learning Lab coach visits each breakout room throughout the tutoring session to offer tips and help to the university student. At the end of the session, the tutor and student re-enter the main Zoom room, where the student logs out of zoom and contacts their teacher for further instruction. Finally, the Learning Lab coach and tutor debrief as they wait for more students to log in for tutoring.

Community embedded approaches such as the Learning Lab offer authentic learning and increase pre-service personnel's self-efficacy in working in inclusive and diverse learning environments. Remote community-embedded experiential learning enhances students' understanding of real-world environments, expands their capacity to integrate theory and practice, and broadens their global outlook (Hines et al., 2022). The ability to offer quality real-world experiences in a novel uncomplicated way is valuable in educating the special education workforce in the 21st century.

## COURSEWORK

Four courses in Language Development and Disorders make up the certificate: Language Science, Language Development, Language Development Lab, and Language Disorders Across the Lifespan. Table 1 shows the interdisciplinary nature of the course sequence during students' junior year.

Students take part in the coursework with others outside the field of education, primarily those studying to become speech-language pathologists. The collaboration allows special education majors to have discussion opportunities and access to perspectives beyond those within the special education program. Advisors work across colleges to support students requesting and registering for courses. For exceptional education majors, participation in the language development and disorders coursework represents a new opportunity for professional growth and study not previously available. With a highly competitive CSD program, space in these courses would not be open without the collaborative partnership. Access to the

## Exceptional Education and Language Disorders

*Table 1. Interdisciplinary course sequence for the junior year*

| Learning and Language Track ||
|---|---|
| Junior Year- Fall (15 Credits) | Junior Year- Spring (15 Credits) |
| EEX 4070 – Teaching Exceptional Students | EEX 3221- Assessment of Exceptional Students |
| LIN 3713- Language Science | LIN 3716- Language Development |
| EEX 4601- Introduction to Behavior Management | LIN 3716L- Language Development Lab |
| EEX 4250- Reading Instruction in Special Education | TSL 4080- Theory and Practice of Teaching ESOL Students in Schools |
| SPA4400- Language Disorders Across the Lifespan | EEX 3243- Techniques for Exceptional Adolescents- Adults |

language development and disorders course sequence provides new academic opportunities for special education majors, as seen in the course description and objectives presented in Table 2.

## Newly Created Professional Activities

Besides field-based coursework in special education, the language development and disorders coursework include an applied approach. The stand-alone two-credit-hour lab places students in interdisciplinary groups to collect and analyze a language sample from a "typically developing" child. After completing course modules and learning the skills and language needed for the assignment, students collect and transcribe a language sample, submit analyzes across the semester, and complete a project report with a summary at the end of the semester. The following are instructions for a sample activity for the collaborative case study:

1. Arrange a recording session (30-60 minutes). Video record the sampling session.
2. Transcribe the language sample as explicitly directed in the course text.
3. Type your transcript according to transcription conventions, and number the utterances per the same conventions.
4. Complete pertinent analyzes using the forms in Appendix A of your text on dates as directed in the course schedule and modules.
5. Submit the final transcript, all analyzes, and a written summary of the findings to the instructor. In summary, the team comprehensively discusses the appropriateness of the child's language skills relative to their age and a detailed discussion of what was learned about the child from this language sample analysis experience.

Working in interdisciplinary teams allows prospective special education teachers and speech-language pathologists to share ideas and practice collaboration skills. The certificate allows undergraduate (UG) students not majoring in CSD to learn more about these critical aspects of development. Students enrolled in majors might work collaboratively with SLPs to better understand how language develops in young children and what to look for as a possible disorder.

*Table 2. Course descriptions and learning outcomes in Language Disorder Syllabi*

| | |
|---|---|
| **Language Science (3 hrs)**<br>*Course Description*<br>Principles of linguistic processing and the theoretical and biological foundations of language development.<br>*Learner Outcomes*<br>This course describes factors that "set the stage" for language development. Students are introduced to linguistic theory, and the major linguistic systems individuals acquire during this process. Theoretical approaches to studying and describing language and language development are covered. Fundamentals of the anatomical and neural mechanisms that endow humans with the capacity for language are also reviewed. | Following completing this course, students will be able to:<br>  1. Define language processes and linguistic relationships.<br>  2. State principles of language processing.<br>  3. Define basic grammatical concepts.<br>  4. Cite the basic building blocks of language and language acquisition.<br>  5. Explain fundamental linguistic theories.<br>  6. Describe the history and current approaches to the study of language development and the research designs pertinent to such study.<br>  7. Define the major theoretical approaches to the understanding of language development.<br>  8. State the relationships between language and culture.<br>  9. Explain theories of bilingualism and second language acquisition.<br>  10. Describe the anatomical and physiological precursors to language development and their contributions to the process of language acquisition and use. |
| **Language Development (3 hrs)**<br>*Course Description*<br>Study of the language acquisition process from infancy through adulthood and how meaning is conveyed and apprehended through sounds, written symbols, words, and sentences.<br>*Learner Outcomes*<br>The overall objective of this course is to provide students with empirical knowledge of the process of language development from infancy through adulthood. This information will be a foundation for the scientific and clinical understanding of developmental speech and language disorders in children and adults. Students will learn about patterns of language development and literacy acquisition, individual differences in language and literacy development, the impact of culture and linguistic diversity on communication development, and disordered development as it pertains to the clarification of developmental issues. | The successful student will:<br>  1. Summarize the characteristics of the various stages of language development: prelinguistic, early language development from birth to two years, preschool language development and emergent literacy from 3-5 years, early school-age language and literacy development from 6-8 years, later school-age language and literacy development 9-18 years, and aspects of language development in adulthood<br>  2. Relate the social and cognitive bases of language and literacy development<br>  3. Relate the significant patterns of child development to communication development<br>  4. Summarize the effects of prenatal care, environmental issues, and genetics on communication development<br>  5. Explain relationships between spoken and written language and their acquisitions<br>  6. Integrate knowledge of prelinguistic behaviors, early communicative behaviors, and emergent literacy skills in infants and toddlers and relate it to later communication development<br>  7. Integrate knowledge of the oral language and literacy skills in preschool and early school-age children and relate it to later communication development<br>  8. Explain the impact of culture and linguistic diversity on communication development<br>  9. Describe selected aspects of disordered communication development in special populations |
| **Language Development Lab (2 hrs)**<br>*Course Description*<br>Introduction and practice in procedures for sampling, analyzing, and describing language across the lifespan<br>*Learner Outcomes*<br>This course will offer both written lecture-type content and practice in the sampling and analysis of language production. | The successful student will demonstrate knowledge of:<br>  1. Obtaining language samples<br>  2. Transcribing language samples<br>  3. Numbering language transcripts<br>  4. Analyzing language samples for the following:<br>    a. Semantic content of one-word and multi-word productions<br>    b. Meaning relationships in one-word and multi-word productions<br>    c. Vocabulary diversity (Type Token Ratio)<br>    d. Morpheme analysis<br>    e. Syntactic analysis, including: negation, yes/no questions, who questions, noun phrases, verb phrases, complex sentences<br>    f. Pragmatic analysis<br>    g. Narrative analysis<br>  5. Interpreting results of language analyses<br>  6. The features of standardized tests of language abilities in children and adults |
| **Language Disorders Across the Lifespan (3 hrs)**<br>*Course Description*<br>Etiology, assessment, and management of language disorders in children, adolescents and adults, including those associated with ASD, brain injury, learning disabilities, and dementia.<br>*Course Objectives*<br>The objective of this course is to provide students with introductory knowledge on the nature and management of language disorders in preschool-aged children, school-aged children, and adults. Language delays, differences and disorders will be presented according to specific etiological factors and/or specific language features, with particular focus on linguistic features related to developmental language deficits, language-learning disabilities, aphasia, dementia, traumatic brain injury, ADD/ADHD, and reading disorders. Assessment and management issues pertinent to the various diagnostic categories will be discussed. | Following successful completion of this course, students will be able to:<br>  1. Define language processes and linguistic relationships.<br>  2. State principles of language processing.<br>  3. Define basic grammatical concepts.<br>  4. Cite the basic building blocks of language and language acquisition.<br>  5. Explain basic linguistic theories.<br>  6. Describe the history and current approaches to the study of language development and the research designs pertinent to such study.<br>  7. Define the major theoretical approaches to the understanding of language development.<br>  8. State the relationships between language and culture.<br>  9. Explain theories of bilingualism and second language acquisition.<br>  10. Describe the anatomical and physiological precursors to language development and their contributions to the process of language acquisition and use. |

## Adaptability and Collective Ownership of Goals

The program and partnership between ExEd and CSD were based on the belief that teacher preparation programs should provide a more customizable, diverse, and accessible curriculum to address the great demand to strengthen and diversify the skills of persons working with SWD. As a result, the 62-credit program provides pre-service personnel with a customized learning experience. They embedded a wide range of course options into the program catalog to ensure knowledge and skill acquisition in language, learning, and special education as they align with students' future career plans. Additionally, students can enroll in courses with web or instructional video modes. They conduct these fully online modalities via flexible, asynchronous web-based instruction and collaboration using various technologies.

Students also choose three additional specialization courses in an area of choice related to disability. Some students, for example, select American Sign Language, while others choose areas related to social policies, advocacy, and a wide range of other selections. Those students planning to enter the teaching profession are advised to take elementary or secondary teaching method courses as a specialization. Changes in the traditional curriculum provide individuals interested in the special education workforce the autonomy to create their path during their undergraduate programs. Upon graduation, students can choose between multiple pathways. For example, if they choose, students can complete the certification to teach in a classroom or work as a Speech Language Pathologist Assistant (SLPa). In Florida, students can meet these requirements if they complete additional speech and language courses in phonetics, articulation, therapy, and audiometry as their specialization courses. Similar conditions exist in other states.

## Reflection on Process

Each semester during the initial pilot year, faculty from both disciplines meet to discuss the progress of special education majors in the language development and disorders courses. The faculty examined the grades of the special education scholars to ensure satisfactory progress. These discussions also included the need for refining processes, such as providing enrollment codes for students to register for classes across colleges and holding seats in high-enrollment courses. Hence, special education majors have access to advising needs. One change in the partnership after the first semester was for the special education program to provide a doctoral scholar to support the instructor in the language development and disorders courses to offset the increase in instructor demands with larger class sizes. By embedding doctoral students as Graduate Teaching Assistants (GTAs) in the Language Development and Disorders courses, ExEd students receive individualized feedback that pertains to classroom teaching and fieldwork. This extended support also benefits the field by providing doctoral scholars with additional experience in language development and disorders and ensuring they take with them the urgency and need for interdisciplinary collaboration upon completing a Ph.D.

During the initial reflection period, the CSD faculty teaching most of the courses shared his observations from experience:

*I thought in starting this that there might be some sort of difference in how (special education) students would perform compared to CSD students because at that point of (the program) CSD students when they come into our first class "language" they're usually in their second semester of CSD courses. So, you know, they have some background. I was curious in looking at the (special education) student performance to ensure they were learning, what they tell me they're learning. I didn't find a marked distinc-*

*tion between those two types of students. The (special education) students seemed just as interested in the material as the CSD students. Sometimes I wonder if the (special education) students are even more interested or more excited...they seem really, really interested in learning. It feels like new material to them that they just hadn't experienced before. (J. DiNapoli, personal communication, July 21, 2022)*

Both programs continually work to create a more streamlined approach to the university logistics so that the program can continue to grow. CSD faculty has been efficient at providing students with quality online learning opportunities. Enrollment in the certificate program has been consistent before the 2020 pandemic. They are developing learning experiences that bridge theory to practice and promote deep learning online is paramount in the 21st century. The program faculty has mastered cultivating coursework and experiences relevant to current practices in schools and other facilities serving students with disabilities. The CSD Language Lab and ExEd Learning Lab are skillfully developed to assist pre-service personnel with acquiring key professional competencies through authentic learning.

Additionally, students on this track are receiving valuable lessons in online education. Engaging in this fully online degree program also includes learning online learning pedagogy (He, 2014). From the ideological to the practical, faculty model best practices to enhance students' toolkit and confidence in providing services or instruction to individuals with disabilities virtually. With remote jobs becoming increasingly available (Pelletier et al., 2022), teacher education programs must consider what more is needed for pre-service personnel to be competent and competitive in the post-pandemic job market. The value added to students in the Language and Learning track program is immense. The students on this track are preparing to become highly qualified specialists for the future of special education.

One student representative of the initial cohort, a young woman who works as a job coach for young adults with developmental disabilities and runs a group home, does not plan to teach and shared how she felt the language development and disorders courses benefited her during an informal focus group:

*There were some classes that were just so engaging in the actual coursework that I could apply those small skills that they taught, or those lesson plans that they included, to be able to develop my client's own language, or help them find their own form of communication, even though our courses were online. The good thing for me is that it is online and I could make my own schedule. I work over 50 hours a week but being able to customize my own schedule because it's online and still be able to apply the skills, I felt like I was getting the best of both worlds, especially when it was a global pandemic going on. You know, I saw it as an opportunity that I need to grow my career and work on myself. So, this track really gave me that opportunity. (Current student, personal communication, August 6, 2022)*

Overall, when speaking about the interdisciplinary track, the student stated:

*It's definitely given me the opportunity to understand each individual better. No two individuals are the same, just like every other human here. But it's really giving me the opportunity to be able to find out how they're communicating...how they communicate and what's their form of expressing themselves. So, all of the classes really have shown me and given me those tools to be able to apply day to day in the community. (Current student, personal communication, August 6, 2022)*

## CONCLUSION

Despite the myriad needs of SWD and especially the differences among disabilities served, there remains a lack of teacher preparation programs incorporating interdisciplinary programs, creating specialists working with these students to date. Supporting the needs of students with disabilities requires highly qualified and versatile special educators and service providers. The Learning and Language program described in this chapter models the cross-sectoral collaboration necessary to prepare practitioners for the future of special education. The current special education teacher shortage and the increasing number of children born with severe learning disabilities highlight the need for future specialists to be confident and compete in multiple aspects of special education. Interdisciplinary coursework prepares pre-service personnel with the depth of knowledge and skill acquisition necessary to meet the needs of students with disabilities in various careers.

Graduates of this program are prepared for employment in a broad spectrum of the special education workforce, including but not limited to the public school system. The new track creates a path for graduates to apply for teaching certification but also allows for professional opportunities with nonprofits that serve persons with disabilities and nontraditional education agencies serving students with disabilities.

## REFERENCES

Able-Boone, H., Harrison, M. F., & West, T. A. (2002). Interdisciplinary education of social inclusion facilitators in early childhood settings. *Teacher Education and Special Education*, *25*(4), 407–412. doi:10.1177/088840640202500409

Allen-Meares, P., & Pugach, M. (1982). Facilitating interdisciplinary collaboration on behalf of handicapped children and youth. *Teacher Education and Special Education*, *5*(1), 30–36. doi:10.1177/088840648200500106

American Association of Colleges for Teacher Education (AACTE). (2022). *Colleges of education: A national portrait*. American Association of Colleges for Teacher Education. https://www.aacteconnect360.org/viewdocument/colleges-of-education-a-national-p-1

Barr, H. (2002). Interprofessional education: Today, yesterday and tomorrow. London: Learning and Teaching support Network: Centre for Health Sciences and Practice.

Billingsley, G., Smith, S., Smith, S., & Meritt, J. (2019). A systematic literature review of using immersive virtual reality technology in teacher education. *Journal of Interactive Learning Research*, *30*(1), 65–90.

Briant, S., & Crowther, P. (2020). Reimagining internships through online experiences: Multi-disciplinary engagement for creative industries students. *International Journal of Work-Integrated Learning*, *21*(5), 617–628.

Bronstein, L. R. (2003). A model for interdisciplinary collaboration. *Social Work*, *48*(3), 297–306. doi:10.1093w/48.3.297 PMID:12899277

Catts, H. W., Fey, M. E., Weismer, S. E., & Bridges, M. S. (2014). The relationship between language and reading abilities. In Understanding individual differences in language development across the school years (pp. 158-179). Academic Press.

Compton, L., Davis, N., & Mackey, J. (2009). Field experience in virtual schools—To be there virtually. *Journal of Technology and Teacher Education, 17*(4), 459–477.

Dobbs-Oates, J., & Wachter Morris, C. (2016). The case for interprofessional education in teacher education and beyond. *Journal of Education for Teaching, 42*(1), 50–65. doi:10.1080/02607476.2015.1131363

Florida Education Association. (2022). *Teacher and staff shortage.* https://feaweb.org/issues-action/teacher-and-staff-shortage

Gaudin, C., & Chaliès, S. (2015). Video viewing in teacher education and professional development: A literature review. *Educational Research Review, 16*, 41–67. doi:10.1016/j.edurev.2015.06.001

Grant-Smith, D., Zwaan, L. D., Chapman, R., & Gillett-Swan, J. (2018). 'It's the worst, but real experience is invaluable': Preservice teacher perspectives of the costs and benefits of professional experience. In D. Heck & A. Ambrosetti (Eds.), *Teacher education in and for uncertain times* (pp. 15–33). Springer. doi:10.1007/978-981-10-8648-9_2

He, Y. (2014). Universal Design for Learning in an online teacher education course: Enhancing learners' confidence to teach online. *Journal of Online Learning and Teaching, 10*(2), 283–298.

Hines, R., Glavey, E. M., Hanley, W., & Romualdo, A. (2022). Redesigning teacher preparation. *Preparing Quality Teachers: Advances in Clinical Practice*, 459-477.

Hixon, E., & So, H. J. (2009). Technology's role in field experiences for preservice teacher training. *Journal of Educational Technology & Society, 12*(4), 294–304.

Hofstra University. (n.d.). *Speech-language hearing sciences: Teacher of students with speech- language disabilities advanced certification.* https://www.hofstra.edu/speech-language-hearing-sciences/teacher-advanced-certificate.html

Humes, C. W., & Hohenshil, T. H. (1987). Elementary counselors, school psychologists, school social workers: Who does what? *Elementary School Guidance & Counseling, 22*(1), 37–45.

Hyson, M. (Ed.). (2003). *Preparing early childhood professionals: NAEYC's standards for programs.* National Association for the Education of Young Children.

Kilgo, J., & Bruder, M. B. (1997). Creating new visions in institutions of higher education: Interdisciplinary approaches to personnel preparation in early intervention. *Reforming personnel preparation in early intervention: Issues, models, and practical strategies, 8*, 1-101.

Kilgo, J. L. (2006). Transdisciplinary teaming from a higher education perspective. In J. L. Kilgo (Ed.), *Transdisciplinary teaming in early intervention/early childhood special education: Navigating together with families and children* (pp. 77–80). Association for Childhood Education International.

Lam, S. K. Y. (2005). An Interdisciplinary Course to Prepare School Professionals to Collaborate with Families of Exceptional Children. *Multicultural Education, 13*(2), 38–42.

Landers, M. F., Weaver, R., & Tompkins, F. M. (1990). Interdisciplinary collaboration in higher education: A matter of attitude. *Action in Teacher Education, 12*(2), 25–30. doi:10.1080/01626620.1990.10462745

Mason-Williams, L., Bettini, E., Peyton, D., Harvey, A., Rosenberg, M., & Sindelar, P. T. (2020). Rethinking shortages in special education: Making good on the promise of an equal opportunity for students with disabilities. *Teacher Education and Special Education, 43*(1), 45–62. doi:10.1177/0888406419880352

McDonnell, A. P., Hawken, L. S., Johnston, S. S., Kidder, J. E., Lynes, M. J., & McDonnell, J. J. (2014). Emergent Literacy Practices and Support for Children with Disabilities: A National Survey. *Education & Treatment of Children, 37*(3), 495–529. doi:10.1353/etc.2014.0024

Miller, P. S., & Stayton, V. D. (2006). Interdisciplinary teaming in teacher preparation. *Teacher Education and Special Education, 29*(1), 56–68. doi:10.1177/088840640602900107

National Center for Education Statistics, Institute of Education Services. (2022). *Characteristics of public-school teachers who completed alternative route to certification programs.* Institute of Education Services. https://nces.ed.gov/programs/coe/indicator/tlc

National Center on Birth Defects and Developmental Disabilities, Centers for Disease Control and Prevention. (2018). *Data and statistics on autism spectrum disorder.* Centers for Disease Control and Prevention. https://www.cdc.gov/ncbddd/autism/data.html

Odom, S. L., & Wolery, M. (2003). A unified theory of practice in early intervention/early childhood special education: Evidence-based practices. *The Journal of Special Education, 37*(3), 164–173. doi:10.1177/00224669030370030601

Orange County Public Schools. (2022). *Student enrollment summaries.* https://www.ocps.net/departments/student_enrollment/enrollment_summary)

Pelletier, K., McCormack, M., Reeves, J., Robert, J., Arbino, N., Al-Freih, M., Dickson-Deane, C., Guevara, C., Koster, L., Sanchez-Mendiola, M., Skallerup Bessette, L., & Stine, J. (2022). *2022 EDUCAUSE horizon report teaching and learning edition.* https://www.learntechlib.org/p/221033/

Peterson-Ahmad, M. (2018). Enhancing preservice special educator preparation through combined use of virtual simulation and instructional coaching. *Education Sciences, 8*(1), 10. doi:10.3390/educsci8010010

Prasse, D. P., & Fafard, M. B. (1982). Interdisciplinary training and professional interaction: A training challenge. *Teacher Education and Special Education, 5*(1), 26–29. doi:10.1177/088840648200500105

Project Speech. (2022). S*peech-language pathologists and exceptional educators collaborating for children with high-intensity needs.* https://healthprofessions.ucf.edu/communication-sciences-disorders/project-speech/

Pugach, M. C. (1992). Unifying the preservice preparation of teachers. In W. Stainback & S. Stainback (Eds.), *Controversial issues confronting special education: Divergent Perspectives* (pp. 255–270). Allyn and Bacon.

Pugach, M. C., & Allen-Meares, P. (1985). Collaboration at the preservice level: Instructional and evaluation activities. *Teacher Education and Special Education, 8*(1), 3–11. doi:10.1177/088840648500800101

Russell, A. (2019). *OSEP awards $1.3 million to special education professor to advance interdisciplinary personnel preparation.* NEVADAToday. https://www.unr.edu/nevada-today/news/2019/osep-grant

S.B. 1159, 2022 Arizona Fifty-fifth Legislature 2022 Second Regular Session. (AZ, 2022). https://legiscan.com/AZ/text/SB1159/2022

Shelton, R., Kerschen, K., & Cooper, S. (2020). The impact of a varied field experience on preservice teachers' perceptions of their personal growth: A summer mathematics academy for early learners. *Teacher Educator, 55*(1), 28–46. doi:10.1080/08878730.2019.1618424

Silverman, K., Hong, S., & Trepanier-Street, M. (2010). Collaboration of teacher education and child disability health care: Transdisciplinary approach to inclusive practice for early childhood pre-service teachers. *Early Childhood Education Journal, 37*(6), 461–468. doi:10.100710643-010-0373-5

Smith, J. (2010). An interdisciplinary approach to preparing early intervention professionals: A university and community collaborative initiative. *Teacher Education and Special Education, 33*(2), 131–142. doi:10.1177/0888406409357546

Stayton, V., & Bruder, M. B. (1999). Early intervention personnel preparation for the new millennium: Early childhood special education. *Infants and Young Children, 12*(1), 59–69. doi:10.1097/00001163-199907000-00009

Stayton, V. D. (2015). Preparation of early childhood special educators for inclusive and interdisciplinary settings. *Infants and Young Children, 28*(2), 113–122. doi:10.1097/IYC.0000000000000030

Sutcher, L., Darling-Hammond, L., & Carver-Thomas, D. (2019). Understanding teacher shortages: An analysis of teacher supply and demand in the United States. *Education Policy Analysis Archives, 27*(35), 35. Advance online publication. doi:10.14507/epaa.27.3696

Texas Christian University. (n.d.). *Deaf and hard of hearing: Bring language and understanding to those without access to sound.* https://www.tcu.edu/academics/programs/deaf-and- hard-of-hearing-studies.php#accd17e202-interdisciplinary-focus

Tuncer, C. A. N. (2020). Training preservice english language teachers with 3-D machinima. *The Turkish Online Journal of Educational Technology, 19*(1), 53–65.

U.S. Department of Education. (2017). *Office of civil rights data collection.* https://ocrdata.ed.gov/profile/9/district/31634/studentswith disabilitiesidea

U.S. Department of Education. (2021). *43rd Annual Report to Congress on the Implementation of the Individuals with Disabilities Education Act, 2021.* Author.

Veterans Can Teach, H. B. 573, 2022 Florida House of Representatives. (FL, 2022).

Vu, P., & Fisher, C. E. (2021). Does virtual field experience deliver? An examination into virtual field experience during the pandemic and its implications for teacher education programs. *Open Praxis, 13*(1), 117-125. https://www.proquest.com/scholarly-journals/does-virtual-field-experience-deliver-examination/docview/2550671348/se-2?accountid=10003

Welch, M., & Sheridan, S. (1993). Educational partnerships in teacher education: Reconceptualizing how teacher candidates are prepared for teaching students with disabilities. *Action in Teacher Education, 15*(3), 35–46. doi:10.1080/01626620.1993.10463162

Welch, M., Sheridan, S. M., Fuhriman, A., Hart, A. W., Connell, M. L., & Stoddart, T. (1992). Preparing professionals for educational partnerships: An interdisciplinary approach. *Journal of Educational & Psychological Consultation, 3*(1), 1–23. doi:10.12071532768xjepc0301_1

Wilkens, C., Eckdahl, K., Morone, M., Cook, V., Giblin, T., & Coon, J. (2014). Communication, community, and disconnection: Preservice teachers in virtual school field experiences. *Journal of Educational Technology Systems, 43*(2), 143–157. doi:10.2190/ET.43.2.c

# Chapter 15
# Interdisciplinary Training in Intensive Intervention for Students With Disabilities and Multi-Lingual Youth

**Kristi S. Hagans**
*California State University, Long Beach, USA*

**Catherine Richards-Tutor**
*California State University, Long Beach, USA*

## ABSTRACT

*This chapter describes an interdisciplinary training project funded by OSEP to support school psychology and dual credential teacher candidates to effectively work with and provide inclusive educational supports to students with disabilities, including multilingual youth, with intensive academic needs. The authors describe the need for the project and provide an overview of the conceptual framework and training components, such as didactic and experiential learning, as well as key elements of the project, including evidence-based assessment and instruction and culturally responsive and sustaining practices. Formative and summative measures used to measure candidate outcomes are described, and preliminary results are provided.*

In the United States, 10.2% of public-school students are considered multi-lingual (National Center for Education Statistics, 2021). Of these, approximately 5 million multi-lingual learners (MLLs), or more than 76%, identify as Hispanic/Latinx, with Spanish as the most prevalent language spoken (U. S. Department of Education, 2020). Student with disabilities make up about 10% of students in U. S. public school, and approximately 10% of students who receive special education services are also designated as a MLL (National Council on Disabilities, 2018). This number varies widely by state. For example, in California, 23% of students were designated MLL in 2015-2016, with 31% identified as having a disability. In West Virginia, by comparison, only 7% of students who were designated MLL also received

DOI: 10.4018/978-1-6684-6438-0.ch015

special education services. While Hispanic and Latinx students may qualify under any of the 13 disability categories in Individuals with Disabilities Education Act (IDEA, 2004), data from the Office of Special Education Program (OSEP) show that of students who identify as Hispanic or Latinx with disabilities, 45% have the designation of Specific Learning Disability (OSEP, 2019).

Data from national assessments underscore that the instructional needs of students with disabilities and MLLs are not being met. The most recent results of the National Assessment of Educational Progress (NAEP, 2019) show that 12% of students with disabilities and 10% of MLLs in fourth grade performed at or above proficient in reading compared to 39% of both students without disabilities and non-MLLs in the same grade. In math, 17% of students with disabilities and 16% of MLLs in fourth grade performed at or above proficient in math compared to 45% of students without disabilities and 44% of non-MLLs. Furthermore, the gap in fourth grade reading and math performance between students with disabilities and those without disabilities has been consistent or increased since 2015. Similarly, the gap in fourth grade reading performance between MLLs and mono-lingual youth has remained the same since 2015 and has steadily increased in math since 2003.

Meeting the needs of MLLs who have intense academic needs and/or disabilities is complex. These students are simultaneously learning to speak, listen, read, and write in English. The assessments used to find areas of strength and need are rarely normed on MLL populations and do not consider variations in language and culture (Ortiz, 2019). These challenges coupled with a small research base on effective interventions for MLLs makes meeting the instructional needs of these students difficult. Multi-tiered systems of support (MTSS) is one potential way that states, districts, and schools can support MLLs with intense academic needs and/or with disabilities.

Current OSEP model demonstration projects focus on developing, implementing, and evaluating MTSS models for MLLs: Project Elite2 at University of Texas, Austin; Project Ellipses at American Institutes for Research; and Project Lee at Portland State University (Multitiered Systems of Supports for English Learners, 2020). These model demonstration projects highlight the need for MLLs to have instruction that is evidence-based and culturally responsive. Together the projects outline key features of instruction for MLLs at each tier of MTSS. For example, Tier 1 core instruction for MLLs should include high quality differentiated instruction in language and literacy; culturally responsive pedagogy; meaningful opportunities for students to practice listening, speaking, reading, and writing; and first language supports. Tier 1 also includes English as a second language instruction and supports, as well as having teachers who are knowledgeable about native and second language development (Multitiered System of Supports for English Learners, 2020). For Tier 2 supplemental supports and Tier 3 intensive supports, instruction for MLLs should include all elements of Tier 1 as well as a focus on oral language and academic language development, and regular use of data for instructional decision-making.

To effectively meet the instructional needs of students with disabilities and MLLs in inclusive education environments via an MTSS model, schools need highly trained teachers and student support specialists who can collect and interpret instructionally relevant data, and design and deliver intensive, evidence-based and culturally responsive instruction (Project Elite2, Project Ellipses, & Project Lee, 2018). Although special education teachers and school psychologists are uniquely positioned to identify and support struggling learners, their training has not traditionally focused on serving all learners, they have received little training and practice in interdisciplinary collaboration, and their roles in schools tend to be narrowly focused. In a recent survey of school psychology practitioners, for example, almost 90% of respondents reported spending a "great deal of time" engaged in special education related assessments whereas 22% reported spending "quite a bit" or a "great deal of time" providing academic intervention

(Farmer et al., 2021). This contrasts with the National Association of School Psychologists' (NASP) Model for Comprehensive and Integrated School Psychological Services (2020), which serves to guide pre-service training and enhance recognition of school psychologists' skills and expertise, which includes collaborative consultation, data-based decision making, and academic instruction.

While there is a great need for highly prepared special education teachers, there is a specific need to have dual licensed teachers who are prepared to work with all students in inclusive school settings. Dual licensed teachers are distinctly trained to meet the needs of all learners across school settings and are highly trained to provide interventions through MTSS models (Brownell et al., 2019; Richards-Tutor et al., 2021). Collaboration is a necessary skill for teachers working in a MTSS framework and is considered a high leverage practice for special education teachers (McLeskey et al., 2017). Additionally, dual licensed teachers have unique training and clinical practice experiences in that they learn to collaborate from the role of a general education and special education teacher. However, it is rare that, in these experiences, they collaborate regularly with school psychologists.

This chapter describes an interdisciplinary training program designed and co-directed by special education and school psychology faculty at California State University, Long Beach (CSULB) to advance the training of dual credentialed general and special education teachers and school psychologists to meet the intensive instructional needs of students with disabilities and MLLs. The project was developed to address the following practice and personnel needs: 1) gap in service for students with disabilities and MLLs who are in need of intensive, evidence-based, data-driven instruction; 2) lack of interdisciplinary collaboration across general and special education teachers and school psychologists to meet the complex instructional needs of students with disabilities and MLLs; and 3) increase the number of school psychologists and dual credentialed teachers who are skilled in providing evidence-based, intensive academic intervention within a MTSS service delivery model. The training program is based on the NASP Model for Comprehensive and Integrative School Psychological Services (2020); Council for Exceptional Children Initial Preparation Standards (2015); and resources developed by the National Center on Intensive Intervention; and Innovation Configurations developed by the Center on Collaboration for Effective Educator Development, Accountability, and Reform.

## Conceptual Framework

Children and youth with disabilities who have high intensity needs often require the combined expertise of numerous professionals. Despite this, school personnel primarily serve children with disabilities in traditional ways using discipline-specific practices (Pfeiffer, et al., 2019). Discrepancies between desired and provided services are likely due to several reasons, such as differing professional cultures and philosophical orientations, perceived responsibilities, stereotypical views of professional roles, and lack of communication (Weist et al., 2012). Additionally, educator preparation programs rarely provide didactic and experiential opportunities to learn with and about other professionals and disciplines other than their own (Miller et al., 2014), making it less likely that school professionals will engage in interdisciplinary practices in schools.

Interdisciplinary approaches to personnel preparation, often referred to as inter-professional education (IPE), provide students opportunities to work alongside and learn about professionals they are likely to encounter in employment settings (Bridges et al., 2011; Rosenberg et al., 2015). IPE models generally consist of cross-disciplinary coursework, shared field work experiences, interdisciplinary courses, case study discussions, and role plays and simulations to develop a team-based, collaborative approach to service delivery (Chen et al., 2022). The interdisciplinary training project at CSULB reflects a combination of two best practice models of IPE described by Bridges et al. (2011): didactic and community-based learning. While both models emphasize a commitment to understanding one's professional identity, a simultaneous focus is on awareness, appreciation, and knowledge of other school professionals' roles. (Timm & Schnepper, 2021; Wharton & Burg, 2017).

In the present project, pre-service dual credential and school psychology candidates engaged in didactic learning experiences that included cross-disciplinary course work in the dual credential and school psychology programs, and completion of modules developed by the National Center on Intensive Intervention (e.g., *Taxonomy of Intervention Intensity*) and IRIS Center (e.g., *Teaching English Language Learners: Effective Instructional Practices*). Candidates also attended monthly interdisciplinary seminars where topics included team building, common roles of participating pre-service professionals, shared values and ethics, and common and complementary skill sets. Community-based IPE experiences included year-long interdisciplinary fieldwork placements in partner schools where students were provided supervised opportunities to engage in interdisciplinary practices, such as planning and implementing data collection protocols; collaboratively identifying intervention targets and developing lesson plans; and attending grade-level and leadership meetings to further plan and problem-solve with school teams.

## Interdisciplinary Training Foci

To prepare school psychologists and dual credentialed teachers to engage in interdisciplinary collaboration and design and deliver individualized, data-informed, evidence-based tiered instruction to improve outcomes for students with disabilities and MLLs, the following scholar competency areas guided the design, delivery, and evaluation of the interdisciplinary training project:

1. Intensive and individualized academic assessment and intervention
2. Culturally and linguistically responsive instructional practices
3. Interdisciplinary collaboration

**Intensive and individualized academic assessment and intervention.** To effectively engage in instructionally useful assessment practices and implement intensive, evidence-based academic instruction, training focused on three competencies: 1) data-based decision making; 2) tiered instructional models; and 3) intensive assessment and intervention strategies.

*Data-based problem solving.* Problem solving is a systemic approach to identifying, analyzing, and finding solutions to problems based on data. Key steps in problem solving include: 1) identifying if a problem exists; 2) analyzing the problem; 3) implementing solutions; and 4) evaluating the effectiveness of solutions (Shinn, 2008). To effectively engage in problem-solving, educators need to be able to identify the type of data (e.g., individual, school-wide), assessment method (e.g., General Outcome Measure, Mastery Measure), and assessment tool (e.g., DIBELS; AIMSweb) appropriate for use at each phase of problem-solving. Practitioners also need to be skilled in collecting and analyzing data to identify who needs intervention and their instructional needs, apply evidence-based solutions, and evaluate their effects (Deno & Fuchs, 1987).

***Tiered instructional models.*** To successfully advocate for and implement services and supports in inclusive settings that meet the needs of all students, including students with disabilities and MLLs, practitioners need to be well-versed in assumptions and components of a tiered service delivery model, as well as principles of effective instructional design and delivery and research-validated practices and strategies (Archer & Hughes, 2010; Hughes et al., 2018). With this knowledge, teachers and school psychologists can effectively collaborate in implementing and evaluating tiered instructional activities and adjust instruction to meet the intensive academic needs of students with disabilities and MLLs. Knowledge and experience in using tools to monitor intervention fidelity (e.g., observation, checklist protocols) and use of specific strategies to increase fidelity across tiers of instruction (e.g., intervention scripts, performance feedback) are more likely to lead to evidence-based interventions implemented as planned (Collier-Meek et al., 2020; Noell et al., 2017).

***Intensive evidence-based assessment and instruction in reading and math.*** To support students with intensive academic needs, practitioners need to know how children's reading and math skills develop, skills to target for intervention, evidence-based instructional practices, and how to identify skill gaps to inform instructional planning (National Center for Intensive Intervention, 2016; St. Martin et al., 2020; Weingarten et al., 2019). In so doing, teachers and school psychologists need to know how to identify and collect instructionally-relevant data to identify gaps in student skills and knowledge, conduct functional academic assessments (e.g., Brief Experimental Analysis, error analysis) to identify and validate factors that may explain a student's response to instruction (e.g., skills vs. performance problem; missing prerequisite skills), collect progress monitoring data to adjust and individualize intervention, and increase intervention intensity by increasing the frequency of intervention, opportunities to respond, and/or alignment between skills taught and instructional needs (Austin, Vaughn, & McClelland, 2017; Fuchs et al., 2017; Lemons et al., 2014; Powell & Stecker, 2014).

**Culturally responsive and sustaining instructional practices.** For students from diverse cultural and linguistic backgrounds, learning can be challenging because the "culture" of school may be in contrast with their cultural experiences (Aceves & Orosco, 2014). Educators who use culturally responsive and sustaining practices (CRSPs; Ladson-Billings, 1995; Paris, 2012) value students' cultures and see culture as an asset rather than a deficit to learning. CRSPs are not a set, or checklist, of practices that teachers "do" but a set of beliefs and values about teaching and learning, and about students, families, and communities (Howard, 2020). CRSPs provide a lens for viewing students' cultural and linguistic skills and abilities as assets in which to build from while emphasizing increased student academic achievement (Howard, 2020). An essential element of CRSP is that student experiences, prior knowledge, and interest are utilized to support instruction. This culture-cognition connection is used to inform instructional practices (Hammond, 2014), increase understanding of a student's culture, and viewculture, including language, as an asset to designing and implementing effective instruction and interventions for MLLs.

***Instructional supports for multi-lingual learners.*** To appropriately and effectively incorporate language acquisition and development techniques into instruction, practitioners need to attend to tiered instructional elements specific to meeting the needs of MLLs, including implementing evidenced-based instructional strategies and supports for MLLs, viewing a students' first language as an asset, building social connections with students, and having a deep understanding of students' multiple identities, including race, culture, ethnic and social identities, including disability (Linan-Thompson et al., 2018). For example, Project Lee, a model demonstration research project on MTSS for MLLs, endorses six important principles in designing interventions for MLLs: a) relevant content that reflect students' cultural and linguistic backgrounds, b) students' prior knowledge and lived experiences, c) active and equitable participation in instruction, d) high-quality linguistic input, and (e) structured language practice and high-quality instructional discourse (Multitiered Systems of Supports for English Learners, 2020).

## Interdisciplinary Collaboration

Interdisciplinary collaboration is defined as a mutual, reciprocal effort among professionals, families, and other caregivers to deliver effective interventions to children for their increased physical, emotional, and academic well-being (see Dettmer et al., 1996). In the field of public health, a growing body of literature suggests that pre-professional healthcare workers who engage in interdisciplinary educational experiences engage in more collaborative practice behaviors that result in greater professional satisfaction and improve client outcomes than those who do not participate in interdisciplinary training (Buelow et al., 2008; Reeves et al., 2011). Opportunities to learn *with*, *from* and *about* various school disciplines is necessary to foster collective responsibility, interprofessional communication, and appreciation of how other disciplines fit within and complement one's 'home' discipline (Zanotti et al., 2015). Knowledge of professional roles and shared values, ethics, and skill sets are needed to engage in cooperative and respectful interdisciplinary collaboration.

*System change.* To implement assessment and intervention practices that improve outcomes for students with disabilities and MLLs, school-based practitioners need to know how to implement and support implementation of evidence-based innovations at a school-wide level. Drawing from implementation science, it is necessary for practitioners to engage in activities that increase the likelihood of successful implementation of innovations, such as forming and supporting an implementation team, assessing contextual fit of a proposed innovation in a local education setting, and co-learning and designing implementation practices (Metz et al., 2020). Additionally, knowledge of attitudes such as trust, motivation, and commitment to equity that help build the capacity of systems to effectively implement evidence-based practices and improve outcomes for all learners are necessary pre-requisites if practitioners are to engage in innovative practices to increase outcomes for students with disabilities and MLLs.

## Interdisciplinary Training Components

This project has three key training components that allow scholars to experience working and learning in team environments like those in which they are likely to work once employed in the field (Smith, 2010). In the following section, we describe these components (e.g., cross-discipline coursework, monthly seminars and activities, and school-based interdisciplinary fieldwork) and share specific examples from the first cohort of students who completed the program.

**Shared coursework.** Scholars in the project take two courses together: one from the dual credential program and one from the school psychology program. The course in the dual credential program, EDUC 454 Supporting the Academic and Language Development of English Language Learners, focuses on culturally responsive pedagogy and understanding connections between language and disability. In school psychology, EDP 536 Collaborative Consultation in Schools, focuses on forming partnerships in school settings to solve problems. We chose these specific courses based on the knowledge and skills scholars would gain from the content as well as the assignments and activities they are required to complete in the courses. Scholars take EDUC 454 in their first year of their program. This course is foundational to understanding the needs of MLLs and the instructional and assessment practices most effective for these students. In the course, scholars collect student data using both language and academic assessments and design a lesson plan using the Sheltered Instruction Observation Protocol (SIOP, Echevarria et al., 2017).

In EDP 536, completed during either the second or third year of their respective programs, centers on theories (e.g., Behavioral Consultation, Multi- and Cross-cultural Consultation) and practices of collaborative consultation in schools, and personal competencies related to effective collaboration (e.g., communication, interpersonal skills). Students are required to complete a case study where they engage in a collaborative partnership with a school professional (e.g., teacher) or parent to address an identified problem (e.g., academic, behavioral, social-emotional). Consultation logs and a final case study report are submitted.

**Project seminar activities.** Project participants attend monthly interdisciplinary seminars together across their 3 years in their respective programs. Each month, scholars complete readings and/or modules related to intensive intervention and culturally responsive instruction and interventions. For example, all scholars receive the book *Response to Intervention and English Learners: Using the SIOP Model* (Echevarria et al., 2014) which walks readers through the steps of academic intervention for MLLs, from data collection through intervention to referral for special education. Materials and modules from the National Center on Intervention (https://intensiveintervention.org), Multi-tiered Systems of Support for English Learners (https://www.mtss4els.org), and IRIS Center (https://iris.peabody.vanderbilt.edu/) supplement content delivered in seminar.

During seminar, scholars engage in both small and large group discussions on topics related to MTSS, intensive intervention, meeting the instructional needs of MLLs, and how to apply what they are learning in real-world school settings. Seminars also are used to directly support scholars' interdisciplinary fieldwork. For example, several seminar sessions are devoted to training scholars on administering, scoring, and interpreting Curriculum-based Measures (CBM) and collecting and analyzing benchmark and progress monitoring data to inform instruction. Seminars that follow are used to examine data, consider instructional changes, develop lesson plans, and problem solve in teams.

**School-based interdisciplinary fieldwork.** Scholars complete weekly interdisciplinary field work hours, typically 4 hours per week, in addition to the practica and fieldwork hours they complete for their respective programs. Fieldwork placements include 3-5 school sites in districts that partner closely with the dual credential program. Scholars are put into teams at each site that are then broken into cross program dyads or triads who collaborate in data collection and intervention implementation at the school site. One example of this is the partnership we formed with Palomar Elementary School (a pseudonym). At Palomar, faculty project directors met with the school principal to identify classrooms or grade levels with the greatest academic needs. After discussion, it was decided that the project would focus on third grade. Two dyads (one school psychology student and one dual credential student) were assigned to the school and delivered intervention Mondays and Fridays; specifically, one dyad on Monday and the other on Friday. Dyads collaborated weekly to ensure screening, diagnostic, and progress monitoring data were collected, and appropriate intervention was provided as seamlessly as possible. Specifically, scholars collected and shared reading benchmark data (e.g., DIBELS) on all third-grade students with teachers and collaborated on forming intervention groups based on need and identify intervention targets. Dyads worked together to develop weekly intervention lessons and progress monitor students in intervention biweekly for the duration of the school year.

## Assessment of Project Scholar Competencies

Formative and summative assessments are used across phases of the project to evaluate the short and long-term effects of the project on scholars' acquisition of competencies. Many of the measures assess more than one scholar competency, include both qualitative and quantitative data, and include multiple informants.

**Formative assessments.** To assess scholars' initial and developing knowledge and skills related to intensive assessment and intervention and culturally- and linguistically- responsive practices, observations of project scholars engaged in interdisciplinary fieldwork settings are conducted, intervention data are reviewed and discussed in seminar, and end-of-semester case study presentations are conducted. Written evaluations completed by dual credential master teachers/university supervisors and school psychology practica and internship supervisors are used to evaluate scholars' acquisition and attainment of competencies related to assessment and instruction, culturally- and linguistically responsive instruction, and interdisciplinary collaboration. An informal survey regarding scholars' interdisciplinary collaboration experiences also is conducted.

*Observations.* As described above, project scholars provide both small group targeted intervention for 2 years to students with disabilities and MLLs in an elementary school setting. Each month project faculty observe intervention sessions and provide feedback to scholar dyads regarding their use of explicit instructional strategies, opportunities for students to respond to instruction, appropriateness of skills targeted for intervention, and student engagement during lessons. Following intervention, oral and/or written feedback is provided to scholars regarding what went well and what could be improved upon. Problem-solving and assistance in modifying lesson plans and obtaining needed resources, if needed, also are provided.

*Interdisciplinary collaboration survey.* At the end of the year, scholars complete an anonymous survey regarding their perceptions of the interdisciplinary work they engaged in over the course of a year. Scholars are asked, "What did you learn from working with your peers across programs?" "What was challenging about that work?" and "How do you think it will benefit you in your future position?"

*Data reviews.* During monthly project seminar meetings, often in small groups, project scholars informally share student intervention data and problem-solve with project faculty and peers regarding the effectiveness of implemented interventions. Data collected during problem identification and analysis phases of problem-solving (e.g., extant data, error analysis data) as well as formative evaluation data (e.g., progress monitoring data) are discussed. This informal assessment often coincides with observations of intervention groups and is used to provide feedback to individual scholars and dyads regarding their assessment and intervention activities. Data reviews also serve to prepare dyads for the end-of-semester case study presentations.

*End-of-semester case study presentations.* At the end of fall and spring semesters, each scholar dyad presents information regarding the targeted student or student group they provided intervention, including relevant student characteristics, instructional strategies implemented and rationale for their use, and any modifications made. Dyads are also required to summarize data collected during each phase of the problem-solving process using tables and graphs and compare student performance to pre-intervention and similar peers (e.g., grade, English language proficiency). At the end of fall, specifically, and based on data presented, dyads provide an action plan detailing targeted skills and instructional strategies to be implemented the following semester. At the end of the academic year, student progress monitoring data over the entire school year are presented and conclusions regarding students' overall response to intervention, what worked, challenges experienced, and what they would do differently are discussed.

*Master teacher and university supervisor evaluations.* In the dual credential program, students in their second year complete 1 year of student teaching with a master teacher, with one semester working with a general education teacher and the other semester with a special education teacher. Student teachers are observed a minimum of six times during a semester by both a university supervisor and their master teacher using an observation protocol used to inform mid-semester and end-of-semester evaluations. Evaluations are based on high leverage practices in special education (McLeskey et al., 2017) and state standards for the teaching profession (Commission on Teacher Credentialing, 2009). The evaluation tool consists of five items that reflect competencies targeted in this project: 1) create safe, inclusive, culturally responsive learning environments; 2) address the needs of MLLs and students with special needs to provide equitable access to the content; 3) collect and analyze assessment data from a variety of sources and use those data to inform instruction and review data, both individually and with colleagues, to monitor student learning; 4) select, adapt, and use a repertoire of evidence-based instructional strategies to advance learning; and 5) collaborate with colleagues and engage in the broader professional community to support teacher and student learning. Each skill is rated on a 4-point scale: (1) not meeting expectations for novice educators, (2) developing skills to meet expectations of a novice educator, (3) meeting expectations as a novice educator, and (5) exceeding expectations of a novice educator.

*School psychology practica and internship supervisor evaluations.* School psychology project scholars are rated by their fieldwork supervisors on a variety of skills at the end of their 2$^{nd}$ and 3$^{rd}$ years in the program. On both the practica and internship supervisor evaluations, three items reflect competencies targeted by the project: 1) effectively collaborates to plan, implement, problem-solve, and make decisions regarding instruction, interventions, and services; 2) implements and evaluates evidence-based academic instruction and programs; and 3) effectively engages in activities to support MLLs. Each skill is rated on a 3-point scale: (1) minimally, developing, (2) developing, (3) well-developed, and (4) outstanding.

**Summative Assessments.** Summative assessments of project scholars' skills related to the above competencies include a final fieldwork intervention case study report, effect size estimates using intervention case study progress monitoring data.

*Intervention case study – school psychology.* During their final fieldwork experience, school psychology scholars complete an academic intervention case study with an individual or group of students. Case study requirements include collecting reliable, valid, and functional academic assessment data to operationalize the problem and obtain baseline data on a targeted academic behavior; implementing or collaborating on the implementation of targeted, appropriate, evidence-based academic intervention; measuring the fidelity intervention implementation; collecting and graphing progress monitoring data; and on-going review of progress monitoring data to inform and tailor intervention based on student need. An intervention case study rubric modeled after a scoring guide developed by NASP to evaluate candidate portfolios for National Certification in School Psychology (NCSP) is used to score and provide feedback to scholars.

*Intervention case study – dual credential.* In their first year, second semester of the program students in the dual credential program conduct an intervention case study project that includes a small group of 3-6 students. The case study assignment requires students to collect data using curriculum-based reading measures, identify students' areas of need, collaborate with peers to develop appropriate reading intervention lessons that are culturally responsive, and monitor student progress throughout the intervention. A rubric guided by high leverage practices (McLeskey et al., 2017) and state standards

(Commission on Teacher Credentialing, 2009) was developed by dual credential program faculty and is used to score case study projects.

*Effect size estimates.* To examine the impact of school psychology scholars on PreK-12 student learning, effect size estimates are calculated using data from the intervention case study. Baseline and progress monitoring data for each targeted skill to calculate percent non-overlapping data (PND), a widely used statistic to calculate effect size in single case designs (Hagans & Powers, 2015). PND is calculated by determining the proportion of progress monitoring data points that exceed the largest baseline datum. PND is easy to interpret in that it closely mirrors grade percentages. According to Scruggs and Mastropieri (1998), PND scores above 85% indicate a significant effect; scores between 65% and 84% indicate a moderate effect; and scores below 64% are of questionable impact. Although not without limitations, such as being oversensitive to atypical baseline data because all data in a baseline phase are not included in the calculation, PND is a simple method for calculating impact on student academic outcomes (Busse, Kratochwill, & Elliot, 1995; Wolery et al., 2010).

*System change project.* Through readings and discussion, scholars learn of the multiple factors that influence successful implementation of an innovation and use this information to complete a system change project at their final fieldwork placement (e.g., internship or student teaching). Specifically, scholars form an implementation team, and conduct a needs assessment (e.g., *Self-Assessment of Problem-Solving Implementation,* Florida Problem-Solving/RtI Statewide Project; *MTSS Self-Assessment*, Panorama Education) to identify how their site is meeting the instructional needs of their students, particularly students with disabilities and MLLs. Based on these data and with their implementation team, project scholars identify and define an innovation to implement at their school site that shows promise in improving achievement outcomes. Scholars collect baseline data, draft a year-end goal, and support school staff in implementing the innovation via professional development and coaching, and collecting data to inform implementation (Collier-Meek et al., 2016). Permanent products for the system change project include two sets of minutes from implementation team meetings and a PowerPoint presentation identifying core features of the targeted innovation, baseline data and goals, current stage of system change implementation, challenges and sources of support, and next steps.

## Scholar Outcomes

Formative and summative outcome data for both school psychology and dual credential scholars and discussion of implications for subsequent interdisciplinary training projects are provided. It should be noted that the timing of assessments for each group of scholars may differ due to varied program requirements in the two respective programs.

**Intervention case studies and effect size data**. The first cohort of school psychology students (n=3) completed the academic intervention case study at their internship placement in fall 2021 or spring 2022. One school psychology project participant in the first cohort left the project and program after the second year for family reasons and thus, did not complete the intervention case study. Although a small sample size, all school psychology scholars received a proficient score (e.g., 3 or 4) on each section of the case study and received an overall passing score (e.g., 23 or above) on the rubric, range 24-26. See Appendix A for NCSP Case Study Rubric. Targeted academic behaviors included accurate and fluent decoding, fluency in reading connected text, and math computation. PND estimates indicate scholars had a significant (e.g., 100%) to moderate (71%) effect on targeted academic behaviors.

Due to school closures from the COVID-19 pandemic, dual credential students in the first and second cohorts either were unable to complete the intervention case study during their student teaching or left the project and program altogether for family, financial, and/or personal reasons (N=6). Intervention case study data are provided, instead, for two dual credential teacher candidates from the third cohort who completed the intervention case study in spring 2022. Both achieved a proficient score on each section of the case study rubric (e.g., score of '3' or '4') and received an overall passing score (e.g., 35 or above) on the rubric, range 40-42. See Appendix A for Urban Dual Credential Program Literacy Intervention Case Study Rubric. Effects size estimates for both case studies indicate scholars had a significant (100% PND) to moderate (67% PND) effect on students' academic achievement. Both case studies focused on increasing elementary students' reading skills.

**Master teacher and field supervisor evaluations.** Evaluations of dual credential and school psychology scholars by their respective field supervisor or master teacher are summarized below.

*Dual credential scholars.* Data across three cohorts of dual credential teacher scholars who completed both semesters of student teaching (N=5) indicated that project scholars either met (3) or exceeded (4) expectations on all five items related to the project: learning environments, needs of MLLs, assessment, evidence-based practices, and collaboration. Overall mean rating across items was 3.8, range 3.6-4.0. These data include responses from both master teachers and university supervisors. There were no differences in ratings across master teachers and university supervisors on these items.

*School psychology scholars.* Fieldwork supervisor evaluations for the first cohort of school psychology scholars (N=3) during their practica (year 2) and internship (year 3) were reviewed. At the end of practica, scholar mean ratings for collaboration was 3.0; implements evidence-based interventions was 2.6; and supports MLLs was 2.6; range 2.0-4.0. Mean end-of-year ratings of school psychology interns by fieldwork supervisors was 4.0 for collaboration; 3.5 for implements evidence-based intervention; and 4.0 for supports MLLs; range 3.0-4.0. As expected, practica students received lower ratings compared to interns considering they had not received the full 3-years of project and program training.

**Interdisciplinary collaboration survey.** In an anonymous survey conducted in year 3 of the project, school psychology and dual credential project scholars in cohorts 1-3 overwhelmingly indicated that the interdisciplinary collaboration aspect of the project was the "best part" of the project and that they not only "learned about each other's roles and benefited from each other's experiences and expertise," but felt that "collaboration benefitted the students in the schools they served." The survey also highlighted challenges in finding time for collaboration across disciplines to develop intervention lessons each week. Almost every scholar positively endorsed that interdisciplinary work will benefit them in their positions in schools, they have tools to collaborate with others, and have a better understanding of who they can collaborate with to help students succeed.

## Conclusions

The goals of this project were to provide training to increase school psychology and dual credential candidates' knowledge and experience in interdisciplinary collaboration to provide intervention to students with disabilities and MLLs who have intensive academic support needs in inclusive school settings. The project focused on training scholars to engage in data-based decision making and deliver evidence-based, culturally responsive academic intervention in an MTSS model. Project scholars participated in interprofessional educational experiences known to be effective in increasing interdisciplinary collaboration, including didactic learning, such as cross-discipline course work and interdisciplinary seminars, and experiential learning, such as year-long interdisciplinary fieldwork.

Overall, data sources show that scholars are positively impacting the academic achievement of school-age youth, as evidenced by effect size calculations, and meeting or exceeding project-related competencies in fieldwork, as seen in master teacher and supervisor evaluations. While these data are useful in making tentative conclusions regarding the influence of the interdisciplinary project on scholar outcomes, there are several limitations. The small sample size due to the number of scholars participating in the training project each year (e.g., four school psychology scholars, four dual credential scholars over 3 years) and the number of scholars who dropped out of the program and project significantly impact conclusions regarding project-related outcomes. Challenges related to COVID-19, including disruptions to school- and home-life, financial stability, and health and well-being, significantly limited scholars' ability to successfully complete course and fieldwork requirements, and likely contributed to scholars leaving the project and program. While the pandemic may be receding, project faculty plan to increase scholar support via structured peer and faculty mentorship and scheduling shorter but more frequent opportunities to meet with school dyads for planning and problem-solving.

Another limitation of the data presented is lack of a comparison group. Project faculty will be examining intervention case study, effect size, and fieldwork supervisor data at the program level to examine differences, if any, between program completers who did and did not participate on the training project. While causal conclusions cannot be made regarding the effects of the project, results will be used to inform program planning.

There are many other indicators of project impact that will be examined in the coming years as scholars who graduate move to employed positions in their respective professions. Data collected from employers will provide a clearer picture of the influence of the training project on scholar practices in schools. While the quantitative data collected are useful, it is also valuable to understand the perspectives of the scholars both while they are in the project and working in the field.

## REFERENCES

Aceves, T. C., & Orosco, M. (2014). *Culturally responsive teaching* (Document No. IC-2). Retrieved from University of Florida, Collaboration for Effective Educator, Development, Accountability, and Reform Center website: https://ceedar.education.ufl.edu/tools/innovation-configurations/

Archer, A. L., & Hughes, C. A. (2010). *Explicit Instruction: Effective and efficient teaching*. Guilford Press.

Austin, C. R., Vaughn, S., & McClelland, A. M. (2017). Intensive reading interventions for inadequate responders in grades k–3: A synthesis. *Learning Disability Quarterly*, *40*(4), 191–210. doi:10.1177/0731948717714446

Bridges, D. R., Davidson, R. A., Odegard, P. S., Maki, I. V., & Tomkowiak, J. (2011). Interprofessional collaboration: Three best practice models of interprofessional education. *Medical Education Online*, *16*, . doi:10.3402/meo.v16i0.6035

Brownell, M. T., Benedict, A. E., Leko, M. M., Peyton, D., Pua, D., & Richards-Tutor, C. (2019). A continuum of pedagogies for preparing teachers to use high-leverage practices. *Remedial and Special Education, 40*(6), 338–355. doi:10.1177/0741932518824990

Buelow, J., Downs, D., Jorgensen, K., Karges, J., & Nelson, D. (2008). Building interdisciplinary teamwork among allied health students through live clinical case simulations. *Journal of Allied Health, 37*(2), e109–e123. PMID:19753390

Busse, R. T., Kratochwill, T. R., & Elliott, S. N. (1995). Meta-analysis for single-case consultation outcomes: Applications to research and practice. *Journal of School Psychology, 33*(4), 269–285. doi:10.1016/0022-4405(95)00014-D

Chen, H. W., O'Donnell, J. M., Chiu, Y. J., Chen, Y. C., Kang, Y. N., Tuan, Y. T., Kuo, S. Y., & Wu, J. C. (2022). Comparison of learning outcomes of interprofessional education simulation with traditional single-profession education simulation: A mixed-methods study. *BMC Medical Education, 22*(1), 651. doi:10.118612909-022-03640-z PMID:36042449

Collier-Meek, M. A., Sanetti, L. M., Fallon, L., & Chafouleas, S. (2020). Exploring the influences of assessment method, intervention steps, intervention sessions, and observation timing on treatment fidelity estimates. *Assessment for Effective Intervention, 46*(1), 3–13. doi:10.1177/1534508419857228

Collier-Meek, M. A., Sanetti, L. M. H., & Boyle, A. M. (2016). Providing feasible implementation support: Direct training and implementation planning in consultation. *School Psychology Forum, 10*, 106–119. https://www.nasponline.org/publications/periodicals/spf/volume-10/volume-10-issue-1-(spring-2016)/providing-feasible-implementation-support-direct-training-and-implementation-planning-in-consultation

Commission on Teacher Credentialing. (2009). *California Standards for the Teaching Profession.* Retrieved from https://www.cde.ca.gov/pd/ps/

Council for Exceptional Children & CEEDAR Center. (n.d.). Retrieved from https://ceedar.education.ufl.edu/wp-content/uploads/2017/07/CEC-HLP-Web.pdf

Council for Exceptional Children Initial Preparation Standards. (2015). *What every special educator must know: Professional Ethics and Standards.* Retrieved from https://exceptionalchildren.org/standards/initial-special-education-preparation-standards

Deno, S. L., & Fuchs, L. S. (1987). Developing curriculum-based measurement systems for data-based special education problem solving. *Focus on Exceptional Children, 19*(8), 1–16. doi:10.17161/foec.v19i8.7497

Dettmer, P., Thurston, L. P., & Dyck, N. (1996). *Consultation, collaboration, and teamwork: For students with special needs* (2nd ed.). Allyn & Bacon.

Echevarria, J. E., Vogt, M. E., & Richards-Tutor, C. (2014). *Response to intervention and English learners: Using the SIOP model* (2nd ed.). Pearson.

Echevarria, J. E., Vogt, M. E., & Short, D. (2017). *Making content comprehensible for English learners: The SIOP model* (5th ed.). Pearson.

Farmer, R. L., Goforth, A. N., Kim, S. Y., Naser, S. C., Lockwood, A. B., & Affrunti, N. W. (2021). Status of School Psychology in 2020, Part 2: Professional Practices in the NASP membership survey. *NASP Research Reports, 5*(3).

Fuchs, L. S., Fuchs, D., & Malone, A. S. (2017). The taxonomy of intervention intensity. *Teaching Exceptional Children, 50*(1), 35–43. doi:10.1177/0040059917703962

Hagans, K., & Powers, K. (2015). Measuring credential candidates' impact on student achievement. *Action in Teacher Education, 37*(4), 355–374. doi:10.1080/01626620.2015.1078755

Hammond, Z. (2014). *Culturally responsive teaching and the brain: Promoting authentic engagement and rigor among culturally and linguistically diverse students*. Corwin Press.

Howard, T. C. (2020). *Why race and culture matter in schools: Closing the achievement gap in America's classrooms* (2nd ed.). Teachers College Press.

Hughes, C. A., Riccomini, P. J., & Morris, J. R. (2018). Use explicit instruction. In J. McLeskey, L. Maheady, B. Billingsley, M. T. Brownell, & T. J. Lewis (Eds.), *High leverage practices for inclusive classrooms*. Routledge. doi:10.4324/9781315176093-20

Individuals with Disabilities Education Act, 20 U.S.C. § 1400 (2004)

Ladson-Billings, G. (1994). *The dreamkeepers: Successful teachers of African American children*. Jossey-Bass.

Ladson-Billings, G. (1995). Toward a theory of culturally relevant pedagogy. *American Educational Research Journal, 32*(3), 465–491. doi:10.3102/00028312032003465

Lemons, C. J., Kearns, D. M., & Davidson, K. A. (2014). Data-based individualization in reading: Intensifying interventions for students with significant reading disabilities. *Teaching Exceptional Children, 46*(4), 20–29. doi:10.1177/0040059914522978

Linan-Thompson, S., Lara-Martinez, J. A., & Cavazos, L. O. (2018). Exploring the intersection of evidence-based practices and culturally and linguistically responsive practices. *Intervention in School and Clinic, 54*(1), 6–13. doi:10.1177/1053451218762574

Margolis, L., Rosenberg, A., Umble, K., & Chewning, L. (2013). Effects of interdisciplinary training on MCH professionals, organizations, and systems. *Maternal and Child Health Journal, 17*(5), 949–958. doi:10.100710995-012-1078-8 PMID:22798078

McLeskey, J., Barringer, M. D., Billingsley, B., Brownell, M., Jackson, D., Kennedy, M., Lewis, T., Maheady, L., Rodriguez, J., Scheeler, M. C., Winn, J., & Ziegler, D. (2017). *High-leverage practices in special education*. Council for Exceptional Children & CEEDAR Center.

Metz, A., Louison, L., Burke, K., Albers, B., & Ward, C. (2020). *Implementation support practitioner profile: Guiding principles and core competencies for implementation practice*. National Implementation Research Network, University of North Carolina at Chapel Hill. Retrieved from https://nirn.fpg.unc.edu/resources/implementation-support-practitioner-profile

Miller, R., Combes, G., Brown, H., & Harwood, A. (2014). Interprofessional workplace learning: A catalyst for strategic change? *Journal of Interprofessional Care*, *28*(3), 186–193. doi:10.3109/13561820.2013.877428 PMID:24428770

Multitiered System of Supports for English Learners. (2020). *Meeting the needs of English learners with and without disabilities: Brief 2, Evidence-based Tier 2 intervention practices for English learners*. Washington, DC: U.S. Office of Special Education Programs. Retrieved from https://www.mtss4els.org/files/resource-files/Series2-Brief2_Final.pdf

NAEP. (2019). *The nation's report card: NAEP data explorer*. Retrieved from https://nces.ed.gov/nationsreportcard/data/

National Association of School Psychologists. (2020). *Model for comprehensive and integrated school psychological services*. Retrieved from https://www.nasponline.org/standards-and-certification/nasp-practice-model

National Center for Education Statistics. (2019). *National Assessment of Educational Progress: An overview of NAEP*. National Center for Education Statistics, Institute of Education Sciences, U.S. Department of Education.

National Center for Education Statistics. (2021). *English learners in public schools*. Retrieved from https://nces.ed.gov/programs/coe/indicator/cgf/english-learners

National Center on Intensive Intervention. (2016). *Principles for designing intervention in mathematics*. Washington, DC: Office of Special Education, U.S. Department of Education. Retrieved from https://intensiveintervention.org/sites/default/files/Princip_Effect_Math_508.pdf

National Council on Disabilities. (2018). *English learners and students from low income families*. Retrieved from https://ncd.gov/sites/default/files/NCD_EnglishLanguageLearners_508.pdf

Noell, G. H., Gansle, K. A., Mevers, J. L., Knox, R. M., Mintz, J. C., & Dahir, A. (2014). Improving treatment plan implementation in schools: A meta-analysis of single subject design studies. *Journal of Behavioral Education*, *23*(1), 168–191. doi:10.100710864-013-9177-1

Ortiz, S. O. (2019). On the measurement of cognitive abilities in English learners. *Contemporary School Psychology*, *23*(1), 68–86. doi:10.100740688-018-0208-8

OSEP. (2019). *OSEP Fast Facts: Hispanic and/or Latino Children with Disabilities*. Retrieved from https://sites.ed.gov/idea/osep-fast-facts-hispanic-latino-children-disabilities-20/

Paris, D. (2012). Culturally sustaining pedagogy: A needed change in stance, terminology, and practice. *Educational Researcher, 41*(3), 93–97. doi:10.3102/0013189X12441244

Powell, S. R., & Stecker, P. M. (2014). Using data-based individualization to intensify mathematics intervention for students with disabilities. *Teaching Exceptional Children, 46*(4), 31–37. doi:10.1177/0040059914523735

Project ELITE2, Project ELLIPSES, & Project LEE. (2018). *Meeting the needs of English learners with and without disabilities: Brief 1, Multitiered instructional systems for ELs*. U.S. Office of Special Education Programs. Retrieved from https://www.mtss4els.org/files/resource-files/Series2-Brief1_Final.pdf

Reeves, S., Goldman, J., Gilbert, J., Tepper, J., Silver, I., Suter, E., & Zwarenstein, M. (2011). A scoping review to improve conceptual clarity of interdisciplinary intervention. *Journal of Interdisciplinary Care, 25*(3), 167–174. doi:10.3109/13561820.2010.529960 PMID:21182439

Richards-Tutor, C., Barber, B. R., Benedict, A. E., Brownell, M., Martinez-Vargas, L., & Gates, J. (2021). Using high leverage practices to organize practice-based opportunities: Academic and behavioral examples from inclusive educational contexts. In P. Chandler & L. Barron (Eds.), *Rethinking school-university partnerships: A new way forward*. Information Age Publishers.

Rosenberg, A., Margolis, L. H., Umble, K., & Chewning, L. (2015). Fostering intentional interdisciplinary leadership in developmental disabilities: The North Carolina LEND experience. *Maternal and Child Health Journal, 19*(2), 290–299. doi:10.100710995-014-1618-5 PMID:25366097

Scruggs, T. E., & Mastropieri, M. A. (1998). Summarizing single-subject research: Issues and applications. *Behavior Modification, 22*(3), 221–242. doi:10.1177/01454455980223001 PMID:9722473

Shinn, M. (2008). Best practices for using curriculum-based measurement in a problem-solving model. In A. Thomas & J. Grimes (Eds.), *Best practices in school psychology IV* (pp. 243–262). National Association of School Psychologists.

Smith, J. (2010). An interdisciplinary approach to preparing early intervention professionals: A aniversity and community collaborative Initiative. *Teacher Education and Special Education, 33*(2), 131–142. doi:10.1177/0888406409357546

St. Martin, K., Vaughn, S., Troia, G., Fien, H., & Coyne, M. (2020). *Intensifying literacy instruction: Essential practices*. Lansing, MI: MiMTSS Technical Assistance Center, Michigan Department of Education. Retrieved from https://intensiveintervention.org/resource/intensifying-literacy-instruction-essential-practices

Timm, J. R., & Schnepper, L. L. (2021). A mixed-methods evaluation of an interprofessional clinical education model serving students, faculty, and the community. *Journal of Interprofessional Care, 35*(1), 92–100. doi:10.1080/13561820.2019.1710117 PMID:32013630

U.S. Department of Education, National Center for Education Statistics. (2020). *The Condition of Education 2020* (2020-144). Retrieved from https://nces.ed.gov/pubs2020/2020144.pdf

U.S. Department of Education, National Center for Education Statistics. (2021). *The Condition of Education 2021* (2021-144). Retrieved from https://nces.ed.gov/programs/coe/indicator/cgf

Weingarten, Z., Bailey, T. R., & Peterson, A. (2019). *Strategies for scheduling: How to find time to intensify and individualize intervention*. Washington, DC: National Center on Intensive Intervention, Office of Special Education Programs, U.S. Department of Education. Retrieved from https://intensiveintervention.org/sites/default/files/NCII-Scheduling-508.pdf

Weist, M. D., Mellin, E. A., Chambers, K. L., Lever, N. A., Haber, D., & Blaber, C. (2012). Challenges to collaboration in school mental health and strategies for overcoming them. *The Journal of School Health*, 82(2), 97–105. doi:10.1111/j.1746-1561.2011.00672.x PMID:22239135

Wharton, T., & Ann Burg, M. (2017). A mixed-methods evaluation of social work learning outcomes in interprofessional training with medicine and pharmacy students. *Journal of Social Work Education*, 53(Suppl 1), S87–S96. doi:10.1080/10437797.2017.1288592 PMID:30774279

Wolery, M., Busick, M., Reichow, B., & Barton, E. E. (2010). Comparison of overlap methods for quantitatively synthesizing single-subject data. *The Journal of Special Education*, 44(1), 18–28. doi:10.1177/0022466908328009

Zanotti, R., Sartor, G., & Canova, C. (2015). Effectiveness of interprofessional education by on-field training for medical students, with a pre-post design. *BMC Medical Education*, 15(1), 1–8. doi:10.118612909-015-0409-z PMID:26220412

# APPENDIX A

## School Psychology Program

Intervention Case Study Rubric

*Table 1. Section 1: Elements of an Effective Case Study*

|  | Effective | Needs Development |
|---|---|---|
| 1.1 | Demographics of the case are adequately described (e.g., age, type of class/school, grade, SES, disability, etc.). | Demographic information does not include sufficient information. |
| 1.2 | Assessment, intervention, and/or consultation practices identify and address unique individual characteristics. | Assessment, intervention, and/or consultation practices DO NOT identify and address unique individual characteristics. |
| 1.3 | Collaboration with relevant stakeholders (e.g., parents, teachers, and other professionals) is evident throughout the process. | Collaboration with relevant stakeholders (e.g., parents, teachers, and other professionals) is NOT evident throughout the process. |
| 1.4 | Steps of the problem-solving process are implemented coherently (i.e., sequential, goal directed, and flow logically based on evidence). | The steps of the problem-solving process are not followed. |
| 1.5 | Professional practices of writing style, formatting, and graphing are present in the case study (i.e., clear succinct and well written text with clearly labeled graphs). | Errors in writing convention, style, and graphing interfere with readability and interpretation of data. |
| 1.6 | Personal identifying information of the case study subject is redacted from the report. | Personal identifying information is not sufficiently redacted from the report. |
| RATING | **EFFECTIVE** | **NEEDS DEVELOPMENT** |

To pass, the candidate must receive a rating of "Effective" on 4/6 items above.
Score: /6

*Table 2. Section 2: Problem Identification*

|   | **Effective** | **Needs Development** |
|---|---|---|
| 2.1 | Information is gathered from multiple sources [e.g., Record review, Interview, Observation, and Testing (RIOT)]. | Data are not gathered from multiple sources. The following are missing:<br>Record Review Interview Observation<br>Testing |
| 2.2 | The problem is operationally defined in observable, measurable terms (i.e., the referral concern is restated as an observable, measurable dependent variable). | The problem is not operationally defined. (e.g., it is reported as a categorical/descriptive cause such as Autism, Depression, ADHD; or terms such as aggression, anxiety or hyperactivity). |
| 2.3 | Expectations for the identified behavior are stated based upon an appropriate source for comparison (e.g., grade level standards, peer performance, normative data, etc.).<br>AND<br>The difference between actual and expected levels of performance is explicitly stated. | Expected performance is not based on an appropriate source for comparison or is not included<br>OR<br>The difference between actual and expected levels of performance is not explicitly stated. |
| 2.4 | Baseline data are graphed<br>AND<br>Clearly establish a discrepancy (e.g., level, trend) between actual and expected levels of performance<br>AND<br>Use an appropriate comparison standard. | Baseline data are not graphed<br>AND/OR<br>Do not clearly establish a discrepancy (e.g., level, trend) between actual and expected levels of performance<br>AND/OR<br>Do not use an appropriate comparison. |
| RATING | **EFFECTIVE** | **NEEDS DEVELOPMENT** |

*Table 3. Section 3: Problem Analysis*

|   | **Effective** | **Needs Development** |
|---|---|---|
| 3.1 | The problem behavior is stated as a skill or performance deficit | The problem behavior is not stated as a skill or performance deficit. |
|   | Multiple hypotheses are formulated to address the problem across one or more of the following areas: curriculum, instruction, and environment.<br>AND<br>All hypotheses are testable. | Multiple hypotheses are not developed<br>AND/OR<br>Hypotheses are untestable. |
| 3.3 | Hypotheses are stated in observable/measurable terms. | Hypotheses are NOT stated in observable/measurable terms. |
| 3.4 | Proposed hypotheses are empirically tested<br>AND<br>Appropriate sources of data are used to confirm or reject each hypothesis. | Hypotheses are not tested<br>AND/OR<br>Appropriate sources of data are not used to confirm or reject each hypothesis. |
| 3.5 | A conclusive statement that formally describes the cause of the problem is included<br>AND<br>☐ Leads to a logical intervention. | A conclusive statement formally describing the cause of the problem is not included<br>AND/OR<br>☐ Does not lead to a logical intervention. |
| RATING | **EFFECTIVE** | **NEEDS DEVELOPMENT** |

*Table 4. Section 4: Intervention*

|  | **Effective** | **Needs Development** |
| --- | --- | --- |
| **4.1** | A single evidence-based intervention is implemented AND Is linked to preceding sections. | Multiple interventions are implemented simultaneously. AND/OR The intervention is not evidence-based. AND/OR The intervention is not linked to preceding sections of the report. |
| **4.2** | Acceptability of the intervention by one or more stakeholders (e.g., caregivers, teachers, etc.) is verified. | Acceptability of the intervention by one or more stakeholders is not verified. |
| **4.3** | The intervention is replicable: Intervention components [i.e., independent and dependent variable(s)] are clearly described AND Logistics are reported (e.g., who will implement, setting, duration and frequency of sessions, etc.) | The intervention is not replicable: Intervention components [i.e., independent and dependent variable(s)] are not clearly described AND/OR Logistics are missing (e.g., who will implement, setting, duration and frequency of sessions, etc.) |
| **4.4** | A skill or performance goal is stated. AND Described using the same metric as the dependent variables AND Is linked to baseline data AND Achievable based on research or other data. | A skill or performance goal is NOT stated. AND/OR Is not described using the same metric as the dependent variables AND/OR Is not linked to baseline data AND/OR Is not achievable based on research or other data. |

*Table 5. Section 4: Intervention (Continued)*

|  | **Effective** | **Needs Development** |
| --- | --- | --- |
| **4.5** | Progress monitoring data are presented. | Progress monitoring data are not presented. |
| **4.6** | Treatment integrity/fidelity data are: Reported AND Used in the interpretation of intervention efficacy. | Treatment integrity/fidelity data are not: Reported AND/OR Are not used in the interpretation of intervention efficacy. |
| RATING | **EFFECTIVE** | **NEEDS DEVELOPMENT** |

*Table 6. Section 5: Evaluation*

|  | **Effective** | **Needs Development** |
| --- | --- | --- |
| 5.1 | A single graph is depicted for the target behavior and includes the following elements:<br>Baseline data<br>AND<br>Goal/Target indicator or aimline AND<br>Treatment/progress monitoring data with a trend line. | A single target behavior is presented on multiple graphs<br>AND/OR<br>Relevant graphs are not included.<br>AND/OR<br>The following components are not included in the graph:<br>Baseline data<br>Goal/Target indicator or aim line<br>Treatment/progress monitoring data with a trend line. |
| 5.2 | Adequate intervention data are collected to meaningfully interpret the results of the intervention.:<br>At least 7 data points collected over<br>AND<br>a minimum of 6 weeks | Insufficient intervention data are collected to meaningfully interpret the results of the intervention.<br>Less than 7 data points<br>AND/OR<br>Less than 6 weeks |
| 5.3 | Visual analysis of the level, trend and variability and/or statistical analyses (e.g., effect size) were used<br>AND<br>The intervention was effective. | Visual or statistical analyses were not used<br>OR<br>The intervention was ineffective. |
| 5.4 | Strategies for generalizing outcomes to other settings are included. | Strategies for generalizing outcomes to other settings are not included. |
| 5.5 | Strategies for follow-up are included. | Strategies for follow-up are not included. |
| RATING | **EFFECTIVE** | **NEEDS DEVELOPMENT** |

*Table 7. Urban Dual Credential Program Preliminary Multiple Subject and Education Specialist Credential Literacy Intervention Project Rubric*

| Criteria | Exceeds expectations | Meets expectations | Meets some expectations | Does not meet expectations | Unable to score; incomplete or missing work | Final Score / Notes |
|---|---|---|---|---|---|---|
| 1. Student Descriptions (P1) | Clear, detailed description of each student is provided, including literacy strengths and areas of need, English Language level, reading level. Baseline data are included. | Description of each student is provided, including literacy areas of strengths and areas of need, English Language level, reading level. Baseline data are included. | Description of each student is provided but one or more key elements of the description is not included. | Vague description of students is provided. Two or more elements of the description are not included. | Student descriptions are missing or so incomplete as to be unable to score. | |
| | 10-9 pts | 8-7 pts | 6-4 pts | 3-1 pts | 0 pts | /10 |
| 2. Description of intervention (P1) | Strong, logical rationale for the area of literacy targeted during intervention is provided and information about student baseline data is included. Research-based intervention is clearly described and direct evidence (at least 2 citations) to support intervention is included. | Rationale for the targeted areas of literacy is provided and information from student baseline data is included. Research-based intervention is described and evidence to support the intervention is included (at least 2 citations). | Rationale for the targeted area of literacy is provided but may not be clear or appropriate. Intervention is described but may not be research-based or evidence is not provided, or inappropriate evidence is used to support the use of the intervention. | Area of literacy to be addressed is unclear; rationale is unclear or missing. No citations are provided. | Area of literacy to be addressed/ rationale is missing or incomplete as to be unable to score. | |
| | 10-9 pts | 8-7 pts | 6-4 pts | 3-1 pts | 0 pts | /10 |
| 3. Description of assessment (P1) | Clear, detailed description of the assessment tool is provided along with a rationale regarding why it was selected. Clear explanation of how it was used to collect baseline and progress monitoring data. At least one citation provided to explain assessment method. | Description of assessment tool is provided. Explanation of how tool was used to collect data is provided. At least one citation is included to provide support for assessment method used. | Description of assessment tool is provided but may adequate information is not included. Unclear explanation regarding data collection. At least one citation is included but may or not be appropriate. | Description of assessment tool is difficult to follow or is inappropriate for the targeted skill. Explanation of how it will be used to collect progress monitoring data is vague or incomplete. No citation. | Assessment description/ rationale is missing or incomplete and unable to score. | |
| | 10-9 pts | 8-7 pts | 6-4 pts | 3-1 pts | 0 pts | /10 |
| 4. Scope and Sequence (P1) | Clear and concise narrative description of the scope and sequence of intervention sessions is included. Intervention sessions follow an appropriate developmental sequence. | Narrative scope and sequence of intervention is provided, and sessions follow an appropriate developmental sequence. | Narrative is included but may not include an adequate description of the scope and sequence. Intervention session may not be sequenced developmentally. | Narrative description of scope and/or sequence of intervention are unclear. | Narrative description of scope and/or sequence is poorly presented as to be unable to grade or is missing. | |
| | 10-9 pts | 8-7 pts | 6-4 pts | 3-1 pts | 0 pts | /10 |
| 5. Intervention Lessons (P1) | 8 lesson plans are included and provide quality detail and follow a logical sequence for the given intervention lesson. | 8 lesson plans are included and provide sufficient detail and follow a logical sequence for the given intervention lesson. | 8 lesson plans are included but are not detailed enough to be completely understandable; intervention lesson plans may not follow a logical sequence. | Lesson plans are incomplete, or some are missing. | Lesson plans are not included. | |
| | 15-13 pts | 12-19 pts | 9-5 pts | 4-1 pts | 0 pts | /16 |
| 6. Description of student outcomes (P2) | Baseline and progress monitoring data for each student are clearly presented in a table; individual student goals are appropriate; summary of each student includes written interpretation accurately reflecting intervention data, including strengths, needs, and strategies to meet needs. | Each student's baseline, individual goals, and progress monitoring data are clearly presented in a table; there is a brief written description of intervention data, including strengths, needs, and strategies to meet needs. | Individual tables are created but are missing one or more component. Individual student data are not clearly presented and/or explained and may be missing strengths, needs and strategies. | Data are not presented in individual table form. Descriptions of student outcomes following intervention are unclear or missing two or more components. Reflection lacks depth. | Data on student progress are missing or are so poorly presented as to be unable to grade. Reflection is missing or is so poorly presented as to be unable to grade. | |
| | 20-16 pts | 15-12 pts | 11-7 pts | 7-1 pts | 0 pts | /20 |
| 7. Narrative Reflection (P2) | Detailed reflection includes what was learned from designing and implementing intervention, including the collaborative planning process, data collection and actual implementation. Clearly describes intervention successes and at least three ideas for improvement in future implementation. Discussion is clear and appropriate and based on data outcomes. | Reflection includes what was learned from designing and implementing intervention, including the collaborative planning process, data collection and actual implementation. Includes description of intervention successes and discusses at least two ideas for improvement in future implementation. Discussion is based on data outcomes. | Reflection includes what was learned from designing and implementing intervention, including all but one of these components: collaborative planning process, data collection, and actual implementation. Includes description of intervention successes, and discusses at least one idea for improvement in future implementation. Discussion is mostly based on data outcomes. | At least two reflection components are missing, or reflection is so poorly written that it cannot be understood. | Reflection is missing and cannot be scored. | |
| | 25-21pts | 20-16pts | 15-10 pts | 9-1 pts | 0 pts | 24 |
| | | | | | Sections 1- 7 Total | /100 |

# Chapter 16
# Preparing Pre-Service Teachers to Work With English Learners With Special Education Needs

**Mariana Alvayero Ricklefs**
https://orcid.org/0000-0002-2237-3268
*Northern Illinois University, USA*

## ABSTRACT

*This chapter reports a mixed methods research study with preservice teachers (PSTs) enrolled in different teacher credentialing programs at a public university in the Midwestern United States. The purpose of the study is twofold: to explore PSTs' self-efficacy and outcome expectancy beliefs to teach and assess English Learners with special education needs and to explore the relationship between PSTs' self-efficacy and outcome expectancy beliefs and with demographic and experiential factors. The findings of the study demonstrate that most PSTs did not feel capable or prepared to teach and assess English Learners with disabilities. The chapter ends with implications for collaborative teacher education and research.*

## INTRODUCTION

Under civil rights laws, American schools are obligated to ensure that English Learners have equal access to education (NCELA, 2011). English Learners[1] are children who speak a different language at home and are learning English as an additional language at school. Equal access to education is not only about attending school but also refers to these children receiving good quality education based on their strengths and needs (Ricklefs, 2021a, 2022a). This is important, considering that English Learners currently represent over 10% of the public-school K–12 population in the United States. Specifically, the percentage of students identified as English Learners increased from 9.2% (4.5 million students) in 2010 to 10.4% (5.1 million students) in 2019 (NCES, 2022a). This percentage is expected to continue growing along with global migration trends, including groups of refugees and asylum seekers. These English Learners and their families often arrive in the US, leaving behind poverty, violence, or war in their homelands. These students have faced interrupted formal schooling and traumatic experiences (Rick-

DOI: 10.4018/978-1-6684-6438-0.ch016

lefs, 2019). The intersection of various factors and identity categories—culture, language, immigration status, interrupted schooling, and dis/ability—increases the vulnerability of these students, as attested by the overidentification of minorities in special education programs (Cavendish et al., 2015; Klingner et al., 2016; Umansky et al., 2017). Considering that English Learners are the fastest-growing subgroup of students in American public schools, all teachers will likely work with English Learners without and *with* disabilities throughout their professional careers (Ortiz & Robertson, 2018).

Teacher education programs[2] need to ensure that candidates are prepared to work effectively with English Learners with disabilities. The literature shows that teacher candidates or preservice teachers (PSTs) often feel insufficiently prepared to identify, assess, and teach these students, whether issues are related to second language acquisition, cultural differences, learning disabilities, or a combination of all these factors (Umansky et al., 2017; Waitoller & Artilles, 2013).

Teacher preparation needs to combine interdisciplinary considerations to train PSTs to work effectively with English Learners with disabilities and create inclusive classrooms for all students. However, institutions of higher education tend to prepare PSTs in separate parallel program tracks (e.g., special education, general education, English as a second language) and even in different departments, limiting opportunities for interdisciplinary and collaborative approaches between faculty and PSTs (Martínez-Alvarez, 2020; Ortiz & Robertson, 2018).

The complex nature of teacher preparation also brings to the foreground issues about teachers' self-efficacy (i.e., beliefs to be able to cope successfully with one's tasks and challenges as a teacher) and outcome expectancy (i.e., beliefs to be able to positively influence students' learning), which can be important in student achievement (Bandura, 1997, 1999; Zimmerman, 1999). Addressing teachers' beliefs is relevant in teacher education, because overlooking the study of self-efficacy beliefs may affect PSTs' preparation as future schoolteachers (McHatton & Parker, 2013).

Teachers' self-efficacy influences their orientation toward the classroom environment, choice of instructional activities, expectations of students' performance, and discipline methods (Bandura, 1997). Teachers with high levels of self-efficacy are less likely to view diverse students' backgrounds as limitations (Brownell & Pajares, 1999; Klingner et al., 2016). Teachers' self-efficacy can also affect students' self-evaluations, goals, and learning in school (Bandura, 1999; Klingner et al., 2016; Zimmerman, 1999).

Considering all these issues, the purpose of the current research study is twofold: (1) to explore PSTs' self-efficacy and outcome expectancy beliefs to teach and assess English Learners with special education needs, and (2) to explore the relationship between PSTs' self-efficacy and outcome expectancy beliefs, and with demographic and experiential factors.

## THEORETICAL FRAMEWORK

The theoretical perspective of self-efficacy forms the framework of this study. Albert Bandura coined the term "self-efficacy" in the late 1970s. The term was part of his psychological theory to explain human behavior and, in particular, "fearful and avoidant behavior" (Bandura, 1977, p. 193). In Bandura's early work, self-efficacy beliefs and outcome expectancies were explained in a causal relationship so that peoples' beliefs about what they can do (i.e., self-efficacy) would determine the outcomes they expect to obtain (i.e., outcome expectancy) with their actions (Bandura, 1991). Years later, Bandura rejected the existence of a simple cause-effect association between the constructs of self-efficacy and outcome expectancy. Bandura (1997) posited that various patterns of efficacy beliefs and outcome expectations existed, which could *interact in various ways* in specific domains. More recently, Bandura (2004) expanded his theory by asserting that social, experiential, and structural factors could influence one's self-efficacy beliefs as well.

According to socio-cognitive theory, self-efficacy can be studied based on four relevant properties (Zimmerman, 1999). The first property is the *judgment* of one's abilities to perform certain activities, rather than real physical characteristics or psychological traits. The second property is that self-efficacy beliefs are *complex* and *multidimensional* rather than a single disposition. The third property is that one's self-efficacy is *context-dependent* and thus varies per situation. The fourth property involves self-efficacy measures based on a *mastery* criterion of performance rather than normative criteria. The author uses the first three properties based on the study's purpose.

Regarding the work of teachers, in this study self-efficacy is defined as teachers' beliefs to be able to cope successfully with tasks, obligations, and challenges related to their professional role (Caprara et al., 2006). Hassan and Tairab (2012) considered that teachers' self-efficacy also relates to their expectations regarding their influence on students' outcomes in connection with what the teachers believe they have learned, which they think would be able to use or control in the classroom.

Importantly, teachers' self-efficacy influences their orientation toward the classroom environment, choice of instructional activities, expectations of students' performance, and discipline methods (Bandura, 1997). Teachers with high levels of self-efficacy are less likely to view diverse students' backgrounds as limitations (Brownell & Pajares, 1999; Klingner et al., 2016). Teachers' self-efficacy can also affect students' self-evaluations, goals, and learning in school (Bandura, 1999; Klingner et al., 2016; Zimmerman, 1999).

In summary, the socio-cognitive theoretical perspective of self-efficacy is appropriate for this study because investigating teachers' beliefs about how capable and prepared they feel to work with English Learners with disabilities may influence the instruction of these students in inclusive classrooms. Researchers should investigate the self-efficacy beliefs of teacher candidates and related factors, consider ways to influence positively PSTs' beliefs through teacher preparation programs, and move the field toward inclusive models of education.

## LITERATURE REVIEW

Research on PSTs' self-efficacy beliefs about working with English Learners with disabilities is very limited. These areas have been studied separately. That is, scholars have researched the efficacy of PSTs to work either with students with special needs only (e.g., McHatton & Parker, 2013; Stites et al., 2018; Gehrke & Cocchiarella, 2013) or with English Learners only (de Jong et al., 2013; Hutchinson, 2013; Walker & Stone, 2011). This trend seems to follow actual common practice in schools in which these students spend more time in segregated settings, such as either in cross-categorical special education or in English-as-a-second language (ESL) pull-out than in inclusive classrooms. Only one research study (Martinez-Alvarez, 2021) addressed PSTs' beliefs about working with English Learners with disabilities. But the PSTs were doing fieldwork in dual-language classrooms in elementary schools, not in general education classrooms.

Nevertheless, the literature demonstrates that PSTs benefit from learning about different aspects of language acquisition and special education to effectively serve English Learners with disabilities. First, regarding language acquisition, PSTs in teacher preparation profit from developing sociolinguistic awareness accompanied by attention to language diversity and an inclination to advocate for English Learners and other linguistically diverse students (Ricklefs, 2021a, 2021b, 2022a, 2022b; de Jong et al., 2013; Hutchinson, 2013). PSTs also need to know about stages of the second language acquisition process, different levels of language proficiency and related standards, linguistic scaffolding, and how to identify and teach to language demands in the content areas (e.g., social studies, mathematics, science) (Lucas & Villegas, 2013). Concerning special education, the literature shows that PSTs often confuse language differences with learning disabilities or mistake culturally oriented conduct and attitudes for attention deficits or behavioral disorders in English Learners (Chitiyo et al., 2020; Waitoller & Artilles, 2013).

Lastly, the literature shows that English Learners' difficulties in learning may be related to cultural differences or linguistic aspects, and not to disabilities per se. PSTs should be able to discern between differences and disabilities. PSTs also need to learn how to work with English Learners who indeed have special education needs and how to incorporate them effectively in inclusive classrooms (Klingner et al. 2016; Martínez-Alvarez, 2020).

## METHOD

### Research Design

This investigation used a mixed-method research design, which was appropriate because such design is concerned "with the conceptualization of reality at different levels and with multiple dimensions and how knowledge of the object of study can be produced using both quantitative and qualitative methodologies" (Riazi & Candlin, 2014, p. 141). There are numerous types of mixed-method designs, which correspond to different intents. These designs are visualized following a notation system commonly used in the mixed methods literature (Creswell et. al., 2003). Specifically, this study used a mixed-method research design that can be visualized as follows: *QUAN® qual=explain*. According to Creswell and Plano Clark (2018) such notation signifies an explanatory sequential design in which the researcher implements two strands in a sequence, the quantitative methods occur first and have a greater emphasis on addressing the study's purpose, and the qualitative methods follow to help explain the quantitative results.

### Research Questions

The following research questions guided the current study:
　　RQ1: What are PSTs' self-efficacy beliefs and outcome expectancy beliefs about working with English Learners with special education needs?
　　RQ2: What is the relationship between PSTs' self-efficacy and outcome expectancy and with demographic and experiential factors?
　　See Table 1 which shows the alignment between research questions, data collection sources and procedures, and data analysis types and procedures.

### Participants

Fifty-three PSTs were invited to participate in this research study. These PSTs were enrolled in two sections of an ESL teaching methods course at a university in the US Midwest, where this study took place.

*Table 1. Alignment of Research Questions with Data Collection and Analysis Procedures*

| Research Questions | Data Collection Procedures | Data Analysis Procedures |
|---|---|---|
| RQ1: What are PSTs' self-efficacy beliefs and outcome expectancy beliefs about working with English Learners with special education needs? | • PSTs' answers to Likert-scale survey items<br>• PSTs' answers to open-ended questions<br>• PSTs' reflection papers | • Statistical tests of Likert-scale survey data using SPSS<br>• Coding and theaming of data from open-ended questions and reflection papers |
| RQ2: What is the relationship between PSTs' self-efficacy and outcome expectancy and with demographic and experiential factors? | • PSTs' answers to Likert-scale survey items<br>• PSTs' answers to open-ended questions<br>• PSTs' reflection papers | • Statistical tests of Likert-scale survey data using SPSS<br>• Coding and theaming of data from open-ended questions and reflection papers |

The author was the course instructor. This course is required for all PSTs in any education program at the university and it is also required for the ESL credential, which can be added to the initial teacher licensure. However, the ESL credential includes other courses to complete the 18 credits mandatory in the state.

Of these PSTs, 30 provided written consent and answered the anonymous survey, and 19 of them decided to continue participating in the full study, which is a 35.85% response rate. Most PSTs were female, white, and English primary speakers. Many students were in their third year (juniors) or fourth year (seniors) of different teacher education programs at the time of the study. Table 2 presents details about the participants' profiles.

## Data Collection Sources and Procedures

The mixed-method design in this study served to answer the research questions and for explanatory and triangulation purposes. Triangulation is a "validity strategy" by which the researcher uses "data drawn from several sources or several individuals" (Creswell & Plano Clark, 2018, p. 217). After obtaining Institutional Review Board approval and the participants' consent, the data were collected through the survey's Likert-scale items, open-ended questions, and reflection papers of the participants to answer the research questions. Table 1 displays the alignment of the research questions with the data collection procedures and data analysis procedures.

Using the *QUAN® qual=explain* research design (Creswell & Plano Clark, 2018), the quantitative method occurred first which included survey data. The scale items of the survey utilized in this study were obtained from the survey created by Chu and Garcia (2014), who reported a validity score of Cronbach's alpha = .95, which is above the minimum criterion of .70 (Chu, 2013). The survey included a total of 40 items organized in four sections described in the following paragraphs.

The first section of the survey included 10 multiple-choice items about PSTs' demographic and experiential information. These items addressed the PSTs' gender, age, race, ethnicity, primary language, teacher education program, year in the program, ESL courses taken, and being enrolled in clinical placement or student teaching. At the university where this study took place, *clinical placement* was the label referring to the fieldwork experience that PSTs complete in schools before their student teaching semester. Each clinical placement gradually increases the number of clock hours and involvement in the classroom required of the PSTs.

The second section of the survey corresponded to 10 items about self-efficacy beliefs (Chu & Garcia, 2014). These items were self-appraisal statements of one's abilities to perform certain activities, rather than real characteristics or psychological traits. Examples of these survey items are the following: I

*Table 2. Profiles of the Participating PSTs*

| Variable | Level | Percentage |
| --- | --- | --- |
| Gender | Female | 78.75% (*n*=15) |
|  | Male | 21.05% (*n*=4) |
| Age | 18–20 | 36.84% (*n*=7) |
|  | 21–23 | 52.63% (*n*=10) |
|  | 24 or older | 10.53% (*n*=2) |
| Race/Ethnicity | African American | 10.53% (*n*=2) |
|  | Asian/Pacific Islander | 5.26% (*n*=1) |
|  | Latino | 26.32% (*n*=5) |
|  | White | 57.89% (*n*=11) |
|  | Other | 0% (*n*=0) |
| Primary Language | English | 73.68% (*n*=14) |
|  | Other than English | 26.32% (*n*=5) |
| Bilingual | No | 73.68% (*n*=14) |
|  | Yes | 26.32% (*n*=5) |
| Major/Program Focus | Early Childhood | 31.58% (*n*=6) |
|  | Elementary Education | 36.84% (*n*=7) |
|  | Middle School | 15.79% (*n*=3) |
|  | High School | 5.26% (*n*=1) |
|  | Special Education | 10.53% (*n*=2) |
| Enrollment Type | Undergraduate student | 100.00% (*n*=19) |
|  | Graduate student | 0% (*n*=0) |
| Year in Program | Freshman | 0% (*n*=0) |
|  | Sophomore | 10.53%% (*n*=2) |
|  | Junior | 26.32% (*n*=5) |
|  | Senior | 63.16% (n=12) |
| Previous ESL Courses | Yes | 36.84% (*n*=7) |
|  | No | 63.16% (*n*=12) |
| School Practice/Field Work | Clinical Placement | 26.32% (*n*=5) |
|  | Student Teaching | 52.63% (*n*=10) |
|  | None | 21.05% (*n*=4) |

*Note.* N=19

am able to distinguish if English Learners' issues in achievement are related to English acquisition or learning disabilities; I am able to design lesson plans for English Learners with disabilities; I am able to assist English Learners with special education needs to be successful by supporting their home/native language. The items in this section utilized a Likert-type scale with five-point values: strongly disagree (1), disagree (2), neither agree nor disagree (3), agree (4), and strongly agree (5).

The third section of the survey encompassed 10 items about outcome expectancy beliefs (Chu & Garcia, 2014). These items were self-appraisal statements of one's ability to deal with certain situations based on what has been learned through training or past learning experiences. Examples of these survey items are the following: I have learned how to distinguish between English Learners' language acquisition issues and learning disabilities; I have learned how to distinguish between English Learners' language proficiency issues and learning disabilities; I have learned about different types of assessment for English Learners with special education needs. The items in this section also utilized a Likert-type scale with five-point values, which varied as follows: strongly disagree (1), disagree (2), neither agree nor disagree (3), agree (4), and strongly agree (5).

The fourth and last section of the survey comprised 10 items, which were open-ended questions about teacher self-efficacy. The open-ended questions addressed properties of self-efficacy (Zimmerman, 1999), as these pertained to how able and prepared the PSTs felt to teach and assess English Learners with disabilities. Examples of questions are the following: How able do you feel to teach English Learners with specific learning disabilities, and why? What experiences have you had teaching or assessing English Learners with and without disabilities in school classrooms? What do you think are your strengths when it comes to working with English Learners who have special education needs? In what areas would you need improvement?

As part of the *QUAN® qual=explain* research design (Creswell & Plano Clark, 2018) the qualitative method followed the quantitative method for an explanatory purpose. The qualitative method included data from the PSTs' answers to the survey's open-ended questions and reflection papers that they wrote throughout the semester. Both the survey and papers were embedded in the ESL course. The reflection papers covered topics related to specific strategies and resources to teach English Learners with and without special education needs. These topics were part of the content of the ESL course that the PSTs were taking at the time of this investigation. Each reflection paper was three to five pages long and was based on specific course readings and requirements. Each of the participating PSTs wrote three reflection papers throughout the course.

## Data Analysis Procedures

Given that this was a mixed-method research study (Creswell & Plano-Clark, 2018), the author analyzed different types of data from different sources for triangulation purposes.

The author used descriptive statistics (Tables 3 and 4) for demographic data obtained with the survey and utilized inferential statistical tests (Tables 5, 6, and 7) for the self-efficacy and outcome expectancy items of the survey. The author conducted all statistical tests with the SPSS computer software. Spearman (rho) correlation tests were run because these are appropriate for the statistical analysis of data from ordinal variables, namely Likert-scale ratings.

In addition, the author analyzed qualitative data from the open-ended questions and reflection papers with coding and theming of data via inductive analysis (Emerson et al., 2011). The study's research questions and theoretical framework (i.e., self-efficacy socio-cognitive theory) guided the coding of data. First, open coding consisted of the initial sorting of data. The author carefully read the PSTs' answers to open-ended questions and their reflection papers to identify major codes or patterns of data. Next, focused coding involved a fine-grained analysis of the initial sorting of data and patterns, which were further developed into categories of themes and subthemes. Some examples of themes and (subthemes) that emerged from the data analysis are the following: assessment issues (linguistic complexity, cultural

Table 3. *Participants' Answers to Items with the Highest Mean in the Self-Efficacy (SE) Section of the Survey and the Outcome Expectancy (OE) Section of the Survey*

| Survey Item | Q1SE | Q8SE | Q8OE | Q9OE |
|---|---|---|---|---|
| Highest Mean (M) | 4.26 | 4.43 | 4.25 | 4.52 |
| Standard Deviation (SD) | .449 | .507 | .448 | .730 |
| Rating 4 (Agree) | 73.9% | 56.5% | 39.1% | 34.8% |
| Rating 5 (Strongly Agree) | 26.1% | 43.5% | 13.0% | 60.9% |

*Note.* The Likert scale consisted of 5 rating values: Strongly Disagree (1), Disagree (2), Neither agree nor disagree (3), Agree (4), and Strongly Agree (5). The percentages are of participants selecting a specific rating for the Likert-scale items in the survey.

bias, accommodations, modifications, and the different types of assessments' advantages and disadvantages), differentiation (differentiated teaching, differentiated assessment, levels of language proficiency, and curriculum), and preparedness to work with English Learners with disabilities (not feeling capable, having doubts and contradictory beliefs, lack of knowledge, and lack of experience).

# FINDINGS

## PSTs' Positive Beliefs

The first research question (RQ1) was: What are PSTs' self-efficacy beliefs and outcome expectancy beliefs about working with English Learners with special education needs? The statistical analysis of the survey's Likert-scale items demonstrated that PSTs' self-efficacy was positive or high (with the highest value on the scale being 5) regarding the use of different instructional materials to meet the needs and interests of English Learners (M = 4.26, SD = .449) and using assessment accommodations (M = 4.43, SD = .507), as shown in Table 3. The statistical analysis of survey data also showed that PSTs' outcome expectancy was high about having learned how to use different types of informal assessments (M = 4.25) (SD = .448) and being aware that standardized tests may be culturally biased against English Learners (M = 4.52, SD = .730), as presented in Table 3.

The findings from the open-ended questions align with and expand PSTs' answers to the Likert-scale survey items (Table 3). Regarding teaching and instructional resources, and meeting students' interests and needs, PSTs reported feeling able to teach English Learners but feeling less confident about working with them if they had disabilities. As an illustration, one PST stated, "I feel capable to write lesson plans that appeal to the interests of English Learners in my clinical placement and teaching them in an additive way and not the subtractive way." Another PST agreed:

*I feel confident being able to make a lesson, teach the lesson, use different teaching resources, and offer as much support as possible when teaching. I think I have learned many strategies in the ESL courses on how to work with students who are English Learners but maybe not with disabilities.*

Similarly, the findings from the open-ended questions and reflection papers concur with and develop the PSTs' answers to the Likert-scale survey items about self-efficacy and outcome expectancy beliefs

*Table 4. Participants' Answers to Surveys Items with the Lowest Mean in the Self-Efficacy (SE) Section of the Survey and the Outcome Expectancy (OE) Section of the Survey*

| Survey Item | Q3SE | Q10SE | Q6OE | Q1ØOE |
|---|---|---|---|---|
| Lowest Mean (M) | 3.57 | 3.47 | 3.39 | 3.39 |
| Standard Deviation (SD) | .843 | .697 | 1.033 | .941 |
| Rating 2 (Disagree) | 13.0% | 10.5% | 26.1% | 21.7% |
| Rating 3 (Neither Agree nor Disagree) | 39.1% | 31.6% | 21.7% | 26.1% |
| Rating 4 (Agree) | 52.2% | 57.9% | 39.1% | 43.5% |

*Note.* The Likert scale consisted of 5 rating values: Strongly Disagree (1), Disagree (2), Neither agree nor disagree (3), Agree (4), and Strongly Agree (5). The percentages are of participants selecting a specific rating for the Likert-scale items in the survey.

(Table 3) regarding their knowledge and use of assessment instruments and procedures. For instance, the PSTs were aware of issues in standardized tests if used as the only instruments to assess English Learners and felt able to use assessment accommodations and modifications. However, whether the teacher candidates knew the differences between the last two was unclear. For example, one of the PSTs said, "I feel capable to use formative and informal assessments with English Learners. I understand that accommodations may need to be used." Another PST explained, "I think that traditional standardized test results are often used for accountability purposes but can affect academic performance. For English Learners, the outcome of these standardized tests can be affected by linguistic complexity and cultural bias." Another PST commented,

*I feel confident in using informal assessments because I have experience with them. I feel semi-confident in using formative or standardized assessments because I have never done them before, so I do not have any prior hands-on experience with them. I feel semi-confident because I know that just because a student has a learning disability does not mean that they are unable to learn the information. I believe that it would just take some modifications, but it depends on the student to determine to what extent things need to be modified.*

## PSTs' Negative Beliefs

Continuing with the findings for RQ1—What are PSTs' self-efficacy beliefs and outcome expectancy beliefs about working with English Learners with special education needs?—the statistical analysis of the survey's Likert-scale data demonstrated that the PSTs' self-efficacy was low, or negative, regarding their ability to design lesson plans for English Learners with disabilities (M = 3.47, SD = .697) and communicating with English Learners with disabilities (M = 3.57, SD = .843), as shown in Table 4. The PSTs' outcome expectancy was also low about having learned strategies to teach English Learners with disabilities (M = 3.39, SD = 1.03) and about how different disabilities manifest in English Learners (M = 3.39, SD = .941), as presented in Table 4.

The findings from the PSTs' answers to the open-ended questions concur with the findings displayed in Table 4 and provide more insights into their self-efficacy and outcome expectancy beliefs. Specifically, 68.42% of the PSTs expressed not feeling able to distinguish whether English Learners have learning disabilities or language acquisition issues. Some of them even considered not being able to detect "signs" to discern between these two different situations. For instance, a PST commented, "I think I need to look more into English Learners with disabilities and how you can determine if there is a disability causing the problems or if they are not able to understand the English language." Another PST concurred saying,

*I do not know yet how to establish the learning disabilities that English Learners might have and how that might affect their learning. I think I need to know more about how learning disabilities affect an English Learner and how that would look in the classroom.*

*I need improvement in students who have learning disabilities that are also English Learners. I feel that I have a lack of knowledge on making the distinction between certain signs that may arise in both and which road to take to best help that student if it is a language problem or a learning problem.*

In addition, findings from the PSTs' answers to the open-ended questions agree with the results portrayed in Table 4 regarding their self-efficacy and outcome expectancy beliefs about working with English Learners *with* learning disabilities. Approximately 94.74% expressed not feeling confident or unprepared to teach or assess these students. An interesting result was that the PSTs commented about having learned about issues that English Learners might experience and issues that students with disabilities might experience, but separately in different teacher preparation programs, not together. For example, three PSTs stated the following: "I feel that my ability to work with English Learners who have learning disabilities would be a 6 out of 10 because I am not very confident in teaching in that area." "I am nervous and less confident in assessing English Learners with learning disabilities." "I have learned how to assess English Learners and students with disabilities, but separately in different courses. I have not learned how to assess both English Learners who also have learning disabilities. So, I feel less confident with this." Another PST concurred,

*I feel unprepared to work with English Learners with learning disabilities. I feel that we learn about English Learners and special education students in separate classrooms and very seldom mixed and would love more information on this to help me become more prepared.*

## PSTs' Mixed and Contradictory Beliefs

The second research question (RQ2) was: What is the relationship between PSTs' self-efficacy and outcome expectancy? The statistical analysis of the survey data demonstrated that the highest correlation ($\rho = .755$, $\alpha = .01$) was between the PSTs feeling able to identify when English Learners' behaviors were related to their cultural backgrounds and not to learning disabilities (self-efficacy) and the PSTs learning to distinguish between English Learners' cultural issues and disabilities (outcome expectancy), as shown in Table 5.

The findings also indicated that the lowest (and statistically significant) correlation ($\rho = .415$, $\alpha = .05$) was between the PSTs' feeling able to distinguish whether English Learners' issues in academic achievement were related to English language acquisition or learning disabilities (self-efficacy) and PSTs' having learned how to distinguish between English Learners' language proficiency issues and learning disabilities (outcome expectancy), as shown in Table 5.

Interestingly, a statistically significant negative correlation ($\rho = -.442$, $\alpha = .05$) was observed (Table 5) between the PSTs' feeling able to identify English Learners' issues due to cultural differences and

Table 5. Spearman (rho) Correlation Coefficients that are Statistically Significant between Items of Self-Efficacy (SE) and Items of Outcome Expectancy (OE) in the Likert-scale Survey

| Survey Item | Q1SE | Q2SE | Q3SE | Q4SE | Q5SE | Q6SE | Q7SE | Q8SE | Q9SE | Q1ØSE |
|---|---|---|---|---|---|---|---|---|---|---|
| Q1OE |  | .443* |  |  |  |  |  | .548** |  |  |
| Q2OE |  |  |  | .495* | .415* |  |  |  |  |  |
| Q3OE |  |  |  |  |  |  |  |  |  |  |
| Q4OE |  |  |  |  |  |  | -.442* |  |  |  |
| Q5OE | .541** | .539** |  | .589** |  | .421* | .549** | .630** |  |  |
| Q6OE |  |  |  |  |  |  |  |  |  |  |
| Q7OE |  |  |  |  | .432* |  | .755** |  |  |  |
| Q8OE | .538** |  |  |  |  |  |  |  |  |  |
| Q9OE |  |  |  | .461* |  |  |  | .525* |  |  |
| Q1ØOE |  |  |  |  |  |  |  |  |  |  |

Note. The correlation is statistically significant at the *.05 level and the **.01 level

not to learning disabilities (self-efficacy item) and the PSTs' having learned how to work with English Learners with disabilities (outcome expectancy item). This finding could be interpreted as follows: what the PSTs thought they lacked in learning may have hindered their level of confidence in teaching English Learners with disabilities.

This negative correlation (quantitative data analysis) might also be explained and amplified by the PSTs' answers to open-ended questions (qualitative data analysis). That is, the PSTs appeared to have contradictory beliefs because they felt that they had knowledge in theory or "on paper" but had no experience themselves or had not observed these situations in "real" classrooms. For example, a PST commented, "I feel capable of teaching English Learners, and I can assess English Learners with learning disabilities. But I am not used to distinguishing whether English Learners have learning disabilities or if they have problems with acquiring English." Another PST explained, "I can do everything 'on paper.' I know how to teach English Learners...I know different techniques to adjust lessons and assessments, but I have not seen these applied in a real classroom." Another PST added details about paying attention to "a lot of areas," which would make teaching more difficult. She stated,

*I feel capable of teaching English Learners with learning disabilities but would like to learn more. I feel like it is hard to teach or assess English Learners who have learning disabilities because, as a teacher, I will have to be paying attention to a lot of areas in a student and not just what they are learning.*

Furthermore, one aspect of the PSTs' outcome expectancy correlated with different self-efficacy items. That is, the outcome expectancy item about PSTs' having learned how to adjust teaching to students who come from culturally and linguistically diverse backgrounds correlated positively (Table 5) with the following self-efficacy items: PSTs' feeling able to use different instructional materials with English Learners ($\rho = .541$, $\alpha = .01$), differentiate instruction for English Learners based on their English proficiency level ($\rho = .539$, $\alpha = .01$), design appropriate instruction for English Learners ($\rho = .589$, $\alpha = .01$), use various types of assessment with English Learners ($\rho = .421$, $\alpha = .05$), distinguish English

Learners' cultural issues and learning disabilities (ρ = .549, α = .01), and use accommodations when assessing English Learners (ρ = .630, α = .01).

The findings from the open-ended questions and reflection papers (qualitative data analysis) confirm and expand the results in Table 5 (quantitative data analysis). The PSTs showed an awareness of English Learners' various cultural and linguistic backgrounds and how these may influence these children's assessments. The PSTs also provided examples of culturally and linguistically responsive teaching and assessment. One PST explained,

*Teachers have to be patient with English Learners because they come from different cultural backgrounds and education situations, whether it be from a rural school to war-torn schooling. When teachers plan their lessons, they need to make sure they are engaging all students. I have experienced an opportunity like this in my clinical placement. One of the classes was on the American government, which could be hard for English Learners to connect with and learn, but the teacher was able to make it interesting and enjoyable for all. She was able to have those students participate in discussions on how their countries would do certain things or how their government was made up. Those English Learners were able to feel that they belonged in the class and were able to connect anything they learned before about their country.*

Another PST explained that various forms of assessments should be employed with English Learners. The PST highlighted the use of performance-based assessments as follows,

*It is important to use alternate forms of assessments for English Learners such as performance-based assessments. The reason is that these are not affected by unnecessary linguistic complexity. I think this is important to remember when assessing English Learners because an over-reliance on language-based tests can be inaccurate in testing their actual knowledge. This is why it is important to use performance-based assessments to properly evaluate students who may not have the English language tools necessary to show their understanding and knowledge.*

## Influence of Demographic and Experiential Factors on PSTs' Beliefs

The *second part* of RQ2 involves the relationship between PSTs' self-efficacy and outcome expectancy *and with demographic and experiential factors*. The study's findings demonstrated that some demographic and experiential factors (i.e., being bilingual, having taken ESL courses, and fieldwork in schools) correlated with PSTs' self-efficacy and outcome expectancy in various ways.

### Influence of Language on PSTs' Beliefs

PSTs' language skills influenced their self-efficacy beliefs, specifically, being bilingual correlated with PSTs' self-efficacy for designing appropriate instruction for English Learners with disabilities (ρ = .548, α = .01), about the ability to distinguish between English Learners' cultural issues and learning disabilities (ρ = .420, α = .05), and about the ability to use accommodations to assess English Learners (ρ = .754, α = .01), as shown in Table 6.

Moreover, PSTs' language skills also influenced their outcome expectancy beliefs as shown in Table 7. Being bilingual correlated with PSTs reporting having learned how to distinguish between English Learners' language acquisition issues and learning disabilities (ρ = .443, α = .05), that standardized

Table 6. *Summary of Statistically Significant Correlations (rho) between PSTs' Demographic and Experiential Factors and PSTs' Self-Efficacy (SE) Likert-scale Items of the Survey*

| Self-Efficacy Item | Demographic and Experiential Factors ||||
|---|---|---|---|---|
| | Being Bilingual | ESL courses | Clinical Placement | Student Teaching |
| Q1SE | No | No | No | No |
| Q2SE | No | Yes .383* | Yes -.625** | No |
| Q3SE | No | No | No | No |
| Q4SE | Yes .548** | No | No | No |
| Q5SE | No | No | No | No |
| Q5SE | No | No | No | No |
| Q6SE | No | Yes .540** | No | No |
| Q7SE | Yes .420* | No | No | No |
| Q8SE | Yes .754** | No | No | No |
| Q9SE | No | No | No | No |
| Q1ØSE | No | No | No | No |

*Note.* The correlation is statistically significant at the *.05 level and the **.01 level

tests may be biased against English Learners ($\rho = .514$, $\alpha = .05$), and that various disabilities were not the same as language acquisition issues ($\rho = .413$, $\alpha = .01$).

Findings from the open-ended questions and reflection papers provided additional insights regarding the data displayed in Tables 6 and 7. That is, the PSTs explained that being bilingual themselves, or hav-

Table 7. *Summary of Statistically Significant Correlations (rho) between PSTs' Demographic and Experiential Factors and PSTs' Outcome Expectancy (OE) Likert-scale Items of the Survey*

| Outcome Expectancy Item | Demographic and Experiential Factors ||||
|---|---|---|---|---|
| | Being Bilingual | ESL Courses | Clinical Placement | Student Teaching |
| Q1OE | Yes .443* | No | No | No |
| Q2OE | No | No | No | No |
| Q3OE | No | No | No | Yes -.523* |
| Q4OE | No | No | No | No |
| Q5OE | No | No | No | No |
| Q5OE | No | No | No | No |
| Q6OE | No | No | No | No |
| Q7OE | No | No | No | No |
| Q8OE | No | No | No | No |
| Q9OE | Yes .514* | No | No | No |
| Q1ØOE | Yes .413* | No | No | No |

*Note.* The correlation is statistically significant at the *.05 level and the **.01 level

ing attended an ESL or bilingual program at school when they were children, helped them to understand and empathize with the needs and struggles of these students. For example, one PST explained, "I am confident in being able to relate to ELs, as I was one myself. My first language is Spanish, and English is my second language. I am bilingual." One more PST commented on the disadvantage of not having experienced inclusion as a young EL child: "growing up as an EL, and being bilingual in school, I can relate to other ELs. It's hard. I had limited exposure to rich academic vocabulary because I was placed in ESL classes at a young age." Contrarily, another PST recalled good teaching practices from her bilingual classroom. Unlike the previous PST's comments, her experience had been positive and encouraged her to become an effective teacher for English Learners. She said,

*[From] my bilingual education experience when I was in elementary school, I recall a particular bilingual teacher who [resembles the] effective teaching that we discussed in class last week. The [bilingual] teacher made sure that the learning environment was positive and supporting [for us]. She would give us rigorous tasks that were meaningful and pertained to the content, and she provided scaffolding... Becoming an educator is one thing but being an effective one that will make sure that his or her English Learner students are successful and reach their full potential, is another thing. I want to be like that good bilingual teacher.*

## Influence of ESL Courses on PSTs' Beliefs

The study's findings demonstrated that having taken ESL courses positively correlated with PSTs' self-efficacy beliefs (Table 6). Specifically, taking ESL courses increased their feeling of being able to differentiate instruction based on English Learners' language proficiency level ($\rho = .383$, $\alpha = .05$) and to use various assessments with English Learners ($\rho = .540$, $\alpha = .05$).

It is important to clarify here that only 36.84% of the PSTs had taken other ESL courses in addition to the course they were enrolled in at the time of this investigation. Thus, the findings discussed in this section pertain to these participants.

PSTs' assertions in the survey open-ended questions and reflection papers (qualitative data analysis) concur and help to explain the quantitative data (Table 6). For instance, one PST asserted that the ESL courses she had taken helped her become aware of the complexity of the second language acquisition process, that language proficiency has different levels, and the importance of diverse cultural backgrounds:

*As I began taking ESL courses at [university], I wasn't aware of what to expect. I feel these courses helped prepare me to work with English Learners. This specific course emphasized the importance of continuing to develop our understanding of how English Learners acquire a second language. This course also helped me to understand how background knowledge and experiences shape English Learners so that teachers can match curriculum and assessments to students' language proficiency and cultural knowledge.*

Another PST commented on the use of appropriate methods and techniques to teach English Learners, that she had learned in ESL courses:

*Before taking the ESL courses, the idea of teaching English Learners used to be completely terrifying, being a native English speaker with no background in any language or Spanish, the most popular second language spoken in the United States. I felt for a long time I would fail the students of a minority language because I wouldn't know how to help them. I am thankful for the ESL courses I have taken at [university] and to have resources and techniques to better prepare me for when that step comes.*

Interestingly, another PST asserted that the ESL courses she had taken at the university, helped her to become aware of issues of achievement gaps between English Learners and mainstream students. These courses also helped her to realize that ineffective teaching can negatively influence students' learning and achievement. This PST said,

*I was never an EL [English Learner] student, so this was a new concept to me...I have taken ESL courses and learned more about ELs...I have realized [that there is an] achievement gap between ELs and non-ELs. I feel like it is easy for teachers to forget about ELs or not to include them. I noticed growing up that many ELs in my classes (I understand now that they were ELs), were not included in class or group discussions. These students seemed to just exist in the class. This is disappointing and as I have learned in my ESL courses at [university] that this method of teaching is not helpful."*

## Influence of Fieldwork on PSTs' Beliefs

Considering the influence of fieldwork practice on the PSTs' self-efficacy beliefs in the form of *clinical placement* in schools (Table 6), the findings from the open-ended questions and reflection papers (qualitative data analysis) either confirmed or contradicted the negative correlation (quantitative data analysis) between this factor and self-efficacy ($\rho = -.625$, $\alpha = .01$). PSTs complained about what they observed in their clinical placements regarding assessments for English Learners with and without disabilities. This complaint confirms the negative correlation previously mentioned. This PST said,

*I have not seen many project-based or formative assessments used with English Learners in my clinical placements, and not all of them [had] the same level of English proficiency. They have mostly been tested in the traditional way using multiple-choice and essay-based tests. This method has its place in school, but I feel that it should not be the only way that students are assessed because of the benefits that can be gained by using project-based assessments and authentic assessments.*

By contrast, a PST who was in the third clinical placement commented on the good influence of fieldwork. This contradicted the negative correlation previously discussed. The fact that this was her *third* clinical placement in schools a that she had the opportunity to observe an effective bilingual teacher, might explain her positive take on fieldwork. This PST explicated how such fieldwork had influenced her self-efficacy beliefs, particularly about assessments in the primary language of English Learners:

*This is my third clinical placement. I feel now that I have a good understanding of when my English Learners have learning disabilities. Assessing them in their first language using informal assessments is key. I have had the opportunity to observe a bilingual teacher assessing English Learners in their first language, Spanish, to find out if the problems were about learning English or about learning disabilities.*

Interestingly, other quantitative data about fieldwork (Table 7) showed a negative correlation between the influence of *student teaching* and outcome expectancy beliefs ($\rho = -.523$, $\alpha = .05$). Findings from the PSTs' answers to the open-ended questions and reflection papers (qualitative data) contradicted the said negative correlation. This is the situation of a PST whose student teaching fieldwork had been helpful to observe a teacher creating a welcoming environment and using instructional scaffolding with English Learners. The PST explicated,

*As a student teacher, I have been observing my cooperating teacher, and now that I think about it, and after our class discussion, [I can tell that] her teaching is good for English Learners because they know [her] expectations and feel safe, [they are] in a very safe environment. I see a lot of English Learners taking risks, for example, if the teacher asks a question, even the students who are nonverbal raise their hands. They know the teacher supports them with visuals, asks them more questions, or uses prompts to get to what they are trying to say.*

One other PST reflected on the benefits of being exposed to differentiation practices for English Learners in her student teaching fieldwork. Yet, she added that her experience with English Learners who have disabilities has been limited. A side note is that these findings concur with previous findings about PSTs expressing to have learned how to write lesson plans for English Learners, but not for English Learners with disabilities. This PST commented on her student teaching as follows:

*I am very comfortable teaching English Learners in my student teaching. I am very fortunate to be in a classroom where the ratio of L1 [first or primary language] English speakers to L1 Spanish speakers is 50:50. This has forced me to become good at differentiating for these students. But I am less comfortable working with English Learners who also have disabilities. I have only ever had one student whose L1 was different from English and who had a learning disability. However, I have gotten an opportunity recently with another student who is an English Learner, whose L1 is Spanish, and who has multiple disabilities. I think this will allow me to become more exposed to differentiating for this student.*

Finally, a PST commented that the student teaching experience had been helpful for her to use culturally responsive teaching practices with an English Learner who had special education needs. Yet, it was unclear how this PST worked in an RTI model. This PST said,

*In my student teaching, I have the opportunity to work with students in an RTI [response to intervention] format where I work with three special education students, [and] one of them [is] an English Learner. To provide this student with proper support, he is allowed to make personal connections and explain examples that are relevant to him and his life and culture rather than following a simple prompt that each student responds to. This allows the English Learner to make connections on a more personal level.*

## Additional Insights: Influence of PSTs' Disabilities on Their Beliefs

Findings from the PSTs' answers to the open-ended questions and reflection papers (dis)confirmed results from the Likert-scale survey items, which aligns with the study's purpose and the *QUAN®qual=explain* mixed-method research design. However, an in-depth analysis of qualitative data also provided additional insights into other factors that influenced PSTs' self-efficacy beliefs. These factors had not been initially considered in the study, nor included, in the survey, which made these findings an interesting discovery from the set of qualitative data itself regarding the participating PSTs. For instance, the qualitative findings showed that having a disability themselves was an important factor in helping PSTs to empathize with English Learners with disabilities. One PST asserted, "since the age of 10, I was diagnosed with ADHD and that led to many learning difficulties in school. So, I feel [that] because... of this... I am very able to teach English Learners who have learning disabilities." Another PST agreed and spoke about specific assessment accommodations that would work with English Learners and students with disabilities. Yet these were considered isolated "categories" (being an English Learner or having a disability) in her comment. This PST said,

*I have never been an English Learner, but I can connect to how assessment results can be influenced by academic limitations. I was on an IEP throughout my whole education...[Like] the English Learners' language barrier, I had to have my learning disability considered when I [had to take] standardized tests or other assessments. To adjust exams for me, I was given a word bank, extra time, or fewer questions. These adjustments would also be beneficial to an English Learner student.*

## Additional Insights: PSTs' Conflicting Views on Assessment

The in-depth analysis of qualitative data also provided additional insights about PSTs' conflicting views regarding issues of assessment. PSTs were concerned about assessment instruments commonly utilized in schools but that might yield inaccurate results, which in turn can influence the over-representation of English Learners in special education programs.

As an illustration, a PST student expressed concern about the use of standardized tests as the only assessment instrument for English Learners:

*High-stakes standardized tests that are used throughout the United States can often not be sensitive to the needs of English Learners. This can make the outcomes of these tests unreliable and invalid for these students. This means that important decisions regarding the future education of these students can be based on bad test results. They can go to special education classrooms when they may not need that.*

PSTs spoke of standardized tests as being insufficient to understand English Learners' outcomes because these assessments can be affected by extraneous variables such as linguistic complexity and cultural bias. A PST said,

*Traditional standardized tests may not be enough to meet the needs of English Learners. The results of these tests may not be useful. Traditional standardized tests are often used for accountability purposes. When it comes to English Learners, the outcomes of the assessments can be affected by linguistic complexity and cultural bias in standardized tests.*

PSTs were also concerned about how self-assessment could be effectively employed with English Learners with disabilities. PSTs viewed self-assessment as a practice that would align with standards. A PST shared conflicting views on self-assessment as an ideal practice for *all* students, yet difficult to carry out in some cases:

*Any assessment for English Learners should meet the same standards and assessments made for English native speakers. This has to be done to have fair assessments for all, and students should be involved in their assessments. It is a student's job to perform the tasks of the assessment and provide evidence of their learning, however, it is also their job to self-assess. I think this is especially important for English Learner students because they have a lot to learn, the lessons being taught in school as well as another language. On top of that if they are disabled like autistic too, how can they self-assess?*

As can be noted, the PSTs participating in the study were concerned about different issues related to the assessment of English Learners who also have special education needs. PSTs' self-efficacy pertained not only to instructing these children but also accurately and fairly assessing them. Teacher preparation programs would need to consider multidimensional issues, which will be addressed in the following sections of this chapter.

## DISCUSSION AND CONCLUSIONS

The purpose of this study was to explore PSTs' self-efficacy and outcome expectancy beliefs about working with English Learners with special education needs, and what demographic and experiential factors may influence these beliefs. In response to such purpose, the findings of the study demonstrated that more than half of the PSTs (68.42%) expressed not feeling capable of distinguishing between language acquisition issues and specific learning disabilities, and the rest of PSTs had mixed or contradictory beliefs. These findings speak of the judgment and multidimensional properties of self-efficacy beliefs (Zimmerman, 1999). PSTs' beliefs reflect the complex appraisal of their abilities. According to self-efficacy theory, the judgment of one's abilities is subjective and might not always relate to factual psychological traits (i.e., intelligence, and aptitudes). This also explains the malleability of self-efficacy beliefs, which is an important feature to consider in teacher preparation programs to positively change PSTs' negative beliefs.

The study's findings also allude to the importance of including *language* considerations in teacher education programs to prepare PSTs to work with linguistically diverse children, such as English Learners. Language considerations are relevant concerning sociolinguistic awareness of and attention to language diversity, second language acquisition stages, standards for English language development (commonly known as WIDA[3] standards) of English Learners, language demands of the content areas, and linguistic scaffolding (de Jong et al., 2013; Hutchinson, 2013; Lucas & Villegas, 2013).

In addition, 94.74% of the PSTs expressed feeling unprepared to properly assess or teach English Learners with disabilities. These findings concur with extant literature (Klingner et al., 2016; Umansky et al., 2017; Waitoller & Artiles, 2013) regarding PSTs' lack of preparedness and beliefs. These findings attest to the need to prepare PSTs to work with this increasing subgroup of the school population.

The current investigation provided interesting details about the low self-efficacy beliefs of the participants in this study. The PSTs did not believe that they could design and implement lesson plans for English Learners with disabilities or communicate effectively (self-efficacy beliefs) with these students. The PSTs did not believe to have learned enough strategies or to have gained enough experience to teach English Learners with disabilities to be able to positively influence these children's learning (outcome expectancy beliefs). These findings allude to the context-dependent property of self-efficacy (Zimmerman, 1999). According to socio-cognitive theory, self-efficacy beliefs are specific to certain situations or contexts. In this study, most PSTs expressed feeling capable of teaching English Learners, based on what they had learned from ESL courses at the university. These self-efficacy beliefs were specific to being able to write and teach lessons for English Learners, considering different levels of English language proficiency. However, the PSTs did not feel capable of, or had contradictory beliefs about, teaching English Learners who *have disabilities*. The PSTs did not feel fully prepared or able to cope with the challenges that this specific situation represents.

There was also a disconnect between what the PSTs were learning in the university courses and what they observed or encountered in their school fieldwork. The reality of school classrooms did not always match what "theory", or the literature says regarding effective teaching practices for English Learners in general, and English Learners with disabilities in particular. This disconnection might result in gaps in PSTs' knowledge and practice and might influence their motivation about becoming future practicing teachers.

This situation was aggravated by the fact that the PSTs were enrolled in different teacher education programs that operated *separately* from each other, namely, early childhood education, elementary education, secondary education, special education, and ESL credential programs. However, children do not come to school with "separate" selves. Different identity categories intersect and influence children's learning and achievement. The intersection of culture, language, race, and ability categories increase the vulnerability of English Learners with special education needs (Cavendish et al., 2015; Klingner et al., 2016). This is concerning, considering that these students are the fastest-growing subgroup of minority pupils in American K–12 schools, and all teachers will likely work with them throughout their professional careers.

## LIMITATIONS AND IMPLICATIONS

### Limitations

One limitation of this research is that the exploratory case study design does not allow for grand generalizations. The conclusions pertain to a particular sample of PSTs at a university in a Midwestern state of the US. The small target group (fifty-three students) and final sample of students who consented to continue participating in the study to its conclusion (nineteen PSTs), and short-term data collection (one semester) are other limitations. In addition, observations of PSTs' fieldwork in schools were not included in the analysis because not all participants were enrolled in clinical placements or student teaching at the time the study took place. The survey utilized to collect data only allowed participants to indicate whether they were or were not engaged in fieldwork in schools. These limitations could be considered and resolved in future investigations.

### Implications for Future Research

Research could be conducted on PSTs' self-efficacy beliefs by employing a larger sample of participants and with a long-term time frame for data collection. Large-scope investigations would offer more generalizable findings. Long-term studies would provide insights into PSTs' developmental trajectories in teacher education programs. Future research might also consider how the COVID-19 pandemic and online teaching has affected English Learners (which is beyond this study's scope) and what are thus the repercussions for teacher preparation.

It is necessary to continue investigating PSTs' self-efficacy beliefs about teaching and assessing English Learners with special education needs. Research could include multidisciplinary teams addressing the "whole" child, instead of examining only some aspects of their development and learning. Scholars could leave their isolated research silos and seek instead to conduct more interdisciplinary research.

Finally, future research could address models of interdisciplinary collaboration among K–12 school personnel so that school practice, along with teacher preparation programs, become more aligned, comprehensive, and inclusive.

## Implications for Teacher Preparation Programs and Teacher Educators

The preparation of PSTs could incorporate interdisciplinary considerations to adequately prepare future teachers who can move the field of special education toward more inclusive and equitable models. Some specific strategies are described in the following paragraphs, though future research could address the use of tangible strategies.

### Implications for Teacher Preparation Programs

Teacher preparation programs could provide interdisciplinary training for PSTs who will be future teachers for English Learners with disabilities who are present in general education classrooms, special education settings, and second language support services in schools. That is, input from different disciplines, such as psychology (i.e., teacher self-efficacy), multicultural education in general education (i.e., cultural differences, culturally responsive teaching), second language learning (i.e., second language acquisition, linguistically responsive teaching), and various areas of special education knowledge and skills, would be most beneficial.

Teacher preparation programs could also use an interdisciplinary approach to guide PSTs from different credentialing programs in collaborative coursework and tasks. In such coursework, PSTs could learn how to use different lenses (e.g., an ESL lens, a special education lens) to ask pertinent questions that would help them obtain a deeper understanding of the whole child. By using concurrently different lenses, PSTs could discuss together the strengths and areas that need improvement of English Learners who have disabilities. PSTs could also be provided with opportunities to use different lenses to discuss possible accommodations and modifications pertinent to different case studies of students with special education needs who are English Learners.

Teacher preparation programs may include interdisciplinary fieldwork in schools. Field experiences in schools are relevant to connect theory with practice. Practicums in schools enable PSTs' deeper understanding and learning. As such, teacher preparation programs may search for and place PSTs in K-12 school settings that use an interdisciplinary model to work with English Learners who have disabilities. In this manner, PSTs could observe directly, and become involved gradually, in real-life effective and interdisciplinary teaching for this increasing population of children in American schools.

### Implications for Teacher Educators

Teacher educators from different disciplines could learn from one another by exchanging information and resources related to teaching English Learners with special education needs. This is relevant because teacher educators are often products of "siloed" training programs themselves. Teacher educators may have to leave their comfort zones and become more teachable and vulnerable amid, and against, the often competitive and individualistic environment of academia.

Teacher educators from different credentialing programs (e.g., ESL, special education, general education) could design shared assignments that necessitate continued collaboration among themselves and the PSTs taking their courses. Teacher educators could design together course content and co-teach PSTs. Teacher educators might consider using an interdisciplinary approach in all teacher preparation programs, not only ESL, special education, and general education.

In this manner, experts from various fields could support the development and delivery of content and fieldwork practicums in teacher preparation. Teacher educators using an interdisciplinary approach would also model for the PSTs how this type of collaboration works and how to solve issues that might arise in this concerted process. As Ortiz and Robertson (2018) affirmed, "teacher educators must engage in interdisciplinary collaboration to ensure that their candidates, regardless of certification area, graduate prepared to provide effective language and literacy instruction to ELs [English Learners]" (p. 8) and to English Learners with special education needs.

## REFERENCES

Bandura, A. (1977). Self-efficacy: Toward a unifying theory of behavioral change. *Psychological Review*, *84*(2), 191–215. doi:10.1037/0033-295X.84.2.191 PMID:847061

Bandura, A. (1991). Social cognitive theory of self-regulation. *Organizational Behavior and Human Performance*, *50*(2), 248–287. doi:10.1016/0749-5978(91)90022-L

Bandura, A. (1997). *Self-efficacy: The exercise of control*. W.H. Freeman & Company.

Bandura, A. (2004). Health promotion by social cognitive means. *Health Education & Behavior*, *31*(2), 143–164. doi:10.1177/1090198104263660 PMID:15090118

Brownell, M. T., & Pajares, E. (1999). Teacher efficacy and perceived success in mainstreaming students with behavior and learning problems. *Teacher Education and Special Education*, *22*(3), 154–164. doi:10.1177/088840649902200303

Caprara, G. V., Barbaranelli, C., Steca, P., & Malone, P. S. (2006). Teachers' self-efficacy beliefs as determinants of job satisfaction and students' academic achievement: A study at the school level. *Journal of School Psychology*, *44*(6), 473–490. doi:10.1016/j.jsp.2006.09.001

Cavendish, W., Artiles, A. J., & Harry, B. (2015). Tracking inequality 60 years after Brown: Does policy legitimize the racialization of disability? *Multiple Voices for Ethnically Diverse Exceptional Learners*, *14*(2), 1–11.

Chitiyo, J., Chitiyo, A., & Dombek, D. (2020). Preservice teachers' understanding of problem behavior. *International Journal of Curriculum and Instruction*, *12*(2), 63–74. https://ijci.wcci-international.org

Chu, S., & García, S. (2014). Culturally responsive teaching efficacy beliefs of in-service special education teachers. *Remedial and Special Education*, *35*(4), 218–232. doi:10.1177/0741932513520511

Creswell, J. W., & Plano Clark, V. L. (2018). *Designing and conducting mixed methods research* (3rd ed.). SAGE.

Creswell, J. W., Plano Clark, V. L., Gutmann, M., & Hanson, W. (2003). Advanced mixed methods research designs. In A. Tashakkori & C. Teddlie (Eds.), *Handbook of mixed methods in social and behavioral research* (pp. 209–240). SAGE.

de Jong, E. J., Harper, C. A., & Coady, M. R. (2013). Enhanced knowledge and skills for elementary mainstream teachers of English Language Learners. *Theory into Practice, 52*(2), 89–97. doi:10.1080/00405841.2013.770326

Emerson, R., Fretz, R., & Shaw, L. (2011). *Writing Ethnographic Fieldnotes.* The University of Chicago Press. doi:10.7208/chicago/9780226206868.001.0001

Every Student Succeeds Act (ESSA). (2015). US Government. https://www.ed.gov/essa

Gehrke, R. S., & Cocchiarella, M. (2013). Preservice special and general educators' knowledge of inclusion. *Teacher Education and Special Education, 36*(3), 204–216. doi:10.1177/0888406413495421

Hassan, A., & Tairab, H. (2012). Science teaching self-efficacy and outcome expectancy beliefs of secondary school teachers in UAE. *International Journal for Research in Education, 32,* 1–22.

Hutchinson, M. (2013). Bridging the gap: Preservice teachers and their knowledge of working with English Language Learners. *TESOL Journal, 4*(1), 25–54. doi:10.1002/tesj.51

Individuals with Disabilities Education Improvement Act. (IDEIA). (2004). US Government. https://sites.ed.gov/idea/

Klingner, J., Brownell, M., Mason, L., Sindelar, P., Benedict, A., Griffin, C., Lane, K., Israel, M., Oakes, W., Menzies, H., Germer, K., & Park, Y. (2016). Teaching students with special needs in the new millennium. In D. H. Gitomer & C. A. Bell (Eds.), *Handbook of Research on Teaching* (5th ed., pp. 639–716). American Educational Research Association. doi:10.3102/978-0-935302-48-6_10

Lucas, T., & Villegas, A. M. (2013). Preparing linguistically responsive teachers: Laying the foundation in preservice teacher education. *Theory into Practice, 52*(2), 37–41. doi:10.1080/00405841.2013.770327

Martínez-Alvarez, P. (2020). Essential constructs in the preparation of inclusive bilingual education teachers: Mediation, agency, and collectivity. *Bilingual Research Journal, 43*(3), 304–322. doi:10.1080/15235882.2020.1802367

Martínez-Alvarez, P. (2021). *Teacher education for inclusive bilingual contexts: Collective reflection to support emergent bilinguals with and without disabilities.* Routledge. doi:10.4324/9781003112259

McHatton, P. A., & Parker, A. (2013). Purposeful preparation: Longitudinally exploring inclusion attitudes of general and special education preservice teachers. *Teacher Education and Special Education, 36*(3), 186–203. doi:10.1177/0888406413491611

National Center for Education Statistics. (2022a). *English Learners in Public Schools. Condition of Education.* U.S. Department of Education, Institute of Education Sciences. https://nces.ed.gov/programs/coe/indicator/cgf

National Center for Education Statistics. (2022b). *Students with Disabilities. Condition of Education.* U.S. Department of Education, Institute of Education Sciences. https://nces.ed.gov/programs/coe/indicator/cgg

National Clearinghouse for English Language Acquisition. (2011). *What legal obligation do schools have to English Language Learners?* https://ncela.ed.gov/faqs/view/6

Ortiz, A. A., & Robertson, P. M. (2018). Preparing teachers to serve English learners with language- and/or literacy-related difficulties and disabilities. *Teacher Education and Special Education, 41*(3), 176–187. doi:10.1177/0888406418757035

Riazi, A. M., & Candlin, C. N. (2014). Mixed-methods research in language teaching and learning: Opportunities, issues, and challenges. *Language Teaching, 47*(2), 135–173. doi:10.1017/S0261444813000505

Ricklefs, M. A. (2019). Teachers' conceptualizations and expectations of culturally and linguistically diverse young students. *International Journal of Diversity in Education, 19*(2), 33–44. https://doi.org/10.18848/2327-0020/CGP/v19i02/33-44

Ricklefs, M. A. (2021a). Functions of language use and raciolinguistic ideologies in students' interactions. *Bilingual Research Journal, 44*(1), 90–107. https://doi:10.1080/15235882.2021.1897048

Ricklefs, M. A. (2021b). Variables influencing ESL teacher candidates' language ideologies. *Language and Education.* https://doi.10.1080/09500782.2021.1936546

Ricklefs, M. A. (2022a). "Politics at its finest!": Language management and ideologies affecting the education of minoritized students. *SN Social Sciences, 2*(61). https://doi.org/10.1007/s43545-022-00359-y

Ricklefs, M. A. (2022b). "¡Échale ganas!": Latina mothers use their cultural community wealth to enhance their children's education. *International Journal of Cultural Studies, 17*(2), 63–73. https://doi.org/10.18848/2327-008X/CGP/v17i02/63-73

Stites, M. L., Rakes, C. R., Noggle, A. K., & Shah, S. (2018). Preservice teacher perceptions of preparedness to teach in inclusive settings as an indicator of teacher preparation program effectiveness. *Discourse in Communication for Sustainable Education, 9*(2), 21–39. doi:10.2478/dcse-2018-0012

Umansky, I. M., Thompson, K. D., & Díaz, G. (2017). Using an ever–English Learner framework to examine disproportionality in special education. *Exceptional Children, 84*(1), 76–96. doi:10.1177/0014402917707470

Vespa, J., Medina, L., & Armstrong, D. A. (2020). *Demographic turning points for the United States: Population projections for 2020 to 2060. Current Population Reports.* US Census Bureau.

Waitoller, F., & Artiles, F. (2013). A decade of professional development research for inclusive education: A critical review and notes for a research program. *Review of Educational Research, 83*(3), 319–356. doi:10.3102/0034654313483905

Walker, C. L., & Stone, K. (2011). Preparing teachers to reach English language learners: Preservice and in-service initiatives. In T. Lucas (Ed.), *Teacher preparation for linguistically diverse classrooms: A resource for teacher educators* (pp. 127–142). Routledge.

Zimmerman, B. J. (1999). Self-efficacy and educational development. In A. Bandura (Ed.), *Self-efficacy in changing societies* (pp. 202–231). Cambridge University Press.

## ENDNOTES

[1] The author is aware of other identity categories (e.g., emergent bilinguals, multilingual learners, translinguals, dual-language learners) commonly utilized by scholars in the field but uses *English Learners* because it is the term employed in the legislation currently in effect in the United States (ESSA, 2015).

[2] Even though several states have teacher preparation standards for educators who will teach English Learners, such as the state where this study took place, none of these standards address English Learners who also have disabilities. One set of standards targets English Learners only. Another set of standards targets students who have disabilities only. There is no convergence of these teacher preparation standards.

[3] WIDA stands for Word-Class Instructional Design and Assessment. The WIDA consortium is a group of states dedicated to the design and implementation of standards, assessment instruments, and teaching guidelines for English Learners in the United States. The state where this investigation took place is part of this consortium.

# Chapter 17
# Interdisciplinary Preparation to Meet the Emotional and Behavioral Health Needs of Diverse Students

**Sara Kupzyk**
https://orcid.org/0000-0002-6721-8659
*University of Nebraska, Omaha, USA*

**Philip D. Nordness**
*University of Nebraska, Omaha, USA*

## ABSTRACT

*Although interdisciplinary teaming within a multi-tiered system of support is valuable, barriers to collaboration exist among professionals because of competing standards, lack of understanding roles, and lack of common language. These challenges may relate to how pre-service training is arranged. Training is usually provided in separate programs with little overlap in courses and field experiences. Interprofessional education (IPE) is a potential means of addressing the siloed approach. The goal of this chapter is to describe an IPE preparation program designed to develop scholars to meet the emotional and behavioral health needs of diverse students. Participating scholars complete a plan of study that includes shared coursework and courses that are unique to their field, participate in a weekly professional seminar, and take part in an interdisciplinary practicum experience. The authors also offer recommendations for university programs seeking to create interdisciplinary opportunities for pre-service professionals.*

School district administrators indicate that the mental health and behavioral needs of students are among their top concerns (Deliberti & Schwartz, 2022). The focus on behavioral health needs is warranted since two out of five youth will meet criteria for a mental health disorder by age 18 (Bitsko et al., 2022). Furthermore, in the School Pulse Panel, a national survey of 846 school public school leaders, over 80

DOI: 10.4018/978-1-6684-6438-0.ch017

*Interdisciplinary Preparation to Meet the Emotional and Behavioral Health Needs of Diverse Students*

percent of the leaders reported that the behavioral and socioemotional development of students had been negatively impacted by the COVID-19 pandemic (U.S. Department of Education, Institute for Education Sciences, 2022). In addition, over 50 percent of school leaders reported an increase in classroom disruptions and tardiness, and over 30 percent reported an increase in fights between students and student verbal abuse on teachers and staff. To address these issues, 70 percent of school leaders said they need more training to support students' socioemotional development and 51 percent reported the need for more training on behavior management strategies.

Even before the pandemic, the mental health and behavioral needs of children and youth were not being met as schools struggled to keep up with demand and barriers to access across diverse populations prevented many students from receiving the services they need (U.S. Department of Education, Office of Special Education and Rehabilitative Services, 2021). In fact, only half of youth with a mental health disorder receive treatment, with schools being the most common site services are delivered (Whitney & Peterson, 2019). Untreated mental health concerns can lead to behavior challenges in classrooms that are linked to high student dropout rates, later unemployment, incarceration, and homelessness (Kataoka et al., 2002). Overall, there is a pressing need to increase the number of school professionals that receive training to effectively and collaboratively address behavioral challenges presented by students.

The current approach to addressing the behavioral challenges of students is often fragmented. Within schools, there are a number of professionals, including teachers, counselors, school psychologists, special educators, and behavior analysts that are trying to address the behavioral needs of students, however they often work independently of each other without collaborating across disciplines (Adelman & Taylor, 2021). This results in a siloed approach to meeting the needs of students and is less effective in supporting the generalization of academic and behavioral skills (Adelman & Taylor, 2021). In the absence of collaborative services and supports for these students, challenging behaviors are often dealt with through punitive discipline procedures or referral to special education. This is problematic when we consider the racial disparities in student discipline rates, particularly exclusionary discipline practices (Barrett et al., 2018; Skiba et al., 2011).

As an alternative to this siloed approach, schools need to consider a multi-tiered system of support (MTSS) to address educational and behavioral health needs of students (U.S. Department of Education. Office of Special Education and Rehabilitative Services, 2021). MTSS is an integrated framework for organizing a continuum of evidence-based practices for addressing the academic, behavioral, and socioemotional needs of children and youth. Within this framework interdisciplinary expertise can by leveraged to guide implementation of integrated practices and promote effective decision making across each tier. The MTSS framework includes universal screening, differentiation of goals and objectives, tiered social and academic interventions, and ongoing progress monitoring. Successful MTSS implementation addresses the academic and behavioral needs of every student, regardless of their ability, eligibility, or cultural background, and can be addressed by integrating assessment and intervention within a multi-tiered approach (March & Mathur, 2020). When implementing an MTSS framework the goal is to identify and address the differing needs of the students and to match them with the supports across the tiers.

An effective MTSS framework prioritizes primary prevention at tier 1 by establishing a routine to provide an environment that is predictable, safe, and emphasizes pro-social behaviors that we want students to display (I-MTSS Research Network, 2022). Tier 1 includes a universal, evidenced based core curriculum that can typically address the diverse behavioral and academic needs of most children. This can include universal expectations for behavior, evidenced based instruction, and screening to measure student progress. The middle tier (tier 2) is intended to provide secondary prevention which may include more focused and targeted supports for those students who may be struggling with the academic or behavioral expectations from tier 1. These students may benefit from additional instruction that may address school readiness skills, provide remedial instruction, or address social skills that may enable them to be more successful in the general education setting. The final tier includes tertiary prevention and it is intended for students who may need more intensive and targeted interventions to meet their unique needs. At this tier decisions related to specialized instruction or special education may be considered depending on the amount of supports needed for student success. The key to effectively implementing an MTSS framework is to make certain that it is a problem solving, data driven decision making process that matches the needs of the child with the supports available at each tier (Averill & Rinaldi, 2013).

An effective approach to MTSS is grounded in the merging of interdisciplinary practices which can be integrated in inclusive settings to meet the diverse needs of all students (Grisham-Brown & Hemmeter, 2017). This approach emphasizes a responsive as well as a preventative approach to students' behavioral needs, as well as academic performance (Marsh & Mathur, 2020). Within an MTSS framework, specialty service providers, such as special educators, school psychologists, and behavior analysts are well-positioned to collaborate on school-wide efforts to implement MTSS.

Special education teachers provide specialized instruction through the use of accommodations and modifications to curriculum to meet the unique needs of the student. As the professional responsible for the individualized education program (IEP), the special education teacher collaborates with professionals across disciplines to coordinate services to ensure the child has access to a free appropriate education in the least restrictive environment. School psychologists often provide comprehensive evaluation to aid in determining disability status, consultation to support teachers and related providers in developing and delivering interventions, direct services to students to support their success, and progress monitoring of services and supports. To address intensive behavioral issues within schools many school districts have started employing Board Certified Behavior Analysts (BCBA). A BCBA is a professional who specializes in Applied Behavior Analysis (ABA) and has been credentialed by the Behavior Analysis Certification Board (BACB). Applied behavior analysts engage in a data driven process to examine the role of antecedents and consequences on behavior and thereby development interventions to improve students' outcomes.

Although interdisciplinary teaming is recognized as a key component of MTSS, barriers to effective collaboration exist including competing policies/standards across disciplines, lack of understanding roles and responsibilities, lack of common language, and logistical barriers (Manor-Binyamini, 2007; O'Keeffe & McDowell, 2004). Challenges such as these may be related to how pre-service training is arranged. Specifically, team members typically receive their pre-service training from separate programs that provide limited overlap in coursework and field experiences and little exposure to the roles, competencies, and strengths of other educational professionals (Dobbes-Oates & Morris, 2016). To address the importance of interdisciplinary teaming and decrease the use of a siloed approach in practice, university and college programs can adopt an interprofessional education (IPE) approach.

The World Health Organization (2010) defines IPE as "When students from two or more professions learn about, from and with each other to enable effective collaboration and improve health outcomes." The concept of IPE has been used in healthcare fields since the 1960s as a means to increase collaboration across fields and enhance the quality and coordination of healthcare. In more recent years, the value of IPE has been demonstrated in education-related fields. For example, programs have been developed that provide training for special educators and physical therapists (George & Oriel, 2009), early childhood educators and social workers (Anderson, 2013), special educators and school counselors (Dobbs-Oates &

Morris, 2016), and school psychologists and speech language pathologists (DeVeny & Mckevitt, 2021). Similar to findings in healthcare, results show benefits to student trainees who participate in the training and benefits to the systems where they work. For example, trainees report (a) more positive perceptions of their own profession and other disciplines, (b) increased awareness of the roles, responsibilities, and contributions of professionals from other disciplines, and (c) higher perception of the value of IPE and teaming (Anderson, 2013; Dobbs-Oates & Morris, 2016; DeVeney & McKevitt, 2021). Larger systemic benefits include improved care outcomes and enhanced staff morale (WHO, 2010). Overall, one means to encourage meaningful interdisciplinary collaboration in practice with an MTSS framework is to provide opportunities for collaboration across disciplines through coursework and field experiences. These collaborative efforts in turn might improve and lead to more equitable student outcomes.

## PERSONNEL DEVELOPMENT PROGRAM

Given the value and potential positive outcomes of IPE, our team developed an interdisciplinary personnel preparation training project for school-based professionals to increase capacity to meet the behavioral needs of students. The project involved three disciplines at the graduate-level: applied behavior analysis, special education, and school psychology. In this section, we describe the development of the project, goals, activities, and evaluation methods.

### Project Development

As described above, many professionals are involved in supporting students within an MTSS framework and special education, yet most professionals do not receive training in how to effectively collaborate across disciplines. Although members of our faculty team often participated on each other's student research committees and students had opportunities to take coursework across the programs, our efforts were not specifically aimed to increase interdisciplinary practice and the students did not have shared practicum opportunities. Overall, we recognized that although we had an understanding and appreciation for related fields, this was not systematically communicated or demonstrated with our students. Therefore, we decided to create an IPE training program to facilitate interdisciplinary collaboration and leadership skills to meet the diverse needs of students with behavioral concerns.

We identified the Personnel Development Grant funding opportunity through the U.S. Department of Education, Office of Special Education and Rehabilitation Programs and developed a team to write a proposal. Our team began preparing materials for the grant approximately a year in advance. In writing and implementing the grant, we identified project goals, competencies, activities, and evaluation procedures. Each is described below.

### Project Goals and Aims

The long-term goal of the project was to increase the pool of trained behavioral interventionists who can effectively implement systemic behavioral interventions in school settings to improve behavioral and academic outcomes for children and adolescents with or at-risk for behavioral issues. Increasing the number of trained professionals is important to address the significant shortages in special education

(AAEE, 2022; U.S. Department of Education, 2021), school psychology (Goforth et al., 2017; NASP, 2021), and behavior analysis (BACB, 2022).

The specific objective was to provide interdisciplinary leadership training for preservice providers in our applied behavior analysis master's program, school psychology educational specialist program, and special education master's program so that they may effectively implement systemic behavioral interventions in school settings. The primary aims were to: (a) establish an interdisciplinary training program focused on systemic behavioral intervention in school settings for youth with significant behavioral issues; (b) recruit and retain high quality masters level scholars in applied behavior analysis, school psychology, and special education to complete an interdisciplinary program focused on systemic behavioral intervention in school settings for youth with significant behavioral issues; and (c) train scholars to competence in evidence-based behavioral intervention and leadership skills needed for systemic implementation to address the multifaceted needs of children and adolescents with and at-risk for significant behavioral concerns.

## Project Competencies

To accomplish these goals, we outlined core competencies for all of the scholars from the three graduate training programs. This task was accomplished by reviewing preparation standards from each of the disciplines (i.e., National Association of School Psychologists Blueprint for Training and Practice, Council for Exceptional Children Professional Preparation Standards, Behavior Analyst Certification Board Task List) and components related to delivery of MTSS. We agreed on the following eight competencies that included knowledge and skill indicators: (1) child and adolescent development, (2) applied behavior analysis, (3) family-centered services, (4) intensive instruction, (5) identification of behavioral health needs, (6) functional behavioral assessment, (7) data-based decision making, and (8) systems-change and leadership. We also used the interdisciplinary collaborative practice competencies identified by the Interprofessional Education Collaborative (IPEC, 2016) that are organized within four domains: values and ethics, roles/responsibilities, interdisciplinary communication, and teams/teamwork. Content and discussion related to cultural responsiveness (i.e., using cultural characteristics and experiences to enhance intervention outcomes) and humility (i.e., an ongoing process of self-reflection to enhance partnerships) were embedded within the competencies and across the project activities (Beaulieu & Jimenez-Gomez, 2022). We found that it was important to establish agreement on the competencies because they were used to inform our program activities. See Figure 1 for an overview of the competencies and activities.

## Project Activities

When discussing potential scholar activities, we wanted to provide balance between coursework/instruction, discussion, and shared fieldwork experiences. Therefore, we decided that scholars would participate in individual program-specific coursework, shared coursework, a weekly professional seminar and practicum. In addition, to promote and encourage continued leadership development, upon graduation, scholars were invited to participate in alumni activities including sharing their experiences from working in the community and their new place of employment. These presentations have been effective in helping scholars understand the relationship between research to practice.

*Figure 1. Overview of the competencies and activities*

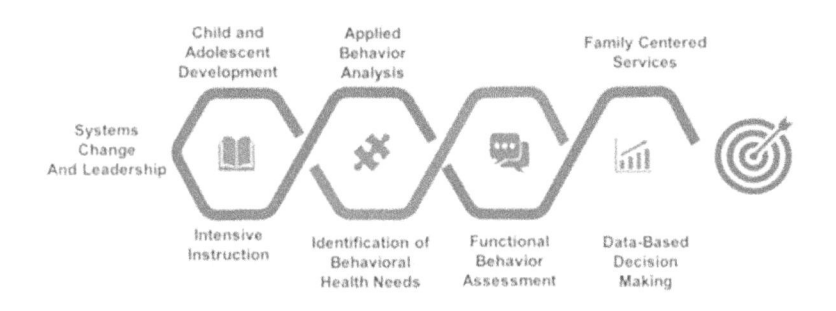

**Coursework**
- Unique to program
- Shared

**Professional Seminar**
- Clinical topics
- Leadership and skill-building
- Speakers from the community
- Literature discussions
- Case presentations

**Alumni Activities**
- Lead presentation/discussions for new scholars
- Faculty available for consultation

**Interdisciplinary Practicum**
- Interdisciplinary teams
- Collaborative efforts with other professional fields
- Conduct behavioral assessments
- Review and write Individualized Education Programs and Behavior Intervention Plans
- Write treatment protocols
- Train educators to implement protocols
- Monitor progress toward goals
- Participate in school/district leadership team meetings
- Supervision on-site and with project faculty

## Coursework

Scholars completed required program/discipline-specific coursework as well as shared coursework. This helped scholars to develop their own area of expertise (i.e., school psychology, special education, ABA) and joint expertise. The shared coursework for this program focused on applied behavior analysis so that all of the scholars developed extensive knowledge and skills to prevent, intervene, and evaluate behavioral concerns. In the first semester, all of the scholars took a Proseminar Learning course together that provided a foundation for an approach to understanding behavior and principles of learning. Other shared courses included (a) Behavior Analysis and Intervention that addresses behavioral assessment (including FBAs) and behavioral interventions, (b) Small-n Research that provides a basis for evaluating interventions in schools; and (c) Psychotherapeutic Interventions that discusses mental health disorders and related treatment.

Once the courses were selected, we conducted a review of the courses to determine where each competency was addressed in coursework and areas that should be of primary emphasis within the proseminar. This task was also completed by an expert reviewer who had significant experience in research, training, policy and practice related to advancing school mental health, and recommendations were incorporated into the training program.

## Professional Seminar

The goals of the professional seminar were to cover content related to the competencies (with emphasis on areas that received less attention across the required courses for each program) and provide opportunities for leadership development through discussion and presentations. The seminars included presentations by program faculty, invited presentations from community members and leaders in each respective field, journal club discussions (i.e., scholar-led discussions about current topics and literature), and interdisciplinary case presentations. In addition to selecting topics for the seminar based on the competencies, as the grant progressed, we also sought scholar input. Topics included roles of each profession, implementation science, family engagement strategies, explicit instruction, program evaluation, behavioral assessment, etc.

For example, in the area of family engagement and cultural responsiveness, we established a collaboration with our local University Center for Excellence in Developmental Disabilities (UCEDD) to create opportunities for the scholars to learn directly with parents of children with disabilities. The UCEDD provides support for Parent Resource Coordinators (PRC) which are parents of children with disabilities who receive training to provide support and assistance to other families who have children with disabilities or complex health needs. With a small group of PRCs, we created a seminar series that included (a) scholars attending a panel discussion with families of children with disabilities, (b) meeting with a family for more in-depth discussion, and (c) discussion of problem-based scenarios with faculty and parents. For the panel, we invited scholars to submit questions in advance and developed questions that the PRCs thought would be helpful for the scholars to learn about from a family-perspective. The questions ranged from benefits of peer-to-peer support, to ways to support families after receiving a diagnosis for their child, to systems-level concerns for children with disabilities. The more individualized family meetings provided an opportunity for the scholars to gain a deeper understanding about an individual family's story, challenges, and success related to special education services for their child. We provided a list of questions to facilitate conversation, but scholars and families were invited to talk about areas that were of greatest interest to them. Lastly, the problem-based scenarios were developed to explore implicit biases and strategies to enhance family-school partnerships, with a focus on engaging diverse families (e.g., language, ethnicity, socioeconomic status). The scholars learned about additional barriers (e.g., language, parental disregard, resources, deficit-based perspectives) to collaboration often experienced by culturally and linguistically diverse families within the scenarios (Burke & Goldman, 2018). The scenarios provided a safe space for scholars to ask questions, increase their understanding of family perspectives and evaluate strategies to better address family and child needs. The scholars and parents reported that the series was mutually beneficial and that they would strongly recommend the experiences to others. The scholars described that they gained a better understanding of family perspectives and improved confidence in partnering with families.

In addition to instruction and discussion, the seminar proved to be a beneficial time for team building and leadership development. We allocated time for the scholars to share experiences from the practicum sites and problem solve with one another. In the first years of the grant, each scholar presented on their own case to develop presentation and leadership skills; however, we later modified this plan to place greater emphasis on interdisciplinary collaboration in practice. In later years, the scholars prepared paired case presentations (partner scholars from different disciplines) and highlighted the unique contributions of each profession and collaborative efforts to address individual student concerns. The scholars also delivered team presentations and facilitated discussion about a class or school-wide project they completed. All of the faculty provide feedback to the scholars based on a project-specific rubric.

## Practicum

Within practicum, scholars used the title "Interdisciplinary Behavioral Consultant." For the interdisciplinary practicum, scholars were placed in teams within local high-needs partnering school districts with a site supervisor. The scholars work with students from diverse backgrounds, including those with significant intellectual and developmental disabilities. For this project, we selected site supervisors who had their BCBA and provided behavioral supports within their district. At one practicum site, the supervisors were employed within the district as behavioral facilitators. At the other site, the supervisors provided behavioral supports through a contract with the school district. In addition to meeting regularly with their site supervisor, the scholars met in teams (a mix of scholars from each practicum site) with an interdisciplinary faculty pair for supervision, discussion, and problem solving. During ongoing supervision, scholars engage in self-awareness activities and use a problem-solving approach to explore cultural considerations and potential bias within assessment and intervention programming (for sample self-awareness activities see Beaulieu & Jimenez-Gomez, 2022; for a description of the use of problem solving to enhance equity see McIntosh et al., 2018).

The specific placements ranged from preschool through high school settings and efforts are made to provide a variety of opportunities during the scholars' training. The scholars participated in a range of activities in practicum across the MTSS tiers. For example, at tier 1, the scholars collaborated as a site-based team to develop, implement, and evaluate a class or school-wide project each year. Projects have included training for paraeducators, developing instructional programming for an alternative curriculum classroom, and conducting reviews of programs and interventions to fulfill needs identified through interviews and data collection. At tier 2, the scholars conducted assessments to identify students at-risk for behavioral concerns and collaborated with teams to develop targeted interventions. At tier 3, the scholars have conducted more in-depth functional behavioral assessments to inform the development of individualized interventions, provided training and coaching to school staff on the implementation of individualized student plans, directly implemented intervention plans with students, and evaluated student progress. At the systems-level, students have participated in MTSS leadership team meetings and attended local and state conferences.

Due to the length of their programs, scholars in ABA and special education participated in the project for two years (ABA scholars complete 48-51 credits depending on selection of thesis or research other than thesis; special education complete 51 credits), whereas scholars in school psychology participated for three years (complete 72-78 credits depending on whether or not they seek the BCBA credential). During the third year of training, scholars in school psychology completed an advanced practicum that included continued services within partner schools as well as engagement in activities to increase leadership and system-change knowledge and skills. We collaborated with our state-level MTSS team to create experiences for the scholars to participate in their meetings, review materials and documents, and create training materials and documents to be used in future school-level social-emotional-behavioral learning trainings.

## Alumni Activities

After completing their programs, scholars were invited to be part of an alumni project network to encourage application of the interdisciplinary teaming in practice and to give the scholars an opportunity to share information from the field with new scholars. These unique interdisciplinary experiences allow scholars to learn more about the roles and contributions of other professionals, achieve similar competencies for addressing emotional and behavioral needs of students, and understand language from other professions. The faculty team also remained available for consultation with the alumni.

## Project Evaluation

The evaluation plan involved an iterative process in which qualitative and quantitative data are collected, reviewed, and changes made to enhance training. To assess scholars' knowledge and skills for each competency, they completed a pre and post self-assessment. In addition, at the end of each semester, the scholars and site supervisors rated the level of independence the scholar demonstrated with skills related to each competency. The scholars also provide feedback about their practicum supervisors. For the professional seminar, an expert consultant reviewed the syllabus and provided feedback; recommendations were incorporated into the plan. Each semester, the scholars completed a course evaluation and were invited to note topics of interest to them for future seminars.

At the end of each year, a focus group was also conducted by our external evaluator. In the fall following graduation, the scholars were contacted by the evaluator for an individual interview which allowed for more in-depth discussion about the impact of the training as they began their professional career (i.e., internship year for scholars in school psychology). All of the information available was reviewed at the end of each semester, problems and successes discussed, and solutions to problems identified and then evaluated in the following semester. To date, seven scholars have completed the IPE training program. Training will continue for the next two years as part of the grant funding. Following this time, we have plans to maintain the program and collaboration across disciplines.

## INSIGHTS AND RECOMMENDATIONS FOR INTERDISCIPLINARY PROGRAMMING

In this section, we share insights for university teams who plan to develop similar IPE programs and enhance collaborative practices at the university-level. The recommended steps are outlined in Table 1 and described below. Although we present the steps in a linear manner, the steps may need to be rearranged or the team may need to return to specific steps to make modifications as the program is developed.

## Steps for Program Development

### Step 1: Identify Programs Serving Common Goals

Faculty can start the process of developing an interdisciplinary program by exploring programs on their campus or within a university system that have goals similar to the ones in their program. Faculty might also consider who professional graduates of their program work with on a regular basis (e.g., graduates of the school psychology program often work with general and special educators, counselors, speech language pathologists, etc.). In our case, we found overlap in training and professional practice related to meeting the needs of students with emotional and behavioral disorders between school psychologists, behavior analysts, and special educators. Having a common goal provided us with a strong foundation for our collaborative work. Once training programs are identified, faculty can reach out to faculty in those programs to develop relationships, discuss goals, and identify potential overlap in projects and programming. It can be useful to start with smaller efforts such as being committee members on thesis or student research committees, providing feedback on writing projects, conducting joint research, etc. Efforts like these provide opportunities to learn more about the other discipline, communicate respect for their contributions, and create trusting relationships (IPEC, 2016). In addition, the efforts can provide demonstrations of the value of working across disciplines to create larger societal impact.

### Step 2: Seek Administrative Support for Interdisciplinary Programming

Similar to the development and implementation of MTSS, gaining administrative support is imperative to the success of interdisciplinary programming. Program and departmental chairs are often involved in making decisions about courses that are required and taught, pre-requisites, and enrollment numbers which can all be impacted by programming across disciplines. College deans should be involved in discussions to encourage collaboration across colleges related to student recruitment, political elements, economic aspects, resource allocation, faculty appointments, and potential program impact and match with university and community stakeholder goals (see Scherer et al., 2020 and Lakofsky, 2020 for additional considerations). In addition, their support is integral for grant submission and allocation of grant funds across colleges. In conversations with administrators, we encourage leaders to emphasize the (a) success of current partnerships (see Step 1); (b) benefits of interdisciplinary programming which might include increased enrollment, course offerings, and increased success of graduates in practice; and (c) the potential for enhanced community partnerships. Overall, establishing buy-in from key administrative personnel will help facilitate the remaining steps.

### Step 3: Further Exploration of Program Values and Language

Further exploration of program values and language use is beneficial to create increased knowledge of the approach each program takes to meeting the needs of students and their families (IPEC, 2016). Values might include discussion of initiatives within each field at the national-, state-, and program-levels. Another area to consider is the theory or conceptual foundations of the field. If the theories differ, faculty can share about the approach and commonalities and differences discussed. In our case, a behavioral approach was consistent across the programs, but we discussed slight differences that existed (e.g., behavior analytic, ecological behavioral systems). Language is another area for discussion because

use of jargon can be a barrier to communication in practice (Anderson, 2013). Oftentimes jargon can be avoided and translated into everyday terms, but when this is not possible, individuals can provide a brief explanation of the term to improve understanding. When a trusting and respectful relationship is established, it is also easier for individuals on the team to pause and ask for clarification of jargon that might be unintentionally used.

## Step 4: Review and Outline Joint Competencies

Outlining joint competencies (i.e., knowledge and skills) for students participating in interdisciplinary education is important for informing development of activities and methods for evaluation of the program. This can be accomplished through review of training standards within the field and discussion of knowledge and skills to meet specific needs of students in schools. Once the list of competencies is developed, experts in each field and other key stakeholders (e.g., families, individuals with disabilities, principals, etc.) might be asked to review the competencies and provide feedback. The feedback can be integrated to refine the competencies and being a continuous improvement process based on data collected (Patton, 2008).

## Step 5: Identify Possible Shared Coursework

The joint competencies provide a basis for identifying possible shared coursework. Syllabi from the courses included in the program of study for each discipline can be reviewed to determine what competencies are addressed in each course. Next, the faculty team can use the list of courses and competencies to see where programs already overlap. For example, if students in school psychology need electives in special education, then team might select a few courses that target the competencies in special education for students participating in interdisciplinary training to take. If there is not already possible overlap, the team can determine if there are additional classes that would be particularly valuable for interdisciplinary training. Through our experience, we found that adding courses can pose challenges to students related to their cost of attendance, course load, and graduation timeline. This can also create challenges at the college-level for related to faculty workload and funding across colleges. Therefore, we recommend added courses only when it absolutely necessary. In cases when students from one department take courses in another department, efforts can be made to "equalize" courses taken in each department to decrease impact on enrollment and funds going to each department. In general, it is important to have administrative support for students taking courses in other departments. After reviewing the courses, faculty teams might notice that some competencies are not sufficiently addressed in the coursework. The team can then explore how to address the competencies through creation of new courses, professional seminars, or experiences.

## Step 6: Develop Shared Applied Experiences

Most programs related to education have applied experiences that students complete during their training, but these experiences are often not coordinated across training programs. For example, students in special education might complete student teaching, those in school psychology might complete practicum placements and internships, and those in behavior analysis complete fieldwork experiences. Although these experiences are valuable for developing skills in practice, having shared applied experiences can increase knowledge and appreciation of the roles of other professions and skills in collaborating with other professionals. Faculty teams can outline current applied experiences including timing of the experience (e.g., year and semester in program when students complete the experience), duration (e.g., semesters or number of hours), goals (e.g., specific learning objectives), and community partners/sites where experiences are completed. If overlap is found, it can provide a base for creation of shared experiences.

Shared experiences might involve having teams of students across disciplines in the same site completing activities that are similar across the roles (e.g., conducting functional behavioral assessment [FBA] analyses and developing behavior intervention plans) or completing activities unique to their future role and then collaborating to develop goals, create a plan, implement and monitor progress. For example, a school psychology student might conduct assessments related to behavior, cognitive, academic, adaptive skills; a special education student might collect information about academic functioning and teaching strategies; and a behavior analyst might conduct an FBA, including direct observations. The student team would then review the information gathered (similar to an MDT) and to develop a plan. After the plan is developed, each member would continue to collaborate: the special education student might implement the plan in the classroom and collect data; the school psychologist might provide training support and deliver small-group skills intervention, and the behavior analyst might provide ongoing coaching for implementation supports and collect treatment integrity data. Overall, the students are encouraged to work together to support students, sharing in decision making and implementation.

## Step 7: Identify and Apply for Funding

Although funding may not be necessary, it is helpful for starting and implementing an interdisciplinary training program. Potential funding is available through several organizations including the Department of Education Office of Special Education and Rehabilitative Programs (e.g., Personnel Preparation Program or Personnel Leadership Program) and Health Resources and Services Administration (HRSA). In addition, faculty can explore funding through national and local foundations or through their university. Funding is useful for supporting faculty time and funding student participation. Bottom of FormFaculty time might include activities such as recruitment of students to the program, delivery of new courses or seminars, organization of field experiences, oversight of the program, and program evaluation. Providing funding opportunities for students to obtain degrees in education-related fields can help to address shortages and barriers to access to higher education and increase the pool of diverse students applying for such programs (Washington et.al., 2020). We have found that at the graduate-level, it is helpful to provide funding for tuition and a stipend for participation in the grant activities. It is also important to understand how grant funding might impact student access to other financial aid options.

When looking for possible grant or other funding opportunities, faculty teams should work closely with their grants office to determine timelines, create a budget, complete any relevant internal forms, and submit the proposal. If the faculty team has limited experience with grant applications, it can be productive to identify a mentor who has more grant experience to assist with the planning and application process. Mentors might be identified through university or professional connections or through contacting individuals who have received similar grants to the one they plan to apply for. Once a grant competition is identified, the faculty team should carefully review the request for application/proposals/notice of award (RFA/RFP/NOA), attend information sessions if offered, and contact the program officer with questions that arise.

### Step 8: Outline Evaluation Process

Within a grant application, faculty teams are typically required to describe how the proposed program will be evaluated, which often involves collaboration with an external evaluator. The evaluator can provide guidance on quantitative and qualitative methods for formative and summative assessment. We recommend seeking feedback on the program from expert consultants, students participating in the program, field or site supervisors, and other school staff that students interact with during practicum. For example, an expert consultant can give feedback on materials developed for the training program. Students can complete self-assessments of their knowledge and skills for identified competencies, provide feedback on site supervision, complete course evaluations, participate in focus groups or interviews, and submit portfolios with samples of their works. Field or site supervisors can evaluate student progress toward independent use of knowledge and skills for each competency. School staff (e.g., teachers, paraeducators), students, and their familsies can also be asked to provide feedback on the quality of services received. Teams might also collect data from students receiving typical training (i.e., completing only their individual program requirements; not participating in IPE) on some of the above measures to evaluate the unique impact of the IPE training.

Once the program begins, it is essential for the team to engage in data-based decision making. The data can be used to determine the effectiveness of the program and to inform changes needed to improve program success. Teams can apply a systematic improvement process by identifying issues, understanding the issue using the data, diagnosing a cause, planning actions, taking actions, and evaluating the plan (Patton, 2008).

## CONCLUSION

Interdisciplinary collaboration is an important component to effective implementation of MTSS to meet the needs of diverse students in an equitable manner, yet in practice school professionals often work independently of each other (Adelman & Taylor, 2021). This siloed approach is likely related to barriers that exist for collaborating across disciplines (e.g., competing policies, lack of understanding of roles, lack of common language; Manor-Binyamini, 2007; O'Keeffe & McDowell, 2004). One way to begin overcoming these barriers is for university and college programs to provide IPE programs. IPE programs can provide pre-service students with unique opportunities to learn about the roles and responsibilities of related fields, skills in collaborative teaming, and other program-specific competencies. Demonstrations of IPE in education thus far show positive outcomes for participating students. More research is needed to determine the impact of IPE programs on student outcomes, family engagement, and teacher/professional retention, etc. Our IPE program provided training to scholars in applied behavior analysis, special education, and school psychology with the goal of increasing the pool of interdisciplinary behavioral interventionists who can effectively implement systemic behavioral interventions to improve behavioral and academic outcomes for children and adolescents with or at-risk for behavioral issues. We hope that the program description and steps outlined spur faculty interest in IPE and provide guidance for developing such programs.

## REFERENCES

Adelman, H., & Taylor, L. (2021). *New directions for school counselors, psychologists, & social workers.* University of California at Los Angeles: The Center for Mental Health in Schools & Student/Learning Supports. http://smhp.psych.ucla.edu/pdfdocs/report/framingnewdir.pdf

Anderson, E. M. (2013). Preparing the next generation of early childhood teachers: The emerging role of interprofessional education and collaboration in teacher education. *Journal of Early Childhood Teacher Education, 34*(1), 23–35. doi:10.1080/10901027.2013.758535

Averill, & Rinaldi, C. (2013). *Research brief: Multi-tier system of supports.* Urban Special Education Leadership Collaborative. https://www.urbancollaborative.org/

Barrett, N., McEachin, A., Mills, J. N., & Valant, J. (2018). *Disparities in student discipline by race and family income.* https://educationresearchalliancenola.org/files/publications/010418-Barrett-McEachin-Mills-Valant-Disparities-in-Student-Discipline-by-Race-and-Family-Income.pdf

Beaulieu, & Jimenez-Gomez, C. (2022). Cultural responsiveness in applied behavior analysis: Self-assessment. *Journal of Applied Behavior Analysis, 55*(2), 337–356. doi:10.1002/jaba.907

Bitsko, R. H., Claussen, A. H., Lichtstein, J., Black, L. J., Everett Jones, S., Danielson, M. D., Hoenig, J. M., Davis Jack, S. P., Brody, D. J., Gyawali, S., Maenner, M. M., Warner, M., Holland, K. M., Perou, R., Crosby, A. E., Blumberg, S. J., Avenevoli, S., Kaminski, J. W., & Ghandour, R. M. (2022). Surveillance of Children's Mental Health – United States, 2013 – 2019. *MMWR, 71*(Suppl-2), 1–42. doi:10.15585/mmwr.su7102a1

Burke, & Goldman, S. E. (2018). Special education advocacy among culturally and linguistically diverse families. *Journal of Research in Special Educational Needs, 18*(S1), 3–14. doi:10.1111/1471-3802.12413

DeVeney, S. L., & McKevitt, B. (2021). Interprofessional experience for future education professionals: School psychology and speech-language pathology students. *Teaching and Learning in Communication Services & Disorders, 5*(1). Advance online publication. doi:10.30707/TLCSD5.1.1624982519.476871

Diliberti, M. K., & Schwartz, H. L. (2022). *District leaders' concerns about mental health and political polarization in schools: Selected findings from the Fourth American School District Panel Survey.* RAND Corporation. https://www.rand.org/pubs/research_reports/RRA956-8.html

Dobbs-Oates, J., & Morris, C. W. (2016). The case for interprofessional education in teacher education and beyond. *Journal of Education for Teaching, 42*(1), 50–65. doi:10.1080/02607476.2015.1131363

George, C., & Oriel, K. (2009). Interdisciplinary learning experience: Two years of experience with an interdisciplinary learning engagement for physical therapy and special education students. *Journal of Allied Health, 38*(1), 22E–28E. PMID:19753409

Grisham-Brown, J., & Hemmeter, M. L. (2017). *Blended practices for teaching young children in inclusive settings* (2nd ed.). Paul H. Brookes.

I-MTSS Research Network. (2022). *Overview: Integrated multi-tiered systems of support*. Retrieved July 16, 2022, from https://mtss.org/overview/

Interprofessional Education Collaborative. (2016). *Interprofessional Education Collaborative releases revised set of core competencies*. https://www.ipecollaborative.org/news-releases.html

Kataoka, S., Zhang, L., & Wells, K. (2002). Unmet need for mental health care among U.S. children: Variation by ethnicity and insurance status. *The American Journal of Psychiatry, 159*(9), 1548–1555. doi:10.1176/appi.ajp.159.9.1548 PMID:12202276

Lakofsky. (2020). *Understanding Interdisciplinary Science Graduate Programs at the University of Delaware*. ProQuest Dissertations Publishing.

Manor-Binyamini, I. (2007). Meaning of language differences between doctors and educators in collaborative discourse. *Journal of Interprofessional Care, 21*(1), 31–43. doi:10.1080/13561820601049468 PMID:17365372

Marsh, R. J., & Mathur, S. R. (2020). Mental health in schools: An overview of multitiered systems of support. *Intervention in School and Clinic, 56*(2), 67–73. doi:10.1177/1053451220914896

McIntosh, K., Ellwood, K., McCall, L., & Girvan, E. J. (2018). Using Discipline Data to Enhance Equity in School Discipline. *Intervention in School and Clinic, 53*(3), 146–152. doi:10.1177/1053451217702130

O'Keefe, M. J., & McDowell, M. (2004). Bridging the gap between health and education: Wordsare not enough. *Journal of Paediatrics and Child Health, 40*(5-6), 252–257. doi:10.1111/j.1440-1754.2004.00359.x PMID:15151577

Patton, M. Q. (2008). *Utilization-focused evaluation* (4th ed.). Sage.

Scherer, M., Moro, R., Jungersen, T., Contos, L., & Field, T. A. (2020). Gaining administrative support for doctoral programs in counselor education. *The Professional Counselor, 10*(4), 632–647. doi:10.15241/rs.10.4.632

Skiba, R. J., Horner, R. H., Chung, C.-G., Rausch, M. K., May, S. L., & Tobin, T. (2011). Race is not neutral: A national investigation of African American and Latino disproportionality in school discipline. *School Psychology Review, 40*(1), 85–107. doi:10.1080/02796015.2011.12087730

U.S. Department of Education, Institute of Education Sciences. (2022). *School responses to COVID-19*. https://ies.ed.gov/schoolsurvey/

U.S. Department of Education, Office of Special Education and Rehabilitative Services. (2021). *Supporting child and student social, emotional, behavioral, and mental health needs*. https://www2.ed.gov/documents/students/supporting-child-student-social-emotional-behavioral-mental-health.pdf

Washington, T., Truscott, S., & Franklin, A. (2020). Using grant funding to enhance school psychology training. *Psychology in the Schools, 57*(8), 1309–1326. doi:10.1002/pits.22389

Whitney, D. G., & Peterson, M. D. (2019). US national and state-level prevalence of mental health disorders and disparities of mental health care use in children. *JAMA Pediatricatics*, *173*(4), 389–391. doi:10.1001/jamapediatrics.2018.5399 PMID:30742204

World Health Organization. (2010). Framework for action on interprofessional education and collaborative practice (No. WHO/HRH/HPN/10.3). World Health Organization.

## KEY TERMS AND DEFINITIONS

**Applied Behavior Analyst:** An individual certified by the Behavior Analyst Certification Board who engages in a data driven process to examine the role of antecedents and consequences on behavior to inform development interventions to improve students' outcomes.

**Cultural Humility:** A process of ongoing self-reflection to enhance partnerships.

**Cultural Responsiveness:** Using cultural characteristics, perspectives, and experiences to enhance intervention outcomes.

**Interprofessional Education:** Education that involves students from more than one discipline with the purpose to enhance knowledge of roles and increase skills to effectively collaborate.

**Multi-Tiered System of Supports:** A tiered approach to delivering evidence-based interventions to address unique needs of students as indicated through an ongoing data-based problem-solving approach.

**School Psychologist:** Provide comprehensive evaluation, consultation to support teachers and related providers in developing and delivering interventions, direct services to students to support their success, and progress monitoring of services and supports.

**Special Education Teacher:** Provide specialized instruction through the use of accommodations and modifications to curriculum to meet the unique needs of the student outlined in their individualized education program.

## APPENDIX

*Table 1. Recommended Steps for Development of an Interdisciplinary Education Program*

| Steps | Key Tasks/Points to Consider |
|---|---|
| Step 1: Identify Programs Serving Common Goals | • Identify programs with similar goals<br>• Develop relationships, goals for collaboration<br>• Partner on smaller projects (e.g., student research, feedback on writing, conducting joint research) |
| Step 2: Seek Administrative Support for Interdisciplinary Programming | • Discuss potential benefits of IPE<br>• Explore how programming might impact enrollment, courses, pre-requisites, etc. |
| Step 3: Further Exploration Program Values and Language | • Explore initiatives of within each collaborating field<br>• Discuss theoretical approach used within instruction and to guide intervention<br>• Use common language; when jargon is used, provide a definition |
| Step 4: Review and Outline Joint Competencies | • Review training standards and roles/responsibilities for each discipline<br>• Outline knowledge and skills for all scholars to meet<br>• Invite expert reviewers and other key stakeholders (e.g., community partners, families, individuals with disabilities) for feedback on the competencies<br>• Refine competencies based on feedback |
| Step 5: Identify Possible Shared Coursework | • Review all syllabi included in the program of study for each discipline for overlap and where competencies outlined are addressed<br>• Identify which shared coursework (i.e., courses all students in a cohort across disciplines would take together)<br>• Obtain administrative support for promoting identified shared coursework |
| Step 6: Develop Shared Applied Experiences | • Outline current applied experiences available to students in each discipline and identify areas of overlap (e.g., community partner sites, timing of experience, goals)<br>• Identify the goals and activities of possible shared applied experiences |
| Step 7: Identify and Apply for Funding | • Identify funding opportunities<br>• Outline how the funding would be used to develop and implement IPE (e.g., faculty time, student tuition/stipends)<br>• Work closely with the grants office<br>• If needed, obtain a mentor with expertise in grant writing to provide support in the process<br>• Allocate sufficient time for grant writing and coordination |
| Step 8: Outline Evaluation Process | • Consider multiple methods of data collection including qualitative and quantitative methods<br>• Collect formative and summative data<br>• Engage in data-based decision making and use of a systematic improvement process |

# Chapter 18
# Interdisciplinary Special Educator and School Counselor Preparation:
## Supporting Equitable Student Outcomes in the COVID-19 Era

**Kristin M. Murphy**
*University of Massachusetts, Boston, USA*

**Laura Hayden**
*University of Massachusetts, Boston, USA*

**Amy Cook**
https://orcid.org/0000-0002-0221-2846
*University of Massachusetts, Boston, USA*

**Christopher Denning**
*University of Massachusetts, Boston, USA*

**Angi Stone-MacDonald**
*California State University, San Bernadino, USA*

## ABSTRACT

*The purpose of this chapter is to provide readers with a rationale and blueprint for interdisciplinary programs like Project TLC, which prepare preservice special educators alongside school adjustment counselors. First, the authors discuss the rationale for Project TLC, including the current state of K-12 student mental health and social emotional learning, particularly in the context of public health and racial pandemics and issues pertaining to personnel shortages and attrition in both teaching and counseling. Then, the authors outline the blueprint of an interdisciplinary program including strategies for recruitment and retention of diverse students and a plan for shared coursework, fieldwork, and other learning opportunities that buoy graduate student development and preparation for serving students as collaborative colleagues. Throughout, the authors present the Project TLC blueprint with considerations for how this interdisciplinary training approach that utilizes faculty expertise and partnerships within local school communities can be translated into other communities.*

DOI: 10.4018/978-1-6684-6438-0.ch018

The COVID-19 pandemic caused abrupt and profound changes for teachers and counselors, as it stripped away opportunities for school-based practitioners and children, including our most vulnerable children, to exist in shared learning environments. The most marginalized children were left behind with severe consequences for academic achievement and mental health (Meherali et al., 2021). These stressors, compounded by the stressors associated with the public health and racial pandemics that have swept the nation, laid bare existing inequities in education, and created new wily stressors for educators and students.

As the country watched this disaster unfold and bore witness to the resultant increase in adverse consequences for students and school staff alike, the authors of this chapter looked for opportunities to capitalize on existing school-based resources with an aim of tending to the social and emotional needs of young people with and at risk for emotional and behavioral disorders (EBDs) who attend Boston Public Schools. To do so, the authors, who are colleagues at a Northeastern public university, formed a collaboration across the programs of Special Education and Counseling (with a concentration in School Adjustment Counseling), given the shared expertise in socio-emotional learning within both programs. This collaboration was formed to rethink the ways in which they were preparing graduate students for collaborative roles in schools that are rapidly evolving in the wake of the COVID-19 pandemic, set against the backdrop of a long history of racial inequities in education. With funding from the U.S. Department of Education's Office of Special Education Programs, the authors embarked on a 5-year Interdisciplinary Personnel Preparation grant funded project titled Project Teachers Learning with Counselors (TLC) in Fall 2021.

Project Teachers Learning with Counselors (TLC) was launched with the goal of ensuring the interdisciplinary preparation of 15 master's level candidates across two disciplines: Special Education (SE) and School Adjustment Counseling (SAC) at a public research university in the Northeast. In Massachusetts, the term school adjustment counselor is used to denote school mental health counselors. The authors of this chapter, representing the Special Education and Counseling (with a concentration in SAC) programs at a university, collaborated to prepare personnel to support academic outcomes for students with emotional and behavioral disorders (EBDs), with particular attention on social-emotional learning (SEL) by way of shared coursework, group assignments, coordinated field experiences, and structured joint activities.

## PURPOSE OF CHAPTER

The purpose of this chapter is to provide readers with a rationale and blueprint for interdisciplinary personnel preparation program like Project TLC, which prepare preservice special educators alongside preservice school adjustment counselors to enhance outcomes for students with disabilities, notably with EBDs. First, the authors discuss the rationale for Project TLC, including the current state of K-12 student mental health and SEL, particularly in the context of a public health pandemic, and issues pertaining to personnel shortages and attrition in both teaching and counseling. Then, the authors outline the blueprint of an interdisciplinary program (developed using data-informed best practices), including strategies for recruitment and retention of diverse students, and a plan for shared coursework, fieldwork, and other learning opportunities that buoy graduate student development and preparation for serving students as collaborative colleagues. Throughout, the authors present the Project TLC blueprint with considerations for how this particular interdisciplinary training approach that utilizes faculty expertise and partnerships within local school communities can be translated into other communities.

## RATIONALE FOR PROJECT TLC

In this section, the authors provide an overview of relevant literature highlighting the need for Project TLC. The authors share research on student mental health, particularly as it has been impacted by COVID-19, the importance of collaboration between school-based practitioners (i.e., special educators and school adjustment counselors), and the need for high quality school-based practitioners in the field of Special Education and School Counseling. This literature guided the development of Project TLC as an initiative to train pre-service Special Education teachers and School Adjustment counselors to recognize and respond to mental health needs for children with disabilities, especially with EBDs, through school-based collaboration.

### Personnel Preparation and Student Mental Health

In recent years, there has been an increased focus on school mental health and attention to addressing non-academic challenges to learning. According to the National Institute of Mental Health (NIMH, 2017), 22.5% of adolescents aged 13-18 have experienced a severe mental health disorder in their life. A systematic meta-analysis of research studies examining the impact of the COVID-19 pandemic on children and adolescents' mental health identified persistent adverse impacts, particularly anxiety and depression (Meherali et al., 2021). Therefore, preparing special educators and counselors to support students' social-emotional development alongside academics is essential. SEL promotes positive outcomes across social and emotional skills, attitudes toward self and others, positive social behavior, conduct problems, emotional distress, and academic performance (Taylor et al., 2017; Weissberg, 2019). In turn, children and adults are proficient in the tools they need to successfully navigate roles, routines, tasks, and challenges encountered across school, work, and life.

Although school mental health services have expanded, students' mental health needs frequently remain under-identified and unmet, making systems-level and school-wide mental health initiatives a priority (August et al., 2018). Students who live under adverse social conditions, particularly in urban areas, encounter unique vulnerabilities. Difficult social and emotional experiences are a common part of childhood and adolescence, particularly for urban youth who are at a greater risk of exposure to adverse life events, such as violence (Kliewer & Lepore, 2014), trauma (Accomazzo et al., 2015), and loss (Finkelhor et al., 2005; Seal et al., 2014). There are various issues associated with living and learning in under-resourced and/or impoverished contexts, and their manifestation in schools and communities requires counselors and educators to prioritize youths' mental health (Lepiéce et al., 2015). Neighborhood and community have a direct effect on an individual's mental health, and some urban neighborhoods are at a disadvantage when it comes to social and economic resources, with poverty presenting as a substantial risk factor for mental illness (Lepiéce et al., 2015). Moreover, youth and families may not readily seek and/or may encounter barriers to accessing mental health services, which consequently adds to the experience of chronic mental health issues and stress-related disorders.

To support children's mental health and academic learning needs, collaboration among school-based counselors (e.g., school adjustment counselors) and special educators is imperative (Barrow & Mamlin, 2016), with researchers supporting the need for counselor education programs to include special education in their curricula (e.g., Hall, 2015, Goodman-Scott et al., 2019). Goodman-Scott and colleagues (2019) found exposure to disability-specific course content and activities allowed school counselor trainees to better understand and more confidently provide services to students with disabilities (Goodman-Scott et al., 2019).

## Student Mental Health and COVID-19

Practitioners and researchers are only scratching the surface of how these issues will heighten in intensity and prevalence with the evolution of the COVID-19 pandemic. The U. S. Surgeon General issued a Surgeon General's Advisory Report focused on youth mental health, which noted that the pandemic has exacerbated existing mental health crises for children and adolescents in the U.S., with heightened prevalence and consequences for the most vulnerable children, including those who are low income, racially and ethnically diverse, homeless, involved in the juvenile justice system, and/or have disabilities (Office of the Surgeon General, 2021). The consequences of increased stress, including personal and economic loss, leaves children with an increased risk of maltreatment and heightened mental health challenges (Golberstein et al., 2019). Children are living through a public health crisis characterized by social distancing and isolation. Nearly all 55 million children in grades PreK through 12 across the United States were affected by the transition of schools to remote delivery that occurred in mid-March 2020, with many shutting their doors for the entire school year (Golberstein et al., 2020) during the 2020-2021 academic year. These needs and disparities are likely to be significantly magnified when focusing on students with EBDs as the pandemic unfolds and assumes new shapes, especially in urban communities, such as Boston.

The dual pandemics have disproportionately affected communities of color (Martinez et al., 2021; U.S. Department of Education, 2021). Researchers argue that practitioners must turn their attention toward evidence-based strategies to support the multifaceted and complex needs of all students and staff (Kearney & Childs, 2021). In particular, practitioners must cultivate safe and supportive learning environments that support the social, emotional, and mental health needs of underserved students who have experienced disproportionate consequences during the pandemic (U.S. Department of Education, 2021).

## COLLABORATION OF SCHOOL-BASED PROFESSIONALS

Researchers (e.g., Scruggs et al., 2007) recommend facilitating improved conditions and outcomes for students through initiating an intentional focus on collaborations among school-based colleagues. The ability to collaborate is an essential skill to ensure that the individualized needs of each student with a disability are met; however, special educators often experience difficulties when it comes to collaboration due to a lack of preparation and practice (Driver et al., 2018). Leading scholars in special education recommend that preservice special educator programs have a strong foundation in special education high leverage practices, including collaboration to improve outcomes for students (McLeskey et al., 2017). Unfortunately, teacher preparation coursework all too often focuses more on theoretical aspects of teaching, thus resulting in a large gap between theoretical learning in a university classroom and application of skills once preservice teachers graduate and enter their first K-12 setting (McLeskey & Brownell, 2015). Theoretical course content about collaboration is important, but hands-on experience remains an essential component to a powerful learning experience (Leko et al., 2015).

To foster competence and confidence in teaching skills and mental health awareness, preservice teachers and school-based counselors need sustained and ongoing opportunities to practice what they are learning through structured, scaffolded, and supervised experiences. Providing collaboration and consultation to teachers are primary roles of school-based counselors to best assist students with individualized needs (Dickstein-Fischer et al., 2019). School-based counselors are better able to assist children with disabilities and mental health needs when they collaborate with special education teachers, yet efficacious counselor training in the area of consultation and collaboration with teachers is lacking (Barrow & Mamlin, 2016, Dickstein-Fischer et al., 2019). Therein lies the potential of Project TLC. Project TLC aims to strengthen collaboration and consultation gaps in special educator training and practice, and foster social-emotional competencies (SECs), which may affect their capacity to cultivate collaborative relationships and instructional and student outcomes (Jennings & Greenberg, 2009).

## Teacher Shortages

Teacher preparation programs are an essential component of both understanding and addressing teacher shortages across the country. Student populations are increasing, while the teacher labor force experienced an estimated 8% attrition annually, and enrollment in teacher education programs dropped 35% from 2009 to 2014 (Sutcher et al., 2016). In addition, 98% of school districts across the country are experiencing a special educator shortage (U.S. Department of Education, 2021), and teacher attrition is increasing at a rate parallel to the growth of the U.S. population of students with disabilities eligible for special education (National Education Association, 2019). COVID-19 has further intensified teacher shortages as educators decide to retire or leave the profession (Garcia & Weiss, 2020). To ensure teaching quality, the education field needs a robust pipeline of well-prepared teachers, which begins by improving the ability to develop confident and competent teachers during teacher preparation.

Since the passage of P. L. 94-142 in 1975, the U.S. has experienced an inadequate supply of qualified special educators. At the national level, higher education is experiencing continually declining enrollment rates in teacher preparation programs, coupled with teachers leaving the profession (Mason-Williams et al., 2020). A report from the National Center for Education Statistics cites enrollment in teacher preparation programs to be lower than at any point since they began collecting enrollment data (Billingsley & Bettini, 2017). Prior to the pandemic, approximately 17% to 29% of special educators were leaving their positions each year, primarily due to attrition (Sullivan et al., 2017). When examining reasons for attrition, two-thirds of attrition is due to voluntary reasons. Many special educators started leaving the classroom due to feeling unprepared for poor working conditions and a lack of resources to support students (Billingsley & Bettini, 2017; Sutcher et al., 2016). This is amplified in urban settings, with more urban special educators leaving than their suburban colleagues, and with teachers of color leaving at higher rates than their White colleagues (Kohli, 2018).

In Massachusetts, teacher attrition will contribute to the available supply of special educators. Shortages are predicted to have a greater impact on our most vulnerable students in urban and rural high poverty districts (Levin et al., 2015). In high-poverty urban districts, students of color are more likely to have unqualified teachers (Mason-Williams, 2015) and teachers who are not representative of the school community's population. For example, in 2019, 86% of the Boston Public Schools (BPS) student population identified as Black, Hispanic, Asian, or Multiracial/other; 5% had a first language other than English; 29% were English Language Learners; 21% were eligible students with disabilities; and 72% were economically disadvantaged (BPS, 2019). Conversely, 59.7% of teachers and school counselors employed by BPS are White (BPS, 2019). Now more than ever, teacher educators must reconsider how to recruit new special education teachers.

## Counselor Shortages

At the national level, one in five youth struggles with an emotional, mental, or behavioral disorder, and access to mental health services is limited, particularly for children from low-income backgrounds who are likely to be underinsured and have difficulty accessing evidence-based treatment (National Center for Children in Poverty, 2019; U.S. Department of Health and Human Services, 2016). Schools offer the potential to improve accessibility; however, many schools in under-resourced communities often lack sufficient resources and personnel to provide comprehensive interventions to meet the mental health needs of children with EBD (Cummings et al., 2013). Researchers have identified shortages in school-based counselors at the national level and in the Northeastern U.S. that are expected to continue through 2025 (American Association for Employment in Education, 2016). While the American School Counselor Association (ASCA) recommends a ratio of 250 students per counselor, the actual ratio across all U.S. schools is 464:1 (Education Trust, 2019).

According to the Education Trust (2019), there are substantial national shortages of counselors and unequal access to counseling services in communities with majority students of color and low-income students. Almost 8 million children do not have access to a school-based counselor, and 3 million of those children do not have access to other mental health professionals (e.g., social worker, school psychologist). In PreK-12 public schools across the nation, 38 states are providing unequal access to school counseling services to students of color and students from low-income families, including Massachusetts (Education Trust, 2019). Limited diversity in the workforce contributes to this problem, with researchers and policymakers making calls for diversifying the profession (Meyers, 2017).

Counselors have the expertise to assist children with mental health and other special needs in school settings; however, culturally diverse counselors are underrepresented within the counseling workforce, as 70.6% are White (Deloitte, 2018). In addition, there are substantial shortages of bilingual mental health professionals to meet the needs of diverse populations (Henderson, 2015). This discrepancy between the cultural and linguistic diversity of the counseling workforce and the population of children served in schools continues to grow.

In Massachusetts, on average, one school counselor is responsible for providing academic, socio-emotional, and vocational supports to approximately 410 students (ASCA, 2019). This far exceeds ASCA's recommended ratio of 1:250. Even more urgently needed are School Adjustment Counselors (SACs), who are trained in child mental health to serve youth with EBD and other special needs.

## BLUEPRINT OF PROJECT TEACHERS LEARNING WITH COUNSELORS (TLC)

Project TLC was launched in Fall 2021, with the first year serving as a planning year, with the goal of ensuring interdisciplinary preparation of master's level candidates across the two disciplines of SE and SAC at one public Northeastern university. Four invested faculty members from the two graduate programs collaborated to prepare personnel to support academic outcomes for students with emotional and behavioral disorders (EBD), with particular attention on social-emotional learning (SEL), by way of shared coursework, group assignments, coordinated field experiences, and structured joint activities. Project TLC welcomed the first cohort of 8 students (6 students in SE; 2 students in SAC) in Summer 2022, working toward its ultimate goal of preparing 15 scholars with a master's degree in order to increase the number and improve the quality of personnel serving our nation's youth. Project TLC provides ongoing opportunities for active interdisciplinary learning through joint classes and activities, including mixed reality simulations (MRS), described below, and urban fieldwork opportunities.

MRS, like those offered by Mursion™, offers an innovative alternative to traditional role-play activities and provide SET and SAC candidates opportunities to engage in deliberative practice with avatars before and alongside field-based practice opportunities. MRS can take place on campus or remotely via Zoom. Similar to flight simulators used to train airline pilots prior to flying an actual airplane, researchers have begun to examine the benefits of virtual and MRS for teacher preparation (Dieker et al., 2014) as an intermediary step that allows teacher preparation candidates to practice their newly learned teaching skills with avatars playing the role of K-12 students, staff, or families before or as a complement to field-based practice. When participating in simulations, students stand individually or in a small team in front of a large-scale monitor where the avatars are displayed. MRS uses human-in-the-loop technology, meaning there is a human "behind the curtain" controlling the movements and speech of the avatars. If students are unsure of what to do, they can "pause" the mixed reality simulation and receive on-the-spot coaching from their professor and peers. MRS takes complex interactions and tasks new teachers often experience for the first time in isolation into a safe, supportive environment. Preservice students can safely make mistakes, practice, and wonder aloud with their peers and professors (Murphy et al., 2018).

## Guiding Competency Areas and Interdisciplinary Domains

Using both existing best practices *and* the mission of the university's SE program and Counseling program (with a concentration in SAC) as a guide, Project TLC covers five major competency areas: (a) promoting high expectations; (b) differentiating instruction; (c) providing intensive individualized instruction and intervention(s); (d) providing instruction or intervention(s) in person and through distance learning technologies; and (e) collaborating with parents, families, and diverse stakeholder using an interdisciplinary team-based approach designed to improve learning and developmental outcomes; ensure access to and progress in academic achievement stands, as appropriate; lead to successful transition to college and care for children with disabilities; and maximize the use of effective technology, including assistive technology, to deliver instruction, interventions, and services. We accomplish these competencies through our TLC interdisciplinary domains, determined based on best practices, required competencies in the profession, and university and program values: (1) consultation and team-based collaboration; (2) evidence-based practice (EBP) and research; (3) social-emotional learning (SEL) and behavior; and (4) professionalism and ethics. TLC scholars are assessed on these competencies as project outcome measures. These practices are reflective of both programs and explicitly outlined in multiple ways in the shared coursework discussed later in this chapter.

(1) **Consultation and Team-Based Collaboration.** Engaging in consultation and team-based collaboration are key components of providing equitable and data-informed counseling and special education practices (ASCA, 2016; McLeskey et al., 2017). Personnel preparation in special education and counseling is monitored and guided by organizations striving to maintain the highest standards of professional practice (i.e., CEC, ASCA, and ACA). The demands placed on personnel preparation programs present challenges to ensure coursework is applied to fieldwork and that preservice practitioners can demonstrate research-to-practice in their work with children and youth. The authors maintain that consulting with teachers and families, as well as engaging in team-based

collaboration, can meet professional standards and support thoughtful, reflective practitioners in the field who are well-prepared to celebrate the successes and resolve the challenges facing children.

(2) **Evidence-Based Practice and Research.** Evidence-based practice and research sits at the core of high quality personnel preparation programs. In Project TLC, the authors track the efficacy of treatment plans and interventions for children, in accordance with best practices in both SE and SAC. Delivering evidence-based practice ensures that practitioners are providing high quality treatment and services to young people and that students are held accountable to their discipline and the students *they* serve. Project TLC uses evidence to determine students' needs, appropriate interventions to address those needs, and the effectiveness of those interventions (Dimmitt et al., 2007).

(3) **Social-Emotional Learning and Behavior.** The development of SEL is a vital component of child development (Berger et al. 2011). SEL is the process by which children acquire knowledge, skills, and attitudes necessary to understand and manage emotions, set and achieve positive goals, feel and show empathy for others, establish and maintain positive relationships, and make responsible decisions (Collaborative for Academic, Social and Emotional Learning [CASEL], 2020; Dusenbury et al. 2015). SEL functions as a framework to support healthy interactions between children and their environments. TLC project goals focus on SEL skill delivery to promote positive youth development and academic outcomes.

(4) **Professionalism and Ethics.** TLC scholars must know and demonstrate professionalism and adherence to the code of ethics in their disciplines. They shall use self-reflection, professional development and seek feedback to stay up-to-date in their field (i.e., CEC Code of Ethics, 2015; ACA Code of Ethics, 2014).

## Project TLC Planning Year

The first twelve months of the project were dedicated to program planning with funding for TLC scholars beginning in summer of the first year. Program planning activities included collaboration with an Advisory Board to finalize the details of TLC activities. The Advisory Board includes ten professionals in practice and research positions supporting students with EBD across special education and school-based counseling in K-12, higher education, and after school settings. Other planning activities included finalizing agreements and details with programs and schools that serve as sites for coordinated clinical experiences, revising group assignments to ensure delivery of the interdisciplinary content and activities, training instructors on MRS delivery, and developing and piloting five Mursion MRS scenarios that TLC scholars use for interdisciplinary learning. The authors used this planning time to develop structured joint activities, including orientation meetings, visits to the library, virtual mentoring, and summer institutes, and to develop recruitment materials and meetings with potential scholars. Importantly, this planning year was used to recruit high quality diverse and nontraditional students into Project TLC. The authors collaborated with leaders across various institutes and departments within the university, which is the only American Pacific Islander-Serving Institution (AANAPISI) research university in New England. Furthermore, the authors engaged in recruitment efforts in the Boston Public School to attract diverse, high-quality students by attempting to recruit educators seeking educational advancement. These efforts yielded 8 scholars for the inaugural class, including 6 scholars in the SE program and 2 scholars in the SAC concentration of the Counseling program. All scholars are currently employed in the Boston Public Schools while completing their Masters degree.

## Shared Coursework and Coordinated Field Experiences

All TLC scholars participate in joint interdisciplinary activities in ethical and legal issues and a series of joint courses that prepare them to collaborate to support students with EBD, including COUNSL 632: Collaborative Consultation in the Schools, SPEG 621: Introduction to Disabilities for Education Professionals, SPEG 633: Legal and Political Aspects of Special Education/COUNSL 633: Professional, Ethical, and Legal Issues in School Counseling, and SPEG 607: Behavior and Classroom Management.

In small interdisciplinary groups, TLC scholars engage in shared clinical experiences. Project faculty collaborate with Boston Public Schools partners to provide field experiences that facilitate interdisciplinary learning focused upon providing support and improving outcomes for students with EBD. Scholars from both programs have a combination of pre-practicum, practicum, and internship experiences in school-based settings with students and school-based professionals who collaborate to support students. Mentoring, reflective supervision and practice are built into both programs' coursework.

**Special education (SE) fieldwork.** Starting in their first semester, SE students begin engaging in pre-practicum experiences as a part of every course. During the practicum semester, students spend the full semester engaged in a 300-hour practicum in which they are required to spend at least 75 hours delivering special education services in an inclusive classroom setting. Candidates receive mentorship and feedback from their university supervisor and field-based supervising practitioners, one of whom must be certified as a general educator and one certified as a special educator. During the semester, candidates complete the Massachusetts Candidate Assessment of Performance (CAP) portfolio to be assessed on their overall readiness to teach at the conclusion of their preparation experience across six essential elements: well-structured lessons; adjustments to practice; meeting diverse needs; safe learning environment; high expectations; and reflective practice (e.g., journaling).

**School adjustment counseling (SAC) fieldwork.** Initial fieldwork activities for counseling students enrolled in the SAC concentration includes completion of a 100-hour school counseling practicum in the first spring semester, during which graduate students shadow a counselor and are introduced to various counseling practices, including individual counseling, group counseling, classroom guidance, teacher consultation, observing meetings with parents, such as pre-referral or team meetings, and conducting interviews with various school personnel. In the second year of the program, SAC students are required to complete a full-time internship, totaling 1350 hours, of which 540 hours include direct service to students, families, and teachers, via counseling and consultation. A university supervisor and a licensed SAC at the site work together to ensure close supervision. During this practicum course, all TLC scholars will spend one day in each other's internship setting. This full-day experience will be counted for their total practicum hours. All scholars will write a reflection based on their experience.

Across fieldwork experiences, we ask students to engage in photovoice and reflective journaling about their fieldwork experiences with a specific focus on the TLC core competencies: Consultation and Team-Based Collaboration; Evidence-Based Practice and Research; Social-Emotional Learning and Behavior; and Professionalism and Ethics. Photovoice is a research approach that integrates photography and critical discussion to examine issues from the perspective of "resident experts" with the goal of promoting change at the personal and community level, and to promote a sense of empowerment (Murphy, 2019).

TLC scholars are tasked with taking pictures with their smartphones that illuminate their experience of learning and practicing the core competencies as a part of their preparation for their future collaborative roles supporting students with EBD. The photographs serve as an artifact to facilitate critical discussion and understanding about the topic at hand during the summer institute. One of the most common ways to structure the discussion is utilizing the SHOWeD method (Wang, 2006). The SHOWeD method allows students to start by reflecting on the most surface-level questions about what they literally see, or do not see, in the photo. They gradually transition to deeper questions about what is really happening in the photo, what it has to do with them, and finally, envisioning ways to strive for personal and community change with regards to the guiding research question. The addition of photographs adds a level of depth to conversations and findings, and facilitates a different level of dissemination, access, and interaction with the findings to UMB, OSEP, and any parties interested in preservice interdisciplinary preparation of special educators and school adjustment counselors. TLC scholars are encouraged to showcase their findings at UMB, conferences, and in publications.

## Structured Joint Activities

In addition to shared course work, group assignments, and coordinated field experiences, TLC scholars actively engage in structured joint activities that are scheduled throughout their program of study. Structured joint activities include: (1) attending orientation meetings, (2) visiting the university library for various training opportunities, (3) engaging in a book club and potluck, (4) receiving virtual mentoring to receive information on the program requirements and complete paperwork, and (5) attending a summer institute focused on in-depth learning activities for SEL for students with EBD and interdisciplinary collaboration between special educators and SACs. Project faculty organize orientation meetings for scholars during the summer. Scholars meet with faculty from two programs and learn about the required coursework, group assignments, coordinated field activities, and structured joint activities. They also learn all the requirements of the federal grant supporting their studies, including their service obligation commitment, and disbursing scholar support. Project faculty invite keynote speakers from professional organizations to support scholars' ongoing professional development.

## Induction opportunities and mentoring support

Project TLC faculty provide multiple ongoing induction opportunities and mentoring support to TLC scholars throughout the program. They are introduced to professional organizations in their field and encouraged to participate in conferences and ongoing activities. TLC scholars receive ongoing mentoring regarding coursework progression and required timelines for milestones including practicum and internship, licensure, and graduation. Furthermore, faculty train scholars to be ready for their field after graduation. TLC scholars receive information and participate in activities and training pertaining to MTEL test-taking support, job fairs, guidance on resume development, writing statement of interest letters for job applications, and mock interviews. In addition, faculty provide mentoring support to scholars regarding the licensure applications in their fields.

**Collaboration with appropriate partners.** TLC scholars have ongoing and varied opportunities to engage with a wide range of stakeholders in representing higher education, K-12, and families across coursework, field-based opportunities, summer institutes, and professional organization engagement across the year. Coursework includes fieldwork-based opportunities and guest speakers. The Advisory Board, consisting of research and practice-based professionals with rich and varied expertise in culturally responsive SEL-driven practice and research for students with EBD, will be engaged in ongoing planning, delivery, and evaluation of TLC. TLC scholars have membership to CCBD throughout their time in the program and receive annual subscriptions to CCBD's peer reviewed journals *Behavioral Disorders* and *Beyond Behavior,* and CCBD's membership newsletter, *Behavior Today.*

## Project Evaluation

One critical component of high-quality interdisciplinary training within special education is project evaluation. Indeed, the authors can assume intentions and best laid plans are sufficient for seeing results, but purposeful evaluation allows researchers to identify areas of strength, recognize spaces for improvement, and affords researchers an opportunity to make formative adjustments throughout the program to ensure we are providing high quality, interdisciplinary, data-informed training to scholars. The authors use a mixed-methods design to explore the extent to which the objectives of Project TLC have been met, including the project processes and outcomes. The methods of evaluation produce quantitative and qualitative data for objective performance measures connected to the TLC outcomes. Project performance measures are designed to convey specific information about how much change is expected, by whom, and when. Ongoing evaluation inform and guide continuous quality improvement and increase the authors' capacity to achieve project outcomes and impact.

Evaluation activities focus on two overarching questions: 1) Did the project fulfill its mission to increase the number and improve the quality of personnel who are fully credentialed to serve children with disabilities? and 2) Did the project produce intended short, intermediate, and long-term outcomes? The data collection schedule follows a systematic approach and is consistent with reporting requirements and naturally occurring time periods. Data are collected each semester and at the conclusion of the academic year to ensure sufficient information is available for program improvement purposes and for reporting to funders. After each year, formative reports are shared with the Advisory Board, Department Chair, and project faculty for feedback purposes. This allows project faculty to make decisions and address needs as a team. In addition, ongoing data collection activities are aggregated on the percentage of TLC scholars who complete the program and/or are employed in high-need districts/in the field of special education and SAC for at least two years; the percentage of TLC scholars who complete the preparation program and who are rated effective by their employers to assess the quality and effectiveness of program graduates. Results of the overall evaluation are used as a basis for improving the proposed project to prepare personnel to provide (a) focused instruction, and (b) intensive individualized intervention(s) in an interdisciplinary team-based approach to improve outcomes of children with disabilities.

## CONCLUSION

Given the increase in mental health issues, coupled with national personnel shortages, Project TLC adopts an interdisciplinary and evidence-informed curricula, joint learning opportunities, high quality mentorship, and field work experiences, to provide a training experience to prepare future practitioners for the demands of serving our nation's youth. In this chapter, the authors share the literature supporting the rationale for this project, followed by the blueprint of the project. The goal of the chapter is to support other programs around the country in building and sustaining their own interdisciplinary programs supporting preservice special educators and school adjustment counselors to become collaborative colleagues who are prepared and committed to support mental health and academic outcomes of students with disabilities in their school communities.

# REFERENCES

Accomazzo, S., Israel, N., & Romney, S. (2015). Resources, exposure to trauma, and the behavioral health of youth receiving public system services. *Journal of Child and Family Studies, 24*(11), 3180–3191. doi:10.100710826-015-0121-y

American Association for Employment in Education. (2016). *Educator supply and demand report 2015-16: Executive summary*. https://aaee.org/resources/Documents/2015-16_AAEE_Supply_Demand_Summary.pdf

American Counseling Association. (2014). *ACA code of ethics*. Alexandria, VA: Author. https://www.counseling.org/resources/aca-code-of-ethics.pdf

American School Counselor Association. (2016). *The school counselor and school-family-community partnerships*. https://www.schoolcounselor.org/asca/media/asca/PositionStatements/PS_Partnerships.pdf

American School Counselor Association. (2019). *ASCA school counselor professional standards & competencies*. Alexandria, VA: Author. https://www.schoolcounselor.org/asca/media/asca/home/SCCompetencies.pdf

August, G. J., Piehler, T. F., & Miller, F. G. (2018). Getting "SMART" about implementing multi-tiered systems of support to promote school mental health. *Journal of School Psychology, 66*, 85–96. doi:10.1016/j.jsp.2017.10.001 PMID:29429498

Barrow, J., & Mamlin, N. (2016). Collaboration between professional school counselors and special education teachers. *VISTAS, 42*, 1-7. https://www.counseling.org/docs/default-source/vistas/article_427cfd25f16116603abcacff0000bee5e7.pdf?sfvrsn=e2eb452c_4

Berger, C., Alcalay, L., Torretti, A., & Milicic, N. (2011). Socio-emotional well-being and academic achievement: Evidence from a multilevel approach. *Psicologia: Reflexão e Crítica, 24*(2), 344–351. doi:10.1590/S0102-79722011000200016

Billingsley, B., & Bettini, E. (2017). Factors influencing the quality of the special education teacher workforce. In Handbook of Special Education. Abingdon, UK: Routledge.

Boston Public Schools. (2019). *Boston Public Schools at a glance 2019-20*. https://www.bostonpublicschools.org/cms/lib/MA01906464/Centricity/Domain/187/BP S%20at%20a%20Glance%202019-20_FINAL.pdf

Collaborative for Academic, Social, and Emotional Learning (CASEL). (2020). *Core SEL competencies*. https://casel.org/core-competencies/

Council for Exceptional Children. (2015). *What every special educator must know: Professional ethics and standards*. CEC.

Cummings, J. R., Wen, H., & Druss, B. G. (2013). Improving access to mental health services for youth in the United States. *Journal of the American Medical Association, 309*(6), 553–554. doi:10.1001/jama.2013.437 PMID:23403677

Deloitte. (2018). *Data USA: Counselors*. https://datausa.io/profile/soc/counselors

Dickstein-Fischer, L., Scott, K., & Connally, J. (2019). Potential benefits of school counselor consultation to enhance student social emotional learning. *The Practitioner Scholar: Journal of the International Trauma Training Institute, 1*, 40–60.

Dieker, L. A., & Rodriguez, J. A., Lignugaris/Kraft, B., Hynes, M. C., & Hughes, C. E. (2014). The potential of simulated environments in teacher education: Current and future possibilities. *Teacher Education and Special Education, 37*, 21–33. doi:10.1177/0888406413512683

Driver, M., Zimmer, K., & Murphy, K. M. (2018). Using mixed reality simulations to prepare preservice special educators for collaboration in inclusive settings. *Journal of Technology and Teacher Education, 26*(1), 57–77. https://www.learntechlib.org/primary/p/181153/

Dusenbury, L., Calin, S., Domitrovich, C., & Weissberg, R. P. (2015). *What does evidence-based instruction in social and emotional learning actually look like in practice?* Collaborative for Academic, Social, and Emotional Learning. http://www.casel.org/wp-

Education Trust. (2019). *School counselors matter*. https://www.schoolcounselor.org/asca/media/asca/Publications/ASCAEdTrustRHFactSheet.pdf

Finkelhor, D., Ormrod, R., Turner, H., & Hamby, S. L. (2005). The victimization of children and youth: A comprehensive national survey. *Child Maltreatment, 5*, 5–25. https://doi.org/10.1177/1077559504271287

Garcia, E., & Weiss, E. (2020). *A policy agenda to address the teacher shortage in U.S. public schools. Perfect storm in the teacher labor market series*. Economic Policy Institute. https://www.epi.org/publication/a-policy-agenda-to-address-the-teacher-shortage-in-u-s-public-schools/

Golberstein, E., Gonzales, G., & Meara, E. (2019). How do economic downturns affect the mental health of children? Evidence from the National Health Interview Survey. *Health Economics, 28*(8), 955–970.

Golberstein, E., Wen, H., & Miller, B. F. (2020). Coronavirus disease 2019 (COVID-19) and mental health for children and adolescents. *JAMA Pediatrics*.

Goodman-Scott, E., Bobzien, J., & Milsom, A. (2019). Preparing preservice school counselors to serve students with disabilities: A case study. *Professional School Counseling, 22*, 1–11. https://doi.org/10.1177/2156759x19867338

Hall, J. G. (2015). The school counselor and special education: Aligning training with practice. *The Professional Counselor, 5*, 217–224. https://doi.org/10.15241/JGH5..2.217

Henderson, T. (2015). States look for help with bilingual mental health. PEW Charitable Trusts. https://www.pewtrusts.org/en/research-and-analysis/blogs/stateline/2015/11/04/states-look-for-help-with-bilingual-mental-health

Jennings, P. A., & Greenberg, M. T. (2009). The prosocial classroom: Teacher social and emotional competence in relation to student and classroom outcomes. *Review of Educational Research, 79*(1), 491–525.

Kearney, C. A., & Childs, J. (2021). A multi-tiered systems of support blueprint for re-opening schools following COVID-19 shutdown. *Children and Youth Services Review, 122*. doi:10.1016/j.childyouth.2020.105919

Kliewer, W., & Lepore, S. J. (2015). Exposure to violence, social cognitive processing, and sleep problems in urban adolescents. *Journal of Youth and Adolescence*, *44*(2), 507–517. https://doi.org/10.1007/s10964-014-0184-x

Kohli, R. (2018). Behind school doors: The impact of hostile racial climates on urban teachers of color. *Urban Education*, *53*, 307–333. doi:10.1177/0042085916636653

Leko, M. M., Brownell, M. T., Sindelar, P. T., & Kiely, M. T. (2015). Envisioning the future of special education personnel preparation in a standards-based era. *Exceptional Children*, *82*(1), 25–43.

Lepiéce, B., Reynaert, C., Jacques, D., & Zdanowicz, N. (2015). Poverty and mental health: What should we know as mental health professionals? *Psychiatria Danubina*, *1*, S92–S96. https://www.ncbi.nlm.nih.gov/pubmed/26417741

Levin, J., Berg-Jacobson, A., Atchison, D., Lee, K., & Vontsolos, E. (2015). *Massachusetts Study of Teacher Supply and Demand: Trends and Projections*. American Institutes for Research.

Martínez, M. E., Nodora, J. N., & Carvajal-Carmona, L. G. (2021). The dual pandemic of COVID-19 and systemic inequities in US Latino communities. *Cancer, 127*, 1548-1550. doi:10.1002/cncr.33401

Mason-Williams, L., Bettini, E., Peyton, D., Harvey, A., Rosenberg, M., & Sindelar, P. T. (2020). Rethinking shortages in special education: Making good on the promise of an equal opportunity for students with disabilities. *Teacher Education and Special Education*, *43*(1), 45–62.

McLeskey, J., Barringer, M-D., Billingsley, B., Brownell, M., Jackson, D., Kennedy, M., Lewis, T., Maheady, L., Rodriguez, J., Scheeler, M. C., Winn, J., & Ziegler, D. (2017, January). *High-leverage practices in special education.* Arlington, VA: Council for Exceptional Children & CEEDAR Center.

McLeskey, J., & Brownell, M. (2015). *High-leverage practices and teacher preparation in special education* (Document No. PR-1). Retrieved from University of Florida, Collaboration for Effective Educator, Development, Accountability, and Reform Center website: https://ceedar.education.ufl.edu/tools/best-practice-review/

Meherali, S., Punjani, N., Louie-Poon, S., Rahim, K. A., Das, J. K., Salam, R. A., & Lassi, Z. S. (2021). Mental health of children and adolescents amidst COVID-19 and past pandemics: A rapid systematic review. *International Journal of Environmental Research and Public Health*, *26*, 3432. https://doi.org/10.3390/ijerph18073432

Meyers, L. (2017). Making the counseling profession more diverse. *Counseling Today*. https://ct.counseling.org/2017/10/making-counseling-profession-diverse/

Murphy, K. M. (2019). Working with Avatars and High Schoolers to Teach Qualitative Methods to Undergraduates. *LEARNing Landscapes*, *12*, 183–203. https://doi.org/10.36510/learnland.v12i1.987

Murphy, K. M., Cash, J., & Kellinger, J. J. (2018). Learning with avatars: Exploring mixed reality simulations for next-generation teaching and learning. In *Handbook of Research on Pedagogical Models for Next-Generation Teaching and Learning* (pp. 1–20). IGI Global.

National Center for Children in Poverty. (2019). *Children's mental health: What every policymaker should know.* NCCP. http://www.nccp.org/publications/pub_929.html

National Education Association. (2019). *Special education.* https://ra.nea.org/search/special+education/

National Institute of Mental Health. (2017). *Transforming the understanding and treatment of mental illnesses.* NIMH. https://www.nimh.nih.gov/health/statistics/mental-illness.shtml

Office of the Surgeon General. (2021). *Protecting Youth Mental Health: The US Surgeon General's Advisory.* https://www.hhs.gov/sites/default/files/surgeon-general-youth-mental-health-advisory.pdf

Scruggs, T. E., Mastropieri, M. A., & McDuffie, K. A. (2007). Co-teaching in inclusive classrooms: A metasynthesis of qualitative research. *Exceptional Children, 73*(4), 392–416.

Seal, D., Nguyen, A., & Beyer, K. (2014). Youth exposure to violence in an urban setting. *Urban Studies Research.* doi:10.1155/2014/368047

Sullivan, K., Barkowski, E., Lindsay, J., Lazarev, V., Nguyen, T., Newman, D., & Lin, L. (2017, December). *Trends in teacher mobility in Texas and associations with teacher, student, and school characteristics* (REL Report No. 2018-283). Regional Educational Laboratory Southwest. Retrieved from https://files.eric.ed.gov/fulltext/ED578907.pdf

Sutcher, L., Darling-Hammond, L., & Carver-Thomas, D. (2016). *A coming crisis in teaching? Teacher supply, demand, and shortages in the US.* Learning Policy Institute.

Taylor, R. D., Oberle, E., Durlak, J. A., & Weissberg, R. P. (2017). Promoting positive youth development through school-based social and emotional learning interventions: A meta-analysis of follow-up effects. *Child Development, 88,* 1156–1171. https://doi.org/10.1111.cdev.12864

United States Department of Education. (2021). *COVID-19 Handbook: Roadmap to reopening safely and meeting all students' needs.* Retrieved from https://www2.ed.gov/documents/coronavirus/reopening-2.pdf

U.S. Department of Health and Human Services. (2016). *Access to adolescent mental health care.* HHS.gov. https://www.hhs.gov/ash/oah/adolescent-development/mental-health/access-to-mental-health-care/index.html

Wang, C. C. (2006). Youth participation in photovoice as a strategy for community change. *Journal of Community Practice, 14,* 147–161. https://doi.org/10.1300/J125v14n01_09

Weissberg, R. P. (2019). Promoting the social and emotional learning of millions of school children. *Perspectives on Psychological Science, 14,* 65–69. https://doi.org/10.1177/1745691618817756

# Chapter 19
# Collaborative Preparation in Equity-Based Practices to Support Minoritized Students With High-Intensity Needs

**Elizabeth D. Cramer**
https://orcid.org/0000-0002-8874-114X
*Florida International University, USA*

**Andy V. Pham**
*Florida International University, USA*

**Liana Gonzalez**
*Florida International University, USA*

**Rosalia F. Gallo**
*Florida International University, USA*

**Ana Paula Fabian Freire**
*Florida International University, USA*

## ABSTRACT

*The purpose of this chapter is to provide an overview of the development and implementation of a currently running, interdisciplinary program between school psychology and special education within a Hispanic-serving institution. Due to critical shortages of school psychologists and special educators across the country, novel practices in interdisciplinary collaborative training may aid in recruitment and retention efforts while enhancing service delivery for racially, ethnically, and linguistically diverse (RELD) students with high intensity needs. The chapter highlights approaches and components including (1) focus on an equity-based and integrated framework for personnel preparation, (2) recruitment and retention activities to attract diverse scholars, (3) planning and delivery of shared collaborative coursework and field experiences, (4) reflection of the lessons learned, and (5) recommendations to other preparation programs in providing interdisciplinary training and support to RELD personnel.*

DOI: 10.4018/978-1-6684-6438-0.ch019

## INTRODUCTION

The critical shortage of school psychologists and special educators across the nation has been a long-standing issue, along with the need to diversify the professions. Students who receive special education services make up approximately 15% of the total public-school population (NCES, 2022). The shift in demographics in the United States (U.S.) is also evident in the overall school age population of public-school students with disabilities from 2000–2020. In 2000, approximately 63% were White, 20% Black and 14% were Hispanic; whereas, in 2020 47% were White, 18% were Black and 26% were Hispanic (NCES, 2022). The change in demographics has significantly impacted the public-school population. Personnel working with students with disabilities are often not credentialed (e.g., teaching special education with a degree in business; not passing state department of education subject area [special education] test) to teach them. They also do not have the necessary advanced skills and in-depth knowledge to implement practices (e.g., application of evidence-based or high leverage practices [HLPs]) that result in positive outcomes for students with disabilities with the most complex educational needs (McLeskey et al., 2019) such as those provided through an advanced degree, and are not representative of the change in US demographics (National Center for Education Statistics [NCES], 2020) that is found in large urban settings. The divergence between the cultural and linguistic characteristics of special education personnel and the school-age children they serve continues to grow. Demographics from a national survey (Goforth et al., 2021) indicate significant underrepresentation of racially, ethnically, and linguistically diverse (RELD) school psychologists in the workforce: 86% are White, 4% are Black/African American, and 8% are Hispanic/Latinx which differs sharply from the student population (Irwin et al., 2021). This is similar to the demographics of classroom teachers: 79% are White, 7% are Black/African American, and 9% are Hispanic/Latinx (NCES, 2020). In fact, as Scott et al. (2022) point out, RELD students with disabilities can complete an entire public school career without having an educator from an RELD background. As research has documented the academic, social, and emotional benefits of a more diverse teacher workforce on this population (Redding, 2019), attracting a diverse workforce is pivotal for optimal student outcomes.

Of similar importance is a workforce that is well-prepared to professionally collaborate. School psychologists traditionally collaborate with educators, parents, and other professionals to create safe, healthy, and supportive learning environments for students with disabilities by providing services in assessment, intervention, and consultation. Special educators are responsible for designing and implementing instructional supports to students with disabilities while also providing accommodations and interventions to assist student learning. However, many educators may have limited knowledge and understanding of the specific roles of school psychologists other than assessment-related activities (Gilman & Medway, 2007). It is essential that these respective disciplines cultivate a collaborative relationship by sharing common values and perspectives, as well as leveraging their expertise to foster learning and positive behavior of students with disabilities (Margison & Shore, 2009). Engaging in interdisciplinary collaboration is also an essential part of the professional socialization process early on in their training. Welcoming opportunities and acknowledging adaptations for graduate training can greatly enhance curricular and cultural understanding, while providing an integrated approach to training and service delivery (Pham et al., 2021).

Interdisciplinary or interprofessional collaboration is not new in education or healthcare (e.g., Hinshaw & DeLeon 1995; Margison & Shore, 2009). Interdisciplinary collaborative training in graduate school may be a purposeful way to promote equity-based practices by (a) increasing understanding of one another's professional roles, (b) developing trust and respect among students, supervisors, and faculty, (c) distributing power equitably when making decisions related to educational planning, (d) expanding competencies, skill sets, and training to serve underserved populations, and (e) self-examining and evaluating outcomes on a regular basis to achieve mutual goals (Hinshaw & DeLeon, 1995).

Thus, the purpose of this chapter is to discuss practices and innovations in the development and implementation of a currently running, collaborative preparation program with school psychology and special education at a Hispanic-Serving Institution. The chapter will (a) outline an equity-based and integrated framework for personnel preparation, (b) detail recruitment and retention activities to attract and retain diverse scholars, (c) discuss planning and delivery of shared collaborative coursework and field experiences, (d) share lessons learned, and (e) provide recommendations to other preparation programs wanting to develop interdisciplinary collaboration to support RELD students with disabilities.

## BACKGROUND

As the U.S. Department of Education's Office of Civil Rights (2016) and over 40 years of research demonstrate, racial and ethnic disparities in the identification and inclusion of students with disabilities persist (Skiba et al., 2014; Sullivan, 2013; Zhang et al., 2014). Students from RELD backgrounds are identified for special education at much higher rates than their White peers (Fish, 2016; Office of Special Education and Rehabilitative Services [OSERS], 2018). The number of emerging bilinguals or those who speak more than one language in the United States has increased steadily in K-12 schools. According to data from the U.S. Census Bureau in 2018, over 67 million residents ages 5 or older speak a language other than English at home (Zeigler & Camarota, 2019), which equates to more than 20% of students, with and without disabilities. Educators have struggled to properly identify special education eligibility among this group, in large part due to the challenge of distinguishing learning or language disabilities from developing English proficiency or second language acquisition (Kangas, 2020). Despite the high numbers of students from RELD backgrounds in special education and the federal mandate for schools to use evidence-based practices to maximize student learning and behavioral outcomes (Individuals with Disabilities Education Improvement Act [IDEA], 2004), there is evidence that students from RELD backgrounds are inadequately served. Compared to White peers, RELD students with disabilities consistently have lower academic achievement and higher dropout rates (Faircloth et al., 2016; Rueda & Stillman, 2012). Special education categories with disproportionate numbers of students of color (e.g., emotional and behavioral disorders) are also those associated with some of the poorest long-term outcomes (Kauffman & Landrum, 2018). Inappropriate identification and ineffective special education services perpetuate these inequities (Carey et al., 2018). Thus, there exists a dire need to improve the quality of the workforce to work with RELD students in both who and how educator preparation programs prepare.

While recruitment efforts have attempted to attract RELD individuals into graduate education programs, novel practices in interdisciplinary collaborative training may aid in recruitment and retention efforts while also enhancing service delivery for students with disabilities, particularly those with high intensity needs such as persistent learning and behavioral challenges. Although graduate students from RELD backgrounds are increasing, many encounter barriers such as limited financial supports, low sense of belonging, and lack of multicultural training that affect academic persistence (Clark et al., 2012). National standards as outlined by the National Association of School Psychologists (NASP, 2020) emphasize that school psychologists work collaboratively with other school personnel to create and maintain a multi-tiered continuum of services to support students' attainment of academic and behavioral goals. Despite the myriad of resources available on multi-tiered instruction, there is no comprehensive national definition on what these supports must encompass (Hauerwas et al., 2013) or how they should be intensified for students with disabilities who have more severe or persistent challenges (Artiles, 2015). Moreover, the implementation of Response to Intervention (RTI) has been diverse and lacking focus in fidelity and procedural integrity (Noelle & Gansle, 2016; Ruble et al., 2018). National data demonstrate inconsistencies on the level of education and support provided to both school psychologists and special educators who work in schools where a significant number of students require multi-tiered supports to be successful (Al Otaiba et al., 2019; Hauerwas et al., 2013), and there is an absence of support systems (nationally and at state levels) for educators who work with these populations. Moreover, data patterns show that up to 30% of students from RELD and low socio-economic strata are identified as having disabilities as they enter school (Artiles, 2015), yet it is generally teachers who work with these students that report the least expertise on how to effectively target students with high intensity needs (Al Otaiba et al., 2019; Snell et al., 2012) through individualized multi-tiered support systems.

## DESCRIPTION OF PROJECT SPECIAL

Project SPECIAL (School Psychologists and Educators: Collaborative Interventions for All Learners) was conceptualized to respond to a critical need for school psychologists and special educators who are highly effective in collaboratively implementing equity-based, evidence-based academic and behavioral interventions for students with high intensity needs at the national, state, and local levels. This Office of Special Education Programs (OSEP) funded project prepares interdisciplinary professionals to work collaboratively with RELD students with disabilities who require intensive, multi-tiered interventions. The project's equity-based framework, the Integrated Learning Model (ILM; Cramer et al., 2014), combines elements of Gay's (2018) components of culturally responsive teaching and Frattura and Capper's (2006) integrated comprehensive services model to create a model that incorporates equitable approaches to teaching and learning in an interdisciplinary fashion with equitable environments and access to education. The ILM focuses on: (a) equity of environments in culturally pluralistic settings; (b) equitable, diverse, and interdependent communities of learners; (c) systems change through critical cultural consciousness; and (d) equitable access to multicultural curriculum with culturally congruent instructional strategies. Figure 1 is a visual representation of the ILM.

As depicted, the ILM addresses various school-related constructs that affect the learning potential of students, particularly RELD students, with documented risk for negative educational outcomes or special education services. This model is meant to facilitate integrated quality instruction across disciplines and professional roles, promote student learning, and increase academic potential and continued school engagement within inclusive urban settings (Cramer et al., 2014). This model lends itself to critical interdisciplinary work such as Project SPECIAL as it cuts across environments, creates collaborative communities of diverse individuals, promotes culturally sustaining instruction, and encourages team building to solve critical social issues. Further, it overlaps with Hinshaw and DeLeon's (1995) recommended interdisciplinary practices by increasing understanding, trust, self-awareness, collaboration, and equity.

Beyond this conceptual grounding, Project SPECIAL emphasizes skills and competencies for scholars to promote high expectations and address individualized needs for RELD students with high intensity needs using an interdisciplinary approach. These competencies are demonstrated across the

*Figure 1. Integrated Learning Model*

[Figure: Four-quadrant diagram with "Integrated Learning Model" at center, surrounded by: Focusing on Equity of Environments in Culturally Pluralistic Settings; Establishing Equitable, Diverse, and Interdependent Communities of Learners; Implementing Change through Critical Cultural Consciousness; Providing Access to Multicultural Curriculum with Culturally Congruent Instructional Strategies]

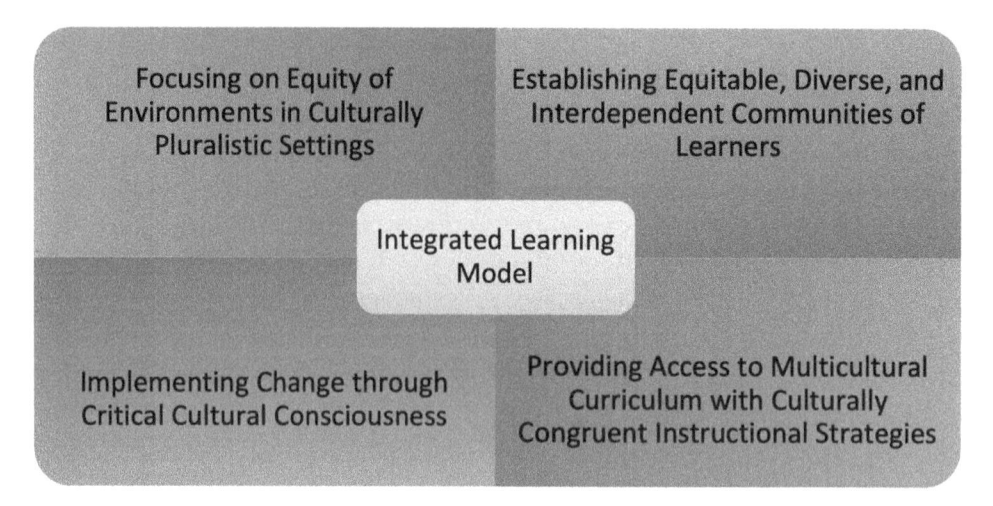

*Table 1. Intended Project Outcomes to Promote High Expectations and Address Individualized Needs for RELD Students with High Intensity Needs Using an Interdisciplinary Approach*

| Program Outcomes |
| --- |
| 1. Expand collaboration across disciplines, departments, and with families |
| 2. Expand scholars' knowledge-base in culturally-sustaining and effective inclusive practices |
| 3. Create collaborative communities of learners via mentorship and shared experiences |
| 4. Promote application of data-based research to practice methods and evidence-based interventions |

project coursework and shared experiences beyond courses, yielding intended project outcomes that are highlighted in Table 1.

## Recruitment of Diverse Scholars

SPECIAL focuses on recruitment of scholars from typically underrepresented groups to be highly effective in the provision of individualized and multi-tiered academic and behavior supports. Various recruitment strategies to recruit diverse scholars include disseminating information through social media and virtual webinars, networking through the program's advisory board, posting diversity statements, and using a holistic admissions process. Importantly, retention of scholars includes providing financial and academic support, ongoing mentorship, professional learning communities, and networking opportunities within the local districts and professional conferences. Scholars subsequently develop professional identities during the program while acquiring educational and applied experiences to foster professional growth.

Grapin et al. (2016) and Scott (2018) provided recommendations to assist programs on recruitment and retention of RELD scholars in school psychology and special education. These frameworks have been used to guide project recruitment and retention efforts.

## Commitment from Project Faculty in Recruitment of an Inclusive Student Body

Project faculty and personnel openly and publicly acknowledge recruitment of RELD scholars as a priority and afford adequate time and resources to contribute to recruitment efforts (Vasquez et al., 2006). These acknowledgements are stated publicly on program webpages, program handbooks, and other recruitment materials.

## Diversity Statements

Bidell and colleagues (2007) indicated that higher multicultural content in recruitment materials is associated with higher enrollment of RELD students. Diversity statements posted on program and project websites can highlight several components: (a) commitment to equity, diversity, inclusion, and social justice, (b) anti-discrimination policies, (c) identification of RELD faculty members, (d) specific minority-focused research and training opportunities, (e) dedication to recruitment of diverse students, and (f) financial and social supports (Smith et al., 2016).

## Reaching out to other Minority Serving Institutions (MSI)

The field of school psychology is often underrepresented in undergraduate coursework; therefore, many individuals may be unaware of the field (Bocanegra et al., 2015). Project faculty and scholars assist in presenting graduate school opportunities via in-person and virtual presentations to student organizations, undergraduate classes in MSIs, conferences, and recruitment fairs.

## Contact the Local Community

Project flyers and brochures are often distributed to public and private schools and agencies in the local communities. Project personnel and scholars also meet with potential applicants who express interest or have questions about the project. Interpersonal interaction with a school psychologist has been found to be a significant predictor of entering the profession (Bocanegra et al., 2016). The large network of practicing school psychologists and special educators from RELD from the local public school districts who are alumni of the institution also serves to promote support for new programs in the local community.

## Project Advisory Board

The advisory board's networking capabilities can support recruitment efforts. The diverse membership of the board, including core program faculty, consultants, parents, and community experts allow for increased dissemination of the project within school districts and community.

## Using Technology and Social Media

The Pew Research Center (2021) reported that amongst those who are 18-29 years of age, 84% actively engaged in social networking. Moreover, approximately 80% of Hispanic/Latinx, and 77% of Black/African American use at least one social media site, compared to 69% of White respondents. Information can be disseminated via various technologies, such as the project website that highlight faculty and successes of program graduates, online videos (e.g., YouTube), podcasts, program newsletters, webinars, online chats, email invitations sent to undergraduate programs at FIU, and postings through social media such as Facebook and Twitter. Current graduate students from RELD backgrounds and program alumni have been instrumental in networking with interested applicants through social media.

The project engages in culturally responsive approaches to ensure retention of RELD scholars:

## Ongoing Faculty and Collaborative Mentorship

Mentoring programs have proven highly effective in increasing RELD student retention and graduation (Risko & Reid, 2019). Project faculty provide ongoing individual advising and mentoring of scholars, with the purpose of encouraging a greater sense of belonging (Bowie et al., 2018). Doctoral peer mentors in Special Education, who have accumulated academic and field experiences as special educators or school psychologists, provide insights on current practices in the field. Peer mentorships are organized in small collaborative groups to foster a closer professional learning community of support. Each group was created purposively by the project directors to comprise both special education and school psychology majors who met as a small group a minimum of three times across the semester under the guidance of the doctoral students.

## Financial and Academic Support

The recruitment and retention of underrepresented students is facilitated by opportunities for financial and academic support (Scott, 2018). The project provides tuition support to scholars and stipends to support conference travel for presenting research projects or professional development, and registration for national certification exams.

## Field Experiences in Diverse Settings and with Diverse Students and their Families

Project faculty design and coordinate collaborative field experiences in schools and clinical settings to ensure scholars demonstrate competencies needed to serve RELD students with disabilities and families. The project provides opportunities for scholars throughout their training to work with a wide variety of populations, particularly those matching their own cultural and linguistic background (Blake et al., 2016). There is a clear emphasis provided on how scholars of color can contribute to their own communities to improve lives of RELD students with disabilities and families (Pham et al., 2021; Proctor et al., 2014).

## Cohort Model to Promote Group Cohesiveness and Sense of Belonging

The project operates on a cohort model to promote sense of belonging, group cohesiveness, peer collaboration, and motivation to perform at an optimal level (Unzueta et al, 2010). A prescribed sequence of courses is provided to each scholar before they start their program of study.

## **Interdisciplinary Program Highlights**

The preparation program entailed modifying separately existing special education master's and school psychologist specialist programs to provide emphasis on interdisciplinary and collaborative training in intensive, multi-tiered interventions for RELD students with high intensity needs. The project features tailored curriculum based on expressed needs from partnerships with Miami-Dade County Public Schools (MDCPS), the fourth largest school district in Florida, and one of the most diverse in the country. Through shared hybrid coursework, supervised fieldwork in highly diverse settings, faculty/peer mentorship with a diverse cadre of professionals, and virtual seminars, scholars receive comprehensive interdisciplinary training in evidence-based practices to address academic learning, social-emotional, and behavioral needs for RELD students with high intensity needs.

Six key shared experiences, anchored around components of the ILM provided the foundation for intensive interdisciplinary training across equitable environments, interdependent communities of learners, critical awareness leading to change, and culturally sustaining instructional strategies:

1. *Collaborative Communities of Learners and Mentorship.* The project uses a cohort-based approach as well as various online and social-media technologies to extend the learning community beyond coursework. Various forms of videoconferencing and social media (e.g., Zoom, Facebook, Twitter, Whatsapp, webinars) are used throughout and after their program to enable scholars to maintain contact with each other and have access to induction support. Research indicates that communities of learners can be enhanced through online communication processes (Martin & Bolliger, 2018). Programs that enlist both professional development and mentoring have shown reduced attrition rates of teachers (Risko & Reid, 2019). Supported teachers have higher job satisfaction, display greater commitment, and show fewer signs of stress and burnout (Vittek, 2015). A systematic mentoring plan details a shared vision, clear roles and responsibilities, and effective resources and supports for graduates of the program. The small interdisciplinary groups of school psychology and special education scholars under the supervision of a mentor meet regularly through videoconferencing with a minimum of three communications per semester. These groups enhance the opportunities for network and connection for the scholars across disciplines and are designed to support them while in training and beyond.

2. *Interdisciplinary Specialization in Intensive, Individualized Multi-Tiered Supports.* Through intensive courses in the summer, scholars enroll in collaborative coursework encompassing prevention, early intervention, universal screening, social-emotional learning, progress monitoring, application of evidence-based practices, and matching the intervention and levels of support to students' needs (Fuchs et al., 2017). Across two summers, students earn 12 credits of coursework with this specialized emphasis. Training special educators and school psychologists together in these practices prepares them to understand the role of each in providing and special emphasis is placed on the scholars understanding their complementary roles in this process, particularly as it relates to assessment and data-based decision making to guide interventions. Group activities were developed to emphasize both the special educator's and school psychologist's roles in curriculum-based assessment, progress monitoring, graphing and analyzing data, and intervention implementation and evaluation at a classroom, small-group, and individual student level.

3. *Action Research.* There is a growing body of evidence of the positive effects of educators engaging in action research. Greater awareness of their teaching options and possibilities for change can provide them greater confidence (Ulvik & Riese, 2016). Scholars complete action research projects under the supervision of a professor and supported by their mentors. Small groups of interdisciplinary scholars collaborate to design the research projects. These are implemented by the special educators in urban classrooms or other appropriate settings and school psychology students are

partnered with their peers to support in the process. The projects are aimed at implementing positive change in diverse classrooms. Upon completion of their projects, students have opportunities to collaboratively disseminate their findings in local or national conferences.

4. *Family-School Collaboration.* The project highlights the importance of collaboration between schools, RELD families, and communities. Parents of students with disabilities are valuable resources to educators by providing unique insights into their experiences and sharing their stories (Garbacz et al., 2018). Project faculty working in schools and communities engage in best practices on consultation and collaboration with families to ensure student success. While best practices in working with families are infused across the curricula and content, all scholars also complete a stand-alone course together on family collaboration taught by the parent of a child with a disability who is also one of the project directors. Special attention to the complementary roles of school psychologists and special educators in the identification notification of disability process as well as in familial support is provided to scholars.

5. *Culturally Responsive Pedagogy.* When documenting the educational outcomes for students who are racially, ethnically, and linguistically diverse, researchers have found that many students have not received culturally responsive instruction in either a special education or general education setting. Gay (2018) outlined strategies that show how educators can provide culturally responsive supports in the classroom. Moreover, it is possible to teach in such a way that educators can apply a critical pedagogy approach in their teaching and learning by remaining abreast of current research in working with RELD exceptional learners; examining their own racial, cultural, and linguistic realities, values, and beliefs; and collaborating with families to understand their history and needs. The entire project is grounded in culturally responsive pedagogy across courses, assignments, and seminars; however, all scholars further complete a stand-alone course together (across disciplines) on advanced issues in the education of RELD students with disabilities with a heavy emphasis on culturally responsive and culturally sustaining (Alim et al., 2020) pedagogies and how school psychologists and special educators alike can professionally implement these pedagogies while working with RELD families.

6. *Collaborative Field Experience.* A unique opportunity within the program is engaging in field experience with world-renowned Florida International University (FIU) Center for Children and Families (CCF) Summer Treatment Program. The Summer Treatment Program is a comprehensive, evidence-based program for children with disruptive behavior disorders, which focuses on addressing behaviors through child's peer relations, the child's academic/classroom functioning, and the caregivers' parenting skills (Pelham & Hoza, 1996). Scholars receive collaborative, interdisciplinary training in data-based decision-making and classroom observations to effectively gather data, identify behaviors, and implement interventions in interdisciplinary teams. Case consultation was done in small groups to analyze behavioral data collaboratively, and to communicate results and recommendations to parents to monitor progress at home. Scholars complete field hours together while receiving field supervision and feedback about their data collection and analysis skills.

## Summer Institute Interventions

A key and unique preparation practice for the interdisciplinary scholars is the Project SPECIAL Summer Institute which extends over a two-year summer period. The Project SPECIAL Summer Institute for Cohort 1 was initiated in summer 2020 and scholars completed the first summer institute in August of 2021. Cohort 2 will begin the institute in May 2023 and conclude in August 2024.

Scholars from both school psychology and special education are enrolled in two courses each summer for a total of 12 credits over the two-year period. The focus of the institute is the application of collaborative skills to address the needs of RELD students with disabilities through the implementation of the Council for Exceptional Children High Leverage Practices pillars (assessment, instruction/intervention, social/emotional learning, and collaboration; McLeskey et.al., 2019). The summer institute course content (e.g., assignments, field experiences) prepares scholars to develop specially designed instruction for students with disabilities who have learning and behavioral challenges. Scholars have the opportunity to research, observe, and apply evidence-based interventions and practices through the summer institute's interdisciplinary course content. Through an enhanced understanding of what constitutes academic and behavioral evidence-based practices and interventions and the use of specific websites (e.g., What Works Clearinghouse) as resources, scholars apply evidence-based practices, approaches, and interventions to specific individual student/classroom case studies selected by course professors and present their research to peers. These evidence-based approaches, practices, and interventions include but are not limited to data-based individualization, progress monitoring, academic and behavioral task analysis, positive behavioral supports, the Orton-Gillingham Approach to reading, systematic and explicit instruction, and the Gradual Release Model. Through the implementation of such evidence-based practices within the context of collaborative tiered-support teams, scholars gain a deep understanding of the importance of each interdisciplinary role in addressing the individual needs of RELD students with disabilities in general and special education settings.

One of the course requirements in the summer institute is a field experience (20 hours) at FIU's CCF Summer Treatment Program that provides children ages 6-12 with attention deficit hyperactivity disorder (ADHD) and related behavioral, emotional, and learning challenges with an eight-week comprehensive summer camp. The Summer Treatment Program implements evidence-based (e.g., daily report card) interventions while conducting state-of-the-art funded research (e.g., Institute of Education Sciences, National Institute of Child Health and Human Development). Scholars participate together across disciplines in the Summer Treatment Program field experience by collaboratively collecting data on student behavior and engaging in multidisciplinary clinical supervision meetings related to the implementation of a student's daily report card. The combination of course content and the Summer Treatment Program field experience provide scholars with a research-to-practice experience which is rare in personnel preparation program and unique to Project SPECIAL.

## Project Status

As of July 2022, the first of two cohorts have completed their training and the second cohort has been recruited and is poised to begin. While the global pandemic raised unforeseen challenges in recruiting and administering the program, the first cohort was indeed diverse (out of 26 scholars, 24 scholars identify as either Black or Hispanic), and highly successful in completing program requirements. The chapter will provide evaluative information about the recruitment and training efforts of Cohort 1 as well as information on adjustments to be made for Cohort 2 due to continuous evaluation and monitoring.

The first cohort for Project Special consisted of 17 special educators and 9 school psychology candidates that started the program in May 2020 with the Project SPECIAL Summer Institute. Both groups had shared classes each semester which, according to their own account, were invaluable courses to understand each other's profession, making a great and positive impact in terms of the collaboration and interdisciplinary approach within the project. These shared, interdisciplinary courses taken each semester consisted of assignments, projects, and seminars that focused on targeted interventions for RELD families and children with high intensity needs. The importance of these interdisciplinary courses is clear, as they aim to prepare a new generation of special educators and school psychologists with tools that will help them in working with students who are RELD to ensure positive and relevant outcomes. The scheduling of classes for these graduate students also takes into consideration the fact that the special educators are mostly full-time teachers and therefore classes are held online or in the evening, after K-12 school hours.

In the summer of 2021, the scholars completed the second half of their summer institute and participated in joint practica at the Center for Children and Families. Sixteen students in the first special education cohort completed their action research projects and graduated in May 2022. The first cohort of school psychology will complete their internships and graduate in May 2023. Doctoral student mentors supported and continue to support the SPECIAL scholars throughout their studies. These mentors have been providing academic guidance and support through virtual meetings and group chats. Such supports consist of guidance on assignments and research projects, time management skills, as well as moral and emotional support for the scholars.

Recruitment for the second cohort for school psychology occurred in 2021, and 10 new school psychology scholars were admitted. This group started their studies in August 2022. Recruitment for the second cohort of special educators is underway, and it is expected that the program will admit 23 new special educators by January 2023. Recruitment sessions happened via zoom meetings, with prospective candidates meeting with professors from the special education and school psychology programs, where they had the opportunity to ask questions and interact with faculty.

## FINDINGS AND RECOMMENDATIONS

Project SPECIAL was designed to improve educational and pro-social outcomes for students with disabilities by targeting the community of teachers and clinical support systems that work with and for them. Lessons learned will be grounded on direct scholar feedback as it relates to program quality, application of the cohort model, and mentoring components. The scholars' perceptions were transcribed using naturalized language to state the lessons learned in their voices and from their perspectives in Table 2.

### Program Quality

Project SPECIAL focused on improving the quality of collaboration among special education teachers and school psychologists. While both play potentially significant roles in the student's academic and pro-social development, quality collaborations that result in the development of joint interventions are generally lacking (McClain et al., 2020) outside of clinical settings (e.g., Early Intervention Centers, Centers for Children and Families, etc.). The students noted that Project SPECIAL changed their perspectives on teaching and collaboration as well as increased their appreciation of what teachers do. As a lesson learned, this reaffirms the project's inter-agency approach, whereby the special educator and school psychologist candidate go beyond the required collaboration dictated by Individualized Education Plan (IEP) protocols, that often focus on assessment and placement but stop short of developing joint

Table 2. *Direct quotes of scholar perceptions are provided around overarching themes*

| Theme | Scholar Perceptions |
| --- | --- |
| Program Quality | "The program changed my perspectives about teaching and on collaborating."<br>"Program made me more appreciative of the work teachers do."<br>"I was able to dissect the content, study more deeply aspects of the law, policy, teaching strategies, impact of RTI/MTSS."<br>"Comfortable in position, have more knowledge now to speak up and contribute, as they are able to disseminate information backed by recent evidence/data"<br>"More invested in what they do; do not just follow directions without understanding why the interventions are necessary but understand now that they have to be done."<br>"APA in the beginning of program. In the first semester, have one assignment in each class that will be thoroughly checked for APA, to know from day one what to expect."<br>"Expectations for writing APA style because it was very technical, it was very difficult as we didn't have experience. Suggestion: a 'workshop' at the very beginning of the program with the basics of APA."<br>"Caught by surprise about the rigor expected in the research classes. Prior experience with writing would help. Great rubric from the professor who always offered support, but many felt they needed more help. Appreciated how structured and clear she was, pleased that they knew the expectations of the course, but it was a hard class."<br>"Able to put into practice the theory and research learned in the classes, e.g.: action-research (intensive but helpful process where they learned a lot; understand the necessity for the practice as special educator, especially for data collection, where they learned many different methods to collect data)" |
| Cohort Model | "Working together as a cohort was meaningful; had refreshed perspectives"<br>"Cooperation and collaboration among us were very positive"<br>"Stress the importance to make the commitment, as this is a program that will take time from their families, from social life; however, very worth it. Our group, being together helped with this, to balance." |
| Mentoring Component | "Frequently motivational quotes from mentors; provided much needed academic and emotional guidance"<br>"Very appreciative of mentors. They would proof-read the papers, provide direction and support, help with APA"<br>"It was because of my mentor that I went through with it (the program)"<br>"Those who did not interact with mentors regret not doing it, not asking for help."<br>"Did not ask mentor for help because of being embarrassed to show own writing, did not feel good about maybe being critiqued." |

interventions. Two of Project SPECIAL's principal investigators from different disciplines (i.e., school psychology and special education) co-taught a course that focused on reviewing multi-disciplinary team reports, identifying academic and pro-social interventions within the context of evidence-based practices, and establishing inter-agency collaboration protocols. The shared courses (six courses, 18 credits) across the program anchored the interdisciplinary preparation. In addition to scholars being exposed to the content of their respective disciplines, scholars were able to collaborate on course projects, fully participate in discussions that reflected the perspective of a professional from a different expertise, and see first-hand how content can be applied to complementary roles in serving RELD students with disabilities and their families. Since the scholars were in interdisciplinary groups from the outset of the training, they have come to develop deeper appreciation of one another's diverse roles relating to implementation and evaluation of interventions during their graduate preparation. The hope is that this natural understanding and collaboration will follow the scholars as they graduate and work interdependently with interdisciplinary colleagues in schools. The ILM (Cramer et al., 2014) guided development in content and pedagogy as to establish such equitable, diverse, and interdependent communities of learners. The students expressed feeling empowered by understanding why mandates, in this case related to evidence-based interventions, must be applied as well as understanding the theory and practice and the need to work collaboratively in implementing these interventions.

The overall quality of a program is inherently tied to the components of the coursework provided in both content and pedagogy. The need to establish a foundational seminar to foster and apply writing dispositions for graduate students was a critical lesson learned within the context of areas for improvement. The students' feedback overwhelmingly indicated the need to address writing competency at the very onset of the program, in particular the application of American Psychological Association (APA) style. Having access to their professors for support, as well as unlimited virtual and physical access to the university's writing lab, were not sufficient nor successful as a means of addressing their emerging skillset in professional writing. The group's feedback underscored the need to establish consistency among rubrics to address writing competency in all courses and incorporating a writing seminar as a foundational tenet of future projects. The support systems needed to foster writing dispositions for graduate students must become an integral feature of the coursework for future projects.

In reflecting upon this area for growth as a valuable lesson learned, it is crucial to acknowledge that most scholars in Cohort 1 (more than 92%) were from RELD backgrounds. Higher education has pervasively assumed that language and cultural differences do not permeate beyond aspects related to language proficiency (Mahalingappa et al., 2021) and their respective impact on reading and writing. Scholars from RELD backgrounds can also benefit from assistance to navigate the institution's culture. As documented, scholars from RELD backgrounds are less likely to seek out support from professors for areas of need or to use writing labs and similar resources (Mahalingappa et al., 2021). Project SPECIAL is committed to acknowledging these multi-cultural aspects of teaching and learning in the future, and to providing more actionable and culturally relevant support.

In the last decade significant and generally positive strides were made toward implementing a more inclusive and equitable model of teaching and delivering school-based supports to students with disabilities (Choi et al., 2020; Da Fonte & Barton-Artwood, 2017). Yet, potentially crucial cultural components and in-depth specialized content knowledge did not evolve alongside the policy and related mandates (Freeman-Green et al., 2021; Lemons et al., 2018). Project SPECIAL implemented the ILM to incorporate the endemic role of culture on educational practices and the specialized and empirically vetted pedagogical approaches and clinical supports indigenous to special education (Scott et al., 2021), but often lost with the propagation of universally designed curricula. The scholars were receptive to the ILM framework and expressed a deeper understanding of the interplay between policy, practice, and teaching strategies as well how these inform the academic and pro-social tenets of multi-tiered support models.

Fostering leadership skills by increasing the scholars' ability to evaluate and apply research was another lesson learned. The students reported increasing their comfort level during professional conversations where in-depth understanding of the topic and a robust understanding of research trends in special education were required. As conveyed by the students, their knowledge of data collection procedures to design interventions using appropriate methodologies increased. Project SPECIAL sought to increase quality interagency collaboration between special education teachers and school psychologists and succeeded by creating better prepared professionals that can potentially prompt and sustain systemic change.

## The Cohort Model

The significant support systems that cohort models have the potential to foster emerged as a key lesson learned. The COVID-19 pandemic impacted Project SPECIAL's first cohort by limiting the number of face-to-face courses and potentially decreasing the meaningful interactions that often result organically in the classroom setting. While the pandemic affected 70% of the student cohort by either personally having the virus or caring for a close relative who did, little to no mention of its impact was made during the exit interviews and debriefing procedures. The students did generally address the need to explicitly inform future cohorts of the program's intensity and the impact it can have on family and social life but noted that it was worth it. Despite the COVID-19 pandemic not emerging as a focal point based on the students' perspectives, while it was propagating during May 2020, some students did indicate stress and overall personal hardship. The Project Directors created student teams within the Zoom platform where students could contact a group member for missed information. Additionally, most assignments were based on group collaboration as to lessen the impact of students being absent after becoming ill and having to make up large quantities of work that would have potentially been exceedingly difficult to accomplish. The implementation of Zoom conferencing for teaching purposes was fairly innovative when the project began, and the faculty were still learning key features of the platform that would later facilitate information via recordings and transcripts accessible to all despite potential disability status.

In August 2021, when Florida's Department of Education required schools to reopen in the state, more than half of the student cohort indicated significant stress and difficulty focusing on their coursework due to feelings of uncertainty, anxiety, and frustration based on what was taking place in the schools. It is important to note that some of the special education teachers who were in Project SPECIAL's first cohort work with children with moderate to severe disabilities, thus adding an extra level of difficulty acclimating the students back to school and to adhering to safety precautions related to COVID-19. Moreover, as vested stakeholders working in urban settings and teaching students from RELD backgrounds, they were concerned about the quality of education their students were receiving. This was especially true for those with remote access to the classroom. There is a vast digital schism for students from RELD backgrounds (Correia, 2020) and disability status can turn it into an abyss.

The Project Director responded to by scheduling the student cohort in at least one course with a faculty member from Project SPECIAL's team per semester. The deadlines in this course were more flexible and implemented the Zoom-based teams approach described. The students defined these experiences as being meaningful and adding new perspectives. Moreover, they labeled their collaborations as very positive and supportive. Project SPECIAL's students demonstrated resiliency and the group consensus was indicative of the robust system of support provided by the cohort model as implemented by the Project SPECIAL team.

## Mentoring Component

Project SPECIAL's mentoring framework was conceptualized by combining tenets of the ILM (Cramer et al., 2014) and the project's established competencies addressing learning expectations and student needs (see Table 1). The ensuing results were overall positive. The students reported feeling supported and motivated by their interactions with the mentors. Overall perceptions of feeling academically and emotionally supported were also documented. The use of inspirational quotes by some mentors was also credited as having a positive impact, and one student even credited mentorship as the catalyst for graduating. In line with the cohort's perceptions, previous studies show that RELD graduate students rate feeling like they belong to a group as key to their success (Holloway-Friesen, 2021; Rudolph et al., 2015).

There is a documented need for more nuanced insights into the various aspects of the graduate student experience (Holloway-Friesen, 2021), particularly as it relates to RELD scholars given their generally low representation in graduate programs (Okahana & Zhou, 2017). Project SPECIAL's team will capitalize on the success of the mentoring model implemented to increase the individualization of supports for RELD graduate students. Specifically, the qualitative competencies credited by the student cohort as being impactful will be actionable tenets of future mentoring initiatives. The missed opportunities within the context of mentoring will also be addressed, as some students expressed regret over not maximizing mentoring supports due to fearing potential criticism of writing ability by mentors.

Motivational teaching strategies which include using inspirational quotes, has been a highly rated tenet of effective teaching at the university level, along with content expertise and willingness to help (Feng &Wood, 2012; Holloway-Friesen, 2021). Similarly, adding academic supports within the mentoring model significantly impacts how RELD graduate students view the program faculty's willingness to offer ongoing and individualized academic support (Curtin et al., 2016; Lunsford, et al., 2017). Writing ability is considered a high-tiered manifestation of expressive language ability. In the case of RELD scholars where language acquisition and application may vary, there are alternate ways to gauge competency and mastery. It is recommended that writing-centered assessments be differentiated as to best measure concept attainment and that overall product quality be emphasized when offering corrective feedback on the written component (Yilmaz & Granema, 2021).

As a lesson learned, project SPECIAL's faculty commit to the implementation of motivational quotes (Feng &Wood, 2012; Holloway-Friesen, 2021), academic coaching teams within the mentoring model (Holloway-Friesen, 2021), and the effective use of positive to corrective feedback ratios (Yilmaz & Granema, 2021) for RELD students as it relates to specified areas of need. Addressing these tenets aligns with the overall iterative nature of the ILM as it addresses the more nuanced cultural aspects of teaching and learning that can impact student success.

## Recommendations to Develop Equity-Based Interdisciplinary Projects

Programs seeking to develop equity-based interdisciplinary preparation programs may consider the description provided of and lessons learned from Project SPECIAL in guiding their program development and implementation. Further recommendations include the following:

1. Involve diverse and qualified professionals across disciplines as key collaborators in program development from initial planning stages. Any disciplines participating in this work should be equal partners from the outset.
2. Consider RELD learners in all parts of the process including program design, recruitment efforts, course design, structure and implementation, scholar supports (e.g., mentors, writing supports, financial supports), and program evaluation.
3. Ensure a community of acceptance where faculty and staff are free to engage in dialogue about their differences in perceptions and language based on professional or life experiences. Recognize and respect the value that this diversity of perspectives brings to the community.
4. Remain nimble as this work is not easy work and will often require flexibility and shifting of plans or schedules. Use feedback from scholars and teammates to be ready to make real-time adjustments as necessary.
5. Keep the end in mind. Regardless of the discipline, all scholars being prepared in these types of programs have a common goal of improving the educational outcomes for diverse learners and their

families. Staying committed to this shared purpose is a common ground that all collaborations can build from.

## CONCLUSION

As the public-school populations of students with disabilities continues to grow and diversify, there is a critical need to cultivate a culturally responsive and diverse educator workforce with proper preparation to collaboratively work to assess, identify, support, and educate these students. Project SPECIAL was carefully designed to attract and support a diverse cadre of scholars to meet the demands of high needs RELD students with disabilities in diverse and inclusive urban settings. From its creation, Project SPECIAL was carefully designed to incorporate culturally sustaining, evidence-based practices that would serve to both connect with potential graduate students and yield professionals who are well prepared to implement the research-to-practice for RELD students with high intensity needs in inclusive settings.

The collaborative aspects of the program such as shared evidence-based coursework, interdisciplinary preparation, shared field work, supported cohorts, and small group interdisciplinary mentoring yielded a group of professionals who are poised to meet the demands and challenges of today's public schools, even in a time of growing racial tensions and a global pandemic. While the process has not been without its challenges- for the project faculty and scholars alike- a shared commitment to the improved outcomes of RELD children with high intensity needs and their families continues to grow and shape this team effort. Hopefully these program improvements will continue well beyond the life of Project SPECIAL and well beyond the reach of one institution.

## ACKNOWLEDGMENT

This research was supported by the US Department of Education, Office of Special Education Programs grant number H325K190116.

## REFERENCES

Al Otaiba, S., Baker, K., Lan, P., Allor, J., Rivas, B., Yovanoff, P., & Kamata, A. (2019). Elementary teacher's knowledge of response to intervention implementation: A preliminary factor analysis. *Annals of Dyslexia*, *69*(1), 34–53. doi:10.100711881-018-00171-5 PMID:30617942

Alim, H. S., Paris, D., & Wong, C. P. (2020). Culturally sustaining pedagogy: A critical framework for centering communities. In *Handbook of the Cultural Foundations of Learning* (pp. 261–276). Routledge. doi:10.4324/9780203774977-18

Artiles, A. J. (2015). Beyond responsiveness to identify badges: Future research culture in disability and implications for Response to Intervention. *Educational Review*, *67*(1), 1–22. doi:10.1080/00131911.2014.934322

Blake, J. J., Graves, S., Newell, M., & Jimerson, S. R. (2016). Diversification of school psychology: Developing an evidence base from current research and practice. *School Psychology Quarterly*, *31*(3), 305–310. doi:10.1037pq0000180 PMID:27617533

Bowie, S. L., Nashwan, A. J. J., Thomas, V., Davis-Buckley, R. J., & Johnson, S. L. (2018). An assessment of social work education efforts to recruit and retain MSW students of color. *Journal of Social Work Education*, *54*(2), 270–286. doi:10.1080/10437797.2017.1404531

Carey, R. L., Yee, L. S., & DeMatthews, D. (2018). Power, penalty, and critical praxis: Employing intersectionality in educator practices to achieve school equity. *The Educational Forum*, *82*(1), 111–130. doi:10.1080/00131725.2018.1381793

Choi, H. C., McCart, A. B., & Sailor, W. (2020). Achievement of students with IEPs and associated relationships with an inclusive MTSS framework. *The Journal of Special Education*, *54*(3), 157–168. doi:10.1177/0022466919897408

Clark, C. R., Mercer, S. H., Zeigler-Hill, V., & Dufrene, B. A. (2012). Barriers to the success of ethnic minority students in school psychology graduate programs. *School Psychology Review*, *41*(2), 176–192. doi:10.1080/02796015.2012.12087519

Correia, A. P. (2020). Healing the digital divide during the COVID-19 pandemic. *Quarterly Review of Distance Education*, *21*(1).

Cramer, E. D., Pellegrini-Lafont, C., & Gonzalez, L. (2014). Towards Culturally Responsive and Integrated Instruction for All Learners: The Integrated Learning Model. *Interdisciplinary Journal of Teaching and Learning*, *4*, 110–124.

Curtin, N., Malley, J., & Stewart, A. (2016). Mentoring the next generation of faculty: Supporting academic career aspirations among doctoral students. *Research in Higher Education*, *57*(6), 714–738. doi:10.100711162-015-9403-x

Da Fonte, M. A., & Barton-Artwood, S. M. (2017). Collaboration of general and special education teachers: Perspectives and strategies. *Teaching Education*, *53*(2), 99–106.

Faircloth, S., Toldson, I., & Lucio, R. (2016). *Decreasing dropout rates for minority male youth with disabilities from culturally and ethnically diverse backgrounds.* Monograph prepared for Office of Special Education Programs. https://files.eric.ed.gov/fulltext/ED575729.pdf

Feng, S., & Wood, M. (2012). What makes a good university lecturer? Students' perceptions of teaching excellence. *Journal of Applied Research in Higher Education*, *4*(2), 142–155. doi:10.1108/17581181211273110

Fish, R. E. (2016). The racialized construction of exceptionality: Experimental evidence of race/ethnicity effects on teachers' interventions. *Social Science Research*, *62*, 317–334. doi:10.1016/j.ssresearch.2016.08.007 PMID:28126108

Frattura, E. M., & Capper, C. A. (2007). *Leading for social justice: Transforming schools for all learners*. Corwin Press.

Freeman-Green, S., Driver, M. K., Wang, P., Kamuru, J., & Jackson, D. (2021). Culturally sustaining practices in content area instruction for CLD students with learning disabilities. *Learning Disabilities Research & Practice*, *36*(1), 12–25. doi:10.1111/ldrp.12240

Fuchs, L. S., Fuchs, D., & Malone, A. S. (2017). The taxonomy of intervention intensity. *Teaching Exceptional Children*, *50*(1), 35–43. doi:10.1177/0040059917703962

Garbacz, S. A., Hirano, K., McIntosh, K., Eagle, J. W., Minch, D., & Vatland, C. (2018). Family engagement in schoolwide positive behavioral interventions and supports: Barriers and facilitators to implementation. *School Psychology Quarterly*, *33*(3), 448–459. doi:10.1037pq0000216 PMID:29154555

Gay, G. (2018). *Culturally responsive teaching: Theory, research, and practice* (3rd ed.). Teachers College Press.

Gilman, R., & Medway, F. J. (2007). Teachers' perceptions of school psychology: A comparison of regular and special education teacher ratings. *School Psychology Quarterly*, *22*(2), 145–161. doi:10.1037/1045-3830.22.2.145

Goforth, A. N., Farmer, R. L., Kim, S. Y., Naser, S. C., Lockwood, A. B., & Affrunti, N. W. (2021). Status of school psychology in 2020: Part 1, demographics of the NASP membership survey. *NASP Research Reports, 5*(2), 1-17.

Grapin, S. L., Bocanegra, J. O., Green, T. D., Lee, E. T., & Jaafar, D. (2016). Increasing diversity in school psychology: Uniting the efforts of institutions, faculty, students, and practitioners. *Contemporary School Psychology*, *20*(4), 345–355. doi:10.100740688-016-0092-z

Hauerwas, L. B., Brown, R., & Scott, A. N. (2013). Specific learning disability and response to intervention: State-level guidance. *Exceptional Children*, *80*(1), 101–120. doi:10.1177/001440291308000105

Hinshaw, A. S., & DeLeon, P. H. (1995). Toward achieving multidisciplinary professional collaboration. *Professional Psychology, Research and Practice*, *26*(2), 115–116. doi:10.1037/0735-7028.26.2.115

Holloway-Friesen, H. (2021, January). The role of mentoring on Hispanic graduate students sense of belonging and academic self-efficacy. *Journal of Hispanic Higher Education*, *20*(1), 46–58. doi:10.1177/1538192718823716

Individuals with Disabilities Education Act, 20 U.S.C. § 1400 (2004).

Irwin, V., Zhang, J., Wang, X., Hein, S., Wang, K., Roberts, A., ... Purcell, S. (2021). *Report on the Condition of Education 2021*. NCES 2021-144. National Center for Education Statistics. Retrieved from:https://files.eric.ed.gov/fulltext/ED612942.pdf

Kangas, S. E. (2020). Counternarratives of English learners with disabilities. *Bilingual Research Journal*, *43*(3), 267–285. doi:10.1080/15235882.2020.1807424

Kauffman, J. M., & Landrum, T. J. (2018). *Characteristics of emotional and behavioral disorders of children and youth* (11th ed.). Pearson.

Lemons, C. J., Vaughn, S., Wexler, J., Kearns, D. M., & Sinclair, A. C. (2018). Envisioning an improved continuum of special education services for students with learning disabilities: Considering intervention intensity. *Learning Disabilities Research & Practice, 33*(3), 131–143. doi:10.1111/ldrp.12173

Lunsford, L. G., Crisp, G., Dolan, E. L., & Wuetherick, B. (2017). Mentoring in higher education. In D. A. Clutterbuck, F. K. Kochan, L. G. Lunsford, N. Dominguez, & J. Haddock-Millar (Eds.), *The SAGE handbook of mentoring* (pp. 316–334). Sage. doi:10.4135/9781526402011.n20

Mahalingappa, L., Kayi-Aydar, H., & Polat, N. (2021). Institutional and faculty readiness for teaching linguistically diverse international students in educator programs in the U.S universities. *TESOL Quarterly, 55*(4), 1247–1277. doi:10.1002/tesq.3083

Margison, J. A., & Shore, B. M. (2009). Interprofessional practice and education in health care: Their relevance to school psychology. *Canadian Journal of School Psychology, 24*(2), 125–139. doi:10.1177/0829573509336537

Martin, F., & Bolliger, D. U. (2018). Engagement matters: Student perceptions on the importance of engagement strategies in the online learning environment. *Online Learning, 22*(1), 205–222. doi:10.24059/olj.v22i1.1092

McClain, M. B., Shahidullah, J. D., Mezher, K. R., Haverkamp, C. R., Benallie, K. J., & Schwartz, S. E. (2020). School-clinic care coordination for youth with ASD: A national survey of school psychologists. *Journal of Autism and Developmental Disorders, 50*(9), 3081–3091. doi:10.100710803-019-03985-3 PMID:30877418

McLeskey, J., Billingsley, B., Brownell, M. T., Maheady, L., Lewis, T. J., Billingsley, B. S., & Maheady, L. J. (2019). What are high-leverage practices for special education teachers and why are they important? *Remedial & Special Education, 40*(6), 331–337. doi:10.1177/0741932518773477

National Association of School Psychologists (NASP). (2020). *Model for comprehensive and integrated school psychological services, 2020*. Retrieved from https://www.nasponline.org/standards-and-certification

National Center for Education Statistics. (2020). *Race and ethnicity of public school teachers and their students*. U.S. Department of Education, Institute of Education Sciences. Retrieved from: https://nces.ed.gov/pubs2020/2020103/index.asp

National Center for Education Statistics. (2022). *Students With Disabilities. Condition of Education*. U.S. Department of Education, Institute of Education Sciences. Retrieved from https://nces.ed.gov/programs/coe/indicator/cgg

Noell, G. H., & Gansle, K. A. (2016). Assuring the response to intervention process has substance: Assessing and supporting intervention implementation. In *Handbook of Response to Intervention* (pp. 407–420). Springer. doi:10.1007/978-1-4899-7568-3_24

Office of Special Education and Rehabilitative Services. (2018). *40th Annual Report to Congress on the Implementation of the Individuals with Disabilities Education Act*. Author.

Okahana, H., & Zhou, E. (2017). *Graduate enrollment and degrees: 2006 to 2016*. Council of Graduate Schools.

Pelham, W. E. Jr, & Hoza, B. (1996). Intensive treatment: A summer treatment program for children with ADHD. In E. D. Hibbs & P. S. Jensen (Eds.), *Psychosocial treatments for child and adolescent disorders: Empirically based strategies for clinical practice* (pp. 311–340). American Psychological Association. doi:10.1037/10196-013

Pew Research Center. (2021). *Social Media Fact Sheet*. Retrieved from: https://www.pewresearch.org/internet/fact-sheet/social-media/?menuItem=2fc5fff9-9899-4317-b786-9e0b60934bcf

Pham, A. V., Lazarus, P., Costa, A., Dong, Q., & Bastian, R. (2021). Incorporating social justice advocacy and interdisciplinary collaborative training in the recruitment and retention of diverse graduate students. *Contemporary School Psychology*, *25*(3), 344–357. doi:10.100740688-020-00322-9

Proctor, S. L., Simpson, C. M., Levin, J., & Hackimer, L. (2014). Recruitment of diverse students in school psychology programs: Direction for future research and practice. *Contemporary School Psychology*, *18*(2), 117–126. doi:10.100740688-014-0012-z

Redding, C. (2019). A teacher like me: A review of the effect of student–teacher racial/ethnic matching on teacher perceptions of students and student academic and behavioral outcomes. *Review of Educational Research*, *89*(4), 499–535. doi:10.3102/0034654319853545

Risko, V. J., & Reid, L. (2019). What really matters for literacy teacher preparation? *The Reading Teacher*, *72*(4), 423–429. doi:10.1002/trtr.1769

Ruble, L. A., McGrew, J. H., Wong, W. H., & Missall, K. N. (2018). Special education teachers' perceptions and intentions toward data collection. *Journal of Early Intervention*, *40*(2), 177–191. doi:10.1177/1053815118771391 PMID:30774283

Rudolph, B. A., Castillo, C. P., Garcia, V. G., Martinez, A., & Navarro, F. (2015). Hispanic graduate students' mentoring themes: Gender roles in a bicultural context. *Journal of Hispanic Higher Education*, *14*(3), 191–206. doi:10.1177/1538192714551368

Rueda, R., & Stillman, J. (2012). The 21st century teacher: A cultural perspective. *Journal of Teacher Education*, *63*(4), 245–253. doi:10.1177/0022487112446511

Scott, L. A. (2018). Recruiting and retaining Black students for special education teacher preparation inclusion programs. *Inclusion*, *6*(2), 143–157. doi:10.1352/2326-6988-6.2.143

Scott, L. A., Cormier, C. J., & Boveda, M. (2022). Critical issues for the preparation and workforce development of racialized special educators. *Teacher Education and Special Education*, *45*(1), 5–7. doi:10.1177/08884064211070571

Scott, L. A., Evans, I., & Berry, R. (2021). Recommendations for teacher education programs to prepare practitioners for diverse urban schools. *Intervention in School and Clinic*, 1–8.

Skiba, R. J., Chung, C. G., Trachok, M., Baker, T. L., Sheya, A., & Hughes, R. L. (2014). Parsing disciplinary disproportionality: Contributions of infraction, student, and school characteristics to out-of-school suspension and expulsion. *American Educational Research Journal*, *51*(4), 640–670. doi:10.3102/0002831214541670

Smith, L. V., Blake, J. J., Graves, S. L. Jr, Vaughan-Jensen, J., Pulido, R., & Banks, C. (2016). Promoting diversity through program websites: A multicultural content analysis of school psychology program websites. *School Psychology Quarterly*, *31*(3), 327–339. doi:10.1037pq0000149 PMID:27054285

Snell, M. E., Berlin, R. A., Voorhees, M. D., Stanton-Chapman, T. L., & Hadden, S. (2012). A survey of preschool staff concerning problem behavior and its prevention in Head Start classrooms. *Journal of Positive Behavior Interventions*, *14*(2), 98–107. doi:10.1177/1098300711416818

Sue, D. W., Alsaidi, S., Awad, M. N., Glaeser, E., Calle, C. Z., & Mendez, N. (2019). Disarming racial microaggressions: Microintervention strategies for targets, White allies, and bystanders. *The American Psychologist*, *74*(1), 128–142. doi:10.1037/amp0000296 PMID:30652905

Sullivan, A. L., & Bal, A. (2013). Disproportionality in special education: Effects of individual and school variables on disability risk. *Exceptional Children*, *79*(4), 475–494. doi:10.1177/001440291307900406

Ulvik, M., & Riese, H. (2016). Action research in pre-service teacher education–a never-Ending story promoting professional development. *Professional Development in Education*, *42*(3), 441–457. doi:10.1080/19415257.2014.1003089

Unzueta, C. H., Moores-Abdool, W., & Vazquez Donet, D. (2010). Perceptions of special education professors and culturally linguistically diverse doctoral students on cohorts. *Teacher Education and Special Education*, *33*(2), 169–182. doi:10.1177/0888406409360009

Vittek, J. E. (2015). Promoting special educator teacher retention: A critical review of the literature. *SAGE Open*, *5*(2), 1–6. doi:10.1177/2158244015589994

Yilmaz, Y., & Granena, G. (2021). The implicitness and explicitness in cognitive abilities and corrective feedback. *Studies in Second Language Acquisition*, *43*(3), 523–550. doi:10.1017/S0272263120000601

Zeigler, K., & Camarota, S. A. (2019). 67.3 million in the United States spoke a foreign language at home in 2018. Center for Immigration Studies.

Zhang, D., Katsiyannis, A., Ju, S., & Roberts, E. (2014). Minority representation in special education: 5-year trends. *Journal of Child and Family Studies*, *23*(1), 118–127. doi:10.100710826-012-9698-6

## KEY TERMS AND DEFINITIONS

**Collaborative Communities of Learners:** A group of students who work together to support each other through the learning process.

**Cultural Responsiveness:** The ability to learn from and relate respectfully with students from various racial, ethnic, linguistic, or cultural backgrounds.

**High Intensity Needs:** The special needs of students with severe and persistent learning and behavior challenges, often requiring individualized and targeted interventions to make adequate academic, social, and behavioral progress.

**Inclusive Practices:** Teaching approaches that recognize and respect the differences between students and use this knowledge to ensure that all students can access educational content and participate fully in their learning alongside their peers.

**Integrated Learning Model (ILM):** A model that combines elements of Gay's (2018) components of culturally responsive teaching and Frattura and Capper's (2006) integrated comprehensive services model to create equitable approaches to teaching and learning with equitable environments and access for education.

**Intensive, Multi-Tiered Interventions:** The most intensive tier in tiered interventions, often referred to as Tier 3, whereby data-based individualization is used to plan for supports to assist students in learning who have not made progress using other whole-class or small group approaches.

**Minority Serving Institutions:** Universities that primarily serve students from minoritized backgrounds and often have missions around providing access and opportunities for traditionally underrepresented and low-income students in higher education.

**Personnel Preparation:** Training and preparation specifically designed at preparing educators for their roles.

**Racially, Ethnically, and Linguistically Diverse (RELD):** A broad term used to describe communities or individuals whose races, ethnic backgrounds, languages, and other cultural factors differ from the culture of power.

**Underrepresented Groups:** A term referring to groups who have been denied access or opportunity and/or suffered past institutional discrimination in the US. This has often included people who are Black, Asian American, Latinx, Native American, and individuals with disabilities.

# Chapter 20
# Interdisciplinary Support Teams to Enhance Social Emotional and Behavioral Outcomes for Students With Disabilities:
## Project BEAMS

**Katina M. Lambros**
*San Diego State University, USA*

**Bonnie Kraemer**
*San Diego State University, USA*

**Jennica L. Paz**
*San Diego State University, USA*

**Teresa Tran**
*San Diego State University, USA*

**Jasmine Kaur Lehal**
*San Diego State University, USA*

## ABSTRACT

*This chapter highlights Project BEAMS (Behavioral Emotional and Mental Health Supports in Schools), an interdisciplinary personnel preparation program at San Diego State University. Project BEAMS is a five-year training grant funded by the Office of Special Education Programs (OSEP) to improve the preparation of school psychologists (SP) and special educators (SE) to deliver intensive, yet coordinated, interventions to address behavior and mental health. This chapter describes the training components and collaborative learning activities (e.g., core research-based courses, monthly project seminars, clinical practicum, summer institutes, and co-attendance at research conferences) that enable special educators and school psychologists to form teams that enhance academic, social-emotional, and behavioral outcomes for students with disabilities.*

DOI: 10.4018/978-1-6684-6438-0.ch020

## CHAPTER MISSION

This chapter highlights Project *BEAMS* (*Behavioral Emotional and Mental Health Supports in Schools*), an interdisciplinary personnel preparation program at San Diego State University. Project BEAMS is a 5-year training grant funded by the Office of Special Education Programs (OSEP) to improve the preparation of school psychologists (SP) and special educators (SE) to deliver intensive, yet coordinated, interventions to address behavior and mental health. This chapter describes the training components and collaborative learning activities (e.g., core research-based courses, monthly project seminars, clinical practicum, summer institutes, and co-attendance at research conferences) that enable special educators and school psychologists to form teams that enhance academic, social-emotional, and behavioral outcomes for students with disabilities.

## MENTAL HEALTH NEEDS IN AMERICA'S SCHOOLS

Mental health is a fundamental component of children and adolescents' overall health and wellbeing and is integral to academic achievement and school success (MHSOAC, 2020; OSG, 2021). Mental health includes the mental, emotional, and behavioral functioning of youth, and impacts how individuals view themselves, respond to their environments, and socially interact with others. Children need mental and emotional stability to achieve their academic potential and thrive in school. Unfortunately, nearly 20% of children and adolescents experience mental health challenges in a given school year, and recent reports indicate significant increases in debilitating mental health disorders such as anxiety, depression, and suicide ideation. In a 10-year span from 2009 to 2019, there was a 40% increase in high school students reporting continual feelings of sadness or hopelessness (OSG, 2021). Younger children (aged 2–8 years) also experience psychological distress, with nearly 18% having a diagnosed mental, behavioral, or developmental disorder (CDC, 2020). In fact, prior to the COVID-19 pandemic, mental health challenges were the leading cause of disability and poor outcomes in our youth, and this crisis has exponentially magnified in recent years with our shift to social distancing and online learning.

Exacerbated by the COVID-19 pandemic, several leading national children's health organizations (US Surgeon General, American Academy of Pediatrics, American Academy of Child and Adolescent Psychiatry, Children's Hospital Association) declared a state of emergency in 2021 due to the rise in youth mental health crises, including increases in hospitalizations for suicide attempts (ASCA, 2022). Understandably, there is an urgent call to address COVID-19 health disparities and social justice advocacy due to the higher mental health needs, especially among students with increased vulnerability due to family and community exposure to the virus and systemic inequity (Sullivan et al., 2021). In a meta-analytic study assessing global prevalence of mental health symptoms in children and adolescents, more than 29 studies provide evidence to suggest a considerable spike in youth-reported symptoms of anxiety and depression, from 11-12% pre-pandemic, to 24-25% across depression and anxiety, respectively (Racine, et al., 2021). An investigation of mental health, suicidality, and connectedness among high school students during the COVID-19 pandemic revealed that 37% reported experiencing poor mental health, with 44% indicating persistent feelings of sadness or hopelessness, nearly 20% indicating serious suicidal ideation, and 9% had attempted suicide (Jones et al, 2022). Importantly, findings suggest that among students who reporting feeling closer (connected) to persons at school had significantly lower prevalence rates of mental health symptoms compared to students with lower levels of school connectedness (Jones et al., 2022). With skyrocketing mental health needs and a return to in-person schooling, we know that many children and adolescents will likely be identified and treated within school settings (Ahrnsbrak, 2017) where they may benefit from opportunities for increased school connectedness, an important protective factor for student mental health following the COVID-19 pandemic. As a result, significant attention has focused on *school-based mental health services* (Barrett et al., 2013; Hunter et al., 2005; IDEA, 2004) to deliver evidence-based interventions.

Within schools, students receiving special education also experience significant mental health needs and demonstrate complex behavior and co-occurring disorders, in addition to deficits in academic achievement (Hallahan et al., 2018; Kaufman & Landrum, 2017; Lambros et al., 2016; McIntrye, 2011). Due to their high intensity needs, these students may be receiving related services under one of several disability categories, including, but not limited to, Serious Emotional Disturbance, Autism, Intellectual Disability, and Other Health Impairments. Garland and colleagues (2001) found the highest prevalence rates of diagnosable mental health disorders in children served in special education settings, as compared to primary care, juvenile justice, or specialty mental health sectors. These are not new issues for children receiving special education, but have been longstanding challenges that significantly impact school performance. As a group, these students perform below grade level, fail academic courses, have high absence rates, more grade retentions, and higher dropout rates in comparison to students without disabilities (Hallahan et al., 2018). Additionally, school-age students with disabilities receive higher rates of exclusionary discipline than other students. They represent 13% of total student enrollment but received nearly 21% of one or more in-school suspensions and 25% of one or more out-of-school suspensions. Preschool students receiving special education represent 23% of total preschool enrollment but 57% of preschool expulsions (OSG, 2022). Furthermore, overrepresentation of males and students of color characterizes many of the special education categories that serve youth with high intensity behavioral needs (Skiba et al., 2014; US DOE, 2016). Unfortunately, a myriad of negative post-school outcomes are associated with mental health challenges, including substance abuse, employment instability, and incarceration (Wagner, 2014).

The provision of appropriate educational and mental health services for this group is paramount, yet often challenging, for school systems. In a study investigating educators' perceptions of youth mental health, 93% reported a high level of concern for student mental health needs and 85% indicated a pressing need for further training in mental health (Moon et al., 2017). Nearly 50% of children with a mental health disorder do not receive needed treatment from a mental health professional, and this prevalence rate varies widely (from 29-72%) depending on their state of residence (CDC, 2020). All too often in schools, mental health services are un- or underfunded and designated mental health or behavioral support staff are not available to implement interventions (Gamble & Lambros, 2014). Thus, classroom teachers, school psychologists, and other related services staff, undertake intervention efforts to address problem behavior and mental health needs. Within the state of California, Assembly Bill 114 (*Educationally Related Mental Health Services*) requires school districts to be solely responsible for ensuring that students with disabilities, as specified by their IEP, receive the necessary mental health services. Previously, county mental health departments provided these services. This makes it especially important for school personnel to learn about evidence-based practices in school mental health.

Strong advocacy has emerged for more *integrated* educational and mental health services within multitiered systems (MTSS) of prevention and intervention to better enhance learning outcomes (Adelman & Taylor, 2020; Atkins et al., 2010; Kataoka et al., 2009). This requires that professional practices in special education classrooms becomes more coordinated, integrating expertise from professionals across multiple disciplines, in order to improve the quality of services provided to children and adolescents with high-intensity mental health needs. While substantial progress has been made in the school-based services literature on positive behavioral support and evidence-based interventions for youth with intensive mental health needs (Walker & Gresham, 2014; Webster-Stratton et al., 2004; Weist et al., 2014), the extent to which these intervention strategies are used in classrooms remains unknown (Forman et al., 2009; Hunter et al., 2005). In order to use high-quality practices more consistently and with greater fidelity, school personnel must adopt interdisciplinary, team-based models of service delivery.

## Chronic/Critical Shortages of Educational Personnel

Critical shortages of school psychologists (SP) have been a persistent reality since the 1980s (Curtis et al., 2004; Fagan, 2004), and are present today at national, state, and local levels (Castillo et al., 2014). For decades, these SP shortages have been the focus of conferences, journal special issues, and professional associations (D'Amato et al., 2004); and data projected these shortfalls would peak in 2010 and last through 2015. Unfortunately, a pertinent study indicates that the field of school psychology will continue to suffer critical personnel shortages well through 2025 and beyond (Castillo et al., 2014). Despite enduring shortages in today's schools, SPs must provide comprehensive psychological services across 10 practice domains (NASP, 2020). Unfortunately, high caseloads make this broad level of service delivery challenging and highlight gaps in services. More specifically, the National Association of School Psychologists (NASP) recommends one SP to 500 students when providing secondary or tertiary services. The state of California well exceeds this ratio with 1:921, and only 2.6% of students attend districts that meet the ideal ratios of school psychologists to students (NASP, 2021).

Critical shortages of SPs who are also culturally and linguistically diverse, has also been a longstanding challenge for the field of SP. In order to provide culturally affirming learning environments, schools need diverse educators to promote intercultural understanding, serve as role models and mentors, enlist parent participation, and reduce bias in decision-making (Green et al., 2009). For decades, the majority of our nation's school personnel have been predominantly monolingual, white females (Goforth et al., 2021), while students in today's schools continue to become increasingly diverse.

Currently across the nation, the need for fully credentialed special education teachers to serve children and adolescents with disabilities exceeds the available supply (Boe et al., 2013; Carver-Thomas & Darling-Hammond, 2017). This influx of underprepared teachers required to fill acute staffing needs, may hold dire consequences for students with disabilities, especially those with severe learning and behavior challenges. Also, such shortages will likely disproportionately impact low-income and minority students in high needs schools (Carver-Thomas & Darling-Hammond, 2017). The loss of special education teachers following the COVID-19 pandemic has been particularly profound (Powell et al., 2022), with many teachers retiring and/or choosing other professions. Districts are desperate to find special education teachers to fill their classrooms, and often must result to hiring teachers on intern credentials or short-term staffing permits. These are teachers who do not hold valid teaching credentials, often earning their credential while being the teacher of record for a caseload of students with disabilities. The negative implications of these untrained teachers, who often support students with the most severe needs, are immense.

## Specialization in Positive Behavioral Supports and Mental Health

Supported by a strong evidence-base (Mayer et al., 2018), the demand for applied behavior analysis (ABA) and positive behavioral supports has increased in educational settings. Behavioral strategies have long been implemented in schools to address instructional and learning outcomes (both academic and behavioral) with diverse student groups, especially those with disabilities. In accordance with this, training competent, ethical, and culturally responsive ABA professionals has become a national, state, and local need. In the past decade, demand for behavior analysts with BCBA/BCBA-D certification has increased by 5,852%, with the highest demand in the state of California (BACB, 2022). While this increase for the BCBA certification grows, it has become commonplace for some school districts to hire one BCBA to serve the entire caseload of special education students (Applied Behavioral Strategies, 2012) or to cover students across multiple school sites. This approach makes it difficult to form interdisciplinary teams that can consistently work together to serve the mental health and behavioral needs of students at their sites. Additionally, the educational setting is rather unique and BCBAs must also be familiar with educational law, instructional curricula, state learning standards, and psychoeducational assessment (Layden, 2022). There is an imperative need for more behavioral specialization within our school personnel (teachers, school psychologists, counselors) to address student mental health.

## Project BEAMS: Behavioral Emotional and Mental Health Supports in Schools

Project BEAMS was designed to increase the interdisciplinary training opportunities across both the SE and SP training programs within the College of Education at San Diego State University. The project has four overarching goals: (1) to increase the number and diversity of SPs and SEs who are highly qualified to address mental health and behavioral challenges in schools; (2) to deliver interdisciplinary specialization so graduating SP and SE's are better prepared to provide coordinated, intensive, and individualized mental health services in classrooms; (3) to enhance educational outcomes (academic, behavioral and social) for students with disabilities having high intensity behavioral and mental health needs and; (4) to disseminate project components and outcomes, and build leadership capacity in the area of school-based mental health and behavioral support.

### Scholar Recruitment

Project BEAMS capitalizes on and leverages the unique strengths of both the SP and SE training programs. The SDSU School Psychology (SP) program prepares psychologists to provide comprehensive school service delivery; the program is nationally known for expertise in cultural competence and social justice. The SDSU Special Education (SE) Department has an ABA focus woven throughout its programs of study and has successfully prepared qualified teachers in this area for many years. The masters in autism degree embeds a BCBA approved verified course sequence, in addition to providing opportunities to receive supervised fieldwork hours required to sit for the BCBA exam.

In order to be eligible for the BEAMS grant, scholars were first admitted to one of the two graduate programs (School Psychology or Special Education). The School Psychology Program receives 130-150 applications annually; invites the top third to a daylong interview consisting of small group tasks resembling collaborative teaching-learning experiences in the program, and offers admissions to 15. The Special Education Program (MA Emphasis in Autism) uses *a flexible admissions process* to select 25 students annually (from over 60 applications). Applicants must submit a Teaching Background Form, Statement of Purpose, Letters of Recommendation, transcripts, and GRE scores.

## BEAMS Traineeships

The pool of prospective scholars included all 25 students in the 1st year admitted Special Education MA Autism program and 30 students in 1st and 2nd years of the School Psychology program (to ensure attainment of the internship credential prior to project's end). Selection criteria included: (a) good academic standing in the graduate program (data source: transcript); (b) experience (and commitment to) working with students with Autism, and/or mental health/behavioral disorders (data source: resume, application); (c) interpersonal skills (data source: group interview/activity/application); (d) commitment to fulfill their responsibilities on the project (data source: affidavit); (e) priority for applicants with ABA training, skills and experience (data source: application).

## Competencies of Effective Interdisciplinary Teams and Inclusive Service Delivery

BEAMS uses a unique cross-disciplinary, cross-cohort learning community modeled after the Professional Learning Communities (DuFour et al., 2016) that provides effective professional development in the schools. Each respective discipline has something to offer the other, and shared experiences in the schools provide a context for meaningful learning and problem-solving challenges to effective practice (Friend & Cook, 2021). The model empowers scholars to develop new competencies, which in turn, are shared between the professions and reflect contributions of one discipline to the other. As part of Project BEAMS training, the SDSU SPs benefit from taking courses in special education and integrating clinical experiences with SEs. SE scholars benefit from a deeper understanding in cultural reciprocity and responsivity while working with diverse students in multicultural schools. Furthermore, research has identified a national need for special educators to improve implementation of screening and progress monitoring practices consistent with a multi-tiered system of supports (MTSS) framework, and the school psychologists are well positioned to support them in this process (Vujnovic et al; 2014). Project BEAMS represents the union of these two strong training programs to build capacity for interdisciplinary training of SP & SE personnel.

As shown in Figure 1, the BEAMS conceptual framework of a school educator as a *Collaborative Professional* was adapted from a model of teacher training at Columbia College (Division of Education, 2012). Each *supportive BEAM* in the framework comprises one of four broad, overarching competencies that are needed to become a collaborative professional who can deliver effective, inclusive, and coordinated teaching practices. Data from a comprehensive review of identified competencies needed to support interdisciplinary practice in school mental health (Ball et al., 2010) informed this conceptual model. Knowledge in one's respective discipline, along with specialized understanding of behavior and mental health are core foundations. This knowledge alone, however, is insufficient for becoming an effective, collaborative educator. It is also necessary to cultivate *interdisciplinary perspectives and models of collaboration* (BEAM 1), enhance *communication and consultation skills* (BEAM 2), understand *evidenced- based practices* in school-based mental health and their application with culturally diverse students (BEAM 3), and engage in *critical inquiry, coupled with action research* in order to provide effective and inclusive practices (BEAM 4). In combination, these four competency areas constitute effective and inclusive teaching practices.

## Individual Scholar Competencies

The BEAMS learning community model empowers scholars, while developing new competencies that are shared between the professions and reflect contributions of one discipline to the other. Figure 2 outlines the individual scholar competencies within each supportive BEAM. These individual competencies were drawn from previous research conducted by Ball and colleagues (2010), identifying a total of 51 competencies across seven domains to support interdisciplinary practice in school mental health. These domains include policies and laws; inter-professional collaboration; cross-systems collaboration; academic, social-emotional and behavioral supports; data-based decision making; personal and professional growth; and cultural competence.

## Collaborative Learning Activities

Two cohorts of scholars were supported on Project BEAMS for a 2-year training cycle. Each cohort was composed of 7 SPs and 7 SEs. In addition to completing the coursework and practica requirements for their respective degrees, each cohort of SPs and SEs was involved in interdisciplinary training and opportunities for shared collaboration across the following activities:

### BEAMS Summer Institutes

Institutes occurred in the summer between the first and second training year for each 2-year cohort, and targeted evidence-based mental health interventions for students with high-intensity needs. The Institutes ensured consistent exposure to content, practices, and skills, and created a common language for BEAMS scholars. Day one of each Institute hosted a nationally recognized expert to present current research and practice; day two invited school counselors and marriage and family therapist trainees to create round-table discussions with our SPs and SEs on relevant issues in school-based mental health. Within this forum, it was important for scholars to interact with other mental health providers in the schools and community to gain their perspectives on barriers to providing quality mental health support. The BEAMS summer institute for the first cohort of 14 scholars (2018–2020) was entitled, *Building Family-School Partnerships to Support School-Based Mental Health Services,* and highlighted a research-supported home-school model for identifying and addressing mental health challenges in schools. The BEAMS summer institute for the second cohort of 14 scholars (2020–2022) was entitled *Using Ci3T to Support School-Based Mental Health,* and focused on how special education teachers and school psychologists can provide integrated, three-tiered models of prevention and intervention to avert and address learning and behavior challenges in school environments.

### BEAMS Interdisciplinary Collaboration Seminars

Scholars contribute to each other's learning by teaching, leading, coaching, and mentoring across disciplines, across cultural groups, and across cohorts. Project BEAMS rejected the dated "expert model" of information transfer (from professor to student) in favor of student-driven discovery, contextualized learning, and outcomes that are linked to practice. Scholars learned effective school-based practices through inter-disciplinary collaboration, project-based learning, and critical inquiry and reflection. These principles served as the catalysts for achieving instructional excellence and effectiveness. This inter-professional seminar was highly structured and included specifically designed scholar roles. Each semester in the four-semester sequence had predictable activities: cross-discipline presentations, discussions of readings, collaborative conversations, and project reflections. Additionally, each semester focused on a competency area as a theme, with seminar texts, readings, and presentations targeting those specific competencies.

## BEAMS Clinical Practicum in Collaborative School-Based Mental Health

During their second year on the project, BEAMS scholars engaged in a collaborative, school-based practicum to learn how to coordinate services by working alongside one another in a classroom. This practicum experience occurred after the first year of co-training, whereby scholars had built solid relationships and trust with one another. Scholars were paired (1 SP with 1 SE) and worked together in the special educator's assigned classroom. Because the SE scholars already had their preliminary special education teaching credential and were returning for their Master's degree in Autism, they were already working in classrooms across districts, schools, and grade levels. Scholarly dyads were required to work together at least four hours weekly (for two semesters) on integrated positive behavioral support and mental health interventions. Scholar pairs conducted a needs assessment in each class to determine the intervention targets, priorities, and intensity, and were responsible for providing collaborative, evidence-based, small-group instruction for students struggling with appropriate behavior. During the first year of the training cycle, the project PIs built relationships with the school administration in advance of the clinical practicum year. Additionally, scholar dyads had opportunities to collaborate with related services staff (e.g., site school psychologists, behavior support specialists, etc.) and parents at the respective schools. They monitored progress, adjusted interventions as needed, and evaluated outcomes using effect sizes. Data collection and analyses, along with progress monitoring to improve interventions for the purpose of enhancing student outcomes, were central to this experience.

One of the greatest challenges many graduate students face in becoming a Board Certified Behavior Analyst (BCBA) is getting the required supervised fieldwork hours by a BCBA level supervisor, as there are relatively few of them working in school districts. As part of BEAMS, a BCBA level supervisor provided supervision using a combination of onsite, remote, and technology enhanced formats. Scholars used their clinical supervision stipend to pay for one to two hours of contracted BCBA supervision bi-weekly over the course of the practicum. The BCBA supervisors were a previous SE graduates who had obtained their Master's degree in Autism, passed the BCBA exam, and had two to three years of special education teaching experience. We recruited these supervisors from a pool of trained university supervisors, currently providing supervision for other practica within the Special Education Department. Project BEAMS used various technologies to enhance supervision between the BCBA supervisor and scholar (especially during COVID-19, when access to classrooms were limited) that offered opportunities for instructional coaching. Scholar dyads submitted segments of teaching videos to be reviewed by the BCBA supervisor, who, in turn, identified sound practices, as well as offered constructive feedback and suggestions for improvement. All BEAMS scholars used the BCBA feedback to reflect on their own professional behavior.

## Core Coursework

Central to BEAMs training is shared coursework, most of which is part of the SE BCBA-approved course sequence and included the following:

**Issues in Autism.** This course assisted educators working with children and students with autism spectrum disorder (ASD) to obtain an understanding of the current issues debated by experts and to enhance the ability to select relevant, effective, and evidence-based educational strategies for individuals with ASD.

**Ethics and Law for Educators.** This course examined professional issues in education-related disciplines such as school psychology, special education, applied behavioral analysis, and mental health. Course content covers principles of professional ethics, ethical dilemmas, and relevant legislation and case law necessary for the delivery of ethically and legally sound educational and psychological services.

**Advanced Behavioral Health Supports.** This course provided a study of advanced approaches to dealing with behavioral crises and health issues in the classroom. Positive behavioral supports are presented based on principles of applied behavior analysis and functional assessment methodologies.

**School-Based Mental Health.** This course examined strategies implemented primarily in school contexts directed toward the prevention and intervention of behavioral, emotional, and other mental health problems of childhood and adolescence. Strength-based and culturally affirming strategies were considered within a multi-tier model that moves from universal prevention to interventions that are more intensive that involve school-community partnerships. The course included instruction and supervision by a licensed clinical and credentialed school psychologist and provided the opportunity to crosswalk between clinical diagnoses and special education eligibility classification.

**Advanced Applied Behavioral Analysis.** This course introduced students to scientifically validated applications and theory of behavior analysis to intervention for learners with autism and related disorders.

## Professional Conference Attendance

Requiring project scholars to learn together about state-of-the-art research was important for competency development across all areas. Each cohort of scholars was required to attend (as a group with the PIs) one professional development conference each year. This conference was determined at the project retreat (start of each year) and selected from conferences related to applied behavioral analysis (ABAI Autism, CalABA), school-based mental health (CSMH, TECBD) or special education/school psychology (CEC, NASP/CASP).

## Technology to Support Scholar Learning

BEAMS scholars received training in facilitative and assistive technology to support access to the curriculum and enhance learning outcomes for students. This technology supported academic access and inclusion (e.g., iPads, text to speech, talking word processors, computer assisted instruction), as well as behavioral support (e.g., video modeling/video self-monitoring, behavior charts, vision boards, talk light, music players, reminder timer/watches, prompting devices) (Browder et al., 2014; Parette et al., 2007).

## Technical Assistance Centers

Project BEAMS scholars accessed research, resources, and supporting materials from the *National Center on Intensive Interventions* (NCII), funded by the U.S. Department of Education's Office of Special Education Programs (OSEP). This center is part of OSEP's Technical Assistance and Dissemination Network (TA&D). Additionally, CEEDAR, which stands for *Collaboration for Effective Educator Development, Accountability and Reform,* is a technical assistance center that provides intensive, targeted, and universal assistance to states and institutes of higher education to reform their teacher and leader preparation programs (https://ceedar.education.ufl.edu/). Resources from these centers supported BEAMS seminars and clinical practicum experiences.

We also accessed training materials from the *National Professional Development Center on Autism Spectrum Disorder,* as a resource on evidence-based practices for children with autism. Evidence-based practice briefs, fidelity checklists, and AFIRM modules were used to support core content in the BEAMS courses, as well as seminar and practica.

## Incorporating Clinical Training in Mental Health for Educators

Educational systems must prioritize and attend to evolving and complex mental health needs and centralize efforts to foster optimal academic and social-emotional functioning among diverse learners. With the existing need-service gap concerning unmet mental health needs, schools are a natural environment for school psychologists and special educators to meet students where they are to provide comprehensive mental health prevention and treatment services, which require specialized intensive clinical training and supervision within their graduate preparation. Special educators often spend the most time with students, and with specialized clinical training, they have the ability to identify areas of mental health and support the development of individualized mental health treatment plans. The training and preparation surrounding the use of culturally affirming interventions and strengths-based assessment reflect promising best practice approaches for implementing multi-tiered systems of support (MTSS) to promote wellbeing. These clinical practices centralize resiliency among today's youth who present with collective experiences of trauma due to the global pandemic and the rising unmet mental health and behavioral needs.

It is imperative for school-based providers to expand the scope of their practice from identifying and referring out youth who present with mental health difficulties, to taking a proactive approach to appropriately respond to a student's mental health needs as a first-line, safe adult. Given that nearly all of today's school-age youth have encountered traumatic events brought about by the global pandemic, publicized mass shootings and racial violence, among others, educators should consider moving beyond a trauma-informed "understanding" to enact positive and proactive strategies to bolster resilience, wellbeing, and educational success through strengths-focused and healing-centered educational practices (Wilson & Richardson, 2020). Strengths-based assessment, positive behavioral support, and positive psychological interventions provide resources for promoting healing-centered clinical and educational practices.

## Clinical Mental Health Training Structure

Across many of the project components, Project BEAMS scholars received specialized training in clinical psychology with a focus on childhood and adolescent mental health assessment, diagnoses, and school-based interventions. BEAMS scholars also participated in a clinical practicum with hands-on collaboration that allowed them to practice (under a supervisor) identification of mental health needs, as well as coordination of services and implementation of evidence-based interventions,

Core learning objectives relevant to clinical mental health training were established to support scholars in acquiring the knowledge and skills necessary to understand and address mental health needs in schools today. In a reciprocal and learner-centered environment, scholars were trained in assessment practices (diagnosis and special education eligibility) through intervention. The evidenced-based interventions were presented within a multi-tier/systemic model (MTSS) that moved from universal prevention programming to more intensive interventions involving home-school-community partnerships. The training embedded consideration of co-occurring disabilities, trauma, and healing-centered practices, strength-based assessment, positive psychological interventions, and incorporation of student/family cultural assets. More specifically, training integrated an analysis of strengths, protective factors, cultural assets, and adaptive functions that contribute to a student's complete mental health profile, as well as issues in conceptualizing mental health and mental health disorders across cultural contexts.

Scholars were introduced over several weeks to Tier I school-based mental health practices promoting wellbeing across whole school settings (e.g., population-based frameworks, strengths-based assessment policy, culturally affirming school climate factors, dual-factor mental health screenings). Subsequently, scholars investigated Tier II interventions and technology-based apps to support student mental health suitable for delivery in the classroom or small group setting (e.g., evidenced-based programs, social-emotional learning curriculum, positive psychological interventions, culturally relevant programs). Students also received specialized training in the identification of mental health diagnoses in children and adolescents, and Tier III evidenced-based interventions aligned with each diagnosis (e.g., Trauma-Focused Cognitive Behavioral Therapy, Coping Cat, self-monitoring, problem-solving training). Scholars examined strategies implemented primarily in school systems directed toward the prevention, early detection, and intervention of behavioral, social-emotional, and other mental health challenges occurring in childhood and adolescence. Particular attention was given to processes and challenges involved with implementing interventions, including an emphasis on multicultural and diversity considerations and the impact of traumatic childhood experiences on service delivery. Effectiveness issues were also explored. Clinical classification systems of mental health disorders were critically examined (i.e., DSM-V and ICD-11) and intersections with IDEIA disability classifications and issues of equity and disparities among BIPOC youth.

## Training Year Five

Project BEAMS is currently beginning training year five. Training in this year is markedly different from years one through four. In this year, we focus on two main priorities: (a) Dissemination of project findings on national, state and local levels, and, (b) Building leadership capacity around school-based mental health. In grant-funded training preparation programs, *project sustainability* and *institutionalization* beyond the lifespan of the grant is challenging. With this in mind, we designed a final training year consisting of several activities aimed at long-term sustainability, program integration, and dissemination.

The scholars (returning and new students) funded during year five will form the BEAMS *Mental Health Leadership Team (MHLT)*, which will engage in a series of dissemination and leadership activities. This team is charged with developing and planning a College of Education *Speaker Series* focused on school-based mental health that will be open to COE students and faculty. Second, this team will create a *Mental Health Leadership Counsel* that includes school district and community representatives interested in supporting behavioral and mental health (e.g., behavioral support specialists, teachers, psychologists, a parent of a child with a mental health disability, or a school based BCBA). Meetings will be used to network across districts, share roles and resources, and discuss relevant issues, challenges, and trends that are occurring in schools around the delivery of mental health services. It is our hope that once established, this counsel will have built momentum and will continue to meet after the grant has ended. The MHLT will work together to develop a mental health website to disseminate project findings and create a lasting compendium of resources for districts, schools, parents, and community members. Lastly, this team will present Project BEAMS findings at national and state conferences, and work collaboratively to further develop those presentations into a manuscript for publication.

## OVERVIEW OF SCHOLARS, MEASURES, AND OUTCOMES

### Scholars

Project BEAMS has supported two cohorts of 14 scholars each (28 scholars in total). Each cohort was composed of 7 SP and 7 SE scholars who were together for a 2-year training cycle. Scholars were primarily female (79%) and diverse, with more than 70% of the scholars being students of color. As shown in Table 1, many scholars also spoke a second language, with 57% being bilingual, the majority of which were bilingual Spanish.

### Measures

Outcome measures focused on ensuring that scholars and graduates have the competencies (i.e., knowledge and skills) to provide high-quality, collaborative interventions for students with intensive needs. Multiple tools assessed competency development from first semester through "on the job" performance following graduation.

Outcome measures included scholar completion of the *Evidence-Based Practice Inventory* (CSESA, 2018) pre- and post-training cycle, scholar completion of a BEAMS evaluation following each of the four semesters within the 2-year training cycle, and BCBA supervisor ratings of scholar acquisition of BEAMS competencies during their clinical practicum. Scholars also showed competence through presentations, intervention case studies, and in seminars. To assess the impact on students with disabilities, goal attainment scaling (GAS) was used in scholars paired clinical practicum to assess behavioral, social-emotional, and academic targets following intervention implementation (Ruble et al., 2012). Finally, an employer survey was sent to the employers of the first cohort one year after, following graduation and completion of BEAMS to assess the real-world implementation and generalization of BEAMS competencies.

### Outcomes

*The Evidence-Based Practice Inventory* (*EBPI*) lists all 27 EBPs from Wong et al. (2015) and asks respondents to rate both frequency of use and skill level. Data from the *Evidence-Based Practice Inventory* for both cohorts of scholars indicated an increase in both frequency of use of the 27 EBPs identified, as well as skill in implementing the practices. Based on a 3-point scale on frequency of use with 1 being *not at all,* 2 being *sometimes,* and 3 being *very often,* the mean increased from 1.91 to 2.23. Overall, scholars reported using evidence-based practices in their work and practicum settings more frequently. The specific practices that were implemented more frequently (operationally defined as a mean increase of more than 0.5 from pre to posttest), following BEAMS were: Cognitive Behavioral Interventions, Functional Behavioral Assessment (FBA), Functional Communication Training (FCT), Reinforcement, Social Skills Training, and Visual Supports. The scholars also reported a significant increase in their skill level in implementing Evidence Based Practices following participation in BEAMS. Based on a 3-point scale with 1 being *novice,* 2 being *practitioner,* and 3 being *expert,* the overall mean score for skill increased from 1.41 to 2.15. The EBPs that increased the most were: Antecedent-Based Interventions, Differential Reinforcement of Alternative Behavior, Exercise, Extinction, FBA, FCT, Modeling, Peer-Mediated Interventions, Prompting, Reinforcement, Self-Management, Social Narratives, Social Skills Training, Structured Play Groups, Technology Aided Instruction, Time Delay, and Visual Supports.

At the completion of the 2-year training cycle, scholars were asked to complete a BEAMS evaluation, which was a mix of a 5-point Likert scale (scale ranging from 1 = *no contribution* to 5 = *substantial contribution*) and open-ended questions. Both Spring 2020 and Spring 2022 graduates overwhelmingly reported that participation in BEAMS helped them in multiple areas. Scholars reported increased knowledge and understanding of how to use action research to address problems in the classroom, with 92% reporting an above average or substantial contribution. A quote from a 2020 SE graduate illustrates this growth:

*BEAMS definitely contributed to my knowledge on single case studies and interpreting graphs when it comes to action research. Prior to BEAMS, it was very difficult for me to understand graphs and I tended to skip over them. Having a school psychologist as a partner definitely contributed to this knowledge. As a dyad, we looked up research in the area of self-monitoring and took that information to implement in the classroom.*

BEAMS also contributed to increased knowledge and understanding of how to use and model different modes of inquiry, including single-case design, small group design, and functional assessment (81% rated above average or substantial contribution), as well as increased knowledge and understanding of how to use and communicate about multiple, appropriate, formative and summative assessments, including data collection sheets and SMART goals (77% rated above average or substantial contribution). A quote from a SP 2020 graduate illustrates growth in these areas:

*Project BEAMS provided me with many opportunities to review educational research and to better understand the different methodologies that can be employed based upon the nature of the topic I was seeking to understand. The readings covered a number of different models of behavior and mental health service delivery in schools across different states and RTI models. Through this information, I was able to develop my knowledge of what variables to investigate if I was looking to conduct research on a system-wide level. In terms of the classroom, close collaboration with a special education teacher and BCBA supervisor allowed me to identify needs and conduct research in real time. These experiences were invaluable.*

Lastly, scholars reported an increased knowledge and understanding of: (a) how to develop students' critical thinking and problem solving skills (88% rated above average or substantial contribution); (b) how to integrate technology to support students' learning, including use of assistive communication devices (73% rated above average or substantial contribution) and; (c) how to develop learning environments that are inclusive and have a positive impact on student learning (92% rated above average or substantial contribution). The following quotes illustrate two scholars' increased understanding of developing positive and inclusive learning environments:

*Through BEAMS retreats and practicum, I have developed a strong understanding of inclusive and positive learning environments. There were many valuable practicum discussions that expanded my knowledge on antecedent strategies and evidence-based practices. For example, we had several conversations in which SPED and school psychologists could elaborate on their practicums and environments while sharing strategies and interventions. I found these discussions essential to developing my knowledge while also helping me formulate new ideas for interventions in my classroom (2022 SE Graduate).*

*BEAMS is amazing at addressing different cultural issues and how to create culturally and linguistically diverse interventions. We discuss at length the differences in needs within specific communities and families and the biases that might come with Special Education in different communities and how to address those biases (2020 SP Graduate).*

Data collected from the clinical practicum included BCBA supervisor observations of scholars related to the BEAMS competencies. BCBA supervisors were asked to rate their supervisees on their acquisition of the four BEAMS competency bands, shown in Figure 1. The supervisors were asked to rate the scholars from 0 to 3, with 0 being *Not Seen*, 1 being *Emerging Skill*, 2 being *Established Skill*, and 3 being *Integrated Skill*. By the end of the final semester on the grant, all scholars, with the exception of one, were rated as having *Integrated Skills* across the four competency areas. This means that the supervisors viewed the scholars as having knowledge and demonstrating skills flexibly as part of an overall repertoire to support the behavioral and mental health needs of the students they were supporting.

Scholars also worked together to complete a culminating project as part of the clinical practicum. Across the two cohorts of scholars, the Special Education and School Psychologist dyads implemented several evidence-based practices across 44–48 students (individual/small group/class wide). The practices included task analysis, chaining, video modeling; differential reinforcement procedures; exercise/physical activity; cognitive behavioral therapy; contingency management; the Mind-Up curriculum; behavioral modeling, reinforcement and extinction; self-monitoring, and peer support procedures. Due to the COVID-19 pandemic, and schools shutting down for in-person instruction in March 2020, the first cohort of scholars were not able to complete their interventions or collect outcome data. However, the second cohort of scholars, who graduated in May 2022, collected data on their intervention participants and were able to utilize goal attainment scaling (GAS) to assess student progress (Ruble et al., 2012). Data indicated a significant change in target behaviors across the student participants.

In order to assess the generalization of competencies into the natural work settings of scholars, one year following completion of BEAMS, employers of Cohort 1 graduates were asked to complete a brief survey that focused on the scholars ability to implement behavioral and mental health interventions with the students they serve. Of the 14 BEAMS scholars that graduated in Spring 2020 (Cohort 1), six employers completed the survey. (Note: the small sample size for the employer survey was because most of the school psychology Cohort 1 scholars went into an internship year and, thus, were not yet working).

All employers rated the scholars as *very knowledgeable* about student mental health needs and ways to support these needs. One employer responded:

*Scholar A was a valuable member on campus during the COVID closures to help with student supports and needs. Two students in particular, who are both diagnosed with autism and struggle to learn from home, worked weekly with her on thinking out of the box and being flexible. Scholar A also did trainings for my instructional aid staff in order to help them better understand behaviors, mental health needs, and how to work with specific students depending on what they were displaying.*

They also rated them as very knowledgeable on evidence-based practices and about student behavioral needs and ways to support these needs:

*Though access to functional behavioral assessment and drafting Behavior Intervention Plans was limited due to COVID protocols related to distance learning, Scholar B was able to utilize other assessment information and/or teacher and parent feedback to understand behavioral needs. With this information, he provided recommendations to support increased positive behavior across school settings.*

Finally, when employers were asked to report on the scholars' knowledge and ability to implement interdisciplinary practices, they reported a high level of skill in this area, "Scholar C consistently consulted and collaborated with all stakeholders involved to identify an appropriate plan to support student needs."

## LESSONS LEARNED

Several lessons were learned across the grant training activities that may be helpful to future projects and graduate preparation programs.

### Changes to BEAMS Training Due to COVID-19

The COVID-19 pandemic is understood to have exacerbated pre-existing difficulties in young people's lives and results indicate the most alarming and negative impacts were observed among youth with disabilities, and racial and ethnic minorities (OSG, 2021). This global pandemic occurred at the end of the first BEAMS 2-year training cycle (cohort 1) and into the second training cycle (cohort 2), forcing us to change the format for delivering interdisciplinary training across all program components.

Like many of the universities across the nation, SDSU pivoted to an online mode of course instruction utilizing ZOOM, TEAMS, and other means of video conferencing. Project BEAMS held start-up retreats, seminars, and other collaboration meetings online. We also continued to meet online for team building events (e.g., trivia nights, project retreats). To foster more collaboration and engagement, we held a cross-grant workshop that included grant scholars from BEAMS and two other OSEP-funded grants in the areas of trauma-informed care for foster youth and social and emotional learning for dual language learners. This online event offered a day-long opportunity to hear about current research and also connect with scholars from different projects to hear about their training goals and generate ways to collaborate in schools.

Interruptions to the clinical practicum also occurred, making it impossible for the first cohort of scholars to finish implementing targeted interventions and data collection. Instead, scholars began consulting about innovative ways to connect with students and families to offer support. As schools shifted to fully online instruction, clinical practicum dyads and BCBA supervisors met online to discuss student/classroom needs. As the pandemic continued, the focus of these online meetings moved from individual student support to supporting teachers and schools at the broader level.

## Areas of Program Specialization

Training grants can be particularly helpful for creating areas of program specialization that deepen candidate preparation. BEAMS scholars shared information they learned from the project in other courses and with their cohort members that were not on the grant. Course instructors also tapped BEAMS students to share school-based mental health resources and knowledge in related courses. The interdisciplinary training on project BEAMS also helped individual degree programs identify gaps in their own program. Once the BEAMS leadership team worked with scholars across the respective programs and learned more about their training, it became clear where additional training was needed. For the school psychology program, needs emerged for more practicum/fieldwork placements in moderate and severe educational settings. The SP scholars communicated how important the BEAMS clinical practicum sites were to their competency development with this group of diverse learners that was not as well represented in the regular SP training program (most practicum placements serve general education and mild/mod settings). As a result, the SP university supervisors are now pursuing partnerships/supervisors that offer more opportunities to work with moderate/severe special education students. Similarly, additional coursework in school-based mental health has been identified as a gap in the SE department. More content around the types of mental health issues that often manifest in classrooms and the co-occurrence of mental health challenges in students with disabilities is an area where more programming is needed.

## Invest in Graduate Students' Mental Health and Wellbeing

A resounding lesson from the previous four years on Project BEAMs centered on paying attention to and investing in the wellbeing and mental health of our scholars. If we expect our graduates to address mental health in schools, we must center care and understanding that supports their own wellbeing at the *training level*. Programming for scholar self-care, cross-disciplinary conversations centered on ways educators can prioritize and enhance their own health, and on creating supportive peer networks that foster wellbeing, which is critical. While some of our scholars felt supported as new teachers and trainees by their school administration, others did not. Creating space for scholars to discuss and work together on burdensome and complex cases helped these new teachers develop a network of peer support.

## Build Relations with School Sites Early

BEAMS leadership also learned that it is critical for project success to invest in the partnership school sites. Taking time to hold meetings, explain the training components, and set expectations for the clinical practicum (in Year 1 of training) was helpful in gaining approval and access to SE classrooms (in Year 2). By design, these activities took place the year before the clinical practicum, which facilitated execution of the service-learning agreements (SLAs), and onboarding paperwork and clearance of the SPs.

## Scaling Up the Training Model

The collaborative and cross-disciplinary design of Project BEAMS enabled our respective programs to continue aspects of this training past the life of the grant. For example, the Special Education Department is considering adding the school-based mental health course to their program of study or offering it as an elective. Additionally, the success of Project BEAMS made it possible to consider partnerships with other educational degree programs within our college (e.g., Department of Dual Language Education, School Counseling), but also with other programs across the University (e.g., Social Work). Consulting with PIs on existing collaborative grants such as Project BEAMS may help programs considering new interdisciplinary partnerships navigate important areas such as: a) student schedules in programming for shared coursework; b) ways to manage a shared clinical practicum involving students from both programs and; c) making space for students to share disciplines with one another, and for collaborative planning in the content area.

Disseminations of grant outcomes (i.e., student evaluations, clinical interventions, competency ratings) is important to raise the visibility of successful interdisciplinary training partnerships. Lastly, sharing outcomes with University and College administration so they are aware of the benefits of interdisciplinary training may increase the likelihood that future collaborations are supported and sustained.

## REFERENCES

Adelman, H., & Taylor, L. (2020). Embedding mental health as schools change. *Annals of Psychiatry and Mental Health*, *8*(2), 1147–1154.

Ahrnsbrak, R., Bose, J., Hedden, S. L., Lipari, R. N., & Park-Lee, E. (2017). *Key substance use and mental health indicators in the United States: Results from the 2016 National Survey on Drug Use and Health.* Center for Behavioral Health Statistics and Quality, Substance Abuse and Mental Health Services Administration. https://www.samhsa.gov/data/ sites/default/files/NSDUH-FFR1-2015/NSDUH-FFR1-2015/NSDUH-FFR1-2015.pdf

Applied Behavioral Strategies. (2012, November 13). *The Very Busy BCBA*. https://applied behavioralstrategies.wordpress.com/2012/11/13/the-very-busy-bcba/

Association of California School Administrators (ASCA). (2022). *Addressing the youth mental health crisis*. https://bit.ly/3EBUH4D

Atkins, M. S., Hoagwood, K. E., Kutash, K., & Seidman, E. (2010). Toward the integration of education and Mental Health in Schools. *Administration and Policy in Mental Health*, *37*(1-2), 40–47. doi:10.100710488-010-0299-7 PMID:20309623

Ball, A., Anderson-Butcher, D., Mellin, E. A., & Green, J. H. (2010). A cross-walk of professional competencies involved in expanded school mental health: An exploratory study. *School Mental Health*, *2*(3), 114–124. doi:10.100712310-010-9039-0

Barrett, S., Eber, L., & Weist, M. (2013). Advancing education effectiveness: Interconnecting school mental health and school-wide positive behavior support [MTSS-ISF Monograph]. *Center on PBIS: Positive Behavioral Interventions & Supports.* https://bit.ly/3dC5gt7

Behavior Analyst Certification Board. (2022). *US employment demand for behavior analysts: 2010–2021.* Author.

Boe, E. E., deBettencourt, L. U., Dewey, J., Rosenberg, M., Sindelar, P., & Leko, C. (2013). Variability in demand for special education teachers: Indicators, explanations, and impacts. *Exceptionality, 21*(2), 103–125. doi:10.1080/09362835.2013.771563

Browder, D. M., Wood, L., Thompson, J., & Ribuffo, C. (2014). *Evidence-based practices for students with severe disabilities* (CEEDAR Document NO. IC-3). CEEDAR Center. https://bit.ly/3CfeDtb

Carver-Thomas, D., & Darling-Hammond, L. (2017). *Addressing California's growing teacher shortage: 2017 update.* Learning Policy Institute. https://bit.ly/3dN7hmA

Castillo, J. M., Curtis, M. J., & Tan, S. Y. (2014). Personnel needs in school psychology: A 10-year follow-up study on predicted personnel shortages. *Psychology in the Schools, 51*(8), 832–849. doi:10.1002/pits.21786

Centers for Disease Control and Prevention. (2020). *Youth risk behavior surveillance data summary & trends report: 2009-2019.* https://bit.ly/3c1Es5n

Curtis, M. J., Hunley, S. A., & Grier, E. C. (2004). The status of school psychology: Implications of a major personnel shortage. *Psychology in the Schools, 41*(4), 431–442. doi:10.1002/pits.10186

D'Amato, R. C. E., Sheridan, S. M., Phelps, L. A., & Lopez, E. C. (2004). Psychology in the Schools, School Psychology Review, School Psychology quarterly, and Journal of Educational and Psychological Consultation Editors Collaborate to Chart School Psychology's Past, Present, and "Futures". *Psychological Review, 33*(1), 3–6. PMID:14756583

DuFour, R., DuFour, R., Eaker, R., Many, T. W., & Mattos, M. (2016). *Learning by doing: A handbook for professional learning communities at work* (3rd ed.). Solution Tree Press.

Fagan, T. K. (2004). School Psychology's significant discrepancy: Historical perspectives on personnel shortages. *Psychology in the Schools, 41*(4), 419–430. doi:10.1002/pits.10185

Forman, S. G., Olin, S. S., Hoagwood, K. E., Crowe, M., & Saka, N. (2009). Evidence-based interventions in schools: Developers' views of implementation barriers and facilitators. *School Mental Health, 1*(1), 26–36. doi:10.100712310-008-9002-5

Friend, M., & Cook, L. (2021). *Interactions: Collaboration skills for school professionals* (9th ed.). Pearson.

Gamble, B. E., & Lambros, K. M. (2014). Provider perspectives on school-based mental health for urban minority youth: Access and services. *Journal of Urban Learning, Teaching, and Research, 10*, 25–38.

Garland, A. F., Hough, R. L., McCabe, K. M., Yeh, M. A. Y., Wood, P. A., & Aarons, G. A. (2001). Prevalence of psychiatric disorders in youths across five sectors of care. *Journal of the American Academy of Child and Adolescent Psychiatry*, *40*(4), 409–418. doi:10.1097/00004583-200104000-00009 PMID:11314566

Goforth, A. N., Farmer, R. L., Kim, S. Y., Naser, S. C., Lockwood, A. B., & Affrunti, N. W. (2021). Status of school psychology in 2020: Part 1 demographics of the NASP membership survey. *NASP Research Reports*, *5*(2), 1–17.

Green, T. D., Cook-Morales, V. J., Robinson-Zañartu, C. A., & Ingraham, C. L. (2009). Pathways on a journey to getting it: Multicultural competence training and continuing professional development. In J. Jones (Ed.), The psychology of multiculturalism in schools: A primer for practice, training, and research (pp. 83–113). Academic Press.

Hallahan, D. P., Kauffman, J. M., & Pullen, P. C. (2018). *Exceptional learners: An introduction to special education* (14th ed.). Pearson.

Hunter, H. L., Evans, K., Weist, S., & Smith, M. (2005). *Working together to promote academic performance, social and emotional learning, and mental health for all children*. Center for the Advancement of Children's Mental Health at Columbia University.

Jones, S. E., Ethier, K. A., Hertz, M., DeGue, S., Le, V. D., Thornton, J., Lim, C., Dittus, P. J., & Sindhura Geda, S. (2022, April). Mental health, suicidality, and connectedness among high school students during the COVID-19 pandemic—Adolescent behaviors and experiences survey, January–June 2021. *MMWR Supplements*, *71*(3), 16–21. doi:10.15585/mmwr.su7103a3 PMID:35358165

Kataoka, S. H., Rowan, B., & Hoagwood, K. E. (2009). Bridging the divide: In search of common ground in mental health and education research and policy. *Psychiatric Services*, *60*(11), 1510–1515. doi:10.1176/ps.2009.60.11.1510 PMID:19880470

Kauffman, J. M., & Landrum, T. J. (2017). *Characteristics of emotional and behavioral disorders of children and Youth* (11th ed.). Pearson.

Lambros, K., Kraemer, B., Wager, J. D., Culver, S., Angulo, A., & Saragosa, M. (2016). Students with dual diagnosis: Can school-based mental health services play a role? *Journal of Mental Health Research in Intellectual Disabilities*, *9*(1–2), 3–23. doi:10.1080/19315864.2015.1091055

Layden, S. J. (2022). Creating a professional network: A statewide model to support school-based behavior analysts. *Behavior Analysis in Practice*, 1–14. doi:10.100740617-022-00700-0 PMID:35371415

Mayer, G. R., Sulzer-Azaroff, B., & Wallace, M. (2018). *Behavior analysis for lasting change* (4th ed.). Sloan Publishing.

McIntyre, L. L. (2011). Dual diagnosis and families: Introduction to the special issue. *Journal of Mental Health Research in Intellectual Disabilities*, *4*(3), 135–139. doi:10.1080/19315864.2011.606596

Mental Health Services Oversight & Accountability Commission. (2020). *Every Young Heart and Mind: Schools as Centers of Wellness*. https://mhsoac.ca.gov/wp-content/uploads/ schools_as_centers_of_wellness_final-2.pdf

Moon, J., Williford, A., & Mendenhall, A. (2017). Educators' perceptions of youth mental health: Implications for training and the promotion of mental health services in schools. *Children and Youth Services Review, 73*, 384–391. doi:10.1016/j. childyouth.2017.01.006

National Association of School Psychologists. (2020). *The professional standards of the national association of school psychologists.* https://www.nasponline. org/x55315.xml

National Association of School Psychologists. (2021, April). *Student to school psychologist ratio 2019–2020* [infographic]. https://www.nasponline.org/research-and-policy/policy-priorities/critical-policyissues/shortage-of-school-psychologists

National Professional Development Center on Inclusion. (2011). *Research synthesis points on practices that support inclusion.* The University of North Carolina, FPG Child Development Institute. https://npdci.fpg.unc.edu/sites/npdci.fpg.unc.edu/files/ resources/NPDCI-ResearchSynthesisPointsInclusivePractices-2011_0.pdf

Office of the Surgeon General (OSG). (2021). *Protecting youth mental health: The U.S. surgeon general's advisory.* https://pubmed.ncbi.nlm.nih.gov/34982518/

Parette, H. P., Jr., Crowley, E. P., & Wojcik, B. W. (2007). Reducing overload in students with learning and behavioral disorders: The role of assistive technology. *Teaching Exceptional Children Plus, 4*(1). https://files.eric.ed.gov/ fulltext/EJ967467.pdf

Plavnick, J. B., Fleury, V. P., & Schiltz, T. R. (2015). Evidence-based practices for children, youth, and young adults with autism spectrum disorder: A comprehensive review. *Journal of Autism and Developmental Disorders, 45*(7), 1951–1966. doi:10.100710803-014-2351-z PMID:25578338

Powell, C., Scott, L. A., Oyefuga, E., Dayton, M., Pickover, G., & Hicks, M. (2022). COVID-19 and the special education teacher workforce. *COVID-19 and the Classroom: How Schools Navigated the Great Disruption,* 263.

Racine, N., McArthur, B. A., Cooke, J. E., Eirich, R., Zhu, J., & Madigan, S. (2021). Global prevalence of depressive and anxiety symptoms in children and adolescents during COVID-19: A meta-analysis. *JAMA Pediatrics, 175*(11), 1142–1150. doi:10.1001/jamapediatrics.2021.2482 PMID:34369987

Ruble, L., McGrew, J. H., & Toland, M. D. (2012). Goal attainment scaling as an outcome measure in randomized controlled trials of psychosocial interventions in autism. *Journal of Autism and Developmental Disorders, 42*(9), 1974–1983. doi:10.100710803-012-1446-7 PMID:22271197

Skiba, R. J., Middelberg, L. V., & McClain, M. B. (2014). *Multicultural issues for schools and students with emotional and behavioral disorders: Disproportionality in discipline and special education. In Handbook of Evidence-Based Practices for Emotional and Behavioral Disorders: Applications in Schools.* Guilford Press.

Sullivan, A. L., Harris, B., Miller, F. G., Fallon, L. M., Weeks, M. R., Malone, C. M., Kulkarni, T., Proctor, S., Johnson, A. H., Rossen, E., Nguyen, T., & Shaver, E. (2021). A call to action for school psychology to address COVID-19 health disparities and advance social justice. *The School Psychologist, 36*(5), 410–421. doi:10.1037pq0000463 PMID:34410800

U.S. Department of Education, Office of Special Education and Rehabilitative Services. (2016, October). *38th Annual Report to Congress on the implementation of the "Individuals with Disabilities Education Act," 2016*. https://files.eric.ed.gov/fulltext/ ED572027.pdf

Vujnovic, R. K., Fabiano, G. A., Morris, K. L., Norman, K., Hallmark, C., & Hartley, C. (2014). 38th Annual Report to Congress on the Implementation of the "Individuals with Disabilities Education Act," 2016. *Exceptionality*, *22*(3), 129–140. doi:10.1080/09362835.2013.865530

Wagner, M. (2014). *Longitudinal outcomes and post-high school status of students with emotional or behavioral disorders. In Handbook of Evidence-Based Practices for Emotional and Behavioral Disorders: Applications in Schools*. Guilford Publications.

Walker, H. M., & Gresham, F. M. (2014). *Handbook of Evidence-Based Practices for Emotional and Behavioral Disorders: Applications in Schools*. Guilford Publications.

Webster-Stratton, C., Reid, M. J., & Hammond, M. (2004). Treating children with early-onset conduct problems: Intervention outcomes for parent, child, and teacher training. *Journal of Clinical Child and Adolescent Psychology*, *33*(1), 105–124. doi:10.1207/S15374424JCCP3301_11 PMID:15028546

Weist, M., Lever, N. A., Bradshaw, C. P., & Owens, J. S. (Eds.). (2014). Handbook of school mental health: Research, training, practice, and policy. Springer US.

Wilson, A., & Richardson, W. (2020). All I want to say is that they don't really care about us: Creating and maintaining healing-centered collective care in hostile times. *Occasional Paper Series*, *2020*(43). https://educate.bankstreet.edu/occasional-paper-series/vol2020/iss43/8

Wong, C., Odom, S. L., Hume, K. A., Cox, A. W., Fettig, A., Kucharczyk, S., Brock, M. E., Plavnick, J. B., Fleury, V. P., & Schiltz, T. R. (2015). Evidence-Based Practices for Children, Youth, and Young Adults with Autism Spectrum Disorder: A Comprehensive Review. *Journal of Autism and Developmental Disorders*, *45*(7), 1951–1966. doi:10.100710803-014-2351-z PMID:25578338

Wright, P. W. (2004). *Individuals with disabilities education improvement act of 2004*. www.wrightslaw.com/idea/idea

# APPENDIX

*Table 1. Scholar Demographics*

| Demographic Information | n | % |
|---|---|---|
| Gender identity | | |
| Male | 2 | 7.1 |
| Female | 11 | 39.3 |
| Gender neutral | 1 | 3.6 |
| Failed to report | 14 | 50 |
| Race/Ethnicity | | |
| LatinX | 9 | 32.1 |
| White | 8 | 28.6 |
| Asian / Pacific Islander | 6 | 21.4 |
| African American | 4 | 14.3 |
| Native Hawaiian / Other Pacific Islander | 1 | 3.6 |
| Languages spoken | | |
| English only | 13 | 46.4 |
| English + Spanish | 8 | 28.6 |
| English + Asian languages | 3 | 10.7 |
| English + Swedish | 1 | 3.6 |
| English + Other | 2 | 7.1 |
| English + Spanish + Asian languages | 1 | 3.6 |
| Sexual orientation | | |
| Heterosexual | 11 | 39.3 |
| Queer | 2 | 7.1 |
| Failed to report | 15 | 53.6 |

*Figure 1. School Educator as a Collaborative Professional*
Note. Adapted from a model of teacher training at Columbia College (Division of Education, 2012).

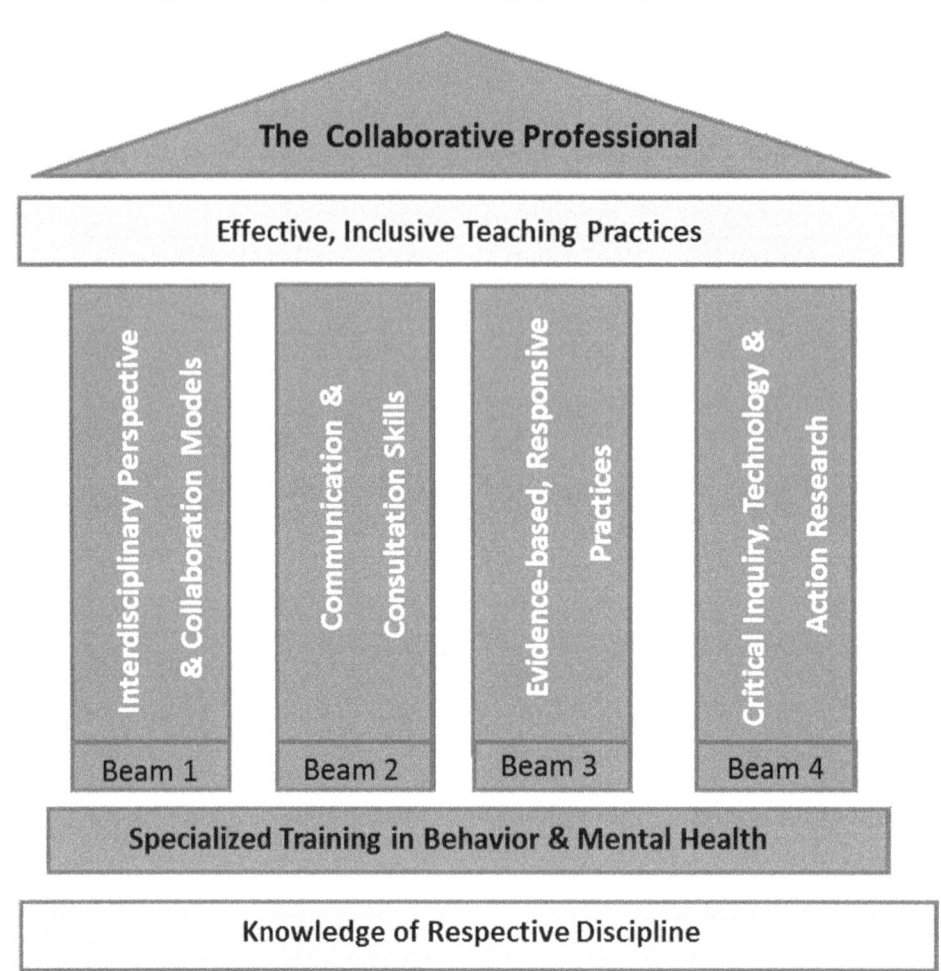

*Figure 2. BEAMS Identified Competencies*

| Scholar Competencies Needed ||||
|---|---|---|---|
| Interdisciplinary Perspective & Models of Collaboration (BEAM 1) | Communication & Consultation (BEAM 2) | Evidence-Based Practices in Mental Health & Behavior (BEAM 3) | Critical Inquiry, Technology & Action Research (BEAM 4) |
| *Conduct Consistent with Ethical Guidelines and Standards of Practice* ||||
| Cross-Discipline Knowledge | Active Listening & Reflection | Universal Design Learning | Data-Based Decision Making |
| Integrative Thinking | Cross-Cultural Communication | Intensive Instruction, Small Groups | Technology for Learning |
| Community Resources | Consultation Models & Skills | Cultural Adaptations | Critical Thinking & Inquiry |
| Family systems | Conflict Resolution Skills | EBPs in Mental Health & Behavior | Behavioral Assessment |
| Systems Level Support | Problem Solving Orientation | MTSS for Mental Health | Action Research |

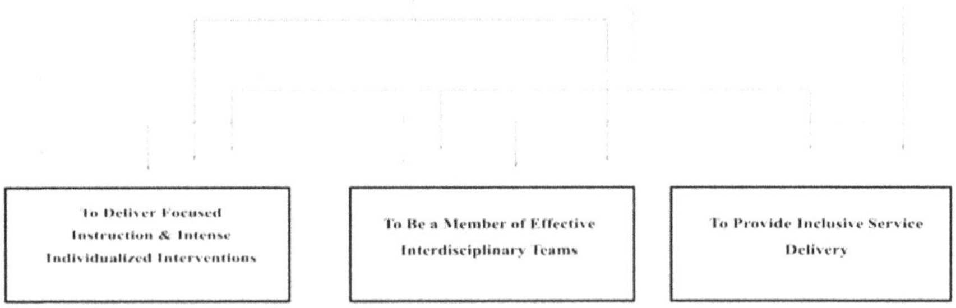

| To Deliver Focused Instruction & Intense Individualized Interventions | To Be a Member of Effective Interdisciplinary Teams | To Provide Inclusive Service Delivery |
|---|---|---|

# Chapter 21
# Creating and Sustaining Collaborative Professional Development in Special Education:
## Lessons From the Interdisciplinary Training Project in Special Education and School Psychology (SP2)

**Seth A. King**
University of Iowa, USA

**Ann Marie Santos**
University of Iowa, USA

**Matthew J. O'Brien**
University of Iowa, USA

**Allison L. Bruhn**
University of Iowa, USA

**Shawn Datchuk**
University of Iowa, USA

## ABSTRACT

*Shortages in personnel qualified to address the academic, behavioral, and mental health needs of people with disabilities are well documented. The limited interdisciplinary training professionals in special education and related disciplines receive greatly exacerbates the challenges faced by exceptional populations, particularly in regions that have historically struggled to provide sufficient access to special education services. This chapter describes the Interdisciplinary Training Project in Special Education and School Psychology (SP2), a federally funded, interdisciplinary program that combines elements of the School Psychology, Special Education, and Applied Behavior Analysis programs at the University of Iowa. Specific sections describe the national and state-level context supporting the development of SP2, identify the components designed to promote interdisciplinary knowledge and competence, and delineate challenges associated with creating and maintaining interdisciplinary programs.*

DOI: 10.4018/978-1-6684-6438-0.ch021

## INTRODUCTION

Shortages in personnel with appropriate qualifications threaten to limit the ability of children with disabilities to access services. Schools increasingly lack the requisite numbers of school psychologists needed to address student social-emotional needs, interpret student assessments, and support school-wide prevention strategies in behavior and academics (Castillo, et al 2014; NASP, 2021; Strein et al., 2014). The scarcity of school psychologists compounds the limited supply of special educators. Well-documented teacher shortages and attrition are more pronounced in rural areas such as those comprising much of the Midwestern US (Berry et al., 2012; NASP 2017). The shortage of special educators is worsened by the difficulty K-12 schools have in finding special educators who are qualified to address the high-intensity needs of students with disabilities (American Association for Employment in Education, 2016).

The number of students who currently receive special education services under the Individuals with Disabilities Education Act (IDEA) exceeds 6.4 million (United States Department of Education [USDOE], 2020). The proportion of students exhibiting problem behavior or otherwise requiring treatment for social-emotional issues at the national level has also increased dramatically (Kauffman & Badar, 2018). Of every 10,000 individuals between the ages of 3 and 21 served under IDEA between 2016 and 2017, 13 were removed to an alternative placement; 73 out of every 10,000 were expelled or suspended for more than 10 days (USDOE, 2020). The supply of school psychologists and special educators falls well short of the demand for services. The National Association of School Psychologists (NASP) recommends a ratio of 500 to 700 for every school psychologist (NASP, 2020). Only 37.2% of school psychologists reported ratios that met the NASP standard (NASP, 2020; Walcott, et al., 2018), with the actual ratio of students to psychologists in the US estimated to be 1,381 to 1. Boe and colleagues (2008, 2013) noted declines in the numbers of special education teachers and attrition (10%) at levels double those of general educators. The Learning Policy Institute identified special education as "the number one field with severe shortages" (Sutcher et al., 2016, p. 10).

The demand for special educators more generally has coincided with an increase in need for services specifically associated with autism spectrum disorders (ASD). ASD refers to a range of developmental disorders evident in early childhood characterized by impairments in communication, social interactions, and restricted interests and stereotyped behavior (American Psychiatric Association, 2013). Recent prevalence estimates indicate that ASD occurs in 1 in 44 children (Maenner et al., 2021). Service providers ideally address skill deficits associated with the disorder using procedures and interventions supported by substantial empirical research (Anderson & Carr, 2021; Eikeseth et al., 2002; Granpeesheh et al., 2009; Matson & Smith, 2008). Interventions based on the principles of applied behavior analysis (ABA) represent a range of approaches demonstrated to develop functional skills (e.g., communication, play), decrease dangerous behavior, and improve overall levels of functioning (Anderson & Carr, 2021; Peters-Scheffer et al., 2011; Sallows & Graupner, 2005). Yet the demand for ABA services far exceeds the availability of people that are qualified (e.g., board-certified behavior analysts) to oversee and implement important elements of individualized treatment plans (Ferguson et al., 2019; McGee & Morrier, 2005; Scheurmann et al., 2003). The resulting shortage of effective training opportunities for staff and families represents a serious problem for consumers seeking effective ABA services. As people with disabilities enter a wider range of settings (e.g., inclusive schools), the absence of effective staff training has (a) resulted in a disparity between research-based guidance and actual service administration (Dillenburger, 2017) and (b) has the potential to delay learning.

Regardless of disability, special educators and school psychologists increasingly encounter students who exhibit intensive difficulties across a range of behavioral and academic domains. The intensive academic, behavioral, and social-emotional issues of students with disabilities continue to result in adverse outcomes for this population. Researchers suggest students with disabilities benefit from a collaboration of informed specialists in school psychology and special education (Shahidullah et al., 2020; Splett, et al., 2013). Within the typical education context, school psychologists potentially play an important role in establishing district- and school-wide systems of academic support, managing assessment systems, and training staff in strategies related to mental and behavioral health (Kasky-Hernandez & Cates, 2015). Likewise, special educators contribute to social-emotional assessments frequently associated with school psychology and can design academic instruction for students who require psychological services (Maras et al., 2015). Consequently, the most effective programs for children with disabilities, in terms of both prevention and intervention, increasingly capitalize on the cooperation between professionals from different disciplines.

Special educators and school psychologists require interdisciplinary training to (a) function within team-based approaches to interventions across academic, behavioral, and mental health domains; (b) meet the high standards of practice from leading organizations within each discipline; and (c) improve outcomes for students with disabilities who require intensive intervention. Establishing such programs is no small feat, and requires an understanding of community needs and institutional capacity as well as a strong vision for content and methods of instruction. Maintaining an interdisciplinary program also gives rise to an array of unique challenges. The purpose of this chapter is to describe the Interdisciplinary Training Project in Special Education and School Psychology ($SP^2$). $SP^2$ is a federally funded, interdisciplinary program that partners the School Psychology and Special Education graduate programs at the University of Iowa. The program includes coursework emphasizing competencies within respective disciplines and the transdisciplinary concepts and practices of ABA, which contributes many active components of effective intervention in special education (e.g., Ardoin et al., 2016) and psychology (e.g., cognitive-behavioral therapy, acceptance-commitment therapy; e.g., Jimenez, 2012; Sturmey, 2022). Specific chapter objectives include (a) describe the national and state-level context supporting the need for interdisciplinary training, (b) delineate the specific elements of the program designed to promote interdisciplinary knowledge and competence, and (c) indentify challenges to creating and maintaining interdisciplinary programs.

## THE NEED FOR INTERDISCIPLINARY TRAINING

The demand for interdisciplinary training is naturally inspired by the larger national context. However, each program must be offered in a specific place and address more immediate concerns. Interdisciplinary programs in special education could potentially relate to a wide range of disciplines including social work, rehabilitation counseling, and occupational therapy. The decision to combine special education with school psychology stemmed from an assessment of the needs in Iowa as well as an understanding of the University of Iowa's capabilities as an institution. This section describes the circumstances in Iowa that led to the development of an interdisciplinary program with combined emphases in special education, school psychology, and ABA, as well as the program strengths leveraged in the creation of $SP^2$.

## Challenges Specific to Iowa

Attempts to improve interdisciplinary training must account for state and local challenges to providing effective services for students with disabilities. SP$^2$ was developed due to specific challenges observed in Iowa. Twenty percent of Iowa's youth, ages 13 to 18, have a mental disorder, with less than half of those receiving treatment. The academic performance of students with disabilities in Iowa likewise reveals issues with state special education services. A low percentage of Iowa students with IEPs—approximately 27% to 35%—scored proficient or above on the language arts and mathematics subtests administered in grades 3-11 (Iowa Department of Education, 2019). In addition to assessment performance, 17% of students with disabilities aged 14 through 21 in the US dropped out of school between 2016 and 2017 (USDOE, 2020), and 19% of students with disabilities in Iowa dropped out of school during 2016-2017.

Iowa is in a challenging situation considering both the high need for mental health services and the lack of trained professionals. The dearth of professionals who are qualified to address the behavioral and mental health challenges of people with disabilities is striking. Data collected by NASP at the state level suggests a greater shortage in Midwestern states, which average 1,505 students per psychologist (NASP, 2011). The numbers are even more disproportionate in Iowa. With 517,322 students and approximately 280 school psychologists, Iowa has a ratio of 1,732 students for every one school psychologist. A consequence of the shortage is that many families in Iowa report that mental health assistance is not available, particularly in rural areas, and that their children are often placed on waitlists for needed services (Child Welfare Policy and Practice Group, 2018).

Teacher shortages and attrition have historically been more salient in rural areas such as those comprising much of the Midwestern US, including Iowa (Berry et al., 2012; Fall & Billingsley, 2011). Yet the lack of special educators in Iowa has been especially pronounced, with all areas of special education licensure experiencing shortages during 2021-2022 (IDOE, 2022). Rates of turnover for educators in rural-serving districts are high. Despite convening a special task force to address special education shortages in 2018, the number of unfilled special education positions in Iowa has increased by 680% since 2017 (IDOE, 2021b). The shortage of special educators coincides with the shortage of applied behavior analysts, which presents serious challenges for families who require ABA services (Dillenburger, 2017; Ludlow, 2015). Iowa has one of the lowest ratios of BCBAs to potential clients in the United States; consequently, consumers frequently report difficulty in accessing services and travel up to 200 miles to attend treatment sessions (Iowa Autism Council, 2018). Currently, professionals in related fields (e.g., special education, psychology) may become qualified to provide ABA services through supplementary academic and clinical training; however, few of Iowa's universities have the capacity to provide these services.

Increasing the number of practitioners in special education, school psychology, and ABA who have interdisciplinary experience is also important due to Iowa's non-categorical approach to identifying and serving students who are eligible to receive special education services. That is, Iowa does not require school psychologists or other professionals to link the needs of an eligible student to a specific disability category found under IDEA. People found to have a disability in Iowa are said to be eligible for special education services and are referred to as "eligible individuals" (Iowa Department of Education, July 2019). This approach can prevent many of the unintended consequences associated with labeling, such as the emphasis on student deficits (e.g., Bianco, 2005). However, communication, collaboration, and an understanding of school personnel roles and functions is essential in K-12 settings when diagnoses and related supports are not summarized through conventional categories. Interdisciplinary training helps to collapse professional silos by exposing and expanding the knowledge of school personnel.

## Program Strengths

In addition to addressing shortages in related professions, the decision to create an interdisciplinary training program in the areas of school psychology, special education, and ABA stemmed from an assessment of the strengths of programs offered by the University of Iowa. The purpose of describing the strengths of our setting is not to deter programs with fewer resources, in terms of material and personnel, from establishing interdisciplinary training. The need for practitioners whose expertise spans across disciplines is too great to limit interdisciplinary curricula to flagship universities in each state. However, choices regarding the disciplines addressed by the program, as well the manner in which scholars are engaged with the content, should stem from a candid assessment of the cooperating programs' capabilities.

The School Psychology and Special Education programs at the University of Iowa have important connections with practical settings throughout Iowa. Placements within school systems for school psychology graduate students and first year special education scholars are completed in collaboration with Iowa's Area Education Agencies (AEAs). Iowa has nine AEAs across the state to provide services for communities for children from birth to age 21. AEAs are regional service agencies that provide educational and media resources to all 327 Iowa public school districts and to all accredited, 180 non-public schools in Iowa. Educational and media services can take the form of professional development, instructional technology, curricular resources, and technology. Special education resources can include the services of school psychologists, school social workers, speech and language therapists, and academic and behavior consultants. A vast percentage of school psychologists serving Iowa school children in the K-12 setting are employed by one of the AEAs. Through these networks, scholars are placed within a variety of practicum placements, including high-need local education agencies (e.g., high poverty).

Scholars also have access to intensive interdisciplinary clinical placements involving children with intensive behavioral needs through the Stead Family Children's Hospital (SFCH). SFCH is the only comprehensive care hospital providing treatment for children across Iowa and other areas of the Midwest. SFCH encompasses the Division of Developmental Pediatrics, which provides clinical care for children with a variety of challenges and difficulties, including developmental delays, intellectual disabilities, ASD, and disruptive behavior disorders. The Division has been a national leader in research using ABA to treat severely challenging behavior. SFCH provides an environment for exceptional patient care and education and routinely facilitates supervised implementation of intensive interventions by graduate students. In addition, the Division of Developmental Pediatrics is recognized as Iowa's University Center for Excellence in Developmental Disabilities, which works to ensure that all Iowans with disabilities have the opportunities, services, and supports they need to be independent and productive members of their home communities. Scholars also have access to a world-renowned center for gifted, talented, and twice exceptional education (i.e., the Belin Blank Center: Gifted Education and Talent Development). Iowa's recent selection of the University of Iowa's College of Education as the state's epicenter for school mental health research, professional development, and clinical services has also increased opportunities for all graduate students to learn, research, and receive funding.

The program was also fortunate to have access to nationally recognized experts in skills relevant to interdisciplinary treatment. Faculty in special education and school psychology involved in planning the program had a record of scholarship in areas specific to effective intervention for students with disabilities.

These areas include: (1) collaboration and consultation (e.g., Bruhn et al., 2019; Lerman, O'Brien, et al., 2020; Schieltz et al., 2017); (2) data-based decision-making and assessment (e.g., Bruhn et al., 2019; King et al., 2012; Schieltz et al., 2018); (3) social-emotional-behavioral practices (e.g., Bruhn et al., 2015; Ledford et al., 2018; Schieltz et al., 2017; Vogelgesang et al., 2016); and (4) intervention in academic skills (e.g., literacy, mathematics; Datchuk & Rodgers, 2019; Datchuk et al., 2020; King et al., 2016).

## SPECIFIC PROGRAM ELEMENTS

Considering the many challenges facing service recipients in Iowa as well as the resources available at the University of Iowa, planning for SP$^2$ occurred through the continued collaboration of faculty in special education and school psychology, many of whom hold dual specializations in ABA. The planning group was immediately confronted by the two questions facing any committee attempting to conceive of an interdisciplinary training effort: (1) What does the program teach? and (2) How is it taught? This section provides a description of competencies targeted in SP$^2$ and the program's approach to promoting interdisciplinary competencies among trainees, with explicit detail regarding program components and their underlying conceptual structure. Throughout, changes are described in context of the special education and school psychology programs as they existed prior to the creation of the interdisciplinary program.

### What to Teach: Program Competencies

Professional standards for special educators, school psychologists, and applied behavior analysts increasingly acknowledge the importance of interdisciplinary collaboration in service provision. For instance, The Council for Exceptional Children's (CEC) Preparation Standards (2015) emphasize the importance of collaboration in ensuring safe and inclusive environments and conducting assessment for the purposes of decision making. Similarly, NASP emphasizes collaboration and engaging in instructional activities traditionally associated with special education (2010a). As part of a professional preparation program, the School Psychology program is tasked with adherence to the NASP Professional Standards and its 10 Practice Model Domains (NASP, 2022, July 19). Two practice domains (i.e., Domain 2: Consultation and Collaboration; Domain 7: Family School and Community Collaboration) specifically address collaboration between and among various professionals and concerned parties (NASP, 2022, Domain Section). Many professionals in ABA receive training in education or psychology, which potentially facilitates collaboration within and across these disciplines (Beaulieu et al., 2019). Additionally, the task list of the Behavior Analyst Certification Board (BACB, 2017) defines collaboration as one of the skills behavior analysts must learn before taking the certification exam. Despite these recommendations, professionals in both special education (Fowler et al., 2019) and school psychology (McNamara et al., 2019) suggest they are either unprepared to engage in interdisciplinary collaboration or rarely provided the opportunity for such experiences in practice. Collaboration is frequently identified as an issue with which behavior analysts struggle in practice (e.g., Brodhead, 2015).

Leaving aside the clear guidelines regarding the importance of interdisciplinary training, creating a cohesive set of objectives for a single program spanning multiple distinctive disciplines presented a serious challenge. The program was therefore designed to emphasize the competencies special educators and school psychologists need to address the academic and behavioral needs of students with disabilities. The nine competencies, which represent a synthesis of training guidelines set forth by professional organizations in special education (CEC, 2015) and school psychology/psychology (NASP, 2020, 2010a, 2010b), lead to improved outcomes for students with disabilities who have intensive needs. Specific competencies include:

1. Demonstrate a foundation in theories, models, and research guiding inclusion, differentiated academic instruction and social-emotional-behavioral intervention
2. Collect and use data for individualized instructional and intervention decision making as well as service evaluation
3. Use valid and reliable assessment techniques for the purpose of diagnosis and the assessment of goals and objectives
4. Assess quality of research to select, develop, implement and evaluate evidence-based practices;
5. Use technology, including assistive technology, to enhance service delivery and decision making
6. Enhance outcomes for children with disabilities through high expectations, differentiation of instruction, application of evidence-based intervention, and systematic adaptation of existing services
7. Explain important concepts and demonstrate key practices to non-specialists (e.g., families, caregivers) in an accessible manner
8. Collaborate across groups of professionals and community stakeholders using interdisciplinary, team-based approaches for purposes of assessment, intervention development, and implementation
9. Reflect an understanding and respect for diversity and advocate for all service recipients\

The competencies cover a wide range of skills related to the promotion of high expectations, differentiation of instruction, and delivery of effective individualized intervention (i.e., competencies 1-6) as well as interdisciplinary collaboration (i.e., competencies 7-9). Once defined, the list of competencies facilitated the recognition of elements of the extant training programs that could be combined to assist scholars obtain targeted skills. Program faculty were also able to identify areas in need of new courses and fieldwork opportunities.

## How to Teach: Active Elements of the SP² Program

After defining the competencies at the core of the program, the next task was to develop curriculum and related experiences pursuant to their acquisition. Effective training programs are typically unified through an explicit, conceptual framework. SP² is guided by principles of effective direct instruction as well as established models of adult professional development. Training concerning specific skills generally involves a verbal rationale and description of the practice, followed by instructional models, and cycles of guided practice and feedback across multiple contexts until skills (e.g., explicit math instruction, development of behavior support plans) are acquired (e.g., Hogan et al., 2015). More broadly, SP² creates collaborative learning environments centered around meaningful activities. Both knowledge and skill acquisition involve processes of reflective practice, authentic learning, sustained engagement, and collaborative inquiry in relation to foundational content, case studies, and practical experiences.

Reflective practice requires scholars to recognize and examine the influence of their beliefs, social positions, and prior experiences on their engagement with colleagues, service recipients, and community stakeholders. This process is coupled with authentic learning opportunities, which include experiences provided throughout SP² in planning, implementing, and reflecting on the intervention process in interdisciplinary practical contexts (i.e., schools, clinics). Sustained engagement refers to sufficiently prolonging practical experiences to an extent that will promote fluency in implementation, generalization over multiple contexts, and reflection. Collectively, these adult learning strategies are designed to build scholars' knowledge, skills, and self-efficacy. SP² provides distinct experiences, in terms of content and skills required, over multiple courses and supervised fieldwork as means of ensuring scholars' sustained engagement. Finally, collaborative inquiry engages scholars in the process of developing practice through project-based learning, progress monitoring, and group discussion and reflection. SP² courses, field experiences, and other enrichment activities promote this approach across special education and school psychology.

## Interdisciplinary Course Sequence

Central to SP² is an interdisciplinary sequence of courses that provides content pertaining to the foundational knowledge and collaborative dispositions valued in each discipline. Shared background knowledge can facilitate mutual understanding and meaningful collaboration in professional settings. SP² includes coursework emphasizing project competencies as applied within respective disciplines. Consequently, scholars obtain a firm grasp of the theoretical and methodological knowledge increasingly identified as active components of effective intervention in special education and school psychology.

Scholars complete the interdisciplinary course sequence comprising SP² in addition to the typical courses within Special Education and School Psychology programs. The sequence is intended to increase the number of practitioners in each discipline who make data-based decisions regarding treatment, problem-solve within a team-based context, and who can alter the intensity of academic and behavioral interventions based on the unique needs of each student. To keep the course load to a minimum and avoid creating additional classes, the interdisciplinary coursework spanning both programs use existing courses from each sequence whenever possible. Courses comprising the original course sequences and the interdisciplinary core appear in Table 1.

Longstanding program offerings provided the basis for the interdisciplinary course sequence. The School Psychology program is a terminal doctoral program with an integrated Ed.S. degree. The program follows the training guidelines of both the American Psychological Association and NASP's standards for graduate education. Students who pursue the Ed.S. in school psychology typically complete 61 coursework hours emphasizing skills in different forms of counseling, child development, and research. The additional content extends the 3-year school psychology sequence by an additional year, with the final year occupied by an internship.

The Special Education program offers undergraduate and graduate licensure in multiple areas (e.g., behavior disorders, learning disabilities). The 32 hours of coursework included in the original sequence emphasize foundations of special education, ABA, and intensive academic intervention. Scholars can pursue credentials related to K-8 special education, K-12 special education, or specialized licensure related to services for students with learning disabilities or emotional/behavioral disorders. Time to completion of the MA degree is typically two years, with the final semester of the program dedicated to student teaching. Interdisciplinary activities effectively increase the length of the program by an additional semester. The special education department also offers a distinct ABA course sequence consisting of seven courses.

The ABA course sequence was developed immediately prior to creation of SP² as a graduate certificate available to students who already possessed a graduate degree. Select ABA courses already appeared in either the school psychology program (e.g., EDTL 5963: Ethics), special education program (e.g., EDTL

*Table 1. Overview of Courses and Interdisciplinary Activities for SP²*

| | School Psychology | Interdisciplinary Core | Special Education |
|---|---|---|---|
| **COURSEWORK** | PSQF 6235 Multicultural Counseling (3) | EDTL 4900 FND of SPED (3) | PSQF 6200 Educational Psych[b](3) |
| | PSY 5212 FND in Behavioral and Cognitive Neuroscience (4) | EDTL 6975 Explicit Instruction* (3) | EPLS: 3000 FND of Education[b](3) |
| | PSY 6370 Principles of Neuropsych (3) | EDTL 4908 SPED Literacy (3) | EDTL 4934 Parent-Teacher Communication (3) |
| | PSQF 6281 Cognitive Theories of Learning (3) | EDTL 5966: Advanced ABA* (3) | EDTL 3002 Technology in the Classroom (3) |
| | PSQF 7367 Social Psych & Social Systems (3) | EDTL 7953 Single Subject* (3) | |
| | PSQF 6206 Advanced Child Development (3) | EDTL 5961 FND of ABA* (3) | EDTL 3103 ASMT Instructional Planning & Practice (3) |
| | PQSF7310 Intelligence ASMT (3) | PSQF 5218 FND of School Psych (4) | |
| | PSQF 6243 Intermediate Stats (4) | EDTL 4950 Behavioral & Social Interventions* (3) | EPLS 4180 Human Relations for the Classroom Teacher (3) |
| | PSQF 7342 Research Project (4) | EDTL 5963 Ethics in ABA and Psychology (3) | |
| | PSQF 6238 ASMT of Learning Differences (3) | PEDS 7264 Clinical Applications of ABA* (3) | EDTL 4984 Academic Skills for Students with Special Needs (3) |
| | PSQF 6263 Consultation Theory & Practice (3) | | |
| **FIELDWORK** | PSQF 7237 Beginning Practicum (6) | | EDTL 6906 Practicum with Exceptional Persons Supervised TCH (3) |
| | PSQF 7337 Advanced Practicum (3) | | EDTL 6950 Strategist 1: Student TCH ELM[a] (5) OR EDTL 6953: Strategist II: TCH ELM/EDTL 6953: Strategist II: TCH Secondary[b] (5) |
| | PSQF 7437 Internship in School Psychology (1 Yr) | | EDTL 6909 Seminar of Supervised TCH (1) |
| **INTERDISCIPLINARY ACTIVITIES** | *Teacher Leader Certification: Individuals with Disabilities Track* – Series of competencies and experiences in assessment, technology and diversity offered through the UI REACH. Consists of 6 workshops and 40 hours of relevant community service<br><br>*Expert Scholar Series* – A sequence sessions facilitated by university partnerships with experts in special education and school mental health. Six sessions, accompanied by readings and other resources, are offered each year. Scholars are required to attend four sessions each year. | | |

Courses listed as coursework and fieldwork have substantial classroom and fieldwork requirements. Courses listed in the fieldwork segment alone represent dedicated practicum courses. Scholars within each program complete interdisciplinary activities within the first two years following enrollment. Solid box denotes courses originally derived from the special education program. Dashed box denotes courses derived from the school psychology program. Dotted box denotes courses new to each sequence. All other interdisciplinary courses were incorporated into both sequences prior to the creation of SP2. Note. ASMT = Assessment; Psych = Psychology; FND = Foundations; ABA = Applied Behavior Analysis; SPED = Special Education; TCH = Teaching; ELM = Elementary. *Part of verified course sequence required for eligibility as a certified behavior analyst. aK-8 Special Education or 5-12 Special Education Only bK-12 Behavior Disorders and Learning Strategist Only

6975: Explicit Instruction) or both programs combined (e.g., EDTL 4950: Behavioral and Social Interventions). Due to the presence of common behavioral concepts across disciplines (e.g., reinforcement) as well as the frequent application of behavior analytic methods in practice (e.g., functional behavioral assessment; Ardoin et al., 2016; Cooper et al., 2020), ABA represents a natural point of convergence for the two disciplines. The transdisciplinary concepts and practices, combined with the need for ABA services in Iowa, provided a sufficient rationale for having these courses serve as the bulk of the courses in the interdisciplinary sequence. From a more practical standpoint, using existing courses already required in one or both programs allowed for the formulation of the interdisciplinary sequence without placing an undue burden on students or faculty.

Prominently featuring ABA courses in the interdisciplinary core allows students to take content related to foundational activities and content of special education and school psychology (e.g., functional behavior assessment, ethics) while simultaneously satisfying the course requirements for certification in behavior analysis. Courses on the foundations of ABA emphasize the shared theoretical assumptions and practices in special education and school psychology. Subsequent courses directly link this content to data-based, individualized intervention for students with disabilities who have intensive needs. One of the ABA courses (PEDS 7264: Clinical Applications of ABA) is taught in the context of a clinical behavioral treatment setting. Taught by a clinical behavioral psychologist, the course teaches scholars about the continuum of clinical service activities from referral to discharge (i.e., case preparation, clinical interviewing, behavioral assessment and treatment, report writing). Scholars learn specific behavioral assessment and treatment procedures (e.g., functional analysis, functional communication training) and gain an awareness of the benefits and limitations of clinical service models, particularly for children and adolescents who exhibit severe and challenging behavior.

In addition to the ABA course sequence, scholars also take two separate foundations courses in special education and school psychology. While the former is typically required in most school psychology programs, many special educators do not have the opportunity to take a course dedicated to the profession and practice of school psychology. The introductory graduate course provides an overview of the history, role and functions of school psychologists, professional issues and standards, and contemporary issues and challenges in the field. The course further encompasses numerous topics including the historical development of the psychology specialty, roles and functions of school psychologists, and the relationship of school psychology to other specialties in psychology and education. The foundations of school psychology course is offered in a discussion format with opportunities for students to engage with course readings, lecture presentations, and their professional experiences. This dialogue is essential to the students' development and understanding of how the different disciplines can contribute to the overall well-being and success of the populations served. Across all courses, content is related to a series of signature assignments, many of which entail fieldwork that requires application of concepts across the continuum of potential placements in special education.

## Fieldwork, Experience, and Other Activities

SP$^2$ further provides scholars with experience in the collaborative implementation of intensive intervention in clinical and school settings that resemble likely locations of post-graduation employment. SP$^2$ expands scholars' exposure to academic interventions in school settings and clinical experiences involving K-12 students who may exhibit severe aggression, feeding disorders, and other critical behavior problems. Although the school setting is their primary professional destination, all scholars participate in coursework and training experiences related to clinical behavioral assessment and treatment. Unfortunately, professional practice across settings is often performed in isolation, even though children with problem behaviors frequently require comprehensive services as they transition between clinical and school settings (Farmer, 2013). Thus, the purpose of the clinical education and training provided within the SP² program is to create a "bridge" that allows scholars to develop more integrated professional practice that combines both clinical and school service models. The framework includes fieldwork that provides practical experiences in interdisciplinary planning and implementation. While describing the full range of fieldwork embedded in courses and extracurricular activity is beyond the scope of this chapter, the following section provides specific examples administered throughout the duration of the program.

**Job shadowing.** To increase scholars' exposure to professional dispositions within the field, the foundations of school psychology course includes an experiential component. Specifically, scholars are required to visit local schools and observe a variety of educational and psychological practices through a 50 clock-hour minimum job shadow experience. Scholars are paired with a credentialed and seasoned school psychologist working in the K-12 setting and spend a minimum of six full days in the school setting observing various psychoeducational activities. Observations occur in different grade-levels within general and special education settings, team meetings, and counseling sessions depending on the specific role and function of each individual school psychologist. Scholars compose daily logs of their experience reflecting on what new information they learned from the experience and its implication for their future professional practice. In addition to observations, faculty expect scholars to engage in tasks to learn about the school environment and collaborative service provision.

Activities completed during the job-shadow experience are not limited to observation, as scholars interview school personnel (e.g., school social workers and guidance counselors), administrators, and teachers. Interviews are designed to promote inquiry into the working relationships amongst various school professionals, including special educators and school psychologists. Scholars are encouraged to consider how the day-to-day practices of school psychologists embody best practices and identify barriers to best practice in schools. The job shadow experience serves as an introduction to the school setting and school psychology practice. The special education graduate scholars who take part begin to understand the role and function of school psychologists and how this can impact the daily work of special education professionals. Scholars in the school psychology program, on the other hand, obtain first-hand experience working alongside professionals from a different background.

**Clinical observation.** Scholars also apply what they learn in their coursework by working directly with people who have severe and challenging behavior in a tertiary care clinic at SFCH. These opportunities are partially linked to one of the ABA certification courses, which promotes observation of common assessments and interventions. Interdisciplinary training within a medical setting increases scholars' awareness of the interplay between communication deficits, various biomedical conditions, and challenging behavior. Within the clinical setting, scholars acquire first-hand experience in conducting advanced behavioral assessment and treatment procedures, which increasingly occur in the school setting. In addition to interdisciplinary training experiences within the clinic, many scholars develop supervision skills as they work with new applicants entering their clinical training. This training approach serves the dual purpose of advancing scholars' proficiency in critical clinical techniques and leadership skills. The clinic is co-staffed by a behavioral psychologist, speech and language pathologist, and medical professional (i.e., physician or physician assistant), which affords scholars additional exposure to interdisciplinary service models. These experiences provide scholars with extensive exposure to appropriate practice and prolonged opportunities for supervised implementation.

**Transition experience.** The University of Iowa hosts UI REACH, a comprehensive transition program that provides integrated college experience and support for people with intellectual, cognitive, and learning disabilities. SP$^2$ scholars are assigned to UI REACH workshops targeting assistive technology, academic and behavioral supports, team-based problems solving, family and caregiver collaboration, life skills, and current issues and trends in disability services. Additionally, scholars commit 40 hours to engage in one-on-one social activities with UI REACH students (i.e., college students with intellectual, cognitive, and learning disabilities). Volunteer experiences and related reflections are tracked through an online portal. This field experience is specifically designed to provide scholars a range of opportunities to observe, engage, and reflect on their work with students with disabilities and their interdisciplinary colleagues. Completion of the program results in a Teacher Leader Certification in Individuals with Disabilities.

**Behavior intervention planning.** As part of one of the ABA courses concerning behavior and social interventions, scholars work in interdisciplinary teams of 3-4 over an entire semester. In tandem with a cooperating K-12 teacher within a high-needs school, scholars conduct a functional behavior assessment and then design a behavior intervention plan in accordance with an established, evidence-based process (e.g., Bruhn et al., 2015). Scholars then train the cooperating teacher to implement the intervention for a K-12 student with intense behavioral needs and evaluate outcomes, implementation fidelity, and consumer satisfaction. With permission from the local Iowa City Community School District, the scholar teams collect data, discuss progress, and engage in data-based decision making. Then, they present their findings to the cooperating K-12 teacher, K-12 student, and to the class.

**Expert scholar series.** SP$^2$ scholars also attend a series of professional development sessions offered by an assembled team of experts in special education and school psychology. Speakers in this expert scholar series hosts professionals with expertise in state and local education, schoolwide behavioral intervention systems, and student mental health. Prior to each session, experts suggest one peer-reviewed article for scholars to read that highlights an interdisciplinary approach to intensive intervention. Experts then deliver a 30–45-minute presentation and participate in a 30-minute live question and answer session. Presentation topics for the series, which consists of 6 presentations per year, include multi-tiered systems of support, equity and diversity, academic interventions (e.g., reading, math), behavior interventions, and assessment. The goal of this Expert Scholar Series is to further expose SP$^2$ scholars to evidence-based practices and interdisciplinary research from renowned scholars in the field. This series provides scholars with an opportunity to engage in discussion on critical and current issues related to serving students with intense intervention needs.

## CHALLENGES TO CREATING AND MAINTAINING INTERDISCIPLINARY PROGRAMS

The final section of this chapter describes challenges encountered in establishing and maintaining an interdisciplinary graduate program, as well as efforts undertaken to surmount these challenges. Note that this section is not exhaustive—each program may face highly specific challenges related to licensure, scheduling, or other matters that were less critical to the execution of SP$^2$. Whenever possible, solutions or potential approaches toward mitigating the issue are also described. As of this writing, the first cohort of SP$^2$ students has yet to graduate. The success of the program ultimately depends on the performance of graduates in their placements. In the interim, metrics such as student performance in courses, testimonials, and faculty evaluations collected throughout the year suggest the program is providing effective preparation in interdisciplinary special education.

It is important to note that much of the commentary in this section is made possible through the program review process implemented by faculty. The review culminates with a formal evaluation meeting at the end of each year and includes an overview of scholar performance and systematic feedback mechanisms (e.g., scholar surveys, interviews, and advisor-advisee consultation sessions). Feedback and course evaluation comments from scholars provide evidence of favorable attitudes towards the program and specific field experiences. Scholars further suggest that the program has enhanced their understanding of school psychology and special education, and provided them with a greater awareness of the need for collaboration amongst school professionals. SP$^2$ scholars and faculty have nonetheless identified issues that emerged before and after the formal development of the program. The ability to identify and solve problems with program implementation represents an important aspect of any interdisciplinary undertaking and deserves as much consideration as program content itself.

## Barriers to Program Development

The dearth of interdisciplinary programs is potentially a consequence of siloing that has persisted both in preparation programs and at the professional level. Consequently, many faculty may be unacquainted with interdisciplinary collaboration. The demands of any faculty position further impede the dedication of time to the development of novel programs in the absence of internal or external support. Additionally, the budget models of many universities allocate funds based on enrollment within individual departments. This promotes adversarial relationships between disciplines, competition for students, and conflict regarding which program receives credit for students enrolled in specific courses—all factors antithetical to sustained collaboration. It is also important to consider the extent to which the program has established relationships with the community needed to offer effective training.

### Potential Solutions

The experience of SP$^2$ faculty suggests that ongoing, frequent communication is key. Including professionals within each department or entity with the ability to make decisions and credibly speak for the department is of critical importance. The barriers to combining programs and procuring resources for faculty and students in nascent interdisciplinary programs demand that those hoping to establish a program seek the assistance of an administrator. Obtaining buy-in from colleagues and figures with the ability to surmount bureaucratic obstacles is critical to ensuring the program will survive. A willingness to engage with colleagues and leverage networks to identify new opportunities is also important. Services offered to students can emerge and grow in exciting ways when networking routinely crosses disciplinary boundaries.

## Community Building

The preparation of special education personnel in the two years following the COVID-19 pandemic was characterized by remote instruction and a general inability to place teacher candidates in practical settings. These features also impede the interaction and opportunities for collaboration that (a) appear to effortlessly emerge in more conventional arrangements and (b) are fundamental to the objective of interdisciplinary programs. It may be tempting to discount the challenge of building meaningful relationships between students from different backgrounds as the restrictions associated with COVID-19 become less commonplace. SP² scholars who entered the program in the latter half of 2021 and witnessed the relaxation of health restrictions nonetheless identified several barriers to cross-disciplinary communication. One issue with little relation to course format is the disparity in experience and age between MA-level students in the Special Education program and the Ed.S. students in the School Psychology program. Whereas many of the aspiring special educators reported having limited exposure to practical settings, students in the School Psychology program often had several years of experience in schools. This tended to result in 'cliques' composed entirely of students from one program or the other, even in intradisciplinary classes designed to promote collaboration. The problem was worsened by the initial design of many of SP² activities. Much like service provision in authentic education settings, it was possible for students from the two programs to engage with a task concurrently without collaborating.

## Potential Solutions

The experience of transitioning SP² into more conventional, in-person arrangements, as well as feedback from scholars, indicates that establishing a community between two disparate disciplines should remain an ongoing priority for SP² and similar programs. SP² faculty proposed a variety of approaches to addressing the situation. Orientation activities should be extended beyond an initial meeting and include informal gatherings as well as more content-based events (e.g., a speaker series). Additionally, course- and fieldwork should be reconceptualized to require interdisciplinary collaboration whenever possible. Although typical group arrangements for class assignments might be based on scholar preference, revised activities should erode barriers between the disciplines whenever possible.

## Program Intensity

Special educators and school psychologists have a variety of professional requirements unique to their programs that simply must be met irrespective of any interdisciplinary content. This creates challenges in terms of course scheduling. The need to account for discipline-specific and interdisciplinary content likewise presents students with a dismal choice: either take as many hours as possible during the semester, or schedule courses during the summer—a period often not covered by scholarships. The intensive nature of interdisciplinary programs often makes it difficult to maintain employment while completing the program, which prohibits many people from historically underserved populations from enrolling.

## Potential Solutions

In collecting feedback regarding challenges related to the program, students have repeatedly identified the intensity of the program as a barrier to success. Given the demands of credentialing, there are no easy solutions to this problem. Faculty should carefully schedule program content to avoid simultaneous administration of the most demanding requirements. Another option is to reduce the number of required courses by reconciling courses with similar content—however, this may require a great deal of planning and collaboration, particularly when external certification agencies are involved. SP² was fortunate to be able to capitalize on a history of integrating school psychology and special education and to consider offering supplementary, on-campus employment at the University of Iowa as a means of making the intense program of study more amenable to a more diverse range of candidates. Universities interested in offering interdisciplinary training are strongly encouraged to consider how to meet the material, emotional, and professional needs of historically underserved groups.

## CONCLUSION

Students with disabilities, particularly those who require intensive academic and behavioral supports, benefit from personnel who possess a comprehensive understanding of interdisciplinary service provision. The extent to which specific training programs facilitate meaningful training experiences involving special educators and the range of relevant service disciplines will vary based on the community context and resources available to each program. As a result, the implementation and creation of SP² for scholars in special education and school psychology may not be directly relevant in all cases. Nonetheless, the detail regarding the rationale for the program, activities completed by scholars, and the challenges faced should be helpful for those either offering or planning to offer interdisciplinary training.

## REFERENCES

American Psychiatric Association. (2013). *Diagnostic and statistical manual of mental disorders* (5th ed.). Author.

American Psychological Association. (2022, July 19). *APA Accreditation*. https://www.accreditation.apa.org/

Anderson, A., & Carr, M. (2021). Applied behaviour analysis for autism: Evidence, issues, and implementation barriers. *Current Developmental Disorders Reports*, 8(4), 1–10. doi:10.100740474-021-00237-x

Ardoin, S. P., Wagner, L., & Bangs, K. E. (2016). Applied behavior analysis: A foundation for response to intervention. In K. C. Stoiber & M. Gettinger (Eds.), *Handbook of response to intervention* (2nd ed., pp. 29–42). Springer. doi:10.1007/978-1-4899-7568-3_3

Beaulieu, L., Addington, J., & Almeida, D. (2019). Behavior analysts' training and practices regarding cultural diversity: The case for culturally competent care. *Behavior Analysis in Practice*, 12(3), 557–575. doi:10.100740617-018-00313-6 PMID:31976264

Behavior Analyst Certification Board. (2017). *BCBA talk list* (5th ed.). Author.

Berry, A. B., Petrin, R. A., Gravelle, M. L., & Farmer, T. W. (2012). Issues in special education teacher recruitment, retention, and professional development: Considerations in supporting rural teachers. *Rural Special Education Quarterly*, 30(4), 3–11. doi:10.1177/875687051103000402

Bianco, M. (2005). The effects of disability labels on special education and general education teachers' referrals for gifted programs. *Learning Disability Quarterly*, 28(4), 285–293. doi:10.2307/4126967

Boe, E. E., Cook, L. H., & Sunderland, R. J. (2008). Teacher turnover: Examining exit attrition, teaching area transfer, and school migration. *Exceptional Children*, 75(1), 7–31. doi:10.1177/001440290807500101

Boe, E. E., deBettencourt, L. U., Dewey, J., Rosenberg, M., Sindelar, P., & Leko, C. (2013). Variability in demand for special education teachers: Indicators, explanations, and impacts. *Exceptionality*, *21*(2), 103–125. doi:10.1080/09362835.2013.771563

Brodhead, M. T. (2015). Maintaining professional relationships in an interdisciplinary setting: Strategies for navigating nonbehavioral treatment recommendations for individuals with autism. *Behavior Analysis in Practice*, *8*(1), 70–78. doi:10.100740617-015-0042-7 PMID:27703885

Bruhn, A., McDaniel, S., & Kreigh, C. (2015). Self-monitoring interventions for students with behavior problems: A systematic review of current research. *Behavioral Disorders*, *40*(2), 102–121. doi:10.17988/BD-13-45.1

Bruhn, A. L., Estrapala, S., Mahatmya, D., Rila, A., & Vogelgesang, K. (2019). Professional Development on Data-Based Individualization: A Mixed Research Study. *Behavioral Disorders*, •••, 0198742919876656. doi:10.1177/0198742919876656

Bruhn, A. L., Wehby, J. H., & Hasselbring, T. S. (2020). Data-based decision making for social behavior: Setting a research agenda. *Journal of Positive Behavior Interventions*, *22*(2), 116–126. doi:10.1177/1098300719876098

Castillo, J. M., Curtis, M. J., & Tan, S. Y. (2014). Personnel needs in school psychology: A 10-year follow-up study on predicted personnel shortages. *Psychology in the Schools*, *51*(8), 832–849. doi:10.1002/pits.21786

Child Welfare Policy and Practice Group. (2018). *Iowa Department of Human Services fidelity assessment – Iowa family team meeting process*. Iowa Department of Human Services. https://dhs.iowa.gov/sites/default/files/CWPPG_IA_RPT_12.18.pdf?051620201458

Cooper, J., Heron, T., & Heward, W. (2020). *Applied behavior analysis* (3rd ed.). Pearson. doi:10.26741/abaespana/2020.cooper3e

Council for Exceptional Children. (2015). *What every special educator must know: Professional ethics and standards*. Author.

Datchuk, S. M., & Rodgers, D. B. (2019). Text writing within simple sentences: A writing fluency intervention for students with high-incidence disabilities. *Learning Disabilities Research & Practice*, *34*(1), 118–118. doi:10.1111/ldrp.12185

Datchuk, S. M., Wagner, K., & Hier, B. O. (2020). Level and trend of writing sequences: A review and meta-analysis of writing interventions for students with disabilities. *Exceptional Children*, *86*(2), 174–192. doi:10.1177/0014402919873311

Dillenburger, K. (2017). Staff training. In *Handbook of treatments for autism spectrum disorder* (pp. 95–107). Springer. doi:10.1007/978-3-319-61738-1_7

Eikeseth, S., Smith, T., Jahr, E., & Eldevik, S. (2002). Intensive behavioral treatment at school for 4-to 7-year-old children with autism: A 1-year comparison controlled study. *Behavior Modification*, *26*(1), 49–68. doi:10.1177/0145445502026001004 PMID:11799654

Fall, A. M., & Billingsley, B. S. (2011). Disparities in work conditions among early career special educators in high-and low-poverty districts. *Remedial and Special Education*, *32*(1), 64–78. doi:10.1177/0741932510361264

Farmer, T. W. (2013). When universal approaches and prevention services are not enough: The importance of understanding the stigmatization of special education for students with EBD a response to Kauffman and Badar. *Behavioral Disorders*, *39*(1), 32–42. doi:10.1177/019874291303900105

Ferguson, J., Craig, E. A., & Dounavi, K. (2019). Telehealth as a model for providing behaviour analytic interventions to individuals with autism spectrum disorder: A systematic review. *Journal of Autism and Developmental Disorders*, *49*(2), 582–616. doi:10.100710803-018-3724-5 PMID:30155578

Fowler, S. A., Coleman, R. B., & Bogdan, W. K. (2019). *The state of the special education profession survey report*. Council for Exceptional Children. doi:10.1177/0040059919875703

Hogan, A., Knez, N., & Kahng, S. (2015). Evaluating the use of behavioral skills training to improve school staffs' implementation of behavior intervention plans. *Journal of Behavioral Education*, *24*(2), 242–254. doi:10.100710864-014-9213-9

Iowa Autism Council. (2019). *Moving Iowa forward: Summary of accomplishment in 2018 and priorities and recommendations for 2019*. https://educateiowa.gov/pk-12/special-education/programs-and-services/autism-spectrum-disorder/iowa-autism-council#Legislative_Reports

Iowa Department of Education. (2019a). *2019 annual report: Condition of education*. Author. https://educateiowa.gov/sites/files/ed/documents/2020-01-23ConditionOfEducation2019.pdf

Iowa Department of Education. (2019b). *Special education eligibility and evaluation standards*. Author. https://educateiowa.gov/sites/files/ed/documents/SpecialEducationEligibilityand EvaluationStandardsJuly2019.pdf

Iowa Department of Education. (2021b). *Input into Iowa's State performance plan for special education*. https://educateiowa.gov/sites/files/ed/documents/2021-12-14%20Input%20SPP-Personnel%20Shortagesv2.pdf

Iowa Department of Education. (2022a). *2021 report on the state of educator preparation in Iowa*. https://educateiowa.gov/sites/files/ed/documents/2021ReportontheStateofEducatorPreparationinIowa11-17-21.pdf

Jiménez, F. J. R. (2012). Acceptance and commitment therapy versus traditional cognitive behavioral therapy: A systematic review and meta-analysis of current empirical evidence. *International Journal of Psychology & Psychological Therapy*, *12*, 333–358.

Kasky-Hernández, L., & Cates, G. L. (2015). Role of psychologists in interdisciplinary relations in special education. In J. P. Bakken & F. E. Obiakor (Eds.), *Interdisciplinary connections to special education: Important aspects to consider*. Emerald. doi:10.1108/S0270-40132015000030A019

Kauffman, J. M., & Badar, J. (2018). *The scandalous neglect of children's mental health: What schools can do*. Routledge. doi:10.4324/9781351165808

King, S. A., Lemons, C. J., & Hill, D. R. (2012). Response to intervention in secondary schools: Considerations for administrators. *NASSP Bulletin*, *96*(1), 5–22. doi:10.1177/0192636511430551

Ledford, J. R., King, S., Harbin, E. R., & Zimmerman, K. N. (2018). Antecedent social skills interventions for individuals with ASD: What works, for whom, and under what conditions? *Focus on Autism and Other Developmental Disabilities*, *33*(1), 3–13. doi:10.1177/1088357616634024

Lerman, D. C., O'Brien, M. J., Neely, L., Call, N. A., Tsami, L., Schieltz, K. M., Berg, W. K., Graber, J., Huang, P., Kopelman, T., & Cooper-Brown, L. (2020). Remote coaching of caregivers via telehealth: Challenges and potential solutions. *Journal of Behavioral Education*, *29*(2), 195–221. doi:10.100710864-020-09378-2 PMID:36093285

Ludlow, B. L. (2015). Virtual reality: Emerging applications and future directions. *Rural Special Education Quarterly*, *34*(3), 3–10. doi:10.1177/875687051503400302

Maenner, M. J., Shaw, K. A., Bakian, A. V., Bilder, D. A., Durkin, M. S., Esler, A., Furnier, S. M., Hallas, L., Hall-Lande, J., Hudson, A., Hughes, M. M., Patrick, M., Pierce, K., Poynter, J. N., Salinas, A., Shenouda, J., Vehorn, A., Warren, Z., Constantino, J. N., ... Cogswell, M. E. (2021). Prevalence and characteristics of autism spectrum disorder among children aged 8 years—Autism and developmental disabilities monitoring network, 11 sites, United States, 2018. *MMWR. Surveillance Summaries*, *70*(11), 1–16. doi:10.15585/mmwr.ss7011a1 PMID:34855725

Maras, M. A., Thompson, A. M., Lewis, C., Thornburg, K., & Hawks, J. (2015). Developing a tiered response model for social-emotional learning through interdisciplinary collaboration. *Journal of Educational & Psychological Consultation*, *25*(2-3), 198–223. doi:10.1080/10474412.2014.929954

Matson, J. L., & Smith, K. R. (2008). Current status of intensive behavioral interventions for young children with autism and PDD-NOS. *Research in Autism Spectrum Disorders*, *2*(1), 60–74. doi:10.1016/j.rasd.2007.03.003

McGee, G. G., & Morrier, M. J. (2005). Preparation of autism specialists (Vol. 2). Handbook of Autism and Pervasive Developmental Disorders. Academic Press.

McNamara, K. M., Goforth, A., Walcott, C. M., Rossen, E., & Hyson, D. (2019). *Results from the NASP 2015 membership survey, part two: Professional practices in school psychology*. National Association of School Psychologists.

National Association of School Psychologists. (2010a). *Model for comprehensive and integrated school psychological services*. Author.

National Association of School Psychologists. (2010b). *Standards for graduate preparation of school psychologists*. Author.

National Association of School Psychologists. (2011). *Ratio of students per school psychologist by state: Data from the 2009-2010 and 2004-2005 NASP membership surveys*. Author.

National Association of School Psychologists. (2021). Shortages in school psychology: Challenges in meeting the growing needs of U.S. students and schools (Research Summary). Author.

National Association of School Psychologists. (2022, July 19). *NASP 2020 Domains of Practice*. https://www.nasponline.org/standards-and-certification/nasp-2020-professional-standards-adopted/nasp-2020-domains-of-practice

Peters-Scheffer, N., Didden, R., Korzilius, H., & Sturmey, P. (2011). A meta-analytic study on the effectiveness of comprehensive ABA-based early intervention programs for children with autism spectrum disorders. *Research in Autism Spectrum Disorders*, 5(1), 60–69. doi:10.1016/j.rasd.2010.03.011

Sallows, G. O., & Graupner, T. D. (2005). Intensive behavioral treatment for children with autism: Four-year outcome and predictors. *American Journal of Mental Retardation*, 110(6), 417–438. doi:10.1352/0895-8017(2005)110[417:IBTFCW]2.0.CO;2 PMID:16212446

Scheuermann, B., Webber, J., Boutot, E. A., & Goodwin, M. (2003). Problems with personnel preparation in autism spectrum disorders. *Focus on Autism and Other Developmental Disabilities*, 18(3), 197–206. doi:10.1177/10883576030180030801

Schieltz, K. M., Graber, J. E., & McComas, J. (2017). Consultation Practices: Training Parents and Families. In Applied Behavior Analysis Advanced Guidebook (pp. 229-257). Academic Press.

Schieltz, K. M., Romani, P. W., Wacker, D. P., Suess, A. N., Huang, P., Berg, W. K., Lindgren, S. D., & Kopelman, T. G. (2018). Single-case analysis to determine reasons for failure of behavioral treatment via telehealth. *Remedial and Special Education*, 39(2), 95–105. doi:10.1177/0741932517743791

Schieltz, K. M., Wacker, D. P., & Romani, P. W. (2017). Effects of signaled positive reinforcement on problem behavior maintained by negative reinforcement. *Journal of Behavioral Education*, 26(2), 137–150. doi:10.100710864-016-9265-0

Schmitz, S. L., Clopton, K. L., Skaar, N. R., Dredge, S., & VanHorn, D. (2021). Increasing school-based mental health services with a "Grow Your Own" school psychology program. *Contemporary School Psychology*, 1–12. PMID:33500839

Shahidullah, J. D., McClain, M. B., Azad, G., Mezher, K. R., & McIntyre, L. L. (2020). Coordinating autism care across schools and medical settings: Considerations for school psychologists. *Intervention in School and Clinic*, 56(2), 107–114. doi:10.1177/1053451220914891

Splett, J. W., Fowler, J., Weist, M. D., McDaniel, H., & Dvorsky, M. (2013). The critical role of school psychology in the school mental health movement. *Psychology in the Schools*, 50(3), 245–258. doi:10.1002/pits.21677 PMID:30774154

Strein, W., Kuhn-McKearin, M., & Finney, M. (2014). Best practices in developing prevention strategies for school psychology practice. In P. L. Harrison & A. Thomas (Eds.), *Best 216 practices in school psychology: Systems-level services* (pp. 137–148). National Association of School Psychologists.

Sturmey, P. (2022). Individual Therapies for Violence and Aggression: I. Cognitive and Behavioral Therapies. In P. St (Ed.), *Violence and Aggression. Advances in Preventing and Treating Violence and Aggression*. Springer. doi:10.1007/978-3-031-04386-4_16

Sutcher, L., Dzarling-Hammond, L., & Carver-Thomas, D. (2016). *A coming crisis in teaching? Teacher supply, demand, and shortages in the U.S*. Learning Policy Institute. doi:10.54300/247.242

United States Department of Education. (2020). *41st annual report to Congress on the implementation of the Individuals with Disabilities Education Act, 2019*. Author.

Vogelgesang, K. L., Bruhn, A. L., Coghill-Behrends, W. L., Kern, A. M., & Troughton, L. C. (2016). A single-subject study of a technology-based self-monitoring intervention. *Journal of Behavioral Education*, *25*(4), 478–497. doi:10.100710864-016-9253-4

Walcott, C. M., McNamara, K., Hyson, D., & Charvat, J. L. (2018). *Results from the NASP 2015 membership survey, part one: Demographics and employment conditions*. National Association of School Psychologists.

# Chapter 22
# Lessons Learned:
## Equipping Interdisciplinary Scholars to Provide a Continuum of Mental and Behavioral Health Supports

**R. Lanai Jennings**
https://orcid.org/0000-0001-8408-398X
*Marshall University, USA*

**Sandra S. Stroebel**
*Marshall University, USA*

## ABSTRACT

*This chapter outlines important lessons learned while implementing Marshall University's interdisciplinary personnel development program. Motivated by the intense needs of youth with disabilities in Appalachia and the shortage of qualified personnel to address these needs, the program employed evidence-based models to train school counselors, school psychologists, and special educators. Factors found to be essential include finding evidence-based interventions appropriate for all disciplines, early intense training, while acknowledging differences in entry skills and knowledge of interdisciplinary scholars, exposing scholars to a continuum of tiered school-based supports including working together across disciplines, modeling and attending to self-care of scholars, and acquiring partnerships for sustainability. These factors were important in successfully training the scholars to provide services to children with intensely complex social, emotional, and behavioral needs. Also included are suggestions for improving training based on the authors' reflections and feedback from scholars.*

## INTRODUCTION

The chapter aims to highlight important practices or "lessons learned" from an interdisciplinary personnel development grant, which is currently in its fourth year of preparing preservice school counselors, special educators, and school psychologists to participate in a variety of evidence-based interventions

DOI: 10.4018/978-1-6684-6438-0.ch022

## Lessons Learned

for the purposes of facilitating positive social, emotional, and behavioral outcomes for young children with high-intensity disabilities. The authors' motivation to obtain the grant was due to a shortage of qualified school personnel in their area to serve school-aged students with disabilities who had intensely complex social, emotional, and behavioral needs. The number of students with these needs had been increasing due to societal issues such as prenatal substance exposure, complex traumatic stress, adverse childhood experiences (ACEs), and adverse community environments. Yet, the number of individuals entering school-based employment to address these issues was declining.

The grant project employed best-practice, evidence-based models (e.g., Prevent Reaffirm Evaluate Provide and Respond Examine School Crisis Prevention and Intervention Training [PREPaRE] and teacher-child interaction training/parent-child interaction training [TCIT/PCIT]) and trauma-informed care to prepare interdisciplinary scholars in two biennial cohorts for what they encountered when working with school-aged children in West Virginia (WV) who have both a complex array of disabilities (e.g., multiple cognitive, physical, sensory, emotional, learning, or processing disabilities, and/or autism, dyslexia) and high-intensity needs (e.g., persistent learning or behavioral challenges, traumatic stress, significant needs for self-regulation and healthy attachments). Marshall's Scholars Program, entitled Special Education and Resiliency (SEAR) project, prepared graduates to implement these specialized evidenced-based models, which are not routinely provided or accessible in most special education settings for children in WV, for the purposes of supporting mental and behavioral health outcomes while also promoting high expectations and collaborating with all disciplines to include students with disabilities with high-intensity needs in least-restrictive and natural environments in public schools.

Through their direct experiences, the authors determined five practices that were important guiding principles for their work with the scholars. These include finding evidence-based interventions appropriate for all disciplines involved, early intense training while acknowledging differences in entry skills and knowledge of interdisciplinary scholars, exposing scholars to a continuum of tiered school-based supports including working together across disciplines, modeling and attending to self-care of Scholars, and acquiring partnerships for sustainability. After detailing these practices, the authors reflect on improvements to their model that would be helpful with future trainings.

## BACKGROUND

In terms of overdose mortality rates, no state has been more negatively affected than WV. Age-adjusted overdose mortality rates from 2014 through 2020 illustrate that WV led the nation each year, and increased to an all-time high of 81.4 deaths per 100,000 in 2020 (CDC - National Center for Health Statistics, 2022). As educators, the deleterious consequences of parental substance abuse disorders (SUD) on children are well-known. These adverse effects can range from the neurodevelopmental impact of in-utero exposure and neonatal abstinence syndrome (NAS) to the toxicity and paralysis of addiction, which can upend a family's routines, the typical parent-child interactions, and ultimately, the family's sense of security. WV's Department of Health and Human Resources (DHHR) (2018) reported prenatal substance exposure in 143 per 1,000 (14.3%) of infants and of those babies 50.6 per 1,000 experienced NAS, representing 5% of infants. This rate of NAS was more than five times the national rate. Consequences of SUD and opioid use, in particular, can similarly involve child neglect, abuse, and even trafficking. For many children an associated adversity was the catastrophic loss of a parent(s) and/or parental figures to arrest, hospitalization or death. Unsurprisingly, then, the number of children removed to foster placements increased with the opioid epidemic, and children tended to remain in these placements for longer durations (Winstanley & Stover, 2019). Presently, nearly 7,000 WV children and adolescents are no longer in their parent's care, and many of them are placed out-of-home due to parental substance abuse and related issues (WV DHHR, 2022). DHHR data on children in state custody show that approximately 85% of those placed have a parent with a SUD (Todd, 2019).

As stated above, children of drug abusing parents are exposed to chaotic home environments. The trauma these youth experience leads to elevated levels of behavior problems, emotional distress, physical problems, and inattention. Behaviors consistent with a diagnosis of attention deficit hyperactivity disorder, especially in boys, are frequently seen. Often, children from alcohol and drug-using families have difficulty developing positive peer relationships and are at a higher risk of substance use (Barnard & McKeganey, 2004). Children from families with substance abuse have significantly lower school grade averages and are more at risk of dropping out of school (Frederiksen et al., 2022).

It was in the context of the opioid epidemic that Marshall University's interdisciplinary preparation project emerged. School personnel were seeking behavioral interventions and strategies to assist the children and adolescents who experienced, firsthand, the instability, and trauma that addiction can radiate. In one study, as many as two-thirds of WV educators surveyed endorsed that they did not have the appropriate resources available to help children prenatally exposed to alcohol or other drugs (Mickey, 2019). In a larger statewide survey of WV school professionals, only one in every 10 teachers reported feeling confident that they could assist children whose parents use drugs ("WVU researchers investigate," 2019). Knowing that high percentages of certified teachers reported a lack of self-efficacy with this population of children, many of whom have high-intensity disabilities, a sense of urgency existed to better arm or equip future school-based professionals with robust interventions in an interdisciplinary training context for the work ahead. Toward this end, faculty from Marshall University's psychology, school psychology, school counseling, and special education departments crafted the SEAR project along with the University's Wellness Director, who now oversees the Marshall Center of Excellence for Recovery.

Added to the issue of school personnel not feeling qualified to support children suffering from the opioid epidemic, was the personnel shortages. As the authors were beginning to write and conceptualize the interdisciplinary training program, teacher shortages in WV spiraled into a crisis. Within two years, vacancies skyrocketed from 400 to 718, with one-third (238) in special education (WV Department of Education [DE], 2017a). Furthermore, 55 of 57 WV local education agencies reported distinct shortages in special education, including autism, multicategorical, severe disabilities, specific learning disabilities, and visually impaired (United States Department of Education, 2017). Because higher salaries are available in neighboring states, WV's shortages are intensified. Shortages are also evident in school psychology. While the National Association of School Psychologists recommends a ratio of one practitioner per 500-700 school-age children (National Association of School Psychologists [NASP], 2021), the WV ratio is one per 2,148 children (WVDE, 2017b; WVDE, 2017c). A school psychology "support certificate" in WV was cited in 10 of the last 11 school years on the US Department of Education's annual publication, Teacher Shortage Areas Nationwide Listing (United States Department of Education, 2017), meaning WV has an ongoing significant shortage of qualified personnel. School psychology personnel projections (Castillo et al., 2014) indicated the South Atlantic Region (inclusive of WV) would experience the most critical shortages of practitioners: -5.5% deficit in 2020 and 2025 (-4.8% deficit in 2025. Finally, the demand for school counselors is also going unmet, although the shortages of counselors in WV's schools was trending in a more positive direction, as compared to special educators and school psychologists. The American School Counselor Association (ASCA) recommends a counselor-to-student ratio of 1 to

250. Meanwhile the U.S. Department of Education (2013-14), reported a national average of 1 to 490. The National Association for College Admission Counseling (NACAC) and ASCA aggregated data on counselor-to-student ratios from 2004 to 2015 nationally and within states. Over this period, WV experienced ratios of one counselor to 416 students in 2004-2005 and one Counselor to 373 students in 2014-2015, a negative 10% change (NACAC, 2018).

Chronic personnel shortages in rural areas are largely attributed to systematic deficits, aging or retiring workforce, and relocation of school personnel to bordering states with higher salaries. Often service professionals in large rural districts are the sole providers of their kind, resulting in barriers to early career supervision and support systems for skill development, along with very high levels of burnout and attrition. In 2019, Marshall University's Department of School Psychology conducted a survey with special education directors in 30 of WV's 55 counties to assess shortages. During the 2018-2019 school year, 28% of the counties had unfilled school psychology vacancies and 14% reported unfilled special education teacher vacancies. For the subsequent 2019-2020 school year, 21% of counties predicted they would be unable to fill a school psychology and a school counselor vacancy, while 18% predicted at least one unfilled special education vacancy. Many districts reported difficulty recruiting applicants: 73% reported difficulty recruiting school psychologists, 47% reported difficulty recruiting school counselors, and 67% reported difficulty recruiting special education teachers. All counties reported better numbers in retaining school psychologists (37%), school counselors (17%), and special education teachers (34%), indicating personnel are likely to stay if programs can place them in high need areas (S. Stroebel, personal communication, 2019).

While the consequences of the opioid epidemic on children and the challenges of the personnel shortages served as the stimulus for the SEAR project, the true imperative was to ensure the SEAR scholars exited their respective graduate programs equipped to provide the necessary supports, including trauma –informed practices within multi-tiered systems of support. Children whose parents have substance use disorders are often traumatized. When school professionals use approaches that realize the behavioral and educational problems can be addressed by addressing the trauma, students have better academic outcomes. Additionally, efforts need to be made to avoid retraumatization of children by the practices used in schools (Dombo & Sabatino, 2019). It is important that teachers create connections with youth while remaining calm, consistent, and regulated. Teachers need to strive to create positive experiences with children and work to build trust. Youth need to feel safe, and this is done by providing clear expectations, well-defined routines, choices when possible, and attuned teachers. Research in the area of trauma-informed schools has, moreover, revealed that changes to strategies used in schools help not only children who have directly experienced trauma, but their classmates as well (Dombo & Sabatino, 2019).

## MAIN FOCUS OF CHAPTER

### Practice One: Select an Evidenced-Based Intervention

The first lesson-learned is to select an evidenced-based intervention that is appropriate for implementation in schools by all scholars, regardless of their discipline. In this section, the authors will outline the core intervention for the SEAR project, but also why selection is so important, given the different scope of practice scholars will have in the schools with respect to mental and behavioral health.

In the case of the authors' interdisciplinary grant, this core intervention is TCIT. TCIT was adapted from PCIT, an empirically-supported behavioral parent training program developed for two to seven-year-olds, although it extends upward for children up to age 10 who exhibit externalizing behaviors (McNeil & Hembree-Kigin, 2010). PCIT is distinct in therapeutic model for using immediate in-person feedback to parents who are utilizing newly acquired skills.

The school-based model, TCIT, serves to improve teacher skills (Tiano & McNeil, 2006). TCIT incorporates the core principles of PCIT, while adapting it to the unique dynamics of the classroom. TCIT is designed to improve teacher-child relationships, decrease inappropriate behaviors in the classroom, and increase academic achievement. The theoretical basis of the model includes a combination of attachment theory, social learning theory, and operant conditioning (McNeil & Hembree-Kigin, 2010). Teachers are taught the importance of establishing a positive relationship with the child. They are trained to understand the function of behavior and methods to use to obtain the desired behavior. TCIT retains many core elements of PCIT such as the two phases which the authors will describe below, the individualized coaching sessions in live interactions, coding of the adult-child interactions during coaching sessions, assignment of homework between sessions, and using standardized assessment instruments. There are adaptations including a group training format, emphasis on skill use with multiple children at once, use of a classroom setting, and using more of a collaborative approach for discipline procedures (Tiano & McNeil, 2006).

As with PCIT, TCIT has two phases, that is, one where the child takes the lead, which is Child directed interaction (CDI), and another where the adult directs the session, appropriately named teacher directed interaction (TDI). During the CDI phase, the focus is on increasing positive communication between the teacher and the child. This is accomplished by allowing the child to make decisions in the classroom and having the teacher be more responsive to the child. During CDI, teachers learn new strategies taken from play therapy models for establishing a positive relationship with the child. Teachers learn skills that build self-esteem, encourage communication, and facilitate initiative in children. During the second phase, TDI, the teacher is trained on behavioral management strategies to address problematic behaviors. Some of these strategies may already be familiar to teachers, but the training helps refine their skills and ensure they are being implemented correctly. Teachers provide praise when they want to see an increase in a behavior and planned ignoring when they want a behavior to decrease. Teachers also learn to communicate commands in a more effective manner and to refrain from excessive questions (Tiano & McNeil, 2006).

The "Do" skills taught during CDI make up the acronym PRIDE: Praise, reflect, imitate, describe, and enjoy. The scholars, comprised of preservice special education teachers, school psychologists, and school counselors, received an initial two-day training on TCIT and learned to use PRIDE skills. These skills can later be used with individual students, small groups or the whole class. Each scholar was required to obtain mastery of PRIDE skills, which necessitated the provision of 10 specific labeled praises, 10 reflections, and 10 behavioral descriptions in a five-minute CDI session with no more than three questions, commands or critical statements. Scholars were coached during the training to use differential reinforcement to increase prosocial behavior and ignore or redirect minor behavioral concerns during play situations, while avoiding asking questions, giving commands, and using critical statements (i.e., the Don't skills) (McNeil & Hembree-Kigin, 2010). The scholars enjoyed these interactive and hands-on sessions. Scholars were given immediate feedback on their performance. They were given frequent opportunities to role-play a teacher, a child, and coach with scholars from different disciplines. Thus, while scholars were perfecting their implementation of PRIDE skills, they, in turn, achieved an ancillary benefit of strengthening relationships with scholars from other programs. Data from the sessions revealed that all scholars were able to obtain mastery.

For another component of determining mastery, scholars were evaluated using PCIT's dyadic parent-child interaction coding system (dpics) clinical manual, fourth edition (Eyberg et al., 2014). DPICS is a coding system that assesses the quality of adult-child interactions. This system has been thoroughly researched and shown to accurately evaluate the quality of overt and nonverbal behaviors during adult-child interactions. Numerous studies document the reliability and validity of the DPICS categories (McNeil & Hembree-Kigin, 2010). Areas assessed by DPICS include reciprocity, nurturance, and adult control. DPICS permits a quantifiable baseline to be obtained and then enables ongoing measurement of progress as adult-child interaction patterns are improved through TCIT. After evaluating scholars with DPICS, they were taught to use it so that they could evaluate the teachers they were working with in schools. During the trainings, Scholars engaged in DPICS coding exercises. Feedback through interrater reliability ratings with a certified TCIT trainer was given to enhance skill development. Data were collected to document attainment of coding skills.

TDI training was given to scholars in a similar manner, as CDI training, in an optional virtual or in-person format by a TCIT certified trainer. Scholars were taught behavior management strategies which could be used in the classroom. These included giving effective commands, providing time for compliance, time-out warning statements, and use of time-out. Being sensitive to schools' policies was discussed with regard to time-out. Some teachers may feel more comfortable using the terms "thinking chair" or "sit and watch area," rather than a time-out chair. Scholars also learned about additional discipline strategies that will likely reduce the usage of time-out.

Generalization of skills was achieved by giving scholars assignments to use their newly learned skills in schools. Each scholar was required to complete a case study which involved identifying a student or group of students, observing the student(s), and interviewing the student(s)' teacher. Teachers were asked to complete rating scales in order to help determine the target behavior and behavioral goals for the student. Baseline observations were conducted prior to implementation of the PRIDE skills. PRIDE skills were administered by scholars either directly to students or indirectly via consultation with teachers. Data were collected postintervention and scholars graphed all their data. Scholars then presented their case studies in class. This permitted them to experience TCIT interventions with different aged youth and varying behavioral issues. Faculty and a certified TCIT trainer gave feedback to the scholars after presentations. These data provided us with a way to document benefits to the students with disabilities who were receiving the interventions.

The trainings for the scholars involved both didactic training, hands-on experiences, and coaching sessions in-person and via Zoom to enable them to achieve mastery. The pandemic necessitated more online trainings than was originally planned. The authors found that many scholars appreciated this option due to their busy schedules. A TCIT certified trainer was available to visit schools in person or virtually provide support as scholars developed their skills. Based on data from the trainings, the online sessions were just as effective as the in-person trainings in helping the participants obtain the needed skills, as all who graduated from the first cohort were able to meet mastery criteria.

The interdisciplinary project team considered four important factors in their selection of interventions. First, they wanted to make sure it was evidence-based. PCIT has been shown to be successful in promoting parent competence and decreasing child behavior problems in over 300 articles in peer reviewed journals (McNeil & Hembree-Kigin, 2010). While fewer studies have been done with TCIT, all studies to date have shown beneficial outcomes for children (Tiano & McNeil, 2006). The faculty wanted the intervention to have been shown to be effective in the literature with children similar to the ones with which scholars would be working. Studies have shown that, when teachers use TCIT, there are improved behaviors in children and increased teacher satisfaction (Budd et al., 2016; Campbell, 2011; Fawley et al., 2020; Fernandez et al., 2015). TCIT has been shown to be effective in a single-subject case study with one teacher and one preschool student (McIntosh, 2010) and with an entire classroom (Garbacz et al., 2014). It has also been shown to be effective when used in consultation (Hubel et al., 2020). TCIT has been shown to be effective in reducing problem behaviors in children when used by teachers after a single training (Budd et al., 2016). It has also reduced problematic behaviors in students with disabilities, children exposed to maltreatment, and children in rural settings (Davidson et al., 2021, Fawley et al., 2020, Kanine et al., 2018).

A second important factor to consider when selecting skills to teach was that it would be appropriate for all the disciplines involved in our grant. Although other mental health interventions, such as cognitive behavioral therapy (CBT), would be ideal for the preservice candidates in school psychology and school counseling, they would have been inappropriate for implementation by teachers. Therefore, interdisciplinary programs must be thoughtful in their intervention selection given the diverse roles of their scholars in supporting mental and behavioral health in school settings. TCIT was appropriate for the School Psychologists and School Counselors as they consulted with teachers regarding student concerns in the classroom. They were able to train teachers in the model and then provide support. Special education teachers used the skills in their own classrooms and also coached other special education teachers in their building on the use of TCIT.

A third important factor in intervention selection was that the technique must include a skill that could be easily learned and immediately implemented. TCIT provided specific skills that scholars were able to learn one day and start practicing the next day in schools to support children with disabilities. For the purpose of emphasizing what scholars can immediately implement, let's consider just one subcomponent of TCIT, behavior specific praise. After receiving their initial training on TCIT, SEAR scholars have demonstrated the ability to provide up to 8-13 more specific praises in a one, five-minute session above and beyond their baseline rates as illustrated in Figure 1. Significantly increasing the frequency of specific praise by scholars has the potential to translate into considerable increases in prosocial behavior and academic engagement of school-age children with and without disruptive behaviors, as is widely documented in the literature (Sutherland et al., 2000). Research demonstrates that when specific praise is stated in a manner that solidifies the link between the desired behavior and positive evaluation, children are better able to identify which behaviors are appropriate, thus increasing the likelihood that the desired behaviors will occur more frequently into the future (Cooper et al., 2020). Yet, despite its effectiveness, behavior specific praise remains underutilized in schools, including classrooms for children with emotional behavioral disorders (Chalk & Bizo, 2004; Wehby et al., 1995).

A fourth factor was that TCIT was able to be taught using high-quality trainings that included in-class practice, performance feedback, and continued skill building. The SEAR project included a TCIT certified trainer who could deliver the trainings to the scholars. Follow-up support was delivered through half-day sessions wherein scholars could join with graduate students from other disciplines to refine their TCIT skills. In addition to receiving whole group, direct instruction from the expert trainer, scholars frequently participated in small group practice with coaching support from the faculty. The certified trainer was available join the scholars in their schools either in-person or virtually to coach live TCIT implementation. Scholars could similarly record themselves and receive feedback. The certified training and faculty incorporated valid and reliable measures, in the form of DPICS, they could use to verify the

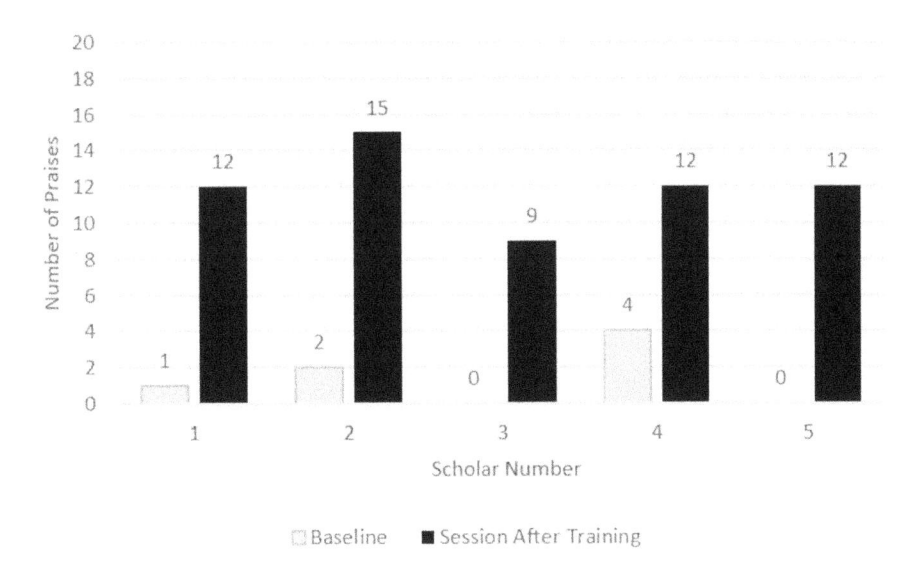

*Figure 1. Frequency of Scholar Use of Behavior Specific Praise in 5-Minute Sessions*

mastery of TCIT skills. Finally, faculty provided feedback as scholars led case discussions to share their successes and obstacles with TCIT implementation in the schools.

TCIT was the programs' core intervention. It met all the factors the program considered important. Scholars mastered the skills and delivered them in schools. They are currently collecting and analyzing data to document the effectiveness of these skills in improving student outcomes in schools. The authors are confident that they will have positive outcomes, due to the literature which supports this.

Initial data collected from the scholars indicate that 92% rated the TCIT workshop as very important or extremely important. With regard to receiving individual or small group follow up, 88% indicated they were very receptive to the idea. When asked what the scholars liked about the training a sample of comments included "These were helpful strategies I can use in the classroom," "It was very engaging and easy to follow," "Clear thorough explanations of topics, practicing with classmates and instructors, video examples of core concepts," "There were lots of opportunities to participate and be active in the group even with it being virtual.," and "Loved the learn and practice format, really helped me apply the strategies."

## Practice Two: Train Early and Intensely While Also Planning for Different Entry Level Knowledge, Skills, and Perceptions by the Interdisciplinary Scholars

Training scholars from three programs necessitates a comingling of three departments with varied recruitment practices, admission standards, plans of study, sequence of courses, and credit hours (Boden, et al., 2011). In addition to the basic procedural and structural differences, interdisciplinary training requires a convergence of cultures, role expectations, and methods for scholars if the program is, in fact, expecting scholars to work outside their silos to utilize and integrate these cross disciplinary approaches (Borrego & Cutler, 2010; Stokols et al., 2008) to support children in the schools. Enhancing preservice educator skills through interdisciplinary training holds great potential. A primary prospect is that interdisciplinary scholars will better have the capacity to go on to solve our most difficult and perennial problems (Borrego & Cutler, 2010) in school settings.

One of the perpetual problems faced by schools is the research-to-practice gap and the lack of evidenced-based interventions (EBIs) (Kerns et al., 2016). Institutes of higher education, however, support many graduate candidates in allied career tracks who will be responsible for the delivery of EBIs in hospital, school, and/or community settings after graduation. Kerns et al.'s (2016) *University of Washington Workforce Initiative* targeted the lack of preparation on EBIs by introducing an interdisciplinary training forum to increase EBI training across disciplines aimed specifically at supporting children's mental health needs. This monthly lecture series was found to have promising results with growth in both participant reported skills and self-efficacy. Similar interdisciplinary initiatives to train on EBIs can help meet the increasing demand for children's mental and behavioral health services (Cree et al., 2018; NASP, 2021; Whitney & Peterson, 2019). Initiatives designed to disseminate EBIs that prevent or treat mental health difficulties are needed as school districts across the United States face shortages in school psychologists, school social workers, school counselors, particularly when considering high poverty, rural or traditionally underserved locations (Boulden & Schimmel, 2021; Castillo et al., 2014; Kepley & Streeter, 2018; Prothero, 2022; Sutfin, 2021).

Although significant capacity exists in interdisciplinary programs to actualize solutions comparable to the proliferation of EBIs in schools, these programs are not absent obstacles. Borrego and Cutler (2010) purported that such graduate programs in engineering and science fields often have a paucity of associated scholarly work to guide curriculum development, Scholar outcomes, and assessment on how effective scholars were in communicating, interacting, and learning in an interdisciplinary context. Through an investigation of funded National Science Foundation's grant projects, Borrego and Cutler found that one preferred learning outcome for the majority of applications was a broader learner perspective. The archival proposals, however, ranged in the extent to which that breadth was defined. This brings about another complication, the trade-off between breadth and depth of skills in interdisciplinary initiatives. While the SEAR project's aim is to foster knowledge transfer across fields, it also necessitates training to a depth that all learners can demonstrate the desired repertoire or skillsets.

Within the faculty's interdisciplinary grant application for the Office of Special Programs' (OSEP) H325K competition, the faculty team struggled with several of these same concepts, including the range of learning outcomes and how to strike a balance between the breadth and depth of the proposed content. As a matter of fact, the authors' "lessons learned" surrounding depth are primarily grounded in learning through implementation. Preceding our first cohort of scholars, the core faculty team planned curriculum to provide prerequisite knowledge for scholars through monthly seminars for the first six months prior to scholars receiving the intensive, expert provided, training on TCIT. Although the content was necessary to support knowledge transfer regarding trauma, development, least restrictive environment, and case study requirements (e.g., how to collect direct observation data, prioritize target behaviors, and write behavioral definitions), the SEAR project faculty subsequently reflected that the informational content could better be trained alongside TCIT. At most, scholars remain in the SEAR project for no more than two years and their overall program for three years. Because there is a limited window of opportunity to facilitate practice and growth, training early on the core intervention with expert trainers is imperative. SEAR grant candidates now receive the two day TCIT training during the fall or spring semester, in which they enter our program.

Connected to the discussion of learning outcomes is scholar knowledge and skill level at entry. Scholars did enter the SEAR project with different knowledge and skills. On the behavioral principles pretest, the school psychology scholars, on average, performed 15 percentage points higher than the school counseling and special education scholars. Although school psychology scholars' posttest scores generally remained higher than their school counseling and special education counters parts, clearly both school counseling and special education scholars gained more knowledge throughout the interdisciplinary grant on behavioral principles. The SEAR project faculty also observed their school counseling scholars seek out more faculty support while constructing and submitting their case studies. Grant faculty attributed these disparities to differences in exposure at the undergraduate level on single subject design, learning theory, and applied behavior analysis. The prerequisites for scholar entry into the school psychology program demand that candidates take a psychology of learning course and either a research methods or experimental course, which are linked specifically to principles of applied behavior analysis and include single subject design. Moreover, scholars in both school psychology and special education had additional graduate assignments and courses above and beyond the SEAR project to facilitate growth in these domains.

This discussion of entry and exit performance begets larger evaluation questions. Is success of an interdisciplinary training program measured by attainment of mastery performance at program termination? Or should success be measured from a growth mindset? From an intraindividual growth perspective, scholars who enter with high achievement levels would need to exit with even significantly higher performance levels compared to their own baseline performance. Similarly, scholars who enter programs with lower knowledge and skill levels still may be deemed successful if they reach their own benchmark, and not necessarily one for scholars with high preprogram performance. While the authors are still reflecting on these same accountability questions that vex education programs, in general, they think the answers are contingent upon each interdisciplinary program's goals, and the level of integration and joint work desired by the initiative. For descriptions and goals of multidisciplinary, interdisciplinary, and transdisciplinary see Rosenfield (1992) and Stokols et al. (2008).

One unanticipated attributional difference emerged among scholars that could be highly salient to treatment, as well as interactions with parents, for a program aimed to serve substantial numbers of children with disabilities whose parents have SUD. In our SEAR project preprogram questionnaire, the grant team surveyed scholars on a variety of topics prior to their participation. This questionnaire included some questions adopted from an unpublished survey developed by Anderson and colleagues who conducted a statewide survey on the effects of the opioid epidemic on West Virginia educators ("WVU researchers investigate," 2019). Three of these questions addressed the extent that educators believe addiction is a choice, disease, or a moral deficiency. School psychology scholars believed that addiction was less of choice and not the result of a moral deficiency when compared to both their counseling and special education scholars' counterparts. Counseling and special education scholars were less likely to endorse addiction as a disease in relation to the school psychology scholars. Although these data are limited by a relatively small "n" size, they are likely, at least partially, a result of educational experiences and orientation prior to beginning graduate school.

As the authors stated previously, the Marshall University School Psychology admission requirements at the Master's level outline prerequisite courses. Examination of Marshall Counseling admission requirements do not limit their candidates to specific prerequisites prior to entry, and a non-educator entry Master's route exists for the special education scholars. This, in hindsight, illuminates the need to expose all scholars in the SEAR project to the role of classical conditioning, environmental cues in drug addiction, tolerance and relapse (Siegel, 2005). Such exposure to addiction science can support all scholars in working from a common framework wherein addiction is viewed as a disease. Viewing addiction as a disease can help Scholars move away from an "inaccurate, outdated view of addiction as a character flaw or moral failing deserving of punishment, toward that of a treatable chronic disease requiring long-term treatment" (Zgierska et al., 2021 p. 3) In doing so, scholars can reduce potential stigma in the schools, use appropriate person-first language, and increase positive interactions with parents with SUDs who are supporting children with disabilities. Although this belief across scholars is critically important, it was captured somewhat inadvertently through the SEAR project grant evaluation. The SEAR project faculty actually intended to examine scholars' perceptions in contrast to those of public educators. Yet, this key difference points to the importance of perception data being included in the evaluation process, an argument we will return to as we discuss readiness for crisis prevention and intervention in schools.

Finally, a caveat, while planning for growth in knowledge, skill and perceptions is that uniformity is not always desired or practical in scholar outcomes at program exit. Although school counselors, psychologists, and special educators certainly share some overlapping job roles, they likewise maintain unique functions linked to their job descriptions. Thus, the diversity and expertise of each participating discipline should be recognized and valued in interdisciplinary initiatives. For example, a school psychologist does not need to match a special educator's command over content standards and objectives and the preparation and implementation of individualized and small group instruction. Instead, multidisciplinary team members can and should rely on the special educator's instructional acumen. In their interdisciplinary training, the faculty frequently hear other candidates voice high esteem for the educators in our program. Granted that the regard for special educators was not formally assessed, in the authors' view it is an extremely positive by-product of their program, as respect for teachers and the profession appears to be declining and is often linked to teacher shortages (Christensen et al., 2019).

By way of illustration, the authors can think of developing an interdisciplinary initiative as similar to planning a meadow garden. They want to plan for species with common characteristics such as deer resistance, disease resistance, sun tolerance, pollinator-friendly, and self-perpetuating including naturalizing perennials or self-sowing annuals and biennials. Translated to the SEAR project, these common qualities embody their scholars' TCIT skills, their knowledge of behavioral principles, and a desire to support a child's least restrictive environment and advocate for children and families, especially "when it is difficult to do so" (Jacob et al., 2016, p. 20). Yet, in that same meadow garden, they want to benefit from diversity by selecting flowers with varied bloom times, tolerance to moisture and drought, and other specialized properties which allow different species to thrive in niches where other species simply do not. Thus, in interdisciplinary training context, as with later practice in the schools, the children and adolescents benefit from the school counselor's unique understanding of developmental guidance and planning for postsecondary careers, the school psychologists' understanding of the social, emotional, and cognitive basis of behavioral and academic issues in the schools, and the special educator's instructional expertise.

## Practice Three: Exposure to a Continuum of Tiered School-Based Supports

When targeting mental and behavioral health outcomes, exposure to a continuum of tiered school-based supports is necessary, including an introduction to how interdisciplinary personnel can function together in school crisis prevention and intervention teams.

Although TCIT is a foundational component of our interdisciplinary personnel preparation grant, this practice alone would be insufficient without addressing a larger framework for mental health supports in the schools. As with evidenced-based academic interventions in the schools, mental health supports, including behavioral and crisis interventions, are best designed and implemented through multitiered and interconnected systems framework (Brock et al., 2016; Sugai & Horner, 2009), and should be instructed as such in an interdisciplinary training program. Multitiered systems of support (MTSS) adhere to longstanding prevention models that originated in public health, but later were adapted to schools as triangle or pyramid-like models (Merrell & Buchanan, 2006). MTSS cultivated its roots primarily through the context of response to intervention (RTI) and positive behavioral interventions and supports (PBIS) (Sugai & Horner, 2009).

At its core, MTSS assumes that children necessitate varying levels of academic, behavioral, and mental health supports. Generally-speaking, the base of the triangle or pyramid signifies the instruction and supports that *all* students require. In the academic realm, this bottom rung or tier constitutes the core curriculum. The second or middle tier(s) represent intervention and supports that *some* students will need in addition to the core curriculum to be successful. The secondary supports are tailored to students' unmet needs and often involve more explicit instruction within a smaller group setting in addition to the support provided to all students. For example, within a three-tier reading model, a school or district might utilize a *Read Naturally* intervention as a standard treatment protocol to target increased fluency. The district might similarly offer a variety of other evidenced-based strategies at the secondary level to facilitate fluency that are not necessarily associated with a commercial intervention program. Finally, the top tier or tertiary level, characterizes those interventions and supports required for the *fewest* number of students to be successful. The interventions and practices at the top of the triangle or pyramid are the most intense, explicit, and sustained; moreover, they are delivered in the smallest group settings to be highly individualized (Avant & Swerdlik, 2016; Stoiber, 2014).

While the instruction and interventions within each tier are essential, the true centerpiece of MTSS is matching the supports to student need. The matching process entails assessment, which comes in the form of universal screening for all students and ongoing progress monitoring scheduled with different frequency for a subset of children and adolescents with more intense needs. After the assessment data are collected, multidisciplinary teams are needed to process the assessment data collaboratively through a problem-solving and data triangulation process. The teams interpret the data to facilitate goal setting, intervention priorities, and intervention implementation. Consequently, the team nature of MTSS frameworks renders MTSS highly compatible with interdisciplinary professional preparation (Shinn & Walker, 2010).

In the case of the Marshall University SEAR project, the interdisciplinary project was largely focused on behavioral and mental health outcomes. Each scholar was initially exposed to MTSS models in their respective course work within the special education, school psychology, and school counseling programs. However, the SEAR project complemented the individual programs of study by providing field assignments and specialized training that spanned the tiers. Faculty tasked the first cohort to initially partner with a scholar from a different discipline to research universal design for learning (UDL) principles through the CEEDAR Center modules, as well as trauma-sensitive practices and trauma-informed care through other technical assistance sites such as the National Child Traumatic Stress Network and the scholarly literature. After researching definitions and practices, scholars were asked to consider how UDL and trauma-sensitive practices can operate in tandem to reduce learning barriers for children with disabilities, and/or trauma, as well as their non-disabled peers who may be at risk for future trauma or mental health challenges. The partner pairs conducted classroom observations and interviews to assess for UDL and trauma-informed practices that permeated the classrooms. Although the culminating activity of consulting with a teacher to develop a plan to increase the number of UDL and trauma-informed practices was stalled due to the pandemic, scholars were able to share many examples of existing Tier 1 supports and UDL practices through this partner activity. Notably, two groups worked in classrooms within schools using PAX Good Behavior Game as a universal prevention program. Other partnering scholars reported on their schools implementation of PBIS; environmental calming spaces, sensory rooms, or schools' Handle with Care approaches. In all, this interdisciplinary assignment resulted in scholars being trained by other scholars on numerous evidenced-based interventions, approaches, and accompanying UDL practices that should comprise our universal wellness and prevention supports in the schools.

While the faculty partners additionally contributed to the teaching of universal, secondary, and tertiary supports, it is beyond the scope of this chapter to list and describe all such interventions and treatments. The authors want to challenge other interdisciplinary training initiatives to consider the benefits of exposing scholars to evidence-based, school crisis prevention and intervention curriculum and threat assessment guidelines when targeting mental health outcomes. The National Association of School Psychologists' PREPaRE curriculum (Brock et al., 2016) and Cornell's (2018) *Comprehensive School Threat Assessment Guidelines: Intervention and Support to Prevent Violence* are two such evidenced-based processes uniquely developed for implementation in schools by multidisciplinary teams.

As we craft this chapter, school safety and threat assessment protocols are at the forefront of our minds, with the Uvalde, Texas school shooting not two months removed. Although the Robb Elementary incident, resulting in the death of two teachers, 19 children, and the 18-year-old assailant, is the $27^{th}$ school shooting in the nation this year (Diaz, 2022), the reality is that crises–though not necessarily mass fatality events–are occurring in school communities every day across America. Be it a death by suicide, a natural disaster, a car accident with injuries or a bomb threat, the preservice professionals who are trained for the schools can facilitate more successful response and recovery efforts if they are knowledgeable of these multidisciplinary efforts. Toward this end, the authors would like to share more about Brock et al.'s (2016) PREPaRE curriculum and Cornell's (2018) threat assessment process within the context of Marshall University's SEAR grant.

## National Association of School Psychologists's PREPaRE Model

The PREPaRE developers deem multidisciplinary teams "essential" and state that skill sets are "best utilized when they are embedded within a multidisciplinary team that engages in all aspects of crisis preparedness" (Brock, et al., 2016, p. 3). The PREPaRE curriculum provides the learner background knowledge including relevant federal requirements, crisis types and consequences, and related crisis models. The PREPaRE curriculum then subdivides the content into two workshops. The first workshop, Workshop 1, *Comprehensive School Safety Planning: Prevention Through Recovery*, is a seven-hour, one-day training. It focuses on comprehensive school safety planning, and spotlights prevention and preparedness. Addressing both physical and psychological safety, concepts such as environmental design, collaboration with partners, safe schools, and climate assessment are introduced. The safe schools thread of the training, again, illuminates MTSS and specifically Tier 1, wherein PBIS, social-emotional learning, and prevention programs dominate.

The second PREPaRE training, Workshop 2, *Mental Health Crisis Intervention: Responding to an Acute Traumatic Stressor in Schools*, supports school teams in responding to crisis events in and about school settings. All Marshall University SEAR grant scholars participated in this 13-hour training. Workshop 2 helps scholars learn about the common crisis reactions and warning signs while concomitantly studying variables which assist responders in anticipating the number of affected students, staff, and school community members who may require intervention. This is, in part, accomplished through evaluation of crisis type, consequences, warning signs and risk factors like physical and emotional proximity. Other risks delineated in the curriculum are internal and external vulnerabilities. PREPaRE outlines eight and seven pretrauma internal and external vulnerabilities, respectively. While the external vulnerabilities that predate the crisis event include inadequate family, fiscal, and community social supports and resources, the preexisting internal vulnerabilities involve variables such as social withdrawal, low cognition, preexisting mental, and physical health issues (Brock, et al., 2016, pp. 195-220). Given the nature of these vulnerabilities, who better than a child's special education teacher or case manager to have individual knowledge of what internal and external vulnerabilities, if any, may place students with disabilities at greater risk for psychological trauma following an acute traumatic stressor? Special educators work to plan goals, instruction, accommodations, and services through Individualized Education Programs (IEPs). They, therefore, may not only be directly servicing students for health impairments or academic deficits related to cognitive and/or social skill deficits, but special educators are required by the Individuals with Disabilities Education Act (IDEA 2004) to obtain input and interact in meaningful ways with families. These interactions result in special educators who have expertise on a family's overall functioning and wellbeing, as well as any self-disclosed economic hardships, family history of illness, and lack of social supports. School counselors and school psychologists, conversely, may know more about an individual's student's difficulties from individual testing, counseling sessions, and student assistance team meetings, and are well positioned to support students given their overall mental health expertise.

The PREPaRE Workshop 2 ultimately provides the multidisciplinary team members instruction on several mental health crisis interventions in a tiered format after introducing steps to evaluate psychological trauma. Similarly, noteworthy is the fact that teachers, including special educators, who desire to provide crisis intervention, can do so for the large number of interventions comprising the PREPaRE Model at the Tier 1 and Tier 2 level, with the exception of Group Crisis Intervention, which requires more intensive training on therapeutic techniques compatible with the role of school counselors and school psychologist. In fact, the PREPaRE authors recommend that teachers *ideally* facilitate classroom meetings, and maintain an active role in student psychoeducational groups. The curriculum provides roles and suggestions for teachers and school mental health providers to cooperatively deliver effective services, whatever the crisis intervention, understanding that a flexible approach is necessary when school-based professionals may also be overwhelmed or otherwise negatively impacted by the crisis.

As part of the SEAR interdisciplinary project, the PREPaRE Workshop 2 pretest and posttest data collected online by NASP immediately before and after the 13 hours of direct instruction and related activities was utilized. The evaluation further included an 8-12-month follow-up assessment to evaluate scholar maintenance that was nearly identical in format to the posttest. Scholars exhibited significant improvement in knowledge scores from the pretest to the posttest $t(47) = 1.61, p = 0.26$. However, after 8-12 months passed, the average scholar demonstrated slippage or regression in knowledge of the PREPaRE specific concepts and interventions. Faculty partially attributed slippage to the pandemic and the fact that only one in every five scholars had the opportunity to implement PREPaRE interventions and only approximately 12% of scholars reported being able to use the material at least 5 times. Another explanation of slippage was the heavy reliance of specific PREPaRE Workshop 2 terminology in the evaluations. It is possible that participants had difficulty recalling the exact terminology and corresponding definitions. Yet, they could possibly maintain the necessary skills to implement the training material when presented with an acute traumatic stressor (Williams, 2022). Regardless, the slippage underscores the importance of sustained, continuing professional development during a training grant and throughout one's career that provides sufficient opportunities for practice, feedback, and reflection (Darling-Hammond et al., 2017).

Prior PREPaRE research (Nickerson et al., 2019) indicates that trainee characteristics such as motivation to implement PREPaRE skills to the schools, self-efficacy, and learner readiness influence the transfer of skills to school settings along with work environment variables, such as peer support and supervisor support, and opportunity to use skills. Fortunately, for this reason, the NASP pre- and posttests contain a few perception items along with the knowledge items. For Marshall SEAR candidates, self-reported anxiety and fear of implementing crisis interventions in schools decreased, on average, between the pre- and posttest, and remained lower at follow-up. The trend regarding scholar confidence in implementing PREPaRE crisis prevention and intervention, however, was somewhat opposite. A higher percentage of scholars indicated *very confident* at pretest, as compared to posttest. One possible explanation provided by the external evaluator is "a phenomenon regularly observed in pre-post survey research–prior to exposure to a training attendees may rate themselves higher, but once they have the exposure, they realize their knowledge/confidence was not as high as they initially thought" (Censeo Strategic Solutions, 2022, p. 50).

Finally, when reflecting "big-picture" upon perceptions and the degree to which self-efficacy and other beliefs can affect transfer of skills, the authors wish to strengthen this portion of the SEAR grant evaluation in future iterations by adding perception items. For example, items that assess the extent to which scholars believe 1) crisis prevention and intervention is part of their desired job role and 2) they could effectively work in multidisciplinary teams to engender positive outcomes for students in the crisis aftermath would be beneficial. The authors believe that scholar affirmation of the desire to engage in crisis prevention and intervention in the schools would likely far outweigh any minor knowledge loss from the posttest to follow-up, as desire to participate will likely yield opportunities for first hand practice in the schools.

## Comprehensive School Threat Assessment Guidelines: Intervention and Support to Prevent Violence

Marshall University SEAR scholars had an opportunity to participate, along with their field supervisors, in a state virtual mini-conference, which hosted Dr. Dewey Cornell for a three hour CSTAG overview in January 2022. Cornell's (2018) CSTAG provides a manualized process with a decision-tree for responding to threats to determine if they are *transient or substantive*. The CSTAG has evolved from Cornell and colleagues Virginia Student Threat Assessment Guidelines (Cornell, 2018).

Burnette et al.'s (2018) research findings from 339 schools using the VSTAG are presented in Cornell's 2018 CSTAG. Burnette et al. reviewed 844 school threats and found that 35% of threat assessments involved children and adolescents with disabilities, resulting in considerable overrepresentation. When threats are made in the school setting, these students with disabilities are at risk for significant disciplinary consequences such as out-of-school suspensions and expulsions. It is important to note that training grants for the Interdisciplinary Preparation in Special Education, Early Intervention, and Related Services are tasked by grant priorities to collaborate with stakeholders using an interdisciplinary team-based approach for the purposes of yielding improved outcomes while also advocating for the inclusion of children with disabilities in the least restrictive and natural environments to the maximum extent appropriate. Cornell's process supports both grant priorities by 1) calling on multidisciplinary teams to participate in the threat assessment process and 2) not treating all threats as equal. When teams

*Lessons Learned*

deem a threat as transient, they define that threat as one wherein no "lasting intent to harm someone" exists Cornell, 2018, p. 20). This, as opposed to substantive threats, end in apologies and often a quick return to the natural setting if any consequence is imposed. With this regard, CSTAG can be considered as a suspension alternative or "suspension reducer" when transient threats are involved. According to Burnette et al. (2018), the vast majority (78%) of the 844 threats were found to be transient.

The presence of a comprehensive and interdisciplinary process for threat assessment in the schools strengthens the continuum of mental health services. Although some school counselors and school psychologists routinely participate in threat assessment across the nation, research shows few state educational agencies have state policies and standards linked to threat assessment and only one state specifically mandates threat assessment (Woitaszewski et al., 2018). Additionally, many schools do not have access to a school-based team to respond to a threat (Gray, 2009). For these reasons, districts often outsource evaluations to community mental health agencies or rely on a sole, school-based professional to conduct an evaluation. Conversely, teachers can participate as a core member of the threat assessment team, though they rarely do because of their classroom obligations (Cornell, 2018, p. 13). Yet, the teacher of the child making a threat is always an integral part of the interview process, as a teacher often knows the child best (Cornell, 2018, p. 45). Importantly, teachers, when trained, can identify potential warning signs and the need for mental health support (Brock et al., 2016) before threats are ever made.

Given this context, participating on a school threat assessment team may a serve as a boundary-spanning role for some school counselors, school psychologists, and special educators wherein an evidenced-based protocol is not already established. Research in school psychology suggests that increased "boundary-spanning activities" enables practitioners to have input on the planning and delivery of services, and even the allocation of funding, leads to increased job satisfaction (Brown & Sobel, 2021, p. 42; Jerrell, 1984), as compared to practitioners with fewer boundary spanning opportunities. School psychologists experience higher job satisfaction when they are able to include more consultative and system services in their practice, both of which are also highly integrated into the threat assessment process, whereas school psychologists experience frequent burnout when almost singularly focused on assessment with high caseloads (Brown & Sobel, 2021). In general, research on boundary-spanning roles suggests that individuals who frequently fulfill such roles do so because they too receive satisfaction from participating in the challenging and valued activities, and boundary spanning by other team members is a protective factor against "role overload" of any one team member (Marrone et al., 2007, p. 1433). This notion of increased satisfaction is paramount, knowing that recruitment, retention, and shortages currently place our children at risk for being underserved in the schools (NASP, 2021).

## Practice Four: Modeling and Attending to Self-Care While Creating Flexibility for Scholar Participation in Monthly Meetings

An obstacle faced during early grant implementation was COVID-19. Several scholars lost loved ones and all scholars already placed in schools reported difficulty maintaining a work/life balance as they transitioned to online classrooms during the early stages of the pandemic. Several of them experienced significant illness. Testing positive twice during the first 1.5 years of COVID-19 appeared to be the norm for many of our Scholars working in the schools. Therefore, the grant planning team worked hard to create a positive interdisciplinary environment during our monthly seminar meetings, while being responsive to scholars' needs and ensuring flexibility in assignment completion when they lacked in-person experiences with K-12 students in the schools. Facing significant educator and substitute shortages in our state, several districts were unable to release Scholars from their teaching duties to attend in-person sessions. Therefore, most monthly seminar meetings were moved to virtual format, and many were rescheduled to afterschool hours. It was also important to provide dates as early as possible so that scholars could plan ahead for monthly seminar meetings. The importance of attendance was stressed, because the interaction between the scholars with each other and with faculty was important for skill development and appropriate mindset.

Even without the looming issue of the pandemic, professionals working in schools and as mental health professionals are at a higher risk for burnout and stress (Maslach & Leiter, 2016). Pakenham (2015) recommended that self-care instruction should be introduced in training programs in order to better prepare mental health providers and educators. Self-care can be defined as self-initiated practices which promote personal health and well-being (Colman et al., 2016).

The SEAR scholars were working with children who have been exposed to ACEs, these children confide in their teachers, school counselors and school psychologists. When they do, scholars may experience secondary traumatization and may not realize it (Hydon et al., 2015). Lesh (2020) suggested that, because students with disabilities have a higher rate of ACEs, those working with them in the schools are more likely to experience secondary or vicarious trauma. Scholars were informed of this phenomenon in order to help them be aware and take steps to engage in self-care. Lesh (2020) recommended the self-care strategies of gratitude journaling, meditating, exercising, having a confident, finding the balance between work and leisure, and developing a stress management plan.

The SEAR project addressed the self-care issue by adding it to their monthly seminar meetings as needed. For example, in a presentation on counseling interventions to support mental health in elementary aged children, the faculty presenter spent time at the beginning stressing that scholars needed to care for themselves prior to caring for others. Stress reduction strategies were discussed. Examples of self-care strategies were presented. Faculty shared their own strategies to model appropriate self-care for Scholars. Then, scholars engaged in a discussion on current stress reduction strategies being used by them, barriers to self-care, and ideas on overcoming barriers. This permitted scholars to process the information and apply it to themselves.

Faculty also incorporated self-care in coursework. For example, in the shared course on violence, loss and trauma, while scholars learned about trauma, its effect on children and families, and different treatment techniques, they were also instructed on self-care. During the course, scholars read a white paper which emphasized self-care and resilience. As scholars were discussing trauma, they were taught some skills for dealing with their own trauma histories if needed. They were also taught to process their emotions and regain a sense of self. They were encouraged to support each other through discussion threads.

Self-care is additionally important because of the high burnout rate for those working in schools. This has been especially documented for special education teachers (Park & Shin, 2020). Factors contributing to burnout include the intensity of the students' needs, less education, and lack of administrative support. Park and Shin (2020) found that teachers self-efficacy and coping capacities reduced burnout. These findings provided additional support for the need to educate our Scholars in self-care.

The SEAR project faculty wanted to not only teach the skills of self-care, model it for our scholars, but also to practice it when making decisions that affected the scholars. When scholars faced difficult situations in their personal lives, the faculty were willing to make accommodations such as permitting them to listen to recordings of required class meetings or allowing extensions for submission of assignments. The faculty strived to maintain the quality of the experience, while showing flexibility during difficult life experiences. They reached out to scholars individually when they were experiencing difficult life situations and needed additional support.

## Practice Five: Partnerships for Sustainability

As recognized in implementation science, the engagement of community partners and stakeholders is a necessity in scaling-up and sustaining EBIs (Milat et al., 2015). In keeping with this pillar of sustainability, numerous partnerships occurred in connection with the SEAR project H325K grant. Several of those partnerships centered on training mentor teachers and clinical field supervisors on TCIT. Each partner-sponsored professional development session supported the capacity for Scholars to implement TCIT assignments and practice in the schools. If field supervisors and mentor teachers have the responsibility of being competent role models (Guiney, 2019), they must develop a growing awareness of TCIT, themselves, in order to provide feedback to their scholars or mentees and advocate for TCIT use within the school settings.

Toward this end, during the 2019-2020 school year, the Opioid Response Network and Central East Addiction Technology Transfer Center funded a three-day TCIT training for mentor teachers, faculty members, and one WV Department of Education partner representative. The Director of Marshall University's Center of Excellence for Recovery connected the core grant team to the response network and transfer center. Additionally, 20 field supervisors participated in a one-day training this same year geared at increasing mental health supports and behavioral strategies in the schools through TCIT at Marshall University. Given that the initial trainings were very well received, the WV School Psychologists Association hosted a TCIT session at its fall conference in October 2022, which reached reach 85-90% of the school psychology practitioners in the state.

In terms of sustaining TCIT/PCIT within the College of Education and Professional Development, three MU faculty additionally received a five-day intensive PCIT clinical training to build capacity within the grant for supervising and guiding scholars in TCIT implementation and coaching in the schools. This training was provided as part of a WV State Opioid Response grant designed to enhance services for children and families affected by the opioid crisis. It allowed two faculty to further pursue PCIT certification. The grant covered the five-day initial training, a two-day advanced training, twice monthly consultation calls for nearly two years, all books and manuals, an equipment kit, and allowed attendees the opportunity to become certified in PCIT. This two-year training and supervision process afforded by the State Opioid Response Grant will enable PCIT and hence TCIT practices to be sustained when H325K monies are no longer available to support the expert coach.

Similar partnerships were formed to scale up NASP's PREPaRE training throughout the state. The WV Department of Education funded a collaborative to offer four PREPaRE training sessions to school counselors, school psychologists, and other WV educators along with the WV School Psychologists Association and a Marshall University trainer. Approximately, 140 WV Educators were trained in NASP's PREPaRE Workshop 2, 3rd Edition *Mental Health Crisis Intervention: Responding to an Acute Traumatic Stressor in Schools.* Although the WV Department of Education provided all monies to implement the training, the WV School Psychologists Association coordinated participants' registration, materials, and Zoom access. This state school psychology association includes the dissemination of PREPaRE as one of its chief priorities in its strategic plan to support crisis prevention and intervention across the state.

The final state partnership with respect to EBIs for the SEAR project is the WV Project SCOPE Echo Series. WV Project Scope is a collaboration with the School of Medicine and Center for Excellence in

Disabilities at WV University and the College of Education and Professional Development and Department of Psychology at Marshall University. WV Project SCOPE offered six sessions, and extended this opportunity to SEAR scholars. SCOPE topics are all opioid crisis related topics, including an overview of the opioid crisis and social determinants of health, neonatal abstinence syndrome, neurodevelopmental outcomes, peer support and stigma, intergenerational trauma and infant-mental health, and traumatic stress and the long term effects in young children. The format of project SCOPE webinars work well for scholars as they are relatively brief, held at the end of a work day, and are recorded online for later viewing. WV Project SCOPE is a partnership with the Nisonger Center at The Ohio State University and the University of Cincinnati Center for Excellence in Developmental Disabilities.

Although the SEAR project focused largely on state or regional partnerships for EBIs scale up initiatives thus far, they would be remiss if we failed to mention the importance of collaborating with OSEP's technical assistance centers and other similar federal resources such as the Substance Abuse and Mental Health Services Administration (www.samhsa.gov/), the National Child Traumatic Stress Network (www.nctsn.org/). These technical centers not only supply immediate, high quality modules and resources to interdisciplinary preparation training grants, they similarly supply scholars important access to materials and resources, such as EBI locators or search engines. Moreover, they are typically no cost resources at the local level, which again promotes sustainability.

Lastly, partnering for recruitment is another important consideration. Indeed, district special education administrators, state education agencies, parent organizations and training centers, as well as undergraduate institutions, are all valuable partners in the recruitment of qualified candidates. While each partner can support the advertising of interdisciplinary training initiatives, district representatives with shortages have the capacity to offer more individualized incentives while recruiting. For example, programs with internships sometimes pose obstacles for candidates returning for a Master's degree. Yet, we have observed some districts promise candidate's internship salaries that are equivalent to their current pay scale. This allows scholars to return for an advanced degree and obtain additional skills or certifications without creating a hardship with a reduced salary during the internship or clinical experience. Some teacher residency programs offer similar benefits wherein residency students are able to work and receive pay for a certain proportion of their hours. Other districts ensure that returning candidates and program scholars are able to attend in-person training on campus while taking paid professional leave days.

Another key partner for the SEAR project was the WV Higher Education Policy Commission. Two state level grants from the West Virginia Higher Education Policy Commission have worked in tandem with the OSEP grant to recruit a pipeline of undergraduates with an interest in behavioral health careers, including school psychology and school counseling. The first grant funded recruitment trips and dissemination of program pamphlets to undergraduate psychology, counseling, social work, and other behavioral health programs in southern WV, as well as similar trips to high schools within the same region. The activities were intended to raise awareness of, and commitment to, careers in behavioral health in WV. The second state funded grant from the West Virginia Higher Education Policy Commission aimed to recruit school psychology candidates in northern WV. Funding was used to purchase additional psychological test kits and digital assessment technologies to facilitate participation from candidates who live further from the Marshall Campus to fill chronic shortages. The additional funds afforded candidates the opportunities to participate in synchronous class meetings via Zoom while also be enrolled in the SEAR project.

## FUTURE RESEARCH DIRECTIONS

Many areas of interdisciplinary programming are ripe for future research with respect to mental health. Research designs that can truly assess the "value-added" nature of an interdisciplinary program are needed. These designs require matched or comparison groups and extend well beyond simple preposttest evaluation. However, before these designs are attempted, faculty and researchers must have the right outcomes and variables measured. As an example, the SEAR project faculty and evaluators learned that tracking PRIDE skill mastery for scholars from program entry to exit was equally important to obtaining case study results and a behavioral principles pre- and posttest. Just as graduate programs in the STEM fields have a paucity of associated scholarly work to guide interdisciplinary outcomes, assessment, and curriculum development (Borrego & Cutler, 2010), so do interdisciplinary graduate preparation programs in special education and related service areas that are designed to support children and adolescents with high intensity disabilities. Consequently, academics working with interdisciplinary programs are frequently learning by trial-and-error in the initial stages of grant implementation.

Another point of interest is the long term effects of interdisciplinary training. Do scholars who graduated from interdisciplinary programs remain in education careers longer? Are they able to use skills learned in everyday practices? Do they demonstrate higher levels of teaming and leadership skills? If scholars are more readily providing trauma-informed practices and other EBIs within tiered systems of support, what is their overall effectiveness in producing desired results for children with disabilities, as compared to professionals without interdisciplinary training?

## CONCLUSION

While working with scholars, some experiences went as planned. Providing training with evidence-based, best practice interventions yielded improved skills in our scholars. Feedback from scholars indicated these were useful practices that could be immediately implemented in classrooms. The authors saw firsthand the value of scholars sharing their experiences in schools which enabled scholars from other disciplines to learn from each other. Additionally, selecting faculty colleagues with similar goals and work ethic resulted in positive working relationships and shared responsibilities. The faculty from the counseling, school psychology, and special education programs were able to model for the scholars positive interdisciplinary working relationships.

Other experiences yielded some "aha" moments when they examined their data. Responding to the limitations of the pandemic taught that a majority of the trainings could be delivered effectively in a virtual format. Utilizing an external evaluation team gave data that highlighted the differences in entry skill and knowledge levels of the authors' interdisciplinary scholars. We determined that education was needed to make sure that children of parents who suffer from SUD are not stigmatized, and there is equal treatment of all students. Efforts were made to educate scholars concerning the adverse effects of stigma on children suffering from the effects of SUD, and youth who have experienced trauma. Educating them about these groups will help the scholars examine their practices including their language when talking about or speaking to students who have high ACEs. Stigma results in increased bullying, lowered self-esteem, diminished confidence, and deficits in social development (Mi An et al., 2020). Studies have shown that teachers can be educated on empirically based strategies to implement that can reduce stigma in the classroom (Salinger, 2019).

Overall, the SEAR project is meeting the grant's goals of training school psychologists, school counselors, and special education teachers with the skills to address the needs of children with intensely complex social, emotional and behavioral needs. Although the time commitment was challenging for the scholars, especially during the pandemic, feedback from them was consistently positive regarding the usefulness of the trainings. Linking together the already existing university resources and grants to the authors' training needs enabled them to do more and ensure that some trainings will continue. Graduate students not part of the grant expressed interest in obtaining similar trainings and the faculty's hope is to try and provide these to them.

## ACKNOWLEDGMENT

This article was based on an interdisciplinary program supported through the Office of Special Education Programs in the U.S. Department of Education under award H325K190039. Any opinions and findings expressed in this article are those of the authors and do not necessarily reflect those of the Office of Special Education Programs.

## REFERENCES

Avant, D. W., & Swerdlik, M. E. (2016). A collaborative endeavor: The roles and functions of school social workers and school psychologists in implementing multi-tiered system of supports/response to intervention. *School Social Work Journal*, *41*(1), 56. https://search-ebscohostcom.proxy1.ncu.edu/login.aspx?direct=true&db=edo&AN=121705552&site=eds-live

Barnard, M., & McKeganey, N. (2004). The impact of parental problem drug use on children: What is the problem and what can be done to help? *Addiction (Abingdon, England)*, *5*(5), 552–559. doi:10.1111/j.1360-0443.2003.00664.x PMID:15078229

Boden, D., Borrego, M., & Newswander, L. K. (2011). Student socialization in interdisciplinary doctoral education. *Higher Education*, *62*(6), 741–755. doi:10.100710734-011-9415-1

Borrego, M., & Cutler, S. (2010). Constructive alignment of interdisciplinary graduate curriculum in engineering and science: An analysis of successful IGERT proposals. *Journal of Engineering Education (Washington, D.C.)*, *99*(4), 355–369. doi:10.1002/j.2168-9830.2010.tb01068.x

Boulden, R., & Schimmel, C. (2021). More than just an internship: One university's collaboration with a rural school district to attract, develop, and retain school counselors. *Rural Educator*, *42*(3), 56–62. doi:10.35608/ruraled.v42i3.1237

Brock, S. E., Nickerson, A. B., Louvar Reeves, M. A., Conolly, C. N., Jimerson, S. R., Pesce, R. C., & Lazzaro, B. R. (2016). *School crisis prevention and intervention: The PREPaRE model* (2nd ed.). National Association of School Psychologists.

Brown, T. J., & Sobel, D. (2021). School psychologists' job attitudes: A systematic review. *Contemporary School Psychology*, *25*(1), 40–50. doi:10.100740688-019-00241-4

Budd, K. S., Garbacz, L. L. & Carter, J. S. (2016). Collaborating with public school partners to implement teacher-child interaction training (TCIT) as universal prevention. *School Mental Health: A Multidisciplinary Research and Practice Journal, 8*(2), 207-221.

Burnette, A. G., Datta, P., & Cornell, D. (2018). The distinction between transient and substantive student threats. *Journal of Threat Assessment and Management, 5*(1), 4–20. doi:10.1037/tam0000092

Campbell, C. B. (2011). *Adapting an evidence-based intervention to improve social and behavioral competence in head start children: Evaluating the effectiveness of teacher-child interaction training* [Doctoral dissertation]. University of Nebraska-Lincoln, Psychiatry and Psychology Commons.

Castillo, J. M., Curtis, M. J., & Tan, S. Y. (2014). Personnel needs in school psychology: A 10-year follow-up study on predicted personnel shortages. *Psychology in the Schools, 51*(8), 832–849. doi:10.1002/pits.21786

CDC - National Center for Health Statistics. (2022, March 1). *Drug overdose mortality by state*. https://www.cdc.gov/nchs/pressroom/sosmap/drug_poisoning_mortality/drug_poisoning.htm

Censeo Strategic Solutions. (2022). *Marshall University's SEAR Project Mid Grant Report* [Unpublished program evaluation].

Chalk, K., & Bizo, L. A. (2004). Specific praise improves on-task behaviour and numeracy enjoyment: A study of year four pupils engaged in the numeracy hour. *Educational Psychology in Practice, 20*(4), 335–351. doi:10.1080/0266736042000314277

Christensen, S. S., Davies, R. S., Harris, S. P., Hanks, J., & Bowles, B. (2019). Teacher recruitment: Factors that predict high school students' willingness to become teachers. *Education Sciences, 9*(4), 282. doi:10.3390/educsci9040282

Colman, D. E., Echon, R., Lemay, M. S., McDonald, J., Smith, K. R., Spencer, J., & Swift, J. K. (2016). The efficacy of self-care for graduate students in professional psychology: A meta-analysis. *Training and Education in Professional Psychology, 10*(4), 188–197. doi:10.1037/tep0000130

Cooper, J. O., Heron, T. E., & Heward, W. L. (2020). *Applied behavior analysis* (3rd ed.). Pearson Education. doi:10.26741/abaespana/2020.cooper3e

Cornell, D. (2018). *Comprehensive school threat assessment guidelines: Intervention and support to prevent violence*. School Threat Assessment Consultants LLC.

Cree, R. A., Bitsko, R. H., Robinson, L. R., Holbrook, J. R., Danielson, M. L., Smith, C., Kaminsky, J. W., Kenny, M. K., & Peacock, G. (2018). Health care, family, and community factors associated with mental, behavioral, and developmental disorders and poverty among children aged 2–8 years—United States, 2016. *Morbidity and Mortality Weekly Report, 67*(50), 1377–1383. doi:10.15585/mmwr.mm6750a1 PMID:30571671

Darling-Hammond, L., Hyler, M. E., & Gardner, M. (2017). *Effective teacher professional development*. Learning Policy Institute., doi:10.54300/122.311

Davidson, B. C., Davis, E., Cadenas, H., Barnett, M., Luis Sanchez, B. E., Gonzalez, J. C., & Jent, J. (2021). Universal teacher-child interaction training in early special education: A pilot cluster-randomized control trial. *Behavior Therapy*, *52*(2), 379–393. doi:10.1016/j.beth.2020.04.014 PMID:33622507

Diaz, J. (2022, May 25). *27 school shootings have taken place so far in 2022*. https://www.npr.org/2022/05/24/1101050970/2022-school-shootings-so-far

Dombo, E. A., & Sabatino, C. A. (2019). *Creating trauma-informed schools: a guide for school social workers and schools*. doi:10.1093/oso/9780190873806.001.0001

Eyeberg, S. M., Chase, R. M., Fernandez, M. A., & Nelson, M. M. (2014). *Dyadic parent-child interaction coding system (DPICS) clinical manual* (4th ed.). PCIT International.

Fawley, K. D., Stokes, T. F., Rainear, C. A., Rossi, J. L., & Budd, K. S. (2020). Universal TCIT improves teacher-child interactions and management of child behavior. *Journal of Behavioral Education*, *29*(4), 635–656. doi:10.100710864-019-09337-6

Fernandez, M. S., Adelstein, J. S., Miller, S. P., Areizaga, M. J., Gold, D. C., Sanchez, A. L., Rothschild, S. A., Hirsch, E., & Gudino, O. G. (2015). Teacher-child interaction training: A pilot study with random assignment. *Behavior Therapy*, *46*(4), 463–477. doi:10.1016/j.beth.2015.02.002 PMID:26163711

Frederiksen, K. S., Hesse, M., Brummer, J., & Pedersen, M. U. (2022). The impact of parental substance use disorder and other family-related problems on school related outcomes. *Drug and Alcohol Dependence Reports*, *3*, 100041. doi:10.1016/j.dadr.2022.100041

Garbacz, L. L., Zychinski, K. E., Feuer, R. M., Carter, J. S., & Budd, K. S. (2014). Effects of implemented Teacher-Child Interaction Training (TCIT) on teacher ratings of behavior change. *Psychology in the Schools*, *51*(8), 850–865. doi:10.1002/pits.21788

Gray, R. (2009). *Columbine 10 years later: the state of school safety today*. http://www.campussafetymagazine.com/Channel/School-Safety/Articles/2009/03/Columbine-10-Years-Later-The-State-of-School-Safety-Today.aspx

Guiney, M. C. (2019). *The school psychology supervisor's toolkit*. Routledge.

Hubel, G. S., Cooley, J. L., & Moreland, A. D. (2020). Incorporating evidence-based behavioral teaching training into Head Start mental health consultation: Description and initial outcomes of a large-scale program. *Psychology in the Schools*, *57*(5), 735–756. doi:10.1002/pits.22348 PMID:33833474

Hydon, S., Wong, M., Langley, A. K., Stein, B. D., & Kataoka, S. H. (2015). Preventing secondary traumatic stress in educators. *Child and Adolescent Psychiatric Clinics of North America*, *24*(2), 319–333. doi:10.1016/j.chc.2014.11.003 PMID:25773327

Individuals with Disabilities Education Improvement Act, H.R. 1350, 108th Congress (2004).

Jacob, S., Decker, D. M., & Lugg, E. T. (2016). *Ethics and law for school psychologists* (7th ed.). Wiley.

Jerrell, J. M. (1984). Boundary-spanning functions served by rural school psychologists. *Journal of School Psychology*, *22*(3), 259–271. doi:10.1016/0022-4405(84)90007-4

Kanine, R. M., Jackson, Y., Huffhines, L., Barnett, A., & Stone, K. J. (2018). A pilot study of universal teacher-child interaction training at a therapeutic preschool for young maltreated children. *Topics in Early Childhood Special Education*, *38*(3), 146–161. doi:10.1177/0271121418790012

Kepley, H. O., & Streeter, R. A. (2018). Closing behavioral health workforce gaps: A HRSA program expanding direct mental health service access in underserved areas. *American Journal of Preventive Medicine*, *54*(6), S190–S191. doi:10.1016/j.amepre.2018.03.006 PMID:29779541

Kerns, S. E. U., Cevasco, M., Comtois, K. A., Dorsey, S., King, K., McMahon, R., Sedlar, G., Lee, T. G., Mazza, J. J., Lengua, L., Davis, C., Evans-Campbell, T., & Trupin, E. W. (2016). An interdisciplinary university-based initiative for graduate training in evidence-based treatments for children's mental health. *Journal of Emotional and Behavioral Disorders*, *24*(1), 3–15. doi:10.1177/1063426615583457

Lesh, J. L. (2020). Don't forget about yourself: Words of wisdom on special education teacher self-care. *Teaching Exceptional Children*, *52*(6), 367–369. doi:10.1177/0040059920936158

Marrone, J. A., Tesluk, P. E., & Carson, J. B. (2007). A multilevel investigation of antecedents and consequences of team member boundary-spanning behavior. *Academy of Management Journal*, *50*(6), 1423–1439. doi:10.5465/amj.2007.28225967

Maslach, C., & Leiter, M. P. (2016). Understanding the burnout experience: Recent research and its implications for psychiatry. *World Psychiatry; Official Journal of the World Psychiatric Association (WPA)*, *15*(2), 103–111. doi:10.1002/wps.20311 PMID:27265691

McIntosh, D. (2010). Treating disruptive classroom behaviors of preschoolers through teacher child interaction therapy. In A. A. Drewes & C. E. Schaefer (Eds.), *School-based play therapy* (pp. 197–218). Wiley. doi:10.1002/9781118269701.ch10

McNeil, C. B., & Hembree-Kigin, T. L. (2010). *Parent-child interaction therapy* (2nd ed.). Springer. doi:10.1007/978-0-387-88639-8

Merrell, K. W., & Buchanan, R. (2006). Intervention selection in school-based practice: Using public health models to enhance systems capacity of schools. *School Psychology Review*, *35*(2), 167–180. doi:10.1080/02796015.2006.12087985

Mickey, A. V. (2019). *An assessment of the perceptions of school professionals regarding prenatal substance exposure*. Theses, Dissertations and Capstones. 1229. https://mds.marshall.edu/etd/1229

Milat, A. J., Bauman, A., & Redman, S. (2015). Narrative review of models and success factors for scaling up public health interventions. *Implementation Science; IS*, *10*(1), 113. doi:10.118613012-015-0301-6 PMID:26264351

National Association for College Admission Counseling. (2018). *State-by-state student-to-counselor ratio report*. https://www.nacacnet.org/news--publications/Research/state-by-state-student-to-counselor-ratio-report2/

National Association of School Psychologists. (2021). *Shortages in school psychology: Challenges to meeting the growing needs of U.S. students and schools.* https://www.nasponline.org/resources-and-publications/resources-and-podcasts/school-psychology/shortages-in-school-psychology-resource-guide

Nickerson, A. B., Cook, E. E., Cruz, M. A., & Parks, T. W. (2019). Transfer of school crisis prevention and intervention training, knowledge, and skills: Training, trainee, and work environment predictors. *School Psychology Review*, *48*(3), 237–250. doi:10.17105/SPR-2017-0140.V48-3

Pakenham, K. I. (2015). Training in acceptance and commitment therapy fosters self-care in clinical psychology trainees. *Clinical Psychologist*, *21*(3), 186–194. doi:10.1111/cp.12062

Park, E.-Y., & Shin, M. (2020). A meta-analysis of special education teachers' burnout. *SAGE Open*, *10*(2). Advance online publication. doi:10.1177/2158244020918297

Prothero, A. (2022). School counselors and psychologists remain scarce even as needs rise. *Education Week*, *41*(24).

Rosenfield, P. L. (1992). The potential of transdisciplinary research for sustaining and extending linkages between the health and social sciences. *Social Science & Medicine*, *35*(11), 1343-1357. doi:10.1016/0277-9536(92)90038-R

Salinger, R. (2019). Empirically based practices to address disability stigma in the classroom. *Journal of Applied School Psychology*, *36*(3), 324–345. doi:10.1080/15377903.2020.1749203

Shinn, M. R., & Walker, H. M. (2010). *Interventions for achievement and behavior problems in a three-tier model including RTI.* National Association of School Psychologists.

Siegel, S. (2005). Drug tolerance, drug addiction, and drug anticipation. *Current Directions in Psychological Science: A Journal of the American Psychological Society*, *14*(6), 296-300. doi:10.1111/j.0963-7214.2005.00384.x

Stoiber, K. C. (2014). A comprehensive framework for multitiered systems of support in school psychology. In P. L. Harrison & A. Thomas (Eds.), *Best practices in school psychology: Data-based and collaborative decision making* (pp. 41–70). National Association of School Psychologists.

Stokols, D., Hall, K. L., Taylor, B. K., & Moser, R. P. (2008). The science of team science: Overview of the field and introduction to the supplement. *American Journal of Preventive Medicine*, *35*(2, 2S), S77–S89. doi:10.1016/j.amepre.2008.05.002 PMID:18619407

Sugai, G., & Horner, R. H. (2009). Responsiveness-to-intervention and school-wide positive Behavior supports: Integration of multi-tiered system approaches. *Exceptionality: The Official Journal of the Division for Research of the Council for Exceptional Children*, *17*(4), 223–237. doi:10.1080/09362830903235375

Sutfin, E. A. (2021). School psychology shortages in West Virginia. *Theses, Dissertations and Capstones*. 1347. https://mds.marshall.edu/etd/1347

Sutherland, K. S., Wehby, J. H., & Copeland, S. R. (2000). Effect of varying rates of behavior-specific praise on the on-task behavior of students with EBD. *Journal of Emotional and Behavioral Disorders*, *8*(1), 2–8. doi:10.1177/106342660000800101

Tiano, J., & McNeil, C. (2006). Training head start teachers in behavior management using parent-child interaction therapy; A preliminary investigation. *Journal of Early and Intensive Behavior Intervention: JEIBI, 3*(2), 220–233. doi:10.1037/h0100334

Todd, R. (2019, October 9). *Inside West Virginia's overwhelmed foster care system*. https://www.marketplace.org/2019/10/09/inside-west-virginias-overwhelmed-foster-care-system/

United States Department of Education. (2017). *Teacher shortage areas nationwide listing: 1990-1991 through 2017-2018*. https://www2.ed.gov/about/offices/list/ope/pol/tsa.html

Wehby, J. H., Symons, F. J., & Shores, R. E. (1995). A descriptive analysis of aggressive behavior in classrooms for children with emotional and behavioral disorders. *Behavioral Disorders, 20*(2), 87–105. doi:10.1177/019874299502000207

West Virginia Department of Education. (2017a). *Teacher vacancies reach crisis level*. https://wvmetronews.com/2017/02/20/teacher-vacancies-reach-crisis-level/

West Virginia Department of Education. (2017b). *Personnel data report*. https://wvde.us/finance-and-administration/school-finance/financial-and-certified-list-reports/

West Virginia Department of Education. (2017c). *Second month enrollment count*. https://zoomwv.k12.wv.us/Dashboard/portalHome.jsp

West Virginia Department of Health and Human Resources. (2018). *DHHR releases neonatal abstinence syndrome data for 2017*. https://dhhr.wv.gov/News/2018/Pages/DHHR-Releases-Neonatal-Abstinence-Syndrome-Data-for-2017-.aspx

West Virginia Department of Health and Human Resources. (2022). *West Virginia celebrates national foster care month*. https://dhhr.wv.gov/News/2022/Pages/West-Virginia-Celebrates-National-Foster-Care-Month.aspx

Whitney, D. G., & Peterson, M. D. (2019). U.S. national and state-level prevalence of mental health disorders and disparities of mental health care use in children. *JAMA Pediatrics, 173*(4), 389–391. doi:10.1001/jamapediatrics.2018.5399 PMID:30742204

Williams, T. M. (2022). *Preservice candidate's knowledge of crisis preparedness in schools: The prepare model* [Unpublished program evaluation]. Marshall University.

Winstanley, E. L., & Stover, A. N. (2019). The impact of the opioid epidemic on children and adolescents. *Clinical Therapeutics, 41*(9), 1655–1662. doi:10.1016/j.clinthera.2019.06.003 PMID:31303278

Woitaszewski, S., Crepeau-Hobson, F., Conolly, C., & Cruz, M. (2018). Rules, requirements, and resources for school-based threat assessment: A fifty state analysis. *California School Psychologist, 22*(2), 125–134. doi:10.100740688-017-0161-y

*WVU researchers investigate the impact of the statewide opioid crisis on teachers.* (2019, March 13). https://wvutoday.wvu.edu/stories/2019/03/13/wvu-researchers-investigate-the-impact-of-the-statewide-opioid-crisis-on-teachers

Zgierska, A. E., Miller, M. M., Rabago, D. P., Hilliard, F., McCarthy, P., Cowan, P., & Salsitz, E. A. (2021). Language matters: It is time we change how we talk about addiction and its treatment. *Journal of Addiction Medicine, 15*(1), 10–12. https://doi.org/10.1097/ADM.0000000000000674

## ADDITIONAL READING

Barnard, M., & McKeganey, N. (2004). The impact of parental problem drug use on children: What is the problem and what can be done to help? *Addiction, 5*(5), 552–559. doi:10.1111/j.1360-0443.2003.00664.x PMID:15078229

Brock, S. E., Nickerson, A. B., Louvar Reeves, M. A., Conolly, C. N., Jimerson, S. R., Pesce, R. C., & Lazzaro, B. R. (2016). *School crisis prevention and intervention: The PREPaRE model* (2nd ed.). National Association of School Psychologists.

Cornell, D. (2018). *Comprehensive school threat assessment guidelines: Intervention and support to prevent violence*. School Threat Assessment Consultants LLC.

McNeil, C. B., & Hebree-Kigin, T. L. (2010). *Parent-child interaction therapy* (2nd ed.). Springer. doi:10.1007/978-0-387-88639-8

Woitaszewski, S., Crepeau-Hobson, F., Conolly, C., & Cruz, M. (2017). 2018;). Rules, requirements, and resources for school-based threat assessment: A fifty state analysis. *California School Psychologist, 22*(2), 125–134. doi:10.100740688-017-0161-y

## KEY TERMS AND DEFINITIONS

**Burnout:** Feelings of emotional and physical exhaustion, cynicism, ineffectiveness, and detachment often due to continual stress in the workplace.

**Evidence-Based Intervention:** A strategy or practice that has been proven to be effective by objective data from research.

**Interdisciplinary:** Relating to two or more academic disciplines or areas of study.

**Partnerships:** Two or more people, groups or organizations working together to achieve a common goal.

**Self-Care:** Being cognizant of one's needs and taking action to sustain or improve one's well-being health, and happiness.

**Threat-Assessment:** The process of determining the credibility and seriousness of a threat and deciding whether the threat will become a reality.

**Trauma:** An experience that is very distressing or disturbing and can generate a variety of emotional, behavioral, physical, and/or cognitive reactions in an individual.

# Chapter 23
# Social Emotional Development and Early Childhood Mental Health:
## Special Education and Social Work Collaboration

**Maryssa Kucskar Mitsch**
https://orcid.org/0000-0002-9285-3478
*San Francisco State University, USA*

**Brett Collins**
*San Francisco State University, USA*

**Amber Friesen**
*San Francisco State University, USA*

**Jocelyn Clare Reyno Hermoso**
https://orcid.org/0000-0001-7472-5504
*San Francisco State University, USA*

## ABSTRACT

*This chapter describes Project Adversity and Resiliency Interventions for Social Emotional Development in Early Childhood (Project ARISE), a preservice interdisciplinary training for early childhood special education (ECSE) and social workers (SW) to support young children and their families with high-intensity social emotional needs who require early childhood mental health support (ECMH) through collaborative and inclusive services. One key to understanding why many young children continue to be excluded from inclusive settings is understanding the differences between disciplines, as well as systemic inequities. To address these challenges, the program honors a holistic and interrelated development approach within the tenets of ECMH. This chapter begins with an overview of the program's essential theoretical frameworks. Then, the chapter shares key elements that define the program. Finally, the chapter shares reflections and next steps for interdisciplinary programmatic development.*

## INTRODUCTION

Experiences and interactions in early childhood impact overall development, leaving a lasting impression on learning, physical, and mental health outcomes of young children (Center for the Developing Child at Harvard University [CDCHU], 2016). Developmentally appropriate practice recognizes children as part of families and their communities, where young children begin to develop a sense of self, identity, and belonging, while beginning to construct ideas of differences (Derman-Sparks et al., 2020; National Association for the Education of Young Children [NAEYC], 2020a). In the early years, it is vital young children have enriching learning experiences and supportive, nurturing adults to support them in acknowledging and valuing differences in others. Moreover, high-quality early childhood learning environments and practitioners can support this by fostering positive self-awareness, comfort, and joy with human diversity in themselves and others (Derman-Sparks & Edwards, 2019).

Equipping practitioners with the knowledge, skills, and dispositions to support the holistic interrelated development of young children with disabilities and their families who are from culturally and linguistically diverse (CLD) backgrounds is critical. Practitioners, institutions of higher education (IHEs), and governing bodies share a responsibility to prioritize and promote high-quality early childhood education for all young children, regardless of race, ethnicity, native language, gender, ability, socioeconomic, and other characteristics (American Federation of State, County, Municipal Employees et al., 2020). A component of professional preparation is the theoretical frameworks included in programs (e.g., antibias education); other essential pieces include opportunities for practice and feedback throughout their program. Practitioners must have opportunities to learn with and about individuals of different personal (e.g., disability, race) and professional backgrounds (e.g., training field, experiences) to equitably provide positive early learning experiences for young CLD children with disabilities and their families (NAEYC, 2019).

With limited to no training in preservice preparation programs, it is unreasonable to expect new practitioners to know best practices for collaboration and working with related fields once they enter the workforce. It is time for IHEs and disciplines who work with young children with disabilities and their families to remove discipline silos so they can embrace the healthy development of disciplinary identities that includes the spirit of collaboration and partnership. Interdisciplinary personnel preparation is more important than ever to serve young children with disabilities and their families from CLD backgrounds in inclusive learning environments. Collaborative efforts must shift to a more equity-empowered and interdisciplinary focus (Blanchard et al., 2021; NAEYC, 2019). The Project Adversity and Resiliency Interventions for Social Emotional Development in Early Childhood (Project ARISE) values and mission align with the empowerment of families and other practitioners to have strong partnerships within and across interdisciplinary teams.

The Project ARISE program at San Francisco State University (SF State) is a 325K personnel preparation grant funded through the Office of Special Education Programs (OSEP) in the U.S. Department of Education. The purpose of Project ARISE is to provide preservice interdisciplinary training for early childhood special education (ECSE) and social workers (SW) to support young children and their families with high-intensity social emotional needs who require early childhood mental health support (ECMH) through collaborative and inclusive services. Project ARISE is an equity-focused interdisciplinary preparation program that forged a new cross-college collaboration that is the first of its kind at SF State. Project ARISE seeks to address state and nationwide shortages of high-quality professionals trained to deliver family centered, racially and culturally responsive, and child welfare-focused services for young children with social emotional needs who are from diverse backgrounds and exposed to adverse experiences. To do this, Project ARISE has committed to: (a) recruiting scholars from nontraditional (e.g., career switchers, para-educators) and unrepresented backgrounds (e.g., race, ethnicity, native language), (b) providing shared coursework, (c) providing shared learning experiences (e.g., institutes/conferences), (d) providing coordinated field experiences, and (e) ongoing scholar support.

Project ARISE was created to address the shortage of ECSE and SW practitioners in which highly qualified, culturally competent ECSE and SW professionals are in great demand. Early childhood is defined as the education of young children from birth through age 8 (NAEYC, 2020a). Practitioners from both ECSE and SW play critical roles in assessment, intervention, inclusion, child welfare, and family support. Together, they can address ECMH and social emotional support needs that are foundational for later development, growth, and learning for young children with disabilities and their families. By providing interdisciplinary training and funding to scholars, Project ARISE will add 36 practitioners (18 ECSE and 18 SW from 2022–2027) to the field by the end of the program. Through intentionally curated content, Project ARISE scholars will engage in: (a) shared coursework, (b) shared supplemental learning opportunities, and (c) coordinated field experiences that center ECMH and inclusion. These three pillars of Project ARISE train scholars to be equipped with the knowledge, skills, and dispositions to work as part of interdisciplinary teams providing high-quality services for young CLD children with high-intensity social emotional needs and their families.

This chapter presents the shared frameworks that ground Project ARISE, an equity-focused interdisciplinary preparation program between ECSE and SW programs. These shared frameworks serve as a beacon for Project ARISE, an understanding of the approach to services for young CLD children with high-intensity social emotional needs and their families. This approach includes situating the impact of sustained adversity, trauma, stress, and/or negative impact of systemic inequities and racism, discrimination, and oppression on developmental and life outcomes for individuals, topics that have been historically overlooked or seen as unrelated in ECSE personnel preparation. Accordingly, the elements of Project ARISE are designed to provide a more fluid and interconnected experience and training for equity-driven service providers. An overview of ECMH systems of care is shared to describe how the program approaches the whole child and interrelated development. Following, additional theoretical frameworks, including social justice, antioppressive practices, and antibias education, are examined. These frameworks and critical concepts are shared for readers to reflect on their personnel preparation programs. The chapter transitions to highlight Project ARISE's key elements and foundations of the interdisciplinary preparation. Finally, this chapter shares a reflection on lessons learned in programmatic development and next steps for the future of Project ARISE. Discussion questions are included at the end of the chapter for readers to reflect on their experiences related to shared ECMH concepts and interdisciplinary preparation.

## CURRENT SHORTAGE IN HIGHLY QUALIFIED PRACTITIONERS SERVING YOUNG CHILDREN AND THEIR FAMILIES

Project ARISE was created to address the shortage of ECSE and SW practitioners in the nation's most diverse and populated state, California, in which highly qualified, culturally competent ECSE and SW professionals are in great demand (California Department of Education [CDE], 2020). In this chapter, the term "practitioners" refers to professionals who support the learning, development, care, and overall well-being of young children identified as at-risk and with disabilities and their families, including but not limited to ECSE, SW, and early childhood educators. A growing number of students receive special education under the Individuals with Disabilities Education Act (IDEA; 2004), with 14% or 7.3 million scholars ages 3–21 receiving special education services in 2019–2020 (USDOE, 2021). High quality and effective, individualized services are challenging given the national shortage of highly qualified personnel in special education and related services, including early intervention, early childhood, and social work (American Association for Employment in Education, 2016–2017; Bruder, 2010; U.S. Department of Education [USDOE], 2017; U.S. Bureau of Labor Statistics, 2021b). The rate of child, family, and school SWs are projected to grow significantly faster than the average occupation over the next decade. Nationally, 98% of school districts report a special educator shortage, requiring more than 28,000 additional special educators through 2029; over 181,000 child, family, and school SWs are needed for the same time period (U.S. Bureau of Labor Statistics, 2021a).

A combination of practitioner shortages and practitioner burnout is grave. The practitioner burnout specific to special education (see Brunsting et al., 2014; Nelson et al., 2020) and SW (Lloyd et al., 2009) are well documented. In turn, prevention and awareness of burnout must be considered in recruitment and retention of practitioners. Strategies to improve wellness rarely focus on systemic changes to practitioner preparation. As outlined in *Self-Care in Social Work*, it is vital for practitioners to feel a sense of self-efficacy, which refers to "the judgments we make of our personal capability to carry out particular activities and produce positive results" (Cox & Steiner, 2013, p. 77). Faculty routinely see scholars feel inadequately prepared to manage issues outside their direct area of practice, which greatly impact the well-being of the children they serve. Practice-related challenges have led to a widening of the research-to-practice gap (Teasley, 2016). For example, a center director learns about lead poisoning but feels powerless to address it on a community level; a classroom teacher senses relational strain between a child and their caregiver but does not feel competent to intervene in that domain. Therefore, interdisciplinary collaboration is necessary to break down silos of care preemptively and to increase practitioner confidence and competence in areas of intersectionality that will have a long-term effect on practitioner wellness and retention.

In addressing these shortages and challenges to preparation, there is a need to recruit and retain fully licensed personnel with diverse linguistic and cultural backgrounds representative of the children they serve. This point is particularly relevant as the nation's student population continues to diversify, requiring more highly qualified, culturally competent practitioners. The National Voices Project reported 74% of teachers of all races had received preservice education related to cultural competence (Iruka et al., 2020), but this is not enough. Young children from marginalized populations continue to be placed in special education disproportionately, especially in preschool Part B Section 619 programs (Aratani et al., 2011; Meek et al., 2020). A key to understanding why many young children continue to be excluded from inclusive settings is understanding the philosophical and training differences between disciplines, impact of systemic inequities, and effective personnel preparation that is culturally responsive (Lawrence et al., 2016; Love & Beneke, 2021; Meek et al., 2020; U.S. Departments of Health and Human Services & Education [USHHS & DOE], 2014).

An initial step for Project ARISE was sharing this research and discussing interdisciplinary training solutions with the project's advisory board. Together, they came to a shared understanding of the program's approach and philosophy in centering equity, ECMH, and inclusive services for young CLD children with high-intensity social emotional needs and their families.

## THEORETICAL FRAMEWORKS GUIDING PROJECT ARISE

Multiple theoretical frameworks underpin ECMH and thus were needed to guide the work within Project ARISE. In considering these frameworks, different disciplines can connect their role in preparing the workforce to provide equitable learning experiences for young children with diverse identities and learning needs and their families. Specifically, the frameworks guiding Project ARISE include family systems framework, systems of care in ECMH, social justice framework and antioppressive practices, and antibias education. These frameworks are discussed next.

## Family Systems Framework

Effective models of support for young children recognize the interconnectedness of development and growth within the family, community, and culture in which they live. A whole child perspective acknowledges the uniqueness and complexity of an individual and subsequently considers an array of services and supports including, but not limited to "social, emotional, behavioral, developmental, promotive-protective, prevention, early identification, early intervention, and referrals to community practitioners and resources for intensive care" (Aragon et al., 2020, p. 18).

For young children, the family unit plays an instrumental and often primary role in a child's security, development, and growth. Within this chapter, a family is defined broadly to include anyone identified by each other as a family unit. This unit may include biologically related people but also may account for individuals chosen or joined by other means. Given the importance of early attachment and the necessity of depending on adults, any type of services and support for young children includes practices that involve and empower a child's identified family unit (Division of Early Childhood [DEC], 2014). The DEC (2014) Recommended Practices were developed to provide guidance to practitioners and families regarding effective ways to support learning and development for young children with diagnosed delays and/or disabilities. These practices include:

- Family centered practices are characterized by a respectful, individualized approach that is responsive to a family's unique circumstances, strengths, and goals.
- Family capacity-building practices seek to empower families by strengthening existing knowledge and skills to promote new learning and self-efficacy in their caregiving beliefs and practices.
- Family and professional collaborations center on practices that build relationships between family members and practitioners to support the development of a child and the family.

Honoring a young child and their family can be supported by having a theoretical framework in which to learn about the complexity, fluidity, and goals of a family. The Family Systems Framework, a predominant theoretical perspective in family studies and family therapy (e.g., Broderick, 1993; White et al., 2019), has been used to consider the ways disability can impact the roles, interactions, and functions of a family (Turnbull et al., 1984, 2014). Central to the Family Systems Framework are four core assumptions: (a) all family members are interconnected; (b) a family can be best understood as a whole, or system, rather than individual parts; (c) the family system affects and is affected by the environmental/context in which it resides, and; (d) conceptualizing a family as a system is a way of organizing and understanding a family rather than an actual physical phenomenon (White et al., 2019).

In applying the Family Systems Framework to families that include children with disabilities, Turnbull and colleagues (1984) proposed different components that dynamically interact and change, sometimes visualized as a set of interlocking gears. These components include family characteristics, family interactions, family functions, and family life cycle.

Family characteristics refer to the identities of the individuals in the family unit. This component includes, but is not limited to, each family member's personality, values, beliefs, race, culture, language/communication, disabilities, socioeconomic status, and more. Family characteristics are viewed as inputs into the family system that respond to and influence a family's interactions.

Family interactions are composed of the relationships between the different individuals and subsystems within a family unit, including the extended family, marital, parental, and sibling interactions. These relationships are considered in terms of their adaptability and cohesiveness when faced with change and/or the presence of stressors. The output of these interactions will contribute and respond to the needs, or functions, of the family.

Family functions are composed of the ways a family seeks to meet a wide variety of needs. This component may include needs related to economics, employment, recreation, socialization, education, self-esteem, affection, daily care, health, and more. What a family prioritizes or wants support with regarding how their family functions are deeply contextualized within their experiences, identities, beliefs, culture, and more.

A final component within the Family Systems Framework model is the family life cycle. This cycle addresses the inevitable and constant changes a family experiences over time, which can include a wide array of situations (e.g., the addition or loss of a family member, transitions to new jobs or schools, and relocating to a new community). Change will impact the input (i.e., family characteristics) and outputs (i.e., family functions of a family). Families are complex systems, and no two are alike. It is important to honor the diversity and intricacies of families due to their primary role in the development of young children. In learning from families and understanding their family systems, meaningful systems and supports can emerge, including supporting ECMH.

## Intersection of ECMH and SW

In merging the fields of SW and ECSE, ECMH finds a prominent place. Major theoretical underpinnings of the Project ARISE curriculum include adverse childhood experiences (ACEs), toxic stress, ECMH systems of care, social justice and antioppressive practices, and antibias education—including antiableist pedagogy. Project ARISE commits to the parallel process of improving scholar experience and improving access to higher education for nontraditional and unrepresented scholar–practitioners, increasing overall representation in the ECSE and SW fields.

## Adverse Childhood Experiences and Toxic Stress

As part of Project ARISE, SWs bring specialized knowledge in trauma-informed care and restorative practices, which can be applied across disciplines. Experts continue to call for early intervention to prevent the significant impact of toxic stress on individuals and its long-term effects on society (Harris, 2018; Liming & Grube, 2018; Nelson et al., 2020). More than six out of 10 Americans have experienced one or more adverse childhood experiences (ACEs), potentially traumatic events or environmental aspects that may impact a child's (0–17 years) sense of safety, stability, and bonding (Centers for Disease Control and Prevention [CDC], 2019). ACEs can include an individual's experiences with or witness of abuse, violence, mental illness, and family substance use (CDC, 2019). Depending on the intensity, frequency, and duration of these stressors, sustained adversity or trauma may lead to toxic stress, negatively affecting brain development (CDCHU, 2020). Though the terms trauma and toxic stress are not interchangeable, they are often misused, creating a barrier to effective intervention and policy (Amaya-Jackson et al., 2021). Accordingly, it is vital to promote consistency of understanding and application of interventions across disciplines.

Whereas ECSE tends to focus on intervention on an individual child level, SW can help expand the focus to a systems level. It is critical to recognize young children who are Black, Indigenous, and/or People of Color (BIPOC) have their overall well-being, health, and development negatively impacted by systemic inequities and racism, discrimination, and oppression (CDCHU, 2020; Heard-Garris et al., 2018; USDOE, 2016; USHSS & DOE, 2014). Trauma-informed supports on individual and systemic levels that counterbalance these negative effects are necessary for young children, families, and communities to develop resilience, but practitioners are rarely trained with the competencies required to address both simultaneously. Targeted interventions, positive social interactions, and supportive learning environments are essential for the success of these intersectional and interdisciplinary efforts (Blanchard et al., 2021; CDCHU, 2016; Derman-Sparks & Edwards, 2019; NAEYC, 2019).

## Systems of Care in ECMH

The field of ECMH focuses on emotional, psychological, social, and overall health and well-being, including aspects that impact daily life and routines (CDC, 2022a). With roots in the field of SW and traditional psychotherapy, ECMH has grown to influence and require various sectors and professions. Due to the relational context of social emotional health goals, and the mechanism by which a child's sense of self is developed, it is essential the child-caregiver dyad be the focus of any developmental goal or intervention (Lieberman & Horn, 2005).

Dyadic interventions alone are insufficient to improve the health of the family and the communities to which young children and their families belong. The protective factors framework has been shown to increase children and families' overall well-being and should be promoted in any and all early intervention efforts. Protective factors include: (a) nurturing and attachment; (b) parental/family knowledge for child development; (c) parental resilience; (d) social connections; (e) concrete support for parents/families; and (f) social and emotional competence of children (USDHHS, 2022). Both directly and indirectly, protective factors support the social emotional development of young children, serving as a strong foundation for overall holistic development. Though entwined, elements of social emotional development in the early years are foundational for overall healthy development, including later academic performance, mental health, and relationships (National Scientific Council on the Developing Child, 2004).

There is a necessity to advance policy and systems change for whole child development related to social, emotional, cognitive, physical, psychological, and academic needs (Learning Policy Institute, 2022). Just as child development must be viewed as an interdependent and dynamic process, so must the fields of mental health and early intervention. Though social emotional development, whole child, protective factors, and systems change are all essential components of more equitable early intervention services, they cannot be practiced independently of each other. Interdisciplinary collaboration is essential if preparation programs are to effectively support practitioners and reduce the impact of racism and ableism on the children, families, and communities served.

## Social Justice Framework and Antioppressive Practices

As important as ECMH interventions are, they are not immune to the realities of racism, ableism, and other forms of oppression—often perpetuated by ECMH practitioners themselves. Therefore, social justice framework and antioppressive practices are vital to improve the overall well-being of families and communities and reduce the potential for this harm to occur within personnel preparation training programs and between disciplines. The social justice framework includes actions and beliefs that attempt to address oppression and inequity while promoting access, participation, and freedom for all individuals. Particularly, the social justice framework seeks to evolve policies, practices, curricula, and institutions that oppress groups of individuals (Love & Beneke, 2021). Commitment to a social justice framework within personnel preparation requires individuals to continuously seek to understand and uproot patterns of injustice and hold each other and ourselves accountable. Accountability includes understanding one's actions, thoughts, and beliefs that perpetuate, disrupt, or are passive to unjust policies or practices.

The application of the social justice framework to personnel preparation training programs and interdisciplinary systems can and should also be guided by antioppressive practices (AOP; see Figure 1). AOP recognizes the structural origins of oppression and promotes social transformation by utilizing critical theories, including feminist, Marxist, postmodernist, Indigenous, poststructuralist, anticolonial, and antiracist theories, among others (Baines, 2007). It works to eradicate oppression and challenge power structures through collective institutional and societal changes (Sakamoto & Pitner, 2005). Application of these practices in practitioner preparation is vital to reducing the inherent ableism within IHEs thereby increasing diversity and representation of practitioners in the field. The five critical practice principles of antioppressive practices are:

1. Critical Reflection on Self in Practice
2. Critical Assessment of Service Users' Experiences of Oppression
3. Empowering Service Users
4. Working in Partnership
5. Minimal Intervention (Healy, 2014)

A shared value of both the ECSE and SW programs is intentionality around whose voices are elevated. Project ARISE continues this by inviting individuals with diverse intersecting identities and lived experiences to share their stories with Project ARISE scholars throughout the program. In doing so, Project ARISE works toward and advocates for more equitable service delivery models for young CLD children with social emotional needs and their families. Consequently, Project ARISE commits to ensuring the equity-focused interdisciplinary program is integrated, intensive, collaborative, and includes applications with multiple opportunities for feedback.

## Antibias Education

Practitioners who work with young children in inclusive environments who are culturally responsive and justice-driven are indisputable (Love & Beneke, 2021; USDHHS, 2014). Within these educational and disability spaces sits antibias education and antiableism. As long as a distinction between special education and general education continues, negative perceptions of disability will continue to exist, and scholars with disabilities will continue to be placed in separate learning environments. Antibias education framework seeks to create safe and supportive learning environments for every child with four core goals: identity, diversity, justice, and activism (Derman-Sparks & Edwards, 2019). Lalvani and Bacon (2019) emphasized how "early childhood classrooms should be spaces that reflect the full range of human differences, and in which all dimensions of human variations are valued" (p. 88). Antibias education emphasizes how young children can be supported to feel empowered to do what is right when faced with injustice in themselves or others and honor human diversity without superiority (Derman-Sparks & Edwards, 2019). This same approach could and should be modeled through the educational experiences of practitioners in the field. Individually and together, practitioners must feel comfortable addressing bias and navigating these foundational conversations as learning opportunities arise in classrooms, programs, and support teams to achieve inclusive, equitable settings. Practitioners using social justice, antibias education, and equity-empowered frameworks are essential for the success of shared, inclusive efforts (Blanchard et al., 2021; CDCHU, 2016; Derman-Sparks & Edwards, 2019; NAEYC, 2019).

As long as there continues to be a distinction between special education and general education, negative perceptions of disability will continue to exist and scholars with disabilities will continued to be placed in separate learning environments. Specifically, young children tend to be in more restrictive environments; only 35% of 3-year-olds, 44% of 4-year-olds, and 53% of 5-year-olds receive most of their services in inclusive environments (Meek et al., 2020). Creating the physical space or learning environments for all young children is a start, but merely placing young children in a setting does not ensure all children are able to participate meaningfully in that learning space. Three defining features of high-quality inclusion are access, participation, and support (DEC & NAEYC, 2009), which include individualized accommodations and unique supports for each child.

DEC (2020) named six areas as the focus of their priority issues agenda for the near future: achieving high-quality inclusion; acknowledging and addressing bias; responding appropriately to child behavior; creating and maintaining strong family partnerships; adequately equipping a highly effective workforce; and providing high-quality environments, interactions, instruction, and supports. Project ARISE recognizes these six areas and has aligned the program's interdisciplinary training to them. Recognizing the negative ripple effect of bias and ableism, practitioners must feel confident in cocreating safe and welcoming learning environments with other disciplines that include a diverse range of learning differences. Individually and together, practitioners must feel comfortable addressing bias and navigating these foundational conversations as learning opportunities arise in classrooms, programs, and support teams to achieve inclusive, equitable settings. Practitioners using social justice, antibias education, and equity-empowered frameworks are essential for the success of shared, inclusive efforts (Blanchard et al., 2021; CDCHU, 2016; Derman-Sparks & Edwards, 2019; NAEYC, 2019).

## OVERVIEW OF PROJECT ARISE

Project ARISE is a new cross-college collaboration. The first of its kind at SF State, it brings together expertise between the Master of Social Work (MSW), Pupil Personnel Services Credential (PPSC), and the Master of Arts (MA) and credential program in ECSE. Initial brainstorming from 2021 revealed similarities in content and philosophy in how to approach working with young children and their families with different lived experiences. Thus began Project ARISE's pathway to develop an interdisciplinary program focused on a shared commitment to the family unit, systems of care, social justice, and anti-oppressive practices, antibias education, and inclusion for young CLD children with social emotional

*Table 1. Project ARISE Alignment with Whole Child Policy's Core Recommendations*

| Whole child policy recommendation | Project ARISE component/outcome/goals |
|---|---|
| Building adult capacity and expertise | Practitioner preparation systems that prepare scholars as leaders with the knowledge, skills, and dispositions needed to support whole child developmental needs and support scholars' development of 21st-century skills. |
| Resigning curriculum, instruction, assessments, and accountability systems | Distance and blended learning models that are equity focused, offer personalized instruction, and take advantage of the different settings in which learning can take place. |
| Transforming learning environments | Support relationship-centered learning environments that are designed to facilitate strong relationships and trust among scholars, staff, and families/caregivers. |
| Investing resources equitably and efficiently | Allocate funding to ensure scholars are prepared to support young children with disabilities and their families from CLD backgrounds (when available); Allocate mentoring resources and supports for scholars. |

needs and their families. Project ARISE is a new cross-college collaboration, so the first year of funding (2022–2027) is a dedicated planning year. Prior to and during the planning year, Project ARISE personnel consulted and received feedback from the program's advisory board.

Project ARISE's strengths include: (a) robust ECSE and SW programs; (b) dedicated faculty with area expertise; (c) strong, diverse community partnerships; and (d) the use of technology. The university is a designated Hispanic-serving institution (c) and Asian American Native American Pacific Islander-serving institution (AANAPISI). Situated in a diverse urban center, the program also focuses on training nontraditional and underrepresented CLD scholars. Moreover, it was essential Project ARISE addressed elements of diversity, intersectionality, and culturally sustaining practices (Gay, 2018; Ladson-Billings, 1995, 2014; Paris & Alim, 2017) within the program to support scholars and young children and their families who program graduates would later serve in the field (Harry & Ocasio-Stoutenburg, 2020).

As a foundation for the partnership, Project ARISE agreed on a whole child and family approach to their collaboration, described in Table 1.

Project ARISE's scholar competencies and three key elements build from Table 1. Scholars interact with these competencies within three elements: shared coursework, shared supplemental learning opportunities, and coordinated field experiences. These are discussed in the following sections.

## Competencies

The foundation for Project ARISE competencies are the theoretical frameworks shared throughout this chapter: Family Systems Framework, adverse childhood experiences (ACEs), toxic stress, ECMH systems of care, social justice and antioppressive practices, and antibias education. It is from these frameworks in which we want the six competencies to grow from. There are six Project ARISE competencies detailed in Figure 1. The competencies consist of core knowledge, skills, and dispositions used to evaluate scholars who serve young CLD children with social emotional needs that require ECMH within inclusive early childhood settings and their families: (a) assessment; (b) natural environments and inclusive settings; (c) supports to positive facilitate interactions; (d) teaming and collaboration; (e) professional development

*Figure 1. Six Project ARISE Scholar Competencies*

[Figure showing six competency blocks: Assessment; Equity, Social Justice and Honoring Diversity; Facilitate Positive Interactions; Natural Environments and Inclusive Settings; Professional Development and Leadership; Teaming and Collaboration]

and leadership; and (f) equity, social justice and honoring diversity (CA Center for Infant-Family and ECMH, 2016; Council on Social Work Education [CSWE], 2015; DEC, 2020, 2014).

These competencies were created by integrating content from key professional organizations including DEC (2014, 2022), Council for Exceptional Children/DEC (2020), CSWE (2015), NAEYC (2019, 2020a, 2020b), and cross-disciplinary standards (Bruder et al., 2019). Project ARISE shared coursework, supplemental learning opportunities, and coordinated field experiences were selected, designed, and revised to facilitate practice and mastery of the six key professional competencies by graduation.

It is important for any practitioner preparation program to understand the impact of mental health on individuals, and, specifically, the impact on young children and their families. Specific ECMH resources that may be useful to individuals are shared in Table 2. For example, scholars read and participate in a book club in a shared course using "The Deepest Well: Healing the Long-Term Effects of Childhood Adversity" by Dr. Nadine Burke Harris (2018). Related, see Mitsch et al. (2022) for a detailed list of specific ECSE resources.

## Key Elements

Three key elements were established as part of Project ARISE: (a) shared coursework, (b) shared supplemental learning opportunities, and (c) coordinated field experiences (see Figure 2). These key elements are foundational to Project ARISE because attempts at interdisciplinary services often fall short and default to a multidisciplinary approach, where practitioners from different disciplines have minimal to no interaction (Little, 2020). While practitioners are expected to partner, they are rarely given the opportunity or guidance to develop the skills necessary for successful collaboration (Herrenkohl et al., 2021). The absence of a shared theoretical framework, purpose, ethics of teaming, or shared goals exacerbates these barriers (Bricker et al., 2020; CEC/DEC, 2020). Scholars from each program need to complete their own programmatic requirements, but it is important to have a high frequency of interactions and opportunities to build rapport to strengthen scholars' relationships over time.

*Table 2. Related ECMH Resources*

| Name | Location information |
|---|---|
| Diversity-Informed Tenets for Work with Infants, Children and Families | Irving Harris Foundation Professional Development Network Tenets Working Group https://cascw.umn.edu/wp-content/uploads/2021/10/tenets-2018.pdf |
| Early Childhood Mental Health - | Center for the Developing Child at Harvard University https://developingchild.harvard.edu/science/deep-dives/mental-health/ |
| The Body Keeps Score: Brain, Mind, and Body in the Healing of Trauma | van der Kolk, B. (2014). *The body keeps score: Brain, mind, and body in the healing of trauma.* Penguin |
| "The Brain Architects" Podcast | Center for the Developing Child at Harvard University https://developingchild.harvard.edu/collective-change/communicating-the-science/the-brain-architects-podcast/ |
| The Deepest Well: Healing the Long-Term Effects of Childhood Adversity | Harris, N. B. (2018). *The deepest well: Healing the long-term effects of childhood adversity.* Houghton Mifflin Harcourt Publishing Company. |
| "The Earliest" Podcast | Zero to Three https://www.zerotothree.org/resources/4381-the-earliest-a-new-podcast-from-zero-to-three |
| The National Child Traumatic Stress Network | https://www.nctsn.org/ |
| Positive Behavior Support (PBS) Process, Teaching Tools, and Resources | https://www.pyramidmodel.org/ |
| Think Babies Infant and Early Childhood Mental Health Resource List | https://www.zerotothree.org/resources/2195-think-babies-infant-and-early-childhood-mental-health-resource-list |
| What Happened to You?: Conversations on Trauma, Resilience, and Healing. | Perry, B. D., & Winfrey, O. (2021). *What happened to you?: Conversations on trauma, resilience, and healing.* Flatiron Books. |
| *Whole Child Policy Toolkit* | Learning Policy Institute https://www.wholechildpolicy.org/ |

*Note.* Resources shared alphabetically

## Shared Coursework and Graduate Certificates

Project ARISE scholars enroll in one shared course each semester for a total of four shared courses. The shared courses from each program were revised to ensure they are aligned with evidence-based practices (EBP) and guidance documents in ECSE (e.g., DEC, 2014; CEC/DEC, 2020), SW (e.g., CSWE, 2015), joint professional organizations (Bruder et al., 2019), and state credential requirements. Scholars are paired to work collaboratively on all major assignments in each of the four shared courses to encourage sharing ideas, strategies, and further discourse. As part of the shared coursework, scholars are also required to include evidence of growing competencies. Through facilitated reflective practice (Heffron & Murch, 2010), scholars self-identify learning gaps and adapt their individualized learning goals.

The four shared courses contribute to scholars earning one of two graduate certificates. ECSE scholars complete the Trauma Informed SW Practices graduate certificate that focuses on child welfare practices with young children and families, SW practices in education and natural environments, understanding ACEs, and systemic ECMH strategies to enhance the positive impact of collaboration. SW scholars complete the Supporting Inclusive Early Childhood Practices graduate certificate focusing on inclusive practices for all children, child development and assessment, and family/community partnerships. The ECSE graduate certificate had been previously established in the ECSE program; the Trauma Informed SW Practices graduate certificate was a new initiative that stemmed from the creation of Project ARISE.

*Figure 2. Key Elements of Project ARISE*

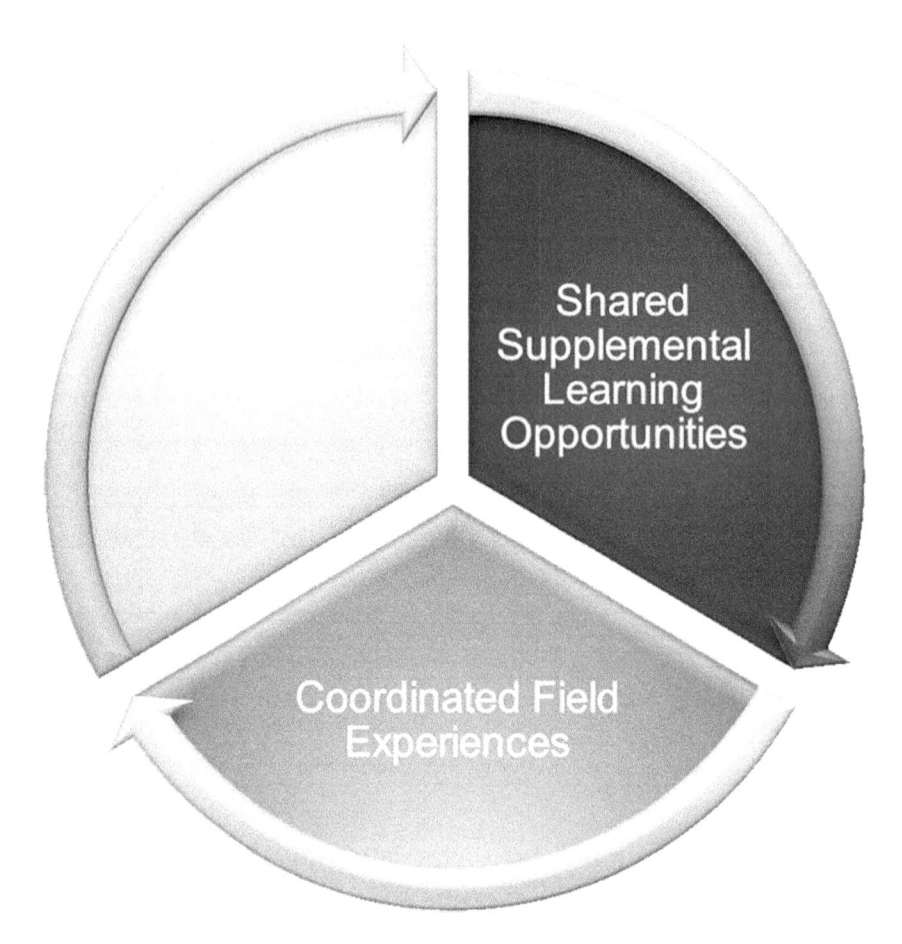

Both programs' coursework is delivered using a hybrid approach that combines on-campus and online coursework, employing small group forums, distance learning strategies, and a variety of technology (e.g., video, modules, interactive tools). In the design of each program's courses, adult learning principles (Rush & Shelden, 2020) and Universal Design for Learning (UDL; CAST, 2018) were used. In all, it would take scholars four (SW) or five semesters (ECSE) for scholars to graduate.

## Shared Learning Experiences

As part of the interdisciplinary Project ARISE program, three shared learning experiences were identified to support the interdisciplinary training of scholars together. Two of the shared learning experiences were long-standing events within the ECSE program, while the SW conference described next was developed as part of Project ARISE. All three shared learning experiences are embedded within shared coursework. When scholars are not enrolled in these specific courses that semester, they are required to participate in the experiences.

Every fall, the ECSE program hosts a Partnering with Families Institute. This institute provides an opportunity to bring community partners, families, and current scholars to share expertise and experiences about working with diverse families during a half-day event. Particularly, the event focuses on ensuring participants hear speakers from diverse lived experiences. Examples of speakers include family members with young children who have disabilities from CLD backgrounds, parents who identify as an individual with a disability, disabled individuals sharing their experiences in special education, family advocates and practitioners (e.g., occupational therapists, early interventionists, speech language therapists, SW).

The second shared learning experience is the long-standing Meaningful Collaborations in Early Childhood annual conference. Since 2014, the annual conference has brought together scholars and SF State students, alums, and community partners every spring. The event focused more on ECSE and early childhood educators in the early years. In an effort to grow collaboration across university programs, the event expanded to include speech language therapy and SW programs on campus. The full-day event includes a keynote speaker and interactive workshops led by practitioners (e.g., ECSE, SW, ECMH specialists), alumni (e.g., music and art therapists, ECMH specialists), community partners (e.g., field experience sites, local Parent Training and Information Center), and even university students or Project ARISE scholars. Conferences in the past focused on topics including antiracism, social emotional curriculum, intersectionality, culturally relevant content and pedagogy, equitable representation, and authenticity while re(finding) joy in one's work. Community partners are invited to set up booths to represent their nonprofits, school districts, and/or organizations during the lunch hour. In hopes of further growth and impact, Project ARISE personnel hope to open the event to a broader audience across the state, in particular inviting other ECSE, SW, and related services preparation programs and practitioners.

The third shared learning experience is the ECMH Institute. This event is a new development as part of Project ARISE, and at the time of publication, the envisioned half-day event has not yet taken place. The hope for the ECMH Institute is for the keynote speaker to be a SW leader in the community. Complementary interactive workshops and learning sessions aim to include practicing SWs and practitioners focused on ECMH and related disciplines. Topics for the workshops and sessions may include but are not limited to working with families, macro/micro-level systems change, advocacy, empowerment, and social change for those who have been marginalized, disenfranchised, and oppressed.

After each of the three shared learning experiences, Project ARISE scholars are asked to reflect individually, in small groups, and as a large group. Scholar reflections include written and verbal discussions at the event and/or in their courses. At the end of each event, participants complete evaluation forms used to inform future events and Project ARISE programmatic development. As part of past evaluations, participants shared how the virtual events provided access to individuals who typically would not have been able to participate (e.g., disability, health, work, childcare responsibilities). Though events were switched to virtual delivery due to the COVID-19 global pandemic, the event recordings allow current and future scholars, stakeholders, and partners to view the event as a whole or in parts later. The event recordings were added to online repositories program faculty had initiated (i.e., university learning management site, ECSE program's YouTube channel) as a way to build professional development resources for scholars, alumni, and stakeholders. In the future, Project ARISE's three shared learning experiences will be delivered in a hybrid flexible (HyFlex) format, allowing participants to join in person or synchronously online. Once again, events will be recorded for later viewing and engagement across California.

## Coordinated Field Experiences

The ECSE and SW programs both had extensive field experience requirements grounded in EBPs, providing opportunities to practice newly learned instructional skills and intervention strategies in the field. As part of Project ARISE, scholars complete some required hours (i.e., student teaching, fieldwork) within settings that provide opportunities to apply their knowledge and further their skills related to supporting young children with social emotional needs requiring ECMH support in inclusive settings. To find appropriate placements that simultaneously provide university student mentorship, faculty collaborate with one another and with community partners to meet everyone's needs. The goal is to find placements where Project ARISE scholars work in pairs or small groups of ECSE and SW scholars to apply, share, brainstorm, and reflect in the moment with peers from other disciplinary backgrounds—the essence of collaboration. Project ARISE has two dedicated personnel, one from ECSE and one from SW, to complete this goal. The coordinated field experiences expand on course assignments for the scholars and include additional assignments such as cocreating circle time activities and completing authentic assessments that are centered on ECMH and inclusive practices.

Scholars receive support in many ways during the coordinated field experiences: regular check-ins with their university supervisor, on-site mentor (either ECSE or SW practitioner), support from two Project ARISE dedicated-fieldwork personnel, and a one-unit seminar. The seminar provides a space for scholars to debrief their experiences, problem solve, and overall share their student teaching/fieldwork reflections. On-site mentors are current ECSE or SW practitioners who embody the mission and values of Project ARISE. To support ongoing reflective practice (Heffron & Murch, 2010) in these settings, scholars also complete a portfolio.

## Reflective Practice

Reflective practice is woven into all components of Project ARISE, including the three key elements, advising, mentoring and evaluation. Extending the critical consciousness of one's thoughts, beliefs, and actions sits reflective practice. A major component of antioppressive practices is the development of critical consciousness, which can be cultivated through reflective practice. While there are many definitions, in the context of infant and early childhood programs, reflective practice refers to:

*A way of working that spans disciplines and encourages staff members to a) consider the possible implications of their interventions while in the midst of their work; b) slow down, filter their thoughts, and more wisely choose actions and words; c) deepen their understanding of the contextual forces that affect their work; and d) take time afterward to consider their work and the related experiences in a way that influences their next steps. (Heffron & Murch, 2010, p. 6)*

In relation to early childhood, the intentional and ongoing routine of reflective practice is outlined in "Professional Standards and Competencies" by the NAEYC (2020b). Specifically, the document states:

*early childhood educators develop a habit of reflective practices, including integrating their knowledge and practices across all six standards in order to create optimal learning environments, design and implement curricula, use and refine instructional strategies, and interact with children and families whose language, race, ethnicity, culture, and social and economic status may be very different from educators' own backgrounds. (NAEYC, 2020b, p. 11)*

An element of the intersection of reflective practice and social justice is critically examining one's role in advocating for an equitable and inclusive service delivery model. Ableism and racism are deeply embedded within special education and historically, there has been oversight of intersectional identities of families (Harry & Ocasio-Stoutenburg, 2020). Federal data require us to face the impact of these systems on young children and their families, specifically the disproportionality of children from marginalized populations in special education and the higher likelihood they may experience discipline and/or expulsion, including in preschools (Aratani et al., 2011; USDHHS, 2014). Commitment to a social justice framework within personnel preparation requires individuals to continuously seek to understand and uproot patterns of injustice and hold each other and ourselves accountable. Accountability includes understanding one's actions, thoughts, and beliefs that either perpetuate, disrupt, or are passive to unjust policies or practices. Project ARISE is committed to holding each other and ourselves accountable to improve practitioner practices and IHE experiences for students who go on to impact young children and their families.

## Advising and Mentoring

While Project ARISE targets the recruitment of scholars from underrepresented and nontraditional backgrounds, individualizing scholar support is imperative to success. The program has a multipronged approach to scholar advising and mentoring to increase retention, graduation, and success in the field. Project ARISE supports the retention and continued success of all scholars through (a) an induction period, (b) individualized and group advising, (c) mentoring, and (d) fostering a professional learning community (PLC). Having multiple and ongoing supports for scholars allows adaptable advising and mentorship to scholars who are identified as at risk of failing or leaving the program.

Upon acceptance into Project ARISE, all scholars participate in an induction period. In addition to required attendance at college and department orientations, scholars also have Project ARISE responsibilities. The induction period includes the review of paperwork, agreements, and expectations of scholars. An overview of Project ARISE activities (shared coursework, supplemental learning opportunities, and coordinated field experiences) is also reviewed.

Scholars are paired with Project ARISE personnel in their respective ECSE or SW program who serve as their advisor. Scholars and advisors (Project ARISE personnel) have consistent meetings throughout each semester. Project ARISE personnel also teach many, if not all, of the shared courses. This structure provides regular opportunities to check in with scholars. Additionally, an individualized plan will be developed to support scholars needing or seeking further support in collaboration between Project ARISE personnel and the student. In previous projects, this has included weekly or biweekly text messaging, video conferences, and/or on campus check-ins.

For mentoring, incoming scholars are paired with a more advanced student in the program as a means of peer mentoring and contributing to the growth of a collaborative support community. In viewing mentorship as a symbiotic relationship, the pair determines the scholars' needs and frequency of communication. These supports are in addition to the advisor, the advisory board, and other stakeholders that can be called upon, as needed, to support unique student situations.

The PLC consists of Project ARISE personnel, scholars, on-site mentors, university supervisors, and related ECSE and SW faculty. Members of Project ARISE's advisory board are also invited to participate. PLC meetings formally take place two or more times per semester, with additional convenings as needed. PLC agenda items will stem from suggested topics by members and areas of identified need from Project personnel. Although student experiences and goals may differ, emotional support and mutual empathy strengthen resilience as part of a community (Gu & Day, 2007).

## Evaluation

Project ARISE seeks regular feedback from scholars, supervisors/employers, school and community partners, families, and faculty. It is imperative to collect ongoing feedback to identify strengths and areas for growth that inform programmatic improvement. Each of these surveys is tailored to align with the role in the program, including being a scholar participant, teaching, mentoring, and collaborating with program scholars. The program also uses course evaluations as a means of feedback. Course evaluations ask quantitative and qualitative questions that can be analyzed and used with other assessment measures.

It is essential throughout the entirety of their programs, scholars receive timely and ongoing feedback to refine their practice around ECMH and inclusive supports. Therefore, Project ARISE scholars are evaluated on key interdisciplinary assignment rubrics in shared courses and coordinated student teaching/fieldwork rubrics. These evaluative tools seek to support scholars in reflective practice, evaluate their application of core program competencies, and provide information to support programmatic development and improvement. Project ARISE developed a self-reflection tool for scholars to use at least three times throughout their program—the beginning, middle, and end. The self-reflection is used for scholars to share their current understanding of ECMH-related knowledge and skills, inclusionary practices for young children with social emotional and ECMH needs and their families, and cultural competence.

Further Project ARISE scholar support is the facilitation of reflective practice (Heffron & Murch, 2010) in the development of an ePortfolio. An ePortfolio serves as both a formative and summative assessment tool that is reviewed regularly by scholars and their advisors. Its use is institutionalized in the ECSE and SW programs. Students are expected to upload exemplary work completed throughout their programs to reflect their knowledge and skills related to Project ARISE's six competencies and additional expected skills of their ECSE or SW field. Project ARISE scholars will be required to complete an ePortfolio that has additional requirements related to their growing expertise in ECMH and inclusion and alignment to the six competencies.

To date, Project ARISE's interdisciplinary efforts have been supported by feedback from the advisory board, community stakeholders, school partners, and alumni. Without the support of administrators, stakeholders, alumni, and community partners, Project ARISE would be much more challenging to implement. Curriculum support, fieldwork activities, and mentoring would be nonexistent if not for the collective feedback and effort of these external supports. Project ARISE's advisory board has provided ongoing constructive feedback since the beginning, when the personnel brainstormed different concepts for interdisciplinary programs. This open feedback has continued informally and formally. The advisory board includes practitioners with expertise in ECMH, inclusionary practices, AOP and social justice pedagogy, young children with disabilities and their families, early intervention, and antibias curriculum development. The advisory board members were invited to consider the board member role due to their expertise and the intersectional identities they hold. Program faculty wants to ensure the program upholds its commitment to equity and diversity and is reflective of the community Project ARISE scholars serve.

## REFLECTIONS AND LESSONS LEARNED

At the time of publication, Project ARISE is situated in its first year, a planning year scheduled by Project ARISE personnel at the proposal submission stage. Scholars have not yet provided feedback about Project ARISE (i.e., first cohort of scholars is set for Fall 2024). Individual and overall student recruitment, retention, completion, and postgraduation employment will be monitored throughout the duration of the program. Likewise, the authors want to be transparent about the steps taken for the Project ARISE program to begin. To always make improvements, Project ARISE strives for continuous reflection. Described next is a reflection on different components of the program's development and implementation process. Woven throughout this section is advice for others seeking to create or revise an interdisciplinary preparation program.

A theme throughout the collaboration efforts between ECSE and SW programs was the collective disposition of wanting to collaborate to create an innovative interdisciplinary personnel preparation program focused on ECSE and SW practitioners. This collective disposition was a mutual belief between the two programs—interdisciplinary personnel training was essential in preparing ECSE and SW to support CLD young children with social emotional needs and their families in inclusive settings. Though ECSE and SW programs have existing partnerships and interdisciplinary programs with other related fields (e.g., speech language pathology), the opportunity to bring together scholars from ECSE and SW felt vital as mental health; therefore, ECMH continues to be evident as a need in the field nationally and internationally (Tomlinson, 2015; WestEd, 2012). What grounded Project ARISE was shared mutual importance with a clear goal and vision. Coupled with problem solving and leveraging resources, the intrinsic motivation of project personnel was essential to transition the program from just an idea to a tangible and funded program.

Both a strength and a challenge, the ECSE and SW programs were housed in different IHE colleges. Therefore, the interdisciplinary program required support from two deans, two department/school leaders, and two program coordinators. Both programs' content made it evident the two programs should be working together (e.g., both programs cover content in adverse childhood experiences and working with diverse families), but the programs did not traditionally collaborate. Project ARISE personnel had an awareness of potential bureaucracy to overcome when bringing together two distinct programs. Multiple personnel from each program were involved in the brainstorming of this collaboration, and it took the support of a small group of dedicated ECSE and SW faculty to submit to create the proposal, gain support, and make Project ARISE come to fruition.

Project ARISE's aim was to bring together two existing programs, so there was already infrastructure to support the program's goals. This infrastructure included typical elements of a graduate preservice program (e.g., four courses, orientation schedule and materials, websites), as well as particular activities that enhanced the proposed interdisciplinary collaboration, including the Supporting Inclusive Early Childhood Practices graduate certificate, Partnering with Families Institute, and Meaningful Collaborations in Early Childhood annual conference. Though existing fieldwork and student teaching sites were identified that supported ECMH, partnerships with these sites need to be discussed in more specific interdisciplinary preparation detail, and the list of sites needs to be expanded. Personnel wants to ensure the program remains a work in progress and does not become stagnant over time.

Curriculum alignment is time intensive and tedious. Approaching the task of curriculum alignment and mapping requires involved individuals to agree about what the finished product will look like and how it will be used throughout the program. Moreover, prioritizing curriculum mapping is recommended to ensure a robust interdisciplinary program grounded in EBPs reflects both fields. Approaching curriculum mapping and logistics, like course scheduling, together is important to tackle challenges as they surface. For instance, coming to an agreement about the learning modality of shared courses or days of the week courses would be scheduled to avoid conflicts are necessary conversations. If not discussed, logistical barriers may delay the creation or execution of a program. The authors hope to continue to revisit and revise existing curricula to stay updated on EBPs related to interdisciplinary preparation, ECMH and inclusive practices. One way to do this is to revise syllabi using Taylor et al.'s (2019) Social Justice Syllabus Design Tool. This tool supports faculty to reflect on if, how, and when their syllabi support elements of social justice framework and practices within their courses.

There continue to be ongoing check-ins between Project ARISE personnel to ensure alignment on key elements of the collaboration. These check-ins ensure the short and long-term action steps and overarching goals of the program are realistic, feasible, and being met in a timely manner. As with any partnership, consistent and ongoing discussions on topics such as scheduling, time commitment, communication, and responsibilities occur to be transparent and to build trust for a new, delicate program. While in the planning stages of a new interdisciplinary preparation program, understanding faculty's individual and collective capacity is vital in developing goals, a shared vision, timeline, and activities that will occur as part of the collaboration.

To initiate and plan Project ARISE, leaders showed a collective effort and feelings of gratitude, knowing the amount of time and energy needed from multiple individuals to get the program off the ground. Personnel leaned into humility throughout the process, knowing the steps to create an interdisciplinary preparation program would require problem solving and understanding mistakes would be made. Project ARISE personnel attempt to align the concept of professional courtesy to "lovingkindness" (Magee, 2019), showing grace and humility within ourselves and for others we work with throughout the process. Over time, balancing professional and personal roles and responsibilities may be cumbersome and reveal advantages for some individuals (Branch et al., 2021; Hanasono et al., 2019). Individuals must be mindful underrepresented individuals may be overburdened with service responsibilities (Wood et al., 2015). Dividing the overarching pressure and daily responsibilities provides space to tackle other demands while allowing space to reflect on overall programmatic success.

## CONCLUSION

Research over the last few decades continues to direct practitioners to support the ECMH of young children and their families, especially those who are experiencing poverty, sustained adversities, and impacted by systemic inequities and racism, discrimination, and oppression (CDCHU, 2020; Heard-Garris et al., 2018; Tomlinson, 2015; USDOE, 2016; USHSS & DOE, 2014). With 9%–14% of infants and young children experiencing emotional or mental health issues with enough intensity to interfere with their development and learning, the field must fiercely and quickly respond (WestEd, 2012). While the number of young children and their families negatively impacted by ECMH continues to grow, practitioners must consider how to best address the whole child within the context of their family system (CDC, 2022b; Turnbull et al., 2014).

A key element to meeting the unique needs of young CLD children with social emotional needs and their families in inclusive settings includes practitioners who have shared their expertise—individuals who have learned about, from, and with each other to implement effective intervention and improve child and family outcomes. Preservice practitioners are unable to effectively do this with limited or no opportunities to practice and receive feedback in siloed practitioner preparation programs. Though steps have been taken to break down discipline barriers, discipline silos remain in many instances (see Bruder et al., 2019). IHE practitioner preparation programs must respond to develop equity-focused interdisciplinary programs intentionally (Blanchard et al., 2021; NAEYC, 2019).

The authors hope in sharing the steps taken to create Project ARISE, others in ECSE, SW, and related services will consider evaluating their preservice preparation programs. Likewise, examining current in-service and professional development supports will support existing practitioners and teams in the field. The theoretical frameworks, centering of families, systems of care, social justice and antioppression, and antibias education, situate how Project ARISE understands the approach to services for young CLD children with high-intensity social emotional needs and their families. The reflections and lessons learned about interdisciplinary programmatic development seek to support others who are in a position to advocate for change and accountability within and across existing programs. To better serve young children with disabilities and their families, their collective interrelated development and overall well-being must be addressed by practitioners who seek to collaborate to provide more effective intervention and support.

## DISCUSSION QUESTIONS

1. What did you learn throughout this chapter?
2. What do you feel you could apply to your own workplace setting?
3. What do you want to learn more about?
4. What collaborations already exist in your program? How can those be strengthened?
5. What barriers or fears come to mind when you imagine creating or strengthening interdisciplinary collaborations at your institution?
6. What do you continue to have questions about?

## REFERENCES

Amaya-Jackson, L., Absher, L. E., Gerrity, E. T., Layne, C. M., & Halladay Goldman, J. (2021). *Beyond the ACE score: Perspectives from the NCTSN on child trauma and adversity screening and impact*. National Center for Child Traumatic Stress. https://www.nctsn.org/sites/default/files/resources/special-resource/beyond-the-ace-score-perspectives-from-the-nctsn-on-child-tauma-and-adversity-screening-and-impact.pdf

American Association for Employment in Education. (2016–2017). *Educator supply and demand report 2016–17*. https://aaee.org/sites/default/files/content-files/AAEE%20Full%20Report2016_17_%205-11_smr.pdf

American Federation of State, County and Municipal Employees, American Federation of Teachers, Associate Degree Early Childhood Teacher Educators, Child Care Aware of America, Council for Professional Recognition, Division for Early Childhood of the Council for Exceptional Children, Early Care and Education Consortium, National Association for Family Child Care, National Association for the Education of Young Children, National Association of Early Childhood Teacher Educators, National Association of Elementary School Principals, National Education Association, National Head Start Association, Service Employees International Union, & ZERO TO THREE. (2020). *Unifying framework for the early childhood profession.* http://powertotheprofession.org/wpcontent/uploads/2020/03/Power-to-Profession-Framework-03312020-web.pdf

Aragon, J., Arrellano, L. M., Brazzel, P., Cárdenas, J., Catalde, T., Cottrill, M., Giambona, M., Manos, S., McMillian, K., Parsons, J., Peevy, J., Pianta, R., Schroeder, M., Sopp, T. J., Strear, M., Thomas, S., Topalian, J., Uresti, A., Weglarz, L., . . . Zavalza, O. (2020). *Fostering the whole child: A guide to school-based mental health professionals.* California Association of School Social Workers, California Association of School Counselors, California Association of School Psychologists. https://naswcanews.org/wp-content/uploads/2020/11/SBMHP-Guide-Book-final.pdf

Aratani, Y., Wright, V. R., & Cooper, J. L. (2011). *Racial gaps in early childhood: Socio-emotional health, development, and educational outcomes among African American boys* (ED522681). ERIC. https://files.eric.ed.gov/fulltext/ED522681.pdf

Baines, D. (2007). *Doing anti oppressive practice: Building transformative, politicized social work.* Fernwood.

Blanchard, S. B., Newton, J. R., Diderickson, K. W., Daniels, M., & Glosson, K. (2021). Confronting racism and bias within early intervention: The responsibility of systems and individuals to influence change and advance equity. *Topics in Early Childhood Special Education, 41*(1), 1–12. doi:10.1177/0271121421992470

Branch, J., Chapman, M., & Gomez, M. (2021). Investigating the interplay between institution, spousal, parental, and personal demands in tenure track faculty everyday life. *Community, Work & Family, 24*(2), 143–154. doi:10.1080/13668803.2020.1727414

Brandt, K. (2014). *Infant and early childhood mental health: Core concepts and clinical practice.* American Psychiatric Publishing.

Bricker, D. D., Felimban, H. S., Lin, F. Y., Stegenga, S. M., & Storie, S. O. (2020). A proposed framework for enhancing collaboration in early intervention/early childhood special education. *Topics in Early Childhood Special Education, 41*(4), 240–252. doi:10.1177/0271121419890683

Broderick, C. B. (1993). *Understanding family process: Basics of family systems theory.* SAGE Publications.

Bruder, M. B. (2010). Early childhood intervention: A promise to children and families for their future. *Exceptional Children, 76*(3), 339–355. doi:10.1177/001440291007600306

Bruder, M. B., Catalino, T., Chiarello, L. A., Cox Mitchell, M., Deppe, J., Gundler, D., Kemp, P., LeMoine, S., Long, T., Muhlenhaupt, M., Prelock, P., Schefkind, S., Stayton, V., & Ziegler, D. (2019). Finding a common lens: Competencies across professional disciplines providing early childhood intervention. *Infants and Young Children*, *32*(4), 280–293. doi:10.1097/IYC.0000000000000153

Brunsting, N. C., Sreckovic, M. A., & Lane, K. L. (2014). Special education teacher burnout: A synthesis of research from 1979 to 2013. *Education & Treatment of Children*, *37*(4), 681–711. https://www.jstor.org/stable/44683943. doi:10.1353/etc.2014.0032

California Department of Education. (2020). *DataQuest report: Estimated number of teacher hires for 2020-21*. https://dq.cde.ca.gov/dataquest/dqcensus/StfTchHires.aspx?cdcode=3868478&agglevel=District&year=2020-21

Center for the Developing Child at Harvard University. (2016). *From best practices to breakthrough impacts: A science-based approach to building more promising future for young children and families.* http://www.developingchild.harvard.edu

Center on the Developing Child at Harvard University. (2020). *How racism can affect child development.* https://developingchild.harvard.edu/resources/racism-and-ecd/

Centers for Disease Control and Prevention. (2019). *Adverse childhood experiences: Preventing early trauma to improve adult health.* https://www.cdc.gov/vitalsigns/aces/index.html

Centers for Disease Control and Prevention. (2022a). *Children's mental health.* https://www.cdc.gov/childrensmentalhealth/features/understanding-public-health-concern.html

Centers for Disease Control and Prevention. (2022b). *Data and statistics on children's mental health.* https://www.cdc.gov/childrensmentalhealth/data.html

Council for Exceptional Children Division for Early Childhood. (2020). *Initial practice based professional preparation standards for early interventionist/early childhood special educators (EI/ECSE) (Initial birth through age 8).* https://www.decsped.org/ei-ecse-standards

Council on Social Work Education. (2015). *Educational policy and accreditation standards.* https://www.cswe.org/getattachment/Accreditation/Standards-andPolicies/2015-EPAS/2015EPASandGlossary.pdf

Cox, K., & Steiner, S. (2013). *Self-care in social work: A guide for practitioners, supervisors, and administrators*. NASW Press.

Derman-Sparks, L., & Edwards, J. O. (2019). Understanding anti-bias education: Bringing the four core goals to every facet of your curriculum. *Young Children*, *74*(5), 6–13. https://www.jstor.org/stable/26842300

Derman-Sparks, L., Edwards, J. O., & Goins, C. M. (2020). *Anti-bias education for young children and ourselves* (2nd ed.). National Association for the Education of Young Children.

Division for Early Childhood. (2014). *DEC recommended practices in early intervention/early childhood special education 2014.* http://www.dec-sped.org/recommendedpractices

Division for Early Childhood. (2020). *DEC priority issues agenda.* http://www.dec-sped.org/PriorityIssues

Division for Early Childhood. (2022). *Personnel preparation for early intervention/early childhood special education.* https://divisionearlychildhood.egnyte.com/dl/bdmVgW3UAi

Division for Early Childhood and National Association for the Education of Young Children. (2009). *Early childhood inclusion: A joint position statement of the Division for the Early Childhood (DEC) and the National Association for the Education of Young Children (NAEYC).* The University of North Carolina at Chapel Hill, FPG Child Development Institute. https://www.naeyc.org/sites/default/files/globally-shared/downloads/PDFs/resources/position-statements/ps_inclusion_dec_naeyc_ec.pdf

Gay, G. (2018). *Culturally responsive teaching: Theory, research, and practice* (3rd ed.). Teachers College Press.

Gu, Q., & Day, C. (2007). Teachers resilience: A necessary condition for effectiveness. *Teaching and Teacher Education, 23*(8), 1302–1316. doi:10.1016/j.tate.2006.06.006

Hanasono, L. K., Broido, E. M., Yacobucci, M. M., Root, K. V., Pena, S., & O'Neil, D. A. (2019). Secret service: Revealing gender biases in the visibility and value of faculty service. *Journal of Diversity in Higher Education, 12*(1), 85–98. doi:10.1037/dhe0000081

Harris, N. B. (2018). *The deepest well: Healing the long-term effects of childhood adversity.* Houghton Mifflin Harcourt Publishing.

Harry, B., & Ocasio-Stoutenburg, L. (2020). *Meeting families where they are: Building equity through advocacy with diverse schools and communities.* Teachers College Press.

Healy, K. (2014). *Social work theories in context: Creating frameworks for practice.* Bloomsbury Academic. doi:10.1007/978-1-137-02425-1

Heard-Garris, N. J., Cale, M., Camaj, L., Hamati, M. C., & Dominguez, T. P. (2018). Transmitting trauma: A systematic review of vicarious racism and child health. *Social Science & Medicine, 199,* 230–240. doi:10.1016/j.socscimed.2017.04.018

Heffron, M. C., & Murch, T. (2010). Reflective supervision and leadership in infant and early childhood programs. *Zero to Three.*

Herrenkohl, T. I., Scott, D., Higgins, D. J., Klika, J. B., & Lonne, B. (2021). How COVID-19 is placing vulnerable children at risk and why we need a different approach to child welfare. *Child Maltreatment, 26*(1), 9–16. doi:10.1177/1077559520963916 PMID:33025825

Individuals With Disabilities Education Act, 20 U.S.C. § 1400 (2004). https://www.congress.gov/108/plaws/publ446/PLAW-108publ446.pdf

Iruka, I. U., Curenton, S. M., Durden, T. R., & Escayg, K.-A. (2020). *Don't look away: Embracing anti-bias classrooms.* Gryphon House.

Ladson-Billings, G. (1995). Toward a theory of culturally relevant pedagogy. *American Educational Research Journal, 32*(3), 465–491. doi:10.3102/00028312032003465

Ladson-Billings, G. (2014). Culturally relevant pedagogy 2.0: A.k.a the remix. *Harvard Educational Review*, *84*(1), 74–84. doi:10.17763/haer.84.1.p2rj131485484751

Lalvani, P., & Bacon, J. K. (2019). Rethinking "we are all special": Anti-ableism curricula in early childhood classrooms. *Young Exceptional Children*, *22*(2), 87–100. doi:10.1177/1096250618810706

Lawrence, S., Smith, S., & Banerjee, R. (2016). *Preschool inclusion: Key findings from research and implications for policy*. Child Care & Early Education Research Connections, National Center for Children in Poverty. https://www.nccp.org/wp-content/uploads/2020/05/text_1154.pdf

Learning Policy Institute. (2022). *Whole child policy toolkit*. https://www.wholechildpolicy.org/

Lieberman, A. F., & Van Horn, P. (2005). Don't hit my mommy!: A manual for child-parent psychotherapy with young witnesses of family violence. *Zero to Three*.

Liming, K. W., & Grube, W. A. (2018). Wellbeing outcomes for children exposed to multiple adverse experiences in early childhood: A systematic review. *Child & Adolescent Social Work Journal*, *35*(4), 317–335. doi:10.100710560-018-0532-x

Little, C. (2020). Collaboration. In I. Spandagou, C. Little, D. Evans, & M. L. Bonati (Eds.), *Inclusive education in schools and early childhood settings* (pp. 85–92). Springer. doi:10.1007/978-981-15-2541-4_8

Lloyd, C., King, R., & Chenoweth, L. (2009). Social work, stress, and burnout: A review. *Journal of Mental Health (Abingdon, England)*, *11*(3), 255–265. doi:10.1080/09638230020023642

Love, H. R., & Beneke, M. R. (2021). Pursuing justice-driven inclusive education research: Disability critical race theory (DisCrit) in early childhood. *Topics in Early Childhood Special Education*, *41*(1), 31–44. doi:10.1177/0271121421990833

Magee, R. V. (2019). *The inner work of racial justice: Healing ourselves and transforming our communities through mindfulness*. TarcherPerigee.

Meek, S., Smith, L., Allen, R., Catherine, E., Edyburn, K., Williams, C., Fabes, R., McIntosh, K., Garica, E., Takanishi, R., Gordon, L., Jimenez-Castellanos, O., Hemmeter, M. L., Gilliam, W., & Pontier, R. (2020). *Start with equity: From the early years to the early grades*. Children's Equity Project and Bipartisan Policy Center. https://childandfamilysuccess.asu.edu/sites/default/files/2020-07/CEP-report-071520- FINAL.pdf

Mitsch, M. K., Weglarz-Ward, J., & Branch, J. (2022). "I'm new here": Leveraging responsibilities, relationships, and resources for new faculty leaders. *Young Exceptional Children*, 1–14. doi:10.1177/10962506221111362

National Association for the Education of Young Children. (2019). *Advancing equity in early childhood education A position statement of the National Association of the Education of Young Children*. https://www.naeyc.org/resources/position-statements/equity

National Association for the Education of Young Children. (2020a). *Developmentally appropriate practice: A position statement of the National Association of the Education of Young Children.* https://www.naeyc.org/sites/default/files/globally-shared/downloads/PDFs/resources/position-statements/dap-statement_0.pdf

National Association for the Education of Young Children. (2020b). *Professional standards and competencies.* https://www.naeyc.org/sites/default/files/globally-shared/downloads/PDFs/resources/position-statements/standards_and_competencies_ps.pdf

National Association of Social Work. (2012). *Standards and indicators for school social work services.* https://www.socialworkers.org/LinkClick.aspx?fileticket=5qpx4B6Csr0%3d&portaid=0

National Association of Social Work. (2015). *Standards and indicators for cultural competence.* https://www.socialworkers.org/LinkClick.aspx?fileticket=7dVckZAYUmk%3d&portali=0

National Scientific Council on the Developing Child. (2004). *Children's emotional development is built into the architecture of their brains* (Working Paper No. 2). https://46y5eh11fhgw3ve3ytpwxt9r-wpengine.netdna-ssl.com/wp-content/uploads/2004/04/Childrens-Emotional-Development-Is-Built-into-the-Architecture-of-Their-Brains.pdf

Nelson, C. A., Scott, R. D., Bhutta, Z. A., Harris, N. B., Danese, A., & Samara, M. (2020). Adversity in childhood is linked to mental and physical health throughout life. *BMJ (Clinical Research Ed.), 371*, m3048. doi:10.1136/bmj.m3048 PMID:33115717

Paris, D., & Alim, H. S. (Eds.). (2017). *Culturally sustaining pedagogies: Teaching and learning for justice in a changing world.* Teachers College Press.

Rush, D. D., & Shelden, M. L. (2020). *Early childhood coaching handbook* (2nd ed.). Brookes Publishing.

Sakamoto, I., & Pitner, R. O. (2005). Use of critical consciousness in anti-oppressive social work practice: Disentangling power dynamics at personal and structural levels. *British Journal of Social Work, 35*(4), 435–452. doi:10.1093/bjsw/bch190

Taylor, S. D., Veri, M. J., Eliason, M., Hermoso, J. C. R., Bolter, N. D., & Van Olphen, J. E. (2019). Social justice syllabus design tool: A first step in doing social justice pedagogy. *Journal Committed to Social Change on Race and Ethnicity, 5*(2), 133–166. doi:10.15763/issn.2642-2387.2019.5.2.132-166

Teasley, M. L. (2016). Related services personnel and evidence-based practice: Past and present challenges. *Children & Schools, 38*(1), 5–8. doi:10.1093/cs/cdv039

Tomlinson, M. (2015). Infant mental health in the next decade: A call for action. *Infant Mental Health Journal, 36*(6), 538–541. doi:10.1002/imhj.21537 PMID:26514552

Turnbull, A. P., Summers, J. A., & Brotherson, M. J. (1984). *Working with families with disabled members: A family systems approach.* University of Kansas.

Turnbull, A. P., Turnbull, H. R., Erwin, E., Soodak, L., & Shogren, K. (2014). *Families, professionals, and exceptionality: Positive outcomes through partnerships and trust* (7th ed.). Pearson.

U.S. Bureau of Labor Statistics. (2021a). *Social workers.* https://www.bls.gov/ooh/community-and-social-service/social-workers

U.S. Bureau of Labor Statistics. (2021b). *Special education teachers.* https://www.bls.gov/ooh/education-training-and-library/special-education-teachers

U.S. Department of Education. (2016). *Racial and ethnic disparities in special education: A multi-year disproportionality analysis by state, analysis category, and race/ethnicity.* https://www2.ed.gov/programs/osepidea/618-data/LEA-racial-ethnic-disparities-tables/disproportionality-analysis-by-state-analysis-category.pdf

U.S. Department of Education. (2017). *Teacher shortage areas nationwide: Listing 1990–1991 through 2017–2018.* https://www2.ed.gov/about/offices/list/ope/pol/ateachershortageareasreport2017-18.pdf

U.S. Department of Education. (2021). *Individuals with Disabilities Education Act (IDEA) database: Digest of Education Statistics 2020.* Office of Special Education Programs. https://www2.ed.gov/programs/osepidea/618-data/state-level-data-files/index.html#bcc

U.S. Department of Health and Human Services. (2022). *Protective factors and adverse childhood experiences.* https://www.childwelfare.gov/topics/preventing/preventionmonth/about/protective-factors-aces/

U.S. Departments of Health and Human Services & Education. (2014). *Policy statement on expulsion and suspension policies in early childhood* settings. https://www2.ed.gov/policy/gen/guid/school-discipline/policy-statement-ece-expulsions-suspensions.pdf

WestEd. (2012). Early childhood mental health: Raising awareness, taking action. *WestEd's R & D Alert, 13*(3), 1–3. https://www.wested.org/wpcontent/uploads/2016/11/1372730177article_earlychildhoodmentalhealth_20123.pdf

White, J. M., Martin, T. F., & Adamsons, K. (2019). *Family theories* (5th ed.). SAGE Publications.

Wood, J. L., Hilton, A. A., & Nevarez, C. (2015). Faculty of color and white faculty: An analysis of service in colleges of education in Arizona public university system. *Journal of the Professoriate, 8*(1), 85–109.

## KEY TERMS AND DEFINITIONS

**Ableism:** The systemic oppression of individuals with disabilities based on negative biases about normalcy and disability.

**Adverse Childhood Experiences:** Potentially traumatic events or environmental aspects that may impact a child's sense of safety, stability, and bonding with caregivers.

**Antibias Practices:** A framework that seeks to support the development of safe and supporting learning environments for all children, informed by its four core goals of identity, diversity, justice, and activism.

**Antioppressive Practices:** Goal of eradicating oppression and challenging traditional power structures through collective institutional and societal changes.

**Early Childhood and Family Mental Health:** Study and practice of the promotion of positive interrelated development (i.e., emotional, psychological, social, and overall health and well-being) that impact daily life and routines.

**Early Childhood Special Education:** Professionals who offer expertise in learning and curricular needs for young children with disabilities and their families.

**Family:** Any primary caregiver(s) for a child.

**Family Systems Framework:** A theoretical framework that considers the ways disability can impact the roles, interactions, and functions of a family, including the complexities, fluidity, and goals of a family.

**Inclusion:** Practice that promotes access, participation, and support through individualized accommodations and unique supports for each child.

**Interdisciplinary Program:** When two or more professions learn about, from, and with each other over the course of a personnel preparation program to enable effective collaboration and improve outcomes for individuals and families.

**Practitioner:** Professionals who support the learning, development, care, and overall well-being of young children identified as at-risk and with disabilities and their families.

**Reflective Practice:** Actions aimed at practitioners to build in regular opportunities to slow down, deepen their understanding of systematic barriers and the impact they have on their thoughts and actions, mindfulness, and to take time afterward to consider next steps.

**Social Justice Framework:** A theoretical framework that focuses on actions and beliefs that attempt to address oppression and inequity while promoting access, participation, and freedom for all individuals.

**Social Work:** Practice of professionals who have specialized knowledge in early childhood mental health, coping strategies, antioppressive practice, and trauma informed care/restorative practices.

**Toxic Stress:** Sustained, intensive, and/or frequent adversity or trauma that negatively impacts brain development.

**Whole Child Policy Toolkit:** Framework of goals and resources aimed at acknowledging interrelated development of a child's physical, psychological, and academic needs.

# Chapter 24
# Introducing a Collaborative Training Program for Special Educators and School Social Workers

**John Elwood Romig**
*University of Texas at Arlington, USA*

**Ambra L. Green**
*University of Texas at Arlington, USA*

**Jandel Crutchfield**
*University of Texas at Arlington, USA*

## ABSTRACT

*This chapter introduces Project Match Made in Schools (Project MMS). Project MMS is funded by a H325K grant from the U.S. Department of Education, Office of Special Education Programs. The project provides interdisciplinary training for special educators and social workers. Scholars in the special education program pursue initial teacher licensure in special education. Special education and social work scholars share six hours of coursework, are paired together for field experiences, and participate in interdisciplinary research apprenticeships. This chapter describes the components of Project MMS and highlights some challenges and successes the project personnel have experienced.*

This chapter presents Project Match Made in Schools (Project MMS), a collaborative training program between the College of Education and the School of Social work at the University of Texas at Arlington. This project was funded by an H325K grant from the Office of Special Education Programs. Scholars funded by the project receive a master's degree in school social work or special education with initial teacher certification. In this chapter, we intend to provide a rationale for the project, describe the collaborative aspects of the project between social workers and special educators, and identify lessons

DOI: 10.4018/978-1-6684-6438-0.ch024

learned through the project by the principal investigators. Project MMS prepares special educators and social workers; due to the focus of this book, this chapter focuses on the preparation of special educators.

## RATIONALE

The United States of America, and, specifically, the state of Texas desperately need well-trained personnel to serve school-aged children with high-intensity needs. High-intensity needs include students with disabilities, students from historically underserved communities, minoritized students, students from low-income households, and other students who have traditionally underachieved in school. Over the last decade, the number of special education teachers in the USA has declined by 17% while the number of students with disabilities declined by only 1% (Snyder et al., 2019). The National Teacher Shortage Areas Listing annual report lists critical teacher shortages in special education in almost every state, including Texas (see https://tsa.ed.gov/#/reports). In Texas, 635,097 students received special education services in 2020-2021 (Texas Education Agency, 2022b) and just 10,637 special education teachers (by FTE) (Texas Education Agency, 2022d). When examining the percentage of teachers serving in special education in Texas, 21% were not certified in special education (TEA, 2022c). Thus, a large percentage of students are taught by educators who are not trained nor well-prepared to meet their individualized needs.

To meet special education shortages, Texas continues to offer multiple routes to certification. In 2021-2022, over 33% of educators were certified through alternative certification programs (Texas Education Agency, 2022a). Thus, the number of well-prepared teachers continues to decline in Texas as alternative certification and certification-by-exam options are used to quickly certify teachers in this area. Also, of 135 approved educator preparation programs in Texas, only 23 offer advanced preparation (master's level training) and degrees in special education.

Social workers are in similar short supply. For example, 10 million students in the United States are in schools without a social worker (Whitaker et al., 2019). The National Association of School Social Workers (2012) recommended 1 social worker for every 250 students. However, only three states in the United States (i.e., Montana, Vermont, and New Hampshire) met this recommendation; the national average is 1 social worker for every 444 students (Whitaker et al., 2019). Texas averaged 1 social worker for every 434 students (Whitaker et al., 2019).

The field of special education and school social work have personnel shortages in common; another reason for the collaboration between these programs is the significant overlap between students served by social workers and special educators. For example, one analysis of these populations found 17 percent of children who had experienced abuse had disabilities (Baladerian, 1994). Estimates suggested youth with disabilities experience abuse or neglect at 1.5 to 3.5 times the rate of children without disabilities (National Council on Disability, 2008).

Although social workers are highly likely to encounter people with disabilities routinely, most social workers receive little education regarding students with disabilities and the supports necessary for their success (Ogden et al., 2017). Historically, special educators have been less familiar with the field of social work and have viewed social workers as less valuable than other related service professionals (Tower, 1996). The lack of collaboration between fields hinders their respective work. The goal of this project was to increase understanding between fields and to recognize each field as crucial for student success.

## CONCEPTUAL FRAMEWORK

The underpinnings of our program are based on adult learning theory (Merriam, 2008). Adult learning theory attends to the sociocultural context of learning, meaning that learning happens amidst social interconnections (Merriam, 2008). This element of adult learning theory can be challenging to incorporate into an online asynchronous master's program. However, we still believed it to be a foundational element of adult learning theory and incorporated this element by arranging coursework, field experiences, and research apprenticeships so special education and social work scholars could have social interconnections enhancing the learning process.

Adult learning theory considers learning to be multidimensional, meaning learning is more than a cognitive process (Merriam, 2008). It involves the body, mind, and emotions. In other words, learning is active and engages the whole person. Our project incorporated this element by placing a heavy emphasis on field experiences and providing a mentor for each student who could attend to students' emotions differently than a course professor could.

Finally, reflection is an important skill in adult learning theory (Merriam, 2008). In adult learning theory, reflection is connecting new information to previous experience (Merriam, 2008). Several elements of the program – coursework, mentoring workshops, and one-on-one mentoring – were designed to foster students' reflection of what they had learned in course material and field experiences. Courses included specific reflection assignments, asking students to reflect on their field experience or other course material. Workshops prompted students to connect material across courses and semesters. Mentors helped students see connections across all facets of the program and in their own personal lives. In the next section, the specific components of the project are described more thoroughly.

## PROJECT DESCRIPTION

### Planning Year

The first year of the project was a planning year. The special education program at UTA was relatively new (undergraduate program beginning in 2019). When the grant was proposed, we intended for the M.Ed. program to be in its second semester of implementation; however, delays with university and state approval meant that the first Project MMS scholars were the first students in our special education M.Ed. program. Because the M.Ed. program and Project MMS were both new to our special education program, the planning year was crucial for our readiness.

During the planning year, we prioritized recruitment of new scholars. As a new special education program, we could not rely on word-of-mouth recruitment to attract new scholars to the program and did not have recruitment materials ready to be distributed. During this year we developed recruitment brochures, websites, and flyers. We also created distribution lists for sending recruitment materials. We met with many local special education directors to explain the master's program Project MMS and to seek potential applicants. When proposing Project MMS, we intended to host recruitment events at historically black colleges and universities (HBCUs) around Texas, but like so many other things over the past three years, these plans were cancelled due to COVID-19.

To apply, applicants had to complete the UTA graduate student application, educator preparation program application, and Project MMS application. The Project MMS application included an additional writing prompt specific to Project MMS applicants. This writing prompt and accompanying rubric were developed during the planning year. A video interview was also part of the application process for Project MMS scholars. During the planning year, we developed the questions that would be used in the interviews.

During the planning year, we also prepared for the first cohort of students. These activities included submitting approvals for course changes and degree plan changes. Programmatic changes had to go through department, college, and university approval processes. We also ordered technology and other materials to support Project MMS (e.g., iPads and Swivl robots). We planned mentoring workshops and invited external experts to present at the workshops. Finally, we planned for the project evaluation. These activities included identifying and creating pre-program and post-program measures (e.g., surveys, focus group protocols).

## Years Two-Five

In years two-five, our activities were guided by the project's goals. The four goals were (1) recruit and retain high-quality master's students as MMS scholars, (2) build capacity and systems for sustainability beyond the duration of the grant, (3) provide high-quality coursework, field-experiences, and apprenticeships, and (4) evaluate Project MMS's impact on scholars' abilities to meet competencies. The following section describes the activities aligned with these goals.

### Goal 1: Recruit and Retain Scholars

Recruitment and retention of scholars was an ongoing activity for the duration of the program. During the project, the college had turnover in marketing personnel. Each new marketing director brought new strategies and philosophy to marketing the project. The university also underwent multiple website makeovers, which caused our web marketing materials to need frequent updates and revisions. Additionally, partly related to the great resignation in the midst of COVID-19, there was high turnover in local school district administration. This turnover created the need to build new relationships with external personnel frequently.

### Goal 2: Sustainability

The goal of sustainability was largely accomplished in the planning year. The courses and plans of study were approved and can continue in perpetuity.

### Goal 3: Coursework, Field Experiences, and Apprenticeships

**Coursework.** Special education scholars had six hours of shared course work (two graduate courses) with social work scholars in their required degree plan. The shared courses were Applied Behavior Analysis for Teachers (part of the typical special education degree plan, but not typically taken with social work students) and Social Work in Schools (part of the typical degree plan in social work, but not typically taken with special education students). These shared courses allowed special education scholars to hear from professors and students from a social work perspective who bring a more holistic approach to students' well-being than is traditionally presented in special education coursework.

Within the shared courses, we intentionally paired special education scholars with social work scholars on assignments. This partnering allows the future special educators to practice collaboration with school social workers and deepen their understanding of social work principles, perspectives, resources, and supports.

**Field Experiences.** Special education scholars completed over 200 hours of field experiences and spend 60 of those hours paired with a social work scholar in the program. A certified special educator oversees the special education scholars' field experience. Paired field experiences allow scholars from both fields to practice collaboration to meet student needs, much like we would hope they do when fully certified. For example, when allowed, social work and special education scholars can attend IEP meetings for the same students.

**Research Apprenticeships.** Project MMS scholars were required to complete a 200-hour research apprenticeship in addition to the course and field requirements common to most preparation programs. At the beginning of each cohort, faculty advisers presented students with various ongoing research projects for scholars to choose. Scholars ranked their top three preferred projects. Typically, scholars participated in their first or second choice project. Research apprenticeships could be, and often were, cross-disciplinary with special education scholars working on research projects with social work faculty and *vice versa*. Research projects often had multiple scholars working on them from both special education and social work, providing another opportunity for cross-disciplinary preparation.

**Mentoring Workshops.** Three times a year, all project scholars and faculty met for a mentoring workshop. During the workshop, a professional development topic was presented, typically by a guest speaker. This professional development opportunity typically included a collaborative activity engaging scholars from both fields in discussion with one another. Scholars also had opportunity to meet with their faculty adviser and the faculty overseeing their research apprenticeship.

## Goal 4: Evaluation

We used process and outcome evaluation to evaluate progress towards our goals. We identified six competencies expected of Project MMS scholars. The six competencies guiding the evaluation process included scholars' ability to select and conduct evidence-based assessments, address bias, use advanced and evidence-based practices, collaborate, teaching prosocial skills, and effective communication. Formative evaluation focused on four primary components: fidelity, dosage and reach, recruitment, and context (Saunders et al., 2005).

The outcome evaluation included quantitative analysis, a repeated measures design to evaluate changes in knowledge, attitudes, and self-reported behavior. Once scholars consented to participate in the evaluation of the program, they completed a baseline assessment upon initial enrollment and a post-test at the conclusion of the project year, 12 months later. Scholars completed a follow-up assessment 6- and 24-months following program completion. Additional outcome measures included course grades in each of the two interdisciplinary courses included in the program, a final field evaluation completed by field supervisors, and an employer assessment completed by the scholars' employers conducted at 24 months following program completion.

## LESSONS LEARNED

### Goal 1: Recruit and Retain Scholars

Recruitment and retention of scholars has been the most challenging part of the project. In years two-four we did not recruit the number of special education scholars we proposed for the project. Our proposal projected twelve scholars to have graduated by the end of year three; however, we only graduated six. We attributed this challenge to several issues. First, the constraints placed on face-to-face interaction from COVID-19 made it significantly more difficult to recruit participants via traditional means. Second, recruitment to teacher certification programs more broadly has been a challenge. The job of teaching has always been difficult, but the past few years presented unprecedented challenges to the field. In addition to all the challenges brought on by COVID-19, Texas had hotly contested school board elections in many school districts; roiling political battles over critical race theory, books in classrooms, and gender policies; and the resignation of at least 14 superintendents in the North Texas region within six months (as of this writing, there are currently 42 superintendent vacancies across the state https://www.texas-isd.com/superintendent-vacancies). Further, rising inflation made many professionals prioritize salary differently than they may have otherwise. We believe the compounding impact of these issues made many potential teachers reluctant to enter the field. At UTA, Project MMS was not the only program to struggle with recruitment; enrollments in the Curriculum and Instruction department were down nearly 30% from previous years.

Another possible issue hindering recruitment was the timing of cohort starts for years two and three of the project. Our cohorts started in January of spring semesters. Often people think of the fall as the typical time to start new school years. To address this issue, we changed the cohort start date in year three to align with the fall semester calendar.

A lesson we learned about recruitment was that we may have scared some applicants away with how we described the program. We used phrases like "competitive application process," "intense training in special education," and "rigorous research apprenticeship." Our intention was to recruit applicants who would be up for the challenge of completing a master's program in one year; however, we heard anecdotally from some people that they thought they were not qualified enough or that this program was not for them due to how we described the program. We tried to temper this language while still communicating that getting a master's degree in one year was going to be challenging.

Although a smaller issue, retention of scholars was also somewhat challenging. In Texas, nearly half of the teacher workforce is alternatively certified. There is a well-established infrastructure for alternative teacher preparation. Prospective teachers can enroll in these programs relatively inexpensively and be teaching in classrooms as soon as they enroll without needing certification. Questions about the quality of the preparation aside, alternative licensure was an attractive alternative for some of our scholars who were overwhelmed by the workload. We only lost one scholar who had begun courses, but several others withdrew from the program after being admitted but before beginning classes. Most did not cite the workload of the program in their reason for withdrawing, but they had other changes in their life that made the workload of the program difficult to endure.

## Goal 2: Sustainability

Sustainability of the program was largely a success. By getting coursework and degree plans approved, there is very little that must be done to keep the interdisciplinary program running after the project ends. We continue to learn and refine the project as we go along, but the heavy lifting of creating an interdisciplinary program was accomplished. The only limitation to sustainability is recruiting students to fill the courses. However, this limitation is manageable because none of the courses are specific to Project MMS. The courses can meet enrollment numbers by being filled with other special education students who are not Project MMS scholars.

## Goal 3: Coursework, Field Experiences, and Apprenticeships

### Coursework

The special education courses were eight weeks long and delivered online asynchronously. Students completed two courses simultaneously in each session and two sessions per semester (4 courses per semester). This schedule made for an intense course load. Students had short, if any, breaks between sessions. However, course scheduling was outside the control of project personnel. Due to university administrative and finance issues, the project could not offer full semester or face-to-face courses. Because of the shortened courses, it was very important for scholars to stay on top of coursework. Falling behind for even a couple days could significantly impact their performance on the course.

### Field Experiences

Sharing field experiences has been a challenge. Special education preparation programs are familiar with the challenges of identifying high-quality field placements for special education candidates. Project MMS has the added challenge of finding high-quality field placements that also have a high-quality school social worker on-site who is also willing to supervise a clinical placement for a social work scholar. Although identifying these placements was a challenge, we believe there was significant benefit to scholars from both fields being paired for these experiences. When discussing and debriefing their field experiences, both student groups have shared understandings of the school culture, student population, and other contextual variables that deepen their discussion of how best to serve students.

### Apprenticeships

Research apprenticeships were a success of the program. Many scholars were able to substantively contribute to research projects, and some were able to publish with their apprenticeship supervisor. Scholars learned what data collection in school settings looks like, data analysis tools, strategies for conducting systematic reviews, and the peer-review publishing process. Many of them had limited, if any, experience with school-based research before the apprenticeships. By the end of the apprenticeship, some expressed interested in pursuing a PhD or other research-related career.

## Mentoring Workshops

Mentoring workshops were also a success of the program. Students were able to hear from content area experts from around the country who supported the interdisciplinary coursework of the project. Students were able to meet with project staff in-person, something some of scholars said they missed about in-person instruction. These face-to-face connections were important to building relationships with scholars and was energizing for many who attended.

A story from one of the mentoring meetings in particular highlighted the benefits of Project MMS's collaboration between special education and social work. During the workshop, the professional development facilitator presented a case study situation to students and asked the special education scholars to identify suggestions for the situation as a group. Separately, the social workers also discussed suggestions for the situation. When the two groups of scholars reported their discussion in the whole group, it was fascinating to hear the responses. Almost to a word, the social work scholars suggested home and community supports (e.g., asking the parent/guardian about any changes at home, home visits, etc.) and the special education scholars made suggestions that the teacher had in their control (e.g., increase data collection, reviewing IEP information, intensifying intervention, conducting a functional behavior analysis). This discussion early on in the program highlighted the importance of Project MMS. Both fields bring incredible expertise, but if they remain in silos, their powers are limited. When united, the full potential of wraparound services, family and community supports, and individualized instruction can be realized.

## Goal 4: Evaluation

Our evaluation process is ongoing but has largely been a success. We have a systematic process for collecting process (i.e., data collection takes place throughout the semester inside and outside of coursework) and outcome data. We have graduated six scholars who were rated as active participants throughout the program. Although quantitative data are still being analyzed, anecdotal data regarding the graduated scholars' experience have been received. Some scholars described the cross-curricular study as enriching and said it allowed them to learn from students with different backgrounds, especially when working in groups. One scholar said," "Having the opportunity to learn from my peers was beneficial, we were able to discuss different ways we would work on a case, understanding their methods and why they would do something helped broaden my view towards cases. It was most beneficial when I took the course in their background, and they were able to take the lead and help me as I did when we took the course in my background." Scholars also provided suggestions for improvement. One scholar said, "An activity in the courses can be the students with that background showcase their specialty, this is where they can show how proud they are of their specialty and highlight key importance for the students not familiar with their backgrounds, since this may be a new area for the other students. Additionally, in the courses where special education and social work students were combined, those classes should include the importance of working with the other professional so we can get it from both point of views." Although we were unable to address this scholars' concern as it would involve changes to a teacher's course, we did enhance our communication about the importance of collaboration between special education and social work during mentoring workshops. Additional data are being analyzed on an ongoing basis and are being used to refine the program.

## CONCLUSION

Project MMS is a collaborative partnership between the fields of special education and school social work to better prepare our students by receiving cross-disciplinary training in each field. From the special education perspective, a main goal of the partnership with the School of Social Work is that graduating special educators will identify the tools social workers have and see them as a valuable resource when faced with student challenges. We want one of their first questions on the job to be, "Who is the school social worker, and how can I contact them?" The entire program is designed with this in mind. Collaboration in coursework, assignments, field experiences, and research apprenticeships all lead to the goal of these two fields seeing collaboration with each other as second nature, as if they could not do their job effectively without the other field.

## REFERENCES

Baladerian, N. J. (1994). *Abuse and neglect of children with disabilities.* ARCH National Center for Crisis Nurseries and Respite Care Services. https://eric.ed.gov/?id=ED378709

Merriam, S. B. (2008). Adult learning theory for the twenty-first century. *New Directions for Adult and Continuing Education*, *2008*(119), 93–98. doi:10.1002/ace.309

National Association of School Workers. (2012). *NASW Standards for School Social Work Services.* https://www.socialworkers.org/LinkClick.aspx?fileticket=1Ze4-9-Os7E%3D&portalid=0

National Council on Disability. (2008). *Youth with disabilities in the foster care system: Barriers to success and proposed policy solutions.* https://ncd.gov/publications/2008/02262008#_edn8

Ogden, L., Mcallister, C., & Neely-Barnes, S. (2017). Assessment of integration of disability content into social work education. *Journal of Social Work in Disability & Rehabilitation*, *16*(3-4), 361–376. doi:10.1080/1536710X.2017.1392394 PMID:29111955

Saunders, R. P., Evans, M. H., & Joshi, P. (2005). Developing a process-evaluation plan for assessing health promotion program implementation: A how-to guide. *Health Promotion Practice*, *6*(2), 134–147. doi:10.1177/1524839904273387 PMID:15855283

Snyder, T. D., de Brey, C., & Dillow, S. A. (2019). Digest of education statistics (54th ed.). NCES 2020-009. US Department of Education. Institute of Education Sciences.

Texas Education Agency. (2022a). *Employed and Certified Teachers by Preparation Route 2012-13 through 2021-22.* https://tea.texas.gov/sites/default/files/employed-and-certified-teachers-by-preparation-route-2022.pdf

Texas Education Agency. (2022b). *Special Education Reports.* https://rptsvr1.tea.texas.gov/cgi/sas/broker?_service=marykay&_program=adhoc.std_driver1.sas&RptClass=SpecEd&_debug=0&SchoolYr=22&report=StateState&format=html

Texas Education Agency. (2022c). *Out-of-Field Teaching for SY 2021-22 by Grade Level and Subject Area.* https://tea.texas.gov/sites/default/files/out-of-field-2022.pdf

Texas Education Agency. (2022d). 2021-2022 teacher FTE counts and course enrollment reports. https://rptsvr1.tea.texas.gov/cgi/sas/broker

Tower, K. D. (1996). *The attitudes of special educators toward social work as a pupil support service* (Publication no. 9716671) [Doctoral dissertation, University of Nevada, Reno). ProQuest Dissertations Publishing.

Whitaker, A., Torres-Guillén, S., Morton, M., Jordan, H., Coyle, S., Mann, A., & Sun, W. L. (2019). *Cops and no counselors: How the lack of school mental health staff is harming students.* American Civil Liberties Union. Retrieved from https://www.aclu.org/report/cops-and-no-counselors

# Chapter 25
# Teaming for Transition:
## A Model for Interdisciplinary, Collaborative Preparation of Secondary Education Professionals

**Suzanne Kucharczyk**
https://orcid.org/0000-0003-4979-0835
*University of Arkansas, USA*

**Kimberly Frazier**
*University of Arkansas, USA*

**Tameeka Hunter**
https://orcid.org/0000-0003-1566-8532
*Florida International University, USA*

**Kristi L. Perryman**
*University of Arkansas, USA*

**Johanna Thomas**
*University of Arkansas, USA*

**Renee Speight**
*University of Arkansas, USA*

**Ed Bengtson**
*University of Arkansas, USA*

## ABSTRACT

*This chapter, developed by faculty who self-organized as an interdisciplinary, collaborative team in the implementation of these two 325K projects, Teaming for Transition, funded at the University of Arkansas, describes a shared, core focus to better prepare professionals to support youth with disabilities in transition to adulthood. The authors share how across disciplines of Special Education, Communication Disorders, Vocational Rehabilitation, School Counseling, Social Work, and School Administration, the projects Teaming for Transition and Teaming for Transition – Preparing Youth for Work and Community have been designed and implemented around a shared framework, using innovative online learning technologies, with an inquiry-based approach to understanding the challenges of transition for youth in Arkansas and beyond. They share lessons learned and implications for faculty seeking to de-silo across programs, colleges, and disciplines.*

DOI: 10.4018/978-1-6684-6438-0.ch025

Individuals with disabilities with high-intensity support needs (e.g., intellectual disabilities, autism spectrum disorder, multiple disabilities, comorbid mental health concern) experience adult outcomes that are far worse on most indicators (e.g., employment, time with friends, engagement in community, access to internet) compared to people with other disabilities or those with no disability (Trainor et al., 2020; Carter et al., 2012; Newman et al., 2011). Youth with disabilities are underemployed (U.S. Bureau of Labor Statistics, 2020), especially if they have high need disabilities (Bates-Harris, 2012), and undereducated compared to their peers without disabilities (National Center for Education Statistics, 2019). Youth continue to not have access to the lives they and their families desire despite efforts by the field of special education transition and relevant federal laws to mitigate barriers and mandate practices known to impact outcomes (Trainor et al., 2020). Collaboration within school systems and beyond to future systems is known to predict postschool outcomes (Mazzotti et al., 2021).

To impact outcomes of youth, interdisciplinary team members, including educators, related service providers, school administrators, and adult service providers must be prepared to apply evidence-based practices in partnership with students and their families in in-person and virtual learning environments. Practitioners working in concert with educational and allied health professionals have a shared mission to support individuals with high-need disabilities to access systems, develop skills, and develop relationships aligned with their desires and priorities for their future. The goal of interdisciplinary preparation programs is to encourage collaborative learning among future professionals from diverse fields so that scholars acquire attitudes, competencies, and knowledge needed for effective interactions with professionals in their shared field of practice. To impact the outcomes of youth with high-need disabilities, interdisciplinary team members, including educators, related service providers, school administrators, and adult service providers must be prepared to apply evidence-based practices in partnership with students and their families. The critical time for these efforts is in the transition from educational services to adult life.

## Criticality of Interdisciplinary and Interagency Transition Services

While interdisciplinary collaboration is a core component of special education across educational ages, its application during transition planning and service provision is especially critical. Schools are federally mandated to provide transition services beginning by the age of 16 for student with disabilities which include a "coordinated set of activities" (20 U.S.C. 1401 sec. 603[34]) and "must invite to the IEP meeting a representative of any participating agency that is likely to be responsible for providing or paying for transition services" (34 CFR §300.321(b)(3)). These expectations are reinforced in the Workforce Innovation and Opportunities Act of 2015 which requires collaborative activities between vocational rehabilitation and educational systems in support of youth with disabilities through pre-employment transition services. To enact these expectations of federal law interdisciplinary transition teams, inclusive of youth and their families, must collaborate with interagency (beyond school systems) and interdisciplinary partners (within school systems) in the planning and delivery of transition services.

Importantly, beyond compliance with federal law, collaboration within school systems and beyond with future service systems is a known predictor of positive transition outcomes for adults with disabilities (Mazzotti et al., 2021; Oertle & Seader, 2015). The National Technical Assistance Center on

Transition (NTACT): The Collaborative's Taxonomy for Transition 2.0 (Kohler et al., 2016) delineates practices known to be predictive of post-school success of programs engaged in effective collaborative service delivery through collaborative frameworks.

Despite the importance of interagency and interdisciplinary collaboration as described in IDEA and WIOA and evidence of its impact on postschool outcomes, scholars and practitioners remain concerned that opportunities remain to invest in research and preparation efforts in support of more effective collaboration in transition services. Trainor et al. (2020), in their call for inquiry in the field of special education transition to address persistent barriers to success for youth with disabilities, suggest a number of opportunities to better understand interdisciplinary efforts. The researchers note the lack of integration between systems and disciplines supporting all students, with and without disabilities, in support of preparation for adulthood. These include career fairs, service learning and volunteer opportunities, personalized learning, extracurricular activities, career assessments and counseling led by professionals in special education, counseling, social work, vocational rehabilitation, career and technical education among others. Further, the researchers express concern for the lack of research targeting models of interagency collaboration with professionals across educational and adult services necessary to improve outcomes for youth with disabilities.

Opportunities for interdisciplinary and interagency collaboration to leverage current supports across systems and link youth with services are underdeveloped. Despite the critical role of collaboration across disciplines and systems in transition planning, a wide gap exists between expectations for special educators to build and leverage networks of professionals and their preparation to do so effectively (Bumble et al., 2021). Further, collaboration is particularly complicated during transition planning and service provision if members are new to teams and thus haven't established the relationships, clarity across roles, shared goals, and common mission necessary to work together at the level of collaboration necessary to attend to barriers (Plotner et al., 2012). Effective collaboration requires understanding of each discipline's and agency's role, frequent communication, and high levels of collaboration (Plotner et al., 2020). Given the ethical decision making integrated throughout the transition planning process, collaborative partners must be prepared to understand their roles, those of others, and the collective goal of the process and each young person (Brady et al., 2021). Professional preparation programs should prepare professionals across roles to build competencies in transition services and programming, as well as critical skills in collaboration to address the pervasive concerns for youth with disabilities.

## TEAMING FOR TRANSITION

This chapter describes the work of two 325K Personnel Preparation projects funded by the Office of Special Education Programs in the U.S. Department of Education – *Teaming for Transition* (H325K170106; T4T) and *Teaming for Transition – Preparing Youth for Work and Community* (H325K210015). The purpose of the projects is to address the preparation needs of graduate students in preparation programs across disciplines with direct roles in the transition process for youth with disabilities. The goals of these projects are to prepare professionals to understand each other's roles and responsibilities while developing competencies in collaboration skills in the context of the provision of transition planning and services. Combining the expertise and knowledge of faculty in fields including Special Education, Communication Disorders, Vocational Rehabilitation, School Counseling, Social Work, and School Administration, our two 325K Personnel Preparation projects - have been designed and implemented around a shared framework, innovative online learning technologies, and with an inquiry-based approach to understanding the challenges of transition for youth with disabilities. As faculty from across these disciplines we model the work of de-siloing the transition process; attended to challenges to collaborative, interdisciplinary preparation; and identified lessons learned to support effective professional preparation. While a paper is forthcoming on the effectiveness of the model in the preparation of scholars through data evaluating scholar competencies across our goals, here we share approaches to structuring the projects in alignment with effective approaches in interdisciplinary and interagency collaboration transition services, as well as lessons learned and implications for faculty seeking to de-silo across programs of study.

## BUILDING OUR OWN INTERDISCIPLINARY TEAM

A collective vision in support of the individual needs and future desires of youth with disabilities and their families is the primary goal for interdisciplinary transition teams. To address the transition needs of students with disabilities with high intensity needs, university programs must tackle the unique teaming needs of professionals across disciplines for successful transition to adulthood. One essential element of transition involves the integration of multiple perspectives of people who know the student and understand the future environment (e.g. interdisciplinary teaming) (Carter et al., 2014). A network of professionals with access to resources and expanding networks help students prepare to navigate their life after high school. When team members across disciplines are excessively rigid with their roles and responsibilities, they risk building silos of expertise creating boundaries that limit collaboration, communication, and flexibility needed for the essential individualization necessary. Finding ways to remove these boundaries is crucial to transition success.

### Faculty Team

The *Teaming for Transition* projects take an intentional approach in choosing team members across disciplines at the University and beyond as partners in the preparation of professionals across specialties. We gathered faculty who had personal and professional interest in supporting children and youth with disabilities and their families and who valued interdisciplinary collaboration in the preparation of professionals. Faculty in each discipline supporting youth were identified to: 1) advocate from the perspective of that discipline in the development of coursework and collaborative opportunities for scholars, 2) gather resources (e.g., curricula, tools) and individuals engaged in transition service support in their field and across the state, and 3) minimize barriers to scholar preparation across disciplines.

Faculty across the following disciplines contribute to the success of the *Teaming for Transition* projects. We have found that faculty do not have to have specific expertise in transition services and programming. Our alignment of collaborative structures with the Taxonomy for Transition facilitated sufficient knowledge of the critical components of the process to support a shared mission for preparing professionals committed to changing outcomes for youth with disabilities. More critically, we have benefited from partnerships with colleagues who, from the first day of planning share a desire to collaborate and learn. The faculty team shared assumptions that interdisciplinary teaming for effective preparation in transition services:

§ Must be intentional and requires frequent communication.

§ Require recognition of expertise in certain areas of knowledge and willingness,
§ Allow for innovation through flexible sharing of responsibility and expertise in an area of knowledge and being open to other perspectives.
§ At times may not be consistent with the learning structure inherent in higher education thus requiring faculty advocacy for different approaches to budgets, teaching responsibilities and resources across college, department and program lines.
§ Benefit from efficiency ensuring faculty time is focused on high impact work both together and separately.

We outline below contributions to transition services in educational systems from our disciplines.

## Special Education

As transition services in secondary education settings are generally led by special educators our special education faculty lead the *Teaming for Transition* projects and teach the course on transition services and practicum. While special educators are key in leading the transition planning process, they may not have the same nor broad enough perspectives to ensure successful transitions for their students. Special education teachers report feeling less prepared in areas critical for effective transition for students with highly intensive support needs including the transition itself, communication skills, technology and medical support needs of students (Ruppar, Neeper, & Dalsen, et al., 2016). Thus, special education faculty were identified who have expertise in instructional methods for students with high intensity needs, and of course the transition process.

## Communication Sciences Disorders

According to Butler (2016), the expertise that speech-language pathologists (SLPs) offer to transition planning is critical, yet they are often underutilized in the process. Speech and language therapy is one of the most highly utilized services for secondary students with high-needs disabilities (Wei, et al., 2014); however, only 15% of SLPs in the United States work in secondary school settings according to the American Speech-Language-Hearing Association's 2022 Schools Survey, (2022). In primary and secondary school settings, one in 12 children has been diagnosed (Black, et al, 2015) and receives services for a communication disorder (Kayama, et al., 2015). The inclusion of communication sciences and disorders graduate students was crucial to the development of the graduate certificate in transition services (Frazier et al., 2019). Our communication sciences and disorders faculty has expertise in communication needs and related technologies for students with high need disabilities; knowledge of communication skills necessary for self-determined lives; expertise regarding communication needs across settings including school, work, home, and community; and, guidance to the transition team in understanding the importance of functional language across these settings.

## Social Work

The discipline of social work includes collaboration as "a critical link between school, home and community" (National Association of Social Workers [NASW], 2012, p.1). Social Work does not take place in a vacuum as it requires partnerships across professions to ensure we are understanding the whole person and addressing challenges and barriers in the home, community, organization and at the policy level.

Historically, social workers have been underutilized in the transition process, as we are often involved in early intervention and ensuring services for successful academic growth. As children age, social workers tend to become involved as a behavioral or mental health intervention and less as a proactive partner in the transition process (Sherman, 2016; Wei et al., 2014).

In 2013 the Academy of Social Work and Social Welfare identified the 12 grand challenges of social work to bring focus to current practices in the field and to educate and compel other professions to better understand the services they provide (see https://grandchallengesforsocialwork.org/). Our research (Kucharczyk et al., 2021) on the transition experiences of youths with disabilities needing high-intensity supports and their families showed alignment between the Taxonomy for Transition (Kohler et al., 2016) and the grand challenges and identified specific opportunities for social workers in transition, including in predominately rural communities. Our social work faculty have expertise in the work of social workers in school settings and working with families.

## Rehabilitation Counseling

The societal benefits of providing vocational rehabilitation services, including independent living, to persons with disabilities have been clearly established, both from economic and psychosocial perspectives, and codified in the Rehabilitation Act, Americans with Disabilities Act, and the Workforce Innovation Education Act, as well as the mission of the vocational rehabilitation service system. As critical partners in the linkage between school and adult service provision, vocational rehabilitation counselors bridge a chasm experienced by youth and their families (Oertle & Trach, 2007). Preparing vocational rehabilitation counselors to effectively partner with school systems and partners, youth, and families has the potential to build a bridge of support for youth as they transition into adulthood. A review of literature in student engagement in transition services identified specific roles for vocational rehabilitation counselors in this process including building skills in self-determination and self-advocacy necessary to engage in work and in their own transition planning (Kucharczyk et al., 2022). Our rehabilitation counseling faculty have expertise in pre-employment transition service planning and support for families in the transition to adult services including vocational rehabilitation.

## School Counseling

School counselors work closely with other educational professionals to plan for successful outcomes of all students. Our review of the role of school counselors in transition planning (Frazier et al., 2020) focused on the role of school counselors in individual student future planning, advocacy for families and youth, support of family engagement in schools, and identification of students needing specific school-based services as well aligned with the activities of the Taxonomy for Transition (Kohler et al., 2016). The graduate certificate in transition was created as an opportunity to extend the expertise of these unfunded scholars beyond their programs of study, including school counselors, in the first version of *Teaming for Transition*. Our counseling faculty has expertise in the role of counselors across school contexts

## Education Administration

School-level administrators are critical to the success of transition programming and services. Given their role in scheduling the school day, week, and year they have significant opportunities to support necessary interdisciplinary planning. Administrators are critical to communicating expectations and providing supports for ensuring that the right partners are coming together and collaborating effectively. Further, school leaders set the tone and pay attention to the culture of a school. Reinforcing effective interdisciplinary collaboration and minimizing barriers to communication can make a significant impact on a transition plan. Our educational administration faculty have expertise in legal aspects of transition and the role of school leaders in creating cultures for change.

## Advisory Team

Recognizing that the knowledge of transition must begin with the experiences of youth, families, and practitioners, we sought out the support of critical partners to ensure that *Teaming for Transition* projects are well-grounded and aligned with priorities of partners in the field. Two women, both in their 20s, served as a self-advocate for each advisory team, providing their insights based on their own recent transition experiences and understanding of the gaps that could have been addressed through effective support. One self-advocate provided considerable support to coursework through videos of her experience of transition and hopes for her future. These videos are used in coursework for all *Teaming for Transition* scholars to identify the attributes of transition and family engagement which supported her success. The other self-advocate was critical in expanding our perspective on supports for youth. Additionally, family members provided helpful insights, such as parent of a student who was in the process of transitioning from high school to adulthood. Another family member leads family support for a regional agency focused on needs of Arkansans with disabilities and was helpful in gaining insights regarding transition needs across our state.

In addition to self-advocates and families, we sought support from professionals in the field with an interdisciplinary perspective on transition services and planning. Across both *Teaming for Transition* projects we sought out and commissioned a leader in special education transition in Arkansas, a leader of vocational rehabilitation in the state, a local mental health provider, two school district special education directors, two directors of adult services, the principal investigator of the PROMISE grant in Arkansas, and a national leader in transition who serves as external evaluator for the projects. The advisory group met formally once a year and are recruited for support informally as needed throughout the projects.

The *Teaming for Transition* projects extend interdisciplinary collaboration beyond the disciplines of faculty supporting the learning of our scholars by identifying efforts across the state and beyond to support transition services. The *Teaming for Transition* projects extend the state's work between the Arkansas Department of Education's Transition Services department and the National Technical Assistance Center on Transition: The Collaborative (NTACT:C). By partnering with leaders working on initiatives for transition across the state we ensure our scholars are prepared to understand state-level priorities (e.g., collaboration between special education, vocational rehabilitation, and career technical education) and support the use of evidence-based practices identified across these projects (e.g., high leverage practices, inclusive practices). In addition to the partnership with Arkansas Department of Education and NTACT:C we leverage the lessons learned from Arkansas' PROMISE Model Demonstration Project (Williams et al., 2019) which focused on improving employment outcomes for youth with disabilities and validated the evidence-based practices and predictors leading to more positive outcomes for youth with disabilities related to employment. Finally, we build on existing partnerships with high-need, rural high schools, the State's Parent Resource Center, and vocational rehabilitation and social work agencies across the state. These shared priorities and intentional relationships with state and national priorities further model effective transition interdisciplinary planning for our scholars.

## Auxiliary Team

The *Teaming for Transition* faculty team sought to understand the experiences of youth in transition, especially those in Arkansas and in other predominantly rural communities throughout each of the projects. To understand these experiences across the perspectives of the disciplines we conducted focus groups across the state with families, special education administrators, SLPs, occupational therapists and physical therapists, and counselors during our first year of planning our initial project year of *Teaming for Transition*. We asked these groups about their hopes for the future of high schoolers with disabilities, current transition practices, strengths and challenges of current transition processes, outcomes of youth they work with in their various roles. Data from these focus groups helped us focus our course development, practicum experiences, and collaborative experiences for scholars. Ultimately, data from this research were published in *Rural Special Education Quarterly* (Kucharczyk et al., 2021) and highlights the need for families and youth to have access to information about the transition process early and through coordinated, collaborative processes involving other, underutilized disciplines such as social work. The findings from this research helped us develop coursework that shifts the transition process from one that is a compliance driven "ticking of boxes" to a more holistic focus with student and family always at the center of the process.

We are grateful to all participants who took part in the focus groups and interviews for the valuable insights into their perspectives on the transition process and preparation needs for professionals supporting students and their families. We consider these participants as auxiliary team members. They have become ever present voices in our team's decision making and critical reflection on not only our successes and challenges, but for our scholars as well. They, with our advisory partners and faculty team, guide our work.

## Collaborative Structures Across Partners

Through our faculty, advisory partners, and scholars we engage in collaborative structures across levels as described in Table 1, Collaborative Structures Across T4T Projects. Frey et al. (2006) developed a levels of collaboration scale to measure collaboration across stages to clarify the various activities, relationships, and depth of collectivity across partners. We illustrate here how the *Teaming for Transition* projects create collaborative relationships across these levels and activities associated with each. Our goal is to ensure that we seek opportunities to partner across stages and that there is a depth to the collaboration through a movement towards collaboration that is mutual and shared as we believe that is the critical to the effectiveness of teams including transition teams. The *Teaming for Transition* projects include collaborative activities (e.g., sharing of data, identifying shared priorities) and structures (e.g., ongoing meetings, opportunities for feedback) intended to de-silo the work at departmental, college, and state levels by creating shared opportunities for networking, alliance building, partnership, coalition, and collaboration across faculty and with advisors. Further, we recreate these opportunities across collaborative structures for our scholars to develop their collaborative competencies.

*Table 1. Collaborative Structures Across Partners*

|  | **Purpose** | **Across Faculty** | **With Advisors** | **For Scholars** |
|---|---|---|---|---|
| Networking | -Dialogue<br>-Shared understanding<br>-Base of support | - Initial planning for grant<br>-Sharing of partners | -Extending advisors through research with youth and families across state | -Learn to identify resources across state and beyond for transition |
| Cooperation/ Alliance | -Coordinate services<br>-Ensure work is done<br>-Avoid duplication | -Change course offerings to meet needs across disciplines<br>-Share faculty teaching resources<br>-Creation of shared Graduate Certificate | -T4T share evaluation with advisors<br>-Seek feedback on project and adapt | - Share resources with partners<br>- Create community resource map for individual students and families and groups of students |
| Coordination/ Partnership | -Share resources<br>-Merge support base for something new | - Share resources across programs | -Coordinate state priorities with course content<br>-State partners guest lecture | - Identify critical team members<br>- Invest in ongoing partnerships for students |
| Coalition | -Commitment to a new system<br>-Sharing of ideas/resources to create something new | - Merging resources<br>- Partnering on research | - Self-advocates support course content | - Blending of activities and priorities across partners through frequent engagement beyond individual students |
| Collaboration | -Accomplishing shared vision<br>-Interdependence for mutual success | - Shared mission and vision for T4T<br>- Shared coursework | -Participate on shared projects across state<br>-Develop professional development based on resources across partners | - Frequent engagement and communication for shared purposes<br>- Working as one system in support of students in transition across a school or district |

\* Adapted from Frey et al. (2006)

## GROUNDING *TEAMING FOR TRANSITION* PROJECTS IN THE *TAXONOMY FOR TRANSITION*

In order to ensure that faculty, advisory teams, and auxiliary members had shared understanding of the transition planning, programming, and services we grounded the development and implementation of each of the *Teaming for Transition* projects in the Taxonomy for Transition 2.0 (Kohler et al., 2016) and in current priorities of the state in transition services as directed by the Arkansas Transition Services department of the Department of Education and the National Technical Assistance Center on Transition: The Collaborative. As discussed above, the Taxonomy for Transition 2.0 provides concrete strategies and practices for professionals across disciplines and systems to engage across categories critical to effective transition including: student-focused planning, family engagement, student development, program structures, and, most relevant to this chapter, interagency collaboration.

Each of the disciplines represented by our faculty supporting the *Teaming for Transition* projects, has a distinctive perspective on the priorities of transition generally and how to support the individual needs and strengths of students. To build a foundation through which our team of faculty and advisory board members could focus our view of transition, we used the Taxonomy for Transition 2.0 developed by Kohler and colleagues (2016). The Taxonomy is organized around categories and subcategories of transition activities across student development, student-focused planning, family engagement, program structures, and interagency collaboration. Language specific to these areas of application of effective transition strategies are used across shared coursework.

In addition to providing a common language for transition, The Taxonomy for Transition framework has guided our course development, progression of collaboration, and other collaborative experiences for our scholars. While we use the Taxonomy for our decision making, we also utilize it as a framework for our scholars to identify their role, from the perspective of their discipline, on transition services and planning. We advocate (Whitby et al., 2020) for each discipline to use the taxonomy to assess their school-level, team-level, and individual approach to transition services.

In Table 2 we illustrate how the *Teaming for Transition* partnerships are structured in alignment with expectations outlined in the Taxonomy for Transition for transition teams and programs in the "interagency collaboration" component. The Taxonomy for Transition grounds the work of the *Teaming for Transition* projects by supporting a common-language across the project that extends beyond discipline-specific language and thus supports the de-siloing of faculty efforts. As example, faculty have sought co-teaching and created research opportunities for undergraduate and graduate students, funded by the projects and others, from outside their own programs, departments, and colleges to examine their discipline's role in transition services. Importantly, we have advocated as a collaborative group for the sake of the project for flexibility in our various masters programs to adjust when courses are offered and sought workloads to be changed to allow for teaching in needed semesters. Further, we have worked with our state's Department of Education in changing course numbers to ensure that scholars across disciplines are given credit for shared coursework that is also aligned with each of the discipline's' standards and accreditation required competencies.

## COLLABORATIVE COURSEWORK

Over the past three decades, transition practices research has demonstrated that post-school outcomes of students with disabilities improve when educators, families, students, and community members and organizations work together to implement a broad perspective of transition planning (Trainor et al., 2020). The *Teaming for Transition* projects prepare professionals from special education, communication sciences and disorders, school and vocational rehabilitation counseling, and social work to develop competencies in transition planning and services through shared coursework and internship designed collaborative.

To support the development of shared competencies and minimize future barriers to professionals engaging in collaboration in transition planning and services, University scholars in education and health-related fields must be knowledgeable about their own role and the responsibilities of other allied professionals to provide the most effective services possible for their students. Multiple perspectives add depth and individualization to the services our professions provide. *Teaming for Transition* shared coursework stress that the transition process is designed to produce results-oriented plans that provide opportunities for skill development to prepare the students for what lies ahead in their future training and education, employment, and experiences of community living. *Teaming for Transition* takes an innovative, interdisciplinary approach to ease such barriers and support scholar readiness for joint work across disciplines through collaborative field experiences. Scholars are prepared in practice standards specific to their discipline and shared coursework attending to competencies in transition planning and programming, and critically collaboration. Table 3, Collaborative Coursework, describes five shared

*Teaming for Transition*

courses, disciplines leading content development, and the focus on the Taxonomy for Transition targeted in each course.

*Table 2. Teaming for Transition across the Taxonomy for Transition Programming 2.0*

| Taxonomy for Transition<br>*Collaborative Framework* | **Alignment in** *Teaming for Transition* | Taxonomy for Transition<br>*Collaborative Service Delivery* | **Alignment in** *Teaming for Transition* |
|---|---|---|---|
| Coordinating body of relevant stakeholders | Coordinating group of faculty, advisory group, state and national partners | School staff, vocational rehabilitation counselors, community service providers engage in planning meetings | Faculty across these key disciplines have been included in projects |
| Lead agency | Special Education as lead | Coordinated requests for information | Faculty share responsibility for applicants and scholars from across disciplines |
| Contact for each agency | Identified lead faculty across disciplines | Coordinated collection and use of assessment data | Faculty and advisory team evaluate data on project management and scholar objectives annually through shared data collection |
| Shared understanding of policy and procedures | Shared understanding described in 325K goals and management plan | Collaborative funding and staffing of transition services | Opportunities have been sought to create co-teaching options for shared courses; Funding supports faculty endeavors specific to transition but across disciplines |
| Systems barriers minimized | Ongoing identification of systemic barriers and opportunities to minimize | Collaborative consultation between special, general, career technical, and vocational educators | As engagement has been needed from other disciplines not involved, faculty have extended collaboration to career technical and secondary education faculty and students; working with program administrations to create flexibility in course scheduling |
| Established methods of communication | Ongoing meetings; annual advisory meetings; shared communication with scholars | Collaborative program planning and development | Faculty meet bi-monthly; advisory teams meet annually; state partners are engaged at least quarterly |
| Data shared across agencies | Cloud-based folder of data | Collaborative delivery of transition-related services | Faculty share responsibility for teaching, research, and internship support of scholars from across disciplines |
| Cross-agency professional development | All faculty engage in course development and extended collaboration experiences | Student and family linked to appropriate providers as needed | Scholars are encouraged to seek support from faculty across disciplines as desired and needed |
| Interdisciplinary and interagency policy and procedures evaluated annually | Annual review of goals and evaluation data with advisory group | | |

*Table 3. Collaborative Coursework*

| Graduate Certificate in Transition Coursework | Disciplines Leading Content Development | Taxonomy for Transition Focus |
|---|---|---|
| Transition Planning and Services | Special Education and Vocational Rehabilitation | § Student-focused Planning<br>§ Program Structures<br>§ Interagency Collaboration |
| Teaching Students with High Need Disabilities | Special Education | § Student Development<br>§ Student-focused Planning |
| Family and Professional Partnerships | Social Work and School Counseling | § Family Engagement<br>§ Program Structures<br>§ Interagency Collaboration |
| Legal Aspects / Disability Policy | School Administration and Vocational Rehabilitation | § Program Structures<br>§ Interagency Collaboration |
| Internship | All | § Student Development<br>§ Student-focused Planning<br>§ Family Engagement<br>§ Program Structures<br>§ Interagency Collaboration |

## Developing Coursework

In addition to core coursework required in each discipline's program of study each scholar completes a 4-course sequence and shared internship. Courses are co-developed by members of the faculty team with feedback from advisory team and taught by faculty from participating disciplines. Courses were restructured and revised to meet the goals of *Teaming for Transition,* align with the special education, vocational rehabilitation, school counseling, communication sciences and disorders, and social work educator competencies across the Taxonomy for Transition, and embedded with evidence-based distance teaching strategies. All shared courses are delivered online to ensure access for students from online (special education, social work) and on campus (vocational rehabilitation, social work, communication science and disorders, school counseling) programs.

## Course Alignment with Taxonomy for Transition

Courses are designed to address challenges in the field experienced by youth and adults with disabilities, their families, and professionals teaming through the transition planning and programming process. The Transition Planning and Services course explores all aspects of the Taxonomy for Transition with focus on program structures and interagency collaboration to ensure that scholars from across disciplines are able to identify quality features of transition planning regardless of their perspective and are able to advocate for practices. Scholars complete the Predictor Implementation School/District Self-Assessment (https://transitionta.org/pisa-self-assessment/) and develop community resource maps in their own contexts to address competencies in identification of services across domains of education, work, and independent living and identification of programmatic strengths and areas of need. The Teaching Students with High Need Disabilities focuses attention on the critical needs of and relevant practices for students with the most dismal post school outcomes. Having a significant disability is a predictor to the degree to which goals are attained in post school outcomes (Carter et al., 2012). This course attends to the student development and student-focused planning components of the *Taxonomy for Transition* with emphasis on evidence-based practices specific to youth with disabilities requiring individualized supports (see CEEDAR Center Innovation Configurations for students with high intensity support needs; Hume et al., 2021). Given the role of family engagement in transition planning and as a predictor of postschool outcomes (Hirano et al., 2018), the Family and Professional Partnership addresses the family engagement, interagency collaboration, and program structures components. While the Transition Services course address specific collaborative structures and activities, the Families and Professionals course focuses on communication and collaboration competencies – the soft skills of collaboration. Finally, Legal Aspects of Special Education/Disability Policies ensures that scholars, across disciplines, understand the civil rights of people of disabilities and the way these have been addressed through education and adult services. The internship course embeds application of knowledge and competencies from across courses with discipline specific competencies in high schools. These courses prepare scholars to develop competencies in leadership and advocacy through attention to program structures of the Taxonomy for Transition. Together, shared learning through these courses, prepares scholars to full attend to the components of the Taxonomy regardless of their disciplinarily focus.

## Course Delivery

In addition to research-based, relevant, and actionable content, faculty across *Teaming for Transition* have collaborated on innovative approaches to online teaching. With support from the University's Global Campus instructional designers, faculty have researched and incorporated the implementation of various innovative pedagogies intended to optimize collaborative learning in online spaces. *VoiceThread* has been used to create interactive, collaborative engagement for students across disciplines and provide opportunities for deep engagement with guest speakers for scholars learning asynchronously. Such interdisciplinary, graduate-level work requires interdisciplinary learning opportunities, which may be particularly challenging in today's asynchronous, online learning formats. Best practices in online learning emphasize the need to promote student engagement, motivation, and enhance the value of the learning experience through an array of technological tools. Often, the lack of face-to-face contact in an online environment can make collaborative learning challenging. We experimented with two forms of discussion to see if either was more likely to engage graduate students in collaborative behaviors during their coursework. We analyzed the collaborative behaviors of graduate students using both text-based, threaded discussion and *VoiceThread*, assessed perspectives on interdisciplinary engagement through learning and in their future work, and sought perceptions of satisfaction of online coursework. We found *VoiceThread* to be an effective vehicle for not only ensuring students are gaining knowledge and applying course content, but expanding their repertoire of collaborative, interdisciplinary skills.

## Interdisciplinary Field Experiences

Interdisciplinary collaboration in special education involves practitioners working in conjunction to coordinate services and weave together discipline specific practices to facilitate positive outcomes for youth with disabilities (Dillon et al., 2021; Flexer et al., 2022). Service coordination across schools and community settings may prove to be particularly important to promote positive post-secondary outcomes for youth with more significant support needs (Kester et al., 2019). Despite the importance of interdisciplinary collaboration, it can be challenging to create opportunities to enhance scholar readiness for collaboration in preparation programs as such work is often siloed at the institutional level and in the broader community. Additionally, field specific disparities exist around knowledge of transition (Kester et al., 2019). Practicing professionals (i.e., special education, vocational rehabilitation counselors) may demonstrate gaps in understanding across various aspects of transition planning, services, and supports (Kester et al., 2019), which may create additional barriers for professional development of novice practitioners. Yet, to promote successful transition of youth, there is a continued need for professional skill development (Weiss et al., 2020).

Field-based learning experiences often play a critical role in development of novice professionals (Kent et al., 2016). During field experiences, scholars practice applying discipline specific strategies with the support of field supervisors to foster positive outcomes for youth. In addition to gaining knowledge and experience in discipline specific practice, field experiences targeting collaborative competencies can also enhance readiness for interdisciplinary collaboration. Such collaborative field experiences have been shown to increase knowledge of other disciplines, improve acceptance of professional support from others, increase trust of other professionals, and encourage preparedness for collaboration in future work (Weiss et al., 2020). Because of the importance of field-experience in the skill development continuum, *Teaming for Transition* includes an interdisciplinary practicum experience. This practicum leverages actionable content and innovative instructional approaches to prepare scholars for application of evidence-supported practices in transition specific to their disciplines and enhance candidates' readiness for collaboration across disciplines (e.g., social work, special education, vocational rehabilitation).

*Teaming for Transition* faculty collaborate across disciplines to identify tools and experiences for scholars in the practicum to support readiness and foster development of collaboration competencies. The practicum activities encourage scholars to establish professional trust across disciplines, create clear roles and responsibilities in transition planning, share knowledge with each other, and engage in group work (Gerdes et al., 2020). Another tool *Vosaic*, an online platform for video analysis, is used as a reflective tool for scholars as they apply transition-specific practices in their field-based practicum experiences. Because evidence suggest video analysis is a powerful tool to foster ongoing learning and growth of practitioners (Morin et al., 2019), this field-based work supports scholars for their current roles and establishes readiness to adapt their practice as the field and recommended practices continue to evolve. After piloting *Vosaic*, course artifacts revealed candidates used the platform to identify opportunities for improvement in their practice such as "I could have provided more detailed feedback in my responses," and "It was typically the same students responding." Scholars also recognized positive changes to their practice, "…showing an area of improvement in the amount of praise given." This innovative instructional approach supports *Teaming for Transition* scholars in enhancing their skills through self-directed professional development.

It is critical stakeholders across disciplines play an active role in providing supports and identifying services for successful transition of youth with disabilities. Yet without proper preparation and professional development, disparities in knowledge of transition can persist across disciplines and thereby diminish positive outcomes for youth. By targeting skill development in a joint practicum through innovative approaches, *Teaming for Transition* faculty create meaningful field-based learning experiences to support scholars for readiness in their discipline specific practice and enhance critical skills for interdisciplinary collaboration.

## Graduate Certificate in Special Education Transition Services

A Graduate Certificate in Special Education Transition Services was created with the intention of creating multiple pathways for students who were not funded to join funded student scholars in specializing in transition service knowledge and competencies. For scholars interested in transition services, our graduate certificate degree program packages shared coursework and interdisciplinary practicum and is available for those eligible for graduate studies.

## Collaboration Beyond Coursework

In addition to the collaborative coursework and internship described above, scholars across disciplines benefited from additional experiences as they developed their competencies. Early in their program, scholars participated in focused discussions with leaders in transition. These included participating in the Arkansas Department of Education's Transition Summit during which they had the opportunity to sit with transition teams from across the state to hear about the application of the principles and practices they had been learning in their coursework. Scholars also attended the University's symposium which focused on transition services and benefited from sitting together and applying learning from leaders in transition services in the United States and Arkansas. Later, COVID limited these face-to-face opportunities, but created new opportunities to have more frequent opportunities at a distance. For example, Dan Habib, film maker and project director of University of New Hampshire's Institute on Disability, shared his films on transition services across the United States and advocacy for inclusion services in one focused *Teaming for Transition* event. Later in their studies, scholars collaborated on a presentation at the Council for Exceptional Children Convention in 2021. Also in 2021, a now practicing teacher and SLP in high schools, presented at Arkansas' Local Education Administration Conference on transition assessments and engaging youth with high- need disabilities in transition planning, respectively. These same graduated scholars will be presenting their work at the Division of Career Development and Transition Conference in 2022. *Teaming for Transition* is not only preparing high quality practitioners in transition – we are developing leaders and future scholars in the field.

## LESSONS LEARNED IN THE INTERDISCIPLINARY PREPARATION OF PROFESSIONALS

In our development and implementation of *Teaming for Transition* we have gathered a few lessons learned that have informed our newest iteration of the program focusing more broadly on perspectives of interdisciplinary work across our disciplines.

### Lesson 1 – Coursework

Development of collaborative, cross discipline coursework required care. Each discipline is responsible to an accrediting body with a set of standards. We were careful to ensure all coursework would meet each discipline's standards. At times, this process opened us further to opportunities for interdisciplinary scholar preparation as we learned how much we had in common. We worked to understand each other's professional standards, found where we shared practices, values and ethics, and worked from there to create content-inclusive courses and to reduce redundancy. We sought guest speakers for specialized topics, such as how the juvenile justice system impacts transition and future outcomes. As with the academic partners, presenting this information to students is invaluable and critical to their success of supporting students through transition. Allowing room for discussion and dialogue, as well as giving opportunities for group collaborative work was valuable to the students in their understanding of how each discipline approaches a student and family's needs and where each of them fit in the greater system. Further, we ensured that coursework included various examples from perspective of different disciplines to give students a sense of what their work might look like in application.

## Lesson 2 – Collaborative Alignment

Collaborative alignment of both *Teaming for Transition* projects to the Taxonomy for Transition and levels of collaboration created unintended structures for engagement across faculty, our advisory team, scholars. While the attention to these was initially intended to guide scholar preparation, the application of strategies for interagency and interdisciplinary collaboration across our coursework created opportunities to model these structures across our disciplines. Thus, the application of the *Teaming for Transition* projects, necessitated the de-siloing of our teaching, research, and project management. As shown in Tables 1 and 2, our application of collaborative strategies shifted our work and modeled such work for scholars.

These shared activities helped faculty better understand each other's profession, requirements of the faculty and students in those professions, and where we overlap and where we do not. As academics and as practitioners we often rely on other professions to do their part so we can do our part, rather than taking the time to purposefully understand what each of us does and how we can work together to fill needs, reduce gaps, and improve life trajectories, especially for people with differing abilities. As we worked together, we have become more adept at focusing our efforts on modeling a true interdisciplinary team and approach to curricula and practice.

## Lesson 3 – Inclusion of Unfunded Students

The *Teaming for Transition* projects are limited in terms of our ability to fund scholars from all disciplines. We have had to make difficult decisions about how to manage project budgets to benefit scholars most likely to impact adult outcomes as future members on transition teams. Opportunities remain for funding in areas such as school administration and occupational therapy to enhance the learning for all scholars involved, gaining needed interdisciplinary knowledge for serving as a part of the transition team and could have provided opportunities for future administrators to lead efforts in ensuring transition teams are interdisciplinary. While we were not able to provide funding for all potential disciplines in the transition process, we have sought creative avenues for access. Our intention was to provide opportunities for scholars from other disciplines through the Graduate Certificate and use of continuing education units. We found, across our programs, that programs of study have very little flexibility and opportunities for electives. We continue to seek innovative approaches to include students across disciplines.

## Lesson 4 – We Are More Aligned Than We Assume

Through our collaborative work through *Teaming for Transition,* we have found strong alignment across our disciplines with the activities and attitudes needed for effective transition services leading to positive outcomes for students with disabilities. Further, each discipline has identified culturally responsive and sustaining practices embedded across our standards especially those focused on family involvement, school climate, life, social and emotional skills, and student supports. Such alignment offers opportunities for future considerations for student planning and learning and project adaptation. We believe that our work has great promise to prepare professionals across disciplines to better collaborate for effective transitions for youth with high support need disabilities.

## Lesson 5 – Sustainability

As *Teaming for Transition* has moved into its second iteration, we have identified ways in which planned and emergent collaborative structures have been maintained outside of the projects. First, the Graduate Certificate in Transition Services draws students from varied backgrounds who are not scholars in the project. We are seeking opportunities to expand this offering to those studying across broader disciplines. For example, our vocational rehabilitation partners work with faculty in the School of Business who have students interested in exploring how to better prepare businesses and employers to include people with disabilities as consumers, employees, and leaders. Second, we continue to partner with faculty in programs not directly impacted by *Teaming for Transition.* Our communication sciences and disorders and special education faculty are finding opportunities outside of the projects to provide professional development, research, and teach. In the next semester, faculty from across disciplines are planning a special Dean's Seminar for undergraduate and graduate students to participate in on the seemingly intractable challenges of education and creative ways these may be mitigated through interdisciplinary collaboration. Finally, the projects are having an impact on programs and leaders outside of our faculty group. The Dean of the College of Education and Health Professions remarking on her "stealing" our *Teaming* idea in the development of funding opportunities for faculty to engage in shared projects across departments in the College. Most importantly, we are gathering impact our scholars are making on the field in their practice. As of this writing, two scholars, a special educator and a speech-language pathologist will be presenting at the national conference for the Division on Career Development and Transition on practices which incorporate examples of their interdisciplinary collaboration in high school settings postgraduation. This dissemination of effective practice is an example of the most valued marker of the potential and of these projects to impact the challenges of transition in practice to shift the outcomes of youth with disabilities.

## SUMMARY

This chapter described how, across disciplines, *Teaming for Transition* graduate coursework and collaborative experiences were restructured around the core, common vision of preparing professionals to shape the outcomes of youth with disabilities in their adult. This core vision is grounded in the Taxonomy for Transition 2.0 (Kohler et al., 2016) and shapes our intention to model effective interdisciplinary planning and implementation of program change as we expect our students to do in their future and current work with youth. Thus, we are explicit about our roles and responsibilities identify gaps in each other's knowledge, as well as expertise across disciplines. When team knowledge needs are identified *Teaming for Transition* faculty have recognized the questions inherent in these gaps and designed research to engage them. These action inquiries have guided research leading to multiple publications, presentations, and have informed project revision. Our collective research has considered the critical role of speech-language pathologists and school counselors in collaboration with special educators in transition planning and services (Frazier et al., 2020; Frazier et al., 2019). Further, we conducted interviews with Arkansan families and youth to understand their experience of transition (Kucharczyk et al., 2021). Additionally, we conducted a scope of literature to explore the role of vocational rehabilitation counselors in engaging youth and families in transition planning (Kucharczyk et al., 2022). In addition to current research, these investigations have deepened experiences of scholars through relevant, timely content.

As faculty in fields of study and practice with a stake in addressing the post-school outcomes for youth with disabilities, the *Teaming for Transition* projects provide an opportunity to address the research and practice needs identified by Trainor et al. (2020). By de-siloing our teaching, research, and engagement with partners outside our programs these projects have created professionals with shared mission for minimizing the barriers to the adult lives that youth with disabilities and their families desire. Through shared coursework, alignment with the *Taxonomy for Transition,* and engagement in collaboration across faculty and with advisory team and state and national partners we prepare scholars to meet the challenges of their shared field of practice.

## REFERENCES

Bates-Harris, C. (2012). Segregated and exploited: The failure of the disability service system to provide quality work. *Journal of Vocational Rehabilitation, 36*, 39–64. https://doi.org/10.3233/JVR-2012-0581

Black, L. I., Vahratian, A., Hoffman, H. J., & National Center for Health Statistics (U.S.). (2015). *Communication disorders and use of intervention services among children aged 3-17 years: United States, 2012.* Hyattsville, MD: U.S. Department of Health and Human Services, Centers for Disease Control and Prevention, National Center for Health Statistics.

Brady, K. P., Kucharczyk, S., Schaefer Whitby, P., Terrell, E., & Merry, K. E. (2021). A review of critical issues in transition team's decision-making and the importance of ethical leadership. *Journal of Leadership and Instruction, 20*(2), 14–19.

Bumble, J. L., Carter, E. W., & Kuntz, E. M. (2021). Examining the transition networks of secondary special educators: An explanatory sequential mixed methods study. *Remedial and Special Education.* doi:10.1177/07419325211063485

Butler, C. (2016). The effectiveness of the TEACCH approach in supporting the development of communication skills for learners with severe intellectual disabilities. *Support for Learning, 31*(3), 185–201. doi:10.1111/1467-9604.12128

Carter, E. W., Austin, D., & Trainor, A. A. (2012). Predictors of postschool employment outcomes for young adults with severe disabilities. *Journal of Disability Policy Studies, 23*, 50–63. 1044207311414680 doi:10.1177/

Carter, E. W., Brock, M. E., & Trainor, A. A. (2014). Transition assessment and planning for youth with severe intellectual and developmental disabilities. *The Journal of Special Education, 47*, 245–255. doi:10.1177/0022466912456241

Dillon, S., Armstrong, E., Goudy, L., Reynolds, H., & Scurry, S. (2021). Improving special education service delivery through interdisciplinary collaboration. *Teaching Exceptional Children, 54*(1), 36–43. https://doi.org/10.1177/00400599211029671

Flexer, R. W., McMahan-Queen, R., Baer, R., & Sparber, C. (2022). A mixed design evaluation of an interdisciplinary transition graduate program. *Journal of Applied Rehabilitation Counseling, 53*(1), 45–67.

Frazier, K., Perryman, K., & Kucharczyk, S. (2020). Transition services: Building successful collaborations among school professionals. *Journal of School-Based Counseling Policy and Evaluation, 2*(2), 131–141. https://doi.org/10.25774/80b3-kc43

Frazier, K. F., Whitby, P. J. S., Kucharczyk, S., Perryman, K. L., Thomas, J., Koch, L. C., & Bengston, E. (2019). Interprofessional education: Teaming for transition from adolescence to adulthood for people with significant disabilities. *Perspectives of the ASHA Special Interest Groups, 4*(3), 492–501.

Frey, B. B., Lohmeier, J. H., Lee, S. W., & Tollefson, N. (2006). Measuring collaboration among grant partners. *The American Journal of Evaluation, 27*(3), 383–392. https://doi.org/10.1044/2019_PERS-SIG10-2018-0008

Gerdes, G. S. L., Huizinga, M., & de Ruyter, D. (2020). Analytic framework for interdisciplinary collaboration in inclusive education. *The Journal of Workplace Learning, 32*(5), 377–388. doi:10.1108/JWL-08-2019-0099

Hirano, K. A., Shanley, L., Garbacz, S. A., Rowe, D. A., Lindstrom, L., & Leve, L. D. (2017). Validating a model of motivational factors influencing involvement for parents of transition-age youth with disabilities. *Remedial and Special Education, 39*(1), 15–26. https://doi.org/10.1177/0741932517715913

Hume, K., Steinbrenner, J. R., & Odom, S. L. (2021). Evidence-based practices for children, youth, and young adults with autism: Third generation review. *Journal of Autism and Developmental Disorders*. doi:10.1007/s10803-020-04844-2

IEP Team, 34 C.F.R. §300.321 (2017).

Individuals with Disabilities Education Act, 20 U.S.C.A. §§ 1431-1444 (2017).

Kayama, M., Haight, W., Kincaid, T., & Evans, K. (2015). Local implementation of disability policies for "high incidence" disabilities at public schools in Japan and the U.S. *Children and Youth Services Review, 52*, 34–44. doi:10.1016/j.childyouth.2015.02.009

Kent, & Giles, R. M. (2016). Dual Certification in General and Special Education: What is the Role of Field Experience in Preservice Teacher Preparation? *The Professional Educator, 40*(2).

Kester, F. M., Beveridge, S., & Stella, J. (2019). Interdisciplinary Professional Development Needs of Transition Professionals Serving Youth with Autism Spectrum Disorders. *Journal of Rehabilitation, 85*(1), 53–63.

Kohler, P. D., Gothberg, J. E., Fowler, C., & Coyle, J. (2016). *Taxonomy for transition programming 2.0: A model for planning, organizing, and evaluating transition education, services, and programs.* Western Michigan University. Available at www.transitionta.org

Kucharczyk, S., Oswalt, A., Schaefer-Whitby, P., Frazier, K., & Koch, L. (2022). Emerging trends in youth engagement during transition: Youth as interdisciplinary partners. *Rehabilitation Research, Policy, and Education, 36*(1), 71–98. https://dx.doi.org/10.1891/RE-21-16

Kucharczyk, S., Thomas, J. M., & Schaefer-Whitby, P. (2021). "It would have been nice if…": Analysis of Transition Experiences through Grand Challenges. *Rural Special Education Quarterly, 40*(3), 117–131. https://doi.org/10.1177/87568705211027970

Mazzotti, V. L., Rowe, D. A., Kwiatek, S., Voggt, A., Chang, W.-H., Fowler, C. H., Poppen, M., Sinclair, J., & Test, D. W. (2021). Secondary transition predictors of postschool success: An update to the research base. *Career Development and Transition for Exceptional Individuals, 44*(1), 47–64. https://doi.org/10.1177/2165143420959793

Morin, G. J. B., Vannest, K. J., Haas, A. N., Nagro, S. A., Peltier, C. J., Fuller, M. C., & Ura, S. K. (2019). A systematic review of single-case research on video analysis as professional development for special educators. *The Journal of Special Education, 53*(1), 3–14. doi:10.1177/0022466918798361

Newman, L., Wagner, M., Huang, T., Shaver, D., Knokey, A. M., Yu, J., Contreras, E., Ferguson, K., Greene, S., Nagle, K., & Cameto, R. (2011). *Secondary School Programs and Performance of Students with Disabilities. A Special Topic Report of Findings from the National Longitudinal Transition Study-2 (NLTS2)* (NCSER 2012-3000). U.S. Department of Education. Available at: www.nlts2.org/reports/2011_11/nlts2_report_2011_11_rev30113_complete.pdf

Oertle, K. M., & Seader, K. J. (2015). Research and practical considerations for rehabilitation transition collaboration. *Journal of Rehabilitation, 81*, 3–18.

Oertle, K. M., & Trach, J. S. (2007). Interagency collaboration: The importance of rehabilitation professionals' involvement in transition. *Journal of Rehabilitation, 73*(3), 36–44.

Plotner, A. J., Mazzotti, V. L., Rose, C. A., & Teasley, K. (2020). Perceptions of Interagency Collaboration: Relationships Between Secondary Transition Roles, Communication, and Collaboration. *Remedial and Special Education, 41*(1), 28–39.

Plotner, A. J., Trach, J. S., & Shogren, K. A. (2012). Identifying a transition competency domain structure: Assisting transition planning teams to understand roles and responsibilities of community partners. *Journal of Rehabilitation Research, Policy, and Education, 26*, 257–272.

*Schools Survey.* (2022). American Speech-Language Hearing Association. https://www.asha.org/siteassets/surveys/2022-schools-slp-summary.pdf

Trainor, A. A., Carter, E. W., Karpur, A., Martin, J. E., Mazzotti, V. L., Morningstar, M. E., Newman, L., & Rojewski, J. W. (2020). A Framework for Research in Transition: Identifying Important Areas and Intersections for Future Study. *Career Development and Transition for Exceptional Individuals*, *43*(1), 5–17. https://doi.org/10.1177/2165143419864551

U.S. Bureau of Labor Statistics. (2020). *Annual youth labor force participation rate and unemployment rate.* https://www.dol.gov/agencies/odep/research-evaluation/statistics

Wei, X., Wagner, M., Christiano, E. R., Shattuck, P., & Yu, J. W. (2014). Special education services received by students with autism spectrum disorders from preschool through high school. *The Journal of Special Education*, *48*(3), 167–179.

Weiss, C. B., & Eren, R. (2020). Transdisciplinary approach practicum for speech- language pathology and special education graduate students. *Journal of Autism and Developmental Disorders, 50*(10), 3661–3678. doi:10.1007/s10803-020-04413-7

Whitby, P. J. S., Kucharczyk, S., & Fowler, C. (2020). Evidence-based practices in transition. *DADD Express. Focus on Autism and Other Developmental Disabilities*, *31*(2), 1–3. http://www.daddcec.com/uploads/2/5/2/0/2520220/dadd_spring2020_v2b.pdf

Williams, B., Lo, W. J., Hill, J., Ezike, N., & Huddleston, J. (2019). Employment supports in early work experiences for transition-age youth with disabilities who receive supplemental security income (SSI). *Journal of Vocational Rehabilitation*, *51*(2), 159–166. https://doi.org/10.3233/jvr-191035

# Chapter 26
# A Model for Interdisciplinary Preparation in Culturally-Responsive, Evidence-Based Transition Planning

**Kristin Powers**
*California State University, Long Beach, USA*

**Edwin Achola**
*California State University, Long Beach, USA*

## ABSTRACT

*Over the past seven years, we have provided intensive training to cohorts of school psychology and special education graduate students. Through rigorous shared coursework, in-person and virtual learning, coordinated school-based fieldwork, and enhanced study (conference attendance, seminar participation, case study completions) scholars gained the skills to establish and sustain culturally responsive, evidence-based transition services for students with disabilities, including those high-intensity needs. This chapter describes the steps the co-authors took to enhance the training and service delivery of school psychologists and special education teachers to provide effective transition services.*

Students with disabilities generally fair less well in adulthood than those without disabilities (Mazzotti et al., 2021; Newman, 2011; Wagner, et al., 2014; Winsor et al., 2018). For example, the postsecondary completion rates of young adults with disabilities were lower than that of their peers in the general population. Data from a national sample showed that while 51% of similar-age peers in the general population had graduated or completed postsecondary, only 29% of youth with disabilities at 4-year universities completed college (Sanford et al., 2011). Other reports have indicated that these disparities in student outcomes may be influenced by type of disabilities. Newman et al., (2011) noted that in the employment domain for instance, young adults with intellectual and multiple disabilities were less likely

DOI: 10.4018/978-1-6684-6438-0.ch026

to have been employed than young adults with other health impairments, speech/language impairments, learning disabilities, or hearing impairments.

In response to the disparities, schools were mandated by federal law to provide transition planning to better prepare students with disabilities for adult life. For more than 30 years, researchers have reported that special education teachers express being under-prepared across essential areas of transition (Plotner, et al. 2016). This lack of preparation is likely due to a failure by preservice special education programs to prepare teachers to be competent in meeting the transition needs of students with disabilities. As we sought to remedy this omission in special education teacher training, we decided to take an interdisciplinary approach and include school psychology students in this training because they could be strong partners in promoting evidence-based transition services due to their training in consultation, problem-solving and evidence-based interventions. Further, we decided to center the training on culturally-responsive transition services due to the potential to increase students with disabilities' adult outcomes by including families and cultural resources in a more consciousness manner.

## Need for Evidence-based Culturally Responsive and Sustaining Transition Services

Culturally responsive and sustaining transition pedagogy can be described as an outcome-oriented process designed to prepare young adults for successful adulthood considering the unique sociocultural contexts within which all students thrive after high school. Transition educators who engage in culturally responsive and sustaining pedagogies (CRSPs) are known to be effective in promoting post-secondary success by increasing student achievement and reducing opportunity gaps (Achola 2019; Achola & Greene, 2016; Christianakis, 2011). Research suggests that such educators foster academic success, cultural competence, and critical consciousness, and work toward the goal of preserving valued cultural heritages in pluralistic societies (Dickson et al., 2015; Ladson-Billings, 1995b; Morrison et al., 2008; Paris & Alim, 2012). These educators also raise students' consciousness about social justice issues, center on students' funds of knowledge, and provide a challenging transition curriculum tailored to address post-school goals.

More recently, the need for CRSP in transition has been amplified by the glaring inequities observed in student transition outcomes. Over the last 20 years, extensive patterns of racial/ethnic and class-based disparities in post school outcomes have been documented (Aucejo et al., 2020; Baker et al., 2019; Newman et al., 2011). The disparities are particularly prominent in the areas of access to quality transition programming (Landmark & Zhang, 2013), satisfaction with the transition experience, participation in gainful employment (Trainor, 2008; Trainor et al., 2014), and enrollment in post-secondary education (Rueda et al., 2005; Schuster et al., 2003). For example, compared to their peers from dominant communities (65.5%) young adults with disabilities from minoritized communities are more likely to receive individualized transition plans that are not compliant with Indicator 13 (Landmark & Zhang, 2013) and are less likely to be employed up to 8 years after graduating from high school. Similarly, many parents of youth from traditionally minoritized communities tend to be less satisfied with their level of involvement in the transition planning process compared to parents from other backgrounds (Cameto, et al., 2004; Greene, 2011; Rueda et al., 2005); they also struggle to access community resources (Cartledge et al., 2008) and feel that their contributions to the transition planning process are undervalued by school professionals (Geenen et al., 2001).

## Current Trends in Training Special Education Teachers and School Psychologists in Transition Planning

Traditionally, transition planning has always been relegated to special education teachers who often serve as student case carriers and transition specialists. Many of the special education teachers receive their transition related training through standalone courses during pre-service training while others learn about transition services from their peers on the job. Research suggested that the majority of the educators reported their transition training was on-the-job, rather than through comprehensive teacher education (Greene & Kochar-Bryant, 2003). Access to transition content and coursework during pre-service training are largely influenced by state licensure requirements as well as federal and state funding and incentives promoting specialized content. Unfortunately, the present landscape of transition professional development is defined by a lack of clear policies as well as limited systems for planning, delivering, and evaluating professional development (Morningstar & Liss, 2008). In addition, little effort has been placed on teaching emergent evidence-based interventions or systems-level factors leading to change.

School psychologists have many useful skills and knowledge-bases that could facilitate culturally-responsive, evidence-based transition planning and services, such as knowledge of assessments and interventions, consultation, and problem-solving (National Association of School Psychologists, 2020). However, school psychologists are even less likely than special education teachers to have taken a course on transition planning in graduate school. Underwood (2018) found none of the school psychology programs surveyed have a course devoted to transition planning and less than 20% of the programs reported having an assignments or readings related to transition planning in their syllabi, despite a natural fit between the professional skills of a school psychologists and the competencies required to engage in high quality transition planning. Since, pre-service training is associated with better transition planning services and outcomes for students with disabilities (Morningstar & Benitez, 2013; Plotner, et al., 2016; Plotner & Simonsen, 2018) we developed an interdisciplinary training model for school psychology and special education graduate students to provide evidence-based, culturally-responsive transition planning and services.

## The Need for Interdisciplinary Teams to Provide Transition Services

Many scholars have argued that effective transition requires the expertise of cross-disciplinary teams, including related service personnel such as school psychologists working to provide comprehensive, coordinated services (Blalock et al., 2003). Such related service providers with specific training on transition have been shown to be more successful in preparing youth with disabilities for post-school life (Butterworth et al., 2012; Carter et al., 2011). Therefore, it is crucial that preparation of personnel for transition teams include interdisciplinary training focused on the specific post-school needs of youth with disabilities (Cawthon et al., 2014; Plotner & Fleming, 2014)

Even though effective transition planning requires the expertise of cross-disciplinary teams, few training models incorporate such strategies. Fortunately, the US department of education's office of special education programs (OSEP) interdisciplinary personnel preparation grants has created unique opportunities for colleges to establish and promote interdisciplinary transition training models. The

## A Model for Interdisciplinary Preparation in Culturally-Responsive, Evidence-Based Transition Planning

current project centered on training both school psychology and special education scholars through a collaborative interdisciplinary training model focused on transition planning. The project aimed to leverage expertise from both programs to provide scholars with opportunities to collaborate and learn about how to deliver culturally responsive and sustaining transition services for youth with disabilities. The scholars from both programs collaborated in delivering evidenced based transition supports, they also, completed shared coursework, seminars, professional conferences, and fieldwork in multicultural settings. This novel approach to training allowed scholars to develop unique knowledge, insights, and problem-solving skills that came about as a result of extensive contact with peers and trainers from different disciplines.

## TRAINING GRANT COMPONENTS

From 2015 to 2020, 11 school psychology and 18 special education students (aka scholars) received OSEP funded training in culturally responsive, evidence-based transition planning and services. Of the 29 scholars, 45% were White, 38% were Latinx, 14% were Black and 3% were Asian American. One quarter (24%) identified as male. Most of the special education credential scholars received two years of training (equivalent to the length of the special education credential program), though five completed only one or two semesters of training. These special education students dropped out of the grant-funded training program due to either being offered a full-time teaching position or dropping out of the special education credential program. The school psychology scholars received three years of training (equivalent to the length of the school psychology Ed.S. program), which allowed them to take on a leadership role on the training grant in their third year. Grant-supported scholars received scholarships to offset the cost of graduate school, as such they were expected to engage in (1) monthly seminars, (2) 4–6 hours of additional fieldwork experiences per week (including systems change projects in their second year of grant funding), (3) cross-program course enrollment, (4) on-line trainings, (5) attend a national conference each year they were funded, and (6) complete two out-reach activities per year in order to recruit for the special education and school psychology programs and professions.

### Monthly Seminar Activities

The purpose of the monthly seminar was to advance students' knowledge and critical skills in culturally-responsive, evidence-based transition services via immersion in the research literature, large and small group discussions, and direct skill instruction. Topics included self-determination training, quality transition plans, cultural reciprocity, services for students with significant support needs, multi-disciplinary collaboration, professional roles, and inter-agency collaboration. After the first year of training, seminar topics included systems change and program improvement to scale-up culturally-responsive, evidence-based transition practices. As a new cohort of special education and school psychology scholars joined the grant in year three, and we began anew on these topics, the school psychology students in their third year selected one of these topics to present in seminar, which involved assigning readings, preparing a power point and an in-class activity.

During the very first seminar of the first cohort, the students were observed to seat themselves by program, with all the special education scholars seated at the same side of the table as the special education professor and all the school psychology scholars electing to sit on the other side of the table near the school psychology professor. One of the professors shared this observation, and expressed that a goal of this interdisciplinary training grant is to "mix things up" – both literally and figuratively. It was a wonderful starting point and became a theme with this cohort wherein they at first deliberately and then later quite naturally arrange themselves in interdisciplinary groupings. Because the grant seminars were nongraded, discussion-orientated and occurred over many semesters on Friday afternoons, they became a rather communal experience. Establishing interdisciplinary connections through the seminars was furthered by the grant-related fieldwork.

## School-Based Fieldwork Activities

The school psychology and special education scholars on the grant engaged in school-based fieldwork activities over the course of two years, to further develop their knowledge and skills in providing culturally-responsive, evidence-based transition services. School psychology and special education scholars were assigned as dyads (based in part on their availability and geographic location to our training sites) to a self-contained special education classroom in one of four local high schools. The teachers with whom they worked were seasoned teachers who volunteered to host and collaborate with our students. Our students were present in their assigned classroom for 4-6 hours one day a week over the course of two years.

### Individualized Transition Plans

For the first year, the students assisted with gathering data for writing evidence-based, culturally responsive individualized transition plans (ITPs). They began by analyzing the high school students' existing transition plans by applying the "Indicator 13" and "Contextual Fit" rubrics and noting whether the major components outlined in these rubrics were present in the ITP. Indicator 13 is a compliance indicator that measures the percentage of youth with IEPs aged 16 and above with an IEP that includes appropriate measurable postsecondary goals that are based upon age-appropriate transition assessments; transition services, including courses of study, that will reasonably enable the student to meet those postsecondary goals. The contextual fit of an ITP refers to the extent that the procedures of the plan are consistent with the knowledge, values, skills, resources, and administrative support of those who are expected to implement the plan. "Contextual fit" is based on the premise that the match between an intervention and local context affects both the quality of intervention implementation and whether the intervention actually produces the desired outcomes for children and families (Horner, 2014). Often, contextual fit is measured by the perceptions of the practitioners, who implement a plan such as an ITP. Horner further noted that practitioners must have a certain level of motivation, interest, and support for intervention fit to be present.

Project directors adapted the contextual fit for ITP from the contextual fit of behavior support plan (Monzalve & Horner, 2021). The adapted contextual fit for ITPs incorporates eight elements that combine to establish the fit between an ITP and the setting in which it is implemented. These include knowledge of elements in the ITP; skills needed to implement the ITP; values are consistent with elements of the ITP; resources available to implement the plan; administrative support; effectiveness of ITP; and the ITP is in the best interest of the student; the ITP is efficient to implement.

During the first year, all scholars received training on what constitutes quality transition plans and evaluated sample ITPs. At the beginning of year two, the scholars completed transition assessments and collaborated with peers, teachers, youth with disabilities and their families to develop new and revised transition plans. Scholars worked in small groups of two to three students and collected both pre-and post-assessment data to monitor the quality of transition plans developed.

Evidence indicated that students with high quality transition plans are more likely to experience successful transition outcomes especially when it comes to post-secondary education outcomes. Erickson et al. (2013) for example found that transition age students who had high quality ITPs were more likely to enroll in and complete a semester of college or a career training program. Unfortunately, youth from culturally and ethnically diverse communities are less likely to receive high quality ITPs that contain evidence of best practices. Landmark and Zhang (2013) noted that being of African American decent was linked with decreased chances of receiving an ITP that was fully compliant with indicator 13 requirements. In addition, students of African American decent were more likely to have ITPs that did not included family involvement or employment preparation.

Data from the office of Special education programs (OSEP) further indicates that many states are struggling to meet the compliance requirements related to quality transition plans. In California for example, the most recent data shows that the state did not meet the target for both indicator 13 and 14. Indicator 13 focuses on the number of youth aged 16 and above with IEPs that contain each of the required components for secondary transition while indicator 14 highlights the percentage of students enrolled in higher education or competitively employed within one year of leaving high school

Culturally responsive transition programming is one strategy that has been suggested as a promising approach to improve the quality of transition plans for youth from culturally and ethnically diverse background (Achola & Greene, 2016; Cote et al., 2012; Gothberg et al., 2019). Some of the key elements of culturally responsive transition programming that were incorporated in the grant program included highlighting the intersections between disability and "other markers of social difference;" asset-based planning; intercultural development; diversity-informed resource mapping (Achola, 2018); culturally responsive relationships; transition strategies attuned to student and family sociocultural backgrounds, evidence-based transition practices, and critical consciousness.

## Self-Determination Groups

In addition to learning to develop culturally responsive transition plans, the special education/school psychology dyads also facilitated self-determination groups with the students at their grant-related fieldwork site. In consultation with the classroom teacher, the dyads selected students either as a small group or whole class to receive a series of 8 to 10 self-determination lessons. The lessons were selected in consultation with the classroom teacher and were found at no-cost on the Zarrow Center website, which includes the *Choice Makers, Me!,* and *Who's Future is it Anyway?* The dyads administered pre- and post-test *Self-Determination Inventory (SDI) – Student and Teacher Reports*. The administration of a self-determination program allowed the school psychology/special education dyads to practice their consultation skills as they worked with the classroom teacher to select appropriate lessons for the students they served. The dyads also practiced their data-based decision-making skills as they examined together the gains or lack of progress on the SDI. The school psychology and special education faculty also observed the dyads during at least one of their self-determination lessons each year and provided feedback and prompts for reflection. Some areas faculty encouraged the scholars to reflect on were:

- How can you ensure all of the students are engaged?
- How can you increase engagement through culturally-responsive strategies?

- How can you better use the pre-test SDI data to guide your lessons?
- How can you incorporate what you are learning about the students in the self-determination group to develop high quality transition plans for them?
- What do you individually have to offer to the group based on your unique training as a school psychologist or a special educator?

This type of inquiry as applied to practice with students who were training for two different disciplines let to a deeper understanding of not only their own developing skills but also a greater awareness of the developing skills set of their colleagues.

## Systems Change Projects

During the second year of training, the dyads identified a transition-related shortcoming in their school site and put a plan together to address the deficiency. For example, one dyad realized the students in the self-contained class were not participating in extracurricular activities on campus, despite many having a desire to do so. They surveyed the students the classroom they served about their interests and met with club presidents to facilitate their enrollment, resulting in doubling the number of students in that class who participated in a school club that year. After discussing the issue with special and general education teachers and a school administrator it was decided to develop a new position on the student government board for a student to serve as a liaison for students with disabilities in order to sustain their increased access to campus extracurricular activities.

Another dyad helped to establish a Best Buddies club on campus in which students with and without disabilities organized the group, which allowed students with high support needs to experience a leadership role. The scholars increased the number of community activities hosted by the club and paired students with and without disabilities based on their culture and home language. Finally, the scholars established a handbook and identified a teacher to take-over the club when their year was done.

Additional systems-change projects included increasing inter-agency collaboration for a community-based transition program and working with teachers and administrators to increase the inclusion of students with high support needs in the Linked Learning program – a school-wide college and career readiness program from which students with high support needs were largely excluded. Unfortunately, this latter project ran into a number of institutional barriers and was never successful. Yet, whether their projects got off the ground or failed, the school psychology/special education dyads learned to work together on gathering data to support the need for change, resource mapping and proceeding through the first stages of systems change implementation as defined by Fixsen et al. (2005) – *'exploration and adoption' 'program installation'* and in some cases *'initial implementation.'* During the third year of the grant, the third-year school psychology students served as "coaches" to the second cohort of newly admitted special education and school psychology scholars. Like the first cohort, the second cohort completed 4-6 hours of fieldwork in dyads in self-contained classes in the local school districts, but this time with greater support from the school psychology coaches who observed and consulted with the dyads.

All students completed bi-weekly logs detailing the activities and hours they completed at the grant-training fieldwork site. They also indicated the percent of their time devoted to (a) promoting students' future employment; (b) post-secondary education and training; (c) adult living tasks; (d) culturally responsive transition activities and services. We asked students to consider engaging in activities that fall within all four of these categories each week to gain a wide range of experiences. Each student

*A Model for Interdisciplinary Preparation in Culturally-Responsive, Evidence-Based Transition Planning*

*Figure 1. Intercultural Development Continuum*
Note. Adapted from "The Intercultural Development Inventory (IDI): A New Frontier in Assessment and Development of Intercultural Competence," by M. R. Hammer, in M. Vande Berg, M. Paige, R. M., and K. Lou (Eds.), *Student Learning Abroad: What Our Students Are Learning, What They're Not, and What We Can Do About It* (pp. 115–136), 2012, Stylu.

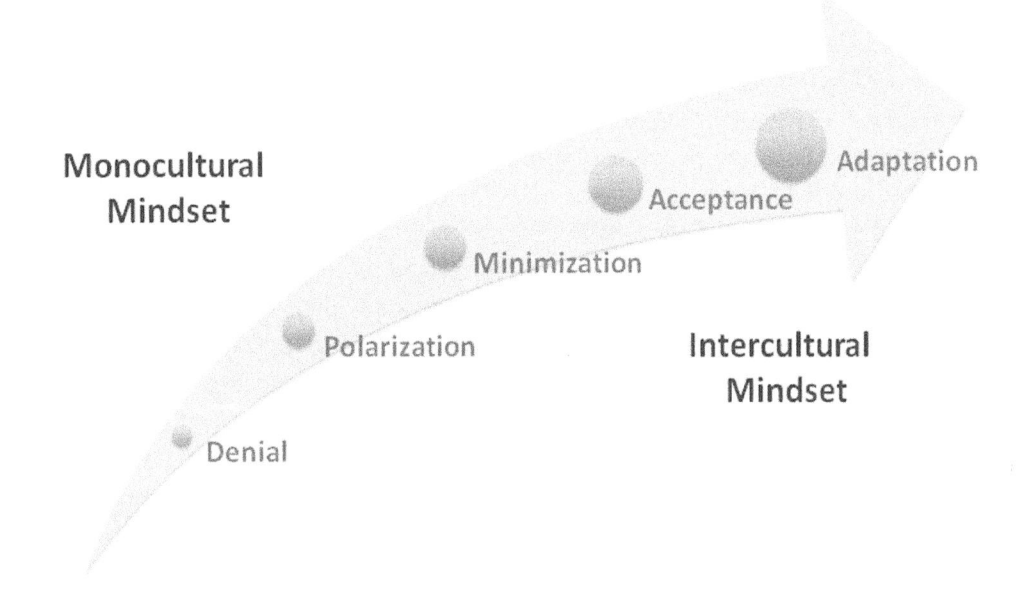

completed their own log and the school psychology professor read the school psychology students' logs and the special education professor read the special education students' logs, thus, faculty were able to hold individual students accountable for meet the fieldwork training objectives.

## Intercultural Development to Enhance Transition Services

The grant program highlighted intercultural development among scholars to enhance their capacity to deliver culturally responsive and sustaining ITPs and other types of transition services. Intercultural development has been linked to improvements in classroom teachers' capacity to respond effectively to students from culturally and ethnically diverse communities (Bird & Mendenhall, 2016; De Leon, 2014). However, there are few training models in transition education that help connect teacher candidates' intercultural development, knowledge of diverse students, and effective transition planning. The application of intercultural development continuum (Bennett, 2016) was one such model useful to preparing teacher candidates to connect intercultural development and effective instruction in diverse settings. The intercultural development continuum describes a set of cognitive (thinking), affective (feeling), and behavioral (doing) skills and orientations towards cultural differences and commonalities that are arrayed along a continuum (Hammer, 2011). The continuum highlights the more monocultural mindsets of denial and polarization through the transitional orientation of minimization to the intercultural or global mindsets of acceptance and adaptation (see Figure 1; Bennett, 2016).

The project directors administered the intercultural development inventory to all scholars and used the results to design training seminars corresponding to the scholar's needs. Thereafter, scholars engaged in discussions focused on linking intercultural development and culturally responsive and sustaining transition planning. The project directors theorized that scholars who applied intercultural or global mindsets were more likely to implement culturally responsive and sustaining practices leading to quality ITPs.

## Cross Program Course Enrollment

Prior to the OSEP funded grant project, school psychology and special education students did not take any core course work together, despite the fact that they would one day work very closely with colleagues from these professions. The students may have crossed paths in a prerequisite child development course, but it would be haphazard and not necessarily bring greater awareness of each other's disciplines. By requiring the school psychology scholars to take *EDP 534 Collaboration and Transition in Special Education* as part of the expectations of the OSEP grant, we emersed the school psychology students in a singularly special education class. We also furthered the school psychology students' knowledge about transition services and it was yet another experience to get to know their special education OSEP grant counter-parts who were also taking the class. Likewise, the OSEP funded special education scholars were expected to take *EDP 536 Collaborative Consultation* as part of their training. In this course, special education students gained knowledge about consultation skills that can be applied in many settings and to multiple types of services, including transition. This course was also one of the few courses that was already inter-disciplinary as school counseling students also take the class as part of their core program. Thus, the grant-funded special education scholars were able to learn and practice consultation skills in a multi-disciplinary course, that also included some of their OSEP grant funded school psychology counter-parts.

Developing a means for shared coursework was somewhat difficult. For the school psychology students, program faculty needed to agree to allow the *Collaboration and Transition in Special Education* class to count toward one of the elective classes required to complete the program. For the special education students, taking the *Collaborative Consultation* class meant taking one more class than needed to complete their credential. Fortunately, many of the special education students found the course to be very beneficial and in fact suggested to the faculty that it should be incorporated into the special education credential program. Interestingly, the *EDP 536 Collaborative Consultation* course was at one-time in the history of our institution a required course for special education credential students, but years ago special education faculty developed a different consultation course for their students that focused more on inclusion of special education students in general education and less on the science and practice of consultation in order to meet their professional standards and the direction they wished to take their program. Though the special education and school psychology programs are housed in the same department within the same college, ongoing curriculum development to meet the unique state and national standards for each discipline has led to more courses that served only one discipline resulting in both programs being "silos" with little to no shared coursework

## On-line Trainings

In addition to the seminars, scholars completed multiple online training modules from the national technical assistance center on transition (NTACT), IRIS center, Transition Coalition, Center for Advanced Studies in Child Welfare, and Project 10: Transition Education Network. Some of the instructional strategies from the in-person seminars that were applied in the online learning environment included discussions, self-directed learning, groupwork, and case studies. The online trainings helped to orientate the scholars to the training grants and to fill-in content that we couldn't cover during seminars.

## National Conference Attendance

The OSEP funded school psychology and special education scholars and the project faculty attended the annual *Division of Career Development and Transition* (DCDT) convention in order to further their knowledge about transition services. Attending this national conference allowed the students and faculty to learn about the most recent research and innovations in transition services. Prior to attending the conference, the faculty curated the conference by highlight specific presentations thought to be particularly relevant to the grant training objectives and /or delivered by someone who is very well established in the field.

Another goal of attending the conference was to introduce students to DCDT with the hopes that some of them may remain active in the organization past their own post-baccalaureate training. Finally, traveling and attending a conference out-of-state with their grant-funded peers led to even more cross-disciplinary relationship building. In fact, many of the students on our training grants formed long-lasting friendships and one school psychology and one special education scholar even fell in love with each other and married last year. The happy couple reported that spending time together in Seattle for the annual DCDT conference was where their spark began. Overall, alumni of the OSEP training grant report feeling much more confident and interested in collaborating with colleagues from the other discipline in their professional lives because of the experiences and friendships they gained by participating in the training grant.

## Recruitment

On August 14, 2022, National Public Radio (NPR) ran a story about the shortage of Black School Psychologists in America. Salhotra (2020) reported that Black men are more likely to play for the NFL than become a school psychologist. Beeks and Graves (2017) interviewed Department Chairs of Historically Black Colleges and Universities (HBCUs) who identified many of the same reasons express in the NPR story for why Black college students don't want to enter the field of school psychology, despite a shortage of school psychologists and ample career opportunities. These reasons included not knowing much about the field of school psychology, lack of representation of Blacks in the field, and the role school psychologists play in assessing students for disabilities and the subsequent over-representation of Black students in special education. In order to address these challenges, scholars on the OSEP grant were tasked with conducting two outreach events per semester to unrepresented communities. Such groups included scholars who identify as male, ethnic and cultural minorities, and those who claim the LGBTQ identity.

Scholars completed several recruitment activities that focused on targeted outreach and asset-based retention strategies. These comprehensive recruitment and retention efforts highlighted social and societal barriers to nontraditional retention, because studies have shown that such factors are more related to attrition than low academic performance (Kalsner, 1991). Examples of recruitment strategies included outreach in unique settings (e.g., barber shops, faith communities, HBCU fairs) known to attract targeted populations, collaboration with cultural liaisons, personal connections, and student-directed recruitment activities. In addition, many of the scholars were matched with educator mentors with similar lived experiences and completed outreach and fieldwork in schools with culturally and ethnically diverse student populations.

A number of the recruitment activities involved presenting on the field of school psychology and special education to classroom aides and paraprofessionals. Classroom aides tend to be more heterogeneous than school psychologists and special education teachers. For example, 34% of paraprofessionals in California (California Department of Education, 2022) are White compared to 86% of school psychologists nation-wide (Goforth et al., 2021). Special education teachers are also predominantly White (US Department of Education, 2021) even though the short and long-term benefits to African American students of having a same-race teacher are well documented (Gershenson et al., 2017).

The outcomes of the recruitment efforts are described next, but it is notable that special education and school psychology scholars on the grant often conducted recruitments in their dyads so they could explain and answer questions about both professions. This experience furthered their mutual understanding and respect for each other's' disciplines.

## OUTCOMES

### Diversifying the Fields

Both programs found the number and diversity of their applicant pools to increase following the implementation of these recruiting activities. Across the project period, applications to the school psychology program increased from 81 applications prior to the project to an average of 148 applications per year thereafter. The education specialist program increased their applications from 29 the previous to an average of 53 applications per year thereafter. In the final year of the grant, 73% of the applicants to the school psychology program were people of color and 15% were male. In the special education program, 70% of the applicants were people of color and 15% were male. Of the 11 school psychology students who trained on the grant, 3 were Black men who now work in the field of school psychology. The 2020 recipient of the Outstanding Student Award for the entire college was a Latina woman who was working as a classroom aide when she was recruited by our first cohort of school psychology and special education students to apply to the school psychology program and to join our grant.

### Strong Sense of Belonging

In addition to intentionally recruiting diverse applicants to the program, the training grant appeared to enhance students' sense of belonging to their program and discipline. Each year students in the school psychology and special education programs completed belonginess surveys and routinely those who participated on the grant reported stronger affiliation to their programs and professions for which they were training, and a stronger sense that they were being adequately prepared to enter that profession. This enhanced sense of belonging may be a result of shared grant-funded experiences such as the monthly seminars, interdisciplinary fieldwork and attending out-of-state conferences.

## Conference Attendance Evaluations

The OSEP grant allowed special education and school psychology scholars to attend national conferences that provide the latest research and best practices on serving students with disabilities. The goal was to attend DCDT each year, but in 2018 we decided to attend the Council on Exceptional Children (CEC) annual conference which is much larger than DCDT. The results presented in Table 1 suggest DCDT actually provided better training on the objectives of the grant than the CEC conference, despite faculty members' attempt to direct students to transition-related workshops, papers and posters at CEC. Table 1 also indicated that students received solid training in transition planning from these conferences but they received less information about systems-change and how to identify practices that may be alienating to families. Fortunately, these were topics of the grant seminars and incorporated into the interdisciplinary field-based activities.

## Improved Training Programs

The grant conceptual framework emphasized commitment to the interdisciplinary training model that challenges prevailing norms of siloed approach to preparing educators. The interdisciplinary training approach was situated in the context of the broadened learning demands of culturally responsive and sustaining transition pedagogy and increased need for collaboration among transition experts with different skillsets. Consequently, scholars developed a greater understanding of each other's disciplines, acquired collaborative skills necessary for culturally responsive and sustaining pedagogies, and established relationships that lasted beyond the life of the program. The benefits of interdisciplinary training also extended to faculty who reported learning about each other's disciplines. The increased expertise as a result of interdisciplinary training contributed to program improvement over time as evidenced by revised training syllabi and enhanced fieldwork experiences.

A third notable outcome of the grant relates to the development of improved ITP evaluation instruments. As noted earlier, scholars in the program used a modified indicator 13 and contextual fit protocols to evaluate the quality of the ITP developed in the fieldwork training sites. The project directors modified the indicator 13 instrument to include two additional questions focused on family engagement and use of CRSP in transition. Scholars used the contextual fit protocol to measure the extent to which ITPs developed were a good fit for the context in which they were implemented. ITPs with higher scores were more likely to be implemented with fidelity.

At the beginning of the programs, scholars randomly selected and evaluated existing ITPs developed by educators at their respective fieldwork sites. These sample ITPs were used in seminars for training scholars in the use of ITP evaluation instruments. Similarly, the sample ITPs were used to train scholars on how to develop quality plans. Findings showed that the majority of the selected ITPs (developed by cooperating teachers) did not meet indicator 13 requirements. Also, most of these ITPs were not a good fit for the contexts in which they were implemented based on the contextual fit for ITP scores. However, almost all of the ITPs developed by scholars post training met indicator 13 compliance requirements and had higher scores on contextual fit protocol. This finding suggests increased knowledge and skills in providing evidence-based, culturally responsive services among scholars.

*Table 1. Scholar Satisfaction with Training*

| CONFERENCE | DCDT | | | CEC | DCDT |
|---|---|---|---|---|---|
| YEAR | 2015 (n=10) | 2016 (n=10) | 2017 (n=15) | 2018 (n=15) | 2019 (n=10) |
| Collaborative Consultation | | | | | |
| Transition related consultation skills | 2.4 | 2.4 | 2.27 | 2.08 | 2.4 |
| Culturally competent consultation skills | 2 | 3.22 | 1.86 | 1.75 | 2.4 |
| Evidence-Based Transition Services | | | | | |
| Developing transition plans that incorporate promising interventions such as self-determination training | 2.4 | 2.25 | 2.67 | 2.33 | 2.4 |
| Developing and assisting in the implementation of targeted evidence-based interventions | 2.2 | 2.4 | 2.33 | 2.25 | 2.7 |
| Person-Family Centered Transition Planning | | | | | |
| How to explore and utilize connections between child and family outcomes in order to develop meaningful ITPs | 2 | 2.5 | 2.4 | 1.75 | 2.6 |
| Strengths-based family empowerment models that recognize family strengths and expertise | 2.1 | 2.6 | 2.67 | 1.58 | 2.5 |
| Recognizing current transition practices that alienate their intended audience because they represent attitudes and practices that some families do not embrace | 1.9 | 2.5 | 1.73 | 1.75 | 2.3 |
| How to develop family-to-family networks | 2.2 | 2.1 | 2.27 | 2.27 | 1.8 |
| Culturally-Responsive Transition Practices | | | | | |
| Ways in which perceptions of transition outcomes and quality of life vary across families | 2.2 | 2.4 | 1.73 | 2 | 2.6 |
| How to apply a flexible approach to transition planning | 2.3 | 2.3 | 2.46 | 2 | 2.4 |
| Systems Change | | | | | |
| Systems change research and/or implementation science | 2.3 | 2.1 | 1.86 | 1.92 | 2.1 |
| Conducting community resource mapping | 2.2 | 2.2 | 2 | 2.42 | 2 |

(None = 1; Acclimation = 2; Competence = 3; Expertise = 4)

## TRANSITION TRAINING GRANTS 2.0

In 2019 project faculty received two more OSEP inter-disciplinary training grants, both focused on preparing school professionals for providing culturally-responsive, evidence-based transition services to students with disabilities. However, they had slightly different foci. One focused on training special education teachers and school psychologist to serve foster involved youth and the other focused on increasing the inclusion of students with disabilities in college and career pathways in middle- and high schools.

## Serving Transitioning Foster Youth

The CASA training project included many of the same activities described above with the addition of a focus on supporting youth experiencing foster care. Thus, the school psychology and special education students were to become Court Appointed Special Advocates (CASA) for transition-age foster youth, which included 30 hours of training by this non-profit organization. They then completed some of their fieldwork hours mentoring their CASA mentee. For this grant, the special education students were graduate students pursuing a master's degree in special education and most worked full time as special education teachers making it difficult to complete the 30 hours of CASA training and meeting weekly with a CASA mentee so they completed alternative online training and mentored a foster youth who attended school at their school site.

## Linked Learning

Many transition educators shared concerns about the exclusion of students with disabilities from access to college and career readiness opportunities. In response to this problem, the training program implemented a system of integrated student support focused on providing equitable access to college and career readiness via Linked Learning pathways in high and middle schools. Linked Learning is a multiyear, comprehensive high school program of integrated academic and technical study organized around an industry sector. Although this program is available in many schools across the country, very few students with disabilities participate in it. Of those who participated, fewer graduate with college and career readiness skills. The grant scholars promoted participation in linked learning for all students with disabilities through an action research-oriented project. First, the scholars collected data to determine the level of involvement of students with disabilities in linked learning pathways and completed a needs assessment at the beginning of their training. Through action research, the scholars examined student course schedules, course selection sheets, and information about general awareness of linked learning pathways. Using these data, each scholar team (dyad) developed an intervention to increase access to linked learning pathway opportunities for students with disabilities. The interventions were tailored to the needs of each fieldwork site.

## LESSONS LEARNED

Seven years of intentional interdisciplinary training has resulted in a number of lessons learned, foremost is the benefits of this training to current and future educators. By and large the project was successful in recruiting, retaining, and graduating highly qualified, diverse individuals to the education specialist and school psychology programs. Across the project period, we observed a marked increase in the number of applicants from communities that are not often represented in the two professions. In fact, our grant scholar population was more culturally and ethnically diverse than what is observed in the college and university. We believe that the diverse background of our candidates and the training focused on culturally responsive pedagogy will go a long way in mitigating the inequities observed in transition programing.

One unanticipated benefit of the program relates to professional development for our district partners. All of our scholars were able to develop and implement culturally responsive individualized transition plans in consultation with the cooperating teachers. As a result, the teachers received professional development through this process especially by collaborating with the scholars and PIs. Generally, our district partners were very collaborative, however, in some cases, it took us longer to complete the processes required to obtain access to school sites for scholars. This barrier was attributed to unanticipated changes in policy and procedures over time. Since the COVID pandemic, this access to securing fieldwork sites has become even more tricky to obtain. We have been able to facilitate access to fieldwork sites by recruiting practicing special education teachers to pursue their master's degree and participate on the training grant, thus, their own classrooms have become the site placements for the dyads.

A second barrier relates to structural challenges that impact service delivery in school sites. Our scholars completed fieldwork hours in sites that had underdeveloped infrastructure for culturally responsive pedagogy. As a result, some scholars experienced pushback while trying to implement culturally responsive transition planning. Finally, the relatively high attrition among the special education scholars due to various reasons (health, offers of paid employment on internship credentials, etc.) posed a challenge.

Some advice we offer to other educators interested in forming interdisciplinary training opportunities for their students include:

a) Take advantage of assets that scholars bring to the program. Our scholars were very successful in diversifying the pool of applicants to the special education and school psychology programs. Many of the scholars leveraged their unique backgrounds and life experiences to reach out to applicants from diverse communities.
b) Develop a community of practitioners in the field who are interested in supporting training goals.
c) Include practicing teachers in grant training opportunities to the maximum extent possible.
d) Align with priorities suggested by school district partners.
e) Plan for unexpected events such as need for medical leave and school closures due to a pandemic.
f) Collaborate closely with program coordinators to design a course of study that does not prolong time-to-graduation.

## CONCLUSION

Graduate school is a formative experience as individuals develop their professional identities and competencies. Working in schools requires interdisciplinary skills such collaborative consultation, problem-solving and knowledge of their colleagues' unique skills and competencies. Interdisciplinary teams for serving students who receive special education is mandated as well as best practices, yet, so many educators work in silos, similar to the institutions that trained them. In large bureaucratic institutions, creating interdisciplinary programs is difficult. The need to meet discipline-specific unique standards for training and credentials further make interdisciplinary training complicated. However, it is possible- particularly with additional resources such as the OSEP grants to fund extra-curricular seminars, fieldwork, conferences, etc. Individuals who pursue careers in teaching, school psychology, school counseling, etc. all want to help students, including special education students, and many realize they can do more together than apart; but it is essential that training programs build-in these opportunities to collaborate in order for true synergism to occur in our schools.

# REFERENCES

Achola, E. O. (2019). Practicing what we preach: Reclaiming the promise of multicultural transition programming. *Career Development and Transition for Exceptional Individuals*, *42*(3), 188–193. doi:10.1177/2165143418766498

Achola, E. O., & Greene, G. (2016). Person-family centered transition planning: Improving post-school outcomes to culturally diverse youth and families. *Journal of Vocational Rehabilitation*, *45*(2), 173–183. doi:10.3233/JVR-160821

Aucejo, E. M., French, J., Ugalde Araya, M. P., & Zafar, B. (2020). The impact of COVID-19 on student experiences and expectations: Evidence from a survey. *Journal of Public Economics, 191*(3). doi:10.1016/j.jpubeco.2020.104271

Baker, J. N., Lowrey, A. K., & Wennerlind, K. R. (2018). Building an inclusive post-secondary education program for young adults with intellectual developmental disability. *Physical Disabilities: Education and Related Services*, *37*(2), 13–33. doi:10.14434/pders.v37i2.25738

Bennett, M. J. (2016). The value of cultural diversity: Rhetoric and reality. *SpringerPlus*, *5*(1), 897. doi:10.118640064-016-2456-2

Bird, A., & Mendenhall, M. E. (2016). From cross-cultural management to global leadership: Evolution and adaptation. *Journal of World Business*, *51*(1), 115–126. doi:10.1016/j.jwb.2015.10.005

Blalock, G., Kochhar-Bryant, C. A., Test, D. W., Kohler, P., White, W., Lehmann, J., Bassett, D., & Patton, J. (2003). The need for comprehensive personnel preparation in transition and career development: A position statement of the Division of Career Development and Transition. *Career Development and Transition for Exceptional Individuals*, *26*(2), 207–226. doi:10.1177/088572880302600207

Butterworth, J., Migliore, A., Nord, D., & Gelb, A. (2012). Improving the employment outcomes of job seekers with intellectual and developmental disabilities: A training and mentoring intervention of employment consultants. *Journal of Rehabilitation*, *78*(2), 20–29.

*California Department of Education.* (2022). *Full-time Equivalent of Classified Staff* [Data Quest]. https://d.cde.ca.gov/dataquest/dqcensus/stfFteclassified.aspx

Cameto, R., Levine, P., & Wagner, M. (2004). *Transition planning for students with disabilities*. SRI International.

Carter, E. W., Austin, D., & Trainor, A. A. (2011). Predictors of postschool employment outcomes for young adults with severe disabilities. *Journal of Disability Policy Studies*, *23*(1), 50–63. doi:10.1177/1044207311414680

Cartledge, G., Gardner, R., & Ford, D. Y. (2009). Diverse learners with exceptionalities: Culturally responsive teaching in the inclusive classroom. Academic Press.

Cawthon, S. W., Schoffstall, S. J., & Garberoglio, C. L. (2014). How ready are postsecondary institutions for students who are d/deaf or hard-of-hearing? *Education Policy Analysis Archives*, *22*, 13. doi:10.14507/epaa.v22n13.2014

Christianakis, M. (2011). Hybrid texts: Fifth graders, rap music, and writing. *Urban Education*, *46*(5), 1131–1168. doi:10.1177/0042085911400326

Cote. (2012). Designing transition programs for culturally and linguistically diverse students with disabilities. *Multicultural Education*, *20*(1), 51–55.

De Leon, N. (2014). Developing intercultural competence by participating in intensive intercultural service learning. *Michigan Journal of Community Service Learning*, *21*(1), 17–30.

Dickson, G. L., Chun, H., & Fernandez, I. T. (2015). The development and initial validation of the student measure of culturally responsive teaching. *Assessment for Effective Intervention*, *41*(3), 141–154. doi:10.1177/1534508415604879

Fixsen, D., Naoom, S., Blasé, K., Friedman, R. M., & Wallace, F. (2005). *Implementation research: A synthesis of the literature*. University of South Florida.

Gaumer Erickson, A. S., Noonan, P. M., Brussow, J. A., & Gilpin, B. J. (2013). The impact of IDEA indicator 13 compliance on postsecondary outcomes. *Career Development for Exceptional Individuals*, *37*(3), 161–167. doi:10.1177/2165143413481497

Geenen, S., Powers, L. E., & Lopez-Vasquez, A. (2001). Multicultural aspects of parent involvement in transition planning. *Council for Exceptional Children*, *67*(2), 265–282. doi:10.1177/001440290106700209

Gershenson, S., Hart, C. M. D., Lindsay, C. A., & Papageorge, N. W. (2017). *The long-run impacts of same-race teachers*. IZA Discussion Paper Series, No. 10630.

Goforth, A. N., Farmer, R. L., Kim, S. Y., Naser, S. C., Lockwood, A. B., & Affrunti, N. W. (2021). Status of school psychology in 2020: Part 1, demographics of the NASP membership survey. *NASP Research Reports*, *5*(2), 1–17.

Gothberg, J. E., Greene, G., & Kohler, P. D. (2018). District implementation of research-based practices for transition planning with culturally and linguistically diverse youth with disabilities and their families. *Career Development and Transition for Exceptional Individuals*, *42*(2), 77–86. doi:10.1177/2165143418762794

Greene, G. (2011). *Transition planning for culturally and linguistically diverse youth. Brookes transition to adulthood series*. Brookes Publishing Company.

Greene, G., & Kochhar-Bryant, C. A. (2003). *Pathways to successful transition for youth with disabilities*. Merrill Prentice-Hall.

Hammer, M. R. (2011). Additional cross-cultural validity testing of the Intercultural Development Inventory. *International Journal of Intercultural Relations*, *35*(4), 474–487. doi:10.1016/j.ijintrel.2011.02.014

Kalsner, L. (1991). Issues in college student retention. *Higher Education Extension Service Review*, *3*(1).

Ladson-Billings, G. (1995b). Toward a theory of culturally relevant pedagogy. *American Educational Research Journal*, *32*(3), 465–491. doi:10.3102/00028312032003465

Landmark, L. J., & Zhang, D. (2012). Compliance and practices in transition planning: A review of individualized education program documents. *Remedial and Special Education*, *34*(2), 113–125. doi:10.1177/0741932511431831

Mazzotti, V. L., Rowe, D. A., Kwiatek, S., Voggt, A., Wen-Huan, C., Fowler, C. H., Poppen, M., Sinclair, J., & Test, D. W. (2021). Secondary transition predictors of postschool success: An update to the research base. *Career Development and Transition for Exceptional Children*, *44*(1), 47–64. doi:10.1177/2165143420959793

Monzalve, M., & Horner, R. H. (2021). The impact of the contextual fit enhancement protocol on behavior support plan fidelity and student behavior. *Behavioral Disorders*, *46*(4), 267–278. doi:10.1177/0198742920953497

Morningstar, M. E., & Liss, J. M. (2008). A preliminary investigation of how states are responding to the transition assessment requirements under IDEIA 2004. *Career Development and Transition for Exceptional Individuals*, *31*(1), 48–55. doi:10.1177/0885728807313776

Morrison, K. A., Robbins, H. H., & Rose, D. G. (2008). Operationalizing culturally relevant pedagogy: A synthesis of classroom-based research. *Equity & Excellence in Education*, *41*(4), 433–452. doi:10.1080/10665680802400006

National Association of School Psychologists. (2020). *The Professional Standards of the National Association of School Psychologists*. Author.

Newman, L., Wagner, M., Knokey, A., Marder, C., Nagle, K. M., Shaver, D., & Wei, X. (2011). *The post-high school outcomes of young adults with disabilities up to 8 years after high school a report from the national longitudinal transition study-2 (NLTS2)*. United States Department of Education. doi:10.13140/RG.2.2.20600.57600

Paris, D., & Alim, S. (2014). What are we seeking to sustain through culturally sustaining pedagogy? A loving critique forward. *Harvard Educational Review*, *84*(1), 85–100. doi:10.17763/haer.84.1.982l873k2ht16m77

Plotner, A. J., & Fleming, A. R. (2014). Secondary transition personnel preparation in rehabilitation counselor education programs. *Rehabilitation Research, Policy, and Education*, *28*(1), 33–44. Advance online publication. doi:10.1891/2168-6653.28.1.33

Plotner, A. J., Mazzotti, V. L., Rose, C. A., & Carlson-Britting, K. B. (2016). Factors associated with enhanced knowledge and use of secondary transition evidence-based practices. *Teacher Education and Special Education*, *39*(1), 28–46. doi:10.1177/0888406415599430

Plotner, A. J., & Simonsen, M. L. (2018). Examining federally funded secondary transition personnel preparation programs. *Career Development and Transition for Exceptional Individuals*, *41*(1), 39–49. doi:10.1177/2165143417742138

Rueda, R., Monzo, L., Shapiro, J., Gomez, J., & Blacher, J. (2005). Cultural models of transition: Latina mothers of young adults with developmental disabilities. *Council for Exceptional Children*, *71*(4), 401–414. doi:10.1177/001440290507100402

Salhotra, P. (2022, August 14). *There's a nationwide shortage of Black male school psychologists*. [Radio Broadcast]. NPR. https://www.npr.org/2022/08/14/1117418891/

Sanford, C., Newman, L., Wagner, M., Cameto, R., Knokey, A.-M., & Shaver, D. (2011). *The Post-High School Outcomes of Young Adults With Disabilities up to 6 Years After High School. Key Findings From the National Longitudinal Transition Study-2 (NLTS2)* (NCSER 2011-3004). SRI International. Available at www.nlts2.org/reports/

Schuster, J. L., Timmons, J. C., & Moloney, M. (2003). Barriers to successful transition for young adults who receive SSI and their families. *Career Development for Exceptional Individuals, 26*(1), 47–66. doi:10.1177/088572880302600104

Trainor, A. A. (2008). Using cultural and social capital to improve postsecondary outcomes and expand transition models for youth with disabilities. *The Journal of Special Education, 42*(3), 148–162. doi:10.1177/0022466907313346

Trainor, A. A., Murray, A., & Kim, H. (2014). *Postsecondary transition and English learners with disabilities: Data from the second national longitudinal transition study.* WCER working paper No. 2014-4. Wisconsin Center for Educational Research.

Underwood, A. (2018). *Preservice preparation in evidence-based and culturally responsive transition services.* Unpublished master's thesis.

U.S. Department of Education. (2022). *State performance plan/Annual performance report: Part B for date formular grant programs under the individual with disabilities education act for reporting FFY2020.* Author.

US Department of Education, National Center of Educational Statistics. (2021). *Schools and staffing survey.* https://nces.ed.gov/surveys/sass/tables/sass1112_20161123001_t1n.asp

Wagner, M. M., Newman, L. A., & Javitz, H. S. (2014). The influence of family socioeconomic status on the post high school outcomes of youth with disabilities. *Career Development and Transition for Exceptional Individuals, 37*(1), 5–17. doi:10.1177/2165143414523980

Winsor, J., Timmons, J., Butterworth, J., Migliore, A., Domin, D., Zalewska, A., & Shepard, J. (2018). *StateData: The national report on employment services and outcomes.* University of Massachusetts Boston, Institute for Community Inclusion.

# Compilation of References

*Schools Survey*. (2022). American Speech-Language Hearing Association. https://www.asha.org/siteassets/surveys/2022-schools-slp-summary.pdf

Able-Boone, H., Harrison, M. F., & West, T. A. (2002). Interdisciplinary education of social inclusion facilitators in early childhood settings. *Teacher Education and Special Education*, 25(4), 407–412. doi:10.1177/088840640202500409

Abu-Rish, E., Kim, S., Choe, L., Varpio, L., Malik, E., White, A. A., & Zierler, B. (2012). Current trends in interprofessional education of health science students: A literature review. *Journal of Interprofessional Care*, 26(6), 444–451. doi:10.3109/13561820.2012.715604 PMID:22924872

Accomazzo, S., Israel, N., & Romney, S. (2015). Resources, exposure to trauma, and the behavioral health of youth receiving public system services. *Journal of Child and Family Studies*, 24(11), 3180–3191. doi:10.100710826-015-0121-y

Aceves, T. C., & Orosco, M. (2014). *Culturally responsive teaching* (Document No. IC-2). Retrieved from University of Florida, Collaboration for Effective Educator, Development, Accountability, and Reform Center website: https://ceedar.education.ufl.edu/tools/innovation-configurations/

Achola, E. O. (2019). Practicing what we preach: Reclaiming the promise of multicultural transition programming. *Career Development and Transition for Exceptional Individuals*, 42(3), 188–193. doi:10.1177/2165143418766498

Achola, E. O., & Greene, G. (2016). Person-family centered transition planning: Improving post-school outcomes to culturally diverse youth and families. *Journal of Vocational Rehabilitation*, 45(2), 173–183. doi:10.3233/JVR-160821

Adams, D., Bittner, M., Lavay, B., & Silliman-French., L. (in-press). Adapted physical education teachers' prior training and current use of action research to monitor student progress. *Palaestra*.

Adams, R. C., Tapia, C., Murphy, N. A., Norwood, K. W. Jr, Adams, R. C., Burke, R. T., Friedman, S. L., Houtrow, A. J., Kalichman, M. A., Kuo, D. Z., Levy, S. E., Turchi, R. M., & Wiley, S. E.Council on Children with Disabilities. (2013). Early Intervention, IDEA Part C Services, and the Medical Home: Collaboration for Best Practice and Best Outcomes. *Pediatrics*, 132(4), e1073–e1088. doi:10.1542/peds.2013-2305 PMID:24082001

Adelman, H., & Taylor, L. (2021). *New directions for school counselors, psychologists, & social workers*. University of California at Los Angeles: The Center for Mental Health in Schools & Student/Learning Supports. http://smhp.psych.ucla.edu/pdfdocs/report/framingnewdir.pdf

Adelman, H., & Taylor, L. (2020). Embedding mental health as schools change. *Annals of Psychiatry and Mental Health*, 8(2), 1147–1154.

Adlof, S. M., & Hogan, T. P. (2019). If we don't look, we won't see: Measuring language development to inform literacy instruction. *Policy Insights from the Behavioral and Brain Sciences, 6*(2), 210–217. doi:10.1177/2372732219839075

Ahrnsbrak, R., Bose, J., Hedden, S. L., Lipari, R. N., & Park-Lee, E. (2017). *Key substance use and mental health indicators in the United States: Results from the 2016 National Survey on Drug Use and Health.* Center for Behavioral Health Statistics and Quality, Substance Abuse and Mental Health Services Administration. https://www.samhsa.gov/data/sites/default/files/NSDUH-FFR1-2015/NSDUH-FFR1-2015/NSDUH-FFR1-2015.pdf

Akbulut, M. S., & Hill, J. R. (2020). Case-based pedagogy for teacher education: An instructional model. *Contemporary Educational Technology, 12*(2), 1-17. doi:10.30935/cedtech/8937

Al Otaiba, S., Baker, K., Lan, P., Allor, J., Rivas, B., Yovanoff, P., & Kamata, A. (2019). Elementary teacher's knowledge of response to intervention implementation: A preliminary factor analysis. *Annals of Dyslexia, 69*(1), 34–53. doi:10.100711881-018-00171-5 PMID:30617942

Alharbi, A. (2018). Perceptions of using assistive technology for students with disabilities in the classroom. *International Journal of Special Education, 33*(1), 129–139.

Alim, H. S., & Paris, D. (2017). What is culturally sustaining pedagogy and why does it matter. In D. Paris & H. S. Alim (Eds.), *Culturally sustaining pedagogies: Teaching and learning for justice in a changing world* (pp. 1–21). Teachers College Press.

Alim, H. S., Paris, D., & Wong, C. P. (2020). Culturally sustaining pedagogy: A critical framework for centering communities. In *Handbook of the Cultural Foundations of Learning* (pp. 261–276). Routledge. doi:10.4324/9780203774977-18

Allen-Meares, P., & Pugach, M. (1982). Facilitating interdisciplinary collaboration on behalf of handicapped children and youth. *Teacher Education and Special Education, 5*(1), 30–36. doi:10.1177/088840648200500106

Alliance for Excellent Education. (2014). On the Path to Equity: Improving the Effectiveness of Beginning Teachers. Alliance for Excellent Education: Washington, D.C.

Almendingen, K., Molin, M., & Šaltytė Benth, J. (2021). Preparedness for interprofessional learning: An exploratory study among health, social care, and teacher education programs. *Journal of Research in Interprofessional Practice and Education, 11*(1), 1–11. doi:10.22230/jripe.2021v11n1a309

Amaya-Jackson, L., Absher, L. E., Gerrity, E. T., Layne, C. M., & Halladay Goldman, J. (2021). *Beyond the ACE score: Perspectives from the NCTSN on child trauma and adversity screening and impact.* National Center for Child Traumatic Stress. https://www.nctsn.org/sites/default/files/resources/special-resource/beyond-the-ace-score-perspectives-from-the-nctsn-on-child-tauma-and-adversity-screening-and-impact.pdf

American Association for Employment in Education. (2016). *Educator supply and demand report 2015-16: Executive summary.* https://aaee.org/resources/Documents/2015-16_AAEE_Supply_Demand_Summary.pdf

American Association for Employment in Education. (2016–2017). *Educator supply and demand report 2016–17.* https://aaee.org/sites/default/files/content-files/AAEE%20Full%20Report2016_17_%205-11_smr.pdf

American Association for Employment in Education. (2021). *Educator supply and demand report 2020-2021.* [Data set]. AAEE.

American Association of Colleges for Teacher Education (AACTE). (2022). *Colleges of education: A national portrait.* American Association of Colleges for Teacher Education. https://www.aacteconnect360.org/viewdocument/colleges-of-education-a-national-p-1

American Counseling Association. (2014). *ACA code of ethics.* Alexandria, VA: Author. https://www.counseling.org/resources/aca-code-of-ethics.pdf

American Federation of State, County and Municipal Employees, American Federation of Teachers, Associate Degree Early Childhood Teacher Educators, Child Care Aware of America, Council for Professional Recognition, Division for Early Childhood of the Council for Exceptional Children, Early Care and Education Consortium, National Association for Family Child Care, National Association for the Education of Young Children, National Association of Early Childhood Teacher Educators, National Association of Elementary School Principals, National Education Association, National Head Start Association, Service Employees International Union, & ZERO TO THREE. (2020). *Unifying framework for the early childhood profession.* http://powertotheprofession.org/wpcontent/uploads/2020/03/Power-to-Profession-Framework-03312020-web.pdf

American Occupational Therapy Association. (2021). Standards of practice for occupational therapy. *The American Journal of Occupational Therapy, 75*(Supplement_3), 7513410030. doi:10.5014/ajot.2021.75S3004 PMID:34939642

American Physical Therapy Association. (2019). *HOD S06-20-35-29: The standards of practice for physical therapy.* APTA. https://www.apta.org/apta-and-you/leadership-and-governance/policies/standards-of-practice-pt

American Psychiatric Association. (2013). *Diagnostic and statistical manual of mental disorders* (5th ed.).

American Psychiatric Association. (2013). *Diagnostic and Statistical Manual of Mental Disorders: Diagnostic and Statistical Manual of Mental Disorders* (5th ed.). American Psychiatric Association.

American Psychological Association. (2022, July 19). *APA Accreditation.* https://www.accreditation.apa.org/

American School Counselor Association. (2016). *The school counselor and school-family-community partnerships.* https://www.schoolcounselor.org/asca/media/asca/PositionStatements/PS_Partnerships.pdf

American School Counselor Association. (2019). *ASCA school counselor professional standards & competencies.* Alexandria, VA: Author. https://www.schoolcounselor.org/asca/media/asca/home/SCCompetencies.pdf

American School Counselor Association. (2022). The school counselor and students with disabilities. *ASCA.* https://www.schoolcounselor.org/Standards-Positions/Position-Statements/ASCA-Position-Statements/The-School-Counselor-and-Students-with-Disabilitie

American Speech-Langauge-Hearing Association. (2004). *Roles and responsibilities of speech-language pathologists with respect to augmentative and alternative communication: Technical report.* ASLHA. https://asha.org/policy

American Speech-Language-Hearing Association. (2006). Guidelines for speech-language pathologists in diagnosis, assessment, and treatment of autism spectrum disorders across the lifespan. *ASHA.* https://www.asha.org/members/deskref-journal/deskref/default

American Speech-Language-Hearing Association. (2016). Scope of Practice in Speech- Language Pathology [Scope of Practice]. *ASHA.* https://www.asha.org/policy/

American Speech-Language-Hearing Association. (2020). Standards and implementation procedures for the certificate of clinical competence in speech-language pathology. *ASLHA*. https://www.asha.org/Certification/2020-SLP-Certification-Standards/

American Speech-Language-Hearing Association. (2021). *Interprofessional practice survey results*. https://www.asha.org/siteassets/surveys/2021-interprofessional-practice-survey-results.pdf

American Speech-Language-Hearing Association. (2022). Strategic pathway to excellence. *ASHA*. https://www.asha.org/about/strategic-pathway/

American Speech-Language-Hearing Association. (n.d.). *Caseload/Workload* (Practice Portal). https://www.asha.org/practice-portal/professional-issues/caseload-and-workload/

Anderson, A., & Carr, M. (2021). Applied behaviour analysis for autism: Evidence, issues, and implementation barriers. *Current Developmental Disorders Reports*, *8*(4), 1–10. doi:10.100740474-021-00237-x

Anderson, E. M. (2013). Preparing the next generation of early childhood teachers: The emerging role of interprofessional education and collaboration in teacher education. *Journal of Early Childhood Teacher Education*, *34*(1), 23–35. doi:10.1080/10901027.2013.758535

Andreatos, A. (2007). Virtual communities and their importance for informal learning. *International Journal of Computers*, *2*(1), 9–47.

Anglim, J., Prendeville, P., & Kinsella, W. (2017). The self-efficacy of primary teachers in supporting the inclusion of children with autism spectrum disorder. *Educational Psychology in Practice*, *34*(1), 1–16. doi:10.1080/02667363.2017.1391750

Ansari, A., & Gottfried, M. A. (2021). The grade level and cumulative outcome of absenteeism. *Child Development*, *92*(4), 548–564. doi:10.1111/cdev.13555 PMID:33739441

Ansari, A., & Pianta, R. C. (2019). School absentee in the first decade of education and outcomes in adolescents. *Journal of School Psychology*, *76*, 48–61. doi:10.1016/j.jsp.2019.07.010 PMID:31759468

Apel, K. (2002). Serving students with spoken and written language challenges. *ASHA Leader*, *7*(1), 6–7. doi:10.1044/leader.FTR1.07012002.6

AphasiaBank. (n.d.) *AphasiaBank*. AphasiaBank. https://aphasia.talkbank.org/

Applied Behavioral Strategies. (2012, November 13). *The Very Busy BCBA*. https://appliedbehavioralstrategies.wordpress.com/2012/11/13/the-very-busy-bcba/

Aragon, J., Arrellano, L. M., Brazzel, P., Cárdenas, J., Catalde, T., Cottrill, M., Giambona, M., Manos, S., McMillian, K., Parsons, J., Peevy, J., Pianta, R., Schroeder, M., Sopp, T. J., Strear, M., Thomas, S., Topalian, J., Uresti, A., Weglarz, L., . . . Zavalza, O. (2020). *Fostering the whole child: A guide to school-based mental health professionals*. California Association of School Social Workers, California Association of School Counselors, California Association of School Psychologists. https://naswcanews.org/wp-content/uploads/2020/11/SBMHP-Guide-Book-final.pdf

*Compilation of References*

Aratani, Y., Wright, V. R., & Cooper, J. L. (2011). *Racial gaps in early childhood: Socio-emotional health, development, and educational outcomes among African American boys* (ED522681). ERIC. https://files.eric.ed.gov/fulltext/ED522681.pdf

Archer, A. L., & Hughes, C. A. (2010). *Explicit Instruction: Effective and efficient teaching*. Guilford Press.

Archibald, D., Trumpower, D., & MacDonald, C. J. (2014). Validation of the interprofessional collaborative competency attainment survey (ICCAS). *Journal of Interprofessional Care*, 28(6), 553–558. doi:10.3109/13561820.2014.917407 PMID:24828620

Archibald, L. M. (2017). SLP-educator classroom collaboration: A review to inform reason-based practice. *Autism & Developmental Language Impairments*, 2. doi:10.1177/2396941516680369

Ardoin, S. P., Wagner, L., & Bangs, K. E. (2016). Applied behavior analysis: A foundation for response to intervention. In K. C. Stoiber & M. Gettinger (Eds.), *Handbook of response to intervention* (2nd ed., pp. 29–42). Springer. doi:10.1007/978-1-4899-7568-3_3

Armstrong, T. (2011). *The power of neurodiversity: Unleashing the advantages of your differently wired brain*. Da Capo Press.

Arner, L., Barreca, J., Cosbey, J., Prasad, A., Schlessman, A., & Stephenson, P. (2022). *Joint statement on interprofessional collaborative goals in school-based practice*. American Occupational Therapy Association, American Physical Therapy Association, American Speech-Language-Hearing Association. Retrieved from https://webnew.ped.state.nm.us/wp-content/uploads/2022/03/Joint-Statement-on-Interprofessional-Collaborative-Goals-in-School-Based-Practice-2022-2-17.pdf

Artiles, A. J. (2015). Beyond responsiveness to identify badges: Future research culture in disability and implications for Response to Intervention. *Educational Review*, 67(1), 1–22. doi:10.1080/00131911.2014.934322

Ashby, I., & Exter, M. (2019). Designing for interdisciplinarity in higher education: Considerations for instructional designers. *TechTrends*, 63(2), 202–208. doi:10.100711528-018-0352-z

Association of California School Administrators (ASCA). (2022). *Addressing the youth mental health crisis*. https://bit.ly/3EBUH4D

Astleitner, H. (2018). Multidimensional engagement in learning-An integrated instructional design approach. *Journal of Institutional Research*, 7(1), 6–32. doi:10.9743/JIR.2018.1

Atkins, C.P. (2007). Graduate SLP/Aud Clinicians on Counseling: Self-Perceptions and Awareness of Boundaries.

Atkins, M. S., Hoagwood, K. E., Kutash, K., & Seidman, E. (2010). Toward the integration of education and Mental Health in Schools. *Administration and Policy in Mental Health*, 37(1-2), 40–47. doi:10.100710488-010-0299-7 PMID:20309623

Aucejo, E. M., French, J., Ugalde Araya, M. P., & Zafar, B. (2020). The impact of COVID-19 on student experiences and expectations: Evidence from a survey. *Journal of Public Economics, 191*(3). doi:10.1016/j.jpubeco.2020.104271

August, G. J., Piehler, T. F., & Miller, F. G. (2018). Getting "SMART" about implementing multi-tiered systems of support to promote school mental health. *Journal of School Psychology*, 66, 85–96. doi:10.1016/j.jsp.2017.10.001 PMID:29429498

Austin, C. R., Vaughn, S., & McClelland, A. M. (2017). Intensive reading interventions for inadequate responders in grades k–3: A synthesis. *Learning Disability Quarterly*, 40(4), 191–210. doi:10.1177/0731948717714446

Autistic Self-Advocacy Network. (2022). About autism. *Autistic Advocacy*. https://autisticadvocacy.org/about-autism/

Avant, D. W., & Swerdlik, M. E. (2016). A collaborative endeavor: The roles and functions of school social workers and school psychologists in implementing multi-tiered system of supports/response to intervention. *School Social Work Journal*, *41*(1), 56. https://search-ebscohostcom.proxy1.ncu.edu/login.aspx?direct=true&db=edo&AN=121705552&site=eds-live

Averill, & Rinaldi, C. (2013). *Research brief: Multi-tier system of supports*. Urban Special Education Leadership Collaborative. https://www.urbancollaborative.org/

Baecher, L. H., & Connor, D. J. (2010). "What do you see?" Using video analysis of classroom practice in a preparation program for teachers of students with learning disabilities. *Insights on Learning Disabilities*, *7*(2), 5–18.

Bagatell, N., & Broggi, M. (2014). Occupational therapy and physical therapy students' perceptions of a short-term interprofessional education module. *Education Special Interest Section Quarterly*, *24*(2), 1–4.

Baines, D. (2007). *Doing anti oppressive practice: Building transformative, politicized social work*. Fernwood.

Baker, B. L., & Blacher, J. (2020). Brief Report: Behavior disorders and social skills in adolescents with autism spectrum disorder: Does IQ matter? *Journal of Autism and Developmental Disorders*, *50*(6), 2226–2233. doi:10.100710803-019-03954-w PMID:30888552

Baker, J. N., Lowrey, A. K., & Wennerlind, K. R. (2018). Building an inclusive post-secondary education program for young adults with intellectual developmental disability. *Physical Disabilities: Education and Related Services*, *37*(2), 13–33. doi:10.14434/pders.v37i2.25738

Baladerian, N. J. (1994). *Abuse and neglect of children with disabilities*. ARCH National Center for Crisis Nurseries and Respite Care Services. https://eric.ed.gov/?id=ED378709

Ball, A., Anderson-Butcher, D., Mellin, E. A., & Green, J. H. (2010). A cross-walk of professional competencies involved in expanded school mental health: An exploratory study. *School Mental Health*, *2*(3), 114–124. doi:10.100712310-010-9039-0

Banach, M., & Couse, L. J. (2012). Interdisciplinary co-facilitation of support groups for parents of children with autism: An opportunity for professional preparation. *Social Work with Groups*, *35*(4), 313–329. doi:10.1080/01609513.2012.671103

Bandura, A. (1971). *Social learning theory*. General Learning Press.

Bandura, A. (1977). Self-efficacy: Toward a unifying theory of behavioral change. *Psychological Review*, *84*(2), 191–215. doi:10.1037/0033-295X.84.2.191 PMID:847061

Bandura, A. (1991). Social cognitive theory of self-regulation. *Organizational Behavior and Human Performance*, *50*(2), 248–287. doi:10.1016/0749-5978(91)90022-L

Bandura, A. (1997). *Self-efficacy: The exercise of control*. W.H. Freeman & Company.

Bandura, A. (2004). Health promotion by social cognitive means. *Health Education & Behavior*, *31*(2), 143–164. doi:10.1177/1090198104263660 PMID:15090118

Banks, T., & Doly, J. (2019). Mitigating barriers to persistence: A review of efforts to improve retention and graduation rates for students of color in higher education. *Higher Education Studies*, *9*(1), 118–131. doi:10.5539/hes.v9n1p118

Barker, R. M., Akaba, S., Brady, N. C., & Thiemann-Bourque, K. (2013). Support for AAC use in preschool, and growth in language skills, for young children with developmental disabilities. *Augmentative and Alternative Communication*, *29*(4), 334–346. doi:10.3109/07434618.2013.848933 PMID:24229337

Barnard, M., & McKeganey, N. (2004). The impact of parental problem drug use on children: What is the problem and what can be done to help? *Addiction (Abingdon, England)*, *5*(5), 552–559. doi:10.1111/j.1360-0443.2003.00664.x PMID:15078229

Barnes, P. E., Friehe, M. J. M., & Radd, T. R. (2003). Collaboration between speech-language pathologists and school counselors. *Communication Disorders Quarterly*, *24*(3), 137–142. doi:10.1177/15257401030240030501

Barnett, L. M., Van Beurden, E., Morgan, P. J., Brooks, L. O., & Beard, J. R. (2009). Childhood motor skill proficiency as a predictor of adolescent physical activity. *The Journal of Adolescent Health*, *44*(3), 252–259. doi:10.1016/j.jadohealth.2008.07.004 PMID:19237111

Barnhill, G. P., Polloway, E. A., & Sumutka, B. M. (2011). A survey of personnel preparation practices in autism spectrum disorders. *Focus on Autism and Other Developmental Disabilities*, *26*(2), 75–86. doi:10.1177/1088357610378292

Barr, H. (2002). Interprofessional education: Today, yesterday and tomorrow. London: Learning and Teaching support Network: Centre for Health Sciences and Practice.

Barr, H., & Low, H. (2012). *Interprofessional education in pre-registration courses: A CAIPE guide for commissioners and regulators of education.* CAIPE. Retrieved from https://www.caipe.org/resources/publications/caipe-publications/caipe-2012-ipe-pre-registration-courses-caipe-guide-commissioners-regulators-eduction-barrh-low-h-howkins-e

Barrett, N., McEachin, A., Mills, J. N., & Valant, J. (2018). *Disparities in student discipline by race and family income.* https://educationresearchalliancenola.org/files/publications/010418-Barrett-McEachin-Mills-Valant-Disparities-in-Student-Discipline-by-Race-and-Family-Income.pdf

Barrett, S., Eber, L., & Weist, M. (2013). Advancing education effectiveness: Interconnecting school mental health and school-wide positive behavior support [MTSS-ISF Monograph]. *Center on PBIS: Positive Behavioral Interventions & Supports.* https://bit.ly/3dC5gt7

Barr, H., Koppel, I., Reeves, S., Hammick, M., & Freeth, D. (2005). *Effective Interprofessional Education*. Blackwell Publishing Ltd., doi:10.1002/9780470776445

Barroso, C. S., McCullum-Gomez, C., Hoelscher, D. M., Kelder, S. H., & Murray, N. G. (2005). Self-reported barriers to quality physical education by physical education specialists in Texas. *The Journal of School Health*, *75*(8), 313–319. doi:10.1111/j.1746-1561.2005.tb07348.x PMID:16179081

Barrow, J., & Mamlin, N. (2016). Collaboration between professional school counselors and special education teachers. *VISTAS, 42,* 1-7. https://www.counseling.org/docs/default-source/vistas/article_427cfd25f16116603abcacff0000bee5e7.pdf?sfvrsn=e2eb452c_4

Bartlett, J. D., & Smith, S. (2019). The role of early care and education in addressing early childhood trauma. *American Journal of Community Psychology*, *64*(3-4), 359–372. doi:10.1002/ajcp.12380 PMID:31449682

Barton, E. E., Moore, H. W., & Squires, J. K. (2012). Preparing speech language pathology students to work in early childhood. *Topics in Early Childhood Special Education*, *32*(1), 4–13. doi:10.1177/0271121411434567

Barton, E. E., & Smith, B. J. (2015). *The preschool inclusion toolbox: How to build and lead a high-quality program.* Brookes Publishing.

Bates-Harris, C. (2012). Segregated and exploited: The failure of the disability service system to provide quality work. *Journal of Vocational Rehabilitation*, *36*, 39–64. https://doi.org/10.3233/JVR-2012-0581

Batey, C. A., Missiuna, C. A., Timmons, B. W., Hay, J. A., Faught, B. E., & Cairney, J. (2013). Self- efficacy toward physical activity and the physical activity behavior of children with and without developmental coordination disorder. *Human Movement Science*, *36*, 258–271. doi:10.1016/j.humov.2013.10.003 PMID:24345354

Battaglia, D., Domingo, R., & Moravcik, G.-M. (2013). Autism related curriculum in New York state graduate speech language pathology programs. *Excelsior (Oneonta, N.Y.)*, *8*(1), 53–64.

Battersby, S. L. (2019). Reimagining music teacher collaboration: The culture of professional learning communities as professional development within schools and districts. *General Music Today*, *33*(1), 15–23. doi:10.1177/1048371319840653

Bauer, K. L., Iver, S. N., Boon, R. T., & Fore, C. (2010). 10 ways for classroom teachers to collaborate with speech-language pathologists. *Intervention in School and Clinic*, *45*(5), 333–337. doi:10.1177/1053451208328833

Beaulieu, & Jimenez-Gomez, C. (2022). Cultural responsiveness in applied behavior analysis: Self-assessment. *Journal of Applied Behavior Analysis*, *55*(2), 337–356. doi:10.1002/jaba.907

Beaulieu, L., Addington, J., & Almeida, D. (2019). Behavior analysts' training and practices regarding cultural diversity: The case for culturally competent care. *Behavior Analysis in Practice*, *12*(3), 557–575. doi:10.100740617-018-00313-6 PMID:31976264

Becirevic, A., Critchfield, T. S., & Reed, D. D. (2016). On the social acceptability of behavior-analytic terms: Crowdsourced comparisons of lay and technical language. *The Behavior Analyst*, *39*(2), 305–317. doi:10.100740614-016-0067-4 PMID:31976979

Beck, A. R., & Verticchio, H. (2018). Effectiveness of a Method for Teaching Self-Compassion to Communication Sciences and Disorders Graduate Students. *American Journal of Speech-Language Pathology*, *27*(1), 192–206. doi:10.1044/2017_AJSLP-17-0060 PMID:29383372

Beck, J. (2002). Emerging literacy through assistive technology. *Teaching Exceptional Children*, *35*(2), 44–48. doi:10.1177/004005990203500206

Beck, S. J., & DeSutter, K. (2020). An examination of group facilitator challenges and problem-solving techniques during IEP team meetings. *Teacher Education and Special Education*, *43*(2), 127–143. doi:10.1177/0888406419839766

Behavior Analyst Certification Board. (2014). Professional and ethical compliance code for behavior analysts. *BACB*. https://www.bacb.com/wp-content/uploads/2020/05/BACB-Complia nce-Code-english_190318.pdf

Behavior Analyst Certification Board. (2017). *BCBA talk list* (5th ed.). Author.

Behavior Analyst Certification Board. (2017). *BCBA task list* (5th ed.). Authors.

Behavior Analyst Certification Board. (2020). Ethics code for behavior analysts. *BACB*. https://bacb.com/wp-content/ethics-code-for-behavior-analysts/

Behavior Analyst Certification Board. (2022). *US employment demand for behavior analysts: 2010–2021*. Author.

Behavior Analyst Certification Board. (n.d.) Board Certified Behavior Analyst. [Data set]. BACB. https://www.bacb.com/bacb-certificant-data/

Bell, S. T. (2007). Deep-level composition variables as predictors of team performance: A meta-analysis. *The Journal of Applied Psychology*, *92*(3), 595–615. doi:10.1037/0021-9010.92.3.595 PMID:17484544

Bennett, M. J. (2016). The value of cultural diversity: Rhetoric and reality. *SpringerPlus*, *5*(1), 897. doi:10.118640064-016-2456-2

*Compilation of References*

Berger, C., Alcalay, L., Torretti, A., & Milicic, N. (2011). Socio-emotional well-being and academic achievement: Evidence from a multilevel approach. *Psicologia: Reflexão e Crítica*, *24*(2), 344–351. doi:10.1590/S0102-79722011000200016

Berry, A. B., Petrin, R. A., Gravelle, M. L., & Farmer, T. W. (2011). Issues in special education teacher recruitment, retention, and professional development: Considerations in supporting rural teachers. *Rural Special Education Quarterly*, *30*(4), 3–11. doi:10.1177/875687051103000402

Beukelman, D., & Mirenda, P. (2013). *Augmentative and alternative communication: Supporting children & adults with complex communication needs* (4th ed.). Paul H. Brookes Publishing. https://www.asha.org/njc/definition-of-communication-and-appropriate-targets/

Beukelman, D. R., & Mirenda, P. (2012). *Principles of assessment in augmentative & alternative communication: Supporting children & adults with complex communication needs* (4th ed.). Paul H. Brookes Publishing.

Beukelman, D. R., & Mirenda, P. (2013). *Augmentative and alternative communication: Supporting children and adults with complex communication needs* (4th ed.). Paul H. Brookes Pub.

Bianco, M. (2005). The effects of disability labels on special education and general education teachers' referrals for gifted programs. *Learning Disability Quarterly*, *28*(4), 285–293. doi:10.2307/4126967

Biddle, S. J., Ciaccioni, S., Thomas, G., & Vergeer, I. (2019). Physical activity and mental health in children and adolescents: An updated review of reviews and an analysis of causality. *Psychology of Sport and Exercise*, *42*, 146–155. doi:10.1016/j.psychsport.2018.08.011

Biggs, E. E., Carter, E. W., & Gilson, C. B. (2018). A scoping review of the involvement of children's communication partners in aided augmentative and alternative communication modeling interventions. *American Journal of Speech-Language Pathology*, *28*(2), 743–758. doi:10.1044/2018_AJSLP-18-0024 PMID:31039322

Billingsley, B. S., Griffin, C. C., Smith, S. J., Kamman, M., & Israel, M. (2009). *A review of teacher induction in special education: Research, practice, and technology solutions.* (NCIPP Doc. RS-1).

Billingsley, B., & Bettini, E. (2017). Factors influencing the quality of the special education teacher workforce. In Handbook of Special Education. Abingdon, UK: Routledge.

Billingsley, B., & Bettini, E. (2019). Special education teacher attrition and retention: A review of the literature. *Review of Educational Research*, *89*(5), 697–744. doi:10.3102/0034654319862495

Billingsley, B., Bettini, E., & Jones, N. D. (2019). Supporting special education teacher induction through high-leverage practices. *Remedial and Special Education*, *40*(6), 365–379. doi:10.1177/0741932518816826

Billingsley, G., Smith, S., Smith, S., & Meritt, J. (2019). A systematic literature review of using immersive virtual reality technology in teacher education. *Journal of Interactive Learning Research*, *30*(1), 65–90.

Binger, C., & Light, J. (2006). Demographics of preschoolers who require AAC. *Language, Speech, and Hearing Services in Schools*, *37*(3), 200–208. doi:10.1044/0161-1461(2006/022) PMID:16837443

Bird, A., & Mendenhall, M. E. (2016). From cross-cultural management to global leadership: Evolution and adaptation. *Journal of World Business*, *51*(1), 115–126. doi:10.1016/j.jwb.2015.10.005

Bitsko, R. H., Claussen, A. H., Lichtstein, J., Black, L. J., Everett Jones, S., Danielson, M. D., Hoenig, J. M., Davis Jack, S. P., Brody, D. J., Gyawali, S., Maenner, M. M., Warner, M., Holland, K. M., Perou, R., Crosby, A. E., Blumberg, S. J., Avenevoli, S., Kaminski, J. W., & Ghandour, R. M. (2022). Surveillance of Children's Mental Health – United States, 2013 – 2019. *MMWR*, *71*(Suppl-2), 1–42. doi:10.15585/mmwr.su7102a1

Black, L. I., Vahratian, A., Hoffman, H. J., & National Center for Health Statistics (U.S.). (2015). *Communication disorders and use of intervention services among children aged 3-17 years: United States, 2012*. Hyattsville, MD: U.S. Department of Health and Human Services, Centers for Disease Control and Prevention, National Center for Health Statistics.

Blake, J. J., Graves, S., Newell, M., & Jimerson, S. R. (2016). Diversification of school psychology: Developing an evidence base from current research and practice. *School Psychology Quarterly*, *31*(3), 305–310. doi:10.1037pq0000180 PMID:27617533

Blalock, G., Kochhar-Bryant, C. A., Test, D. W., Kohler, P., White, W., Lehmann, J., Bassett, D., & Patton, J. (2003). The need for comprehensive personnel preparation in transition and career development: A position statement of the Division of Career Development and Transition. *Career Development and Transition for Exceptional Individuals*, *26*(2), 207–226. doi:10.1177/088572880302600207

Blanchard, S. B., Newton, J. R., Diderickson, K. W., Daniels, M., & Glosson, K. (2021). Confronting racism and bias within early intervention: The responsibility of systems and individuals to influence change and advance equity. *Topics in Early Childhood Special Education*, *41*(1), 1–12. doi:10.1177/0271121421992470

Bock, S. J., Michalak, N., & Brownlee, S. (2011). Collaboration and consultation: The first steps. In C. G. Simpson & J. P. Bakken (Eds.), *Collaboration: A multidisciplinary approach to educating students with disabilities* (pp. 3–15). Prufrock Press.

Boden, D., Borrego, M., & Newswander, L. K. (2011). Student socialization in interdisciplinary doctoral education. *Higher Education*, *62*(6), 741–755. doi:10.100710734-011-9415-1

Boe, E. E., Cook, L. H., & Sunderland, R. J. (2008). Teacher turnover: Examining exit attrition, teaching area transfer, and school migration. *Exceptional Children*, *75*(1), 7–31. doi:10.1177/001440290807500101

Boe, E. E., deBettencourt, L. U., Dewey, J., Rosenberg, M., Sindelar, P., & Leko, C. (2013). Variability in demand for special education teachers: Indicators, explanations, and impacts. *Exceptionality*, *21*(2), 103–125. doi:10.1080/09362835.2013.771563

Boivin, B., Ruane, J., Quigley, S. P., Harper, J., & Weiss, M. J. (2021). Interdisciplinary collaboration training: An example of preservice training series. *Behavior Analysis in Practice*, *14*(4), 1223–1236. doi:10.100740617-021-00561-z PMID:34868824

Boon, R. T., Urton, K., Grunke, M., & Ko, E. H. (2020). Video modeling interventions for students with learning disabilities: A systematic review. *Learning Disabilities (Weston, Mass.)*, *18*(1), 49–69.

Borg, E., & Drange, I. (2019). Interprofessional collaboration in school: Effects on teaching and learning. *Improving Schools*, *22*(3), 251–266. doi:10.1177/1365480219864812

Borrego, M., & Cutler, S. (2010). Constructive alignment of interdisciplinary graduate curriculum in engineering and science: An analysis of successful IGERT proposals. *Journal of Engineering Education (Washington, D.C.)*, *99*(4), 355–369. doi:10.1002/j.2168-9830.2010.tb01068.x

Boston Public Schools. (2019). *Boston Public Schools at a glance 2019-20*. https://www.bostonpublicschools.org/cms/lib/MA01906464/Centricity/Domain/187/BPS%20at%20a%20Glance%202019-20_FINAL.pdf

Boulden, R., & Schimmel, C. (2021). More than just an internship: One university's collaboration with a rural school district to attract, develop, and retain school counselors. *Rural Educator*, *42*(3), 56–62. doi:10.35608/ruraled.v42i3.1237

*Compilation of References*

Bowie, S. L., Nashwan, A. J. J., Thomas, V., Davis-Buckley, R. J., & Johnson, S. L. (2018). An assessment of social work education efforts to recruit and retain MSW students of color. *Journal of Social Work Education, 54*(2), 270–286. doi:10.1080/10437797.2017.1404531

Boyer, E. (1990). Scholarship reconsidered: Priorities of the professoriate. Carnegie Foundations for the Advancement of Teaching. Princeton University Press.

Brady, K. P., Kucharczyk, S., Schaefer Whitby, P., Terrell, E., & Merry, K. E. (2021). A review of critical issues in transition team's decision-making and the importance of ethical leadership. *Journal of Leadership and Instruction, 20*(2), 14–19.

Branch, J., Chapman, M., & Gomez, M. (2021). Investigating the interplay between institution, spousal, parental, and personal demands in tenure track faculty everyday life. *Community, Work & Family, 24*(2), 143–154. doi:10.1080/13668803.2020.1727414

Brandel, J., & Frome Loeb, D. (2011). Program intensity and service delivery models in the schools: SLP survey results. *Language, Speech, and Hearing Services in Schools, 42*(4), 461–490. doi:10.1044/0161-1461(2011/10-0019 PMID:21616986

Brandt, K. (2014). *Infant and early childhood mental health: Core concepts and clinical practice*. American Psychiatric Publishing.

Bransford, J. D., Brown, A. L., & Cocking, R. R. (2000). *How people learn: Brain, mind, experience, and school*. National Resource Council.

Bransford, J., Brown, A. L., & Cocking, R. R. (Eds.). (2000). *How people learn: Brain, mind, experience and schools*. National Academy Press.

Branson, D., & Demchak, M. (2009). The use of augmentative and alternative communication methods with infants and toddlers with disabilities: A research review. *Augmentative and Alternative Communication, 25*(4), 274–286. doi:10.3109/07434610903384529 PMID:19883287

Briant, S., & Crowther, P. (2020). Reimagining internships through online experiences: Multi-disciplinary engagement for creative industries students. *International Journal of Work-Integrated Learning, 21*(5), 617–628.

Bricker, D. D., Felimban, H. S., Lin, F. Y., Stegenga, S. M., & Storie, S. O. M. (2022). A proposed framework for enhancing collaboration in early intervention/early childhood special education. *Topics in Early Childhood Special Education, 41*(4), 240–252. doi:10.1177/0271121419890683

Bridges, D. R., Davidson, R. A., Odegard, P. S., Maki, I. V., & Tomkowiak, J. (2011). Interprofessional collaboration: Three best practice models of interprofessional education. *Medical Education Online, 16*, . doi:10.3402/meo.v16i0.6035

Brinton, B., Fujiki, M., & Robinson, L. A. (2005). Life on a Tricycle: A Case Study of Language Impairment From 4 to 19. *Topics in Language Disorders, 25*(4), 338–352. doi:10.1097/00011363-200510000-00009

Brock, M. E., Huber, H. B., Carter, E. W., Juarez, A. P., & Warren, Z. E. (2014). Statewide assessment of professional development needs related to educating students with autism spectrum disorders. *Focus on Autism and Other Developmental Disabilities, 29*(2), 67–79. doi:10.1177/1088357614522290

Brock, S. E., Nickerson, A. B., Louvar Reeves, M. A., Conolly, C. N., Jimerson, S. R., Pesce, R. C., & Lazzaro, B. R. (2016). *School crisis prevention and intervention: The PREPaRE model* (2nd ed.). National Association of School Psychologists.

Broderick, C. B. (1993). *Understanding family process: Basics of family systems theory*. SAGE Publications.

Brodhead, M. T. (2015). Maintaining professional relationships in an interdisciplinary setting: Strategies for navigating nonbehavioral treatment recommendations for individuals with autism. *Behavior Analysis in Practice*, *8*(10), 70–78. doi:10.100740617-015-0042-7 PMID:27703885

Bronstein, L. (2003). A model for interdisciplinary collaboration. *Social Work*, *48*(3), 297–306. doi:10.1093w/48.3.297 PMID:12899277

Brookfield, S. D. (1986). *Understanding and facilitating adult learning*. Jossey-Bass.

Browder, D. M., Wood, L., Thompson, J., & Ribuffo, C. (2014). *Evidence-based practices for students with severe disabilities* (CEEDAR Document NO. IC-3). CEEDAR Center. https://bit.ly/3CfeDtb

Browder, D. M., Wood, L., Thompson, J., & Ribuffo, C. (2014). *Evidence-based practices for students with severe disabilities* (Document No. IC-3). University of Florida, Collaboration for Effective Educator, Development, Accountability, and Reform Center. https://ceedar.education.ufl.edu/tools/innovation-configurations/

Brownell, M. T., Benedict, A. E., Leko, M. M., Peyton, D., Pua, D., & Richards-Tutor, C. (2019). A continuum of pedagogies for preparing teachers to use high-leverage practices. *Remedial and Special Education*, *40*(6), 338–355. doi:10.1177/0741932518824990

Brownell, M. T., & Pajares, E. (1999). Teacher efficacy and perceived success in mainstreaming students with behavior and learning problems. *Teacher Education and Special Education*, *22*(3), 154–164. doi:10.1177/088840649902200303

Brown, T. J., & Sobel, D. (2021). School psychologists' job attitudes: A systematic review. *Contemporary School Psychology*, *25*(1), 40–50. doi:10.100740688-019-00241-4

Brown, T., Moore, T. H., Hooper, L., Gao, Y., Zayggh, A., Ijaz, S., Elwenspoke, M., Foxen, S. C., Magee, L., O'Malley, C., Water, E., & Summerbell, C. D. (2019). Interventions for preventing obesity in children. *Cochrane Database of Systematic Reviews*, *7*(7). doi:10.1002/14651858.CD001871.pub4 PMID:31332776

Bruce, S. M., & Bashinski, S. M. (2017). The Trifocus Framework and interprofessional collaborative practice in severe disabilities. *American Journal of Speech-Language Pathology*, *26*(2), 162–180. doi:10.1044/2016_AJSLP-15-0063 PMID:28514472

Bruder, M. B., Long, T., & Rhodes, T. (2018). *Cross-disciplinary competencies: Serving the whole child* [PowerPoint slides]. Early Childhood Personnel Center. https://www.aucd.org/docs/webinars/PresentationSlides_ECPC%20Cross%20Disciplinary%20Core%20%20Personnel%20Competencies_.pdf

Bruder, M. B. (2010). Early childhood intervention: A promise to children and families for their future. *Exceptional Children*, *76*(3), 339–355. doi:10.1177/001440291007600306

Bruder, M. B., Catalino, T., Chiarello, L. A., Mitchell, M. C., Deppe, J., Gundler, D., Kemp, P., LeMoine, S., Long, T., Muhlenhaupt, M., Prelock, P., Schefkind, S., Stayton, V., & Ziegler, D. (2019). Finding a common lens: Competencies across professional disciplines providing early childhood intervention. *Infants and Young Children*, *32*(4), 280–293. doi:10.1097/IYC.0000000000000153

Bruder, M. B., Mogro-Wilson, C. M., Stayton, V. D., & Dietrich, S. L. (2009). The national status of in-service professional development systems for early intervention and early childhood special education practitioners. *Infants and Young Children*, *22*(1), 13–20. doi:10.1097/01.IYC.0000343333.49775.f8

*Compilation of References*

Bruder, M., & Dunst, C. (2005). Personnel preparation in recommended early intervention practices: Degree of emphasis across disciplines. *Topics in Early Childhood Special Education*, *25*(1), 25–33. doi:10.1177/02711214050250010301

Bruhn, A. L., Estrapala, S., Mahatmya, D., Rila, A., & Vogelgesang, K. (2019). Professional Development on Data-Based Individualization: A Mixed Research Study. *Behavioral Disorders*, •••, 0198742919876656. doi:10.1177/0198742919876656

Bruhn, A. L., Wehby, J. H., & Hasselbring, T. S. (2020). Data-based decision making for social behavior: Setting a research agenda. *Journal of Positive Behavior Interventions*, *22*(2), 116–126. doi:10.1177/1098300719876098

Bruhn, A., McDaniel, S., & Kreigh, C. (2015). Self-monitoring interventions for students with behavior problems: A systematic review of current research. *Behavioral Disorders*, *40*(2), 102–121. doi:10.17988/BD-13-45.1

Brunsting, N. C., Sreckovic, M. A., & Lane, K. L. (2014). Special education teacher burnout: A synthesis of research from 1979 to 2013. *Education & Treatment of Children*, *37*(4), 681–711. https://www.jstor.org/stable/44683943. doi:10.1353/etc.2014.0032

Bryan, K., Garvani, G., Gregory, J., & Kilner, K. (2015). Language difficulties and criminal justice: The need for earlier identification. *International Journal of Language & Communication Disorders*, *50*(6), 763–775. doi:10.1111/1460-6984.12183 PMID:26344062

Bryan, R. L., Kreutre, M. W., & Brownson, R. C. (2009). Integrating adult learning principles into training for public health practice. *Health Promotion Practice*, *10*(4), 557–563. doi:10.1177/1524839907308117 PMID:18385488

Budd, K. S., Garbacz, L. L. & Carter, J. S. (2016). Collaborating with public school partners to implement teacher-child interaction training (TCIT) as universal prevention. *School Mental Health: A Multidisciplinary Research and Practice Journal, 8*(2), 207-221.

Buell, M., Hallam, R., Gamel-McCormick, M., & Scheer, S. (1999). A survey of general and special education teachers' perceptions and inservice needs concerning inclusion. *International Journal of Disability Development and Education*, *46*(2), 143–156. doi:10.1080/103491299100597

Buelow, J., Downs, D., Jorgensen, K., Karges, J., & Nelson, D. (2008). Building interdisciplinary teamwork among allied health students through live clinical case simulations. *Journal of Allied Health*, *37*(2), e109–e123. PMID:19753390

Bumble, J. L., Carter, E. W., & Kuntz, E. M. (2021). Examining the transition networks of secondary special educators: An explanatory sequential mixed methods study. *Remedial and Special Education*. doi:10.1177/07419325211063485

Burden, R., Tinnerman, L., Lunce, L., & Runshe, D. (2010). Video case studies: Preparing teachers for inclusion. *Teaching Exceptional Children Plus*, *6*(4), 2–11.

Burke, & Goldman, S. E. (2018). Special education advocacy among culturally and linguistically diverse families. *Journal of Research in Special Educational Needs, 18*(S1), 3–14. doi:10.1111/1471-3802.12413

Burnette, A. G., Datta, P., & Cornell, D. (2018). The distinction between transient and substantive student threats. *Journal of Threat Assessment and Management*, *5*(1), 4–20. doi:10.1037/tam0000092

Busse, R. T., Kratochwill, T. R., & Elliott, S. N. (1995). Meta-analysis for single-case consultation outcomes: Applications to research and practice. *Journal of School Psychology*, *33*(4), 269–285. doi:10.1016/0022-4405(95)00014-D

Butler, C. (2016). The effectiveness of the TEACCH approach in supporting the development of communication skills for learners with severe intellectual disabilities. *Support for Learning*, *31*(3), 185–201. doi:10.1111/1467-9604.12128

Butterworth, J., Migliore, A., Nord, D., & Gelb, A. (2012). Improving the employment outcomes of job seekers with intellectual and developmental disabilities: A training and mentoring intervention of employment consultants. *Journal of Rehabilitation, 78*(2), 20–29.

California Commission on Teacher Credentialing. (2016, June). *Preliminary Education Specialist teaching credential preconditions, program standards, and teaching performance expectations*. CTC. https://www.ctc.ca.gov/docs/default-source/educator-prep/standards/adopted-tpes-2016.pdf

California Department of Education. (2008). *California preschool learning foundations, volume 1*. CDE. https://www.cde.ca.gov/sp/cd/re/documents/preschoollf.pdf

California Department of Education. (2020). *DataQuest report: Estimated number of teacher hires for 2020-21*. https://dq.cde.ca.gov/dataquest/dqcensus/StfTchHires.aspx?cdcode=3868478&agglevel=District&year=2020-21

California Department of Education. (2022). California Preschool Learning Foundations. *CDE*. https://www.cde.ca.gov/sp/cd/re/psfoundations.asp

*California Department of Education*. (2022). *Full-time Equivalent of Classified Staff* [Data Quest]. https://d.cde.ca.gov/dataquest/dqcensus/stfFteclassified.aspx

California Department of Education. (2022). *Multi-Tiered System of Supports*. CDE. https://www.cde.ca.gov/ci/cr/ri

Cameto, R., Levine, P., & Wagner, M. (2004). *Transition planning for students with disabilities*. SRI International.

Campbell, C. B. (2011). *Adapting an evidence-based intervention to improve social and behavioral competence in head start children: Evaluating the effectiveness of teacher-child interaction training* [Doctoral dissertation]. University of Nebraska-Lincoln, Psychiatry and Psychology Commons.

Campbell, P. H., & Halbert, J. (2002). Between research and practice: Provider perspectives on early intervention. *Topics in Early Childhood Special Education, 22*(4), 213–226. doi:10.1177/027112140202200403

Campbell, P. H., Milbourne, S., Dugan, L. M., & Wilcox, M. J. (2006). A review of the evidence on practices for teaching young children to use assistive technology devices. *Topics in Early Childhood Special Education, 26*(1), 3–13. doi:10.1177/02711214060260010101

Caprara, G. V., Barbaranelli, C., Steca, P., & Malone, P. S. (2006). Teachers' self-efficacy beliefs as determinants of job satisfaction and students' academic achievement: A study at the school level. *Journal of School Psychology, 44*(6), 473–490. doi:10.1016/j.jsp.2006.09.001

Carey, F. R., Singh, G. K., Brown, H. S. III, & Wilkinson, A. V. (2015). Educational outcomes associated with childhood obesity in the United States: Cross-sectional results from the 2011–2012 National Survey of Children's Health. *The International Journal of Behavioral Nutrition and Physical Activity, 12*(S1), S3. doi:10.1186/1479-5868-12-S1-S3 PMID:26222699

Carey, R. L., Yee, L. S., & DeMatthews, D. (2018). Power, penalty, and critical praxis: Employing intersectionality in educator practices to achieve school equity. *The Educational Forum, 82*(1), 111–130. doi:10.1080/00131725.2018.1381793

Carter Andrews, D. J., Castro, E., Cho, C. L., Petchauer, E., Richmond, G., & Floden, R. (2019). Changing the narrative on diversifying the teaching workforce: A look at the historical and contemporary factors that inform recruitment and retention of teachers of color. *Journal of Teacher Education, 70*(1), 6-12. https:// doi:10.1177/0022487118812418

Carter, E. W., Austin, D., & Trainor, A. A. (2012). Predictors of postschool employment outcomes for young adults with severe disabilities. *Journal of Disability Policy Studies, 23*, 50–63. 1044207311414680 doi:10.1177/

Carter, E. W., Austin, D., & Trainor, A. A. (2011). Predictors of postschool employment outcomes for young adults with severe disabilities. *Journal of Disability Policy Studies, 23*(1), 50–63. doi:10.1177/1044207311414680

Carter, E. W., Brock, M. E., & Trainor, A. A. (2014). Transition assessment and planning for youth with severe intellectual and developmental disabilities. *The Journal of Special Education, 47*, 245–255. doi:10.1177/0022466912456241

Cartledge, G., Gardner, R., & Ford, D. Y. (2009). Diverse learners with exceptionalities: Culturally responsive teaching in the inclusive classroom. Academic Press.

Carver-Thomas, D. (2017). Diversifying the field: Barriers to recruiting and retaining teachers of color and how to overcome them. ERIC. https://files.eric.ed.gov/fulltext/ED582730.pdf

Carver-Thomas, D., & Darling-Hammond, L. (2017). *Addressing California's growing teacher shortage: 2017 update.* Learning Policy Institute. https://bit.ly/3dN7hmA

Carver-Thomas, D., & Darling-Hammond, L. (2017). *Teacher turnover: Why it matters and what we can do about it.* Learning Policy. https://learningpolicyinstitute.org/product/teacher-turnover-report doi:10.54300/454.278

CAST. (2018). *Universal design for learning guidelines, version 2.2.* https://pillars.taylor.edu/cgi/viewcontent.cgi?article=1003&context=ett-conference

Castillo, J. M., Curtis, M. J., & Tan, S. Y. (2014). Personnel needs in school psychology: A 10-year follow-up study on predicted personnel shortages. *Psychology in the Schools, 51*(8), 832–849. doi:10.1002/pits.21786

Catts, H. W., Fey, M. E., Weismer, S. E., & Bridges, M. S. (2014). The relationship between language and reading abilities. In Understanding individual differences in language development across the school years (pp. 158-179). Academic Press.

Cavendish, W., Artiles, A. J., & Harry, B. (2015). Tracking inequality 60 years after Brown: Does policy legitimize the racialization of disability? *Multiple Voices for Ethnically Diverse Exceptional Learners, 14*(2), 1–11.

Cawthon, S. W., Schoffstall, S. J., & Garberoglio, C. L. (2014). How ready are postsecondary institutions for students who are d/deaf or hard-of-hearing? *Education Policy Analysis Archives, 22*, 13. doi:10.14507/epaa.v22n13.2014

CDC - National Center for Health Statistics. (2022, March 1). *Drug overdose mortality by state.* https://www.cdc.gov/nchs/pressroom/sosmap/drug_poisoning_mortality/drug_poisoning.htm

CEEDAR Center. (2020). Preparing and retaining effective special education teachers: Short term strategies for long-term solutions (A policy brief). *CEEDAR Center.* https://ceedar.education.ufl.edu/wp-content/uploads/2020/01/CEEDAR-GTL-Shortages-Brief.pdf

CEEDAR Center. (n.d.) The CEEDAR Center Innovation Configuration Guidelines. *CEEDAR Center.* https://ceedar.education.ufl.edu/wp-content/uploads/2014/08/IC-Guidelines.pdf

Censeo Strategic Solutions. (2022). *Marshall University's SEAR Project Mid Grant Report* [Unpublished program evaluation].

Center for Advancement of Interprofessional Education. (CAIPE; 2002). *Interprofessional education: Today, yesterday, and tomorrow – a review* (Barr, H.). Higher Education Academy, Learning and Teaching Support Network for Health Sciences & Practice, Occasional Paper 1.

Center for Disease Control (n.d.). *Disability impacts Mississippi.* 2022 MS Disability and Health State Profile (cdc.gov). *CDC.*

Center for Disease Control. (2021). Autism prevalence higher in CDC's ADDM Network: Improvements being made in identifying children with autism early. *CDC.* https://www.cdc.gov/media/releases/2021/p1202-autism.html

Center for Disease Control. (2022). Percentage of births born preterm by states. *CDC.* https://www.cdc.gov/nchs/pressroom/sosmap/preterm_births/preterm.htm

Center for Disease Control. (2022). Physical activity guidelines for Americans. *CDC.*

Center for Disease Control. (n.d.). *Disability and health U.S. state profile data for Mississippi (adults 18+ years of age).* [Data set]. https://www.cdc.gov/ncbddd/disabilityandhealth/impacts/mississippi.html

Center for Learning Disabilities. (2017). The State of Learning Disabilities: Understanding the 1 in 5. *CDC.* https://www.ncld.org/wp-content/uploads/2017/03/Executive-Summary.Fin_.03142017.pdf

Center for the Developing Child at Harvard University. (2016). *From best practices to breakthrough impacts: A science-based approach to building more promising future for young children and families.* http://www.developingchild.harvard.edu

Center on Disability. California State University-Northridge. (2018). *Assistive Technology Certificate Program* [Course syllabus]. https://canvas.csun.edu/courses/47382

Center on the Developing Child at Harvard University. (2020). *How racism can affect child development.* https://developingchild.harvard.edu/resources/racism-and-ecd/

Centers for Disease Control and Prevention. (2019). *Adverse childhood experiences: Preventing early trauma to improve adult health.* https://www.cdc.gov/vitalsigns/aces/index.html

Centers for Disease Control and Prevention. (2020). *Youth risk behavior surveillance data summary & trends report: 2009-2019.* https://bit.ly/3c1Es5n

Centers for Disease Control and Prevention. (2020, June 24). Inclusive school physical education and physical activity. *CDC.* https://www.cdc.gov/healthyschools/physicalactivity/inclusion_pepa.htm

Centers for Disease Control and Prevention. (2022a). *Children's mental health.* https://www.cdc.gov/childrensmentalhealth/features/understanding-public-health-concern.html

Centers for Disease Control and Prevention. (2022b). *Data and statistics on children's mental health.* https://www.cdc.gov/childrensmentalhealth/data.html

Centre for the Advancement of Interprofessional Education. (2006). CAIPE re-issues its statement on the definition and principles of interprofessional education. *CAIPE.* www.caipe.org/resources/publications/archived-publications/caipe-2006-re-issues-its-statement-on-the-definition-and-principles-of-interprofessional-education

*Compilation of References*

Chairs, M. J., McDonald, B. J., Shroyer, P., Urbanski, B., & Vertin, D. (2002). Meeting the graduate education needs of Minnesota extension educators. *Journal of Extension*, *40*(4). http://www.joe.org/joe/2002august/rb4.shtml

Chalk, K., & Bizo, L. A. (2004). Specific praise improves on-task behaviour and numeracy enjoyment: A study of year four pupils engaged in the numeracy hour. *Educational Psychology in Practice*, *20*(4), 335–351. doi:10.1080/0266736042000314277

Chang, Y., & Locke, J. (2016). A systematic review of peer-mediated interventions for children with autism spectrum disorder. *Research in Autism Spectrum Disorders*, *27*, 1–10. doi:10.1016/j.rasd.2016.03.010 PMID:27807466

Chang, Y., & Shire, S. (2020). Promoting play in early childhood programs for children with ASD: Strategies for educators and practitioners. *Teaching Exceptional Children*, *52*(2), 66–76. doi:10.1177/0040059919874305

Chen, D., Klein, M. D., & Minor, L. (2009). Interdisciplinary perspectives in early intervention: Professional development in multiple disabilities through distance education. *Infants and Young Children*, *22*(2), 146–158. doi:10.1097/IYC.0b013e3181a030e0

Cheng, Z., Watson, S. L., & Newby, T. J. (2018). Goal setting and open digital badges in higher education. *TechTrends*, *62*(2), 190–196. doi:10.100711528-018-0249-x

Chen, H. W., O'Donnell, J. M., Chiu, Y. J., Chen, Y. C., Kang, Y. N., Tuan, Y. T., Kuo, S. Y., & Wu, J. C. (2022). Comparison of learning outcomes of interprofessional education simulation with traditional single-profession education simulation: A mixed-methods study. *BMC Medical Education*, *22*(1), 651. doi:10.118612909-022-03640-z PMID:36042449

Chesley, M. G., & Jordan, J. (2012). What's missing from teacher prep. *Educational Leadership*, *69*(8), 41–45.

Child Welfare Policy and Practice Group. (2018). *Iowa Department of Human Services fidelity assessment – Iowa family team meeting process*. Iowa Department of Human Services. https://dhs.iowa.gov/sites/default/files/CWPPG_IA_RPT_12.18.pdf?051620201458

Children's Foundation of Mississippi. (2020). *2020 Mississippi kids count factbook*. [Data set]. https://childrensfoundationms.org/research/kidscount2020/

Chitiyo, J., Chitiyo, A., & Dombek, D. (2020). Preservice teachers' understanding of problem behavior. *International Journal of Curriculum and Instruction*, *12*(2), 63–74. https://ijci.wcci-international.org

Chiu, C., Hsu, M., & Wang, E. (2006). Understanding knowledge sharing in virtual communities: An integration of social capital and social cognitive theories. *Decision Support Systems*, *42*(3), 1872–1888. doi:10.1016/j.dss.2006.04.001

Choi, H. C., McCart, A. B., & Sailor, W. (2020). Achievement of students with IEPs and associated relationships with an inclusive MTSS framework. *The Journal of Special Education*, *54*(3), 157–168. doi:10.1177/0022466919897408

Chow, J. C., & Wehby, J. H. (2018). Associations between language and problem behavior: A systematic review and correlational meta-analysis. *Educational Psychology Review*, *30*(1), 61–82. doi:10.100710648-016-9385-z

Christensen, S. S., Davies, R. S., Harris, S. P., Hanks, J., & Bowles, B. (2019). Teacher recruitment: Factors that predict high school students' willingness to become teachers. *Education Sciences*, *9*(4), 282. doi:10.3390/educsci9040282

Christianakis, M. (2011). Hybrid texts: Fifth graders, rap music, and writing. *Urban Education*, *46*(5), 1131–1168. doi:10.1177/0042085911400326

Chunngam, B., Chanchalor, S., & Murphy, E. (2014). Membership, participation and knowledge building in virtual communities for informal learning. *British Journal of Educational Technology*, *45*(5), 863–879. doi:10.1111/bjet.12114

Chu, S., & García, S. (2014). Culturally responsive teaching efficacy beliefs of in-service special education teachers. *Remedial and Special Education*, *35*(4), 218–232. doi:10.1177/0741932513520511

Cihon, J. H., Milne, C. M., Leaf, J., Ferguson, J. L., & Leaf, R. (2020). Fad treatments in autism intervention. *Education and Training in Autism and Developmental Disabilities*, *5*(4), 466–475.

Clark, C. R., Mercer, S. H., Zeigler-Hill, V., & Dufrene, B. A. (2012). Barriers to the success of ethnic minority students in school psychology graduate programs. *School Psychology Review*, *41*(2), 176–192. doi:10.1080/02796015.2012.12087519

Cochran-Smith, M., & Lytle, S. L. (1990). Research on teaching and teacher research: The issues that divide. *Educational Researcher*, *19*(2), 2–11. doi:10.3102/0013189X019002002

Coiro, M. J., Kotchick, B. A., & Preis, J. (2016). Youth social skills groups: A training platform for promoting graduate clinician interprofessional competence. *Journal of Interprofessional Education & Practice*, *4*, 89–92. doi:10.1016/j.xjep.2016.04.004

Colebourn, J. A., Golub-Victor, A. C., & Paez, A. (2017). Developing overhand throwing skills for child with autism with a collaborative approach in school-based therapy. *Pediatric Physical Therapy*, *29*(3), 262–269. doi:10.1097/PEP.0000000000000405 PMID:28654501

Coleman, H. M., Xu, Y., & De Arment, S. (2020). Empowering diverse families. *International Journal of Early Childhood Special Education*, *12*(1), 702077. doi:10.20489/intjecse

Collaborative for Academic, Social, and Emotional Learning (CASEL). (2020). *Core SEL competencies*. https://casel.org/core-competencies/

Collier-Meek, M. A., Sanetti, L. M. H., & Boyle, A. M. (2016). Providing feasible implementation support: Direct training and implementation planning in consultation. *School Psychology Forum*, *10*, 106–119. https://www.nasponline.org/publications/periodicals/spf/volume-10/volume-10-issue-1-(spring-2016)/providing-feasible-implementation-support-direct-training-and-implementation-planning-in-consultation

Collier-Meek, M. A., Sanetti, L. M., Fallon, L., & Chafouleas, S. (2020). Exploring the influences of assessment method, intervention steps, intervention sessions, and observation timing on treatment fidelity estimates. *Assessment for Effective Intervention*, *46*(1), 3–13. doi:10.1177/1534508419857228

Colman, D. E., Echon, R., Lemay, M. S., McDonald, J., Smith, K. R., Spencer, J., & Swift, J. K. (2016). The efficacy of self-care for graduate students in professional psychology: A meta-analysis. *Training and Education in Professional Psychology*, *10*(4), 188–197. doi:10.1037/tep0000130

Colombo-Dougovito, A. M. (2015). "Try to do the best you can:" How pre-service APE specialists experience teaching students with autism spectrum disorder. *International Journal of Special Education*, *30*(3), 160–176.

Commission on Teacher Credentialing. (2009). *California Standards for the Teaching Profession*. Retrieved from https://www.cde.ca.gov/pd/ps/

Compton, L., Davis, N., & Mackey, J. (2009). Field experience in virtual schools—To be there virtually. *Journal of Technology and Teacher Education*, *17*(4), 459–477.

Conner, L. R., Richardson, S., & Murphy, A. L. (2018). Teaching note: Using adult learning principles for evidence-based learning in a BSW research course. *The Journal of Baccalaureate Social Work*, *23*(1), 355–365. doi:10.18084/1084-7219.23.1.355

## Compilation of References

Conners, B., Johnson, A., Duarte, J., Murriky, R., & Marks, K. (2019). Future directions of training and fieldwork in diversity issues in applied behavior analysis. *Behavior Analysis in Practice*, *12*(4), 767–776. doi:10.100740617-019-00349-2 PMID:31976288

Constantino, J. N., Abbacchi, A. M., Saulnier, C., Klaiman, C., Mandell, D. S., Zhang, Y., Hawks, Z., Bates, J., Klin, A., Shattuck, P., Molholm, S., Fitzgerald, R., Roux, A., Lowe, J. K., & Geschwind, D. H. (2020). Timing of the diagnosis of autism in African American children. *Pediatrics*, *146*(3), e20193629. doi:10.1542/peds.2019-3629 PMID:32839243

Conti-Ramsden, G., Durkin, K., Toseeb, U., Botting, N., & Pickles, A. (2018). Education and employment outcomes of young adults with a history of developmental language disorder. *International Journal of Language & Communication Disorders*, *53*(2), 237–255. doi:10.1111/1460-6984.12338 PMID:29139196

Cook, L., & Friend, M. (2010). The state of the art of collaboration on behalf of students with disabilities. *Journal of Educational & Psychological Consultation*, *20*(1), 1–8. doi:10.1080/10474410903535398

Cook, S., & Howell, P. (2014). Bullying in children and teenagers who stutter and the relation to self-esteem, social acceptance, and anxiety. *Perspectives on Fluency and Fluency Disorders*, *24*(2), 46–57. doi:10.1044/ffd24.2.46

Cooper-Duffy, K., & Eaker, K. (2017). Effective team practices: Interprofessional contributions to communication issues with a parent's perspective. *American Journal of Speech-Language Pathology*, *26*(2), 181–192. doi:10.1044/2016_AJSLP-15-0069 PMID:28514473

Cooper, J. O., Heron, T. E., & Heward, W. L. (2020). *Applied behavior analysis*. doi:10.26741/abaespana/2020.cooper3e

Cornell, D. (2018). *Comprehensive school threat assessment guidelines: Intervention and support to prevent violence.* School Threat Assessment Consultants LLC.

Correia, A. P. (2020). Healing the digital divide during the COVID-19 pandemic. *Quarterly Review of Distance Education*, *21*(1).

Costigan, F. A., & Light, J. (2010). A review of preservice training in augmentative and alternative communication for speech-language pathologists, special education teachers, and occupational therapists. *Assistive Technology*, *22*(4), 200–212. doi:10.1080/10400435.2010.492774 PMID:21306066

Cote. (2012). Designing transition programs for culturally and linguistically diverse students with disabilities. *Multicultural Education*, *20*(1), 51–55.

Coufal, K. L., & Scherz, J. (2013). *Interprofessional education in communication sciences and disorders*. Retrieved from https://www.asha.org/enews/accessacademics.html

Council for Clinical Certification in Audiology and Speech-Language Pathology of the American Speech Language Hearing Association. (2018). 2020 standards for the certificate of clinical competence in speech-language pathology. *ASHA*. www.asha.org/certification/2020-slp-certification-standards

Council for Clinical Certification in Audiology and Speech-Language Pathology of the American Speech-Language-Hearing Association. (2018). 2020 Standards for the Certificate of Clinical Competence in Speech-Language Pathology. ASHA. www.asha.org/certification/2020-SLP-Certification-Standards

Council for Exceptional Children & CEEDAR Center. (n.d.). Retrieved from https://ceedar.education.ufl.edu/wp-content/uploads/2017/07/CEC-HLP-Web.pdf

Council for Exceptional Children (CEC). (2015). What every special educator must know: Professional ethics and standards. *CEC*.

Council for Exceptional Children (CEC). (2015). *What every special educator must know: Professional ethics and standards.* CEC..

Council for Exceptional Children (CEC). (2020). *Shortages of Special Education Teachers and Early Intervention Providers: Issue Brief.* Special Education Legislative Summit. https://exceptionalchildren.org/sites/default/files/2020-07/2020-TeacherShortageBrief.pdf

Council for Exceptional Children and The Division for Early Childhood. (2020). Initial practice-based professional preparation standards for early interventionists/early childhood special educators (EI/ECSE) (initial birth through age 8). *Exceptional Children.* https://exceptionalchildren.org/standards/initial-practice-based-standards-early-interventionists-early-childhood-special-educators

Council for Exceptional Children Division for Early Childhood. (2020). *Initial practice based professional preparation standards for early interventionist/early childhood special educators (EI/ECSE) (Initial birth through age 8).* https://www.decsped.org/ei-ecse-standards

Council for Exceptional Children Division for Early Childhood. (2020). Initial practice-based professional preparation standards for early interventionists/early childhood special educators (EI/ECSE) (initial birth through age 8). *Exceptional Children.* https://exceptionalchildren.org/standards/initial-practice-based-standards-early-interventionists-early-childhood-special-educators

Council for Exceptional Children Initial Preparation Standards. (2015). *What every special educator must know: Professional Ethics and Standards.* Retrieved from https://exceptionalchildren.org/standards/initial-special-education-preparation-standards

Council for Exceptional Children. (2015). What every special educator must know: Professional ethics and standards. *CEC.* https://exceptionalchildren.org/standards/professional-practice-guidelines

Council for Exceptional Children. (2020). Initial practice-based professional preparation standards for special educators. *CEC.* https://exceptionalchildren.org/standards/initial-practice-based-professional-preparation-standards-special-educators

Council for Exceptional Children. (2020). *Initial practice-based professional preparation standards for special educators.* Retrieved from https://exceptionalchildren.org/standards/initial-practice-based-professional-preparation-standards-special-educators

Council for Exceptional Children. (n.d.). High Leverage Practices for students with disabilities. *CEC.* https://highleveragepractices.org/

Council of Exceptional Children. (2014). CEC standards for evidence-based practices. *CEC.*

Council on Social Work Education. (2015). Educational Policy and Accreditation Standards. *CSWE.* https://www.cswe.org/accreditation/standards/2015-epas/

Council on Social Work Education. (2015). *Educational policy and accreditation standards.* https://www.cswe.org/getattachment/Accreditation/Standards-andPolicies/2015-EPAS/2015EPASandGlossary.pdf

Council on Social Work Education. (2022). Educational Policy and Accreditation Standards. *CSWE.* https://www.cswe.org/accreditation/standards/2022-epas/

*Compilation of References*

Courchesne, V., Tesfaye, R., Mirenda, P., Nicholas, D., Mitchell, W., Singh, I., Zwaigenbaum, L., & Elsabbagh, M. (2022). Autism Voices: A novel method to access first-person perspective of autistic youth. *Autism*, *26*(5), 1123–1136. doi:10.1177/13623613211042128 PMID:34482746

Cox, M. D. (n.d.). *Faculty learning communities: 16 recommendations for FLCs*. Center for Teaching Excellence. Miami University. https://miamioh.edu/cte/faculty-staff/flcs/index.html

Cox, S., Parmer, R., Strizek, G., & Thomas, T. (2016). Documentation for the 2011–12 Schools and Staffing Survey (NCES 2016-817). U.S. Department of Education. *National Center for Education Statistics*. https://nces.ed.gov/pubsearch

Cox, E. (2015). Coaching and adult learning: Theory and practice. *New Directions for Adult and Continuing Education*, *2015*(148), 27–38. doi:10.1002/ace.20149

Cox, K., & Steiner, S. (2013). *Self-care in social work: A guide for practitioners, supervisors, and administrators*. NASW Press.

Crais, E. R., Boone, H. A., Harrison, M., Freund, P., Downing, K., & West, T. (2004). Interdisciplinary personnel preparation: Graduates' use of targeted practices. *Infants and Young Children*, *17*(1), 82–92. doi:10.1097/00001163-200401000-00010

Cramer, E. D., Pellegrini-Lafont, C., & Gonzalez, L. (2014). Towards Culturally Responsive and Integrated Instruction for All Learners: The Integrated Learning Model. *Interdisciplinary Journal of Teaching and Learning*, *4*, 110–124.

Cratty, B. J. (1989). *Adapted physical education in the mainstream*. Love Publishing Company.

Crawford, S., O'Reilly, R., & Luttrell, S. (2012). Assessing the effects of integrating the reflective framework for teaching in physical education (RFTPE) on the teaching and learning of undergraduate sport studies and physical education students. *Reflective Practice*, *13*(1), 115–129. doi:10.1080/14623943.2011.626025

Cree, R. A., Bitsko, R. H., Robinson, L. R., Holbrook, J. R., Danielson, M. L., Smith, C., Kaminsky, J. W., Kenny, M. K., & Peacock, G. (2018). Health care, family, and community factors associated with mental, behavioral, and developmental disorders and poverty among children aged 2–8 years—United States, 2016. *Morbidity and Mortality Weekly Report*, *67*(50), 1377–1383. doi:10.15585/mmwr.mm6750a1 PMID:30571671

Creswell, J. W., & Plano Clark, V. L. (2018). *Designing and conducting mixed methods research* (3rd ed.). SAGE.

Creswell, J. W., Plano Clark, V. L., Gutmann, M., & Hanson, W. (2003). Advanced mixed methods research designs. In A. Tashakkori & C. Teddlie (Eds.), *Handbook of mixed methods in social and behavioral research* (pp. 209–240). SAGE.

Critchfield, T. S., Becirevic, A., & Reed, D. D. (2017a). On the social validity of behavior-analytic communication: A call for research and description of one method. *Analysis of Verbal Behavior*, *33*(1), 1–23. doi:10.100740616-017-0077-7 PMID:30854284

Critchfield, T. S., Doepke, K. J., & Epting, L. K. (2017). Normative emotional responses to behavior analysis jargon or how not to use words to win friends and influence people. *Behavior Analysis in Practice*, *7*(2), 1–10. doi:10.100740617-016-0161-9 PMID:28630814

Cropanzano, R., & Mitchell, M. S. (2005). Social exchange theory: An interdisciplinary review. *Journal of Management*, *31*(6), 874–900. doi:10.1177/0149206305279602

Cross, A. F., Traub, E. K., Hutter-Pishgahi, L., & Shelton, G. (2004). Elements of successful inclusion for children with significant disabilities. [TECSE]. *Topics in Early Childhood Special Education*, *24*(3), 169–183. doi:10.1177/02711214040240030401

Cummings, J. R., Wen, H., & Druss, B. G. (2013). Improving access to mental health services for youth in the United States. *Journal of the American Medical Association*, *309*(6), 553–554. doi:10.1001/jama.2013.437 PMID:23403677

Cunningham, S. A., Kramer, M. R., & Narayan, K. M. (2014). Incidence of childhood obesity in the United States. *The New England Journal of Medicine*, *370*(5), 403–411. doi:10.1056/NEJMoa1309753 PMID:24476431

Curtin, C., Jojic, M., & Bandini, L. G. (2014). Obesity in children with autism spectrum disorder. *Harvard Review of Psychiatry*, *22*(2), 93–103. doi:10.1097/HRP.0000000000000031 PMID:24614764

Curtin, N., Malley, J., & Stewart, A. (2016). Mentoring the next generation of faculty: Supporting academic career aspirations among doctoral students. *Research in Higher Education*, *57*(6), 714–738. doi:10.100711162-015-9403-x

Curtis, M. J., Hunley, S. A., & Grier, E. C. (2004). The status of school psychology: Implications of a major personnel shortage. *Psychology in the Schools*, *41*(4), 431–442. doi:10.1002/pits.10186

D'Amato, R. C. E., Sheridan, S. M., Phelps, L. A., & Lopez, E. C. (2004). Psychology in the Schools, School Psychology Review, School Psychology quarterly, and Journal of Educational and Psychological Consultation Editors Collaborate to Chart School Psychology's Past, Present, and "Futures". *Psychological Review*, *33*(1), 3–6. PMID:14756583

D'Armour, D., Ferrada-Videla, M., San Martin Rodriguez, L., & Beaulieu, M. (2005). The conceptual basis for interprofessional collaboration: Core concepts and theoretical frameworks. *Journal of Interprofessional Care*, *19*(1), 116–131. doi:10.1080/13561820500082529 PMID:16096150

Da Fonte, M. A., & Barton-Artwood, S. M. (2017). Collaboration of general and special education teachers: Perspectives and strategies. *Teaching Education*, *53*(2), 99–106.

Da Fonte, M. A., & Barton-Arwood, S. M. (2017). Collaboration of general and special education teachers: Perspectives and strategies. *Intervention in School and Clinic*, *53*(2), 99–106. doi:10.1177/1053451217693370

Daley, B. J. (2001). Learning and professional practice: A study of four professions. *Adult Education Quarterly*, *52*(1), 39–54. doi:10.1177/074171360105200104

Daly, R. M. (2007). The effect of exercise on bone mass and structural geometry during growth. *Optimizing Bone Mass and Strength*, *51*, 33–49. doi:10.1159/000103003 PMID:17505118

Darling-Hammond, L., & Berry, B. (2006). Highly qualified teachers for all. *Educational Leadership*, *64*(3), 14–20.

Darling-Hammond, L., Hyler, M. E., & Gardner, M. (2017). *Effective teacher professional development*. Learning Policy Institute., doi:10.54300/122.311

Datchuk, S. M., & Rodgers, D. B. (2019). Text writing within simple sentences: A writing fluency intervention for students with high-incidence disabilities. *Learning Disabilities Research & Practice*, *34*(1), 118–118. doi:10.1111/ldrp.12185

Datchuk, S. M., Wagner, K., & Hier, B. O. (2020). Level and trend of writing sequences: A review and meta-analysis of writing interventions for students with disabilities. *Exceptional Children*, *86*(2), 174–192. doi:10.1177/0014402919873311

Davidson, B. C., Davis, E., Cadenas, H., Barnett, M., Luis Sanchez, B. E., Gonzalez, J. C., & Jent, J. (2021). Universal teacher-child interaction training in early special education: A pilot cluster-randomized control trial. *Behavior Therapy*, *52*(2), 379–393. doi:10.1016/j.beth.2020.04.014 PMID:33622507

Davidson, M. N., & Foster-Johnson, L. (2001). Mentoring in the preparation of graduate researchers of color. *Review of Educational Research*, *71*(4), 549–574. doi:10.3102/00346543071004549

Davis, A. E., Perry, D. F., & Rabinovitz, L. (2020). Expulsion prevention: Framework for the role of infant and early childhood mental health consultation in addressing implicit biases. *Infant Mental Health Journal*, *41*, 327-339.

*Compilation of References*

Dawson, M., Soulières, I., Gernsbacher, M. A., & Mottron, L. (2007). The level and nature of autistic intelligence. *Psychological Science*, *18*(8), 657–662. doi:10.1111/j.1467-9280.2007.01954.x PMID:17680932

De Arment, S., Reed, E., & Wetzel, A. (2013). Promoting adaptive expertise: A conceptual framework for special educator preparation. *Teacher Education and Special Education*, *36*(1), 217–230. doi:10.1177/0888406413489578

de Brey, C., Musu, L., McFarland, J., Wilkinson-Flicker, S., Diliberti, M., Zhang, A., Branstetter, C., & Wang, X. (2019). Status and trends in the education of racial and ethnic groups 2018 (NCES 2019-038). *U.S. Department of Education*. Washington, DC: National Center for Education Statistics. https://nces.ed.gov/pubsearch/

de Jong, E. J., Harper, C. A., & Coady, M. R. (2013). Enhanced knowledge and skills for elementary mainstream teachers of English Language Learners. *Theory into Practice*, *52*(2), 89–97. doi:10.1080/00405841.2013.770326

De Leon, N. (2014). Developing intercultural competence by participating in intensive intercultural service learning. *Michigan Journal of Community Service Learning*, *21*(1), 17–30.

de OliveiraP. S.van MunsterM. D. A.de SouzaJ. V.LiebermanL. J. (2020). Adapted physical education collaborative consulting: A systematic literature review. Journal of Teaching in Physical Education, 39, 165–175.

deBettencourt, L. U., & Nagro, S. A. (2019). Tracking special education teacher candidates' reflective practices over time. *Remedial and Special Education*, *40*(5), 277–288. doi:10.1177/0741932518762573

Dee, T. (2004). Teachers, race and student achievement in a randomized experiment. *The Review of Economics and Statistics*, *86*(1), 195–210. https://www.nber.org/system/files/working_papers/w8432/w8432.pdf. doi:10.1162/003465304323023750

DeKemel, K. P. (2003). *Intervention in language arts: A practical guide for speech-language pathologists*. Butterworth Heinemann.

Deloitte. (2018). *Data USA: Counselors*. https://datausa.io/profile/soc/counselors

DeLuca, C., & Klinger, D. A. (2010). Assessment literacy development: Identifying gaps in teachers candidates' learning. *Assessment in Education: Principles, Policy & Practice*, *17*(4), 419–438. doi:10.1080/0969594X.2010.516643

Deno, S. L., & Fuchs, L. S. (1987). Developing curriculum-based measurement systems for data-based special education problem solving. *Focus on Exceptional Children*, *19*(8), 1–16. doi:10.17161/foec.v19i8.7497

DePaepe, P. A., & Wood, L. A. (2001). Collaborative practices related to augmentative and alternative communication: Currently personnel preparation programs. *Communication Disorders Quarterly*, *22*(2), 77–86. doi:10.1177/152574010102200203

Department of Human Resources for Health. (2010). Framework for action on interprofessional education and collaborative practice (WHO/HRH/HPN/10.3). WHO Press, World Health Organization.

Derman-Sparks, L., & Edwards, J. O. (2019). Understanding anti-bias education: Bringing the four core goals to every facet of your curriculum. *Young Children*, *74*(5), 6–13. https://www.jstor.org/stable/26842300

Derman-Sparks, L., Edwards, J. O., & Goins, C. M. (2020). *Anti-bias education for young children and ourselves* (2nd ed.). National Association for the Education of Young Children.

Dettmer, P., Thurston, L. P., & Dyck, N. (1996). *Consultation, collaboration, and teamwork: For students with special needs* (2nd ed.). Allyn & Bacon.

Dettmer, P., Thurston, L. P., Knackendoffel, A., & Dyck, N. J. (2009). *Collaboration, consultation, and teamwork for students with special needs* (6th ed.). Pearson Education, Inc.

Devecchi, C., & Nevin, A. (2010). Leadership for inclusive schools and inclusive school leadership. *Advances in Educational Administration*, *11*, 211–241. doi:10.1108/S1479-3660(2010)0000011014

Developmental Disabilities Assistance and Bill of Rights Act of. 2000, Pub. L. No. 106-402, § 102(8). https://www.congress.gov/106/plaws/publ402/PLAW-106publ402.pdf

DeVeney, S. L., & McKevitt, B. (2021). Interprofessional experience for future education professionals: School psychology and speech-language pathology students. *Teaching and Learning in Communication Services & Disorders*, *5*(1). Advance online publication. doi:10.30707/TLCSD5.1.1624982519.476871

Diaz, J. (2022, May 25). *27 school shootings have taken place so far in 2022.* https://www.npr.org/2022/05/24/1101050970/2022-school-shootings-so-far

Dickenson, D. K., Golinkoff, R. M., & Hirsh-Pasek, K. (2010). Speaking out for language: Why language is central to reading development. *Educational Researcher*, *39*(4), 305–310. doi:10.3102/0013189X10370204

Dickson, G. L., Chun, H., & Fernandez, I. T. (2015). The development and initial validation of the student measure of culturally responsive teaching. *Assessment for Effective Intervention*, *41*(3), 141–154. doi:10.1177/1534508415604879

Dickstein-Fischer, L., Scott, K., & Connally, J. (2019). Potential benefits of school counselor consultation to enhance student social emotional learning. *The Practitioner Scholar: Journal of the International Trauma Training Institute*, *1*, 40–60.

Dieker, L. A., Lane, H. B., Allsopp, D. H., O'Brien, C., Butler, T. W., Kyger, M., Louvin, L., & Fenty, N. S. (2009). Evaluating video models of evidence-based instructional practices to enhance teacher learning. *Teacher Education and Special Education*, *32*(3), 180–196. doi:10.1177/0888406409334202

Dieker, L. A., & Rodriguez, J. A., Lignugaris/Kraft, B., Hynes, M. C., & Hughes, C. E. (2014). The potential of simulated environments in teacher education: Current and future possibilities. *Teacher Education and Special Education*, *37*, 21–33. doi:10.1177/0888406413512683

Diliberti, M. K., & Schwartz, H. L. (2022). *District leaders' concerns about mental health and political polarization in schools: Selected findings from the Fourth American School District Panel Survey.* RAND Corporation. https://www.rand.org/pubs/research_reports/RRA956-8.html

Dillenburger, K. (2017). Staff training. In *Handbook of treatments for autism spectrum disorder* (pp. 95–107). Springer. doi:10.1007/978-3-319-61738-1_7

Dillon, S., Armstrong, E., Goudy, L., Reynolds, H., & Scurry, S. (2021). Improving special education service delivery through interdisciplinary collaboration. Teaching Exceptional Children, 54(1), 36–43.

Dillon, S., Armstrong, E., Goudy, L., Reynolds, H., & Scurry, S. (2021). Improving special education service delivery through interdisciplinary collaboration. *Teaching Exceptional Children*, *54*(1), 36–43. doi:10.1177/00400599211029671

DiLollo, A., & Neimeyer, R. A. (2022). *Counseling in speech-language pathology and audiology: Reconstructing personal narratives* (2nd ed.). Plural Publishing.

Dingfelder, H. E., & Mandell, D. S. (2011). Bridging the research-to-practice gap in autism intervention: An application of diffusion of innovation theory. *Journal of Autism and Developmental Disorders*, *41*(5), 597–609. doi:10.100710803-010-1081-0 PMID:20717714

Dinnebeil, L. A. (2014). Top-down and bottom-up thinking comprehensively about support for early childhood inclusion. *Young Exceptional Children*, *17*(3), 48–50. doi:10.1177/1096250614542175

Dinnebeil, L., Boat, M., & Bae, Y. (2013). Integrating principles of universal design into early childhood curriculum. *Dimensions in Early Childhood, 41*(1), 3–13.

Dinnebeil, L., Petti-Frontczak, K., & McInerney, W. (2009). A consultative itinerant approach to service delivery: Considerations for the early childhood community. *Language, Speech, and Hearing Services in Schools, 40*(4), 435–445. doi:10.1044/0161-1461(2008/08-0028) PMID:18952808

Division for Early Childhood (DEC). (2014). DEC recommended practices in early intervention/early childhood special education 2014. *DEC.* https://divisionearlychildhood.egnyte.com/dl/7urLPWCt5U

Division for Early Childhood and National Association for the Education of Young Children. (2009). *Early childhood inclusion: A joint position statement of the Division for the Early Childhood (DEC) and the National Association for the Education of Young Children (NAEYC).* The University of North Carolina at Chapel Hill, FPG Child Development Institute. https://www.naeyc.org/sites/default/files/globally-shared/downloads/PDFs/resources/position-statements/ps_inclusion_dec_naeyc_ec.pdf

Division for Early Childhood of the Council for Exceptional Children. (2020). *Initial practice-based professional preparation standards for early interventionists/early childhood special educators (EI/ECSE) (initial birth through age 8).* Retrieved from: https://exceptionalchildren.org/standards/initial-practice-based-standards-early-interventionists-early-childhood-special-educators

Division for Early Childhood. (2014). DEC recommended practices in early intervention/early childhood special education 2014. *DEC.* http://www.dec-sped.org/recommendedpractices

Division for Early Childhood. (2014). *DEC recommended practices in early intervention/early childhood special education 2014.* http://www.dec-sped.org/recommendedpractices

Division for Early Childhood. (2014). *DEC recommended practices in early intervention/early childhood special education 2014.* Retrieved from http://www.dec-sped.org/recommendedpractices

Division for Early Childhood. (2014). DEC recommended practices in early intervention/early childhood special education. *DEC.* http://www.dec-sped.org/recommendedpractices

Division for Early Childhood. (2014). DEC recommended practices. *DEC.* http://www.dec-sped.org/recommendedpractices

Division for Early Childhood. (2020). *DEC priority issues agenda.* http://www.dec-sped.org/PriorityIssues

Division for Early Childhood. (2022). *Personnel preparation for early intervention/early childhood special education.* https://divisionearlychildhood.egnyte.com/dl/bdmVgW3UAi

Division of Early Childhood. (2015). DEC recommended practices: Enhancing services for young children with disabilities and their families. DEC Recommended Practices Monograph Series, 1.

Dobbs-Oates, J., & Wachter Morris, C. (2016). The case for interprofessional education in teacher education and beyond. *Journal of Education for Teaching, 42*(1), 50–65. doi:10.1080/02607476.2015.1131363

Dombo, E. A., & Sabatino, C. A. (2019). *Creating trauma-informed schools: a guide for school social workers and schools.* doi:10.1093/oso/9780190873806.001.0001

Dow, A. W., DiazGranados, D., Mazmanian, P. E., & Retchin, S. M. (2014). An exploratory study of an assessment tool derived from the competencies of the interprofessional education collaborative. *Journal of Interprofessional Care, 28*(4), 299–304. doi:10.3109/13561820.2014.891573 PMID:24593327

Downing, J. E., Hanreddy, A., & Peckham-Hardin, K. D. (2015). *Teaching communication skills to students with severe disabilities* (3rd ed.). Paul H. Brookes Publishing.

Drager, K., Light, J., & McNaughton, D. (2010). Effects of AAC interventions on communication and language for young children with complex communication needs. *Journal of Pediatric Rehabilitation Medicine*, *3*(4), 303–310. doi:10.3233/PRM-2010-0141 PMID:21791864

Drescher, T., & Chang, Y. C. (2022). Benefits of Collaborative Teaching Models in Teacher Education Programs: Sharing disability knowledge and promoting inclusion. *Teacher Development*, *26*(2), 151–165. doi:10.1080/13664530.2022.2032299

Driver, M., Zimmer, K., & Murphy, K. M. (2018). Using mixed reality simulations to prepare preservice special educators for collaboration in inclusive settings. *Journal of Technology and Teacher Education*, *26*(1), 57–77. https://www.learntechlib.org/primary/p/181153/

DuFour, R., DuFour, R., Eaker, R., Many, T. W., & Mattos, M. (2016). *Learning by doing: A handbook for professional learning communities at work* (3rd ed.). Solution Tree Press.

Durkin, K., & Conti-Ramsden, G. (2010). Young people with specific language impairment: A review of social and emotional functioning in adolescence. *Child Language Teaching and Therapy*, *26*(2), 105–121. doi:10.1177/0265659010368750

Dusenbury, L., Calin, S., Domitrovich, C., & Weissberg, R. P. (2015). *What does evidence-based instruction in social and emotional learning actually look like in practice?* Collaborative for Academic, Social, and Emotional Learning. http://www.casel.org/wp-

Dymond, S., & Bentz, J. (2006). Using digital videos to enhance teacher preparation. *Teacher Education and Special Education*, *29*(2), 98–112. doi:10.1177/088840640602900202

Early Childhood Personnel Center. (2020). Cross-disciplinary competencies. *ECPTCA*. https://ecpcta.org/cross-disciplinary-competencies/

Early Childhood Personnel Center. (2020). https://ecpcta.org

Early Childhood Technical Assistance Center. (2020). Part C. *ECTA Center*. https://ectacenter.org/partc/partc.asp

Echevarria, J. E., Vogt, M. E., & Richards-Tutor, C. (2014). *Response to intervention and English learners: Using the SIOP model* (2nd ed.). Pearson.

Echevarria, J. E., Vogt, M. E., & Short, D. (2017). *Making content comprehensible for English learners: The SIOP model* (5th ed.). Pearson.

Education Trust. (2019). *School counselors matter*. https://www.schoolcounselor.org/asca/media/asca/Publications/ASCAEdTrustRHFactSheet.pdf

Edwards, C. C., & Da Font, A. (2012). The 5-point plan: Fostering successful partnerships with families of students with disabilities. *Teaching Exceptional Children*, *44*(30), 6–13. doi:10.1177/004005991204400301

Edwards, S., McGrath Davis, A., Ernst, L., Sitzman, B., Bruce, A., Keeler, D., Almadhoun, O., Mousa, H., & Hyman, P. (2015). Interdisciplinary strategies for treating oral aversions in children. *Journal of Parental and Entreal Nutrition*, *39*(8), 899–909. doi:10.1177/0148607115609311 PMID:26487751

Ehrhardt, K., Curiel, E., Frieder, J., Ross, D., & Summy, S. (2017). *Interdisciplinary Preparation in Autism. Office of Special Education Programs (OSEP) Preparation of Special Education*. Early Intervention, and Related Service Leadership Personnel Grant.

Eikeseth, S., Smith, T., Jahr, E., & Eldevik, S. (2002). Intensive behavioral treatment at school for 4-to 7-year-old children with autism: A 1-year comparison controlled study. *Behavior Modification*, *26*(1), 49–68. doi:10.1177/0145445502026001004 PMID:11799654

Elliott, R., Clayton, J., & Iwata, J. (2014). Exploring the use of microcredentialing and digital badges in learning environments to encourage motivation to learn and achieve. In B. Hegarty, J. McDonald, & S.-K. Loke (Eds.), *Rhetoric and Reality: Critical perspectives on educational technology. Proceedings ascilite Dunedin 2014* (pp. 703–707).

Emerson, R., Fretz, R., & Shaw, L. (2011). *Writing Ethnographic Fieldnotes*. The University of Chicago Press. doi:10.7208/chicago/9780226206868.001.0001

Etscheidt, S., Curran, C. M., & Sawyer, C. M. (2012). Promoting reflection in teacher preparation programs: A multilevel model. *Teacher Education and Special Education*, *35*(1), 7–26. doi:10.1177/0888406411420887

Every Student Succeeds Act (ESSA). (2015). US Government. https://www.ed.gov/essa

Every Student Succeeds Act. (2015). Every Student Succeeds Act. *ESSA*. https://www.ed.gov/essa?src=ft

Eyeberg, S. M., Chase, R. M., Fernandez, M. A., & Nelson, M. M. (2014). *Dyadic parent-child interaction coding system (DPICS) clinical manual* (4th ed.). PCIT International.

Ezell, H. K., & Justice, L. M. (2005). *Shared storybook reading: Building young children's language and emergent literacy skills*. Paul H. Brookes Publishing Co.

Fagan, T. K. (2004). School Psychology's significant discrepancy: Historical perspectives on personnel shortages. *Psychology in the Schools*, *41*(4), 419–430. doi:10.1002/pits.10185

Faircloth, S., Toldson, I., & Lucio, R. (2016). *Decreasing dropout rates for minority male youth with disabilities from culturally and ethnically diverse backgrounds*. Monograph prepared for Office of Special Education Programs. https://files.eric.ed.gov/fulltext/ED575729.pdf

Fall, A. M., & Billingsley, B. S. (2011). Disparities in work conditions among early career special educators in high-and low-poverty districts. *Remedial and Special Education*, *32*(1), 64–78. doi:10.1177/0741932510361264

Farmer, R. L., Goforth, A. N., Kim, S. Y., Naser, S. C., Lockwood, A. B., & Affrunti, N. W. (2021). Status of School Psychology in 2020, Part 2: Professional Practices in the NASP membership survey. *NASP Research Reports*, *5*(3).

Farmer, T. W. (2013). When universal approaches and prevention services are not enough: The importance of understanding the stigmatization of special education for students with EBD a response to Kauffman and Badar. *Behavioral Disorders*, *39*(1), 32–42. doi:10.1177/019874291303900105

Fawley, K. D., Stokes, T. F., Rainear, C. A., Rossi, J. L., & Budd, K. S. (2020). Universal TCIT improves teacher-child interactions and management of child behavior. *Journal of Behavioral Education*, *29*(4), 635–656. doi:10.100710864-019-09337-6

Feng, S., & Wood, M. (2012). What makes a good university lecturer? Students' perceptions of teaching excellence. *Journal of Applied Research in Higher Education*, *4*(2), 142–155. doi:10.1108/17581181211273110

Ferguson, J., Craig, E. A., & Dounavi, K. (2019). Telehealth as a model for providing behaviour analytic interventions to individuals with autism spectrum disorder: A systematic review. *Journal of Autism and Developmental Disorders*, *49*(2), 582–616. doi:10.100710803-018-3724-5 PMID:30155578

Fernandez, M. S., Adelstein, J. S., Miller, S. P., Areizaga, M. J., Gold, D. C., Sanchez, A. L., Rothschild, S. A., Hirsch, E., & Gudino, O. G. (2015). Teacher-child interaction training: A pilot study with random assignment. *Behavior Therapy*, *46*(4), 463–477. doi:10.1016/j.beth.2015.02.002 PMID:26163711

Ferndandes, P. R. S., Jardim, J., & Lopes, M. C. S. (2021). The soft skills of special education teachers: Evidence from the literature. *Education Sciences*, *11*(3), 125. doi:10.3390/educsci11030125

Finkelhor, D., Ormrod, R., Turner, H., & Hamby, S. L. (2005). The victimization of children and youth: A comprehensive national survey. *Child Maltreatment*, *5*, 5–25. https://doi.org/10.1177/1077559504271287

Fink, L. D. (2003). *Creating significant learning experiences: An integrated approach to designing college courses*. Jossey-Bass.

Fischer, K. (2022). The shrinking of higher ed. *The Chronicle of Higher Education*. https://www.chronicle.com/article/the-shrinking-of-higher-ed

Fisher, A., Reilly, J. J., Kelly, L. A., Montgomery, C., Williamson, A., Paton, J. Y., & Grant, S. (2005). Fundamental movement skills and habitual physical activity in young children. *Medicine and Science in Sports and Exercise*, *37*(4), 684–688. doi:10.1249/01.MSS.0000159138.48107.7D PMID:15809570

Fish, R. E. (2016). The racialized construction of exceptionality: Experimental evidence of race/ethnicity effects on teachers' interventions. *Social Science Research*, *62*, 317–334. doi:10.1016/j.ssresearch.2016.08.007 PMID:28126108

Fixsen, D., Naoom, S., Blasé, K., Friedman, R. M., & Wallace, F. (2005). *Implementation research: A synthesis of the literature*. University of South Florida.

Flexer, R. W., McMahan-Queen, R., Baer, R., & Sparber, C. (2022). A mixed design evaluation of an interdisciplinary transition graduate program. *Journal of Applied Rehabilitation Counseling*, *53*(1), 45–67.

Florida Education Association. (2022). *Teacher and staff shortage*. https://feaweb.org/issues-action/teacher-and-staff-shortage

Forgan, J. W. (2002). Using bibliotherapy to teach problem solving. *Intervention in School and Clinic*, *38*(2), 75–82. doi:10.1177/10534512020380020201

Forman, S. G., Olin, S. S., Hoagwood, K. E., Crowe, M., & Saka, N. (2009). Evidence-based interventions in schools: Developers' views of implementation barriers and facilitators. *School Mental Health*, *1*(1), 26–36. doi:10.100712310-008-9002-5

Fowler, S. A., Coleman, R. B., & Bogdan, W. K. (2019). *The state of the special education profession survey report*. Council for Exceptional Children. doi:10.1177/0040059919875703

Fox, L., Dunlap, G., Hemmeter, M. L., Joseph, G. E., & Strain, P. S. (2003). The teaching pyramid: A model for supporting social competence and preventing challenging behavior in young children. *Young Children*, *58*(4), 48–53.

Francois, J. R., Coufal, K. L., & Subramanian, A. (2015). Student preparation for professional practice in early intervention. *Communication Disorders Quarterly*, *36*(3), 177–186. doi:10.1177/1525740114543349

Frankel, E. B. (2006). The knowledge, skills and personal qualities of early childhood resource consultants as agents of change. *Exceptionality Education Canada*, *16*(2), 35–58.

Frattura, E. M., & Capper, C. A. (2007). *Leading for social justice: Transforming schools for all learners*. Corwin Press.

*Compilation of References*

Frauenholtz, S., Mendenhall, A. N., & Moon, J. (2017). Role of school employees' mental health knowledge in interdisciplinary collaborations to support the academic success of students experiencing mental distress. *Children & Schools*, *39*(2), 71–79. doi:10.1093/cs/cdx004

Frazier, K. F., Whitby, P. J. S., Kucharczyk, S., Perryman, K. L., Thomas, J., Koch, L. C., & Bengston, E. (2019). Interprofessional education: Teaming for transition from adolescence to adulthood for people with significant disabilities. *Perspectives of the ASHA Special Interest Groups*, *4*(3), 492–501.

Frazier, K., Perryman, K., & Kucharczyk, S. (2020). Transition services: Building successful collaborations among school professionals. *Journal of School-Based Counseling Policy and Evaluation*, *2*(2), 131–141. https://doi.org/10.25774/80b3-kc43

Frederiksen, K. S., Hesse, M., Brummer, J., & Pedersen, M. U. (2022). The impact of parental substance use disorder and other family-related problems on school related outcomes. *Drug and Alcohol Dependence Reports*, *3*, 100041. doi:10.1016/j.dadr.2022.100041

Freeman-Green, S., Driver, M. K., Wang, P., Kamuru, J., & Jackson, D. (2021). Culturally sustaining practices in content area instruction for CLD students with learning disabilities. *Learning Disabilities Research & Practice*, *36*(1), 12–25. doi:10.1111/ldrp.12240

Frenk, J., Chen, L., Bhutta, Z. A., Cohen, J., Crisp, N., Evans, T., Fineberg, H., Garcia, P., Ke, Y., Kelley, P., Kistnasamy, B., Meleis, A., Naylor, D., Pablos-Mendez, A., Reddy, S., Scrimshaw, S., Sepulveda, J., Serwadda, D., & Zurayk, H. (2010). Health professions for a new century: Transforming education to strengthen health systems in an independent world. *Lancet*, *376*(9756), 1923–1958. doi:10.1016/S0140-6736(10)61854-5 PMID:21112623

Frey, B. B., Lohmeier, J. H., Lee, S. W., & Tollefson, N. (2006). Measuring collaboration among grant partners. *The American Journal of Evaluation*, *27*(3), 383–392. https://doi.org/10.1044/2019_PERS-SIG10-2018-0008

Friend, M., & Cook, L. (2010). *Interactions: Collaboration skills for school professionals* (6th ed.). Pearson.

Friend, M., Cook, L., Hurley-Chamberlain, D., & Shamberger, C. (2010). Co-teaching: An illustration of the complexity of collaboration in special education. *Journal of Educational & Psychological Consultation*, *20*(1), 9–27. doi:10.1080/10474410903535380

Frost, J. S., Hammer, D. P., Nunez, L. M., Adams, J. L., Chesluk, B., Grus, C., Harvison, N., McGuinn, K., Mortensen, L., Nishimoto, J. H., Palatta, A., Richmond, M., Ross, E. J., Tegzes, J., Ruffin, A. L., & Bentley, J. P. (2019). The intersection of professionalism and interprofessional care: Development and initial testing of the interprofessional professionalism assessment (IPA). *Journal of Interprofessional Care*, *33*(1), 102–115. doi:10.1080/13561820.2018.1515733 PMID:30247940

Fuchs, L. S., Fuchs, D., & Malone, A. S. (2017). The taxonomy of intervention intensity. *Teaching Exceptional Children*, *50*(1), 35–43. doi:10.1177/0040059917703962

Gage, N. A., Lierheimer, K. S., & Goran, L. (2012). Characteristics of students with high-incidence disabilities broadly defined. *Journal of Disability Policy Studies*, *23*(3), 168–178. doi:10.1177/1044207311425385

Gamble, B. E., & Lambros, K. M. (2014). Provider perspectives on school-based mental health for urban minority youth: Access and services. *Journal of Urban Learning, Teaching, and Research*, *10*, 25–38.

Ganz, J. B. (2014). Interdisciplinary issues and collaboration in assessment and treatment. In *Aided Augmentative Communication for Individuals with Autism Spectrum Disorders, Autism and Child Psychopathology Series*. Springer Science Business Media. doi:10.1007/978-1-4939-0814-1_4

Ganz, J. B., Earles-Vollrath, T. L., Heath, A. K., Parker, R. I., Rispoli, M. J., & Duran, J. B. (2012). A Meta-Analysis of Single Case Research Studies on Aided Augmentative and Alternative Communication Systems with Individuals with Autism Spectrum Disorders. [ERIC.]. *Journal of Autism and Developmental Disorders*, *42*(1), 60–74. doi:10.100710803-011-1212-2 PMID:21380612

Garbacz, L. L., Zychinski, K. E., Feuer, R. M., Carter, J. S., & Budd, K. S. (2014). Effects of implemented Teacher-Child Interaction Training (TCIT) on teacher ratings of behavior change. *Psychology in the Schools*, *51*(8), 850–865. doi:10.1002/pits.21788

Garbacz, S. A., Hirano, K., McIntosh, K., Eagle, J. W., Minch, D., & Vatland, C. (2018). Family engagement in school-wide positive behavioral interventions and supports: Barriers and facilitators to implementation. *School Psychology Quarterly*, *33*(3), 448–459. doi:10.1037pq0000216 PMID:29154555

Garcia, E., & Weiss, E. (2020). *A policy agenda to address the teacher shortage in U.S. public schools. Perfect storm in the teacher labor market series*. Economic Policy Institute. https://www.epi.org/publication/a-policy-agenda-to-address-the-teacher-shortage-in-u-s-public-schools/

Garland, A. F., Hough, R. L., McCabe, K. M., Yeh, M. A. Y., Wood, P. A., & Aarons, G. A. (2001). Prevalence of psychiatric disorders in youths across five sectors of care. *Journal of the American Academy of Child and Adolescent Psychiatry*, *40*(4), 409–418. doi:10.1097/00004583-200104000-00009 PMID:11314566

Gaudin, C., & Chaliès, S. (2015). Video viewing in teacher education and professional development: A literature review. *Educational Research Review*, *16*, 41–67. doi:10.1016/j.edurev.2015.06.001

Gaumer Erickson, A. S., Noonan, P. M., Brussow, J. A., & Gilpin, B. J. (2013). The impact of IDEA indicator 13 compliance on postsecondary outcomes. *Career Development for Exceptional Individuals*, *37*(3), 161–167. doi:10.1177/2165143413481497

Gay, G. (2010). Acting on beliefs in teacher education for cultural diversity. *Journal of Teacher Education*, *61*(1-2), 143–152. doi:10.1177/0022487109347320

Gay, G. (2018). *Culturally responsive teaching: Theory, research, and practice* (3rd ed.). Teachers College Press.

Geenen, S., Powers, L. E., & Lopez-Vasquez, A. (2001). Multicultural aspects of parent involvement in transition planning. *Council for Exceptional Children*, *67*(2), 265–282. doi:10.1177/001440290106700209

Geer, C., & Hamill, L. E. E. (2007). An online interdisciplinary discussion: Promoting collaboration between early childhood and special education preservice teachers. *Journal of Technology and Teacher Education*, *15*(4), 533–553.

Gehrke, R. S., & Cocchiarella, M. (2013). Preservice special and general educators' knowledge of inclusion. *Teacher Education and Special Education*, *36*(3), 204–216. doi:10.1177/0888406413495421

Geist, L., Erickson, K. A., Greer, C., Hatch, P., & Erwin-Davidson, L. (2016). *Core vocabulary for students with significant cognitive disabilities: Essential tools, teaching strategies and assessment components*. Session presented at the annual meeting of the International Association for Augmentative and Alternative Communication, Toronto, Canada.

George, C., & Oriel, K. (2009). Interdisciplinary learning experience: Two years of experience with an interdisciplinary learning engagement for physical therapy and special education students. *Journal of Allied Health*, *38*(1), 22E–28E. PMID:19753409

Gerdes, G. S. L., Huizinga, M., & de Ruyter, D. (2020). Analytic framework for interdisciplinary collaboration in inclusive education. *The Journal of Workplace Learning*, *32*(5), 377–388. doi:10.1108/JWL-08-2019-0099

*Compilation of References*

Gershenson, S., Hart, C. M. D., Lindsay, C. A., & Papageorge, N. W. (2017). *The long-run impacts of same-race teachers*. IZA Discussion Paper Series, No. 10630.

Gevova, H. M., Arora, A., & Botticeelo, A. L. (2021). *Effects of school closures resulting from COVID-19 in autistic and neurotypical children*. Frontiers in Education., doi:10.3389/feduc.2021.761485

Giangreco, M. F., Pennington, R. C., & Walker, V. L. (2021). Conceptualizing and utilizing board certified behavior analysts as related service providers in inclusion-oriented schools. *Remedial and Special Education*, •••, 1–13. doi:10.1177/07419325211063610

Giles, A. K., Carson, N. E., Breland, H. L., Coker-Bolt, P., & Bowman, P. J. (2014). Use of simulated patients and reflective video analysis to assess occupational therapy students' preparedness for fieldwork. *The American Journal of Occupational Therapy*, *68*(S2), S57–S66. doi:10.5014/ajot.2014.685S03 PMID:25397940

Gilliam, W. S., & Reyes, C. R. (2018). Teacher decision factors that lead to preschool expulsion. *Infants and Young Children*, *31*(2), 93–108. doi:10.1097/IYC.0000000000000113

Gillon, G. (2002). Phonological awareness intervention for children. From the research laboratory to the clinic. *ASHA Leader*, *7*(22), 4–5, 16–17. doi:10.1044/leader.FTR2.07222002.4

Gilman, R., & Medway, F. J. (2007). Teachers' perceptions of school psychology: A comparison of regular and special education teacher ratings. *School Psychology Quarterly*, *22*(2), 145–161. doi:10.1037/1045-3830.22.2.145

Giordano, K., LoCascio, S., & Inoa, R. (2019). Special education placement: An interdisciplinary case study. *Journal of Cases in Educational Leadership*, *22*(2), 14–25. doi:10.1177/1555458919828422

Glover, A., McCormack, J., & Smith-Tamaray, M. (2015). Collaboration between teachers and speech and language therapists: Services for primary school children with speech, language and communication needs. *Child Language Teaching and Therapy*, *31*(3), 363–382. doi:10.1177/0265659015603779

Glowacki-Dudka, M., & Brown, M. P. (2007). Professional development through faculty learning communities. *New Horizons in Adult Education and Human Resource Development*, *21*(1-2), 29–39. doi:10.1002/nha3.10277

Goforth, A. N., Farmer, R. L., Kim, S. Y., Naser, S. C., Lockwood, A. B., & Affrunti, N. W. (2021). Status of school psychology in 2020: Part 1, demographics of the NASP membership survey. *NASP Research Reports,* *5*(2), 1-17.

Goforth, A. N., Farmer, R. L., Kim, S. Y., Naser, S. C., Lockwood, A. B., & Affrunti, N. W. (2021). Status of school psychology in 2020: Part 1 demographics of the NASP membership survey. *NASP Research Reports*, *5*(2), 1–17.

Goforth, A. N., Farmer, R. L., Kim, S. Y., Naser, S. C., Lockwood, A. B., & Affrunti, N. W. (2021). Status of school psychology in 2020: Part 1, demographics of the NASP membership survey. *NASP Research Reports*, *5*(2), 1–17.

Golberstein, E., Wen, H., & Miller, B. F. (2020). Coronavirus disease 2019 (COVID-19) and mental health for children and adolescents. *JAMA Pediatrics*.

Golberstein, E., Gonzales, G., & Meara, E. (2019). How do economic downturns affect the mental health of children? Evidence from the National Health Interview Survey. *Health Economics*, *28*(8), 955–970.

Goldberg, L. R. (2015). The importance of interprofessional education for students in communication sciences and disorders. *Communication Disorders Quarterly*, *36*(2), 121–125. doi:10.1177/1525740114544701

Goldfield, G. S., Raynor, H. A., & Epstein, L. H. (2002). Treatment of pediatric obesity.

González, N., Moll, L. C., & Amanti, C. (Eds.). (2005). Funds of knowledge: Theorizing practices in households, communities, and classrooms. Routledge.

575

Goodley, D. (2016). *Disability studies an interdisciplinary introduction* (2nd ed.). Sage Publications Limited.

Goodman-Scott, E., Bobzien, J., & Milsom, A. (2019). Preparing preservice school counselors to serve students with disabilities: A case study. *Professional School Counseling*, 22, 1–11. https://doi.org/10.1177/2156759x19867338

Goodwin, A. L. (2002). The case of one child: Making the shift from personal knowledge to professionally informed practice. *Teaching Education*, 13(2), 137–154. doi:10.1080/1047621022000007558

Gothberg, J. E., Greene, G., & Kohler, P. D. (2018). District implementation of research-based practices for transition planning with culturally and linguistically diverse youth with disabilities and their families. *Career Development and Transition for Exceptional Individuals*, 42(2), 77–86. doi:10.1177/2165143418762794

Grace, S. (2021). Models of interprofessional education for healthcare students: A scoping review. *Journal of Interprofessional Care*, 35(5), 771–783. doi:10.1080/13561820.2020.1767045 PMID:32614628

Grant-Smith, D., Zwaan, L. D., Chapman, R., & Gillett-Swan, J. (2018). 'It's the worst, but real experience is invaluable': Preservice teacher perspectives of the costs and benefits of professional experience. In D. Heck & A. Ambrosetti (Eds.), *Teacher education in and for uncertain times* (pp. 15–33). Springer. doi:10.1007/978-981-10-8648-9_2

Grapin, S. L., Bocanegra, J. O., Green, T. D., Lee, E. T., & Jaafar, D. (2016). Increasing diversity in school psychology: Uniting the efforts of institutions, faculty, students, and practitioners. *Contemporary School Psychology*, 20(4), 345–355. doi:10.100740688-016-0092-z

Gray, R. (2009). *Columbine 10 years later: the state of school safety today*. http://www.campussafetymagazine.com/Channel/School-Safety/Articles/2009/03/Columbine-10-Years-Later-The-State-of-School-Safety-Today.aspx

Green, D. J. (2019). Are state-level physical education programs aching student learning? Ace Fitness. https://www.acefitness.org/education-and-resources/professional/certified/august-2019/7345/ are-state-level-physical-education-programs-tracking-student-learning/

Green, T. D., Cook-Morales, V. J., Robinson-Zañartu, C. A., & Ingraham, C. L. (2009). Pathways on a journey to getting it: Multicultural competence training and continuing professional development. In J. Jones (Ed.), The psychology of multiculturalism in schools: A primer for practice, training, and research (pp. 83–113). Academic Press.

Greene, G. (2011). *Transition planning for culturally and linguistically diverse youth. Brookes transition to adulthood series*. Brookes Publishing Company.

Greene, G., & Kochhar-Bryant, C. A. (2003). *Pathways to successful transition for youth with disabilities*. Merrill Prentice-Hall.

Greenwood, C. R., Carta, J. J., Goldstein, H., Kaminski, R. A., McConnell, S. R., & Atwater, J. (2014). The center for response to intervention in early childhood: Developing evidence-based tools for a multi-tier approach to preschool language and early literacy instruction. *Journal of Early Intervention*, 36(4), 246-262. https://doi doi:10.1177/1053815115581209

Greer, R. D., & Ross, D. E. (2008). Verbal behavior analysis: Inducing and expanding new verbal capabilities in children with language delays. In Pearson. Foxx, R. M., & Mulick, J. A. (Eds.) (2015). Controversial therapies for autism and intellectual disabilities.

Gregory, R. J., Schwer Canning, S., Lee, T. W., & Wise, J. C. (2004). Cognitive bibliotherapy for depression: A Meta-Analysis. *Professional Psychology, Research and Practice*, 35(3), 275–280. doi:10.1037/0735-7028.35.3.275

Grisham-Brown, J., & Hemmeter, M. L. (2017). *Blended practices for teaching young children in inclusive settings* (2nd ed.). Paul H. Brookes.

*Compilation of References*

Guiney, M. C. (2019). *The school psychology supervisor's toolkit*. Routledge.

Gu, Q., & Day, C. (2007). Teachers resilience: A necessary condition for effectiveness. *Teaching and Teacher Education*, *23*(8), 1302–1316. doi:10.1016/j.tate.2006.06.006

Guralnick, M. (2011). Why early intervention works: A systems perspective. *Infants and Young Children*, *24*(1), 6–28. doi:10.1097/IYC.0b013e3182002cfe PMID:21532932

Guraya, S. Y., & Barr, H. (2018). The effectiveness of interprofessional education in healthcare: A systematic review and meta-analysis. *The Kaohsiung Journal of Medical Sciences*, *34*(3), 160–165. doi:10.1016/j.kjms.2017.12.009 PMID:29475463

Güvendi, B., & İlhan, E. L. (2017). Effects of adapted physical activity applied on intellectual disability students toward level of emotional adjustment, self-managing and the socialization: Parent and teacher interactive research. *Journal of Human Sciences*, *14*(4), 3879–3894. doi:10.14687/jhs.v14i4.4812

Haberman, M. (2005). *Star teachers: The ideology and best practice of effective teachers of diverse children and youth in poverty*. Haberman Educational Foundation.

Hagans, K., & Powers, K. (2015). Measuring credential candidates' impact on student achievement. *Action in Teacher Education*, *37*(4), 355–374. doi:10.1080/01626620.2015.1078755

Hallahan, D. P., Kauffman, J. M., & Pullen, P. C. (2018). *Exceptional learners: An introduction to special education* (14th ed.). Pearson.

Hall, J. (2015). The school counselor and special education: Aligning training with practice. *The Professional Counselor*, *5*(2), 217–224. doi:10.15241/jgh.5.2.217

Hammer, M. R. (2011). Additional cross-cultural validity testing of the Intercultural Development Inventory. *International Journal of Intercultural Relations*, *35*(4), 474–487. doi:10.1016/j.ijintrel.2011.02.014

Hammerness, K., Darling-Hammond, L., & Shulman, L. (2002, April 10-14). *Towards expert thinking: How case-writing contributes to the development of theory-based professional knowledge in student-teachers*. Paper presented at the Annual Meeting of the American Educational Research Association, Seattle, WA.

Hammerness, K., Darling-Hammond, L., Bransford, J., Berliner, D., Cochran-Smith, M., McDonald, M., & Zeichner, K. (2005). How teachers learn and develop. In L. Darling Hammond & J. Bransford (Ed.), Preparing teachers for a changing world: What teachers should learn and be able to do (pp. 358–389). Jossey-Bass.

Hammick, M., Freeth, D., Koppel, S., Reeves, S., & Barr, H. (2007). A best evidence systematic review of interprofessional education: BEME Guide No. 9. *Medical Teacher*, *29*(735), 735–751. doi:10.1080/01421590701682576 PMID:18236271

Hammond, Z. (2014). *Culturally responsive teaching and the brain: Promoting authentic engagement and rigor among culturally and linguistically diverse students*. Corwin Press.

Hanasono, L. K., Broido, E. M., Yacobucci, M. M., Root, K. V., Pena, S., & O'Neil, D. A. (2019). Secret service: Revealing gender biases in the visibility and value of faculty service. *Journal of Diversity in Higher Education*, *12*(1), 85–98. doi:10.1037/dhe0000081

Hanline, M. F. (2010). Preservice teachers' perceptions of field experiences in inclusive preschool settings: Implications for personnel preparation. *Teacher Education and Special Education*, *33*(4), 335–351. doi:10.1177/0888406409360144

Hanna, E. I. (2005). *Inclusive design for maximum accessibility: A practical approach to universal design (PEM research rep. no. 05-04)*. Pearson Educational Measurement.

Harris, N. B. (2018). *The deepest well: Healing the long-term effects of childhood adversity.* Houghton Mifflin Harcourt Publishing.

Harry, B., & Ocasio-Stoutenburg, L. (2020). *Meeting families where they are: Building equity through advocacy with diverse schools and communities.* Teachers College Press.

Hart-Baldridge, E. (2020). Faculty advisor perspectives of academic advising. *NACADA Journal, 40*(1), 10–22. doi:10.12930/NACADA-18-25

Hasnain, R. (2010). Brokering the culture gap. *Forced Migration Review,* (35), 32.

Hassan, A., & Tairab, H. (2012). Science teaching self-efficacy and outcome expectancy beliefs of secondary school teachers in UAE. *International Journal for Research in Education, 32,* 1–22.

Hauerwas, L. B., Brown, R., & Scott, A. N. (2013). Specific learning disability and response to intervention: State-level guidance. *Exceptional Children, 80*(1), 101–120. doi:10.1177/001440291308000105

Hawkins, R. O., Kroeger, S. D., Musti-Rao, S., Barnett, D. W., & Ward, J. E. (2008). Preservice training in response to intervention: Learning by doing an interdisciplinary field experience. *Psychology in the Schools, 45*(8), 745–762. doi:10.1002/pits.20339

Healy, K. (2014). *Social work theories in context: Creating frameworks for practice.* Bloomsbury Academic. doi:10.1007/978-1-137-02425-1

Heard-Garris, N. J., Cale, M., Camaj, L., Hamati, M. C., & Dominguez, T. P. (2018). Transmitting trauma: A systematic review of vicarious racism and child health. *Social Science & Medicine, 199,* 230–240. doi:10.1016/j.socscimed.2017.04.018

Heffron, M. C., & Murch, T. (2010). Reflective supervision and leadership in infant and early childhood programs. *Zero to Three.*

Hein, R., & Els, J. OBrien, K., Anasi, S., Pascuzzi, K., Blanchard, S., & Bollmann, E. (2019). Effectiveness of video modeling in children with Autism Spectrum Disorder (ASD). *American Journal of Occupational Therapy, 73*(S1), NA. http://dx.doi.org.webdb.plattsburgh.edu:2048/10.5014/ajot.2019.73S1-PO3039

Heisler, L. A., & Thousand, J. S. (2021). A guide to co-teaching for the SLP: A tutorial. *Communication Disorders Quarterly, 42*(2), 122–127. doi:10.1177/1525740119886310

Hemmeter, M. L., Ostrosky, M. M., & Fox, L. K. (2021). *Unpacking the Pyramid Model: A practical guide for preschool teachers.* Brookes Publishing.

Hemmeter, M. L., Ostrosky, M., & Fox, L. (2006). Social and emotional foundations for early learning: A conceptual model for intervention. *School Psychology Review, 35*(4), 583–601. doi:10.1080/02796015.2006.12087963

Hemmeter, M. L., Snyder, P. A., Fox, L., & Algina, J. (2016). Evaluating the implementation of the Pyramid Model for Promoting Social-Emotional Competence in early childhood classrooms. *Topics in Early Childhood Special Education, 36*(3), 133–146. doi:10.1177/0271121416653386

Hemphill, D., & Leskowitz, S. (2013). DIY activists: Communities of practice, cultural dialogism, and radical knowledge sharing. *Adult Education Quarterly, 63*(1), 51–77. doi:10.1177/0741713612442803

Henderson, T. (2015). *States look for help with bilingual mental health*. PEW Charitable Trusts. https://www.pewtrusts.org/en/research-and-analysis/blogs/stateline/2015/11/04/states-look-for-help-with-bilingual-mental-health

Hernandez, S. J. (2013). Collaboration in Special Education: Its History, Evolution, and Critical Factors Necessary for Successful Implementation. *Online submission, 3*(6), 480-498.

Herreid, C. F., Schiller, N. A., Herreid, K. F., & Wright, C. (2011). In case you are interested: Results of a survey of case study teachers. *Journal of College Science Teaching, 40*, 7–80.

Herrenkohl, T. I., Scott, D., Higgins, D. J., Klika, J. B., & Lonne, B. (2021). How COVID-19 is placing vulnerable children at risk and why we need a different approach to child welfare. *Child Maltreatment, 26*(1), 9–16. doi:10.1177/1077559520963916 PMID:33025825

He, Y. (2014). Universal Design for Learning in an online teacher education course: Enhancing learners' confidence to teach online. *Journal of Online Learning and Teaching, 10*(2), 283–298.

Higher Education Consortium for Special Education (HECSE) (2021, February). The shortage of special education teachers and higher education faculty. *HECSE.*

Hines, R., Glavey, E. M., Hanley, W., & Romualdo, A. (2022). Redesigning teacher preparation. *Preparing Quality Teachers: Advances in Clinical Practice*, 459-477.

Hinshaw, A. S., & DeLeon, P. H. (1995). Toward achieving multidisciplinary professional collaboration. *Professional Psychology, Research and Practice, 26*(2), 115–116. doi:10.1037/0735-7028.26.2.115

Hirano, K. A., Shanley, L., Garbacz, S. A., Rowe, D. A., Lindstrom, L., & Leve, L. D. (2017). Validating a model of motivational factors influencing involvement for parents of transition-age youth with disabilities. *Remedial and Special Education, 39*(1), 15–26. https://doi.org/10.1177/0741932517715913

Hirst, R. A., Anderson, K. L., Packard, B. W. L., Liotta, L. J., Bleakley, B. H., Lombardi, P. J., & Burkholder, K. C. (2021). Faculty learning at the individual and group level: A multi-year analysis of an interdisciplinary science faculty learning community focused on inclusive teaching and mentoring. *Journal of College Science Teaching, 50*(6), 20–30.

Hixon, E., & So, H. J. (2009). Technology's role in field experiences for preservice teacher training. *Journal of Educational Technology & Society, 12*(4), 294–304.

Hoagwood, K. E., & Kelleher, K. J. (2020). A Marshall plan for children's mental health after COVID-19. *Psychiatric Services (Washington, D.C.), 71*(12), 1216–1217. doi:10.1176/appi.ps.202000258 PMID:32933414

Hoeh, E., Bonati, L. M., Chatlos, S., Squires, M., & Countermine, B. (in press). Stop, collaborate, and listen: A faculty learning community developed to address gaps in pre-service education about interdisciplinary collaboration. *International Journal for the Scholarship of Teaching and Learning*.

Hofstra University. (n.d.). *Speech-language hearing sciences: Teacher of students with speech- language disabilities advanced certification*. https://www.hofstra.edu/speech-language-hearing-sciences/teacher-advanced-certificate.html

Hogan, A., Knez, N., & Kahng, S. (2015). Evaluating the use of behavioral skills training to improve school staffs' implementation of behavior intervention plans. *Journal of Behavioral Education, 24*(2), 242–254. doi:10.100710864-014-9213-9

Holland, A., & Nelson, R. (2020). *Counseling in communication disorders* (3rd ed.). Plural Publishing.

Holland, S. K., & Haegele, J. A. (2020). Socialization experiences of first-year adapted physical education teachers with a master's degree. *Adapted Physical Activity Quarterly; APAQ*, *37*(3), 304–323. doi:10.1123/apaq.2019-0126 PMID:32534449

Holland, S. K., Holland, K., Haegele, J. A., & Alber-Morgan, S. R. (2019). Making it stick: Teaching students with autism to generalize physical education skills. *Journal of Physical Education, Recreation & Dance*, *90*(6), 32–39. doi:10.1080/07303084.2019.1614120

Hollo, A., & Chow, J. C. (2015). Communicative Functions of Problem Behavior for Students with High-Incidence Disabilities. *Beyond Behavior*, *24*(3), 23–30. doi:10.1177/107429561502400304

Holloway, E., & Alexandre, L. (2012). Crossing boundaries in doctoral education: Relational learning, cohort communities, and dissertation committees. *New Directions for Teaching and Learning*, *131*, 85-97.

Holloway-Friesen, H. (2021, January). The role of mentoring on Hispanic graduate students sense of belonging and academic self-efficacy. *Journal of Hispanic Higher Education*, *20*(1), 46–58. doi:10.1177/1538192718823716

Hoover, J. J. (2013). *Linking assessment to instruction in Multi-Tiered Models: A teacher's guide to selecting reading, writing, and mathematics interventions*. Pearson.

Horn, E. M., & Kang, J. (2012). Supporting young children with multiple disabilities: What do we know and what do we still need to learn? *Topics in Early Childhood Special Education*, *31*(4), 241–248. doi:10.1177/0271121411426487 PMID:24574575

Horn, E., Lieber, J., Sandall, S. R., Schwartz, I., & Li, S. (2002). Supporting young children's IEP goals in inclusive settings through embedded learning opportunities. *Topics in Early Childhood Special Education*, *20*(4), 208–223. doi:10.1177/027112140002000402

Horvat, M., Kelly, L., Block, M., & Croce, R. (2019). *Developmental and adapted physical activity assessment* (2nd ed.). Human Kinetics. doi:10.5040/9781718209244

Howard, T. C. (2020). *Why race and culture matter in schools: Closing the achievement gap in America's classrooms* (2nd ed.). Teachers College Press.

Hsiao, Y.-J., Higgins, K., & Diamond, L. (2018). Parent empowerment: Respecting their voices. *Teaching Exceptional Children*, *51*(1), 43–53. doi:10.1177/0040059918790240

Hubel, G. S., Cooley, J. L., & Moreland, A. D. (2020). Incorporating evidence-based behavioral teaching training into Head Start mental health consultation: Description and initial outcomes of a large-scale program. *Psychology in the Schools*, *57*(5), 735–756. doi:10.1002/pits.22348 PMID:33833474

Huete, J., Schmidt, J., & Lopez-Arvizu, D. (2014). Behavioral disorders in young children with autism spectrum disorder. In J. Tarbox, D. R. Dixon, P. Sturmey, & J. L. Matson (Eds.), *Handbook of Early Intervention for Autism Spectrum Disorders* (pp. 717–752). Springer. doi:10.1007/978-1-4939-0401-3_26

Hughes, C. A., Riccomini, P. J., & Morris, J. R. (2018). Use explicit instruction. In J. McLeskey, L. Maheady, B. Billingsley, M. T. Brownell, & T. J. Lewis (Eds.), *High leverage practices for inclusive classrooms*. Routledge. doi:10.4324/9781315176093-20

Hughes, J. (2010). What teacher preparation programs can do to better prepare teachers to meet the challenges of educating students living in poverty. *Action in Teacher Education*, *32*(1), 54–64. doi:10.1080/01626620.2010.10463542

Hull, L., Petrides, K. V., & William, M. (2020). The female autism phenotype and camouflaging: A narrative review. *Review Journal of Autism and Developmental Disorders*, *7*(4), 306–317. doi:10.100740489-020-00197-9

*Compilation of References*

Hume, K., Steinbrenner, J. R., & Odom, S. L. (2021). Evidence-based practices for children, youth, and young adults with autism: Third generation review. *Journal of Autism and Developmental Disorders*. doi:10.1007/s10803-020-04844-2

Humes, C. W., & Hohenshil, T. H. (1987). Elementary counselors, school psychologists, school social workers: Who does what? *Elementary School Guidance & Counseling*, *22*(1), 37–45.

Hung, S., & Cheng, M. (2013). Are you ready for knowledge sharing? An empirical study of virtual communities. *Computers & Education*, *62*, 8–17. doi:10.1016/j.compedu.2012.09.017

Hunter, H. L., Evans, K., Weist, S., & Smith, M. (2005). *Working together to promote academic performance, social and emotional learning, and mental health for all children*. Center for the Advancement of Children's Mental Health at Columbia University.

Hunt, P., Soto, G., Maier, J., Liboiron, N., & Bae, S. (2004). Collaborative teaming to support preschoolers with severe disabilities who are placed in general education early childhood programs. *Topics in Early Childhood Special Education*, *24*(3), 123–142. doi:10.1177/02711214040240030101

Hunt, T., Carter, R., Zhang, L., & Yang, S. (2020). Micro-credentials: The potential of personalized professional development. *Development and Learning in Organizations*.

Hutchinson, M. (2013). Bridging the gap: Preservice teachers and their knowledge of working with English Language Learners. *TESOL Journal*, *4*(1), 25–54. doi:10.1002/tesj.51

Hutzler, Y. S. (2011). Evidence-based practice and research: A challenge to the development of adapted physical activity. *Adapted Physical Activity Quarterly; APAQ*, *28*(3), 189–209. doi:10.1123/apaq.28.3.189 PMID:21725114

Hydon, S., Wong, M., Langley, A. K., Stein, B. D., & Kataoka, S. H. (2015). Preventing secondary traumatic stress in educators. *Child and Adolescent Psychiatric Clinics of North America*, *24*(2), 319–333. doi:10.1016/j.chc.2014.11.003 PMID:25773327

Hyson, M. (Ed.). (2003). *Preparing early childhood professionals: NAEYC's standards for programs*. National Association for the Education of Young Children.

IDEA Data Center. (2022). IDEA Part C: Child count and settings. *IDEA*. https://idc.clicdata.com/v/sqKIRJeKdg2J

IEP Team, 34 C.F.R. §300.321 (2017).

Imazeki, J., & Goe, J. (2009). *The distribution of highly qualified, experienced teachers: Challenges and opportunities. TQ Research and Policy Brief*. National Comprehensive Center for Teacher Quality.

Immigrant Learning Center. (2019). Quick immigration statistics: United States. *ILL*. https://www.ilctr.org/quick-us-immigration-statistics/?gclid=Cj0KCQjw0JiXBhCFARIsAOSAKqCF54aQDel0ea1sGcfe7LgS78q9brz5n12e3mgGbdkdq-8ZLAcrZ2gaAlu9EALw_wcB

I-MTSS Research Network. (2022). *Overview: Integrated multi-tiered systems of support*. Retrieved July 16, 2022, from https://mtss.org/overview/

Individuals with Disabilities Education Act of 2004, 20 U.S.C. 1400 *et seq*. (2004). https://sites.ed.gov/idea/statute-regulations/

Individuals with Disabilities Education Act, 20 U.S.C. § 1400 (2004)

Individuals with Disabilities Education Act, 20 U.S.C. § 1400 (2004).

Individuals With Disabilities Education Act, 20 U.S.C. § 1400 (2004).

Individuals With Disabilities Education Act, 20 U.S.C. § 1400 (2004). https://www.congress.gov/108/plaws/publ446/PLAW-108publ446.pdf

Individuals With Disabilities Education Act, 20 U.S.C. §§ 1400 et seq. (1994; 2006; 2012)

Individuals with Disabilities Education Act, 20 U.S.C.A. §§ 1431-1444 (2017).

Individuals with Disabilities Education Act. (2004). https://sites.ed.gov/idea/about-idea/

Individuals with Disabilities Education Act. (2022). *2021 Annual report to Congress on IDEA*. https://sites.ed.gov/idea/department-submits-the-43rd-annual-report-to-congress-idea

Individuals with Disabilities Education Improvement Act, H.R. 1350, 108th Congress (2004).

Individuals with Disabilities Education Improvement Act, Pub. L. 101-476. 20 U.S.C. § 303.24. (2004). https://sites.ed.gov/idea/regs/c/a/303.24

Individuals with Disabilities Education Improvement Act. (IDEIA). (2004). US Government. https://sites.ed.gov/idea/

Institute of Medicine. (2001). Crossing the Quality Chasm. *Health Systems (Basingstoke, England)*, 21.

International Clinical Educators Learning Center. (2022) *ICE Learning Center*. https://www.icelearningcenter.com/

Interprofessional Education Collaborative Expert Panel. (2011). *Core competencies for interprofessional collaborative practice: Report of an expert panel*. Washington, DC: Interprofessional Education Collaborative. https://ipec.memberclicks.net/assets/2011-Original.pdf

Interprofessional Education Collaborative Expert Panel. (2016). *Core competencies for interprofessional collaborative practice: 2016 update*. Washington, DC: Interprofessional Education Collaborative. https://ipec.memberclicks.net/assets/2016-Update.pdf

Interprofessional Education Collaborative. (2011). *Core competencies for interprofessional collaborative practice: Report of an expert panel*. IEC. https://www.aacom.org/docs/default-source/insideome/ccrpt05-10-11.pdf

Interprofessional Education Collaborative. (2016) Core competencies for interprofessional collaborative practice: 2016 update. *Interprofessional Education Collaborative*. https://ipec.memberclicks.net/assets/2016-Update.pdf

Interprofessional Education Collaborative. (2016). Core competencies for interprofessional collaborative practice: Report of an expert panel. *IEC*. https://www.asha.org/siteassets/uploadedfiles/interprofessional-collaboration-core-competency.pdf

Interprofessional Education Collaborative. (2016). *Interprofessional Education Collaborative releases revised set of core competencies*. https://www.ipecollaborative.org/news-releases.html

Interprofessional Education Collaborative. (2021). Press release: IPEC announces working group members for core competencies revision update of IPEC core competencies to begin June 2021. *IEC*. https://www.ipecollaborative.org/assets/press-release/IPEC_Press-Release_2021-05-04_CCR-WG-Announcement.pdf

Iowa Autism Council. (2019). *Moving Iowa forward: Summary of accomplishment in 2018 and priorities and recommendations for 2019*. https://educateiowa.gov/pk-12/special-education/programs-and-services/autism-spectrum-disorder/iowa-autism-council#Legislative_Reports

Iowa Department of Education. (2019a). *2019 annual report: Condition of education*. Author. https://educateiowa.gov/sites/files/ed/documents/2020-01-23ConditionOfEducation2019.pdf

Iowa Department of Education. (2019b). *Special education eligibility and evaluation standards*. Author. https://educateiowa.gov/sites/files/ed/documents/SpecialEducationEligibilityand EvaluationStandardsJuly2019.pdf

Iowa Department of Education. (2021b). *Input into Iowa's State performance plan for special education*. https://educateiowa.gov/sites/files/ed/documents/2021-12-14%20Input%20SPP-Personnel%20Shortagesv2.pdf

Iowa Department of Education. (2022a). *2021 report on the state of educator preparation in Iowa*. https://educateiowa.gov/sites/files/ed/documents/2021ReportontheStateofEducatorPreparationinIowa11-17-21.pdf

Iris Center. (n.d.). *IRIS & adult learning theory*. IRIS. https://iris.peabody.vanderbilt.edu/_archive/iris-and-adult-learning-theory/

Iruka, I. U., Curenton, S. M., Durden, T. R., & Escayg, K.-A. (2020). *Don't look away: Embracing anti-bias classrooms*. Gryphon House.

Irwin, V., Zhang, J., Wang, X., Hein, S., Wang, K., Roberts, A., ... Purcell, S. (2021). *Report on the Condition of Education 2021*. NCES 2021-144. National Center for Education Statistics. Retrieved from:https://files.eric.ed.gov/fulltext/ED612942.pdf

Israel, M., Ribuffo, C., & Smith, S. (2014). *Universal Design for Learning: Recommendations for teacher preparation and professional development (Document No. IC-7)*. University of Florida, Collaboration for Effective Educator, Development, Accountability, and Reform Center website: https://ceedar.education.ufl.edu/tools/innovation-configurations/

Ivey, C., & Reed, E. (2011). An examination of learning formats on interdisciplinary teamwork knowledge, skills, and dispositions. *Interdisciplinary Journal of Teaching and Learning*, *1*, 43–55.

Jacob, S., Decker, D. M., & Lugg, E. T. (2016). *Ethics and law for school psychologists* (7th ed.). Wiley.

Jacoby, J. W., & Lesaux, N. K. (2017). Language and literacy instruction in preschool classes that serve Latino dual language learners. *Early Childhood Research Quarterly*, *40*, 77–86. doi:10.1016/j.ecresq.2016.10.001

Jamanis, S., & Vogler-Elias, D. (2014). *Examining parent and professional survey results for preservice professional preparation in autism spectrum disorders*. Nazareth College of Rochester.

Jane-Griffiths, A., Alsip, J., Hart, S. R., Round, R. L., & Brady, J. (2021). Together we can do so much: A systematic review and conceptual framework of collaboration in schools. *Canadian Journal of School Psychology*, *36*(1), 59–85.

Jennings, P. A., & Greenberg, M. T. (2009). The prosocial classroom: Teacher social and emotional competence in relation to student and classroom outcomes. *Review of Educational Research*, *79*(1), 491–525.

Jerome, M. K., & Ainsworth, M. K. (2020). Literacy acquisition for students with severe disabilities: Making it happen through assistive technology. *Teaching Exceptional Children*, *53*(1), 80–83. doi:10.1177/0040059920945590

Jerrell, J. M. (1984). Boundary-spanning functions served by rural school psychologists. *Journal of School Psychology*, *22*(3), 259–271. doi:10.1016/0022-4405(84)90007-4

Jiménez, F. J. R. (2012). Acceptance and commitment therapy versus traditional cognitive behavioral therapy: A systematic review and meta-analysis of current empirical evidence. *International Journal of Psychology & Psychological Therapy*, *12*, 333–358.

Jin, J., & Yun, J. (2010). Evidence-based practice in adapted physical education. *Journal of Physical Education, Recreation & Dance*, *81*(4), 50–54. doi:10.1080/07303084.2010.10598465

Jobling, A. (2001). Life be in it: Lifestyle choices for active leisure. *Down's Syndrome: Research and Practice*, *6*(3), 117–122. doi:10.3104/perspectives.102 PMID:11501213

Johnson, A., Soares, L., & Gutierrez de Blume, A. (2021). Professional development for working with students with autism spectrum disorders and teacher self-efficacy. *Georgia Educational Researcher*, *18*(1), 1–25. doi:10.20429/ger.2021.180101

Johnson, R. K., & Prebor, J. (2019). Update on preservice training in augmentative and alternative communication for speech-language pathologists. *American Journal of Speech-Language Pathology*, *28*(2), 536–549. doi:10.1044/2018_AJSLP-18-0004 PMID:31136246

Jones, L., & Wells, K. (2007). Strategies for academic and clinician engagement in community-participatory partnered research. *Journal of the American Medical Association*, *297*(4), 407–410. doi:10.1001/jama.297.4.407 PMID:17244838

Jones, P., & West, E. A. (2010). Moving toward a hybrid teacher education course: Supporting the theory to practice challenge in special education. *Journal of Special Education Technology*, *25*(2), 45–56. doi:10.1177/016264341002500204

Jones, S. E., Ethier, K. A., Hertz, M., DeGue, S., Le, V. D., Thornton, J., Lim, C., Dittus, P. J., & Sindhura Geda, S. (2022, April). Mental health, suicidality, and connectedness among high school students during the COVID-19 pandemic—Adolescent behaviors and experiences survey, January–June 2021. *MMWR Supplements*, *71*(3), 16–21. doi:10.15585/mmwr.su7103a3 PMID:35358165

Jung, L. A. (2007). Writing SMART objectives and strategies that fit the ROUTINE. *Teaching Exceptional Children*, *39*(4), 54–58. doi:10.1177/004005990703900406

Justice, L. M., Jiang, H., & Strasser, K. (2018). Linguistic environment of preschool classrooms: What dimensions support children's language growth? *Early Childhood Research Quarterly*, *42*, 79–92. doi:10.1016/j.ecresq.2017.09.003

Kalsner, L. (1991). Issues in college student retention. *Higher Education Extension Service Review*, *3*(1).

Kameenui, E., & Simmons, D. (1999). *Toward successful inclusion of students with disabilities: The architecture of instruction*. The Council for Exceptional Children. https://files.eric.ed.gov/fulltext/ED429381.pdf

Kamhi, A. G. (2003). The role of the SLP in improving reading fluency. *ASHA Leader*, *8*(7), 6–8. doi:10.1044/leader.FTR1.08072003.6

Kampwirth, T. J., & Powers, K. M. (2016). *Collaborative consultation in the schools: Effective practices for students with learning and behavior problems* (5th ed.). Pearson.

Kangas, S. E. (2020). Counternarratives of English learners with disabilities. *Bilingual Research Journal*, *43*(3), 267–285. doi:10.1080/15235882.2020.1807424

Kanine, R. M., Jackson, Y., Huffhines, L., Barnett, A., & Stone, K. J. (2018). A pilot study of universal teacher-child interaction training at a therapeutic preschool for young maltreated children. *Topics in Early Childhood Special Education*, *38*(3), 146–161. doi:10.1177/0271121418790012

Kantar, L., & Massouh, A. (2015). Case-based learning: What traditional curricula fail to teach. *Nurse Education Today*, *35*(8), e8–e14. doi:10.1016/j.nedt.2015.03.010 PMID:25842004

Kara, A. (2021). Covid-19 pandemic and possible trends for the future of higher education: A Review. *Journal of Education and Educational Development*, *8*(1), 9–26. doi:10.22555/joeed.v8i1.183

Kasari, C., Gulsrud, A. C., Shire, S. Y., & Strawbridge, C. (2021). *The JASPER model for children with autism: promoting joint attention, symbolic play, engagement, and regulation*. Guilford Publications.

Kasari, C., Gulsrud, A. C., Shire, S. Y., & Strawbridge, C. (2021). *The JASPER model for children with autism: Promoting joint attention, symbolic play, engagement, and regulation*. The Guilford Press.

Kasari, C., Kaiser, A., Goods, K., Nietfeld, J., Mathy, P., Landa, R., Murphy, S., & Almirall, D. (2014). Communication interventions for minimally verbal children with autism: A sequential multiple assignment randomized trial. *Journal of the American Academy of Child and Adolescent Psychiatry*, *53*(6), 635–646. doi:10.1016/j.jaac.2014.01.019 PMID:24839882

Kasari, C., Lawton, K., Shih, W., Barker, T. V., Landa, R., Lord, C., Orlich, F., King, B., Wetherby, A., & Senturk, D. (2014). Caregiver-mediated intervention for low-resourced preschoolers with autism: An RCT. *Pediatrics*, *134*(1), e72–e79. doi:10.1542/peds.2013-3229 PMID:24958585

Kasky-Hernández, L., & Cates, G. L. (2015). Role of psychologists in interdisciplinary relations in special education. In J. P. Bakken & F. E. Obiakor (Eds.), *Interdisciplinary connections to special education: Important aspects to consider*. Emerald. doi:10.1108/S0270-40132015000030A019

Kataoka, S. H., Rowan, B., & Hoagwood, K. E. (2009). Bridging the divide: In search of common ground in mental health and education research and policy. *Psychiatric Services*, *60*(11), 1510–1515. doi:10.1176/ps.2009.60.11.1510 PMID:19880470

Kataoka, S., Zhang, L., & Wells, K. (2002). Unmet need for mental health care among U.S. children: Variation by ethnicity and insurance status. *The American Journal of Psychiatry*, *159*(9), 1548–1555. doi:10.1176/appi.ajp.159.9.1548 PMID:12202276

Katsiyannis, A., Counts, J., Popham, M., Ryan, J., & Butzer, M. (2016). Litigation and students with disabilities: An Overview of cases from 2015. *NAASP Bulletin*, *100*(1), 287–298. doi:10.1177/0192636516664827

Katz, L. A., Maag, A., Fallon, K. A., Blenkarn, K., & Smith, M. K. (2010). What makes a caseload (un)manageable? School-based speech language pathologists speak. *Language, Speech, and Hearing Services in Schools*, *41*(2), 139–151. doi:10.1044/0161-1461(2009/08-0090) PMID:19755641

Kauffman, J. M., & Badar, J. (2018). *The scandalous neglect of children's mental health: What schools can do*. Routledge. doi:10.4324/9781351165808

Kauffman, J. M., & Landrum, T. J. (2017). *Characteristics of emotional and behavioral disorders of children and Youth* (11th ed.). Pearson.

Kauffman, J. M., & Landrum, T. J. (2018). *Characteristics of emotional and behavioral disorders of children and youth* (11th ed.). Pearson.

Kayama, M., Haight, W., Kincaid, T., & Evans, K. (2015). Local implementation of disability policies for "high incidence" disabilities at public schools in Japan and the U.S. *Children and Youth Services Review*, *52*, 34–44. doi:10.1016/j.childyouth.2015.02.009

Kearney, C. A., & Childs, J. (2021). A multi-tiered systems of support blueprint for re-opening schools following COVID-19 shutdown. *Children and Youth Services Review, 122*. doi:10.1016/j.childyouth.2020.105919

Kekoni, T., Kainulainen, A., Tiilikainen, E., Mäki-Petäjä-Leinonen, A., Mönkkönen, K., & Vanjusov, H. (2022). Integrative learning through the interdisciplinary social law clinic—Learning experiences of law and social work students. *Social Work Education*, 1–15. doi:10.1080/02615479.2022.2102163

Kelly, L. E. (Ed.). (2019). *Adapted physical education national standards* (3rd ed)Human Kinetics.

Kennedy, M. J., Peeples, K. N., Romig, J. E., Mathews, H. M., & Rodgers, W. J. (2018). Welcome to our new series on high-leverage practices for students with disabilities. https://highleveragepractices.org/welcome-our-new-series-high-leverage-...

Kent, & Giles, R. M. (2016). Dual Certification in General and Special Education: What is the Role of Field Experience in Preservice Teacher Preparation? *The Professional Educator*, *40*(2).

Kent-Walsh, J., Binger, C., & Malani, M. (2010). Teaching partners to support the communication skills of young children who use AAC: Lessons from the ImPAACT program. *Early Childhood Services (San Diego, Calif.)*, *4*(3), 155–170.

Kent-Walsh, J., Murza, K. A., Malani, M. D., & Binger, C. (2015). Effects of communication partner instruction on the communication of individuals using AAC: A meta-analysis. *Augmentative and Alternative Communication*, *31*(4), 271–284. doi:10.3109/07434618.2015.1052153 PMID:26059542

Kepley, H. O., & Streeter, R. A. (2018). Closing behavioral health workforce gaps: A HRSA program expanding direct mental health service access in underserved areas. *American Journal of Preventive Medicine*, *54*(6), S190–S191. doi:10.1016/j.amepre.2018.03.006 PMID:29779541

Kerns, S. E. U., Cevasco, M., Comtois, K. A., Dorsey, S., King, K., McMahon, R., Sedlar, G., Lee, T. G., Mazza, J. J., Lengua, L., Davis, C., Evans-Campbell, T., & Trupin, E. W. (2016). An interdisciplinary university-based initiative for graduate training in evidence-based treatments for children's mental health. *Journal of Emotional and Behavioral Disorders*, *24*(1), 3–15. doi:10.1177/1063426615583457

Kester, F. M., Beveridge, S., & Stella, J. (2019). Interdisciplinary Professional Development Needs of Transition Professionals Serving Youth with Autism Spectrum Disorders. *Journal of Rehabilitation*, *85*(1), 53–63.

Kilgo, J., & Bruder, M. B. (1997). Creating new visions in institutions of higher education: Interdisciplinary approaches to personnel preparation in early intervention. *Reforming personnel preparation in early intervention: Issues, models, and practical strategies*, *8*, 1-101.

Kilgo, E. D., Jennifer, L., Aldridge, J., Vogtle, L., Ronilo, W., & Bruton, A. (2017). Teaming, collaboration, and case-based learning: A transdisciplinary approach to early intervention/education. *Case Studies Journal*, *6*(6), 7–12.

Kilgo, J. L. (2006). Transdisciplinary teaming from a higher education perspective. In J. L. Kilgo (Ed.), *Transdisciplinary teaming in early intervention/early childhood special education: Navigating together with families and children* (pp. 77–80). Association for Childhood Education International.

Kim, N., & Lambie, G. W. (2018). Burnout and implications for professional school counselors. *The Professional Counselor*, *8*(3), 277–294. https://tpcjournal.nbcc.org/burnout-and-implications-for-professional-school-counselors/. doi:10.15241/nk.8.3.277

King, G., Orchard, C., Khalili, H., & Avery, L. (2016). Refinement of the Interprofessional Socialization and Valuing Scale (ISVS-21) and development of 9-item equivalent versions. *The Journal of Continuing Education in the Health Professions*, *36*(3), 171–177. doi:10.1097/CEH.0000000000000082 PMID:27583993

King, S. A., Lemons, C. J., & Hill, D. R. (2012). Response to intervention in secondary schools: Considerations for administrators. *NASSP Bulletin*, *96*(1), 5–22. doi:10.1177/0192636511430551

*Compilation of References*

King-Sears, M. E., Janney, R., & Snell, M. E. (2015). *Collaborative teaming: Teachers' guides to inclusive practices* (3rd ed.). Brookes.

Klawetter, S., & Frankel, K. (2018). Infant mental health: A lens for maternal and child mental health disparities. *Journal of Human Behavior in the Social Environment*, *28*(5), 557–569. doi:10.1080/10911359.2018.1437495

Kleinert, H., Towles-Reeves, E., Quenemoen, R., Thurlow, M., Fluegge, L., Weseman, L., & Kerbel, A. (2015). Where students with the most significant cognitive disabilities are taught: Implications for general curriculum access. *Exceptional Children*, *81*(3), 312–328. doi:10.1177/0014402914563697

Kliewer, W., & Lepore, S. J. (2015). Exposure to violence, social cognitive processing, and sleep problems in urban adolescents. *Journal of Youth and Adolescence*, *44*(2), 507–517. https://doi.org/10.1007/s10964-014-0184-x

Klingner, J., Brownell, M., Mason, L., Sindelar, P., Benedict, A., Griffin, C., Lane, K., Israel, M., Oakes, W., Menzies, H., Germer, K., & Park, Y. (2016). Teaching students with special needs in the new millennium. In D. H. Gitomer & C. A. Bell (Eds.), *Handbook of Research on Teaching* (5th ed., pp. 639–716). American Educational Research Association. doi:10.3102/978-0-935302-48-6_10

Knowles, M. S. (Ed.). (1984). *Andragogy in action*. Jossey-Bass.

Knowles, M. S., Holton, E. E., & Swanson, R. A. (2005). *The adult learner: The definitive classic in adult education and human resource development*. Elsevier. doi:10.4324/9780080481913

Koegel, L. K., Bryan, K. M., Su, P. L., Vaidya, M., & Camarata, S. (2020). Definitions of nonverbal and minimally verbal in research for autism: A systematic review of the literature. *Journal of Autism and Developmental Disorders*, *50*(8), 2957–2972. doi:10.100710803-020-04402-w PMID:32056115

Koegel, R. L., Vernon, T., & Koegel, L. K. (2009). Improving social initiations in young children using reinforcers and embedded social interactions. *Journal of Autism and Developmental Disorders*, *39*(9), 1240–1251. doi:10.100710803-009-0732-5 PMID:19357942

Kohler, P. D., Gothberg, J. E., Fowler, C., & Coyle, J. (2016). *Taxonomy for transition programming 2.0: A model for planning, organizing, and evaluating transition education, services, and programs*. Western Michigan University. Available at www.transitionta.org

Kohl, H. W. III, Craig, C. L., Lambert, E. V., Inoue, S., Alkandari, J. R., Leetongin, G., & Kahlmeier, S.Lancet Physical Activity Series Working Group. (2012). The pandemic of physical inactivity: Global action for public health. *Lancet*, *380*(9838), 294–305. doi:10.1016/S0140-6736(12)60898-8 PMID:22818941

Kohli, R. (2018). Behind school doors: The impact of hostile racial climates on urban teachers of color. *Urban Education*, *53*, 307–333. doi:10.1177/0042085916636653

Korthagen, F. (2001). A reflection on reflection. In *Linking practice and theory* (pp. 67–84). Routledge. doi:10.4324/9781410600523-9

Kosko, K. W., & Wilkins, J. L. (2009). General educators' in-service training and their self-perceived ability to adapt instruction for students with IEPs. *Professional Educator*, *33*(2). https://eric.ed.gov/?id=EJ988196

Koury, K., Hollingsead, C., Fitzgerald, G., Miller, K., Mitchem, K., Tsai, H., & Zha, S. (2009). Case-based instruction in different delivery contexts: The impact of time in cases. *Journal of Interactive Learning Research*, *20*(4), 445–467.

Kucharczyk, S., Oswalt, A., Schaefer-Whitby, P., Frazier, K., & Koch, L. (2022). Emerging trends in youth engagement during transition: Youth as interdisciplinary partners. *Rehabilitation Research, Policy, and Education*, *36*(1), 71–98. https://dx.doi.org/10.1891/RE-21-16

Kucharczyk, S., Thomas, J. M., & Schaefer-Whitby, P. (2021). "It would have been nice if…": Analysis of Transition Experiences through Grand Challenges. *Rural Special Education Quarterly*, *40*(3), 117–131. https://doi.org/10.1177/87568705211027970

Kuntz, E. M., & Carter, E. W. (2021). Effects of a collaborative planning and consultation framework to increase participation of students with severe disabilities in general education classes. *Research and Practice for Persons with Severe Disabilities*, *46*(1), 35–52. doi:10.1177/1540796921992518

Kunze, M., & Machalicek, W. (2022). Interdisciplinary teams: A model to support students with autism. *Psychology in the Schools*, *59*(7), 1350–1362. doi:10.1002/pits.22618

Kutsyuruba, B., & Walker, K. (2015). The role of trust in developing teacher leaders through early-career induction and mentoring programs. *Antistasis*, *5*(1), 32-36. Retrieved from https://journals.lib.unb.ca/index.php/antistasis/article/view/22859 https://www.ncsl.org/research/education/tackling-teacher-and-principal-shortages-in-rural-areas.aspx

Ladson-Billings, G. (1994). *The dreamkeepers: Successful teachers of African American children*. Jossey-Bass.

Ladson-Billings, G. (1995). But that's just good teaching! The case for culturally relevant pedagogy. *Theory into Practice*, *34*(3), 159–165. doi:10.1080/00405849509543675

Ladson-Billings, G. (1995). Toward a theory of culturally relevant pedagogy. *American Educational Research Journal*, *32*(3), 465–491. doi:10.3102/00028312032003465

Ladson-Billings, G. (2014). Culturally relevant pedagogy 2.0: A.k.a the remix. *Harvard Educational Review*, *84*(1), 74–84. doi:10.17763/haer.84.1.p2rj131485484751

Lakofsky. (2020). *Understanding Interdisciplinary Science Graduate Programs at the University of Delaware*. ProQuest Dissertations Publishing.

Lalvani, P., & Bacon, J. K. (2019). Rethinking "we are all special": Anti-ableism curricula in early childhood classrooms. *Young Exceptional Children*, *22*(2), 87–100. doi:10.1177/1096250618810706

Lambe, J., McNair, V., & Smith, R. (2013). Special educational needs, e-learning and the reflective e-portfolio: Implications for developing and assessing competence in pre-service education. *Journal of Education for Teaching*, *39*(2), 181–196.

Lambros, K., Kraemer, B., Wager, J. D., Culver, S., Angulo, A., & Saragosa, M. (2016). Students with dual diagnosis: Can school-based mental health services play a role? *Journal of Mental Health Research in Intellectual Disabilities*, *9*(1–2), 3–23. doi:10.1080/19315864.2015.1091055

Lam, S. K. Y. (2005). An Interdisciplinary Course to Prepare School Professionals to Collaborate with Families of Exceptional Children. *Multicultural Education*, *13*(2), 38–42.

Landers, M. F., Weaver, R., & Tompkins, F. M. (1990). Interdisciplinary collaboration in higher education: A matter of attitude. *Action in Teacher Education*, *12*(2), 25–30. doi:10.1080/01626620.1990.10462745

Landmark, L. J., & Zhang, D. (2012). Compliance and practices in transition planning: A review of individualized education program documents. *Remedial and Special Education*, *34*(2), 113–125. doi:10.1177/0741932511431831

Lapkin, S., Levett-Jones, T., & Gilligan, C. (2013). A systematic review of the effectiveness of interprofessional education in health professional programs. *Nurse Education Today*, *33*(2), 90–102. doi:10.1016/j.nedt.2011.11.006 PMID:22196075

Lavay, B., French, R., & Henderson, H. (2016). *Positive behavior management in physical activity settings* (3rd ed.). Human Kinetics.

*Compilation of References*

Lawrence, S., Smith, S., & Banerjee, R. (2016). *Preschool inclusion: Key findings from research and implications for policy*. Child Care & Early Education Research Connections, National Center for Children in Poverty. https://www.nccp.org/wp-content/uploads/2020/05/text_1154.pdf

Layden, S. J. (2022). Creating a professional network: A statewide model to support school-based behavior analysts. *Behavior Analysis in Practice*. doi:10.100740617-022-00700-0 PMID:35371415

Leader-Janssen, E., Swain, K. D., Delkamiller, J., & Ritzman, M. J. (2012). Collaborative relationships for general education teachers working with students with disabilities. *Journal of Instructional Psychology*, *39*(2), 112–118.

Learning Policy Institute. (2022). *Whole child policy toolkit*. https://www.wholechildpolicy.org/

Leatherman, E., & Wegner, J. (2022). Augmentative and alternative communication in the classroom: Teacher practices and experiences. *Journal of Speech. Language and Hearing in the Schools*, *53*(3), 874–893. doi:10.1044/2022_LSHSS-21-00125 PMID:35699256

Ledford, J. R., King, S., Harbin, E. R., & Zimmerman, K. N. (2018). Antecedent social skills interventions for individuals with ASD: What works, for whom, and under what conditions? *Focus on Autism and Other Developmental Disabilities*, *33*(1), 3–13. doi:10.1177/1088357616634024

Ledford, J. R., Lane, J. D., & Severini, K. E. (2018). Systematic use of visual analysis for assessing outcomes in single case design studies. *Brain Impairment*, *19*(1), 4–17. doi:10.1017/BrImp.2017.16

Lee, A., Poch, R., Smith, A., Kelly, M. D., & Leopold, H. (2018). Intercultural pedagogy: A faculty learning cohort. *Education in Science*, *177*, 1–14.

Leh, A. S. C. (2002). Action research in hybrid courses and their online communities. *Educational Media International*, *39*, 31–38.

Leko, M. M., Brownell, M. T., Sindelar, P. T., & Kiely, M. T. (2015). Envisioning the future of special education personnel preparation in a standards-based era. *Exceptional Children*, *82*(1), 25–43.

Lemons, C. J., Vaughn, S., Wexler, J., Kearns, D. M., & Sinclair, A. C. (2018). Envisioning an improved continuum of special education services for students with learning disabilities: Considering intervention intensity. *Learning Disabilities Research & Practice*, *33*(3), 131–143. doi:10.1111/ldrp.12173

Lemons, C. J., Kearns, D. M., & Davidson, K. A. (2014). Data-based individualization in reading: Intensifying interventions for students with significant reading disabilities. *Teaching Exceptional Children*, *46*(4), 20–29. doi:10.1177/0040059914522978

LeMura, L. M., & Maziekas, M. T. (2002). Factors that alter body fat, body mass, and fat-free mass in pediatric obesity. In *Database of abstracts of reviews of effects (DARE): Quality-assessed reviews*. Centre for Reviews and Dissemination. doi:10.1097/00005768-200203000-00016

Lepiéce, B., Reynaert, C., Jacques, D., & Zdanowicz, N. (2015). Poverty and mental health: What should we know as mental health professionals? *Psychiatria Danubina*, *1*, S92–S96. https://www.ncbi.nlm.nih.gov/pubmed/26417741

Lerman, D. C., O'Brien, M. J., Neely, L., Call, N. A., Tsami, L., Schieltz, K. M., Berg, W. K., Graber, J., Huang, P., Kopelman, T., & Cooper-Brown, L. (2020). Remote coaching of caregivers via telehealth: Challenges and potential solutions. *Journal of Behavioral Education*, *29*(2), 195–221. doi:10.100710864-020-09378-2 PMID:36093285

Lerman, D. C., Vorndran, C. M., Addison, L., & Contrucci Kuhn, S. (2004). Preparing teachers in evidence-based practices for young children with autism. *School Psychology Review*, *33*(4), 510–526.

Lesh, J. L. (2020). Don't forget about yourself: Words of wisdom on special education teacher self-care. *Teaching Exceptional Children*, 52(6), 367–369. doi:10.1177/0040059920936158

Levin, B. B. (2001). *Energizing teacher education and professional development with problem-based learning*. ASCD.

Levin, B. B. (2002). *Case studies of teacher development: An in-depth look at how thinking about pedagogy develops over time*. Erlbaum.

Levin, J., Berg-Jacobson, A., Atchison, D., Lee, K., & Vontsolos, E. (2015). *Massachusetts Study of Teacher Supply and Demand: Trends and Projections*. American Institutes for Research.

Lewin, K. (1946). Action research and minority problems. *The Journal of Social Issues*, 2(4), 34–46. doi:10.1111/j.1540-4560.1946.tb02295.x

Leyfer, O. T., Folstein, S. E., Bacalman, S., Davis, N. O., Dinh, E., Morgan, J., Tager-Flusberg, H., & Lainhart, J. E. (2006). Comorbid psychiatric disorders in children with autism: Interview development and rates of disorders. *Journal of Autism and Developmental Disorders*, 36(7), 849–861. doi:10.100710803-006-0123-0 PMID:16845581

Lieber, J., Horn, E., Palmer, S., & Fleming, K. (2008). Access to the general education curriculum for preschoolers with disabilities: Children's school success. *Exceptionality*, 16(1), 18–32. doi:10.1080/09362830701796776

Lieberman, A. F., & Van Horn, P. (2005). Don't hit my mommy!: A manual for child-parent psychotherapy with young witnesses of family violence. *Zero to Three*.

Light, J., & McNaughton, D. (2014). Communicative competence for individuals who require augmentative and alternative communication: A new definition for a new era of communication? *Augmentative and Alternative Communication*, 30(1), 1–18. doi:10.3109/07434618.2014.885080 PMID:30952185

Light, J., & McNaughton, D. (2015). Designing AAC research and intervention to improve outcomes for individuals with complex communication needs. *Augmentative and Alternative Communication*, 31(2), 85–96. doi:10.3109/07434618.2015.1036458 PMID:25904008

Light, J., McNaughton, D., & Caron, J. (2019). New and emerging AAC technology supports for children with complex communication needs and their communication partners: State of the science and future research directions. *Augmentative and Alternative Communication*, 35(1), 26–41. doi:10.1080/07434618.2018.1557251 PMID:30648902

Lim, D. H., & Yoon, S. W. (2008). Team learning and collaboration between online and blended learner groups. *Performance Improvement Quarterly*, 21, 59–72. doi:10.1002/piq.20031

Liming, K. W., & Grube, W. A. (2018). Wellbeing outcomes for children exposed to multiple adverse experiences in early childhood: A systematic review. *Child & Adolescent Social Work Journal*, 35(4), 317–335. doi:10.100710560-018-0532-x

Linan-Thompson, S., Lara-Martinez, J. A., & Cavazos, L. O. (2018). Exploring the intersection of evidence-based practices and culturally and linguistically responsive practices. *Intervention in School and Clinic*, 54(1), 6–13. doi:10.1177/1053451218762574

Linder, T. (2008). *Transdisciplinary Play-Based Assessment: A Functional Approach to Working with Young Children* (2nd ed.). Paul H. Brookes.

Lindsay, C. A. (2016). Teacher race and school discipline. *Education Next*, 17(1), 72–78. https://www.educationnext.org/teacher-race-and-school-discipline-suspensions-research/

*Compilation of References*

Lindsay, S., Proulx, M., Thomson, N., & Scott, H. (2013). Educators' challenges of including children with autism spectrum disorders in mainstream classrooms. *International Journal of Disability Development and Education*, *60*(4), 347–362. doi:10.1080/1034912X.2013.846470

Linton, S. (1998). *Claiming disability: Knowledge and identity*. New York University Press.

Little, C. (2020). Collaboration. In I. Spandagou, C. Little, D. Evans, & M. L. Bonati (Eds.), *Inclusive education in schools and early childhood settings* (pp. 85–92). Springer. doi:10.1007/978-981-15-2541-4_8

Lloyd, C., King, R., & Chenoweth, L. (2009). Social work, stress, and burnout: A review. *Journal of Mental Health (Abingdon, England)*, *11*(3), 255–265. doi:10.1080/09638230020023642

Locke, J., Lawson, G. M., Beidas, R. S., Aarons, G. A., Xie, M., Lyon, A. R., Stahmer, A., Seidman, M., Frederick, L., Oh, C., Spaulding, C., Dorsey, S., & Mandell, D. S. (2019). Individual and organizational factors that affect implementation of evidence-based practices for children with autism in public schools: A cross-sectional observational study. *Implementation Science; IS*, *14*(29), 29. doi:10.118613012-019-0877-3 PMID:30866976

Lord, C., Charman, T., Havdahl, A., Carbone, P., Anagnostou, E., Boyd, B., Carr, T., de Vries, P. J., Dissanayake, C., Divan, G., Freitag, C. M., Gotelli, M. M., Kasari, C., Knapp, M., Mundy, P., Plank, A., Scahill, L., Servili, C., Shattuck, P., ... McCauley, J. B. (2022). The lancet commission on the future of care and clinical research in autism. *Lancet*, *399*(10321), 271–334. doi:10.1016/S0140-6736(21)01541-5 PMID:34883054

Love, H. R., & Beneke, M. R. (2021). Pursuing justice-driven inclusive education research: Disability critical race theory (DisCrit) in early childhood. *Topics in Early Childhood Special Education*, *41*(1), 31–44. doi:10.1177/0271121421990833

Lucas, T., & Villegas, A. M. (2013). Preparing linguistically responsive teachers: Laying the foundation in preservice teacher education. *Theory into Practice*, *52*(2), 37–41. doi:10.1080/00405841.2013.770327

Ludlow, B. L. (2015). Virtual reality: Emerging applications and future directions. *Rural Special Education Quarterly*, *34*(3), 3–10. doi:10.1177/875687051503400302

Lund, E., Young, A., & Yarbrough, R. (2020). The effects of co-treatment on concept development in children with Down syndrome. *Communication Disorders Quarterly*, *41*(3), 176–187. doi:10.1177/1525740119827264

Lundeberg, M. A., & Yadav, A. (2006). Assessment of case study teaching: Where do we go from here? Part 1. *Journal of College Science Teaching*, *35*(5), 10–13.

Lunsford, L. G., Crisp, G., Dolan, E. L., & Wuetherick, B. (2017). Mentoring in higher education. In D. A. Clutterbuck, F. K. Kochan, L. G. Lunsford, N. Dominguez, & J. Haddock-Millar (Eds.), *The SAGE handbook of mentoring* (pp. 316–334). Sage. doi:10.4135/9781526402011.n20

Luterman, D. (2006). The counseling relationship. *ASHA Leader*, *11*(4), 8–33. doi:10.1044/leader.FTR3.11042006.8

Lynch, E., & Hanson, M. (2011). *Developing cross-cultural competence: A guide for working with children and their families* (4th ed.). Brookes Publishing.

Lyons, P., & Bandura, R. P. (2020). Skills needs, integrative pedagogy and case-based instruction. *Journal of Workplace Learning*, *32*(7), 473–487. doi:10.1108/JWL-12-2019-0140

Lyons, R., & Roulstone, S. (2018). Well-Being and Resilience in Children With Speech and Language Disorders. *Journal of Speech, Language, and Hearing Research: JSLHR*, *61*(2), 324–344. doi:10.1044/2017_JSLHR-L-16-0391 PMID:29374284

Lytle, R., Lavay, B., & Rizzo, T. (2010). What is a highly qualified adapted physical education teacher? *Journal of Physical Education, Recreation & Dance*, *81*(2), 40–50. doi:10.1080/07303084.2010.10598433

Maenner, M. J., Shaw, K. A., Bakian, A. V., Bilder, D. A., Durkin, M. S., Esler, A., Furnier, S. M., Hallas, L., Hall-Lande, J., Hudson, A., Hughes, M. M., Patrick, M., Pierce, K., Poynter, J. N., Salinas, A., Shenouda, J., Vehorn, A., Warren, Z., Constantino, J. N., DiRienzo, M., ... Cogswell, M. E. (2021). Prevalence and Characteristics of Autism Spectrum Disorder Among Children Aged 8 Years - Autism and Developmental Disabilities Monitoring Network, 11 Sites, United States, 2018. *Morbidity and mortality weekly report. Surveillance summaries (Washington, D.C.: 2002)*, *70*(11), 1–16. doi:10.15585/mmwr.ss7011a1

Magee, R. V. (2019). *The inner work of racial justice: Healing ourselves and transforming our communities through mindfulness*. TarcherPerigee.

Magnuson, K. A., & Waldfogel, J. (2005). Early childhood care and education: Effects on ethnic and racial gaps in school readiness. *The Future of Children*, *15*(1), 169–196.

Mahalingappa, L., Kayi-Aydar, H., & Polat, N. (2021). Institutional and faculty readiness for teaching linguistically diverse international students in educator programs in the U.S universities. *TESOL Quarterly*, *55*(4), 1247–1277. doi:10.1002/tesq.3083

Manor-Binyamini, I. (2007). Meaning of language differences between doctors and educators in collaborative discourse. *Journal of Interprofessional Care*, *21*(1), 31–43. doi:10.1080/13561820601049468 PMID:17365372

Maras, M. A., Thompson, A. M., Lewis, C., Thornburg, K., & Hawks, J. (2015). Developing a tiered response model for social-emotional learning through interdisciplinary collaboration. *Journal of Educational & Psychological Consultation*, *25*(2-3), 198–223. doi:10.1080/10474412.2014.929954

March of Dimes. (2021). *Rate of PreTerm Births*. https://www.marchofdimes.org/Peristats/tools/prematurityprofile.aspx?reg=99

Margison, J. A., & Shore, B. M. (2009). Interprofessional practice and education in health care: Their relevance to school psychology. *Canadian Journal of School Psychology*, *24*(2), 125–139. doi:10.1177/0829573509336537

Margolis, L., Rosenberg, A., Umble, K., & Chewning, L. (2013). Effects of interdisciplinary training on MCH professionals, organizations, and systems. *Maternal and Child Health Journal*, *17*(5), 949–958. doi:10.100710995-012-1078-8 PMID:22798078

Marlow, M. (2009). Supporting teacher professional identity through mentoring activities. *Research in Higher Education*, 2.

Marrone, J. A., Tesluk, P. E., & Carson, J. B. (2007). A multilevel investigation of antecedents and consequences of team member boundary-spanning behavior. *Academy of Management Journal*, *50*(6), 1423–1439. doi:10.5465/amj.2007.28225967

Marsh, R. J., & Mathur, S. R. (2020). Mental health in schools: An overview of multitiered systems of support. *Intervention in School and Clinic*, *56*(2), 67–73. doi:10.1177/1053451220914896

Martínez, M. E., Nodora, J. N., & Carvajal-Carmona, L. G. (2021). The dual pandemic of COVID-19 and systemic inequities in US Latino communities. *Cancer, 127*, 1548-1550. doi:10.1002/cncr.33401

Martínez-Alvarez, P. (2020). Essential constructs in the preparation of inclusive bilingual education teachers: Mediation, agency, and collectivity. *Bilingual Research Journal*, *43*(3), 304–322. doi:10.1080/15235882.2020.1802367

Martínez-Alvarez, P. (2021). *Teacher education for inclusive bilingual contexts: Collective reflection to support emergent bilinguals with and without disabilities*. Routledge. doi:10.4324/9781003112259

Martin, F., & Bolliger, D. U. (2018). Engagement matters: Student perceptions on the importance of engagement strategies in the online learning environment. *Online Learning*, *22*(1), 205–222. doi:10.24059/olj.v22i1.1092

Martin, F., Ritzhaupt, A., Kumar, S., & Budhrani, K. (2019). Award-winning faculty online teaching practices: Course design, assessment and evaluation, and facilitation. *The Internet and Higher Education*, *42*, 34–43. doi:10.1016/j.iheduc.2019.04.001

Masi, A., DeMayo, M. M., Glozier, N., & Guastella, A. J. (2017). An Overview of Autism Spectrum Disorder, Heterogeneity and Treatment Options. *Neuroscience Bulletin*, *33*(2), 183–193. doi:10.100712264-017-0100-y PMID:28213805

Maslach, C., & Leiter, M. P. (2016). Understanding the burnout experience: Recent research and its implications for psychiatry. *World Psychiatry; Official Journal of the World Psychiatric Association (WPA)*, *15*(2), 103–111. doi:10.1002/wps.20311 PMID:27265691

Mason-Williams, L., Bettini, E., Peyton, D., Harvey, A., Rosenberg, M., & Sindelar, P. T. (2020). Rethinking shortages in special education: Making good on the promise of an equal opportunity for students with disabilities. *Teacher Education and Special Education*, *43*(1), 45–62.

Mason-Williams, L., Bettini, E., Peyton, D., Harvey, A., Rosenberg, M., & Sindelar, P. T. (2020). Rethinking shortages in special education: Making good on the promise of an equal opportunity for students with Disabilities. *Teacher Education and Special Education*, *43*(1), 45–62. doi:10.1177/0888406419880352

Master Clinician Network. (n.d.) *Master Clinician Network*. https://www.masterclinician.org/

Mathur, S. K., & Rodriguez, K. A. (2021). Cultural responsiveness curriculum for behavior analysts: A meaningful step towards social justice. *Behavior Analysis in Practice*. doi:10.100740617-021-00579-3

Matson, J. L., & Smith, K. R. (2008). Current status of intensive behavioral interventions for young children with autism and PDD-NOS. *Research in Autism Spectrum Disorders*, *2*(1), 60–74. doi:10.1016/j.rasd.2007.03.003

Matzat, U. (2013). Do blended virtual learning communities enhance teachers' professional development more than purely virtual ones? A large scale empirical comparison. *Computers & Education*, *60*(1), 40–51. doi:10.1016/j.compedu.2012.08.006

Mayer, G. R., Sulzer-Azaroff, B., & Wallace, M. (2018). *Behavior analysis for lasting change* (4th ed.). Sloan Publishing.

Mazzotti, V. L., Rowe, D. A., Kwiatek, S., Voggt, A., Chang, W.-H., Fowler, C. H., Poppen, M., Sinclair, J., & Test, D. W. (2021). Secondary transition predictors of postschool success: An update to the research base. *Career Development and Transition for Exceptional Individuals*, *44*(1), 47–64. https://doi.org/10.1177/2165143420959793

Mazzotti, V. L., Rowe, D. A., Kwiatek, S., Voggt, A., Wen-Huan, C., Fowler, C. H., Poppen, M., Sinclair, J., & Test, D. W. (2021). Secondary transition predictors of postschool success: An update to the research base. *Career Development and Transition for Exceptional Children*, *44*(1), 47–64. doi:10.1177/2165143420959793

McCall, R. C., Padron, K., & Andrews, C. (2018). Evidence-based instructional strategies for adult learners: A review of the literature. *Codex: the Journal of the Louisiana Chapter of the ACRL*, *4*(4), 29–47.

McClain, M. B., Shahidullah, J. D., Mezher, K. R., Haverkamp, C. R., Benallie, K. J., & Schwartz, S. E. (2020). School-clinic care coordination for youth with ASD: A national survey of school psychologists. *Journal of Autism and Developmental Disorders*, *50*(9), 3081–3091. doi:10.100710803-019-03985-3 PMID:30877418

McConnell, S. R., & Rahn, N. L. (2016). Assessment in early childhood special education. In *Handbook of early childhood special education* (pp. 89–106). Springer. doi:10.1007/978-3-319-28492-7_6

McConnell, T. J., Parker, J. M., Eberhardt, J., Koehler, M. J., & Lundeberg, M. A. (2013). Virtual professional learning communities: Teachers' perceptions of virtual versus face-to-face professional development. *Journal of Science Education and Technology, 22*(3), 267–277. doi:10.100710956-012-9391-y

McDaniel, E. A. (2020). Faculty collaboration for better teaching: Adult learning principles applied to teaching improvement. *To Improve the Academy, 6*, 94-102.

McDonnell, A. P., Hawken, L. S., Johnston, S. S., Kidder, J. E., Lynes, M. J., & McDonnell, J. J. (2014). Emergent Literacy Practices and Support for Children with Disabilities: A National Survey. *Education & Treatment of Children, 37*(3), 495–529. doi:10.1353/etc.2014.0024

McFadyen, A. K., Webster, V. S., & Maclaren, W. M. (2006). The test-retest reliability of a revised version of the Readiness for Interprofessional Learning Scale (RIPLS). *Journal of Interprofessional Care, 20*(6), 633–639. doi:10.1080/13561820600991181 PMID:17095441

McGee, G. G., & Morrier, M. J. (2005). Preparation of autism specialists (Vol. 2). Handbook of Autism and Pervasive Developmental Disorders. Academic Press.

McGinty, A., & Justice, L. (2006). Predictors of print knowledge in children with specific language impairment: Experiential and developmental factors. *Journal of Speech, Language, and Hearing Research: JSLHR, 52*(1), 81–97. doi:10.1044/1092-4388(2008/07-0279) PMID:18723595

McHatton, P. A., & Parker, A. (2013). Purposeful preparation: Longitudinally exploring inclusion attitudes of general and special education preservice teachers. *Teacher Education and Special Education, 36*(3), 186–203. doi:10.1177/0888406413491611

McIntosh, D. (2010). Treating disruptive classroom behaviors of preschoolers through teacher child interaction therapy. In A. A. Drewes & C. E. Schaefer (Eds.), *School-based play therapy* (pp. 197–218). Wiley. doi:10.1002/9781118269701.ch10

McIntosh, K., Ellwood, K., McCall, L., & Girvan, E. J. (2018). Using Discipline Data to Enhance Equity in School Discipline. *Intervention in School and Clinic, 53*(3), 146–152. doi:10.1177/1053451217702130

McIntyre, L. L. (2011). Dual diagnosis and families: Introduction to the special issue. *Journal of Mental Health Research in Intellectual Disabilities, 4*(3), 135–139. doi:10.1080/19315864.2011.606596

McKerchar, P. M., & Thompson, R. H. (2004). A descriptive analysis of potential reinforcement contingencies in the preschool classroom. *Journal of Applied Behavior Analysis, 37*(4), 431–443. doi:10.1901/jaba.2004.37-431 PMID:15669403

McLaughlin, M. (2002). Examining special and general education collaborative practices in exemplary schools. *Journal of Educational & Psychological Consultation, 13*, 279–283.

McLaughlin, T. W., Budd, J., & Clendon, S. (2017). The Child and Youth Profile: A toolkit to facilitate cross-disciplinary educational planning. *Kairaranga, 18*(1), 3–11. doi:10.54322/kairaranga.v18i1.217

McLean, M. (2016). A history of the DEC Recommended Practices. *DEC Recommended Practices Monograph Series, 1*, 1–10.

McLeskey, J., & Brownell, M. (2015). *High-leverage practices and teacher preparation in special education* (Document No. PR-1). Retrieved from University of Florida, Collaboration for Effective Educator, Development, Accountability, and Reform Center website: https://ceedar.education.ufl.edu/tools/best-practice-review/

McLeskey, J., & Brownell, M. (2015). *High-leverage practices and teacher preparation in special education* (Document No. PR-1). University of Florida, Collaboration for Effective Educator, Development, Accountability, and Reform Center website: https://ceedar.education.ufl.edu/tools/best-practice-review/

McLeskey, J., Barringer, M.-D., Billingsley, B., Brownell, M., Jackson, D., Kennedy, M., Lewis, T., Maheady, L., Rodriguez, J., Scheeler, M. C., Winn, J., & Ziegler, D. (2017). *High-leverage practices in special education.* Council for Exceptional Children and CEEDAR Center. https://highleveragepractices.org/four-areas-practice-k-12/collaboration

McLeskey, J., Barringer, M-D., Billingsley, B., Brownell, M., Jackson, D., Kennedy, M., Lewis, T., Maheady, L., Rodriguez, J., Scheeler, M. C., Winn, J., & Ziegler, D. (2017). High-leverage practices in special education. *Council for Exceptional Children and CEEDAR Center.*

McLeskey, J., Barringer, M-D., Billingsley, B., Brownell, M., Jackson, D., Kennedy, M., Lewis, T., Maheady, L., Rodriguez, J., Scheeler, M. C., Winn, J., & Ziegler, D. (2017, January). *High-leverage practices in special education.* Arlington, VA: Council for Exceptional Children & CEEDAR Center.

McLeskey, J., Barringer, M-D., Billingsley, B., Brownell, M., Jackson, D., Kennedy, M., Lewis, T., Maheady, L., Rodriguez, J., Scheeler, M. C., Winn, J., & Ziegler, D. (2017, January). High-leverage practices in special education. *Council for Exceptional Children & CEEDAR Center.*

McLeskey, J., Billingsley, B., Brownell, M. T., Maheady, L., Lewis, T. J., Billingsley, B. S., & Maheady, L. J. (2019). What are high-leverage practices for special education teachers and why are they important? *Remedial & Special Education, 40*(6), 331–337. doi:10.1177/0741932518773477

McLeskey, J., Barringer, M. D., Billingsley, B., Brownell, M., & Jackson, D. (2017). *High-leverage practices in special education.* Council for Exceptional Children & CEEDAR Center.

McNamara, K. M., Goforth, A., Walcott, C. M., Rossen, E., & Hyson, D. (2019). *Results from the NASP 2015 membership survey, part two: Professional practices in school psychology.* National Association of School Psychologists.

McNamara, S. (2020). Universal design for learning in physical education. *Adapted Physical Activity Quarterly; APAQ, 37*(2), 235–237. doi:10.1123/apaq.2020-0016

McNeil, C. B., & Hembree-Kigin, T. L. (2010). *Parent-child interaction therapy* (2nd ed.). Springer. doi:10.1007/978-0-387-88639-8

McNiff, J. (2017). Action research: All you need to know. *Sage (Atlanta, Ga.).*

McWilliam, P. J. (2000). *Lives in Progress: Case Stories in Early Intervention.* Paul H. Brookes.

McWilliam, R. A. (2010). *Routines-based early intervention: Strategies for supporting young children with disabilities.* Brookes Publishing.

Meek, S., Smith, L., Allen, R., Catherine, E., Edyburn, K., Williams, C., Fabes, R., McIntosh, K., Garica, E., Takanishi, R., Gordon, L., Jimenez-Castellanos, O., Hemmeter, M. L., Gilliam, W., & Pontier, R. (2020). *Start with equity: From the early years to the early grades.* Children's Equity Project and Bipartisan Policy Center. https://childandfamilysuccess.asu.edu/sites/default/files/2020-07/CEP-report-071520- FINAL.pdf

Meherali, S., Punjani, N., Louie-Poon, S., Rahim, K. A., Das, J. K., Salam, R. A., & Lassi, Z. S. (2021). Mental health of children and adolescents amidst COVID-19 and past pandemics: A rapid systematic review. *International Journal of Environmental Research and Public Health, 26,* 3432. https://doi.org/10.3390/ijerph18073432

Mello, L. V. (2016). Fostering postgraduate student engagement: Online resources supporting self-directed learning in a diverse cohort. *Research in Learning Technology, 24*(1). Doi:10.3402/rlt.v24.29366

Meloy, B., & Schachner, A. (2019). *Early childhood essentials: A framework for aligning child skills and educator competencies*. Learning Policy Institute. https://learningpolicyinstitute.org/sites/default/files/product-files/Early_Childhood_Essentials_Framework_REPORT.pdf

Mental Health Services Oversight & Accountability Commission. (2020). *Every Young Heart and Mind: Schools as Centers of Wellness*. https://mhsoac.ca.gov/wp-content/uploads/schools_as_centers_of_wellness_final-2.pdf

Merrell, K. W., & Buchanan, R. (2006). Intervention selection in school-based practice: Using public health models to enhance systems capacity of schools. *School Psychology Review*, *35*(2), 167–180. doi:10.1080/02796015.2006.12087985

Merriam, S. B. (2008). Adult learning theory for the twenty-first century. *New Directions for Adult and Continuing Education*, *2008*(119), 93–98. doi:10.1002/ace.309

Mertler, C. A. (2019). *Action research: Improving schools and empowering educators*. Sage Publications.

Metz, A., Louison, L., Burke, K., Albers, B., & Ward, C. (2020). *Implementation support practitioner profile: Guiding principles and core competencies for implementation practice*. National Implementation Research Network, University of North Carolina at Chapel Hill. Retrieved from https://nirn.fpg.unc.edu/resources/implementation-support-practitioner-profile

Meyers, L. (2017). Making the counseling profession more diverse. *Counseling Today*. https://ct.counseling.org/2017/10/making-counseling-profession-diverse/

Meyer, U., Kriemler, S., Roth, R., Zahner, L., Gerber, M., Puder, J., & Hebestreit, H. (2011). Contribution of physical education to overall physical activity. *Scandinavian Journal of Medicine & Science in Sports*, *23*, 600–606. doi:10.1111/j.1600-0838.2011.01425.x PMID:22151355

Mickey, A. V. (2019). *An assessment of the perceptions of school professionals regarding prenatal substance exposure*. Theses, Dissertations and Capstones. 1229. https://mds.marshall.edu/etd/1229

Milat, A. J., Bauman, A., & Redman, S. (2015). Narrative review of models and success factors for scaling up public health interventions. *Implementation Science; IS*, *10*(1), 113. doi:10.118613012-015-0301-6 PMID:26264351

Miller, G. E., & Nguyen, V. (2014). Family school partnering to support new immigrant and refugee families with children with disabilities. In L. Lo & D. B. Hiatt-Michael (Eds.), *Promising practices to empower culturally and linguistically diverse families of children with disabilities* (pp. 67–84).

Miller, P. S., & Stayton, V. D. (2006). Interdisciplinary teaming in teacher preparation. *Teacher Education and Special Education*, *29*(1), 56–68. doi:10.1177/088840640602900107

Miller, R., Combes, G., Brown, H., & Harwood, A. (2014). Interprofessional workplace learning: A catalyst for strategic change? *Journal of Interprofessional Care*, *28*(3), 186–193. doi:10.3109/13561820.2013.877428 PMID:24428770

Miller, R., & Stein, K. V. (2018). Building competencies for integrated care: Defining the landscape. *International Journal of Integrated Care*, *17*(6), 6. doi:10.5334/ijic.3946

Mills, G. E. (2000). *Action research: A guide for the teacher researcher*. Prentice-Hall, Inc.

Minuchin, S. (1974). *Families and Family Therapy*. Harvard University Press. doi:10.4159/9780674041127

*Compilation of References*

Mississippi Department of Education. (2022, June). *4-year graduation rates*. [Data set]. https://www.mdek12.org/sites/default/files/Offices/MDE/OEA/OPR/2022/grad_dropout_rates_2022_report.pdf

Mitsch, M. K., Weglarz-Ward, J., & Branch, J. (2022). "I'm new here": Leveraging responsibilities, relationships, and resources for new faculty leaders. *Young Exceptional Children*, 1–14. doi:10.1177/10962506221111362

Montgomery, C., & Smith, L. C. (2015). Bridging the gap between researchers and practitioners. *Die Unterrichtspraxis/Teaching German, 48*(1), 100-113.

Monzalve, M., & Horner, R. H. (2021). The impact of the contextual fit enhancement protocol on behavior support plan fidelity and student behavior. *Behavioral Disorders, 46*(4), 267–278. doi:10.1177/0198742920953497

Moon, J., Williford, A., & Mendenhall, A. (2017). Educators' perceptions of youth mental health: Implications for training and the promotion of mental health services in schools. *Children and Youth Services Review, 73*, 384–391. doi:10.1016/j. childyouth.2017.01.006

Moore, B., & Montgomery, J. (2008). *Making a difference for America's children: Speech-Language pathologists in public schools*. Pro-Ed.

Moore, R. (2003). Reexamining the field experiences of teacher candidate. *Journal of Teacher Education, 54*, 31–42. doi:10.1177/ 0022487102238656

Morin, G. J. B., Vannest, K. J., Haas, A. N., Nagro, S. A., Peltier, C. J., Fuller, M. C., & Ura, S. K. (2019). A systematic review of single-case research on video analysis as professional development for special educators. *The Journal of Special Education, 53*(1), 3–14. doi:10.1177/0022466918798361

Morningstar, M. E., & Liss, J. M. (2008). A preliminary investigation of how states are responding to the transition assessment requirements under IDEIA 2004. *Career Development and Transition for Exceptional Individuals, 31*(1), 48–55. doi:10.1177/0885728807313776

Morrison, K. A., Robbins, H. H., & Rose, D. G. (2008). Operationalizing culturally relevant pedagogy: A synthesis of classroom-based research. *Equity & Excellence in Education, 41*(4), 433–452. doi:10.1080/10665680802400006

Mortier, K. (2020). Communities of practice: A conceptual framework for inclusion of students with significant disabilities. *International Journal of Inclusive Education, 24*(3), 329–340. https://doi.org/10.1080/13603116.2018.1461261

Mueller, T. G., Massafra, A., Robinson, J., & Peterson, L. (2019). Simulated Individualized Education Program meetings: Valuable pedagogy within a preservice special educator program. *Teacher Education and Special Education, 42*(3), 209–226. doi:10.1177/0888406418788920

Mukeredzi, T. G. (2014). Re-envisioning teaching practice: Student teacher learning in a cohort model of practicum in a rural South African context. *International Journal of Educational Development, 39*, 100–109.

Mullen, E. M. (1995). *Mullen Scales of Early Learning*. American Guidance Service.

Mullen, R., & Schooling, T. (2010). The National outcomes measurement system for pediatric speech-language pathology. *Language, Speech, and Hearing Services in Schools, 41*(1), 44–60. doi:10.1044/0161-1461(2009/08-0051) PMID:19833827

Multitiered System of Supports for English Learners. (2020). *Meeting the needs of English learners with and without disabilities: Brief 2, Evidence-based Tier 2 intervention practices for English learners*. Washington, DC: U.S. Office of Special Education Programs. Retrieved from https://www.mtss4els.org/files/resource-files/Series2-Brief2_Final.pdf

Murphy, K. M. (2019). Working with Avatars and High Schoolers to Teach Qualitative Methods to Undergraduates. *LEARNing Landscapes*, *12*, 183–203. https://doi.org/10.36510/learnland.v12i1.987

Murphy, K. M., Cash, J., & Kellinger, J. J. (2018). Learning with avatars: Exploring mixed reality simulations for next-generation teaching and learning. In *Handbook of Research on Pedagogical Models for Next-Generation Teaching and Learning* (pp. 1–20). IGI Global.

NAEP. (2019). *The nation's report card: NAEP data explorer*. Retrieved from https://nces.ed.gov/nationsreportcard/data/

Nancarrow, S. A., Booth, A., Ariss, S., Smith, T., Enderby, P., & Roots, A. (2013). Ten principles of good interdisciplinary team work. *Human Resources for Health*, *11*(19), 1–11. doi:10.1186/1478-4491-11-19 PMID:23663329

National Assessment of Educational Progress (2017). *State performance compared to the nation*. State Profiles. nationsreportcard.gov

National Assessment of Educational Progress. (2019). *State performance compared to the nation*. [Data set]. https://www.nationsreportcard.gov/profiles/stateprofile?chort=1&sub=RED&sj=AL&sfj=NP&st=MN&year=2019R3

National Association for College Admission Counseling. (2018). *State-by-state student-to-counselor ratio report*. https://www.nacacnet.org/news--publications/Research/state-by-state-student-to-counselor-ratio-report2/

National Association for the Education of Young Children. (2019). *Advancing equity in early childhood education A position statement of the National Association of the Education of Young Children*. https://www.naeyc.org/resources/position-statements/equity

National Association for the Education of Young Children. (2020a). *Developmentally appropriate practice: A position statement of the National Association of the Education of Young Children*. https://www.naeyc.org/sites/default/files/globally-shared/downloads/PDFs/resources/position-statements/dap-statement_0.pdf

National Association for the Education of Young Children. (2020b). *Professional standards and competencies*. https://www.naeyc.org/sites/default/files/globally-shared/downloads/PDFs/resources/position-statements/standards_and_competencies_ps.pdf

National Association of School Psychologists (NASP). (2020). *Model for comprehensive and integrated school psychological services, 2020*. Retrieved from https://www.nasponline.org/standards-and-certification

National Association of School Psychologists. (2010b). *Standards for graduate preparation of school psychologists*. Author.

National Association of School Psychologists. (2011). *Ratio of students per school psychologist by state: Data from the 2009-2010 and 2004-2005 NASP membership surveys*. Author.

National Association of School Psychologists. (2020). *Model for comprehensive and integrated school psychological services*. Author.

National Association of School Psychologists. (2020). *Model for comprehensive and integrated school psychological services*. Retrieved from https://www.nasponline.org/standards-and-certification/nasp-practice-model

National Association of School Psychologists. (2020). *The Professional Standards of the National Association of School Psychologists*. Author.

National Association of School Psychologists. (2020). *The professional standards of the national association of school psychologists.* https://www.nasponline. org/x55315.xml

National Association of School Psychologists. (2021). Shortages in school psychology: Challenges in meeting the growing needs of U.S. students and schools (Research Summary). Author.

National Association of School Psychologists. (2021). *Shortages in school psychology: Challenges to meeting the growing needs of U.S. students and schools.* https://www.nasponline.org/resources-and-publications/resources-and-podcasts/school-psychology/shortages-in-school-psych ology-resource-guide

National Association of School Psychologists. (2021, April). *Student to school psychologist ratio 2019–2020* [infographic]. https://www.nasponline.org/research-and-policy/policy-priori ties/critical-policyissues/shortage-of-school-psychologists

National Association of School Psychologists. (2022, July 19). *NASP 2020 Domains of Practice.* https://www.nasponline.org/standards-and-certification/nasp-2020-professional-standards-adopted/nasp-2020-domains-of-pra ctice

National Association of School Workers. (2012). *NASW Standards for School Social Work Services.* https://www.socialworkers.org/LinkClick.aspx?fileticket=1Ze4 -9-Os7E%3D&portalid=0

National Association of Social Work. (2012). *Standards and indicators for school social work services.* https://www.socialworkers.org/LinkClick.aspx?fileticket=5qpx 4B6Csr0%3d&portaid=0

National Association of Social Work. (2015). *Standards and indicators for cultural competence.* https://www.socialworkers.org/LinkClick.aspx?fileticket=7dVc kZAYUmk%3d&portali=0

National Board for Professional Teaching Standards. (2022). *ATLAS: Accomplished Teaching, Learning, and Schools.* National Board for Professional Teaching Standards. https://www.nbpts.org/support/atlas/

National Center for Children in Poverty. (2019). *Children's mental health: What every policymaker should know.* NCCP. http://www.nccp.org/publications/pub_929.html

National Center for Education Statistics, Institute of Education Services. (2022). *Characteristics of public-school teachers who completed alternative route to certification programs.* Institute of Education Services. https://nces.ed.gov/programs/coe/indicator/tlc

National Center for Education Statistics. (2019). *National Assessment of Educational Progress: An overview of NAEP.* National Center for Education Statistics, Institute of Education Sciences, U.S. Department of Education.

National Center for Education Statistics. (2020). *Race and ethnicity of public school teachers and their students.* U.S. Department of Education, Institute of Education Sciences. Retrieved from: https://nces.ed.gov/pubs2020/2020103/index.asp

National Center for Education Statistics. (2021). *English learners in public schools.* Retrieved from https://nces.ed.gov/programs/coe/indicator/cgf/english-learn ers

National Center for Education Statistics. (2021). Findings and conclusions: National standards project, phase 2. *Digest of Education Statistics.* https://nces.ed.gov/programs/digest/d21/tables/dt21_204.30.asp

National Center for Education Statistics. (2022). Students With Disabilities Condition of Education. *U.S. Department of Education, Institute of Education Sciences.* https://nces.ed.gov/programs/coe/indicator/cgg

National Center for Education Statistics. (2022). Students With Disabilities. *Condition of Education.* U.S. Department of Education, Institute of Education Sciences. *NCES.* https://nces.ed.gov/programs/coe/indicator/cgg

National Center for Education Statistics. (2022). *Students With Disabilities. Condition of Education.* U.S. Department of Education, Institute of Education Sciences. Retrieved from https://nces.ed.gov/programs/coe/indicator/cgg

National Center for Education Statistics. (2022). *Students With Disabilities. Condition of Education.* U.S. Department of Education, Institute of Education Sciences. Retrieved October 17, 2022, from https://nces.ed.gov/programs/coe/indicator/cgg

National Center for Education Statistics. (2022). Students with disabilities. *NCES.* https://nces.ed.gov/fastfacts/display.asp?id=64

National Center for Education Statistics. (2022, May). Characteristics of public school teachers. *Condition of Education.* U.S. Department of Education, Institute of Education Sciences. *NCES.* https://nces.ed.gov/programs/coe/pdf/2021/clr_508c.pdf

National Center for Education Statistics. (2022a). *English Learners in Public Schools. Condition of Education.* U.S. Department of Education, Institute of Education Sciences. https://nces.ed.gov/programs/coe/indicator/cgf

National Center for Education Statistics. (2022b). *Students with Disabilities. Condition of Education.* U.S. Department of Education, Institute of Education Sciences. https://nces.ed.gov/programs/coe/indicator/cgg

National Center for Educational Research. (2017). Characteristics of public and private elementary and secondary school teachers in the United States: Results from the 2011–12 schools and staffing survey. *NCES 2013-314.* https://nces.ed.gov/

National Center for Learning Disabilities. (2020). Significant disproportionality in special education: Current trends and actions for impact. *NCLD.* https://www.ncld.org/sigdispro/

National Center on Birth Defects and Developmental Disabilities, Centers for Disease Control and Prevention. (2018). *Data and statistics on autism spectrum disorder.* Centers for Disease Control and Prevention. https://www.cdc.gov/ncbddd/autism/data.html

National Center on Intensive Intervention. (2016). *Principles for designing intervention in mathematics.* Washington, DC: Office of Special Education, U.S. Department of Education. Retrieved from https://intensiveintervention.org/sites/default/files/Princip_Effect_Math_508.pdf

National Clearinghouse for English Language Acquisition. (2011). *What legal obligation do schools have to English Language Learners?* https://ncela.ed.gov/faqs/view/6

National Council on Disabilities. (2018). *English learners and students from low income families.* Retrieved from https://ncd.gov/sites/default/files/NCD_EnglishLanguageLearners_508.pdf

National Council on Disability. (2008). *Youth with disabilities in the foster care system: Barriers to success and proposed policy solutions.* https://ncd.gov/publications/2008/02262008#_edn8

National Education Association. (2019). *Special education.* https://ra.nea.org/search/special+education/

National Institute of Mental Health. (2017). *Transforming the understanding and treatment of mental illnesses.* NIMH. https://www.nimh.nih.gov/health/statistics/mental-illness.shtml

National Parent Center on Transition and Employment (2022). Person-Centered Planning. *Pacer.* https://www.pacer.org/transition/learning-center/independent-community-living/person-centered.asp.

National Professional Development Center on Inclusion. (2011). *Research synthesis points on practices that support inclusion.* The University of North Carolina, FPG Child Development Institute. https://npdci.fpg.unc.edu/sites/npdci.fpg.unc.edu/files/resources/NPDCI-ResearchSynthesisPointsInclusivePractices-2011_0.pdf

National Professional Development Center on Inclusion. (2012). [Data set]. NPDCI. https://fpg.unc.edu/projects/national-professional-development-center-inclusion

National Research Council. (2001). *Eager to learn: Educating our preschoolers.* National Academies Press.

National Resource Council. (2001). *Educating children with autism.* National Academy Press.

National Scientific Council on the Developing Child. (2004). *Children's emotional development is built into the architecture of their brains* (Working Paper No. 2). https://46y5eh11fhgw3ve3ytpwxt9r-wpengine.netdna-ssl.com/wp-content/uploads/2004/04/Childrens-Emotional-Development-Is-Built-into-the-Architecture-of-Their-Brains.pdf

Neely, L., Rispoli, M., Gerow, S., & Ninci, J. (2014). Effects of antecedent exercise on academic engagement and stereotypy during instruction. *Behavior Modification, 39*(1), 98–116. doi:10.1177/0145445514552891 PMID:25271070

Neeper, L. S., & Dymond, S. K. (2020). Incorporating service-learning in special education coursework: Experiences of university faculty. *Teacher Education and Special Education, 43*(4), 343–357. doi:10.1177/0888406420912373

Neitzel, J. (2018). Research to practice: Understanding the role of implicit bias in early childhood disciplinary practices. *Journal of Early Childhood Teacher Education, 39,* 232–242.

Nelson, C. A., Scott, R. D., Bhutta, Z. A., Harris, N. B., Danese, A., & Samara, M. (2020). Adversity in childhood is linked to mental and physical health throughout life. *BMJ (Clinical Research Ed.), 371,* m3048. doi:10.1136/bmj.m3048 PMID:33115717

Nevison, C., & Zahorodny, W. (2019). Race/ethnicity-resolved time trends in United States ASD prevalence estimates from IDEA and ADDM. *Journal of Autism and Developmental Disorders, 49*(12), 4721–4730. doi:10.100710803-019-04188-6 PMID:31435818

New York State Education Department. (2006). Syllabus (outline) and application for approval as a provider of training or course work in the needs of children with autism. *NYSED.* https://www.highered.nysed.gov/ocue/documents/appsyllabus.pdf

New York State Interagency Task Force on Autism. (2010). New York state interagency task force on autism. *NYSED.* http://www.opwdd.ny.gov/opwdd_community_connections/autism_platform/interagency_task_force_on_autism

Newman, L., Wagner, M., Huang, T., Shaver, D., Knokey, A. M., Yu, J., Contreras, E., Ferguson, K., Greene, S., Nagle, K., & Cameto, R. (2011). *Secondary School Programs and Performance of Students with Disabilities. A Special Topic Report of Findings from the National Longitudinal Transition Study-2 (NLTS2)* (NCSER 2012-3000). U.S. Department of Education. Available at: www.nlts2.org/reports/2011_11/nlts2_report_2011_11_rev30113_complete.pdf

Newman, L., Wagner, M., Knokey, A., Marder, C., Nagle, K. M., Shaver, D., & Wei, X. (2011). *The post-high school outcomes of young adults with disabilities up to 8 years after high school a report from the national longitudinal transition study-2 (NLTS2)*. United States Department of Education. doi:10.13140/RG.2.2.20600.57600

Nickerson, A. B., Cook, E. E., Cruz, M. A., & Parks, T. W. (2019). Transfer of school crisis prevention and intervention training, knowledge, and skills: Training, trainee, and work environment predictors. *School Psychology Review*, *48*(3), 237–250. doi:10.17105/SPR-2017-0140.V48-3

Noell, G. H., & Gansle, K. A. (2016). Assuring the response to intervention process has substance: Assessing and supporting intervention implementation. In *Handbook of Response to Intervention* (pp. 407–420). Springer. doi:10.1007/978-1-4899-7568-3_24

Noell, G. H., Gansle, K. A., Mevers, J. L., Knox, R. M., Mintz, J. C., & Dahir, A. (2014). Improving treatment plan implementation in schools: A meta-analysis of single subject design studies. *Journal of Behavioral Education*, *23*(1), 168–191. doi:10.100710864-013-9177-1

Noffke, S. E. (1997). Professional, personal, and political dimensions of action research. *Review of Research in Education*, *22*(1), 305–343. doi:10.3102/0091732X022001305

Nolet, V., & McLaughlin, M. (2005). *Accessing the general curriculum: Including students with disabilities in standards-based reform* (2nd ed.). Corwin Press. doi:10.4135/9781483329253

Noonan, M. J., & McCormick, L. (2014). *Teaching Young Children with Disabilities in Natural Environments* (2nd ed.). Brookes Publishing Co., Inc.

Nooteboom, L.A., Mulder, E.A., Vermeiren, R.R. JM, Eilander, J., van den Driesschen

Normand, M. P., & Donohue, H. E. (2022). Behavior analytic jargon does not seem to influence treatment acceptability ratings. *Journal of Applied Behavior Analysis*, *55*(4), 1294–1305. doi:10.1002/jaba.953 PMID:36131368

Nunez, L. (2015). Achieving Quality and Improved Outcomes Through Interprofessional Collaboration. *ASHA Leader Live*. Retrieved from https://leader.pubs.asha.org/do/10.1044/2021-0902-interprofessional-collaboration-outcomes?utm_source=TrendMD&utm_medium=cpc&utm_campaign=The_ASHA_Leader_TrendMD_0

O'Grady, C., & Ostrosky, M. M. (2021). Suspension and Expulsion: Early Educators' Perspectives. *Early Childhood Education Journal*, 1–11.

O'Keefe, M. J., & McDowell, M. (2004). Bridging the gap between health and education: Wordsare not enough. *Journal of Paediatrics and Child Health*, *40*(5-6), 252–257. doi:10.1111/j.1440-1754.2004.00359.x PMID:15151577

O'Keeffe, P. (2013). A sense of belonging: Improving student retention. *College Student Journal*, *47*(4), 605–613.

O'Neill, T., Light, J., & Pope, L. (2018). Effects of interventions that include aided augmentative and alternative communication input on the communication of individuals with complex communication needs: A meta-analysis. *Journal of Speech, Language, and Hearing Research: JSLHR*, *61*(7), 1743–1765. doi:10.1044/2018_JSLHR-L-17-0132 PMID:29931287

Odom, S. L., Vitztum, J., Wolery, R., Lieber, J., Sandall, S., Hanson, M. J., ... Horn, E. (2004). Preschool inclusion in the United States: A review of research from an ecological systems perspective. *Journal of Research in Special Educational Needs*, *4*(1), 17–49. doi:10.1111/J.1471-3802.2004.00016.x

Odom, S. L., & Wolery, M. (2003). A unified theory of practice in early intervention/early childhood special education: Evidence-based practices. *The Journal of Special Education*, *37*(3), 164–173. doi:10.1177/00224669030370030601

Oertle, K. M., & Seader, K. J. (2015). Research and practical considerations for rehabilitation transition collaboration. *Journal of Rehabilitation*, *81*, 3–18.

Oertle, K. M., & Trach, J. S. (2007). Interagency collaboration: The importance of rehabilitation professionals' involvement in transition. *Journal of Rehabilitation*, *73*(3), 36–44.

Ofe, E. E., Plumb, A. M., Plexico, L. W., & Haak, N. J. (2016). School-based speech-language pathologists' knowledge and perceptions of autism spectrum disorder and bullying. *Language, Speech, and Hearing Services in Schools*, *47*(1), 59–76. doi:10.1044/2015_LSHSS-15-0058 PMID:26812936

Office for Civil Rights. (2021). Education in a pandemic: The disparate impact of COVID-19 on America's students. https://www2.ed.gov/about/offices/list/ocr/docs/20210608-impacts-of-covid19.pdf

Office of Special Education and Rehabilitative Services. (2018). *40th Annual Report to Congress on the Implementation of the Individuals with Disabilities Education Act*. Author.

Office of Special Education Programs. (2020). Fast facts: Children identified with autism. *OSEP*. https://sites.ed.gov/idea/osep-fast-facts-children-with-autism-20/

Office of Special Education Programs. (n.d.) Personnel Preparation Program Description. *U.S. Department of Education*. https://www2.ed.gov/print/programs/osepprep/index.html

Office of the Surgeon General (OSG). (2021). *Protecting youth mental health: The U.S. surgeon general's advisory*. https://pubmed.ncbi.nlm.nih.gov/34982518/

Office of the Surgeon General. (2021). *Protecting Youth Mental Health: The US Surgeon General's Advisory*. https://www.hhs.gov/sites/default/files/surgeon-general-youth-mental-health-advisory.pdf

Ogden, L., Mcallister, C., & Neely-Barnes, S. (2017). Assessment of integration of disability content into social work education. *Journal of Social Work in Disability & Rehabilitation*, *16*(3-4), 361–376. doi:10.1080/1536710X.2017.1392394 PMID:29111955

Ogletree, B. T. (2017). Addressing the communication and other needs of persons with severe disabilities through engaged interprofessional teams: Introduction to a clinical forum. *American Journal of Speech-Language Pathology*, *26*(2), 157–161. doi:10.1044/2017_AJSLP-15-0064 PMID:28514471

Ogletree, B. T. (2017). Meaningful moves toward independence. *ASHA Leader*, *22*(2). doi:10.1044/leader.OV.22022017.np

Okahana, H., & Zhou, E. (2017). *Graduate enrollment and degrees: 2006 to 2016*. Council of Graduate Schools.

Okely, A. D., Booth, M. L., & Patterson, J. W. (2001). Relationship of physical activity to fundamental movement skills among adolescents. *Medicine and Science in Sports and Exercise*, *33*(11), 1899–1904. doi:10.1097/00005768-200111000-00015 PMID:11689741

Olson, A. J., & Roberts, C. A. (2020). Navigating barriers as special education teacher educators. *Research and Practice for Persons with Severe Disabilities*, *45*(3), 161–177. https://doi.org/10.1177/1540796920914969

Orange County Public Schools. (2022). *Student enrollment summaries*. https://www.ocps.net/departments/student_enrollment/enrollment_summary)

Orchard, C. A., King, G. A., Khalili, H., & Bezzina, M. B. (2012). Assessment of Interprofessional Team Collaboration Scale (AITCS): Development and testing of the instrument. *The Journal of Continuing Education in the Health Professions*, *32*(1), 58–67. doi:10.1002/chp.21123 PMID:22447712

Oriel, K. N., George, C. L., Peckus, R., & Semon, A. (2011). The effects of aerobic exercise on academic engagement in young children with autism spectrum disorder. *Pediatric Physical Therapy*, *23*(2), 187–193. doi:10.1097/PEP.0b013e318218f149 PMID:21552085

Orlando, A., & Ruppar, A. (2016). *Literacy instruction for students with multiple and severe disabilities who use augmentative/alternative communication* (Document No. IC-16). University of Florida, Collaboration for Effective Educator, Development, Accountability, and Reform Center. https://ceedar.education.ufl.edu/tools/innovation-configurations/

Ortiz, A. A., & Robertson, P. M. (2018). Preparing teachers to serve English learners with language-and/or literacy-related difficulties and disabilities. *Teacher Education and Special Education*, *41*(3), 176–187. doi:10.1177/0888406418757035

Ortiz, S. O. (2019). On the measurement of cognitive abilities in English learners. *Contemporary School Psychology*, *23*(1), 68–86. doi:10.100740688-018-0208-8

OSEP. (2019). *OSEP Fast Facts: Hispanic and/or Latino Children with Disabilities*. Retrieved from https://sites.ed.gov/idea/osep-fast-facts-hispanic-latino-children-disabilities-20/

Osler, J. (2016). Beyond brochures: Practicing "soul care" in the recruitment of teachers of color. *San Francisco: San Francisco Teacher Residency*. http://www.wcstonefnd.org/wp-content/uploads/2016/12/SFTR-SoulCare-Final1.pdf

Osofsky, J. D., & Liebrmam, A. F. (2011). A call for integrating a mental health perspective into systems of care for abused and neglected infants and young children. *The American Psychologist*, *66*(2), 120–128.

Osterholt, D. A., & Barratt, K. (2011). A case for a collaborative classroom. *About Campus: Enriching the Student Learning Experience*, *16*(2), 20–26. doi:10.1002/abc.20057

Østvik, J., Ytterhus, B., & Balandin, S. (2017). Friendship between children using augmentative and alternative communication and peers: A systematic literature review. *Journal of Intellectual & Developmental Disability*, *42*(4), 403–415. doi:10.3109/13668250.2016.1247949

Ouellette, R. R., Pellecchia, M., Beidas, R. S., Wideman, R., Xie, M., & Mandell, D. S. (2019). Boon or Burden: The effect of implementing evidence-based practices on teachers' emotional exhaustion. *Administration and Policy in Mental Health*, *46*(1), 62–70. doi:10.100710488-018-0894-6 PMID:30225662

Pakenham, K. I. (2015). Training in acceptance and commitment therapy fosters self-care in clinical psychology trainees. *Clinical Psychologist*, *21*(3), 186–194. doi:10.1111/cp.12062

*Compilation of References*

Parette, H. P., Jr., Crowley, E. P., & Wojcik, B. W. (2007). Reducing overload in students with learning and behavioral disorders: The role of assistive technology. *Teaching Exceptional Children Plus, 4*(1). https://files.eric.ed.gov/ fulltext/EJ967467.pdf

Paris, D. (2012). Culturally sustaining pedagogy: A needed change in stance, terminology, and practice. *Educational Researcher*, *41*(3), 93–97. doi:10.3102/0013189X12441244

Paris, D., & Alim, H. S. (Eds.). (2017). *Culturally sustaining pedagogies: Teaching and learning for justice in a changing world*. Teachers College Press.

Paris, D., & Alim, S. (2014). What are we seeking to sustain through culturally sustaining pedagogy? A loving critique forward. *Harvard Educational Review*, *84*(1), 85–100. doi:10.17763/haer.84.1.982l873k2ht16m77

Park, E.-Y., & Shin, M. (2020). A meta-analysis of special education teachers' burnout. *SAGE Open*, *10*(2). Advance online publication. doi:10.1177/2158244020918297

Patrick, C. A., Ward, P., & Crouch, D. W. (1998). Effects of holding students accountable for social behaviors during volleyball games in elementary physical education. *Journal of Teaching in Physical Education*, *17*(2), 143–156. doi:10.1123/jtpe.17.2.143

Patti, A. L., & McLeskey, J. (2019). The role of high-leverage practices in Special Education Teacher Preparation. *Teacher Education Division of the Council for Exceptional Children*. https://tedcec.org/wp-content/uploads/2019/11/TED-Brief-1-HLPs-PDF.pdf

Patton, M. Q. (2008). *Utilization-focused evaluation* (4th ed.). Sage.

Payne, R. K. (2005). A framework for understanding poverty (4th ed.). aha! Process.

Pelham, W. E. Jr, & Hoza, B. (1996). Intensive treatment: A summer treatment program for children with ADHD. In E. D. Hibbs & P. S. Jensen (Eds.), *Psychosocial treatments for child and adolescent disorders: Empirically based strategies for clinical practice* (pp. 311–340). American Psychological Association. doi:10.1037/10196-013

Pelletier, K., McCormack, M., Reeves, J., Robert, J., Arbino, N., Al-Freih, M., Dickson-Deane, C., Guevara, C., Koster, L., Sanchez-Mendiola, M., Skallerup Bessette, L., & Stine, J. (2022). *2022 EDUCAUSE horizon report teaching and learning edition.* https://www.learntechlib.org/p/221033/

Pennington, R. (2022). Applied behavior analysis: A valuable partner in special education. *Teaching Exceptional Children*, *54*(4), 315–317. doi:10.1177/00400599221079130

Pentimonti, J. M., Justice, L. M., Yeomans-Maldonado, G., McGinty, A. S., Slocum, L., & O'Connell, A. (2017). Teachers' use of high-and low-support scaffolding strategies to differentiate language instruction in high-risk/economically disadvantaged settings. *Journal of Early Intervention*, *39*(2), 125–146. doi:10.1177/1053815117700865

Pershey, M. G., & Rapking, C. I. (2003). A survey of collaborative speech-language service delivery under large caseload conditions in an urban school district in the United States. *Journal of Speech-Language Pathology and Audiology*, *27*, 211–220.

Personnel Improvement Center. (2011). *Practice brief summer 2011*. Retrieved from http://personnelcenter.org/documents/Special%20Education-Related%20Personnel%20Preparation%20Partnerships-HEADINGS.pdf

Peterson, S., & Neef, N. (2020). Functional behavioral assessment. In J. O. Cooper, T. E. Heron, & W. L. Heward, Applied behavior analysis (3rd Ed.) (pp. 628-654). Pearson.

Peterson-Ahmad, M. (2018). Enhancing preservice special educator preparation through combined use of virtual simulation and instructional coaching. *Education Sciences*, *8*(1), 10. doi:10.3390/educsci8010010

Peters-Scheffer, N., Didden, R., Korzilius, H., & Sturmey, P. (2011). A meta-analytic study on the effectiveness of comprehensive ABA-based early intervention programs for children with autism spectrum disorders. *Research in Autism Spectrum Disorders*, *5*(1), 60–69. doi:10.1016/j.rasd.2010.03.011

Petri, L. (2010). Concept analysis of interdisciplinary collaboration. *Nursing Forum*, *45*(2), 73–82. doi:10.1111/j.1744-6198.2010.00167.x PMID:20536755

Petrus, C., Adamson, S. R., Block, L., Einarson, S. J., Sharifnejad, M., & Harris, S. R. (2008). Effects of exercise interventions on stereotypic behaviours in children with autism spectrum disorder. *Physiotherapy Canada. Physiotherapie Canada*, *60*(2), 134–145. doi:10.3138/physio.60.2.134 PMID:20145777

Pew Research Center. (2021). *Social Media Fact Sheet*. Retrieved from: https://www.pewresearch.org/internet/fact-sheet/social-media/?menuItem=2fc5fff9-9899-4317-b786-9e0b60934bcf

Pfeiffer, D. L., Pavelko, S. L., Hahs-Vaughn, D. L., & Dudding, C. C. (2019). A national survey of speech-language pathologists' engagement in interprofessional collaborative practice in schools: Identifying predictive factors and barriers to implementation. *Language, Speech, and Hearing Services in Schools*, *50*(4), 639–655.

Pfeiffer, D. L., Pavelko, S. L., Hahs-Vaughn, D. L., & Duddinge, C. C. (2019). A national survey of Speech-Language Pathologists' engagement in interprofessional collaborative practice in schools: Identifying predictive factors and barriers to implementation. *Language, Speech, and Hearing Services in Schools*, *50*(4), 639–655. doi:10.1044/2019_LSHSS-18-0100 PMID:31411947

Pham, A. V., Lazarus, P., Costa, A., Dong, Q., & Bastian, R. (2021). Incorporating social justice advocacy and interdisciplinary collaborative training in the recruitment and retention of diverse graduate students. *Contemporary School Psychology*, *25*(3), 344–357. doi:10.100740688-020-00322-9

Phoenix, M., Dix, L., DeCola, C., Eisen, I., & Campbell, W. (2020). Health professional-educator collaboration in the delivery of school-based tiered support services: A qualitative case study. *Child: Care, Health and Development*, *47*(3), 367–376. doi:10.1111/cch.12849 PMID:33432659

Plantiveau, C., Dounavi, K., & Virues-Ortega, J. (2018). High levels of burnout among early-career board-certified behavior analysts with low collegial support in the work environment. *European Journal of Behavior Analysis*, *19*(2), 195–207. doi:10.1080/15021149.2018.1438339

Plavnick, J. B., Fleury, V. P., & Schiltz, T. R. (2015). Evidence-based practices for children, youth, and young adults with autism spectrum disorder: A comprehensive review. *Journal of Autism and Developmental Disorders*, *45*(7), 1951–1966. doi:10.100710803-014-2351-z PMID:25578338

Plotner, A. J., & Fleming, A. R. (2014). Secondary transition personnel preparation in rehabilitation counselor education programs. *Rehabilitation Research, Policy, and Education*, *28*(1), 33–44. Advance online publication. doi:10.1891/2168-6653.28.1.33

Plotner, A. J., Mazzotti, V. L., Rose, C. A., & Carlson-Britting, K. B. (2016). Factors associated with enhanced knowledge and use of secondary transition evidence-based practices. *Teacher Education and Special Education*, *39*(1), 28–46. doi:10.1177/0888406415599430

Plotner, A. J., Mazzotti, V. L., Rose, C. A., & Teasley, K. (2020). Perceptions of Interagency Collaboration: Relationships Between Secondary Transition Roles, Communication, and Collaboration. *Remedial and Special Education*, *41*(1), 28–39.

Plotner, A. J., & Simonsen, M. L. (2018). Examining federally funded secondary transition personnel preparation programs. *Career Development and Transition for Exceptional Individuals*, *41*(1), 39–49. doi:10.1177/2165143417742138

Plotner, A. J., Trach, J. S., & Shogren, K. A. (2012). Identifying a transition competency domain structure: Assisting transition planning teams to understand roles and responsibilities of community partners. *Journal of Rehabilitation Research, Policy, and Education*, *26*, 257–272.

Plowman, S. A., & Meredith, M. D. (2017). *FitnessGram/ActivityGram reference guide* (5th ed.). The Cooper Institute.

Podolsky, A., Kini, T., Darling-Hammond, L., & Bishop, J. (2019). Strategies for attracting and retaining educators: What does the evidence say? *Education Policy Analysis Archives*, *27*(38), 1–47. doi:10.14507/epaa.27.3722

Powell, C., Scott, L. A., Oyefuga, E., Dayton, M., Pickover, G., & Hicks, M. (2022). COVID-19 and the special education teacher workforce. *COVID-19 and the Classroom: How Schools Navigated the Great Disruption*, 263.

Powell, S. R., & Stecker, P. M. (2014). Using data-based individualization to intensify mathematics intervention for students with disabilities. *Teaching Exceptional Children*, *46*(4), 31–37. doi:10.1177/0040059914523735

Powers, L. S. (1965). Interprofessional education and medicolegal conflict as seen from the other side. *Journal of Medical Education*, *40*, 233–244. PMID:14254289

Prasse, D. P., & Fafard, M. B. (1982). Interdisciplinary training and professional interaction: A training challenge. *Teacher Education and Special Education*, *5*(1), 26–29. doi:10.1177/088840648200500105

Pratt, S. M., Imbody, S. M., Wolf, L. D., & Patterson, A. L. (2017). Co-planning in co-teaching: A practical solution. *Intervention in School and Clinic*, *32*(4), 243–249. doi:10.1177/1053451216659474

Pretti-Frontczak, K., & Bricker, D. (2004). *An activity-based approach to early intervention* (3rd ed.). Brookes Publishing.

Proctor, S. L., Simpson, C. M., Levin, J., & Hackimer, L. (2014). Recruitment of diverse students in school psychology programs: Direction for future research and practice. *Contemporary School Psychology*, *18*(2), 117–126. doi:10.100740688-014-0012-z

Professional Education Licensing and Standards Board [PELSB] (2020). *Rules relating to teacher preparation program and unit approval 8705.0100*. PELSB. https://mn.gov/pelsb/board/rulemaking/program-unit-rules/

Project Core. (n.d.). Universal core communication systems. *Project Core*. https://www.project-core.com/communication-systems

Project ELITE2, Project ELLIPSES, & Project LEE. (2018). *Meeting the needs of English learners with and without disabilities: Brief 1, Multitiered instructional systems for ELs*. U.S. Office of Special Education Programs. Retrieved from https://www.mtss4els.org/files/resource-files/Series2-Brief1_Final.pdf

Project Speech. (2022). *Speech-language pathologists and exceptional educators collaborating for children with high-intensity needs*. https://healthprofessions.ucf.edu/communication-sciences-disorders/project-speech/

Prothero, A. (2022). School counselors and psychologists remain scarce even as needs rise. *Education Week*, *41*(24).

Pugach, M. C. (1992). Unifying the preservice preparation of teachers. In W. Stainback & S. Stainback (Eds.), *Controversial issues confronting special education: Divergent Perspectives* (pp. 255–270). Allyn and Bacon.

Pugach, M. C., & Allen-Meares, P. (1985). Collaboration at the preservice level: Instructional and evaluation activities. *Teacher Education and Special Education*, *8*(1), 3–11. doi:10.1177/088840648500800101

Quattrin, T., Liu, E., Shaw, N., Shine, B., & Chiang, E. (2005). Obese children who are referred to the pediatric endocrinologist: Characteristics and outcome. *Pediatrics*, *115*(2), 348–351. doi:10.1542/peds.2004-1452 PMID:15687443

Racine, N., McArthur, B. A., Cooke, J. E., Eirich, R., Zhu, J., & Madigan, S. (2021). Global prevalence of depressive and anxiety symptoms in children and adolescents during COVID-19: A meta-analysis. *JAMA Pediatrics*, *175*(11), 1142–1150. doi:10.1001/jamapediatrics.2021.2482 PMID:34369987

Rafferty, Y., Piscitelli, V., & Boettcher, C. (2003). The impact of inclusion on language development and social competence among preschoolers with disabilities. *Exceptional Children*, *69*(4), 467–479. doi:10.1177/001440290306900405

Rahman, R., Herbst, K., & Mobley, P. (2016). *More than simply "doing good": A definition of changemaker*. Ashoka Changemaker Learning Lab. http://changemakers.com/learning-lab

Randall, D. L., & West, R. E. (2020). Who cares about open badges? An examination of principals' perceptions of the usefulness of teacher open badges in the United States. *Open Learning*, 1–19. doi:10.1080/02680513.2020.1752166

Raspa, M., Hebbeler, K., Bailey, D. B. Jr, & Scarborough, A. A. (2010). Service provider combinations and the delivery of early intervention services to children and families. *Infants and Young Children*, *23*(2), 132–144. doi:10.1097/IYC.0b013e3181d230f9

Ratcliff, A., Koul, R., & Lloyd, L. L. (2008). Preparation in augmentative and alternative communication: An update for speech-language pathology training. *American Journal of Speech-Language Pathology*, *17*(1), 48–59. doi:10.1044/1058-0360(2008/005) PMID:18230813

Redding, C. (2019). A teacher like me: A review of the effect of student–teacher racial/ethnic matching on teacher perceptions of students and student academic and behavioral outcomes. *Review of Educational Research*, *89*(4), 499–535. doi:10.3102/0034654319853545

Redmond, S. M. (2011). Peer victimization among students with specific language impairment, attention-deficit/hyperactivity disorder, and typical development. *Language, Speech, and Hearing Services in Schools*, *42*(4), 520–535. doi:10.1044/0161-1461(2011/10-0078) PMID:21844400

Reed, E. (2012). Education of low income children in US. In J. E. Banks (Ed.), *Encyclopedia of Diversity in Education*. Sage.

Reeves, S., Goldman, J., Gilbert, J., Tepper, J., Silver, I., Suter, E., & Zwarenstein, M. (2011). A scoping review to improve conceptual clarity of interdisciplinary intervention. *Journal of Interdisciplinary Care*, *25*(3), 167–174. doi:10.3109/13561820.2010.529960 PMID:21182439

Regan, K., & Page, P. (2008). "Character" building: Using literature to connect with youth. *Reclaiming Youth and Children: The Journal of Strength-Based Interventions*, *16*, 37–43.

Repko, A. (2011). *Interdisciplinary research: Process and theory* (2nd ed.). Sage Publications.

Riazi, A. M., & Candlin, C. N. (2014). Mixed-methods research in language teaching and learning: Opportunities, issues, and challenges. *Language Teaching*, *47*(2), 135–173. doi:10.1017/S0261444813000505

Richard, A., Gagnon, M., & Careau, E. (2019). Using reflective practice in interprofessional education and practice: A realist review of its characteristics and effectiveness. *Journal of Interprofessional Care*, *33*(5), 424–436. doi:10.1080/13561820.2018.1551867 PMID:30513235

Richards, K. A. R., & Wilson, W. J. (2020). Recruitment and initial socialization into adapted physical education teacher education. *European Physical Education Review*, *26*(1), 54–69. doi:10.1177/1356336X18825278

## Compilation of References

Richardson-Gibbs, A. M., & Klein, M. D. (2014). *Making preschool inclusion work*. Brookes Publishing.

Richards-Tutor, C., Barber, B. R., Benedict, A. E., Brownell, M., Martinez-Vargas, L., & Gates, J. (2021). Using high leverage practices to organize practice-based opportunities: Academic and behavioral examples from inclusive educational contexts. In P. Chandler & L. Barron (Eds.), *Rethinking school-university partnerships: A new way forward*. Information Age Publishers.

Richlin, L., & Cox, M. D. (2004). Developing scholarly teaching and the scholarship of teaching and learning through faculty learning communities. *New Directions for Teaching and Learning*, *2004*(97), 127–135. doi:10.1002/tl.139

Rickels, D. A., & Brewer, W. D. (2017). Facebook band director's group: Member usage behaviors and perceived satisfaction for meeting professional development needs. *Journal of Music Teacher Education*, *26*(3), 77–92. doi:10.1177/1057083717692380

Ricklefs, M. A. (2021b). Variables influencing ESL teacher candidates' language ideologies. *Language and Education*. https://doi.10.1080/09500782.2021.1936546

Ricklefs, M. A. (2022a). "Politics at its finest!": Language management and ideologies affecting the education of minoritized students. *SN Social Sciences, 2*(61). https://doi.org/10.1007/s43545-022-00359-y

Ricklefs, M. A. (2019). Teachers' conceptualizations and expectations of culturally and linguistically diverse young students. *International Journal of Diversity in Education*, *19*(2), 33–44. https://doi.org/10.18848/2327-0020/CGP/v19i02/33-44

Ricklefs, M. A. (2021a). Functions of language use and raciolinguistic ideologies in students' interactions. *Bilingual Research Journal*, *44*(1), 90–107. https://doi:10.1080/15235882.2021.1897048

Ricklefs, M. A. (2022b). "¡Échale ganas!": Latina mothers use their cultural community wealth to enhance their children's education. *International Journal of Cultural Studies*, *17*(2), 63–73. https://doi.org/10.18848/2327-008X/CGP/v17i02/63-73

Rimmer, J. H., Chen, M. D., McCubbin, J. A., Drum, C., & Peterson, J. (2010). Exercise intervention research on persons with disabilities: What we know and where we need to go. *American Journal of Physical Medicine & Rehabilitation*, *89*(3), 249–263. doi:10.1097/PHM.0b013e3181c9fa9d PMID:20068432

Rimmer, J., & Rowland, J. (2008). Physical activity for youth with disabilities: A critical need in an underserved population. *Developmental Neurorehabilitation*, *11*(2), 141–148. doi:10.1080/17518420701688649 PMID:18415819

Rios-Aguilar, C., & Kiyama, J. M. (Eds.). (2018). *Funds of knowledge in higher education: Honoring students' cultural experiences and resources as strength*. Routledge.

Riskiyana, R., Claramita, M., & Rahayu, G. R. (2018). Objectively measured interprofessional education outcome and factors that enhance program effectiveness: A systematic review. *Nurse Education Today*, *66*, 73–78. doi:10.1016/j.nedt.2018.04.014 PMID:29684835

Risko, V. J., & Reid, L. (2019). What really matters for literacy teacher preparation? *The Reading Teacher*, *72*(4), 423–429. doi:10.1002/trtr.1769

Roberts, J., & Styron, R. (2010). Student satisfaction and persistence: Factors vital to student retention. *Research in Higher Education*, *6*(3), 1–18.

Robertson, P. M., García, S. B., McFarland, L. A., & Rieth, H. J. (2012). Preparing culturally and linguistically responsive special educators: It "does" take a village. *Interdisciplinary Journal of Teaching and Learning*, *2*(3), 115–130.

Robertson, P., McCaleb, K. N., & McFarland, L. A. (2022). Preparing all educators to serve students with extensive support needs: An interdisciplinary approach. *New Educator*, *18*(1-2), 87–109. doi:10.1080/1547688X.2022.2055248

Roeser, R. (2002). Bringing a "whole adolescent" perspective to secondary teacher education: A case study of the use of an adolescent case study. *Teaching Education*, *13*(2), 155–178.

Roggman, L. A., Peterson, C. A., Chazan-Cohen, R., Ispa, J., Decker, K. B., Hughes-Belding, K., Cook, G. A., & Wallotton, C. D. (2016). Preparing home visitors to partner with families of infants and toddlers. *Journal of Early Childhood Teacher Education*, *37*, 301–313.

Rolandson, D. M., & Ross-Hekkel, L. E. (2022). Virtual professional learning communities: A case study in rural music teacher professional development. *Journal of Music Teacher Education*, *31*(3), 81–94. doi:10.1177/10570837221077430

Rolider, A., Axelrod, S., & Van Houten, R. (1998). Don't speak behaviorism to me: How to clearly and effectively communicate behavioral interventions to the general public. *Child & Family Behavior Therapy*, *20*(2), 39–56. doi:10.1300/J019v20n02_03

Romski, M., Sevcik, R. A., Barton-Hulsey, A., & Whitmore, A. S. (2015). Early intervention and AAC: What a difference 30 years makes. *Augmentative and Alternative Communication*, *31*(3), 181–202. doi:10.3109/07434618.2015.1064163 PMID:26153901

Roncaglia, I. (2018). Transdisciplinary approaches embedded through PERMA with Autistic individual: A case study. *Psychological Thought*, *11*(2), 224–233. doi:10.5964/psyct.v11i2.306

Ronfeldt, M., Farmer, S. O., McQueen, K., & Grissom, J. A. (2015). Teacher collaboration in instructional teams and student achievement. *American Educational Research Journal*, *52*(3), 475–514. doi:10.3102/0002831215585562

Ronfeldt, M., & McQueen, K. (2017). Does new teacher induction really improve retention? *Journal of Teacher Education*, *68*(4), 394–410. doi:10.1177/0022487117702583

Rosanoff, M. J., Daniels, A. M., & Shih, A. (2015). Autism: A (key) piece of the global mental health puzzle. *Global Mental Health (Cambridge, England)*, *2*, e2. doi:10.1017/gmh.2014.7 PMID:28596851

Rosenberg, A., Margolis, L. H., Umble, K., & Chewning, L. (2015). Fostering intentional interdisciplinary leadership in developmental disabilities: The North Carolina LEND experience. *Maternal and Child Health Journal*, *19*(2), 290–299. doi:10.100710995-014-1618-5 PMID:25366097

Rosenfield, P. L. (1992). The potential of transdisciplinary research for sustaining and extending linkages between the health and social sciences. *Social Science & Medicine*, *35*(11), 1343-1357. doi:10.1016/0277-9536(92)90038-R

Rosen, M., Diazgranados, D., Dietz, A., Benishek, L. E., Thompson, D., Pronovost, P. J., & Weaver, S. J. (2018). Teamwork in healthcare: Key discoveries enabling safer, high-quality care. *The American Psychologist*, *73*(4), 433–450.

Roth, K., Zittel, L., Pyfer, J., & Auxter, D. (2016). *Principles and methods of adapted physical education & recreation*. Jones & Bartlett Learning.

Rothstein, J., & Rouse, C. E. (2011). Constrained after college: Student loans and early-career occupational choices. *Journal of Public Economics*, *91*(1-2), 149–163. doi:10.1016/j.jpubeco.2010.09.015

Ruble, L. A., McGrew, J. H., Wong, W. H., & Missall, K. N. (2018). Special education teachers' perceptions and intentions toward data collection. *Journal of Early Intervention*, *40*(2), 177–191. doi:10.1177/1053815118771391 PMID:30774283

Ruble, L., McGrew, J. H., & Toland, M. D. (2012). Goal attainment scaling as an outcome measure in randomized controlled trials of psychosocial interventions in autism. *Journal of Autism and Developmental Disorders*, *42*(9), 1974–1983. doi:10.100710803-012-1446-7 PMID:22271197

Rudolph, B. A., Castillo, C. P., Garcia, V. G., Martinez, A., & Navarro, F. (2015). Hispanic graduate students' mentoring themes: Gender roles in a bicultural context. *Journal of Hispanic Higher Education*, *14*(3), 191–206. doi:10.1177/1538192714551368

Rueda, R., Monzo, L., Shapiro, J., Gomez, J., & Blacher, J. (2005). Cultural models of transition: Latina mothers of young adults with developmental disabilities. *Council for Exceptional Children*, *71*(4), 401–414. doi:10.1177/001440290507100402

Rueda, R., & Stillman, J. (2012). The 21st century teacher: A cultural perspective. *Journal of Teacher Education*, *63*(4), 245–253. doi:10.1177/0022487112446511

Ruffino, A. G., Mistrett, S. G., Tomita, M., & Hajare, P. (2006). The Universal Design for Play Tool: Establishing validity and reliability. *Journal of Special Education Technology*, *21*(4), 25–38. doi:10.1177/016264340602100404

Ruppar, A. L., Neeper, L. S., & Dalsen, J. (2016). Special education teachers' preparedness to teach students with severe disabilities. *Research and Practice for Persons with Severe Disabilities*, *41*(4), 273–286. doi:10.1177/1540796916672843

Rush, D. D., & Shelden, M. L. (2020). *Early childhood coaching handbook* (2nd ed.). Brookes Publishing.

Russell, A. (2019). *OSEP awards $1.3 million to special education professor to advance interdisciplinary personnel preparation.* NEVADAToday. https://www.unr.edu/nevada-today/news/2019/osep-grant

S.B. 1159, 2022 Arizona Fifty-fifth Legislature 2022 Second Regular Session. (AZ, 2022). https://legiscan.com/AZ/text/SB1159/2022

S.I, Kuiper, C.H.Z. (2022). Practical recommendations for youth care professionals to improve evaluation and reflection during multidisciplinary team discussions: An action research project. *International Journal of Integrated Care*, *22*(1). . doi:10.5334/ijic.5639

Saddler, K. (2012). How prepared are New York's teachers to work with students with autism spectrum disorders? *Exceptional Individuals*, *35*, 8–12.

Sakamoto, I., & Pitner, R. O. (2005). Use of critical consciousness in anti-oppressive social work practice: Disentangling power dynamics at personal and structural levels. *British Journal of Social Work*, *35*(4), 435–452. doi:10.1093/bjsw/bch190

Salhotra, P. (2022, August 14). *There's a nationwide shortage of Black male school psychologists*. [Radio Broadcast]. NPR. https://www.npr.org/2022/08/14/1117418891/

Salinger, R. (2019). Empirically based practices to address disability stigma in the classroom. *Journal of Applied School Psychology*, *36*(3), 324–345. doi:10.1080/15377903.2020.1749203

Sallows, G. O., & Graupner, T. D. (2005). Intensive behavioral treatment for children with autism: Four-year outcome and predictors. *American Journal of Mental Retardation*, *110*(6), 417–438. doi:10.1352/0895-8017(2005)110[417:IBTFCW]2.0.CO;2 PMID:16212446

Sameroff, A. (2009). The transactional model. In A. Sameroff (Ed.), *The transactional model of development: How children and contexts shape each other* (pp. 3–21). American Psychological Association. doi:10.1037/11877-001

Samson, A. C., Phillips, J. M., Parker, K. J., Shah, S., Gross, J. J., & Hardan, A. Y. (2014). Emotion dysregulation and the core features of autism spectrum disorder. *Journal of Autism and Developmental Disorders*, *44*(7), 1766–1772. doi:10.100710803-013-2022-5 PMID:24362795

Sandall, S., Hemmeter, M. L., Smith, B. J., & McLean, M. (2009). *DEC Recommended Practices: A Comprehensive Guide for Practical Application in Early Intervention/Early Childhood Special Education*. Division for Early Childhood of the Council for Exceptional Children. Sopris West.

Sandall, S., & Schwartz, I. (2008). *Building blocks for teaching preschoolers with special needs* (2nd ed.). Brookes Publishing.

Sandoz, J. (2007). Teaching in the 21st century: Pedagogies for the evolving brain. In J. A. Chambers (Ed.), *Selected papers from the 18th international conference on College Teaching and Learning* (pp. 167-187). Jacksonville, FL: Florida State College at Jacksonville.

Sanford, C., Newman, L., Wagner, M., Cameto, R., Knokey, A.-M., & Shaver, D. (2011). *The Post-High School Outcomes of Young Adults With Disabilities up to 6 Years After High School. Key Findings From the National Longitudinal Transition Study-2 (NLTS2)* (NCSER 2011-3004). SRI International. Available at www.nlts2.org/reports/

Santos, J. L., & Haycock, K. (2016). Fixing America's college attainment problems: It's about more than affordability. *The Education Trust*. https://edtrust.org/wp-content/uploads/2014/09/FixingAmericasCollegeAttainmentProblem_EdTrust.pdf

Saunders, R. P., Evans, M. H., & Joshi, P. (2005). Developing a process-evaluation plan for assessing health promotion program implementation: A how-to guide. *Health Promotion Practice*, 6(2), 134–147. doi:10.1177/1524839904273387 PMID:15855283

Sayeski, K., & Paulsen, K. (2012). Student teacher evaluations of cooperating teachers as indices of effective mentoring. *Teacher Education Quarterly*, 39, 117–130.

Scheeler, M. C., Budin, S., & Markelz, A. (2016). The role of teacher preparation in promoting evidence-based practice in schools. *Learning Disabilities (Weston, Mass.)*, 14(2), 171–187.

Scheeler, M. C., Budin, S., & Markelz, A. (2016). The role of teacher preparation in promoting evidence-based practices in schools. *Learning Disabilities (Weston, Mass.)*, 14(2), 171–187. https://files.eric.ed.gov/fulltext/EJ1118433.pdf

Scheibel, G., & Watling, R. (2016). Collaborating with behavior analysts on the autism service delivery team. *OT Practice*, 21(7), 15–19.

Scherer, M., Moro, R., Jungersen, T., Contos, L., & Field, T. A. (2020). Gaining administrative support for doctoral programs in counselor education. *The Professional Counselor*, 10(4), 632–647. doi:10.15241/rs.10.4.632

Scheuermann, B., Webber, J., Boutot, E. A., & Goodwin, M. (2003). Problems with personnel preparation in autism spectrum disorders. *Focus on Autism and Other Developmental Disabilities*, 18(3), 97–206. https://journals.sagepub.com/doi/pdf/10.1177/108835760301800 3080. doi:10.1177/10883576030180030801

Schieltz, K. M., Graber, J. E., & McComas, J. (2017). Consultation Practices: Training Parents and Families. In Applied Behavior Analysis Advanced Guidebook (pp. 229-257). Academic Press.

Schieltz, K. M., Romani, P. W., Wacker, D. P., Suess, A. N., Huang, P., Berg, W. K., Lindgren, S. D., & Kopelman, T. G. (2018). Single-case analysis to determine reasons for failure of behavioral treatment via telehealth. *Remedial and Special Education*, 39(2), 95–105. doi:10.1177/0741932517743791

Schieltz, K. M., Wacker, D. P., & Romani, P. W. (2017). Effects of signaled positive reinforcement on problem behavior maintained by negative reinforcement. *Journal of Behavioral Education*, 26(2), 137–150. doi:10.100710864-016-9265-0

Schmitz, S. L., Clopton, K. L., Skaar, N. R., Dredge, S., & VanHorn, D. (2021). Increasing school-based mental health services with a "Grow Your Own" school psychology program. *Contemporary School Psychology*, 1–12. PMID:33500839

Schmuck, R. A. (1997). *Practical action research for change*. Skylight Training and Publishing.

School Reform Initiative. (2017). *Three levels of text protocol*. https://www.schoolreforminitiative.org/download/three-levels-of-text-protocol/

Schreck, K. A., Karunaratne, Y., Zane, T., & Wilford, H. (2016). Behavior analysts' use of and beliefs in treatment for people with autism: A 5-year follow-up. *Behavioral Interventions*, *31*(4), 355–376. doi:10.1002/bin.1461

Schreck, K. A., & Mazur, K. (2008). Behavior analysts' use of and beliefs in treatments for people with autism. *Behavioral Interventions*, *23*(3), 201–212. doi:10.1002/bin.264

Schreibman, L., Dawson, G., Stahmer, A. C., Landa, R., Rogers, S. J., McGee, G. G., Kasari, C., Ingersoll, B., Kaiser, A., Bruinsma, Y., McNerney, E., Wetherby, A., & Halladay, A. (2015). Naturalistic developmental behavioral interventions: Empirically validated treatments for autism spectrum disorder. *Journal of Autism and Developmental Disorders*, *45*(8), 2411–2428. doi:10.100710803-015-2407-8 PMID:25737021

Schuster, J. L., Timmons, J. C., & Moloney, M. (2003). Barriers to successful transition for young adults who receive SSI and their families. *Career Development for Exceptional Individuals*, *26*(1), 47–66. doi:10.1177/088572880302600104

Sciaraffa, M. A., Zeanah, P. D., & Zeanah, C. H. (2018). Understanding and promoting resilience in the context of adverse childhood experiences. *Early Childhood Education Journal*, *46*, 343–353.

Scott, L. A. (2018). Recruiting and retaining Black students for special education teacher preparation inclusion programs. *Inclusion*, *6*(2), 143–157. doi:10.1352/2326-6988-6.2.143

Scott, L. A., Cormier, C. J., & Boveda, M. (2022). Critical issues for the preparation and workforce development of racialized special educators. *Teacher Education and Special Education*, *45*(1), 5–7. doi:10.1177/08884064211070571

Scott, L. A., Evans, I., & Berry, R. (2021). Recommendations for teacher education programs to prepare practitioners for diverse urban schools. *Intervention in School and Clinic*, 1–8.

Scruggs, T. E., & Mastropieri, M. A. (2017). Making inclusion work with co-teaching. Teaching Exceptional Children, 49(4), 284–293. https://doi.org/10.1177/0040059916685065

Scruggs, T. E., & Mastropieri, M. A. (1998). Summarizing single-subject research: Issues and applications. *Behavior Modification*, *22*(3), 221–242. doi:10.1177/01454455980223001 PMID:9722473

Scruggs, T. E., Mastropieri, M. A., & McDuffie, K. A. (2007). Co-teaching in inclusive classrooms: A metasynthesis of qualitative research. *Exceptional Children*, *73*(4), 392–416.

Seal, D., Nguyen, A., & Beyer, K. (2014). Youth exposure to violence in an urban setting. *Urban Studies Research*. doi:10.1155/2014/368047

Selwyn, N. (2008). Realising the potential of new technology? Assessing the legacy of New Labour's ICT agenda 1997–2007. *Oxford Review of Education*, *34*(6), 701–712. doi:10.1080/03054980802518920

Sexton, D., Snyder, P., Lobman, M., & Daly, T. (2002). Comparing the developmentally appropriate practice (DAP) beliefs of practitioners in general and special early childhood service settings. *Teacher Education and Special Education*, *25*(3), 247–261. doi:10.1177/088840640202500305

Shahidullah, J. D., McClain, M. B., Azad, G., Mezher, K. R., & McIntyre, L. L. (2020). Coordinating autism care across schools and medical settings: Considerations for school psychologists. *Intervention in School and Clinic*, *56*(2), 107–114. doi:10.1177/1053451220914891

Shakman, K., Bailey, J., & Breslow, N. (2017). *A primer for continuous improvement in schools and districts*. Teacher & Leadership Programs.

Shannon, G. S., & Bylsma, P. (2004). *Characteristics of improved school districts: Themes from research*. Washington State Department of Education.

SHAPE America. (2017). National standards for initial physical education teacher education. https://www.shapeamerica.org/accreditation/upload/2017-SHAPE-America-Initial-PETE-Standards-and-Components.pdf

Shaughnessy, A., & Sanger, D. (2005). Kindergarten teachers' perceptions of language and literacy development, speech-language pathologists, and language interventions. *Communication Disorders Quarterly*, *26*(2), 67–84. doi:10.1177/15257401050260020601

Shaw, K. A., Maenner, M. J., Bakian, A. V., Bilder, D. A., Durkin, M. S., Furnier, S. M., Hughes, M. M., Patrick, M., Pierce, K., Salinas, A., Shenouda, J., Vehorn, A., Warren, Z., Zahorodny, W., Constantino, J. N., DiRienzo, M., Esler, A., Fitzgerald, R. T., Grzybowski, A., Hudson, A., & Cogswell, M. E. (2021). Early Identification of Autism Spectrum Disorder Among Children Aged 4 Years - Autism and Developmental Disabilities Monitoring Network, 11 Sites, United States, 2018. *Morbidity and mortality weekly report. Surveillance summaries (Washington, D.C.: 2002)*, *70*(10), 1–14. doi:10.15585/mmwr.ss7010a1

Shaw, T. V., Lee, B. R., & Wulczyn, F. (2012). "I thought I 'hated' data": Preparing MSW students for data-driven practice. *Journal of Teaching in Social Work*, *32*(1), 78–89. doi:10.1080/08841233.2012.640599

Shelton, R., Kerschen, K., & Cooper, S. (2020). The impact of a varied field experience on preservice teachers' perceptions of their personal growth: A summer mathematics academy for early learners. *Teacher Educator*, *55*(1), 28–46. doi:10.1080/08878730.2019.1618424

Shepley, C., Allday, R. A., Crawford, D., Pence, R., Johnson, M., & Winstead, O. (2017). Examining the emphasis on consultation in behavior analyst preparation programs. *Behavior Analysis: Research and Practice*, *17*(4), 381–392. doi:10.1037/bar0000064

Shepley, C., & Grisham-Brown, J. (2018). Applied behavior analysis in early childhood education: An overview of policies, research, blended practices, and the curriculum framework. *Behavior Analysis in Practice*, *12*(1), 235–246. doi:10.100740617-018-0236-x PMID:30918790

Shields, N., Bruder, A. M., & Cleary, S. L. (2021). An exploratory content analysis of how physiotherapists perceive barriers and facilitators to participation in physical activity among adults with disability. *Physiotherapy Theory and Practice*, *37*(1), 149–157. doi:10.1080/09593985.2019.1623957 PMID:31172868

Shinn, M. (2008). Best practices for using curriculum-based measurement in a problem-solving model. In A. Thomas & J. Grimes (Eds.), *Best practices in school psychology IV* (pp. 243–262). National Association of School Psychologists.

Shinn, M. R., & Walker, H. M. (2010). *Interventions for achievement and behavior problems in a three-tier model including RTI*. National Association of School Psychologists.

Shire, S. Y., Shih, W., Chang, Y. C., & Kasari, C. (2018). Short Play and Communication Evaluation: Teachers' assessment of core social communication and play skills with young children with autism. *Autism*, *22*(3), 299–310. doi:10.1177/1362361316674092 PMID:29671644

Shire, S. Y., Shih, W., & Kasari, C. (2018). Brief report: Caregiver strategy implementation—advancing spoken communication in children who are minimally verbal. *Journal of Autism and Developmental Disorders*, *48*(4), 1228–1234. doi:10.100710803-017-3454-0 PMID:29313178

Shoffner, M., & Wachter Morris, C. A. (2010). Preparing preservice English teachers and school counselor interns for future collaboration. *Teaching Education*, *21*(2), 185–197. doi:10.1080/10476210903183894

Shogren, K. A., Luckasson, R., & Schalock, R. L. (2020). Using a multidimensional model to analyze context and enhance personal outcomes. *Intellectual and developmental disabilities, 58*(2), 95-110.

Shonkoff, J. P., & Garner, A. S. (2012). The lifelong effects of early childhood adversity and toxic stress. *Pediatrics, 129*(1), e232–e246.

Shulman, L. S. (1986). Those who understand: Knowledge growth in teaching. *Educational Researcher, 15*(2), 4–14. doi:10.3102/0013189X015002004

Sickel, A., & Hanuscin, D. (2010). A new chapter: How NSTA student chapters can support preservice teachers and prepare them for the challenges ahead. *Science and Children, 48*(2), 71–75.

Siegel, D. H., Smith, M. C., & Melucci, S. C. (2020). Teaching social work students about homelessness: An interdisciplinary interinstitutional approach. *Journal of Social Work Education, 56*(sup1), S59-S71. doi:10.1080/10437797.2020.1741479

Siegel, S. (2005). Drug tolerance, drug addiction, and drug anticipation. *Current Directions in Psychological Science: A Journal of the American Psychological Society, 14*(6), 296-300. doi:10.1111/j.0963-7214.2005.00384.x

Silberman, S. (2013). Neurodiversity rewires conventional thinking about brains. *Wired.* https://www.wired.com/2013/04/neurodiversity/

Silverman, K., Hong, S., & Trepanier-Street, M. (2010). Collaboration of teacher education and child disability health care: Transdisciplinary approach to inclusive practice for early childhood pre-service teachers. *Early Childhood Education Journal, 37*(6), 461–468. doi:10.100710643-010-0373-5

Simpson, R. L. (2004). Finding effective intervention and personnel preparation practices for students with autism spectrum disorders. *Exceptional Children, 70*(2), 135–144. doi:10.1177/001440290407000201

Singh, S., & Keese, J. (2020). Applying systems-based thinking to build better IEP relationships: A case for relational coordination. *Support for Learning, 35*(3), 359–371. doi:10.1111/1467-9604.12315

Sisti M. K., & Robledo, J. A. (2021). Interdisciplinary collaboration practices between education specialists and related service providers. *The Journal of Special Education Apprenticeship, 10*(1), 5.

Sisti, M. K., & Robledo, J. A. (2021). Interdisciplinary collaboration practices between education specialists and related service providers. *The Journal of Special Education Apprenticeship, 10*(1), 1–19. https://scholarworks.lib.csusb.edu/josea/vol10/iss1/5

Sisti, M., & Robledo, J. (2021). Interdisciplinary Collaboration Practices between Education Specialists and Related Service Providers. *The Journal of Special Education Apprenticeship, 10*(1), 1–22.

Skiba, R. J., Chung, C. G., Trachok, M., Baker, T. L., Sheya, A., & Hughes, R. L. (2014). Parsing disciplinary disproportionality: Contributions of infraction, student, and school characteristics to out-of-school suspension and expulsion. *American Educational Research Journal, 51*(4), 640–670. doi:10.3102/0002831214541670

Skiba, R. J., Horner, R. H., Chung, C.-G., Rausch, M. K., May, S. L., & Tobin, T. (2011). Race is not neutral: A national investigation of African American and Latino disproportionality in school discipline. *School Psychology Review, 40*(1), 85–107. doi:10.1080/02796015.2011.12087730

Skiba, R. J., Middelberg, L. V., & McClain, M. B. (2014). *Multicultural issues for schools and students with emotional and behavioral disorders: Disproportionality in discipline and special education. In Handbook of Evidence-Based Practices for Emotional and Behavioral Disorders: Applications in Schools.* Guilford Press.

Smith, J. (2010). An interdisciplinary approach to preparing early intervention professionals: A university and community collaborative initiative. *Teacher Education and Special Education*, *33*(2), 131–142. doi:10.1177/0888406409357546

Smith, L. V., Blake, J. J., Graves, S. L. Jr, Vaughan-Jensen, J., Pulido, R., & Banks, C. (2016). Promoting diversity through program websites: A multicultural content analysis of school psychology program websites. *School Psychology Quarterly*, *31*(3), 327–339. doi:10.1037pq0000149 PMID:27054285

Smith, T. (2001). Discrete Trial Training in the treatment of Autism. *Focus on Autism and Other Developmental Disabilities*, *16*(2), 86–92. doi:10.1177/108835760101600204

Snell, M. E., Berlin, R. A., Voorhees, M. D., Stanton-Chapman, T. L., & Hadden, S. (2012). A survey of preschool staff concerning problem behavior and its prevention in Head Start classrooms. *Journal of Positive Behavior Interventions*, *14*(2), 98–107. doi:10.1177/1098300711416818

Snell, M. E., & Brown, F. (2011). *Instruction of students with severe disabilities*. Pearson.

Snell, M. E., & Janney, R. (2005). *Collaborative teaming* (2nd ed.). Paul H. Brooks Publishing Co.

Snyder, T. D., de Brey, C., & Dillow, S. A. (2019). Digest of education statistics (54th ed.). NCES 2020-009. US Department of Education. Institute of Education Sciences.

Snyder, P., & McWilliam, P. J. (2003). Using case method of instruction effectively in early intervention personnel preparation. *Infants and Young Children*, *16*(4), 284–295. doi:10.1097/00001163-200310000-00003

Solone, C. J., Thornton, B. E., Chiappe, J. C., Perez, C., Rearick, M. K., & Falvey, M. A. (2020). Creating collaborative schools in the United States: A review of best practices. *International Electronic Journal of Elementary Education*, *12*(3), 283–292. doi:10.26822/iejee.2020358222

Sopko, K. (2010). *Workforce preparation to serve children who receive part C services: Brief Policy Analysis*. Project Forum at National Association of School of State Directors of Special Education. https://www.yumpu.com/en/document/view/37973326/here-national-association-of-state-directors-of-special-education

Soto, G., & Zangari, C. (2009). *Practically speaking: Language, literacy, & academic development for students with AAC needs*. Brookes Publishing.

Spencer, E. J., Goldstein, H., & Kaminski, R. (2012). Teaching Vocabulary in Storybooks: Embedding Explicit Vocabulary Instruction for Young Children. *Young Exceptional Children*, *15*(1), 18–32. doi:10.1177/1096250611435367

Splett, J. W., Fowler, J., Weist, M. D., McDaniel, H., & Dvorsky, M. (2013). The critical role of school psychology in the school mental health movement. *Psychology in the Schools*, *50*(3), 245–258. doi:10.1002/pits.21677 PMID:30774154

Springboard to Active Schools. (2017). *Strengthen physical education in schools*. National Network of Public Health Institutes.

Squires, J., & Bricker, D. (2009). Ages & Stages Questionnaires®, Third Edition (ASQ®-3): A Parent-Completed Child Monitoring System. Paul H. Brookes Publishing Co., Inc.

St. Martin, K., Vaughn, S., Troia, G., Fien, H., & Coyne, M. (2020). *Intensifying literacy instruction: Essential practices*. Lansing, MI: MiMTSS Technical Assistance Center, Michigan Department of Education. Retrieved from https://intensiveintervention.org/resource/intensifying-literacy-instruction-essential-practices

*Compilation of References*

Stanley, A. M., Snell, A., & Edgar, S. (2014). Collaboration as effective musical professional development: Success stories from the field. *Journal of Music Teacher Education*, *24*(1), 76–88. doi:10.1177/1057083713502731

Stayton, V. D. (2015). Preparation of early childhood special educators for inclusive and interdisciplinary settings. *Infants and Young Children*, *28*, 113–122.

Stayton, V., & Bruder, M. B. (1999). Early intervention personnel preparation for the new millennium: Early childhood special education. *Infants and Young Children*, *12*(1), 59–69. doi:10.1097/00001163-199907000-00009

Stehle Wallace, E., Senter, R., Peterson, N., Dunn, K. T., & Chow, J. (2022). How to Establish a Language-Rich Environment Through a Collaborative SLP–Teacher Partnership. *Teaching Exceptional Children*, *54*(3), 166–176. doi:10.1177/0040059921990690

Steinberg, D. M., & Vinjamuri, M. K. (2014). Activating adult-learning principles through small groups in preparing social work students to achieve CSWE research competencies. *Journal of Teaching in Social Work*, *34*(4), 363–383. doi:10.1080/08841233.2014.937890

Steinbrenner, J. R., Hume, K., Odom, S. L., Morin, K. L., Nowell, S. W., Tomaszewski, B., Szendrey, S., McIntyre, N. S., Yücesoy-Özkan, S., & Savage, M. N. (2020). *Evidence-based practices for children, youth, and young adults with autism*. The University of North Carolina at Chapel Hill, Frank Porter Graham Child Development Institute, National Clearinghouse on Autism Evidence and Practice Review Team. https://ncaep.fpg.unc.edu/sites/ncaep.fpg.unc.edu/files/imce/documents/EBP%20Report%202020.pdf

Stevens-Smith, D. A., Fisk, W., Williams, F. K., & Barton, G. (2006). Principals' perceptions of academic importance and accountability in physical education. *International Journal of Learning*, *13*(2), 7–20. doi:10.18848/1447-9494/CGP/v13i02/44632

Stites, M. L., Rakes, C. R., Noggle, A. K., & Shah, S. (2018). Preservice teacher perceptions of preparedness to teach in inclusive settings as an indicator of teacher preparation program effectiveness. *Discourse in Communication for Sustainable Education*, *9*(2), 21–39. doi:10.2478/dcse-2018-0012

Stockman, I. J., Boult, J., & Robinson, G. (2004). Multicultural issues in academic and clinical education: A cultural mosaic. *ASHA Leader*, *9*(13), 6–22. doi:10.1044/leader.FTR5.09132004.6

Stoiber, K. C. (2014). A comprehensive framework for multitiered systems of support in school psychology. In P. L. Harrison & A. Thomas (Eds.), *Best practices in school psychology: Data-based and collaborative decision making* (pp. 41–70). National Association of School Psychologists.

Stokols, D., Hall, K. L., Taylor, B. K., & Moser, R. P. (2008). The science of team science: Overview of the field and introduction to the supplement. *American Journal of Preventive Medicine*, *35*(2, 2S), S77–S89. doi:10.1016/j.amepre.2008.05.002 PMID:18619407

Stoll, L., Bolam, R., McMahon, A., Wallace, M., & Thomas, S. (2006). Professional learning communities: A review of the literature. *Journal of Educational Change*, *7*(4), 221–258. doi:10.100710833-006-0001-8

Strein, W., Kuhn-McKearin, M., & Finney, M. (2014). Best practices in developing prevention strategies for school psychology practice. In P. L. Harrison & A. Thomas (Eds.), *Best 216 practices in school psychology: Systems-level services* (pp. 137–148). National Association of School Psychologists.

Sturmey, P. (2022). Individual Therapies for Violence and Aggression: I. Cognitive and Behavioral Therapies. In P. St (Ed.), *Violence and Aggression. Advances in Preventing and Treating Violence and Aggression*. Springer. doi:10.1007/978-3-031-04386-4_16

Sue, D. W., Alsaidi, S., Awad, M. N., Glaeser, E., Calle, C. Z., & Mendez, N. (2019). Disarming racial microaggressions: Microintervention strategies for targets, White allies, and bystanders. *The American Psychologist*, *74*(1), 128–142. doi:10.1037/amp0000296 PMID:30652905

Sugai, G., & Horner, R. H. (2009). Responsiveness-to-intervention and school-wide positive Behavior supports: Integration of multi-tiered system approaches. *Exceptionality: The Official Journal of the Division for Research of the Council for Exceptional Children*, *17*(4), 223–237. doi:10.1080/09362830903235375

Suleman, S., McFarlane, L., Pollock, K., Schneider, P., Leroy, C., & Skoczylas, M. (2014). Collaboration: More than 'working together': An exploratory study to determine effect of interprofessional education on awareness and application of models of specialized service delivery by student speech-language pathologists and teachers. *Canadian Journal of Speech Language Pathology and Audiology*, *37*, 298–307.

Sullivan, K., Barkowski, E., Lindsay, J., Lazarev, V., Nguyen, T., Newman, D., & Lin, L. (2017, December). *Trends in teacher mobility in Texas and associations with teacher, student, and school characteristics* (REL Report No. 2018-283). Regional Educational Laboratory Southwest. Retrieved from https://files.eric.ed.gov/fulltext/ED578907.pdf

Sullivan, A. L., & Bal, A. (2013). Disproportionality in special education: Effects of individual and school variables on disability risk. *Exceptional Children*, *79*(4), 475–494. doi:10.1177/001440291307900406

Sullivan, A. L., Harris, B., Miller, F. G., Fallon, L. M., Weeks, M. R., Malone, C. M., Kulkarni, T., Proctor, S., Johnson, A. H., Rossen, E., Nguyen, T., & Shaver, E. (2021). A call to action for school psychology to address COVID-19 health disparities and advance social justice. *The School Psychologist*, *36*(5), 410–421. doi:10.1037pq0000463 PMID:34410800

Sutcher, L., Darling-Hammond, L., & Carver-Thomas, D. (2016). *A coming crisis in teaching? Teacher supply, demand, and shortages in the US*. Learning Policy Institute.

Sutcher, L., Darling-Hammond, L., & Carver-Thomas, D. (2019). Understanding teacher shortages: An analysis of teacher supply and demand in the United States. *Education Policy Analysis Archives*, *27*(35), 35. Advance online publication. doi:10.14507/epaa.27.3696

Sutcher, L., Dzarling-Hammond, L., & Carver-Thomas, D. (2016). *A coming crisis in teaching? Teacher supply, demand, and shortages in the U.S.* Learning Policy Institute. doi:10.54300/247.242

Sutfin, E. A. (2021). School psychology shortages in West Virginia. *Theses, Dissertations and Capstones*. 1347. https://mds.marshall.edu/etd/1347

Sutherland, K. S., Wehby, J. H., & Copeland, S. R. (2000). Effect of varying rates of behavior-specific praise on the on-task behavior of students with EBD. *Journal of Emotional and Behavioral Disorders*, *8*(1), 2–8. doi:10.1177/106342660000800101

Swayze, S., & Jakeman, R. C. (2014). Student perceptions of communication, connectedness, and learning in a merged cohort course. *The Journal of Continuing Higher Education*, *62*(2), 102–111.

Sylvester, L., Ogletree, B. T., & Lunnen, K. (2017). Cotreatment as a vehicle for interprofessional collaborative practice: Physical therapists and speech-language pathologists collaborating in the care of children with severe disabilities. *American Journal of Speech-Language Pathology*, *26*(2), 206–216. doi:10.1044/2017_AJSLP-15-0179 PMID:28514475

Symon, J. B., Bruinsma, Y., & McNerney, E. M. (2019). Antecedent Strategies, In Bruinsma, Y., Boettcher, M. Stahmer, A., Schreibman, L., (Eds.). Naturalistic Developmental Behavioral Interventions: An Overview and Practical Application. Brookes Publishing Co.

Syracuse University. (2022). Disability Studies at Syracuse University. *Syracuse University*. https://soe.syr.edu/disability-studies/

Tabors, P. O. (2008). *One child, two languages: A guide for early childhood educators of children learning English as a second language* (2nd ed.). Brookes Publishing.

Tager-Flusberg, H., & Kasari, C. (2013). Minimally verbal school-aged children with autism spectrum disorder: The neglected end of the spectrum. *Autism Research*, *6*(6), 468–478. doi:10.1002/aur.1329 PMID:24124067

Taggart, G. L., & Wilson, A. P. (1999). Promoting reflective thinking in teachers: 44 action strategies. *Quality Assurance in Education*.

Taheri, A., Perry, A., & Minnes, P. (2017). Exploring factors that impact activity participation of children and adolescents with severe developmental disabilities. *Journal of Intellectual Disability Research*, *61*(12), 1151–1161.

Tang, K. S., Fortner, K. M., & Morgan, R. D. (2021). School counselors and special education teachers involvement in leadership activities at their school sites. *Journal of Leadership, Equity, &. Research*, *7*(3), 1–17.

Taylor, R. D., Oberle, E., Durlak, J. A., & Weissberg, R. P. (2017). Promoting positive youth development through school-based social and emotional learning interventions: A meta-analysis of follow-up effects. *Child Development*, *88*, 1156–1171. https://doi.org/10.1111.cdev.12864

Taylor, S. D., Veri, M. J., Eliason, M., Hermoso, J. C. R., Bolter, N. D., & Van Olphen, J. E. (2019). Social justice syllabus design tool: A first step in doing social justice pedagogy. *Journal Committed to Social Change on Race and Ethnicity*, *5*(2), 133–166. doi:10.15763/issn.2642-2387.2019.5.2.132-166

Teasley, M. L. (2016). Related services personnel and evidence-based practice: Past and present challenges. *Children & Schools*, *38*(1), 5–8. doi:10.1093/cs/cdv039

Technical Assistance Center on Social Emotional Intervention for Young Children (TACSEI). (2018). *Learn about the Pyramid Model*. http://challengingbehavior.fmhi.usf.edu/do/pyramid_model.htm

Teffs, E., & Whitbread, K. M. (2009). Level of Preparation of General Education Teachers to Include Students with Autism Spectrum Disorders. *Current Issues in Education (Tempe, Ariz.)*, *12*, https://cie.asu.edu/ojs/index.php/cieatasu/article/view/172

Tegler, H., Pless, M., Johansson, M. B., & Sonnander, K. (2019). Speech and language pathologists' perceptions and practises of communication partner training to support children's communication with high-tech speech generating devices. *Disability and Rehabilitation. Assistive Technology*, *14*(6), 581–589. doi:10.1080/17483107.2018.1475515 PMID:29790394

Texas Christian University. (n.d.). *Deaf and hard of hearing: Bring language and understanding to those without access to sound*. https://www.tcu.edu/academics/programs/deaf-and- hard-of-hearing-studies.php#accd17e202-interdisciplinary-focus

Texas Education Agency. (2022a). *Employed and Certified Teachers by Preparation Route 2012-13 through 2021-22*. https://tea.texas.gov/sites/default/files/employed-and-certified-teachers-by-preparation-route-2022.pdf

Texas Education Agency. (2022b). *Special Education Reports*. https://rptsvr1.tea.texas.gov/cgi/sas/broker?_service=marykay&_program=adhoc.std_driver1.sas&RptClass=SpecEd&_debug=0&SchoolYr=22&report=StateState&format=html

Texas Education Agency. (2022c). *Out-of-Field Teaching for SY 2021-22 by Grade Level and Subject Area*. https://tea.texas.gov/sites/default/files/out-of-field-2022.pdf

Texas Education Agency. (2022d). 2021-2022 teacher FTE counts and course enrollment reports. https://rptsvr1.tea.texas.gov/cgi/sas/broker

The Office of Special Education Programs. (2011). *Creating Equal Opportunities for Children and Youth with Disabilities to Participate in Physical Education and Extracurricular Athletics*. Office of Special Education and Rehabilitative Services.

Thistlethwaite, J., & Moran, M. (2010). Learning outcomes for interprofessional education (IPE): Literature review and synthesis. *Journal of Interprofessional Care*, *24*(5), 503–513. doi:10.3109/13561820.2010.483366 PMID:20718596

Tiano, J., & McNeil, C. (2006). Training head start teachers in behavior management using parent-child interaction therapy; A preliminary investigation. *Journal of Early and Intensive Behavior Intervention: JEIBI*, *3*(2), 220–233. doi:10.1037/h0100334

Timm, J. R., & Schnepper, L. L. (2021). A mixed-methods evaluation of an interprofessional clinical education model serving students, faculty, and the community. *Journal of Interprofessional Care*, *35*(1), 92–100. doi:10.1080/13561820.2019.1710117 PMID:32013630

Tisdell, E. J. (2002). High tech meets high touch: Cohort learning online in graduate higher education. In R. Orem (Ed.), *Proceedings of the 21st Midwest Research-to-Practice Conference in Adult, Continuing and Community Education, DeKalb, Illinois, October 9-11, 2002* (pp. 114-119). Retrieved from https://www.cedu.niu.edu/reps/Document/Midwest_Conference_Papers_part2.pdf

Todd, R. (2019, October 9). *Inside West Virginia's overwhelmed foster care system*. https://www.marketplace.org/2019/10/09/inside-west-virginias-overwhelmed-foster-care-system/

Tomlinson, M. (2015). Infant mental health in the next decade: A call for action. *Infant Mental Health Journal*, *36*(6), 538–541. doi:10.1002/imhj.21537 PMID:26514552

Tower, K. D. (1996). *The attitudes of special educators toward social work as a pupil support service* (Publication no. 9716671) [Doctoral dissertation, University of Nevada, Reno]. ProQuest Dissertations Publishing.

Townley-Cochran, D., Leaf, J. B., Taubman, M., Leaf, R., & McEachin, J. (2015, September). Observational Learning for Students Diagnosed with Autism: A Review Paper. *Review Journal of Autism and Developmental Disorders*, *2*(3), 262–272. doi:10.100740489-015-0050-0

Trainor, A. A., Murray, A., & Kim, H. (2014). *Postsecondary transition and English learners with disabilities: Data from the second national longitudinal transition study*. WCER working paper No. 2014-4. Wisconsin Center for Educational Research.

Trainor, A. A. (2008). Using cultural and social capital to improve postsecondary outcomes and expand transition models for youth with disabilities. *The Journal of Special Education*, *42*(3), 148–162. doi:10.1177/0022466907313346

Trainor, A. A., Carter, E. W., Karpur, A., Martin, J. E., Mazzotti, V. L., Morningstar, M. E., Newman, L., & Rojewski, J. W. (2020). A Framework for Research in Transition: Identifying Important Areas and Intersections for Future Study. *Career Development and Transition for Exceptional Individuals*, *43*(1), 5–17. https://doi.org/10.1177/2165143419864551

Tripp, T. R., & Rich, P. J. (2012). The influence of video analysis on the process of teacher change. *Teaching and Teacher Education*, *28*, 728–739. doi:10.1016/j.tate.2012.01.011

Trivette, C. M., Dunst, C. J., Hamby, D. W., & O'Herin, C. E. (2009). Characteristics and consequences of adult learning methods and strategies, *Research Brief, 3*(1). Tots n Tech Research Institute.

*Compilation of References*

Trost, S. G. (2005). Report: Discussion paper for the development of recommendations for children's and youth's participation in health promoting physical activity.

Tseng, H., Gardner, T., & Yeh, H.-T. (2016). Enhancing students' self-efficacy, elaboration, and critical thinking skills in a collaborative educator preparation program. *Quarterly Review of Distance Education*, *17*(2), 15–28.

Tuncer, C. A. N. (2020). Training preservice english language teachers with 3-D machinima. *The Turkish Online Journal of Educational Technology*, *19*(1), 53–65.

Turnbull, A. P., Summers, J. A., & Brotherson, M. J. (1984). *Working with families with disabled members: A family systems approach*. University of Kansas.

Turnbull, A. P., Turnbull, H. R., Erwin, E., Soodak, L., & Shogren, K. (2014). *Families, professionals, and exceptionality: Positive outcomes through partnerships and trust* (7th ed.). Pearson.

U.S. Bureau of Labor Statistics. (2020). *Annual youth labor force participation rate and unemployment rate*. https://www.dol.gov/agencies/odep/research-evaluation/statistics

U.S. Bureau of Labor Statistics. (2021a). *Social workers*. https://www.bls.gov/ooh/community-and-social-service/social-workers

U.S. Bureau of Labor Statistics. (2021b). *Special education teachers*. https://www.bls.gov/ooh/education-training-and-library/special-education-teachers

U.S. Census Bureau. (2021). American community survey tables on the foreign born by subject. *USCB*. https://www.census.gov/topics/population/foreign-born/guidance/acs-guidance/acs-by-subject.html

U.S. Congress. (1975, November 29). Education for All Handicapped Children Act of 1975. *Public Law*, •••, 94–142.

U.S. Congress. (1990). Individuals with Disabilities Act 1990. *Public Law*, 101–476.

U.S. Congress. (1997). Individuals with Disabilities Act 1997. *Public Law*, 105–117.

U.S. Congress. (2004). Individuals with Disabilities Act 2004. *Public Law*, 114–195.

U.S. Department of Education, Institute of Education Sciences. (2022). *School responses to COVID-19*. https://ies.ed.gov/schoolsurvey/

U.S. Department of Education, National Center for Education Statistics. (2020). *The Condition of Education 2020* (2020-144). Retrieved from https://nces.ed.gov/pubs2020/2020144.pdf

U.S. Department of Education, National Center for Education Statistics. (2021). *The Condition of Education 2021* (2021-144). Retrieved from https://nces.ed.gov/programs/coe/indicator/cgf

U.S. Department of Education, Office of Special Education and Rehabilitative Services, Office of Special Education Programs. (2020). "IDEA Part B Child Count Collection" 2008-09 to 2011-12, "IDEA Part B Child Count and Educational Environments Collection" 2012-13 to 2018-19. *EDFacts Data Warehouse (EDW)*. https://sites.ed.gov/idea/osep-fast-facts-children-with-autism-20/

U.S. Department of Education, Office of Special Education and Rehabilitative Services. (2016, October). *38th Annual Report to Congress on the implementation of the "Individuals with Disabilities Education Act," 2016*. https://files.eric.ed.gov/fulltext/ ED572027.pdf

U.S. Department of Education, Office of Special Education and Rehabilitative Services. (2021). *Supporting child and student social, emotional, behavioral, and mental health needs*. https://www2.ed.gov/documents/students/supporting-child-student-social-emotional-behavioral-mental-health.pdf

U.S. Department of Education. (2016). *Racial and ethnic disparities in special education: A multi-year disproportionality analysis by state, analysis category, and race/ethnicity*. https://www2.ed.gov/programs/osepidea/618-data/LEA-racial-ethnic-disparities-tables/disproportionality-analysis-by-state-analysis-category.pdf

U.S. Department of Education. (2017). *39th Annual Report to Congress on the Implementation of the Individuals with Disabilities Education Act, 2017*. [Data set]. https://files.eric.ed.gov/fulltext/ED591108.pdf

U.S. Department of Education. (2017). *Office of civil rights data collection*. https://ocrdata.ed.gov/profile/9/district/31634/studentswithdisabilitiesidea

U.S. Department of Education. (2017). *Teacher shortage areas nationwide: Listing 1990–1991 through 2017–2018*. https://www2.ed.gov/about/offices/list/ope/pol/ateachershortageareasreport2017-18.pdf

U.S. Department of Education. (2020). *OSEP fast facts: Children identified with autism. USDE*. https://sites.ed.gov/idea/osep-fast-facts-children-with-autism-20/

U.S. Department of Education. (2021). *43rd Annual Report to Congress on the Implementation of the Individuals with Disabilities Education Act, 2021*. Author.

U.S. Department of Education. (2021). *Individuals with Disabilities Education Act (IDEA) database: Digest of Education Statistics 2020*. Office of Special Education Programs. https://www2.ed.gov/programs/osepidea/618-data/state-level-data-files/index.html#bcc

U.S. Department of Education. (2022). *43rd annual report to Congress on the implementation of the Individuals with Disabilities Education Act, 2021*. https://sites.ed.gov/idea/files/43rd-arc-for-idea.pdf

U.S. Department of Education. (2022). *Fact sheet: The U.S. Department of Education Announces Partnerships Across States, School Districts, and Colleges of Education to Meet Secretary Cardona's Call to Action to Address the Teacher Shortage*. Retrieved from https://www.ed.gov/coronavirus/factsheets/teacher-shortage

U.S. Department of Education. (2022). Office of Special Education and Rehabilitative Services, Office of Special Education Programs, 43rd Annual Report to Congress on the Implementation of the Individuals with Disabilities Education Act. *USDE*.

U.S. Department of Education. (2022). Part C child count and setting. *USDE*. https://www2.ed.gov/programs/osepidea/618-data/static-tables/index.html

U.S. Department of Education. (2022). *State performance plan/Annual performance report: Part B for date formular grant programs under the individual with disabilities education act for reporting FFY2020*. Author.

U.S. Department of Education. OSERS. (2022, March 28). About OSEP. *OSEP*. https://www2.ed.gov/about/offices/list/osers/osep/about.html

U.S. Department of Health and Human Services. (2016). *Access to adolescent mental health care*. HHS.gov. https://www.hhs.gov/ash/oah/adolescent-development/mental-health/access-to-mental-health-care/index.html

U.S. Department of Health and Human Services. (2022). *Protective factors and adverse childhood experiences*. https://www.childwelfare.gov/topics/preventing/preventionmonth/about/protective-factors-aces/

U.S. Departments of Health and Human Services & Education. (2014). *Policy statement on expulsion and suspension policies in early childhood* settings. https://www2.ed.gov/policy/gen/guid/school-discipline/policy-statement-ece-expulsions-suspensions.pdf

U.S. Immigrant Learning Center. (2019). Retrieved from: https://www.ilctr.org/quick-us-immigration-statistics/

Udvari-Solner, A., Causton-Theoharis, J., & York-Barr, J. (2004). Developing adaptations to promote participation in inclusive environments. In *Orelove, F.P., Sobsey, D., & Dilberman, R.K. of Educating children with multiple disabilities: A collaborative approach, 4*. Brookes Publishing.

Ulrich, D. A. (2018). *TGMD-3: Test of gross motor development*. Pro-Ed.

Ulvik, M., & Riese, H. (2016). Action research in pre-service teacher education–a never-Ending story promoting professional development. *Professional Development in Education*, *42*(3), 441–457. doi:10.1080/19415257.2014.1003089

Umansky, I. M., Thompson, K. D., & Díaz, G. (2017). Using an ever–English Learner framework to examine disproportionality in special education. *Exceptional Children*, *84*(1), 76–96. doi:10.1177/0014402917707470

Underwood, A. (2018). *Preservice preparation in evidence-based and culturally responsive transition services*. Unpublished master's thesis.

United Health Foundation. (2018). America's health rankings: Health of women and children report 2018. *UHF*. https://assets.americashealthrankings.org/app/uploads/2018ahrannual_020419.pdf

United Health Foundation. (2021). America's health rankings: Health of women and children report 2021. *UHF*. https://assets.americashealthrankings.org/app/uploads/state-summaries-healthofwomenandchildren-2021.pdf

United Nations Department of Economic and Social Affairs. (1998). Recommendations on statistics of international migration, Revision 1. *United Nations Publication, Sales No. E.98.XVII.14*. https://unstats.un.org/unsd/publication/SeriesM/SeriesM_58rev1E.pdf

United Nations, High Commissioner for Refugees. (1951). Relating to the status of refugees. *UN*. https://www.unhcr.org/en-us/3b66c2aa10

United States Department of Education Office for Civil Rights. (2016). School Climate and Safety. *USDE*. https://www2.ed.gov/about/offices/list/ocr/docs/school-climate-and-safety.pdf

United States Department of Education. (2017). *Teacher shortage areas nationwide listing: 1990-1991 through 2017-2018*. https://www2.ed.gov/about/offices/list/ope/pol/tsa.html

United States Department of Education. (2020). *41st annual report to Congress on the implementation of the Individuals with Disabilities Education Act, 2019*. Author.

United States Department of Education. (2021). *COVID-19 Handbook: Roadmap to reopening safely and meeting all students' needs*. Retrieved from https://www2.ed.gov/documents/coronavirus/reopening-2.pdf

United States., & Job Accommodation Network (U.S.). (2011). *The ADA Amendments Act of 2008*. Morgantown, WV: U.S. Dept. of Labor, Office of Disability Employment Policy, Job Accommodation Network.

University of Kentucky HealthCare. (n.d.). Short and long-term effects of preterm birth. *UKH*. https://ukhealthcare.uky.edu/wellness-community/health-information/short-long-term-effects-preterm-birth

University of the State of New York, The State Education Department. (2010). *Guide to quality Individualized Education Program (IEP) development and implementation*. http://www.p12.nysed.gov/specialed/publications/iepguidance/IEPguideDec2010.pdf

University of Washington. (n.d.). The learning cycle. *Inspire Washington*. https://inspirewashington.edu/index.php/the-learning-cycle/

Unzueta, C. H., Moores-Abdool, W., & Vazquez Donet, D. (2010). Perceptions of special education professors and culturally linguistically diverse doctoral students on cohorts. *Teacher Education and Special Education*, *33*(2), 169–182. doi:10.1177/0888406409360009

US Department of Education, National Center of Educational Statistics. (2021). *Schools and staffing survey*. https://nces.ed.gov/surveys/sass/tables/sass1112_20161123001_t1n.asp

Valle, J., & Connor, D. (2019). *Rethinking disability: A disability studies approach to inclusive practices*. Routledge. doi:10.4324/9781315111209

van Winkelen, C. (2003). Inter-organizational communities of practice. *Henley Knowledge Management Forum*. https://www.elearningeuropa.info/en/article/Inter-Organizational-Communities-of-Practice

Vaughan, M., & Burnaford, G. (2016). Action research in graduate teacher education: A review of the literature 2000–2015. *Educational Action Research*, *24*(2), 280–299. doi:10.1080/09650792.2015.1062408

Vespa, J., Medina, L., & Armstrong, D. A. (2020). *Demographic turning points for the United States: Population projections for 2020 to 2060. Current Population Reports*. US Census Bureau.

Veterans Can Teach, H. B. 573, 2022 Florida House of Representatives. (FL, 2022).

Villa, R. A., Thousand, J. S., & Nevin, A. I. (2008). *A guide to co-teaching: Practical tips for facilitating student learning*. Corwin.

Villa, R. A., Thousand, J. S., & Nevin, A. I. (2010). *Collaborating with students in instruction and decision making*. Corwin.

Villa, R. A., Thousand, J. S., & Nevin, A. I. (2013). *A guide to co-teaching: New lessons and strategies to facilitate student learning* (3rd ed.). Corwin.

Villa, R., & Thousand, J. S. (2016). *A guide to co-teaching PD resources center*. Corwin.

Vittek, J. E. (2015). Promoting special educator teacher retention: A critical review of the literature. *SAGE Open*, *5*(2), 1–6. doi:10.1177/2158244015589994

Vogelgesang, K. L., Bruhn, A. L., Coghill-Behrends, W. L., Kern, A. M., & Troughton, L. C. (2016). A single-subject study of a technology-based self-monitoring intervention. *Journal of Behavioral Education*, *25*(4), 478–497. doi:10.100710864-016-9253-4

Volkers. (2016). Bridging the professional divide: Along with clear benefits, interprofessional collaboration can bring misunderstandings. Six bridge-builders share their strategies. *ASHA Leader, 21*(11), 41-50. doi:10.1044/leader.FTR1.21112016.40

*Compilation of References*

von Tetzchner, S., Brekke, K., Sjøthun, B., & Grindheim, E. (2009). Constructing preschool communities of learners that afford alternative language development. *Augmentative and Alternative Communication, 21*(2), 82–100. doi:10.1080/07434610500103541

Voress, J. K., Maddox, T., & Hammill, D. D. (2012). *Developmental Assessment of Young Children* (2nd ed.). Pearson.

Vu, P., & Fisher, C. E. (2021). Does virtual field experience deliver? An examination into virtual field experience during the pandemic and its implications for teacher education programs. *Open Praxis, 13*(1), 117-125. https://www.proquest.com/scholarly-journals/does-virtual-field-experience-deliver-examination/docview/2550671348/se-2?accountid=10003

Vujnovic, R. K., Fabiano, G. A., Morris, K. L., Norman, K., Hallmark, C., & Hartley, C. (2014). 38th Annual Report to Congress on the Implementation of the "Individuals with Disabilities Education Act," 2016. *Exceptionality, 22*(3), 129–140. doi:10.1080/09362835.2013.865530

Wagner, D. L., Hammerschmidt-Snidarich, S. M., Espin, C. A., Seifert, K., & McMaster, K. L. (2017). Pre-service teachers' interpretation of CBM progress monitoring data. *Learning Disabilities Research & Practice, 32*(1), 22–31. doi:10.1111/ldrp.12125

Wagner, M. (2014). *Longitudinal outcomes and post-high school status of students with emotional or behavioral disorders. In Handbook of Evidence-Based Practices for Emotional and Behavioral Disorders: Applications in Schools*. Guilford Publications.

Wagner, M. M., Newman, L. A., & Javitz, H. S. (2014). The influence of family socioeconomic status on the post high school outcomes of youth with disabilities. *Career Development and Transition for Exceptional Individuals, 37*(1), 5–17. doi:10.1177/2165143414523980

Waitoller, F., & Artiles, F. (2013). A decade of professional development research for inclusive education: A critical review and notes for a research program. *Review of Educational Research, 83*(3), 319–356. doi:10.3102/0034654313483905

Walcott, C. M., McNamara, K., Hyson, D., & Charvat, J. L. (2018). *Results from the NASP 2015 membership survey, part one: Demographics and employment conditions*. National Association of School Psychologists.

Walker, C. L., & Stone, K. (2011). Preparing teachers to reach English language learners: Preservice and in-service initiatives. In T. Lucas (Ed.), *Teacher preparation for linguistically diverse classrooms: A resource for teacher educators* (pp. 127–142). Routledge.

Walker, H. M., & Gresham, F. M. (2014). *Handbook of Evidence-Based Practices for Emotional and Behavioral Disorders: Applications in Schools*. Guilford Publications.

Wallace, E., Senter, R., Peterson, N., Dunn, K. T., & Chow, J. (2020). How to establish a language-rich environment through a collaborative SLP–teacher partnership. *Teaching Exceptional Children*.

Wang, C. C. (2006). Youth participation in photovoice as a strategy for community change. *Journal of Community Practice, 14*, 147–161. https://doi.org/10.1300/J125v14n01_09

Warrier, V., Greenberg, D. M., Weir, E., Buckingham, C., Smith, P., Lai, M. C., Allison, C., & Baron-Cohen, S. (2020). Elevated rates of autism, other neurodevelopmental and psychiatric diagnoses, and autistic traits in transgender and gender-diverse individuals. *Nature Communications, 11*(1), 3959. doi:10.103841467-020-17794-1 PMID:32770077

Washington, T., Truscott, S., & Franklin, A. (2020). Using grant funding to enhance school psychology training. *Psychology in the Schools, 57*(8), 1309–1326. doi:10.1002/pits.22389

Watts, B., & Jones, S. (2000). Inter-professional practice and action research: Commonalities and parallels. *Educational Action Research*, *8*(2), 377–382. doi:10.1080/09650790000200126

Webster-Stratton, C., Reid, M. J., & Hammond, M. (2004). Treating children with early-onset conduct problems: Intervention outcomes for parent, child, and teacher training. *Journal of Clinical Child and Adolescent Psychology*, *33*(1), 105–124. doi:10.1207/S15374424JCCP3301_11 PMID:15028546

Wehby, J. H., Symons, F. J., & Shores, R. E. (1995). A descriptive analysis of aggressive behavior in classrooms for children with emotional and behavioral disorders. *Behavioral Disorders*, *20*(2), 87–105. doi:10.1177/019874299502000207

Weingarten, Z., Bailey, T. R., & Peterson, A. (2019). *Strategies for scheduling: How to find time to intensify and individualize intervention*. Washington, DC: National Center on Intensive Intervention, Office of Special Education Programs, U.S. Department of Education. Retrieved from https://intensiveintervention.org/sites/default/files/NCII-Scheduling-508.pdf

Weiss, C. B., & Eren, R. (2020). Transdisciplinary approach practicum for speech- language pathology and special education graduate students. *Journal of Autism and Developmental Disorders*, *50*(10), 3661–3678. doi:10.1007/s10803-020-04413-7

Weissberg, R. P. (2019). Promoting the social and emotional learning of millions of school children. *Perspectives on Psychological Science*, *14*, 65–69. https://doi.org/10.1177/1745691618817756

Weiss, D., Cook, B., & Eren, R. (2020). Transdisciplinary approach practicum for speech-language pathology and special education graduate students. *Journal of Autism and Developmental Disorders*, *50*(10), 3661–3678.

Weist, M., Lever, N. A., Bradshaw, C. P., & Owens, J. S. (Eds.). (2014). Handbook of school mental health: Research, training, practice, and policy. Springer US.

Weist, M. D., Mellin, E. A., Chambers, K. L., Lever, N. A., Haber, D., & Blaber, C. (2012). Challenges to collaboration in school mental health and strategies for overcoming them. *The Journal of School Health*, *82*(2), 97–105. doi:10.1111/j.1746-1561.2011.00672.x PMID:22239135

Wei, X., Wagner, M., Christiano, E. R., Shattuck, P., & Yu, J. W. (2014). Special education services received by students with autism spectrum disorders from preschool through high school. *The Journal of Special Education*, *48*(3), 167–179. doi:10.1177/0022466913483576 PMID:25419002

Welch, M., & Sheridan, S. (1993). Educational partnerships in teacher education: Reconceptualizing how teacher candidates are prepared for teaching students with disabilities. *Action in Teacher Education*, *15*(3), 35–46. doi:10.1080/01626620.1993.10463162

Welch, M., Sheridan, S. M., Fuhriman, A., Hart, A. W., Connell, M. L., & Stoddart, T. (1992). Preparing professionals for educational partnerships: An interdisciplinary approach. *Journal of Educational & Psychological Consultation*, *3*(1), 1–23. doi:10.12071532768xjepc0301_1

Wenger, E. (2001). Supporting communities of practice: A survey of community-oriented technologies. Retrieved from http://www.ewenger.com/tech/

West Virginia Department of Education. (2017a). *Teacher vacancies reach crisis level*. https://wvmetronews.com/2017/02/20/teacher-vacancies-reach-crisis-level/

*Compilation of References*

West Virginia Department of Education. (2017b). *Personnel data report*. https://wvde.us/finance-and-administration/school-finance/financial-and-certified-list-reports/

West Virginia Department of Education. (2017c). *Second month enrollment count*. https://zoomwv.k12.wv.us/Dashboard/portalHome.jsp

West Virginia Department of Health and Human Resources. (2018). *DHHR releases neonatal abstinence syndrome data for 2017*. https://dhhr.wv.gov/News/2018/Pages/DHHR-Releases-Neonatal-Abstinence-Syndrome-Data-for-2017-.aspx

West Virginia Department of Health and Human Resources. (2022). *West Virginia celebrates national foster care month*. https://dhhr.wv.gov/News/2022/Pages/West-Virginia-Celebrates-National-Foster-Care-Month.aspx

WestEd. (2012). Early childhood mental health: Raising awareness, taking action. *WestEd's R & D Alert, 13*(3), 1–3. https://www.wested.org/wpcontent/uploads/2016/11/1372730177article_earlychildhoodmentalhealth_20123.pdf

Westling, D., Fox, L., & Carter, E. (2015). *Teaching students with severe disabilities*. Pearson.

Wharton, T., & Ann Burg, M. (2017). A mixed-methods evaluation of social work learning outcomes in interprofessional training with medicine and pharmacy students. *Journal of Social Work Education, 53*(Suppl 1), S87–S96. doi:10.1080/10437797.2017.1288592 PMID:30774279

Whinnery, S. B., Whinnery, K. W., & Eddins, D. (2016). A Strategy for Embedding Functional Motor and Early Numeracy Skill Instruction into Physical Education Activities. *Physical Disabilities: Education and Related Services, 35*(1), 17–27. doi:10.14434/pders.v35i1.20499

Whipple, W. (2014). *Key principles of early intervention and effective practices: A crosswalk with statements from discipline-specific literature*. Early Childhood TA Center. https://ectacenter.org/~pdfs/topics/eiservices/KeyPrinciplesMatrix_01_30_15.pdf

Whitaker, A., Torres-Guillén, S., Morton, M., Jordan, H., Coyle, S., Mann, A., & Sun, W. L. (2019). *Cops and no counselors: How the lack of school mental health staff is harming students*. American Civil Liberties Union. Retrieved from https://www.aclu.org/report/cops-and-no-counselors

Whitby, P. J. S., Kucharczyk, S., & Fowler, C. (2020). Evidence-based practices in transition. *DADD Express. Focus on Autism and Other Developmental Disabilities, 31*(2), 1–3. http://www.daddcec.com/uploads/2/5/2/0/2520220/dadd_spring2020_v2b.pdf

Whitcomb, J. A. (2002). Composing dilemma cases: An opportunity to understand moral dimensions of teaching. *Teaching Education, 13*(2), 125–135.

White, J. M., Martin, T. F., & Adamsons, K. (2019). *Family theories* (5th ed.). SAGE Publications.

Whitney, D. G., & Peterson, M. D. (2019). US national and state-level prevalence of mental health disorders and disparities of mental health care use in children. *JAMA Pediatricatics, 173*(4), 389–391. doi:10.1001/jamapediatrics.2018.5399 PMID:30742204

Wiggins, L. D., Durkin, M., Esler, A., Lee, L.-C., Zahorodny, W., Rice, C., Yeargin-Allsopp, M., Dowling, N. F., Hall-Lande, J., Morrier, M. J., Christensen, D., Shenouda, J., & Baio, J. (2020). Disparities in documented diagnoses of autism spectrum disorder based on demographic, individual, and service factors. *Autism Research*, *13*(3), 464–473. doi:10.1002/aur.2255 PMID:31868321

Wilkens, C., Eckdahl, K., Morone, M., Cook, V., Giblin, T., & Coon, J. (2014). Communication, community, and disconnection: Preservice teachers in virtual school field experiences. *Journal of Educational Technology Systems*, *43*(2), 143–157. doi:10.2190/ET.43.2.c

Williams, B., Lo, W. J., Hill, J., Ezike, N., & Huddleston, J. (2019). Employment supports in early work experiences for transition-age youth with disabilities who receive supplemental security income (SSI). *Journal of Vocational Rehabilitation*, *51*(2), 159–166. https://doi.org/10.3233/jvr-191035

Williams, D. S., & Mulrooney, K. (2021). Guardians in the nursery: The role of early childhood educators in fostering infant and young children's positive mental health. *Zero to Three Journal*, *41*(3), 10–16.

Williams, M., Krezman, C., & McNaughton, D. (2008). Reach for the stars: Five principles for the next 25 years of AAC. *Augmentative and Alternative Communication*, *24*(3), 94–206. doi:10.1080/08990220802387851

Williams, T. M. (2022). *Preservice candidate's knowledge of crisis preparedness in schools: The prepare model* [Unpublished program evaluation]. Marshall University.

Wilson, A., & Richardson, W. (2020). All I want to say is that they don't really care about us: Creating and maintaining healing-centered collective care in hostile times. *Occasional Paper Series*, *2020*(43). https://educate.bankstreet.edu/occasional-paper-series/vol2020/iss43/8

Wilson, L., McNeill, B. C., & Gillon, G. T. (2016). A comparison of inter-professional education programs in preparing prospective teachers and speech and language pathologists for collaborative language–literacy instruction. *Reading and Writing*, *29*(6), 1179–1201. doi:10.100711145-016-9631-2

Wilson, L., McNeill, B. C., & Gillon, G. T. (2017). Inter-professional education of prospective speech–language therapists and primary school teachers through shared professional practice placements. *International Journal of Language & Communication Disorders*, *52*(4), 426–439. doi:10.1111/1460-6984.12281 PMID:27624388

Wilson, L., McNeill, B. C., & Gillon, G. T. (2019). Understanding the effectiveness of student speech-language pathologists and student teachers co-working during inter-professional school placements. *Child Language Teaching and Therapy*, *35*(2), 125–143. doi:10.1177/0265659019842203

Winsor, J., Timmons, J., Butterworth, J., Migliore, A., Domin, D., Zalewska, A., & Shepard, J. (2018). *StateData: The national report on employment services and outcomes*. University of Massachusetts Boston, Institute for Community Inclusion.

Winstanley, E. L., & Stover, A. N. (2019). The impact of the opioid epidemic on children and adolescents. *Clinical Therapeutics*, *41*(9), 1655–1662. doi:10.1016/j.clinthera.2019.06.003 PMID:31303278

Witt, J. C., Moe, G., Gutkin, T. B., & Andrews, L. (1984). The effect of saying the same thing in different ways: The problem of language and jargon in school-based consultation. *Journal of School Psychology*, *22*(4), 361–367. doi:10.1016/0022-4405(84)90023-2

Woitaszewski, S., Crepeau-Hobson, F., Conolly, C., & Cruz, M. (2018). Rules, requirements, and resources for school-based threat assessment: A fifty state analysis. *California School Psychologist*, *22*(2), 125–134. doi:10.100740688-017-0161-y

Wolery, M., Busick, M., Reichow, B., & Barton, E. E. (2010). Comparison of overlap methods for quantitatively synthesizing single-subject data. *The Journal of Special Education*, *44*(1), 18–28. doi:10.1177/0022466908328009

Wood, J. L., Hilton, A. A., & Nevarez, C. (2015). Faculty of color and white faculty: An analysis of service in colleges of education in Arizona public university system. *Journal of the Professoriate*, *8*(1), 85–109.

Woodruff, G., & McGonigel, M. J. (1988). *Early intervention team approaches: The transdisciplinary model*. Council for Exceptional Children, Office of Educational Research and Improvement (ED). https://files.eric.ed.gov/fulltext/ED302971.pdf

Woods, A. D., Morrison, F. J., & Palincsar, A. S. (2018). Perceptions of communication practices among stakeholders in special education. *Journal of Emotional and Behavioral Disorders*, *26*(4), 209–224. doi:10.1177/1063426617733716

World Health Organization. (2010). Framework for action on interprofessional education and collaborative practice (No. WHO/HRH/HPN/10.3). World Health Organization.

World Health Organization. (2010). *Framework for action on interprofessional education and collaborative practice*. Retrieved from http://whqlibdoc.who.int/hq/2010/WHO_HRH_HPN_10.3_eng.pdf?ua=1

World Health Organization. (2022). International classification of functioning, disability and health (ICF). *WHO*. https://www.who.int/standards/classifications/international-classification-of-functioning-disability- and-health

Wright, P. W. (2004). *Individuals with disabilities education improvement act of 2004*. www.wrightslaw.com/idea/idea

*WVU researchers investigate the impact of the statewide opioid crisis on teachers*. (2019, March 13). https://wvutoday.wvu.edu/stories/2019/03/13/wvu-researchers-investigate-the-impact-of-the-statewide-opioid-crisis-on-teachers

Yell, M. L., & Bateman, D. F. (2018). Free appropriate public education and Endrew F. v. Douglas County School District (2017): Implication for personnel preparation. *Teacher Education and Special Education*, *42*(1), 6–17. doi:10.1177/0888406417754239

Yell, M. L., & Katsiyannis, A. (2019). The Supreme Court and special education. *Intervention in School and Clinic*, *54*(5), 311–318. doi:10.1177/1053451218819256

Yew, S. G. K., & O'Kearney, R. (2015). The role of early language difficulties in the trajectories of conduct problems across childhood. *Journal of Abnormal Child Psychology*, *43*(8), 1515–1527. doi:10.100710802-015-0040-9 PMID:26105208

Yilmaz, Y., & Granena, G. (2021). The implicitness and explicitness in cognitive abilities and corrective feedback. *Studies in Second Language Acquisition*, *43*(3), 523–550. doi:10.1017/S0272263120000601

Young, D., West, R. E., & Nylin, T. A. (2019). Value of open microcredentials to earners and issuers: A case study of national instruments open badges. *International Review of Research in Open and Distributed Learning*, *20*(5), 104–121. doi:10.19173/irrodl.v20i5.4345

Zagona, A. L., Kurth, J. A., & MacFarland, S. Z. C. (2017). Teachers' views of their preparation for inclusive education and collaboration. *Teacher Education and Special Education*, *40*(3), 163–178. doi:10.1177/0888406417692969

Zambo, D., & Zambo, R. (2007). Action research in an undergraduate teacher education program: What promises does it hold? *Action in Teacher Education*, *28*(4), 62–74. doi:10.1080/01626620.2007.10463430

Zangari, C. (2016). Looking back to move forward: 25 years of thinking about AAC and language. *Perspectives of the ASHA Special Interest Groups*, *1*(12), 144–152. doi:10.1044/persp1.SIG12.144

Zanotti, R., Sartor, G., & Canova, C. (2015). Effectiveness of interprofessional education by on-field training for medical students, with a pre-post design. *BMC Medical Education*, *15*(1), 1–8. doi:10.118612909-015-0409-z PMID:26220412

Zeigler, K., & Camarota, S. A. (2019). 67.3 million in the United States spoke a foreign language at home in 2018. Center for Immigration Studies.

Zgierska, A. E., Miller, M. M., Rabago, D. P., Hilliard, F., McCarthy, P., Cowan, P., & Salsitz, E. A. (2021). Language matters: It is time we change how we talk about addiction and its treatment. *Journal of Addiction Medicine*, *15*(1), 10–12. https://doi.org/10.1097/ADM.0000000000000674

Zhang, D., Katsiyannis, A., Ju, S., & Roberts, E. (2014). Minority representation in special education: 5-year trends. *Journal of Child and Family Studies*, *23*(1), 118–127. doi:10.100710826-012-9698-6

Zilz, W., & Pang, Y. (2021). Application of assistive technology in inclusive classrooms. Disability and Rehabilitation. Assistive Technology, 16(7), 684–686.

Zimmerman, B. J. (1999). Self-efficacy and educational development. In A. Bandura (Ed.), *Self-efficacy in changing societies* (pp. 202–231). Cambridge University Press.

# About the Contributors

**Dena D. Slanda**, Ph.D., is a Research Associate in the College of Community Innovation and Education and serves as the Education Doctoral Program (Ed.D.) Advisor in Exceptional Student Education at the University of Central Florida. She is currently a Co-Principal Investigator or Project Coordinator for federal grants in excess of $7.25 million for research and personnel/leadership development. Dr. Slanda is a published author and has conducted numerous presentations at international, national, regional, and state conferences focused on culturally proactive pedagogy and practices, equitable educational opportunities, inclusive practices, interdisciplinary collaboration, teacher and administrator preparation, intensive interventions, and multi-tier systems of support. Additionally, her research is focused on the intersection of race and disability with particular attention to disproportionality of culturally and linguistically diverse students in special education.

**Lindsey Pike**, M.S.W., is a Doctoral Candidate in the Exceptional Education Track of the College of Community Innovation and Education at the University of Central Florida. She currently serves as a researcher on a federally funded Teacher Quality Partnerships preparation grant project and teaches special education courses to undergraduate education majors. Ms. Pike is a published author of several peer-reviewed journal articles and book chapters, and has presented at numerous international, national, and state conferences. Her research and scholarship centers on teacher preparation, equitable and inclusive practices, and interdisciplinary collaboration. Ms. Pike's work has a particular focus on the intersectionality of disability and other identity markers in education, the disproportionality of culturally and linguistically diverse students in special education, and social justice dispositions in teacher education.

\* \* \*

**Edwin Obilo Achola** is currently an Associate Professor of Special Education at California State University Long Beach. Dr. Achola earned his Ph.D. in Special Education and Disability Policy from Virginia Commonwealth University. In the last 15 years, Dr. Achola has worked as a classroom teacher, teacher educator, and researcher- concentrating primarily on issues of equity for students with disabilities in the United States and Kenya. His research and teaching activities have focused on culturally responsive and sustaining pedagogy in transition planning, personnel development, and higher education for students with disabilities. He has co-authored a number of book chapters and published research articles on various topics in the field of transition planning and diversity. His research themes include meaningful involvement of culturally diverse families in transition planning, transition assessments, development of culturally responsive transition plans as well as post-secondary education success for traditionally marginalized youths.

**David Adams** is an assistant professor within the Department of Applied Health at Cal Poly Humboldt. His Primary responsibilities include preparing future physical education teachers. Dr. Adams also serves as a co-director for an OSEP grant that allows students to complete their special education credential, along with a physical education credential, adapted physical education added authorization, and master's degree in kinesiology. David's research interest include supporting the development motor skills in children with autism spectrum disorder and improving teacher preparation programming for future APE teachers.

**Mariana Alvayero Ricklefs** is an assistant professor in ESL and bilingual education in the College of Education at Northern Illinois University. She has worked with English Learners with and without learning disabilities in various settings for several years. Her research interests include language ideologies, raciolinguistics, identity positioning, critical language awareness, and teacher education. She is a former Fulbright scholar. She has presented her research at professional conferences at the state, national, regional, and international levels.

**Jill Anderson** is an Associate Professor of Kinesiology at Cal Poly Humboldt and holds an MS and PhD in Kinesiology with a focus in Adapted Physical Activity and a MPH with a focus in Health Promotion and Health Behavior. Throughout her career Dr. Anderson has combined these expertise to support her passion for accessible health promotion programming and Adapted Physical Education teacher preparation. Dr. Anderson supports these passions though her research lines and facilitating and supporting accessible and inclusive community programming.

**Wenjing Bao**, M.S., is a doctoral student in the Department of Special Education and Clinical Sciences at the University of Oregon. Her research interests include assessment and intervention for children with developmental disabilities, dissemination and implementation science, and cultural adaptation of interventions. In addition to research, she has experience training teachers and caregivers as well as working with young children in family, school, and clinical settings. She aspires to make services more accessible and appropriate for children and families.

**Ed Bengtson** is an Associate Professor of Educational Leadership at the University of Arkansas where he serves as Department Head of Curriculum and Instruction. He has 22 years in K-12 education, serving as instrumental music teacher, assistant principal and principal. His research interests focus on the socialization of educators, educators' use of data, and the educational doctorate as a professional degree. Dr. Bengtson's teaching areas include qualitative research methods, program evaluation, instructional supervision and the principalship. He has worked with the Carnegie Project on the Education Doctorate (CPED) where he has served as a research team member as a qualitative methodologist.

**Michelle L. Bonati**, Ph.D., is an Associate Professor of Teacher Education at the State University of New York at Plattsburgh. Her research interests include service-learning pedagogy and examining approaches for developing inclusive K-12 schools, universities, and communities. At SUNY Plattsburgh, she teaches undergraduate and graduate courses in the Childhood Education BSEd and Special Education

*About the Contributors*

MSEd programs. Her teaching philosophy embodies inclusive pedagogical approaches and alignment with the principles of Universal Design for Learning. Her co-edited book, People with Intellectual Disability Experiencing University Life is available from Brill. Her 2020 co-authored book, Inclusive Education in Schools and Early Childhood Settings is published by Springer. Michelle previously served as a K-12 special education teacher in Arizona.

**Jennifer Brown** is an Associate Professor and Graduate Coordinator in the Department of Communication Sciences and Special Education at the University of Georgia Mary Frances Early College of Education. Her research focuses on improving communication outcomes for children in natural and inclusive environments through collaborative practices. She has expertise in early intervention, family-guided routines-based intervention, caregiver coaching, cooperative interagency early intervention, and inclusive practices. She is a clinically certified speech-language pathologist and has provided early childhood services to young children with and at-risk for disabilities and their families in a variety of settings. She has been involved with Office of Special Education Programs (OSEP) interdisciplinary master's personnel preparation and doctoral leadership grants as a scholar, project coordinator, key personnel, and co-investigator.

**Allison Bruhn**, a former middle school teacher and a graduate of Vanderbilt University, is a Professor of Special Education at University of Iowa. She has taught courses on elementary classroom management, social and behavioral interventions, and two doctoral seminars. In her role as special education program coordinator, she oversaw all curricular and programmatic decisions, admissions, and student issues. Her current administrative role is serving as the Executive Director of the Scanlan Center for School Mental Health. Dr. Bruhn's research interests include designing, implementing, and evaluating multi-tiered systems of support and using technology-based self-management to help students improve behavior. Bruhn has authored over 80 publications including a book on managing challenging behavior, created two behavioral intervention and assessment mobile apps, and has an extensive record in personnel preparation.

**Sydney A. Bueno** is the Director of Graduate Programs and an Associate Professor at the University of Wisconsin Stevens Point. She currently teaches courses on classroom and behavior management, transition to adulthood, and inclusion. Prior to working in higher education, Dr. Bueno taught K-12 special education for 13 years. Her research interests include graduate programs and curriculum delivery, teacher preparation, and transition for students with disabilities to postsecondary ed.

**Ya-Chih Chang**, Ph.D., is a Professor in the Division of Special Education and Counseling at California State University, Los Angeles. Her research focuses on evidence-based interventions for young children with autism spectrum disorders and other developmental disabilities, including collaboration and implementation of evidence-based strategies with community partners, teachers, and families in diverse and underserved communities.

**Suzannah B. Chatlos** is an Assistant Professor at SUNY Plattsburgh in the psychology department, with a focus on instruction in the school psychology MA/CAS program. Her research focuses on bullying in childhood and adolescence and reducing barriers to adopting and implementing with fidelity evidence-based interventions in the school setting. She is a Nationally Certified School Psychologist (NCSP).

**Brett Collins** (she/her), MSW, LCSW, has served young children and families in many roles (e.g., doula, clinician, educator, part-time San Francisco State University faculty) and across multiple settings (e.g., home, classroom, community), allowing her to view interventions through a blend of person-centered and systemic lenses. Ms. Collins' range of expertise, passions, and experiences center on intersectional, transdisciplinary, and family-driven practices in EC relationships and systems.

**Amy L. Cook**, Ph.D., is an associate professor and the Department Chair of the Counseling and School Psychology Department, College of Education and Human Development, at the University of Massachusetts Boston. She received a Ph.D. in Educational Psychology, with a concentration in Counseling Psychology, from the University of Connecticut Storrs. She has worked in urban schools and community mental health organizations, providing counseling services to students and families. Her research focuses on developing culturally responsive practices that promote youth development and equity-oriented outcomes largely via community-engaged participatory research with youth and educators in partner schools and organizations. Dr. Cook teaches courses in collaborative consultation in schools; professional, ethical, and legal issues; sociocultural considerations in counseling; research in counseling and psychology, and practicum. Through her teaching, she incorporates community engagement and scholarly research outcomes that prepare graduate students to implement transformative programming and practices that elevate the voices and social-emotional lives of youth. She also serves as co-PI on Project Teachers Learning with Counselors (TLC), a personnel preparation grant funded by the U.S. Department of Education, Office of Special Education Programs, along with Kristin Murphy, Ph.D. (PI), Chris Denning, Ph.D. (co-PI), and Laura Hayden, Ed.D. (co-PI). Project TLC focuses on providing interdisciplinary preparation of master's level candidates across Special Education and School Adjustment Counseling programs, with a focus on incorporating transformative social-emotional learning training to master's scholars that support academic outcomes for children with emotional and behavioral disorders.

**Marina Crain**, M.S., CCC-SLP, is a licensed Speech Language Pathologist and AAC specialist currently enrolled as a doctoral student in the Special Education program at University of Oregon. She earned a Master of Science in Speech Language Pathology from University of the Pacific and a Master of Education in Applied Behavior Analysis from Arizona State University. She has 10 years of experience as a speech language pathologist in schools specializing in working with preschool and early elementary students with ASD and students with complex communication needs. Her research interests include AAC implementation in the school setting and early literacy skills for non-speaking preschool and early elementary students. She has also served as a clinical supervisor for undergraduate and graduate Speech Language Pathology students at the University of the Pacific.

**Elizabeth D. Cramer** is a professor of special education, Graduate Program Director of Teaching and Learning at Florida International University, and the director of Project SPECIAL. Her research is focused on the education of high-need children in inclusive urban settings. Her work explores opportunity and achievement gaps; the intersection of race, culture, language, poverty, and disability; collaboration with diverse family and faculty; data-based decision making; and placement issues and educational outcomes for minoritized learners.

**Shawn Datchuk**, a former K-12 special education teacher and director, is an Associate Professor of Special Education at the University of Iowa. He teaches academic intervention courses, including explicit

*About the Contributors*

instruction and academic skills for students with special needs. Dr. Datchuk's research interests include explicit instruction, fluency procedures, and methods to improve the written expression of students with disabilities. Dr. Datchuk has authored over 20 publications including articles in several leading special education journals. He is often recognized by students and colleagues for his teaching and mentorship, including the "Teacher of the Year Award" (2020) in the UI Department of Teaching and Learning.

**Serra De Arment** earned her B.A. and M.T. degrees from the University of Virginia in 2001 and began a 10-year career as a special education teacher in diverse school divisions around Virginia. In 2009 she achieved National Board Certification as an Exceptional Needs Specialist and from 2012-2020 she co-facilitated a regional support program for educators pursuing National Board Certification through the Virginia Commonwealth University's Metropolitan Education Training Alliance. Now as a teacher educator, Dr. De Arment prepares early intervention to preschool (birth to 5) and K-12 special educators for working with children and youth in inclusive settings. She is the coordinator for the Post-Baccalaureate Graduate Certificate Program in Special Education Teaching K-12 and also teaches and advises in the M.Ed. in Special Education, Early Childhood concentration. A teacher at heart, her research interests center on teacher education practices for strengthening the special educator workforce and enhancing student access and inclusion, particularly in under-resourced communities and for students with multiple marginalized identities. She is a member of the Council for Exceptional Children and the American Educational Research Association as well as the local Richmond Early Childhood Association.

**Christopher Denning** is an Associate Professor and Department Chair of Curriculum and Instruction in the College of Education and Human Development at the University of Massachusetts Boston. He received his PhD in Special Education from the University of Virginia with a concentration in Education Sciences. He has worked in residential and public schools with individuals with emotional impairments, intellectual impairments, learning disabilities and autism spectrum disorder (ASD) in inclusive and self-contained settings, and as an Autism Specialist with a regional program serving students ages 2-22 in six counties. He has nine peer-reviewed publications and has written two books focusing on successful inclusion practices and motor development/exercise programs for students with ASD. He's taught courses such as, Introduction to Disabilities, Classroom and Behavior Management, Characteristics of Students with Autism Spectrum Disorders, Student Teaching Seminar, and the Capstone Research Seminar. His work focuses on intervention research to support academic and social skill development, and successful inclusion practices for children with disabilities. He has collaborated with Quincy Public Schools to help preschool and elementary teachers implement programs to support physical activity and motor development. The focus is on partnering with classroom teachers to develop sustainable programs for schools and classrooms. Dr. Denning will assist with the oversight of the project, oversee components across disciplines, and will be primarily responsible for planning, evaluating, and supporting advising and student management systems.

**Maria V. Dixon**, M.A., CCC-SLP, is a Clinical Professor at Arizona State University (ASU). She is a nationally-certified speech-language pathologist (SLP) with 25 years of experience. Ms. Dixon specializes in assessment and intervention for individuals with autism across the lifespan. Her work focuses on assisting individuals with autism to achieve positive life outcomes and ensuring inclusion and equity in their communities. She has been a clinical faculty member at Purdue University and the University of Maryland at College Park. At each university, she has provided clinical education of SLP graduate students engaged in practicum experiences in a variety of practice settings and populations. At ASU, she is the co-lead of an autism translational team which focuses on bringing transdisciplinary research to practice in autism. Ms. Dixon is the co-founder and co-director of an interdisciplinary program to support undergraduate students with autism. She is Multicultural Coordinator for a training grant targeting pre-professional preparation for interprofessional clinical practice between SLPs and special education teachers.

**Kristal Ehrhardt** is the Interim Dean of the Western Michigan College of Education & Human Development and a Professor of Special Education. She has ample experience with funded projects, including serving as a principal investigator on a federally-funded personnel training project, Interdisciplinary Preparation for Autism Services, 2017-2022 $1,134,000, Improving Outcomes for Students with High Incidence Disabilities through Accountable and Reflective School Psychology Practice, 2000-2004, $565,195, and on two federally-funded Early Reading First projects, Promising Beginnings, 2008-2013, $4,024,946 and I CAN Read!, 2006-2010, $3,404,137. She served as the Project Director for the Ohio Early Childhood Intervention Project at the University of Cincinnati. She has co-authored articles and chapters on collaborative consultation, behavioral assessment, and intervention in special education and school psychology.

**Lisa Erwin-Davidson**, Ph.D., CCC-SLP, is an Assistant Professor in the Communication Science & Disorder Department at California State University Fullerton. Lisa is currently the project director in year 3 of a 5-year implementation science project engaged with a district-wide community of learners (Partners4Literacy) to facilitate the uptake of three evidence-based practices and research into regular use by special education classroom educators. Lisa is a Significant Contributor to Project ABC, a federally-funded Office of Special Education project to improve interdisciplinary collaborations between speech-language pathologists and early childhood educators to benefit preschoolers' early language and literacy development. Before entering academia, Lisa was a practicing speech-language pathologist for over 25 years specializing in the assessment and implementation of aided augmentative and alternative communication systems for adults and children presenting with complex communication needs.

**Ana Paula Fabian Freire** is a doctoral student and graduate research assistant at Florida International University. She serves as the grant assistant for Project SPECIAL. Her research interests are bilingualism and language acquisition and development in children with autism and other disabilities.

**Elizabeth (Beth) Foster**, Ph.D., is an associate professor at West Chester University, PA in adapted physical activity/education (APA/E). She is the APA/E program coordinator and graduate coordinator of the APE graduate certificate program. Dr. Foster is a nationally Certified Adapted Physical Educator. She is currently the assistant director for Camp Abilities in Pennsylvania, which is a developmental sports camp for children with sensory loss. Dr. Foster has published and presented internationally and nationally at conferences on research and various application-based topics on blindness/deafblindness, adaptations, and assessment within the field of APA/E and adapted sports. Dr. Foster was named the 2012 Pennsylvania State Association for Health, Physical Education, Recreation, and Dance APE teacher of the year. In addition, Dr. Foster has been involved with various adapted sport organizations and disability organizations promoting physical activities, fitness, adapted sports, and aquatics for all individuals with disabilities.

*About the Contributors*

**Kimberly Frazier**, Ph.D., CCC-SLP, an associate professor at the University of Arkansas, has over 30 years of experience working with children with high-needs disabilities. She frequently presents her research to regional, national and international audiences and has published two textbooks related to communication disorders in children.

**Amber Friesen** (she/her), PhD, is an Associate Professor and Coordinator of the Early Childhood Special Education program, Department of Special Education, at San Francisco State University. Since joining SF State in 2012, her research has focused on promoting inclusive early childhood settings and strong family partnerships. With colleagues in early childhood, she co-created and is the co-coordinator of the Inclusive Early Childhood Practices Graduate Certificate. Dr. Friesen has been the PI on two Office of Special Education Programs (OSEP) grants, including a more recent interdisciplinary grant with speech language therapists.

**Mitch Fryling** is currently Associate Dean in the College of Education at California State University, Los Angeles. Prior to this he was Chair of the Division of Special Education and Counseling and a faculty member in the Applied Behavior Analysis program.

**Rosalia F. Gallo**, Ph.D., is a Research Associate Professor at Florida International University's (FIU) Center for Children and Families and a consultant on Project SPECIAL. Dr. Gallo has over 35 years with the Miami-Dade County Public Schools (M-DCPS) the fourth largest school system in the nation with over four-hundred schools. In that role, she established, created, and monitored programs for students with disabilities including those learning English. She has been a consultant to non-profit agencies, universities, and educational software systems. and a university adjunct faculty at all degreed levels (doctoral, graduate, and undergraduate). She has co-authored federal (e.g., Institute of Education Sciences), state, organizational and local grants which resulted in funds awarded to agencies (e.g., M-DCPS and FIU). She has published articles and a book chapter.

**Liana Gonzalez** is an associate teaching professor of special education at Florida International University and co-director of Project SPECIAL with over 20 years experience teaching students with disabilities and is a member of the disability community as the mother of a son who has autism spectrum disorder. She currently teaches special education and disability-focused courses following both in-person and fully online formats. Her research interests and efforts center around family advocacy within the context of disability and specialized pedagogy to meet the needs of diverse learners.

**Ambra L. Green**, Ph.D., is an Associate Professor of Special Education within the College of Education at The University of Texas at Arlington. Dr. Green's scholarship is focused on diverse learners with and at risk for disabilities and mitigating issues of inequity for vulnerable populations through teacher preparation, multi-tiered systems of support, and policy.

**Kristi S. Hagans** is a professor in the school psychology program at California State University, Long Beach (CSULB). She received her Ph.D. in school psychology from the University of Oregon. Prior to her appointment at CSULB, she worked as a school psychologist in both Oregon and California. Dr. Hagans teaches courses related to assessment for intervention and evidence-based instructional strategies and supervises practica students and interns. She has served as Co-PI on five single- and inter-disciplinary training grants from the Office of Special Education Programs (OSEP). Dr. Hagans' research and publications focus on graduate student training, multi-tiered systems of support, and equity in education.

**Chaiqua A. Harris** is currently a Core Teaching Faculty member at Northwestern University. She has had 8 years of experience as a professor. Also, Dr. Harris has worked as a middle school counselor, high school counselor, private behavior interventionist, and adolescent offender therapist. She obtained a doctorate of philosophy in Counselor Education from Mississippi State University. Her research interests include: academic self-efficacy, ethnic identity, African American women who hold the doctorate, African-American hair, sexual orientations, gender differences, socioeconomic status, academic performance, children/adolescents and the impact of nutrition on mental health, and oppressed populations. She is an AAAA licensed professional school counselor for the state of Mississippi and is also a National Certified Counselor. She has presented at several local, regional, and national counseling conferences as well as published multiple scholarly journal articles.

**Laura Hayden** is an Associate Professor of Counseling and School Psychology in the College of Education and Human Development at UMass Boston. Since joining UMass Boston as a faculty member in 2010, she has held various leadership roles specific to School Counseling, including the role of School Counseling Graduate Program Director (2010-2014, 2017) for online and on-campus programs and Counseling and School Psychology Department Chair (2018-2019). She has revised the School Counseling curriculum to align with state and national standards, managed courses for the program of study, overseen admission, secured field placements for practicum and internship students, obtained program approval through external organizations, and led the program through accreditation reviews. She is the author of over 40 articles and books addressing social, emotional, academic, and physical development of young people, specifically in relation to systemic support and change. She is a leading scholar in the field of school-based physical activity and mental health, launching programs, partnerships, and scholarship exploring the impact of physical activity on mental health and socio-emotional development, specifically with young people of color in urban areas.

**Renee Hepperlen** received a master's degree in clinical social work from the University of Chicago and a Ph.D. from the University of Minnesota. While at the University of Minnesota, she was a fellow in the Leadership Education in Neurodevelopmental and Related Disabilities (LEND) program, an interdisciplinary training program. Her work experience before receiving her Ph.D. included social work practice in interdisciplinary settings, including in health care and education.

**Jocelyn Clare Reyno Hermoso** (she/her/siya), PhD, MSW, is an Associate Professor and Bachelor of Arts in Social Work (BASW) Program Coordinator in the School of Social Work at San Francisco State University. Her interests are in macro and community practice, policy advocacy, community-based research, transnational social work, gender and peacebuilding, and social justice pedagogy. Since joining faculty at SF State in 2006, Dr. Hermoso has taught and mentored MSW and BASW students in honing a practice perspective of working with clients within their micro, meso, and macro contexts informed by anti-oppressive, anti-racist, and trauma-informed principles. Among other awards, Dr. Hermoso is the recipient of the Equity Research Fellowship Hub for BIWOC Associate Professors. Recently, Dr. Hermoso co-developed an interdisciplinary training program for Early Childhood Special Education and Social Work pre-service practitioners.

*About the Contributors*

**Rebecca Hines**, Ph.D., is an Associate Professor in Exceptional Education at the University of Central Florida. She created and oversees the undergraduate Learning & Language program track in exceptional student education program at the University of Central Florida (UCF). She is also the PI on an OSEP personnel preparation grant and Co-PI on three other federally funded projects. In addition to teacher preparation, her research interests include working with students with emotional/behavioral disorders, inclusion, and technology integration.

**Emily Hoeh** is an Associate Professor in the Department of Education at the State University of New York, Plattsburgh. She earned her doctorate (Ph.D.) in Special Education from the University at Buffalo, as an Office of Special Education Programs research fellow. Her professional experience includes teaching special and general education higher education coursework, professional development trainer and a special education classroom teacher for students with a range of disabilities. Emily recently served as a Council for Exceptional Children, Innovations in Special Education Technology Executive Board Member as Member at Large and on the New York State Council for Exceptional Children as President. Her research interests are high incidence disabilities, technology, and curriculum.

**Chris Hopper** is a Professor of Kinesiology at Cal Poly Humboldt. He has degrees from the University of Exeter in England and the University of Oregon. Dr. Hopper is a specialist in adapted physical activity and has led programs designed to promote active lifestyles for children and youth with disabilities. Dr. Hopper has written four books for teachers on how to implement physical activity and nutrition education programs in schools. During his career he has received five personnel preparation grants from the United States Department of Education to prepare adapted physical education teachers.

**Delaney Hughes** is an Education Specialist born in Tucson, Arizona. Her undergraduate degree of Fitness and Wellness was attained from Northern Arizona University in 2017. She moved to Humboldt County, California in 2021 to begin the graduate program for Adapted Physical Education at Cal Poly Humboldt. Delaney is currently teaching special education in the area as she finishes her masters program.

**Tameeka L. Hunter**, Ph.D., LPC, NCC, CRC (she/her), is a licensed professional counselor, nationally certified counselor, and a nationally certified rehabilitation counselor. She is a tenure track assistant professor, an intersectional diversity and social justice scholar, a professional diversity speaker, and a researcher at Florida International University. Her research focuses on the resilience of marginalized and multiply marginalized populations, including people living with disabilities and chronic illnesses, people of color, sexual- and gender-expansive people, and women. Her work examines the impact of resilience and strength-based approaches on marginalized and multiply marginalized populations' psychosocial, educational, and vocational functioning.

**Bonnie Ingelin** is an assistant professor of Early Childhood Special Education (ECSE) at the University of St. Thomas in Minnesota. Dr. Ingelin specializes in both ECSE and autism spectrum disorder (ASD). She received her Ph.D. from Florida State University in 2018 with an emphasis on teaching science, technology, engineering, and math (STEM) to students with ASD. Her research interests are in teaching academic skills to young children with ASD. Dr. Ingelin has published her work on teaching early number sense skills to young children with ASD and understanding gender differences for individuals with ASD. Dr. Ingelin has previously published articles on teaching early number sense skills, listening comprehension, and algebraic word problems to students with ASD under her previous last name Henning.

**Shanna Jamanis**, Ph.D., is a Professor in the School of Education at Nazareth College, where she is also co-director of I-SPAN, the Interdisciplinary Specialty Program in Autism at Nazareth. She is a former special education teacher, integration facilitator, behavior specialist, and coordinator for autism services. Aside from teaching in inclusive schools in the Washington D.C. area and consulting for the Eugene 4J public schools in Oregon, Dr. Jamanis has also worked as an educational consultant at the University of Rochester's Strong Center for Developmental Disabilities Autism Spectrum Disorders program. Her research and professional development interests include Neurodiversity, strength-based planning and support in schools for students on the autism spectrum, and interprofessional preparation of teacher candidates. Dr. Jamanis has presented locally, nationally and internationally on teacher preparation and interdisciplinary preparation in autism.

**Lanai Jennings** is an Associate Professor and Program Director of the Marshall University School Psychology program. Dr. Jennings earned her Ph.D. in School Psychology from Western Michigan University in 2007. She has worked for over 15 years in public education as both a school psychologist and a coordinator at the West Virginia Department of Education. She currently teaches graduate courses in cognitive assessment, prevention, crisis intervention, and ethics. Dr. Jennings also is the project director for Marshall University's Special Education and Resiliency (SEAR) project, an interdisciplinary program supported by award H325K190039 through the Office of Special Education Programs in the U.S. Department of Education.

**Alison R. King**, Ph.D., CCC-SLP, LSLS Cert. AVT, is an Assistant Professor and Graduate Director in the Communication Sciences and Disorders program at Longwood University. She holds a Bachelor's degree from Appalachian State University, a Master's degree from the University of South Carolina, and a Ph.D. from Virginia Commonwealth University. She teaches in the areas of research methods, collaboration, educational settings, and aural habilitation. Her research interests include professional preparation of Speech-Language Pathologists, caregiver coaching in early intervention, and aural habilitation of young children with hearing loss. Dr. King has worked in the public schools, early intervention, and as the Auditory Therapist on the cochlear implant team at VCU. She currently serves on the Virginia Board of Audiology and Speech-Language Pathology, Virginia Board of Health Professions, and the Virginia Early Hearing Detection and Intervention Advisory Board.

**Seth King** is an Associate Professor of Special Education at the University of Iowa where he teaches courses related to behavior management, ABA, and research methods. He has published or co-published 35 articles in areas of developmental disability, behavior intervention, and research design. Dr. King's most recent research involves integrating simulation technology into teacher education programs. He has experience in developing and coordinating verified ABA course sequences and mentoring graduate level students pursuing careers in special education and behavior analysis.

**Bonnie R. Kraemer** is a Professor and Board-Certified Behavior Analyst in the Department of Special Education at San Diego State University. Her areas of teaching and research are in severe intellectual disabilities and autism, with a specific focus on families, instruction, transition, quality of life, and applied

*About the Contributors*

behavior analysis. Dr. Kraemer has been the Project Director or Co-Project Director on multiple OSEP funded Personnel Preparation grants that focus on preparing teachers and master's degree candidates in the areas of autism, behavior, and secondary transition.

**Suzanne Kucharczyk** is Associate Professor of Special Education and Program Coordinator of Inclusive Education and Clinical Programs at the University of Arkansas in the Department of Curriculum and Instruction. Dr. Kucharczyk is Principal Investigator on two 325K grants and a 325D grant from the Office of Special Education Programs through the Department of Education. She teaches and studies the transition experiences of youth and their families, as well as supports for special educators in implementation of evidence-based transition services and programs through interdisciplinary teams.

**Sara Kupzyk** received her Master's degree in Applied Behavioral Science at the University of Kansas (KU) and Doctoral degree in School Psychology at the University of Nebraska-Lincoln (UNL). She completed her pre-doctoral internship and post-doctoral experience at the Munroe-Meyer Institute (MMI). She is a Licensed Psychologist and Certified Behavior Analyst. She provided outpatient behavioral health services for eight years at MMI to children and families with varied concerns including learning problems, autism spectrum disorder, and internalizing and externalizing behavior disorders. She is currently a faculty member in the Psychology Department at the University of Nebraska Omaha. She teaches courses in the joint MMI/UNO Applied Behavior Analysis Master's Program. She is the primary investigator on a personnel preparation grant funded through the Office of Special Education and Rehabilitative Services, Department of Education. The grant provides training on interdisciplinary behavioral consultation in schools to scholars in applied behavior analysis, school psychology, and special education. She is also actively involved in research with a focus on home-school collaboration, behavioral consultation, and treatment integrity.

**Kate LaLonde** is an Assistant Professor in Special Education and Literacy Studies at Western Michigan University and is a doctoral-level Board Certified Behavior Analyst (BCBA). Her teaching and research focus on evaluating instructional strategies in special education teacher preparation programs and increasing pre-and-in-service teachers' fidelity in implementing academic assessment, intervention, and data-based decision-making. She is also evaluating innovative teacher preparation pedagogies and their effect on diversifying the teaching force. She has published in the areas of autism, early intervention, interdisciplinary collaboration, and language and imitation skills.

**Katina Lambros**, PhD, BCBA-D, is the Director of the School Psychology Program at San Diego State University in the Department of Counseling and School Psychology (CSP). She is a School Psychologist and Board Certified Behavior Analyst specializing in ecobehavioral assessment-intervention for academic and socio-emotional problems in school-aged populations. Dr. Lambros directs Project BEAMS, a 5-year $1.25 million dollar grant funded by the Office of Special Education (OSEP) to co-train school psychologists and special educators to serve diverse students with behavioral, emotional, and mental health challenges in California's public schools Her research to date focuses on three broad areas: (1) improving mental health services and positive behavioral support in schools with an emphasis on students with emotional and behavioral difficulties; (2) promoting the use of evidence-based practices and data-based decision making in schools; and (3) increasing access to school-based service use and culturally responsive services for diverse learners.

**About the Contributors**

**Jasmine Lehal** is a School Psychology Trainee in the School Psychology Program at San Diego State University (SDSU) in the Department of Counseling and School Psychology (CSP). Jasmine is a Graduate Assistant for Project BEAMS - a grant federally funded by the Office of Special Education (OSEP). Project BEAMS assists with the training of school psychology trainees and special educators to service diverse students with behavioral, emotional, and mental health challenges in California's public schools. Jasmine is also a member of the School Psychology Student Association (SPSA) and served as the former Diversity Chair. She is currently the President-Elect and will serve as the association's President in the upcoming academic year. As the only international student in the School Psychology program at SDSU, Jasmine works to bring diverse and unique perspectives to the program.

**Rebecca Lieberman-Betz** is an Associate Professor of Special Education in the Department of Communication Sciences and Special Education at the University of Georgia. She is co-Director of the Birth Through Kindergarten Program and Coordinator of the Preschool Special Education endorsement at UGA. Prior to becoming faculty at UGA, her professional experiences included work as an early interventionist serving families of infants and toddlers with disabilities and as a preschool special education teacher. Dr. Lieberman-Betz's scholarship focuses on play and communication in young children with disabilities, Part C early intervention, and interdisciplinary personnel preparation.

**Paige McCloud**, M.L.A., is a Ph.D. scholar in Exceptional Education at the University of Central Florida. Paige's research focuses on the learning disabilities-to-prison pipeline. Specifically, on the differential treatment hypothesis and how schools handle behavioral referrals of students with emotional and behavioral disorders or ADHD to law enforcement.

**Aja McKee** is an Associate Professor at California State University, Fullerton (CSUF) in the Department of Special Education. She has worked in the public education system since 1998. Her work as a special educator and administrator in special education provides her with practical experience she shares with her credentialing, masters, and doctoral students. Aja's research examines inclusion of all individuals regardless of perceived severity of disability, autism (with an emphasis on those who are non-speaking), and early childhood special education.

**Maryssa Kucskar Mitsch** (she/her), PhD, is an Assistant Professor in the Early Childhood Special Education program and Coordinator of the Special Education Minor at San Francisco State University. Her research focuses on inclusive practices, strategies for effective ECSE personnel preparation, social skills interventions, and partnerships with CLD families. Dr. Mitsch teaches undergraduate, graduate, and doctoral students in Early Childhood Special Education and Special Education. Dr. Mitsch led the co-development of an interdisciplinary training program for Early Childhood Special Education and Social Work pre-service practitioners. In her time at SF State since Fall 2017, she has been awarded the Presidential Award for Development of Probationary Faculty and the First-Year Experience Teaching Award, as well as numerous grants.

**Danica Moise**, M.A., BCBA, is a Ph.D. scholar in Exceptional Education at the University of Central Florida. Danica's current graduate work focuses on preparing teachers and practitioners entering the special education workforce.

*About the Contributors*

**Erika Moore** is a Ph.D. scholar in the Exceptional Education program at the University of Central Florida. Erika's research agenda includes preparing educators for inclusion and promoting equitable opportunities for students with cognitive disabilities in education.

**Kristin Murphy** is an Associate Professor of Special Education at UMass Boston. She earned her Ph.D. in Special Education from the University of Florida. Dr. Murphy's scholarship focuses on preservice and professional learning opportunities for special educators, mixed reality simulations as an active learning tool, and issues pertaining to exclusionary school settings serving students with emotional and behavioral disorders. Dr. Murphy is a former special educator of students with emotional and behavioral disorders for the NYC Department of Education and she has served in various special education-focused teaching, research, and policy roles for nearly twenty years. Locally, Dr. Murphy has provided professional development to over 600 Boston Public Schools teachers on special education law and serves in an active leadership role with the MA DESE in MRS development for teacher education programs across the state. On a national level, she serves as co-chair of the Professional Development Committee for CEC's Division for Emotional and Behavioral Health. Dr. Murphy has received several awards in recognition of exemplary teaching and dedication to students including the 2018 Face-to-Face Innovation in Teaching Award, a UMass Boston-wide award, and the 2020 Manning Prize for Excellence in Teaching, a University of Massachusetts system-wide award. She is currently the Principal Investigator for Project Teachers Learning with Counselors, an interdisciplinary personnel preparation program for future special educators and school adjustment counselors funded by the US DOE's Office of Special Education Programs.

**Janice Myck-Wayne**, Ed.D., is a Professor and the Early Childhood Special Education Credential Coordinator in the Department of Special Education at California State University, Fullerton (CSUF). She has been the principal investigator for three US Department, Office of Special Education Programs, Personnel Training grants that focus on inclusive practices. She teaches assessment and intervention courses, working with families and foundations in ECSE. Her research focuses on young children and play, working with families, inclusion and very young children, and teacher education. Dr. Myck-Wayne has presented her research at many national and international conferences. Her work has been published in a variety of books and journals.

**Bergen Nelson**, MD, MS, is an Associate Professor at the VCU School of Medicine, a primary care pediatrician and a researcher with a specialty in early childhood development and systems of care for children with developmental and behavioral concerns.

**Brandi L. Newkirk-Turner**, Ph.D., CCC-SLP, is the Associate Provost for Academic Affairs at Jackson State University and a professor in the Department of Communicative Disorders. Her research examines issues that are relevant to speech-language assessment of child speakers of African American English; best practices in preparing graduate students to serve culturally and linguistically diverse populations; and barriers, opportunities, and potential impacts in reducing or eliminating equity gaps of underserved student populations in higher education.

**Matthew O'Brien** is a Clinical Associate Professor of Pediatrics at University of Iowa Stead Family Children's Hospital. He completed his doctorate in Psychological and Quantitative Foundations from the

University of Iowa and completed postdoctoral fellowships in neuropsychology and behavioral psychology at the University of Iowa Hospitals and Clinics. Dr. O'Brien serves as the Director of Biobehavioral Services. In addition, he is the Director of Research and Psychology for the Iowa Leadership Education in Neurodevelopmental and Related Disabilities program, a graduate training initiative designed to expand interdisciplinary competence in aspiring clinical service providers. Dr. O'Brien is the Principal Investigator on a multisite R01 research grant funded by NIH evaluating behavioral assessment through telehealth and conducts research related to functional analysis of severe and challenging behavior in individuals with autism and other neurodevelopmental disorders.

**Miyoko Patricelli** serves as a clinical supervisor for the Communication Disorders and Sciences graduate program in the Augmentative and Alternative Communication (AAC) Clinic. She is licensed by the Oregon Board of Examiners in Speech-Language Pathology and by the American Speech-Language-Hearing Association (ASHA). She has served as a Speech Language Pathologist across an array of settings. She began her career as a school-based Speech Language Pathologist in preschool through high school before transitioning to combined-setting medical positions that included outpatient pediatric and adult therapy, inpatient rehab, and adult acute care. She enjoys the opportunity to be able to work with a variety of patient populations and especially loves how AAC allows her to support individuals across the lifespan. In addition to providing direct intervention as a Speech Language Pathologist, Miyoko has also served as the hospital representative for the Pediatric Rehab Operations Committee within her hospital network.

**Jennica Paz**, PhD, is an Assistant Professor in the Department of Counseling and School Psychology at San Diego State University. Passionate about ensuring high-quality service delivery, her work focuses on positive youth development, strengths-based assessment, resiliency among foster youth, school-based mental health, school safety, and assessment and intervention among CLD students.

**Whitney Perkins** is a Mississippi native who received her bachelor's in Speech and Hearing Sciences from the University of Southern Mississippi (USM), master's in Deaf Education from USM, master's in Communicative Disorders from Jackson State University (JSU), and doctorate in Early Childhood Education from JSU. She currently serves as the interim chairperson and graduate program director at JSU's Communicative Disorders department.

**Kristi Perryman** is an Associate Professor of Counseling at the University of Arkansas. Her experience includes working as a special education teacher as well as an elementary and middle school counselor and an RPT-S and an LPC-S in private practice. She is the founder of the Missouri State University Institute for Play Therapy and the University of Arkansas Office of Play Therapy Research and Training. Research foci include play therapy, school counseling and the use of creative arts in counseling and in supervision.

**Stephanie M. Peterson**, Ph.D., is Professor Psychology and Associate Dean of the College of Arts and Sciences at Western Michigan University, previously serving as the Chair of the Department of Psychology for 8 years. She earned her doctorate in Special Education at The University of Iowa in 1994. Previously, she taught at Gonzaga University, Utah State University, The Ohio State University, and Idaho State University. Her primary research interests are helping to decrease chronic severe behavior problems in children with developmental disabilities. Specifically, she studies choice making in the

*About the Contributors*

treatment of problem behavior, functional communication training, reinforcement-based interventions for children with problem behavior, concurrent schedules of reinforcement in the treatment of severe problem behavior, functional analysis of problem behavior, and teleconsultation. She also has interests in applications of behavior analysis to educational interventions and teacher/behavior analyst training. She has served on a variety of editorial boards, including the Journal of Applied Behavior Analysis and Behavior Analysis in Practice and is currently the editor of Behavior Analysis in Practice. She also served as a Senior Editor for Education and Treatment of Children for many years. She served two 3-year terms on the Board of Directors for the Behavior Analyst Certification Board and was appointed by the Governor of Michigan to the Michigan Board of Behavior Analysts, Michigan's licensing board for behavior analysts. She served as the President of the Board for two years.

**Andy V. Pham**, PhD, is an associate professor of school psychology at Florida International University. Dr. Pham's research interests include examining the intersection of neurocognitive and sociocultural variables on academic and mental health outcomes of diverse youth. He aims to reduce disparities in mental health and education by implementing cultural humility and cultural responsiveness in research and practice.

**Al Poling** is a Professor of Psychology at Western Michigan University. He received his B.A. from Alderson-Broaddus College, his M.A. from West Virginia University, and his Ph.D. from the University of Minnesota. A Fellow of the Association for Behavior Analysis International and Divisions 3, 25, and 28 of the American Psychological Association, Al has published 12 books and over 350 articles and book chapters and served as the research advisor of 38 Ph.D. recipients. With them and other colleagues Al has conducted research and done conceptual work in several areas, including behavioral pharmacology, clinical psychopharmacology (with special emphasis on the effects of psychotropic drugs in people with autism spectrum disorder), applied behavior analysis, gender issues, animal welfare, quantitative analysis, learning processes, research methods, and scent detection. Their work has been published in more than 50 different journals. Al was recognized as a Distinguished Faculty Scholar at Western Michigan University in 1996 and as a Distinguished Alumnus of West Virginia University in 1999. In 2003, he received the Western Michigan University College of Arts and Sciences Outstanding Achievement in Research and Creative Activity Award. In 2016, he received a Lifetime Achievement Award from the California Association of Behavior Analysis, a Translational Research Award from the Association for Behavior Analysis International, and an International Humanitarian Award from the American Psychological Association. In 2019 he received the SEAB Don Hake Translational Research Award from the American Psychological Association.

**Kristin Powers** is a professor of school psychology and director of the Community Clinic for Counseling and Educational Services at California State University, Long Beach. She is coauthor of the text book Collaborative Consultation in the Schools 5th Edition and has published on transition planning for students with disabilities, multi-tiered systems of support, and preparing school psychology candidates for the field. She has been PI and Co-PI on seven Office of Special Education Programs (OSEP) personnel preparation grants. She began her career as a school psychologists for Long Beach Unified School District.

**Sarah Kye Price** is Professor in the School of Social Work at Virginia Commonwealth University.

**Seb Prohn**, PhD, is the Assistant Director-Research & Evaluation at Virginia's University Center for Excellence in Developmental Disabilities, the Partnership for People with Disabilities at VCU. Seb holds a PhD in psychology and has over a decade of experience evaluating programs and projects that address wellness, quality of life and community participation for people with intellectual and developmental disabilities (IDD). Many of his current projects employ participatory methods to actively engage people with IDD in the knowledge creation and translation.

**Catherine (Cara) Richards-Tutor** completed her Ph.D in 2004 at University of California, Santa Barbara in Special Education, Risk, and Disability Studies. Prior to completing her doctorate, she taught in both general and special education classrooms and worked with families as a behavior specialist. Her research and publications focus on interventions for students at-risk for learning disabilities and multilingual youth. Dr. Richards-Tutor has served as Co-PI for several large-scale studies and is currently Co-PI on two interdisciplinary training grants from the Office of Special Education Programs (OSEP). Dr. Richards-Tutor works with local schools to develop and implement Multi-tiered Systems of Support, including RTI and PBIS. She serves on the executive board for the Council for Exceptional Children's Division of Research.

**John Elwood Romig** is an Assistant Professor of Special Education at the University of Texas at Arlington. His research interests include writing instruction for students with disabilities, curriculum-based measurement, and effective professional development offerings.

**Erin Rotheram-Fuller** is an Associate Professor at ASU. She is a Board Certified Behavior Analyst as well as a licensed psychologist and provides consultation to schools and agencies on how to best support children with disabilities who are struggling within the classroom or home. Dr. Rotheram-Fuller has been working in schools for over 20 years, across multiple urban school districts, to examine interventions and environmental factors impacting student behavior, academic, and social success.

**Kalyn Ruland** is an Adapted Physical Education Professional in California. She has an education specialist credential with an Added Authorization in Adapted Physical Education and a Masters of Science in Kinesiology.

**Ann Santos** is a Clinical Associate Professor and Program Coordinator of the School Psychology program at the University of Iowa, where she is primarily responsible for curricular decisions, accreditation processes, and practicum supervision and placement. Dr. Santos is a Licensed Psychologist and Licensed Specialist in School Psychology (LSSP). She has extensive experience working as a school psychologist and LSSP across the country, including Texas, Iowa, and Maryland. She is a member of the National Association of School Psychologists (NASP) and the American Psychological Association (APA). Additionally, Dr. Santos serves as an active site visitor for the Commission on Accreditation (CoA) of the American Psychological Association. For over 20 years, Dr. Santos has provided direct service to students in public and private school settings for students displaying academic, social, emotional, and behavioral difficulties. Her research interests include effective supervision practices, school consultation, and improving school psychology training.

*About the Contributors*

**Stephanie Shire** is an Assistant Professor in Early Intervention and Early Childhood Special Education. Her research interests focus on the development, adaptation, and real world effectiveness of intervention programs for children with autism and other neurodevelopmental disorders examined through community partnerships in both low and high resource settings. She is interested in the use of effectiveness-implementation hybrid designs (e.g., Shire et al., 2017), and Sequential Multiple Assignment Randomized Trials (SMARTs) to examine both the implementation of the intervention through community practitioners as well as children's development.

**Renee Speight**, PhD, BCBA-D, is a Teaching Assistant Professor at the University of Arkansas. Dr. Speight's expertise and research interests are in multi-tiered systems of positive behavior support to improve outcomes of children and youth with emotional, behavioral, and mental health support needs; and professional development of in-service and preservice teachers to support their implementation of inclusive practices. Dr. Speight serves on the editorial board for *Journal of Special Education Technology*.

**Christine Spence** is an assistant professor of Early Childhood Special Education at Virginia Commonwealth University. She has worked primarily in the early intervention field as an educator and music therapist in multi-disciplinary teams, and as a professional development provider. Due to this background, her research focuses on 1) analyzing personnel preparation and professional development focused on culturally appropriate and responsive teaching and learning; 2) hearing the voices of families engaged in and impacted by these services and systems; and 3) investigating the systems themselves, particularly focused on collaboration between and across systems (i.e., developmental and medical, educational and child welfare).

**Maureen E. Squires**, Ed.D., is an Associate Professor of Teacher Education and Department Chair at the State University of New York at Plattsburgh, in Plattsburgh, N.Y. She earned an Ed.D. in Educational Theory and Practice (2011) and a C.A.S. in Educational Leadership (2008) from Binghamton University, an M.S.Ed. in Special Education (2003) from LeMoyne College, and a B.A. in English (2001) with a concentration in Secondary Education from Nazareth College. She holds multiple New York State teaching and leadership certifications. Her professional career began as an English teacher. Currently, she teaches graduate courses and supervises teacher candidate fieldwork. Her areas of interest and research include teacher preparation, special education, mother-scholars/leaders in academia, and ethics and education.

**L. Lynn Stansberry Brusnahan** is a Professor at the University of St. Thomas in Minnesota. At the university, she is former chair of the Department of Special Education and coordinates the autism spectrum disorder and developmental cognitive disabilities programs. Lynn is coauthor of Do Watch Listen Say: Social and Communication Intervention for Autism Spectrum Disorder. She was the 2012 Autism Society of America Professional of the Year. Dr. Stansberry Brusnahan has a Ph.D. from University of Wisconsin-Milwaukee in Urban Education. Lynn serves on the Council for Exceptional Children's (CEC) Division on Autism and Developmental Disabilities (DADD) board. Lynn is the parent of an adult with autism.

**Angi Stone-MacDonald** is a Professor and Department Chair in the Department of Special Education, Rehabilitation, and Counseling at California State University, San Bernardino. Until July 2022, she was the Associate Dean of Grants and Research for the College of Education and Human Development and Associate Professor at the University of Massachusetts Boston in the Early Education and Care in Inclusive Settings program. She received her doctorate from Indiana University in Special Education. Dr. Stone-MacDonald has worked with people with disabilities for the last two decades as a paraprofessional, teacher, consultant, and researcher. Her areas of research include early intervention, international special education for children with developmental disabilities, and teacher preparation for early intervention. Her current research agenda includes early intervention personnel preparation and inclusive early childhood education in Tanzania. She has received several grants to support her research from her university, the Massachusetts Department of Early Education and Care, and the US Department of Education. Dr. Stone-MacDonald serves her field and children and families with disabilities at the local, state, and national levels on a variety of committees and projects. She has published three books and several articles on her research and completed a Fulbright Scholar grant in Zanzibar, Tanzania during 2016-2017. Angi serves her field and children and families with disabilities at the local, state, and national levels on a variety of committees and projects. She has been actively involved in state and local committees, organizations, and grant work with the state government to promote inclusion and adequate teacher preparation to work with children with disabilities in early childhood. Most recently, she services on the Higher Education Early Intervention Task Force and Personnel Prep Committee and the board of the Massachusetts Association of Early Childhood Teacher Educators.

**Sandra Stroebel** is the Associate Dean for the College of Education and Professional Development. She is a Professor in the School Psychology program. Dr. Stroebel earned her Ph.D. in School Psychology from the University of South Carolina in 1988. She holds a dual license in psychology and school psychology. In collaboration with peers, she has received several federal and state grants pertaining to mental health shortages in the state. She serves on the West Virginia School Psychology Executive Board. Due to her longstanding service to WVSPA and school psychology, she received the Fred Jay Krieg Lifetime Achievement Award in 2020. She has numerous presentations and peer-reviewed publications related to the topic of mental health in children and youth. Dr. Stroebel was appointed to the WV Board of Examiners of Psychologists in January 2015 and was elected as chair in 2019. Dr. Stroebel provides therapy to children and youth in Charleston as part of her community service.

**Sarah Summy** is a Professor at WMU within the Department of Special Education and Literacy Studies. Her research areas include: teacher preparation, challenging behaviors, and children and youth with emotional/behavioral disorders.

**Jennifer B. Symon**, PhD, BCBA-D, is a Professor in the Division of Special Education and Counseling at Cal State LA. She coordinates the graduate programs in autism and conducts research in the areas of social communication intervention, family support, and collaboration between team members for individuals with Autism Spectrum Disorders (ASD).

**Heather Taylor** is an associate professor and the Education Specialist program coordinator in the College of Education and Integrative Studies at Cal Poly Pomona. Prior to earning her doctorate, Dr. Taylor taught K-12 general and special education. Her area of expertise is in supporting students with high-incidence disabilities in inclusive settings. Dr. Taylor is Director of a United States Department of Education, Office of Special Education programs personnel development 325K grant. Her current

*About the Contributors*

research interests include effective, culturally-sustaining teacher preparation and effective new teacher mentoring. Dr. Taylor holds a Ph.D. in Education from Claremont Graduate University.

**Johanna Thomas**, Ph.D., is an Associate Professor and Director in the School of Social Work at The University of Arkansas and a Licensed Certified Social Worker (LCSW) in the State of Arkansas. Her research interests include early childhood truancy prevention and intervention, school social work, prevention and intervention with students with high need disabilities, specifically autism, gun violence prevention, political advocacy and policy implementation and evaluation. Dr. Thomas has over a decade of experience in program implementation and evaluation and is currently the external evaluator or PI / Co-PI on numerous federally funded grants from the Substance Abuse and Mental Health Services Administration, the Department of Justice - Bureau of Justice Assistance, and The Department of Education. Programs range in size and area including, but not limited to, Truancy Intervention Programs, Individual Development Accounts programs, Temporary Assistance to Needy Families programs, Community Mental Health Centers, Certified Community Behavioral Health Centers, Adult Drug Treatment Courts and Veterans Treatment Courts. In addition to her research, she teaches both BSW and MSW students.

**Jacqueline Towson**, PhD, CCC-SLP, is Associate Director of the School of Communication Sciences and Disorders and Associate Professor in Communication Sciences and Disorders at the University of Central Florida.

**Teresa Tran** is a second year graduate student in the School Psychology Ed.S Program at San Diego State University in the Department of Counseling and School Psychology. As a trainee, she is currently working at an elementary school in the Chula Vista Elementary School District as part of her practicum fieldwork. She is also a scholar on Project BEAMS, a grant funded by the Office of Special Education (OSEP) to provide interdisciplinary training of school psychologists and special educators to serve culturally diverse students with behavioral, emotional, and mental health challenges. Her areas of interest in school psychology include school-based mental health, social-emotional learning, and improving equity in schools for culturally and linguistically diverse learners.

**Cynthia Vail** received her Ph.D. from Florida State University and has been on the faculty of the University of Georgia in since 1989. She developed the Early Childhood Special Education undergraduate and graduate programs at UGA and recently served as the Department Head for the Department of Communication Sciences and Special Education (2015-2021). Dr. Vail directed numerous federally funded DOE, Office of Special Education Program grants. She currently directs the Georgia Sensory Assistance Project (GSAP), and Co-Directs two personnel preparation grants in early childhood special education. Her research interests include teacher collaboration through peer coaching, partnering with families, and fostering play in young children with challenging behaviors. She has published in The Journal of Early Intervention, Teacher Education and Special Education, Exceptional Children and other scholarly journals. Her recent national service activities include serving on the task force to develop national ECSE/EI personnel standards and serving as the President for the Higher Education Consortium for Special Education (HECSE). She also provides leadership in Georgia as the personnel preparation representative for the State Interagency Coordinating Council for Early Intervention Programs.

**Joanne M. Van Boxtel** is an Interim Associate Dean in the Collage of Education and Integrative Studies at California Polytechnic State University, Pomona. Dr. Van Boxtel is the Co-PI of a personnel development 325K grant. Her research interests include teacher education and special education, teaching and learning for students with disabilities, Universal Design for Learning (UDL), and international inclusive education. She holds a Ph.D. in Disability Studies from Chapman University.

**Rena VanDerwall** is a certified special education teacher, Board Certified Behavior Analyst and Assistant Professor in Special Education at Western Michigan University. Prior to coming to Western Michigan University, she worked as a special education teacher, teacher consultant, behavior support staff, and Dean of Specialized Services in both Chicago, Illinois and Kalamazoo, Michigan. Dr. VanDerwall's teaching and research focuses on teacher preparation, applied behavior analysis, positive behavior supports, and supporting students with emotional and behavioral disorders.

**Dawn Vogler-Elias**, Ph.D., is a Professor of Speech-Language Pathology at Nazareth College and co-directs the Interdisciplinary Specialty Program in Autism at Nazareth College (I-SPAN). She is also the Speech-Language Pathology Discipline Coordinator at the University of Rochester's Leadership in Neurodevelopment and Related Disabilities (LEND) program. Her clinical and research interests include the assessment and intervention of language and social communication for children with developmental disabilities, including autism spectrum disorder. She has presented research locally and nationally on interdisciplinary professional preparation in autism, service-learning pedagogy, and social communication assessment and intervention.

**Sarah Wiegand** is an assistant professor of early childhood and special education at New Mexico State University. She recently completed her doctoral program at the University of Georgia, where she studied special education with areas of emphasis in autism spectrum disorder, early intervention, and professional development. Prior to pursuing her doctorate Dr. Wiegand worked in Minneapolis, Minnesota as an early intervention provider and autism specialist for children birth to three and their families. While attending the University of Georgia Dr. Wiegand was the graduate assistant to the Preparing Interdisciplinary Providers Project, a grant funded through the U.S. Department of Education Office of Special Education Programs focused on preparing highly qualified special education teachers and speech-language pathologists to work with young children with complex needs and their families. Dr. Wiegand's research centers around improving policies and practices and promoting equity in early intervention through examining screening practices, professional development, and personnel preparation.

**Jennifer Wiles** received her Bachelor of Science in Speech and Hearing Sciences from the University of Southern Mississippi and her Doctorate of Audiology from the University of Memphis. Following graduation, she obtained certification as a Listening and Spoken Language Specialist. She has provided aural rehabilitation and family coaching services to diverse populations across the state of Mississippi. She has also taught, advised, mentored, and supervised both undergraduate and graduate students across Communication Disorders and Oral Deaf Education programs. She is currently employed at Jackson State University in the Department of Communicative Disorders.

**Maris Wyatt**, with a passion for students and families and a love for Special Education and the ability to bring that love to the University level and K-12 world of education, brings 26 years of special

*About the Contributors*

education experience to the table along with a Ed.S in Administration and Supervision allows for a blending of both worlds.

**Yaoying Xu** is Professor in Counseling and Special Education Department and Director of the International Educational Studies Center at Virginia Commonwealth University School of Education. Her research focuses on social and language skills of culturally and linguistically diverse children and interdisciplinary personnel preparation. As PI/co-PI, she has received a number of federal, state, and university research awards investigating impacts of social and cultural factors on children's developmental and educational outcomes as well as the impact of interdisciplinary personnel preparation on children and family outcomes, generating over $11 million. She currently directs two interdisciplinary grants sponsored by the U.S. Department of Education Office of Special Education Programs (OSEP). She is Associate Editor for the Journal of Child and Family Studies.

**Dana Yarbrough** is the associate director of the Partnership for People with Disabilities, Virginia's university center for excellence in developmental disabilities located at Virginia Commonwealth University. Annually, Dana serves as a principal investigator of 10+ grants and contracts totaling over $1.2 million. She holds a master's degree in special education secondary transition from The George Washington University and a master's degree in transformational nonprofit leadership from New England College.

# Index

## A

Ableism 474-476, 483, 494
Action Research 18, 40, 65-66, 71-73, 76, 78-79, 82-84, 93, 177, 211, 275, 381, 384, 394, 401, 408, 539
Adapted Physical Education 65-67, 79-89, 108-109
Adult Learning Strategies 252, 427
Adverse Childhood Experiences 3, 19, 441, 473, 477, 485, 489, 493-494
Adverse Experiences 469, 491
Advocacy 68-69, 79, 106, 166, 170, 173, 289, 355, 393, 397-398, 481, 490, 509-510, 517, 519
Analyzing Data 35, 65, 72, 75, 299, 381, 447
Antibias Practices 494
Antioppressive Practices 470, 472-473, 475-477, 482, 494
Applied Behavior Analysis 80, 132-135, 139, 143, 149, 151, 153, 165, 177-178, 181, 196-197, 283, 344-347, 354-355, 400, 404, 420-421, 428, 434-435, 438, 449, 461, 498
Applied Behavior Analyst 188, 261, 357
Apprenticeship 40, 110, 235, 274, 499-501
Augmentative and Alternative Communication (AAC) 99, 182, 185, 199, 258, 267
Autism 3, 13-14, 18, 20, 35, 38, 63, 67, 69, 80-81, 83, 111-112, 117, 123, 126-132, 135-136, 148-153, 155-162, 164-166, 168-178, 182, 185-187, 189-190, 192-197, 202, 205, 221-222, 224, 229, 235, 245, 261, 269-275, 278, 281, 283, 293, 392, 398, 400-401, 403-405, 410, 415-416, 421, 423, 434-438, 441-442, 506, 523, 525
Autism Spectrum Disorders 111, 126-127, 148, 150-153, 173-175, 177-178, 182, 192, 229, 271, 283, 421, 437-438, 523, 525

## B

Board Certified Behavior Analyst 130, 148, 403
Burnout 132, 134, 147, 152, 235, 381, 440, 443, 455-456, 463-464, 466, 471, 489, 491

## C

Case-Based Instruction 17, 240, 251-252
Case-Based Learning 7-8, 14, 17, 239, 251
Changemaker 161, 175-176
Children with Disabilities 2-4, 6-7, 10-11, 14, 18, 23, 42-45, 47-50, 52-57, 59, 61, 67-69, 78, 87, 112, 114, 122, 131, 160, 177-178, 180-183, 190, 194, 205, 209, 211-212, 216, 219-226, 228-229, 231-232, 242, 250, 255-256, 258, 279-281, 293, 298, 311, 348, 361, 363, 365, 369, 421-422, 426, 446, 449-451, 454, 459, 469-470, 472, 484, 487, 494, 503
Collaboration 1-3, 5, 8-18, 21-30, 32-43, 46-47, 49, 54, 57-59, 61-63, 69, 77-78, 81, 85-88, 92, 94, 98, 100-101, 104, 106-110, 113, 119, 121, 124-125, 131, 134-135, 138-140, 143-144, 147, 149, 155, 158-160, 164, 169-

*Index*

170, 173-195, 198-199, 202, 204-206, 209, 214, 226-227, 231-233, 235, 237-245, 247, 249-251, 254-257, 261-266, 268-281, 283-284, 286-287, 289, 291, 293-294, 297-299, 301-303, 306-308, 312, 337-338, 342, 344-345, 348-351, 354-355, 360-363, 366-368, 370-372, 375-377, 380, 382-387, 390-391, 401-403, 405-406, 408, 410, 413, 422-427, 431-433, 437, 452, 457, 460, 468-469, 471, 474, 476-479, 481-483, 485-486, 488, 491, 494, 496, 499, 502-503, 506-509, 511-514, 516, 518-524, 529, 532, 534-535, 537

Collaborative Clinical Experiences 219, 226, 228, 231, 261-262

Collaborative Communities of Learners 381, 394

Committee on Special Education (CSE) 22, 41

Communication 7, 12-13, 20, 25, 28, 30, 32-34, 36, 40, 44, 53-54, 56, 66, 68-69, 78-79, 99-100, 102, 106, 110-115, 117-121, 123, 125-129, 131, 156-159, 170, 176-178, 180, 182-187, 190, 195-219, 221, 224, 227, 229-234, 241-242, 244-246, 254-268, 270-275, 277-278, 281-285, 290, 295, 298, 301-302, 340, 346, 352, 355, 381, 401, 408-409, 421, 423, 429-430, 432-433, 443-444, 473, 483, 486, 499, 502, 505, 507-509, 511, 514, 516-517, 521-522, 524

Communication Disorders 111-112, 127, 205, 213, 219, 221, 230-231, 233-234, 270-275, 277-278, 281, 284, 505, 507, 522

Communication Skills 25, 32, 66, 78, 102, 177, 185, 187, 201-202, 210, 214-215, 255, 257, 260-263, 266, 509, 522

Community Programming 65, 76, 78, 84

Competency Based Assessment 63

Counselor Shortage 359

Coursework 5, 7-8, 10-11, 39, 54, 66, 71, 91, 104, 106, 111-115, 117, 120, 122-125, 132-136, 139-140, 143-146, 158, 160, 168, 170-171, 177-178, 182-184, 188, 190-191, 198, 202-206, 209-210, 212, 219, 223-224, 226, 230, 238, 241, 248, 259, 262, 277, 281-282, 285-287, 290-291, 299, 301, 337, 342, 344-348, 352, 359-360, 362, 364-365, 367-368, 374, 376, 378-379, 381, 386-387, 389, 402, 404, 411-412, 422, 427-430, 456, 469-470, 477-480, 483, 495, 497-498, 501-503, 508, 511-512, 514, 516-517, 519-522, 526, 528-529, 534

Critical Shortage 2, 255, 374-375

Cultural Humility 2, 63, 357

Cultural Responsiveness 151, 342, 346, 348, 355, 357, 374, 394

Culturally and Linguistically Sustaining Practices 51-52, 63

Culturally Responsive and Sustaining Practices 296, 300, 521, 534

Culturally-Responsive 526-531, 538

# D

Data Collection 12, 65, 72, 74, 78, 93, 105, 119, 132, 139, 143-144, 146, 179, 182, 187, 294, 299, 302, 321-322, 336, 349, 369, 382, 386, 393, 403, 408, 411, 501-502

Digital Badges 42, 47, 50, 58-59, 63

Disabilities 1-4, 6-15, 17-18, 22-30, 32-33, 36-39, 43-45, 47-50, 52-63, 66-69, 76-79, 81-89, 91-93, 97, 99-101, 104, 106-110, 112-114, 121-122, 127-129, 131-133, 135, 138, 141, 143, 145, 148-153, 157, 160, 164, 173-175, 177-184, 188, 190, 194-197, 199-203, 205, 207-209, 211-217, 219-226, 228-235, 237-238, 242, 250, 252, 255-259, 268, 270-273, 275, 277-283, 290-301, 303, 305-306, 309-311, 318-321, 323-330, 332-337, 339-341, 348-349, 352, 360-363, 365, 367, 369, 371-372, 375-377, 380, 382-387, 389-392, 395-400, 406-407, 410-411, 413-414, 416, 420-427, 429, 431, 434-435, 437-442, 445-446, 449-451, 453-454, 456, 458-459, 462, 469-470, 472-473, 475-476, 481, 484, 487, 490, 493-494, 496, 503, 505-512, 514, 516-519, 521-530, 532, 535, 537-539, 541-544

# E

Early Childhood 2-4, 10, 14-20, 42-45, 47, 54-59, 63, 108, 111-115, 117, 121, 123, 126-127, 129, 133, 135, 139, 150, 153, 177-179, 181, 183-184, 188, 192, 195-199, 201-203, 205, 207-210, 213-218, 229, 237-239, 251, 278, 280-282, 291-294, 336, 344, 355, 421, 463, 468-472, 476-477, 479, 481-482, 485, 488-494

Early Childhood and Family Mental Health 468, 494

Early Childhood Special Education 2, 15-17, 19, 42-43, 55-57, 63, 111-112, 126-127, 129, 135, 150, 153, 177-178, 181, 188, 195-196, 198-199, 213-214, 237-238, 251, 281, 292-294, 463, 468-469, 488-491, 494

Early Intervention 2, 4-5, 12, 14-16, 19, 34, 40, 43, 46, 57, 63, 87, 111-114, 118, 121-123, 125-127, 129, 131, 150, 153, 185, 189, 195, 199, 211, 213-214, 216-218, 220, 237-243, 248-252, 274, 278, 280, 292-294, 311, 381, 384, 393, 438, 454, 471-474, 484, 488-490, 510

Education 1-4, 6, 8-9, 11, 13-30, 32-34, 36-47, 50,

653

52, 54-63, 65-72, 77, 79-89, 92, 94, 97-100, 105-114, 121-122, 125-136, 138-141, 143-155, 157-161, 164, 166-167, 169-179, 181-182, 184, 186-191, 193-206, 209-210, 213-217, 220-226, 228, 232-240, 242, 250-251, 254-259, 262, 265, 268-287, 289-295, 297-298, 301-302, 304-305, 307-312, 317-327, 329, 331, 333-340, 342-349, 352-358, 360-378, 380-387, 389-406, 408-409, 411-416, 418, 420-439, 441-444, 446, 448-449, 451, 453-454, 456-465, 468-473, 475-479, 481, 483, 487-507, 509-514, 516-525, 527-544

English as a Second Language 217, 297, 318-319

Evidence-Based Intervention 43, 94, 306, 426, 440, 461, 466

Experiential Learning 57, 125, 164, 240, 252, 286, 296, 307

## F

Faculty Learning Community (FLC) 22-23, 30-31, 33, 41

Family 3-4, 10, 12, 23, 25, 27, 32, 49-50, 52-53, 61, 78, 92, 94, 114, 128, 132, 140, 156, 160-161, 164, 170, 172, 181-185, 187, 197, 200, 205-206, 220, 227, 242-245, 247-248, 250, 252, 281, 305-306, 348, 354-355, 370, 382, 387, 391, 394, 397, 402, 406, 424-425, 431, 435, 441, 453, 461, 468-474, 476-477, 479, 481, 487-488, 491, 493-494, 502, 510-514, 517, 520-521, 531, 537, 544

Family Systems Framework 472-473, 477, 494

Field Experience 10, 46, 54-55, 59, 63, 285-286, 292, 294, 382-383, 431, 481-482, 497, 499, 523

Fieldwork 5, 10-11, 38, 78, 92-93, 106, 136, 139, 142-144, 147, 149, 177, 179-180, 182, 186-187, 190, 192-193, 201, 204-205, 209, 211-212, 281, 289, 299, 301-307, 320, 322, 329, 332-333, 336-338, 346, 352, 359-360, 365, 367, 381, 400, 403, 411, 426-430, 433, 482, 484-485, 526, 529-533, 536-537, 539-540

## H

High Intensity Needs 112, 118, 130-131, 144, 220, 250, 255, 258-259, 268, 298, 374, 376-378, 381, 384, 389, 395, 398, 508-509

High School 93, 131, 175, 221, 228, 349, 397, 414, 461, 508, 511, 521, 525, 527, 530-531, 539, 543-544

Higher Education 6, 17, 20, 22-23, 36, 46, 50, 58, 60, 86-87, 107-108, 110, 148, 150, 152, 155, 157-158, 164, 166, 169-171, 174, 191, 193, 216, 224, 251, 279, 285, 292-293, 319, 353, 363, 366, 368, 386, 390-393, 395, 405, 448, 458, 460, 469, 473, 490, 509, 531, 542

High-Intensity Needs 1-4, 8-10, 13, 32, 121, 125, 131-135, 198, 202, 206, 208, 220, 231, 237-238, 241, 250, 255, 257-258, 260-261, 263, 283, 293, 374, 402, 421, 441, 496, 526

High-Leverage Practices 38-39, 60, 85-86, 89-90, 106-107, 109-110, 126, 196, 308-309, 372, 392

High-Need Disabilities 505-506

## I

Immigrants 42, 44, 48, 51, 53, 57

Inclusion 2, 18, 35, 37, 69, 86, 88, 105-106, 108-110, 114, 148, 155, 161, 163, 170-171, 195, 200, 204, 206, 209, 212-217, 224, 242, 257, 281-282, 291, 331, 339, 376, 379, 393, 404, 415, 426, 454, 468, 470, 476, 484, 490-491, 494, 509, 519-520, 532, 534, 538, 544

Inclusive Practices 35, 38, 175, 205, 281, 374, 395, 402, 479, 482, 486, 511

Institutional Support 155, 170, 254-255, 259, 263

Integrated Learning Model (ILM) 395

Intensive, Multi-Tiered Interventions 377, 381, 395

Interdisciplinary 1-17, 20-30, 32-45, 47-54, 56-61, 63, 65-66, 69-72, 76-79, 81, 84-89, 92-93, 97-100, 104-107, 109-114, 117-125, 130-146, 148-150, 155, 157-160, 162, 164, 169-170, 172-180, 182-188, 190-195, 198-200, 203-205, 207, 209-210, 212, 219-222, 226-227, 231-232, 235, 237-239, 241-245, 247-250, 252, 255, 269-274, 277-287, 289-299, 301-303, 305-309, 311, 319, 337-338, 342-346, 348-356, 358-360, 364-369, 374-378, 380-385, 388-390, 393, 396-397, 399-402, 410-412, 420, 422-431, 433-437, 440-442, 444-455, 458-460, 463, 466, 468-471, 474-476, 478, 480, 484-487, 494-495, 499, 501-502, 505-508, 511-512, 514, 517-521, 523-524, 526-530, 536-537, 539-540

Interdisciplinary Collaboration 3, 5, 22, 24-25, 27-30, 32-35, 37-41, 49, 69, 78, 81, 87, 92, 106, 109-110, 131, 138, 140, 144, 149, 155, 158-160, 170, 173, 175-176, 178-179, 182-188, 190-195, 204, 232, 235, 237, 239, 241, 243, 249-250, 274, 277-278, 281, 284, 289, 291, 293, 297-299, 301, 303, 306, 337-338, 342, 345, 349, 354, 368, 375-376, 402, 425-426, 432-433, 437, 471, 474, 485, 506-508, 511, 517-518, 520-521, 523

Interdisciplinary Competencies 10, 42-43, 46, 48, 193, 425

Interdisciplinary Curriculum 35, 65

*Index*

Interdisciplinary Education 22-23, 43, 46, 65, 69, 79, 84, 239, 291, 352, 358

Interdisciplinary Personnel Preparation 1-2, 8-9, 14-15, 46-47, 58, 111, 200, 219, 231, 237-239, 241-242, 281, 294, 345, 360, 396-397, 450, 469, 485, 528

Interdisciplinary Practice 10, 13, 49, 63, 113, 142, 164, 239, 255, 345, 401-402

Interdisciplinary Preparation 2, 27, 43, 46-47, 50, 69, 132, 148, 150, 160, 170, 220, 238, 280-281, 342, 360, 364, 368, 385, 388-389, 442, 454, 458, 469-470, 485-486, 495, 506, 508, 519, 526

Interdisciplinary Professional Education 342

Interdisciplinary Program 46, 66, 70-72, 76, 78-79, 86, 135, 139, 146, 170, 172, 220, 281, 283, 346, 351, 359-360, 374, 380, 420, 422, 425, 449, 459-460, 475-476, 485-486, 494, 501

Interdisciplinary Service Delivery 85, 88, 92

Interdisciplinary Teams 2, 13, 28, 66, 107, 112-113, 119, 123, 135, 144, 157, 159, 222, 237, 242-243, 245, 250, 272, 287, 382, 400-401, 431, 469-470, 528, 540

Interprofessional Clinical Practice (IPCP) 254-255

Interprofessional Competencies 42-43, 47, 56-57, 63, 256, 259

Interprofessional Education (IPE) 62, 254, 281, 342, 344

Interprofessional Education Collaborative (IPEC) 43, 63

Interprofessional Training 46, 56-57, 237-238, 241, 243, 252, 255, 259, 267, 312

Intervention for English Learners 296

## L

Language 12-14, 19, 24-25, 28, 39, 50, 77, 87, 112-113, 118, 120, 123-124, 127, 129, 141, 159, 172-173, 175, 180, 182-184, 188, 190-191, 195-199, 201-205, 207-212, 214-218, 220-230, 233-235, 238, 241-242, 246, 251, 256-261, 265, 269-278, 281-285, 287-292, 294, 296-297, 299-303, 319-327, 329-330, 332-340, 342, 344-345, 348, 350-351, 354, 356, 363, 376, 384, 386, 388, 394, 402, 407, 410, 412, 423-424, 430, 450, 459, 466, 469, 473, 481, 483, 485, 500, 509, 514, 525, 527, 532

## M

Medical Model of Disability 176

Mental Health 2-3, 16-17, 19-20, 45, 67, 80, 151, 274, 312, 342-343, 347-348, 355-357, 359-364, 369-373, 396-416, 420, 422-424, 431, 436, 438, 446, 448, 450-453, 455-459, 461-463, 465, 468-469, 474, 478, 485-486, 488-489, 491-494, 504, 506, 510-511

Mentoring Workshops 497-499, 502

Micro Credentials 42, 47, 50-52, 63

Midwest 20, 321, 424

Minority Serving Institutions 379, 395

Mixed Methods Research 318, 338-339

Motor Development 3, 74, 84, 87, 92

MTSS 133-135, 296-298, 300, 302, 305-306, 310-311, 343-346, 349, 351, 354, 356, 390, 398, 401, 405-406, 451-452

Multidisciplinary 21, 23-24, 27-28, 32, 40-41, 43, 65-66, 68-69, 71, 75-79, 84, 132, 149, 191, 255, 336, 383, 391, 449-454, 461, 478

Multidisciplinary Collaboration 24, 27, 41, 43

Multidisciplinary Teams 27-28, 65-66, 69, 71, 78, 84, 336, 451-452, 454

Multilingual Learners 341

## N

Neurodiversity 155, 161-162, 169, 173, 175-176, 232

## O

Observation 72-74, 147, 228-230, 300, 302, 304, 308, 430, 448, 530

Office of Special Education Programs (OSEP) 43, 111-112, 129, 131, 150, 198, 238, 279, 377, 396-397, 405, 469, 528, 531

## P

Partnerships 3, 28, 35, 55, 106, 114, 125, 140, 148, 171, 193, 214, 241, 259, 263-266, 275, 280-281, 295, 301, 311, 346, 348, 351, 357, 359-360, 370, 381, 402, 404, 406, 411-412, 440-441, 457-458, 466, 469, 476-477, 479, 485, 493, 508-509, 511, 514

Personnel Preparation 1-4, 8-9, 11, 14-15, 46-47, 58-59, 109, 111-113, 126, 130-131, 148, 152-154, 159, 161, 169, 175, 198-200, 213, 219, 231, 237-239, 241-243, 245, 248-249, 252, 271, 280-281, 283, 292, 294, 298, 345, 353, 359-361, 365-366, 372, 374, 376, 383, 395-397, 438, 450, 469-471, 475, 483, 485, 490, 494, 505, 507, 528, 541, 543

Physical Education 15, 65-67, 79-89, 108-109, 135, 171

Practitioner 25, 310, 371, 408, 442, 471, 475, 478, 482-483, 487, 494

Preservice Professional Preparation 174, 277

Preservice Training 47, 59, 149, 178, 189, 198, 201,

655

213, 215, 238-239

Preservie Training 198

Preverbal 112, 129, 185

Professional Preparation 9, 16, 21-22, 27, 33-35, 47, 58, 108, 155, 157-158, 160, 173-174, 176, 251, 269-270, 277, 280, 346, 425, 451, 469, 489, 507-508

Professional Standards 25, 43, 87, 135-138, 144, 238-239, 241, 253, 255, 281, 366, 370, 415, 425, 482, 492, 519, 534, 543

Program Development 194, 351, 388, 420, 432

## R

Racially, Ethnically, and Linguistically Diverse (RELD) 374-375, 395

Recruitment 66, 77, 83, 141, 146, 149, 151, 162, 170, 182, 232, 270, 351, 353, 359-360, 366, 374, 376, 378-380, 383-384, 388, 393, 400, 434, 447, 455, 458, 461, 471, 483, 485, 497-500, 535-536

Reflection of Data 72, 76

Reflective Practice 7, 15, 23, 262, 274, 367, 426, 479, 482-484, 494

Refugees 44, 48, 50, 53, 57, 62, 318

Regulation 29, 112, 114-115, 117, 120, 125, 127, 129, 185, 196

Reporting Data 72, 75, 78, 140

Retention 141-142, 146, 148-149, 151-152, 189, 205, 210, 212, 270, 354, 359-360, 374, 376, 378, 380, 393-394, 434, 455, 471, 483, 485, 498, 500, 535, 542

Rural Education 420

## S

School Counselors 219, 222-225, 228, 231-233, 235-236, 281, 344, 355, 363, 370-371, 402, 440, 442-444, 446, 448, 450, 453, 455-457, 460, 464, 488, 510, 522

School Psychologist 32, 353, 357, 364, 379-381, 384, 404, 408-409, 415, 421, 423, 430, 437, 450, 453, 465-466, 532, 535, 538

School Psychology 17-18, 30, 32-34, 36, 174, 188, 197, 233, 281, 296-299, 301-311, 313, 338, 345-347, 349-356, 370, 374, 376, 378-381, 383-385, 390-394, 396, 399-401, 404, 409, 411, 413-415, 420, 422-435, 437-438, 442-443, 446, 449, 451, 455, 457-464, 526-537, 539-540, 542

School-Based Mental Health 396, 398, 400-404, 406, 411-414, 438, 488

Secondary Education 336, 505, 509

Self-Care 135, 229, 258, 411, 440-441, 455-456, 461, 463-464, 466, 471, 489

Self-Efficacy Beliefs 318-322, 325-326, 329, 331-333, 335-336, 338

Shared Coursework 5, 7-8, 10, 115, 117, 139, 178, 182-184, 188, 204-206, 212, 219, 226, 301, 342, 346-347, 352, 359-360, 364-365, 367, 404, 412, 469-470, 477-480, 483, 514, 519, 522, 526, 529, 534

Skill Development 8, 48, 56, 67, 94, 143, 179, 225, 240, 262-263, 278, 443, 445, 456, 514, 518

Social Communication 112, 114-115, 117-120, 129, 131, 177-178, 185, 197, 202, 210

Social Engagement 114, 117, 119, 129, 256

Social Justice Framework 472, 475, 483, 486, 494

Social Model of Disability 176

Social Work 2, 4, 7, 9, 15, 19, 35, 42-43, 54-56, 58, 60-61, 63, 135, 157, 159, 161, 173, 240, 252, 269, 281, 291, 312, 390, 412, 422, 458, 460, 468, 471, 476, 478, 488-492, 494-499, 501-505, 507, 509-512, 514, 516, 518

Special Education 1-4, 8-9, 11, 13, 15-17, 19-24, 26-30, 32-34, 36-43, 52, 54-57, 59-60, 63, 65-67, 79-81, 84-87, 94, 98-100, 106-107, 109-114, 121-122, 125-136, 138-141, 143-151, 153-155, 157-161, 166-167, 169, 173, 175, 177-179, 181-182, 184, 186, 188, 193-196, 198-199, 202-203, 205, 209, 213-214, 217, 220, 223-226, 234-238, 242, 250-251, 254-257, 268, 270, 274-287, 289-294, 297-298, 302, 304, 308-312, 318-321, 323-327, 333-340, 343-349, 352-357, 360-363, 365-367, 369-378, 380-387, 389-394, 396-406, 408-409, 411-416, 420-438, 441-444, 446, 449, 451, 453-454, 456, 458-460, 462-464, 468-471, 475-476, 481, 483, 488-491, 493-503, 505-507, 509, 511-512, 514, 516-519, 521-540, 542-544

Special Education Teacher 8, 16, 24, 32, 52, 56, 86, 109-110, 126, 131-132, 139, 145, 147, 149, 203, 270, 291, 298, 304, 344, 357, 370, 391, 393, 408, 415, 434, 443, 453, 463, 489, 527

Special Educator Personnel Preparation 359

Special Educators 16, 20, 24, 26-27, 29, 32, 45, 47, 50-51, 54, 56, 58, 61, 65-66, 69, 108, 112, 114, 121, 131-132, 134-135, 138, 143, 146-147, 190-191, 198, 203, 208, 247, 251, 255, 257, 270, 281, 283, 291, 294, 343-344, 351, 359-363, 368-369, 371, 374-375, 377, 379-384, 393, 396-397, 401, 405, 421-423, 425, 429-430, 433-434, 436, 440, 442, 450, 453, 455, 471, 489, 495-496, 499, 503-504, 507, 509, 522, 524

Speech and Language Pathologist 198, 430

Speech-Language Pathology (SLP) 12, 220, 238, 254

## Index

Students With Disabilities 8, 13, 22, 24-30, 33, 36, 38, 50, 58, 66-67, 69, 78-79, 82, 85-87, 97, 99-101, 104, 106-108, 131, 133, 145, 149-151, 157, 179, 209, 214-216, 221-224, 230, 233, 235, 255, 257, 259, 268, 272-273, 277-280, 282, 290-291, 293, 295-301, 303, 305-306, 311, 327, 334, 339, 360, 362-363, 369, 371-372, 375-377, 380, 382-386, 389, 392, 396-400, 407, 411, 421-426, 429, 431, 434-435, 441, 445-446, 453-454, 456, 496, 508, 514, 521, 524, 526-528, 532, 537-539, 541-542

## T

Teacher Candidates 7-8, 16, 69, 86, 97-98, 107, 147, 179, 199, 209, 212, 295-296, 306, 318-320, 326, 340, 432, 533

Teacher Education 2, 4, 8, 14, 16-20, 26, 30, 34, 37, 39, 59, 61-62, 69-70, 83-86, 88, 108, 110, 149, 151-152, 154, 158, 182, 195, 206, 215, 217, 222, 240, 271, 276, 279-280, 282-283, 290-295, 309, 311, 318-319, 322, 335-336, 338-340, 355, 363, 371-372, 393-394, 490, 528, 543

Teacher Education Programs 14, 70, 158, 195, 279, 282, 290, 294, 318-319, 322, 335-336, 363, 393

Teacher Preparation 7-8, 16, 26, 37, 39, 54, 61, 65-69, 71, 77-79, 83, 85-86, 88, 101, 106-107, 109-110, 132, 141-142, 146, 152, 215, 280-281, 285-286, 289, 291-293, 319-320, 327, 335-338, 340-341, 362-363, 365, 372, 393, 495, 500, 523

Teacher Shortage 131, 145, 147, 275, 291, 359, 371, 413, 442, 465, 493, 496

Threat Assessment 440, 452, 454-455, 461, 465-466

Toxic Stress 3, 19, 473, 477, 494

Transactional Model of Child Development 114, 129

Transdisciplinary 20, 23-25, 40, 120, 184, 196, 242, 251, 275, 280, 292, 294, 422, 429, 449, 464, 525

Transition 13-14, 30, 34, 68, 92-93, 100, 105, 109, 123, 242-243, 245, 362, 365, 368, 430-431, 485, 505, 507-512, 514-529, 531-535, 537-544

Transition Planning 34, 68, 92, 242, 506-507, 509-510, 513-514, 516-519, 522, 524, 526-529, 533, 537, 540-542

Transition Services 68, 506-511, 513-514, 517, 519, 521, 523, 526-530, 533-535, 538, 544

Trauma 3-4, 14, 45, 51-52, 227, 231, 361, 370-371, 405-406, 440, 442-443, 448, 451, 453, 456, 458-459, 467, 470, 473, 479, 487, 489-490, 494

## U

Undergraduate Exceptional Student Education 283
Underrepresented Groups 190, 378, 395
United States 18, 40, 60-61, 79-80, 87, 128, 131, 134, 151, 153, 155, 157, 174, 202, 236, 250, 255, 268, 274, 294, 296, 318, 331, 334, 340-341, 355, 362, 370, 373, 375-376, 394, 412, 421, 423, 437, 439, 442, 448, 461, 465, 496, 509, 519, 522, 543
Urban Schools 393

## V

Video Modeling 21, 26, 29-30, 33-34, 36-38, 41, 404, 409
virtual learning communities 42, 47, 52, 60
Virtual Learning Community 47, 49, 64

## W

Western Michigan University 130-131, 135, 524
Whole Child Policy Toolkit 491, 494

# Recommended Reference Books

IGI Global's reference books are available in three unique pricing formats:
Print Only, E-Book Only, or Print + E-Book.

Shipping fees may apply.

**www.igi-global.com**

---

**Participatory Pedagogy: Emerging Research and Opportunities**
ISBN: 9781522589648
EISBN: 9781522589655
© 2021; 156 pp.
List Price: US$ **155**

**Transformative Pedagogical Perspectives on Home Language Use in Classrooms**
ISBN: 9781799840756
EISBN: 9781799840763
© 2021; 282 pp.
List Price: US$ **185**

**Advancing Online Course Design and Pedagogy for the 21st Century Learning Environment**
ISBN: 9781799855989
EISBN: 9781799856009
© 2021; 382 pp.
List Price: US$ **195**

**Deep Fakes, Fake News, and Misinformation in Online Teaching and Learning Technologies**
ISBN: 9781799864745
EISBN: 9781799864752
© 2021; 271 pp.
List Price: US$ **195**

**Enhancing Higher Education Accessibility Through Open Education and Prior Learning**
ISBN: 9781799875710
EISBN: 9781799875734
© 2021; 252 pp.
List Price: US$ **195**

**Connecting Disciplinary Literacy and Digital Storytelling in K-12 Education**
ISBN: 9781799857709
EISBN: 9781799857716
© 2021; 378 pp.
List Price: US$ **195**

---

**Do you want to stay current on the latest research trends, product announcements, news, and special offers?**
Join IGI Global's mailing list to receive customized recommendations, exclusive discounts, and more.
Sign up at: **www.igi-global.com/newsletters**.

---

Publisher of Timely, Peer-Reviewed Inclusive Research Since 1988

**IGI Global**
PUBLISHER of TIMELY KNOWLEDGE

www.igi-global.com | Sign up at www.igi-global.com/newsletters | facebook.com/igiglobal | twitter.com/igiglobal | linkedin.com/igiglobal

# Ensure Quality Research is Introduced to the Academic Community

# Become an Evaluator for IGI Global Authored Book Projects

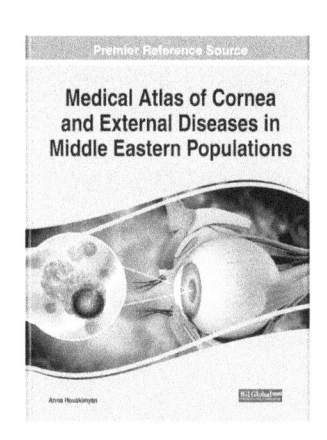

**The overall success of an authored book project is dependent on quality and timely manuscript evaluations.**

## Applications and Inquiries may be sent to:
development@igi-global.com

Applicants must have a doctorate (or equivalent degree) as well as publishing, research, and reviewing experience. Authored Book Evaluators are appointed for one-year terms and are expected to complete at least three evaluations per term. Upon successful completion of this term, evaluators can be considered for an additional term.

If you have a colleague that may be interested in this opportunity, we encourage you to share this information with them.

Easily Identify, Acquire, and Utilize Published
Peer-Reviewed Findings in Support of Your Current Research

# IGI Global OnDemand

Purchase Individual IGI Global OnDemand Book Chapters and Journal Articles

**For More Information:**
www.igi-global.com/e-resources/ondemand/

## Browse through 150,000+ Articles and Chapters!

Find specific research related to your current studies and projects that have been contributed by international researchers from prestigious institutions, including:

- Massachusetts Institute of Technology
- HARVARD UNIVERSITY
- COLUMBIA UNIVERSITY IN THE CITY OF NEW YORK
- Australian National University

- Accurate and Advanced Search
- Affordably Acquire Research
- Instantly Access Your Content
- Benefit from the InfoSci Platform Features

*It really provides an excellent entry into the research literature of the field. It presents a manageable number of highly relevant sources on topics of interest to a wide range of researchers. The sources are scholarly, but also accessible to 'practitioners'.*

- Ms. Lisa Stimatz, MLS, University of North Carolina at Chapel Hill, USA

## Interested in Additional Savings?

Subscribe to

**IGI Global OnDemand** *Plus*

**Learn More**

Acquire content from over 128,000+ research-focused book chapters and 33,000+ scholarly journal articles for as low as US$ 5 per article/chapter (original retail price for an article/chapter: US$ 37.50).

# 6,600+ E-BOOKS.
# ADVANCED RESEARCH.
# INCLUSIVE & ACCESSIBLE.

## IGI Global e-Book Collection

- **Flexible Purchasing Options** (Perpetual, Subscription, EBA, etc.)
- Multi-Year Agreements with **No Price Increases** Guaranteed
- **No Additional Charge** for Multi-User Licensing
- No Maintenance, Hosting, or Archiving Fees
- Transformative **Open Access Options** Available

*Request More Information, or Recommend the IGI Global e-Book Collection to Your Institution's Librarian*

## Among Titles Included in the IGI Global e-Book Collection

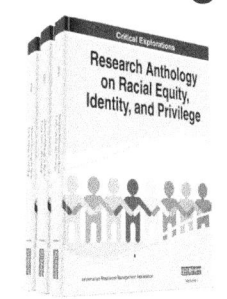

**Research Anthology on Racial Equity, Identity, and Privilege (3 Vols.)**
EISBN: 9781668445082
Price: US$ 895

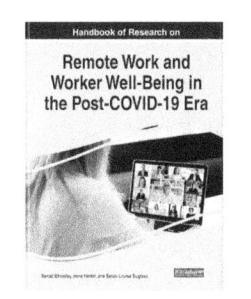

**Handbook of Research on Remote Work and Worker Well-Being in the Post-COVID-19 Era**
EISBN: 9781799867562
Price: US$ 265

**Research Anthology on Big Data Analytics, Architectures, and Applications (4 Vols.)**
EISBN: 9781668436639
Price: US$ 1,950

**Handbook of Research on Challenging Deficit Thinking for Exceptional Education Improvement**
EISBN: 9781799888628
Price: US$ 265

### Acquire & Open

When your library acquires an IGI Global e-Book and/or e-Journal Collection, your faculty's published work will be considered for immediate conversion to Open Access *(CC BY License)*, at no additional cost to the library or its faculty *(cost only applies to the e-Collection content being acquired)*, through our popular **Transformative Open Access (Read & Publish) Initiative**.

**For More Information or to Request a Free Trial, Contact IGI Global's e-Collections Team:** eresources@igi-global.com | 1-866-342-6657 ext. 100 | 717-533-8845 ext. 100

# Have Your Work Published and Freely Accessible
# Open Access Publishing

With the industry shifting from the more traditional publication models to an open access (OA) publication model, publishers are finding that OA publishing has many benefits that are awarded to authors and editors of published work.

- Freely Share Your Research
- Higher Discoverability & Citation Impact
- Rigorous & Expedited Publishing Process
- Increased Advancement & Collaboration

## Acquire & Open

When your library acquires an IGI Global e-Book and/or e-Journal Collection, your faculty's published work will be considered for immediate conversion to Open Access *(CC BY License)*, at no additional cost to the library or its faculty *(cost only applies to the e-Collection content being acquired)*, through our popular **Transformative Open Access (Read & Publish) Initiative**.

- Provide Up To **100%** OA APC or CPC Funding
- Funding to Convert or Start a Journal to **Platinum OA**
- Support for Funding an **OA Reference Book**

IGI Global publications are found in a number of prestigious indices, including Web of Science™, Scopus®, Compendex, and PsycINFO®. The selection criteria is very strict and to ensure that journals and books are accepted into the major indexes, IGI Global closely monitors publications against the criteria that the indexes provide to publishers.

WEB OF SCIENCE™ | Compendex | Scopus | PsycINFO® | IET Inspec

**Learn More Here:**

For Questions, Contact IGI Global's Open Access Team at openaccessadmin@igi-global.com

IGI Global
PUBLISHER of TIMELY KNOWLEDGE
www.igi-global.com

# Are You Ready to Publish Your Research?

**IGI Global**
PUBLISHER of TIMELY KNOWLEDGE

IGI Global offers book authorship and editorship opportunities across 11 subject areas, including business, computer science, education, science and engineering, social sciences, and more!

### Benefits of Publishing with IGI Global:

- Free one-on-one editorial and promotional support.
- Expedited publishing timelines that can take your book from start to finish in less than one (1) year.
- Choose from a variety of formats, including Edited and Authored References, Handbooks of Research, Encyclopedias, and Research Insights.
- Utilize IGI Global's eEditorial Discovery® submission system in support of conducting the submission and double-blind peer review process.
- IGI Global maintains a strict adherence to ethical practices due in part to our full membership with the Committee on Publication Ethics (COPE).
- Indexing potential in prestigious indices such as Scopus®, Web of Science™, PsycINFO®, and ERIC – Education Resources Information Center.
- Ability to connect your ORCID iD to your IGI Global publications.
- Earn honorariums and royalties on your full book publications as well as complimentary copies and exclusive discounts.

### Join Your Colleagues from Prestigious Institutions, Including:

- Australian National University
- Massachusetts Institute of Technology
- Johns Hopkins University
- Tsinghua University
- Harvard University
- Columbia University in the City of New York

**Learn More at:** www.igi-global.com/publish
or Contact IGI Global's Aquisitions Team at: acquisition@igi-global.com

Lightning Source UK Ltd.
Milton Keynes UK
UKHW030841040123
414788UK00008B/122